MASTER VISUALLY®

Dreamweaver® MX and Flash™ MX

by Sherry Kinkoph and Mike Wooldridge
Contributions by Kyle Bowen

From

maranGraphics®

&

Wiley Publishing, Inc.

Master VISUALLY® Dreamweaver® MX and Flash™ MX

Published by
Wiley Publishing, Inc.
909 Third Avenue
New York, NY 10022

Published simultaneously in Canada

maranGraphics, Inc.
5755 Coopers Avenue
Mississauga, Ontario, Canada
L4Z 1R9

Library of Congress Control Number: 2002110243

ISBN: 0-7645-3696-6

Manufactured in the United States of America

10 9 8 7 6 5 4 3 2 1

1V/RY/QZ/QS/IN

Trademark Acknowledgments

Important Numbers

For U.S. corporate orders, please call maranGraphics at 800-469-6616 or fax 905-890-9434.

For general information on our other products and services or to obtain technical support please contact our Customer Care Department within the U.S. at 800-762-2974, outside the U.S. at 317-572-3993 or fax 317-572-4002.

Permissions

maranGraphics

Certain text and Illustrations by maranGraphics, Inc., used with maranGraphics' permission.

U.S. Corporate Sales

Contact maranGraphics at (800) 469-6616 or fax (905) 890-9434.

U.S. Trade Sales

Contact Wiley at (800) 762-2974 or fax (317) 572-4002.

Praise for Visual books...

"If you have to see it to believe it, this is the book for you!"
–PC World

"I would like to take this time to compliment maranGraphics on creating such great books. I work for a leading manufacturer of office products, and sometimes they tend to NOT give you the meat and potatoes of certain subjects, which causes great confusion. Thank you for making it clear. Keep up the good work."
–Kirk Santoro (Burbank, CA)

"I write to extend my thanks and appreciation for your books. They are clear, easy to follow, and straight to the point. Keep up the good work! I bought several of your books and they are just right! No regrets! I will always buy your books because they are the best."
–Seward Kollie (Dakar, Senegal)

"What fantastic teaching books you have produced! Congratulations to you and your staff."
–Bruno Tonon (Melbourne, Australia)

"Compliments To The Chef!! Your books are extraordinary! Or, simply put, Extra-Ordinary, meaning way above the rest! THANKYOUTHANKYOU THANKYOU! for creating these. They have saved me from serious mistakes, and showed me a right and simple way to do things. I buy them for friends, family, and colleagues."
–Christine J. Manfrin (Castle Rock, CO)

"A master tutorial/reference — from the leaders in visual learning!"
–Infoworld

"Your books are superior! An avid reader since childhood, I've consumed literally tens of thousands of books, a significant quantity in the learning/teaching category. Your series is the most precise, visually appealing and compelling to peruse. Kudos!"
–Margaret Rose Chmilar (Edmonton, Alberta, Canada)

"You're marvelous! I am greatly in your debt."
–Patrick Baird (Lacey, WA)

"Just wanted to say THANK YOU to your company for providing books which make learning fast, easy, and exciting! I learn visually so your books have helped me greatly – from Windows instruction to Web page development. I'm looking forward to using more of your Master Books series in the future as I am now a computer support specialist. Best wishes for continued success."
–Angela J. Barker (Springfield, MO)

"A publishing concept whose time has come!"
–The Globe and Mail

"I have over the last 10-15 years purchased $1000's worth of computer books but find your books the most easily read, best set out and most helpful and easily understood books on software and computers I have ever read. You produce the best computer books money can buy. Please keep up the good work."
–John Gatt (Adamstown Heights, Australia)

"The Greatest. This whole series is the best computer learning tool of any kind I've ever seen."
–Joe Orr (Brooklyn, NY)

maranGraphics is a family-run business
located near Toronto, Canada.

At maranGraphics, we believe in producing great computer books – one book at a time.

maranGraphics has been producing high-technology products for over 25 years, which enables us to offer the computer book community a unique communication process.

Our computer books use an integrated communication process, which is very different from the approach used in other computer books. Each spread is, in essence, a flow chart – the text and screen shots are totally incorporated into the layout of the spread. Introductory text and helpful tips complete the learning experience.

maranGraphics' approach encourages the left and right sides of the brain to work together – resulting in faster orientation and greater memory retention.

Above all, we are very proud of the handcrafted nature of our books. Our carefully-chosen writers are experts in their fields, and spend countless hours researching and organizing the content for each topic. Our artists rebuild every screen shot to provide the best clarity possible, making our screen shots the most precise and easiest to read in the industry. We strive for perfection, and believe that the time spent handcrafting each element results in the best computer books money can buy.

Thank you for purchasing this book. We hope you enjoy it!

Sincerely,

Robert Maran
President
maranGraphics
Rob@maran.com
www.maran.com

CREDITS

Acquisitions, Editorial, and Media Development

Project Editor
Jade Williams

Acquisitions Editor
Jen Dorsey

Product Development Supervisor
Lindsay Sandman

Copy Editors
Jill Mazurczyk
Marylouise Wiack

Technical Editor
Kyle D. Bowen

Permissions Editor
Laura Moss

Media Development Specialist
Megan Decraene

Editorial Manager
Rev Mengle

Manufacturing
Allan Conley
Linda Cook,
Paul Gilchrist
Jennifer Guynn

Production

Book Design
maranGraphics®

Project Coordinator
Dale White

Layout and Graphics
Melanie DesJardins
Joyce Haughey, LeAndra Johnson
Kristin McMullan, Heather Pope

Screen Artists
Mark Harris
Jill A. Proll

Illustrators
Ronda David-Burroughs
David E. Gregory

Proofreader
Christine Pingleton

Quality Control
Laura Albert, John Bitter
Andy Hollandbeck, Susan Moritz

Indexer
Liz Cunningham

Special Help
Macromedia, Inc.

GENERAL AND ADMINISTRATIVE

Wiley Technology Publishing Group: Richard Swadley, Vice President and Executive Group Publisher; Bob Ipsen, Vice President and Executive Publisher; Barry Pruett, Vice President and Publisher; Joseph Wikert, Vice President and Publisher; Mary Bednarek, Editorial Director; Mary C. Corder, Editorial Director; Andy Cummings, Editorial Director.

Wiley Production for Branded Press: Debbie Stailey, Production Director

ABOUT THE AUTHORS

Sherry Willard Kinkoph has written more than 40 books over the past eight years covering a variety of computer topics ranging from hardware to software, from Microsoft Office programs to the Internet. Her recent titles include *Teach Yourself VISUALLY Premiere 6, Master VISUALLY Dreamweaver 4 and Flash 5,* and *Master VISUALLY FrontPage 2002.* Sherry's never-ending quest is to help users of all levels master the ever-changing computer technologies. No matter how many times the software manufacturers and hardware conglomerates throw out a new version or upgrade, Sherry vows to be there to make sense of it all and help computer users get the most out of their machines.

Mike Wooldridge is a Web developer in the San Francisco Bay Area. He has authored or co-authored seven other Visual books, including *Teach Yourself VISUALLY Dreamweaver 4* and *Teach Yourself VISUALLY Photoshop 7.*

AUTHORS' ACKNOWLEDGMENTS

Sherry Kinkoph: Special thanks go out to acquisitions editor, Jennifer Dorsey, for allowing us the opportunity to work on this project; to project editor, Jade Williams, for shepherding the book from start to finish, never missing a beat; to copy editor, Jill Mazurczyk, for ensuring that all the i's were dotted and t's were crossed; to technical editor, Kyle Bowen, for checking everything over for accuracy and offering his skilled observations; and finally to the production team at Wiley for their efforts in creating such a visual masterpiece.

Mike Wooldridge: Thanks to project editor Jade Williams and everyone else at Wiley who worked on this book. Also thanks to Sherry Kinkoph for being so easy to work with.

To my mother, Patricia Willard, for her on-going support and encouragement for all of life's little projects.
-- Sherry

To Linda, for understanding while I worked late nights and weekends to finish this book.
--Mike

DREAMWEAVER® MX AND FLASH™ MX

I USING DREAMWEAVER MX BASICS

II ADDING DESIGN ELEMENTS

III ENHANCING YOUR WEB SITE

IV MANAGING YOUR FINISHED SITE

WHAT'S INSIDE

V CREATING A DYNAMIC SITE

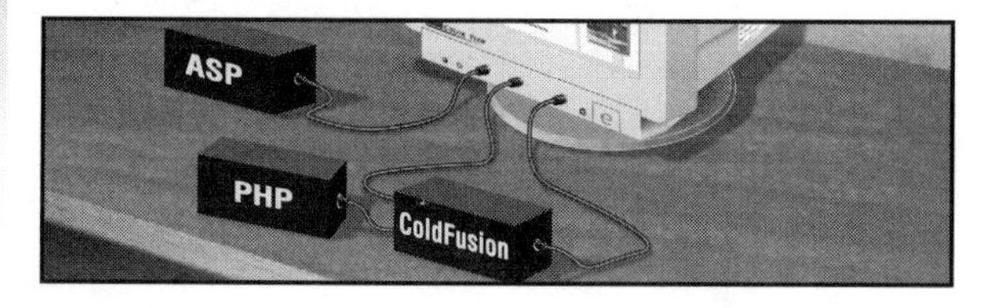

VI MASTERING FLASH MX BASICS

VII ADDING MOVIE ELEMENTS

VIII ANIMATING IN FLASH

IX BUILDING INTERACTIVE ELEMENTS

X FINALIZING YOUR PROJECT

XI ADVANCED FLASH

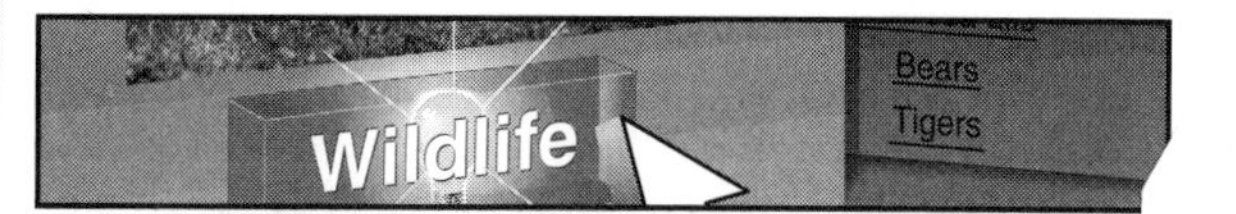

1 USING DREAMWEAVER MX BASICS

1) GETTING STARTED WITH DREAMWEAVER MX

2) EXPLORING DREAMWEAVER BASICS

3) WORKING WITH HTML

4) SETTING UP YOUR WEB SITE

2 ADDING DESIGN ELEMENTS

5) FORMATTING TEXT

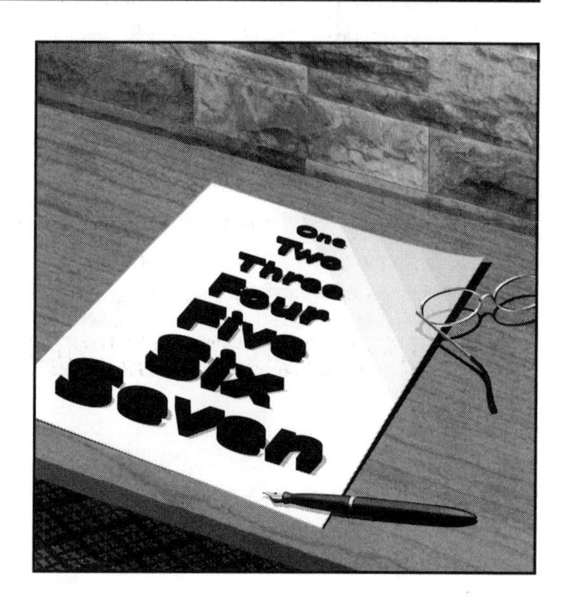

6) WORKING WITH IMAGES AND GRAPHICS

7) CREATING HYPERLINKS

8) CREATING TABLES

TABLE OF CONTENTS

9) CREATING FORMS

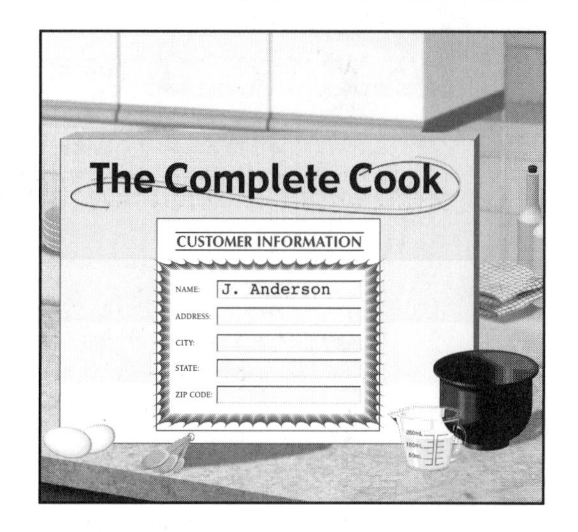

10) DESIGNING WITH FRAMES

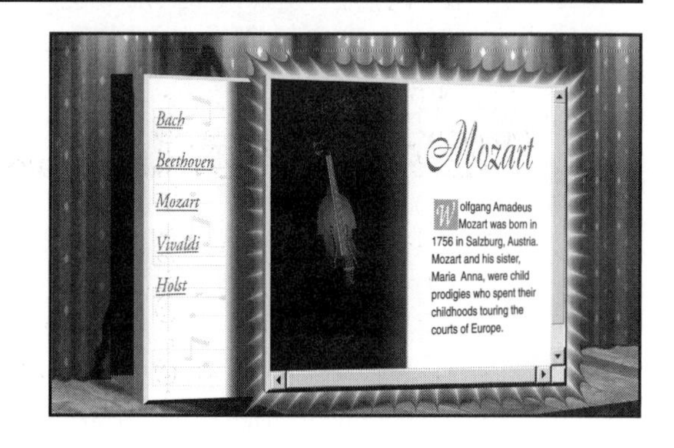

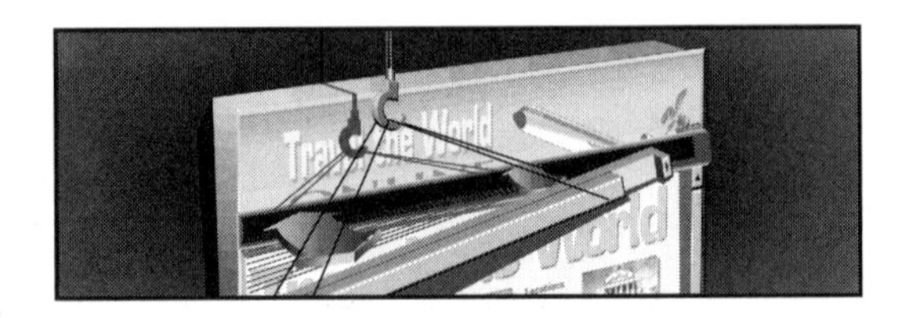

3 ENHANCING YOUR WEB SITE

11) USING SNIPPETS, LIBRARY ITEMS, AND TEMPLATES

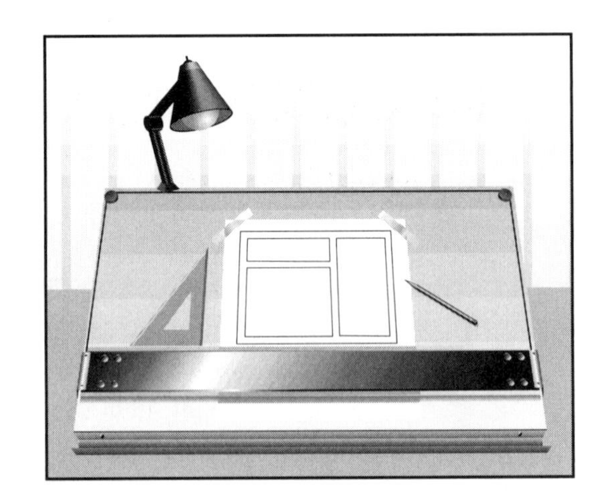

12) IMPLEMENTING STYLE SHEETS AND LAYERS

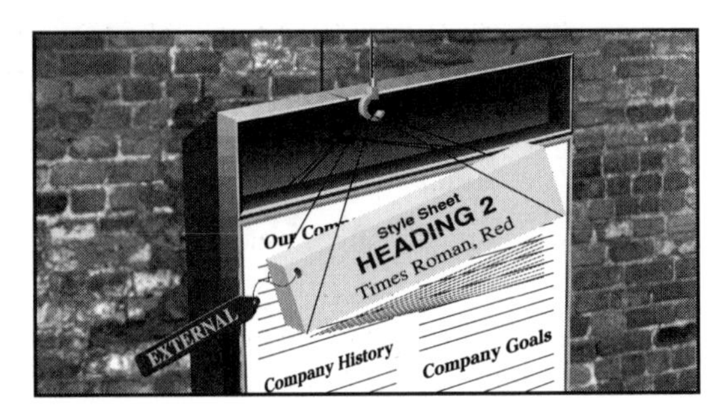

TABLE OF CONTENTS

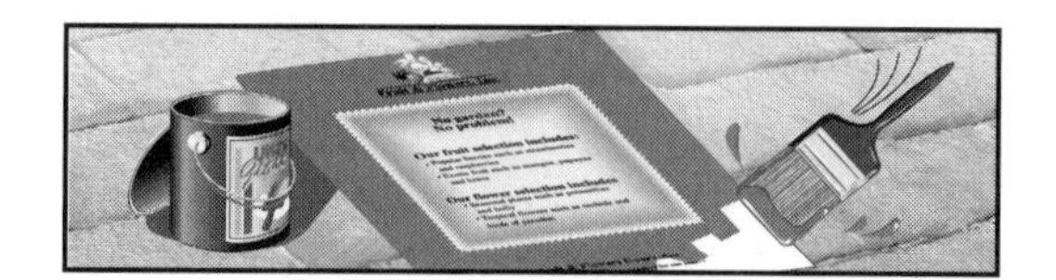

13) IMPLEMENTING BEHAVIORS

14) IMPLEMENTING TIMELINES

4 MANAGING YOUR FINISHED SITE

15) PUBLISHING A WEB SITE

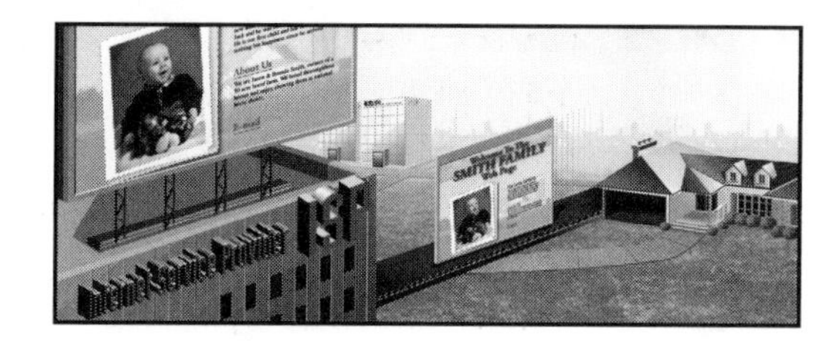

5 CREATING A DYNAMIC SITE

TABLE OF CONTENTS

19) ADVANCED DYNAMIC TOPICS

6 MASTERING FLASH MX BASICS

20) GETTING STARTED WITH FLASH MX

21) CREATING SHAPES AND OBJECTS

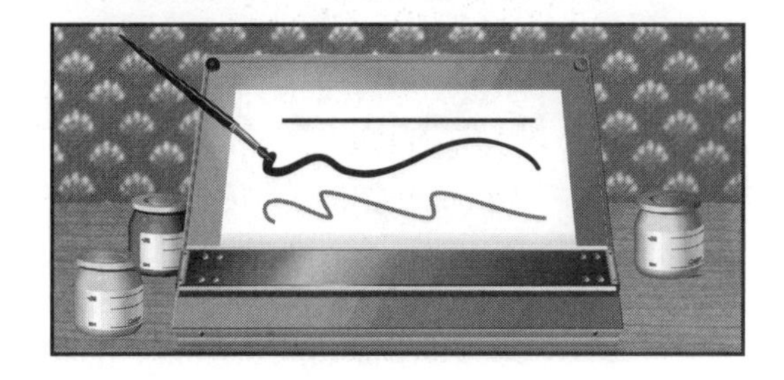

22) ENHANCING AND EDITING OBJECTS

23) WORKING WITH IMPORTED GRAPHICS AND VIDEO

24) WORKING WITH TEXT

TABLE OF CONTENTS

7 ADDING MOVIE ELEMENTS

25) WORKING WITH LAYERS

26) WORKING WITH FLASH SYMBOLS AND INSTANCES

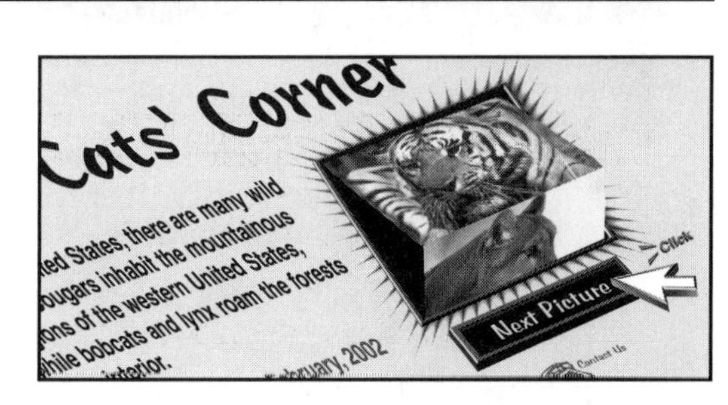

27) CREATING INTERACTIVE BUTTONS

28) ADDING SOUND

8 ANIMATING IN FLASH

29) CREATING ANIMATION IN FLASH

30) CREATING ANIMATION BY TWEENING

9 BUILDING INTERACTIVE ELEMENTS

31) ADDING FLASH ACTIONS

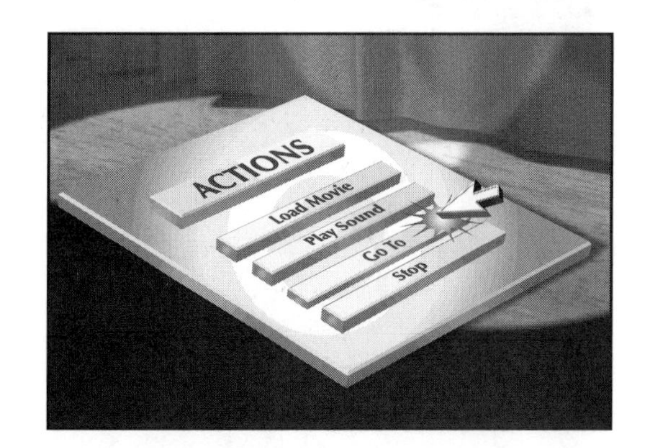

32) MAKING INTERACTIVE MOVIES

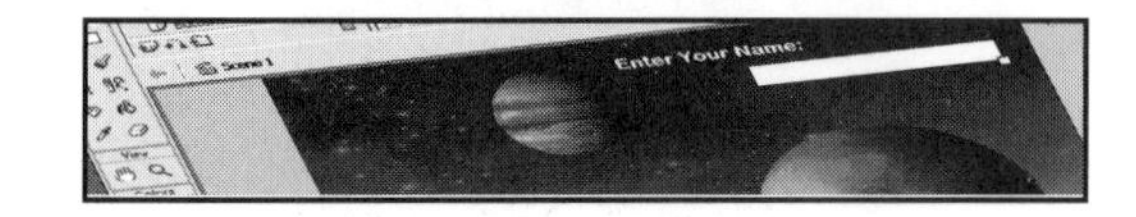

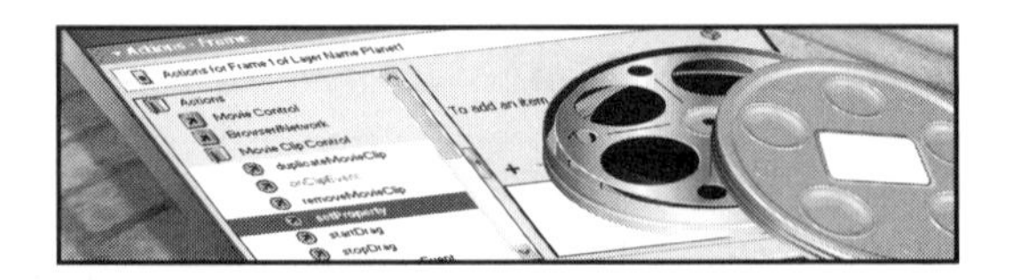

33) WORKING WITH FLASH MX COMPONENTS

10 *FINALIZING YOUR PROJECT*

34) DISTRIBUTING FLASH MOVIES

TABLE OF CONTENTS

11 ADVANCED FLASH

35) BUILDING INTERFACE CONTROLS

36) ENHANCING INTERACTIVITY WITH FLASH

37) CREATING SPECIAL EFFECTS IN FLASH

APPENDIX

SECTION I

1) GETTING STARTED WITH DREAMWEAVER MX

2) EXPLORING DREAMWEAVER BASICS

3) WORKING WITH HTML

4) SETTING UP YOUR WEB SITE

EXPLORE THE WORLD WIDE WEB

The *World Wide Web*, or *Web*, is a global collection of documents located on Internet-connected computers that you can access by using a Web browser. You usually view these documents in the form of Web pages, which are connected to one another by clickable hyperlinks.

Web pages can include text and images, as well as multimedia content such as sound and video. Web pages can also include animated, interactive features created in Flash.

Dreamweaver and the Web

Dreamweaver is a program that enables you to build and create Web pages that feature text, images, and multimedia. Dreamweaver provides an environment in which to organize your Web pages and link them together. Dreamweaver also includes tools that let you transfer the finished files to a Web server where others can view them. Developers who want to create complex, dynamic sites can use Dreamweaver to connect their pages to databases and retrieve information.

HTML Format

HTML, or *Hypertext Markup Language*, is the formatting language you use to create Web pages. Every Web page you see has an associated page of HTML that gives it its structure. You can use Dreamweaver to create Web pages without knowing HTML, because Dreamweaver writes the HTML for you behind the scenes. For more information on HTML, see Chapter 3.

Web Browser

A *Web browser* is a program that downloads Web documents from the Internet, interprets their HTML, and then displays the Web page text and any associated images and multimedia as a Web page. Two popular Web browsers are Microsoft Internet Explorer and Netscape Navigator.

Web Server

A *Web server* is an Internet-connected computer that makes Web documents available to Web browsers. Each Web page that you view on the World Wide Web comes from a Web server somewhere on the Internet. When you are ready to publish your pages on the Web, Dreamweaver can connect to a Web server and transfer your files to it. See Chapter 15 for more information on publishing a Web site.

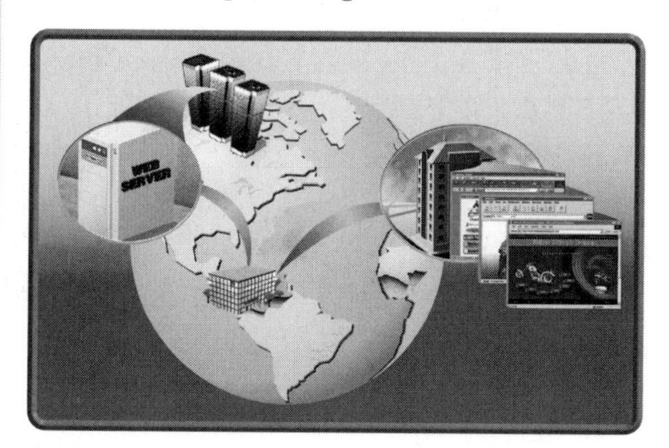

Web Site

A *Web site* is a collection of linked Web pages stored on a Web server. Most Web sites have a *home page* that describes the information located on the Web site and provides a place where people can start their exploration of the site. The pages of a good Web site are intuitively organized and have a common theme. To learn about how to set up a Web site, see Chapter 4.

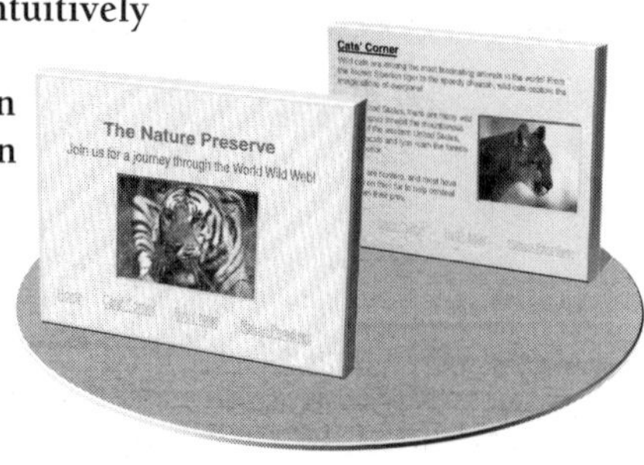

Web Application

A *Web application* is a more advanced type of Web site whose pages are built dynamically as they are requested by a user, instead from static HTML documents. In a Web application, pages are made up of a combination of HTML and additional code, such as ColdFusion Markup Language, Java, or PHP. This extra code allows the pages to serve up different information depending on the type of user accessing the page, the pages visited previously, and other factors. In Web applications, information needed to create a page is often retrieved from a database and then integrated into HTML to create the final page.

TOUR A WEB PAGE

You can communicate your message on the Web in a variety of ways. The following are some of the common elements found on Web pages.

Text

Text is the simplest type of content you can publish on the Web. Perhaps the best thing about text is that practically everyone can view it, no matter what type of browser or Internet connection they have, and it downloads very quickly. Dreamweaver lets you change the size, color, and font of Web-page text and organize it into paragraphs, headings, and lists. See Chapter 5 for information on formatting text in Dreamweaver.

Images

You can digitize photographs, drawings, and logos using a digital camera or scanner and then save them for the Web in image editing programs such as Adobe Photoshop and Macromedia Fireworks. You can then place the images on your Web pages with Dreamweaver. Graphics are a must if you want your pages to stand out visually; complementing your text information with images can help you inform, educate, and entertain with your site. See Chapter 6 for more information on images and graphics.

Hyperlinks

Often simply called *links*, a hyperlink is text or an image that you associate with another file. You can access the other file by clicking the hyperlink. Hyperlinks usually link to other Web pages, but they can also link to other locations on the same page or to other types of files. Text hyperlinks are usually colored and underlined. You can design image hyperlinks in an image editor so that they look like pushable buttons.

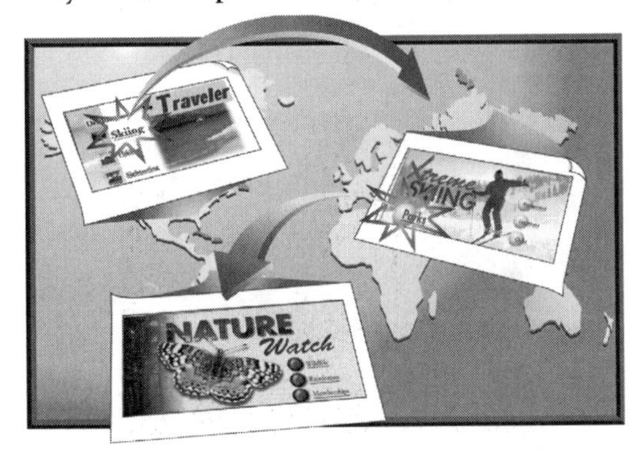

Tables

Tables organize information in columns and rows on your Web page. You can use tables to organize text, images, forms, and other page elements. By turning off a table's borders and setting it to span an entire page, you can use a table to invisibly organize the layout of a page. Dreamweaver's commands give you an easy way to create complex tables. See Chapter 8 for more on tables.

Softball Standings

Team	Games	Wins	Losses	Ties	Points
The Chargers	10	9	1	0	18
Sluggers	10	8	1	1	17
The Champs	10	7	2	1	15
The Eagles	10	5	5	0	10
Barry's Battalion	10	3	7	0	6
The Professionals	10	2	8	0	4
Baseball Bombers	10	1	9	0	2

Forms

Forms reverse the information flow on Web sites — they enable your site's visitors to send information back to you. This information can then be processed using programs called *form handlers*, which can forward the information to an e-mail address, insert it into a database, or use it in other ways. Dreamweaver lets you create forms that include text fields, drop-down menus, radio buttons, and other elements. See Chapter 9 for more information on forms.

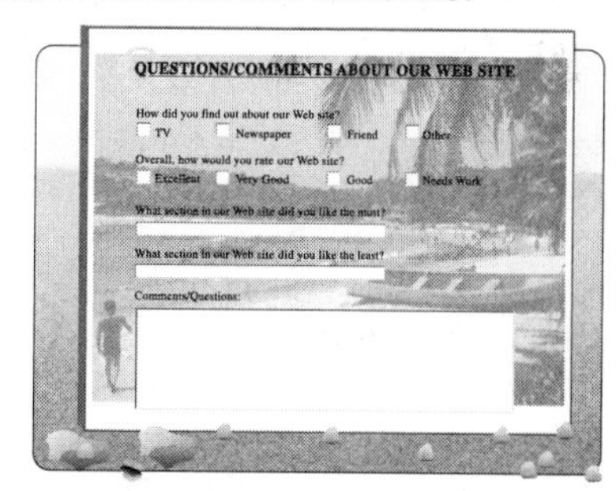
QUESTIONS/COMMENTS ABOUT OUR WEB SITE

How did you find out about our Web site?
TV Newspaper Friend Other

Overall, how would you rate our Web site?
Excellent Very Good Good Needs Work

What section in our Web site did you like the most?

What section in our Web site did you like the least?

Comments/Questions:

Frames

In a framed Web site, the browser window is divided into several rectangular frames, and a different Web page is loaded into each frame. Users can scroll through content in each frame independently of the content in the other frames. You can create hyperlinks that open up pages in other frames. Dreamweaver offers visual tools for building frame-based Web sites. You can learn about those tools in Chapter 10.

Advanced Features

Dreamweaver offers tools that enable you to integrate some of the more advanced Web technologies on your pages. You can apply style sheets, which allow you to customize Web-page text. You can use layers to precisely position and overlap content on a page. You can use JavaScript programming, which can add interactivity to a site. Dreamweaver also has tools for inserting video, sound clips, and Flash animation into Web pages. See Chapter 12 for more on style sheets and layers, Chapter 13 for more on JavaScript programming, and Chapters 29 and 30 for more on Flash animation.

PLAN YOUR WEB SITE

No one would consider building a house without first drawing up blueprints, sourcing construction materials, and doing other preparations. Similarly, doing some offline work on your Web site before you start opening pages, laying out text, and inserting images in Dreamweaver is a very good idea. This preparation helps ensure that your finished Web site looks good and is well organized, and that you have a place to put the Web site online when you are finished building it.

Organize Your Ideas

Build your site on paper before you start building it in Dreamweaver. Make a list of the topics that you want to cover in your site and try to organize those topics into categories that you can then assign to Web pages. Sketching out a site map, with rectangles representing Web pages and arrows representing hyperlinks, helps you visualize the size and scope of your project. Applications such as Microsoft Visio offer advanced tools for diagramming a potential Web site.

Gather Your Content

After you decide what types of Web pages you want to create, you have to generate content to appear on them. This process may involve writing text, shooting and scanning photos, and designing graphics, and may also involve producing multimedia content such as audio and video files. Having lots of content to choose from makes it easier to create pages that are interesting to read and look at. If you do not have the time or inclination to create all the art yourself, you can license images, artwork, and other digital media for use on your site from content distributors. Many of these companies allow you to download licensed content online.

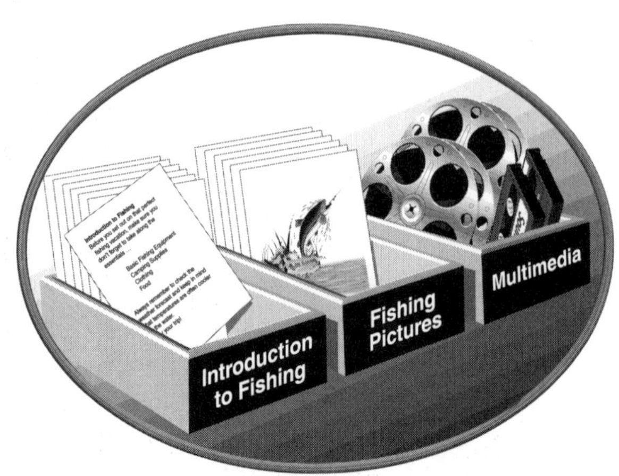

Define Your Audience

Carefully defining your audience helps you decide what kind of content to offer on your Web site. Some advanced Dreamweaver features — such as cascading style sheets and layers — can be viewed using only the most recent versions of Web browsers. Some multimedia content involves files that are too large for users on dial-up modems. Knowing how technologically advanced your audience is can help you decide whether to include more advanced features on your pages.

Choose an Application Platform

If you are creating a dynamic Web site that retrieves information from a database, you need to select and set up certain technologies before you can develop your site. This includes an application server, such as Macromedia ColdFusion or Microsoft .NET, that can process the dynamic code in your pages, plus a database, such as Microsoft Access or Oracle, that stores your dynamic content. See Chapter 17 for more information on setting up a dynamic Web site.

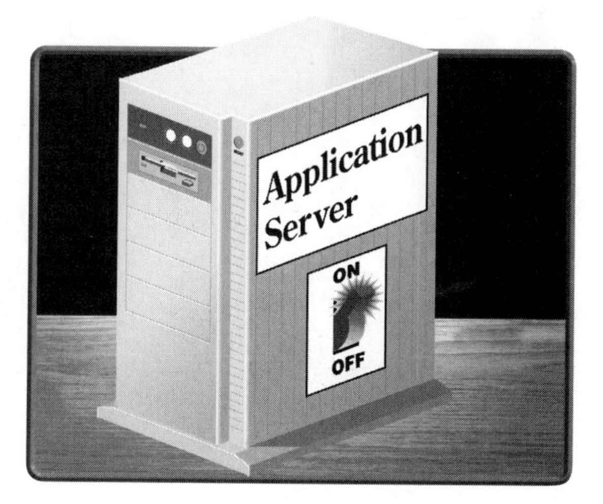

Host Your Finished Web Site

For a user to have access to your finished site on the Web, you need to store, or *host*, the site on a Web server. Most people host their Web sites on a Web server at a commercial *Internet service provider* (ISP) or at their company. Most ISPs charge a monthly fee for a set amount of storage space on their Web servers. Other ISPs offer free hosting to customers in exchange for the ability to place advertising on the Web pages that they serve. If you are deploying a Web application, you will have to find an ISP that runs software that supports your type of application.

DREAMWEAVER FLOATING-WINDOWS WORKSPACE ON A PC

You build Web pages in Dreamweaver on a PC using various windows, panels, and inspectors. In the floating-windows workspace, also known as the Dreamweaver 4 workspace, these elements are displayed as windows that you can arrange by clicking and dragging. To switch Windows workspaces, see page 18.

You build a page by inserting and arranging elements in the main Document window. Other accessory windows allow you to format and stylize those elements.

Insert Panel

Enables you to add images, tables, and media to your Web pages without opening menus.

Menus

Contain the commands for using Dreamweaver. Dreamweaver duplicates many of these commands in windows, panels, and inspectors.

Panel

Enables you to manage a feature of your Web page or apply particular types of commands.

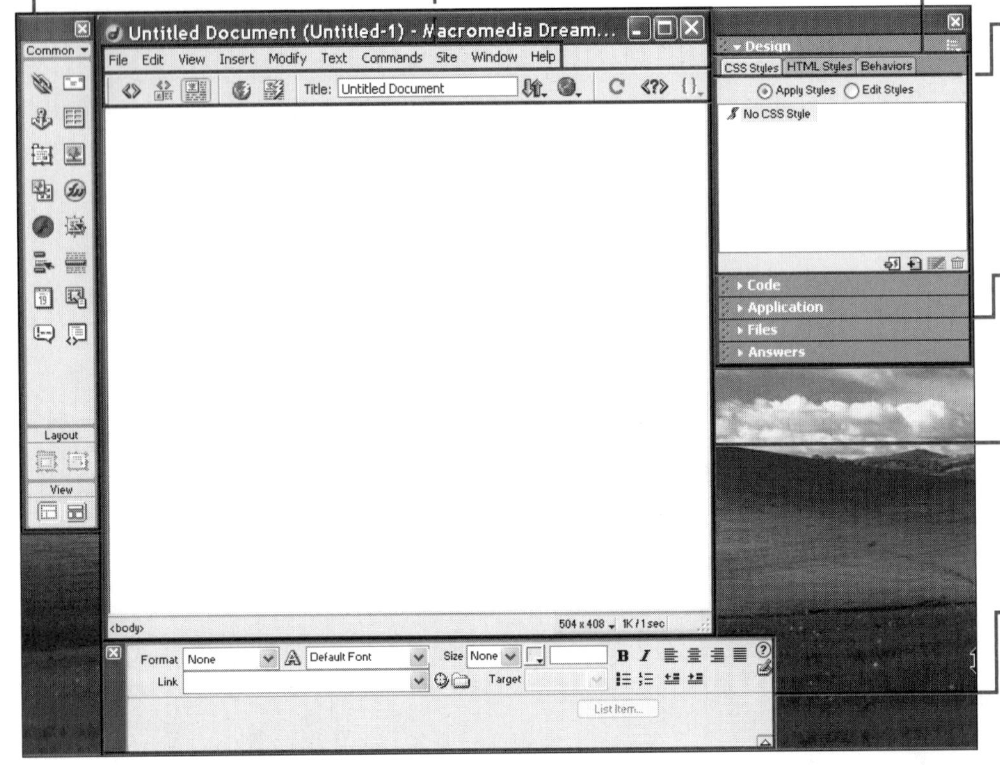

Document Toolbar

Enables you to switch views of the Document window. Also contains shortcuts to many Document window commands and a text field where you can type a page's title.

Panel Headings

Organize similar types of panels into groups. You click the heading titles to view or hide the panels.

Document Window

Area where you insert and arrange text, images, and other elements of your Web page.

Properties Inspector

Enables you to view and modify properties of text and other objects that are selected in the Document window.

DREAMWEAVER MX WORKSPACE ON A PC

You build Web pages in Dreamweaver on a PC using various windows, panels, and inspectors. In the MX workspace, these elements are integrated into one larger application window. To switch Windows workspaces, see page 18.

You build a page by inserting and arranging elements in the main Document window. Other accessory windows allow you to format and stylize those elements.

Menus

Contain the commands for using Dreamweaver. Dreamweaver duplicates many of these commands in windows, panels, and inspectors.

Insert Bar

Enables you to add images, tables, and media to your Web pages without opening menus. It also allows you to switch layout views.

Document Toolbar

Allows you to switch views of the Document window. Also contains shortcuts to many Document window commands and a text field where you can type a page's title.

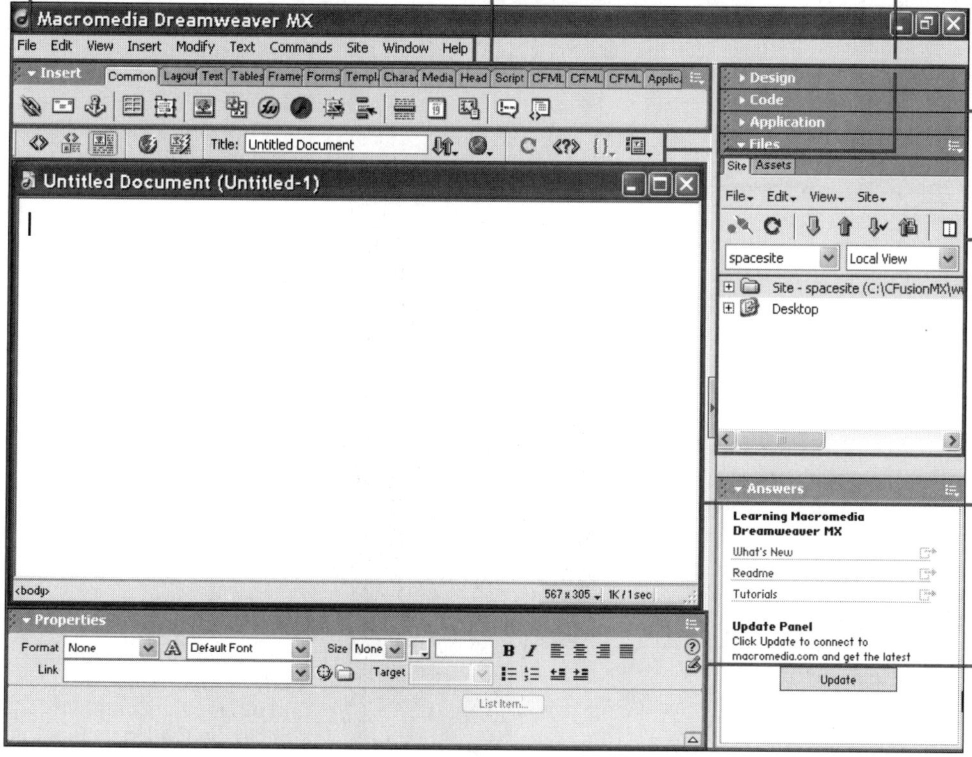

Panel Headings

Organize similar types of panels. You click the headings to view or hide the panels.

Panel

Allows you to manage a feature of your Web page or apply particular types of commands.

Document Window

Area where you insert and arrange the text, images, and other elements of your Web page.

Properties Inspector

Enables you to view and modify properties of text and other objects that are selected in the Document window.

DREAMWEAVER WORKSPACE ON A MACINTOSH

You build Web pages in Dreamweaver on a Macintosh using various windows, panels, and inspectors. On the Macintosh, you are limited to the floating-windows interface. In Windows, you have a choice between the floating-windows workspace and the MX workspace.

You build a page by inserting and arranging elements in the main Document window. Other accessory windows allow you to format and stylize those elements.

Menus

Contain the commands for using Dreamweaver. Dreamweaver duplicates many of these commands in windows, panels, and inspectors.

Insert Panel

Enables you to add images, tables, and media to your Web pages without opening menus. It also allows you to switch layout views.

Document Toolbar

Allows you to switch views of the Document window. Also contains shortcuts to many Document window commands and a text field where you can type a page's title.

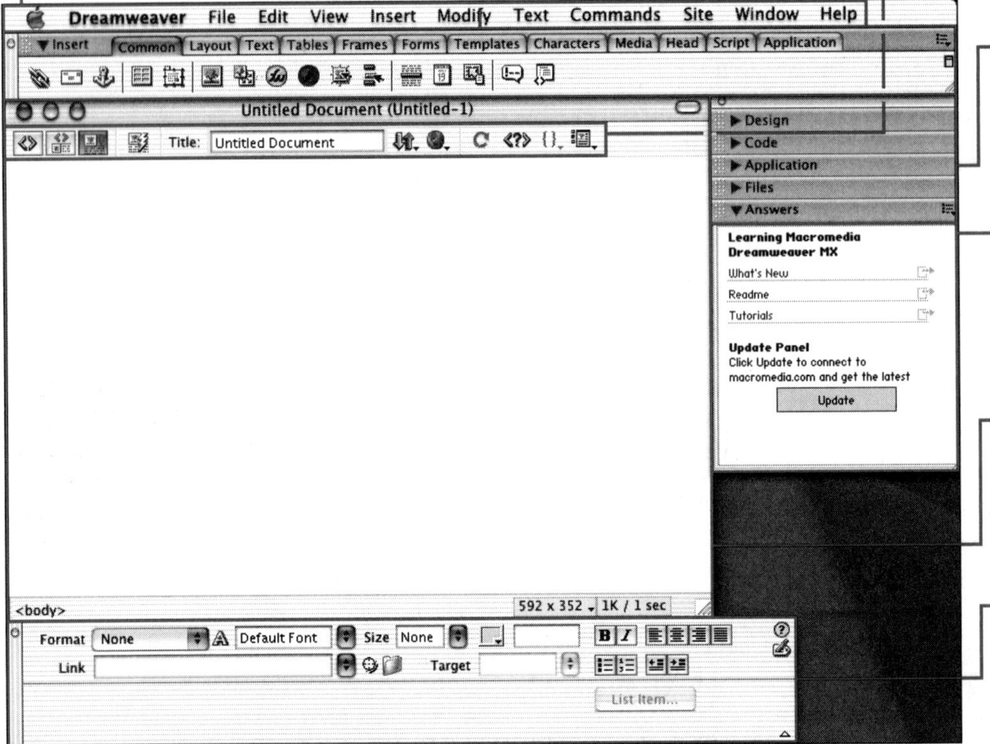

Panel Headings

Organize similar types of panels. You click the headings to view or hide the panels.

Panel

Allows you to manage a feature of your Web page or apply particular types of commands.

Document Window

Area where you insert and arrange the text, images, and other elements of your Web page in this window.

Properties Inspector

Enables you to view and modify properties of text and other objects that are selected in the Document window.

START DREAMWEAVER ON A MACINTOSH

You can start Dreamweaver on a Macintosh and begin creating documents that you can publish on the Web. The default place to install Dreamweaver on a Macintosh is in the root folder of your computer's startup hard drive.

Starting Dreamweaver opens a blank Document window, which serves as a blank canvas on which you can add text, images, and other elements for your Web page. You can access accessory windows, known as panels and inspectors, under the Window menu.

If you are new to Dreamweaver, you can become familiar with the application by completing one or more tutorials. You can access the tutorials under the Help menu. Tutorials take you step-by-step through common Web-design techniques such as designing a page layout with tables, creating an image map, and formatting text with style sheets.

In addition to running on the Macintosh OS X platform, Dreamweaver MX also runs on Macintosh OS 9. Running the application on Macintosh requires at least 96MB of RAM and 275MB of hard disk space.

START DREAMWEAVER ON A MACINTOSH

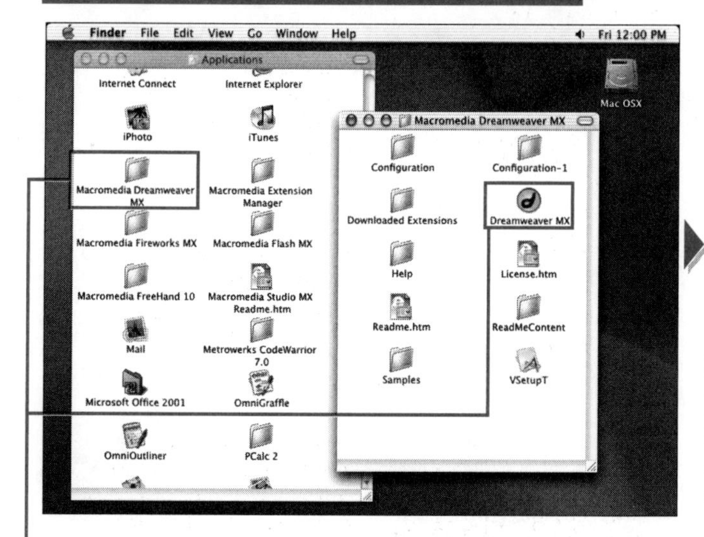

1 Open the Macromedia folder on your hard drive.

2 Double-click the Dreamweaver MX icon (●).

Note: The location of the Dreamweaver folder depends on how you installed your software.

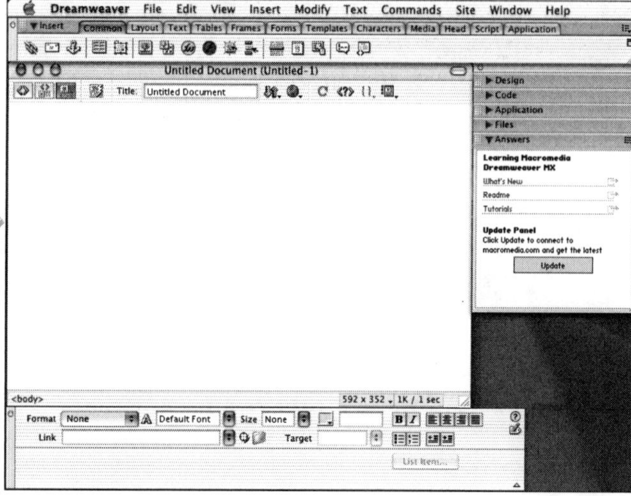

■ Dreamweaver launches an untitled Web page in a Document window.

START DREAMWEAVER ON A PC

You can start Dreamweaver on a PC and begin creating documents that you can publish on the Web. If you installed Dreamweaver's files in the default locations, you should be able to access the program in the Macromedia folder under the All Programs menu in the Start menu.

Starting Dreamweaver opens a blank Document window, that serves as a blank canvas on which you can add text, images, and other elements for your Web page. You can access accessory windows, known as panels and inspectors, under the Window menu.

If you are new to Dreamweaver, you can become familiar with the application by completing one or more tutorials. You can access the tutorials under the Help menu. Tutorials take you step-by-step through common Web-design techniques such as designing a page layout with tables, creating an image map, and formatting text with style sheets.

Windows 98, 2000, NT, ME, and XP all support Dreamweaver MX. Running the application on Windows requires at least 96MB of RAM and 275MB of hard disk space.

START DREAMWEAVER ON A PC

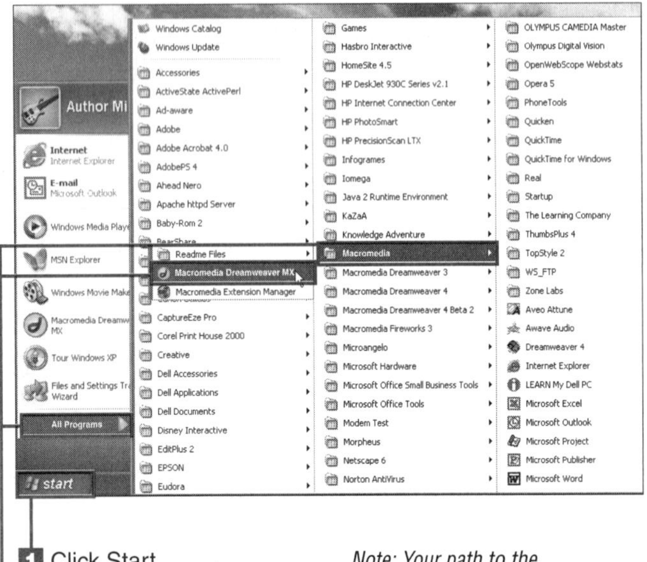

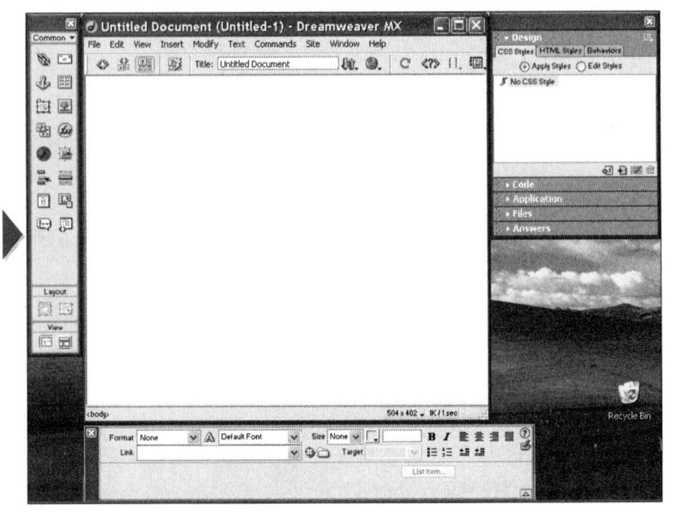

1 Click Start.

2 Click All Programs.

3 Click Macromedia.

4 Click Macromedia Dreamweaver MX.

Note: Your path to the Dreamweaver application may vary depending on how you installed your software.

■ Dreamweaver launches an untitled Web page in a Document window.

GET ANSWERS ONLINE

The Answers panel gives you quick access to useful Dreamweaver information from the Macromedia support site. The panel enables you to download up-to-date information from Macromedia and view it in the Dreamweaver application. You can click the Update button in the panel to retrieve the latest information.

After you update the Answers panel, a drop-down menu appears, letting you choose from various help categories. *Getting Started* features local support documents and tutorials that help you begin using Dreamweaver. *TechNotes* connects you to frequently asked questions about technical topics on the Macromedia site. It also enables you to search the Macromedia support site from Dreamweaver. *Extensions* accesses the most recent Dreamweaver extensions available online, and also lets you search Macromedia's library of extensions. Written by third parties, extensions are software add-ons that enhance the functionality of Dreamweaver.

You can configure the search functionality in the Answers panel under the *Settings* category. You can specify that the panel displays search results in the panel itself, or in a separate browser window.

GET ANSWERS ONLINE

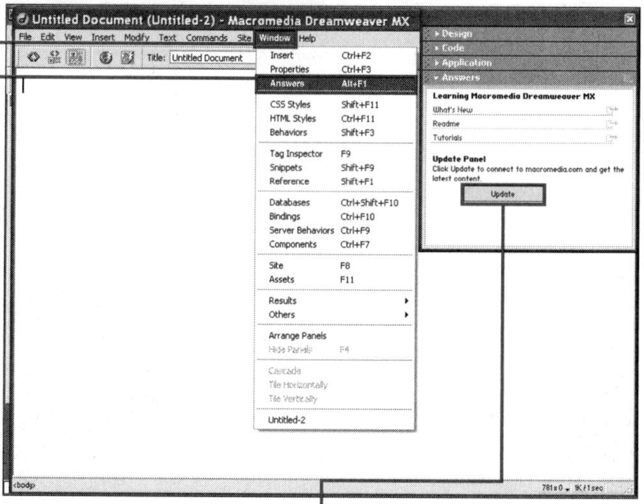

1 Click Window.

2 Click Answers.

■ The Answers panel opens.

3 Click Update.

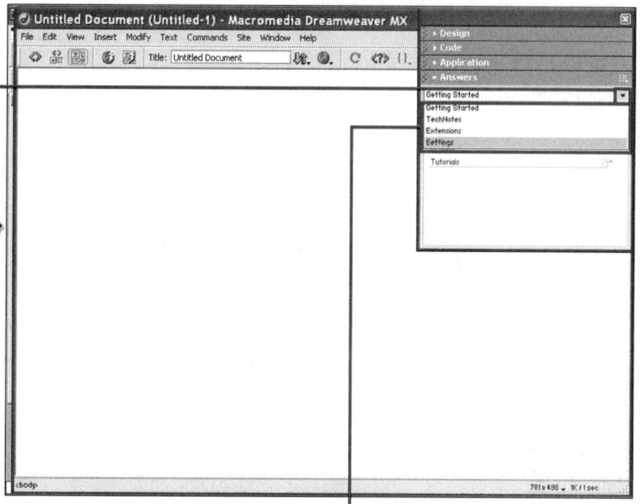

■ Dreamweaver connects to the Macromedia Web site and downloads the latest support information.

4 Click ▾.

5 Click a category.

■ Dreamweaver displays links to online support information.

GET HELP

Dreamweaver comes with extensive Help documentation that is installed along with the application. After opening the Help documentation, you can switch back and forth between Dreamweaver and the Help window to answer questions you may have, learn new functions, and solve many of the problems that may arise when you are using the application.

The Help documentation is tightly integrated into the application. Clicking the Help command in the different window menus opens up information specific to that window.

In addition to the Help documentation, the What's New feature offers an interactive overview of just-introduced Dreamweaver topics, including using the application's new design and coding tools, and creating dynamic Web sites that interact with databases. Click Help and then What's New to access this feature.

You can also hone your Web-building skills with Tutorials, which take you step-by-step through common tasks you may encounter when building a Web site. Click Help and then Tutorials to access them.

If you find it more convenient to have hard-copy information to refer to as you use Dreamweaver, you can click the print button at the top of the Help pages to print topics on your printer.

GET HELP

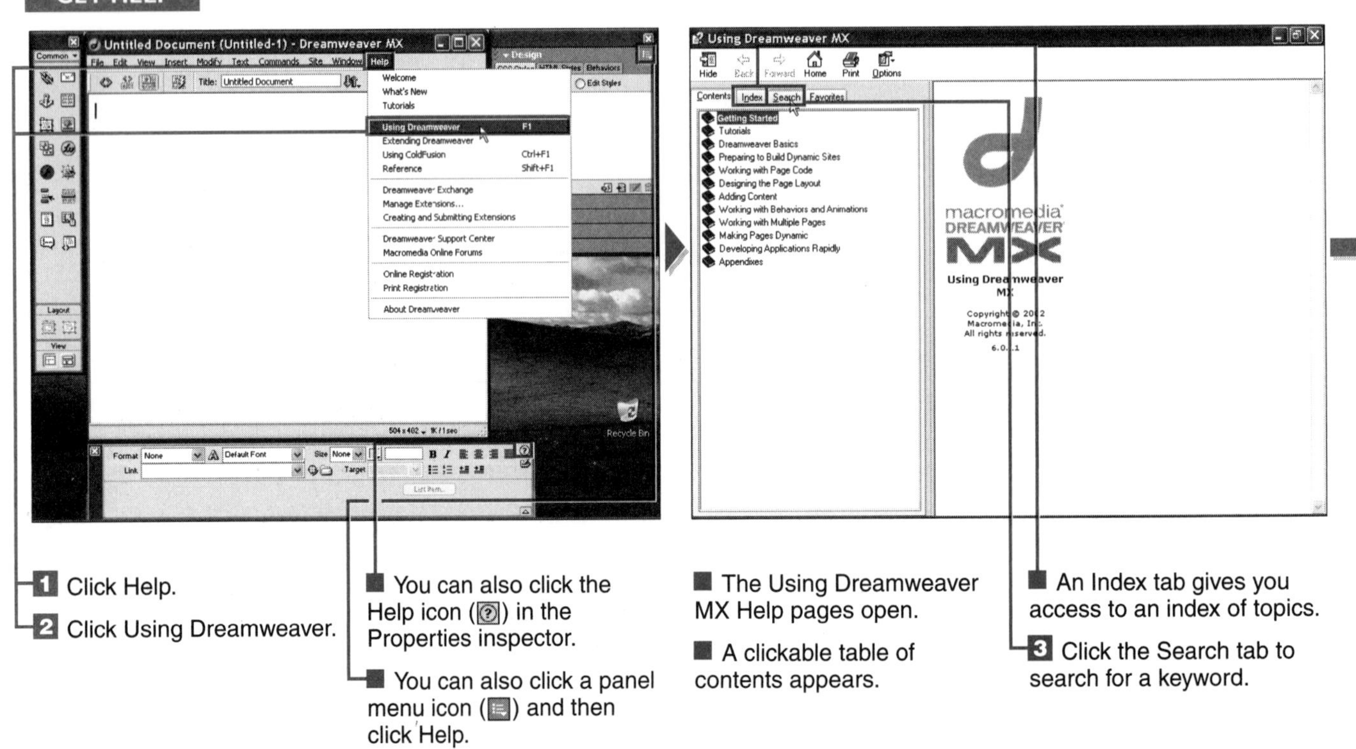

1 Click Help.

2 Click Using Dreamweaver.

■ You can also click the Help icon (?) in the Properties inspector.

■ You can also click a panel menu icon (≡) and then click Help.

■ The Using Dreamweaver MX Help pages open.

■ A clickable table of contents appears.

■ An Index tab gives you access to an index of topics.

3 Click the Search tab to search for a keyword.

How can I find help online?

✔ Visiting Macromedia's Web site is the best way to get the most up-to-date information about Dreamweaver support as well as reports of any bugs that may exist in the program. You can click Help and then Dreamweaver Support Center to view online help.

How can I learn about extending Dreamweaver's capabilities?

✔ Users who know how to program in JavaScript or C can create custom objects, commands, and other features in Dreamweaver. Click Help and then Extending Dreamweaver to learn more. You can also obtain add-ons that other programmers have written for Dreamweaver at Macromedia's Dreamweaver Exchange. You can access this by clicking Help and then Dreamweaver Exchange.

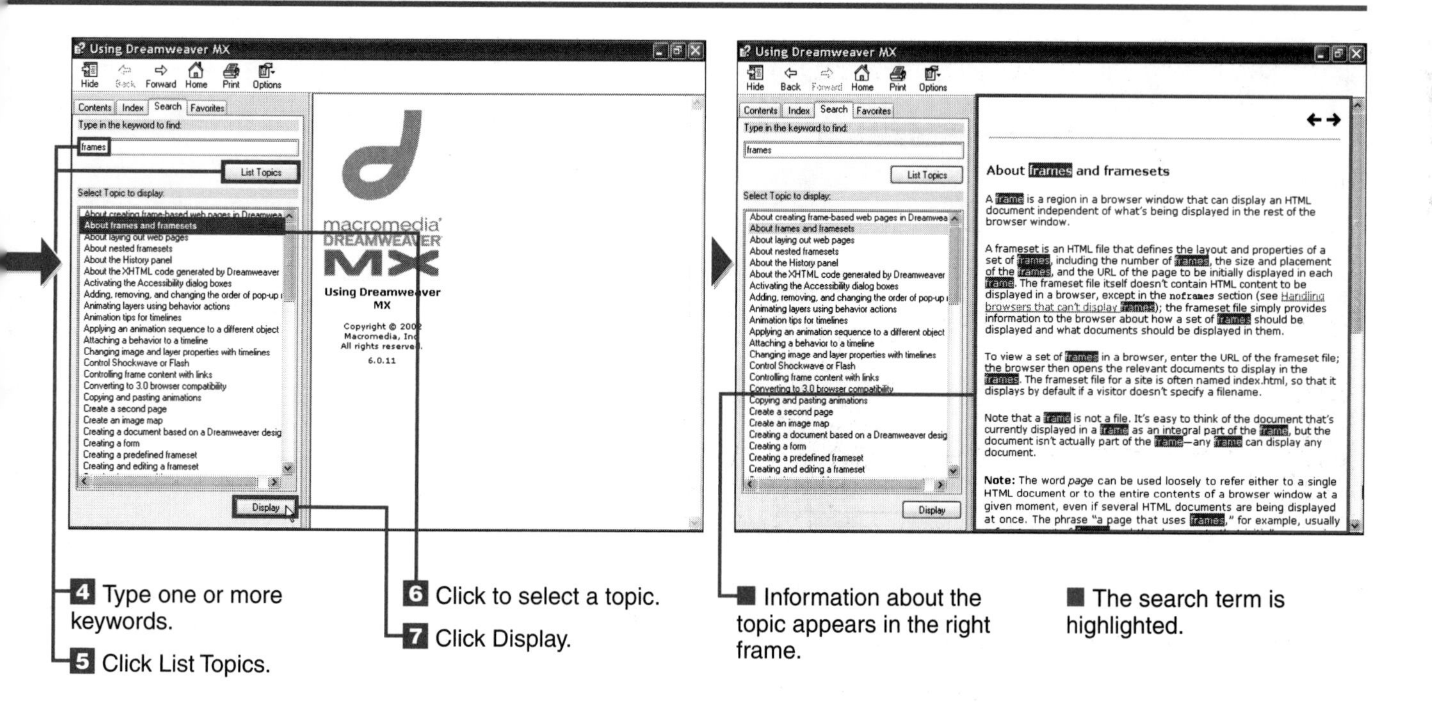

4 Type one or more keywords.

5 Click List Topics.

6 Click to select a topic.

7 Click Display.

■ Information about the topic appears in the right frame.

■ The search term is highlighted.

SWITCH DREAMWEAVER WORKSPACES ON A PC

When you start Dreamweaver MX on a PC for the first time, a window appears allowing you to choose between two Dreamweaver workspaces. The floating-window workspace, also known as the Dreamweaver 4 workspace, features windows and panels arranged in free-floating windows. The Dreamweaver MX workspace features windows and panels integrated into a larger application window.

After initially selecting a workspace to build pages in, you can switch to the other workspace in Preferences. Users who are accustomed to working with Dreamweaver 4 may find it easier working in the floating-window workspace, which was the standard in version 4.

In Dreamweaver MX on the Macintosh, only the floating-window workspace is available. The user does not have a choice of workspaces. The look and feel of the Dreamweaver MX workspace is shared with Macromedia Flash MX and Fireworks MX, so working across these applications can be easier. One of the noticeable changes in the MX workspace is the Insert Panel buttons, which are organized horizontally across the top of the Document window.

SWITCH DREAMWEAVER WORKSPACES ON A PC

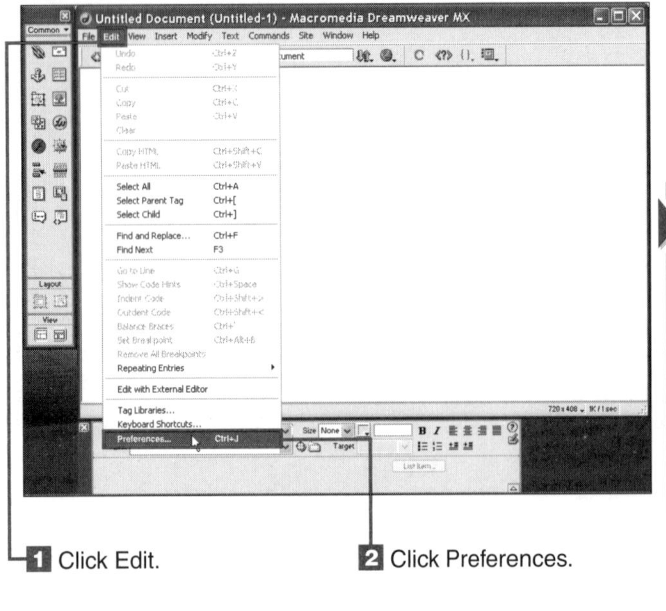

1 Click Edit.

2 Click Preferences.

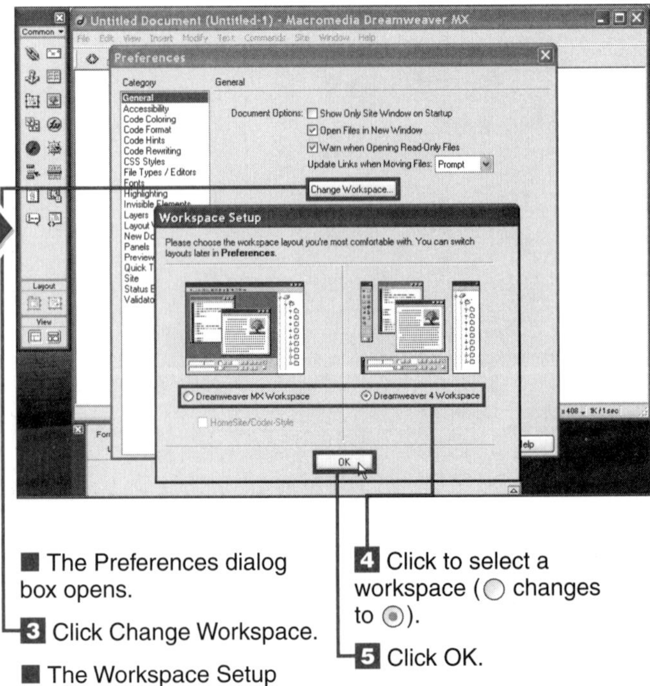

■ The Preferences dialog box opens.

3 Click Change Workspace.

■ The Workspace Setup dialog box appears.

4 Click to select a workspace (○ changes to ◉).

5 Click OK.

What is HomeSite/Coder-Style?

✔ The Dreamweaver MX HomeSite/Coder-Style workspace option is similar to the regular Dreamweaver MX interface but with the panel groups docked on the left. This is similar to the interface used by Macromedia HomeSite and Macromedia ColdFusion Studio. The Document window also shows Code View by default in the document window. This workspace can be useful for HomeSite or ColdFusion Studio users who want a familiar workspace layout.

How do I switch between documents in the MX workspace?

✔ Just like in the Dreamweaver 4 workspace, you can use the Window menu to switch between open documents. If the documents are not maximized, they float as independent windows and you can click the windows to switch between them. If the documents are maximized, there is a tab in the lower left corner for each document that is open. You click the tabs to switch documents.

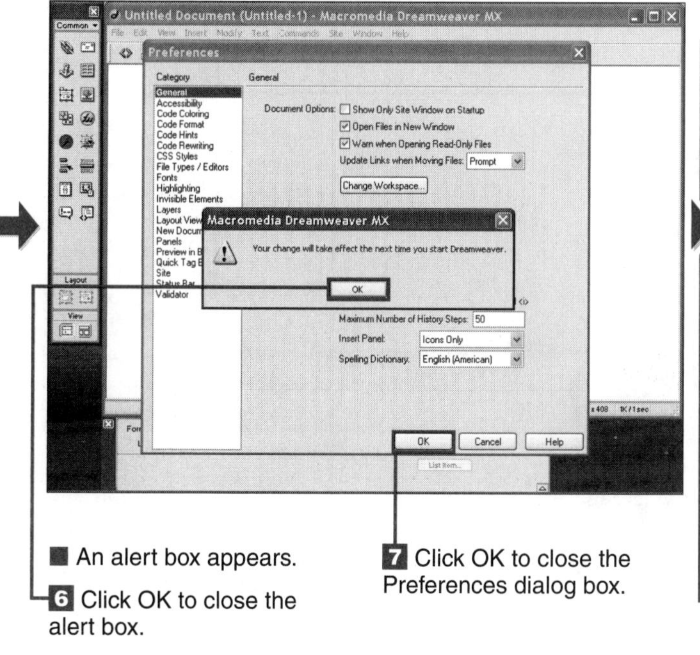

■ An alert box appears.

6 Click OK to close the alert box.

7 Click OK to close the Preferences dialog box.

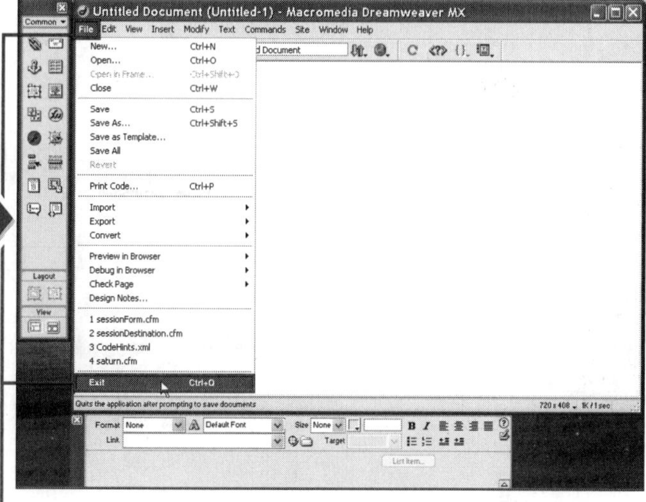

8 Click File.

9 Click Exit.

10 Restart Dreamweaver.

Note: To start Dreamweaver, see page 13 or 14.

ACCESS DREAMWEAVER WINDOWS

You work in a variety of windows when building Web pages in Dreamweaver. The main window is the Document window, where you insert and arrange the different elements of your Web pages. Dreamweaver also has accessory windows, called *inspectors* and *panels*, that display information and hold commands specific to different elements on your Web page.

When you are designing a page, you most likely keep the Document window open at all times and open and close the inspectors and panels as you need them. Dreamweaver has commands for opening and closing all the inspectors and panels under the Window menu.

Dreamweaver organizes its panels, of which there are dozens, into tabbed groups. You can display or hide a group of panels by clicking the group title bar that appears across the top of the panels. You can detach a group of panels from the other groups by clicking and dragging the group heading. To reorganize the different panel groups, see page 27 for more information.

Note that Dreamweaver arranges windows slightly differently depending on which workspace you work in. See pages 10-12 for details about workspaces.

ACCESS DREAMWEAVER WINDOWS

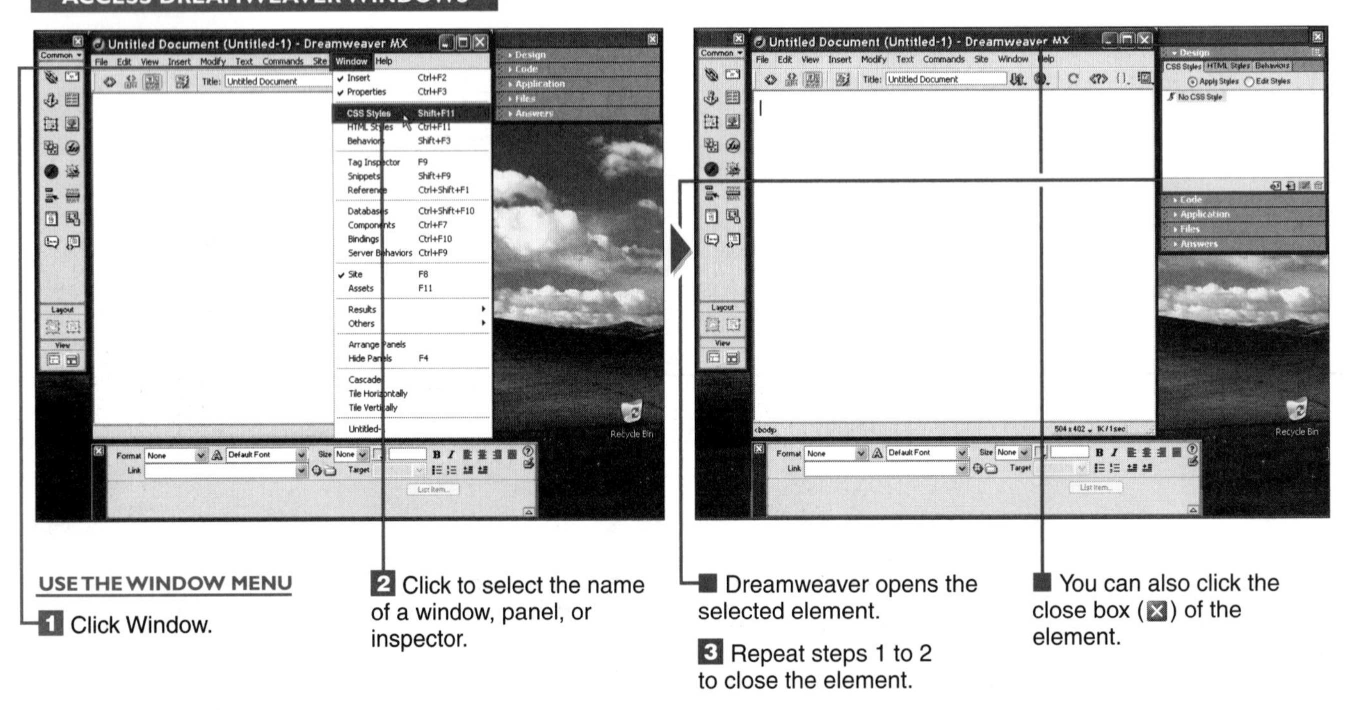

USE THE WINDOW MENU

1 Click Window.

2 Click to select the name of a window, panel, or inspector.

■ Dreamweaver opens the selected element.

3 Repeat steps 1 to 2 to close the element.

■ You can also click the close box (☒) of the element.

How do I move or resize windows, panels, and inspectors?

✔ You can move windows, panels, and inspectors by clicking and dragging their title bars. You can resize them by clicking and dragging their edges.

Is there a quick way to reorganize the elements in my workspace?

✔ You can click Window and then Arrange Panels to automatically rearrange the windows, panels, and inspectors to their default positions in the Dreamweaver workspace.

What is the Launcher?

✔ The Launcher is a set of buttons that appears on the right side of the Document window status bar. Clicking the buttons enables you to view and hide commonly used panels. You can open the Launcher by clicking the Show Icons in Panels and Launcher check box in the Panels category of the Preferences dialog box. See page 32 for more information.

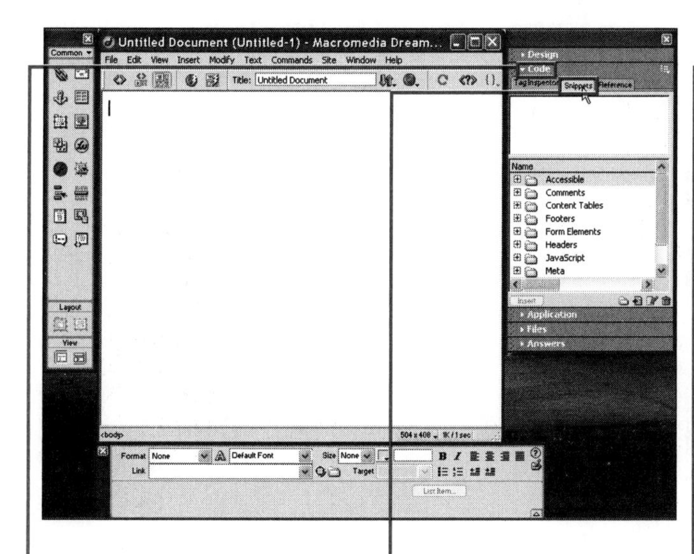

USE A PANEL TITLE BAR

1 Click the title of a panel group.

■ The group of panels opens.

2 Click a panel tab.

■ The panel moves to the front of the group for viewing.

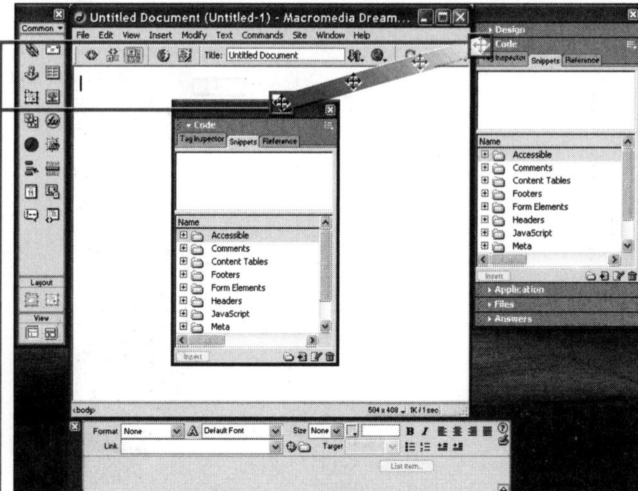

MAKE A PANEL GROUP FREE-FLOATING

1 Click the left edge of a panel group title bar.

■ The cursor changes to ✥.

2 Drag the title bar.

■ The panel group detaches from the other groups.

Note: You can detach a panel from a panel group by clicking and dragging its tab.

EXPLORE AND ADJUST THE DOCUMENT WINDOW

The Document window is the main workspace in Dreamweaver, where you insert and arrange the text, images, and other elements of your Web page. For every page you open in Dreamweaver, you have a Document window.

The Document window has two views. Most of your work is probably done in Design view. In Design view, the Document window displays a WYSIWYG — What Your See Is What You Get — version of your Web page, letting you work with your page in approximately the form it takes when displayed in the browser. You can also switch to Code view, in which you view and work with raw HTML in the Document window. Dreamweaver also has a Code and Design view, where you see both the Design view and Code view at the same time. Learn more about the different views in Chapter 3.

To help make sure your Web pages conform to commonly used monitor settings, you can automatically set the height and width of your Document window using the status bar. You can also turn rulers on in the Document window to help keep track of Web page dimensions.

EXPLORE AND ADJUST THE DOCUMENT WINDOW

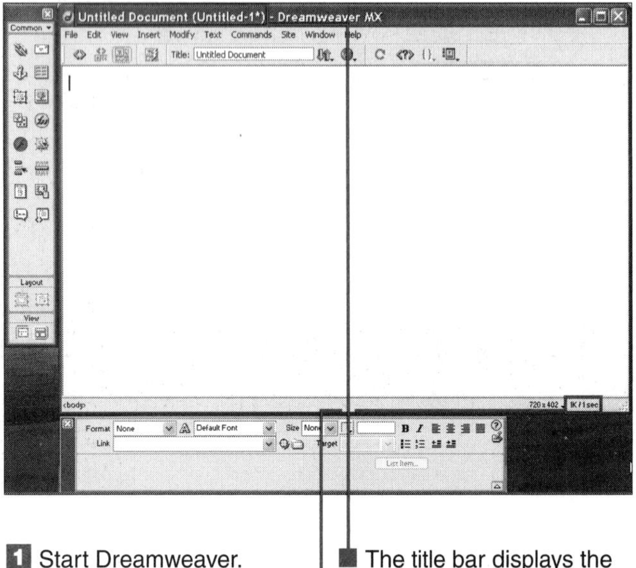

1 Start Dreamweaver.

Note: To start Dreamweaver, see page 13 or 14.

■ A blank Document window opens.

■ The title bar displays the title and filename of the document.

■ The status bar displays the file size and estimated download time for the page.

2 Click inside the Document window.

3 Type some text.

■ The text appears in the Document window approximately as it does when you open the page in a Web browser.

4 Click the Document window size menu.

■ The menu lists preset sizes that mimic the dimensions of Web browser windows at common monitor settings.

5 Click to select a window size.

How can I customize my view of the Document window?

✔ In addition to using the commands found in the toolbar, you can use various commands in the View menu. For example, commands in the Visual Aids submenu let you turn on and off table, layer, and frame borders; image map information; and invisible elements such as named anchors and layer icons. Commands under the Tracing Image submenu enable you to load an image beneath your page content to serve as a layout guide. This lets you design a page mock-up in an image editor and then use it as a guide for your Dreamweaver design.

What are some of the Web-page features that do not appear in Dreamweaver as they do in a Web-browser window?

✔ Some of the features that do not appear as they do in a browser include behaviors and images that are referenced on an external Web server. Also, hyperlinks appear colored and underlined in the Document window but are not clickable. To view and test these features, preview your page in a Web browser. See page 58 for more information.

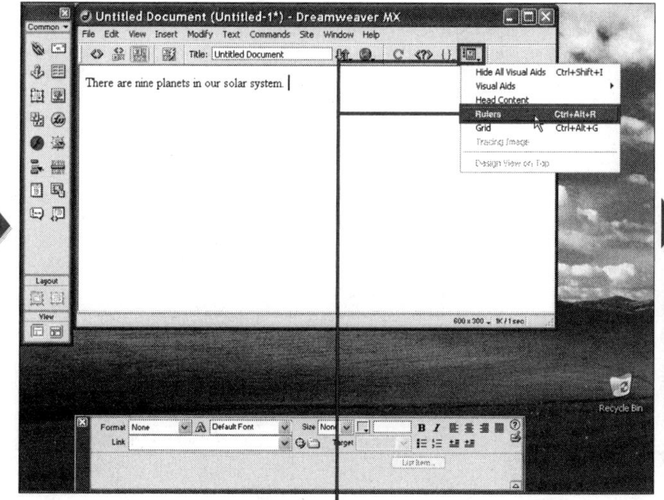

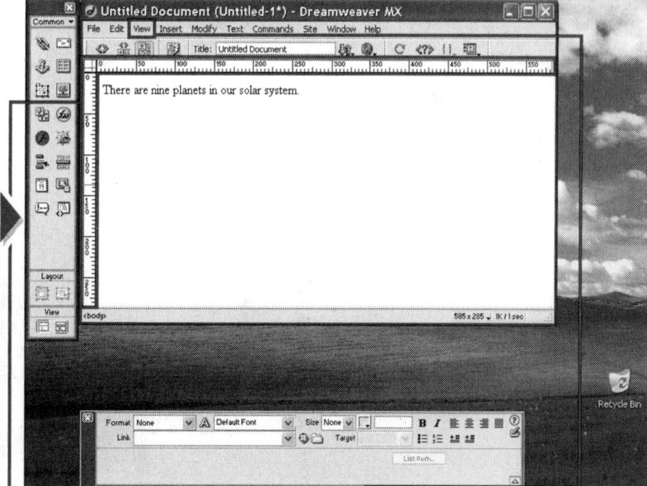

■ The window readjusts its dimensions to the selected setting.

■ The toolbar at the top of the Document window gives you easy access to various commands.

6 Click the View Options button ( ).

7 Click Rulers.

■ Rulers appear at the top and on the side of the Document window. The ruler units are set to pixels.

■ You can change the ruler units by clicking View, Rulers, and then a units setting.

USING THE PROPERTIES INSPECTOR

The Properties inspector enables you to view the properties associated with the object or text currently selected in the Document window. Text fields, drop-down menus, buttons, and other form elements in the Properties inspector allow you to modify these properties.

The appearance of the Properties inspector changes as you select different elements of your page, because different elements have different properties. For example, text elements have different properties than image elements.

The Properties inspector has two modes: standard and expanded. The standard mode shows only the most commonly used properties for a selected element. In most cases, the expanded version shows all of an element's properties. The screen shots in this book show the Properties inspector in expanded mode.

How do I access help in the Properties inspector?

✔ For more information about different properties, you can click the Question Mark (?) in the inspector to open the help documentation for Dreamweaver.

How do I switch between the standard and expanded modes?

✔ You can click ▾ in the lower right corner to switch between the standard and expanded modes.

USING THE PROPERTIES INSPECTOR

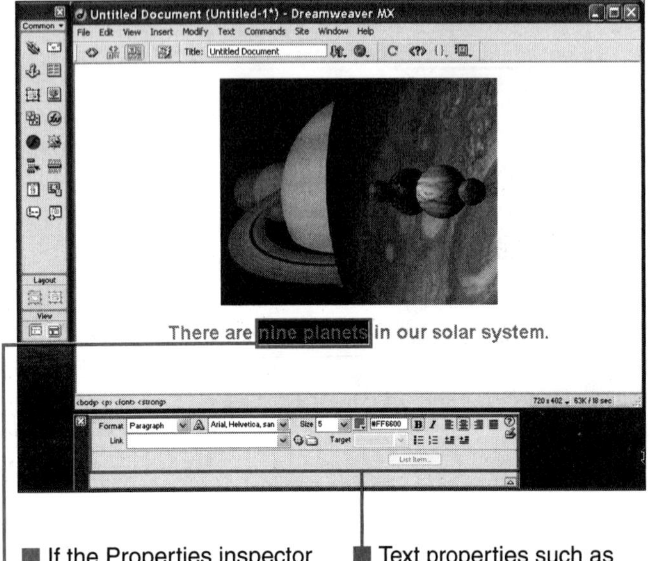

■ If the Properties inspector is not open, click Window and then Properties to open it.

1 Click and drag to select some text.

■ Text properties such as format, size, and alignment appear.

■ You can change options in the inspector to modify the text.

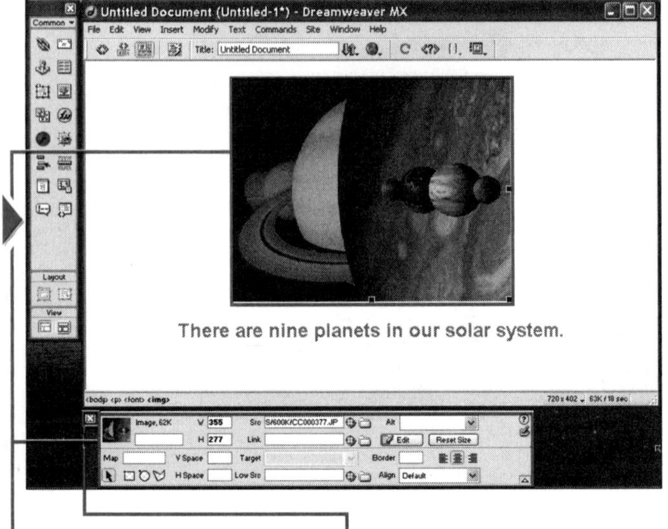

2 Click an image.

■ Image properties such as dimensions, filename, and alignment appear.

■ You can change options in the inspector to modify the image.

3 Click the Close button (☒) in the upper-left corner of the Properties inspector to close it.

USING THE INSERT PANEL

The Insert panel enables you to create objects such as images, tables, and layers and then insert them into the Document window. The panel has a drop-down menu at the top, allowing you to view different sets of object-insertion buttons.

For most Web-building tasks, you use the buttons under the *Common* category that enable you to insert images, tables, layers, and other common objects. For more advanced HTML features you can switch to the *Frames*, *Forms*, or *Head* categories.

If you write HTML by hand, the Text category gives you shortcuts for inserting common HTML tags. For dynamic Web sites, there is an *Application* category that enables you to insert dynamic elements such as recordsets, dynamic tables, and dynamic text into your Web page.

Most of the time, a dialog box appears after you click an Insert panel button, allowing you to specify the characteristics of the object that you are inserting.

In the Dreamweaver MX workspace, the Insert panel buttons appear in the Insert bar, which stretches horizontally above the Document window.

Can I bypass the dialog box that appears when I click an Insert panel button?

✔ You can bypass this dialog box and insert a generic object by holding down the Ctrl (Option) key when you click the panel button. This works for some, but not all, objects.

USING THE INSERT PANEL

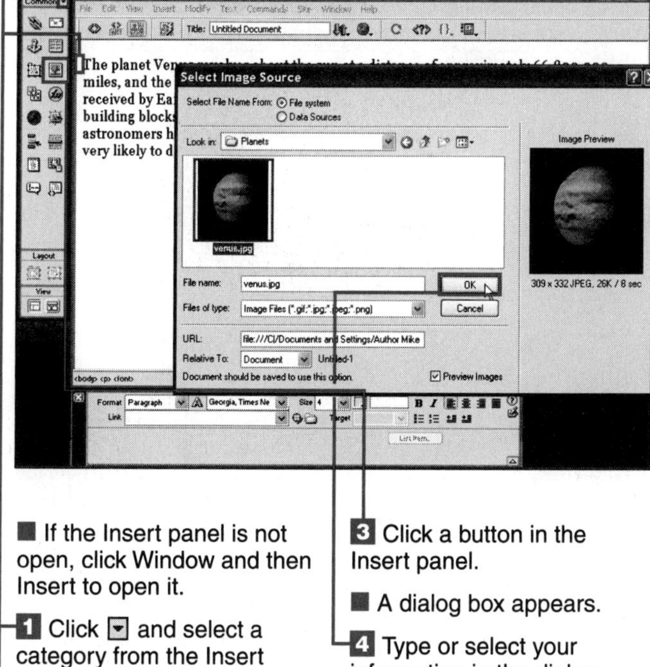

■ If the Insert panel is not open, click Window and then Insert to open it.

1 Click ▾ and select a category from the Insert panel menu.

2 Click inside the Document window where you want to insert an object.

3 Click a button in the Insert panel.

■ A dialog box appears.

4 Type or select your information in the dialog box and click OK.

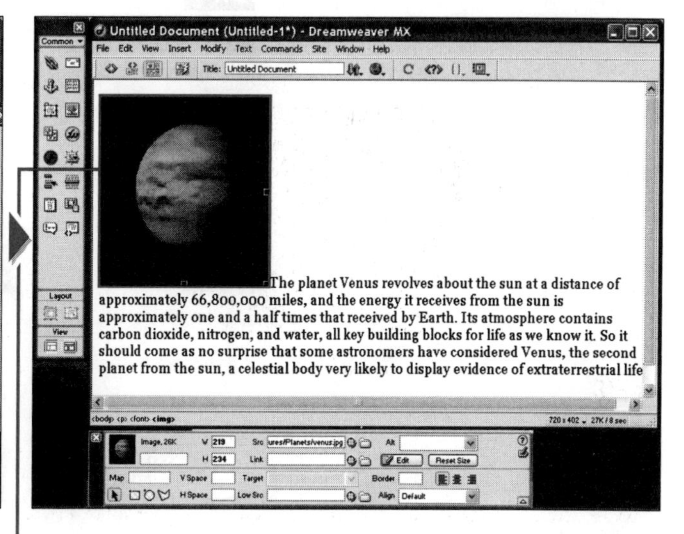

■ Dreamweaver inserts the object into the Document window.

■ You can click and drag the corner of the panel to change its dimensions.

UNDO COMMANDS WITH THE HISTORY PANEL

The History panel keeps track of the commands you perform in Dreamweaver and allows you to return your page to a previous state by backtracking through those commands. The History panel gives you a convenient way to correct errors or to revert your page to an earlier version if you do not like the modifications you have made.

When you backtrack to undo several steps in the History panel, the Document window content reverts to the state it was prior to performing the steps. The steps that were undone are grayed out in the History panel list. You can redo the steps if necessary. If you perform new commands, Dreamweaver erases any grayed-out commands.

While the History panel saves the commands you perform in Dreamweaver, it keeps separate history lists for different Document windows and frames. You can click inside the different windows or frames to see their respective histories.

You can select a sequence of commands in the History panel and turn them into a custom command. See page 28 for more information.

UNDO COMMANDS WITH THE HISTORY PANEL

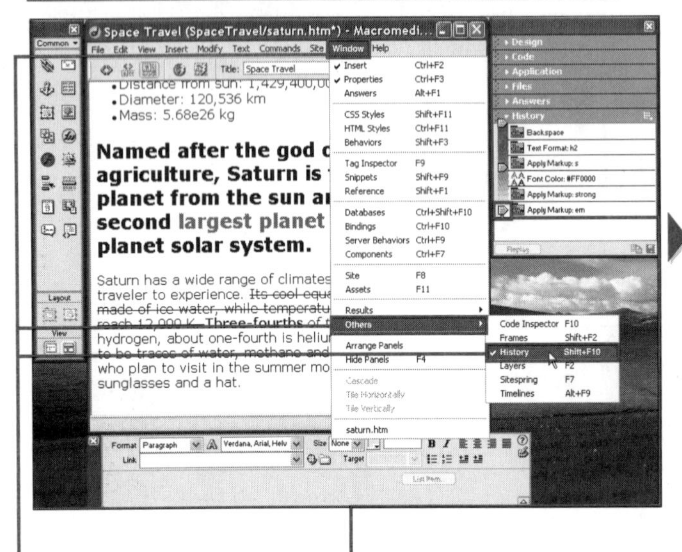

1 Click Window.

2 Click Others.

3 Click History.

■ The History panel records the commands you perform in Dreamweaver.

4 To undo one or more commands, click and drag the slider (▷) upward.

■ The page reverts to its previous state.

■ To redo the commands, drag the slider (▷) downward.

5 Click ☰ and then Close Panel Group when you are done using the History panel.

REARRANGE PANELS

Dreamweaver has more than a dozen panels that you can use to build Web pages and manage your Web site. To keep your on-screen workspace from getting cluttered, Dreamweaver combines similar panels into tabbed groups. You can view and hide groups of panels, and click the tabs of a group to switch between different panels.

Dreamweaver comes with the panels already organized in groups. For example, the CSS Styles panel shares a window with the HTML Styles and Behaviors panels. This group is named Design. You can modify these arrangements with the commands in the panel menu to rearranges the tools in ways that work best for you.

The different windows in Dreamweaver snap to the sides of one another and also to the edges of your screen. This makes it easy to arrange windows efficiently in your workspace.

You can also ungroup a panel from its current group and place it by itself in a new group. This can be helpful if you want to use two panels in the same group for a number of alternating tasks. Ungrouping enables you to arrange the panels where you can access both of them easily.

REARRANGE PANELS

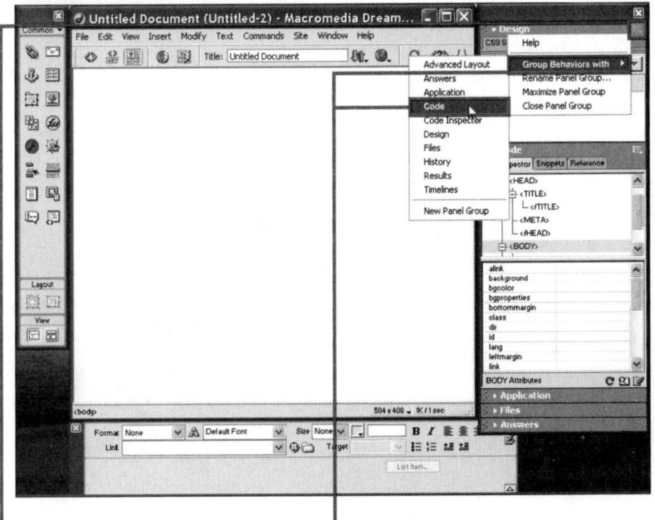

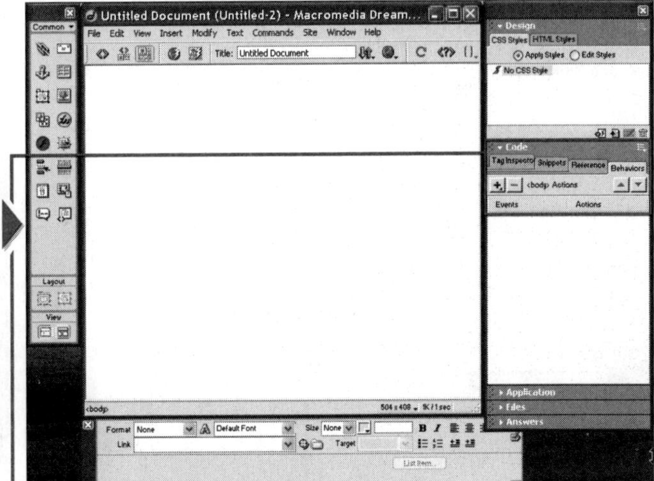

1 Open two panels.

Note: To open and close panels, see page 20.

2 Click on one of the panels.

3 Click Group "Panel," where "Panel" is the name of the panel you want to group.

4 Click a panel group.

Note: In this example, the Behaviors panel is being grouped with the Code panel.

■ The first panel is grouped with the other panel group.

■ You can select among the different tools in the window by clicking the tabs.

■ You can ungroup a panel by clicking New Panel Group under the Group "Panel" submenu, where "Panel" is the name of the panel you want to ungroup.

CREATE A COMMAND WITH THE HISTORY PANEL

You can select a sequence of commands that the History panel has recorded and save that sequence as a custom command. The new command appears under the Commands menu.

You should consider saving any sequence of commands that you plan to perform over and over on your Web site. This saves you time and physical effort, and ensures that the settings you apply are identical each time.

Dreamweaver stores saved commands as a JavaScript or HTML file in the Commands folder located in the Dreamweaver application's Configuration folder. This allows commands to be saved permanently between the times you exit and restart Dreamweaver. If you are familiar with JavaScript, you can edit commands by hand by opening the files in the Commands folder.

Note that the commands that you see in the History panel are specific to the current Document window and, if you are working on a framed site, to the current frame. If you switch to a different Document window or frame, a different history list appears in the panel.

CREATE A COMMAND WITH THE HISTORY PANEL

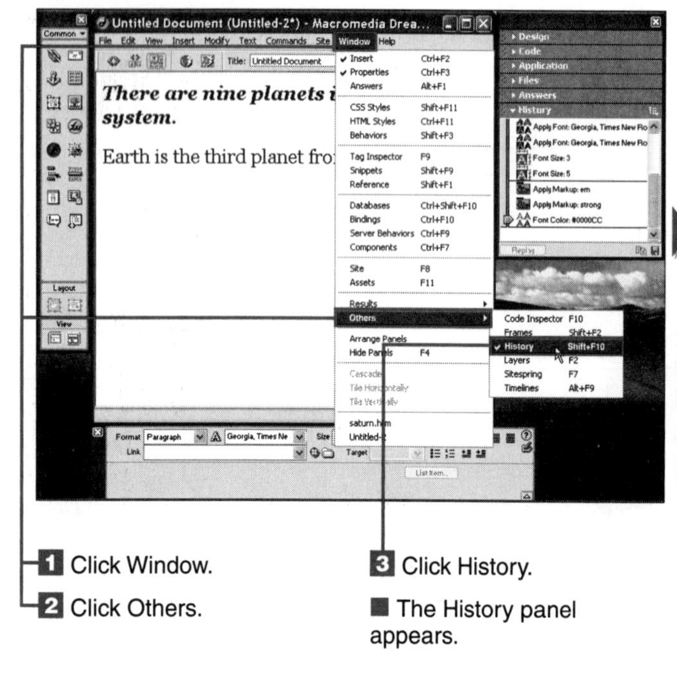

1 Click Window.

2 Click Others.

3 Click History.

■ The History panel appears.

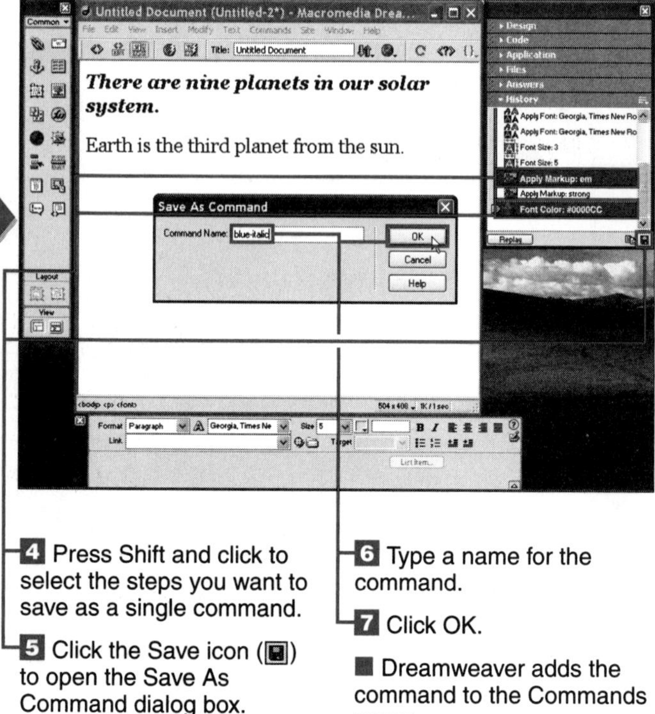

4 Press Shift and click to select the steps you want to save as a single command.

5 Click the Save icon (▣) to open the Save As Command dialog box.

6 Type a name for the command.

7 Click OK.

■ Dreamweaver adds the command to the Commands menu.

Can I rearrange the steps that appear in the History panel?

✔ No, you cannot rearrange the steps in the History panel. Dreamweaver lets you go back in history, but Dreamweaver does not let you rewrite history!

Why would I want to reduce the number of steps recorded by the History panel?

✔ Reducing the maximum number of steps you record, which you can do in Preferences, reduces the amount of memory Dreamweaver uses. Reducing the steps may also improve Dreamweaver's performance, especially if you do not have a lot of RAM installed on your computer.

What happens to the History panel when I close a document?

✔ Dreamweaver erases the history list for that document. Commands created from the History panel, however, are not erased.

Can I copy History information between Document windows?

✔ Yes. You can press Shift and then click to select the steps and use the Copy Steps command in the History panel menu. Then you can paste the commands into another Document window's History. You can also paste the steps into a text editor and view the JavaScript that defines them.

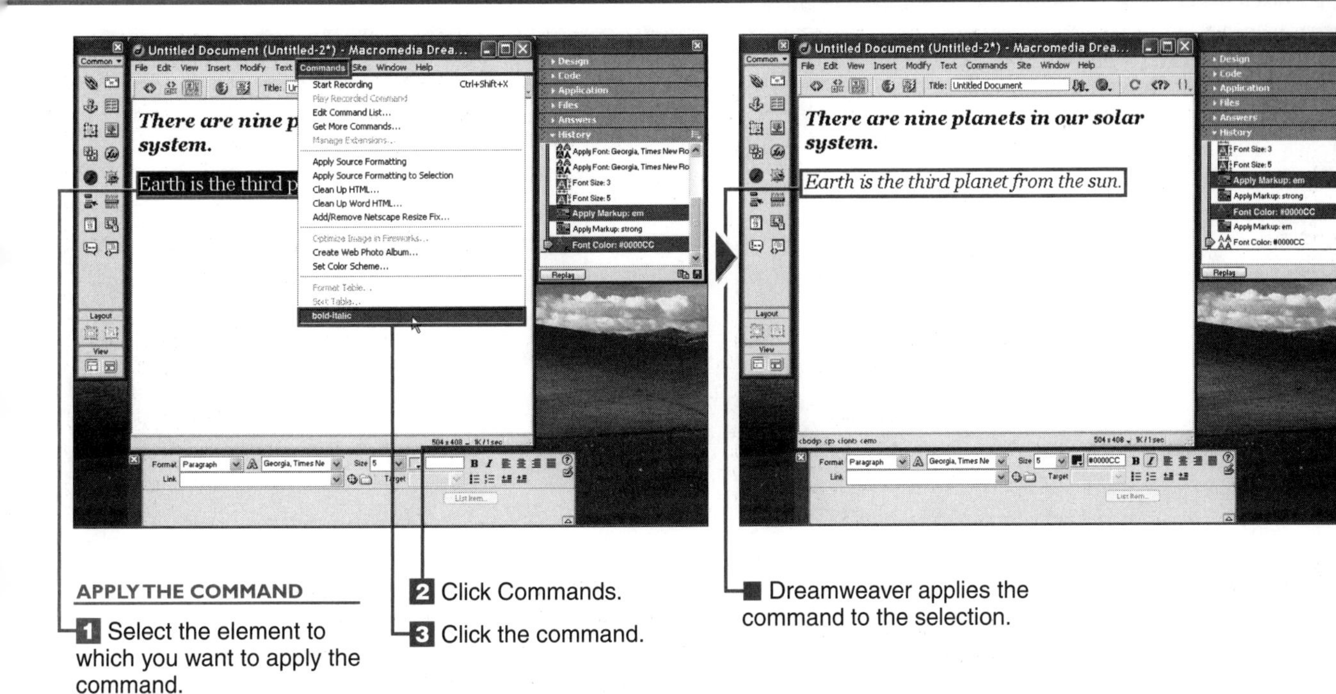

APPLY THE COMMAND

1 Select the element to which you want to apply the command.

2 Click Commands.

3 Click the command.

■ Dreamweaver applies the command to the selection.

CREATE A KEYBOARD SHORTCUT

You can use the Keyboard Shortcut Editor to define your own shortcut commands or edit existing shortcuts. This allows you to assign easy-to-remember keyboard combinations to commands that you use often in Dreamweaver.

To start defining your own shortcuts in Dreamweaver, you first have to create your own custom set, which you can do by duplicating an existing set.

The Keyboard Shortcuts Editor includes several predefined sets, which are complete collections of keyboard combinations mapped to Dreamweaver's commands. The default set is Macromedia Standard, which is the standard set of shortcuts for Dreamweaver MX. If you are more familiar with an older version of Dreamweaver, you can load the set of shortcuts from Dreamweaver 3 with the editor and use the application with those.

You can also load sets from other Web editors, including HomeSite, a Windows text-based editor, and BBEdit, a Macintosh text-based editor. These sets map shortcuts from the other applications to equivalent Dreamweaver commands. Where there are no equivalents, such as where Dreamweaver has commands that the other applications do not, Dreamweaver uses the Macromedia Standard shortcuts.

CREATE A KEYBOARD SHORTCUT

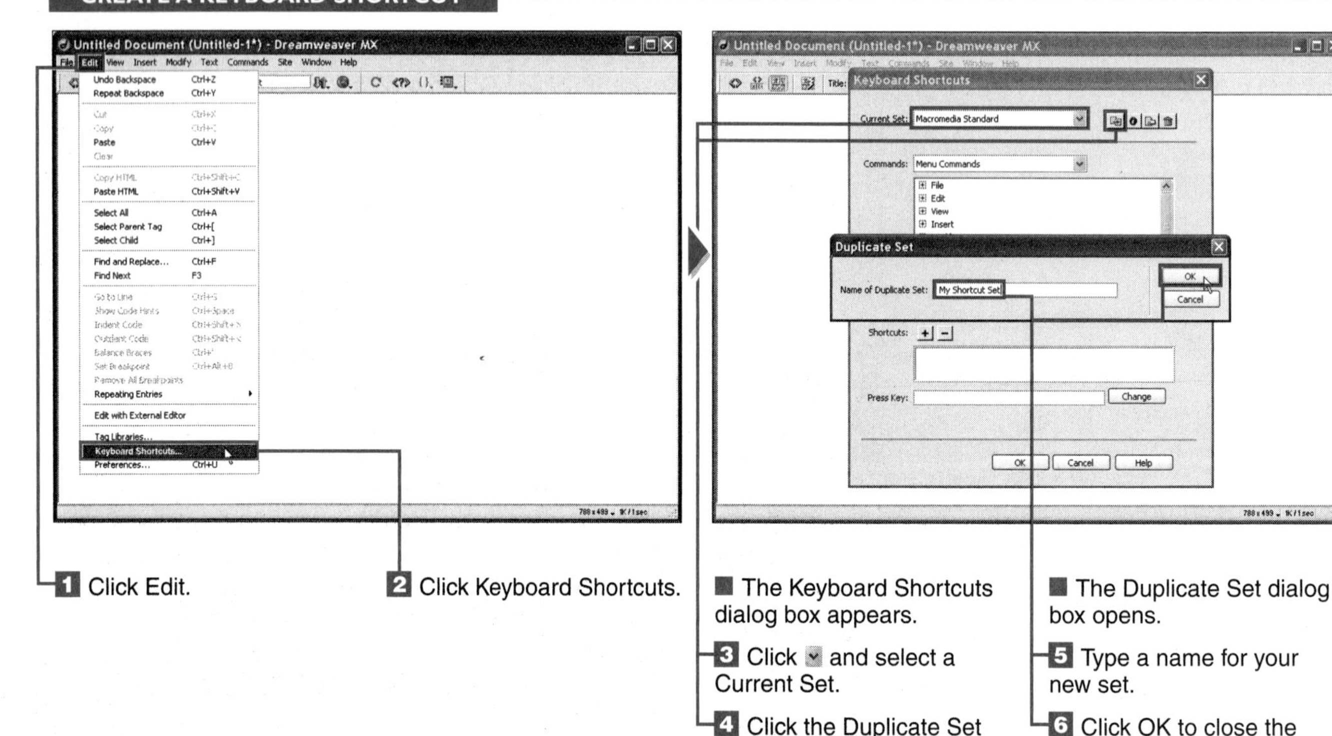

1 Click Edit.

2 Click Keyboard Shortcuts.

■ The Keyboard Shortcuts dialog box appears.

3 Click ▾ and select a Current Set.

4 Click the Duplicate Set button (▣).

■ The Duplicate Set dialog box opens.

5 Type a name for your new set.

6 Click OK to close the dialog box.

Can I reassign a keyboard shortcut?

✔ Yes. Dreamweaver warns you that you are already using the keyboard shortcut, but you can dismiss the warning and reassign the shortcut.

How can I print out a list of the assigned shortcuts of a set for reference?

✔ Click [print] button in the Keyboard Shortcuts dialog box.

Can I edit the keyboard shortcut sets that come preinstalled?

✔ No. This is why you need to duplicate an existing shortcut set before you create any new shortcuts or make any modifications to existing shortcuts. Keeping the installed sets intact allows you to revert back to them if needed.

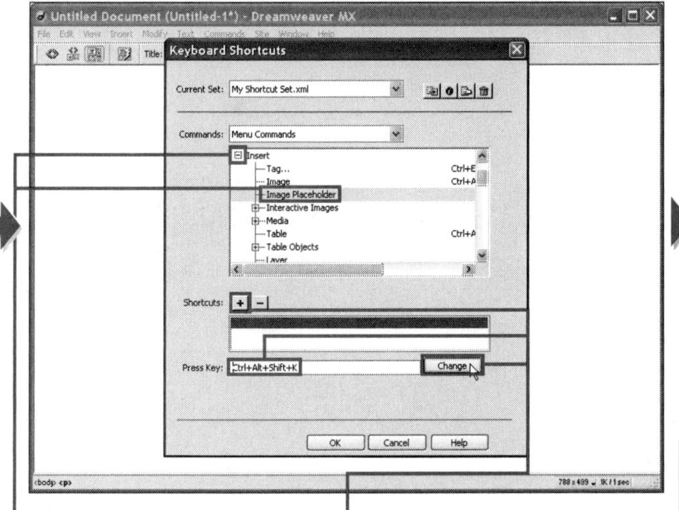

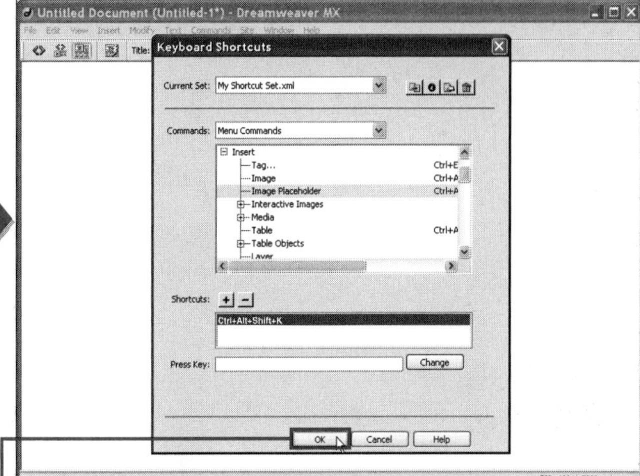

7 In the menu window, open the menu with the desired command by clicking the plus sign (⊞) next to the name of the menu (⊞ changes to ⊟).

8 Click to select a command.

9 Click the Plus button (⊞).

10 Press the keystroke combination that you want to use for the command.

■ The combination appears in the Press Key field.

11 Click Change.

■ The keystroke is assigned to the command.

12 Click OK.

■ To execute a keyboard shortcut, click inside the Document window, select an object if necessary, and press the keystroke combination. The command executes.

SET PREFERENCES

You can easily change the default appearance and behavior of Dreamweaver by specifying settings in the Preferences dialog box. Preferences let you modify the user interface of Dreamweaver to better suit how you like to work. They allow you to specify the default type of documents that open in new windows and the default browser Dreamweaver uses to test documents. You can also use Preferences to change the way Dreamweaver writes HTML, how it generates page elements such as style sheets and layers, and a wide variety of other features.

The Preferences dialog box consists of a list of categories on the left side, and configurable menus, text fields, check boxes, and other elements on the right. The options available on the right change depending on the category selected on the left. For help in configuring a particular set of preferences, you can click the Help button at the bottom of the box to open Dreamweaver's help documentation.

When you change most preferences in Dreamweaver, the program's behavior changes immediately after you click OK in the Preferences dialog box. An exception is when you change the Dreamweaver workspace, which requires you to exit and restart Dreamweaver.

SET PREFERENCES

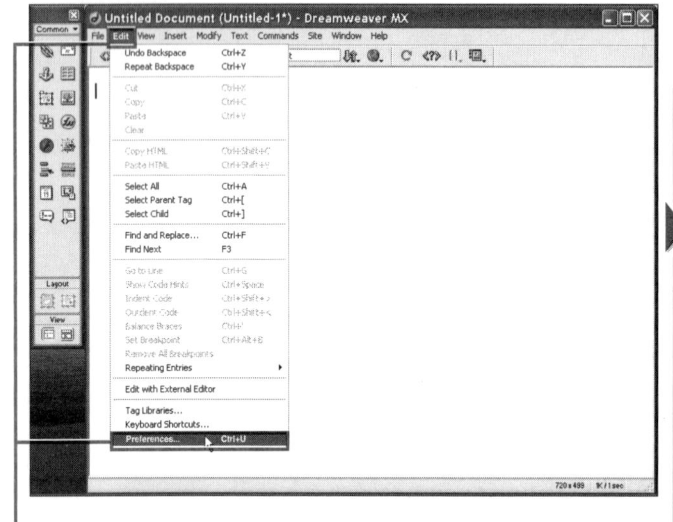

1 Click Edit.

2 Click Preferences.

■ The Preferences dialog box appears.

3 Click a Preferences category.

■ Options for the category appear.

How do I customize the information available in the status bar of the Document window?

✔ By selecting options under the Status Bar category in Preferences, you can add window sizes to the drop-down menu on the status bar and specify the connection speed it uses to determine the displayed download speed.

Can I change the default font styles and size for Design and Code views?

✔ Yes. Click the Fonts category in Preferences to display the options. You can further customize the look and formatting of the text in Code view under the Code Coloring and Code Format categories.

How do I ensure that Dreamweaver does not rewrite my HTML or other code?

✔ You can select options under the Code Rewriting category in Preferences to ensure that Dreamweaver does not automatically correct or modify your code. You can turn off its error-correcting functions, specify files that should not be rewritten based on file extension, or disable its character encoding features.

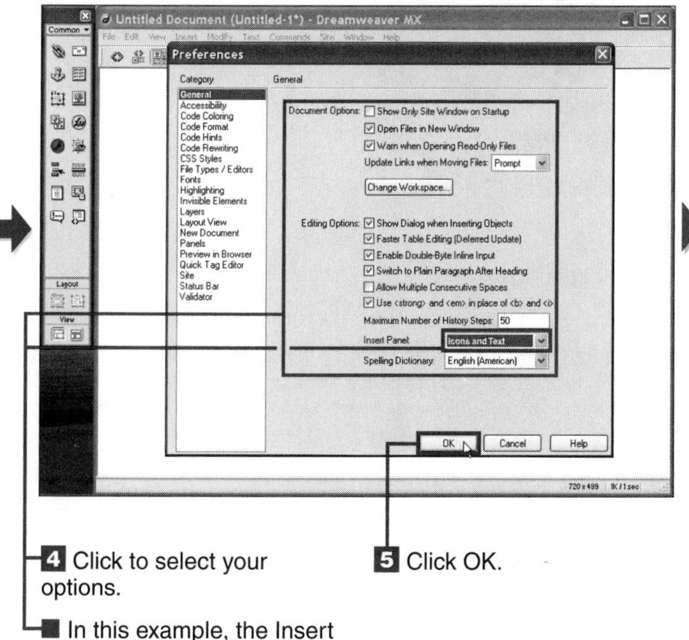

4 Click to select your options.

■ In this example, the Insert panel is set to display both icons and text descriptions.

5 Click OK.

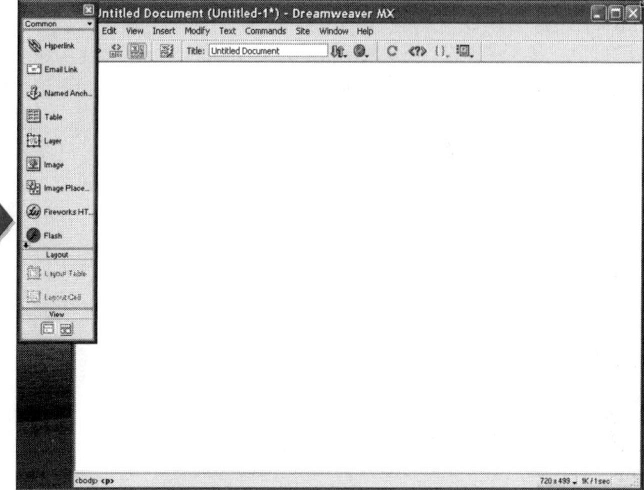

■ The preference changes take effect.

INTRODUCTION TO HTML

Hypertext Markup Language, or HTML, is the formatting language that you use to create Web pages. When you open a Web page in a browser, its HTML code tells the browser how to display the text, images, and other content on the page. At its most basic level, Dreamweaver is an HTML-writing application, although it can write different code and do many other things as well.

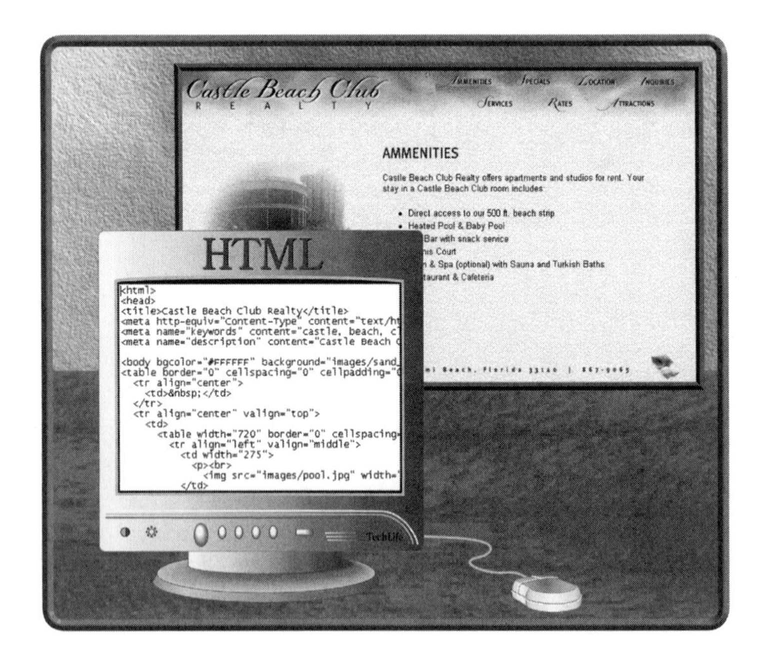

Official Standard

The official HTML standard is maintained by the World Wide Web Consortium (W3C), an international body made up of members from industry, academia, and government. The consortium makes recommendations as to what new HTML features should be adopted. Developers of browsers, servers, and HTML editors, such as Dreamweaver, can then follow these guidelines when building their products. As of this writing, the current HTML standard is version 4.01, which you can view at www.w3c.org.

HTML Tags

The basic unit of HTML is a *tag*. You can recognize HTML tags by their angle brackets:

```
<p>Today the weather was
<b>nice</b>.<br>Tomorrow it may
<i>rain</i>.</p>
```

Some HTML tags work in twos — opening and closing tags surround content in a document and control the formatting of the content. For example, the <b> tags above cause text to be bold. Closing tags are distinguished by a forward slash (/). Other tags can stand alone. For example, the <br> tag adds a line break. HTML tags are not case sensitive — they can be uppercase, lowercase, or mixed case.

HTML Attributes

You can modify the effect of an HTML tag by adding extra information known as *attributes*. Attributes are name/value pairs, such as `align="right"`, that live inside the HTML angle brackets to the right of the tag name. As an example, you can add the align attribute to a <p> (paragraph) tag to align a paragraph in various ways:

```
<p align="right">I think I will
go for a walk today instead of
typing on the computer. The sun
is shining and there is a warm
breeze.</p>
```

The HTML above would cause the two-sentence paragraph to be aligned to the right side of the Web browser window.

HTML Documents

Because HTML documents are plain text files, you can open and edit them with any text editor. In fact, in the early days of the Web, most people created their pages with simple editors such as Windows' Notepad and Macintosh's SimpleText. But writing HTML by hand can be a slow, tedious process, especially when creating advanced HTML elements, such as tables, forms, and frames.

Access to Code

Dreamweaver gives you direct access to the raw HTML code if you want it. This can be an advantage for people who know HTML and want to do some formatting of their page by typing tags. The Code View mode, Code inspector, and Quick Tag Editor in Dreamweaver enable you to edit your page by adding HTML information manually. Access to the code also means you can add HTML features that Dreamweaver does not yet support, such as newly approved HTML tags.

Create Web Pages

Dreamweaver streamlines the process of creating Web pages by giving you an easy-to-use, visual interface with which to generate HTML. You specify formatting with menu commands and button clicks, and Dreamweaver takes care of writing the HTML code behind the scenes. When you build a Web page in the Document window, you see your page as it appears in a Web browser, instead of as HTML.

Style Sheets

Although HTML provides the nuts and bolts that give a Web page its primary structure, there are also other types of code that play a part in making a Web page what it is. *Style sheets*, also known as Cascading Style Sheets or CSS, is a language that allows you to specify how text and other elements appear visually on a Web page. Here is some style-sheet code:

```
h1 {font-style: italic; color: red}
```

Style sheets allow you to implement much more elaborate formatting than you can with HTML. For more information on style sheets, see Chapter 12.

XML

Extensible Markup Language, or *XML*, is another type of markup language for creating digital documents. It is similar to HTML in that it involves formatting text with surrounding tags and attributes. But it is more flexible than HTML in that it lets you define your own custom tags. For example, in XML, you can define a `<price>` tag that you can use to distinguish price information in your XML documents.

Dreamweaver has tools to convert your HTML documents to XHTML, which is a modified version of HTML that complies with the stricter rules of XML. XHTML has advantages in that it can be interpreted by newer browsers just as HTML can, but can be interpreted by XML-compliant devices as well.

VIEW AND EDIT THE SOURCE CODE

For Web developers who like to build their Web site the old-fashioned way — by writing HTML by hand — Dreamweaver gives users several ways to edit a page's source code. You can open up a document's code in a separate window called the Code inspector. Or you can switch to Code View mode in the Document window, which replaces Dreamweaver's What You See Is What You Get (WYSIWYG) Design View with the current page's raw HTML. Dreamweaver also allows you to split the Document window in two, and view the Design View and Code View simultaneously.

As you make changes in Code View or in the Code inspector, a page's Design View changes in concert. The synchronization between the views makes Dreamweaver a useful environment for learning HTML. You can switch between views to see which tags do what. Dreamweaver also color codes the different HTML tags for easy reading and can also highlight HTML mistakes.

Code View is also useful when you want to manually edit other types of code present in Web documents, such as Cascading Style Sheet code, JavaScript, or server-side languages such as PHP.

VIEW AND EDIT THE SOURCE CODE

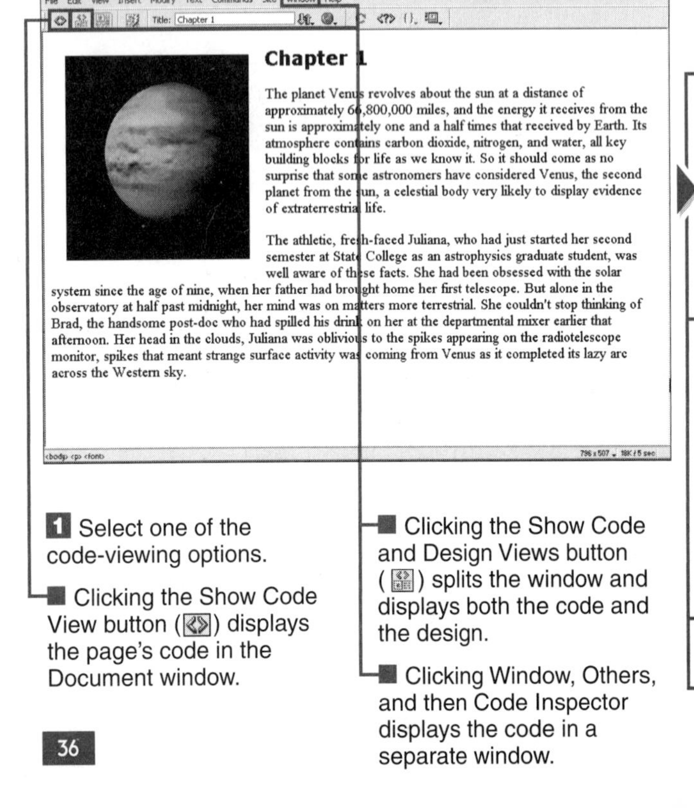

1 Select one of the code-viewing options.

■ Clicking the Show Code View button (◇) displays the page's code in the Document window.

■ Clicking the Show Code and Design Views button (▣) splits the window and displays both the code and the design.

■ Clicking Window, Others, and then Code Inspector displays the code in a separate window.

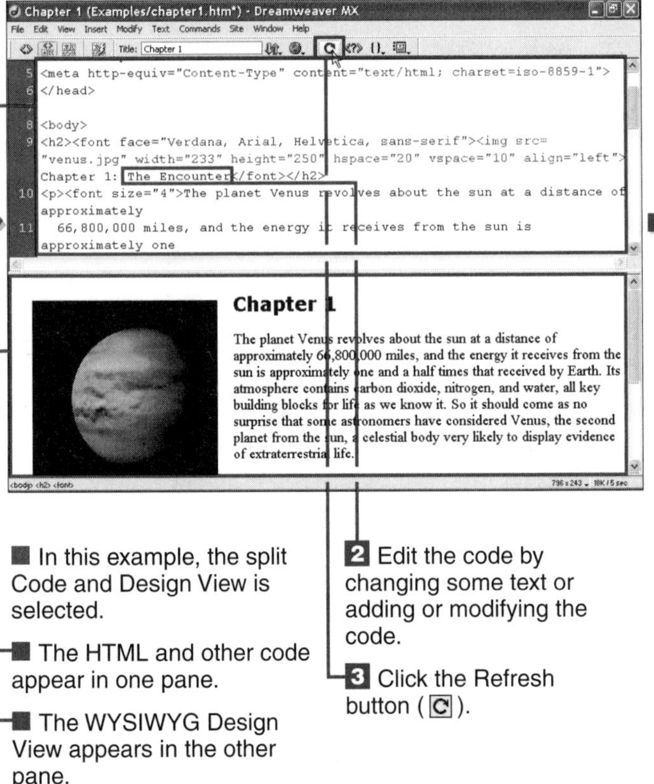

■ In this example, the split Code and Design View is selected.

■ The HTML and other code appear in one pane.

■ The WYSIWYG Design View appears in the other pane.

2 Edit the code by changing some text or adding or modifying the code.

3 Click the Refresh button (C).

How do I make code wrap at the right edge of the window?

✔ To make the code wrap on the right in Code View, click the View Options button (▤) at the top of the Document window and then click Word Wrap.

How does Dreamweaver display errors in my HTML?

✔ If you click View, Code View Options, and then Highlight Invalid HTML, Dreamweaver displays suspected HTML errors in yellow highlighting. Errors Dreamweaver flags include orphaned closing tags and opening and closing tags that do not match. Note that Dreamweaver *does not* flag HTML tags that it does not recognize, because these could be valid new HTML tags that it simply is not aware of, or tags of a different type of code such as XML.

How do I change the color coding of my HTML?

✔ Click Edit (Dreamweaver in Mac OS X) and then Preferences. In the Preferences dialog box, click the category Code Coloring. From there, you can change how Dreamweaver colors your HTML.

What is Live Data View?

✔ Live Data View is similar to Design View except that Dreamweaver replaces dynamic code, such as ColdFusion Markup Language, Java, or PHP, that is in your pages with the appropriate dynamic content. Live Data View is useful when you are developing Web applications that generate pages using a database. Click the Live Data button (▦) to switch to Live Data View.

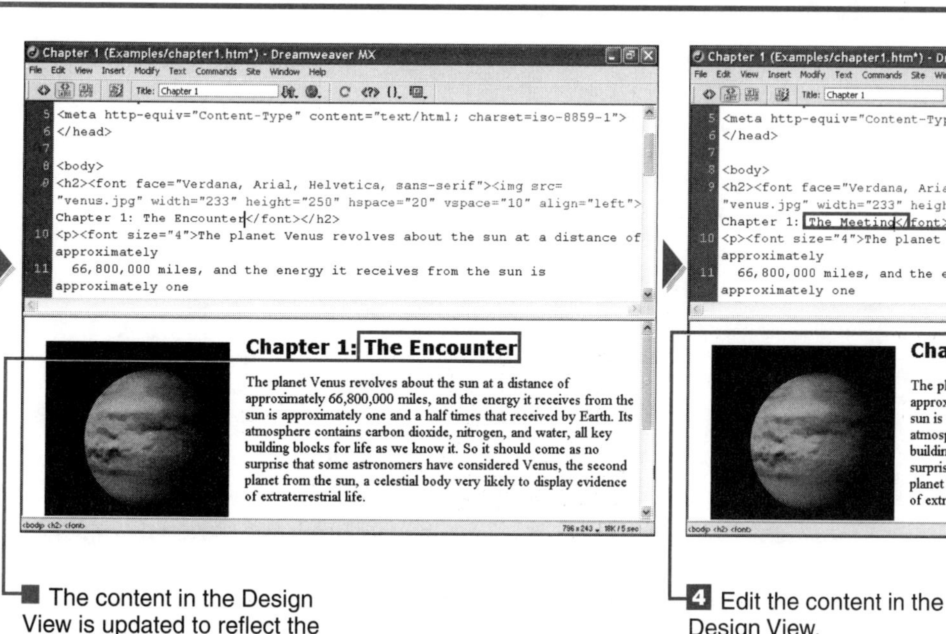

■ The content in the Design View is updated to reflect the code changes.

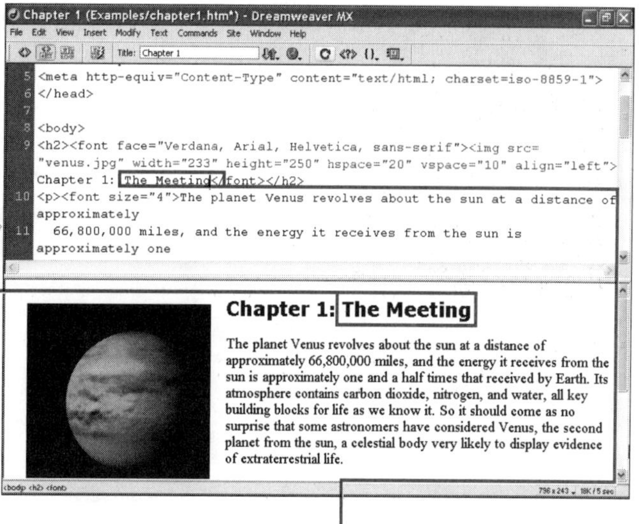

4 Edit the content in the Design View.

■ The text in the Code View updates dynamically as you make your changes.

CLEAN UP YOUR HTML

Dreamweaver offers commands that optimize the HTML in your Web page by deleting extraneous or nonfunctional tags. This can decrease a page's file size and make the source code easier to read in Code View.

You can use the Clean Up HTML command to remove empty and redundant HTML tags as well as HTML comments. You can specify that Dreamweaver-generated comments be ignored; this ensures that template information and library items, which depend on special comments in the code, remain intact. The command also lets you automatically remove particular HTML tags in your code.

It is useful to clean up your HTML as a final step before uploading your pages to a remote Web server. It can also be useful when editing files originally built in other Web editors, which can sometimes write inefficient code and add their own proprietary tags.

The Clean Up Word HTML, also under the Commands menu, removes extraneous tags that Microsoft Word adds when saving a Word document as a Web page. This command works on Web pages generated by Word 97 and later versions.

CLEAN UP YOUR HTML

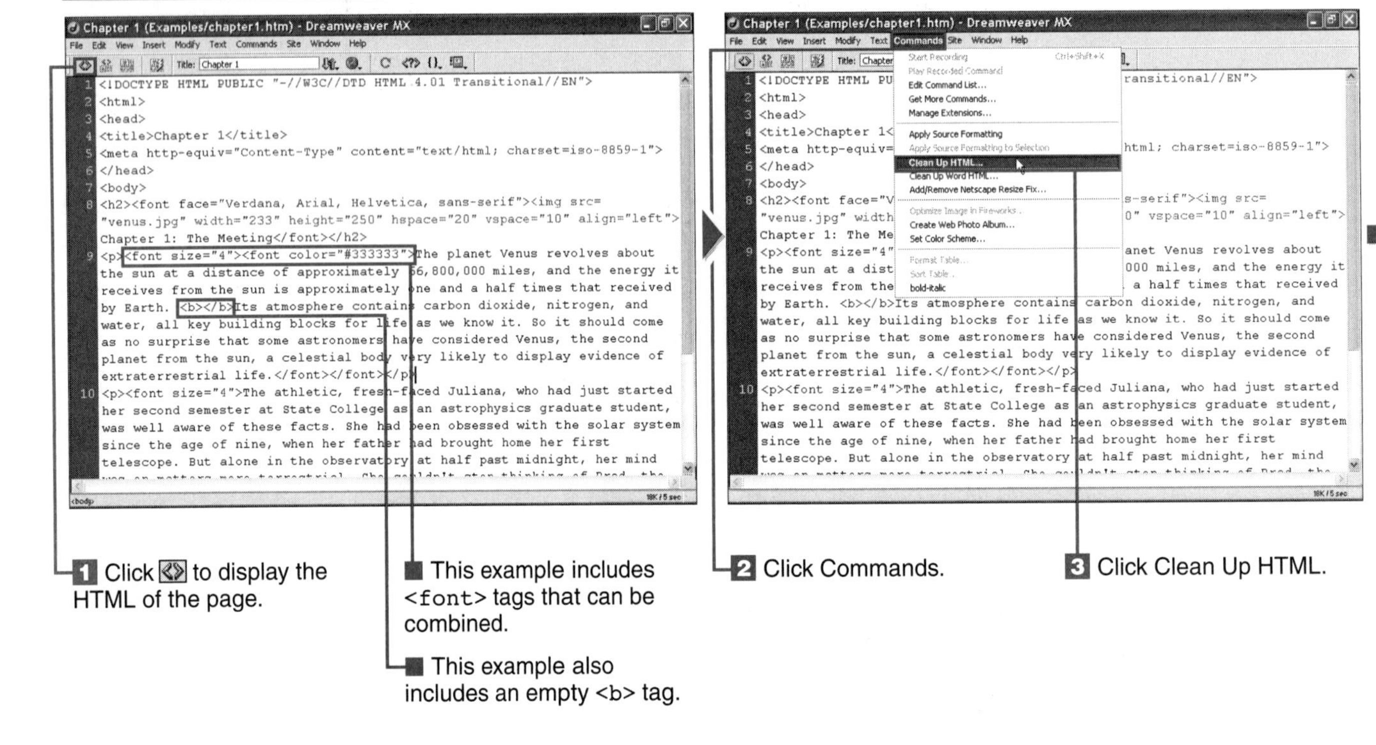

1 Click [icon] to display the HTML of the page.

■ This example includes <font> tags that can be combined.

■ This example also includes an empty <b> tag.

2 Click Commands.

3 Click Clean Up HTML.

How do empty tags end up appearing in Dreamweaver's HTML?

✔ Sometimes if you heavily edit Web-page text in the Document window, such as cutting and pasting sentences, reformatting words, and so on, Dreamweaver inadvertently removes text from inside tags without removing the tags themselves.

What does the Clean Up Word HTML command do?

✔ This command, which is also under the Commands menu, removes the extra head information, style-sheet rules, and XML tags that Microsoft Word adds when saving a document as a Web page. Most of these tags are added so that the HTML document can be displayed correctly in Word itself.

How can I make my code more readable in Code View?

✔ In addition to using the Clean Up HTML command, you can use Apply Source Formatting, also under the Commands menu. This applies the code settings such as indent size and wrapping frequency that you specify under the Code Format category of Preferences. You can also specify capitalization settings under Code Format. This determines how Dreamweaver formats HTML tags when you insert objects in Design View. For more information about settings Preferences, see page 32.

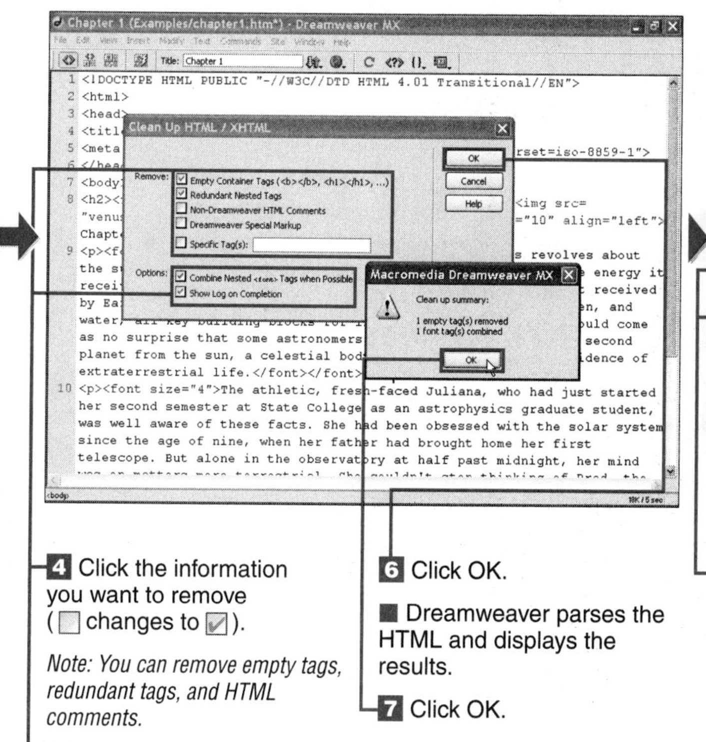

4 Click the information you want to remove (☐ changes to ☑).

Note: You can remove empty tags, redundant tags, and HTML comments.

5 Click these options (☐ changes to ☑).

6 Click OK.

■ Dreamweaver parses the HTML and displays the results.

7 Click OK.

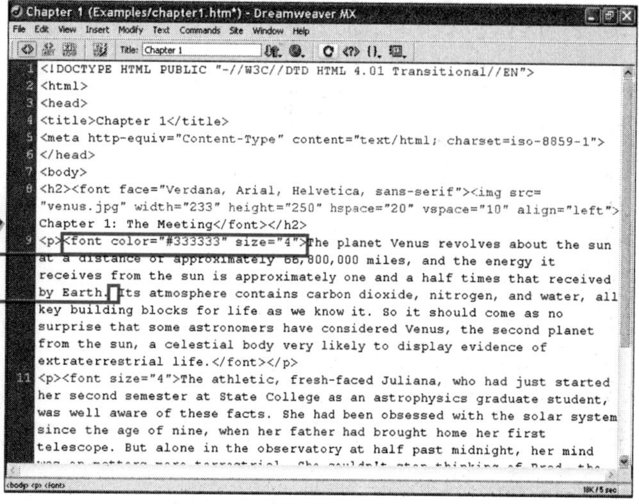

■ The cleaned up HTML appears in the Document window.

USING THE QUICK TAG EDITOR

Dreamweaver's Quick Tag Editor gives you easy access to HTML code without having to open the Code inspector or switch to Code View. You can open it when you are working inside the Document window and use it to add or modify HTML tags.

The Quick Tag Editor can work in any of three modes: Edit, Insert, or Wrap. Which mode it opens in depends on what you select in the Document window. For example, if you select an existing HTML tag in Code View, the Editor opens in Edit Tag mode. If you select plain text in Design View, it opens in Wrap Tag mode. If you do not select anything, the cursor appears between page elements and the Editor opens in Insert Tag mode.

The Quick Tag Editor includes a help feature for those who are not familiar with all the available HTML tags and their attributes. If you pause after opening the editor, it displays a drop-down menu listing all the available HTML tags. After you select a tag, it displays a menu listing the attributes available for that tag.

USING THE QUICK TAG EDITOR

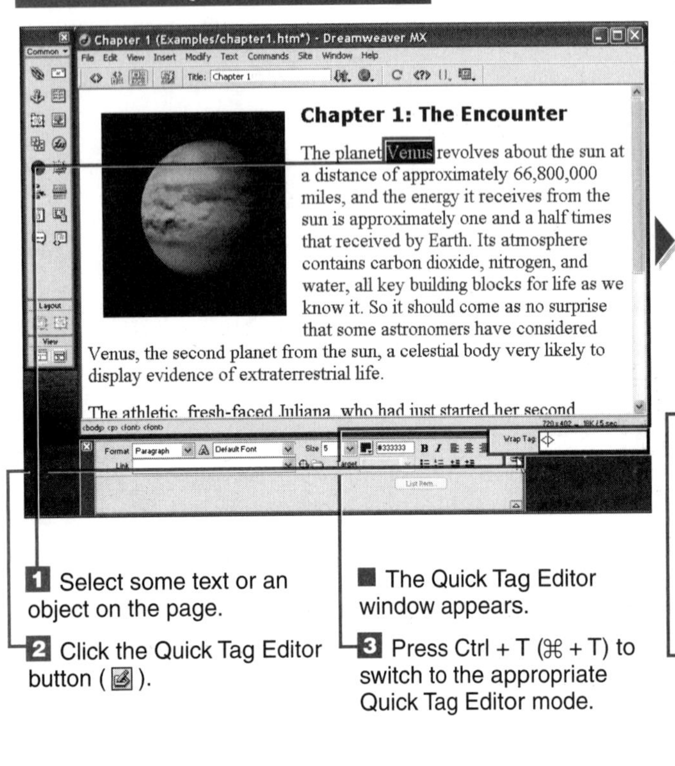

1 Select some text or an object on the page.

2 Click the Quick Tag Editor button (📝).

■ The Quick Tag Editor window appears.

3 Press Ctrl + T (⌘ + T) to switch to the appropriate Quick Tag Editor mode.

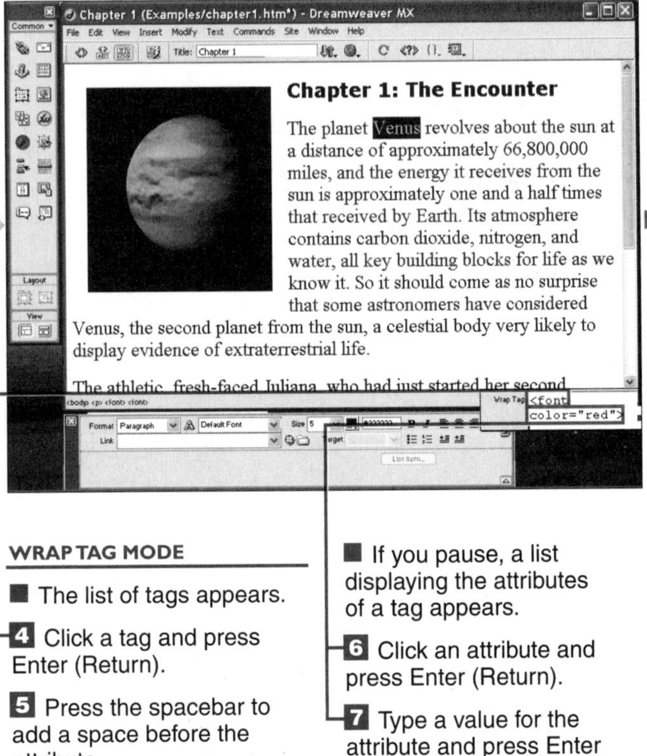

WRAP TAG MODE

■ The list of tags appears.

4 Click a tag and press Enter (Return).

5 Press the spacebar to add a space before the attribute.

■ If you pause, a list displaying the attributes of a tag appears.

6 Click an attribute and press Enter (Return).

7 Type a value for the attribute and press Enter (Return).

How can I customize the Quick Tag Editor?

✔ Click Edit and then Preferences. In the Preferences dialog box, click the Quick Tag Editor category. Here you can choose whether the tag information that you enter in the editor is applied immediately as you type it. You can also specify how long it takes for the drop-down help list to appear.

How do I exit the editor without applying changes?

✔ You can press Esc to exit without applying changes.

Does the Quick Tag Editor allow me to enter incorrect HTML?

✔ While the Quick Tag Editor helps you create well-formed HTML by adding the appropriate closing tags and quoted attributes, it does not try to correct HTML tags or attributes that it does not understand. Because HTML is an evolving language, Dreamweaver assumes that it may not know all the HTML tags that are currently being used. You can also use the Quick Tag Editor to enter XML, which includes user-defined tags.

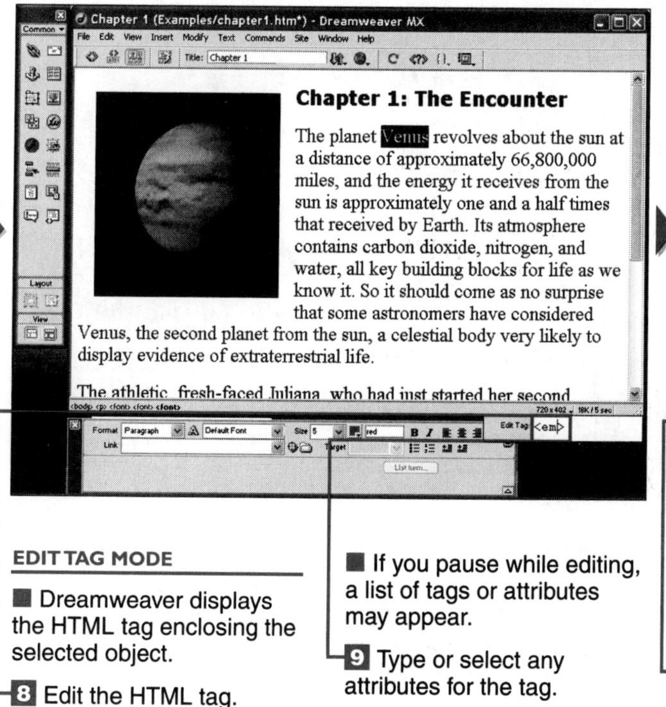

EDIT TAG MODE

■ Dreamweaver displays the HTML tag enclosing the selected object.

8 Edit the HTML tag.

■ If you pause while editing, a list of tags or attributes may appear.

9 Type or select any attributes for the tag.

10 Press Enter (Return) when you are done editing.

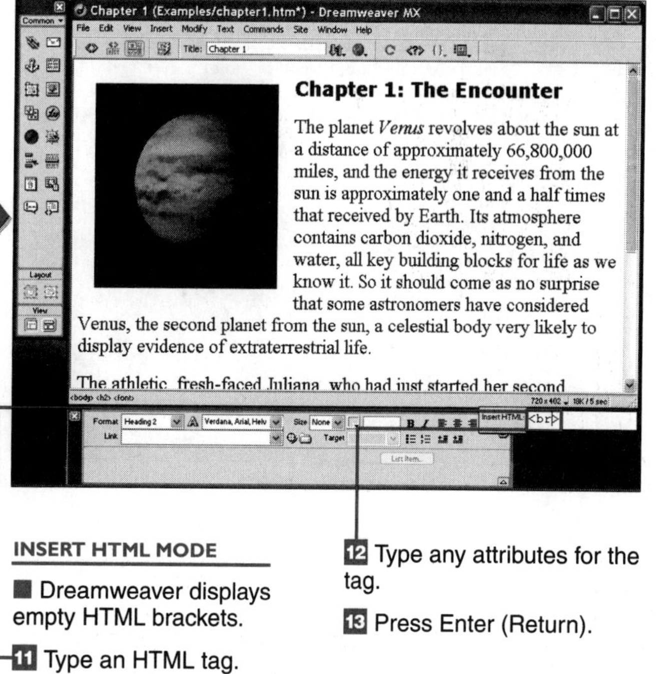

INSERT HTML MODE

■ Dreamweaver displays empty HTML brackets.

11 Type an HTML tag.

12 Type any attributes for the tag.

13 Press Enter (Return).

VIEW AND EDIT HEAD CONTENT

Near the beginning of every HTML document is a section of head content, defined by opening and closing <head> tags, where special information related to the Web page is stored. Dreamweaver gives you various ways to view, add to, and edit this information. Since head content does not exist inside the body area of an HTML page, it does not appear in the browser window.

Information in a document's head includes the page title, JavaScript variables and functions, and style-sheet rules. It also can include optional *meta* information that describes the page to Web browsers and search engines.

When you create a new page in Dreamweaver, a meta tag is automatically added that specifies the type of content in your document such as text/html.

Other types of information that you can add to a page using meta tags include a description, keywords, and code that automatically refreshes the page or forwards the user to a new address.

Dreamweaver gives you an easy way to add head information through buttons in the Insert Panel. You can also add head information by hand via the Code View or in the Code inspector.

VIEW AND EDIT HEAD CONTENT

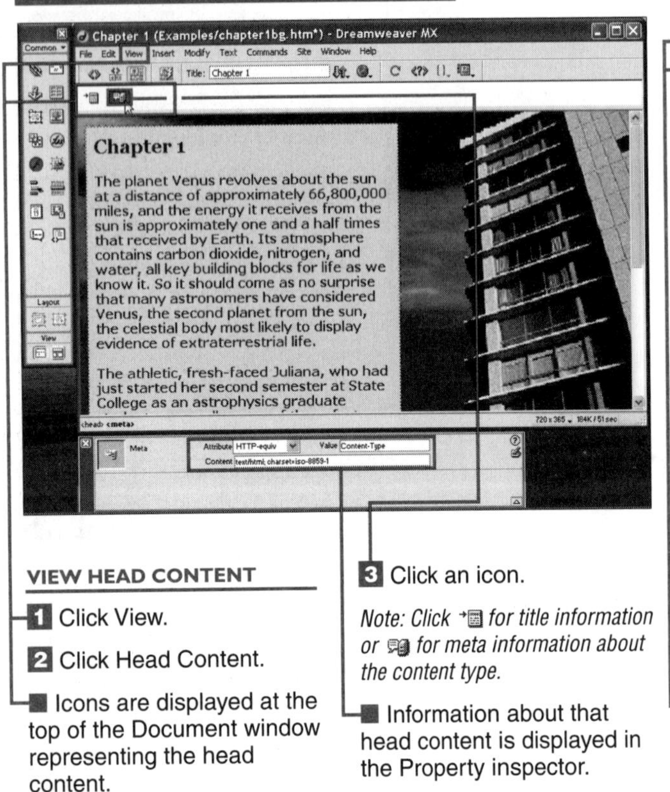

VIEW HEAD CONTENT

1 Click View.

2 Click Head Content.

■ Icons are displayed at the top of the Document window representing the head content.

3 Click an icon.

Note: Click for title information or for meta information about the content type.

■ Information about that head content is displayed in the Property inspector.

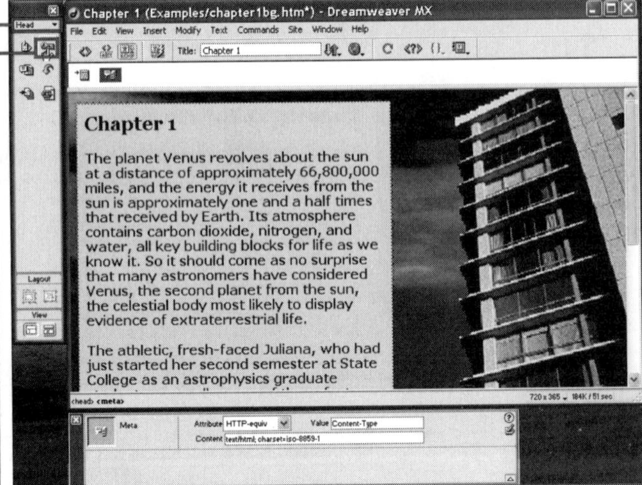

INSERT HEAD CONTENT

1 Click the Insert Panel and select Head from the menu that appears.

2 Click the button of the type of content that you want to insert.

- Meta information
- Meta description
- Base URL
- Meta keywords
- Page Refresh
- Relationship to another file

How is description and keyword information in a Web page useful?

✔ When cataloguing information from Web pages, search engines give greater importance to the optional description and keyword information in the head content of HTML documents. You can influence how search engines rank your pages by making sure you add concise descriptions and relevant keywords to the head content of each page you create.

How do I make a page automatically refresh, or reload, after a certain length of time?

✔ Add refresh instructions to the page's head content by using the Refresh button (C) in the Insert panel. If you want, you can instruct the page to forward to a different Web address when it refreshes. Refreshing can be useful if your page content changes often, or if you move your content to a different Web site and want to redirect visitors there.

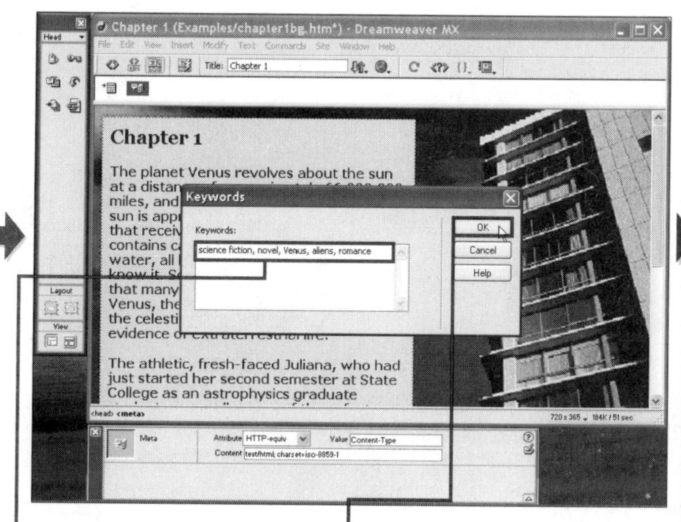

■ A dialog box appears for the type of head content you chose.

3 Type the head content that you want to add.

Note: If you insert keywords, type the keywords that are relevant to the page. Remember to separate the keywords with commas.

4 Click OK.

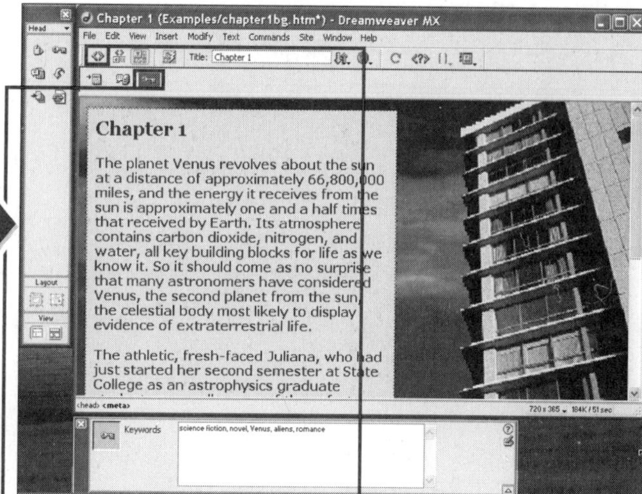

■ The new head content is represented by a new icon in the Document window's head section.

■ To see the HTML code for the new head content, click the Show Code View button ( ). Look near the top of the page, inside the <head> tag.

USING THE REFERENCE PANEL

You can get quick access to reference information about HTML tags and their attributes from the Reference panel. For each HTML tag, the Reference panel provides a basic definition, information about appropriate usage, and some sample code. The Reference panel is an excellent resource for Dreamweaver users who are used to building pages visually but are not familiar with the intricacies of HTML.

The Reference panel tells you which browsers and browser versions support each HTML tag. In the panel, NN represents Netscape Navigator, and IE represents Microsoft Internet Explorer. This can help you decide whether to avoid certain features if your audience tends to use older browsers.

You can also use the Reference panel to look up information about style sheets, JavaScript, and various Web application languages such as ColdFusion Markup Language. The style sheet information includes many examples of style rules that you can insert into your page if you are familiar with coding style sheets by hand. The JavaScript material is more technical and offers insight into how JavaScript objects work and how the language is organized.

USING THE REFERENCE PANEL

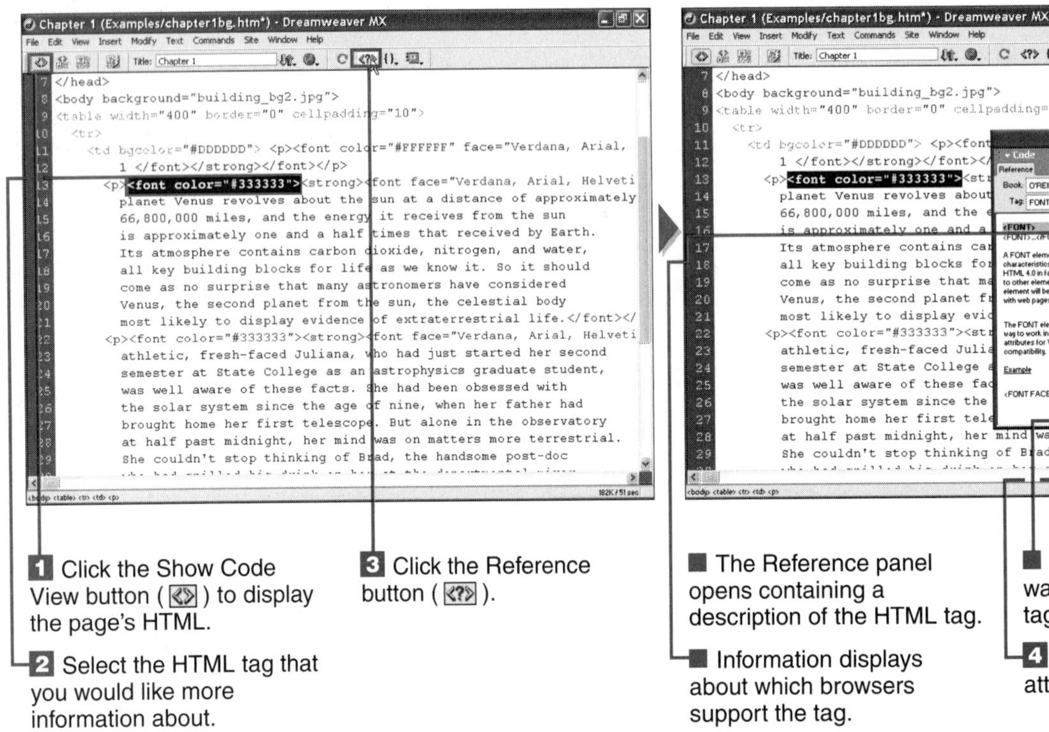

1 Click the Show Code View button ( ) to display the page's HTML.

2 Select the HTML tag that you would like more information about.

3 Click the Reference button ( ).

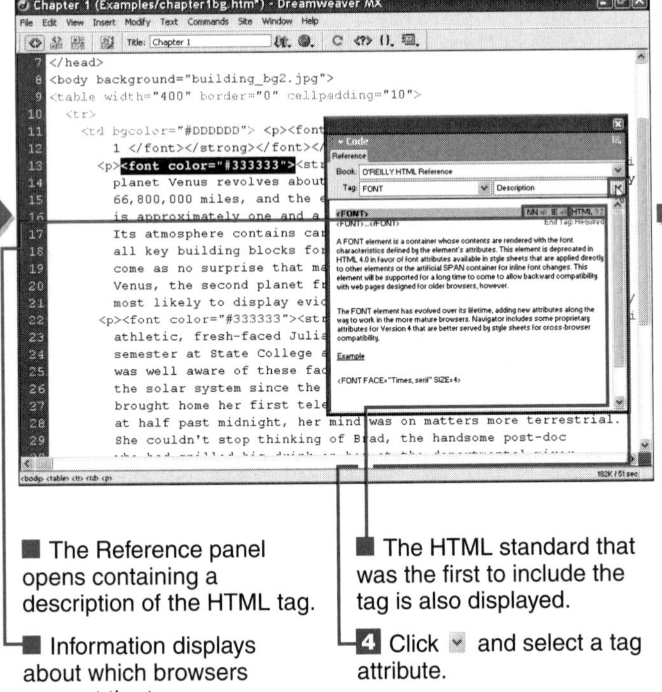

■ The Reference panel opens containing a description of the HTML tag.

■ Information displays about which browsers support the tag.

■ The HTML standard that was the first to include the tag is also displayed.

4 Click and select a tag attribute.

Does Dreamweaver have commands for creating all the tags listed in the Reference panel?

✔ No. Commands allow you to integrate *most* of the tags listed in the Reference Panel, in particular the most widely used tags. But there are tags listed that Dreamweaver does not offer commands for at this time. For example, you cannot insert the **<thead>** tag with any of Dreamweaver's table commands. Many of these unsupported tags are specific to only Netscape or Microsoft browsers, making them less useful. Tags that Dreamweaver does not support with commands can be inserted by hand in the Code View mode or in the Code inspector.

How can I find out how to make my Web site accessible to all users?

✔ You can click UsableNet Accessibility Reference under the Reference panel's Book menu for information about Web accessibility issues. This section features tips on how to code your HTML so that all users, no matter what type of browser device they are using, can experience all the content on your site. Accessibility is especially important for users with disabilities who may not be able to view images or hear sounds on the Web. Coding for accessibility includes measures such as adding ALT attributes to image tags to provide accompanying text descriptions.

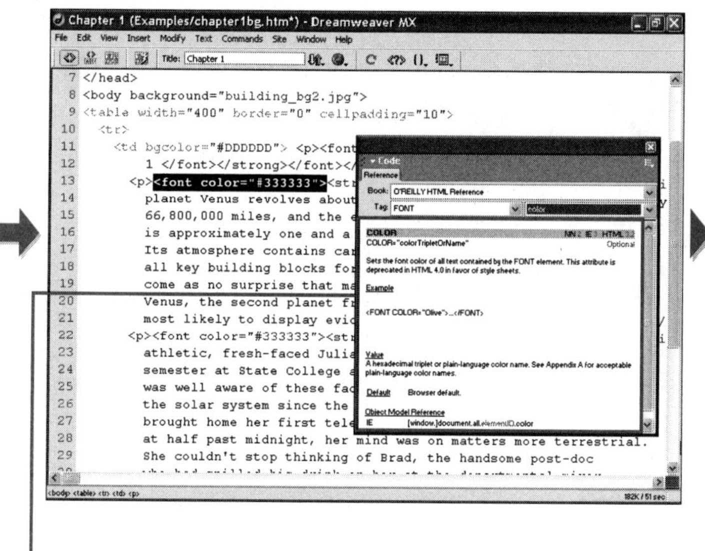

■ Information displays about the attribute.

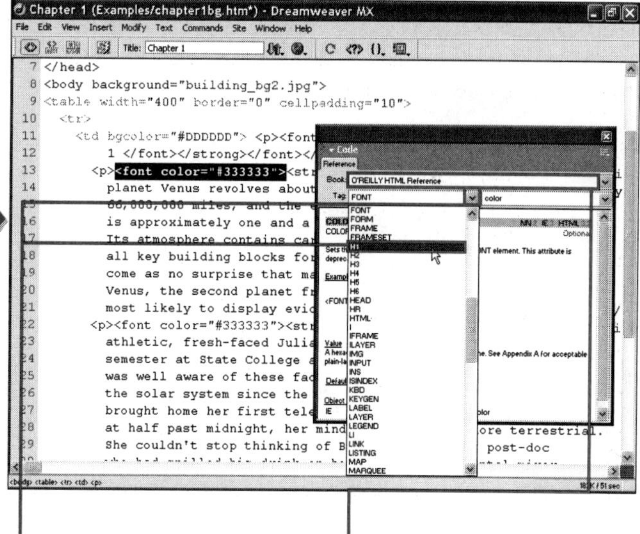

■ To look up a different HTML tag, click ▾ and select that tag.

■ To get information about JavaScript objects, style sheet rules, and other subjects, click the Book ▾.

EDIT CODE WITH THE TAG EDITOR

You can edit HTML tags using an easy-to-use interface — instead of by hand typing in the Code View — with the Tag Editor. The Tag Editor lets you change attributes for a particular tag using text fields and menus in a dialog box, similar to the way you modify objects on your page in the Properties inspector.

You open the Tag Editor by right-clicking any object in the Document window and selecting Edit Tag. To edit a specific tag for an object, you can first click an HTML tag in the tag selector on the left side of the status bar before right-clicking. You can access the Tag Editor in both Design View and Code View.

The details that appear in the Tag Editor depend on the type of tag you edit. With some more complex tags, such as `<table>`, you can edit attributes and styles for the tag as well as browser-specific features and JavaScript events. After you make changes to the tag properties in the Tag Editor and click OK, Dreamweaver adds or edits the appropriate HTML code in your page. You can view the edited code in Code View.

EDIT CODE WITH THE TAG EDITOR

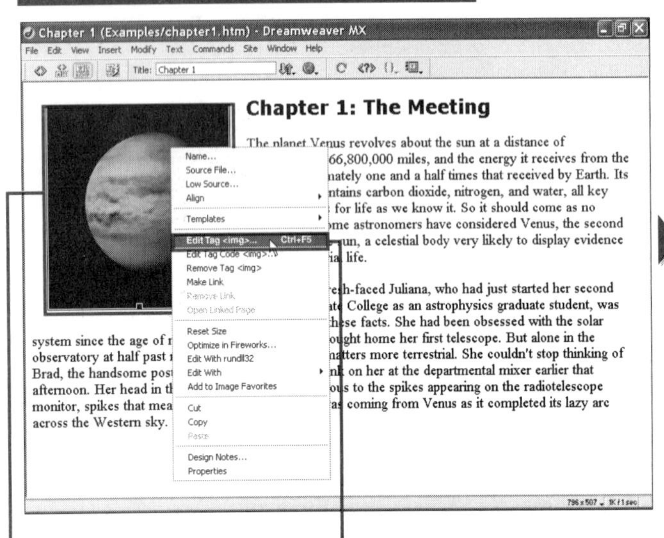

1 Right-click (Control-click) an object in the Document window.

■ If you are in Code View, you can right-click (Control-click) an HTML tag.

2 Click Edit Tag.

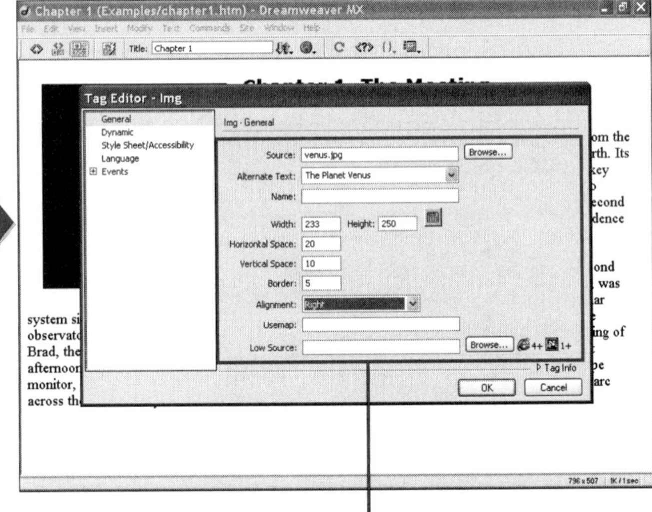

■ The Tag Editor opens.

3 Specify attribute values for the tag.

How do I delete an HTML tag without leaving the Design View?

✔ You can right-click (Control-click) a tag in the tag selector on the left side of the Document window status bar and click Remove Tag. You can also use the tag selector to edit the attributes of tags by hand or add style classes, or IDs to a tag.

How can I get detailed reference information about a tag from the Tag Editor?

✔ Click Tag Info in the lower-right corner to access the information from the Reference panel for that tag. See page 44 for more information.

Can I edit non-HTML tags in the Tag Editor?

✔ The Tag Editor supports only HTML tags. If you try to edit other tags, such as user-defined XML tags, the Edit Tag option will be grayed out when you right-click. You can still edit those tags in Code View or using the Quick Tag Editor. See page 40 for details.

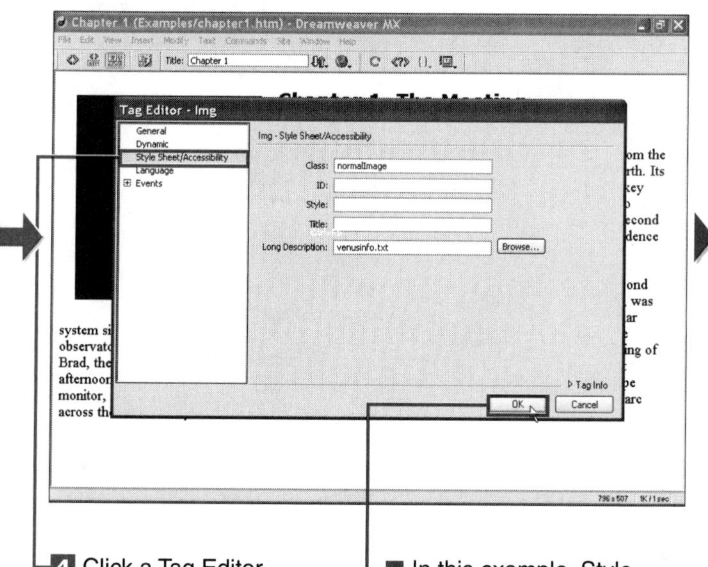

4 Click a Tag Editor category.

Note: The categories that are available depend on the tag edited.

■ In this example, Style Sheets/Accessibility allows you to apply styles to your tag and add information to improve accessibility.

Note: For information about applying styles, see page 200.

5 Click OK.

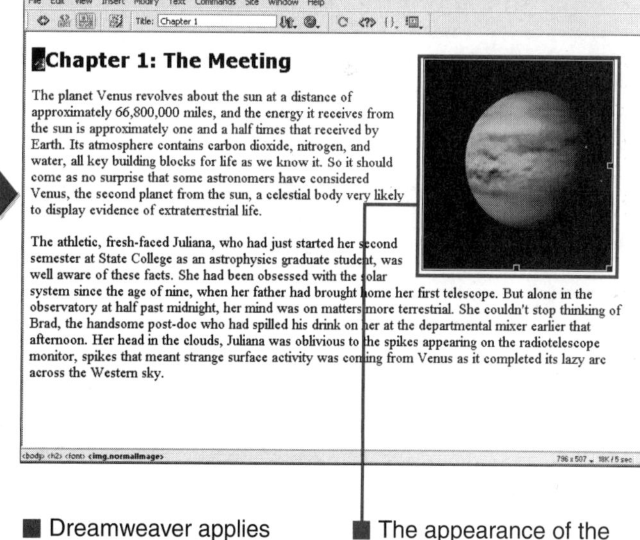

■ Dreamweaver applies your edits to the object's HTML.

■ The appearance of the object in the Design View changes accordingly.

SET UP A LOCAL FOLDER

Before creating pages for your site, you need to define a local folder. Defining a local folder enables you to pick a convenient place to store your Web project files on your computer. Creating a local folder also tells Dreamweaver where to store certain accessory files, such as templates and library items, that help you maintain your pages efficiently. After defining your local folder, you can manage your files in the site window. See page 252 for information on managing your files.

You need to set up a different local folder for each Web site you build in Dreamweaver. You may want to create a folder named Sites somewhere on your hard drive and create a subfolder for each Dreamweaver site that you create.

After you have created the Web pages in your local folder, you can transfer those files to your remote folder, where the rest of the world can then view them. The remote folder usually exists on a Web server maintained by your Internet service provider. For details about setting up a remote folder, see page 254.

SET UP A LOCAL FOLDER

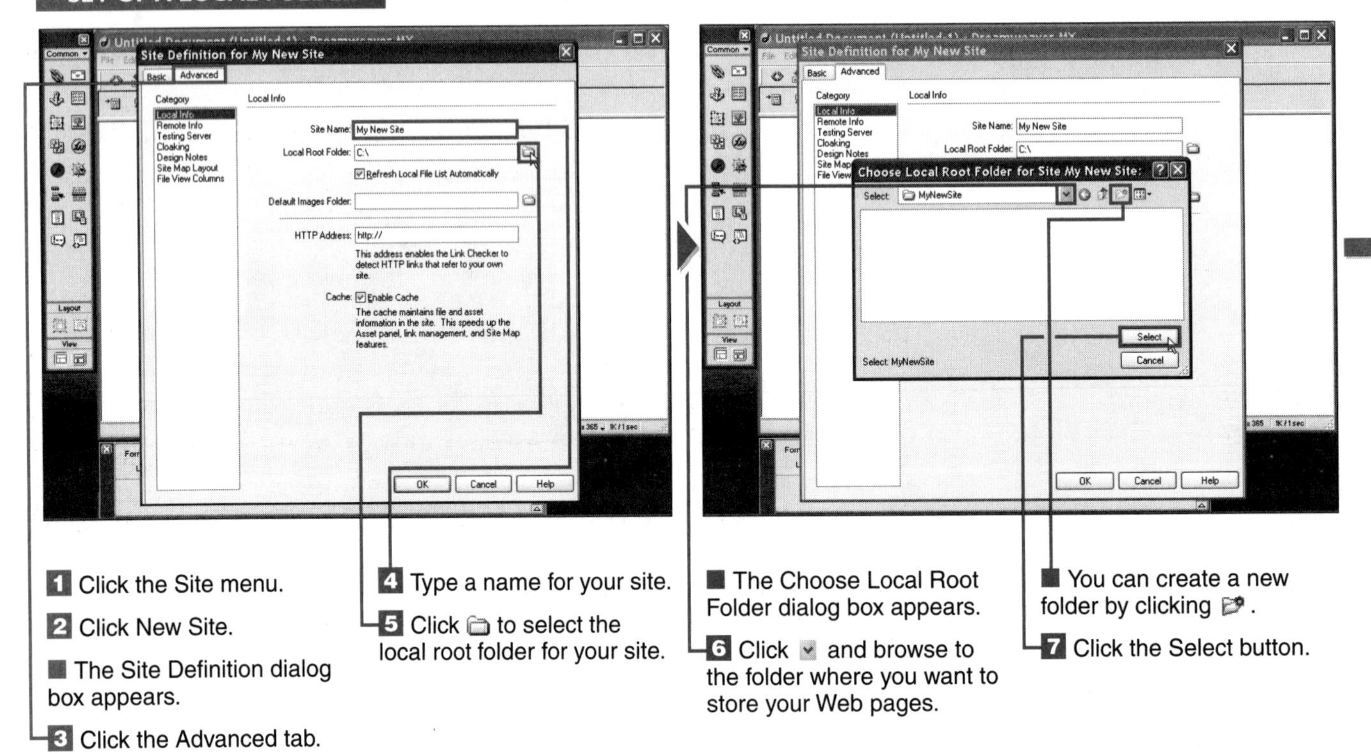

1 Click the Site menu.

2 Click New Site.

■ The Site Definition dialog box appears.

3 Click the Advanced tab.

4 Type a name for your site.

5 Click 🗀 to select the local root folder for your site.

■ The Choose Local Root Folder dialog box appears.

6 Click ▾ and browse to the folder where you want to store your Web pages.

■ You can create a new folder by clicking 🗀.

7 Click the Select button.

Why is it important to keep all my Web site's files in a single folder on my computer?

✔ Keeping everything in the same folder enables you to easily transfer your site files to the Web server without changing their organization. If you do not organize your site files on the Web server the same way they appear on your local computer, hyperlinks will not work and images will not display properly.

Will the name that I give my site appear anywhere on my finished Web site?

✔ No. The name is used only for keeping track of different sites in Dreamweaver. It appears in the Site drop-down list at the top of the Site window.

How does Dreamweaver use a default images folder?

✔ If you specify a default images folder for your new site, Dreamweaver will place new images that you add to your site in that folder unless you explicitly put the images elsewhere. For example, if you drag an image from the Desktop into the Document window, Dreamweaver will place a copy of the image in the default folder.

What is the Basic option for setting up a new site?

✔ If you click the Basic tab at the top of the Site Definition window, Dreamweaver will guide you through the steps required to create a new site. This can be useful if you are new to developing Web sites.

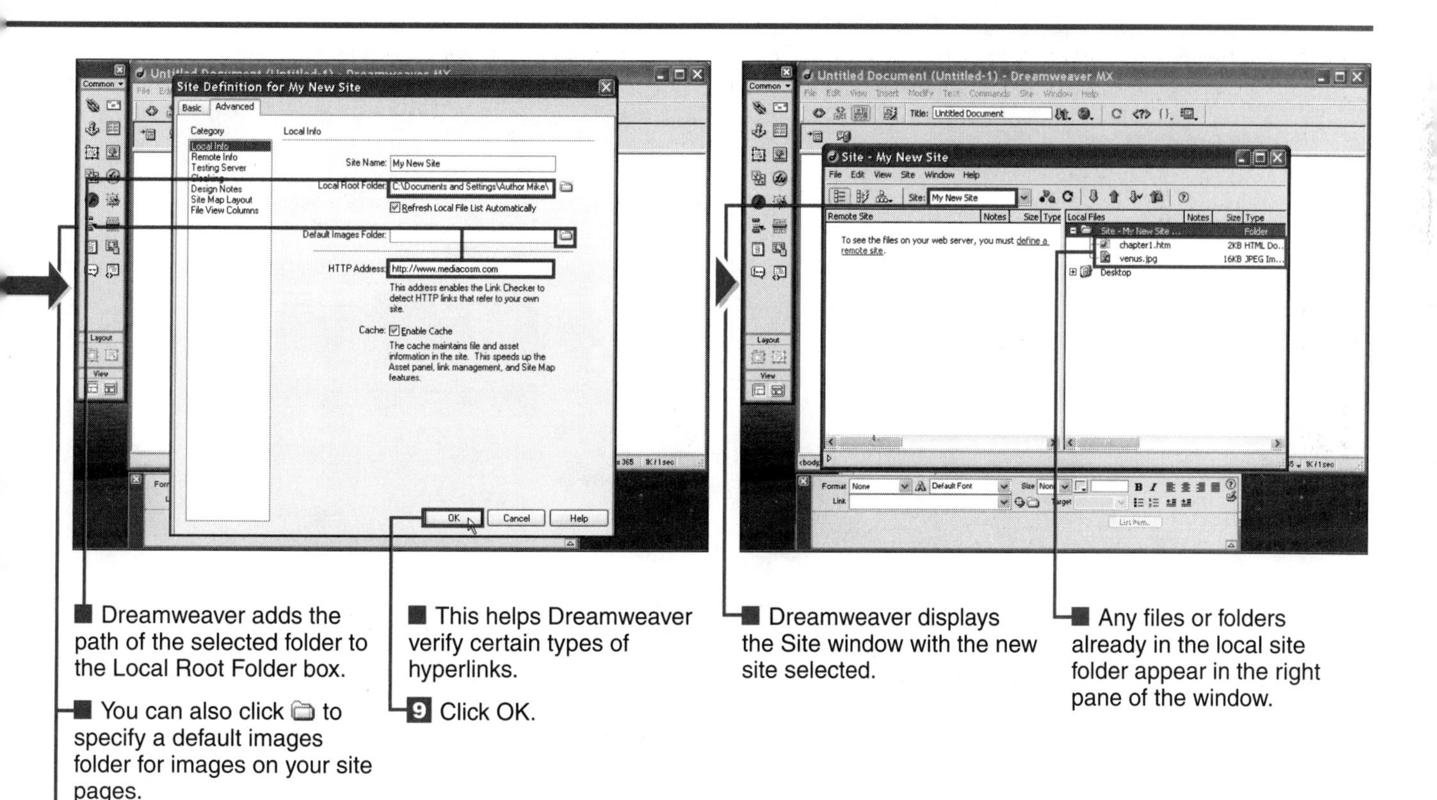

■ Dreamweaver adds the path of the selected folder to the Local Root Folder box.

■ You can also click 🗀 to specify a default images folder for images on your site pages.

8 Type the online address of your Web site.

■ This helps Dreamweaver verify certain types of hyperlinks.

9 Click OK.

■ Dreamweaver displays the Site window with the new site selected.

■ Any files or folders already in the local site folder appear in the right pane of the window.

OPEN A WEB PAGE

You can open an existing Web page in Dreamweaver to view its structure and modify it. To do this, you open the document containing the HTML code that defines the page. When you open a page, Dreamweaver displays the text content, tables, forms, and other HTML features of the page in the Document window. Dreamweaver also displays any images that have been inserted into the page, as long as the image files are part of the local site. What you see in the Document window is what you see when you open the page in a Web browser.

Dreamweaver does not display any images that have remote addresses in the Document window. To see these, you have to preview the page in a Web browser.

You can have multiple Web pages open at once in Dreamweaver and even drag and drop content between open pages.

To open a Web page based on a template is slightly more complicated than opening a regular Web page. See Chapter 11 for details.

OPEN A WEB PAGE

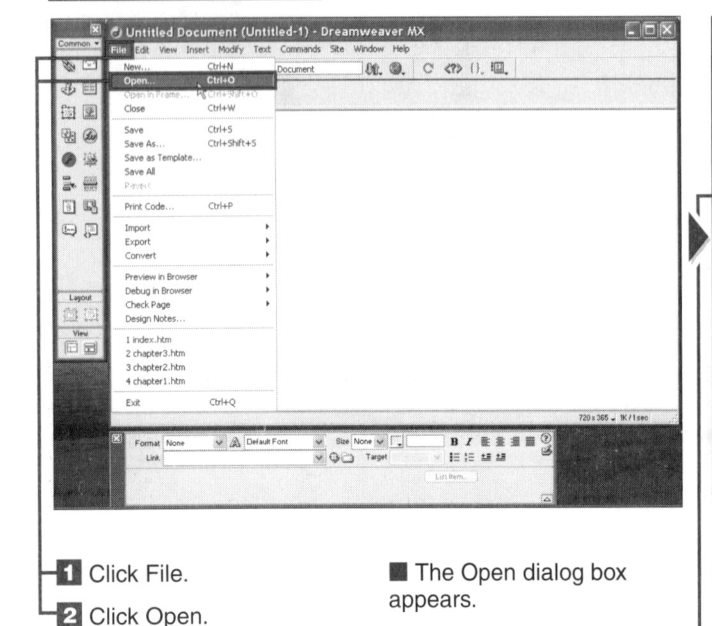

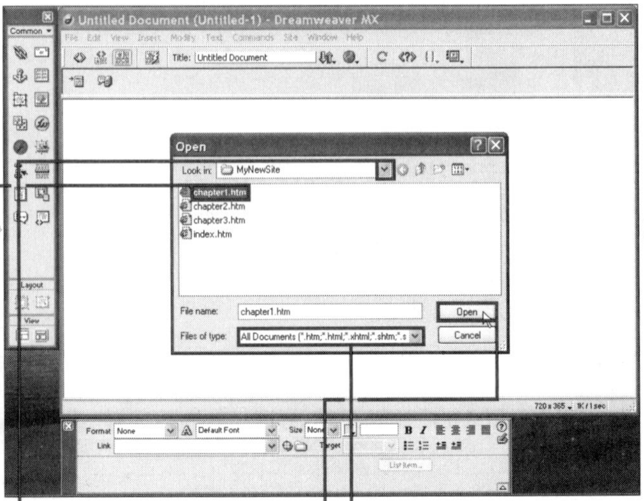

1 Click File.

2 Click Open.

■ The Open dialog box appears.

3 Click ▾ and browse to the folder containing the Web page you want to open.

4 Click the filename of the Web page.

Note: Most Web page filenames have an .htm or .html file extension.

■ You can use the Files of type menu (Show menu on the Mac) to limit the types of files displayed in the dialog box.

5 Click Open.

Can I open Web pages created in other HTML editors?

✔ Yes. Dreamweaver can open any HTML file, no matter where it was created. It can also open non-HTML text files, and dynamic Web files that are a mix of HTML and other languages, such as .cfm (ColdFusion) and .jsp (Java server page) files.

How do I open a page that I find on the Web in Dreamweaver?

✔ You can open any page on the Web in Dreamweaver by first saving that page's HTML source code as a local file. You can do this by opening the page in a Web browser and using the browser's Save command. Then open the saved page as described in this section.

How can I keep multiple Document windows from opening?

✔ Click Edit, click Preferences, and then make sure that the General category is highlighted. Uncheck Open Files in New Window and then click OK. Any new page you open will now appear in the current Document window. The current page open in the window closes. Setting this preference can help keep your workspace from getting cluttered.

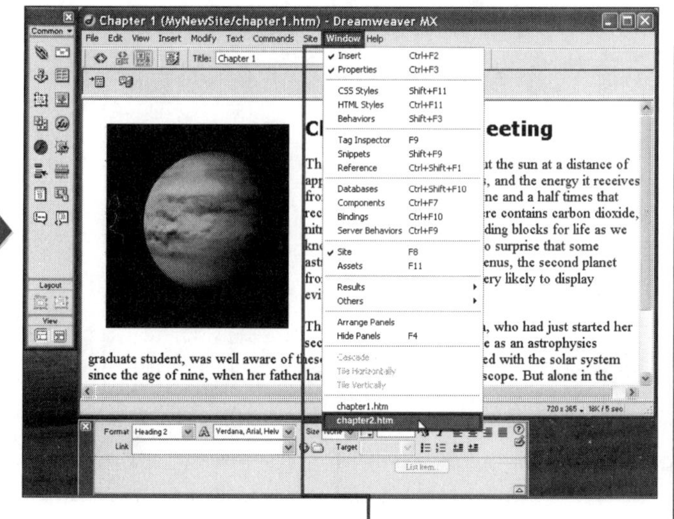

■ Dreamweaver opens the file in a Document window.

■ You can switch between open Web pages by clicking Window and then a filename.

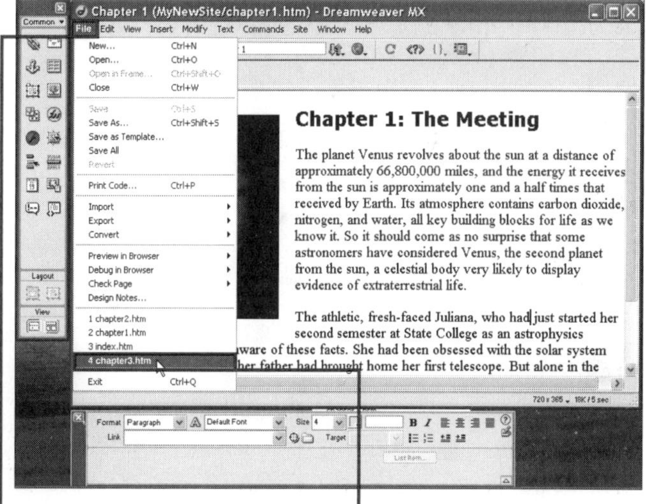

OPEN A RECENTLY OPENED PAGE

1 Click File.

■ Dreamweaver displays the last four files that you opened.

2 Click the file that you want to open.

OPEN A PREDEFINED WEB PAGE

Dreamweaver comes with numerous predefined Web pages that help you create starter pages for a number of different types of sites. Using such ready-made designs can save you time and keep the pages within your site consistent.

The predefined pages are grouped into different categories. *Commerce* designs are useful for creating pages that showcase products on an e-commerce Web site. *Image* designs are also helpful when creating product showcases, as well as online photo albums and slide shows of digital photographs. For more about inserting images, see page 88.

Text designs give you predefined layouts for online newsletters and magazines. *UI* designs offer standard forms that you can use to collect information from your site visitors. For more about forms, see Chapter 9.

OPEN A PREDEFINED WEB PAGE

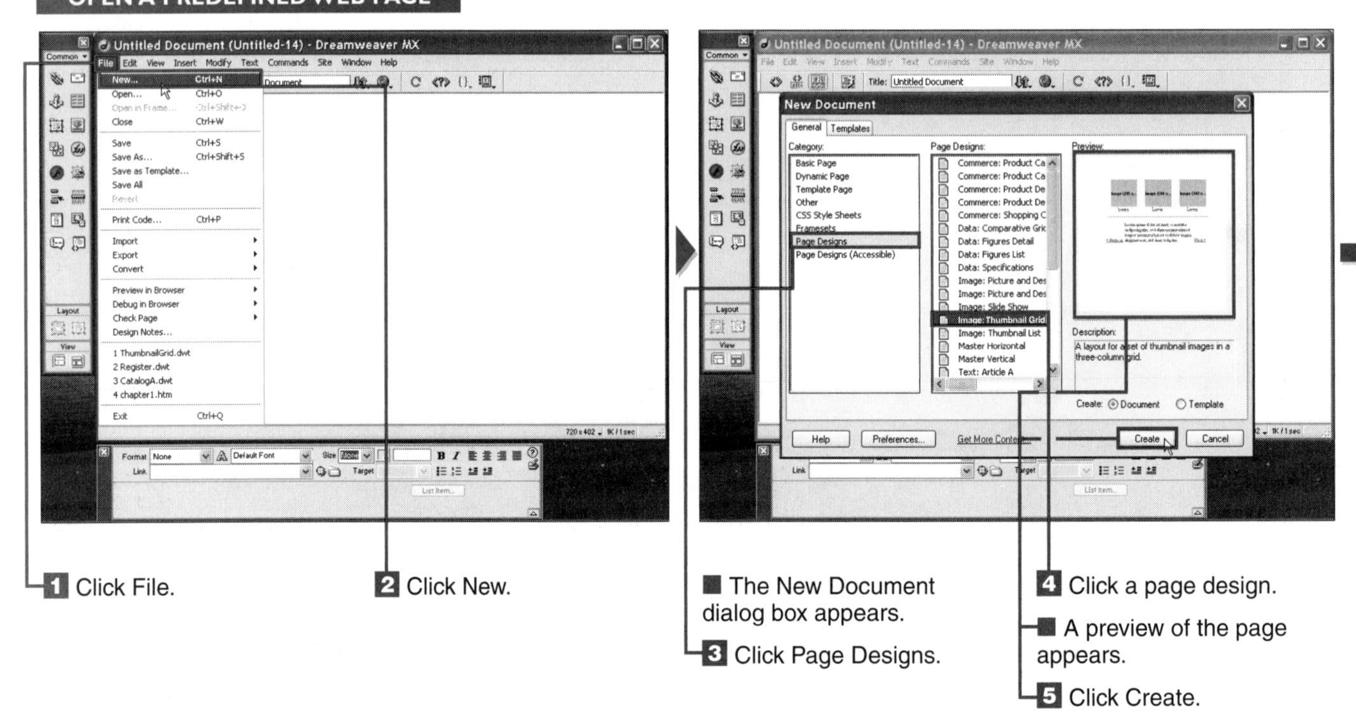

1 Click File.

2 Click New.

■ The New Document dialog box appears.

3 Click Page Designs.

4 Click a page design.

■ A preview of the page appears.

5 Click Create.

What is the Get More Content link?

✔ Clicking this link connects you with the Macromedia Web site, where you can download additional page designs to use with Dreamweaver.

What is the difference between a predefined page and a template?

✔ *Template* has special meaning in Dreamweaver. Dreamweaver templates are special starter pages that you can use to create, and then maintain, similar pages across a site. When you update an original template page, all the pages based on the template update as well. You can turn a predefined page into a template by clicking Template in the New Document window. See Chapter 11 for more about templates.

What is the Page Designs category?

✔ The Page Designs (Accessible) category features layouts and HTML code that can be interpreted by the wide variety of browser types that access the Web. The regular page designs work fine in the major browsers such as Microsoft Internet Explorer and Netscape Navigator, but they may not work so well in specialized browsers for users who, for example, cannot view graphics. If you expect such users to be part of your audience, you may want to consider using the accessible designs.

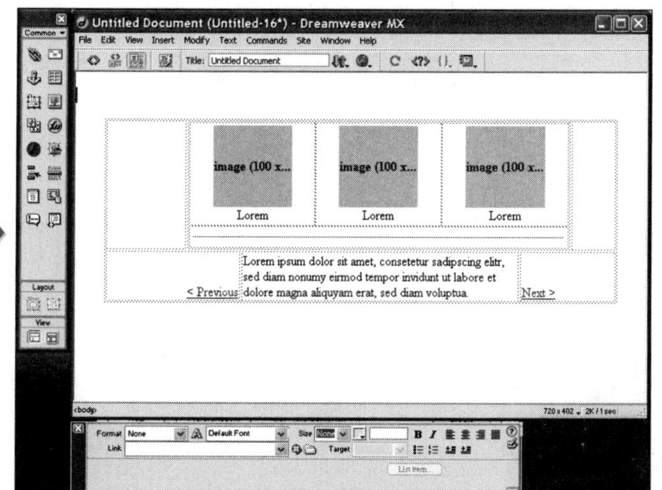

■ Dreamweaver opens the predefined page in a Document window.

■ The page includes generic text and placeholder images as filler in content areas.

■ You can replace text and images, and make other changes to create your own page.

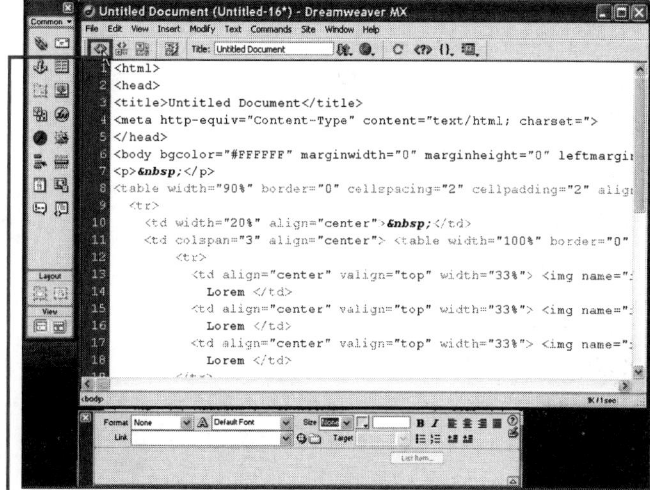

VIEW THE PAGE CODE

1 Click ◇.

■ Dreamweaver displays the HTML code for the predefined page.

Note: For information on editing the code, *see page 36.*

CREATE A BLANK WEB PAGE

You can open a new, blank page in Dreamweaver and then add text, images, and other elements to create a new Web page design. This is an alternative to opening up an existing Web page or a predefined page and using it as a starting point.

From an HTML standpoint, a blank page is not completely empty. If you click Window and then Code inspector with a blank page open, you see a few rudimentary HTML tags. These include the <html>, <head>, <title>, and <body> tags, which almost all HTML pages include. See Chapter 3 for details on working with HTML tags.

You can also create a blank page by simply starting the Dreamweaver application. A blank page appears automatically at startup.

See Chapter 11 to find out how you can also use the Dreamweaver template feature to start your new pages.

CREATE A BLANK WEB PAGE

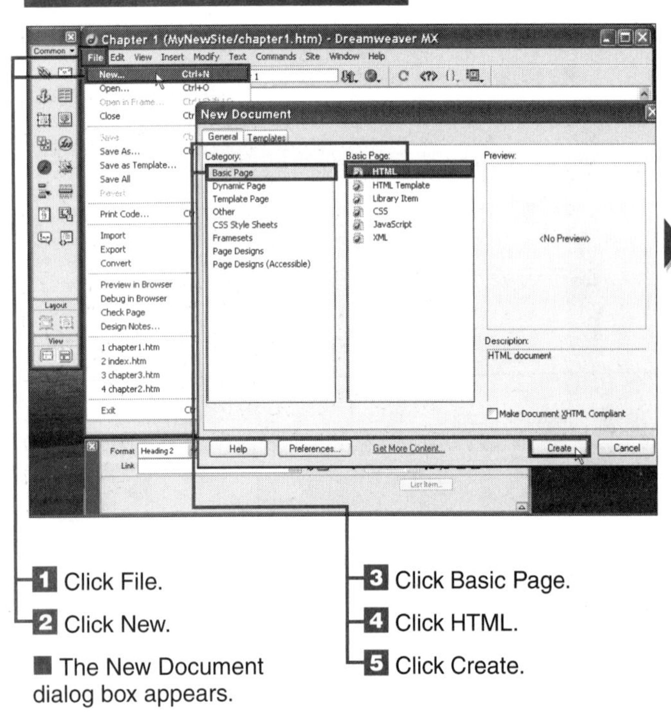

1 Click File.

2 Click New.

■ The New Document dialog box appears.

3 Click Basic Page.

4 Click HTML.

5 Click Create.

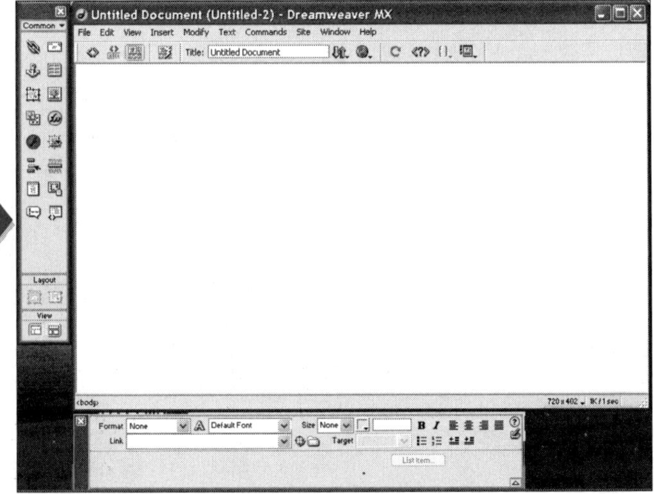

■ Dreamweaver opens an empty Document window. The page name and filename are untitled until you save the page.

ADD A TITLE TO A WEB PAGE

The title of a Web page appears in the title bar when the page opens in a Web browser. Adding a title enables you to tell viewers what they can expect to see on your Web page. The title of the page also appears as a placeholder when a viewer adds a Web page to a Favorites list in Microsoft Internet Explorer, or Bookmarks in Netscape Navigator. It also appears in a browser's History list.

Some search engines give greater weight to the information in the title when indexing a Web page. If you are interested in getting your pages top placement on search engines, it is important to include titles on your pages that are descriptive and that include keywords that are the most relevant to your pages.

The Document window includes a text field that allows you to define a page's title. You can also define the title in the Page Properties dialog box, accessible under the Modify menu.

ADD A TITLE TO A WEB PAGE

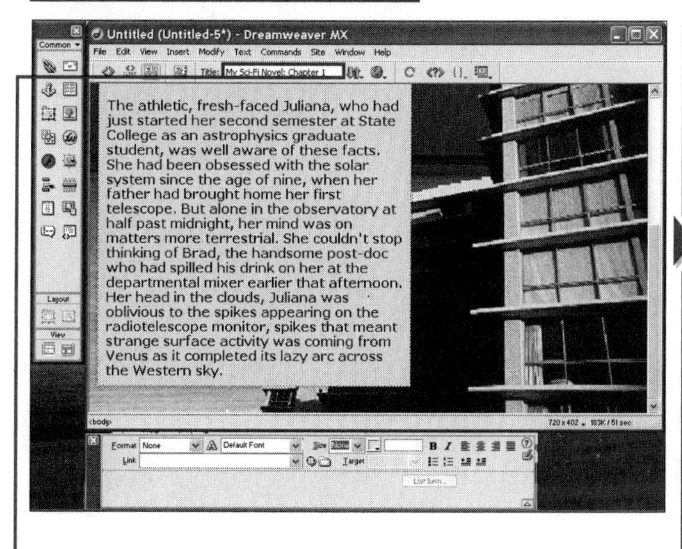

1 Type a title for your page.

2 Press Enter (Return).

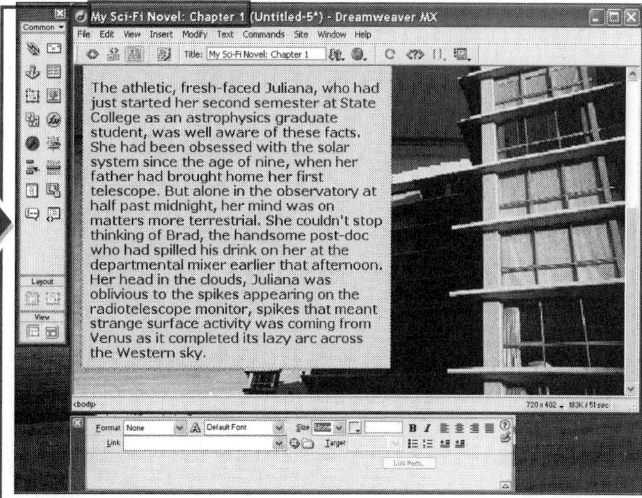

■ The title appears in the title bar of the Document window.

SAVE A WEB PAGE

Before closing your Web page files or transferring files to your remote site, save your files. This ensures the files you have stored on your computer or on your remote site are up to date. It is also a good idea to save all your files frequently to prevent work from being lost due to power outages or system failures.

When you save a document for the first time, Dreamweaver displays a dialog box that allows you to name the file and choose its location. It is best to limit yourself to letters, numbers, hyphens, and underscores when naming your Web page files. Avoid using spaces, special characters such as é, ç, or ¥, and punctuation such as colons, slashes, or periods. Many servers convert these characters during upload, which can cause links to the files to break. If you try to exit Dreamweaver and have unsaved documents open, you will receive a prompt asking whether you want to save your files.

SAVE A WEB PAGE

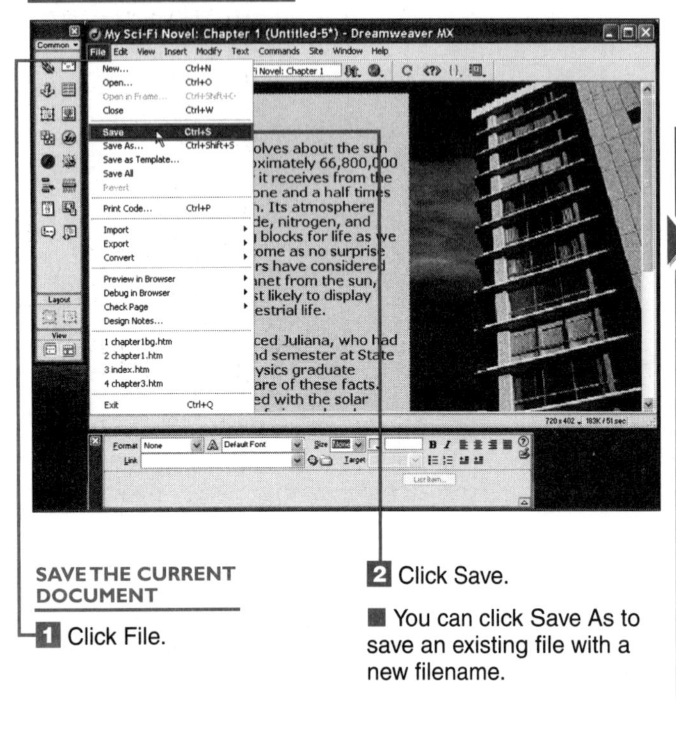

SAVE THE CURRENT DOCUMENT

1 Click File.

2 Click Save.

■ You can click Save As to save an existing file with a new filename.

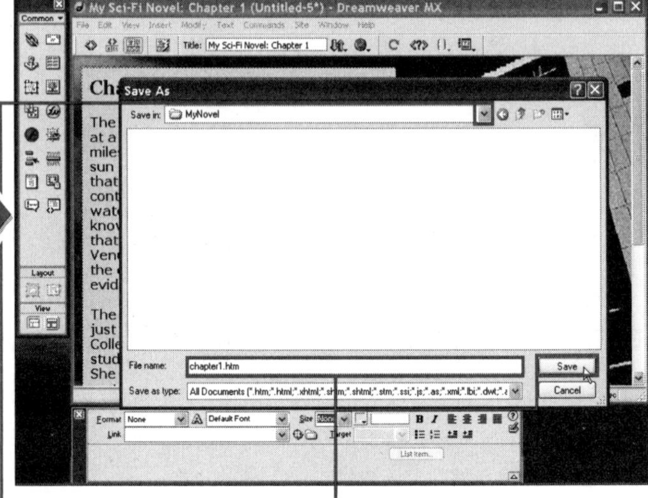

■ If you are saving a new file for the first time, Dreamweaver prompts you to name the file.

3 Click ▾ and browse to the folder where you want to save the document.

Note: To save the file in your local folder, see page 48.

4 Type a filename for the page.

5 Click Save.

What extension should I use for my Dreamweaver files?

✔ Most non-dynamic Web pages that consist of static HTML will require the .htm or .html extension. If you are creating dynamic Web pages that interact with an application server and database, you will need to use an extension specific to the application server, such as .cfm (ColdFusion Markup file), .jsp (Java server page), or .php.

What is the keyboard shortcut for saving a page?

✔ You can save the current page by pressing Ctrl + S (⌘ + S).

How can I make a duplicate of the current page?

✔ Make sure that the current page is saved. Then save it again by clicking File and then Save As and giving the file a different filename.

Does Dreamweaver have an auto-save feature?

✔ No. You need to save your files using the menu commands or keyboard shortcuts.

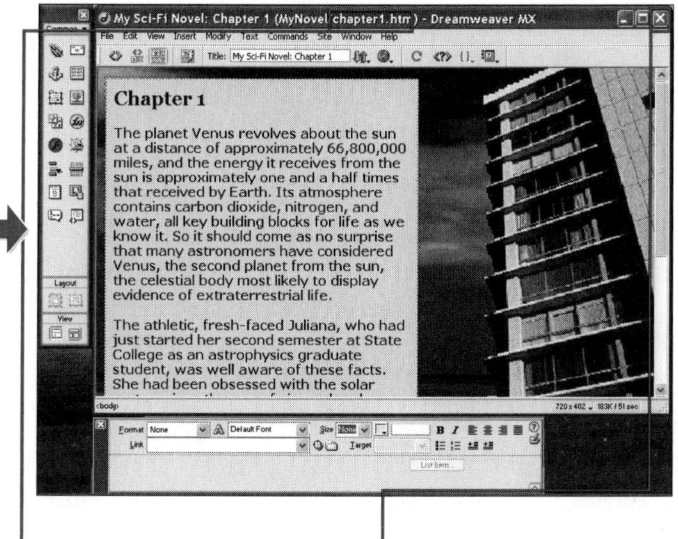

■ Dreamweaver saves the file. The filename appears in the title bar.

Note: After you have saved and named your page, you can save any subsequent changes by performing steps 1 to 2.

■ You can click ☒ to close the page.

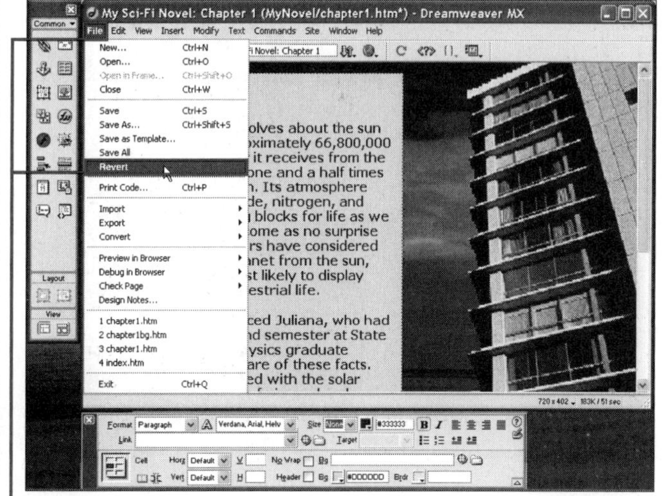

REVERT A PAGE TO THE LAST SAVED VERSION

1 Click File.

2 Click Revert.

■ Dreamweaver reverts the page to the previously saved version. All the changes made since you last saved the page will be lost.

PREVIEW A WEB PAGE IN A BROWSER

You can see how your page looks online by previewing it in a Web browser. Dreamweaver's Preview in Browser command works with the Web browsers already installed on your computer. Dreamweaver does not come with browser software.

Previewing your pages before uploading is important because you cannot see all of Dreamweaver's features in action when you create them in the Document window. These features include hyperlinks and some behaviors such as rollover image effects and form validation. You can see how these features behave when you open the pages in a browser.

It is also a good idea to preview your pages in several different browser types and versions before posting the pages live. This can help you catch features that Microsoft Internet Explorer and Netscape Navigator display differently or that one browser supports and the other does not. There are also features that are supported in newer browsers but not in older browsers, such as style sheets, Timeline animations, and layers.

PREVIEW A WEB PAGE IN A BROWSER

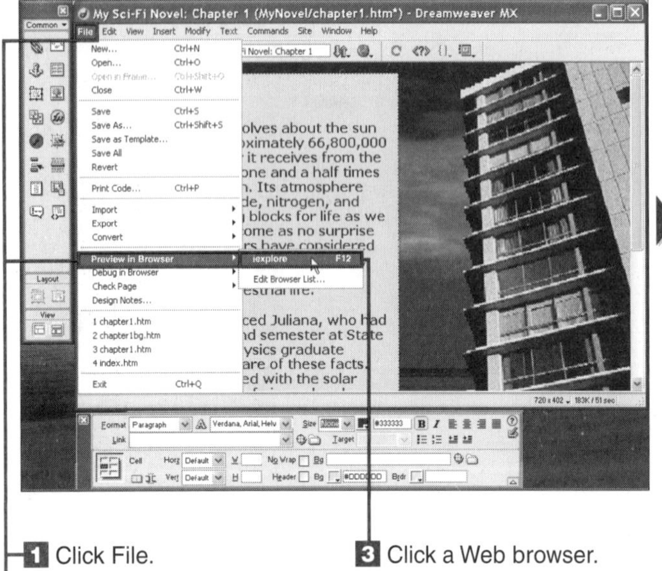

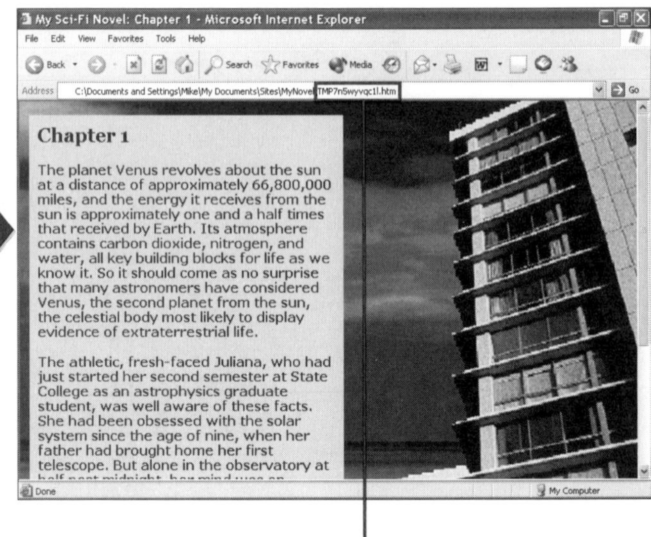

1 Click File.

2 Click Preview In Browser.

3 Click a Web browser.

■ You can also preview the page in your primary browser by pressing F12.

■ Dreamweaver launches the Web browser and opens the current page inside it.

■ The file is given a temporary filename for viewing in the browser.

Why does Dreamweaver create a temporary file when I preview?

✔ Dreamweaver usually needs to modify your page so that the content appears correctly in the browser. For example, if you define your images using root-relative paths, Dreamweaver changes those paths to document-relative paths. The modified page is stored as a temporary file, which the browser opens.

How do I define which browser is considered primary?

✔ Click File, Preview in Browser, and then Edit Browser List. Select the browser you want to define as primary, and click Primary Browser (☐ changes to ☑).

How do I make my pages appear consistently in all browsers?

✔ Building a page compatible with *every* browser is probably unfeasible, given the multitude of browsers and browser versions in use on the Web. But if you want to achieve consistency in *most* browsers, especially older versions, it is a good idea to avoid advanced features such as behaviors, Timeline animations, style sheets, and layers.

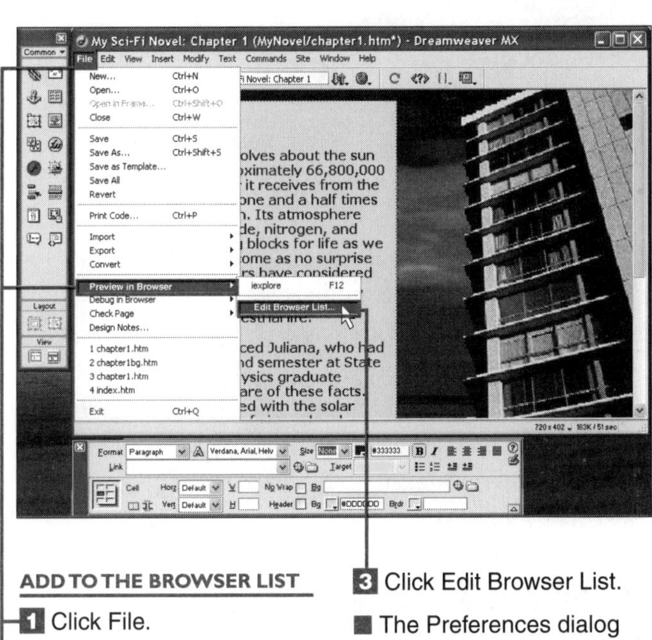

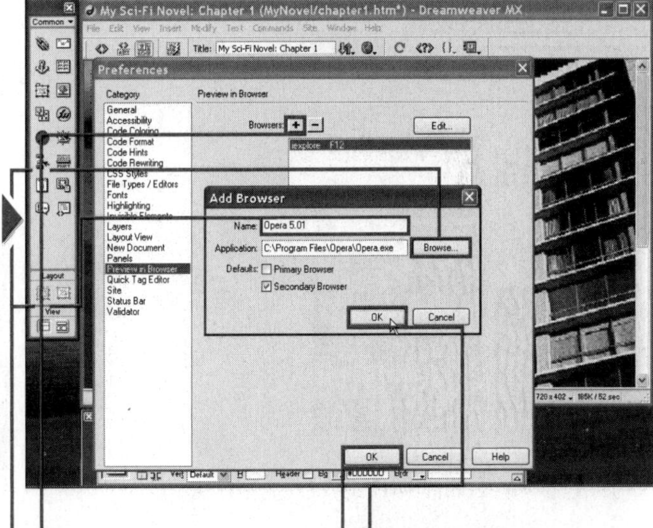

ADD TO THE BROWSER LIST

1 Click File.

2 Click Preview In Browser.

3 Click Edit Browser List.

■ The Preferences dialog box appears.

4 Click ⊞.

5 Type a name for the new browser.

6 Click Browse and select the browser application on your computer.

■ You can also define the browser as primary or secondary.

7 Click OK.

8 Click OK in the Preferences dialog box.

■ The browser is added to the browser list.

SECTION II

5) FORMATTING TEXT

6) WORKING WITH IMAGES AND GRAPHICS

7) CREATING HYPERLINKS

ADDING DESIGN ELEMENTS

8) CREATING TABLES

9) CREATING FORMS

10) DESIGNING WITH FRAMES

CREATE A PARAGRAPH

You can organize text on your Web page by creating and aligning paragraphs. When you put text into its own paragraph, Dreamweaver separates the text from the content above and below it with line space. To create a new paragraph, you simply insert the cursor where you want the paragraph to begin and press Enter (Return).

Aligning a paragraph involves selecting it and then clicking one of Dreamweaver's alignment buttons in the Properties inspector. Equivalent commands exist in the Text menu under the Alignment submenu. Center aligning a one-line paragraph at the top of a page is one way to add a title to your Web page. Center aligning a paragraph at the bottom lets you create a footer.

You can add more elaborate formatting to your paragraphs, such as different line spacing with style sheets. See Chapter 12 for more information on style sheets.

To remove paragraph formatting, you can right-click a paragraph and select Remove Tag <p> from the menu that appears. To create a new line in the flow of your text without adding paragraph spacing, see page 66.

CREATE A PARAGRAPH

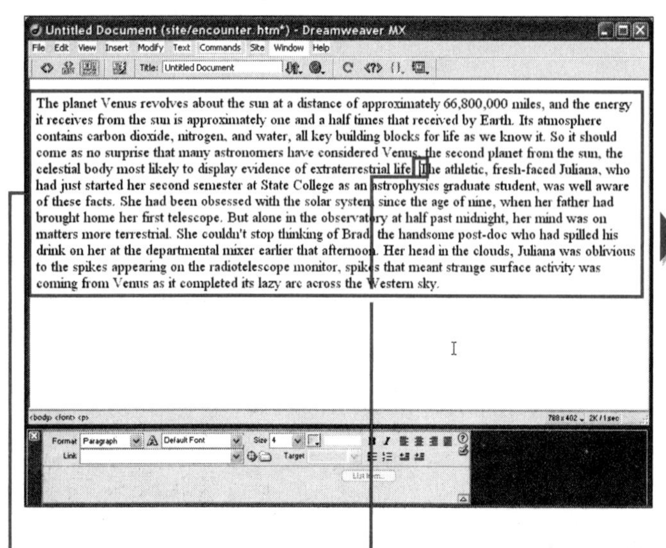

1 Type the text of your Web page into the Document window.

2 Position the cursor where you want a paragraph break.

3 Press Enter (Return).

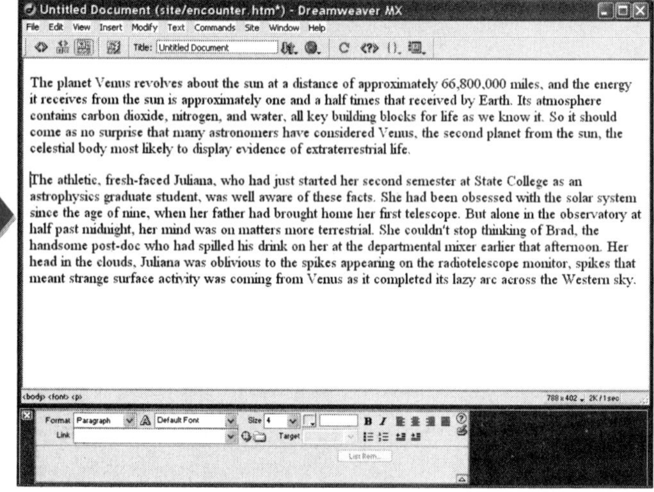

■ A blank line appears between the blocks of text, separating them into paragraphs.

What controls the width of the paragraphs on my Web page?

✔ The width of your paragraphs depends on the width of the Web browser window. When a user changes the size of the browser window, the width of the paragraphs also changes.

Can I give my paragraph a fixed width?

✔ You can fix a paragraph's width, so that it does not change with a change in the size of the browser window, by placing it inside a fixed-width table. See pages 134 to 138 for more information on creating a fixed-width table. You can also put paragraphs inside layers to fix their widths.

Can I put an image inside a paragraph by itself?

✔ Yes, you can put an image inside a paragraph by pressing Enter (Return) before and after the image on your page. Then you can align the image using the paragraph alignment commands. You can also mix images and text in the same paragraph.

How do I remove paragraph formatting?

✔ To remove paragraph formatting, right-click (Control-click) the paragraph and select Remove Tag <p> from the menu that appears.

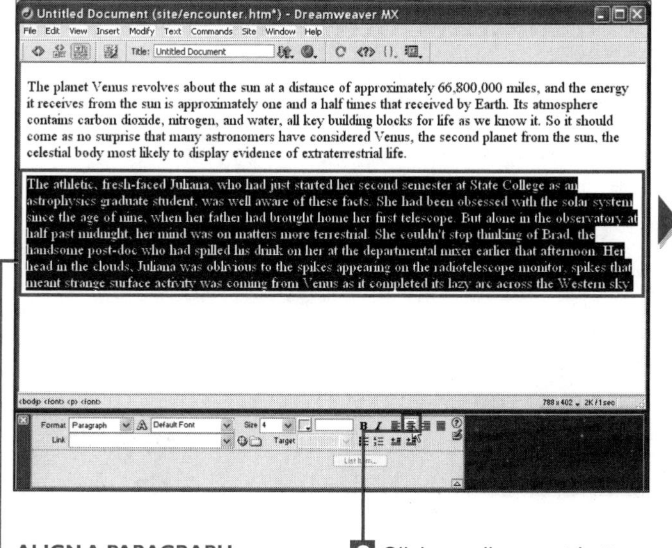

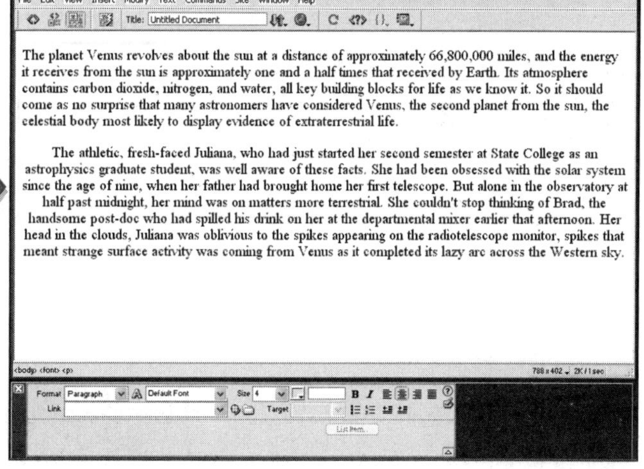

ALIGN A PARAGRAPH

1 Click and drag to select a paragraph of text.

■ Left alignment is the default for paragraph text.

2 Click an alignment button in the Properties inspector.

- Right-align
- Center-align
- Left-align

■ The alignment of the paragraph changes.

CREATE A HEADING

You can define text on your Web page as a heading to give it emphasis and to set it off from other text. You can define six different levels of headings. *Heading 1* creates the largest heading and *Heading 6* creates the smallest. The text in all six levels has a bold style and is separated from the other text in your page by extra space, similar to paragraphs.

Headings enable you to organize the information on your Web page hierarchically, with level-1 headings defining the initial headline text and other levels defining the different levels of subheadings.

You align a heading the same way you align a paragraph: You select it and then click one of Dreamweaver's alignment buttons in the Properties inspector. You can also use the Properties inspector to change the color of a heading. See page 80 for details.

As part of the earliest HTML specifications, headings used to be one of the only ways to give your text nondefault formatting. Nowadays, Web page authors can style their text in a variety of ways using various font commands as well as style sheets.

CREATE A HEADING

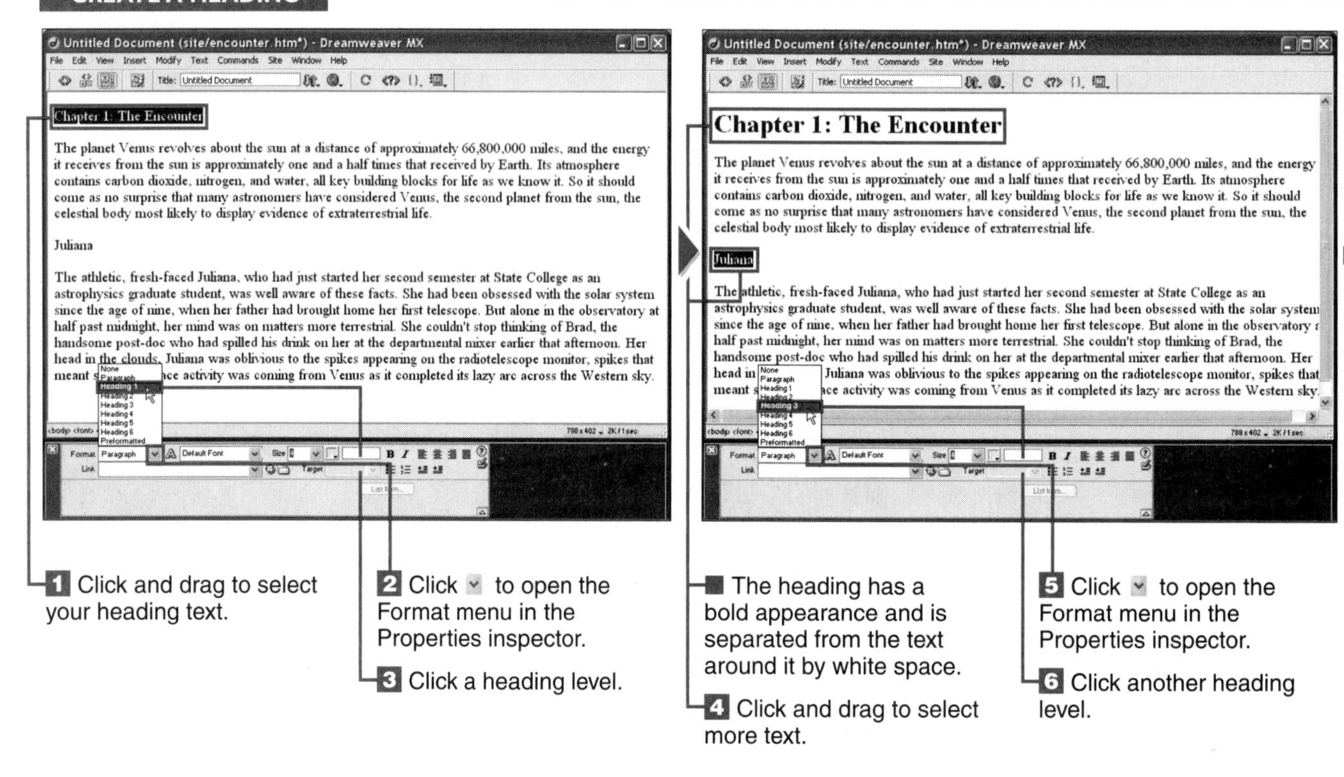

1 Click and drag to select your heading text.

2 Click ▾ to open the Format menu in the Properties inspector.

3 Click a heading level.

■ The heading has a bold appearance and is separated from the text around it by white space.

4 Click and drag to select more text.

5 Click ▾ to open the Format menu in the Properties inspector.

6 Click another heading level.

Do larger headings take longer to download than smaller headings?

✔ No. The same amount of HTML code is required to create headings, regardless of the heading level. So downloading text takes the same amount of time whether you format it as a large level-1 heading or as a small level-6 heading.

What are some common uses for level-5 and level-6 headings?

✔ You can use these heading styles to set copyright and disclaimer information apart from the rest of the page content.

Can I make my headings a different font or color?

✔ Yes. You can customize your headings the same way you customize regular text. See page 74 and 80.

How do the sizes of headings compare to paragraph text?

✔ Most browsers display level-4 headings the same size as regular bolded paragraph text. Consequently, levels 1, 2, and 3 create larger-than-default bolded text, and levels 5 and 6 create smaller-than-default bolded text.

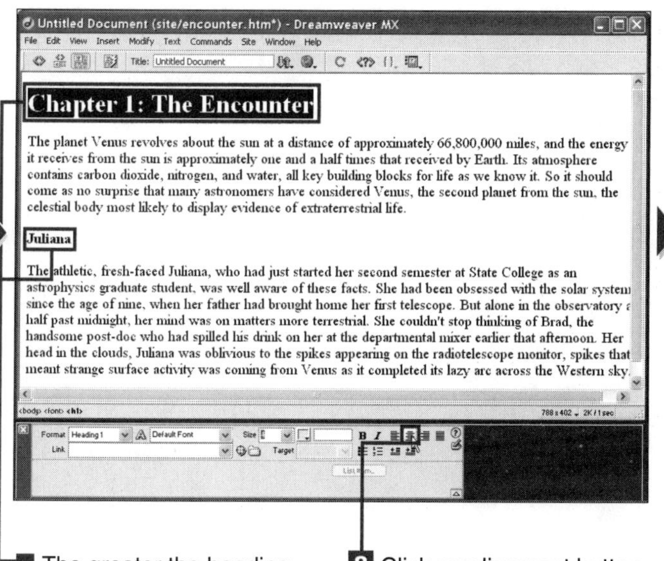

■ The greater the heading level, the smaller the heading text.

7 Click and drag to select some heading text.

8 Click an alignment button in the Properties inspector.

- ☰ Right-align
- ☰ Center-align
- ☰ Left-align

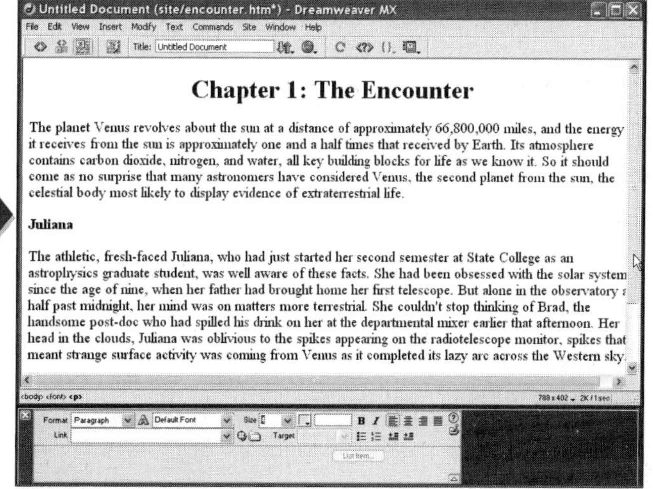

■ The alignment of the heading changes.

CREATE A LINE BREAK

Adding line breaks to your page enables you to keep adjacent lines of related text close together. *Line breaks* are an alternative to paragraph breaks, which add more space between lines of text. See page 62. Line breaks can be useful when displaying content such as addresses and poetry.

You can use line breaks with nontext elements as well. Putting a line break between images, tables, or form fields can ensure that the elements stay close together, which can help you fit more information onto a Web page.

Inserting line breaks inside a paragraph does not affect the alignment of the text inside the paragraph. For example, if you right-align paragraph text and add a new line break, the text before and after the break stays right-aligned.

You can easily add lots of vertical space on your page by adding multiple line breaks. The amount of space added with each break you insert depends on the size of the text right before the first break.

CREATE A LINE BREAK

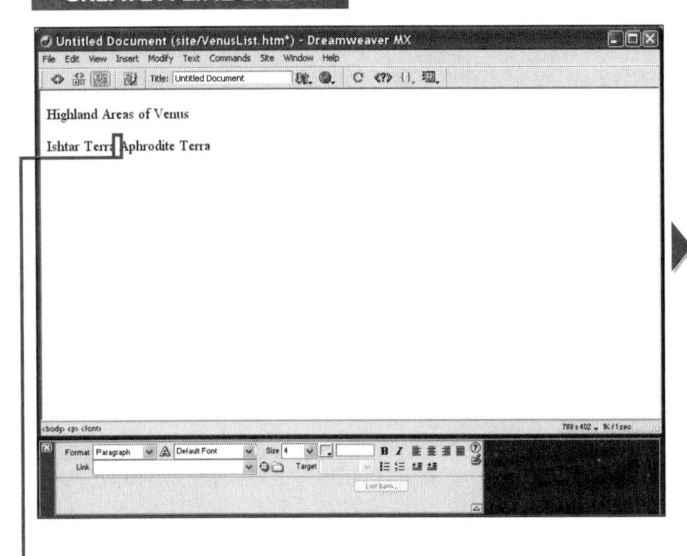

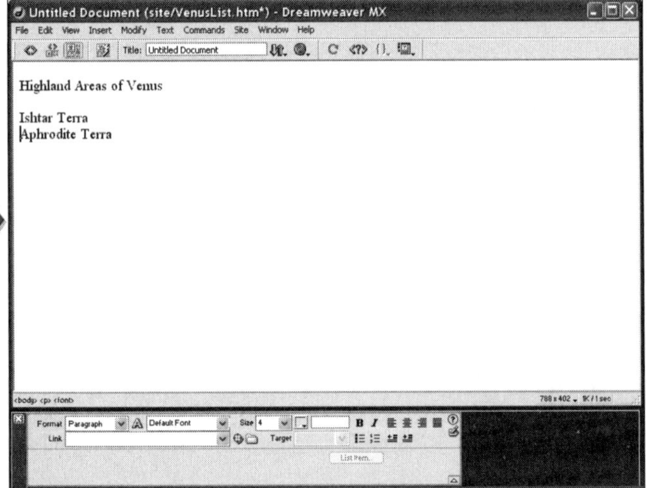

1 Postion your cursor where you want the line to break.

2 Press Shift + Enter (Shift + Return).

■ Dreamweaver adds a line break.

ADD EXTRA BLANK SPACE

You can insert more than one blank space between characters by using a special command. Extra blank space is ignored in HTML code, which means you can usually insert only one space between the characters on your page using the space bar.

The character that you add with the special command is called a *nonbreaking space*. Nonbreaking means if you put more than one of these spaces in a row, they wrap as a single unit when they hit the right edge of a browser window, just like characters in a word do.

You can use extra spaces to indent the first line at the beginning of your paragraphs; you can also use them for artistic purposes, such as spreading words and letters at uneven horizontal intervals on your page.

Nonbreaking spaces can also serve a purpose when inserting tables that include empty cells. Some Web browsers do not render table cells that are empty. Adding a nonbreaking space to such cells is a way to force a browser to render them, but still keep such cells empty of visible content.

You can achieve a similar effect with style sheets, which let you precisely define the spacing between the letters of your text. See Chapter 12 for more information.

ADD EXTRA BLANK SPACE

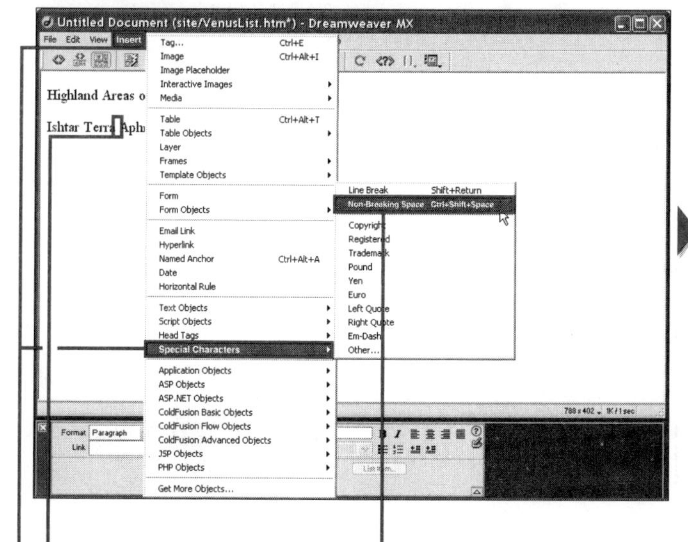

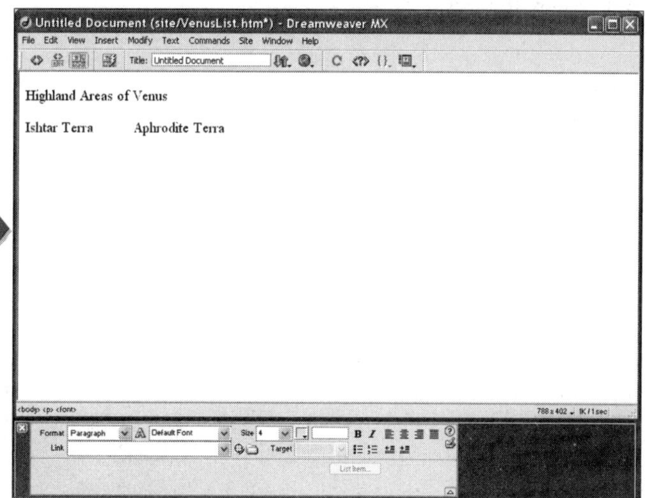

1 Postion your cursor where you want to add an extra blank space.

2 Click Insert.

3 Click Special Characters.

4 Click Non-Breaking Space.

■ You can also add an extra blank space by pressing Ctrl + Shift + Space (⌘ + Shift + Space).

■ Dreamweaver adds additional space between the characters.

CREATE AN UNORDERED LIST

You can organize text items on your Web page into *unordered lists*, which display the items indented and bulleted. Unordered lists are useful for organizing elements that need to be grouped but in no particular order. Bulleting a series of sentences can make information stand out on a text-heavy page. There is no size limit to the length of each list item — items can be single words or long passages. To create lists that are numbered instead of bulleted, see page 70.

You can *nest* unordered lists, which means you can have a list inside another list. In such a case, Dreamweaver indents the inside list further and gives it differently styled bullets. Dreamweaver uses hollow circles for the secondary list and solid squares for any lists nested inside that. Nested lists can be useful when creating an outline.

Unordered lists are created in HTML with the <ul> and <li> tags. See page 36 for more information about viewing a page's HTML.

CREATE AN UNORDERED LIST

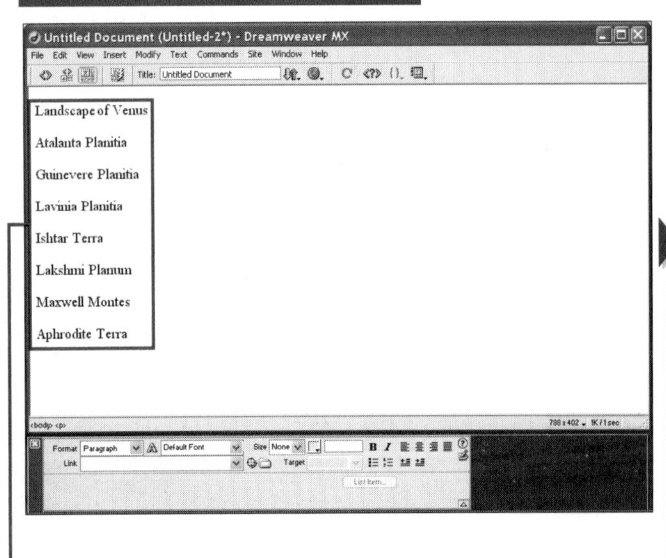

1 Type your list items into the Document window.

2 Position each item on a separate line by pressing Enter (Return) between the items.

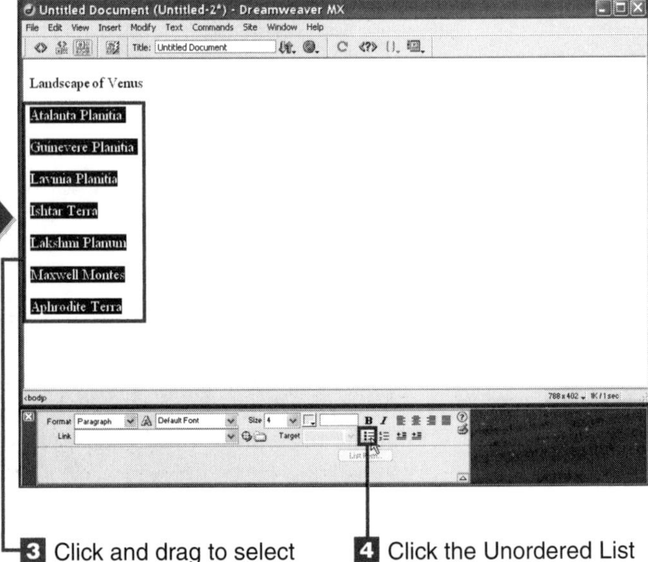

3 Click and drag to select all the list items.

4 Click the Unordered List button (☰) in the Properties inspector.

How do I modify the bullets in my unordered list?

✔ You can modify the style of a bullet by highlighting an item in the list and clicking Text, List, and then Properties. You can also click the List Item button in the Properties inspector. A dialog box enables you to select different bullet styles for your unordered list.

How do I add extra space between my list items?

✔ By default, Dreamweaver single-spaces your list items. To add more space, insert line breaks by pressing Shift + Enter (Shift + Return) at the end of each item.

How do I create differently colored bullets?

✔ When you create your list using Dreamweaver commands, you cannot change the color of the bullets — you are stuck with black. But you can create custom images to serve as bullets in an image editor and then insert them as Web-page images. See page 86 for information on inserting images.

How do I indent content on my page without bulleting it as a list?

✔ Select the text and click the Indent button ( )in the Properties inspector. The ( ) reverses the effect.

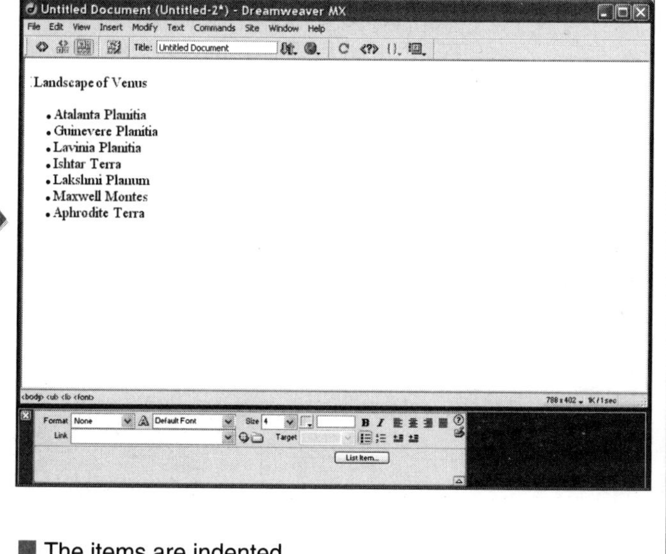

■ The items are indented and bulleted.

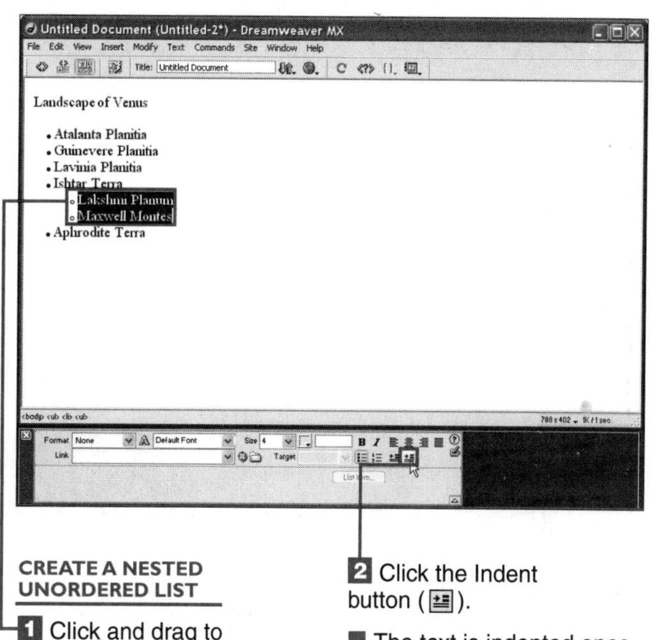

CREATE A NESTED UNORDERED LIST

1 Click and drag to select the list items you want to nest.

2 Click the Indent button ( ).

■ The text is indented once again with differently styled bullets.

CREATE AN ORDERED LIST

You can display step-by-step instructions on your Web page by organizing text items into an ordered list. *Ordered lists* have items that are indented and numbered.

Ordered lists are useful for displaying driving directions, test questions, or recipes on your Web pages. There is no size limit to the length of each item. Items can be single words or long passages. To create lists that are bulleted instead of ordered, see page 68.

You can *nest* ordered lists, which means you can place a list inside another list. In such cases, Dreamweaver indents the inside list and restarts its numbers at 1. When it comes to updating, using the ordered list feature can save you time because you do not have to number items by hand. When you add a new item to an ordered list, Dreamweaver does the renumbering for you.

A feature that ordered lists do not include, however, is a way to add letter modifiers to list items, such as 1a, 1b, and so on. If you want that style of numbering, you have to order your list by hand.

Unordered lists are created in HTML with the <ol> and <li> tags. See Chapter 3 for more information about viewing a page's HTML.

CREATE AN ORDERED LIST

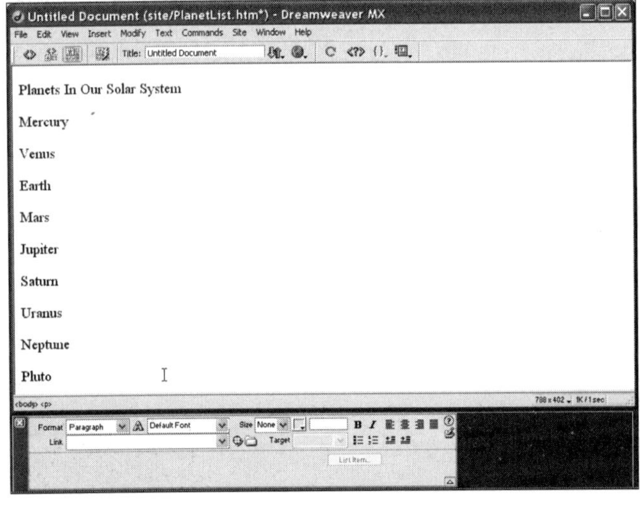

1 Type your list items into the Document window.

2 Position each item on a separate line by pressing Enter (Return) between the items.

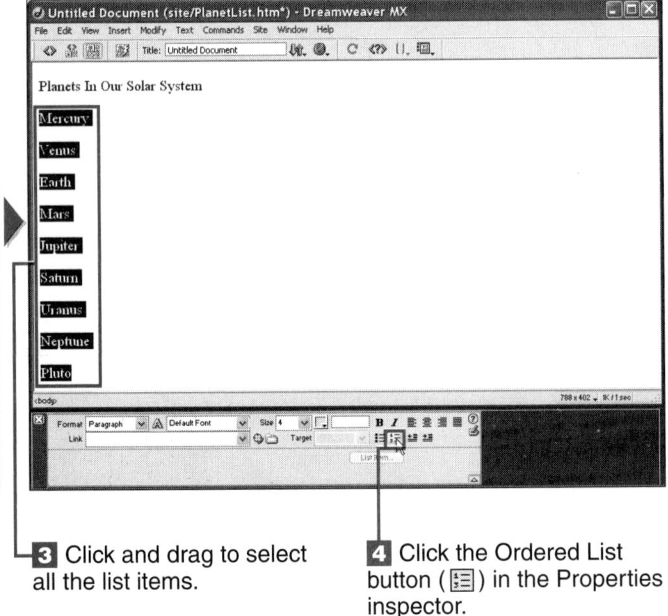

3 Click and drag to select all the list items.

4 Click the Ordered List button (☰) in the Properties inspector.

Can I bold or italicize the numerals in my list?

✔ Not when you create your list using Dreamweaver commands — you are stuck with the default text style. For fancier numbering, you have to create your lists from scratch on your pages, using regular text for numbering. You can then style the numbers all you want.

How do I align my list?

✔ Select some or all of your list items and then click [align left], [align center], or [align right] in the Properties inspector. The selected items are aligned.

How do I modify the numerals in my ordered list?

✔ You can modify the numerals by highlighting an item in the list and selecting Text, List, and then Properties. You can also click the List Item button in the Properties inspector. A dialog box enables you to select different numbering schemes, including Roman numerals (upper and lower case) and alphabetical styles. It also lets you begin a list with a number other than 1 (the default), or reset the count in the middle of the list.

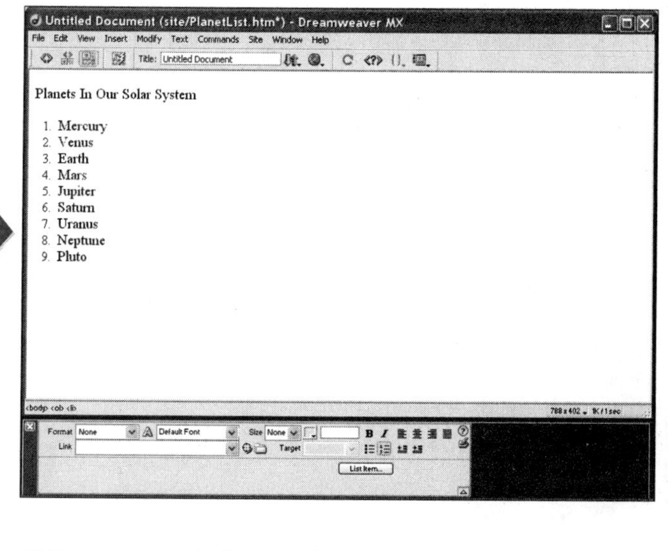

■ Dreamweaver indents and numbers the items.

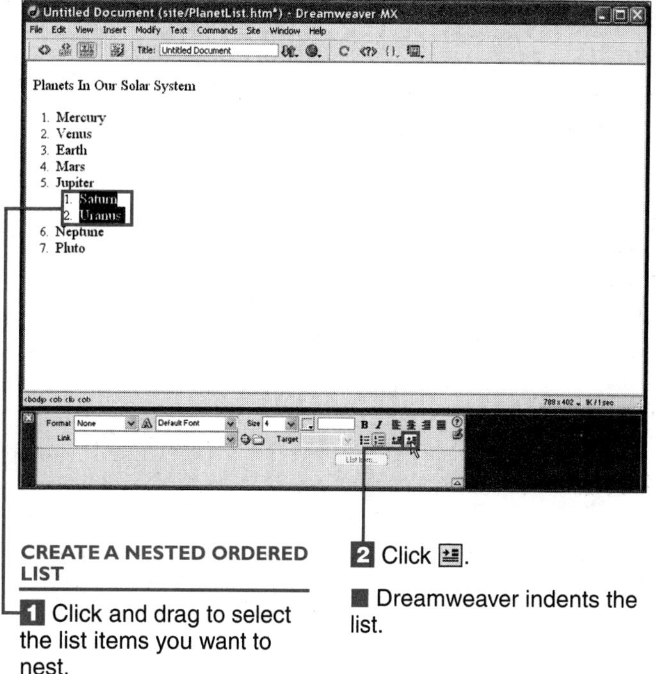

CREATE A NESTED ORDERED LIST

1 Click and drag to select the list items you want to nest.

2 Click [indent].

■ Dreamweaver indents the list.

INSERT SPECIAL CHARACTERS

You can insert special characters that do not appear on your keyboard by using buttons from the Insert panel. Characters available in the panel include currency symbols, trademark and copyright symbols, non-English language characters, and mathematical symbols.

Dreamweaver adds the characters to your page by inserting special codes, also known as *entities*, into the HTML of the page. All the special codes begin with an ampersand (&) and end with a semicolon (;). In between the ampersand (&) and semicolon (;) are a set of either letters or numbers preceded by a number sign. For the copyright symbol and trademark symbols, for example, Dreamweaver inserts `©` and `™` respectively. You can see the special codes after you insert the characters by viewing a page's HTML. See Chapter 3 for more about HTML.

When you copy and paste text that contains special characters from another text application, Dreamweaver inserts the special codes automatically. If you want to paste special characters into your page and you do not want them converted, you can paste the characters into the page code in Code View.

INSERT SPECIAL CHARACTERS

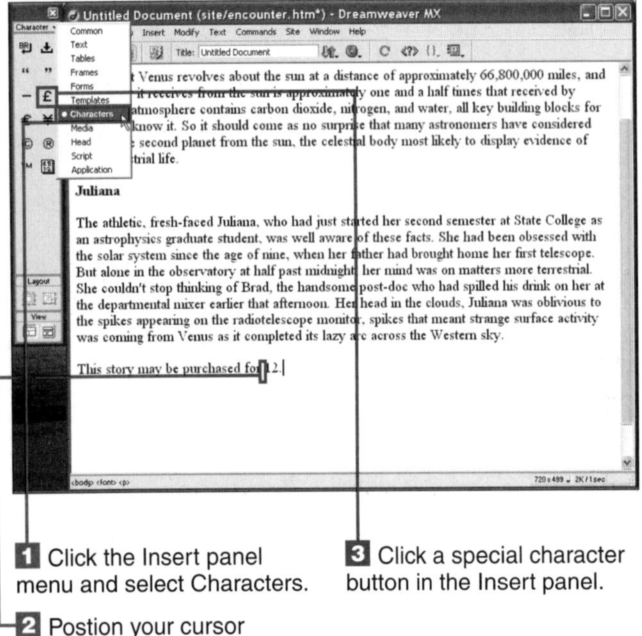

1 Click the Insert panel menu and select Characters.

2 Postion your cursor where you want to insert the special character.

3 Click a special character button in the Insert panel.

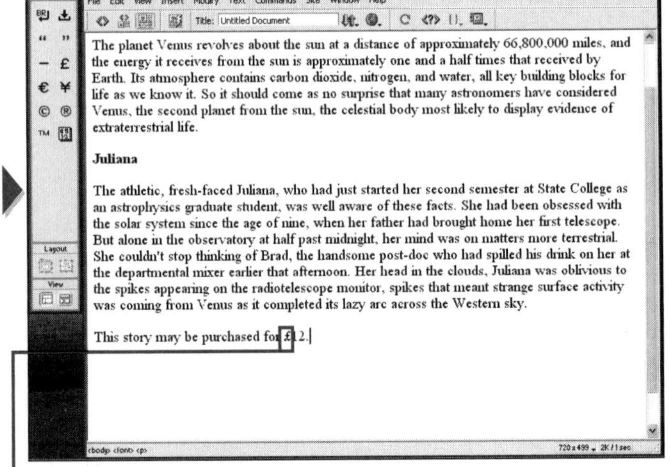

■ Dreamweaver inserts a special character into your Web page.

How can I make HTML tags display in the text of my Web page?

✔ HTML tags have to be coded differently if they are to be displayed on a Web page. This is because when a browser encounters an HTML tag in a page's code — for example a `<P>`, which is a paragraph tag — it interprets it as a formatting command and not something it should display for the viewer. So the viewer never sees it.

To actually display HTML tags on a Web page, you need to use special character codes for the angle brackets (< and >). To display a paragraph tag, you must code the tag as `<P>` in HTML. The `<` and `>` are the special codes for displaying angle brackets.

How do I insert an en dash or em dash symbol into my page text?

✔ The Insert Other Character dialog box lets you insert both characters. You can also insert them by typing `–` or `—` into your HTML code.

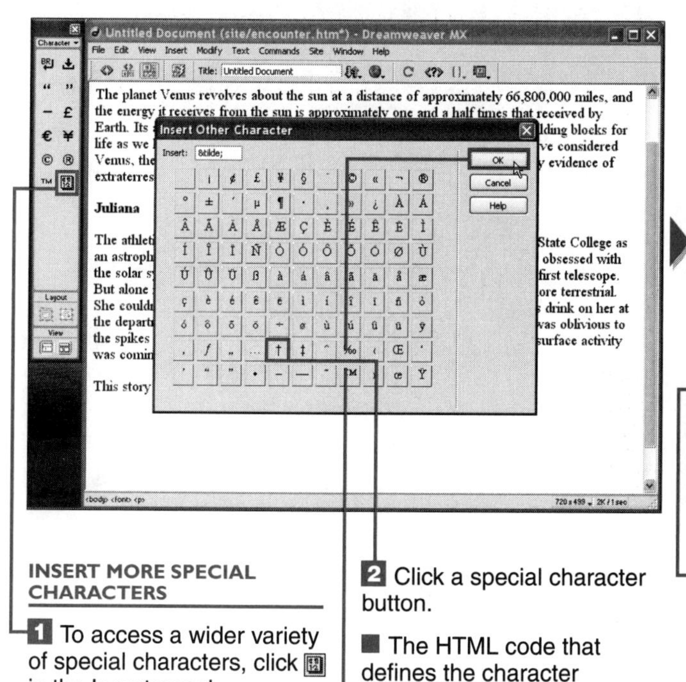

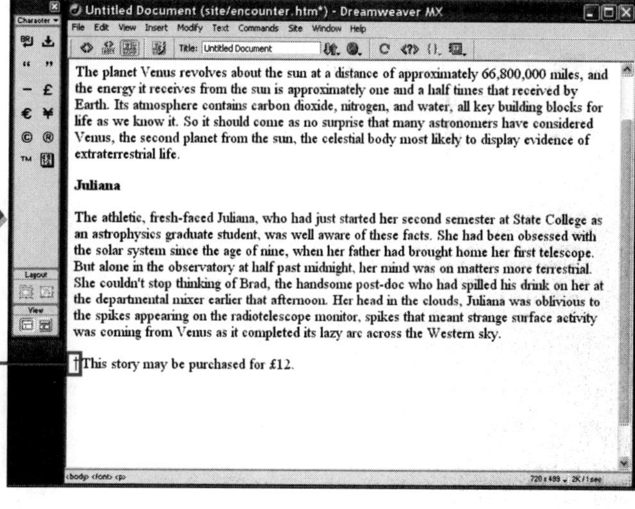

INSERT MORE SPECIAL CHARACTERS

1 To access a wider variety of special characters, click [icon] in the Insert panel.

2 Click a special character button.

■ The HTML code that defines the character appears in the text field.

3 Click OK.

■ Dreamweaver inserts a special character into your Web page.

CHANGE A FONT

You can make the text on your Web page look more interesting by changing its font. If you do not specify a particular font, most browsers display text on your Web page in Times New Roman (Times).

You can specify any style of font that you want in Dreamweaver; however, Web browsers can display only fonts that are installed on the computer on which they are running. Because of this, you most likely want to limit your font choices to the more popular ones, such as Arial, Verdana, Georgia, Comic Sans, and Courier.

To ensure that a viewer sees the style of text that you want them to see, you can specify more than one font choice for your text. If your first choice is available on the viewer's computer, the Web browser displays text using that font. If your first choice is not available, and you have specified a second choice, the browser tries to display it using that font, and so on. If the computer has none of the font choices, the default font for the browser displays. The default font can usually be changed in the Options or Preferences for the browser.

CHANGE A FONT

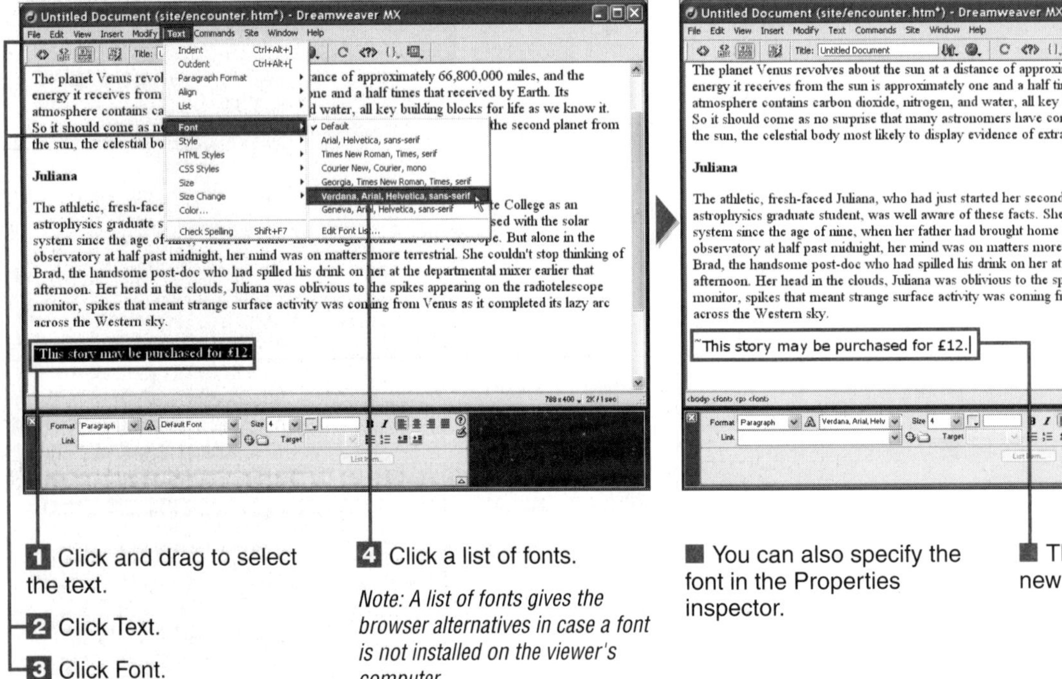

1 Click and drag to select the text.

2 Click Text.

3 Click Font.

4 Click a list of fonts.

Note: A list of fonts gives the browser alternatives in case a font is not installed on the viewer's computer.

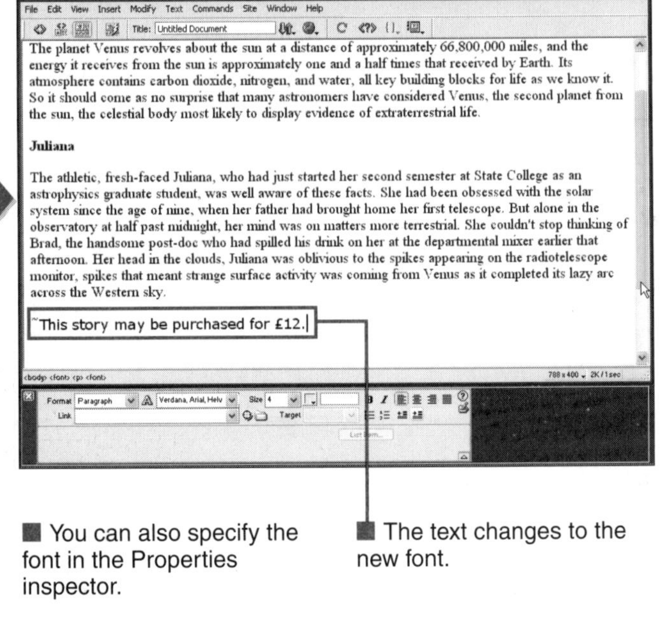

■ You can also specify the font in the Properties inspector.

■ The text changes to the new font.

What are serif and sans serif?

✔ *Serif* and *sans serif* are common font classifications. Serifs are the tiny decorations that appear on the ends of many traditional fonts such as Times New Roman, Georgia, and Palatino, and the text you are reading now. Sans serif means *without serifs*. Fonts in this category include Arial, Verdana, and Helvetica.

How do I create text that looks like typewriter text on my Web page?

✔ Use a monospaced font style such as Courier. *Monospaced* means that each letter in the font style has the same width, similar to typewriter text.

Can I specify a font category instead of a specific font name?

✔ Yes. Most browsers recognize serif, sans-serif — hyphen required — and mono for monospaced. Some browsers also recognize cursive and fantasy. When you specify a font category, the browser displays the default font for that category. For example, the default sans-serif font for Windows is Arial; for Macintosh, it is Helvetica.

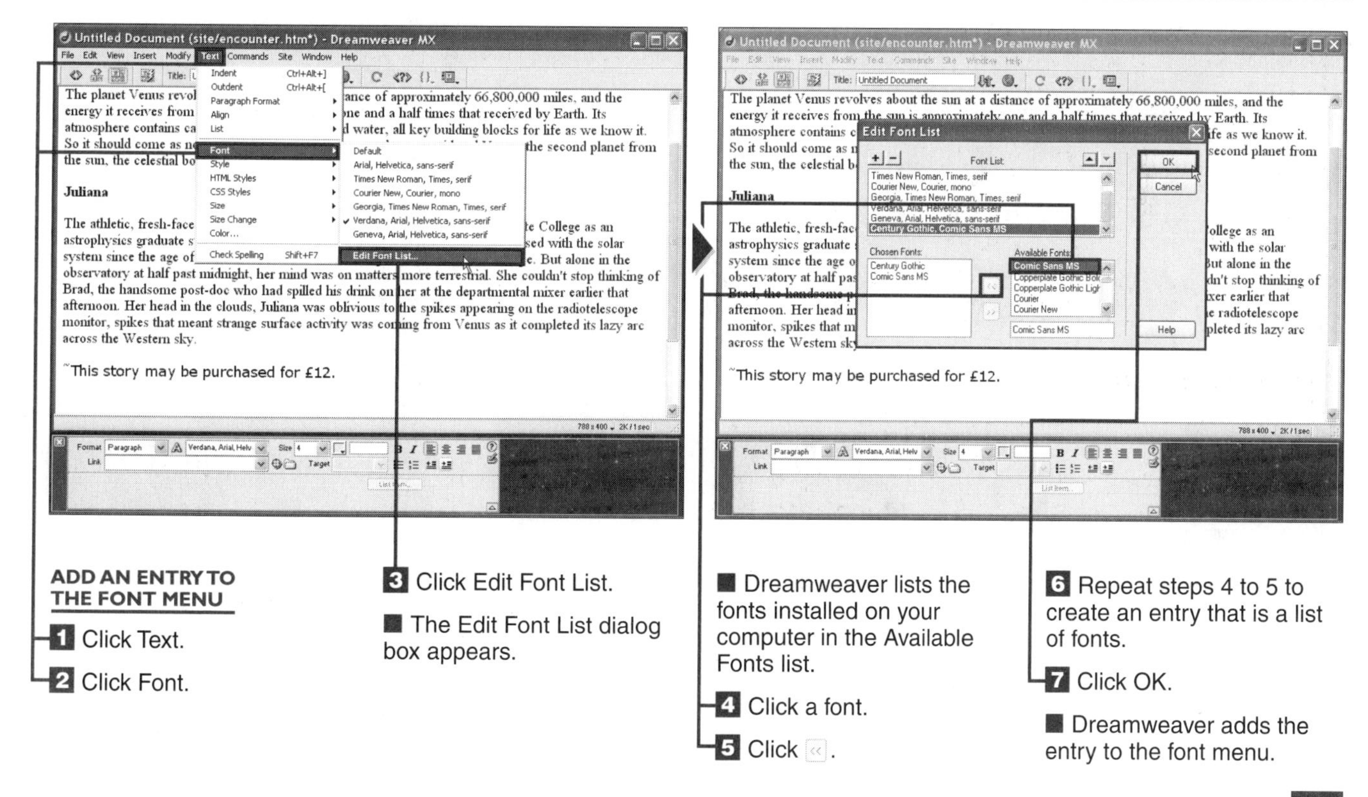

ADD AN ENTRY TO THE FONT MENU

1 Click Text.

2 Click Font.

3 Click Edit Font List.

■ The Edit Font List dialog box appears.

■ Dreamweaver lists the fonts installed on your computer in the Available Fonts list.

4 Click a font.

5 Click «.

6 Repeat steps 4 to 5 to create an entry that is a list of fonts.

7 Click OK.

■ Dreamweaver adds the entry to the font menu.

FORMAT TEXT

You can emphasize text on your Web page with a number of HTML-based style commands. You can access two of the most commonly used commands, Bold and Italic, via the Properties inspector.

You can find other styles in the Text menu under the Style submenu. The Strong and Emphasis styles have the same visual effect as the Bold and Italic styles, respectively. The Teletype style displays text in a typewriter-style font. Underline does just what you would expect, while Strikethrough crosses out text on your page.

In Preferences, you can specify that Dreamweaver use the Strong and Emphasis HTML tags when you click the Bold and Italic buttons in the Properties inspector. See page 32 for more about setting Preferences. This setting is turned on by default when you install Dreamweaver.

You can combine text styles to create more complicated effects. For example, a line of text can have bold, italic, and underline styles applied to it all at once. If you use certain style combinations a lot, you can create shortcuts for them in the HTML Styles panel. See page 83 for more information.

FORMAT TEXT

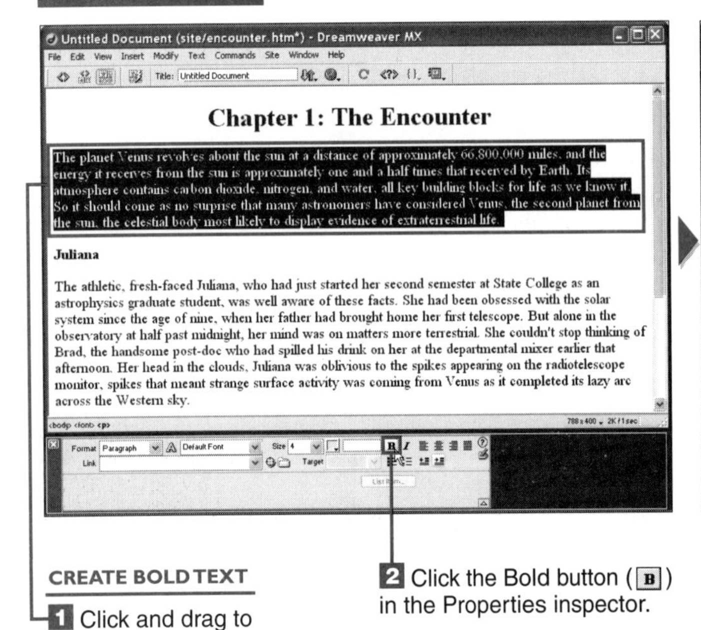

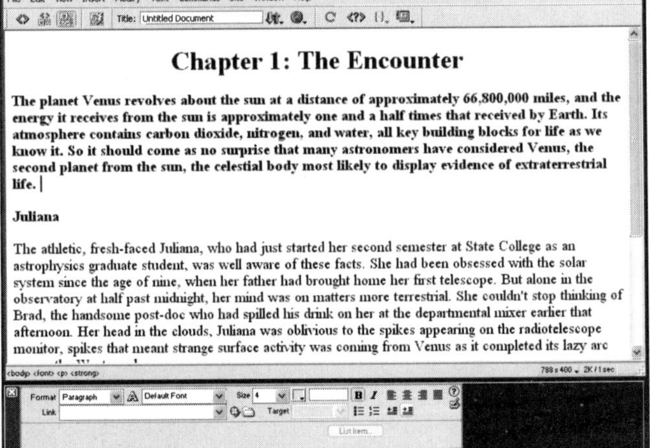

CREATE BOLD TEXT

1. Click and drag to select the text.
2. Click the Bold button (B) in the Properties inspector.

■ The text appears in a heavier weight.

If Italic and Emphasis produce the same visual effect on my page, which command should I use to produce italic text?

✔ A technical difference exists between the two commands. HTML tags such as <I>,which is the result of the Italic command, are known as physical appearance tags. Tags such as <EM>, which is the result of the Emphasis command, are known as structural meaning tags. Structural meaning commands tend to be preferred by HTML purists, the reason being physical appearance tags may be ignored by nonvisual Web browsers.

Is it better to use bold or italic formatting to emphasize words in my page?

✔ Some fonts are more legible in bold, others in italics. The font size and platform you are viewing the page on can also make a difference. For example, the default Times font on Macintosh browsers can be very hard to read when italicized. You should test your completed pages in several different Web browsers to see what your audience will see.

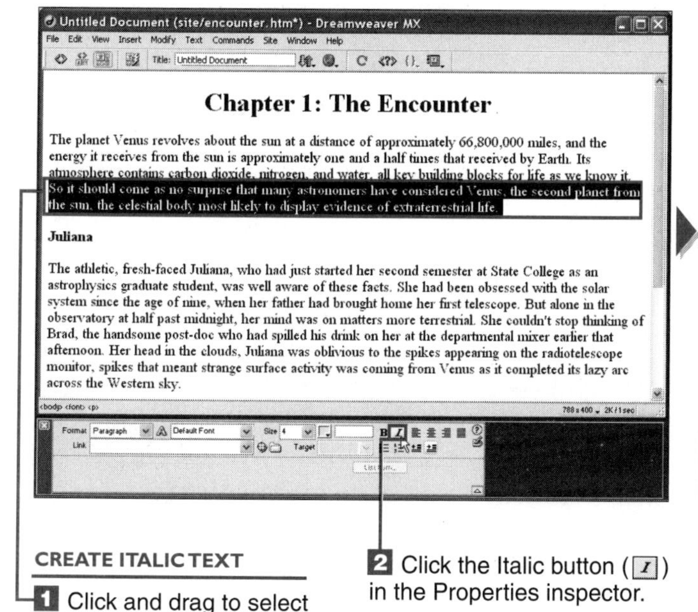

CREATE ITALIC TEXT

1 Click and drag to select the text.

2 Click the Italic button (*I*) in the Properties inspector.

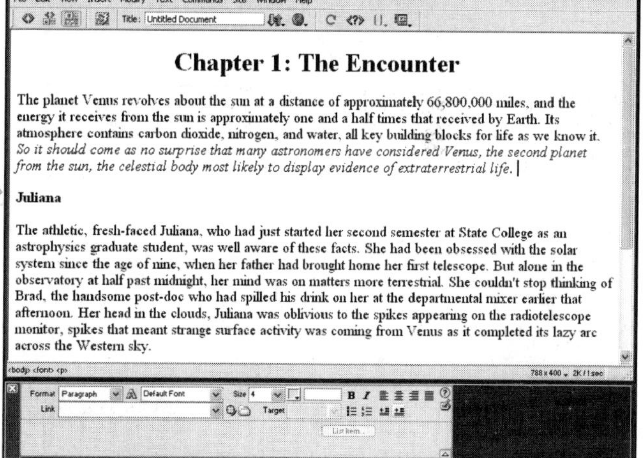

■ The selected text is italicized.

CHANGE FONT SIZE

You can change the size of the font on your Web page to emphasize or de-emphasize sections of text. You can specify an absolute size from 1 to 7 for your font — 3 is equivalent to the default text size. You can also specify a relative size, such as +1 or -2, and the font increases or decreases relative to its current size.

You often use sizes 5 and 6 for titles and headlines. Size 1 text is often used for copyright and disclaimer text. Sans-serif type, such as Arial, Helvetica, and Verdana, is relatively easy to read at small sizes and can usually be used as body text at size 2. This can help you fit more words in a browser window.

Note that the numeric value bears no relation to actual physical units of measurement such as picas, points, inches, and so on. To size your text using physical units, you can use style sheets. To learn more about style sheets, see Chapter 12. Also, the size of text that a viewer sees varies depending on the default font settings in the Web browser.

CHANGE FONT SIZE

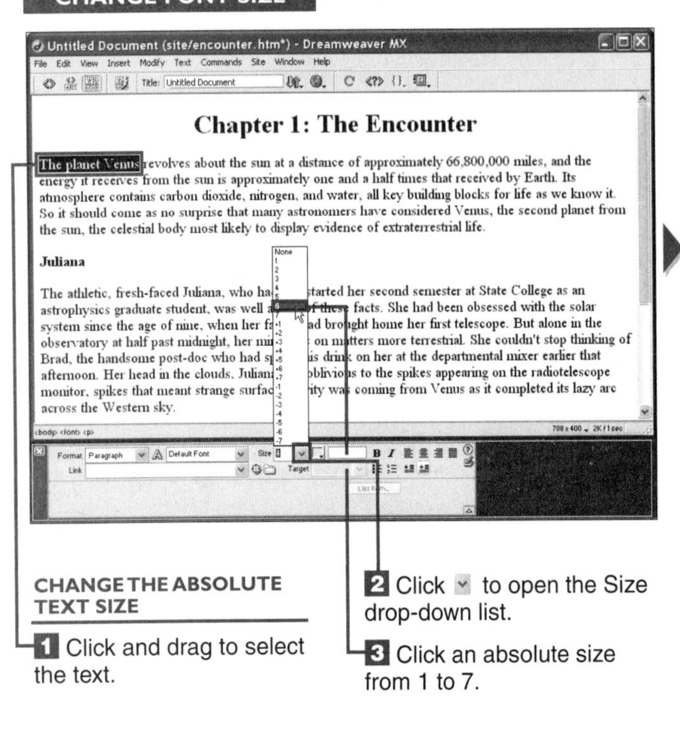

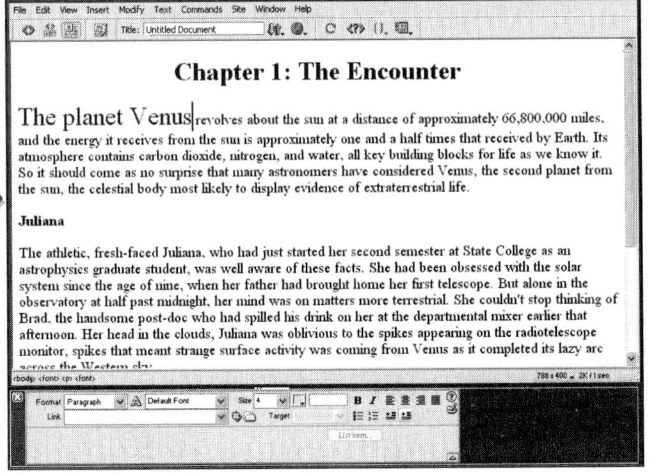

CHANGE THE ABSOLUTE TEXT SIZE

1 Click and drag to select the text.

2 Click ▾ to open the Size drop-down list.

3 Click an absolute size from 1 to 7.

■ The text changes size.

Can I change the size of individual characters?

✔ Yes. Simply select the character and follow the steps in this section. Increasing the size of the character that begins a passage can give a page a traditional feel.

How do I create text that is bigger than size 7 or smaller than size 1?

✔ One way is to format your text using style sheets, which give you an almost unlimited range of sizes when formatting text. You can also create the text in an image editor and then add it to your Web page as an image. See page 86.

Should I use a larger font size or a heading to create the headlines on my page?

✔ It is up to you. Creating a level-1 or level-2 heading produces relatively large text, but it also gives text a bold appearance and adds space above and below it. Experimenting with different font sizes as well as different headings can give you a variety of looks to choose from. For more information about headings, see page 64.

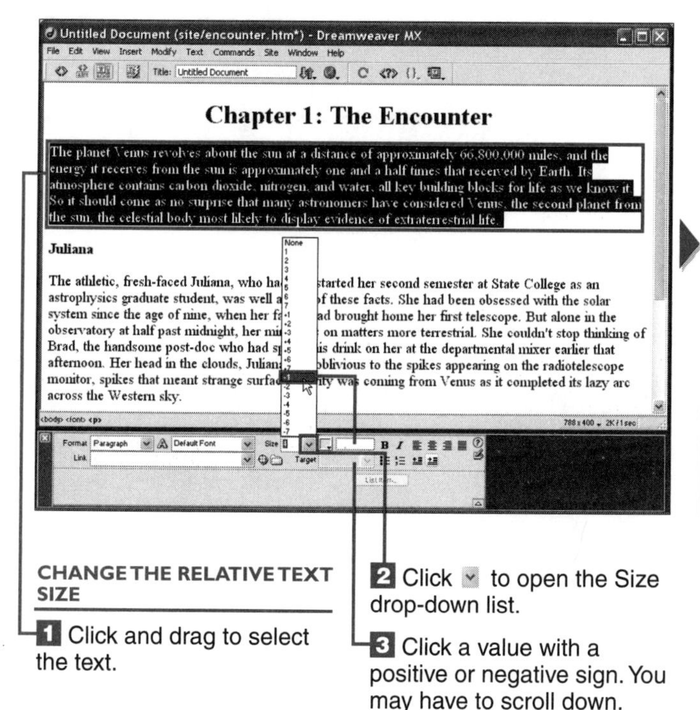

CHANGE THE RELATIVE TEXT SIZE

1 Click and drag to select the text.

2 Click ▾ to open the Size drop-down list.

3 Click a value with a positive or negative sign. You may have to scroll down.

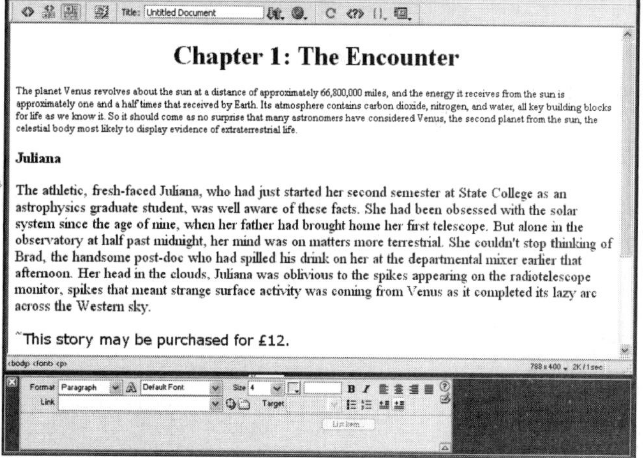

■ The text changes size.

Note: To adjust text size by creating a heading, see page 64.

CHANGE FONT COLOR

You can change the color of text on all or part of your Web page to make it more visually interesting. You change the color by selecting the text in the Document window and then selecting from the color menu in the Properties inspector. The default color for text on a Web page is black.

Dreamweaver provides an easy-to-access palette of Web-safe colors that you can apply in the Properties inspector. *Web-safe* means the colors display accurately no matter what browser, platform, and monitor setting the viewer uses.

You can also choose the color of you text by accessing a standard color-picker dialog box, or by typing the color's common name or hexadecimal code. *Hexadecimal codes* are six-digit combinations of letters and numbers that define the amount of red, blue, and green mixed to produce a color.

To ensure that the text is readable, make sure its color contrasts with the background color or background image of your Web page. To adjust the background color or background image of your Web page, see page 96.

CHANGE FONT COLOR

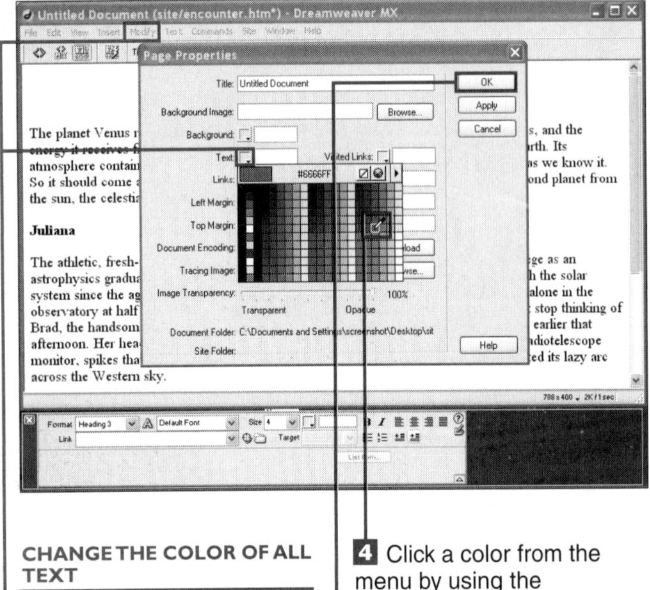

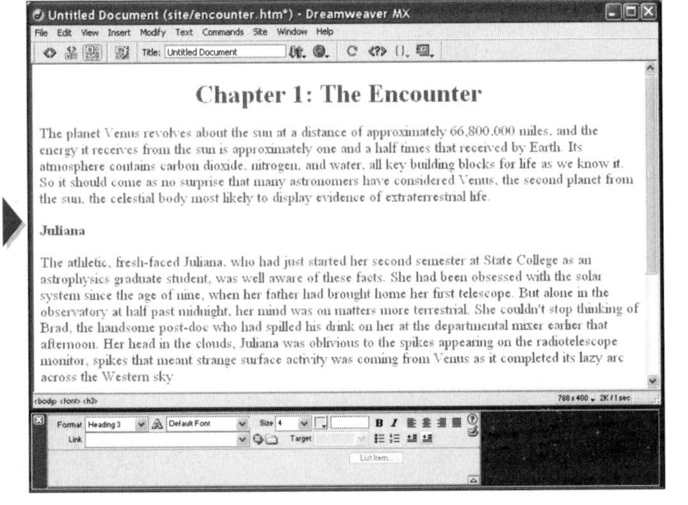

CHANGE THE COLOR OF ALL TEXT

1 Click Modify.

2 Click Page Properties.

3 Click the Text color menu.

4 Click a color from the menu by using the eyedropper tool that appears.

5 Click OK.

■ The default color of text on a Web page is black.

■ All the text on your Web page displays in the new color.

What are the letter and number combinations that show up in Dreamweaver's color fields when I define a color?

✔ HTML defines colors using six-digit codes called *hexadecimal codes*, which show up in the color field when you select from Dreamweaver's color menu. Hex codes are preceded by a pound sign (#). Instead of ranging from 0 through 9, hex-code digits range from 0 through F, with A equal to 10, B equal to 11, and so on through F, which is equal to 15. This special numbering scheme lets a pair of digits define 255 values, instead of the 99 available with decimal numbering. The first two digits in a hex code specify the amount of red in the selected color, the second two digits specify the amount of green, and the third two digits specify the amount of blue.

What are some examples of hex codes and the colors they stand for?

✔ #000000 represents black. #FFFFFF represents white. Using six of the same digit between 0 and F (for example, #666666) produces a shade of gray. The primary colors — red, green, and blue — are represented by #FF0000, #00FF00, and #0000FF.

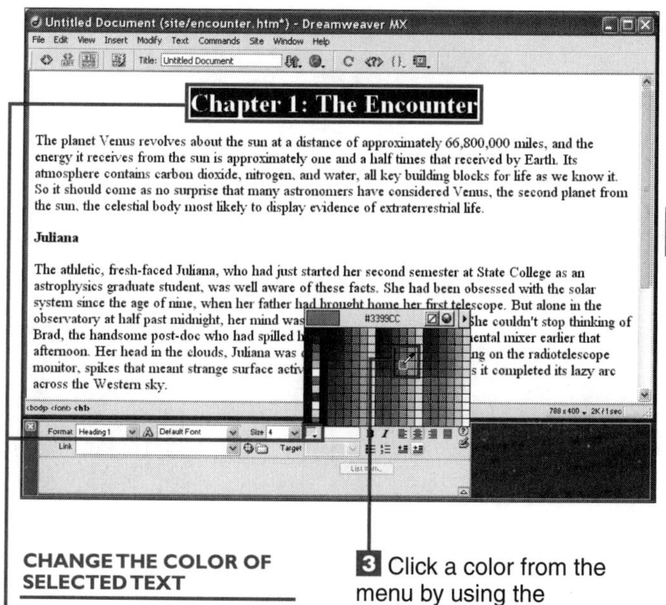

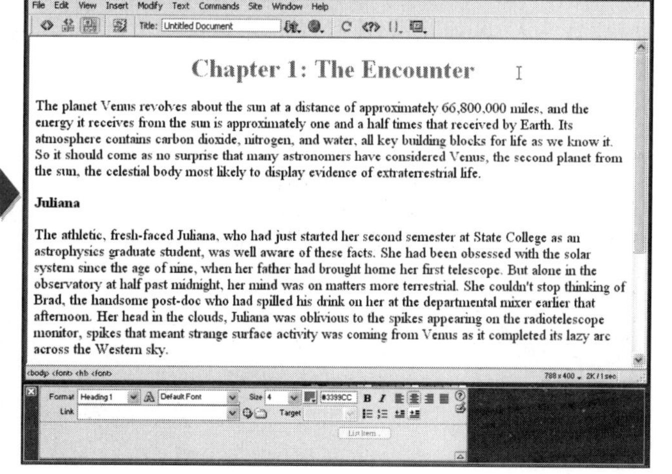

CHANGE THE COLOR OF SELECTED TEXT

1 Click and drag to select the text.

2 Click the color menu in the Properties window.

3 Click a color from the menu by using the eyedropper tool that appears.

■ The selected text appears in the new color.

CREATE A NEW HTML STYLE

You can save time by creating complicated text styles and adding them to the HTML Styles panel. From the panel, you can apply the styles to content in your page quickly and easily. HTML Styles can help you create titles, subtitles, captions, and other common text features across Web pages.

Style definitions can involve text-level definitions, such as size, color, and boldness, as well as paragraph-level definitions, such as heading level and alignment. When you define a new style, you specify whether you want it applied to just selected text or to the entire paragraph. You also specify whether the style should replace any current styles or be added to any current styles.

Note that if you decide to redefine a style in the HTML Styles panel, the new definition is not applied to places where you have applied the style previously. This is in contrast to style sheets, which let you make changes to style definitions and then update previously-styled text.

CREATE A NEW HTML STYLE

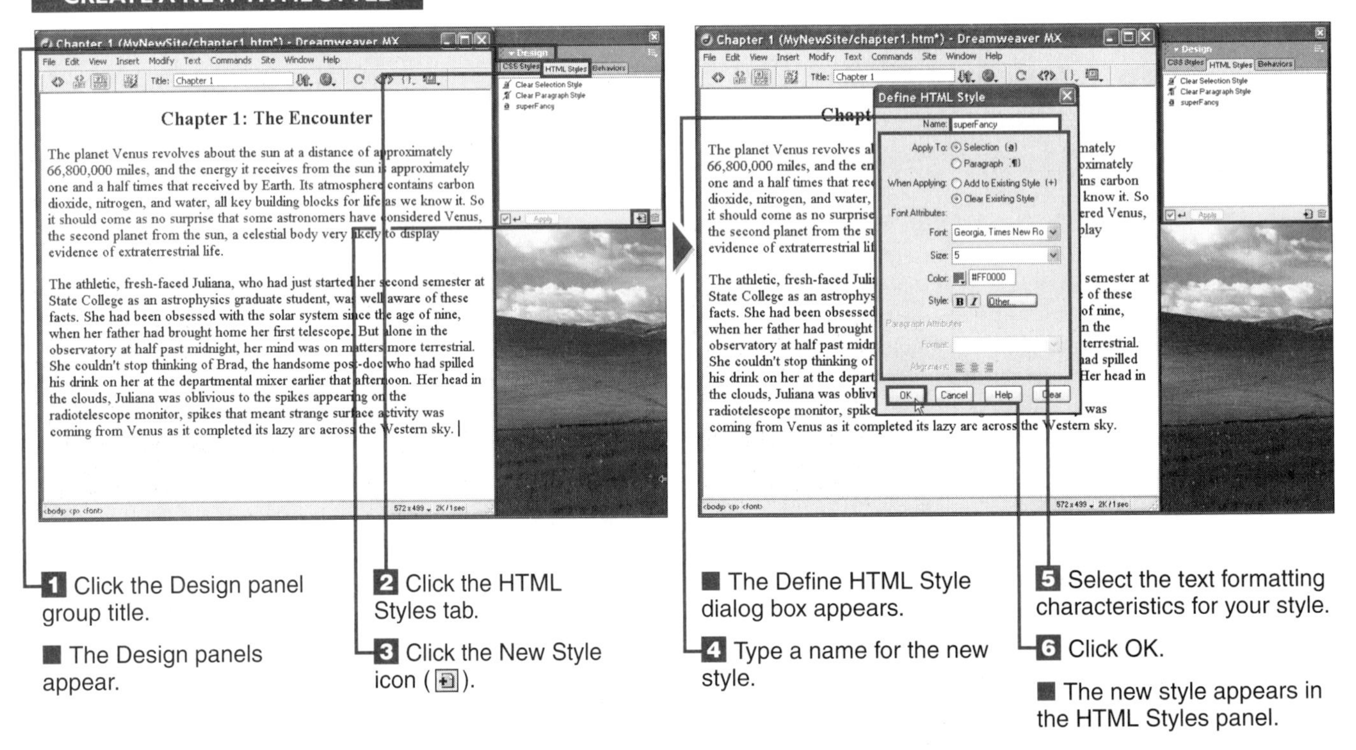

1 Click the Design panel group title.

■ The Design panels appear.

2 Click the HTML Styles tab.

3 Click the New Style icon ( ).

■ The Define HTML Style dialog box appears.

4 Type a name for the new style.

5 Select the text formatting characteristics for your style.

6 Click OK.

■ The new style appears in the HTML Styles panel.

APPLY AN HTML STYLE

You can format text by using the HTML Styles panel, which enables you to apply complicated styles with a single click. The panel is a timesaver when applying styles that appear many times on a page or throughout a site.

Style definitions can involve text-level definitions, such as size, color, and boldness, as well paragraph-level definitions, such as heading level and alignment.

Before you can apply an HTML style, you need to define it by setting text formatting, paragraph formatting, and alignment characteristics. Text formatting can include font face, size, and color formats, bold and italic formatting, and other formats such as underlining. Paragraph formats can include heading definitions and paragraph formatting. To define a custom HTML style, see "Create a New HTML Style.

HTML Styles can either add to the existing styles on a page or replace the existing styles. What they do depends on how they are defined. Adding to existing styles gives you the option of combining different HTML styles on a single block of text.

Dreamweaver HTML styles are an alternative to style sheets, which allow you to create more complicated styles and apply them to your pages. See Chapter 12 for more information on style sheets.

APPLY AN HTML STYLE

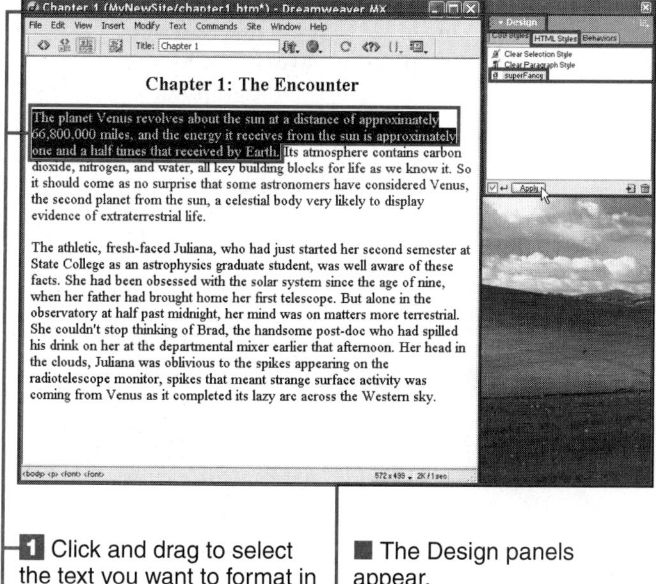

■1 Click and drag to select the text you want to format in the Document window.

■2 Click the Design panel group title.

■ The Design panels appear.

■3 Click the HTML Styles tab.

■4 Click to select a style from the list.

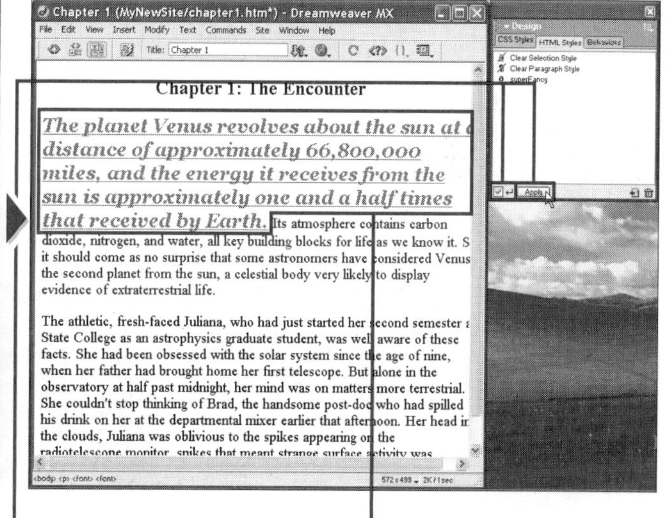

■5 Click Apply.

■ If the check box is selected, Dreamweaver applies the style automatically.

■ Dreamweaver formats the selected text according to the style.

INCORPORATE IMAGES AND GRAPHICS

Adding images and graphics to your pages is a great way to add color to your site and complement text and other non-graphical elements. Dreamweaver's commands let you insert images, align them on your page, add borders, and turn them into clickable hyperlinks. For an image to be viewable on a Web page, it has to be in a format that Web browsers can display. All the popular Web browsers can display JPEG and GIF images, and some can also display PNG images. Dreamweaver does not have image-editing capabilities, so if you want to customize the images that you use on your Web pages, you need an image editing program such as Macromedia Fireworks, which is included on the CD-ROM, or Adobe Photoshop.

Images

You can get images for your Web pages from a variety of sources. A flatbed scanner lets you digitize hand-drawn illustrations, photographic prints, and other paper-based content. Digital cameras let you skip the scanning step and shoot digital photos for your pages directly. You can also get a variety of images and graphics from clip art collections, which are available online and in computer stores. If the images you scan, shoot, or buy are not in a format appropriate for the Web (JPEG, GIF, or PNG), you have to convert them in an image editor before placing them on your pages in Dreamweaver.

GIF Images

GIF, which stands for *Graphics Interchange Format*, is the preferred Web image format for illustrations and other images that contain a lot of solid color. You can also animate GIF images by saving multiple frames in a single file. GIF images can only contain up to 256 colors, which is why the format is less suitable for photographic images. Saving your GIF images using a minimum number of colors can help keep your file sizes small. GIF is a *lossless* image format, which means quality does not degrade when you save as GIF. GIF files have a .gif extension.

JPEG Images

JPEG, which stands for *Joint Photographic Experts Group*, is the preferred Web image format for photos and other images that contain a broad range of colors. This is because JPEG files support 16.7 million colors in a single image, which is many more colors than GIF. When you save images as JPEGs, you specify the amount of JPEG compression to be applied. The more compression you apply, the smaller the resulting file size, but the lower the quality of the resulting image. JPEG is a *lossy* image format, which means some quality is lost when you save as JPEG. JPEG files have a .jpg or .jpeg extension.

Download Time

One potential drawback to inserting images in your Web pages is that they can add to the total file size of a page, making it slower to download. That is why it is important to optimize your images to make them as small as possible before placing them on your page. Image editing programs such as Macromedia Fireworks have special tools to help you create very compact GIF, JPEG, and PNG images. To see how images are affecting the file size of your page, you can look at the status bar of the Document window in Dreamweaver, which tells you the total size of your Web page. As a rule, it is a good idea to keep your Web pages below 50K if you are designing your pages for an audience using 56K modems. You may have to remove images or split one page into several pages to keep page sizes low.

PNG Images

PNG, which stands for *Portable Network Graphics*, is a relatively new Web image format. This format combines some of the advantages of both JPEG and GIF — it supports 16.7 million colors and is a lossless format. However, because many older Web browsers do not support PNG, the format is still much less popular than GIF and JPEG.

INSERT AN IMAGE INTO YOUR WEB PAGE

You can insert different types of images, including clip art, digital camera images, and scanned photos, into your Web page. Adding images can complement your text and make your Web page more visually interesting. But images can also significantly increase the download time for a page. You should store the images that you want to add to your Web pages inside the local folder for your site.

When you add an image to a page, Dreamweaver creates a reference to the image file in the HTML code — it does not actually insert image information into the HTML. When a browser accesses a Web page that includes images, it must download a separate file for each image on the page.

Dreamweaver lets you add borders to your images. You specify the size of the border in pixels, and the border appears around the image in the same color as the default text color on the page. You can change the color of the image border by changing the default text color for a page in the Page Properties. See page 80 for more information.

INSERT AN IMAGE INTO YOUR WEB PAGE

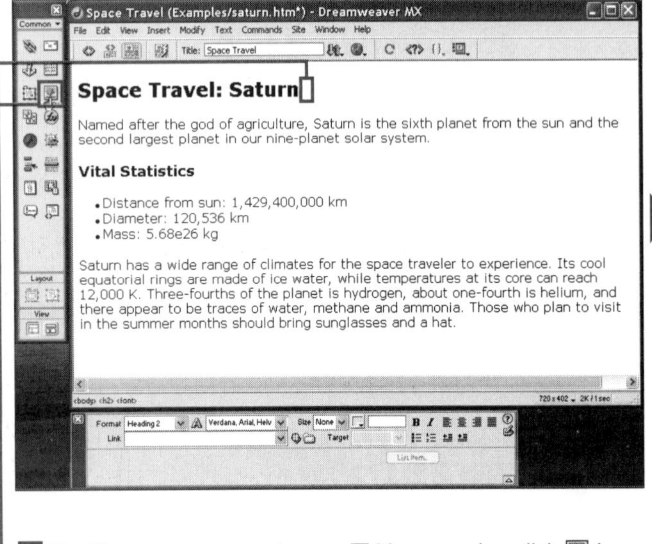

1 Position your cursor where you want to insert the image.

2 Click the Image button ().

■ You can also click in the Objects window to insert an image.

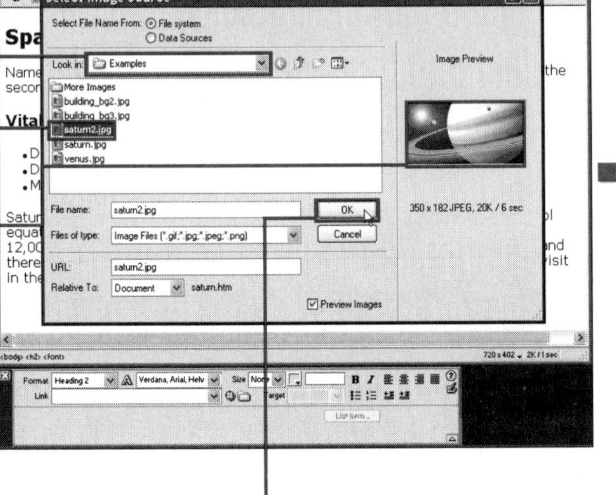

3 Click to select the folder that contains your image.

4 Click the name of your image file.

■ A preview of the image appears.

Note: If you want to insert an image that exists at a Web address on the Internet, you can type the address of the image into the URL field.

5 Click OK.

Where should I store images that I want to use on my Web pages?

✔ You should store your images in the same folder as your HTML files. Keeping your HTML files and image files in the same folder ensures that your Web site works correctly when you transfer it to a live Web server. When your site consists of many files, you may find it more convenient to keep images in a subdirectory called images.

How do I delete an image?

✔ To delete an image that is in a Web page, click the image and press Delete. To delete an image file from a site entirely, open the Site window, click the image file in the local site list, and press Delete. Dreamweaver warns you if any of your Web pages reference the image file. If you delete an image that is referenced on a page, that page displays a broken image icon.

How can I tell how much space my images and text take up on my Web page?

✔ Dreamweaver displays your page's total size in kilobytes (K) on the status bar. This total includes the size of your HTML file, the size of your images, plus the size of anything else on the page. Next to the size is the estimated download time for the page. You can configure the connection speed used to determine this estimate in your Preferences. See page 32 for more information.

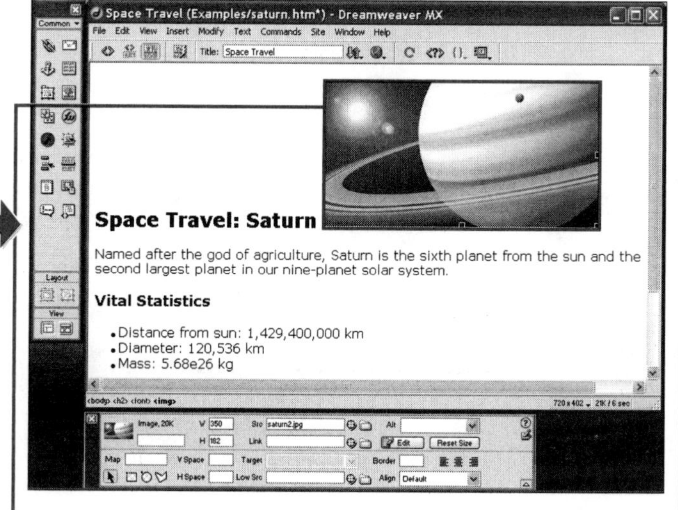

■ The new image appears in the Web page.

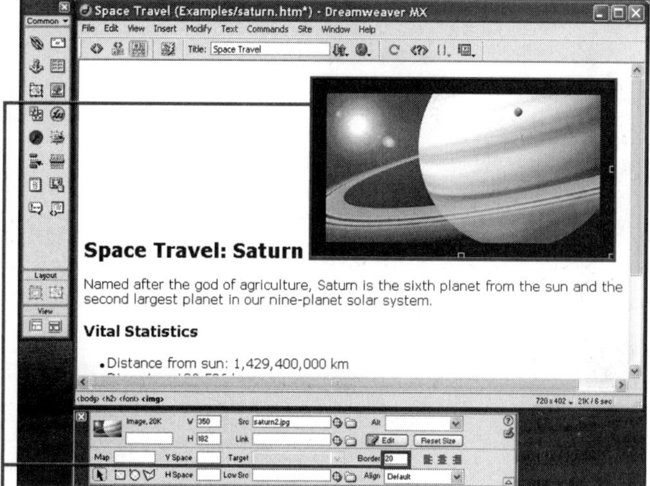

ADD A BORDER TO AN IMAGE

1 Click the image to select it.

2 Type a width (in pixels) into the Border field.

3 Press Enter (Return).

■ A border appears around the image. The color of the border is the same as the default text of your page.

WRAP TEXT AROUND AN IMAGE

You can wrap text around an image to give your Web page a more professional look, as well as fit more information inside the browser window. You wrap text around an image by adjusting the image's alignment. Specifying *left* alignment moves the image to the left of the page and wraps any following text around the right side of the image. *Right* alignment moves the image to the right of the page and wraps text around the image's left side. Wrapping text can decrease unnecessary whitespace on your page by making text fit flush around the sides of an image.

Dreamweaver offers several other alignment options that specify how the preceding or following text abuts the inserted image. Middle, for example, aligns the baseline of the text with the middle of the image. These other settings are typically less useful than the Right and Left settings.

You do not have a simple alignment setting that wraps text around both sides of an image. To place text to the left and right of an image, you can insert a three-column table, place the image in the center cell, and place text in the neighboring cells.

WRAP TEXT AROUND AN IMAGE

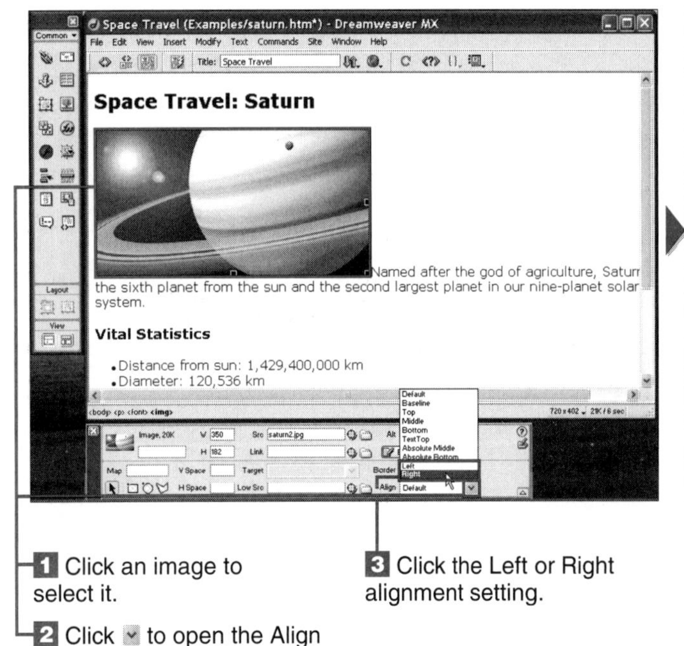

1 Click an image to select it.

2 Click ▾ to open the Align drop-down list.

3 Click the Left or Right alignment setting.

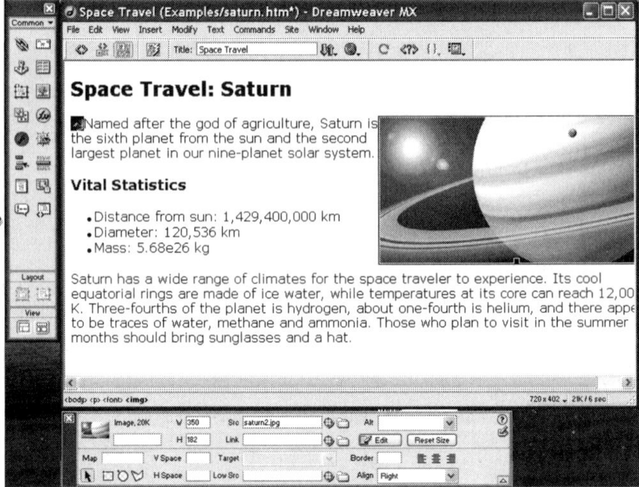

■ Text flows around the image according to the alignment you selected.

CENTER AN IMAGE

Centering an image can give it a photo or banner prominence on your page by setting it off from text or other images above and below it. Dreamweaver makes centering an image easy — you select the image and click a center-align button.

However, the HTML involved behind the scenes is slightly more complicated. No center alignment attribute for the HTML image tag exists, which is why you do not see a Center option in the Align drop-down menu. When you click the center-align button in the Property inspector, Dreamweaver does one of three things: If the image is inside a paragraph, Dreamweaver aligns the entire paragraph to the center. If the image is not in a paragraph, Dreamweaver either adds a `<DIV ALIGN="CENTER">` tag or a `<CENTER>` tag around the image HTML. You can specify which in the Code Format category in your Preferences. The `<DIV>` option is recommended by recent HTML specifications.

Another way to align images and other content on your pages is by using styles sheets. You can create style-sheet rules that specify positioning information, and then apply those rules to an image. See Chapter 12 for more information.

CENTER AN IMAGE

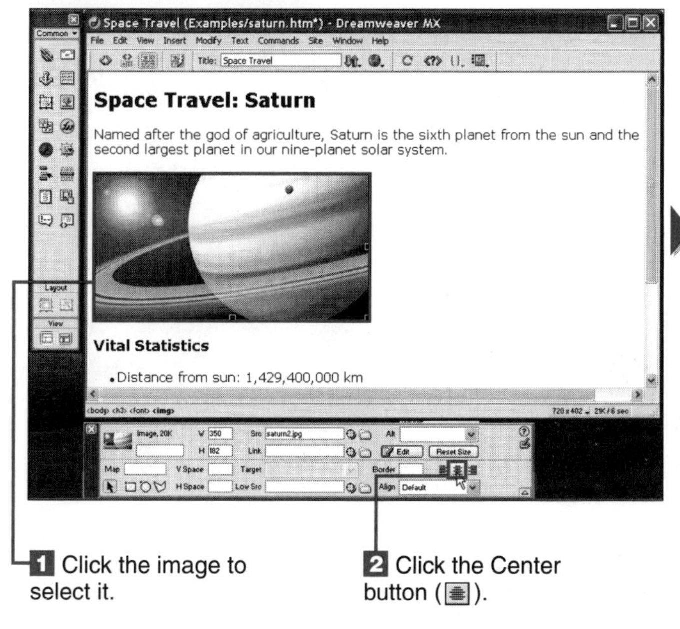

1 Click the image to select it.

2 Click the Center button (▤).

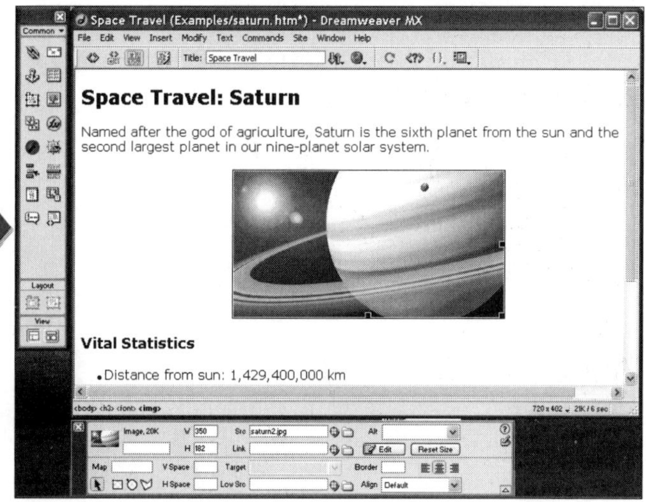

■ Dreamweaver centers the image on the page.

CHANGE THE SIZE OF AN IMAGE

Dreamweaver enables you to change an image's size in several ways. You can change the pixel dimensions by entering new values in height and width fields or by clicking and dragging the corner of the image. You can also define the image as a percentage of the browser window, so that it expands and contracts as the user resizes the browser.

None of these techniques changes the size of the image in the actual image file. To modify the image file, you need to use an image editor. Instead, resizing in Dreamweaver lets you change how the image is presented on your Web page. For example, you can insert a 10 x 10 pixel image into your page in Dreamweaver and specify that it display at 20 x 20 pixels (or at 5 x 30 pixels). The image will be stretched or shrunk for display on the page, but the actual image file will still be 10 x 10 pixels.

Enlarging an image in Dreamweaver can decrease the quality of the image. Shrinking an image in Dreamweaver means that your viewers will be downloading an image file that is larger than it needs to be. For both these reasons, it is usually best to change the size of your images in an image editor.

CHANGE THE SIZE OF AN IMAGE

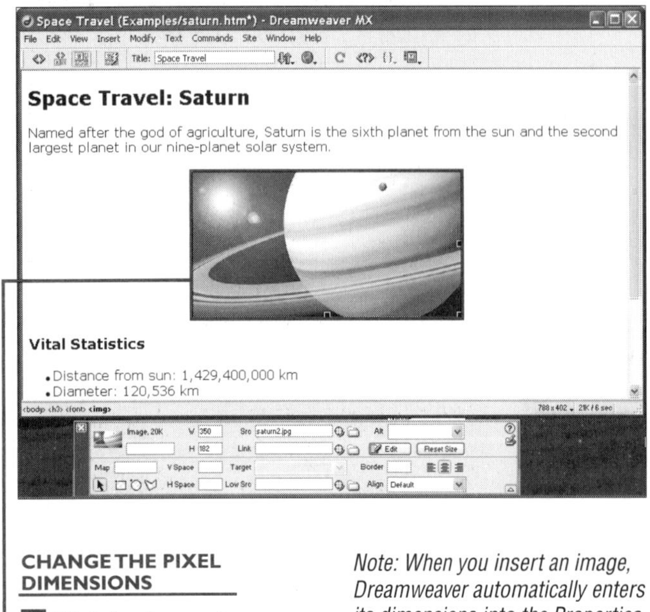

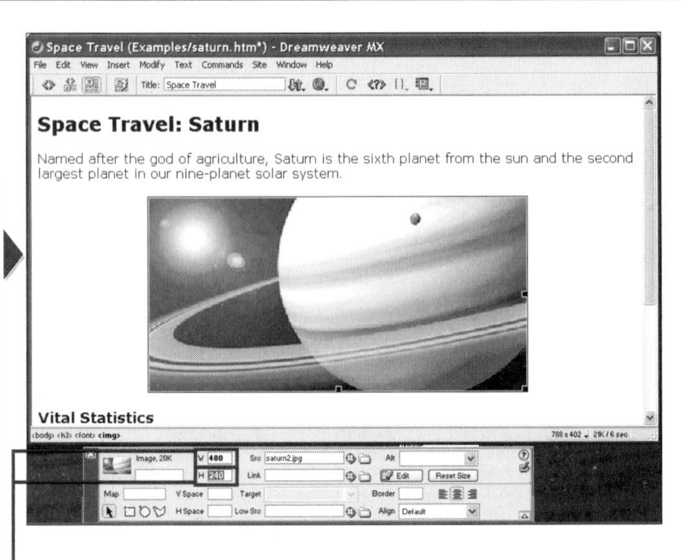

CHANGE THE PIXEL DIMENSIONS

1 Click the image to select it.

Note: When you insert an image, Dreamweaver automatically enters its dimensions into the Properties inspector.

2 Type the width (in pixels) of the image.

3 Press Enter (Return).

4 Type the height (in pixels) of the image.

5 Press Enter (Return).

■ The image displays with its new pixel dimensions.

Is there a limit to how small I can make an image on my page?

✔ Using the handles on the image edges to resize, you can shrink an image to no smaller than 8 x 8 pixels. To decrease the size down to the real minimum of 1 x 1 pixel, you need to enter values in the W and H fields of the Property inspector.

After resizing, how do I return an image to its original dimensions?

✔ You can click the H and W labels in the Property inspector to return the dimensions to their original values.

How do I make an image take up the entire browser window?

✔ Set the W and H fields in the Property inspector both to 100%. The image stretches to fill the entire window, and if the image was small to begin with, it will look very pixelated.

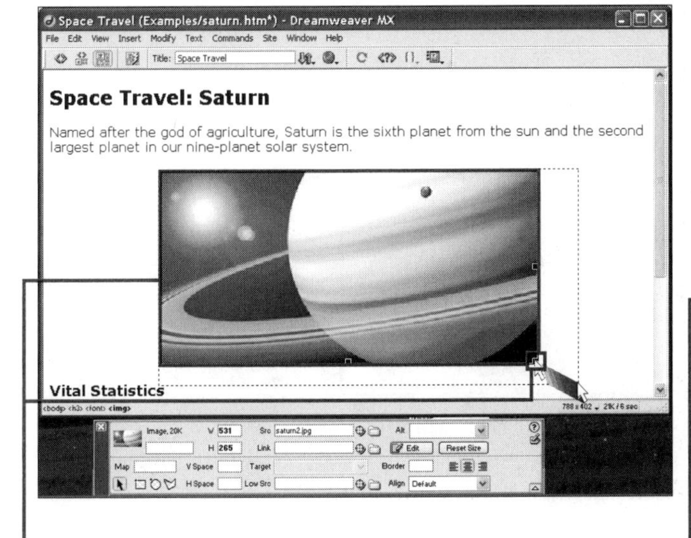

CLICK AND DRAG THE IMAGE

1 Click the image to select it.

2 Drag the handles at the sides or corners of the image.

■ To retain the proportion of the image, hold down the Shift key as you drag a corner.

■ The image expands or contracts to its new dimensions.

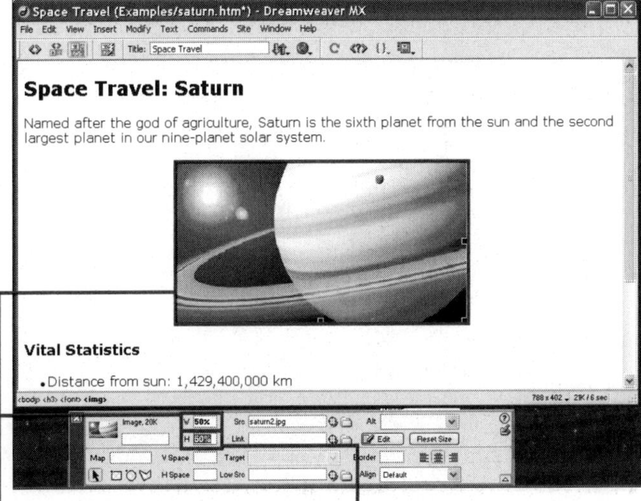

CHANGE THE PROPORTIONAL SIZE

1 Click the image to select it.

2 Type the percentage of the width.

3 Press Enter (Return).

4 Type the percentage of the height.

5 Press Enter (Return).

■ The image displays as a percentage of the browser window, not as a percentage of its original size.

ADD SPACE AROUND AN IMAGE

Adding space around an image can distinguish it from the text and other images on your Web page. You may want to add space if you are wrapping text around an image to make the text easier to read. The added space around an image is measured in pixels.

The techniques described here only let you add a fixed amount to the top and bottom or a fixed amount to the left and right sides. Space on the top and bottom of an image is called *V Space*, or vertical space; space on the left and right sides of an image is called *H Space*, or horizontal space. To add a fixed amount of space to just one side of an image, or to different combinations of sides, you can use style sheets. See Chapter 12 for more information on style sheets.

You can also add space to the sides of your images using an image editor. Just make sure the space you add is transparent or the same color as your page background, or else you will end up with an image border. Note that adding space using an image editor increases the file size of an image.

ADD SPACE AROUND AN IMAGE

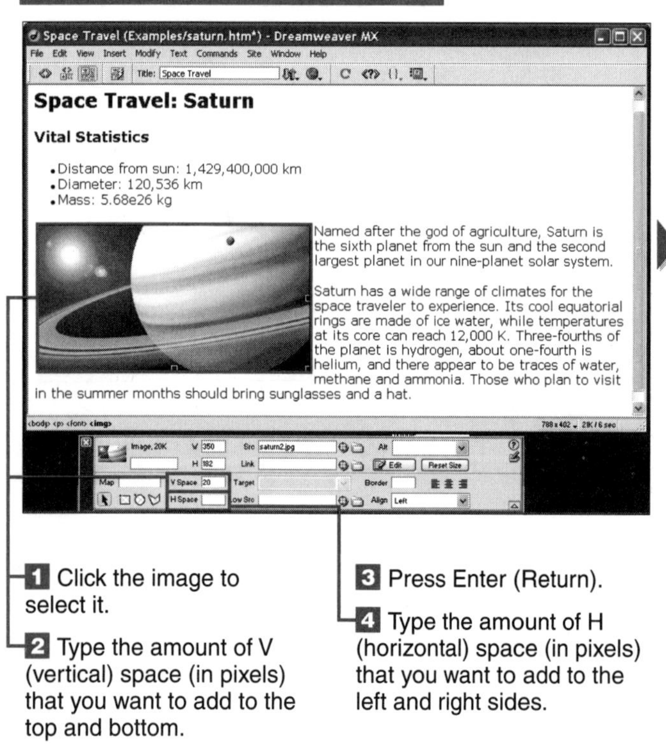

1 Click the image to select it.

2 Type the amount of V (vertical) space (in pixels) that you want to add to the top and bottom.

3 Press Enter (Return).

4 Type the amount of H (horizontal) space (in pixels) that you want to add to the left and right sides.

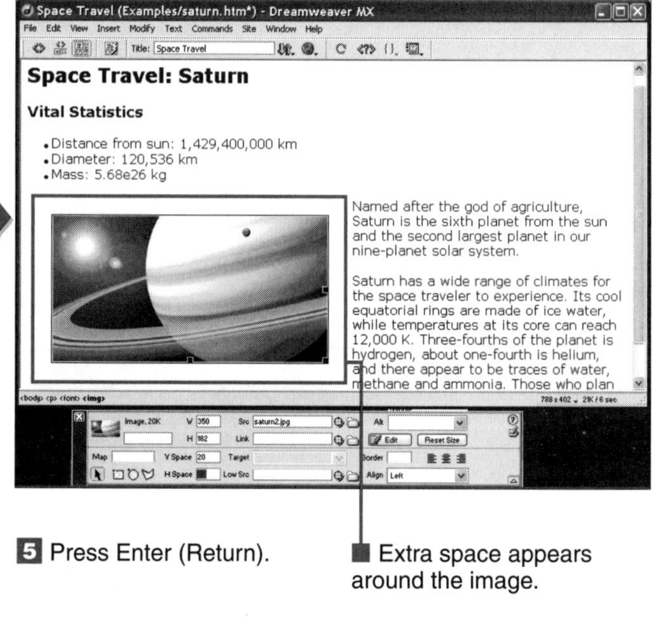

5 Press Enter (Return).

■ Extra space appears around the image.

ADD A HORIZONTAL RULE

You can use thin lines known as *horizontal rules* to your Web page to separate sections of content. Horizontal rules are part of the HTML standard, and it is the Web browser that produces the rules when a page loads; the rules are not separate image files. As a result, horizontal rules may appear slightly different in different types of browsers. An advantage of horizontal rules is that because they are not separate images, they do not affect the overall size of a downloaded page.

You can customize a horizontal rule in various ways. The default horizontal rule stretches to fill the width of the page. Alternatively, you can express the width as an absolute pixel value or a percentage of the browser window. You can also adjust the thickness of your rules.

Rules can have shading turned on, which gives them a 3-D look. Rules without shading are solid gray.

If you are not pleased with the horizontal rules that Dreamweaver gives you, you can always use an image editor to create your own wavy rules, multicolored rules, or dashed rules and insert them as images. See page 86.

ADD A HORIZONTAL RULE

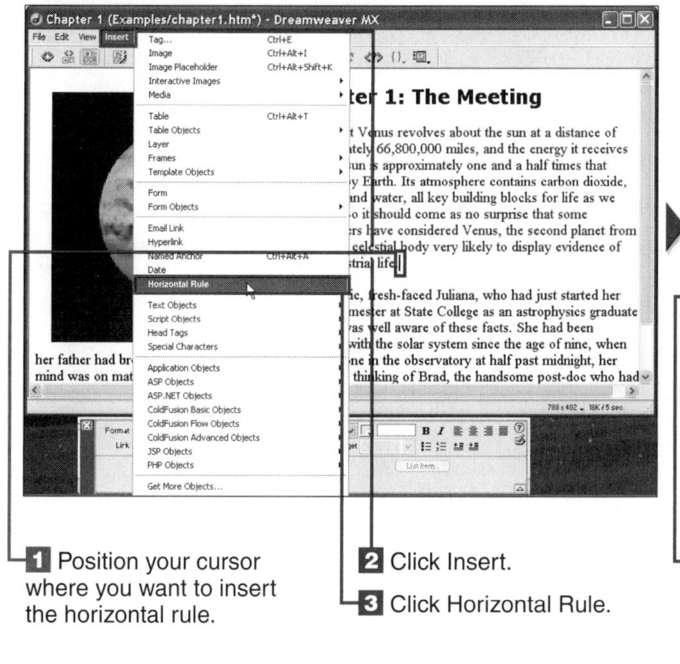

1 Position your cursor where you want to insert the horizontal rule.

2 Click Insert.

3 Click Horizontal Rule.

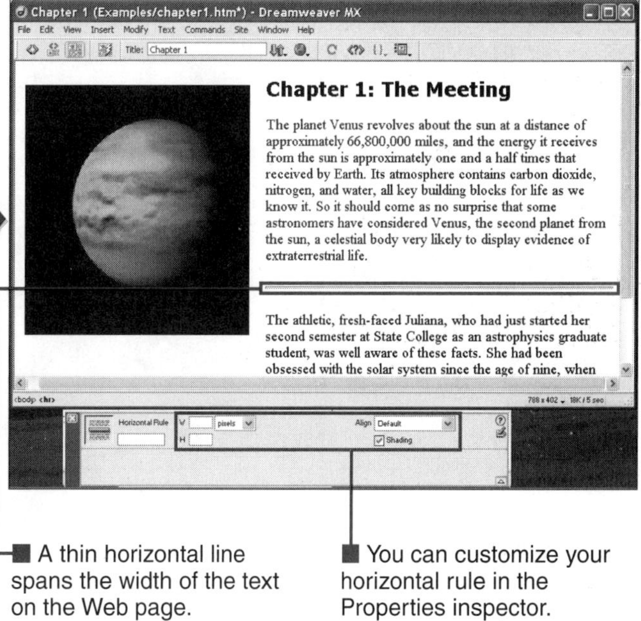

■ A thin horizontal line spans the width of the text on the Web page.

■ You can customize your horizontal rule in the Properties inspector.

ADD A BACKGROUND IMAGE

You can add a background image to your Web page to compliment its theme or to make it more colorful. Dreamweaver enables you to specify an image file in your local folder, or on the Web, to serve as the background image. You can design backgrounds that work with elements in the foreground of your pages. For example, you can make a background that has columns of color that underlay similarly arranged columns of text.

Unless the background image is larger than the browser window, the image tiles horizontally and vertically to fill the entire window. This is an important design consideration, because viewers with different monitor settings can have browser windows with very different sizes. For example, a background that takes up the entire window on a browser, running on a monitor set at 640 x 480 pixels, may end up tiling (repeating) on a browser running on a 1,024 x 768 screen.

Another consideration when creating a background image is to make sure it does not overwhelm content in the foreground. A rainbow-colored background may call attention to a page, but it may also make it impossible to read the words displayed over it.

ADD A BACKGROUND IMAGE

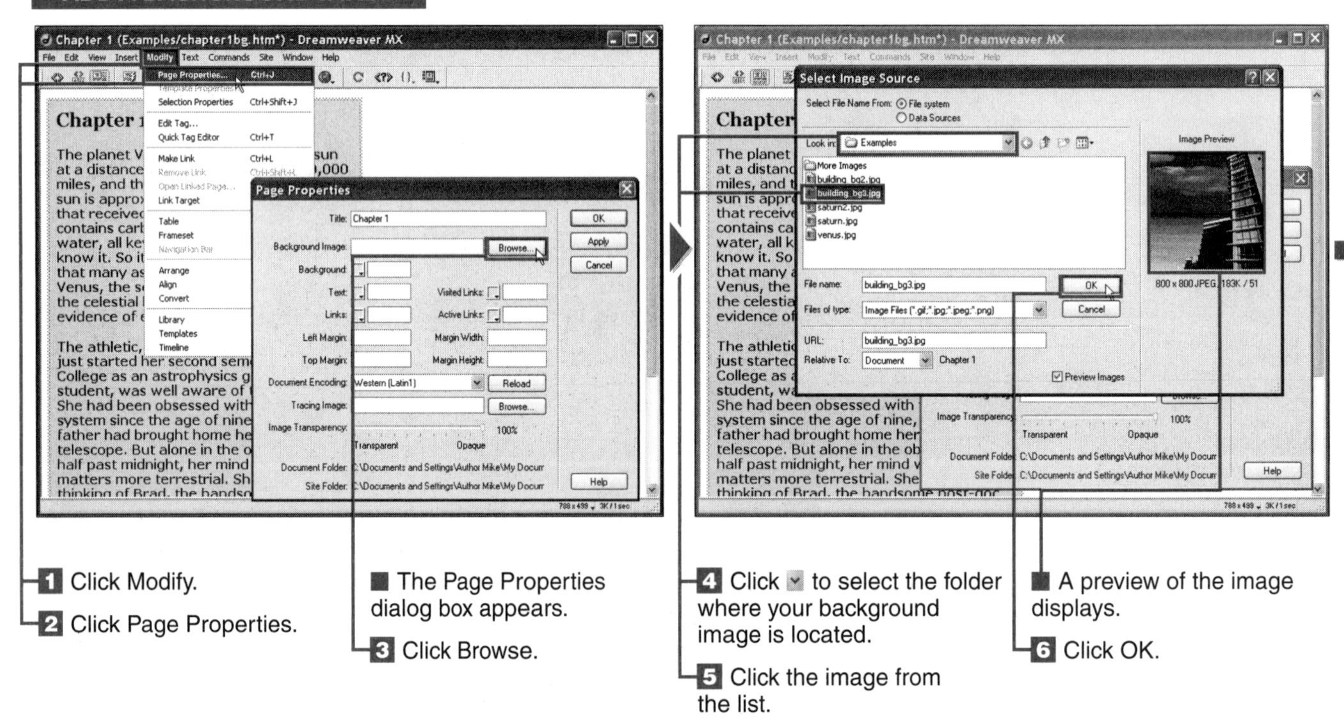

1 Click Modify.

2 Click Page Properties.

■ The Page Properties dialog box appears.

3 Click Browse.

4 Click ▾ to select the folder where your background image is located.

5 Click the image from the list.

■ A preview of the image displays.

6 Click OK.

How do I create a background image that tiles seamlessly?

✔ You can use an image editor, such as Adobe Photoshop or Macromedia Fireworks, to eliminate the seams that can appear when an image tiles. The trick involves offsetting the image horizontally and vertically, and then cleaning up the seams with editing tools. Many books on Web graphics show you how to create seamless tiles.

How do I estimate the browser sizes for monitors at different settings?

✔ Dreamweaver comes with several predefined window settings that mimic what a user sees at different monitor settings. To choose a setting, click on the Dimensions menu on the Document window status bar.

How do I keep my background images from taking up a lot of file space?

✔ Keeping your background image file sizes small is important if you want your pages to download quickly. For GIF backgrounds, try to keep the number of colors in the image to a minimum. For JPEG images, try to increase the amount of compression applied when you save your images.

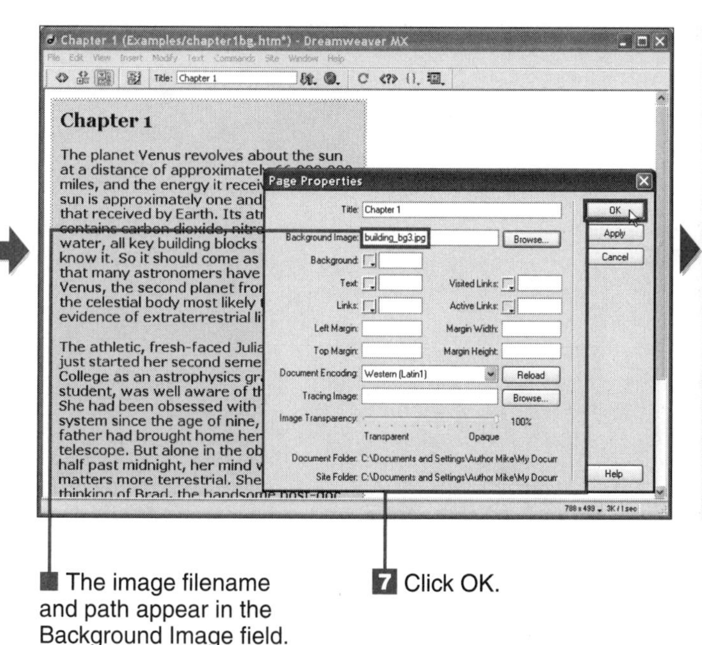

■ The image filename and path appear in the Background Image field.

7 Click OK.

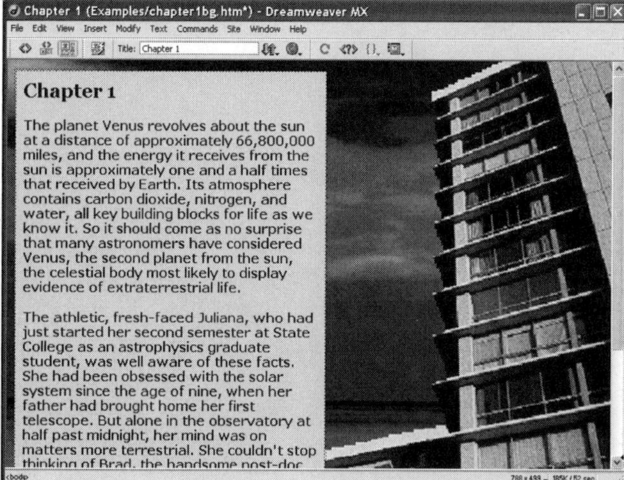

■ The image appears as a background on your Web page. If necessary, it tiles horizontally and vertically to fill the entire window.

■ In this example, the background image appears behind a solid-color table.

CHANGE THE BACKGROUND COLOR

You can give your page a visually striking appearance by changing the background color. A background color also allows you to make your pages more consistent with your company's or organization's identity. The background color appears behind all of the content in your page, including text, images, and layers.

White is the default background color for Web pages created in Dreamweaver. You can choose a different color from a palette of Web-safe colors accessible from the Page Properties dialog box. *Web-safe* means that the colors display accurately on different platforms and monitor settings. You can also specify a background color by name, such as red or green, or with a hex code definition.

Setting a background color has advantages over adding a background image. For example, defining a color uses up practically zero file space whereas adding an image adds that image's file size to your page.

If you set both a background image and background color for your page, the image takes precedence. If for some reason the image cannot load, the background color appears instead.

CHANGE THE BACKGROUND COLOR

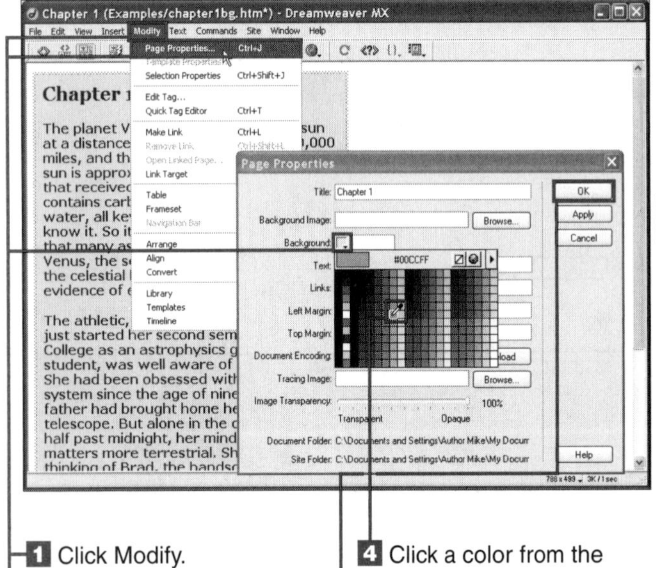

1 Click Modify.

2 Click Page Properties.

3 Click the Background color menu.

4 Click a color from the menu.

5 Click OK.

■ The background changes to the selected color.

■ In this example, the background color appears behind a solid-color table.

ADD ALTERNATE TEXT

You can add alternate text that displays in the place of images for viewers using text-based or non-visual browsers. Alternative, or *alt,* text also displays in the place of images when a visual browser is unable to display image. This happens when users turn off image viewing in their browser options.

Alt text is optional — nothing will break if you do not add it to your Web images. However, alt text should be added if you want your pages to be accessible by the widest audience.

For photographs or illustrations, you usually want the alt information to describe the image you are displaying, for example: Adorable kitten with ball of string. For button graphics, you may want the alt text the same as the label that is on the button, for example: Home or Contact Us.

Some newer browsers, such as Internet Explorer version 5 and greater, display the alt text temporarily when you roll your cursor over an image on a Web page.

Some search engines index the alt text of Web pages. This means adding important key words to your alt information could potentially help your pages score higher in search results.

ADD ALTERNATE TEXT

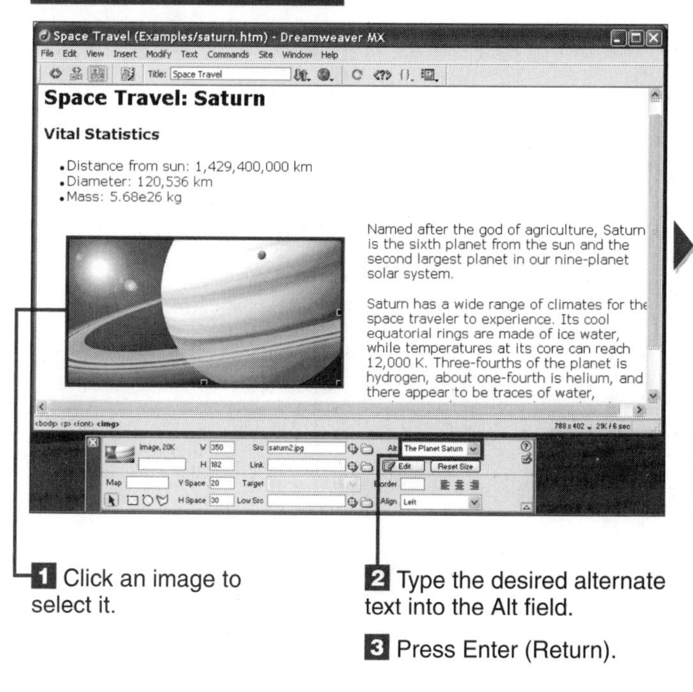

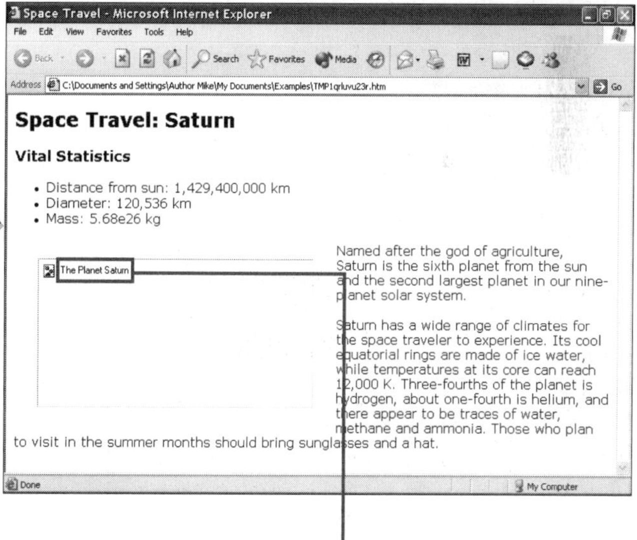

1 Click an image to select it.

2 Type the desired alternate text into the Alt field.

3 Press Enter (Return).

4 Preview your page in a Web browser.

Note: To preview a page in a Web browser, see page 58.

■ The alternate text displays when image loading is turned off.

INSERT A PLACEHOLDER IMAGE

You can add a placeholder image to your Web page to temporarily mark off the space where you will place an image later. A placeholder image can be sized to be the same height and width as your eventual real image. You can set the placeholder's color to blend in with or contrast with the Web page's overall color.

Placeholders can be useful when you are just starting to build a Web site and want to experiment with different text and image layouts. Using placeholders allows you to quickly mark off space and not have to worry about the content of the images distracting you from the overall organization of the page.

When you add a placeholder image, Dreamweaver inserts a normal <img> tag to the HTML of the page. In the case of a placeholder, the src attribute of the <img> is left blank, and a custom style is used to generate the background color, if needed. Because Dreamweaver builds placeholders by using <img> tags, you can align and add space around placeholder images just like you can regular images.

INSERT A PLACEHOLDER IMAGE

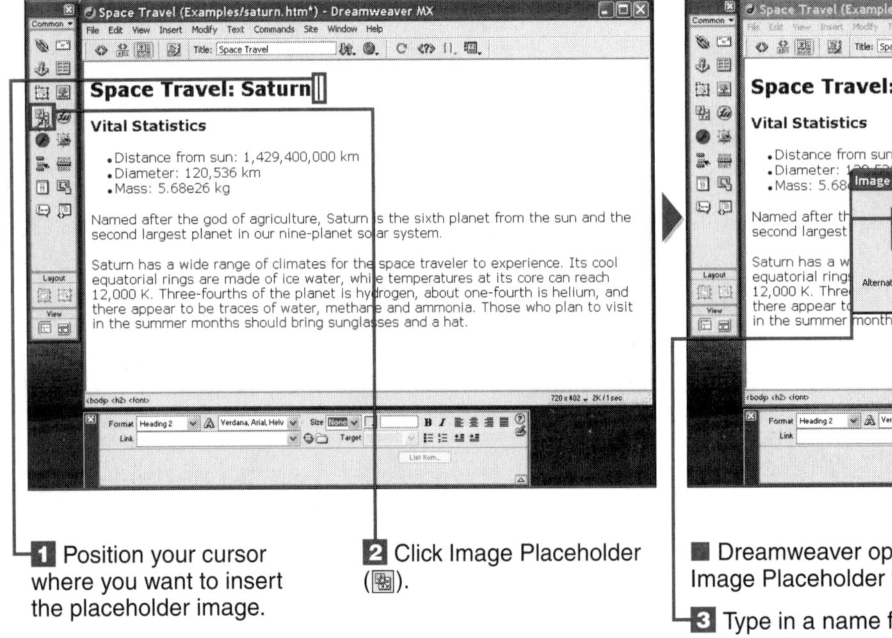

1 Position your cursor where you want to insert the placeholder image.

2 Click Image Placeholder (▦).

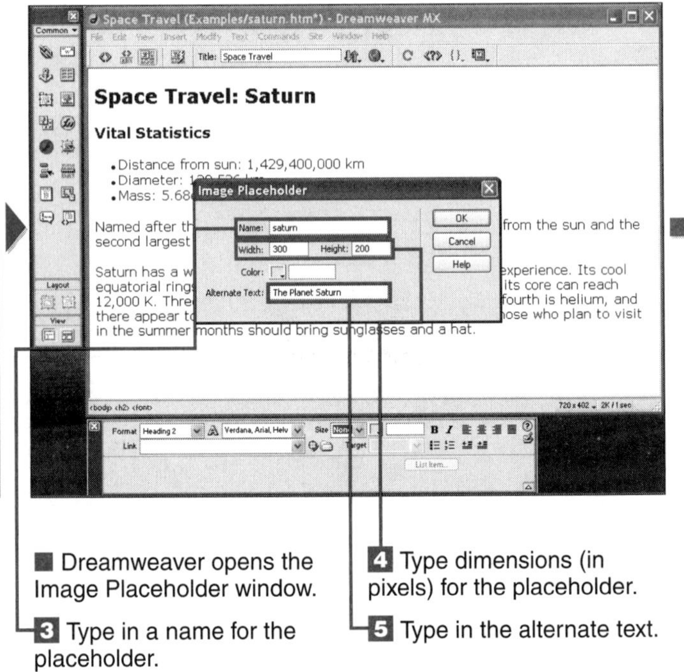

■ Dreamweaver opens the Image Placeholder window.

3 Type in a name for the placeholder.

4 Type dimensions (in pixels) for the placeholder.

5 Type in the alternate text.

How do I edit my image placeholder after I have inserted it?

✔ You can edit your image placeholder just as you can any object on your page. Click the placeholder to select it, and then adjust the settings in the Properties inspector.

How do I replace an image placeholder with a regular image?

✔ Double-click the image placeholder in the Document window. The Insert Image dialog box appears. Select the image to insert and click OK. The placeholder is replaced with the regular image. For more about inserting images, see page 86.

What is another way to temporarily mark off different areas in a Web page?

✔ You can insert an image that is one pixel tall and one pixel wide, and then stretch it using Dreamweaver's image dimension fields to create a solid block on your Web page. If the image that you insert is a transparent GIF, the image block will be invisible to the viewer. Because one-pixel images are of minimum size, they take very little time to download no matter how large you stretch them on the page. See page 90 for more information on resizing.

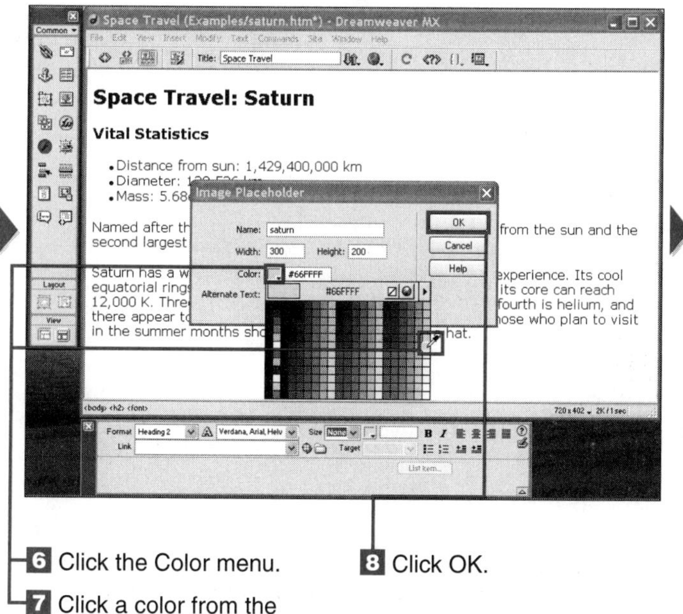

6 Click the Color menu.

7 Click a color from the menu.

8 Click OK.

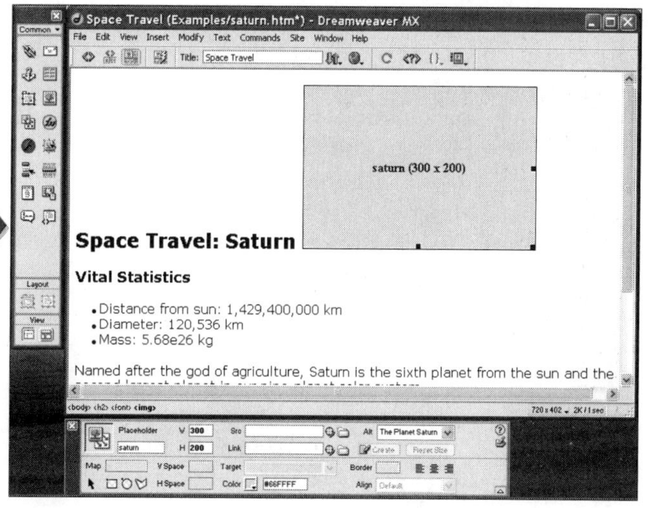

■ Dreamweaver inserts a placeholder image into the page.

CREATING HYPERLINKS

Hyperlinks, or links, are the clickable elements on a Web page that transfer a user to another Web page or file. Creating a link in Dreamweaver is as easy as selecting a piece of text or an image on your Web page and then specifying a destination page or other file.

Text links are distinguished on a Web page by underlining and color. Image hyperlinks can be outlined with color by turning on the image's Border property. Most browsers also change the appearance of the cursor when it is placed over a link.

Hyperlink Code

In HTML, hyperlinks are created with an <A> tag combined with an HREF attribute, which tells a browser where the link should lead. To view a link's HTML in Dreamweaver, you can select the link in the Document window and then open the Code Inspector. Here is an example of HTML code that turns the text My page into a link:

```
<A HREF="mypage.html">My page</A>
```

What the HREF value looks like can vary, depending on the type of addressing used. The three types of addressing, each of which you can use in Dreamweaver, are relative addressing, root-relative addressing, and absolute addressing.

Document-Relative Addressing

Document-relative addressing defines the destination page relative to the page that contains the link. This type of addressing leaves off the Web server information in the HTML, because it is assumed that both files are on the same Web server. In HTML, document-relative addressing looks like this:

```
HREF="folder/file.htm"
```

Document-relative links allow a Web site to be portable. You can move a site from one server to another and not have document-relative links break, because their references are independent of the actual server where files are hosted.

Root-Relative Addressing

Root-relative addressing defines a destination page relative to the Web server's root folder. This root folder is represented by a leading forward slash (/) in the address path. Similar to relative addressing, root-relative addressing leaves off the Web server information, because it is assumed that both files are on the same Web server. In HTML, root-relative addressing looks like this:

```
HREF="/folder/file.htm"
```

Root-relative links allow individual files within a Web site to be portable. You can move a file that contains root-relative addressing to another folder in a site and root-relative links will not break. This is because the root folder does not change.

Absolute Addressing

Links can also be defined absolutely, which means a complete URL is used to define the destination page or file. In HTML, absolute addressing looks like this:

```
HREF="http://www.webserver.com/
folder/file.htm"
```

Absolute links are necessary when you are linking to content on other Web sites, because these pages exist on different Web servers.

Frame Links

Creating links in a framed Web site is slightly more complicated than creating regular links. This is because for links in a framed site, you need to define not just the destination file but also what frame you want that file to open into. You can make a link open content in a particular frame by specifying the frame's name as a *target* for the link. See Chapter 10 for more information.

HYPERLINK TO ANOTHER PAGE

You can create clickable *hyperlinks*, also simply called *links*, on your Web pages that lead to related information on other pages on your site. Well-placed links within your site can help users find the information they need quickly. You create links by selecting text or an image in the Document window and then selecting a destination page from your local site folder.

For navigation purposes you can insert a set of links that lead to the main areas of your site in the same place on every page. It is common practice to place such navigation links along the side or at the bottom of your pages. You can also create a site map page that lists descriptions of all the pages on your site along with links to those pages.

Most of the time when you create links to other pages on your Web site, you will want to use relative addressing. You can specify the type of addressing that Dreamweaver uses for a link in the Select File dialog box that appears when you define the link's destination page.

HYPERLINK TO ANOTHER PAGE

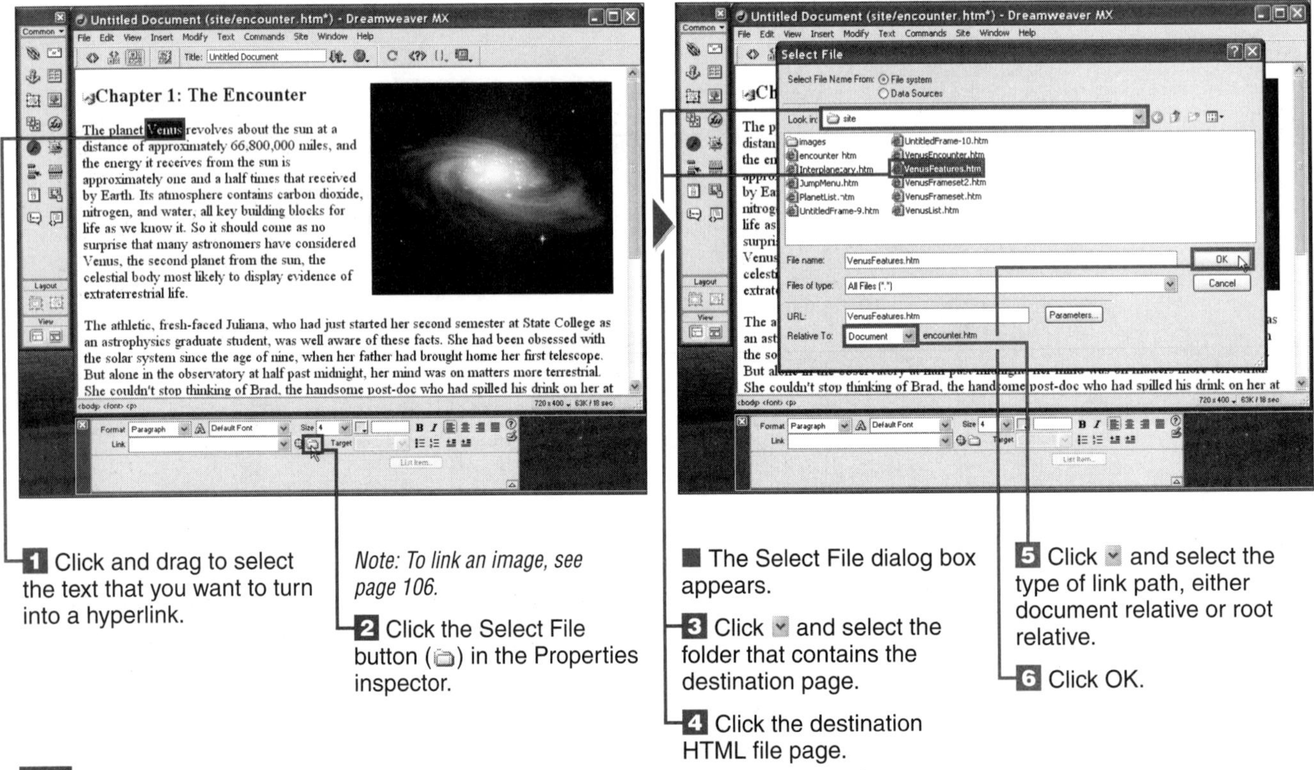

1 Click and drag to select the text that you want to turn into a hyperlink.

Note: To link an image, see page 106.

2 Click the Select File button (📂) in the Properties inspector.

■ The Select File dialog box appears.

3 Click ▾ and select the folder that contains the destination page.

4 Click the destination HTML file page.

5 Click ▾ and select the type of link path, either document relative or root relative.

6 Click OK.

If I rename a page in my site, what happens to hyperlinks that point to that page?

✔ Normally, the links break. But if you rename the page using the Site window. Dreamweaver checks to see whether there are links to that page and, if there are, gives you the opportunity to automatically update them.

How do I organize hyperlinks down the left side of my Web page?

✔ This is a common way to organize a site's navigation. Create a two-column table that fills the entire page with the left column narrower than the right. Then organize the hyperlinks as a list in the left column. If you are going to use the same navigation links on every page, it is a good idea to make the list a library item.

How do I distinguish a row of text hyperlinks?

✔ It is a common convention to distinguish a row of hyperlinks with pipe symbols (|) and brackets. This makes text links look more like buttons:

[Home | Products | Feedback]

You can find the pipe symbol below or next to the Backspace key on your keyboard.

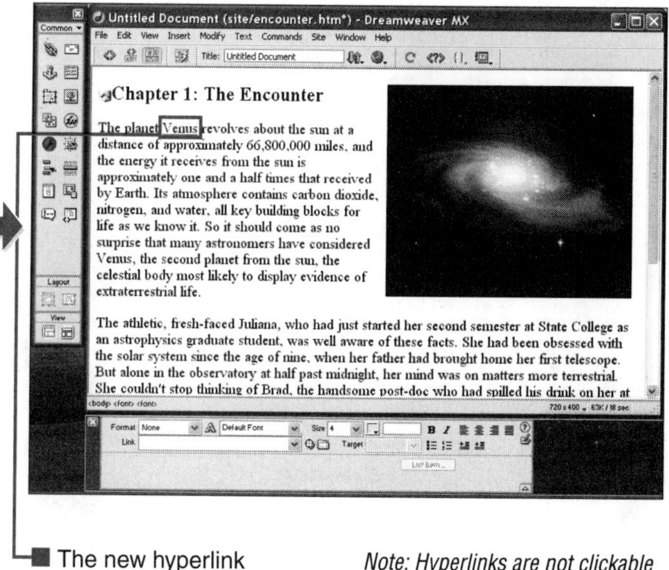

■ The new hyperlink appears colored and underlined.

Note: Hyperlinks are not clickable in the Document window. To test the link in a Web browser, see page 58.

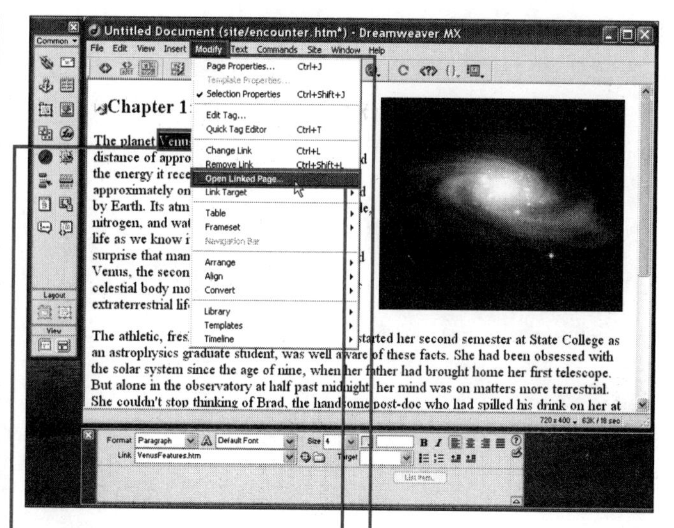

OPEN THE LINKED PAGE

1 Click and drag to select the text of the hyperlink whose destination you want to open.

2 Click Modify.

3 Click Open Linked Page.

■ The link destination opens in a Document window.

HYPERLINK TO ANOTHER WEB SITE

You can create clickable hyperlinks, also simply called links, from pages in your site to external pages elsewhere on the Web. You create such links by selecting text or an image in the Document window and then specifying the destination page's complete Web address, also known as a Uniform Resource Locator, or URL. When visitors click on an external link, they are taken to another Web site.

Links that reference a page using a complete Web address are known as absolute links, because those links contain all the information needed to locate the page from anywhere on the Internet.

You can link to any other page on the Web as long as you know its address. You can get an external Web page's address by opening the page in your Web browser and copying the text that appears in the browser's address field. While no one can stop a person from *linking* to a Web page, access to a page can be blocked by adding password protection. Password protecting pages is usually performed on the server; you can add it if you are using Dreamweaver to create a dynamic Web site.

As a service to their visitors, many Web developers include a list of links to sites that contain information similar to what is on their sites. These lists are simply collections of external links. One way to increase traffic to your site is by linking to similar Web sites and then requesting reciprocal links from those sites.

HYPERLINK TO ANOTHER WEB SITE

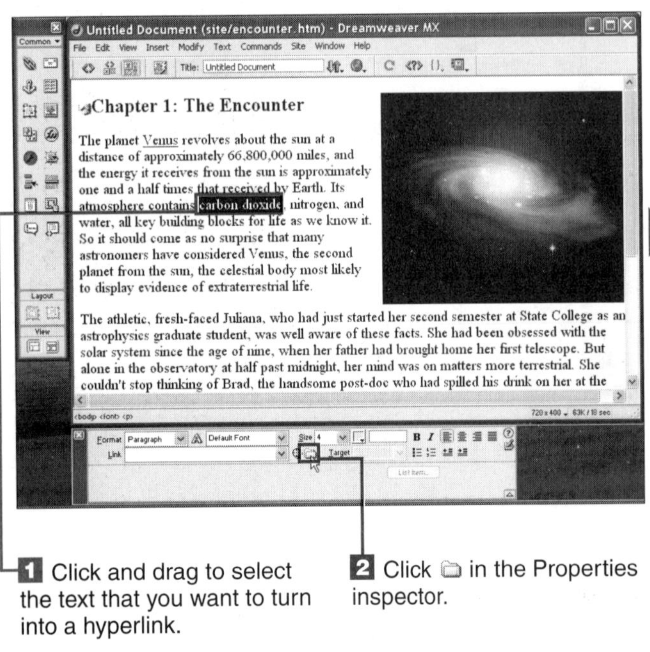

1 Click and drag to select the text that you want to turn into a hyperlink.

2 Click 🗀 in the Properties inspector.

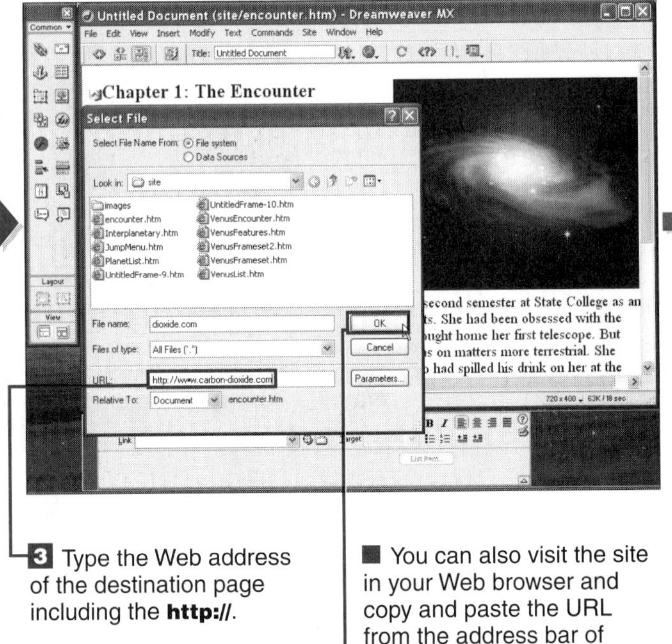

3 Type the Web address of the destination page including the **http://**.

■ You can also visit the site in your Web browser and copy and paste the URL from the address bar of the browser.

4 Click OK.

What happens when an external page is deleted or renamed?

✔ If you have linked to the page, that link breaks. This means a user clicking the link receives an error specifying that the page could not be found. This is one of the challenges of including external links on your site. Ultimately, you do not have control over whether they work or not. This makes testing your site's external links on a regular basis important.

How can I automatically test the external links in my site?

✔ Dreamweaver cannot test external links in your site; it can only check links to pages within your site. See page 119 for more information. But there are other programs that can test external links. To find such a program, do a search for the term *link checker* on your favorite search engine.

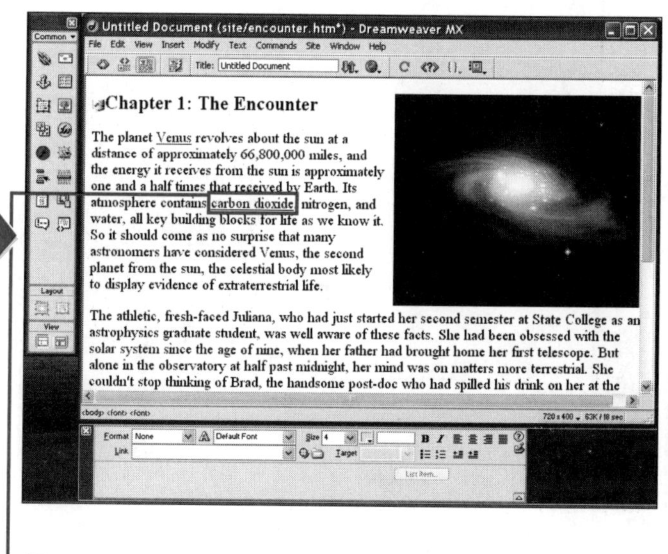

■ The new hyperlink appears colored and underlined.

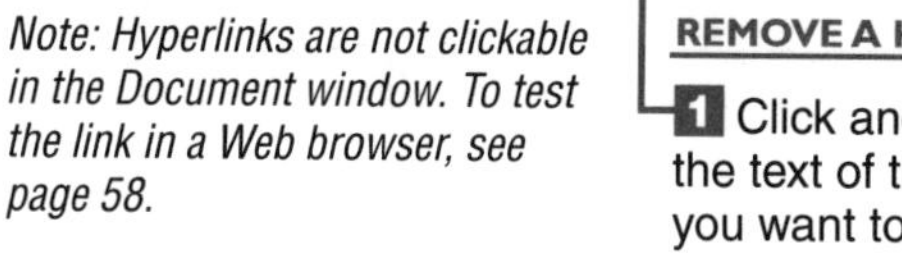

Note: Hyperlinks are not clickable in the Document window. To test the link in a Web browser, see page 58.

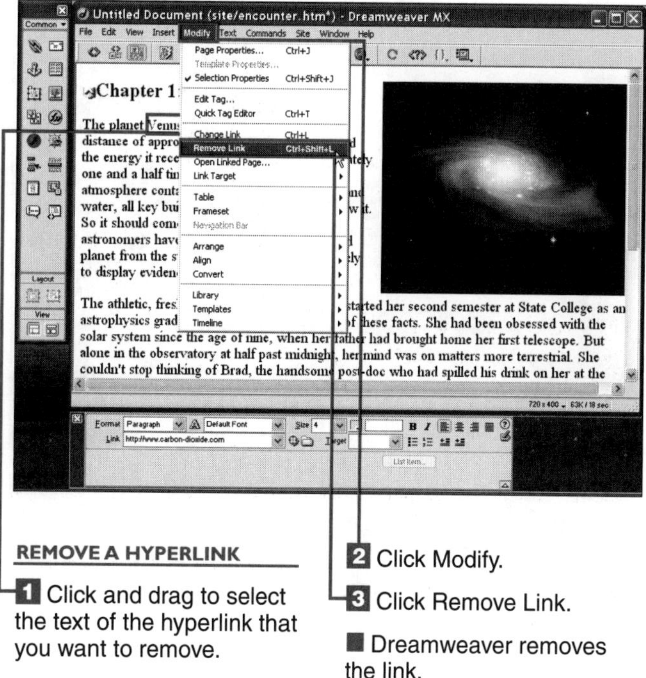

REMOVE A HYPERLINK

1 Click and drag to select the text of the hyperlink that you want to remove.

2 Click Modify.

3 Click Remove Link.

■ Dreamweaver removes the link.

CREATE AN IMAGE HYPERLINK

You can create image hyperlinks that lead to other pages when the user clicks them. You create such links by selecting an image in the Document window and then selecting the destination page from your local site folder. If they are colorful, image hyperlinks can draw more attention than text hyperlinks.

If you pass your cursor over a hyperlinked image in a Web browser, the cursor changes shape. This is one way that hyperlinked images are distinguished from regular images on a Web page.

The stylized navigation buttons you see on many Web pages are usually image files that have been hyperlinked to other pages on the site. You can build such buttons in an image editor such as Adobe Photoshop or Macromedia Fireworks, and then insert them into your page and define them as hyperlinks.

Image hyperlinks can be useful when you want to display very large images on your site. You can make small versions of your image files called thumbnails, which download quickly and give viewers a hint of what the image consists of. You can then hyperlink those thumbnails to the large versions of the image files.

CREATE AN IMAGE HYPERLINK

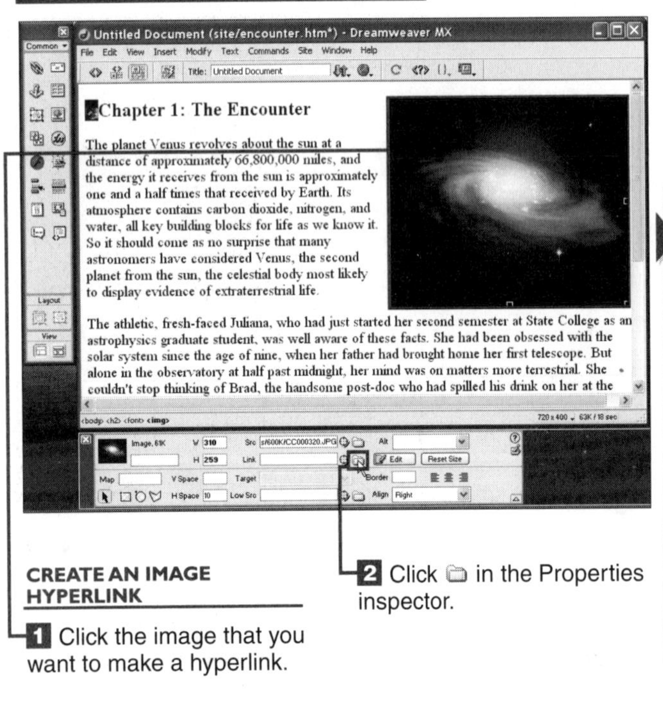

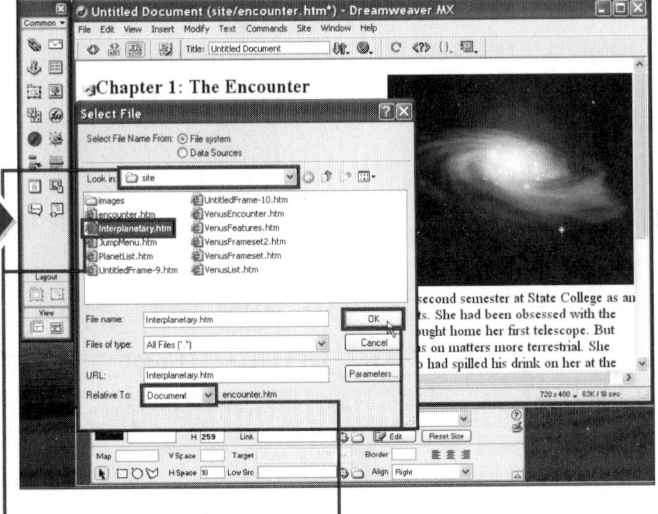

CREATE AN IMAGE HYPERLINK

1 Click the image that you want to make a hyperlink.

2 Click 🗀 in the Properties inspector.

3 Click ⌄ and select the folder that contains the destination page.

4 From the list menu, click the HTML file to which you want to link.

■ You can also enter a Web address in the URL field to link to an external Web page.

5 Click ⌄ and select the type of link path, document relative or root relative.

6 Click OK.

How do I add a colored border to my hyperlinked images?

✔ When you create an image hyperlink, Dreamweaver automatically sets the image border to 0, so the border is turned off. To make a border appear, set the Border field in the Properties inspector to a positive number, which defines the width of the border in pixels. The color of the border is the same as the text hyperlinks on the page. Turning on borders for hyperlinked images is a useful way to indicate that the images are clickable.

How can I obtain navigational buttons and other images that I can use on my Web pages?

✔ You can make them from scratch in an image editor such as Macromedia Fireworks or Adobe Photoshop, get them out of clip-art collections that you can purchase at a computer store or online, or download public-domain art from one of the many Web sites that offer it.

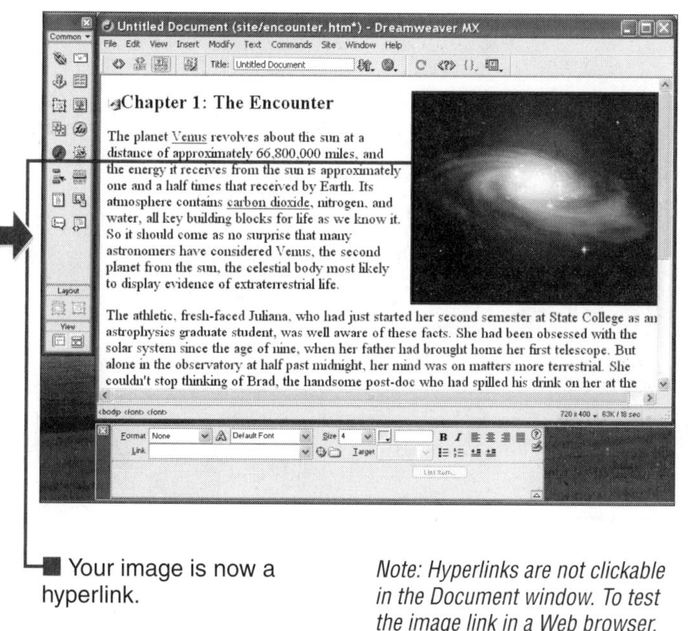

■ Your image is now a hyperlink.

Note: Hyperlinks are not clickable in the Document window. To test the image link in a Web browser, see page 58.

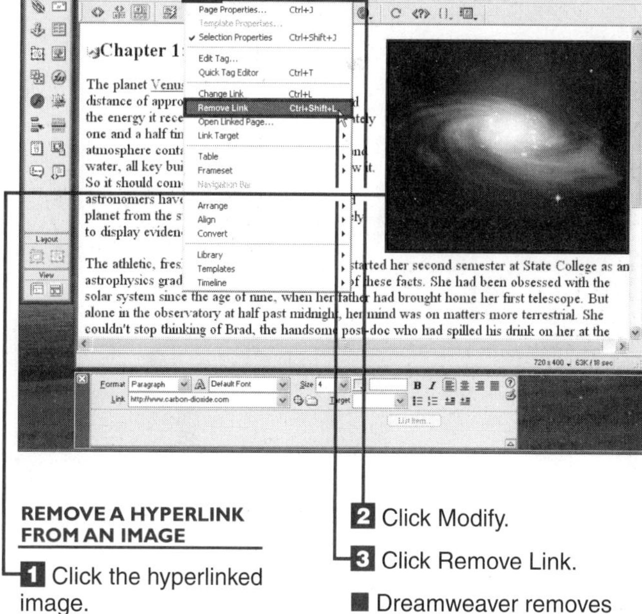

REMOVE A HYPERLINK FROM AN IMAGE

1 Click the hyperlinked image.

2 Click Modify.

3 Click Remove Link.

■ Dreamweaver removes the link.

HYPERLINK WITHIN A WEB PAGE

You can create a clickable hyperlink on a Web page that leads to information on the same page. This can be useful for pages that are extremely long. It saves viewers from having to scroll to find the information that they are interested in.

Creating such an inter-page link is a two-step process. First, you create a *named anchor* at the place on the page that will be the link destination. Then you create a hyperlink that references that anchor. An anchor hyperlink is distinguished from a regular hyperlink in HTML by a # sign preceding the name of the anchor, such as #myanchor.

A glossary page can benefit from named anchor hyperlinks. Listing the alphabet at the top of a glossary and making each letter a link to items below that begin with that letter makes it easy for viewers to find the words they are looking for.

Many times when you create a long page with many anchor links, you want to also create links that send a user back to the top of the page. You can do this by creating an anchor at the very top of the page and referencing it with hyperlinks.

HYPERLINK WITHIN A WEB PAGE

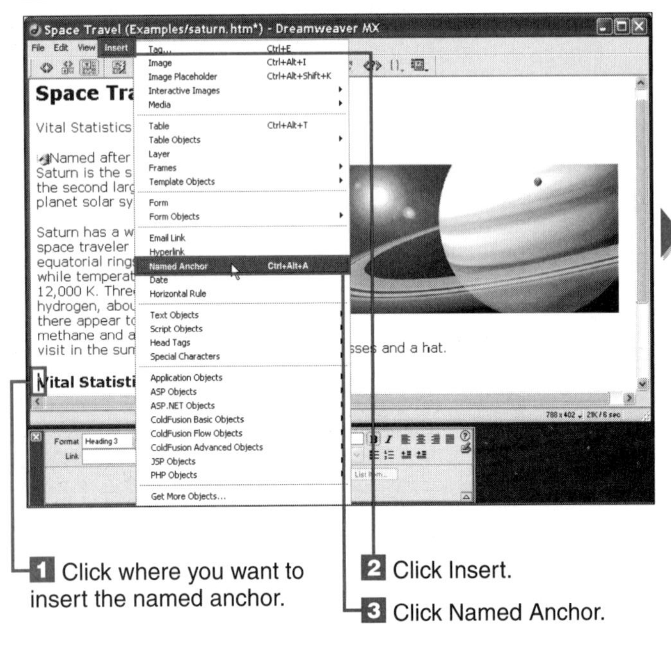

1 Click where you want to insert the named anchor.

2 Click Insert.

3 Click Named Anchor.

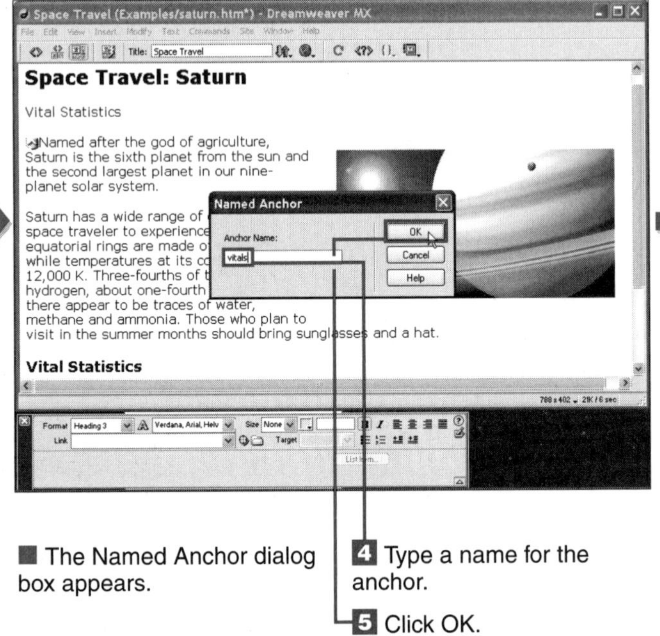

■ The Named Anchor dialog box appears.

4 Type a name for the anchor.

5 Click OK.

Can I link to an anchor that is defined in *another* page?

✔ Yes. First link to the page as you normally would. Then, in the HTML, reference the named anchor using a pound sign (#) at the end of the HREF code, for example:

```
HREF=folder/page.
    html#anchorname
```

When the link is clicked, the destination page opens and then scrolls to the position of the anchor.

How do I link to an anchor using the Link icon?

✔ Select the text or image that you want to be the link. Then click and drag the (⊕), located in the Properties inspector, to the anchor icon in the Document window. You may have to turn on anchor viewing by selecting Invisible Elements under the View menu.

How can I use named anchors to make navigating a long page easier?

✔ At the top, you can create a table of contents for the page that consists of named anchor links. The links can take the user to the different sections of the page further down. This can be a good strategy for creating navigation for glossary pages, where named anchor links can take the user to different sections of the alphabet.

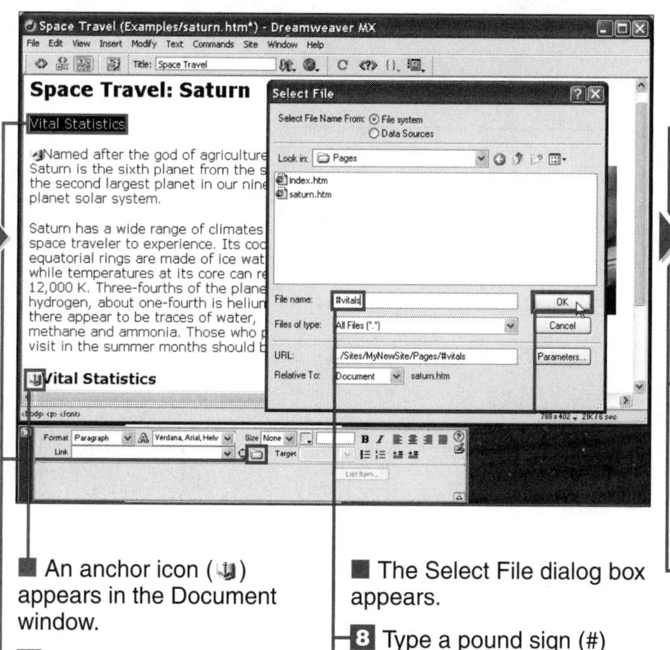

■ An anchor icon (⚓) appears in the Document window.

6 Click and drag to select the text that you want to turn into a hyperlink.

7 Click (📁) in the Properties inspector.

■ The Select File dialog box appears.

8 Type a pound sign (#) followed by the name of the anchor from step 4.

9 Click OK.

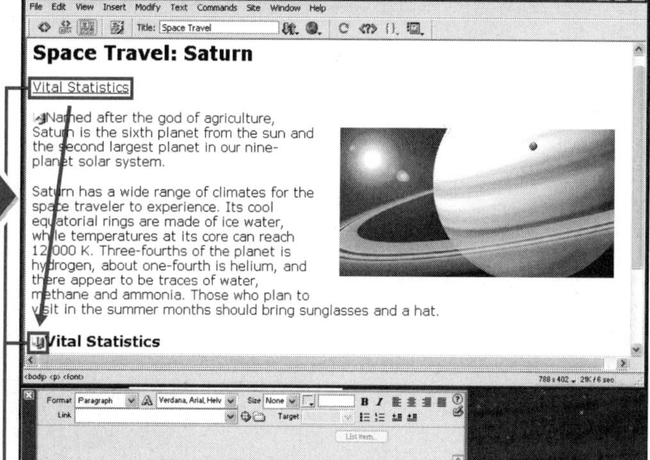

■ The new hyperlink is linked to the named anchor.

Note: The new hyperlink is not clickable in the Document window. To test the link in a Web browser, see page 58.

HYPERLINK TO OTHER FILES

You can create clickable hyperlinks from your site's Web pages to non-HTML documents. This can give your visitors access to information that you may not be able to save in a Web-page format, such as multimedia clips and newsletter layouts.

You create such links by selecting text or an image in the Document window and then defining the destination file's location in the local site folder or its external address on the Web. You can link to any other type of file, including word-processing documents, PDF files, multimedia files, and image files.

What you need to remember about non-HTML documents is that users who click the links need to have the software necessary to view the files installed on their computers. Image files are usually not a problem, because practically all Web browsers can interpret JPEG and GIF files, the most common image files on the Web, and some can even read other image formats such as TIFF and PNG. Multimedia files, such as Flash and QuickTime movies, require that a user have add-on features known as plug-ins installed in their browsers. Other types of files, such as Microsoft Word documents, require that specific standalone applications are installed.

HYPERLINK TO OTHER FILES

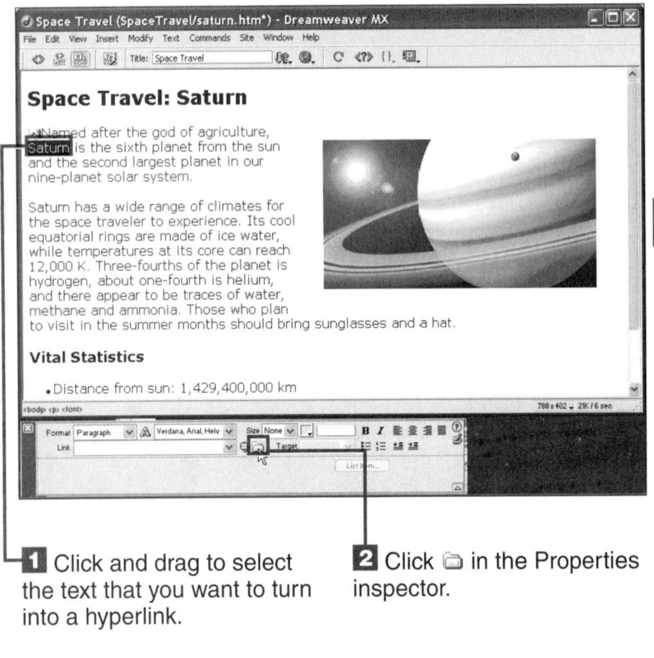

1 Click and drag to select the text that you want to turn into a hyperlink.

2 Click 🗀 in the Properties inspector.

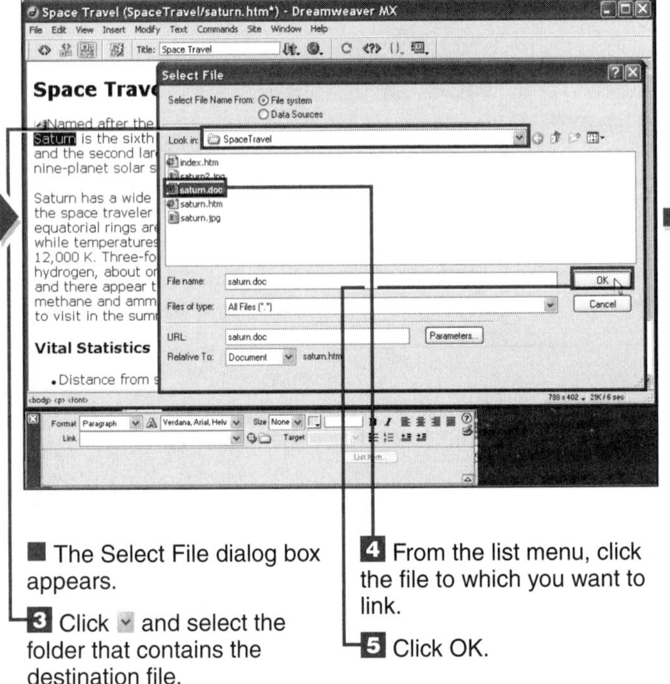

■ The Select File dialog box appears.

3 Click ⌄ and select the folder that contains the destination file.

4 From the list menu, click the file to which you want to link.

5 Click OK.

How can I help ensure that my viewers are able to view the non-HTML file that I put on my site?

✔ Try to present content in file formats that are popular. This way, there is a good chance that viewers have the necessary software installed. For example, if you want to provide users with text in a page-layout form that they can print, it is probably a good idea to present it as a PDF file or as a Microsoft Word document. If you want to make your content *really* accessible, provide it in several different formats, for example, in both PDF *and* Word form. Then the user can click the link that is best for them. Another strategy is to have a Dreamweaver behavior check for plug-ins on the browser, and give users who do not have the necessary plug-ins details about how they can get them.

What happens if a user does not have the required software to view a hyperlinked file?

✔ Usually, the browser presents the user with several options, including saving the file to the computer so the user can view the file later when the required software has been installed, visiting a Web site where the user can download the required software, or canceling the download altogether.

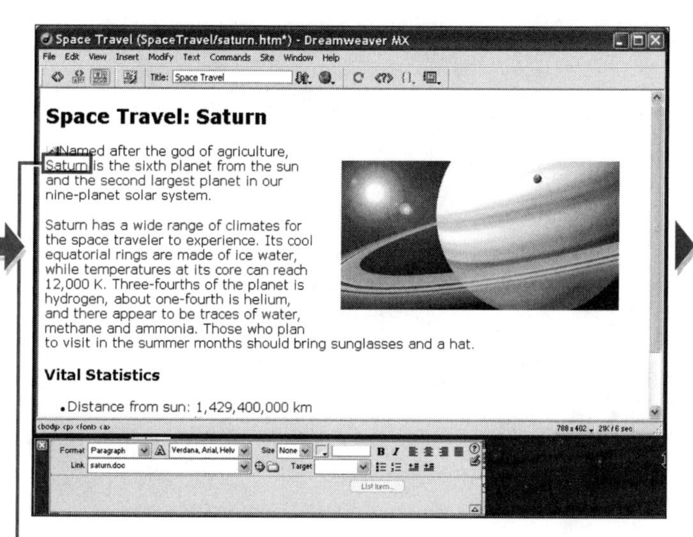

■ The new hyperlink appears colored and underlined.

Note: Hyperlinks are not clickable in the Document window. To test the link in a Web browser, see page 58.

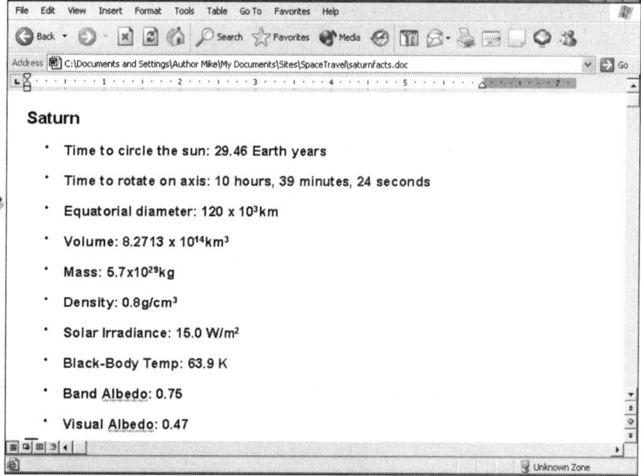

6 Preview your Web page in a browser.

7 Click the link to test it.

■ The browser reads the file and displays it.

Note: If a user clicks a link that points to a type of file that a browser cannot display, the browser will usually ask whether the user wants to open the file with another application or save it.

CREATE MULTIPLE HYPERLINKS WITHIN AN IMAGE

You can assign different hyperlinks to different parts of an image using Dreamweaver's image-mapping tools. This allows you to make a large image serve as a navigational jumping-off point for the rest of your Web site. You can also take a complicated image, such as a geography map, and link different parts of the image to different pages describing each part.

On an HTML level, mapping hyperlinks to specific areas of an image can be complicated. First you have to determine the mathematical coordinates that define the different areas, also called *hotspots*, in the image, and then you have to integrate those coordinates into the HTML.

Dreamweaver makes the process easy. First you click and drag with different shape-making tools to define the different hotspots on your image. Dreamweaver determines the coordinates for those hotspots for you and writes them into the HTML. All you have to do is define a link for each hotspot.

One drawback to creating image maps is that viewers who do not have image-viewing capability cannot access the different hyperlinks unless those hyperlinks are also defined elsewhere on the page.

CREATE MULTIPLE HYPERLINKS WITHIN AN IMAGE

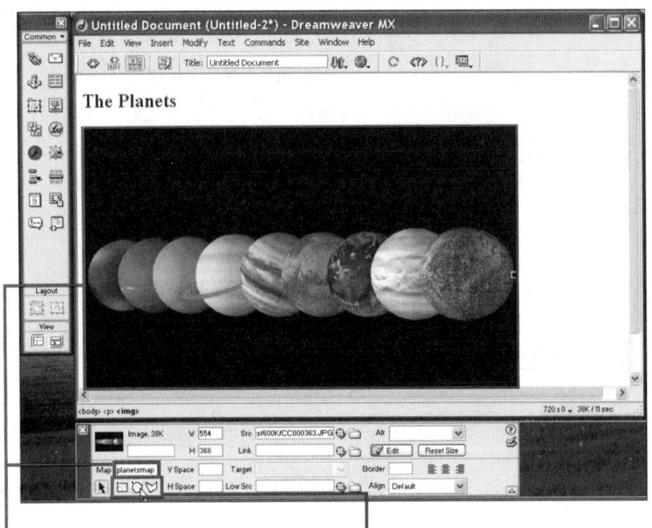

1 Click the image.

2 Type a descriptive name to serve as the name of the image map.

3 Click a drawing tool.

- Rectangular areas
- Circular areas
- Polygons

Note: To create irregularly shaped areas with the tool, click the corner points one at a time.

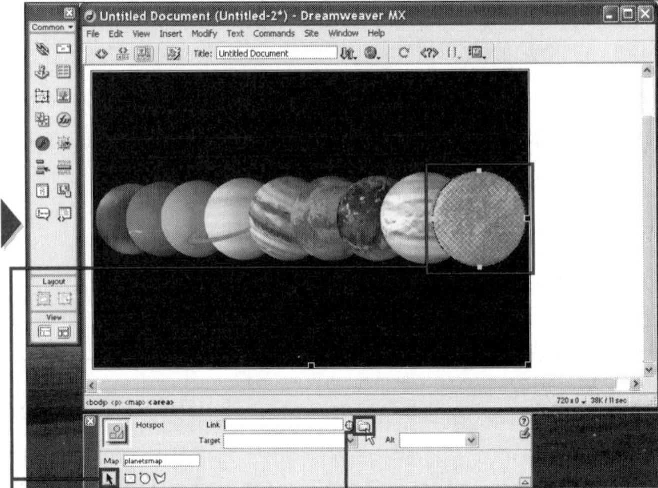

4 Click and drag to draw an area on the image using the selected tool.

■ Using the Pointer tool, you can click and drag the side handles to change size, or click and drag the entire shape to change position.

■ To delete the shape and start over, you can press Delete.

5 Click the .

How can I create an interactive map of the United States with each state having a different hyperlink?

✔ Add a map of the U.S. to your Web page and define a hotspot over each state. You probably want to use the polygon tool to draw around the states. Then assign a different hyperlink to each state.

Where is the information about an image map stored?

✔ Dreamweaver stores the information about image maps inside a `<MAP>` tag in the page's HTML. This type of image map is known as a client-side image map, because the coordinate information is read and interpreted by the browser, also known as the *client*.

How can I create an image map and still accommodate viewers who cannot view images?

✔ Duplicate the links defined in your image map as text hyperlinks elsewhere on the page. For example, if you created an interactive map of the U.S., you might also repeat the text hyperlinks for the states below the map image.

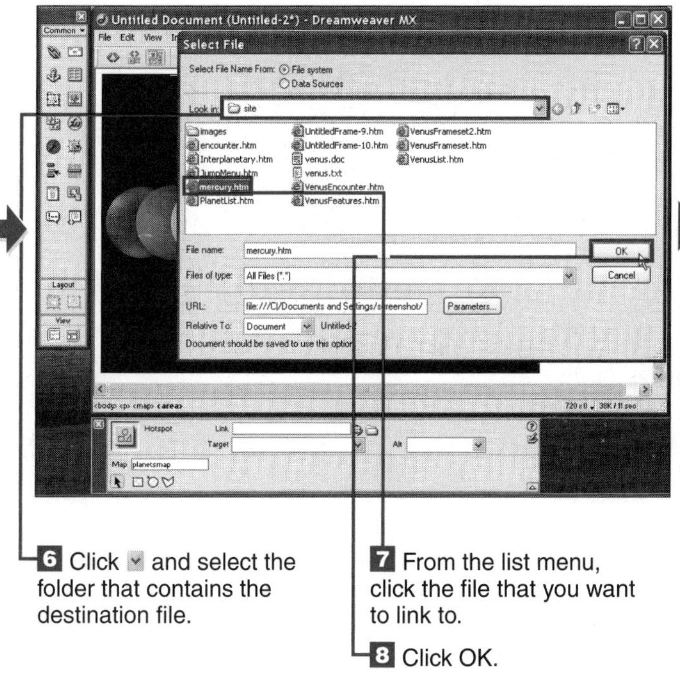

6 Click ▾ and select the folder that contains the destination file.

7 From the list menu, click the file that you want to link to.

8 Click OK.

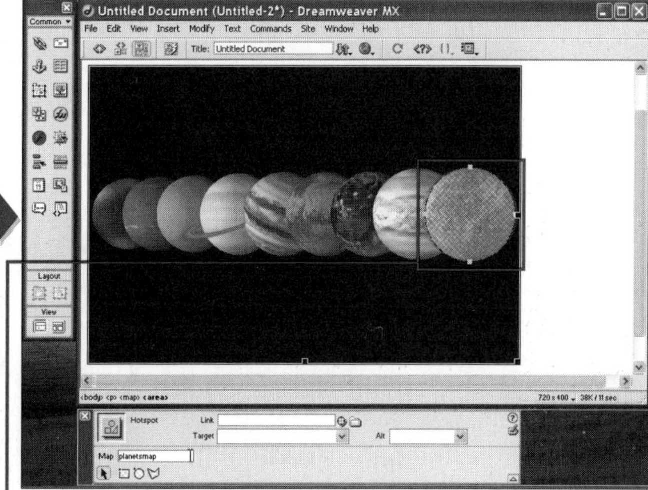

■ The area defined by the shape becomes a hyperlink to the selected file.

■ You can repeat steps 3 to 8 to add other linked areas to your image.

Note: The image-map shapes do not appear when you open the page in a Web browser. To test the links by previewing the page in a Web browser, see page 58.

OPEN A NEW WINDOW WITH A HYPERLINK

You can create a hyperlink that opens a new browser window when a user clicks. The destination specified for the link then opens in the new window. Opening a new browser window involves specifying a target value for the link, in this case a value of _blank. The target of a link also comes into play when creating frames-based sites, because it is necessary to target links to particular frames in the window.

Opening a new browser window can be useful when linking to pages that exist on external Web sites. Creating a new window means the page in the old window remains open on the user's computer, making it easy for the user to return to your site later on.

Opening new windows, however, can also eventually lead to clutter on a user's desktop.

You may want to add a short explanation next to links that open destinations in a new window. This lets users know that they will not be able to click the Back button on their browser to return to the previous page. They will need to close the window.

OPEN A NEW WINDOW WITH A HYPERLINK

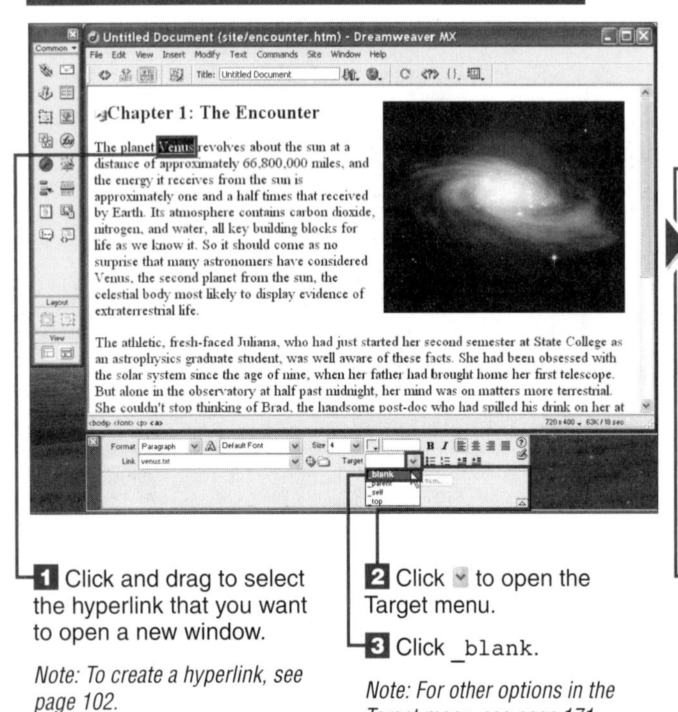

Untitled Document - Microsoft Internet Explorer

C:\Documents and Settings\screenshot\Desktop\site\venus.tx...

1 Click and drag to select the hyperlink that you want to open a new window.

Note: To create a hyperlink, see page 102.

2 Click ▾ to open the Target menu.

3 Click _blank.

Note: For other options in the Target menu, see page 171.

4 Preview the page in a Web browser and click the hyperlink.

Note: To preview a page in a Web browser, see page 58.

■ Dreamweaver displays the hyperlink destination in a new window.

Note: To create a link that opens a browser window with a predefined size and toolbar configuration, see page 230.

HYPERLINK BY USING THE SITE WINDOW

A quick and visual way to create hyperlinks between pages in your Web site is by clicking and dragging to the Site window. This technique lets you avoid navigating to each destination link using a dialog box.

The technique involves selecting the text or image that you want to define as a link, and then clicking and dragging the ⊕ from the Properties inspector to the destination file in the Site window. This technique works best on monitors at high resolution settings, where you can have many windows and panels open and visible at once.

You can create links this way with the Site window in either Site Files or Site Map mode. The Site Map mode provides an additional advantage in that you can create links to external Web addresses if those addresses already exist in the Site Map structure.

The ⊕ is also available next to the Image Source field in the Properties inspector when an image is selected in the Document window. With it, you can similarly specify the source file for an image.

HYPERLINK BY USING THE SITE WINDOW

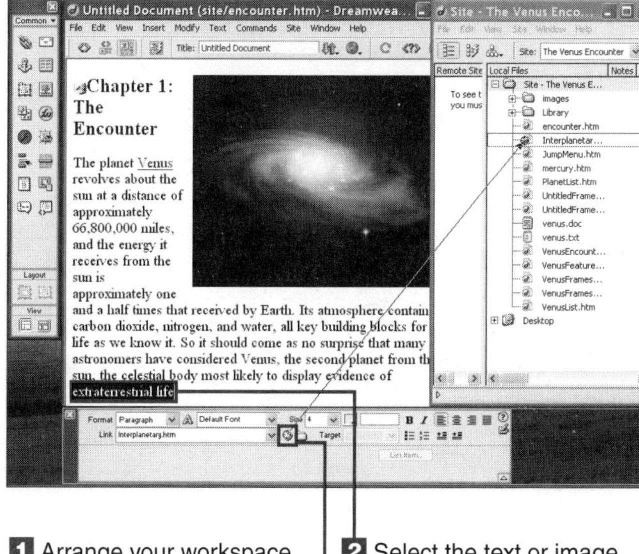

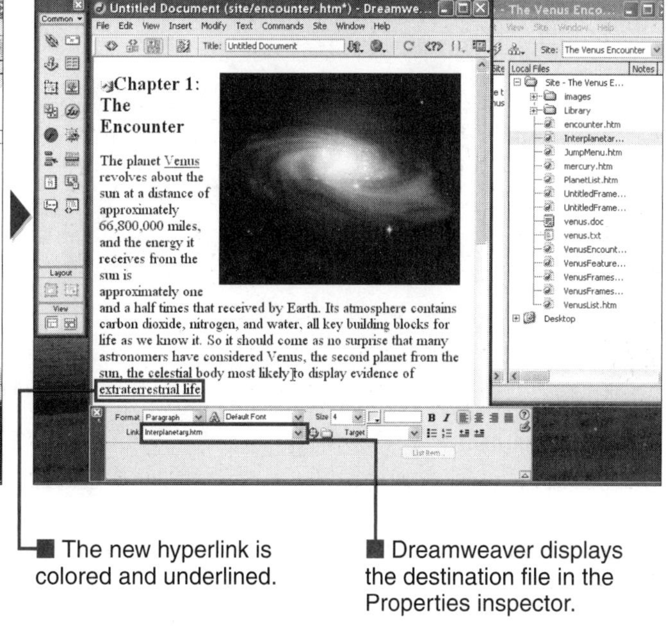

1 Arrange your workspace to make both the Document and Site windows visible.

Note: To open the Site window, see page 251.

2 Select the text or image that you want to turn into a hyperlink.

3 Click and drag the ⊕ to the destination file listed in the Site window.

■ The new hyperlink is colored and underlined.

■ Dreamweaver displays the destination file in the Properties inspector.

CHANGE THE COLOR OF HYPERLINKS

You can change the color of the hyperlinks on your Web page to make them match the visual style of the text and images on your page. Changing link colors also enables you to emphasize important links and de-emphasize unimportant links. You can select a link color by choosing from a palette of colors, specifying a color by name, or by specifying a color with its hexadecimal code.

Dreamweaver lets you specify the color of three different types of hyperlinks: unvisited links, visited links, and active links. Which links are defined as visited is determined by the Web pages in the browser's history cache. A link turns the active color when the cursor clicks on it. You can set the three types of links to different colors, or to the same color so that they never change.

As a rule, it is good to choose link colors that are distinct from the color of the page's regular text so a viewer can pick out the links at a glance. For more information about defining colors, see page 80.

CHANGE THE COLOR OF HYPERLINKS

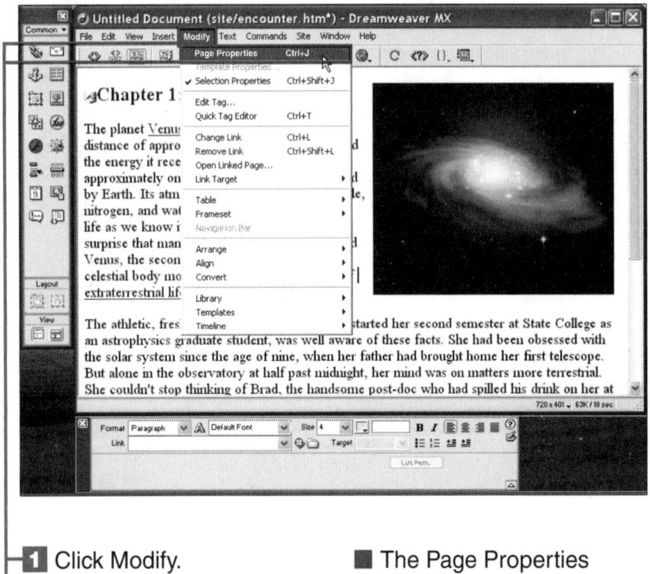

1 Click Modify.

2 Click Page Properties.

■ The Page Properties dialog box lets you change the color of all the links on a page.

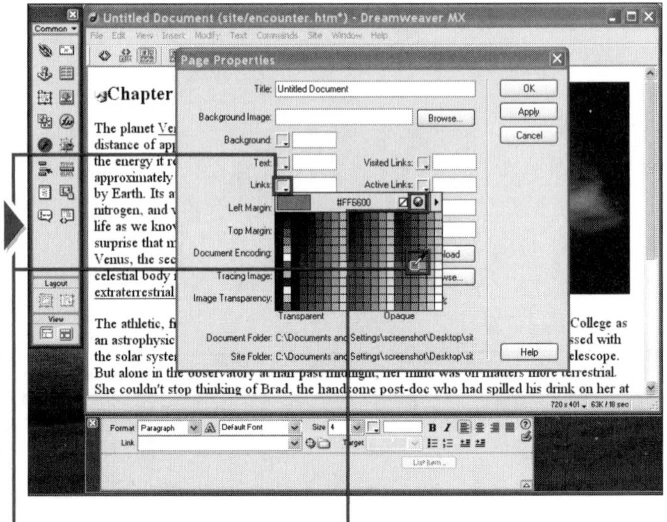

3 Click the Links color button ( ).

4 Click a color from the menu using the eyedropper tool.

■ The changes to an .

■ You can click to select a custom color.

How do I get rid of the underlining on my hyperlinks?

✔ You can specify that links not be underlined by using style sheets. To modify links using style sheets, see page 210. However, doing this may confuse some users, because underlining is such a universal way to distinguish links from regular text.

How can I make my links disappear when they are clicked?

✔ If you set the active color to the same color as the page background, the link disappears when it is clicked. The link reappears when the mouse button is released.

What color do my links appear if I do not specifically define them in Dreamweaver?

✔ In the Dreamweaver Document window, blue is the default link color. What viewers see when the page is opened in a browser depends on the browser settings. By default, most browsers display unvisited links as blue, visited links as purple, and active links as red. Users can override these settings in their browser options.

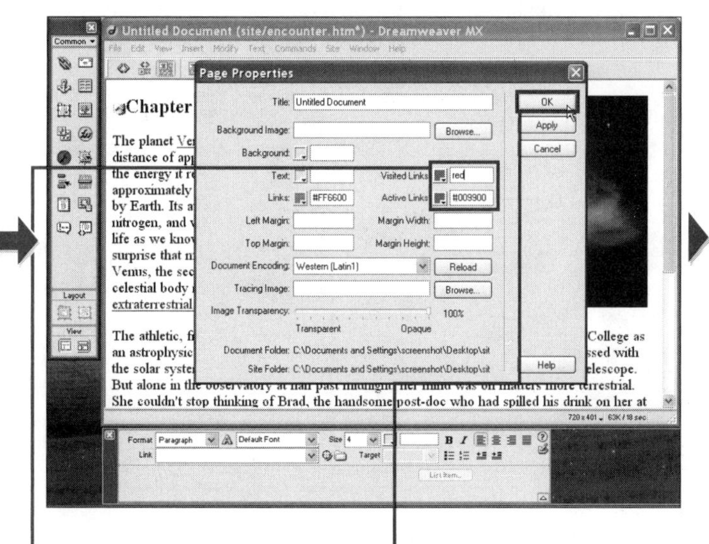

5 Click the for Visited Links and Active Links to define their colors.

6 Click OK.

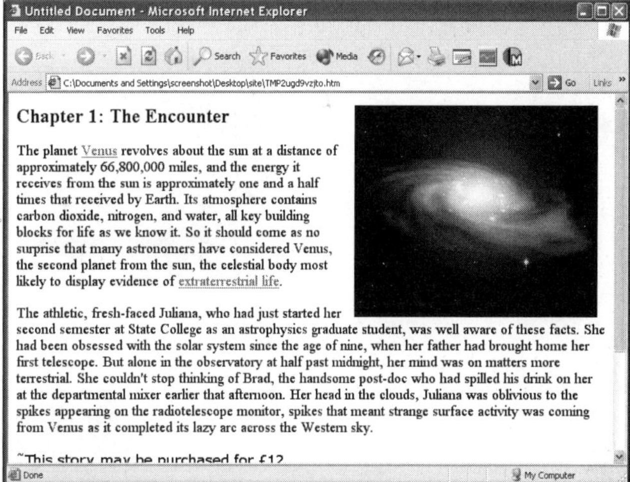

7 Preview the page in a Web browser.

Note: To test links in a Web browser, see page 58.

■ The hyperlinks display in the defined colors.

CREATE AN E-MAIL HYPERLINK

You can create hyperlinks that launch an e-mail composition window when clicked. These are useful when you want to give your viewers a way to send you feedback about your site or request more information about your products or services. The e-mail application automatically opens a new message window, with the To: e-mail address filled in.

When you define an e-mail link, you specify the e-mail address of the intended recipient, for example, `webmaster@mysite.com`. This address is automatically placed in the To field when the e-mail composition window opens.

An e-mail hyperlink is a simpler alternative to a form, which you can also use to allow visitors to send you feedback or other information. To use a form, you must install a form handler on your Web server that processes the entered information. For more information about forms, see Chapter 9.

One drawback to e-mail hyperlinks is that some users may not use browsers that have e-mail capability installed or configured. In such cases, the user may get no response or an error message when the link is clicked. Both Microsoft Internet Explorer and Netscape Navigator, support e-mail links.

CREATE AN E-MAIL HYPERLINK

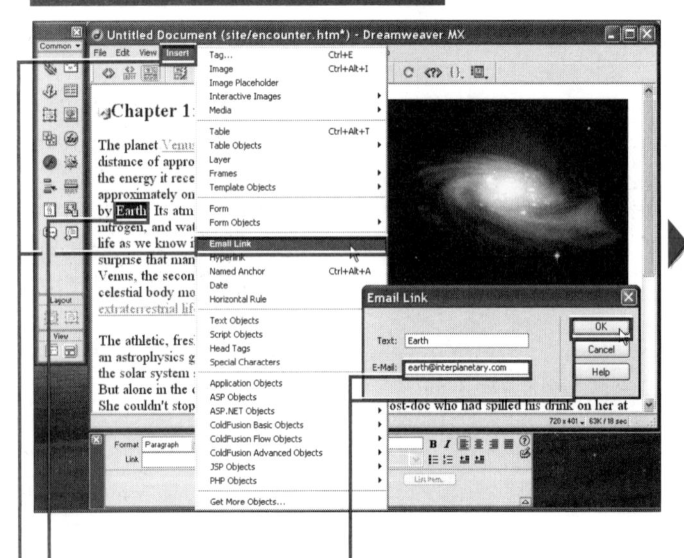

1 Click and drag to select the text you want to turn into an e-mail hyperlink.

2 Click Insert.

3 Click E-mail Link.

■ The selected text appears in the Text field of the Insert E-Mail Link dialog box.

4 In the E-Mail field, type the e-mail address to which you want to link.

5 Click OK.

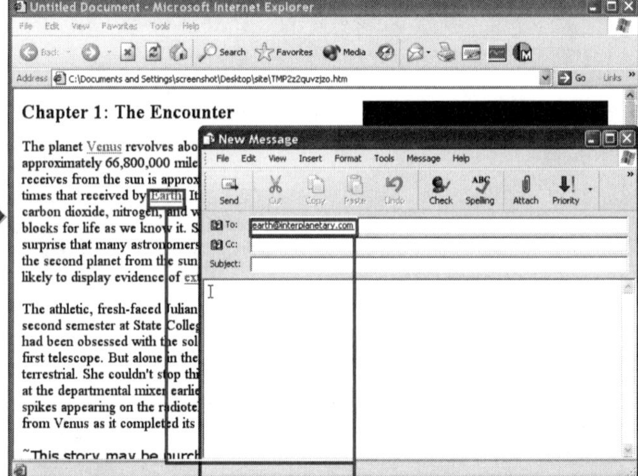

■ The selected text appears underlined and in color.

6 To test the link, preview the page in a Web browser.

Note: To test the link in a Web browser, see page 58.

■ In Web browsers that support e-mail, clicking the hyperlink launches an e-mail composition window.

■ If the browser does not have e-mail capability, clicking the link will have no effect.

CHECK A HYPERLINK

Dreamweaver can automatically check all the links among the pages of your Web site and report whether any are broken. Checking links, along with checking for errors in HTML syntax, is a good final step before you upload your site to a live Web server. This feature is especially useful for large sites, which may contain hundreds or thousands of hyperlinks.

Dreamweaver cannot check hyperlinks to files on external Web sites. For these, you have to check them by hand with a Web browser or use a third-party link checker. To find one, search for "link checker" on your favorite search engine. Dreamweaver also cannot check e-mail links.

Different things can cause hyperlinks to break. A filename might be misspelled in the HTML, the destination file might be deleted, or its name may have changed. When a visitor clicks a broken hyperlink on a site, they receive a "404 error" from the server, indicating that the requested file was not found. You can fix broken links inside Dreamweaver's Link Checker dialog box by changing the spelling of a filename or reselecting the destination file.

CHECK A HYPERLINK

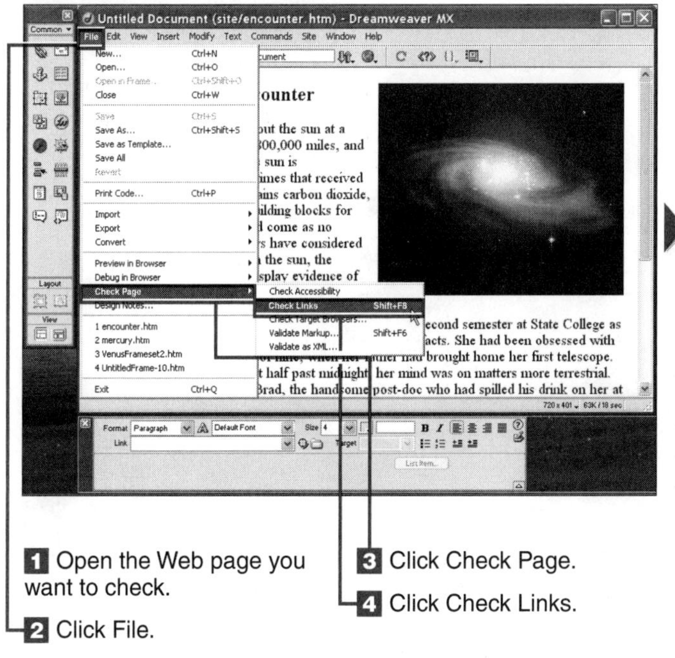

1 Open the Web page you want to check.

2 Click File.

3 Click Check Page.

4 Click Check Links.

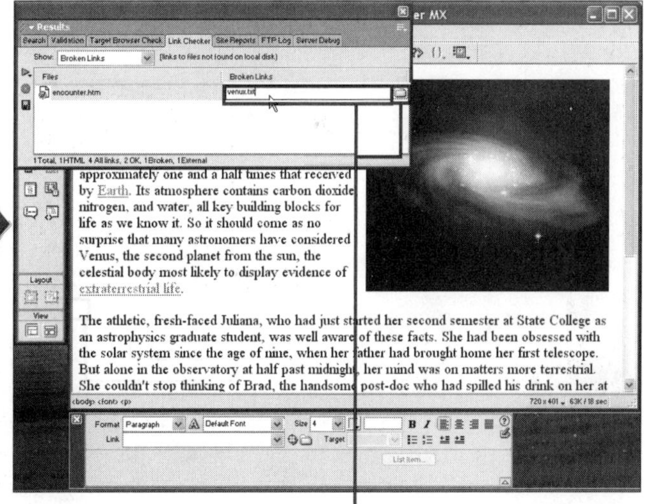

■ Dreamweaver checks the local hyperlinks and lists any broken links it finds.

■ You can edit a broken destination file by selecting it and editing the Broken Links field. You can also click 🗀 to select a new destination for the link.

INSERT A TABLE INTO YOUR WEB PAGE

HTML tables offer you a flexible tool for organizing and positioning information on your Web page. You can use Dreamweaver to create HTML tables to organize text, images, and other information into regular rows and columns on your page.

You can also use tables to determine the overall layout of a page's content. For example, you can use a table to create a narrow side column, where you can organize navigation links, next to a larger area where you can place the page's main content. Frames, discussed in Chapter 10, are another way to organize the layout of your page.

You define a table in Dreamweaver by specifying the number of rows and columns, size, and border characteristics. After you insert a table, you can further customize its structure by merging and splitting its cells, which are the rectangular containers that make up a table, or even inserting another table inside a cell of an existing table.

You can turn on a table's borders to distinguish the individual cells that divide the content. Or you can keep the borders turned off to make the structure invisible to the viewer.

INSERT A TABLE INTO YOUR WEB PAGE

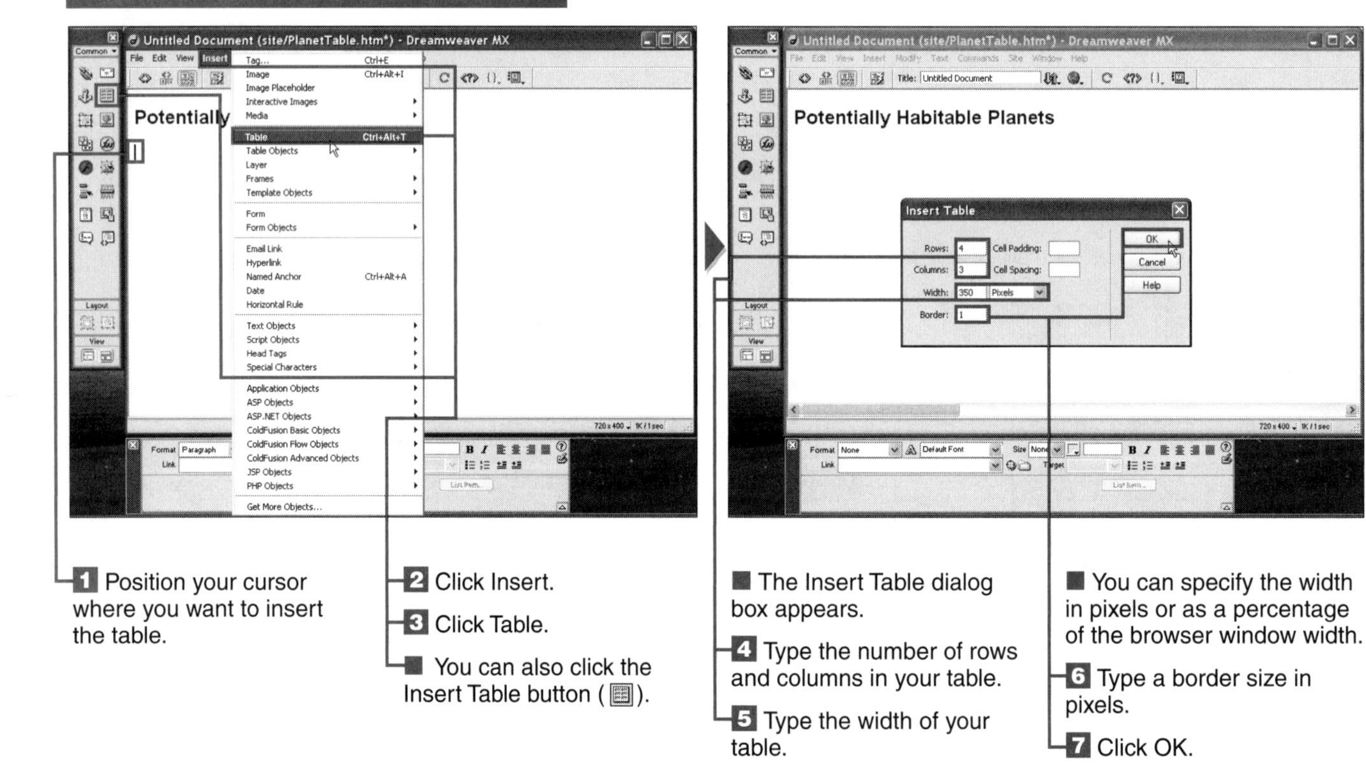

1 Position your cursor where you want to insert the table.

2 Click Insert.

3 Click Table.

■ You can also click the Insert Table button (▦).

■ The Insert Table dialog box appears.

4 Type the number of rows and columns in your table.

5 Type the width of your table.

■ You can specify the width in pixels or as a percentage of the browser window width.

6 Type a border size in pixels.

7 Click OK.

How can I duplicate a table on my Web page?

✔ First, you need to select the table by clicking its upper-left corner. Then, use the Copy and Paste commands under the Edit menu to copy it and paste it elsewhere.

What are the HTML tags that define a table?

✔ The `<table>` tag defines where the table begins and ends in your HTML code, `<tr>` tags define the table rows, and `<td>` tags define the cells within each row. The content displayed in a table sits inside the `<td>` tags.

How do I align a table on a Web page?

✔ Aligning a table is similar to aligning an image. You select the table in Dreamweaver by clicking its upper-left corner. Then, you choose an alignment from the Align menu in the Properties inspector. A left or right alignment wraps other content on the page around the table.

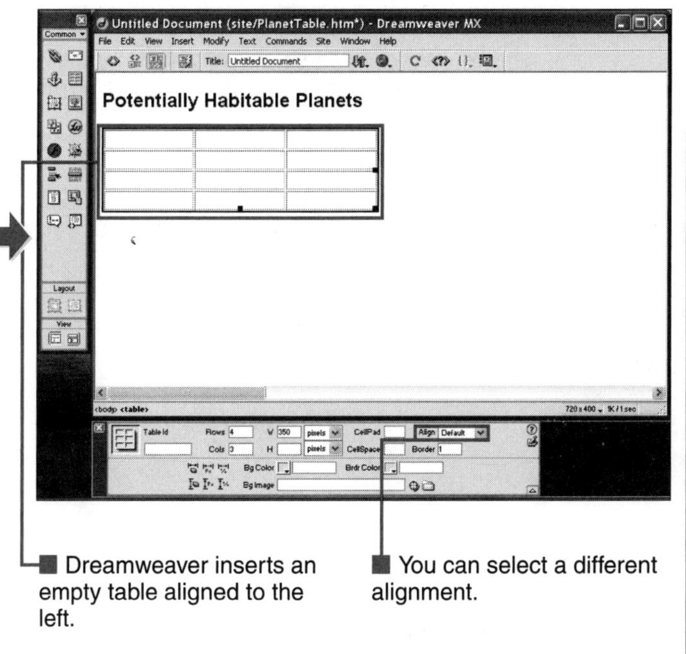

■ Dreamweaver inserts an empty table aligned to the left.

■ You can select a different alignment.

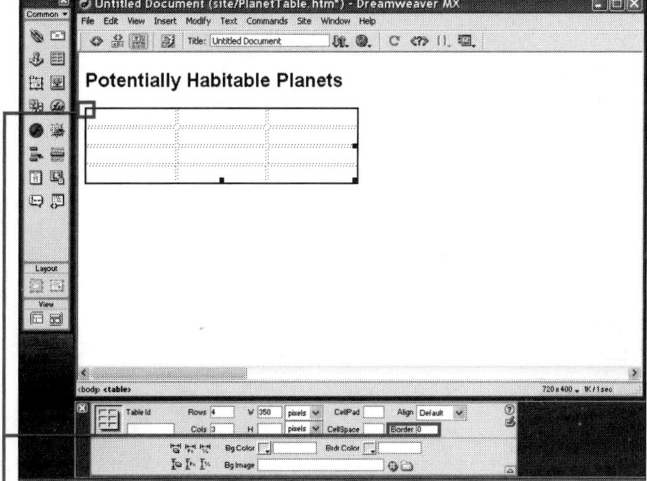

TURN OFF TABLE BORDERS

1 Click the upper-left corner of the table to select it.

2 Type **0** for the border size.

3 Press Enter (Return).

■ Dashed table borders represent the now-invisible table borders.

INSERT CONTENT INTO A TABLE

After you insert a table into your Web page, you can fill the table cells with text, images, form elements, and even other tables. Tables are useful for placing Web-page elements side by side, in table rows, or on top of one another, in table columns.

The cells of a table expand to accommodate whatever content you insert into it. After you insert content, you can adjust the content alignment or add space around the content. See pages 126 and 127 for more information.

You can put entire passages of text inside fixed-width tables to keep the text from rewrapping when a viewer adjusts the browser window size. To create a fixed-width table, see page 132. Tables are also useful for displaying grids of images in photo-gallery sites.

Large tables can also enable you to organize the entire layout of your Web page. For example, you can create a two-column table that features navigation links in one column and the main page content in the other.

INSERT CONTENT INTO A TABLE

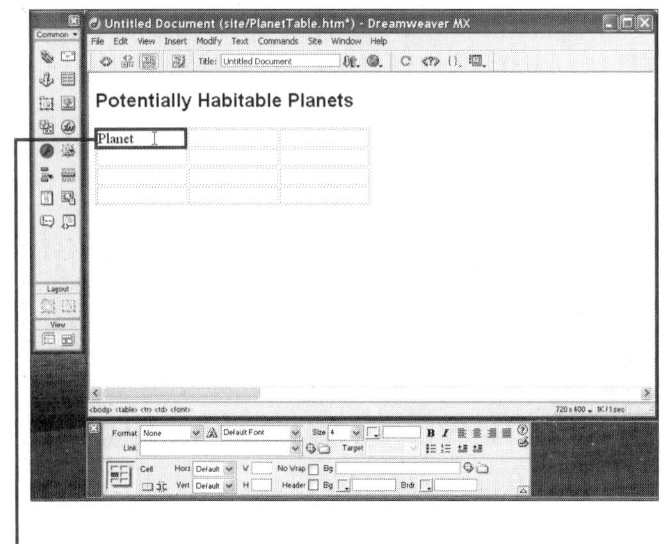

INSERT TEXT

1 Click inside a table cell.

2 Type your text.

Note: To format your text, see Chapter 5.

■ To maneuver between table cells, you can press Tab. To move backwards through the table cells, you can press Shift + Tab.

INSERT AN IMAGE

1 Click inside a table cell.

2 Click the Insert Image button ( ).

3 Click and select the folder that contains your image.

4 Click the name of your image file.

5 Click OK.

How can I add captions to images on my Web page?

✔ The best way to add a caption to the top, bottom, or side of an image is with a two-celled table. Place the image in one cell and the caption in the other. You can then insert the table and adjust its alignment to fit the captioned image in with the rest of your page's content.

How can I use a table to organize my forms?

✔ Often, when you create Web-page forms, you may want the text fields, drop-down menus, and other elements neatly aligned in one column on the page, and the labels for the elements aligned next to them. You can do this by inserting a two-column table and putting a form element and label into the cells of each row. Table borders can be turned on or off, depending on your style preference.

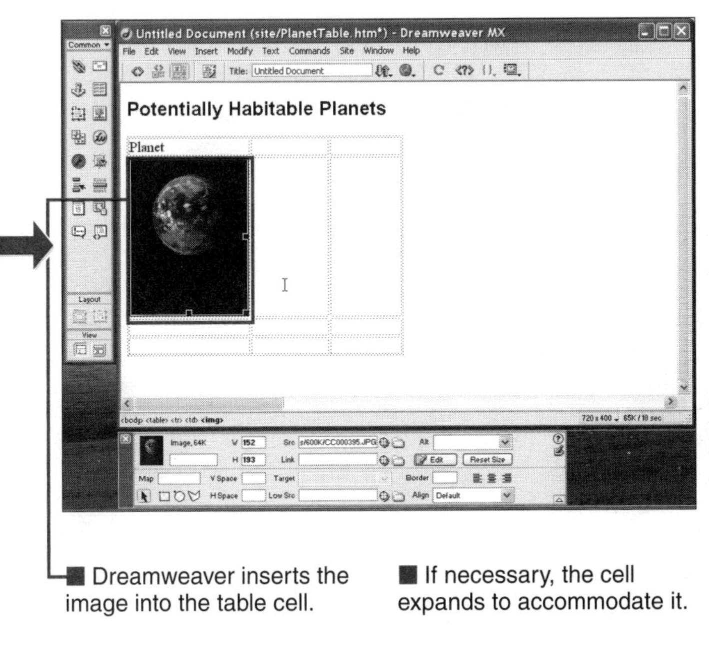

■ Dreamweaver inserts the image into the table cell.

■ If necessary, the cell expands to accommodate it.

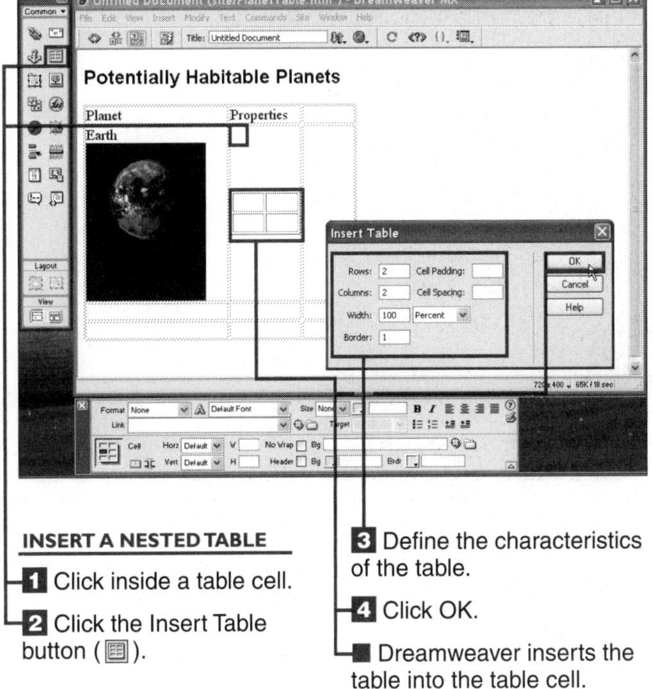

INSERT A NESTED TABLE

1 Click inside a table cell.

2 Click the Insert Table button (▦).

3 Define the characteristics of the table.

4 Click OK.

■ Dreamweaver inserts the table into the table cell.

CHANGE THE BACKGROUND OF A TABLE

You can change the background of a table to make it complement the style of the rest of your Web page. You can change the color of a table's background or specify an image that you want the table background filled with.

To change the background, you can select the table in the Document window and then select a color from a palette in the Properties inspector. You can also specify a color by typing a color name or by specifying a color's hexadecimal code. Adding a background to a table that contains text can distinguish that text from the rest of the page. It offers an alternative to italicizing text or changing the color of text.

In addition to changing the background of the entire table, you can also change just the background of a row, column, or cell. Changing color in this way can highlight a row or column that deserves attention. Alternating the colors of rows or columns can help viewers better distinguish related values in a large table.

CHANGE THE BACKGROUND OF A TABLE

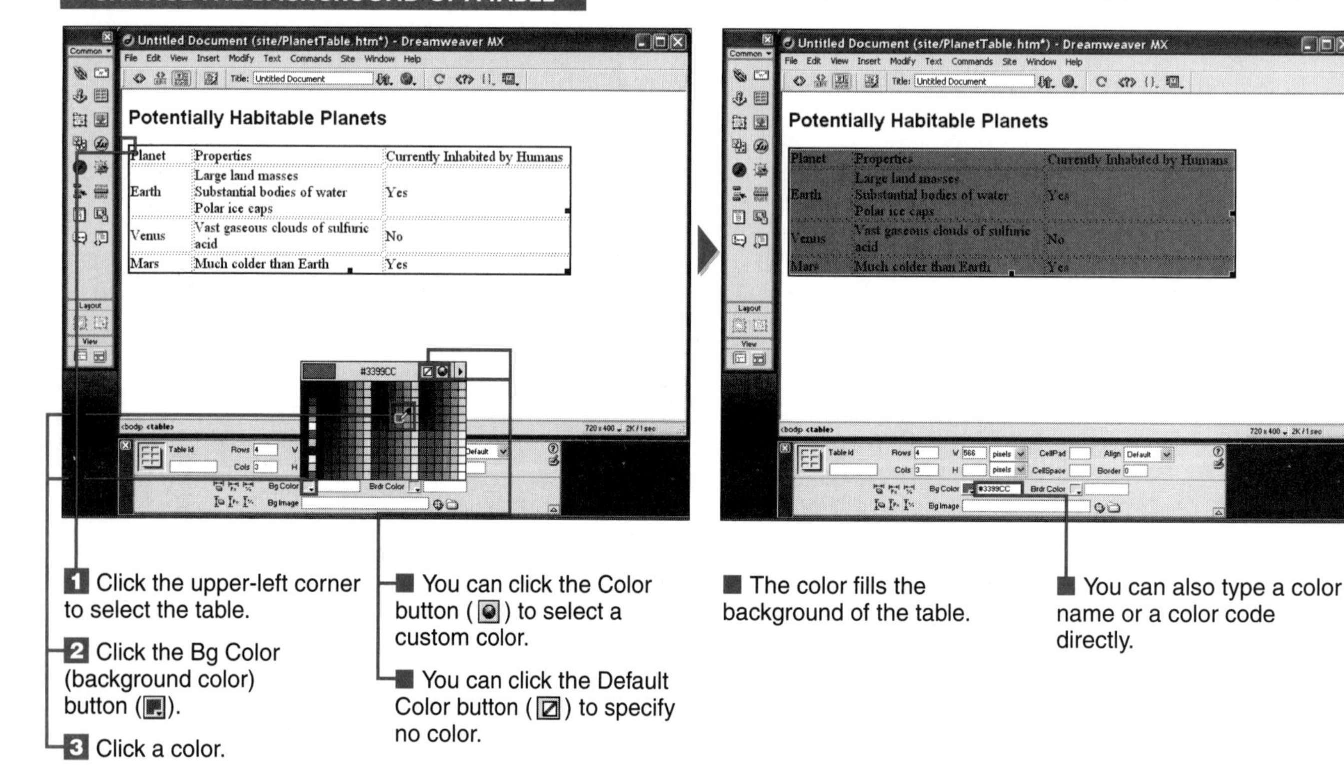

1 Click the upper-left corner to select the table.

2 Click the Bg Color (background color) button (■).

3 Click a color.

■ You can click the Color button (◉) to select a custom color.

■ You can click the Default Color button (☒) to specify no color.

■ The color fills the background of the table.

■ You can also type a color name or a color code directly.

How do I change the color of a single table row or column?

✔ First, click the side edge of the row or top of the column to select it. You can also select a row or column by Ctrl-clicking (Command-clicking) each component cell. Then, click the Bg color swatch in the Properties inspector to select the color for the row or column.

How can I quickly apply an interesting background color scheme to my table?

✔ Select your table by clicking its upper-left corner and click Commands and Format Table. This opens a dialog box that enables you to quickly format your table with a number of preset color schemes. It also lets you format your table's alignment and border.

How do I change the color of the borders of my table?

✔ After selecting your table, you can adjust the border colors using the Brdr, Light Brdr, and Dark Brdr fields in the Properties inspector. You may want to test such effects in different browsers. Some versions of Netscape Navigator and Microsoft Internet Explorer differ in how they apply border colors.

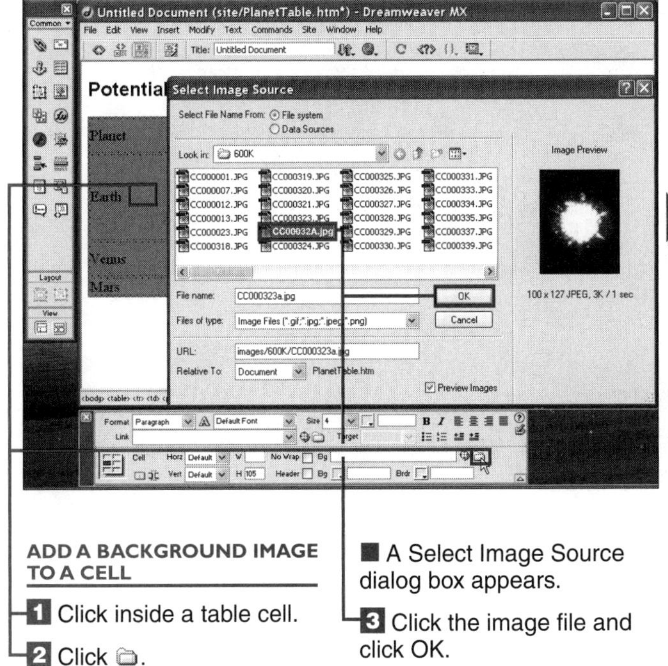

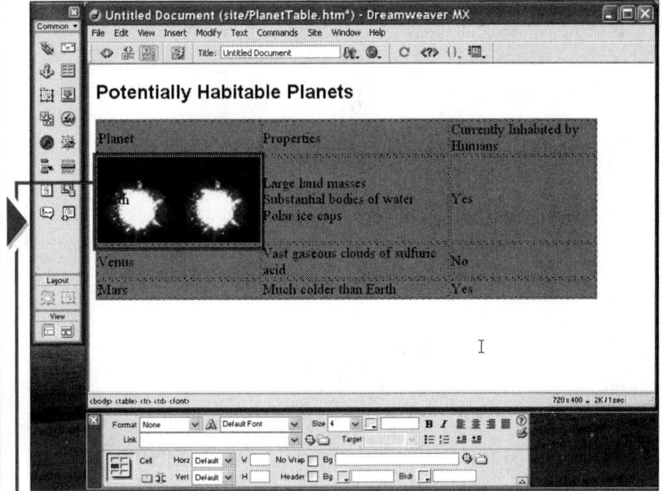

ADD A BACKGROUND IMAGE TO A CELL

1 Click inside a table cell.

2 Click 🗀.

■ A Select Image Source dialog box appears.

3 Click the image file and click OK.

■ The cell background fills with the image.

■ If necessary, the image tiles to fill the entire cell.

CHANGE THE CELL SPACING OR PADDING IN A TABLE

You can emphasize the borders in a table by adjusting the spacing between its different cells. You can also present a table's cell contents more attractively by changing the spacing between the cell content and the cell borders, also known as padding.

You define these settings in pixels in the CellSpace and CellPad fields in the Properties inspector. To see the difference between cell spacing versus cell padding, turn on the borders in a table. When borders are turned off, cell spacing and cell padding produce similar effects; they add space between the contents of the different table cells.

You may want to add some padding to a table to keep the table content from being squished against the table borders. When you do not assign specific values for cell spacing and cell padding, Dreamweaver, Netscape Navigator, and Microsoft Internet Explorer all display a table as if cell spacing were set to 2 and cell padding were set to 1.

CHANGE THE CELL SPACING OR PADDING IN A TABLE

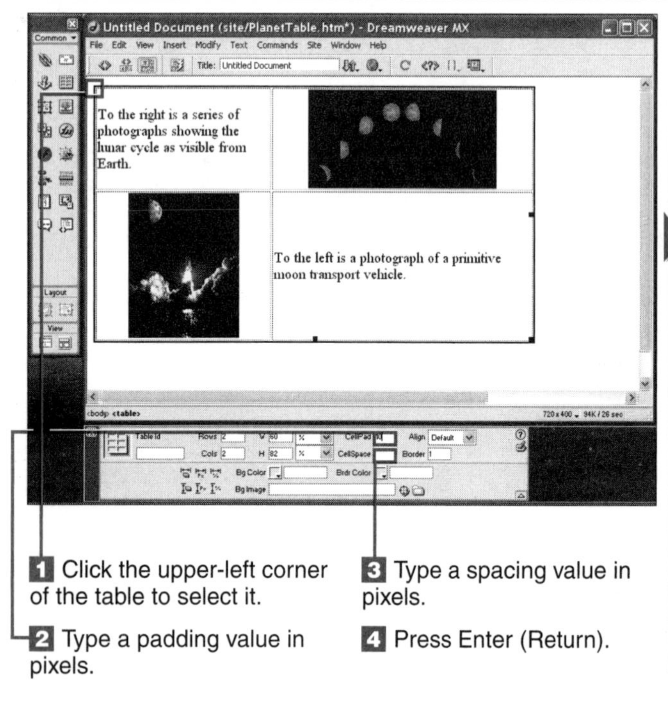

1 Click the upper-left corner of the table to select it.

2 Type a padding value in pixels.

3 Type a spacing value in pixels.

4 Press Enter (Return).

■ Dreamweaver adds padding and spacing to all the table cells.

■ Padding affects the space between the content and the border.

■ Spacing affects the size of the border itself.

Note: Any changes you make to cell padding or spacing will affect the entire table. You cannot define padding or spacing for just a few cells of a table.

CHANGE THE ALIGNMENT OF TABLE CONTENT

You can change the horizontal and vertical alignment in table cells to clearly present the text, images, and other content inside them. You set the alignment for a table's different cells independently of one another. For example, you can have content in the top row of a table center-aligned, while the rest of the table is still set to the default left alignment.

The default alignment for table cells is left horizontal alignment and middle vertical alignment. To set a different alignment, you must select the cells you would like to define and then select alignments using the Horz and Vert menus in the Properties inspector.

When you use a table for layout purposes, you may want to change the vertical alignment in the cells to Top, so that text content in the cell begins at the upper-left corner of the cell. If you use a table to arrange a gallery of images, you may want to center the images horizontally and vertically. This way they have consistent spacing on all their sides.

CHANGE THE ALIGNMENT OF TABLE CONTENT

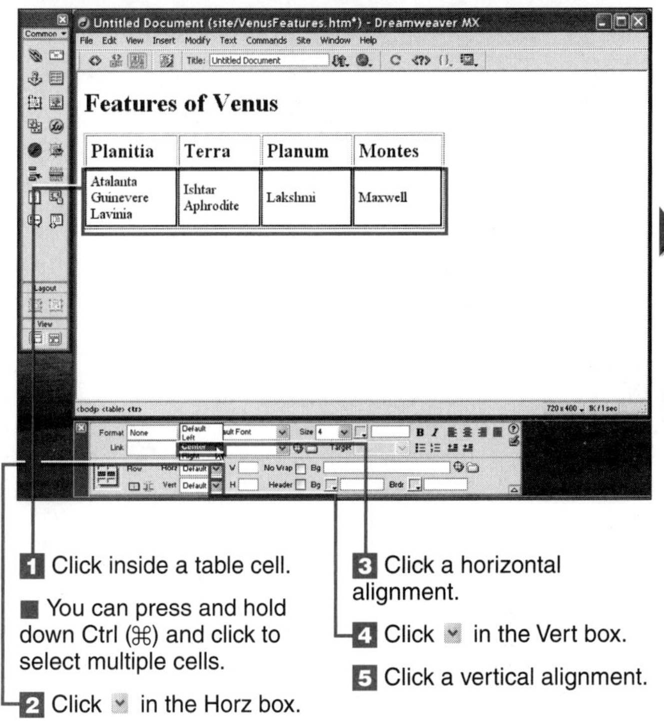

1 Click inside a table cell.

■ You can press and hold down Ctrl (⌘) and click to select multiple cells.

2 Click ▾ in the Horz box.

3 Click a horizontal alignment.

4 Click ▾ in the Vert box.

5 Click a vertical alignment.

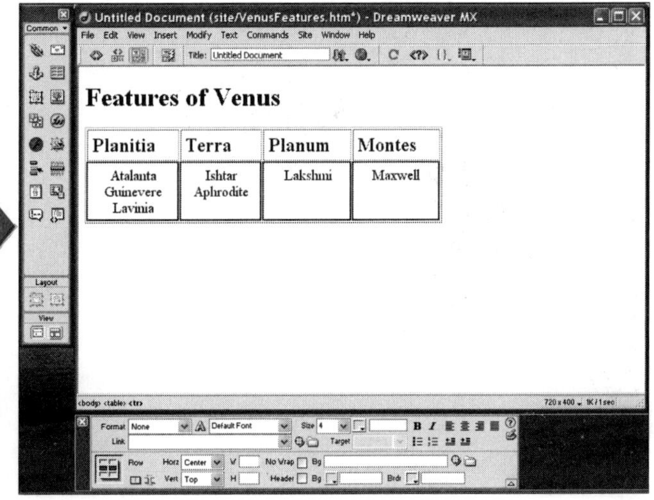

■ Dreamweaver aligns the content inside the selected cells.

INSERT OR DELETE A ROW OR COLUMN

You can add cells to or delete them from your table a row or column at a time. Inserting cells into your table enables you to add additional content, while deleting lets you get rid of empty areas of a table.

You can add or remove rows and columns several ways: You can select a cell and then select one of the Insert or Delete commands under the Modify menu and the Table submenu. You can select the entire table by clicking its upper-left corner, and then change the Rows or Cols value in the Properties inspector. Or you can right-click (Control-click) a table cell and select one of the Insert or Delete commands from the Table menu that appears.

The Insert Rows or Columns command, which is under the Modify menu and the Table submenu, is useful in that it lets you add multiple rows or columns to a table all at once. The command also lets you specify whether to add the rows or columns before or after the current selection.

INSERT A ROW

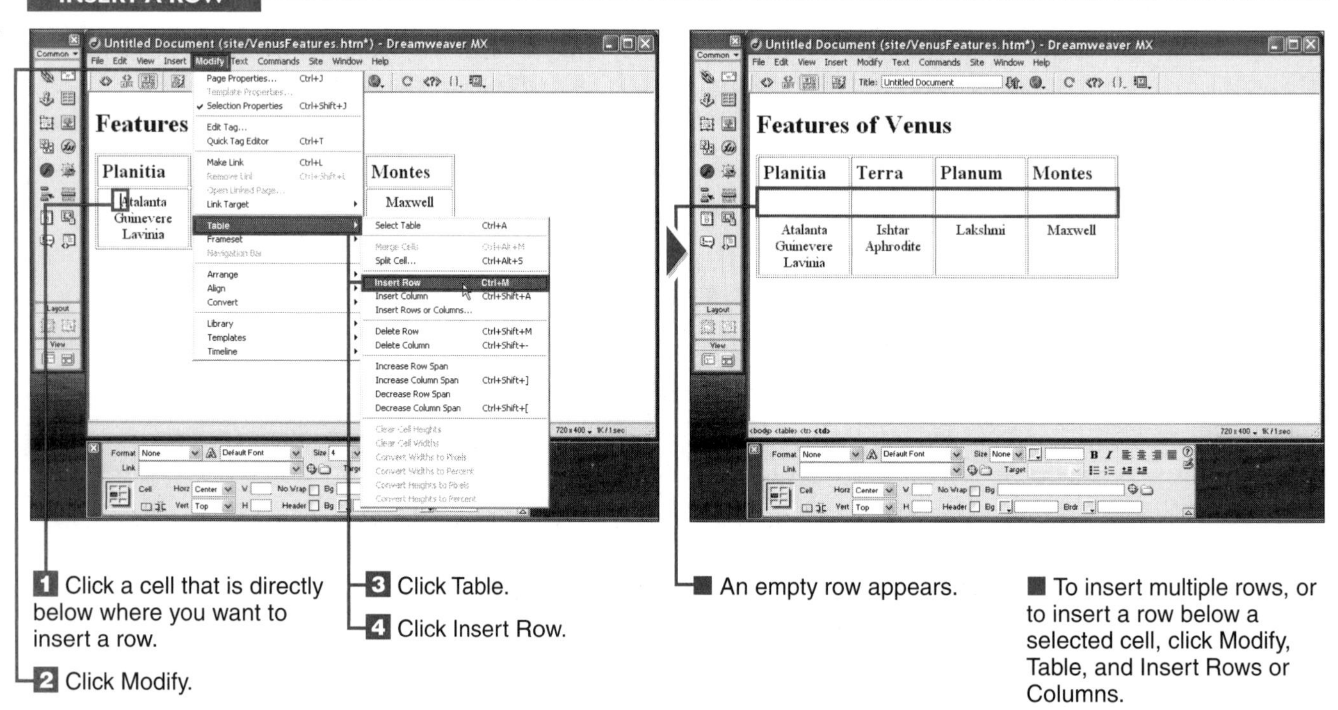

1 Click a cell that is directly below where you want to insert a row.

2 Click Modify.

3 Click Table.

4 Click Insert Row.

■ An empty row appears.

■ To insert multiple rows, or to insert a row below a selected cell, click Modify, Table, and Insert Rows or Columns.

What happens to the content of a deleted cell?

✔ It is deleted as well. Dreamweaver does not warn you if the cells you are deleting contain content. If you accidentally remove content when deleting rows or columns, you can select Edit and then Undo to undo the last command.

How large are new rows or columns after I insert them?

✔ The size of the new row or column takes on the same size as the row or column that you selected before inserting. If you need to, you can resize your table after you have added your rows or columns.

How do I save a copy of the content in a row or column before I delete it?

✔ You can make a copy of the row or column elsewhere on the page. First select the row by clicking its side edge, or the column by clicking its top edge. Select Copy under the Edit menu. Then, click somewhere outside the table and select Paste under the Edit menu to duplicate the content.

DELETE A COLUMN

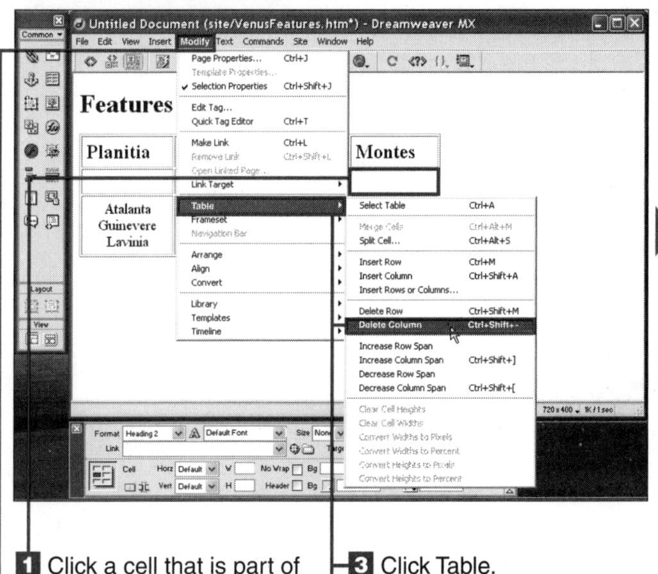

1 Click a cell that is part of the column you want to delete.

2 Click Modify.

3 Click Table.

4 Click Delete Column.

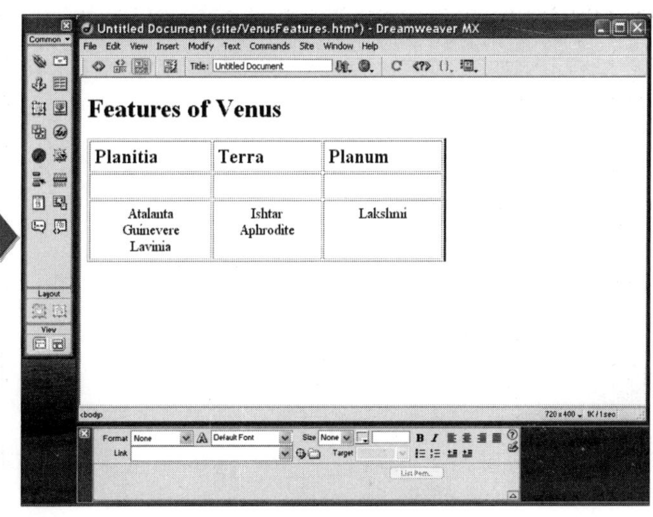

■ The column disappears.

SPLIT OR MERGE TABLE CELLS

You can create a more elaborate arrangement of cells in a table by splitting or merging its cells. *Splitting* turns one cell into two or more cells, either horizontally or vertically arranged. *Merging* cells takes several adjacent table cells and combines them.

You can split a cell by clicking inside it and then selecting Modify, Table, and Split Cell. This brings up a dialog box allowing you to specify whether you want to split the cell into rows or columns, and how many rows or columns. You can also right-click (Control-click) a cell and select Table and Split Cell or click the Split Cells button (⊞) in the Properties inspector. This brings up the same dialog box.

To merge cells, first select the cells to be merged by Ctrl-clicking (⌘-clicking) them. Then, you can either click Modify, Table, and Merge Cells; right-click (Control-click) the cells and select Table and then Merge Cells; or click the Merge Cells button (⊡) in the Properties inspector.

When you split cells, any content in the cell moves to the topmost or rightmost cell. When you merge cells, all content is combined into the merged cell. No content is lost when you split or merge table cells.

SPLIT A TABLE CELL

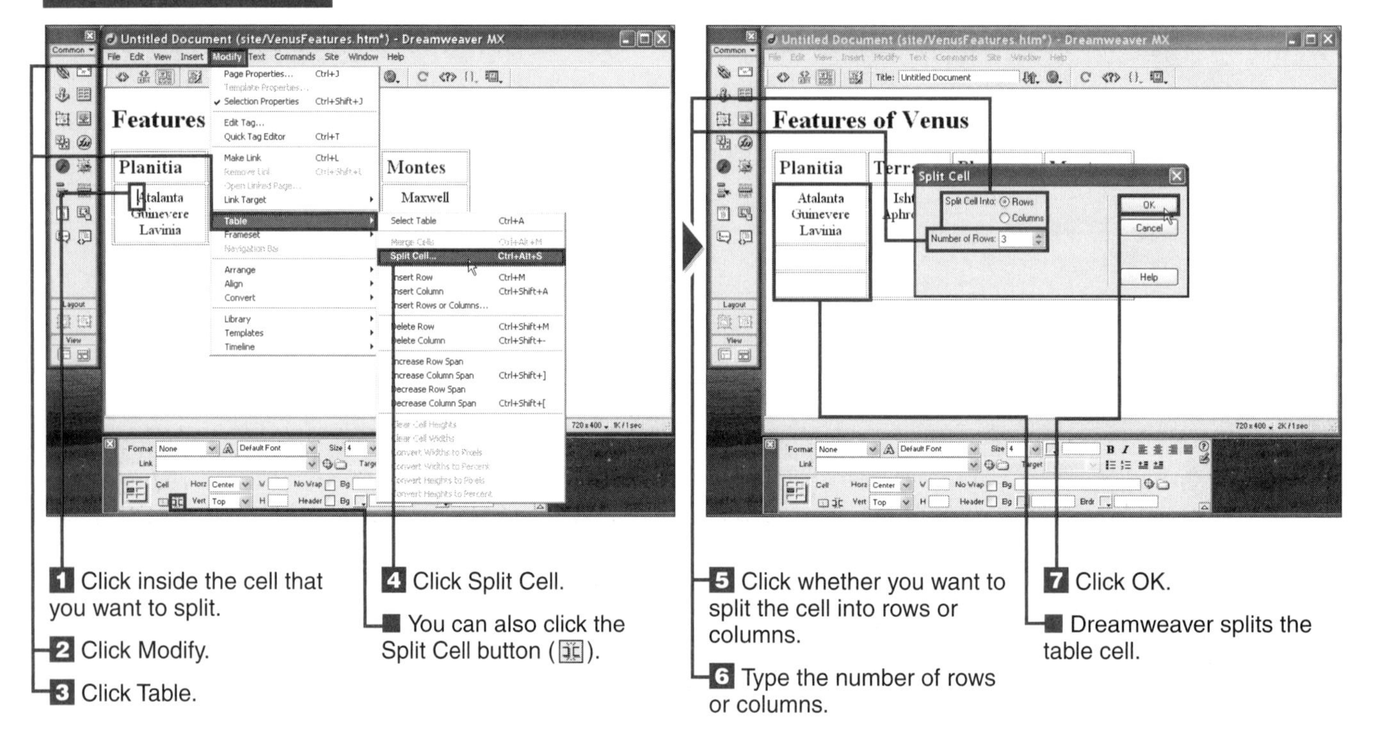

1 Click inside the cell that you want to split.

2 Click Modify.

3 Click Table.

4 Click Split Cell.

■ You can also click the Split Cell button (⊞).

5 Click whether you want to split the cell into rows or columns.

6 Type the number of rows or columns.

7 Click OK.

■ Dreamweaver splits the table cell.

Can I merge any combination of table cells?

✔ No. The cells must have a rectangular arrangement. For example, you can merge all the cells in a two-row-by-two-column table. But you cannot select three cells that form an L shape and merge them into one.

What happens in the HTML code when you split or merge table cells?

✔ When you split or merge table cells, Dreamweaver adds or removes the necessary `<td>` tags, and then it adds `colspan` or `rowspan` attributes to cells that end up spanning more than one neighboring cell after the split or merge.

Can I merge an entire row or column of cells?

✔ Yes. Just click the side of the row or top of the column to select it, and then select a Merge Cells command or click ( ) in the Properties inspector. You can conveniently add a title to your table by merging the cells in a table's first row, typing the title into the row, and then center-aligning the title.

MERGE TABLE CELLS

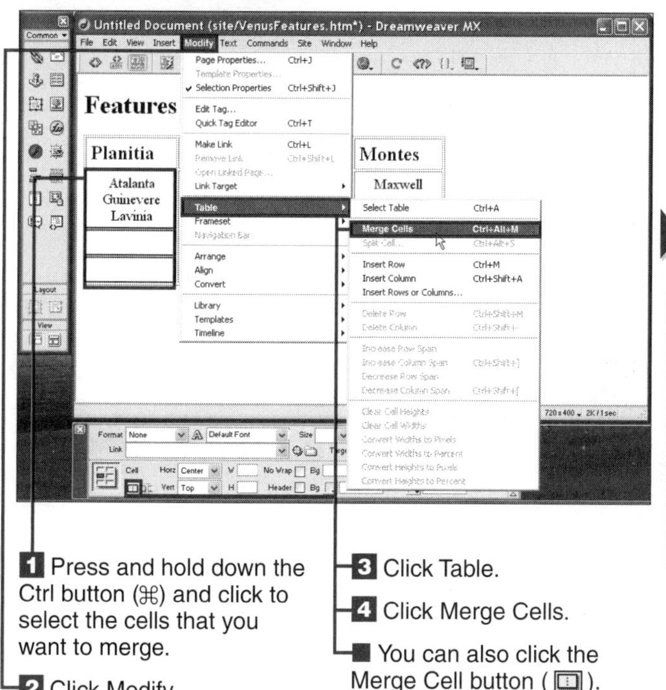

1 Press and hold down the Ctrl button (⌘) and click to select the cells that you want to merge.

2 Click Modify.

3 Click Table.

4 Click Merge Cells.

■ You can also click the Merge Cell button ( ).

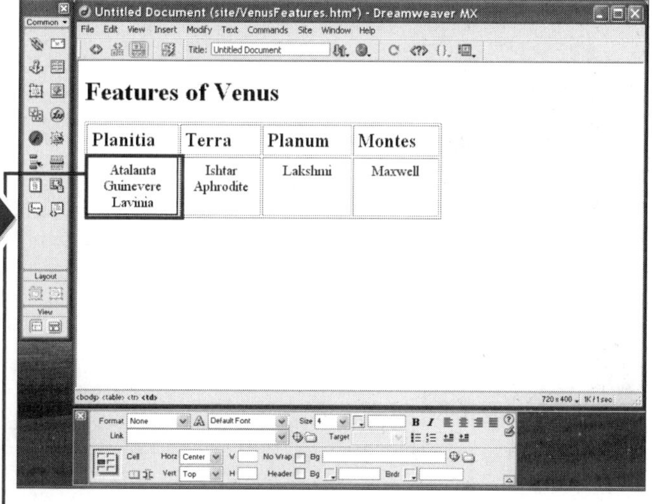

■ Dreamweaver merges the table cells into one.

CHANGE CELL AND TABLE DIMENSIONS

You can change the dimensions of an HTML table in two ways: You can change the dimensions of individual cells, which enables you to allocate different amounts of space to different parts of a table, or you can change the dimensions of the entire table, which lets you best fit a table into the confines of the Web page.

To adjust the dimensions of individual cells, select one or more of the cells by Ctrl-clicking (⌘-clicking). Then change the W, or width, and H, or height, values in the Properties inspector. The W and H values can be defined in pixels, for example, 50, or a percentage, for example, 50%. A percentage specifies the width or height relative to the size of the table.

To change the dimensions of a table, select the table by clicking its upper-left corner. Then enter the desired dimensions of the table in the W and H fields. Drop-down menus enable you to specify a pixel or percentage value for the dimensions. A percentage specifies the width or height relative to the dimensions of the browser window.

If you are specifying dimensions of a table for layout purposes, you may want to design your table in layout mode. See page 134 to create a layout table.

CHANGE CELL DIMENSIONS

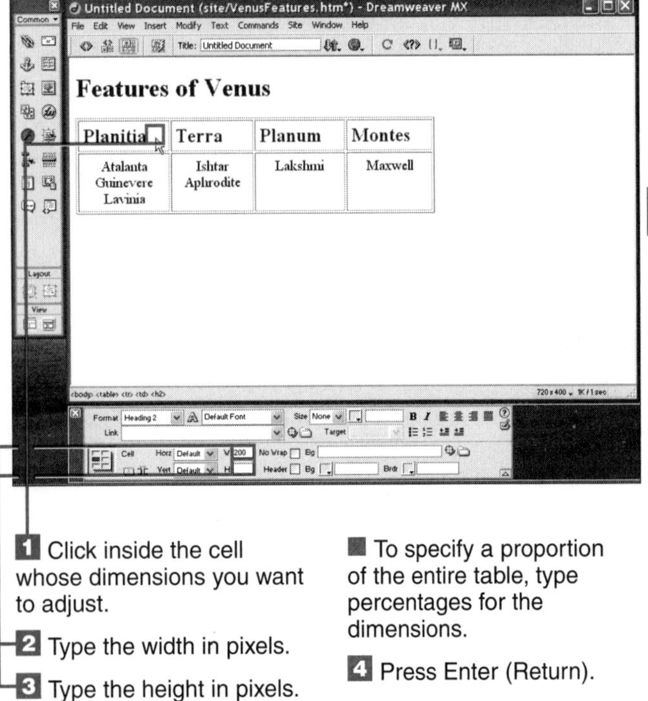

Untitled Document (site/VenusFeatures.htm*) - Dreamweaver MX

Features of Venus

Planitia	Terra	Planum	Montes
Atalanta Guinevere Lavinia	Ishtar Aphrodite	Lakshmi	Maxwell

1 Click inside the cell whose dimensions you want to adjust.

2 Type the width in pixels.

3 Type the height in pixels.

■ To specify a proportion of the entire table, type percentages for the dimensions.

4 Press Enter (Return).

■ The dimensions of the cell change.

■ The dimensions of cells next to it change as well.

Note: A cell will not shrink to less than the size of its content.

How do I make a table span the entire browser window?

✔ Select the table and specify a width (W) of 100% in the Properties inspector. To make it also span the page from top to bottom, specify a height (H) of 100%. Such a table fills the entire page, no matter what the browser window size.

How do I change the dimensions of a row or column?

✔ Select a row or column in a table by clicking the side edge of the row or top edge of the column. Then, change the dimensions as you would a cell — with the W and H fields in the Properties inspector.

Can I use a shortcut for changing cell and table dimensions?

✔ Yes. You can place the cursor over the table borders, which causes the cursor to change shape. Then click and drag to change cell dimensions. To change a table's dimensions, you can select the table and then click and drag the square handles that appear on the table's edges. Clicking and dragging to resize causes the W and H fields in the Properties inspector to change dynamically.

CHANGE TABLE DIMENSIONS

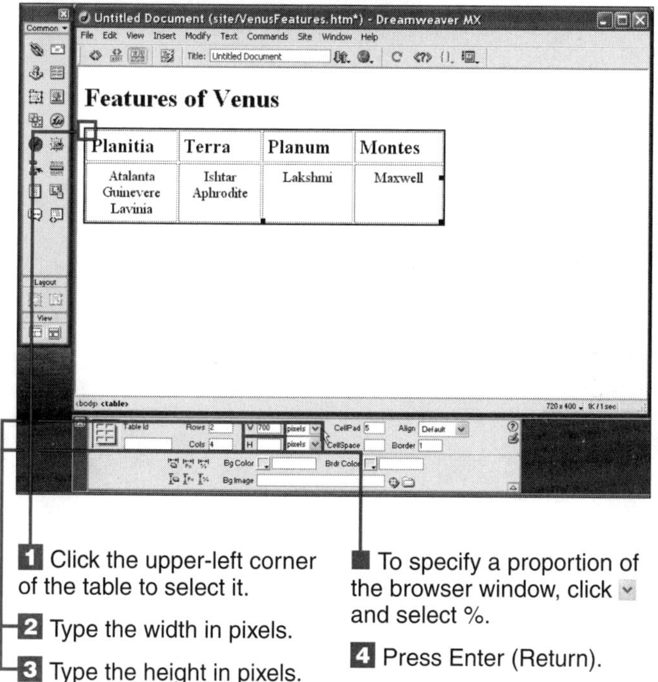

1 Click the upper-left corner of the table to select it.

2 Type the width in pixels.

3 Type the height in pixels.

■ To specify a proportion of the browser window, click ⌄ and select %.

4 Press Enter (Return).

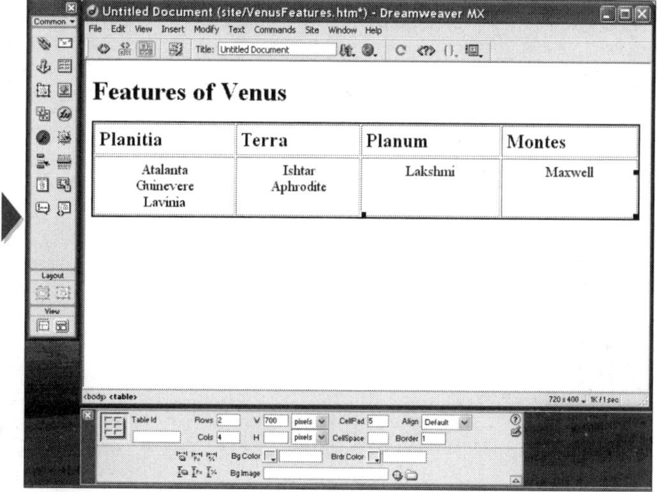

■ The dimensions of the table change.

CREATE A LAYOUT TABLE

A popular method for organizing the layout of information on a Web page is using tables that have their borders turned off. Dreamweaver offers a special Layout View in which you can create such tables and easily format their cells for layout purposes.

From a code standpoint, tables created in Layout View are no different from the tables created in Standard View. Layout View simply enables you to define page layout using a table more efficiently. When you draw new cells inside a table in Layout View, Dreamweaver automatically resizes the cells around them to keep the table structure valid. Layout View also lets you fix the width of some table cells and format others to stretch and contract depending on the size of the browser window. See page 138 for more information.

When you have finished defining the layout of your page, you can switch out of Layout View and format and add content to the tables in the Standard View.

CREATE A LAYOUT TABLE

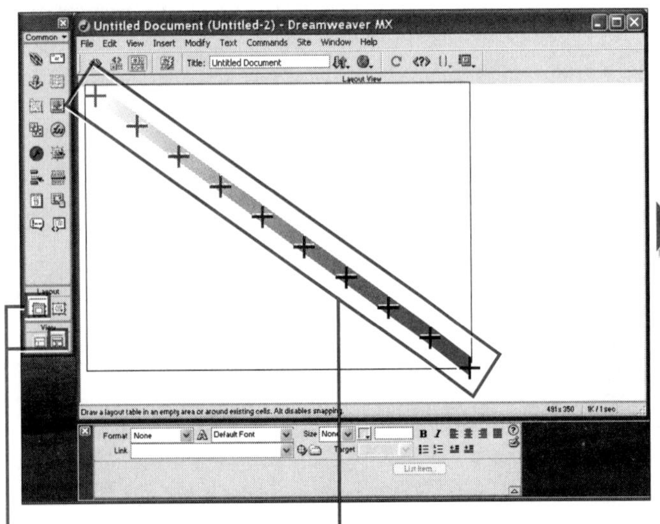

1 Click the Layout View button (▣).

■ This switches you to Layout View.

2 Click the Draw Layout Table button (▣).

■ In the Document window, the cursor changes to +.

3 Click and drag to create a table.

■ The outline of a table is displayed.

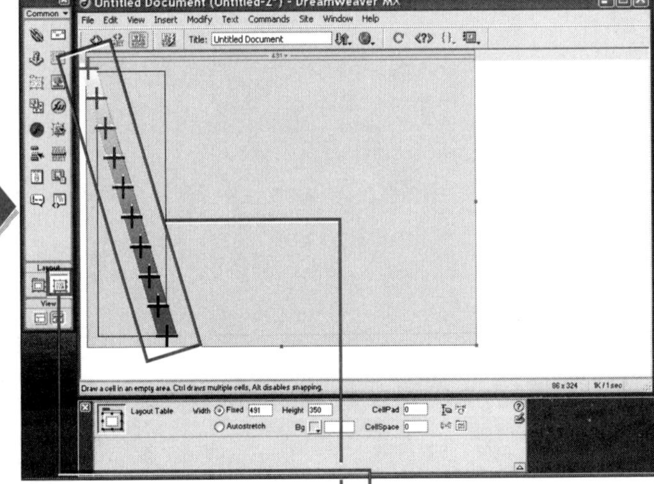

■ To add content to your table in Layout View, you have to first create layout cells.

4 Click the Draw Layout Cell button (▣).

5 Click and drag inside the table to create a Layout Cell.

Can I turn on the grid in the Document window to help me size my layout tables and table cells?

✔ Yes. This is one of the best uses of Dreamweaver's grid feature. You can turn it on by clicking View, Grid, and then Show Grid. To customize the grid, select Grid Settings under the Grid submenu. Options include changing the grid square size, color, and style, and specifying that table and cell edges snap to the grid edges when they are near them.

Can I use a shortcut to create cells in a layout table?

✔ To create a new cell in your layout table without having to click the layout cell button each time, press the Ctrl (⌘) key while you click and drag.

How do I disable the snap-to feature when I am drawing a cell?

✔ To temporarily disable snapping when you get near a table edge, another cell, or a grid line, press Alt (Option).

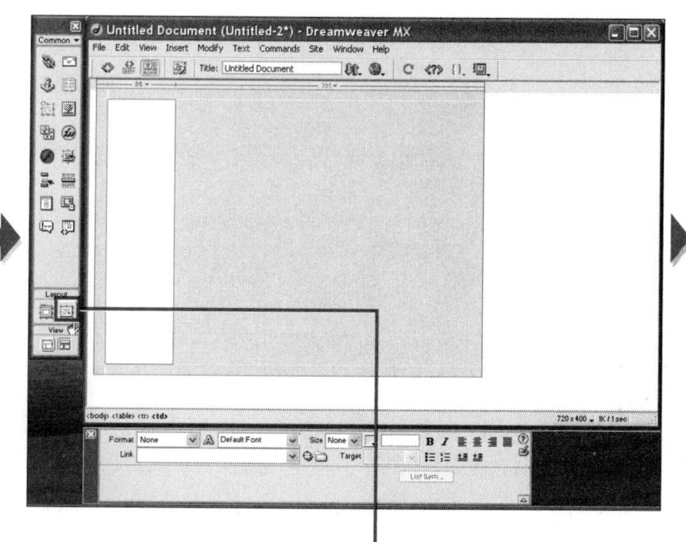

■ You can adjust the size and position of a cell by clicking its edge.

Note: To adjust size and position, see page 136 .

6 Click again to draw more cells.

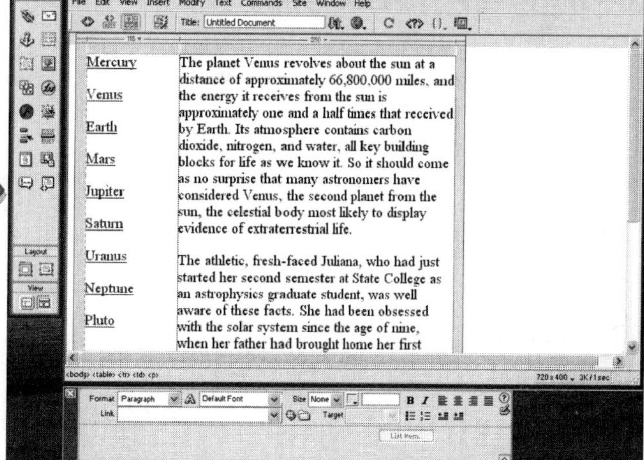

7 Insert content into your cells.

Note: To insert content, see page 122.

■ To change the properties of a table cell, click its edge and use the Properties inspector.

■ Dreamweaver displays the completed layout table.

RESIZE OR MOVE A TABLE CELL

One of the benefits of creating tables in Layout View is the ease with which you can rearrange and change the size of the component table cells.

To change a cell's size in Layout View, click its edge, which causes handles to appear on the corners and sides of the cell. You can then click and drag the handles to change the size. To move a cell, click the edge of the cell and then click and drag the edge. As you resize a cell, Dreamweaver resizes the other undefined cells in the table automatically.

You may run into some limitations with regard to resizing and moving cells: You cannot overlap other cells that you have defined, which means that you may have to resize other cells as you work. Also, a layout cell needs to be at least as large as the content it contains.

To resize or move a layout table, you click the table's tab, which makes handles appear on the edges. Then you click and drag the handles to resize the table, or drag the edge to move the table altogether.

RESIZE A CELL

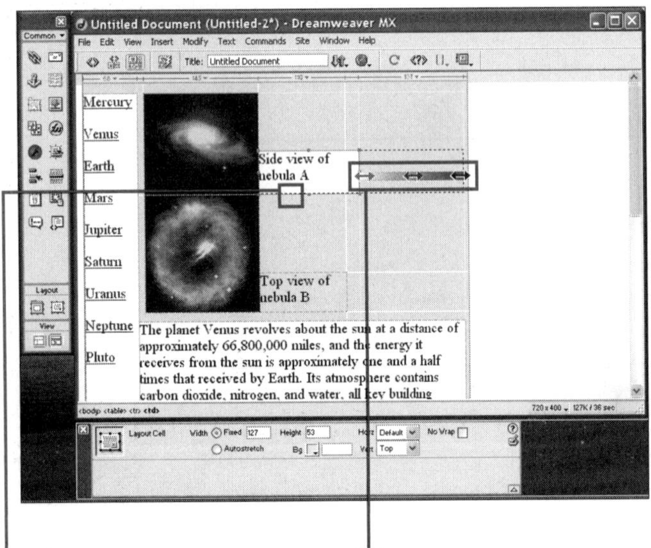

1 Click the edge of a layout cell.

2 Click and drag a side or corner handle.

■ The layout cell resizes.

■ Dreamweaver does not let you overlap other layout cells that you have defined.

How do I delete a layout cell or table?

✔ Select the cell by clicking its edge, and then press Delete. Dreamweaver replaces the space with gray, noneditable cells. Similarly, you can delete a layout table by clicking the table's top tab and pressing Delete.

How do I format a layout cell or table?

✔ To format a layout cell, click the outside edge of the cell. You can then adjust the cell's properties, such as its dimensions, alignment, and background color, in the Properties inspector. To format a table, click the Table tab and adjust the properties.

How do I add content to a layout table?

✔ You add content just like you do to a table in Standard View. However, you can add content only to cells you have defined using the layout cell tool. You cannot add content to the gray cells in a layout table; you must turn them into layout cells first with the layout cell tool.

MOVE A CELL

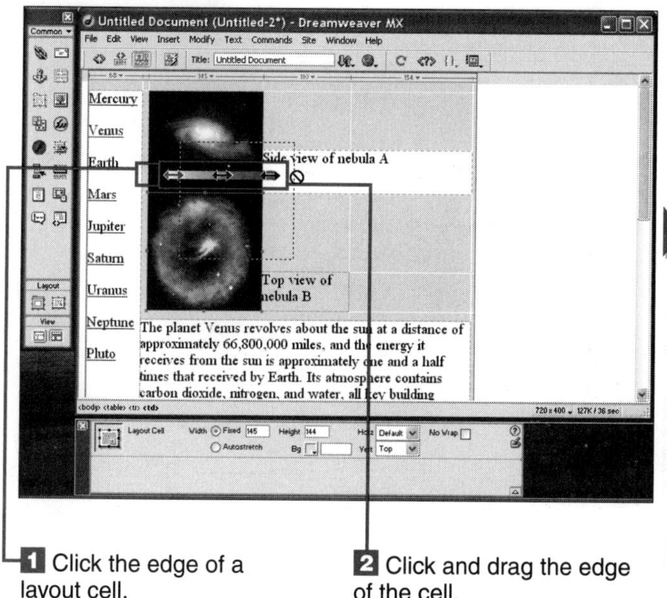

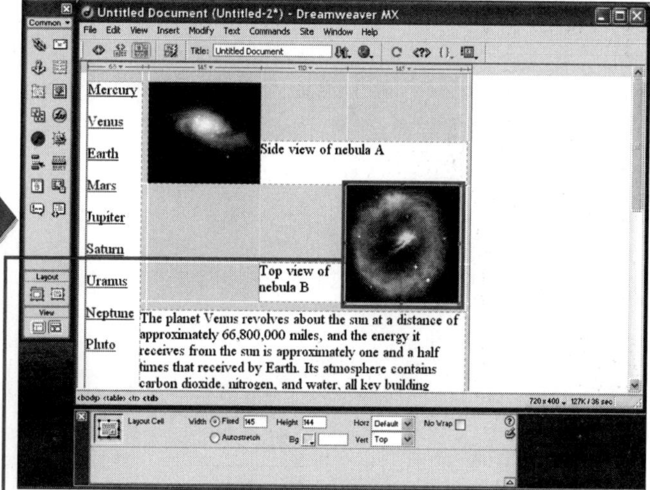

1 Click the edge of a layout cell.

2 Click and drag the edge of the cell.

Note: Do not click and drag a handle.

■ A ⃠ symbol appears when you drag over other layout cells, since you cannot overlap cells.

3 Position the layout cell in its new position.

■ Undefined cells in the table adjust their sizes to make room for the cell's new position.

CREATE COLUMN WIDTH IN A TABLE

In the Layout View, you can specify how a table behaves when the user resizes the browser window. You do this by defining attributes of the widths of the columns of the table. You can define the width of the columns of a layout table as either fixed or autostretch. You define a column as fixed by selecting the Columns drop-down menu and adding a spacer image. You define a column as autostretch by selecting the Make Column Autostretch command in the menu.

Columns with fixed widths are held with *spacers* — transparent images of a fixed width that Dreamweaver inserts into a table's cells. Autostretch columns lack spacers in their cells. They have their widths defined in the HTML as 100 percent so that they stretch to take up any available space on the page.

Only one column in a layout table can be set to autostretch.

You initially define column widths when you draw your layout table cells, with the widths in pixels listed at the top of the table. You can then define the widths as fixed or change them to autostretch by clicking the column heading to open a command menu.

CREATE A FIXED-WIDTH COLUMN

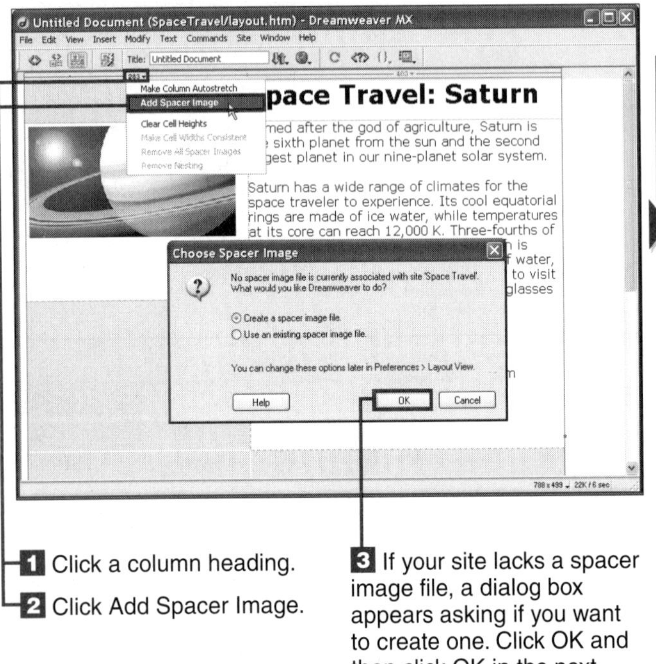

1 Click a column heading.

2 Click Add Spacer Image.

3 If your site lacks a spacer image file, a dialog box appears asking if you want to create one. Click OK and then click OK in the next dialog box that appears.

■ A spacer file is added to your local folder.

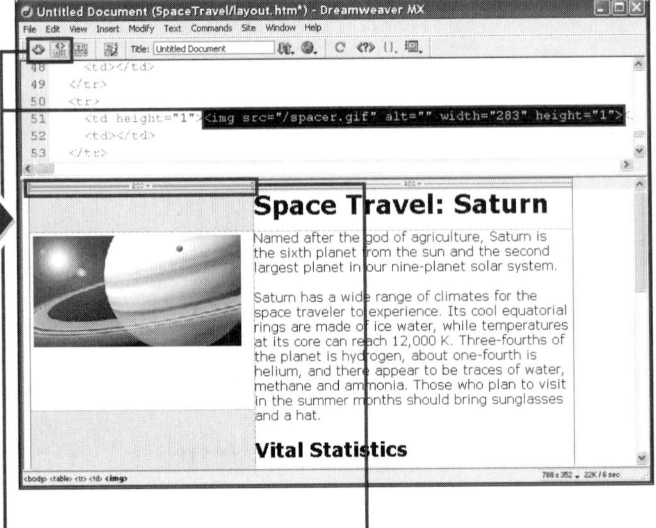

4 Click a Code View button.

■ In the HTML, you can find where Dreamweaver has added the spacer image.

■ Fixed-width columns are given a distinct heading style.

■ After a spacer image is added to your local folder, you can use it with any layout table in your site.

What is a spacer image?

✔ A spacer image is a transparent GIF image file that is one pixel by one pixel in size. Dreamweaver inserts these into tables and then uses HTML code to stretch the images to specific sizes to keep table cells at fixed widths. Because Dreamweaver can stretch a spacer image to any height or width, you only need one such image in your site folder.

What does it mean to make cell widths consistent?

✔ When objects in table cells are larger than the width defined by the HTML, table columns display widths that are different from the HTML-defined widths. You can rectify such conflicts by selecting Make Cell Widths Consistent in a table column header menu.

What happens if spacers are removed from layout table cells?

✔ If a column in a table is set to autostretch, and other columns do not have spacers, those columns may change size when the browser is resized, or even disappear completely if they lack content. This is why spacers are important to keep widths in your layout tables fixed.

CREATE AN AUTOSTRETCH COLUMN

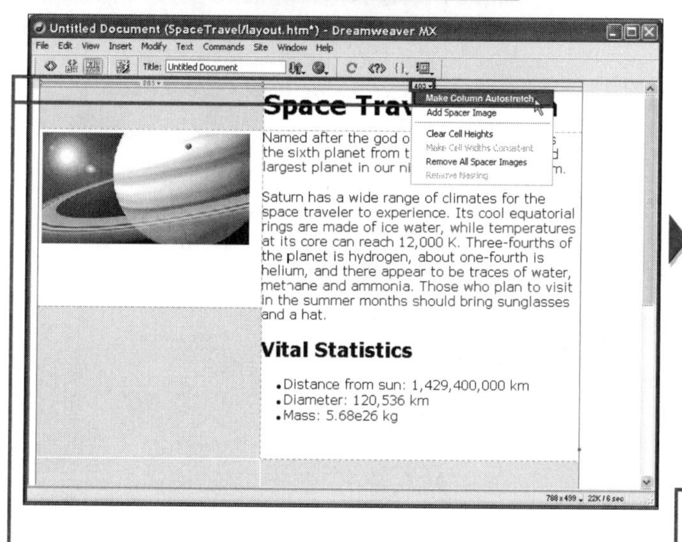

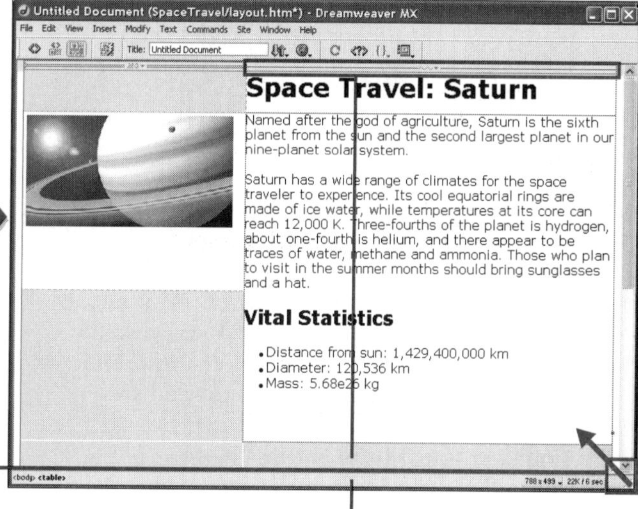

1 Click a column heading.

2 Click Make Column Autostretch.

■ Dreamweaver writes HTML code that stretches the column to take up any available horizontal space in the Document.

■ The autostretch column stretches to fill up any available space.

■ The autostretch column width changes if you resize the window.

■ Autostretch columns are given a distinct heading style.

INTRODUCTION TO FORMS

Adding forms to your Web site makes it more interactive, enabling viewers to enter and submit information to you through your Web pages. Every form works with a separate program called a *form handler,* which processes the form information.

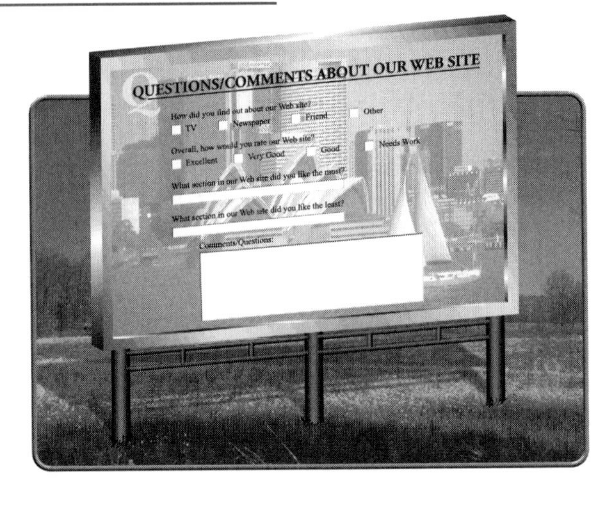

Create a Form

You can construct a form by inserting text fields, pull-down menus, check boxes, and other interactive elements into your page. You can also assign the Web address of a form handler to the form so that the information can be processed. Visitors to your Web page fill out the form and send the information to the form handler by clicking a Submit button.

Choose Your Form Elements

Creating a useful form requires you to think about the information you want to collect as well as how you want to collect it. You can use a variety of input elements to capture the information that you are interested in. Think about whether you want users to send you information in a free-form manner, such as typing into text fields, or in a more controlled manner, such as using menus or check boxes that you prepopulate with information. Make sure that you present the form clearly, with instructions at the beginning and intuitive labels on all the form elements. Also, make sure the form is not too long; not very many people take the time to fill out a long form.

Process the Form Information

The form handler, often known as a *CGI script,* is the program that processes the form information and does something useful with it, such as forwarding the information to an e-mail address or entering it into a database. Form handlers are often written in programming languages such as Perl and C. Your Internet service provider may have form handlers available for you to use with your site. If you are creating a dynamic Web site that interacts with a database, your application server will probably act as your form handler. See Chapter 17 for details about building these types of sites.

Handle the Form Data

The form handler receives the form information as a series of name/value pairs sent by the browser. Each name corresponds to an element in the form, for example, a text field or menu. You define these names when you insert your form elements. Each element name in your form should be unique. The values correspond to the information that the user enters into or attaches to the form element.

SET UP A FORM

You set up a form on your Web page by first creating a container that holds the text fields, menus, and other form elements. This container gets assigned the Web address of the form handler, which is the program that processes the submitted form.

The container also determines how the browser sends form information to the form handler. The POST method embeds form information in the HTTP request sent to the handler. The GET method attaches the form information to the end of the form handler URL.

Dreamweaver defines the form container in the HTML code with opening and closing <form> tags. This container appears as a dashed red box in Dreamweaver so that you can tell where you need to insert the form elements.

If you try to add form elements to a page that does not have a form container, Dreamweaver displays an alert box asking if you want to insert one. Sometimes you do not need to insert a form container into your page if your form elements are interacting with JavaScript code rather than an external form handler.

SET UP A FORM

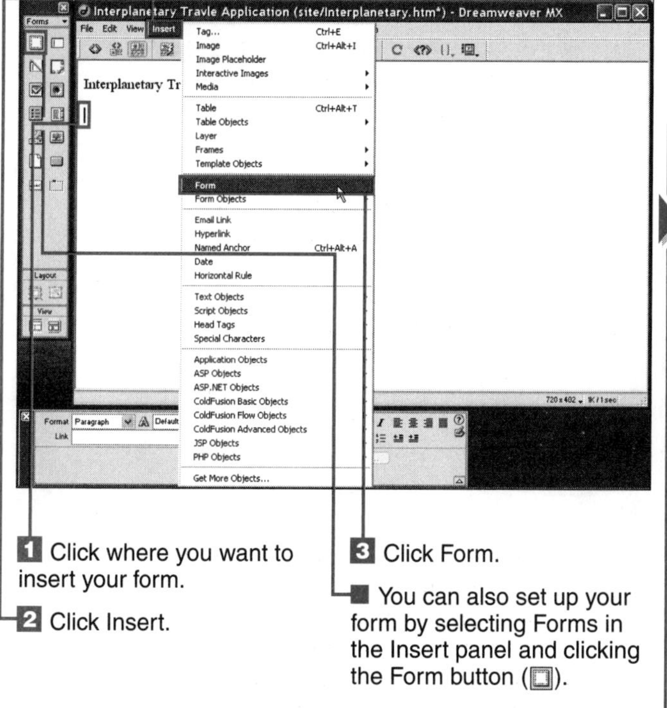

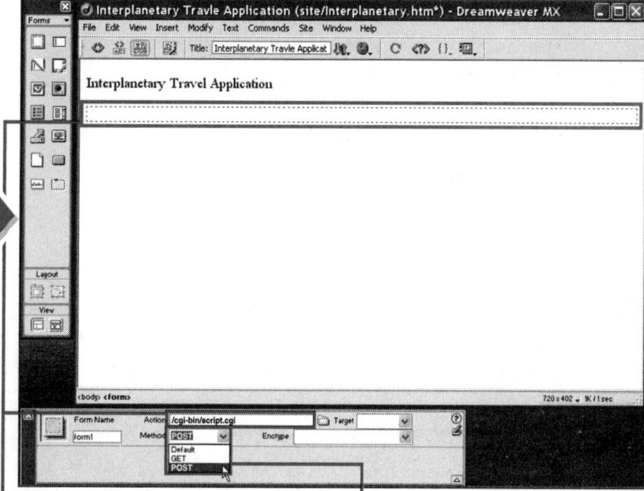

1 Click where you want to insert your form.

2 Click Insert.

3 Click Form.

■ You can also set up your form by selecting Forms in the Insert panel and clicking the Form button (▢).

■ Dreamweaver adds a red, dashed box to the page.

Note: If this box does not appear, click View, Visual Aids, and then Invisible Elements.

4 Type the address of the form handler.

5 Click ▾ to select POST or GET.

Note: Review your form handler's documentation to determine whether to use POST or GET.

■ Your form is ready for text fields, menus, and other elements, which you add inside the red box.

ADD A TEXT FIELD TO A FORM

You can add a *text field* to enable viewers to submit text through your form. Text fields are probably the most common form elements; they enable users to enter names, addresses, brief answers to questions, and other short pieces of text.

You can customize your text field in various ways, such as defining the size of the field or limiting the number of characters it can contain. Utilizing a character limit can sometimes keep users from entering erroneous information. For example, if your form handler can process only five-number postal codes, you may want to limit your form's postal-code text field to a maximum of five characters. To learn more about making sure the input from a form is valid, see page 228.

To give your users the opportunity to enter longer text responses in a form, see page 144.

ADD A TEXT FIELD TO A FORM

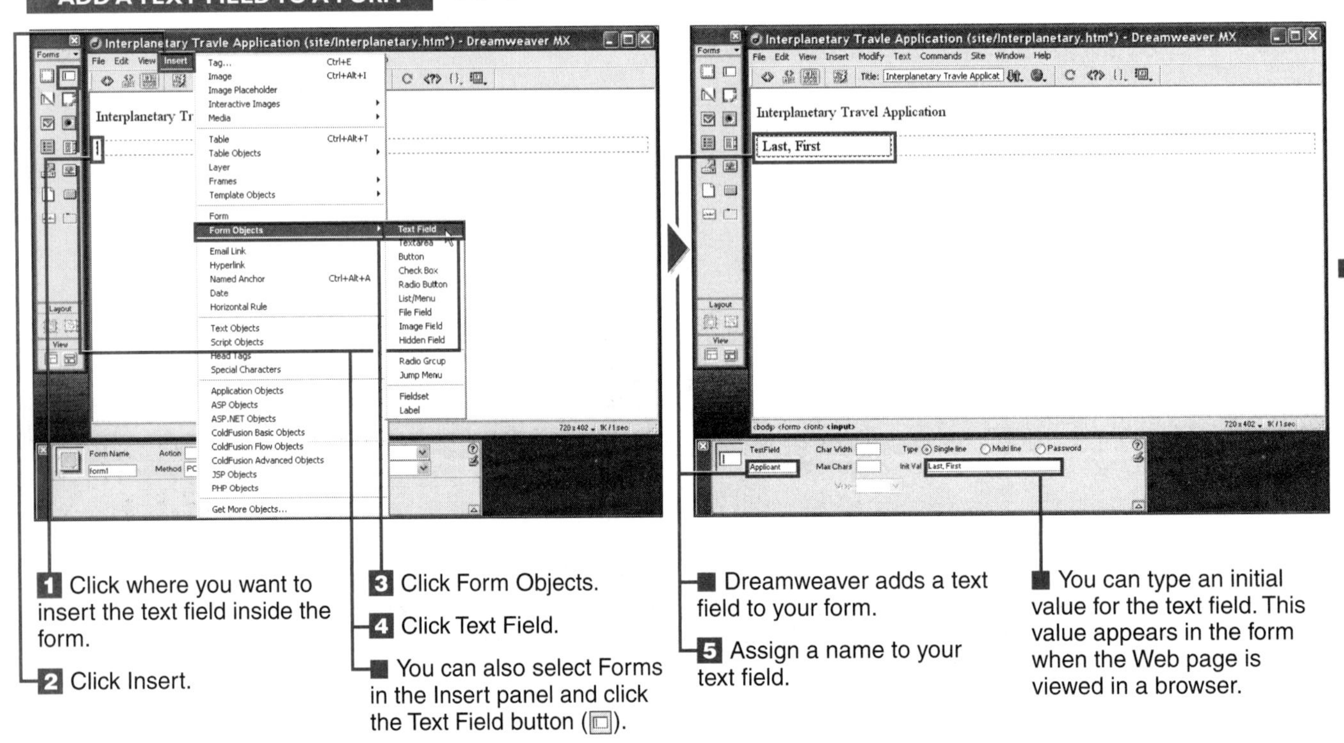

1 Click where you want to insert the text field inside the form.

2 Click Insert.

3 Click Form Objects.

4 Click Text Field.

■ You can also select Forms in the Insert panel and click the Text Field button (▭).

■ Dreamweaver adds a text field to your form.

5 Assign a name to your text field.

■ You can type an initial value for the text field. This value appears in the form when the Web page is viewed in a browser.

What happens if I do not specify an initial value, width, or maximum characters to my text field?

✔ The text field is blank when it appears in the browser, it displays at a default width, and it has no limit as to how much text a user can enter. The default width is usually about 24 characters.

Can I define the style of text that appears in the text field?

✔ Generally, no. The browser determines what style of text appears in the form fields. But you can customize the style of the text labels that you put beside the text fields, just like you can any Web page text.

What is sent to the form handler from a text field?

✔ When a user submits a form, the browser sends the text field's name and the information typed into the field by the user. The form handler distinguishes one text field from another by their unique names, so be sure to give your text fields different names.

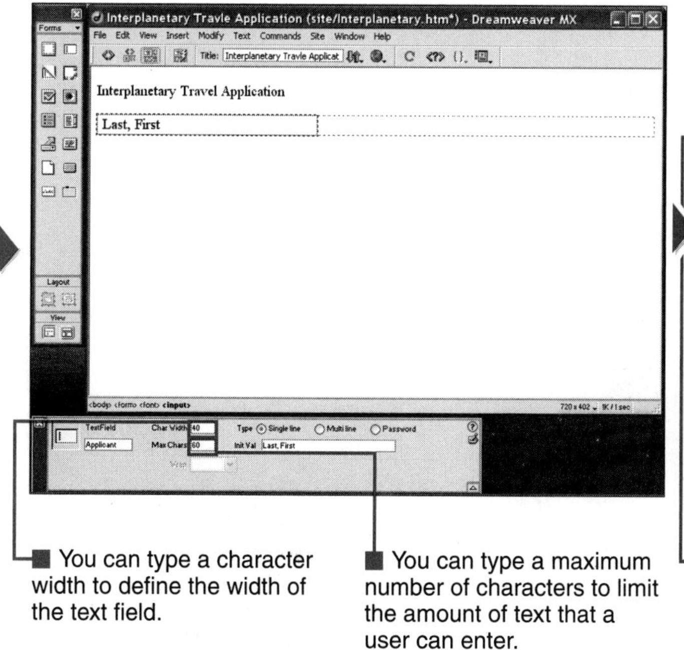

■ You can type a character width to define the width of the text field.

■ You can type a maximum number of characters to limit the amount of text that a user can enter.

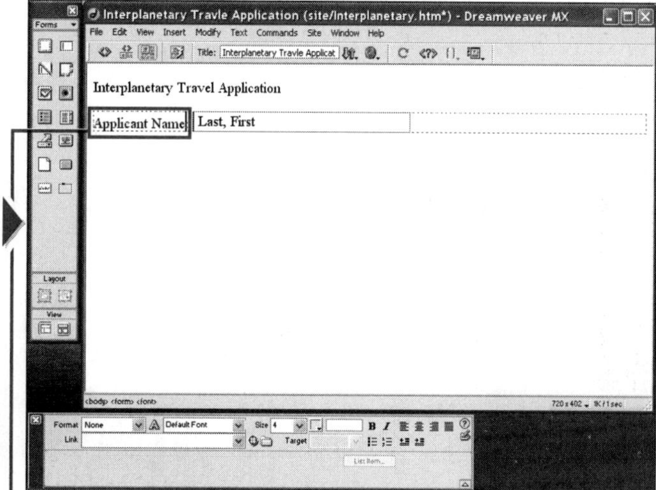

6 Type a label for the text field so that users know what kind of information to enter.

■ The text field is complete.

ADD A MULTILINE TEXT FIELD TO A FORM

Multiline text fields enable users to submit large amounts of text in a form. These fields can be useful if you want viewers to send you lengthy feedback about your site or cut and paste large amounts of text, for example, a resume, into a form.

You define the size of the multiline text field by specifying the number of rows and columns you want to display. If the user adds more information than the text field allows, scroll bars appear on the edges of the text field for viewing all the entered text. You can specify an initial value for the multiline text field, and this value appears in the field when a user opens the page. Unlike single-line text fields, you cannot define a maximum character value for multiline text fields.

Dreamweaver enables you to specify a wrap value for multiline text fields. Doing so tells the browser what should happen when entered text hits the right side of the text-field window.

ADD A MULTILINE TEXT FIELD TO A FORM

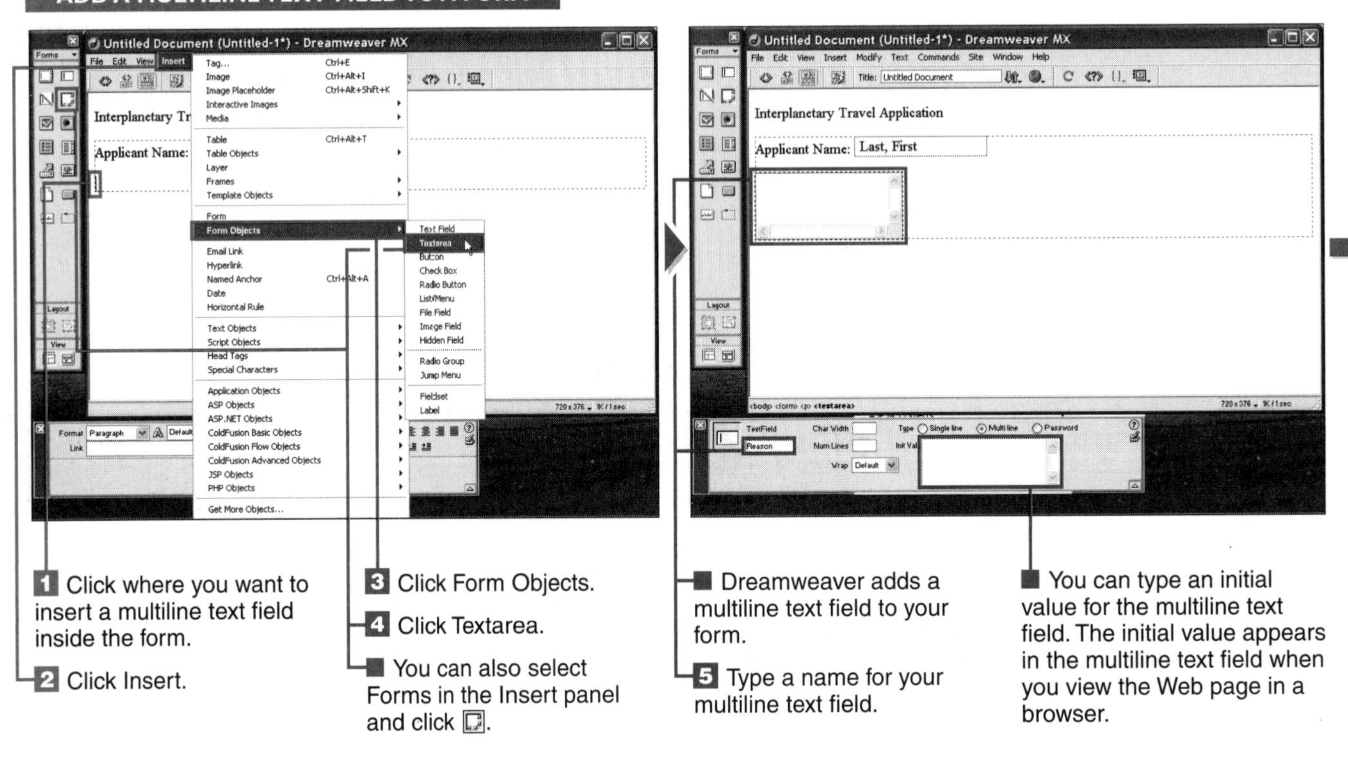

1 Click where you want to insert a multiline text field inside the form.

2 Click Insert.

3 Click Form Objects.

4 Click Textarea.

■ You can also select Forms in the Insert panel and click ▢.

■ Dreamweaver adds a multiline text field to your form.

5 Type a name for your multiline text field.

■ You can type an initial value for the multiline text field. The initial value appears in the multiline text field when you view the Web page in a browser.

Why should I define the wrap attribute of a multiline text field?

✔ In some Web browsers, text typed into a multiline text field does not automatically wrap when it reaches the right edge of the field, which can be annoying for the user. Selecting Virtual or Physical in the Wrap menu ensures that text automatically wraps in a multiline text field.

What is the difference between the wrap values?

✔ Setting wrap to Off turns off word wrapping. Users must add line breaks by pressing Enter (Return) in the multiline text field themselves to wrap the text. The Virtual option automatically wraps the text in the text-field window, but the information is sent to the form handler without line breaks at those places. The Physical option wraps the lines and also sends line-break commands to the form handler. If you specify Default, the user's browser determines the wrapping behavior.

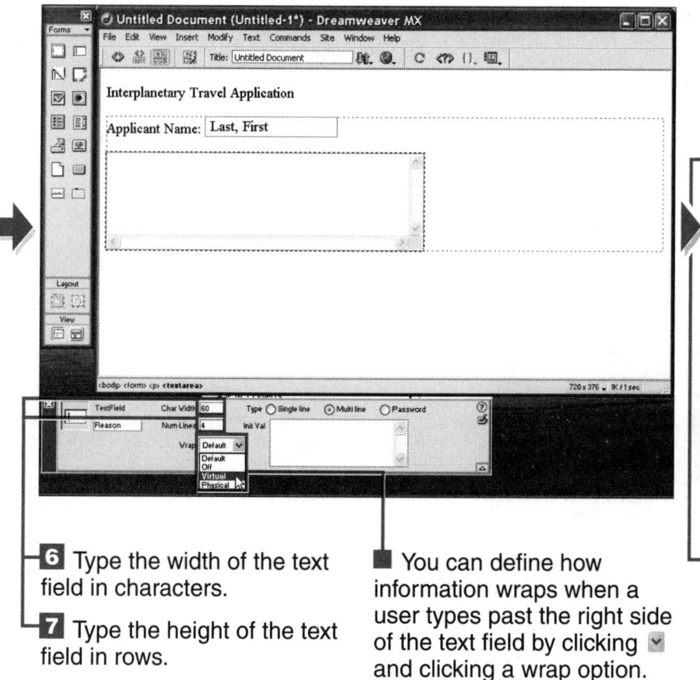

6 Type the width of the text field in characters.

7 Type the height of the text field in rows.

■ You can define how information wraps when a user types past the right side of the text field by clicking ▾ and clicking a wrap option.

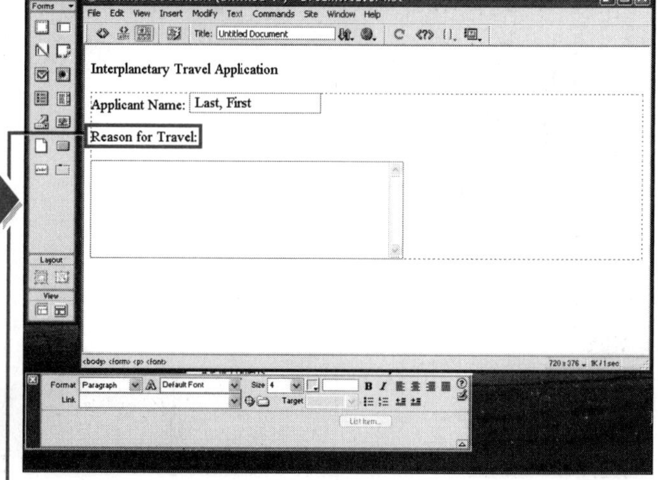

8 Type a label for the multiline text field so that users know what kind of information to enter.

■ The multiline text field is complete.

ADD A PASSWORD FIELD TO A FORM

A *password field* is similar to a text field, except that the text in the field is hidden as the user types it. The characters display as asterisks or bullets, depending on the type of operating system being used to view the page. Password fields are useful for letting users enter passwords or other secure pieces of text.

Just like regular text fields, you can set the length of a password field as well as the maximum characters that can be entered into the field. You can also enter an initial value for the password field.

Often in account-setup forms, a user must choose a password and type it in two different password fields. The two fields allow a form handler to compare the two entries and make sure that users do not make a mistake in entering their password information.

ADD A PASSWORD FIELD TO A FORM

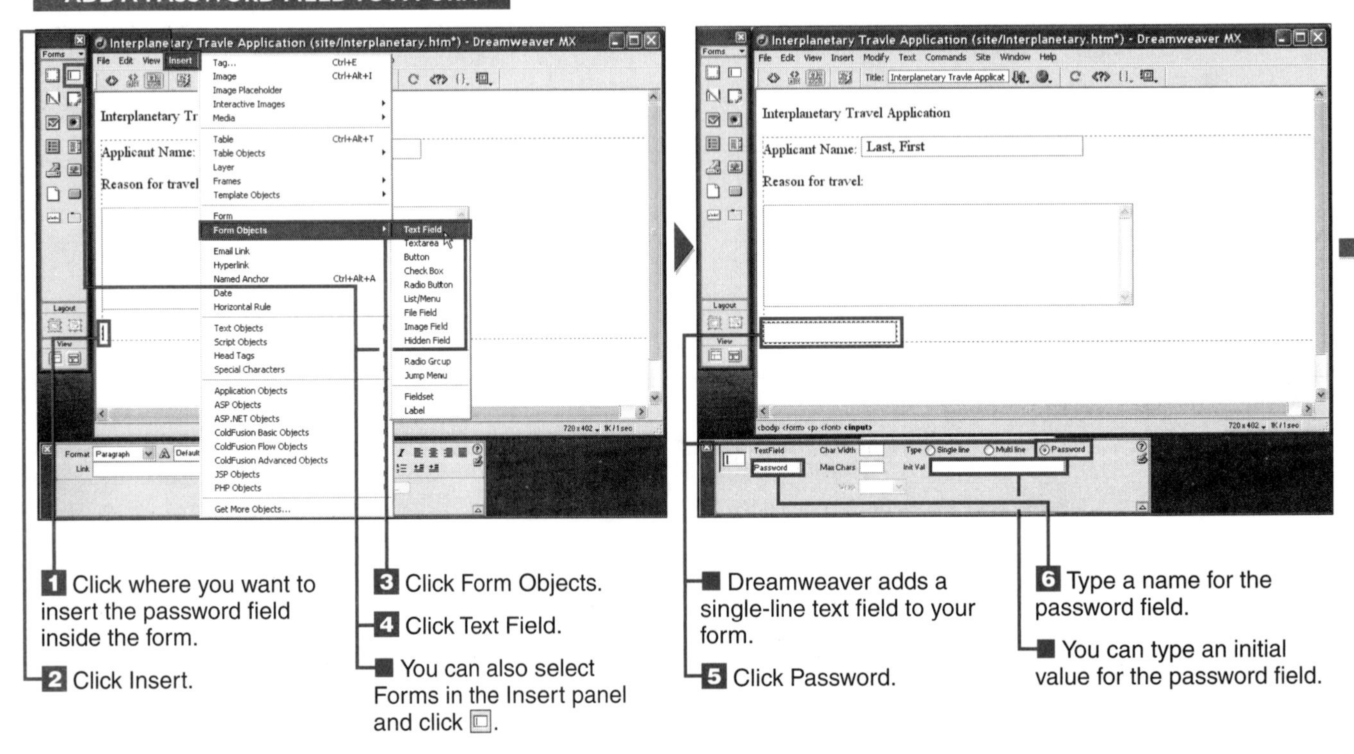

1 Click where you want to insert the password field inside the form.

2 Click Insert.

3 Click Form Objects.

4 Click Text Field.

■ You can also select Forms in the Insert panel and click ▢.

■ Dreamweaver adds a single-line text field to your form.

5 Click Password.

6 Type a name for the password field.

■ You can type an initial value for the password field.

Does the password field protect the entered information as it travels over the Internet?

✔ No. The browser sends the password field information to the form handler as plain text, just like it does everything else in the form. The password field does *not* protect your information from someone intercepting it as it travels between the user's computer and the form handler. To protect your form information during transmittal, you can host your site on a secure Web server, which enables you to encrypt information passed from a user's browser to the server.

Can I specify the character that appears in the password field when the user enters information?

✔ No. Dreamweaver does not let you specify the character that appears. What character appears depends on the operating system the viewer uses.

What is the difference between a password field and a hidden field?

✔ Password fields allow viewers to type information into a form but disguise that information so onlookers cannot see it. Hidden fields let the Web designer add information to a form that does not appear in the browser window. For more information, see the section "Add Hidden Information to a Form."

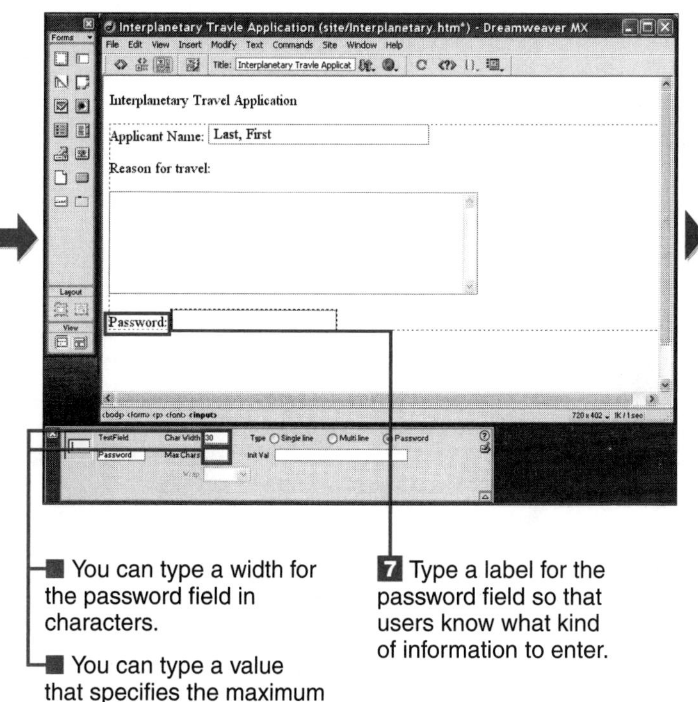

- You can type a width for the password field in characters.
- You can type a value that specifies the maximum number of characters that a user can enter into the field.

7 Type a label for the password field so that users know what kind of information to enter.

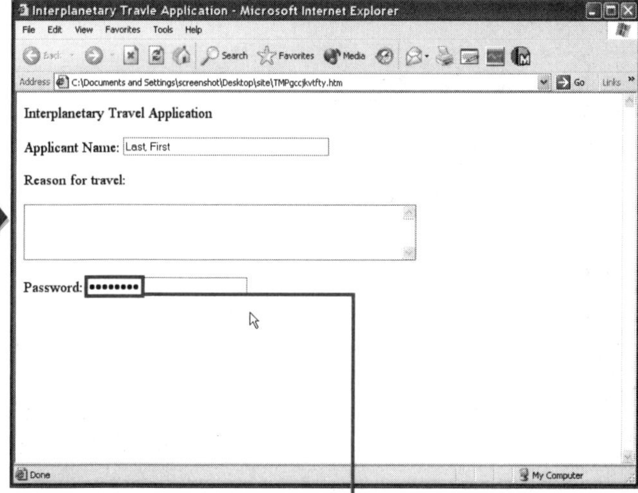

8 Preview the page in a browser.

Note: To preview a page in a Web browser, see page 58.

- When entering text in the password field, asterisks or bullets appear instead of the text.

ADD CHECK BOXES TO A FORM

Check boxes enable you to present multiple options in a form and allow users to select one, several, or none of the options. Check boxes usually appear in a group, with a label next to each check box.

Each check box in a form has a name and a checked value associated with it. The name of each check box should be unique to the form. The checked value should be something similar to "checked," "selected," or "yes" to tell the form handler that the check box was indeed selected. A form handler may need a particular check value to function correctly.

If you want to enable the user to select only a single choice from a group of choices, present the choices as radio buttons or in a menu instead of as check boxes. For more information, see pages 150 to 153.

ADD CHECK BOXES TO A FORM

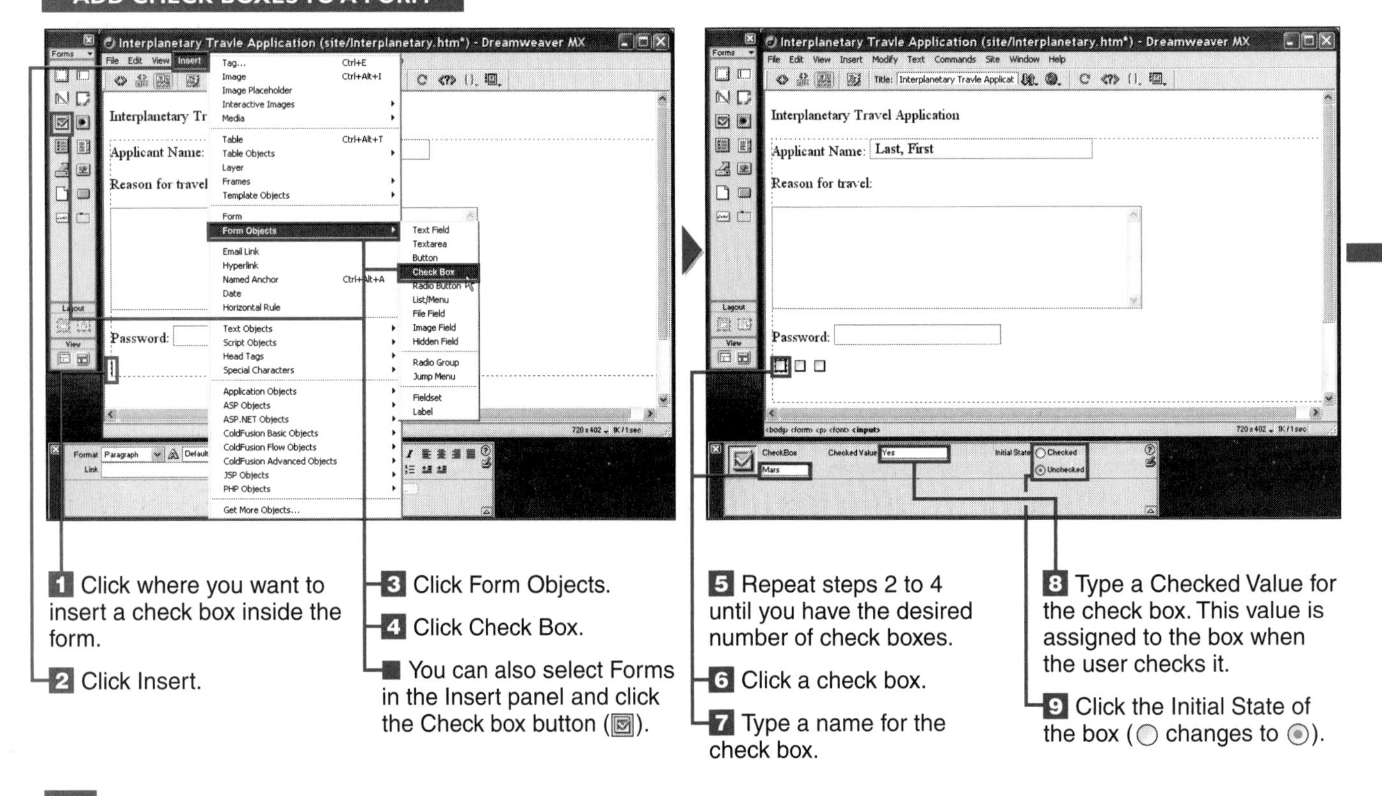

1 Click where you want to insert a check box inside the form.

2 Click Insert.

3 Click Form Objects.

4 Click Check Box.

■ You can also select Forms in the Insert panel and click the Check box button (☑).

5 Repeat steps 2 to 4 until you have the desired number of check boxes.

6 Click a check box.

7 Type a name for the check box.

8 Type a Checked Value for the check box. This value is assigned to the box when the user checks it.

9 Click the Initial State of the box (○ changes to ◉).

What is sent to the form handler from a set of check boxes?

✔ When the user submits a form, the browser sends a name and value for each selected check box to the form handler. It does not send information for check boxes that have not been selected.

Can I use the same checked value for all my check boxes?

✔ Yes. In fact, this is probably a good idea, so that the information that is sent to the form handler is consistent. Remember that the *name* given to each check box should be unique.

Can I have several different groups of check boxes in the same form?

✔ Yes. How you organize the check boxes in a form — in one group, several groups, or each one by itself — is up to you. Because each box has a unique name, how you visually organize the boxes does not matter to the form handler.

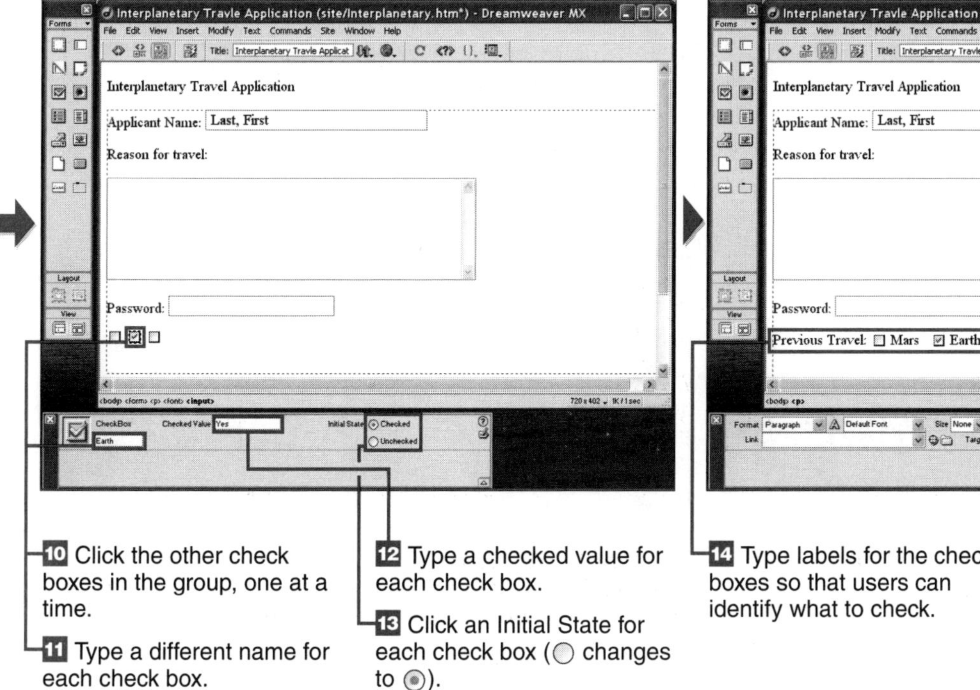

10 Click the other check boxes in the group, one at a time.

11 Type a different name for each check box.

12 Type a checked value for each check box.

13 Click an Initial State for each check box (○ changes to ◉).

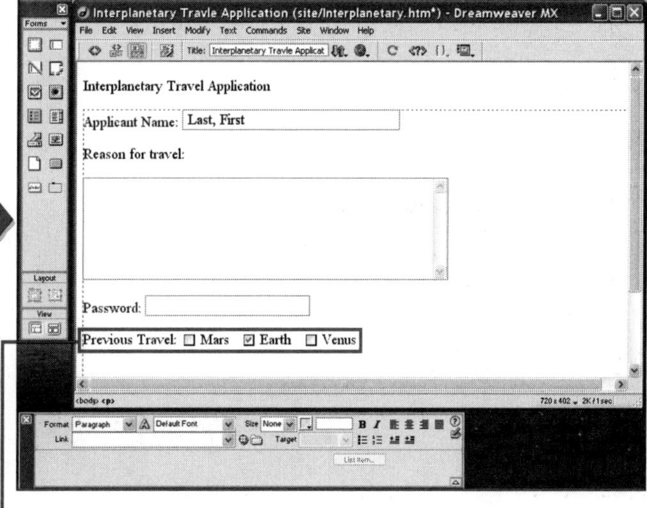

14 Type labels for the check boxes so that users can identify what to check.

■ The check boxes are complete.

ADD RADIO BUTTONS TO A FORM

You can let users select one option from a set of several options by adding a set of *radio buttons* to your form. With radio buttons, a user cannot select more than one option from a set.

Radio buttons get their name from the buttons on old car radios, where pushing in one button would cause the one that was currently selected to pop out.

Each radio button in a form has a name and a checked value associated with it. All the radio buttons in a set should have the same name associated with them, while the checked value for each button should be unique. This is in contrast to check boxes, where the names are unique and the checked values are the same.

If you want to permit the user to select more than one option from a group of options, you should present the options as check boxes. See page 148.

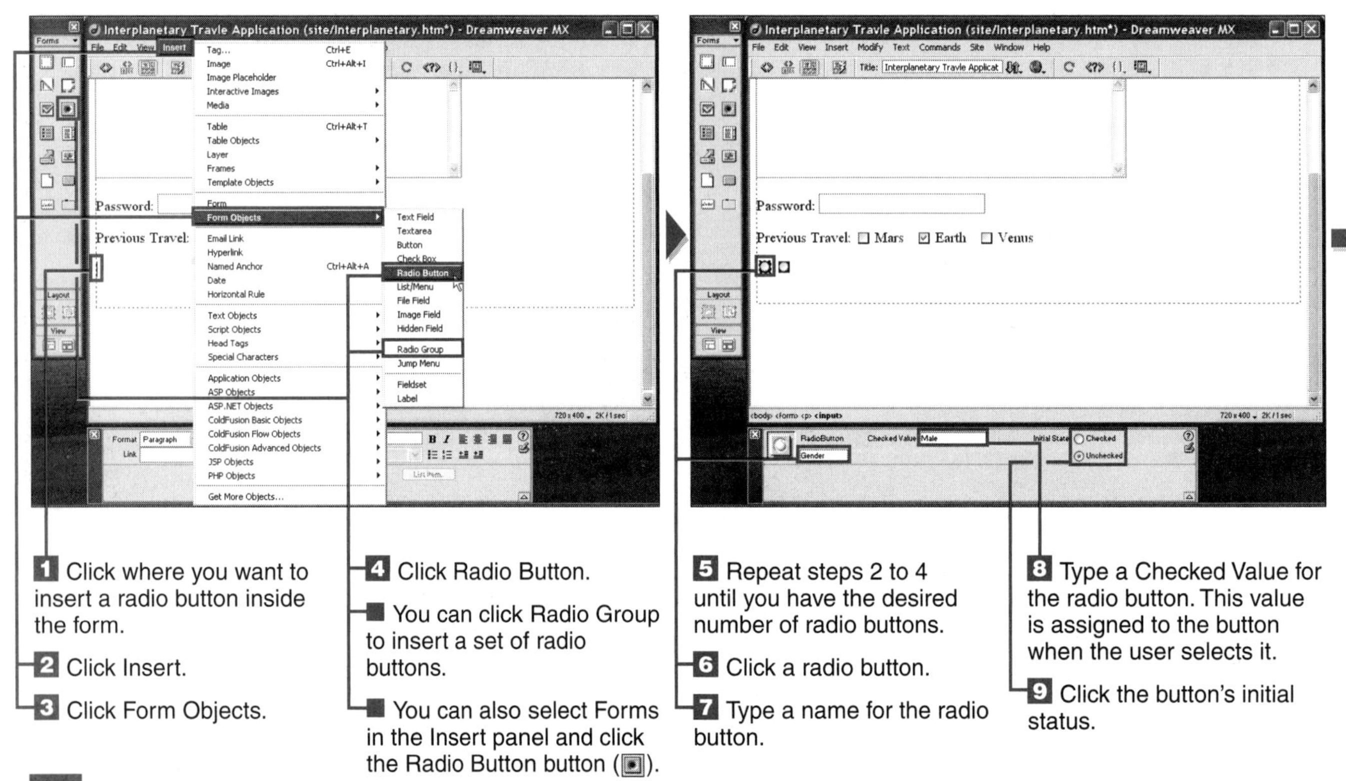

1 Click where you want to insert a radio button inside the form.

2 Click Insert.

3 Click Form Objects.

4 Click Radio Button.

■ You can click Radio Group to insert a set of radio buttons.

■ You can also select Forms in the Insert panel and click the Radio Button button (◙).

5 Repeat steps 2 to 4 until you have the desired number of radio buttons.

6 Click a radio button.

7 Type a name for the radio button.

8 Type a Checked Value for the radio button. This value is assigned to the button when the user selects it.

9 Click the button's initial status.

What information is sent to the form handler from a set of radio buttons?

✔ When the user submits a form, the browser sends the name assigned to the set of buttons and the value of the selected radio button. It does not send information if no buttons have been selected from the group.

Can I have more than one set of radio buttons in a form?

✔ Yes. Just make sure that each set uses a different name.

What happens if I give each radio button in a set a different name?

✔ If you do this, a user can select more than one button at a time, and after a button is selected, the user cannot deselect it. If the user submits the form, information from each selected button is sent to the form handler. This defeats the purpose of radio buttons.

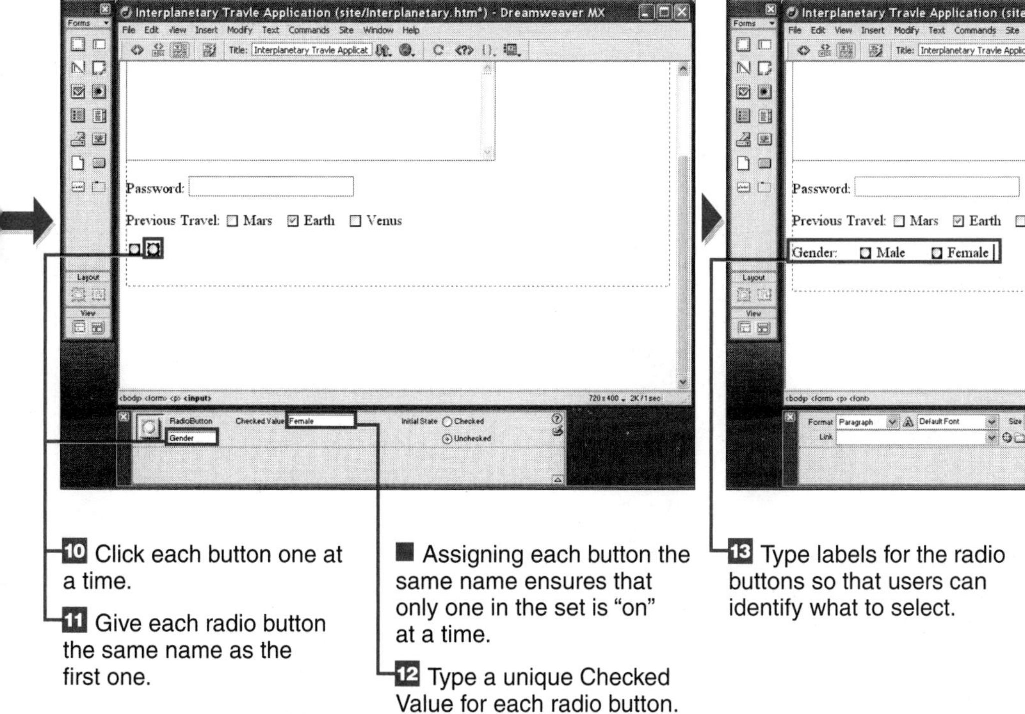

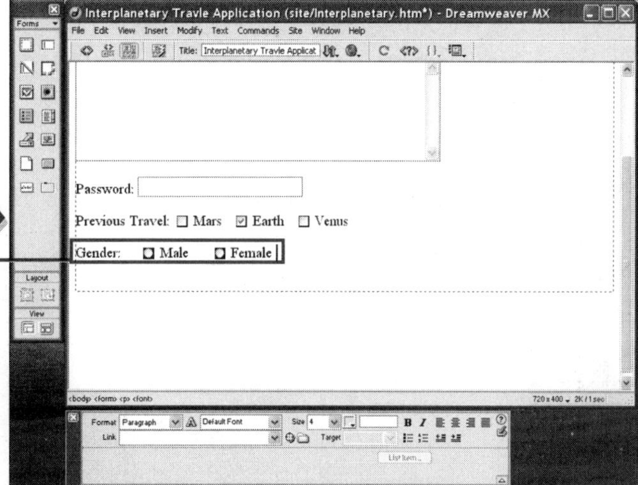

10 Click each button one at a time.

11 Give each radio button the same name as the first one.

■ Assigning each button the same name ensures that only one in the set is "on" at a time.

12 Type a unique Checked Value for each radio button.

13 Type labels for the radio buttons so that users can identify what to select.

■ The radio buttons are complete.

ADD A MENU OR LIST TO A FORM

Menus and *lists* are similar in that they both present users with a set of several options to choose from. A menu lets users choose one of the options, while a list allows users to choose several options, but only if you specifically allow it. Multiple items are selected in a list by clicking the items while pressing Ctrl (Command).

To view the options in a form menu, the user clicks the menu and the options appear in a drop-down arrangement. Items in a list are displayed in a window that a user can scroll through.

One advantage to using menus and lists in your forms is that they let you organize a lot of information in a small space. For example, a menu that lets users select from a list of the fifty U.S. states only takes up one line in the browser window. Organizing this information using radio buttons would require you to display 50 different radio buttons in your form.

A separate Dreamweaver command enables you to create a special *jump menu* that lets a user navigate to other pages. See page 154.

ADD A MENU OR LIST TO A FORM

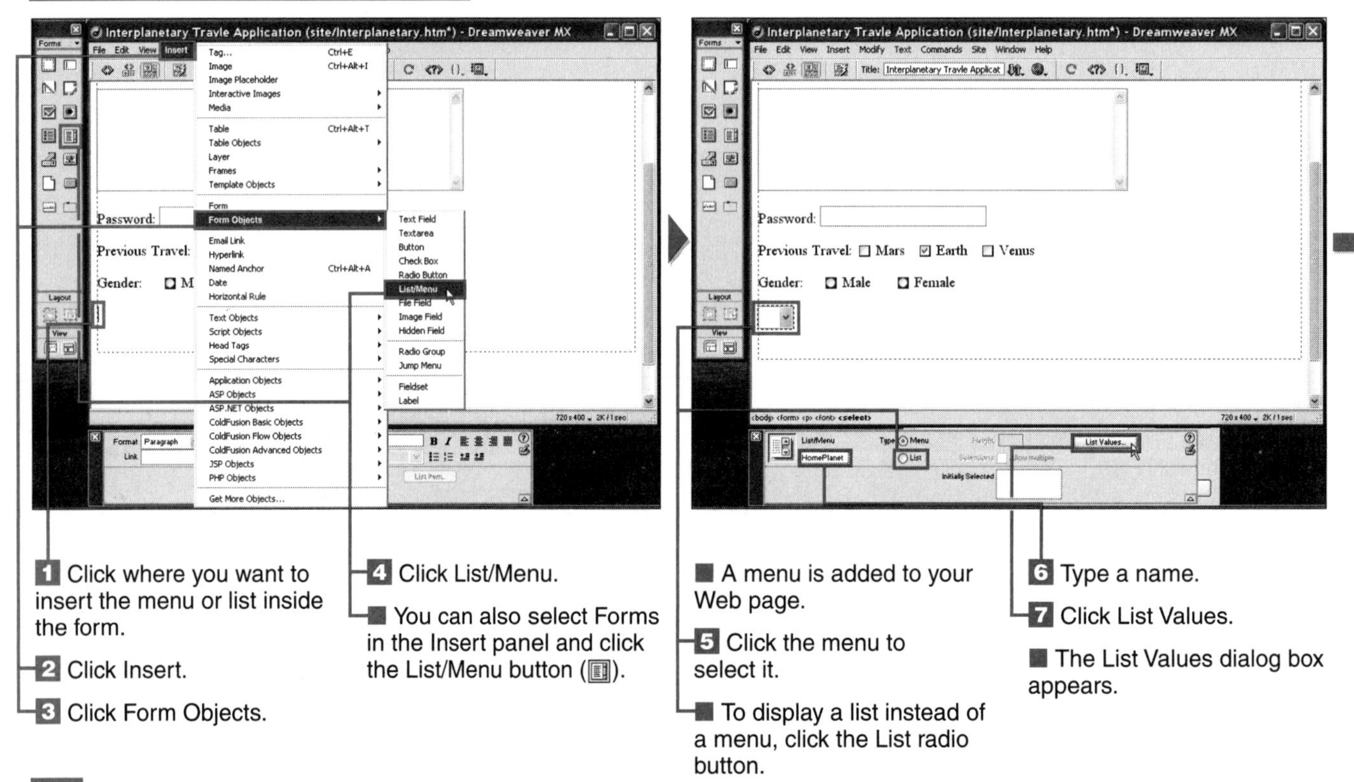

1 Click where you want to insert the menu or list inside the form.

2 Click Insert.

3 Click Form Objects.

4 Click List/Menu.

■ You can also select Forms in the Insert panel and click the List/Menu button (▤).

■ A menu is added to your Web page.

5 Click the menu to select it.

■ To display a list instead of a menu, click the List radio button.

6 Type a name.

7 Click List Values.

■ The List Values dialog box appears.

What is sent to the form handler from a menu or list?

✔ When the user submits the form, the browser sends the name of the menu or list and the value of the option that was selected. If multiple items were selected in a list, multiple name/value pairs are sent.

Can I specify the width of a menu or list?

✔ No. The width of the menu or list is determined by its widest item. To change the width, you can make the items in the list shorter or longer.

When should I use a list instead of check boxes?

✔ Both elements let your viewers choose several options from a set of options in your form. Lists let you combine your set of options into a relatively small space; check boxes let your viewers have a clearer view of all the options that are available. The best choice probably depends on the type of information you are presenting and the space available.

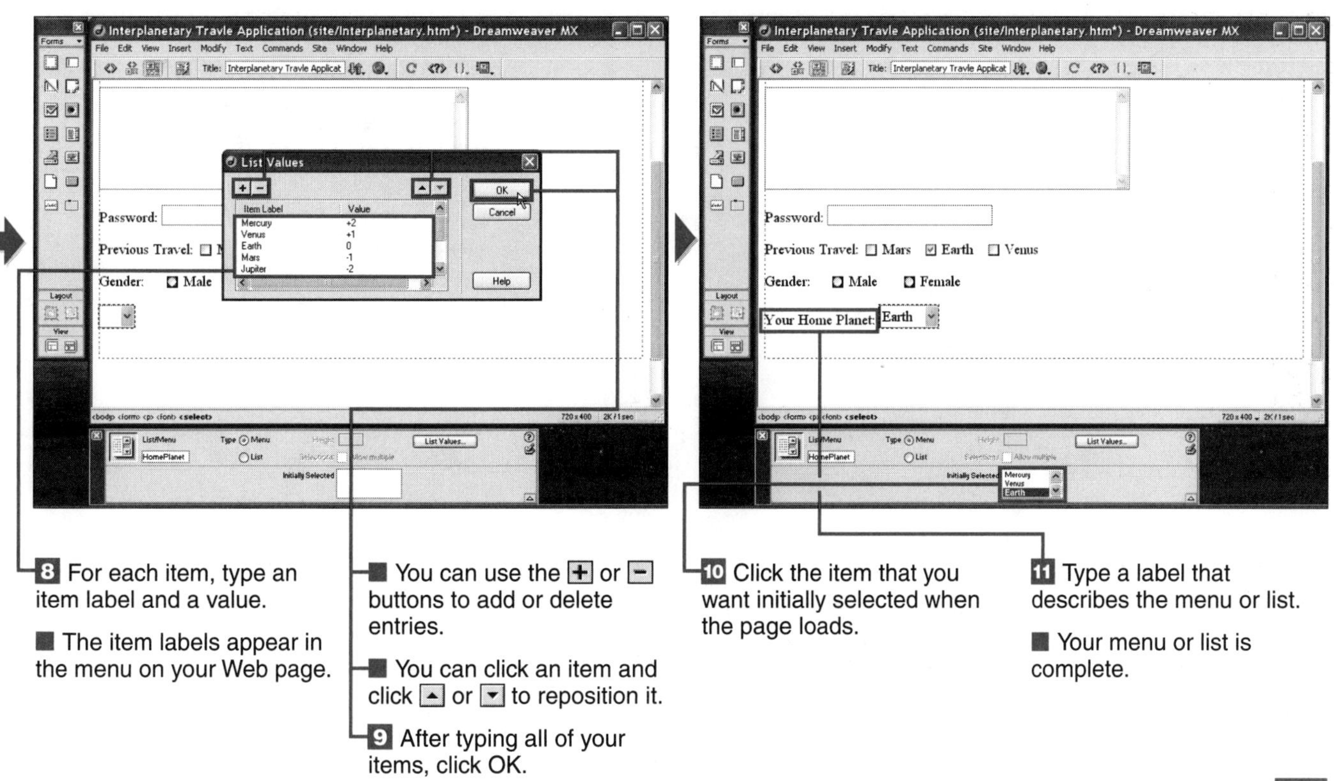

8 For each item, type an item label and a value.

■ The item labels appear in the menu on your Web page.

■ You can use the [+] or [−] buttons to add or delete entries.

■ You can click an item and click [▲] or [▼] to reposition it.

9 After typing all of your items, click OK.

10 Click the item that you want initially selected when the page loads.

11 Type a label that describes the menu or list.

■ Your menu or list is complete.

CREATE A JUMP MENU

A *jump menu* lets users easily navigate to other Web pages using a form menu. You can also let users access non-HTML documents from a jump menu.

A jump menu uses the same HTML code as regular form menus, but it combines that code with JavaScript. The JavaScript reads the selected menu item and then forwards the user to the requested URL. For more information, see page 152.

You can use jump menus in addition to or in place of regular navigation links on your site. Because form menus enable you to hide a lot of information in a small amount of space, you can fit a lot more links in a jump menu than you can as regular text links on a page.

Jump menus can include an optional Go button that the user can click to visit the selected URL. If you do not include the Go button, users are forwarded to the new URL whenever they choose a new item in the menu.

CREATE A JUMP MENU

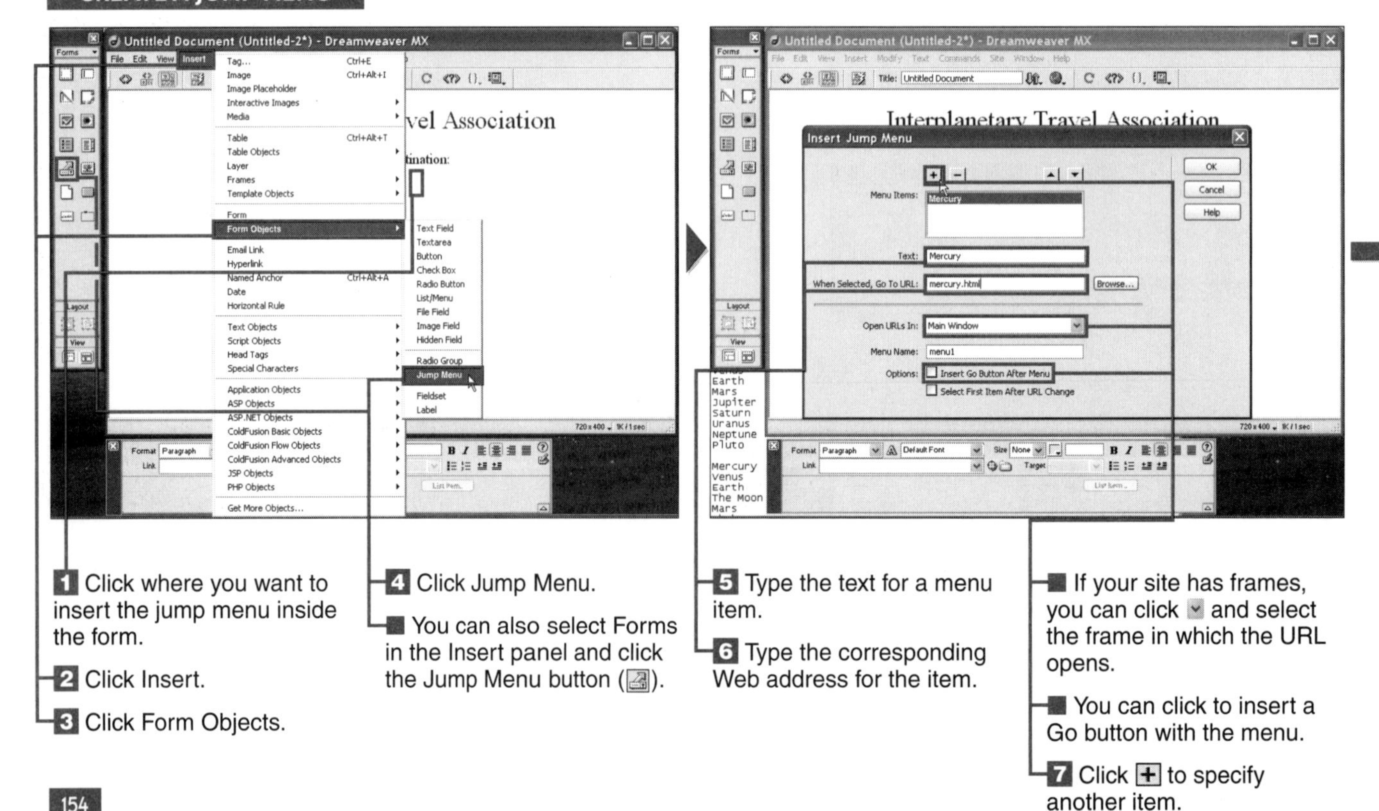

1 Click where you want to insert the jump menu inside the form.

2 Click Insert.

3 Click Form Objects.

4 Click Jump Menu.

■ You can also select Forms in the Insert panel and click the Jump Menu button (▣).

5 Type the text for a menu item.

6 Type the corresponding Web address for the item.

■ If your site has frames, you can click ▾ and select the frame in which the URL opens.

■ You can click to insert a Go button with the menu.

7 Click ⊞ to specify another item.

How do I edit the jump menu items after I have inserted the menu on the page?

✔ You can select the menu and click the List Values button in the Property inspector. Doing this enables you to edit the menu items just as you would a regular form menu. You can also open the Behaviors panel and double-click the Jump Menu item. Jump menus are listed in the Behaviors panel because their functionality requires JavaScript code.

Does a jump menu require a form handler?

✔ No. A form handler does not process the menu information; JavaScript code does. If you view the code used to display a jump menu, you may notice that the `<form>` tag is missing the `action` attribute that usually specifies the form handler.

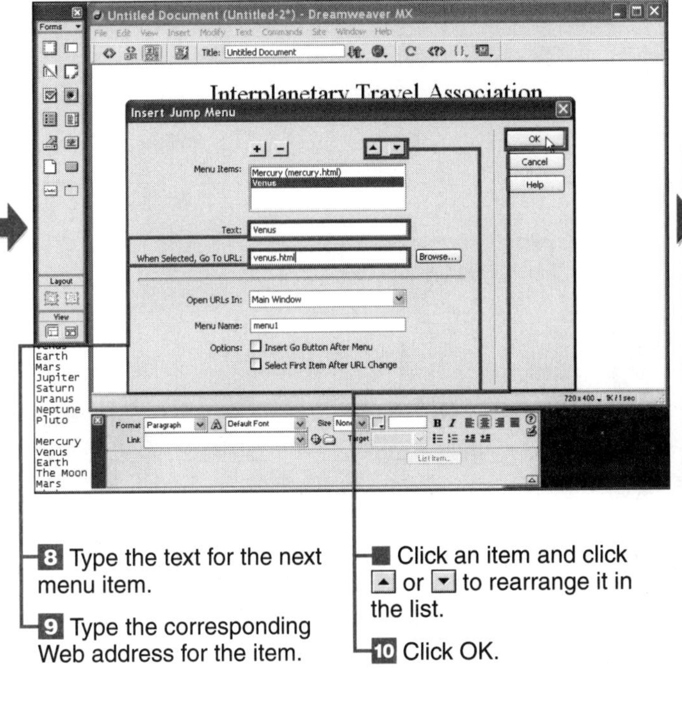

8 Type the text for the next menu item.

9 Type the corresponding Web address for the item.

■ Click an item and click ▲ or ▼ to rearrange it in the list.

10 Click OK.

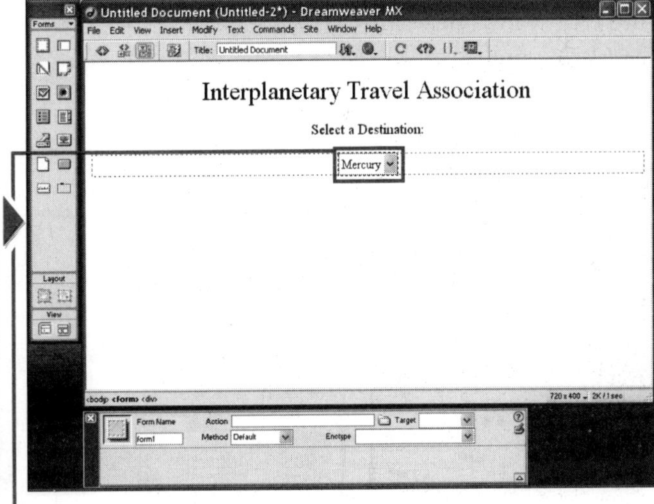

■ The jump menu appears on the page.

■ To test the menu, preview the page in a Web browser.

Note: To preview a page in a Web browser, see page 58.

ADD FILE UPLOADING TO A FORM

You can let users select files from their computer and upload them with the other form information that they submit. File uploading can be a nice feature when you require users to send you a lot of information. For example, you can include a form element that allows users to send you their resumes through a form on a company's job-listing page. File uploading can also let people send you images and other information that cannot be sent using other form elements.

The file-uploading feature inserts a text field and Browse button into the form container. The Browse button enables users to search their hard drives for the file that they want to send. After the user selects the file, the path to it appears in the text field.

Note that if you include a file-upload element in your form, you must set up your form to use the `post` method of sending its information to the form handler. For more information, see page 141.

ADD FILE UPLOADING TO A FORM

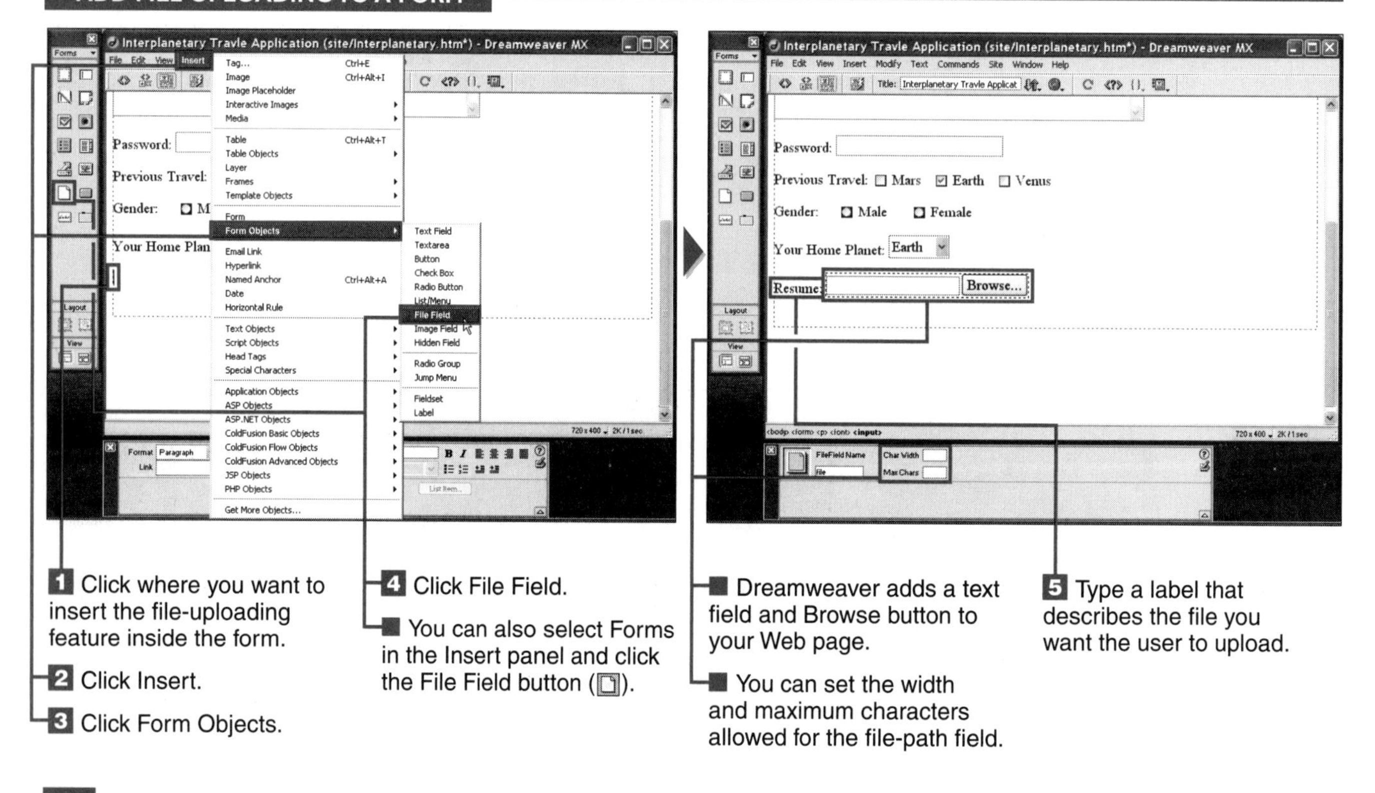

1 Click where you want to insert the file-uploading feature inside the form.

2 Click Insert.

3 Click Form Objects.

4 Click File Field.

■ You can also select Forms in the Insert panel and click the File Field button.

■ Dreamweaver adds a text field and Browse button to your Web page.

■ You can set the width and maximum characters allowed for the file-path field.

5 Type a label that describes the file you want the user to upload.

ADD HIDDEN INFORMATION TO A FORM

You can use hidden form fields to add information to your forms without displaying the information in the browser window. You may want to add hidden information in order to customize the form for use with a particular page or form handler. For example, you may add a hidden field that tells the form handler what URL you want users forwarded to after they submit a form. Users can still view information in a hidden form field if they examine the source HTML for the page.

The information in a hidden field consists of a name/value pair, just as other form elements have names to distinguish them and values that represent the user-added information.

A hidden form field is denoted in the Document window by a special icon. You need to have Dreamweaver's invisible elements turned on to see the icon. Click View, Visual Aids, and Invisible

ADD HIDDEN INFORMATION TO A FORM

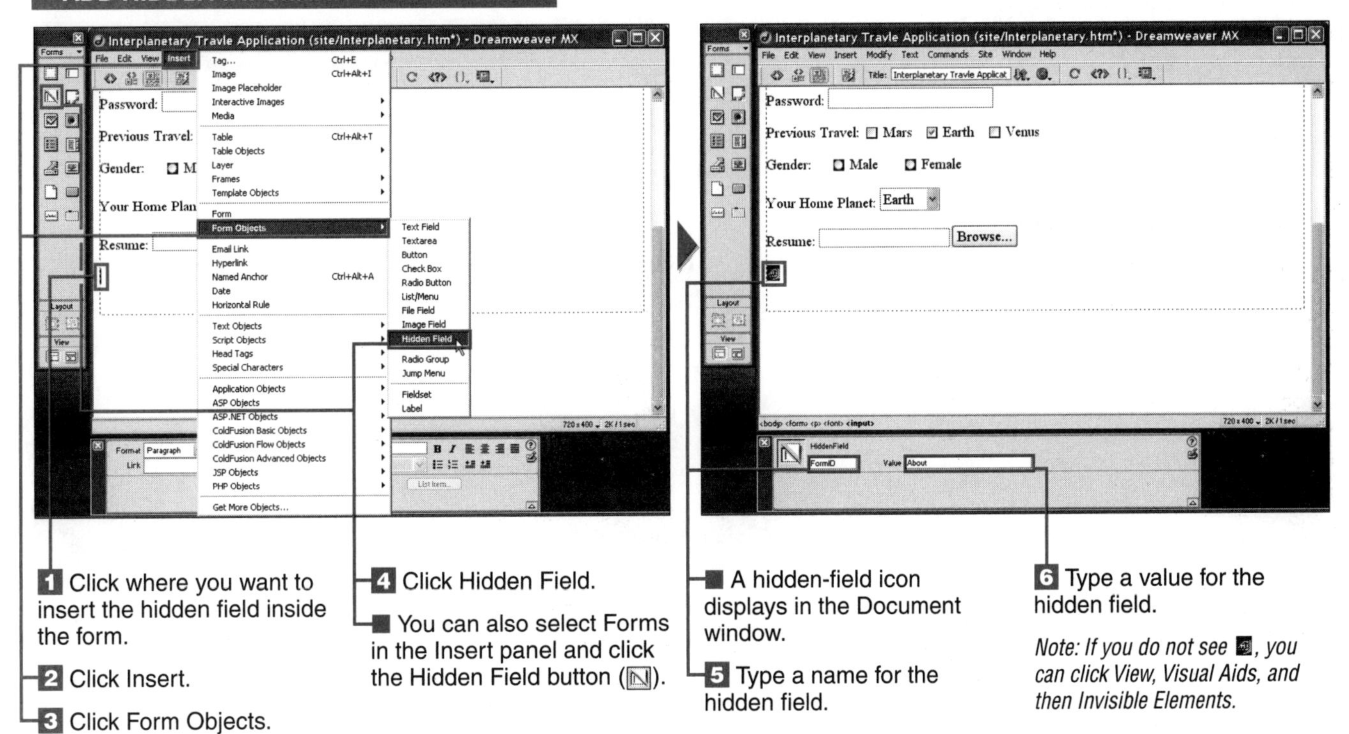

1 Click where you want to insert the hidden field inside the form.

2 Click Insert.

3 Click Form Objects.

4 Click Hidden Field.

■ You can also select Forms in the Insert panel and click the Hidden Field button (▣).

■ A hidden-field icon displays in the Document window.

5 Type a name for the hidden field.

6 Type a value for the hidden field.

Note: If you do not see ▣, you can click View, Visual Aids, and then Invisible Elements.

ADD A SUBMIT BUTTON TO A FORM

You can add a button that enables users to submit a form's information to the specified form handler. To specify a form handler, see page 141.

You can specify the label for the Submit button in the Label field of the Properties inspector. The default label is Submit.

An alternative to the standard HTML button for the Submit button is a custom image button. You can create a custom button in an image editor, such as Macromedia Fireworks or Adobe Photoshop.

How do I add a custom Select button to my form?

✔ You can add a custom Select button to your form by selecting Forms in the Insert panel and clicking [image]. Make sure you insert your image inside the dashed red form box. You must then change the Image Field name in the Properties inspector to Submit for that image. This causes Dreamweaver to use the image as a clickable Submit button.

ADD A SUBMIT BUTTON TO A FORM

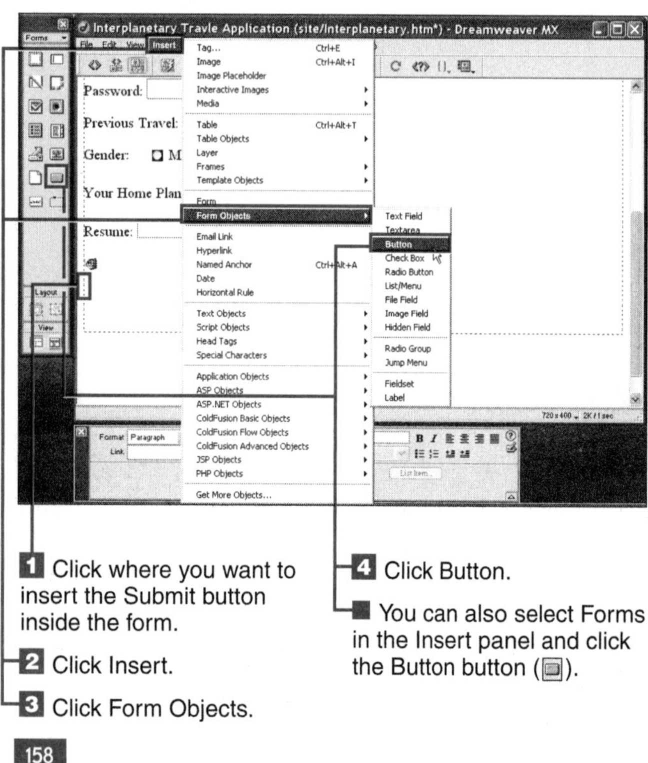

1 Click where you want to insert the Submit button inside the form.

2 Click Insert.

3 Click Form Objects.

4 Click Button.

■ You can also select Forms in the Insert panel and click the Button button ([image]).

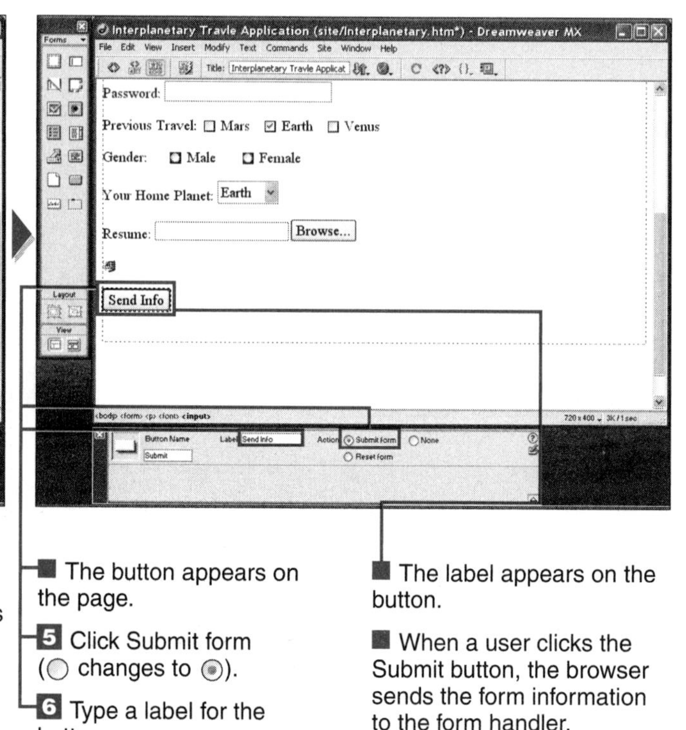

■ The button appears on the page.

5 Click Submit form (◯ changes to ◉).

6 Type a label for the button.

■ The label appears on the button.

■ When a user clicks the Submit button, the browser sends the form information to the form handler.

ADD A RESET BUTTON TO A FORM

You can add a button that enables users to reset all the elements of a form to their initial values. This Reset button lets users quickly erase their form entries so that they can start over again.

You can specify the label that goes on the Reset button in the Label field of the Properties inspector. Reset is the default label.

An alternative to the standard HTML button for the Reset button is a custom image button. You can create a custom button in an image editor, such as Macromedia Fireworks or Adobe Photoshop.

How do I add a custom Reset button to my form?

✔ You can add a custom Reset button to your form by selecting Forms in the Insert panel and clicking ▣. Make sure you insert your image inside the dashed red form box. You must then change the Image Field name in the Properties inspector to Reset for that image. This causes Dreamweaver to use the image as a clickable Reset button.

ADD A RESET BUTTON TO A FORM

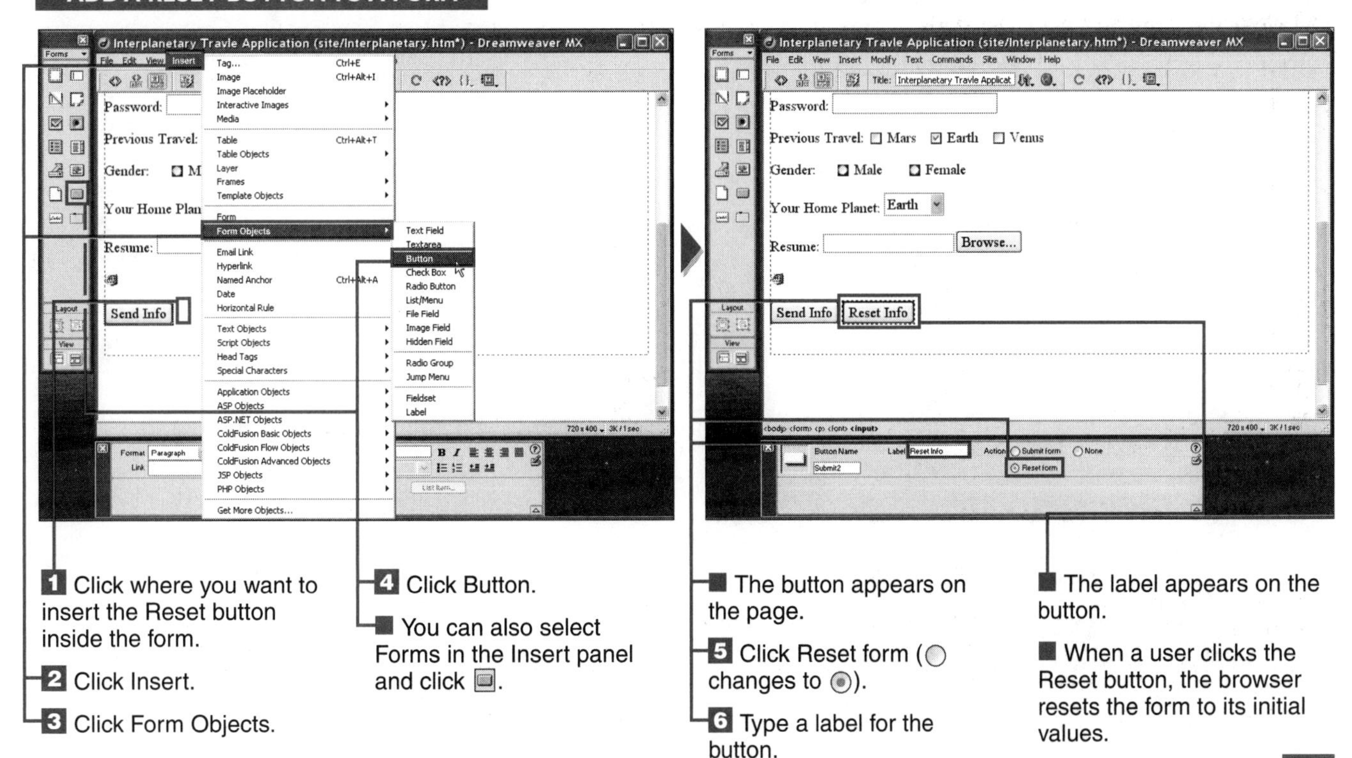

1 Click where you want to insert the Reset button inside the form.

2 Click Insert.

3 Click Form Objects.

4 Click Button.

■ You can also select Forms in the Insert panel and click ▣.

■ The button appears on the page.

5 Click Reset form (○ changes to ◉).

6 Type a label for the button.

■ The label appears on the button.

■ When a user clicks the Reset button, the browser resets the form to its initial values.

INTRODUCTION TO FRAMES

Frames enable you to divide your Web page into several smaller windows and then display a different Web page in each window. The most common use of frames is for organizing a site's navigational links. You can put a list of navigational links in one frame and have the destination pages open in a larger content area. Organizing your site this way means the browser does not have to reload the navigational links each time the user clicks a link. The user can always see the links, as well.

Using Frames

Frames can introduce some complications. Because frames split your site content into more pages, other Web developers may find it difficult to link to specific content on your site. Also, users with older browsers that are not frames-capable or small monitors, which can not display your page at a large window size, can run into problems when viewing framed pages. Additionally, frames mean more work for the developer, who has to keep track of how content is organized in the frameset.

Create Frames

You create a framed Web site by dividing the Document window horizontally or vertically one or more times. You can also choose from one of several predefined frameset templates in Dreamweaver. You then load a Web page into each frame by specifying the page in the Properties inspector. The overall organization of frames in your site is controlled by a separate HTML document called a *frameset page*. You can manage the pages that make up your framed site using Dreamweaver's Frames panel.

Behavior of Framed Pages

Frames allow the pages being viewed to operate independently of one another. As you scroll through the content of a frame, the content in other frames remains fixed. In one frame, you can create hyperlinks that open pages in other frames. Just like in unframed pages, the linked pages can be either part of your site or pages on external Web sites. You can also cause a linked Web page to open on top of any existing frames, thereby taking a user out of the framed version of your site.

DIVIDE A PAGE INTO FRAMES

Creating a framed page enables you to compartmentalize the content on your page. That way, the entire page does not need to change as a user clicks links to other pages on the site. The first step in creating a framed Web page is dividing the Document window into more than one frame.

You can split the Document window horizontally to create a frameset with left and right frames, or you can split it vertically to create a frameset with top and bottom frames. An alternative to splitting the window by hand is choosing one of Dreamweaver's predefined framesets for your site.

Many Web sites consist of a narrow left frame and a wide right frame, with the navigation links appearing on the left and the site's main content appearing on the right. Other site designs may split the window vertically and place the site's title and navigation links across a short top frame and the main content in a taller bottom frame. See page 172 to learn how to resize frames.

For a more complicated framed site, you can continue to split your component frames to create a *nested* frameset. Nested framesets are useful when you want to have many different elements in their own frames. See page 163 for more information.

DIVIDE A PAGE INTO FRAMES

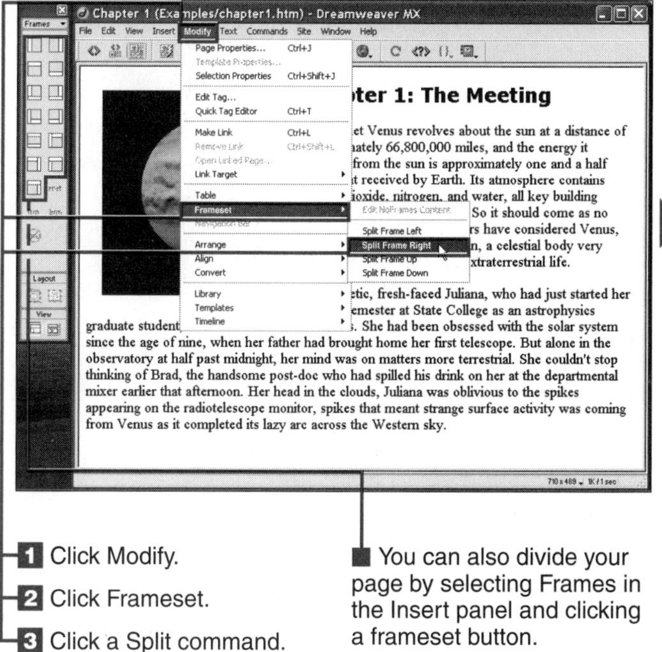

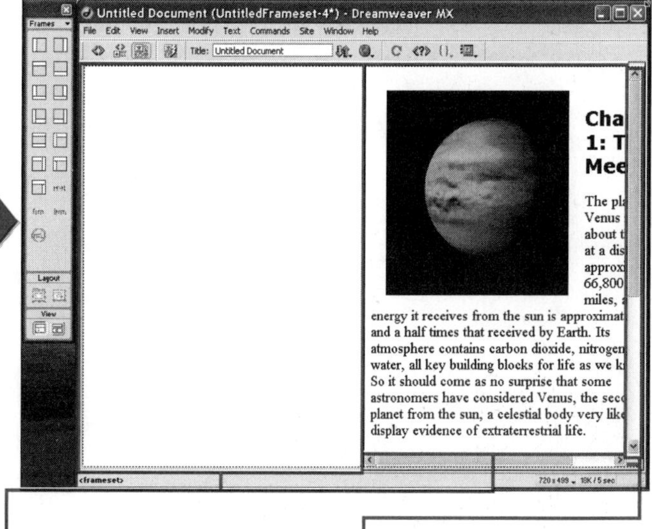

1 Click Modify.

2 Click Frameset.

3 Click a Split command.

■ You can also divide your page by selecting Frames in the Insert panel and clicking a frameset button.

■ The window splits into two frames.

■ If content existed in the original page, it shifts to one of the new frames.

■ A frame appears with scroll bars if the content extends outside its borders.

INSERT A PREDEFINED FRAMESET

Dreamweaver makes it easy to create several different frameset styles with its predefined framesets accessible via the New command. The designs include popular two- and three-panel frameset arrangements that can be opened in a blank Document window.

When you open a new predefined frameset, Dreamweaver automatically gives the frames generic names, such as topFrame, leftFrame, and mainFrame. If you prefer, you can rename your frames to reflect the type of content that is inside them. For more information, see page 169.

Most of the predefined page designs lend themselves to a particular site-navigation scheme. For example, you can place a list of navigational links in the narrow side frame and the main site content in one of the larger frames. Designs that have fixed in their title include some frames that have fixed dimensions, and others whose dimensions will vary depending on the size of the browser window.

After you insert a predefined frameset, you can modify the frameset to suit your needs by subdividing the frames. You can also delete frames in the frameset that you have no use for.

INSERT A PREDEFINED FRAMESET

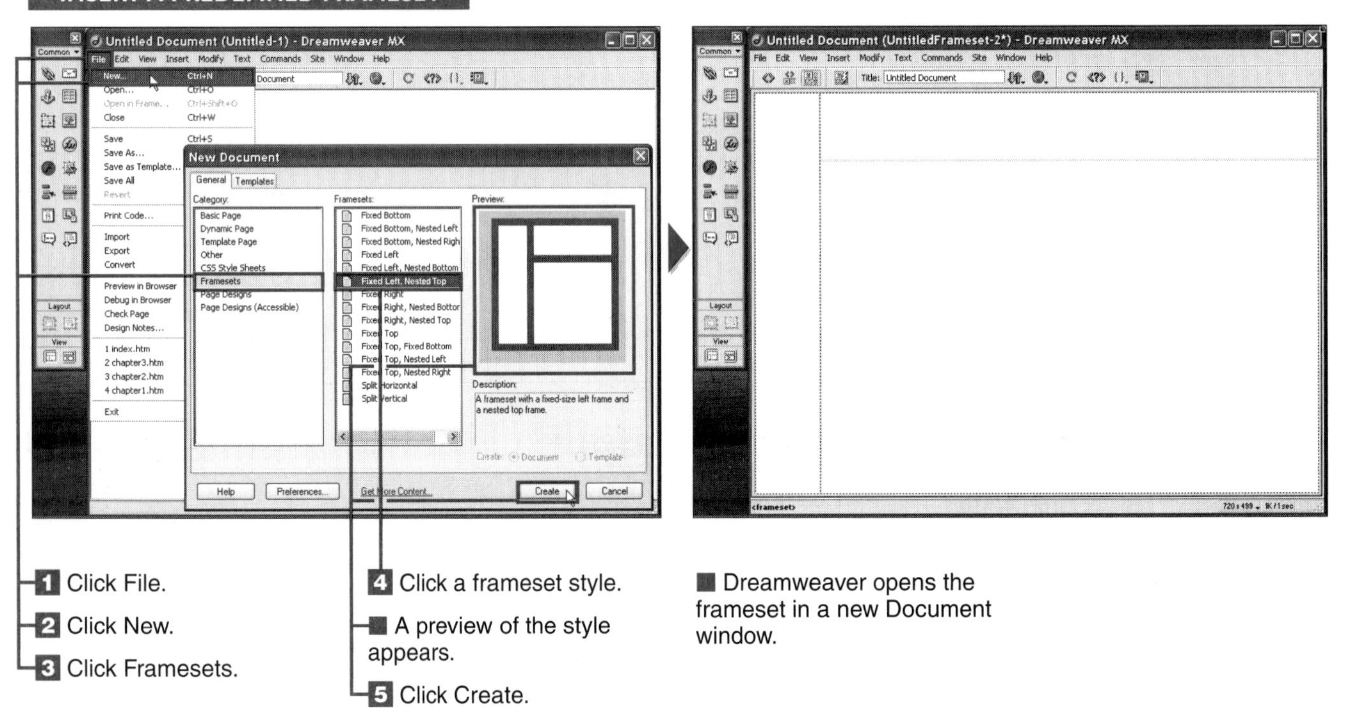

1 Click File.

2 Click New.

3 Click Framesets.

4 Click a frameset style.

■ A preview of the style appears.

5 Click Create.

■ Dreamweaver opens the frameset in a new Document window.

NEST FRAMES

Nested frames give your site a more complex organization and more options regarding where you can insert your page information. Nesting frames involves subdividing the frames of an existing frameset.

To nest frames, you click inside an existing frame and then subdivide that frame horizontally or vertically.

See page 161 for more information. Also, some of the predefined framesets that Dreamweaver offers are nested frameset designs. See page 162.

One drawback to nested framesets is that they can be more difficult to hyperlink to. Make sure you name all of the frames that you plan to link to in your nested frameset.

Can I nest frames using HTML code?

✔ Yes, but you may find nested framesets hard to create using HTML. To see the code for a frameset, select the frameset by clicking on a frame border, and click the Show Code View button on the top of the Document window. You create nested framesets by nesting groups of `<frameset>` and `<frame>` tags.

NEST FRAMES

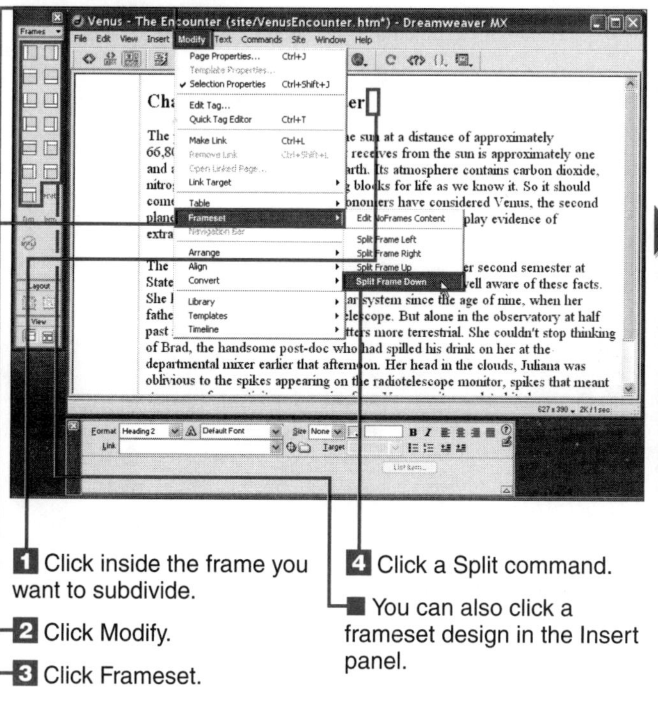

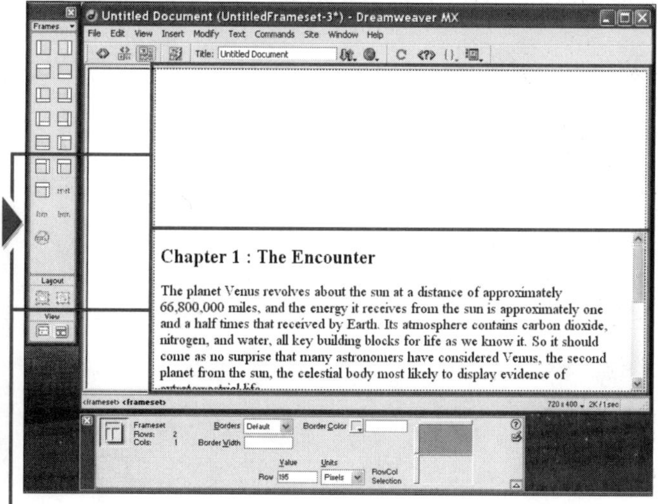

1 Click inside the frame you want to subdivide.

2 Click Modify.

3 Click Frameset.

4 Click a Split command.

■ You can also click a frameset design in the Insert panel.

■ Dreamweaver splits the selected frame into two frames. You now have a frameset inside a frameset.

■ You can add content to the empty frame.

■ You can continue to split your frames into as many frames as you want.

ADD CONTENT TO A FRAME

A new framed Web site is not very interesting without something showing inside the frames. You can add content to a frame by opening up an existing HTML document in the frame. You can also add content by typing text or inserting elements, such as images and tables, just as you do with an unframed page.

Content in a frame behaves just as it does in a normal Document window. Scroll bars appear on the frame if the content extends outside its boundaries. To turn the scroll bars off, see page 176. Text also wraps at the edge of a frame, unless you enclose the text in a fixed width table.

When you design the layout of the content in your framesets, think about how your audience views your site. Framed sites may display differently when viewed on different monitors, depending on the resolution setting. You may want to test your finished framed site at different browser size settings to make sure all the content appears correctly.

ADD CONTENT TO A FRAME

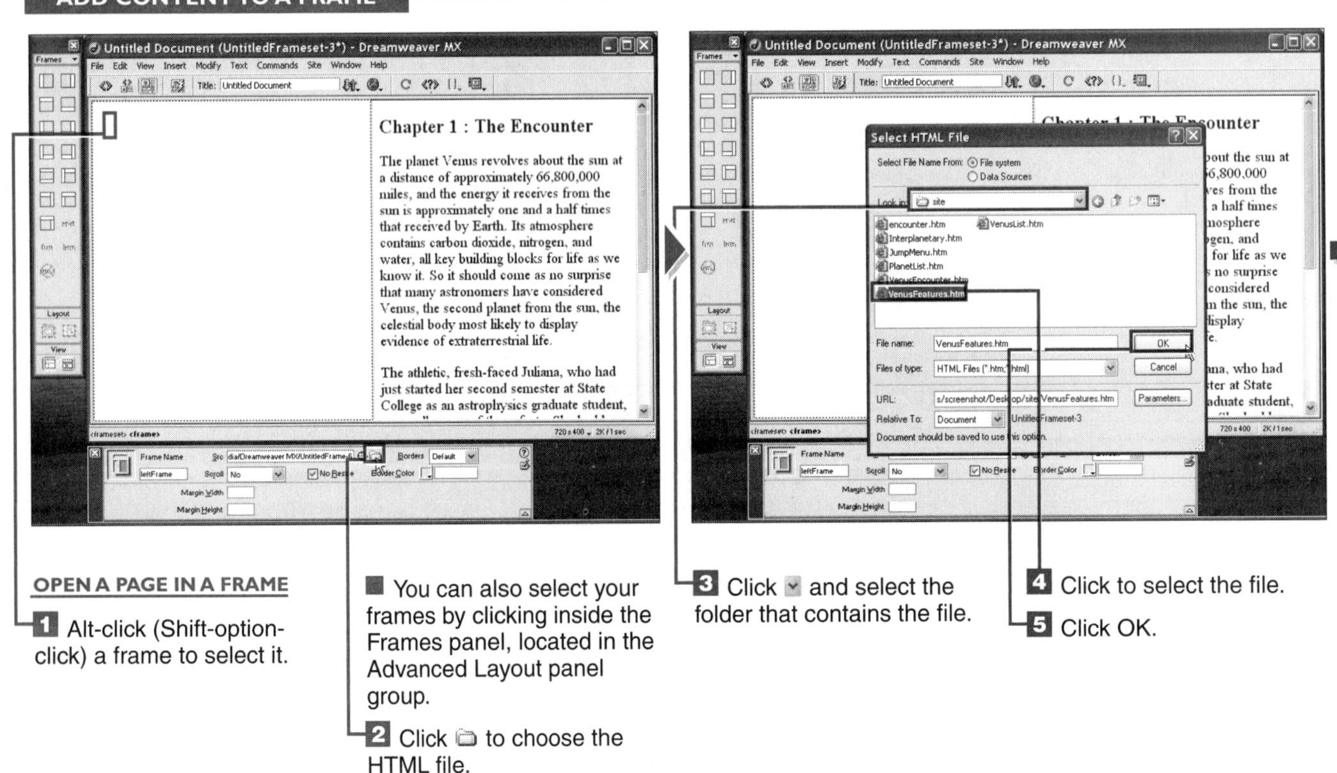

OPEN A PAGE IN A FRAME

1. Alt-click (Shift-option-click) a frame to select it.

■ You can also select your frames by clicking inside the Frames panel, located in the Advanced Layout panel group.

2. Click 🗀 to choose the HTML file.

3. Click ▾ and select the folder that contains the file.

4. Click to select the file.

5. Click OK.

Can I load an image into an empty frame?

✔ Yes. An alternative to loading HTML pages into your frames is loading GIF, JPEG, or PNG images. If the image is smaller than the size of the frame, a blank space appears around it. An image opened in a frame does not tile to fill the entire frame, like a background image does.

What are the HTML tags that define a page's frames?

✔ The <frameset> tag defines the dimensions and organization of the frames of your site. The <frameset> tag encloses <frame> tags, which define what content fills the different frames. The <frameset> and <frame> tags also define the physical characteristics of frames, such as whether they have scroll bars and can be resized. To see the code that defines your frames, select the frameset by clicking the frame border, and click the Show Code View button on the top of the Document window.

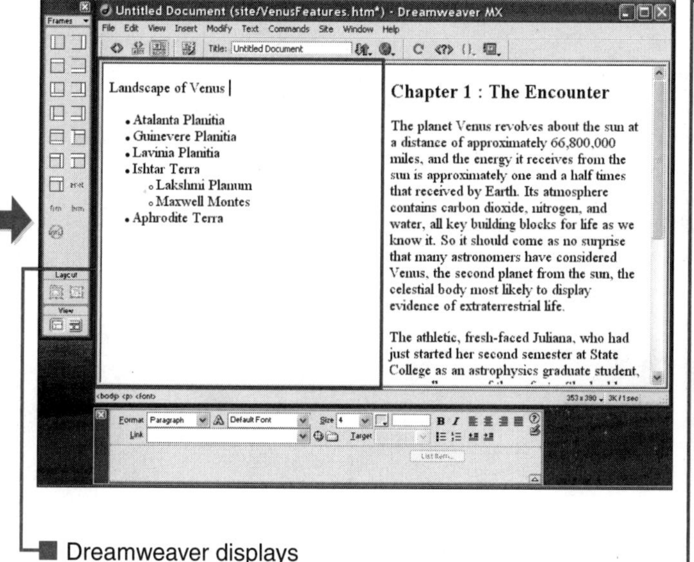

■ Dreamweaver displays the page in the frame.

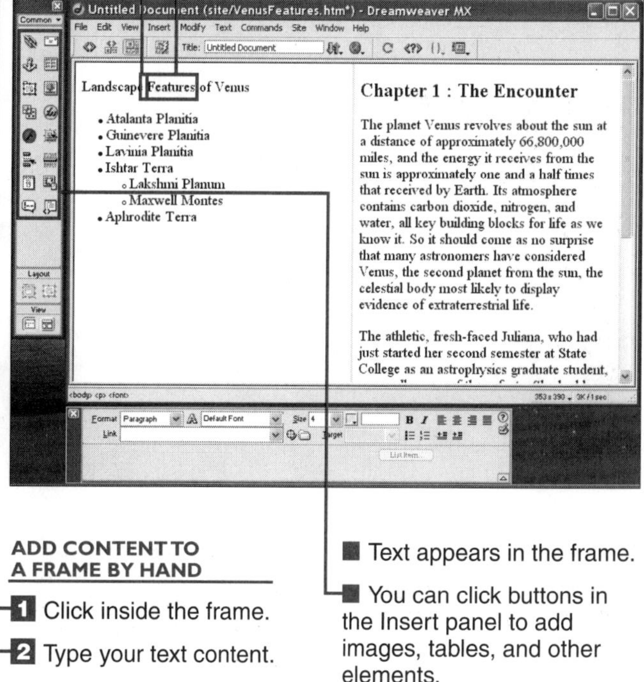

ADD CONTENT TO A FRAME BY HAND

1 Click inside the frame.

2 Type your text content.

■ Text appears in the frame.

■ You can click buttons in the Insert panel to add images, tables, and other elements.

SAVE A FRAMED SITE

Saving a framed site enables you to view your frameset in a Web browser and double check how your framed content displays. Saving framed pages is slightly more complicated than saving regular pages. That is because framed pages are made up of multiple HTML documents, including a frameset document that defines how the frames are organized. All of the documents involved need to be saved for a framed site to display correctly in a browser.

To save a framed page, you click inside the frame that holds it and save it like you do a regular page. Saving a frameset requires selecting the frameset by clicking on the frame border and then selecting the Save Frameset menu command.

You can duplicate an already-saved frameset by selecting it and then clicking File and Save Frameset As. Saving the frameset with a new name creates a duplicate. The duplicate has the same framed pages as the original.

SAVE A FRAMED SITE

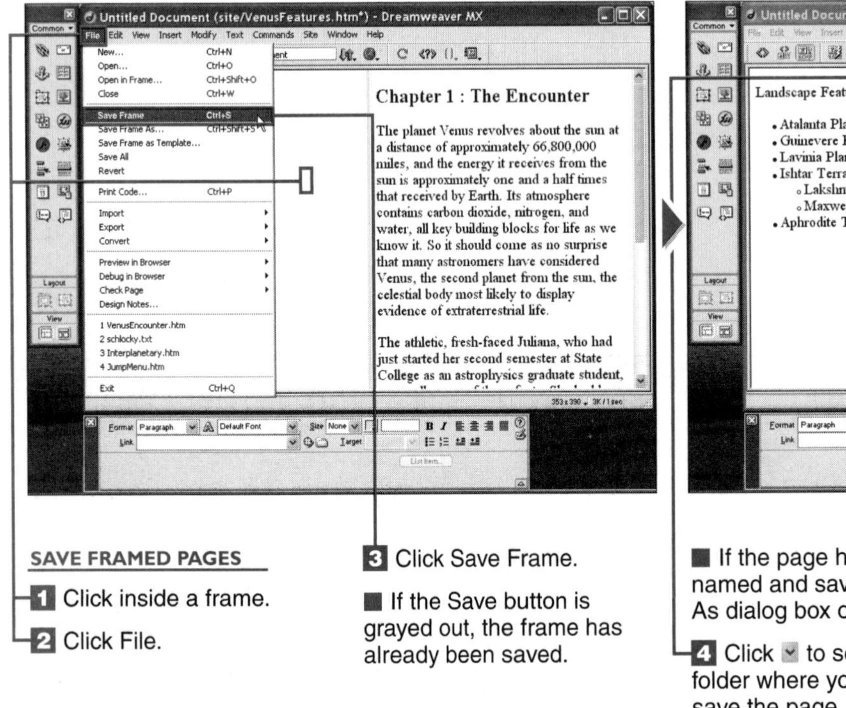

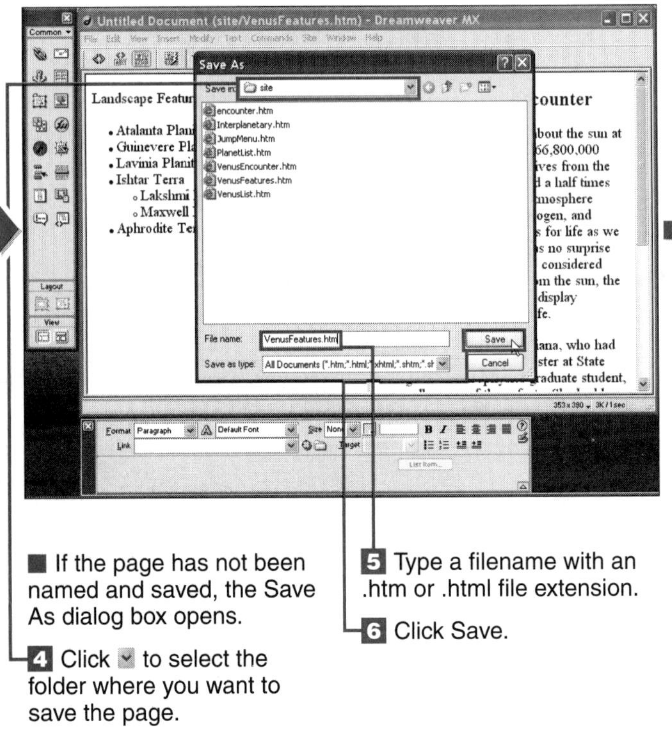

SAVE FRAMED PAGES

1 Click inside a frame.

2 Click File.

3 Click Save Frame.

■ If the Save button is grayed out, the frame has already been saved.

■ If the page has not been named and saved, the Save As dialog box opens.

4 Click ▾ to select the folder where you want to save the page.

5 Type a filename with an .htm or .html file extension.

6 Click Save.

Is there a shortcut for saving all the documents of my framed site?

✔ Yes. You can select File and then Save All Frames. This option saves all the framed pages and framesets that make up your site. This is definitely a timesaver!

Do I have to save framed pages in the same folder?

✔ You usually save frameset files and the pages that they hold in the same folder. But you do not have to do this. You can reference frame contents from the frameset page just like a hyperlink, which means they can exist in another folder or even on another Web site.

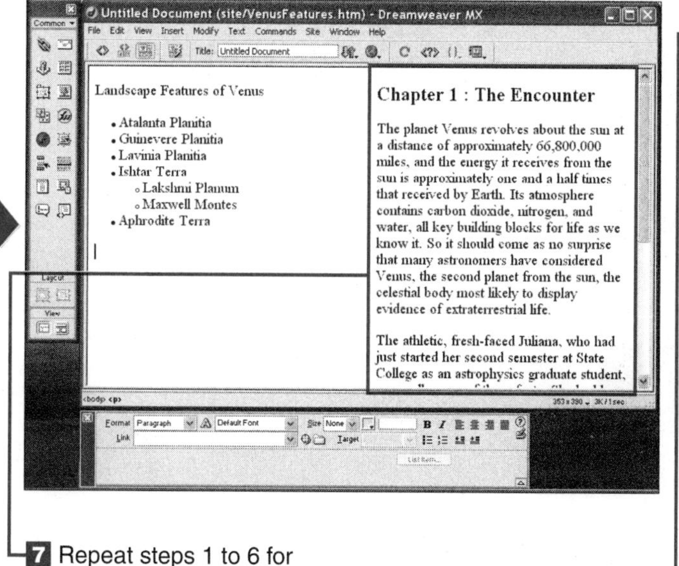

7 Repeat steps 1 to 6 for additional framed pages in your document.

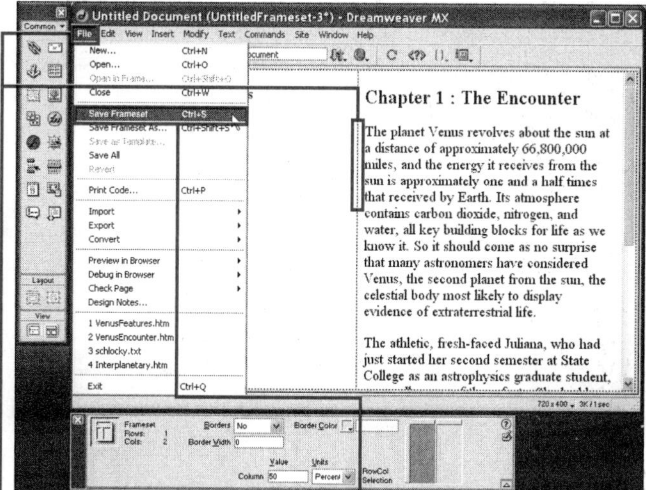

SAVE THE FRAMESET

1 Click the frame border to select the frameset.

■ You can also open the Frames panel and click the frameset border in the panel.

2 Click File.

3 Click Save Frameset.

4 Save the frameset as an .htm or .html file.

■ Dreamweaver saves the frameset.

DELETE A FRAME

Deleting a frame is convenient when you have a nested frameset that has become too complicated. You can delete a frame in Dreamweaver by clicking and dragging the frame's border to the edge of the Document window.

Deleting a frame does not delete the file that is currently open in it if that frame has been saved. If you delete a frame that has not been saved or has unsaved changes, the content or changes are lost.

If you delete a frame from a two-frame site, what is left is a frame inside a frameset. This is not the same as having the page open by itself, because a frameset still encloses the page. If you want to get rid of the frameset, you need to close the Document window and open the content in a regular, unframed window.

DELETE A FRAME

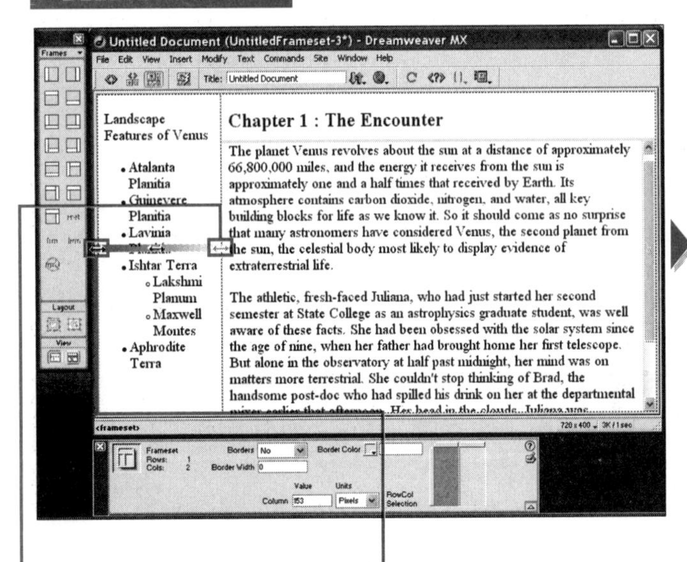

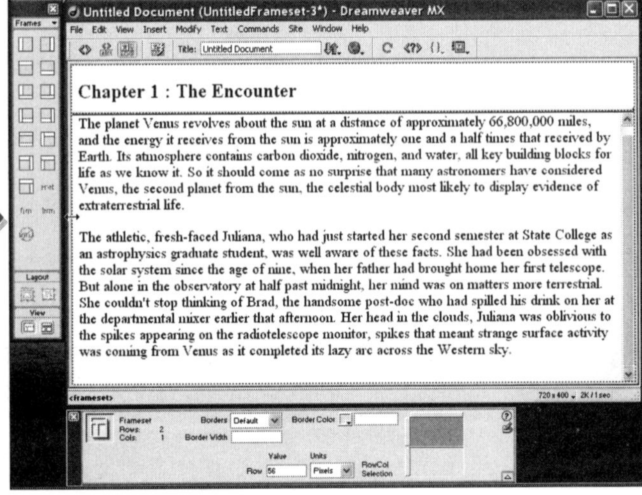

1 Click and drag the border of the frame you want to delete.

2 Drag the border to the edge of the window.

■ The frame is deleted.

NAME A FRAME

To create hyperlinks that can work between your frames, you need to give your frames names. The frame name is what you reference in the target of a hyperlink. The hyperlink target tells a browser where the hyperlink destination should open. You can give your frames descriptive names such as SideNav and Footer to help you identify them when it is time to create hyperlinks.

When you create your frameset manually, your frames are created without names. You have to name them before you can create hyperlinks that target other frames in the frameset.

When you create your frames using a predefined frameset, Dreamweaver automatically gives your frames generic names, such as topFrame, leftFrame, and mainFrame. If you prefer, you can rename your frames to reflect the type of content that is inside them. See page 162 for more information on inserting a predefined frameset.

After you have named your frames, targeting your hyperlinks is easy. The frame names for the frameset appear in the Target drop-down menu in the Properties inspector. For more information about creating links, see page 170.

NAME A FRAME

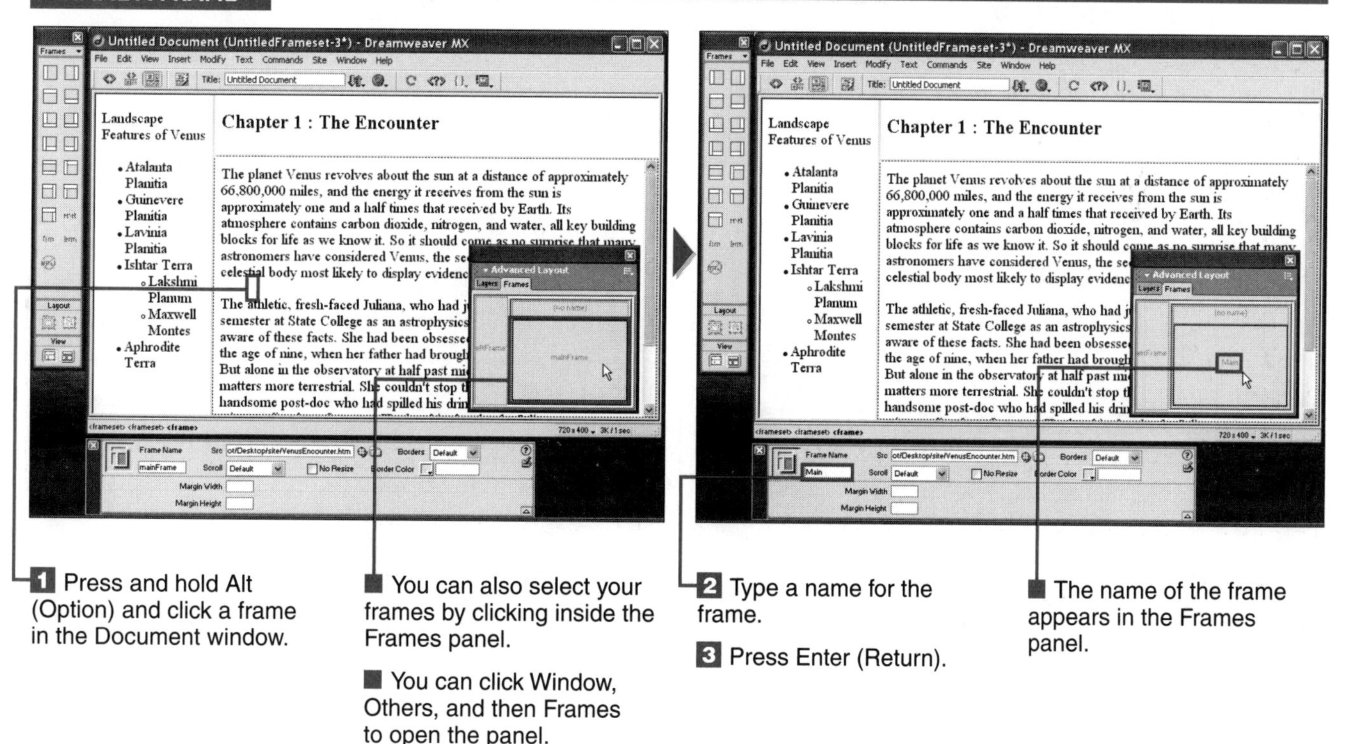

1 Press and hold Alt (Option) and click a frame in the Document window.

■ You can also select your frames by clicking inside the Frames panel.

■ You can click Window, Others, and then Frames to open the panel.

2 Type a name for the frame.

3 Press Enter (Return).

■ The name of the frame appears in the Frames panel.

HYPERLINK TO A FRAME

Hyperlinking from one frame in your site to another allows you to open new content inside your frameset. Site visitors can click a hyperlink in a frame, which triggers the link destination to open in a different frame.

Hyperlinking between frames requires you to give the destination frame a name. After you have named the frame, you can link to it by specifying the name as the hyperlink target. To name a frame, see page 169.

Including target information enables you to create a list of hyperlinks in a left frame and have all the linked content open up in the right frame. This is a useful way to organize glossary or dictionary information on a Web site.

If you do not specify the target of a hyperlink in a framed site, the hyperlink destination opens in the same frame as the hyperlink. If you specify a target name that does not exist, most browsers open up a new window and load the hyperlink destination inside it. You can also specify special keywords as hyperlink targets. These keywords enable you to open hyperlink destinations on top of existing frames.

HYPERLINK TO A FRAME

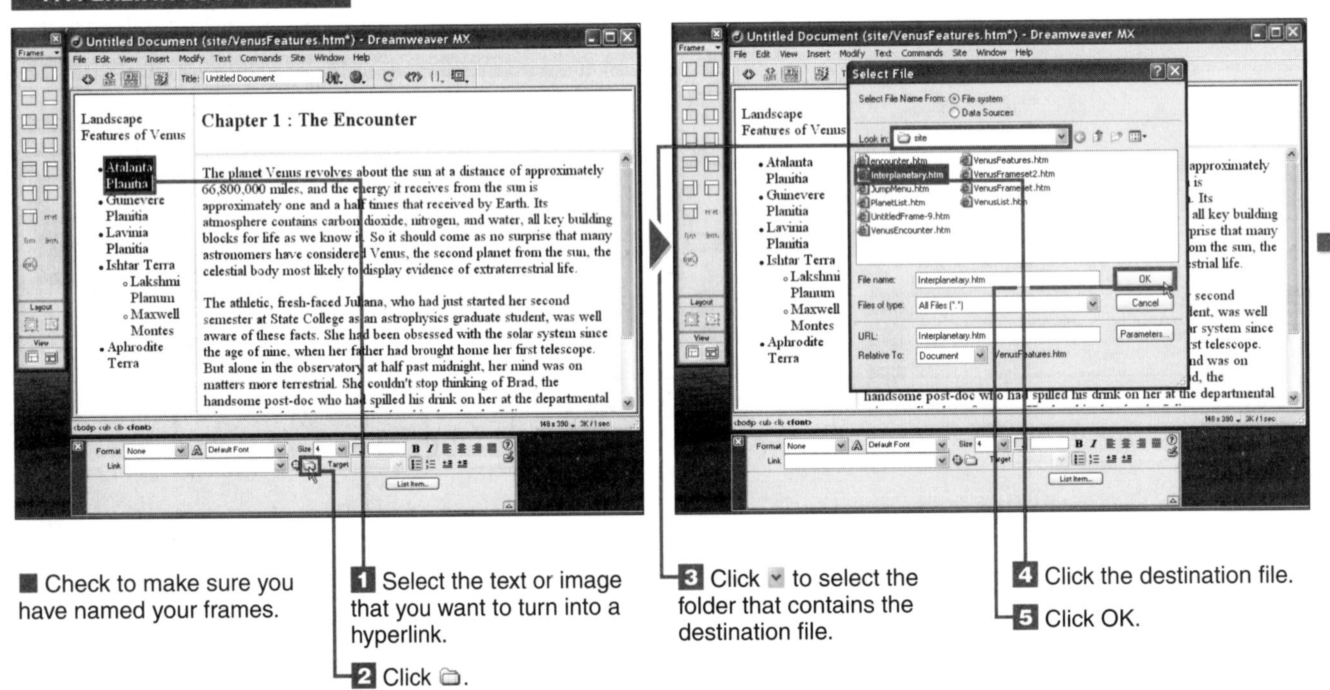

■ Check to make sure you have named your frames.

1 Select the text or image that you want to turn into a hyperlink.

2 Click 🗀.

3 Click ▾ to select the folder that contains the destination file.

4 Click the destination file.

5 Click OK.

What happens if I select _top for my hyperlink target?

✔ Selecting `_top`, instead of a frame name, opens the hyperlink destination on "top" of any existing framesets. This gets rid of a site's existing frameset.

What happens if I select _parent for my hyperlink target?

✔ Selecting `_parent` as the target opens the hyperlink destination over the current frame's parent frameset. A nested frameset has more than one parent. For a non-nested frameset, `_parent` has the same effect as `_top`.

What happens if I select _self for my hyperlink target?

✔ Selecting `_self` as the target opens the hyperlink destination in the same frame as the hyperlink. This is the default behavior for most browsers when you do not specify a target.

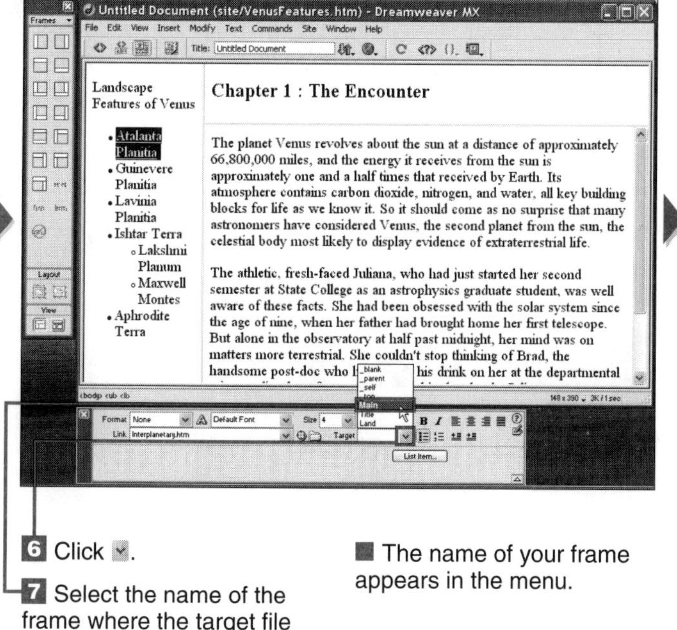

6 Click ▾.

7 Select the name of the frame where the target file opens.

■ The name of your frame appears in the menu.

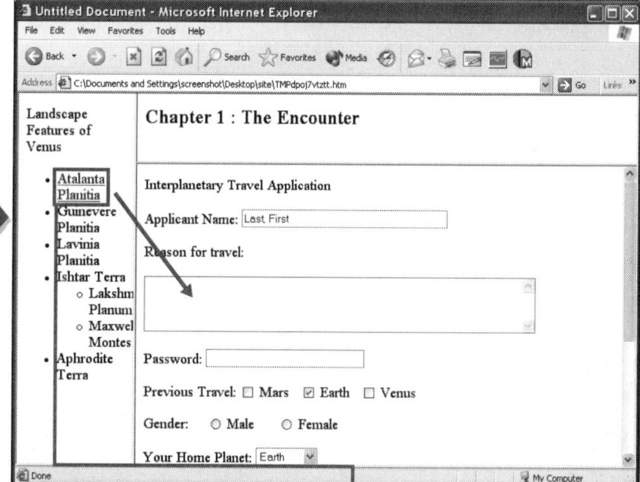

8 Preview the page in a Web browser.

Note: To preview a page in a Web browser, see page 58.

■ When you open the framed page in a Web browser and click the hyperlink, the destination page opens inside the targeted frame.

CHANGE THE DIMENSIONS OF A FRAME

You can change the dimensions of a frame to attractively and efficiently display the information inside it. When you change the height or width of a frame, other frames in the frameset shrink or expand to accommodate the change.

You can define the dimensions of your frames in one of three ways. Defining it in *pixels* lets you specify the exact physical dimensions of a frame. Defining it as a *percentage* lets you specify the frame size as a proportion of the browser window. Giving the frame a *relative* value lets you specify the dimensions relative to the other frames in the frameset.

Different frames in a frameset can be defined using different types of units. In such cases, frames defined using pixels are sized first by the browser, followed by frames defined using percentages, followed by frames defined using relative values.

This precedence means you can create a frameset in which some frames are fixed and others automatically stretch to take up the rest of the available space. For example, for a two-column design, you can specify that the navigation frame on the left take up a fixed width of 80 pixels while the content frame on the right takes up the remaining width in the browser window – 100%.

CHANGE THE DIMENSIONS OF A FRAME

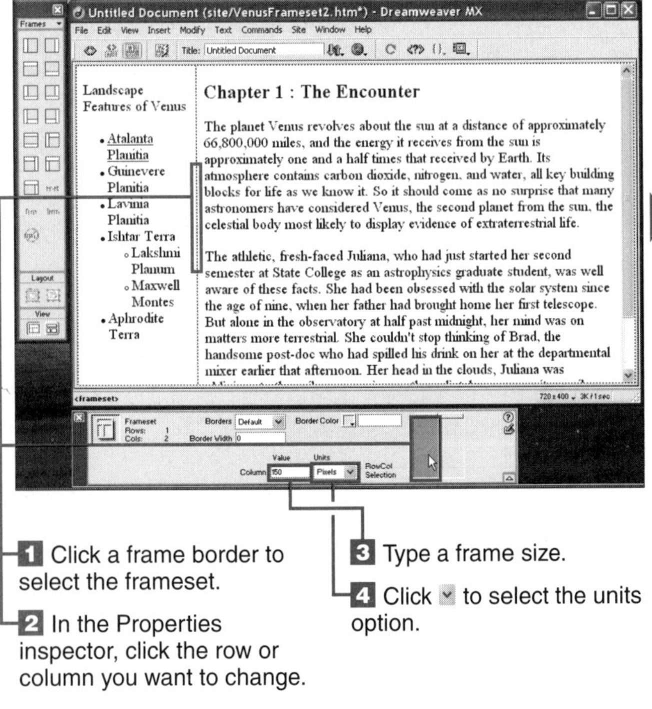

1 Click a frame border to select the frameset.

2 In the Properties inspector, click the row or column you want to change.

3 Type a frame size.

4 Click ▾ to select the units option.

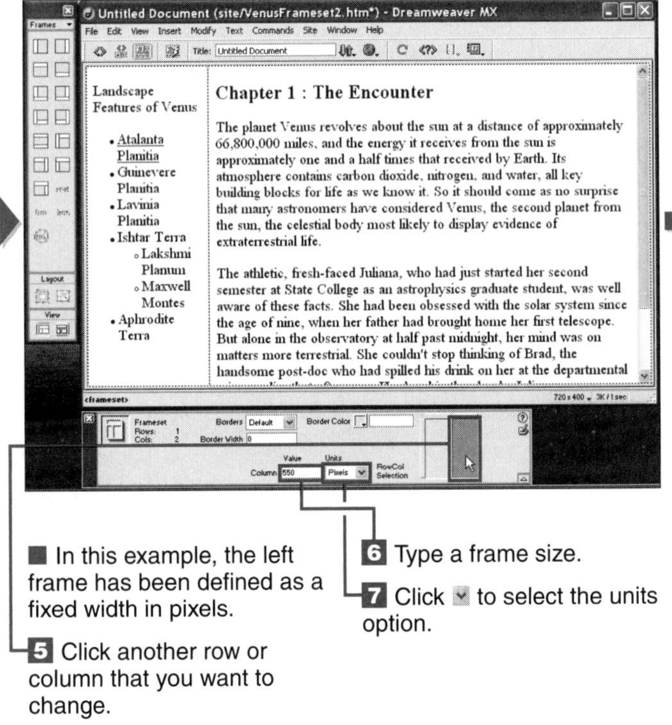

■ In this example, the left frame has been defined as a fixed width in pixels.

5 Click another row or column that you want to change.

6 Type a frame size.

7 Click ▾ to select the units option.

Is there a shortcut for changing the dimensions of frames?

✔ Yes. You can click and drag a frame border to quickly adjust the dimensions of a frameset. The values in the Properties inspector change as you drag.

Are viewers able to resize the frames in the browsers?

✔ Most browsers allow the viewer to resize frames, unless a noresize attribute has been added to the frame's HTML. To control whether or not you can resize frames in a browser, see page 177.

What happens when I specify pixel sizes for my frames that add up to more than the size of the browser window?

✔ Browsers interpret the sizes as relative values. For example, if you define two frames in a frameset as 1000 pixels and 2000 pixels, the browser allocates them ⅓ and ⅔ of the browser space, respectively.

How can I create two frames that assume equal sizes on my page, regardless of the size of the browser window?

✔ Set the size of each frame to 50% or a relative size of 1.

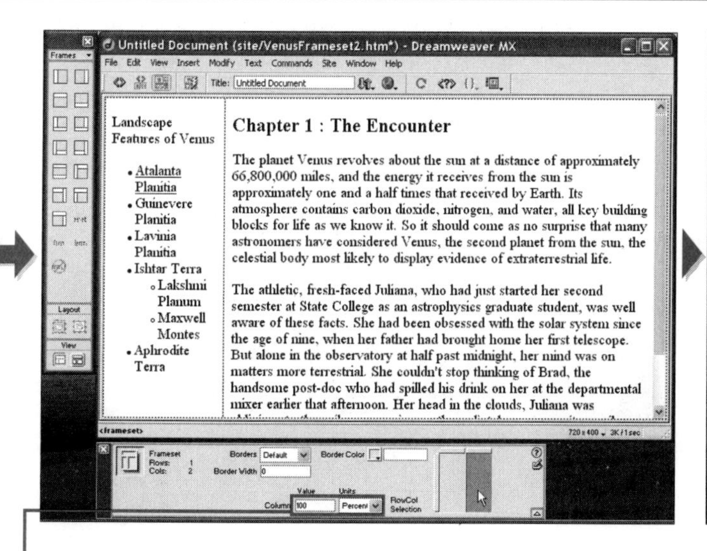

■ In this example, the right frame has been defined as a percentage width. The right frame takes up the remaining space in the browser window.

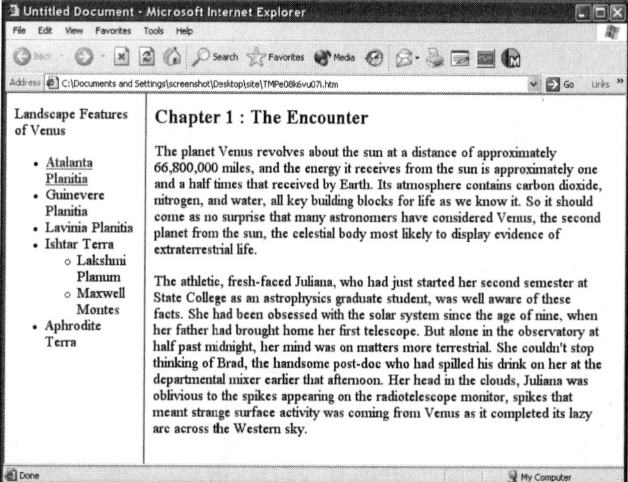

8 Preview the page in a Web browser.

Note: To preview a page in a Web browser, see page 58.

■ The frameset displays as it was defined in Dreamweaver.

FORMAT FRAME BORDERS

You can modify the appearance of your frame borders to make them complement the style of your Web-site content. Using the Properties inspector, you can specify whether borders are turned on or off, as well as the color and width of the borders.

Turning borders off can disguise the fact that you are using frames in the first place. If you want to further disguise your frames, you can set the pages inside your frames to the same background color, so that they blend at the edges. The frames then look like one solid page.

You specify the color of borders just like you do the color of Web page text or the page background by selecting from a pop-up color palette or by specifying the color name or hex code. Remember that in addition to complementing the current content in the frames, the border should also match the hyperlinked pages that open in your frames.

If the frame characteristics for your site are left unspecified, most browsers display frames as turned on, gray in color, and with a width of two pixels.

FORMAT FRAME BORDERS

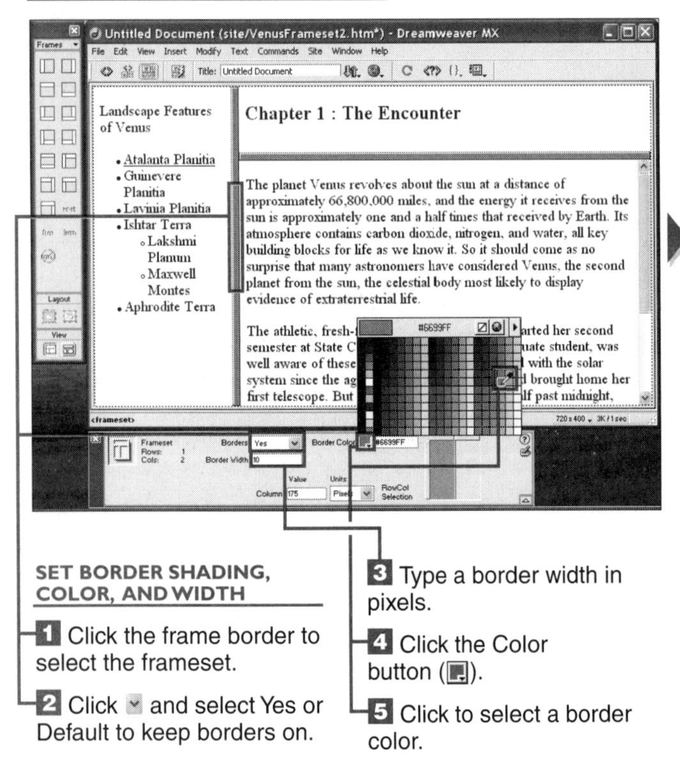

SET BORDER SHADING, COLOR, AND WIDTH

1 Click the frame border to select the frameset.

2 Click ▾ and select Yes or Default to keep borders on.

3 Type a border width in pixels.

4 Click the Color button (▣).

5 Click to select a border color.

■ The frame border displays at the specified settings.

■ You can override settings at the frameset level by pressing Alt-click (Shift-option-click) to select a frame and then specifying formatting in the Properties inspector.

What happens if I set my frames and frameset to different border colors?

✔ In most browsers, border color set at the frame level overrides border color at the frameset level. But to make sure your borders appear the way you expect them to, you should make your border-color settings consistent.

Can I change the spacing between my frame borders and the frame content?

✔ Yes. Select a frame by pressing Alt-click (Shift-option-click), or by clicking in the Frames panel. Specify the spacing using the Margin Width for left and right margins, and Margin Height for top and bottom margins settings.

Is there an easy way to change the background color of a framed page?

✔ You can right-click (Control-click) inside the frame and select Page Properties from the menu that appears. You can define the page background inside the dialog box.

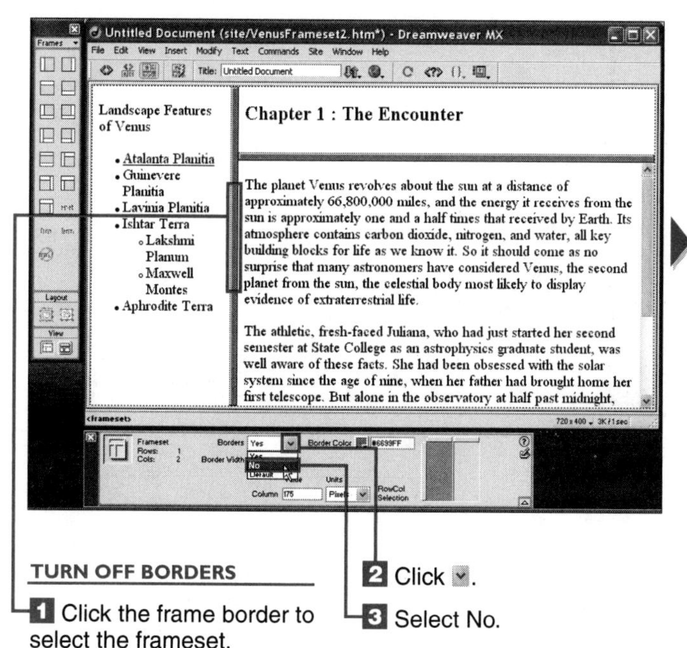

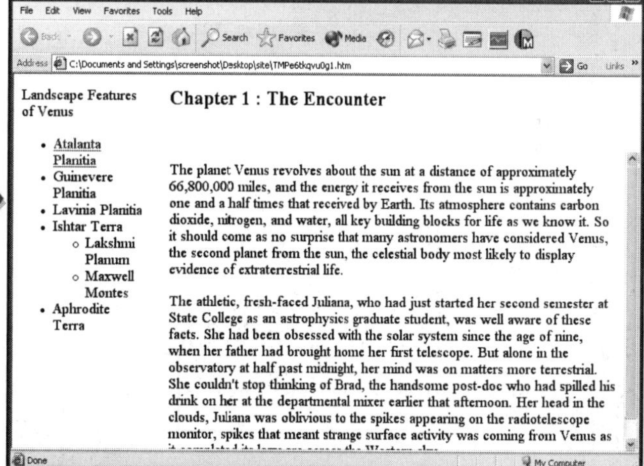

TURN OFF BORDERS

1 Click the frame border to select the frameset.

2 Click ▾.

3 Select No.

4 Preview the page in a Web browser.

Note: To preview a page in a Web browser, see page 58.

■ The frame border does not display.

CONTROL SCROLL BARS IN FRAMES

Because frames can have dimensions that are smaller than the content they contain, controlling whether scroll bars are on or off in your frames is an important design consideration. A browser normally adds scroll bars to frames when the frame content extends outside the borders. A horizontal scroll bar on the bottom edge lets a user scroll horizontally, while a scroll bar on the right side lets a user scroll vertically. In Dreamweaver, you can adjust this default behavior so that scroll bars are always on or always off.

You may want to consider turning your scroll bars off if you are trying to disguise the presence of frames in your site, for example, if you have turned off borders. Even when borders are turned off, scroll bars can appear if content extends outside the frame, unless the scroll bars are explicitly turned off. See page 174 for more information.

CONTROL SCROLL BARS IN FRAMES

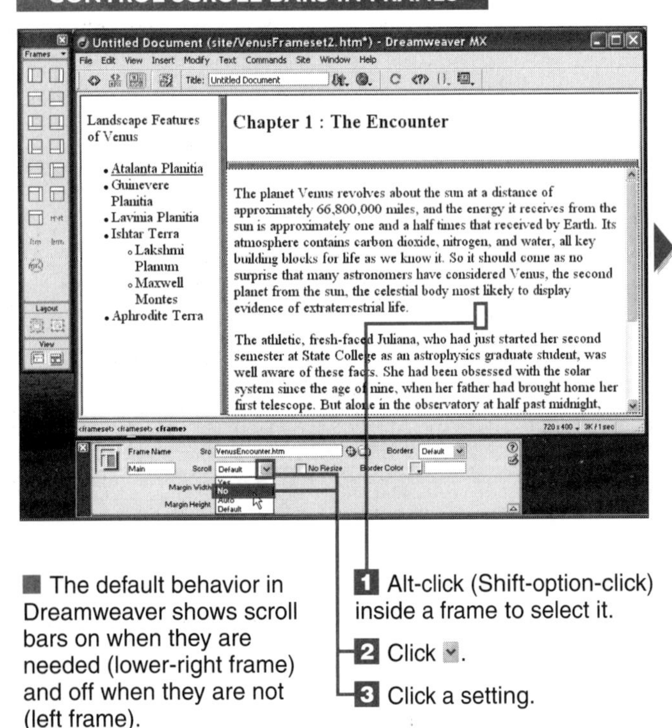

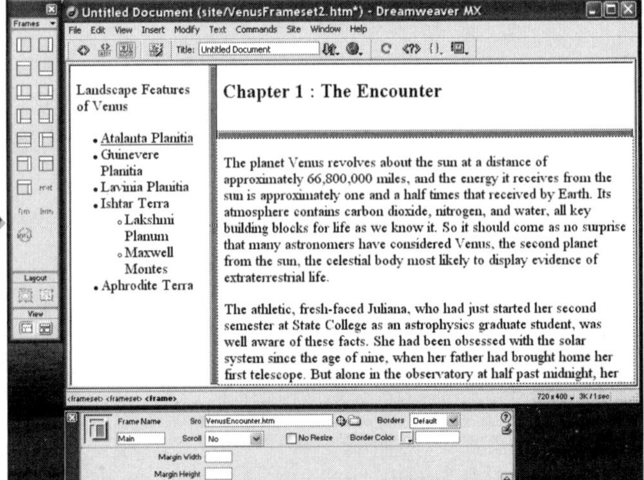

■ The default behavior in Dreamweaver shows scroll bars on when they are needed (lower-right frame) and off when they are not (left frame).

1 Alt-click (Shift-option-click) inside a frame to select it.

2 Click ▾.

3 Click a setting.

■ The frame displays with the new setting.

■ In this example, scroll bars have been turned off in the lower-right frame. The user now has no way to access all of that frame's content.

CONTROL RESIZING IN FRAMES

The default behavior of most browsers lets users resize frames by clicking and dragging the frame borders. The shape of the cursor changes when placed over a border, indicating that the frame can be resized. In Dreamweaver, you can adjust this default behavior so that users cannot resize frames and thereby change the design of the frameset.

Note that you can always change the dimensions of frames in Dreamweaver by clicking and dragging borders in the Document window. The resize setting affects the behavior only when the page is opened in a browser. For more about changing frame dimensions, see page 172.

You may want to turn resizing off if your page layout depends on the size of your frames. This can keep users from changing the dimensions of your frames and causing the content to become disorganized.

Note that, unless resizing has been disabled, a user can still resize borders even if borders have been turned off. In such a case, a user just needs to click and drag where the two frame edges meet.

CONTROL RESIZING IN FRAMES

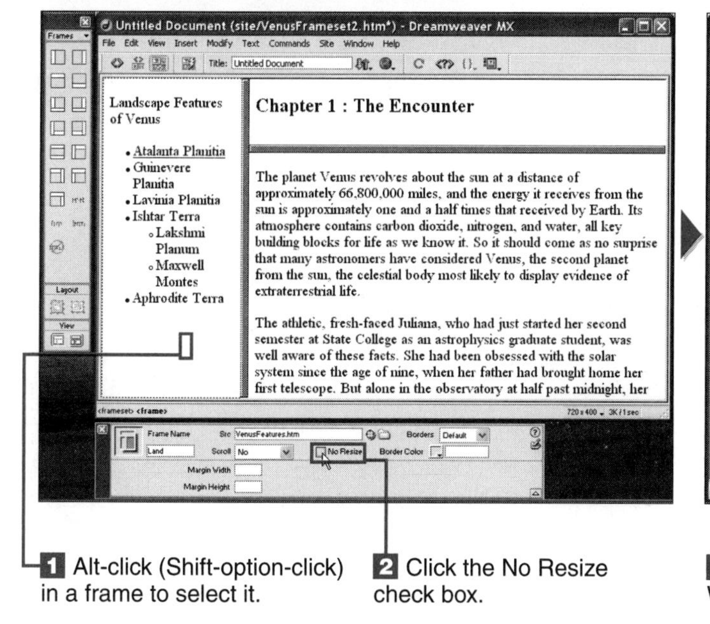

1 Alt-click (Shift-option-click) in a frame to select it.

2 Click the No Resize check box.

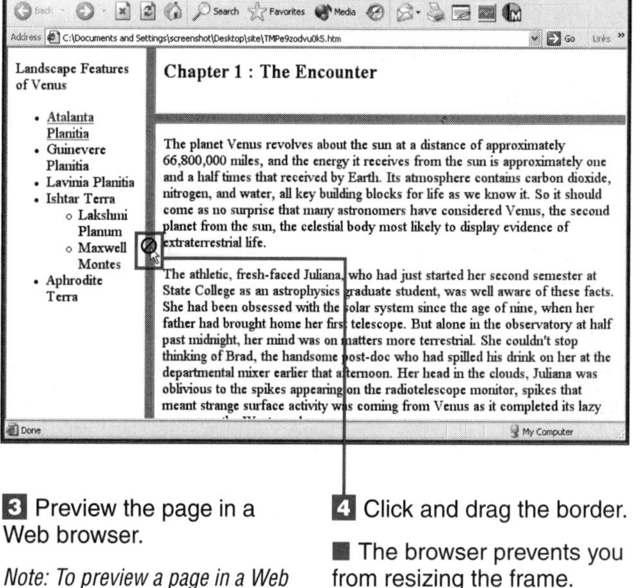

3 Preview the page in a Web browser.

Note: To preview a page in a Web browser, see page 58.

4 Click and drag the border.

■ The browser prevents you from resizing the frame.

SECTION III

11) USING SNIPPETS, LIBRARY ITEMS, AND TEMPLATES

12) IMPLEMENTING STYLE SHEETS AND LAYERS

ENHANCING YOUR WEB SITE

13) IMPLEMENTING BEHAVIORS

14) IMPLEMENTING TIMELINES

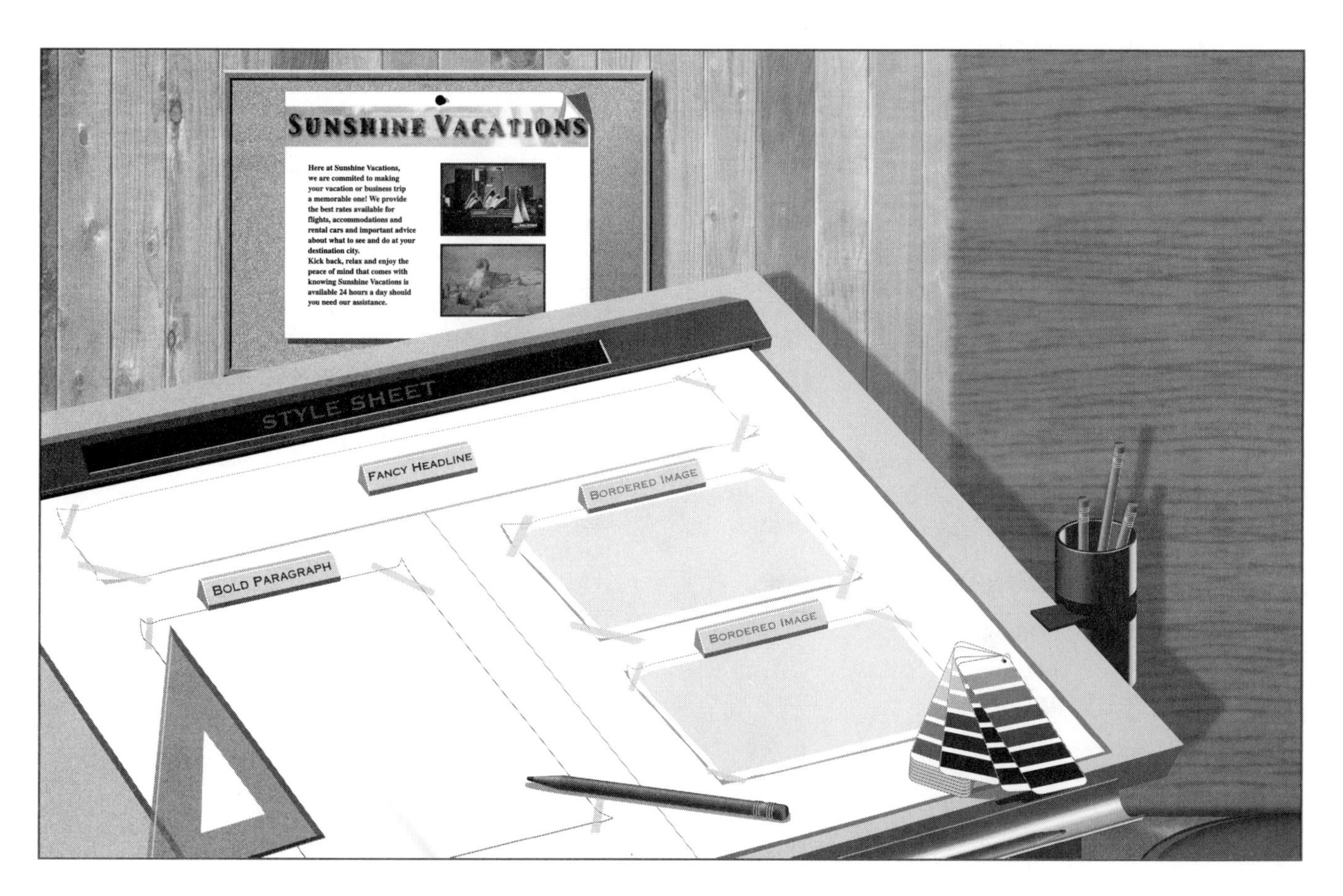

INTRODUCTION TO SNIPPETS, LIBRARY ITEMS, AND TEMPLATES

Many of the pages that you build for your Web site include layouts, content, and code that repeat on some or all of your site pages. Repeated elements are often found in headers, footers, and navigation areas of pages. Dreamweaver has several powerful features that allow you to create such repeating elements once and then insert or apply them as needed across your site. Snippets and library items allow you to create blocks of reusable code and content, while templates let you create layouts that you can use for pages that have similar designs.

Snippets

Snippets let you store pieces of frequently used design elements and code in a central place — the Snippets panel. You can add snippets to the panel for reuse later as you build your pages, which lets you avoid repetitive work when developing your site. Snippets can be shared among all the different sites that you develop in Dreamweaver. Dreamweaver comes with a variety of snippets predefined.

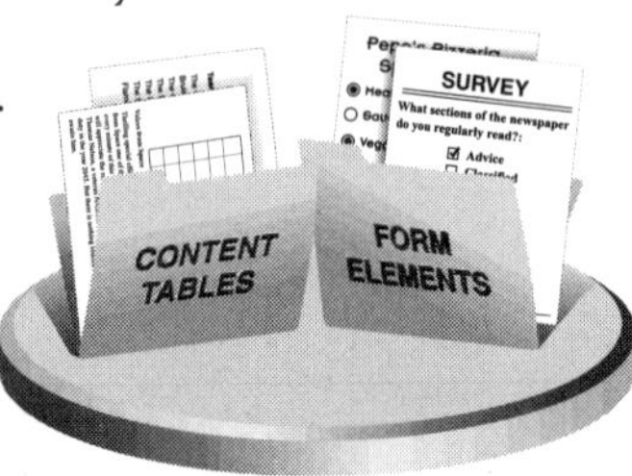

Library Items

You can define parts of your Web pages that are repeated in a particular site as *library items,* so you do not have to create them from scratch over and over. Each time you need a library item, you can just insert it from your library. If you ever make changes to a library item, Dreamweaver automatically updates all the instances of the item across your Web site. Good candidates for library items include advertising banners, company slogans, and any other features that appear many times across a site.

Templates

You can define commonly used Web page layouts as *templates* to save time as you build your pages. Templates can also help you maintain a consistent page design across a site. After you make changes to a template, Dreamweaver automatically updates all your site's pages that are based on that template. If you use just a few page layouts across all the pages in your site, you should consider defining those layouts as templates.

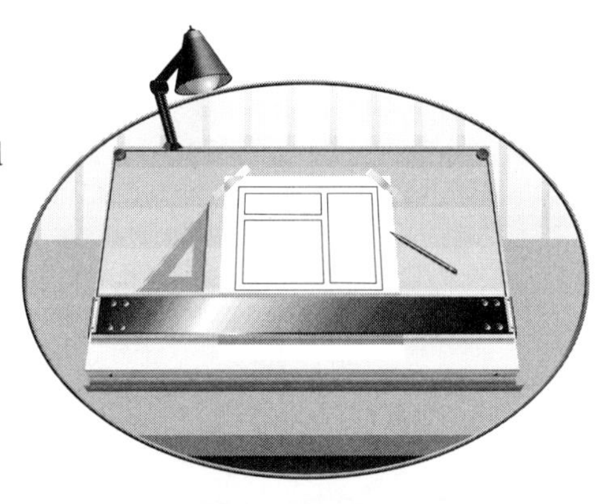

INSERT A SNIPPET

Snippets are convenient pieces of Web page code that can be reused across different pages in a site, or across different sites. Dreamweaver stores these pieces of code in a Snippets panel for easy lookup and insertion into your Web pages. You can add snippets to your pages when you are in Design View or in Code View.

The Snippets panel includes folders and subfolders to categorize your snippets. Some of the predefined folders for content-related snippets include Content Tables, which contains prebuilt HTML tables for organizing rows and columns of text and images, and Form Elements, which contains HTML code for commonly used buttons, date-related drop-down menus, and other form features.

There are also folders with useful snippets for adding sets of links to your pages. The Footers folder features horizontal arrangements of text and links for the bottom of pages. The Headers folder contains horizontal arrangements of text, placeholder images, and links for the top of pages. The Navigation folder features prebuilt sets of navigation links in horizontal, vertical, tabbed, and other arrangements.

Each snippet is stored as a separate file with a .csn extension in the Snippets folder. To add a new snippet to the Snippets panel, see page 182.

INSERT A SNIPPET

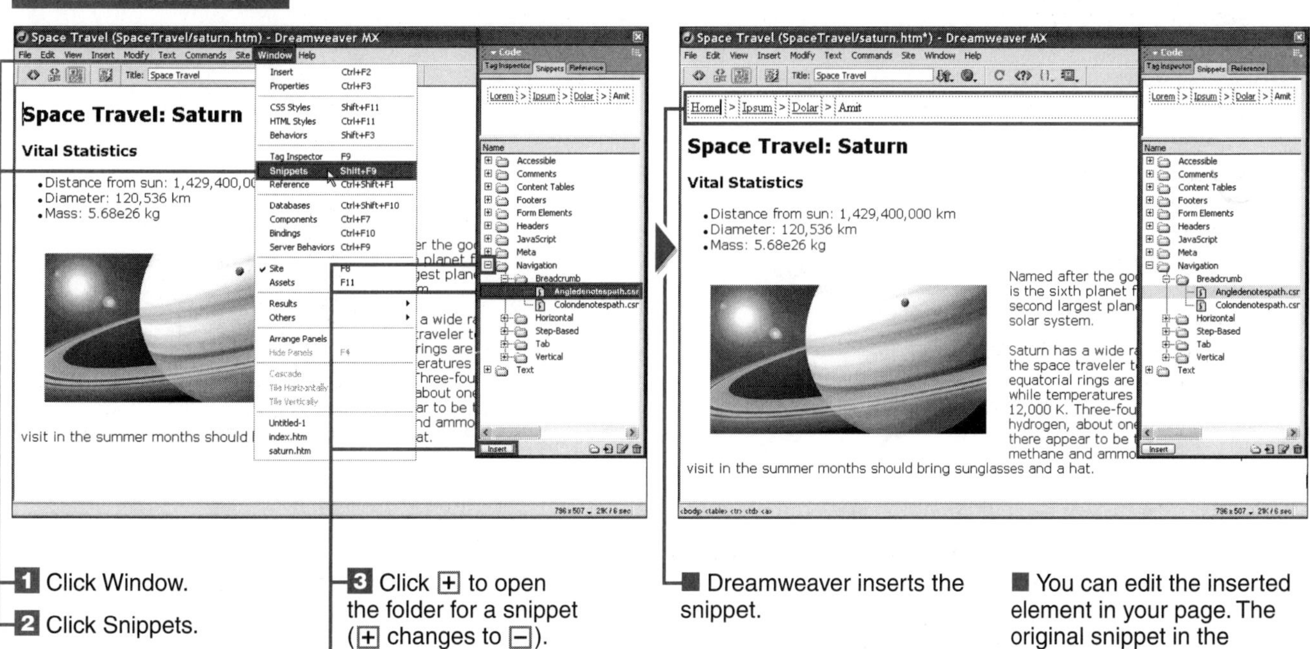

1. Click Window.
2. Click Snippets.

■ The Snippets panel opens.

3. Click ⊞ to open the folder for a snippet (⊞ changes to ⊟).
4. Click a snippet.
5. Click Insert.

■ Dreamweaver inserts the snippet.

■ You can edit the inserted element in your page. The original snippet in the Snippets panel remains unchanged.

SAVE A NEW SNIPPET

If you have a piece of design content or code that you expect to use again on your Web pages, you can save it in the Snippets panel. This can save you time when creating your site. The Snippets panel offers a central place to store and organize reusable elements, including table layouts, form inputs, header designs, and footer designs.

Snippets are not restricted to HTML; they can comprise any type of code that exists in a Web page, including JavaScript, Cascading Style Sheet rules, and Web application code such as ColdFusion Markup Language. You can save an element as a snippet when you are working in Design View or Code View.

You can save two types of snippets: those that wrap a selection and those that are inserted as a single block. A *Wrap Selection snippet* includes a piece that is inserted before the current selection in the Document window and a piece that is inserted after. You define the two pieces in the Snippet dialog box. An *Insert Block snippet* is inserted as a single piece of code and cannot be applied to a selection.

SAVE A NEW SNIPPET

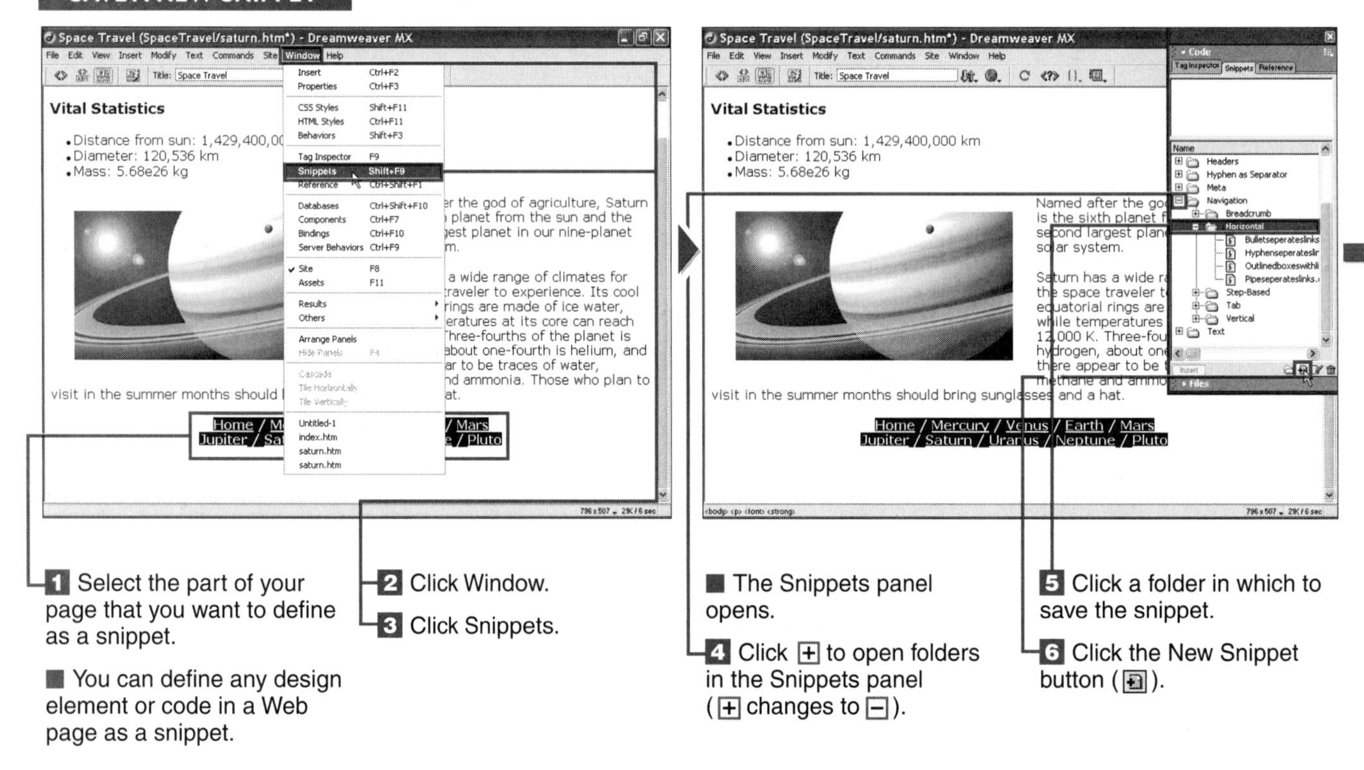

1 Select the part of your page that you want to define as a snippet.

■ You can define any design element or code in a Web page as a snippet.

2 Click Window.

3 Click Snippets.

■ The Snippets panel opens.

4 Click ⊞ to open folders in the Snippets panel (⊞ changes to ⊟).

5 Click a folder in which to save the snippet.

6 Click the New Snippet button ( ).

How are snippets different from library items?

✔ Snippets differ from library items in that they are not specific to a particular Dreamweaver site. You can use the same snippets across all the sites you develop in Dreamweaver. Snippets also do not remain connected to the places where they have been inserted like library items do. Editing a snippet from the Snippets panel has no effect on the places where you have used the snippet previously. See the other sections in this chapter for more about library items.

When should I save a reusable element as a snippet, and when should I save it as a library item?

✔ If your reusable element needs to remain identical across many instances in a particular site, and you think you will need to update the element in the future, you should probably save it as a library item. If you want to use the element across different Dreamweaver sites, and the element needs to vary depending on where you insert it, you should probably save it as a snippet. Remember, you can always save something as a snippet and also define is as a library item for a particular site. This lets you reap the rewards of both features.

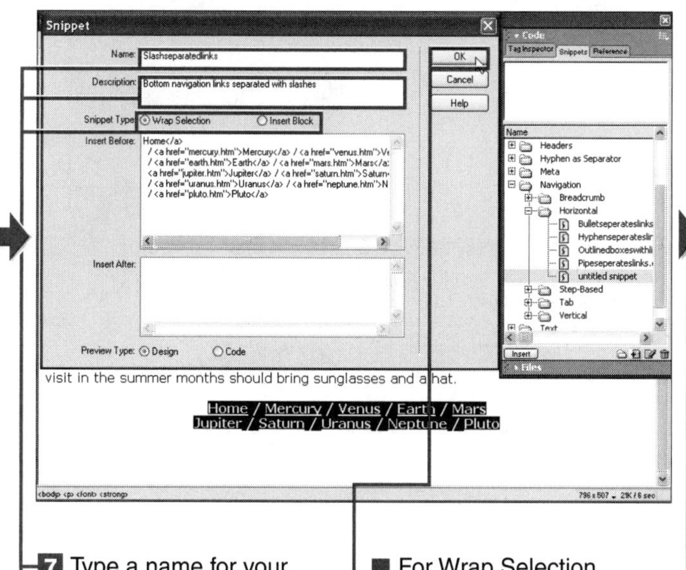

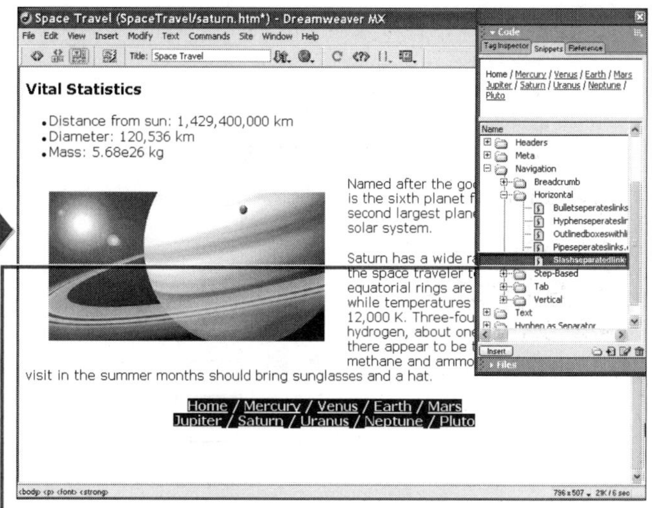

7 Type a name for your snippet.

8 Type a description.

9 Click to select a snippet type (○ changes to a ◉).

■ For Wrap Selection snippets, define the code that should go before and after a selected element.

10 Click OK.

■ Dreamweaver saves the snippet in the Snippets panel.

Note: To insert the snippet, see page 181.

CREATE A LIBRARY ITEM

You can define text, images, and other Dreamweaver objects that you want to appear frequently in your Web site as library items, which are blocks of reusable content. Library items enable you to quickly insert such page elements without having to re-create them from scratch every time. It can be convenient to define headers, footers, and navigation links as library items.

If you ever need to edit your library items, you can change the copies after they are in your site library and have Dreamweaver automatically update the instances of each item across your site. This can save you a lot of time, especially if you maintain a large site that has hundreds of pages.

When you create a library item, Dreamweaver saves the item as a separate file with an .lbi extension. These files are stored in a Library folder inside your local folder. See page 48 for information on setting up a local folder. You can view the library items for a site in the Assets panel. Because library items are specific to a local folder, you cannot use them across different Dreamweaver sites.

CREATE A LIBRARY ITEM

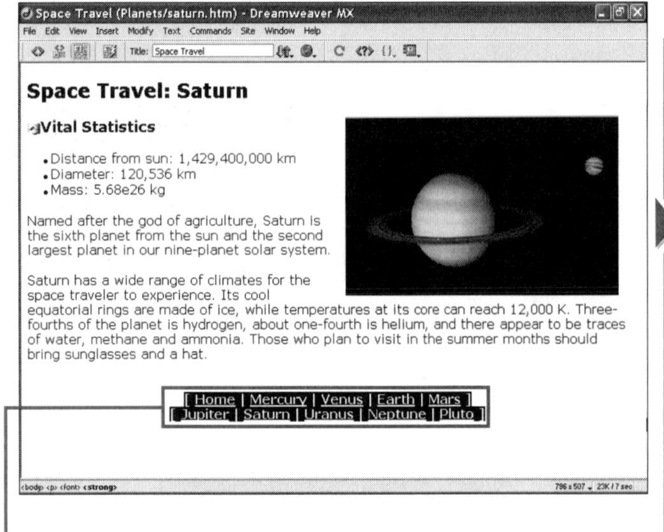

1 Select the part of your page that you want to define as a library item.

■ Library items can be created from any elements that appear in the body of an HTML document, including text, images, tables, forms, layers, and multimedia.

Note: To create library items for your Web pages, you must already have defined a local site. To set up a local folder, see page 48.

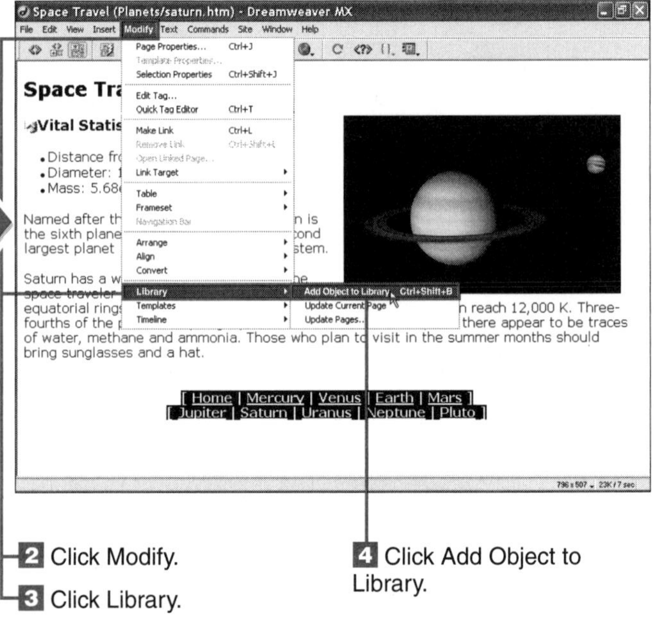

2 Click Modify.

3 Click Library.

4 Click Add Object to Library.

How do I delete a library item?

✔ The correct way to delete a library item is to select the item in the Assets panel and click 🗑. If you delete a library file directly from the Library folder, Dreamweaver does not have the opportunity to properly detach the file from the site, and the file still shows up in the Assets panel, although you can no longer use it. Note that deleting an item from the library does not delete instances of the item that you have already inserted into your pages.

How do I delete an instance of a library item on a page?

✔ Simply click the library item to select it and press Delete.

How can I re-create a library item after I delete it?

✔ If you delete a library item from the Assets panel and later want to use it again, you can select an instance of the old item somewhere in the Document window and click the Re-create button in the Properties inspector. The item is again available in the Assets panel.

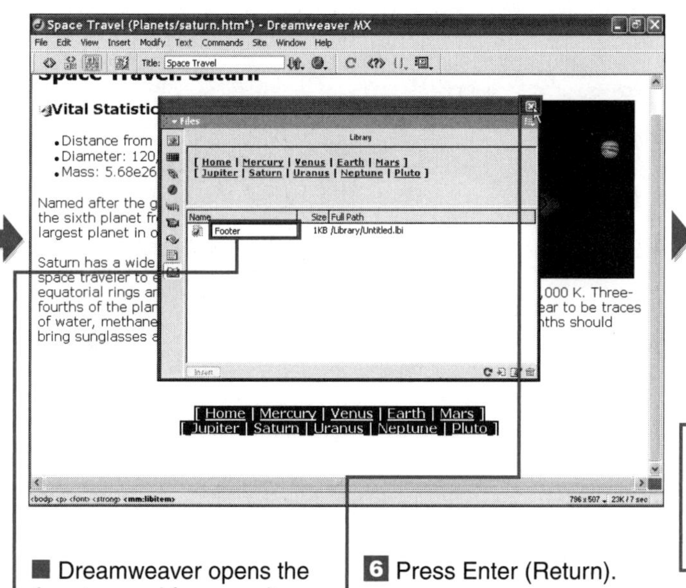

■ Dreamweaver opens the Assets panel for your site and creates a new, untitled library item.

5 Type a name for the library item.

6 Press Enter (Return).

7 Click the Close button ☒ to close the Library window.

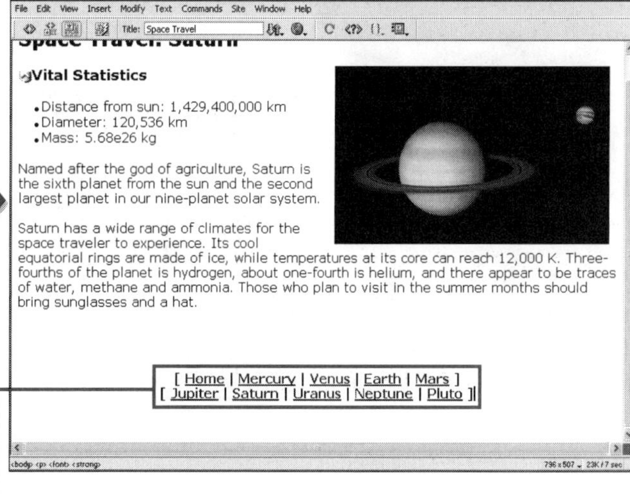

■ The new library item is highlighted in yellow.

Note: To change the highlight color for library items in Preferences, see page 32.

■ Defining an element as a library item prevents you from editing it in the Document window.

Note: To edit library items, see page 188.

INSERT A LIBRARY ITEM

Inserting an element onto your page from the library not only saves you from having to create it from scratch, but also ensures that its design is identical to other instances of that library item in your site. When you are ready to update the item later, you can edit the original in the site Library and have Dreamweaver automatically update all the instances on your pages.

When you insert a library item onto a page, Dreamweaver inserts the item's HTML along with some extra HTML comment information. You can identify HTML comments by their surrounding <!-- and --> characters. The comments identify the information as a library item and let Dreamweaver perform automatic updating in the future. If you remove this comment information, the library item may not work correctly.

Instances of library items are highlighted in yellow in the Document window. You can change the highlighting color in the Preferences dialog box. After you insert a library item into the page, you cannot edit it unless you detach it from the library. See page 190 for more information on editing detached library items.

INSERT A LIBRARY ITEM

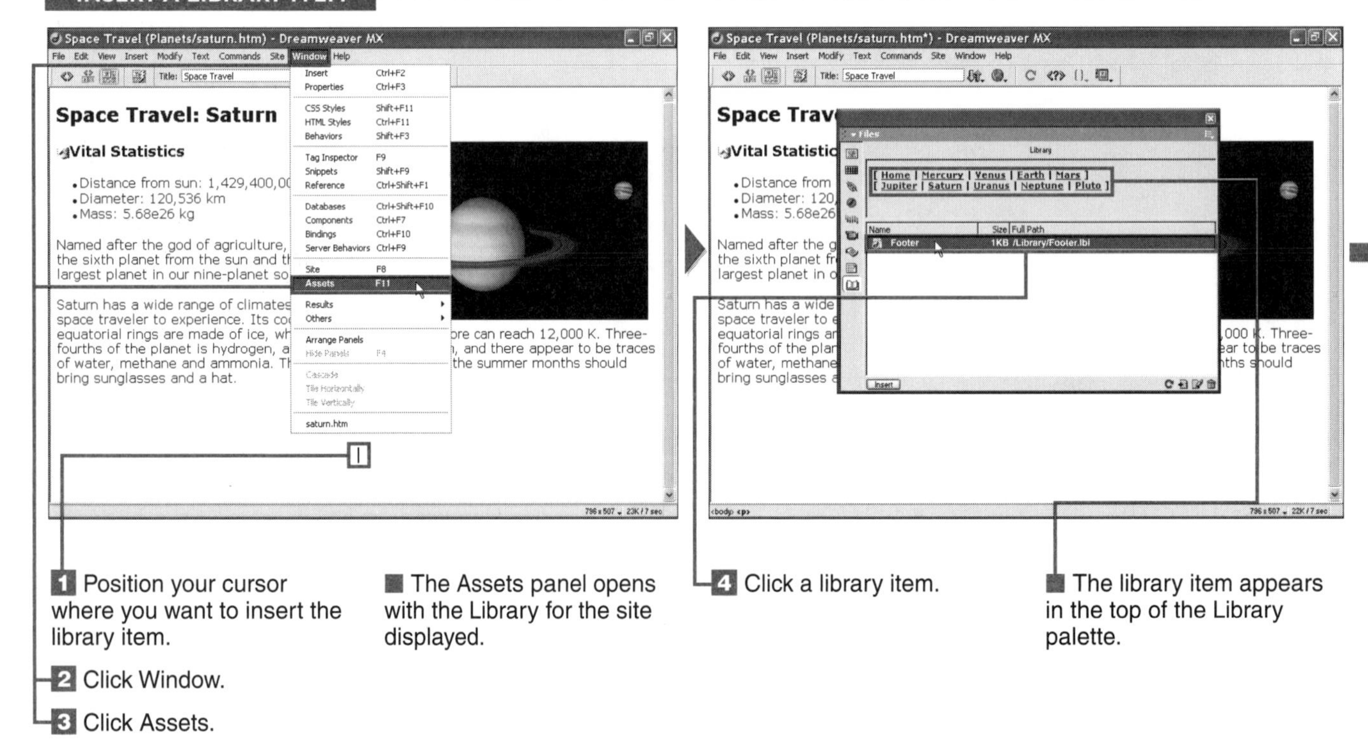

1 Position your cursor where you want to insert the library item.

2 Click Window.

3 Click Assets.

■ The Assets panel opens with the Library for the site displayed.

4 Click a library item.

■ The library item appears in the top of the Library palette.

What kind of content cannot be defined as a library item?

✔ Most content that is defined in the head area of a page's HTML cannot be defined as a library item. This includes style-sheet rules and timelines. You *can* define elements that have behaviors attached to them as library items, even though some of the code for behaviors is stored in the head of a document. When you insert an item that includes a behavior into a page, Dreamweaver adds the necessary JavaScript code into the head to permit the behavior to work.

How can I quickly find the instances of a particular library item in my site?

✔ You can perform a search on the filename of the library item by clicking Edit and then Find and Replace. Library item filenames have an .lbi extension, for example, myitem.lbi. Make sure you search through the Entire Current Local Site and in each file's Source Code. For more information on searching for text, see page 276.

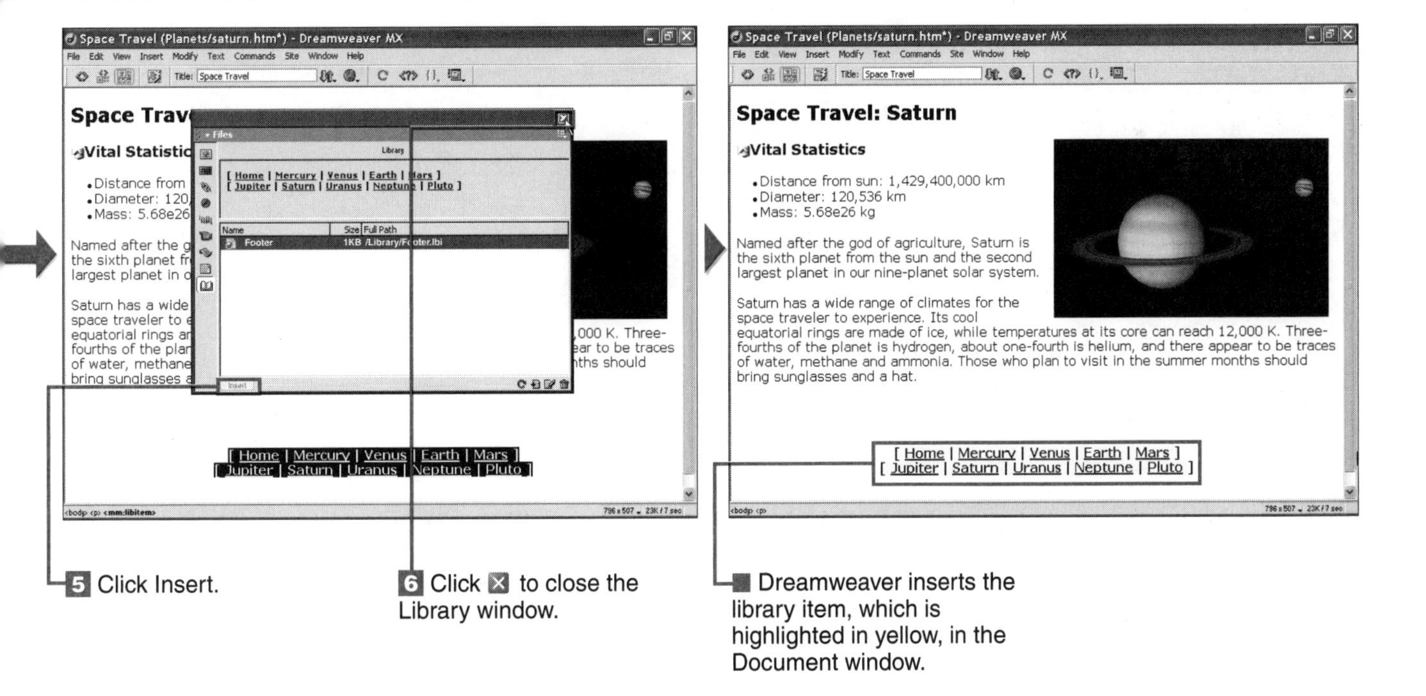

5 Click Insert.

6 Click ☒ to close the Library window.

■ Dreamweaver inserts the library item, which is highlighted in yellow, in the Document window.

EDIT A LIBRARY ITEM AND UPDATE YOUR WEB SITE

If you have a large site, library items can take some of the effort out of maintaining it by streamlining the process of updating elements that appear on multiple pages. When you need to make a sitewide change to a repeating item, you can modify the library item for that element instead of modifying by hand the hundreds of pages that make up your site.

Whenever you modify a library item, Dreamweaver gives you the opportunity to immediately update the site wherever the item appears. You can also make updates to library items manually, using commands under the Library submenu located under the Modify menu. The Update Pages command brings up a dialog box that enables you to select which library items should get updated and on which pages.

The different instances of library items in your site pages reference the original item in a site's Library, which means you cannot edit the instances — only the original. You can detach an instance from the Library, which makes it editable. See page 190 for details.

EDIT A LIBRARY ITEM AND UPDATE YOUR WEB SITE

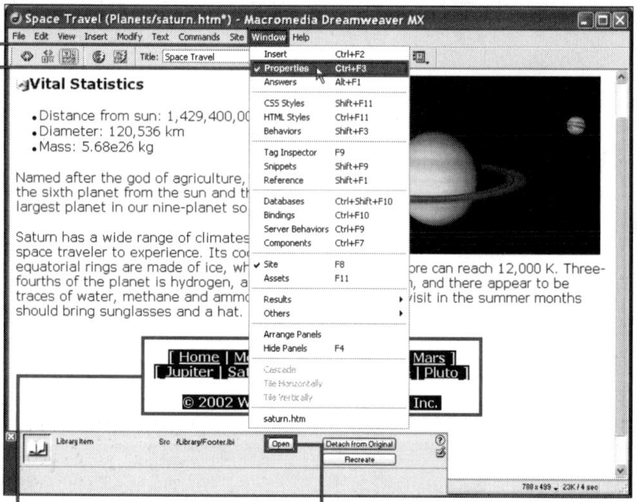

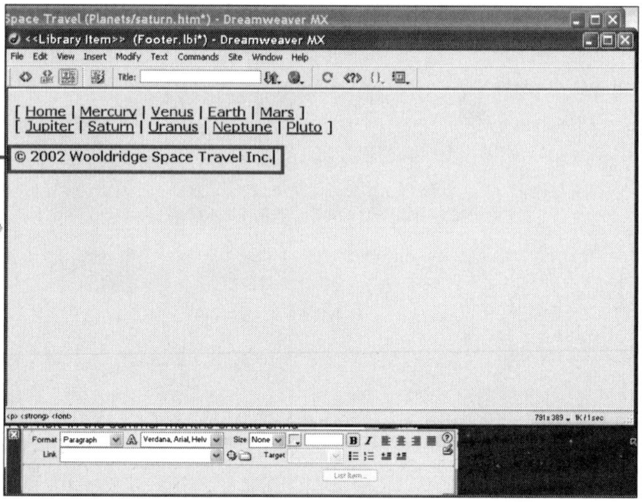

1 Click a library item.

2 Click Window.

3 Click Properties.

■ The Properties inspector opens.

4 Click Open.

■ The library item opens in a new window.

5 Edit the library item.

6 Save the file.

How do I keep particular instances of library items from being changed during the update process?

✔ If you no longer want a particular library item to be changed with all the others on your site, you can detach it from the library. This is useful if you want the old content to remain on a certain page for archival purposes. See page 190. If you want to just keep the item unchanged temporarily and still be able to update it later, you can perform updates for a library item one page at a time. Use the Update Current Page command under the Library submenu under the Modify menu.

What can cause a library item in the site to fail to update?

✔ If somehow the HTML comment code that surrounds and identifies a library item becomes corrupted, Dreamweaver may not be able to correctly update it. For this reason, you may not want to edit library items in Code View if you are unfamiliar with HTML.

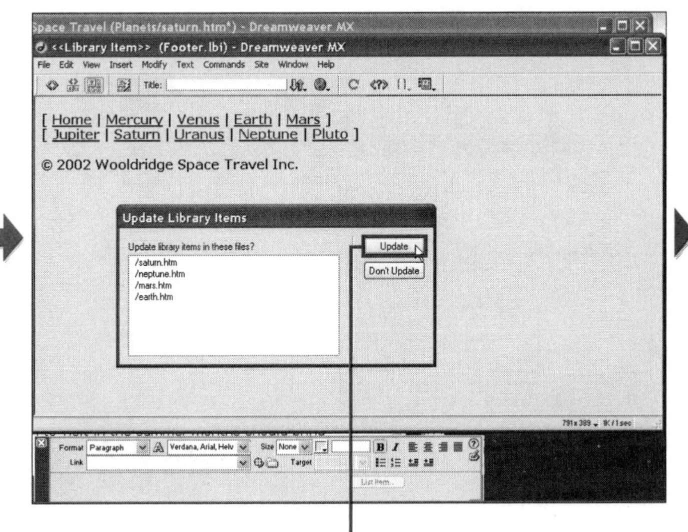

■ An alert box asks if you want to update all the instances of the library item in the site.

7 Click Update.

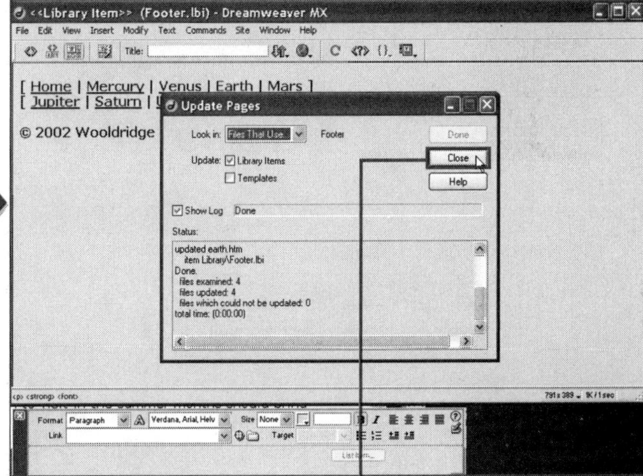

■ A dialog box shows the progress of the updates.

8 After Dreamweaver is finished updating the site, click Close.

DETACH LIBRARY CONTENT FOR EDITING

If you want to edit an instance of a library item in a page, you can detach it from the library. This means the item is no longer associated with the original library item, and it is not updated when that original item is edited. This can be useful if you need one of the pages in your site to deviate from the other pages in some way.

When you detach an instance of a library item, Dreamweaver removes the HTML comment information that defines it as such in the page. With that code gone, the yellow highlighting that denotes an element as a library item in the Document window disappears and you can change the item.

This command is useful if you need to make updates to site elements that diverge from the normal design. For example, if you are adding a holiday theme to your page, and you want the normal header library item on several pages to have extra decorative graphics, you could detach the header on these pages from the library. When the season is over, you can reinsert the normal header library item.

DETACH LIBRARY CONTENT FOR EDITING

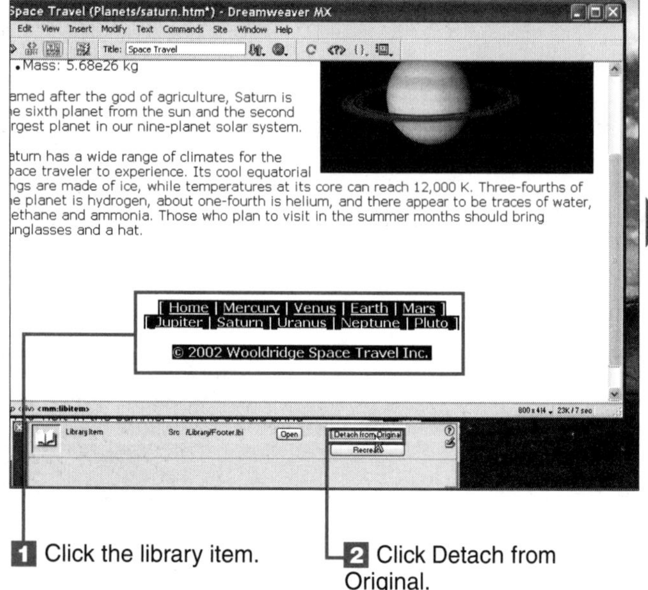

1 Click the library item.

2 Click Detach from Original.

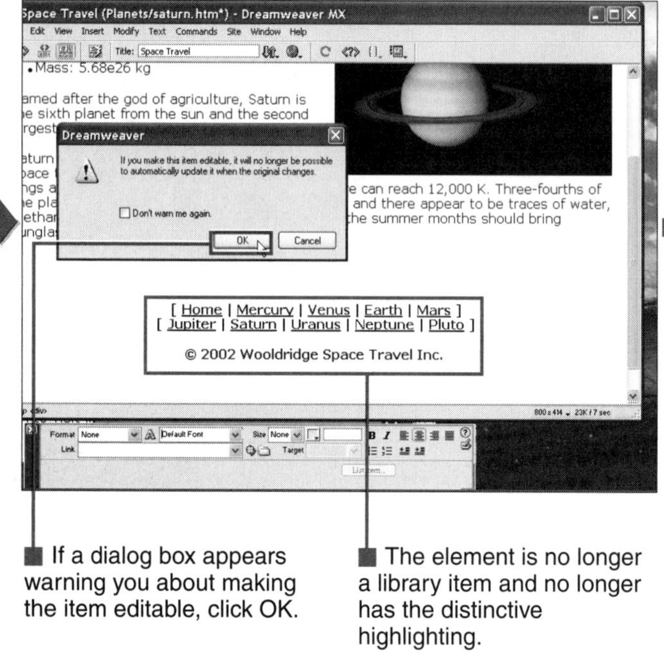

■ If a dialog box appears warning you about making the item editable, click OK.

■ The element is no longer a library item and no longer has the distinctive highlighting.

How do I revert a detached library item back to its undetached state?

✔ While no specific command for doing this exists, you can use the Undo command, located under the Edit menu, if you detached the item with your previous command. Or you can backtrack over several previous commands using the History panel. See Chapter 2 for more information about the History panel.

Why would I want to use the Detach from Original command on a regular basis?

✔ You may want to use this command a lot if you use library items as templates for specific design elements on your pages. For example, if you need numerous captioned images in your Web site, you can create a library item that has a two-cell table with a generic image and caption. To place an image and caption, you insert the library item and then detach the item from the library to make it editable. You can then replace the generic image and caption with appropriate content.

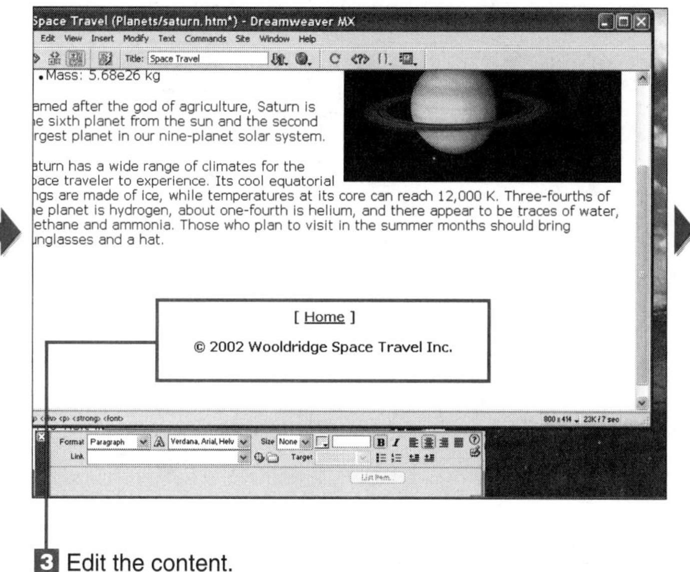

3 Edit the content.

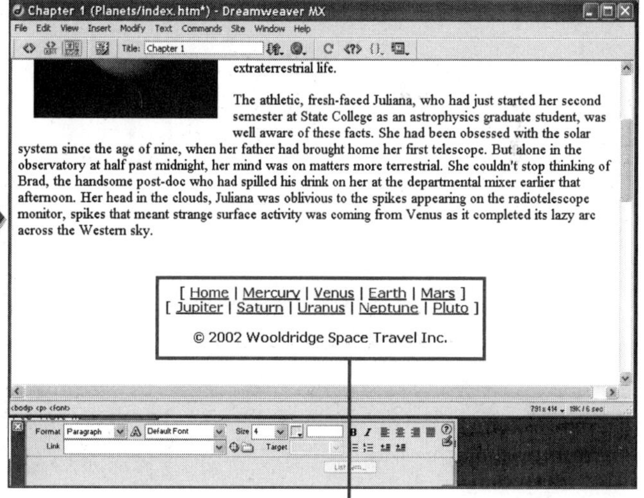

4 Open another page that has the library item.

Note: To open a page, see page 50.

■ Editing the detached library item has no effect on other undetached library items.

CREATE A TEMPLATE

If the pages of your Web site share common design elements — such as navigation links, headers, and footers — you can save time and ensure consistency on the pages by using templates when building them. After you build a template, you can use it as a starting point for new pages.

To make a Dreamweaver template functional, you must define which areas of the page you want to make editable. See page 194 for more information. The rest of the page stays locked and can only be edited by editing the original template.

Similar to library items, when you later make changes to your original template, Dreamweaver can automatically update all the pages in your site that are based on the template. See page 198.

When you create and save a template, Dreamweaver stores the file in a Templates folder inside your local site folder. Templates have a .dwt extension. See Chapter 4 for information about setting up a local site.

CREATE A TEMPLATE

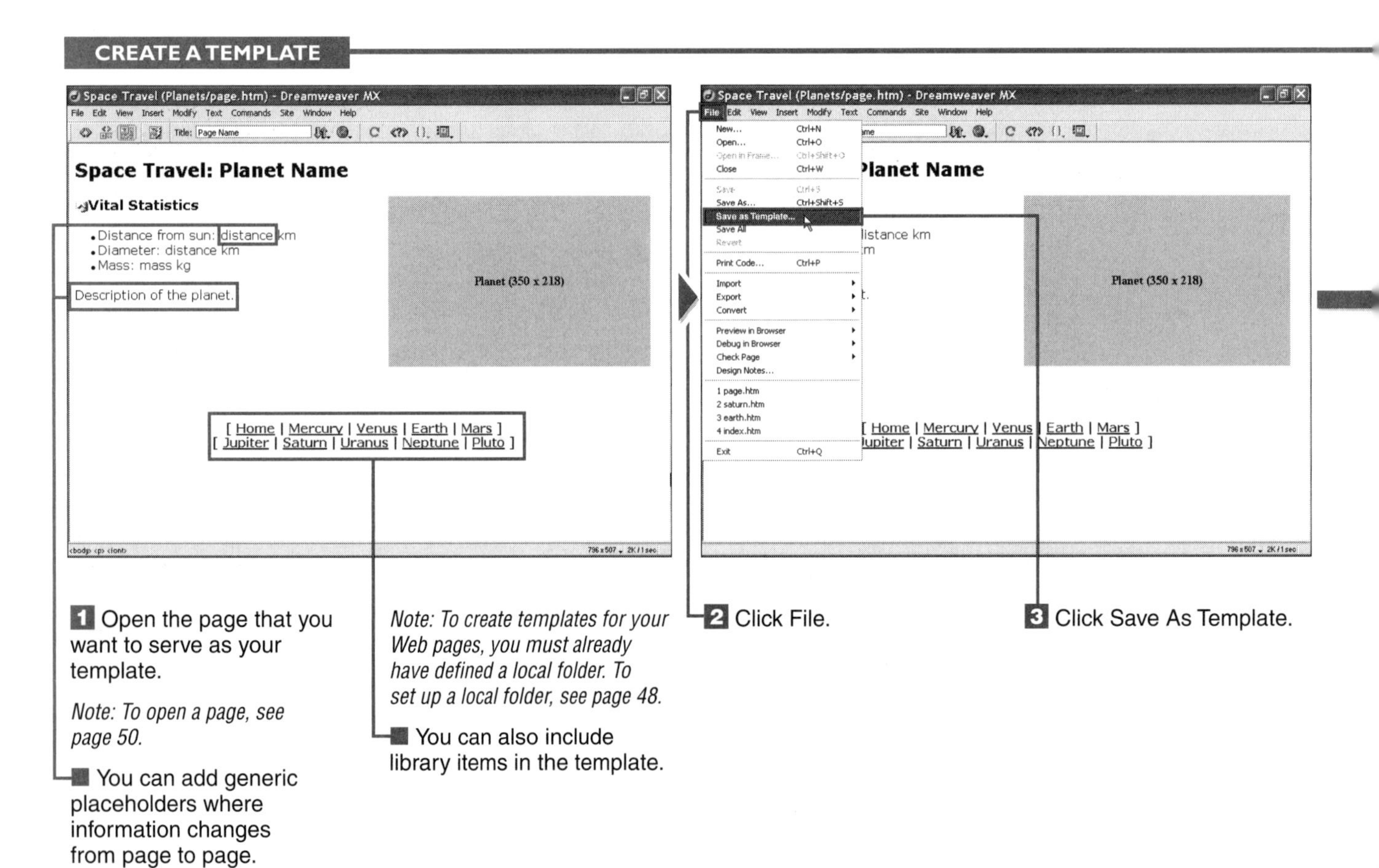

1 Open the page that you want to serve as your template.

Note: To open a page, see page 50.

■ You can add generic placeholders where information changes from page to page.

Note: To create templates for your Web pages, you must already have defined a local folder. To set up a local folder, see page 48.

■ You can also include library items in the template.

2 Click File.

3 Click Save As Template.

How do I delete a template?

✔ The correct way to delete a template is to select it in the Assets panel and click 🗑. If you delete a template file directly from the Library folder, Dreamweaver does not have the opportunity to properly detach the file from the site. The file still shows up in the Assets panel, although you can no longer use it. Note that deleting a template does not delete pages that you have already built using that template.

How can I store notes about a template that other people using the template can access?

✔ You can attach information about a template — such as who created it, when it was created, and tips about using it — with Design Notes, just as you can regular pages. See Chapter 16 for more information on Design Notes.

Can I use placeholder images in templates?

✔ Yes. Placeholder images are useful to use in areas of your template where images will vary from page to page. See page 98 for more on inserting placeholder images.

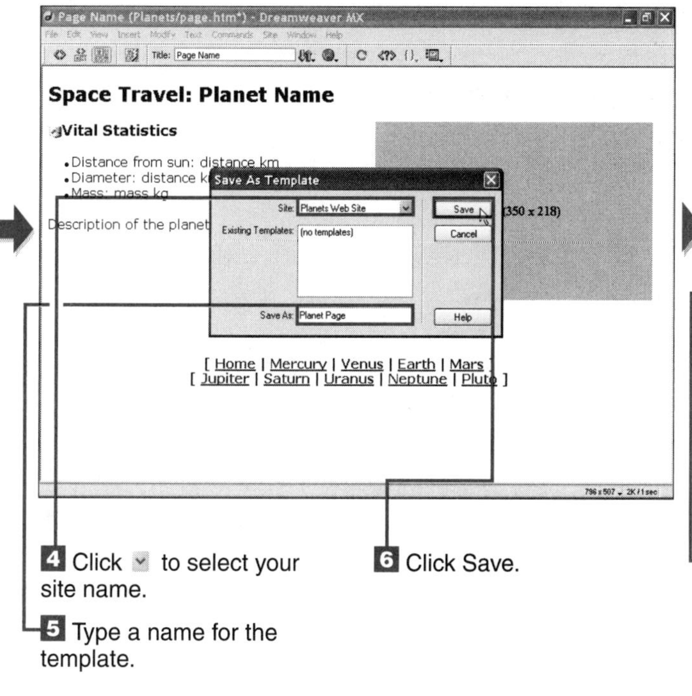

4 Click ⌄ to select your site name.

5 Type a name for the template.

6 Click Save.

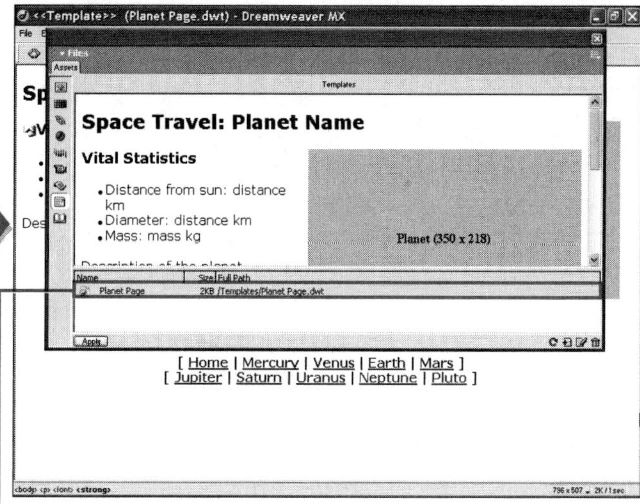

■ Dreamweaver saves the page with a .dwt extension in the Templates folder.

■ You can view your templates in the Assets panel.

Note: For more about the Assets panel, see page 262.

SET A TEMPLATE'S EDITABLE REGIONS

Dreamweaver templates have two types of content: *locked* content, which you can edit only in the original template file, and *editable* content, which you can edit in the original template and in all the files you create based on the template.

After you save a page as a template, you must define which areas of the page are editable. These editable regions appear highlighted in pages that you create using the template. Areas that are not specifically defined as editable remain locked.

You typically define as editable the areas that contain the main content for a page, as well as areas that contain other variable content, such as page headlines and ad banners. Navigation areas, headers, and footers are usually left locked.

You can modify the editable and locked areas of a template further at any time, even after you begin creating pages with the template.

SET A TEMPLATE'S EDITABLE REGIONS

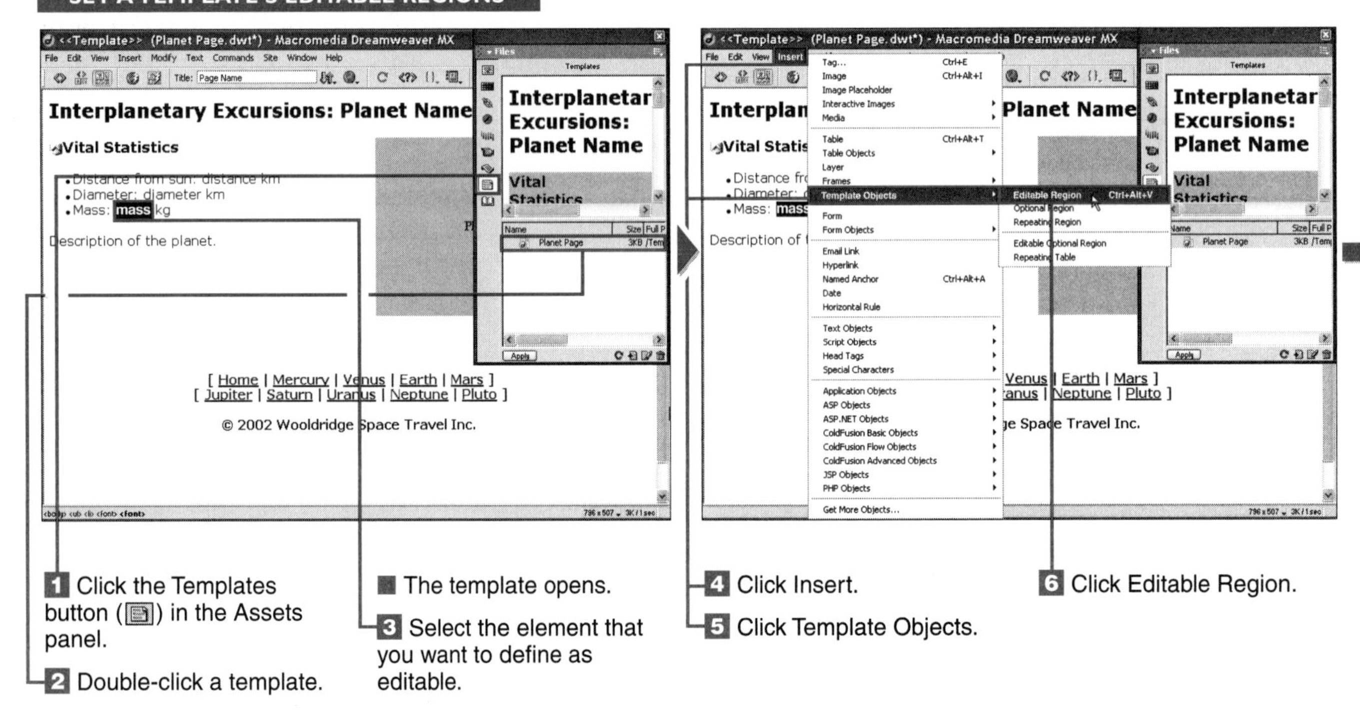

1 Click the Templates button ( ) in the Assets panel.

2 Double-click a template.

■ The template opens.

3 Select the element that you want to define as editable.

4 Click Insert.

5 Click Template Objects.

6 Click Editable Region.

How do I define a table in my page as editable?

✔ You can define an individual cell of a table as an editable area. You can also define an entire table as an editable area. But you can not select several cells of a table and define them as a single editable area — such cells have to be defined as separate editable regions. For more about creating tables, see Chapter 8.

Can I make a layer editable?

✔ Yes, but you have a choice between making the entire layer, including its contents, editable and making just the layer contents editable. If you make just the contents editable, the layer's position in the Document window is locked. If you make the entire layer editable, you can move the layer wherever you want. To make the entire layer editable, click the icon associated with the layer in the Document window. To make just the contents editable, click inside the layer and click Edit, and then Select All.

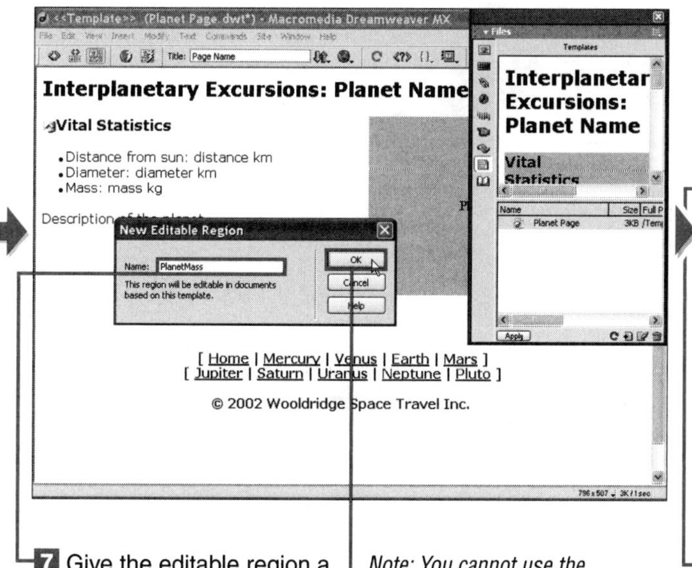

7 Give the editable region a name that distinguishes it from any other editable regions on the page.

Note: You cannot use the characters &, ", ', <, or > in the name.

8 Click OK.

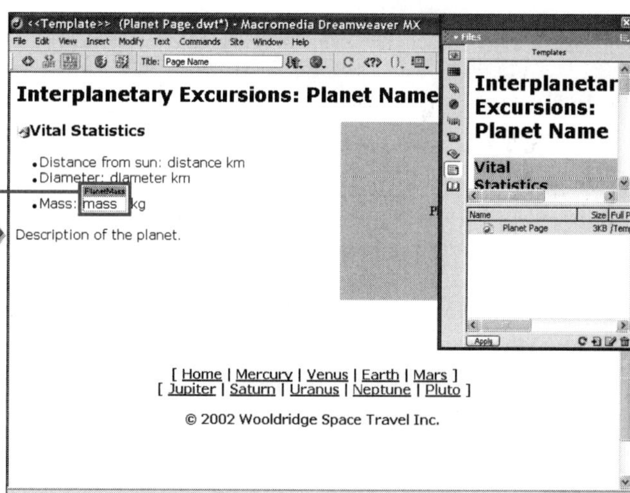

■ The editable region is highlighted on the page. A tab denotes its name.

Note: To change the highlight color in Preferences, see page 32.

9 Repeat steps 3 to 8 for all the regions on the page that you want to make editable in the template.

10 Save the file.

CREATE A PAGE USING A TEMPLATE

Creating a page using a template saves you from having to build from scratch all the generic elements of the page — for example, elements that appear across many pages of your site, such as headers, footers, copyright information, and so on. Using a template also enables you to automatically update the design of the page, as well as other pages based on the template, by editing the original template.

You can create a page from one of the templates that you have already saved for your site with the New from Template command in the File menu. See page 192 for details. You can also open the Assets panel, where you can view a list of all your site's templates and select a template to start with. A third option is to apply a template to an existing Web page by selecting a template from the Assets panel and clicking the Apply button.

When you build a page from a template, you can modify only the areas of the page that you have specifically defined as editable. The editable areas are highlighted in blue.

CREATE A PAGE USING A TEMPLATE

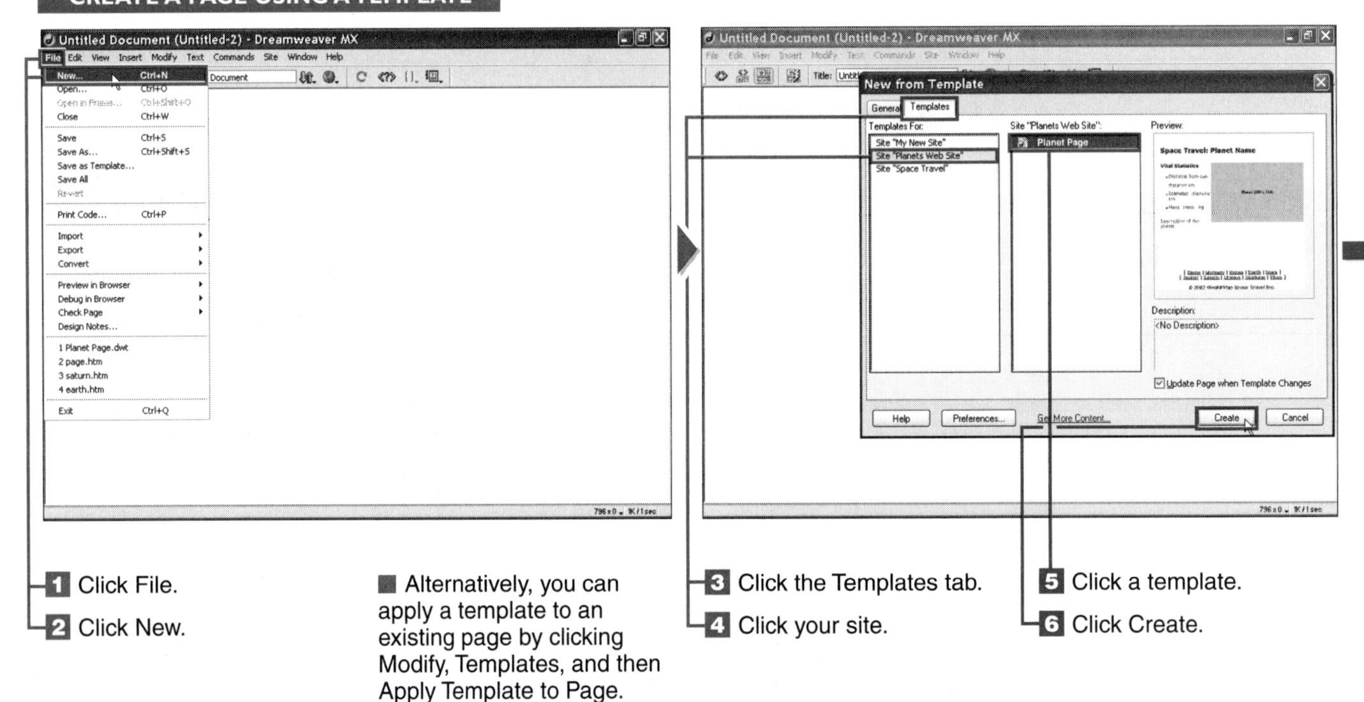

1 Click File.

2 Click New.

■ Alternatively, you can apply a template to an existing page by clicking Modify, Templates, and then Apply Template to Page.

3 Click the Templates tab.

4 Click your site.

5 Click a template.

6 Click Create.

How do I detach a page from a template?

✔ Select the Detach from Template command located under the Templates submenu under the Modify menu. The page becomes a regular document, with its previously locked regions now fully editable. It is no longer updated when the original template is updated.

Can I apply a template to a page that is already based on a different template?

✔ Yes. Open the page and click Modify, Templates, and then Apply Template to Page. Dreamweaver tries to match content in the original document with editable areas that have the same names in the new template. For content that it cannot match, Dreamweaver asks which editable area the content should be placed in.

Are there generic template pages that I can use as a starting point for dynamic Web pages?

✔ Yes. Click File and then New to open the New Document dialog box. Click the Template Page category to view a list of different dynamic page templates. These include templates for ASP, ColdFusion, JSP, and PHP pages. For more information about creating dynamic pages, see Chapter 17.

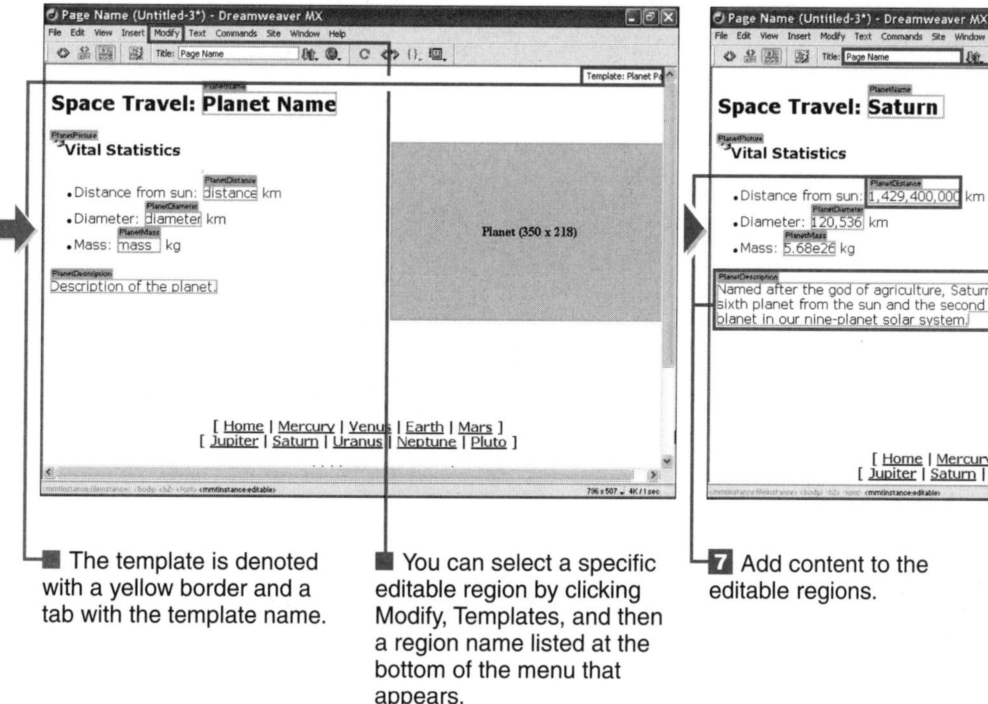

■ The template is denoted with a yellow border and a tab with the template name.

■ You can select a specific editable region by clicking Modify, Templates, and then a region name listed at the bottom of the menu that appears.

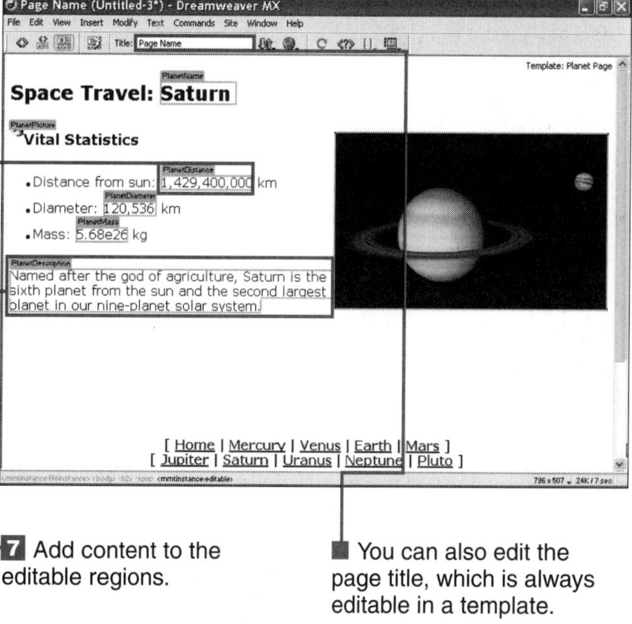

7 Add content to the editable regions.

■ You can also edit the page title, which is always editable in a template.

8 Save the file.

EDIT A TEMPLATE AND UPDATE YOUR WEB SITE

Basing your site's pages on templates can be a tremendous timesaver when maintaining and evolving the design of your site pages. You can make changes to an original template file and then have Dreamweaver update other pages that you based on that template. You can easily make wholesale changes to your site's page design in a matter of seconds, instead of having to open and edit dozens or hundreds of pages one at a time.

In contrast to pages that are based on templates, which can have only their editable regions modified, you can modify everything in the original template file. You can modify the locked regions inside the page body, body properties such as background and link colors, and head properties such as timelines and style sheets. When you save your changes, you can have Dreamweaver update all the files based on that template.

When you update template pages, you have an option of updating library items in those pages at the same time. For more about updating library items, see page 188.

EDIT A TEMPLATE AND UPDATE YOUR WEB SITE

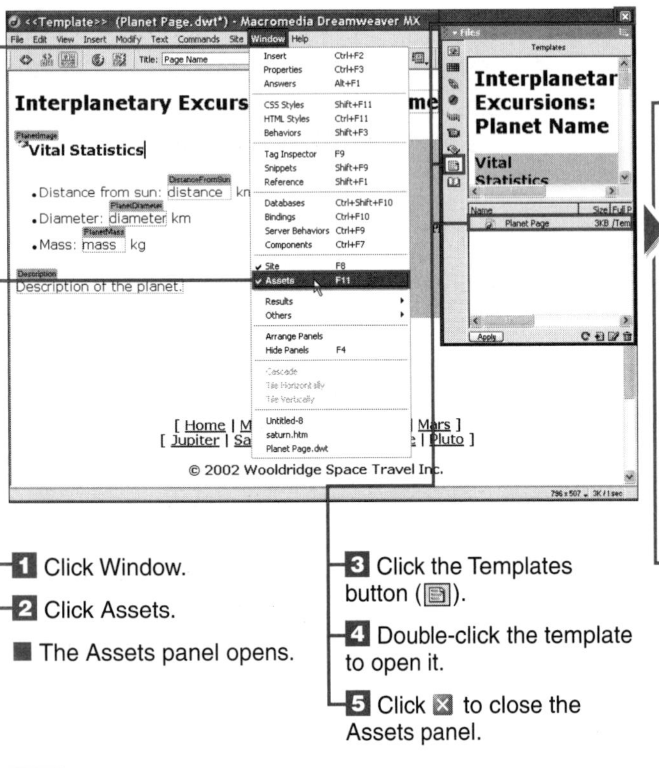

1 Click Window.

2 Click Assets.

■ The Assets panel opens.

3 Click the Templates button (▤).

4 Double-click the template to open it.

5 Click ☒ to close the Assets panel.

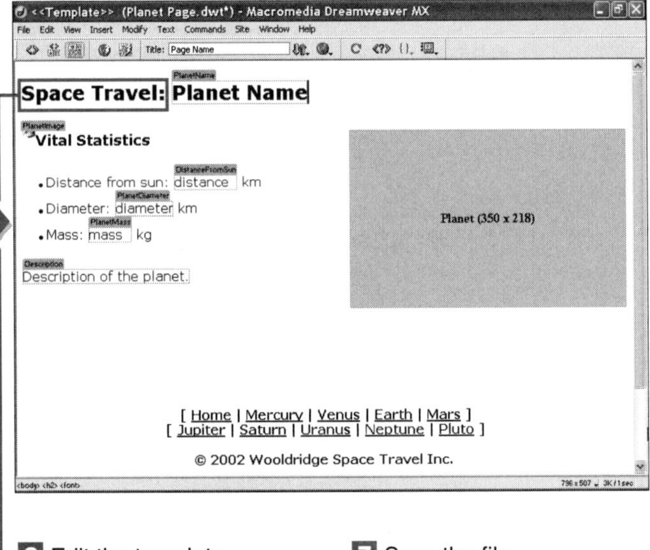

6 Edit the template.

Note: To add, modify, or delete editable or locked content in the page, see page 194.

7 Save the file.

How do I create new links in a template file?

✔ Creating links in an original template is a bit tricky, because template files are located in a subfolder, named Templates, inside the local site, and therefore must have relative links that are different from those in normal pages in the local site folder. You can avoid any problems by clicking the Link 🗀 in the Properties inspector when you need to define your links to other pages in your site, instead of trying to define them in the Link text field by hand. Doing so allows Dreamweaver to build the correct path to the destination page for you.

Can I edit timelines and style sheets in pages based on templates?

✔ Unfortunately, no, because only body content in a document can be defined as editable in a template, and timelines and style sheets are located in a page's head area. To add or modify timelines or style sheets, you need to work with the original template file, or detach the template-based page from the template by clicking Modify, Templates, and then Detach from Template.

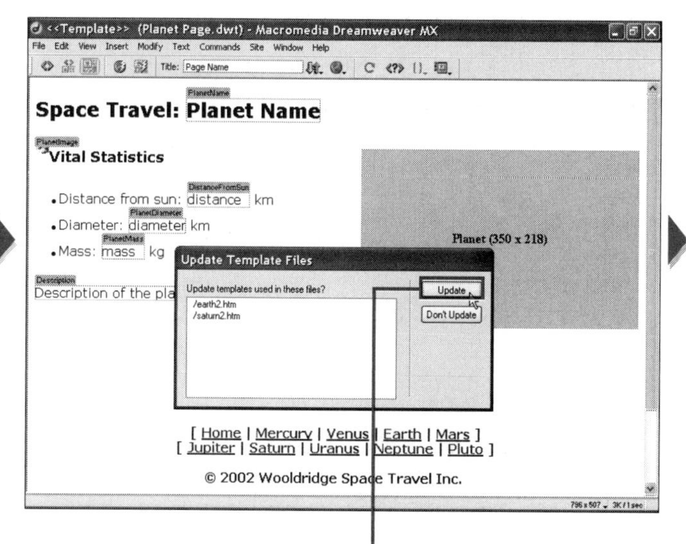

■ An alert box appears asking if you want to update all the pages that are based on the template.

8 Click Update.

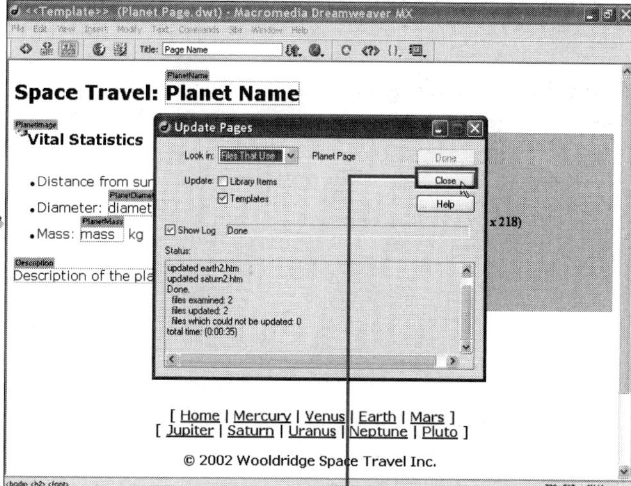

■ A dialog box shows the progress of the updates.

9 After Dreamweaver is finished updating the site, click Close.

INTRODUCTION TO STYLE SHEETS

Style sheets, also called *Cascading Style Sheets* or CSS, enable you to create complex formatting rules for your page content that can be stored in the <head> area of a Web page or in a separate text file. Style sheets offer designers much more power and precision in terms of styling their Web content compared to HTML. They also make maintaining a consistent style across a site easier, because many pages can link to a single set of style rules.

Format Text

A separate standard from HTML, style sheets let you format type, choose different fonts, customize the look of hyperlinks, tailor the colors on your page, and more. You can apply this formatting by using style sheets to customize existing HTML tags or by creating style-sheet *classes* that you can add to your HTML.

Position Web Page Elements

You can use style sheets to position images, text, and other elements precisely on your Web page, something that is not possible with HTML. Dreamweaver's layer feature offers a user-friendly way to apply style sheets' positioning capabilities.

Use Style Sheets Instead of HTML

You can perform many of the HTML-based formatting features discussed in Chapter 5 using style sheets. You can also use style sheets to apply more elaborate formatting to your pages than is possible with regular HTML. Because the World Wide Web Consortium, which sets Web publishing standards, favors the use of style sheets over many HTML style-related tags, you should see style sheets continue to increase in popularity.

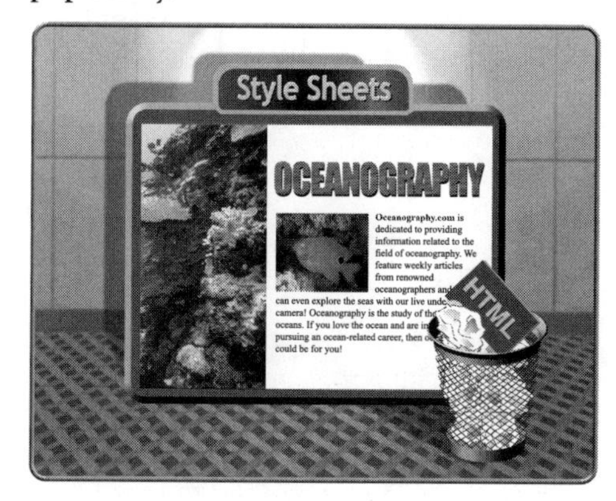

External Style Sheets

You can save style sheets as separate files; these external style sheets exist independently of your HTML pages. Different Web pages can access a common set of style rules by linking to the same external style sheet.

Embedded Style Sheets

A style sheet that is saved inside a particular Web page is called an *embedded style sheet.* Embedded style sheet rules apply only to the page in which they are embedded.

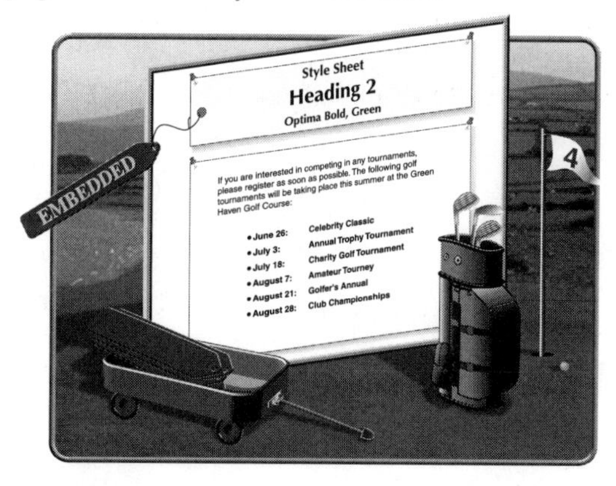

Style Sheets and Browsers

The first Web browsers to begin supporting style sheets were Microsoft Internet Explorer version 3 and Netscape Navigator version 4. However, these browsers supported the standard incompletely and interpreted some style sheet rules differently from one another. Newer browser versions support more style sheet features and support them more consistently. But you should still thoroughly test pages that use style sheets in both browsers before you put them live to ensure that the content displays correctly.

CUSTOMIZE AN HTML TAG

You can use style sheets to customize the style that is applied by an HTML tag. Doing this enables you to add color or font definitions to headings (by customizing the <h> tags), add backgrounds or borders to paragraphs (by customizing the <p> tag), or apply different margin settings to the page body (by customizing the <body> tag).

Designers once had relatively few style options that HTML offered and that browsers supported. Style sheets, in contrast, offer a wide variety of style options and let *you* determine how tags affect your content.

Style sheets make updating customized tags easy. You can make style changes to the <h3> heading in the style sheet and have those changes instantly show up in all instances of the <h3> tag on a page or throughout your entire site, if you define the styles in an external style sheet. See pages 212 to 215.

A drawback to customizing a tag is that a change affects all the instances of a tag. To apply style settings independently of particular HTML tags, see pages 204 to 207.

CUSTOMIZE AN HTML TAG

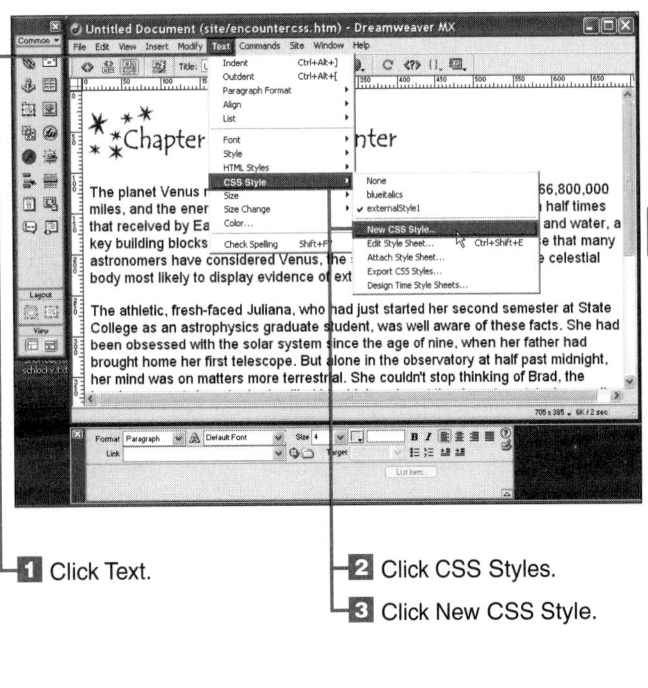

1 Click Text.

2 Click CSS Styles.

3 Click New CSS Style.

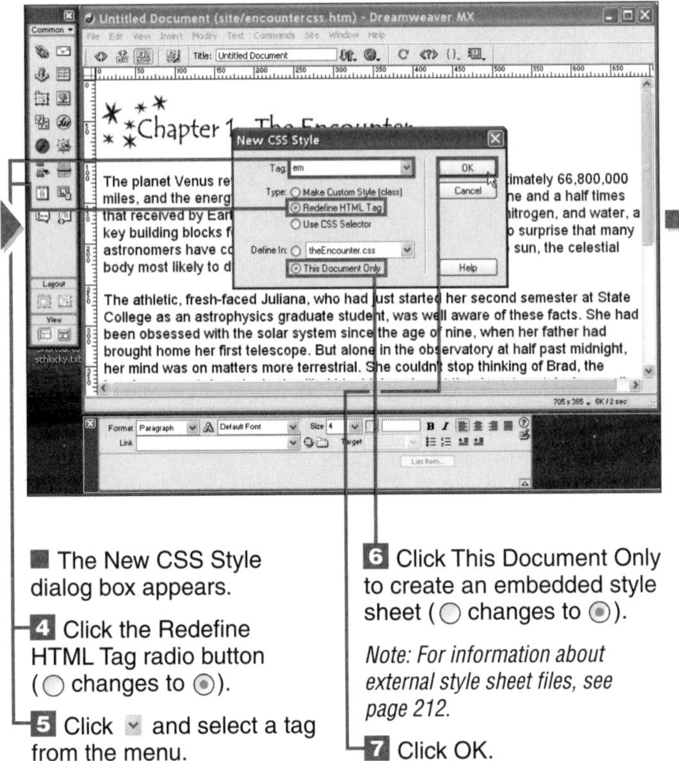

■ The New CSS Style dialog box appears.

4 Click the Redefine HTML Tag radio button (○ changes to ◉).

5 Click ▾ and select a tag from the menu.

6 Click This Document Only to create an embedded style sheet (○ changes to ◉).

Note: For information about external style sheet files, see page 212.

7 Click OK.

Can I use style sheets to make one tag behave exactly like another?

✔ Yes. You can, for example, customize the <b> (bold) tag so that it applies an italic style and no change in weight, just like the <i> (italic) tag.

How do I keep a background image fixed in the browser while content scrolls?

✔ The Background category in the Style Definition dialog box enables you to set an Attachment value. To keep a background fixed, customize the <body> tag and set the Attachment to fixed.

How do I edit the style that I have applied to a tag?

✔ Click Text, CSS Styles, and then Edit Style Sheet. The dialog box that opens displays the current customized tags and style-sheet classes. Click the tag and then click Edit.

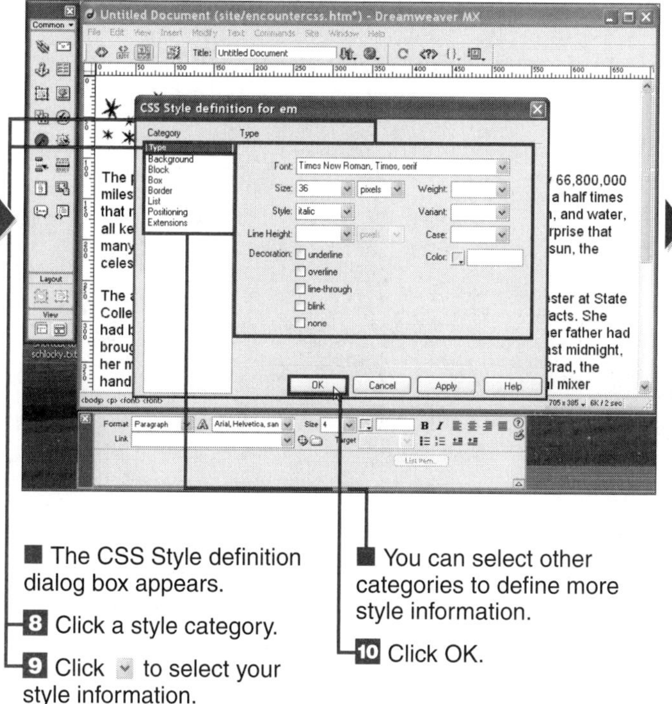

■ The CSS Style definition dialog box appears.

8 Click a style category.

9 Click ▾ to select your style information.

■ You can select other categories to define more style information.

10 Click OK.

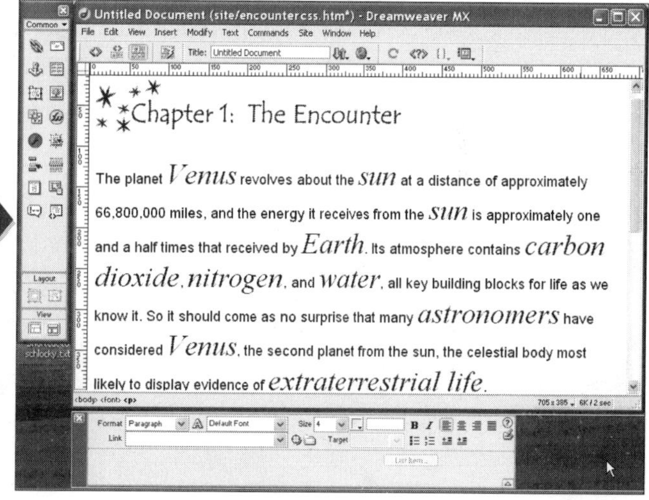

■ Dreamweaver adds the new style to any content formatted with the redefined tag (in this example, the <em> tag).

■ Formatting new content with the tag applies the style as well.

CREATE A CLASS

Style sheet classes let you define custom style rules that you can apply to many different types of content on your page. For example, you can create a class that turns text blue and underlined. You can then apply the class to a paragraph, a heading, or a sentence on the same page.

Creating classes is an alternative to using style sheet rules to customize existing HTMLtags — for example, customizing heading tags to apply a specific color in addition to a size and boldness. For more information, see page 202. Classes exist independently of the HTML tags that they customize on a page.

You can view the classes that you create for your page in the CSS Styles panel by clicking Window and then CSS Styles. These include classes that you have embedded in your page which are accessible only by that page, and classes that you have applied to the page via an external style sheet.

After you create and apply a class, you can edit it. When you save edits to a class, the changes are immediately applied to the instances of that class on your page. See page 208.

CREATE A CLASS

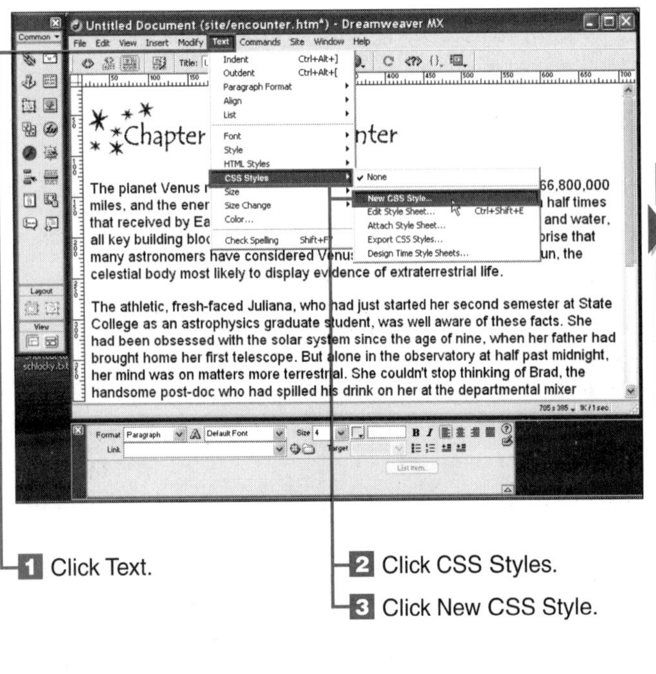

1 Click Text.

2 Click CSS Styles.

3 Click New CSS Style.

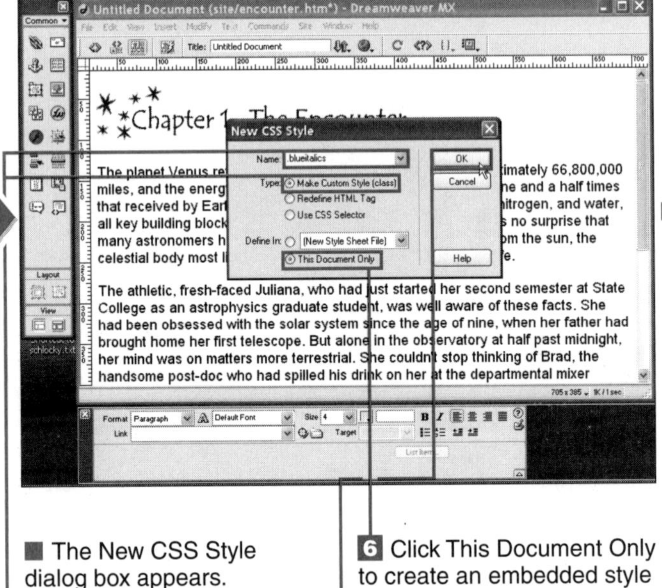

■ The New CSS Style dialog box appears.

4 Click the Make Custom Style (class) radio button (○ changes to ◉).

5 Type a period (.) and the name for the class.

6 Click This Document Only to create an embedded style sheet (○ changes to ◉).

Note: For information about external style sheet files, see page 212.

7 Click OK.

Where can I find sets of predefined classes to use on my pages?

✔ Dreamweaver comes with a variety of predefined sets of classes that you can apply to your pages. Click File and then New to open the New Document dialog box, and then select the CSS Style Sheets category. Clicking an item in the CSS Style Sheets list and then clicking OK opens the CSS code in a new Document window. You can save the code as a CSS file, and then attach the classes to your page as an external style sheet. See the section "Create an External Style Sheet" for more information.

How can I find out about the styles that I can create with style sheets?

✔ You can look at the many options available in the Style Definition dialog box that appears when you create styles. You can also open Dreamweaver's Reference panel and look up style information there. You need to select O'REILLY CSS Reference in the top menu.

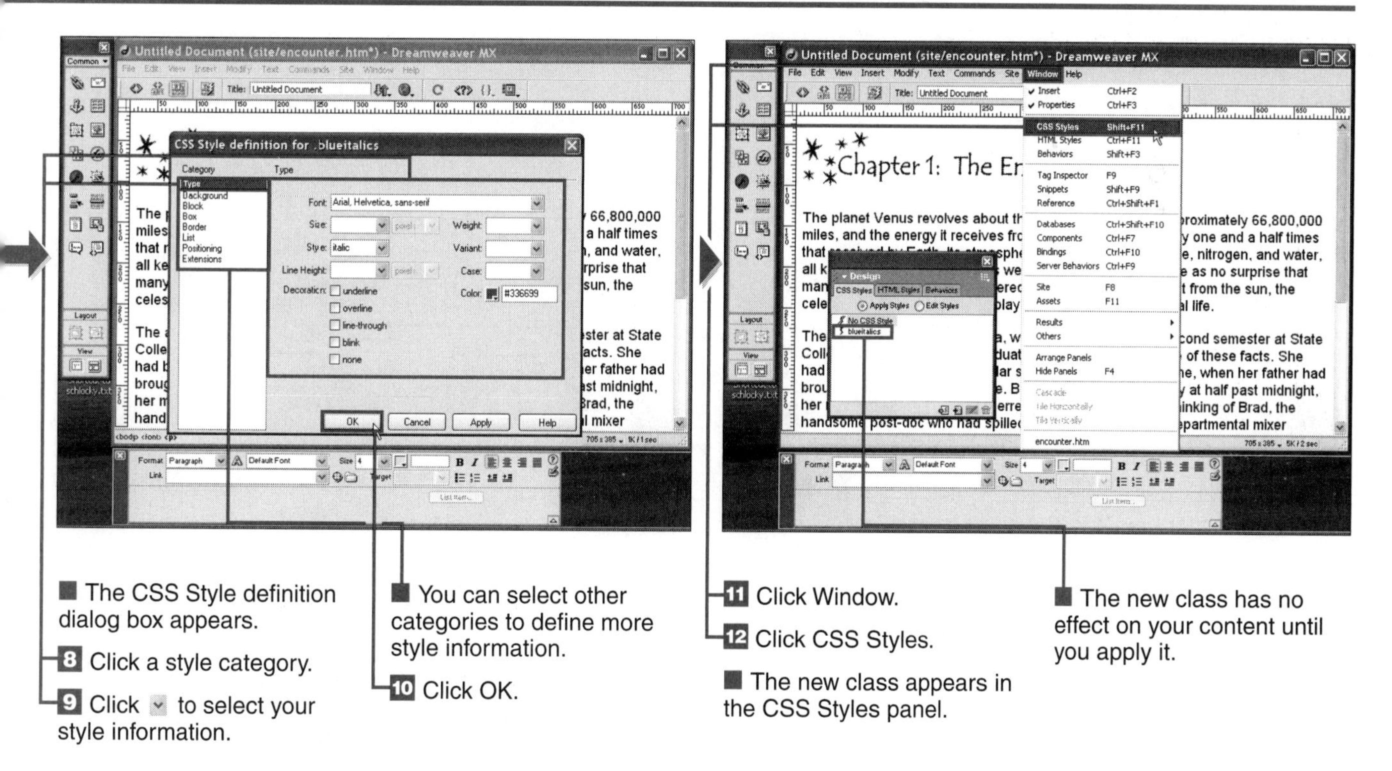

■ The CSS Style definition dialog box appears.

8 Click a style category.

9 Click ⌄ to select your style information.

■ You can select other categories to define more style information.

10 Click OK.

11 Click Window.

12 Click CSS Styles.

■ The new class appears in the CSS Styles panel.

■ The new class has no effect on your content until you apply it.

APPLY A CLASS

CSS Style classes allow you to create complicated style rules and apply those rules to specific objects on your page. Because classes are independent of the tags and other code that makes up your Web page, you must explicitly apply the classes to have an effect. After you select an object in your page, you can apply a class to the object by clicking the class name in the CSS Styles panel.

You can apply more than one class to an element on a page. What effect the combination of classes has depends on how you apply the information. If a conflict between classes exists, the style that is closest to the content in question wins out.

For example, if you give a paragraph a blue style and a sentence inside the paragraph a green style, the sentence appears green while the rest of the paragraph appears blue.

Many of the style rules that you can apply in Dreamweaver are specifically designed for text, which is why you access style sheet commands under the Text menu. But you can also create styles that apply to both text and other page elements. For example, you can create a border style that creates a blue, double-lined border and apply it to both text and images.

APPLY A CLASS

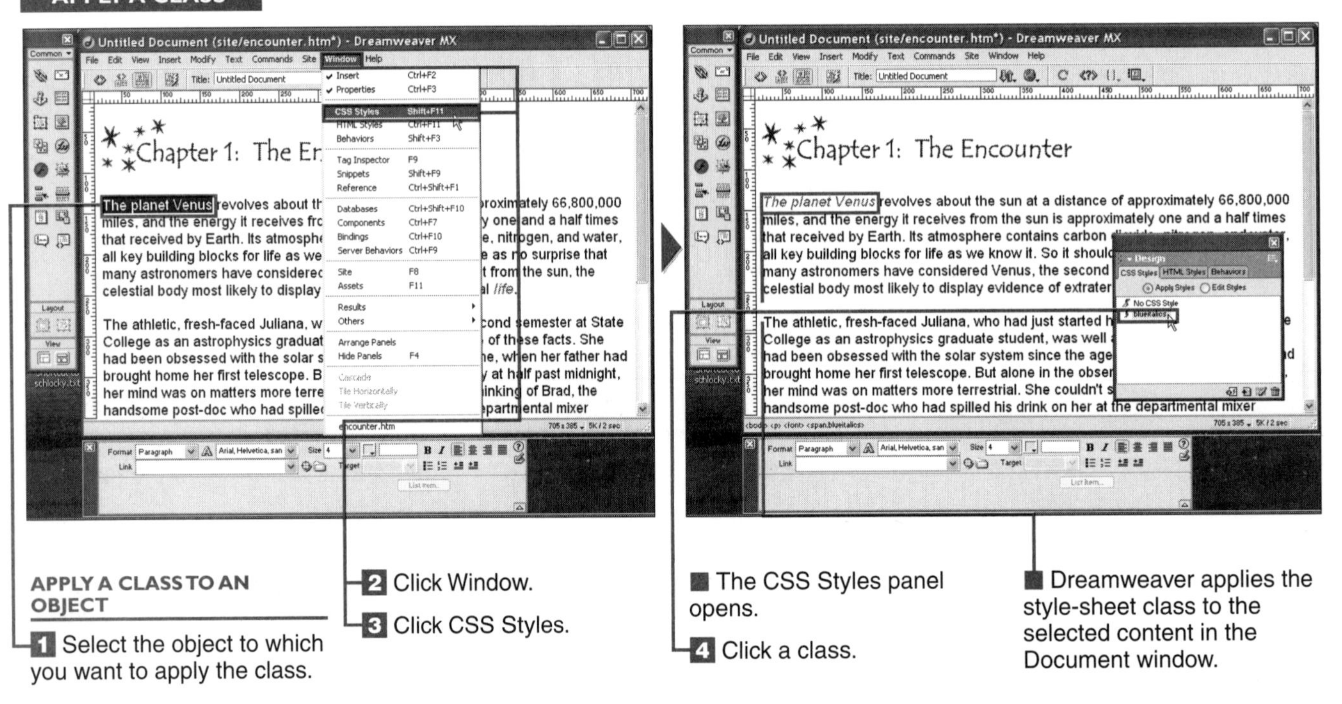

APPLY A CLASS TO AN OBJECT

1. Select the object to which you want to apply the class.
2. Click Window.
3. Click CSS Styles.

■ The CSS Styles panel opens.

4. Click a class.

■ Dreamweaver applies the style-sheet class to the selected content in the Document window.

How can I tell which styles have been applied to an element in my page?

✔ You can select the element and look at the tag selector at the bottom of the Document window. HTML tags and any associated classes are displayed. Applied classes are also highlighted in the CSS Styles panel and checked in the CSS Styles submenu under the Text menu.

How do I remove a style from an element in my page?

✔ Select the element and then click Text, CSS Styles, and None. You can also select the element and click No CSS Style in the CSS Styles panel.

What does the code that defines a class look like?

✔ The code includes the name of the class, which must start with a period (.), plus property/value pairs that determine the style of the class. Here is an example:

```
.myclass {font-weight: bold;
   color: green}
```

The above code creates a class that turns text bold and green. Style sheet code is placed in the <head> area of an HTML document.

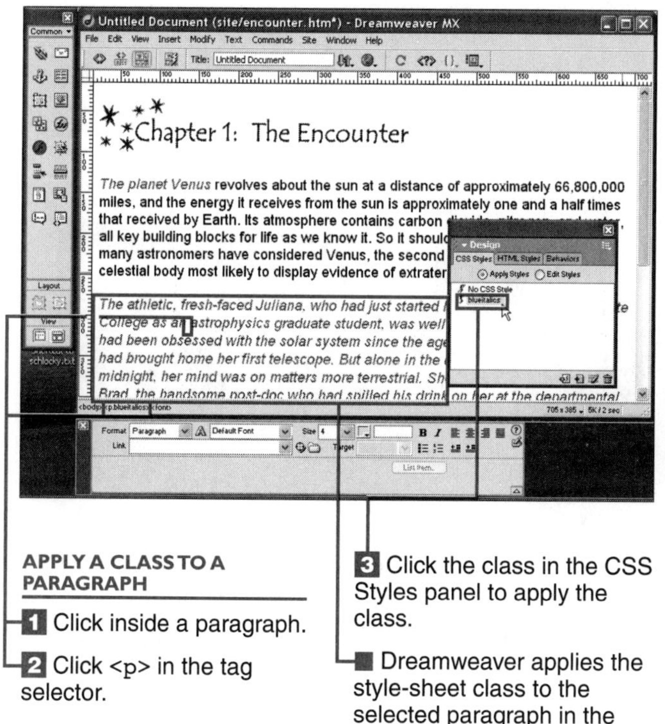

APPLY A CLASS TO A PARAGRAPH

1 Click inside a paragraph.

2 Click <p> in the tag selector.

3 Click the class in the CSS Styles panel to apply the class.

■ Dreamweaver applies the style-sheet class to the selected paragraph in the Document window.

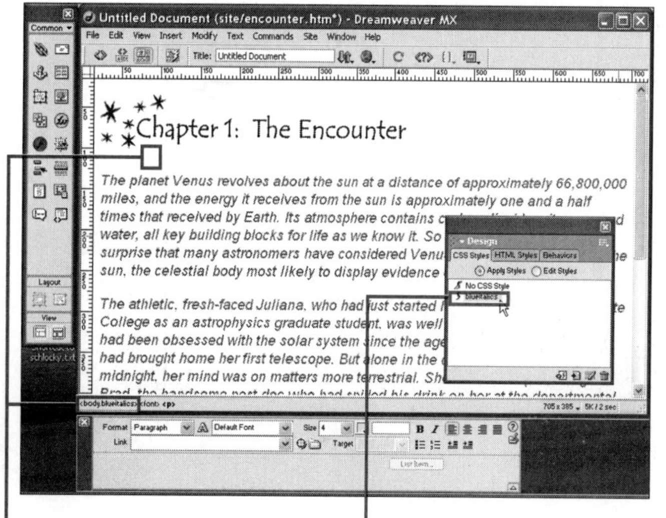

APPLY A CLASS TO THE ENTIRE BODY OF A PAGE

1 Click inside the Document window.

2 Click <body> in the tag selector.

3 Click the class in the CSS Styles panel to apply the class.

■ Dreamweaver applies the style-sheet class to the entire body of the page in the Document window.

EDIT A STYLE SHEET CLASS

Style sheet classes are powerful tools for maintaining the look and feel of a page or an entire site. Classes let you define a collection of style rules that control the formatting of body text, headings, subheadings, headers, and footers in one place. Changing the appearance of all those elements can then be as easy as editing the list of style sheet rules.

When you edit a style, the change takes effect immediately. You do not have to update your styles across your pages like you do library items and templates. Edits also have the same effect no matter when you apply them. The effects that styles have are always tied to the current style sheet rules, not what the rules were when you applied them. For more information about library items and templates, see Chapter 11.

EDIT A STYLE SHEET CLASS

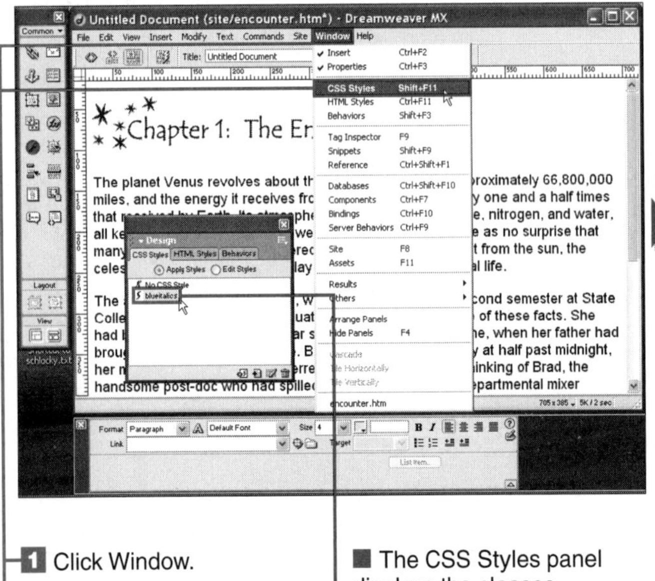

1 Click Window.

2 Click CSS Styles.

■ The CSS Styles panel displays the classes available for that page.

3 Double-click the class you want to edit.

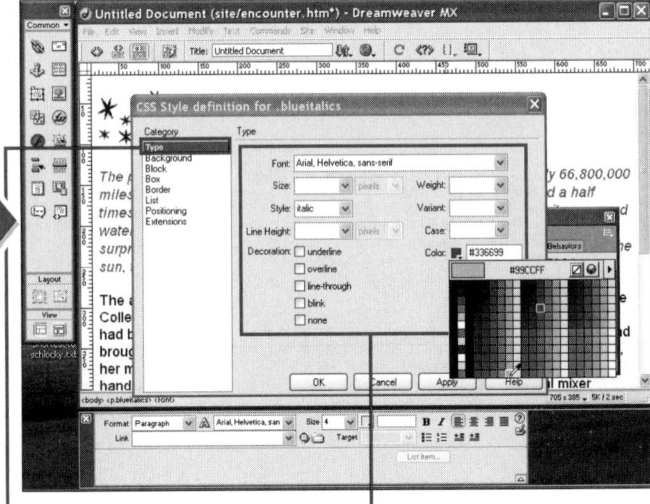

■ The CSS Style definition dialog box appears.

4 Click a style category.

5 Click ▾ to select your style definitions.

■ In this example, the font color has been changed.

How do I indent the first line of my paragraphs?

✔ Create a class that applies a positive Indent value using the settings under the Block category in the Style Definitions dialog box. Then apply the class to the paragraphs that you want to indent. An alternative to creating a class is to use the setting to customize the <p> tag. This indents all the paragraphs on your page. A negative Indent value causes the first line of text to stick out into the margin, which can also provide an interesting effect.

What are some type-based features that I can apply with style sheets that I cannot apply with HTML?

✔ Style sheets let you specify a numeric value for font weight, enabling you to apply varying degrees of boldness, instead of just a single boldness setting as with HTML. Note that this works with only certain fonts. You can also define type size in absolute units (pixels, points, picas, inches, centimeters, millimeters) or relative units (ems, exes, percentage). HTML offers no such choices of units.

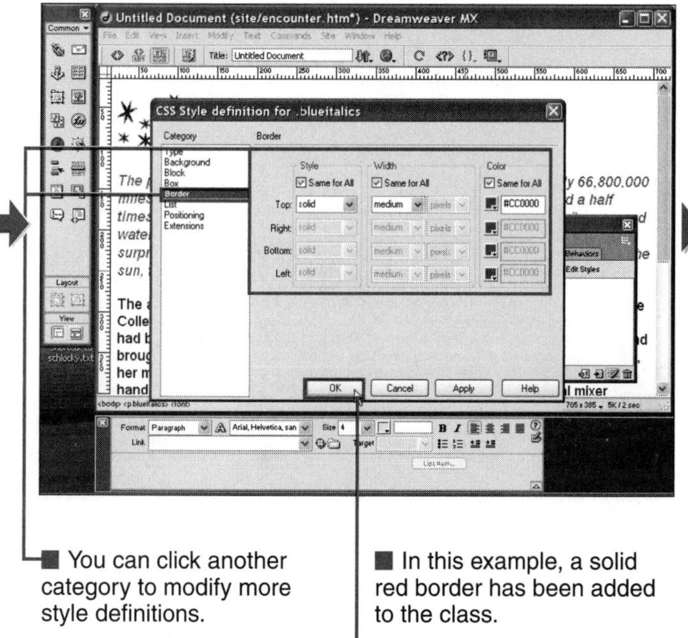

■ You can click another category to modify more style definitions.

■ In this example, a solid red border has been added to the class.

6 Click OK.

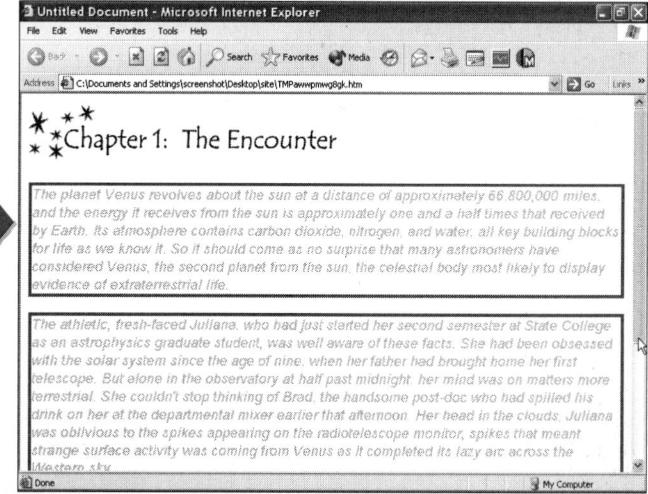

7 Preview the page in a Web browser.

Note: To preview a page in a Web browser, see page 58.

■ The page displays with the edited class information applied.

USING CSS SELECTORS TO MODIFY LINKS

Just as style sheets give you more options when styling regular text on a page, they also offer new ways to style hyperlinks to make them better match the style of the other text and images on your pages. You can style your hyperlinks by defining styles to a style sheet's CSS selectors.

Using regular HTML styles, you can customize only the color of links on a page. See page 216. *CSS selectors* enable you to fully customize hyperlinks — you can specify weight, letter spacing, background color, border, and many other characteristics.

The CSS selectors Dreamweaver makes available are `a:active`, which lets you define the style of clicked links; `a:hover`, which lets you define the style of links when a cursor rolls over them; `a:link`, which lets you define the style of unvisited links; and `a:visited`, which lets you define the style of links that your browser has recently visited.

In contrast to the other selectors, the `a:hover` selector enables you to apply a dynamic effect to your links by making the link style change in response to the cursor position in the browser window.

USING CSS SELECTORS TO MODIFY LINKS

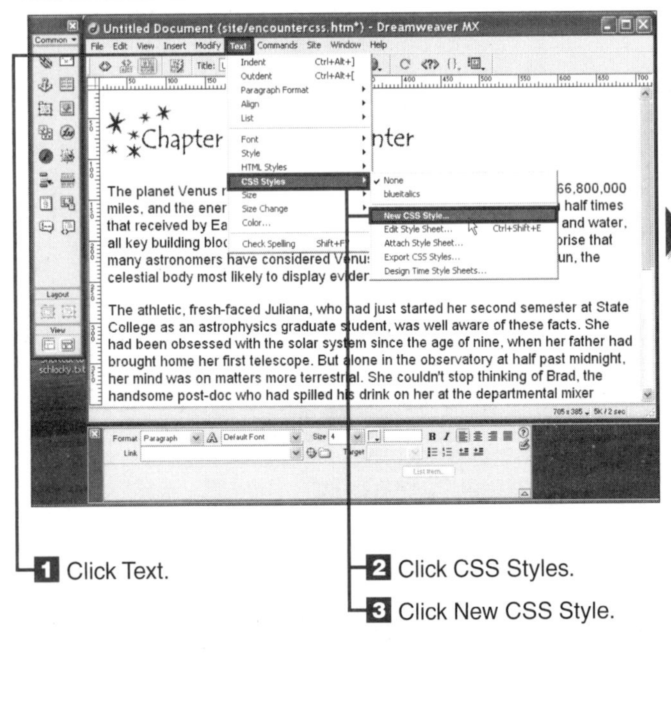

1 Click Text.

2 Click CSS Styles.

3 Click New CSS Style.

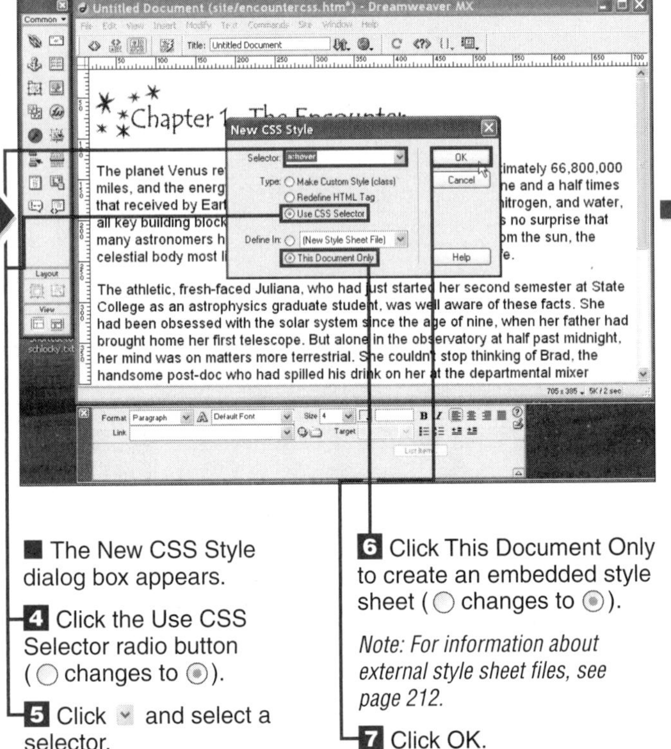

■ The New CSS Style dialog box appears.

4 Click the Use CSS Selector radio button (○ changes to ◉).

5 Click ▾ and select a selector.

6 Click This Document Only to create an embedded style sheet (○ changes to ◉).

Note: For information about external style sheet files, see page 212.

7 Click OK.

What is the overline feature?

✔ The *overline feature* applies a line across the top of your text. It is the stylistic opposite of underlining. The overline style is available under the Type category in the Style Definition dialog box. When used with CSS selectors, overline places a line across the top of your links.

How can I make my links look like they have been marked with a highlighter pen?

✔ Define a bright background color for your links under the Background category in the Style Definition dialog box.

Should I leave my links underlined?

✔ Underlining has long been a visual cue to signal a clickable hyperlink. If you remove the underlining, viewers skimming your page may not recognize all the links. Users on black and white systems, who can see underlining but not changes in color, which also accompanies hyperlinks, are even worse off.

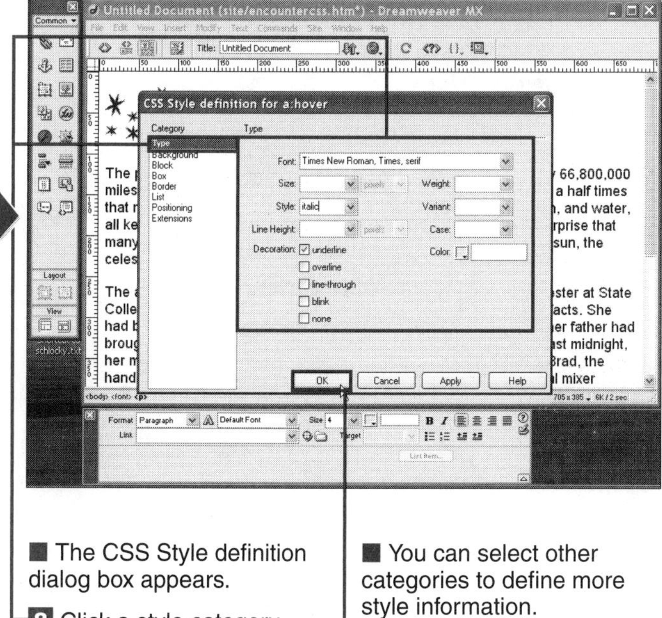

■ The CSS Style definition dialog box appears.

8 Click a style category.

9 Click ▾ to select your style information.

■ You can select other categories to define more style information.

10 Click OK.

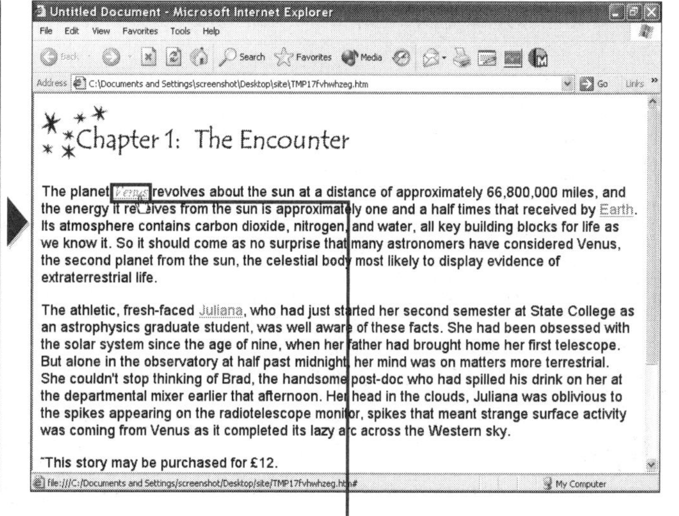

11 Preview the page in a Web browser.

Note: To preview a page in a Web browser, see page 58.

■ Because the `a:hover` selector was set, the style of the links changes when the cursor is placed over them.

■ In this example, the text becomes italicized.

CREATE AN EXTERNAL STYLE SHEET

External style sheets enable you to put a list of style sheet rules in a separate file, which you can save in your local folder. All the pages of your site can access this file, and in turn access the style rules inside it.

An external style sheet can contain all the style information needed to create the look and feel for your Web site. This information can include styles for body text, headings, navigation, captions, and other common site features.

Alternatively, you can organize your site styles into several separate external files, and just link to styles needed for each given page. For example, you can put styles for product pages into one external file, and styles for employee pages into another file. If your site includes many different style sheet files, you may want to store all the files in a separate subfolder.

The code that defines style rules in external style sheets is the same as that in embedded style sheets. Any style you can define in one you can also define in the other.

CREATE AN EXTERNAL STYLE SHEET

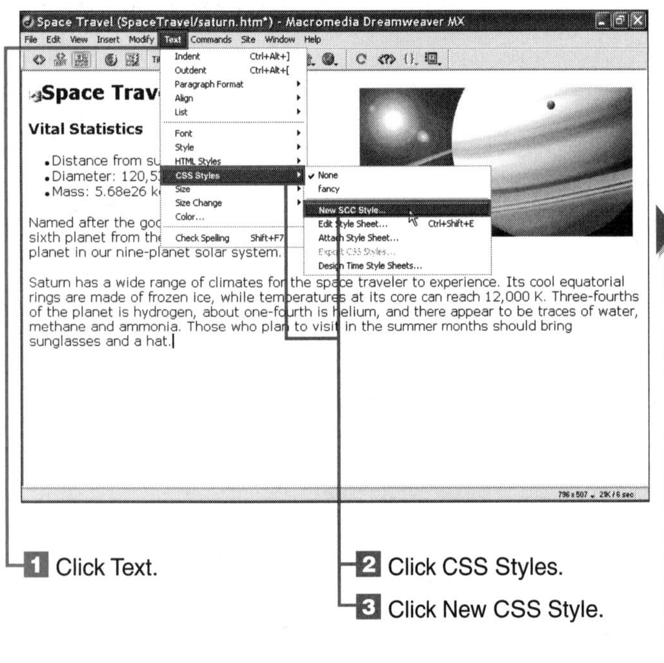

1 Click Text.

2 Click CSS Styles.

3 Click New CSS Style.

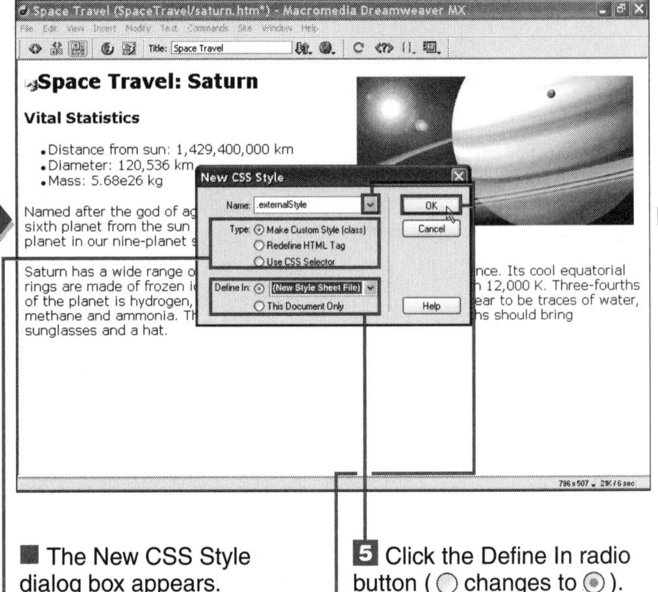

■ The New CSS Style dialog box appears.

4 Click a radio button to select a style type (◯ changes to ◉).

5 Click the Define In radio button (◯ changes to ◉).

6 Click ▾ to select New Style Sheet File.

7 Click OK.

How do I export a set of embedded styles to create an external style sheet?

✔ You can click File, Export, and then Export Styles. This enables you to name a new `.css` file and specify where the file is stored. You can then link to the external file to use those styles in other documents.

What happens when I delete an external style sheet?

✔ All the files that link to the sheet lose the style information that was in the sheet. Before you delete an external style sheet, consider whether you or someone else could be relying on it to format other pages.

Can I reference an external style sheet stored on another Web site?

✔ When you attach a style sheet to a page in Dreamweaver, you can either browse for the file in your local folder or enter a URL. The URL option lets you link to a style sheet on another Web site.

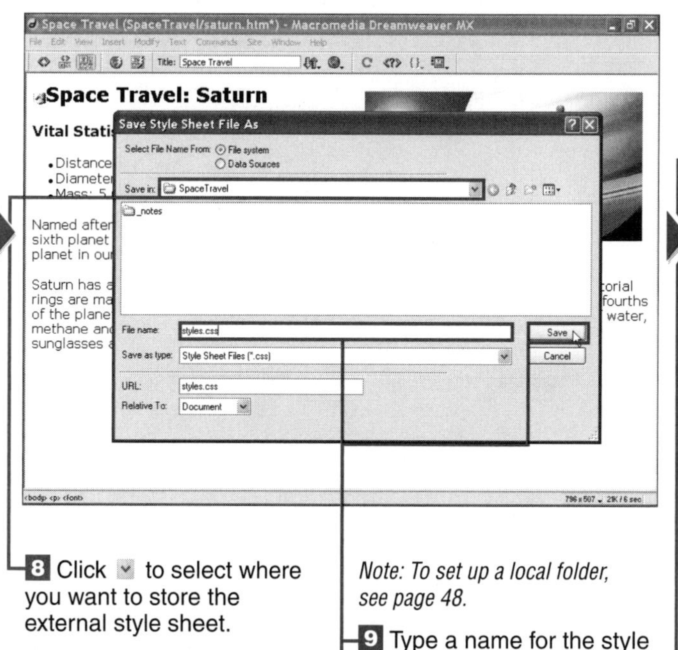

8 Click to select where you want to store the external style sheet.

■ You should store your external style sheet inside your local folder.

Note: To set up a local folder, see page 48.

9 Type a name for the style sheet with a `.css` extension.

10 Click Save.

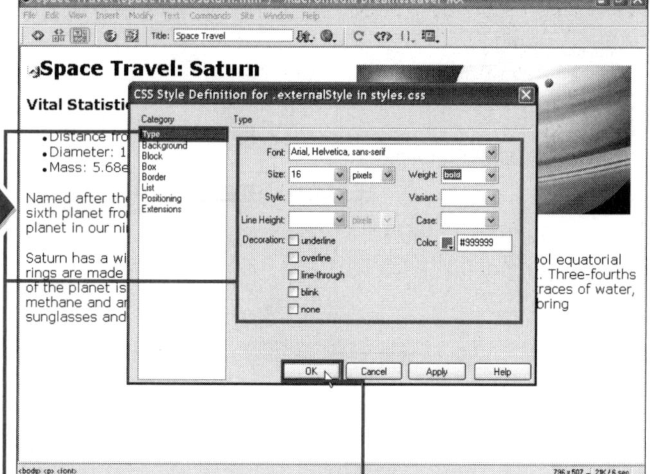

■ The CSS Style Definition dialog box opens, allowing you to add a style to your external style sheet.

11 Click a style category.

12 Click and the check boxes to define your style information.

13 Click OK.

■ You can repeat steps 1 to 6 (selecting the file you just created in step 4) and steps 11 to 13 to add more style rules to the external style sheet.

ATTACH AN EXTERNAL STYLE SHEET

You can attach an external style sheet file to your Web page in order to get access to all the rules defined in the style sheet. This gives you easy access to a variety of styles that you can apply to all the content in your page — all without having to define the styles inside your page. After you attach the style sheet, all of its styles show up in the CSS Styles panel.

Usually, all the files in a site will reference one or more style sheets located in the local folder of the site. However, if your site is one of many departmental sites on a corporate intranet, you may need to use a standard company style sheet. Your site can also reference such an external style sheet somewhere else on the network.

Creating external style sheets offers a big advantage to designers who want to separate style rules for a site from its content. Placing style information in a separate file means that updating page content cannot affect, or corrupt, the styles for that page. Storing style definitions centrally can also help ensure a consistent look and feel across all pages of a site.

ATTACH AN EXTERNAL STYLE SHEET

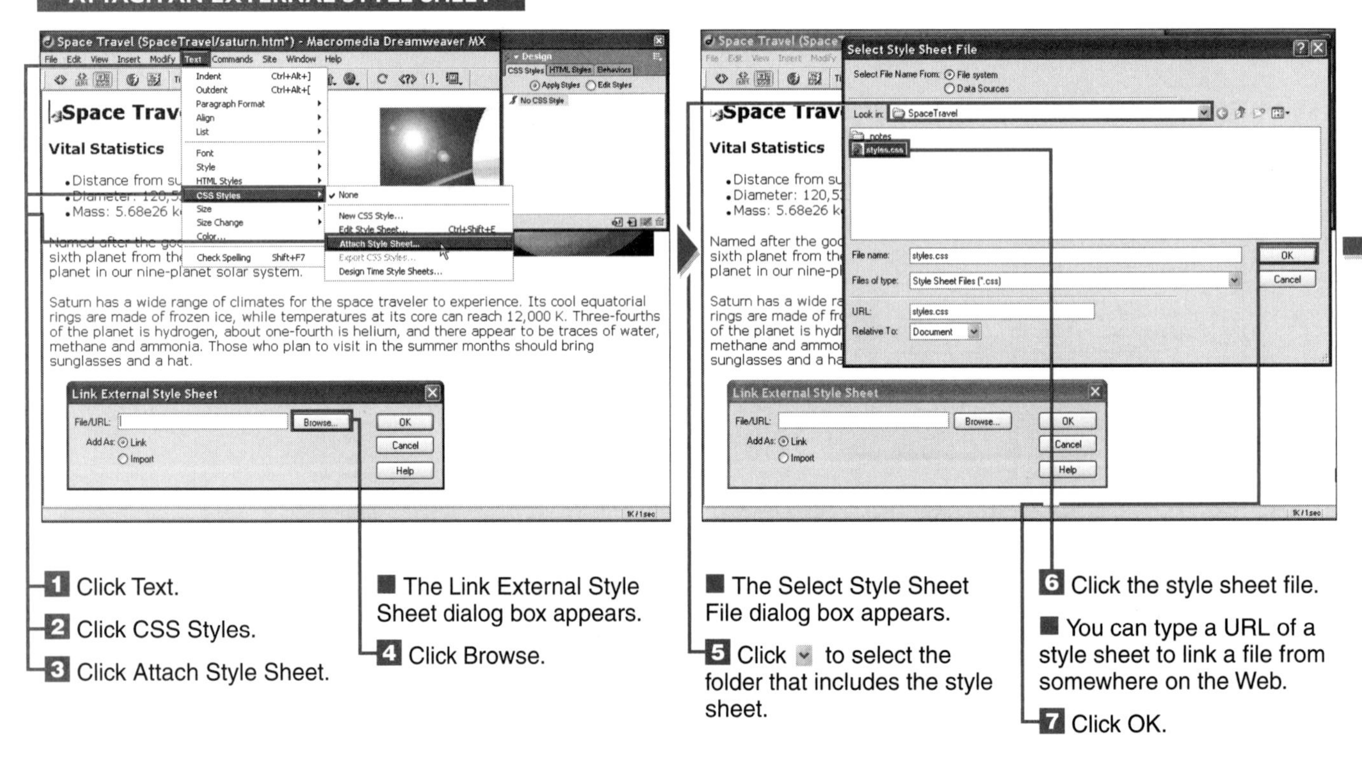

1 Click Text.

2 Click CSS Styles.

3 Click Attach Style Sheet.

■ The Link External Style Sheet dialog box appears.

4 Click Browse.

■ The Select Style Sheet File dialog box appears.

5 Click ▾ to select the folder that includes the style sheet.

6 Click the style sheet file.

■ You can type a URL of a style sheet to link a file from somewhere on the Web.

7 Click OK.

How do I use style sheets to accommodate different browser types?

✔ A common strategy for creating sites that have a consistent look and feel across different browsers is to create multiple style sheets, one for each type of browser you want to support. For example, you can create separate style sheets for Internet Explorer on Windows, Internet Explorer on Macintosh, Netscape Navigator on Windows, and Netscape Navigator on Macintosh. You can then write JavaScript that checks the browser of a user and displays the appropriate style sheet.

How can I turn off style sheets while I design my page?

✔ You can include or exclude linked external style sheets in Dreamweaver by using the Design Time style sheets feature. This can be useful if you want to temporarily apply just the style sheets for a particular browser platform — for example, style sheets for Windows or Macintosh — or turn off style sheets altogether.

After linking your external style sheets, right-click (Alt-click) the CSS Styles panel and select Design Time Style Sheet. Then click the [+] or [−] to specify the CSS files you want included or excluded.

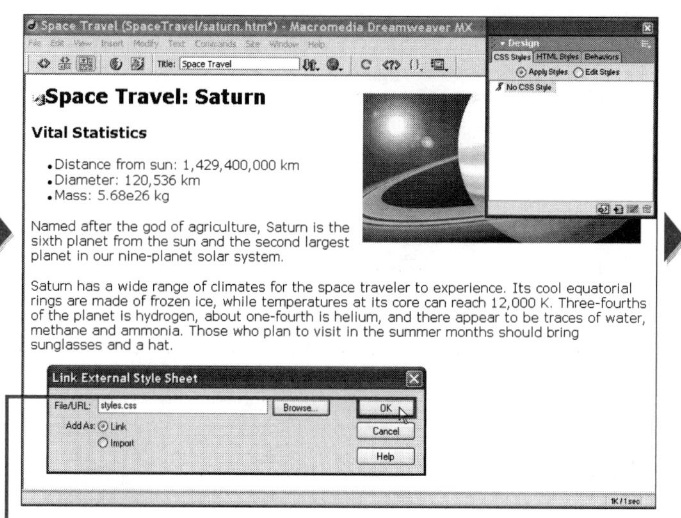

8 Click OK in the Link External Style Sheet dialog box.

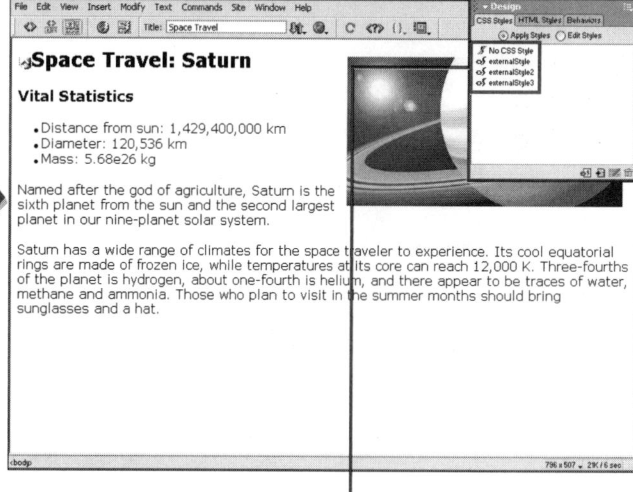

■ Dreamweaver attaches the external style sheet to the Web page.

■ The styles from the style sheet appear in the CSS Styles panel.

CREATE A LAYER

Layers give you the option of creating rectangular areas that float above the other information on your page. You can fill these blocks with different types of content and position them precisely in the browser window. Because layers exist on a page independently of one another, you can also overlap them.

Layers are actually a style sheet phenomenon — they are built using the positioning capabilities afforded by style sheets. When you create a layer in the Document window, Dreamweaver writes the style sheet code behind the scenes that specifies the positioning properties as well as the dimensions of the layer. You can change these properties interactively in the Document window or by typing new values in the Properties inspector. See page 218.

To view layers in a browser, you need Version 4 or later of Microsoft Internet Explorer or Netscape Navigator. But note that even browsers that support layers can sometimes render them unpredictably, especially older Version 4 browsers. This can make layers inappropriate for audiences that do not use up-to-date browsers.

CREATE A LAYER

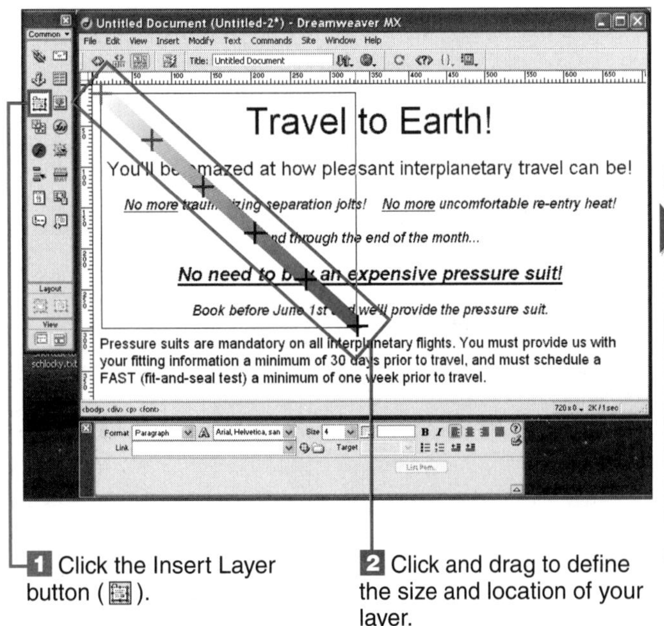

1 Click the Insert Layer button (▣).

2 Click and drag to define the size and location of your layer.

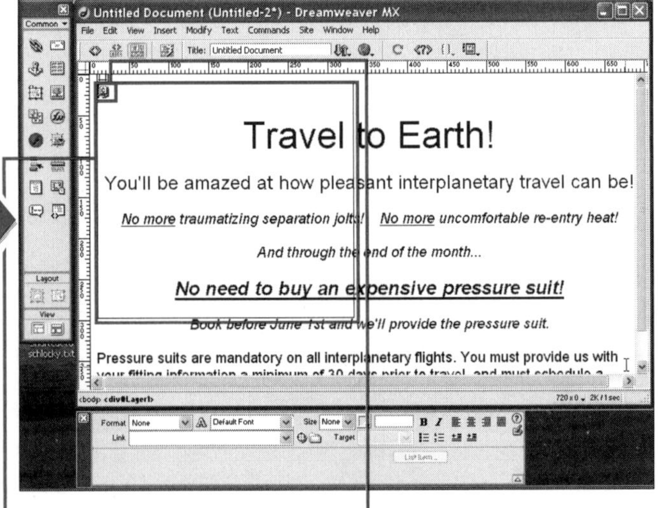

■ A layer is inserted into the page. Layers are removed from the regular flow of content on the page, and can sit on top of other content.

■ An icon represents where you inserted the layer code. You can click the icon to select the layer.

How do I keep layers displaying correctly in Netscape Navigator Version 4?

✔ Netscape Navigator Version 4 has a problem displaying layers correctly when a user resizes the browser window. Dreamweaver can remedy the problem by inserting JavaScript code that forces the Version 4 browser to reload the page if the user resizes the window. You can specify that Dreamweaver add this fix by clicking Netscape 4 Compatibility under the Layers category in Preferences. For more about setting Preferences, see Chapter 2.

How do I nest layers?

✔ Make sure the Nesting check box is selected in Preferences under the Layers category. Click the Object panel layer button and then click and drag inside an existing layer. When you nest a layer inside another, the layer's icon appears inside the enclosing layer.

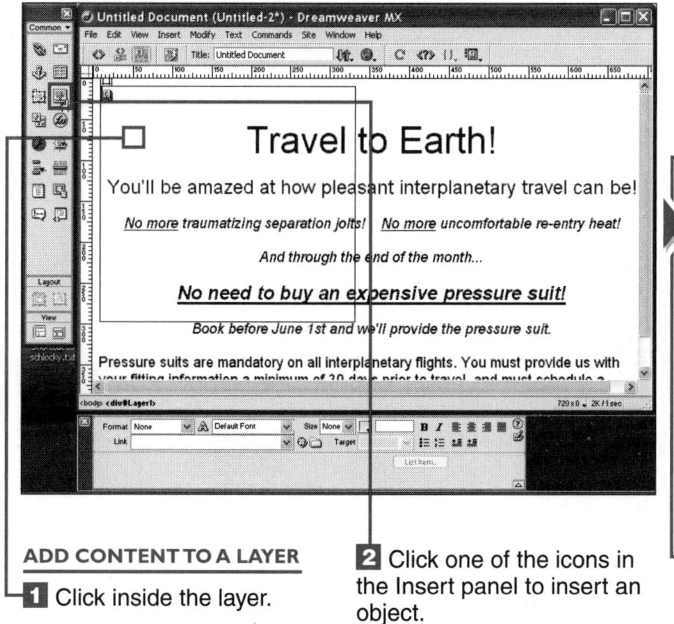

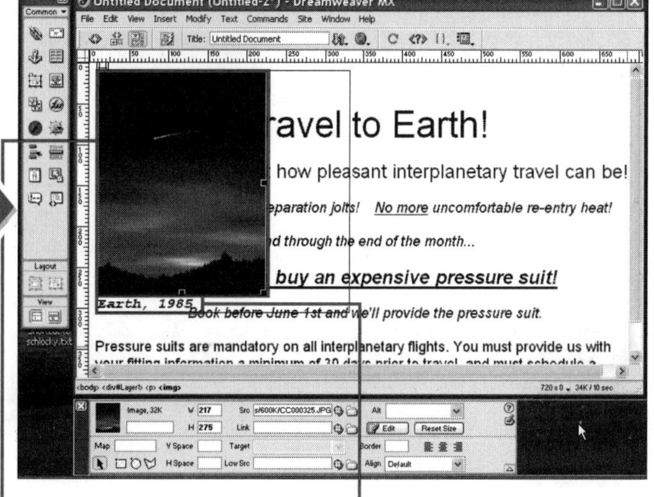

ADD CONTENT TO A LAYER

1 Click inside the layer.

2 Click one of the icons in the Insert panel to insert an object.

■ The object appears inside the layer, floating over any other content on the page.

■ To add text, you can also click inside the layer and type. You can also style the text in a layer.

RESIZE AND REPOSITION LAYERS

Every layer has specific position and dimension settings that define its place in the page. You can adjust these settings to make a layer fit attractively with the rest of the content on your page, or to make it overlap other layers.

When you select the layer, its position coordinates, as well as its dimension values, appear in the Properties inspector. The default unit of measurement is pixels (px), but you can change this to inches (in), centimeters (cm), and even a percentage of the browser window (%). The position of a layer in Dreamweaver is measured from the top left of the browser window.

You can adjust the size of a layer to display the content inside it in different ways. For example, you can stretch a layer horizontally to create a strip across the top of a page or elongate a layer to create a narrow band down the side of a page. The content inside a layer may limit its size. For example, you cannot shrink a layer that contains an image to smaller than the size of the image.

RESIZE AND REPOSITION LAYERS

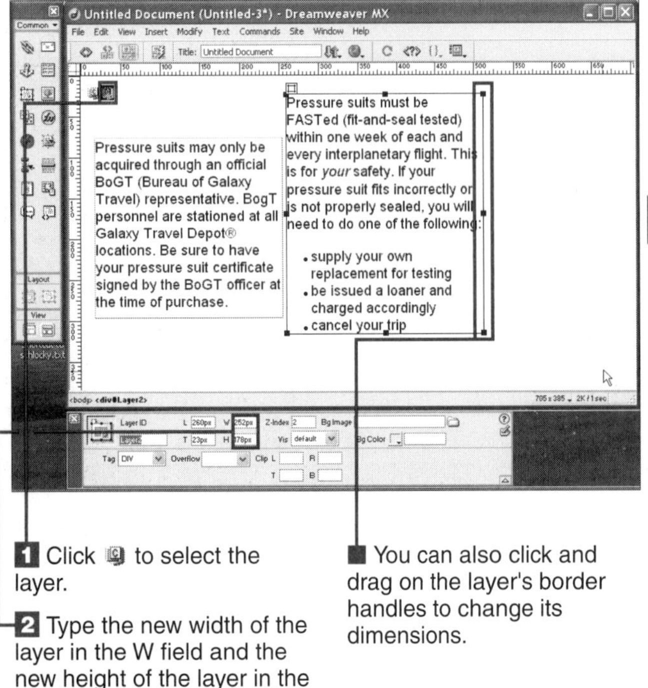

1 Click the layer icon to select the layer.

2 Type the new width of the layer in the W field and the new height of the layer in the H field, followed by **px** for pixels, **in** for inches, or **cm** for centimeters.

■ You can also click and drag on the layer's border handles to change its dimensions.

■ Dreamweaver applies the new dimensions to the layer.

How can I more easily position or resize a layer in a page?

✔ A useful way to control the position and size of your layers as you click and drag them in the Document window is to turn on the grid. Click View, Grid, and Show Grid. Make sure that you set the page content to snap to the grid lines. Click View, Grid, and Snap to Grid.

How do I change the properties of several layers at once?

✔ Select more than one layer in the Document window by shift-clicking. Then change the properties of these layers by adjusting the values in the Properties inspector.

What happens if the L (left) or T (top) values for a layer are larger than the dimensions of the browser window?

✔ The layer is positioned out of sight from your viewers. This is something you should consider if you think your site's visitors may be using small monitors.

How do I make a layer invisible?

✔ Adjust the Vis (Visibility) menu in the Properties inspector. The menu lets you make a layer visible, invisible, or have it inherit its characteristic from its parent (the enclosing layer).

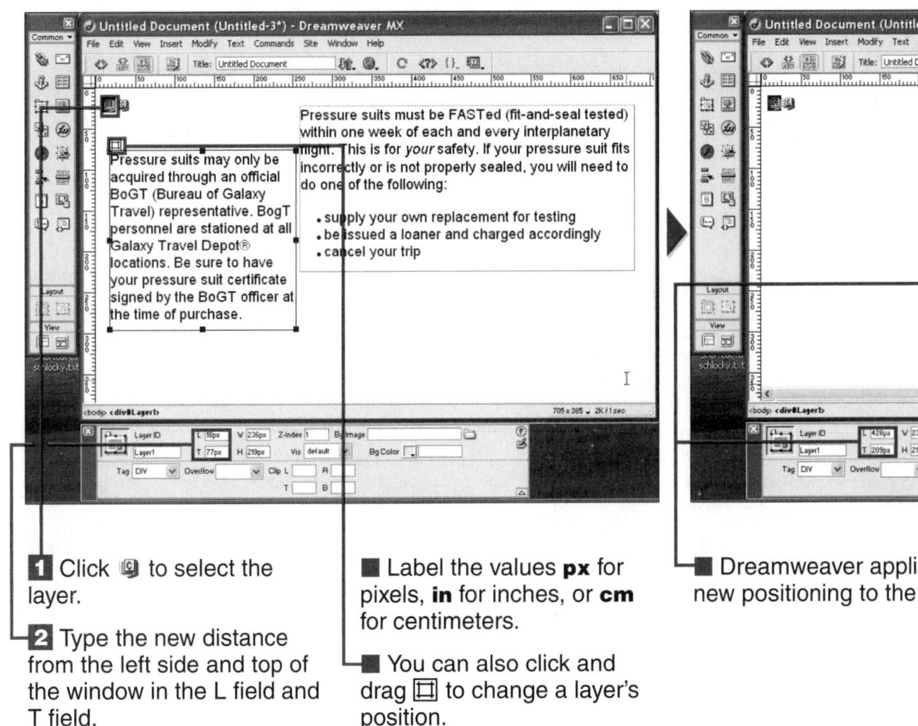

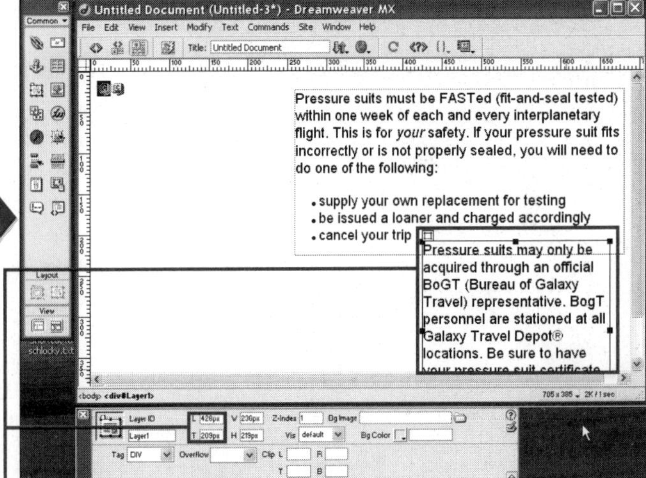

1 Click 🔲 to select the layer.

2 Type the new distance from the left side and top of the window in the L field and T field.

■ Label the values **px** for pixels, **in** for inches, or **cm** for centimeters.

■ You can also click and drag ⊡ to change a layer's position.

■ Dreamweaver applies the new positioning to the layer.

ADD A BACKGROUND COLOR TO A LAYER

Just as you can set the background color of pages and tables, you can set the background color of a layer to make it complement the rest of your page content. Dreamweaver lets you define the color of a layer by selecting from a pop-up color palette in the Properties inspector. You can also define the color by typing a name or hexadecimal code.

Layer backgrounds can prove especially effective when several layers overlap one another on a page. When a background color is absent, the organization of the layers can be unclear, especially when text overlaps other text.

You can also define a background image for a layer. Just as with pages and tables, background images in layers tile horizontally and vertically to fill the entire dimensions of the layer. You can insert images into a layer that already has an image background to create an interesting collage effect.

With timelines, you can create a background color that changes over time. This can result in a colorful flashing effect as the background cycles from one color to another. See Chapter 14 for more about timelines.

ADD A BACKGROUND COLOR TO A LAYER

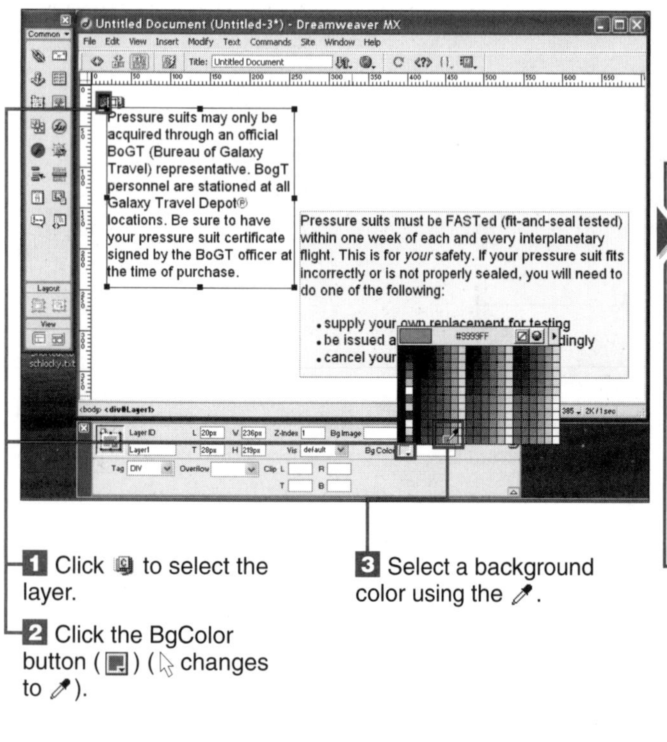

1 Click 🖳 to select the layer.

2 Click the BgColor button (▣) (⇖ changes to 🖉).

3 Select a background color using the 🖉.

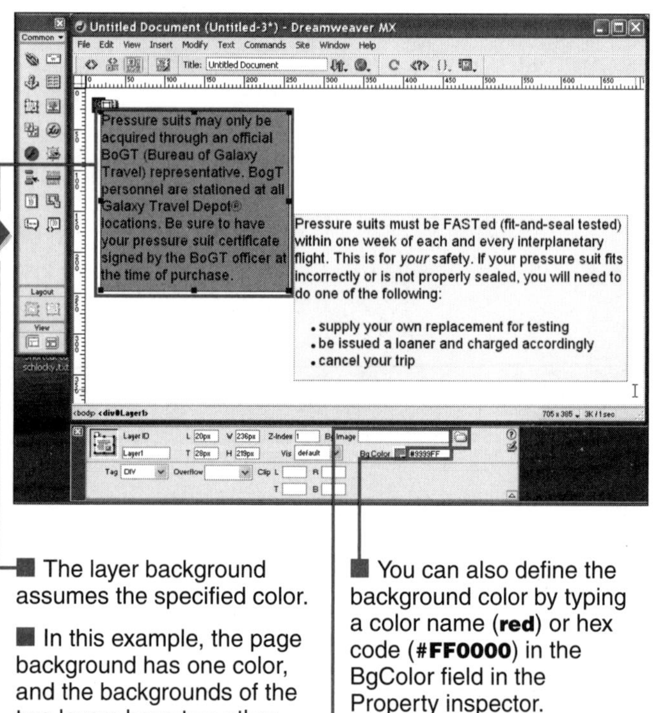

■ The layer background assumes the specified color.

■ In this example, the page background has one color, and the backgrounds of the two layers have two other colors.

■ You can also define the background color by typing a color name (**red**) or hex code (**#FF0000**) in the BgColor field in the Property inspector.

■ Clicking 🗀 lets you select a background image for the layer.

CHANGE THE STACKING ORDER OF LAYERS

Layers that float on top of one another in the Document window have a stacking order. This determines which layer displays on top, and on down through the stack to the bottom. Stacking order is determined by the *z-index* of each layer. The greater the z-index relative to the other layers in a stack, the higher the layer is in the stack.

You can view the stacking order of a page's layers by opening the Layers panel. Layers are ordered in the panel from top to bottom by their z-index. You can click and drag layers up and down in the panel, and Dreamweaver adjusts their z-indexes accordingly. You can also adjust the z-index of a layer by hand in the Layers panel. After you change a z-index, Dreamweaver automatically rearranges the layers to reorder them from highest to lowest, if necessary. A z-index can be positive or negative.

If you click Prevent Overlaps in the Layers panel, Dreamweaver prevents layers from overlapping as you arrange them in the Document window. This effectively renders the z-index moot in a page.

CHANGE THE STACKING ORDER OF LAYERS

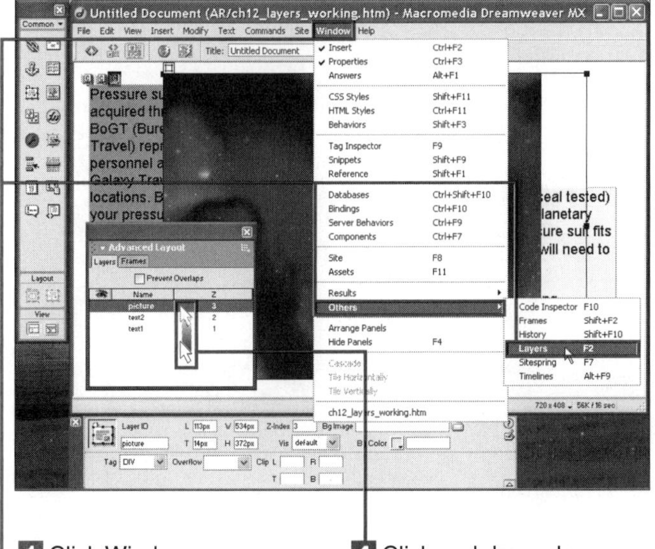

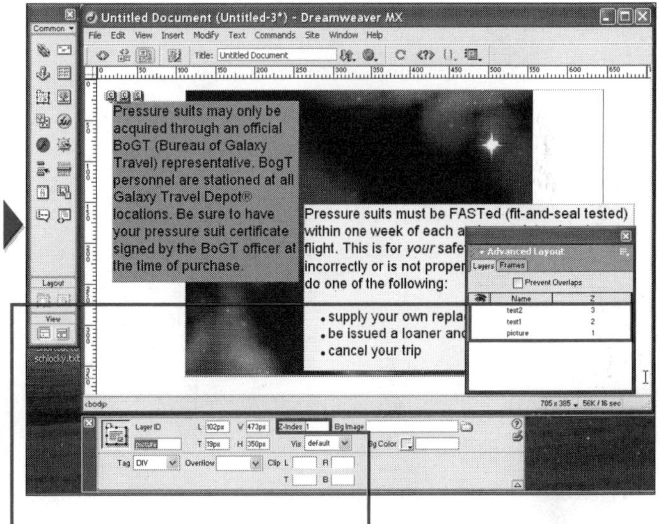

1 Click Window.

2 Click Others.

3 Click Layers.

■ The layers in the page appear in the Layers palette.

4 Click and drag a layer name to change its order in the stack.

■ You can drag the layer name up to move it higher in the stack, or drag down to send it down.

■ Dreamweaver changes the stacking order of the layers.

■ You can also select a layer in the Document window and change its z-index value in the Properties inspector.

INTRODUCTION TO BEHAVIORS

You can add interactivity to your Web pages with *behaviors*. A behavior is a cause-and-effect feature that you set up in your Web page. You specify a user event, such as a mouse click, and the resulting action, such as a pop-up window appearing, that should take place when that event occurs. Dreamweaver lets you create behaviors that produce image rollovers, validate forms, check browser versions, and more.

Build Behaviors with JavaScript

Dreamweaver builds behaviors with *JavaScript*, a popular programming language for adding dynamic features to Web sites. You apply behaviors to specific objects on your Web page using dialog boxes, and then Dreamweaver writes the JavaScript code behind the scenes to create the behaviors. The JavaScript that Dreamweaver writes coexists with your page's HTML code. You can view it by switching to Code view and looking for text enclosed in opening and closing `<script>` tags.

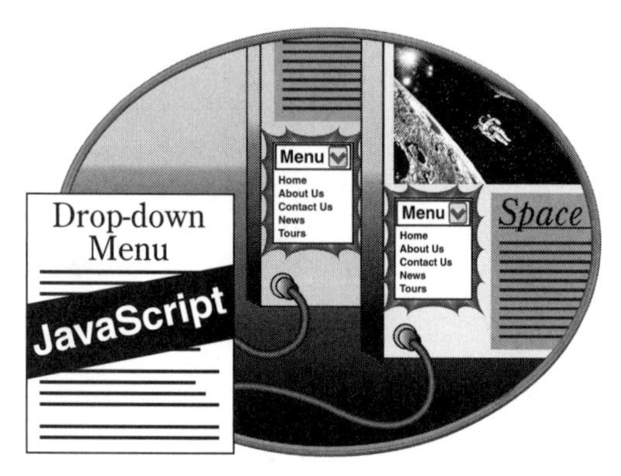

Behaviors and Browsers

Dreamweaver's standard behaviors all work in version 4 or later of Microsoft Internet Explorer and Netscape Navigator. Some of the behaviors also work in earlier browsers. The behaviors are designed such that if they load into browsers that do not support them, they fail without error — the page can still be viewed. Because some browsers still do not support certain JavaScript features and because some users surf the Web with JavaScript turned off, you probably should not make the use of a behavior a prerequisite for browsing your site. For example, you may not want to put critical text that your users need to see inside a pop-up message window that is generated by a behavior.

Create Rollover Images

A *rollover* behavior replaces an image on your page with another in response to a cursor passing over it. You often see the rollover behavior applied to navigation buttons on Web pages. Rollovers can add pizzazz to your page and give users an extra visual cue that such buttons produce an effect when clicked.

Use Form Validation

You can keep users from entering erroneous information on your forms by using a behavior to validate form fields. The behavior generates an alert if invalid data is submitted. Validating form information using behaviors is an alternative to validating it at the form handler, which is the program on the Web server that processes your form information.

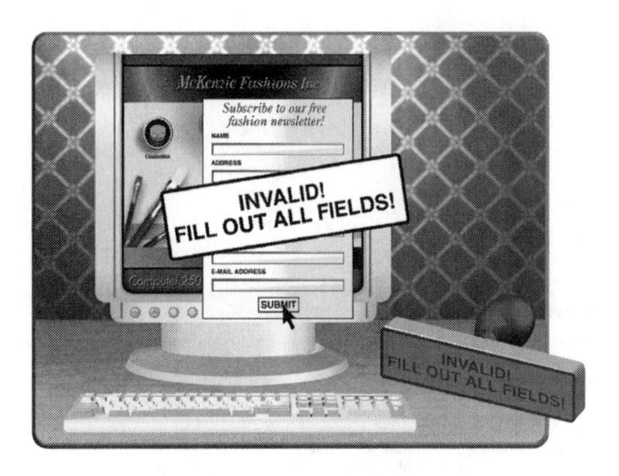

Check Browser Versions

Designing a page that works equally well in all browsers can be difficult, especially if you use advanced features, such as style sheets and layers. You can use a behavior to check the brand of browser, such as Microsoft Internet Explorer or Netscape Navigator, as well as the version. The behavior can then forward a user to a page built specifically for that browser.

CREATE A ROLLOVER IMAGE

A *rollover* behavior replaces an image on your page with another in response to a cursor passing over it. A rollover can add pizzazz to a page, and also give the viewer an extra visual cue that an image produces an effect when clicked. You often apply rollover effects to navigation buttons, where passing your cursor over the button causes it to light up or appear depressed, like a real button.

For a rollover to look its best, you want the images involved to be the same size, because the replacement image appears in the space occupied by the original. If the images differ in size, the replacement image is stretched or shrunk by the browser.

You can specify that the images involved in rollovers preload, which means the original and replacement images load into the browser when the page first appears. With preloading, the rollover effect can appear instantly when triggered. Without preloading, the browser has to load the replacement image off the Web, which can take several seconds, when the rollover event occurs.

CREATE A ROLLOVER IMAGE

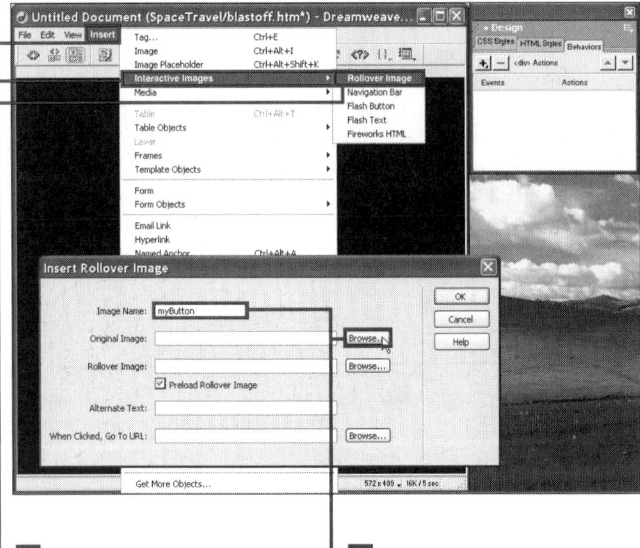

1 Click Insert.

2 Click Interactive Images.

3 Click Rollover Image.

■ The Insert Rollover Image dialog box appears.

4 Type a name for the image.

5 Click Browse to open the Original Image dialog box where you can select an original image.

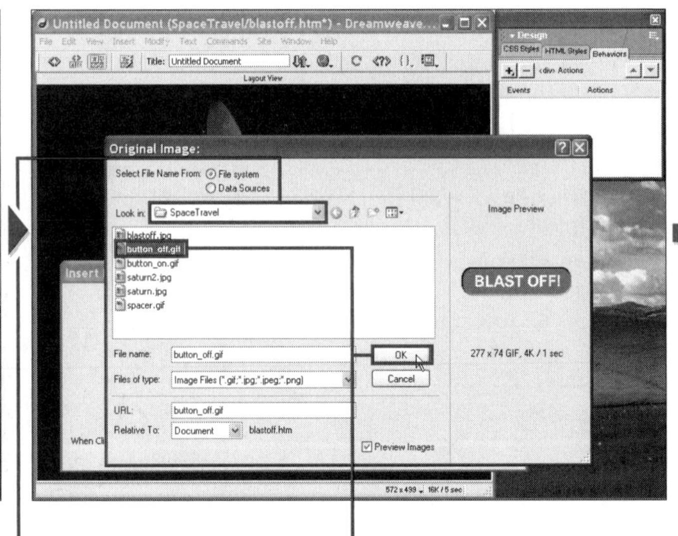

6 Click ⌄ and select the folder that contains the original image.

7 Click the original image file.

8 Click OK.

How do I create interesting rollover buttons for my page navigation?

✔ You can create interesting buttons to use for navigation in an image editor, such as Adobe Photoshop or Macromedia Fireworks. Both programs include commands that let you easily create contoured or colorful shapes that you can then label with text. Some common ways to create the replacement version of a rollover button are to reverse its colors, add a border, or shift the art slightly so it looks like the graphic has been pressed down.

Can I create a rollover using the Behaviors panel?

✔ Yes. The steps in this task show you how to create the behavior using the Rollover Image command. You can alternatively select an image in your page, open the Behaviors panel, and apply the Swap Image action to it. Note that unlike using the Rollover Image command, creating a rollover using the panel lets you swap an image other than the image that is being rolled over.

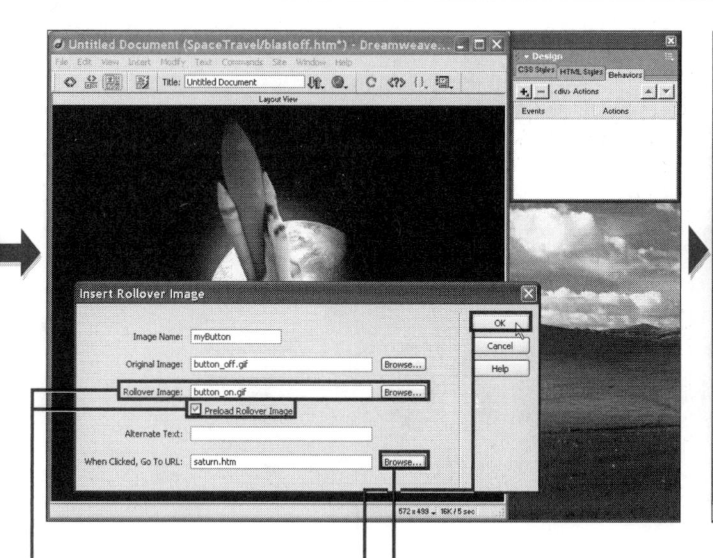

9 Repeat steps 5 to 8 for the rollover, or replacement, image.

10 Click to select the Preload Rollover Image check box (☐ changes to ☑).

11 Click Browse to select the hyperlink destination for the button.

Note: For more about hyperlinks, see pages 100 to 119.

12 Click OK.

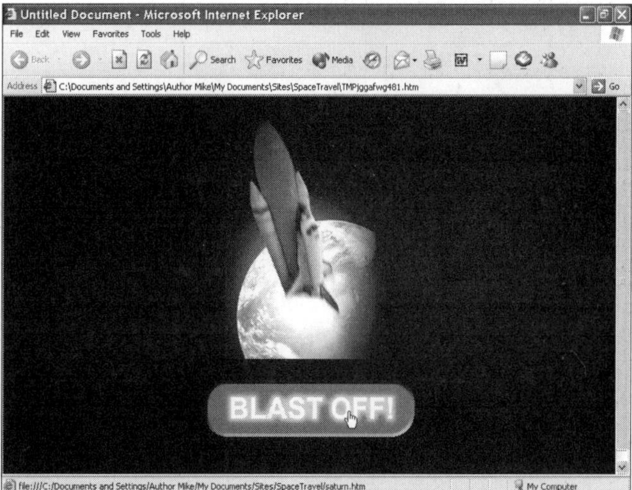

13 Preview the page in a Web browser.

Note: To preview a page in a Web browser, see page 58.

■ When you pass the cursor over the original image, the rollover image replaces it.

CREATE A STATUS BAR MESSAGE

Usually when you pass your cursor over a hyperlink on a page, the destination URL of the hyperlink appears in the status bar of the Web browser. You can use a Dreamweaver behavior to change that status bar message to one of your choosing. For example, you can display a helpful message that describes where the hyperlink takes the user.

You can also do away with the effect altogether by specifying a blank status bar message. This can help hide the file structure of your site by keeping users from seeing the file names and folders that make up your site.

You can also create a status bar message when the user rolls over an image on your page. Just select an image and then attach the status bar behavior. Unlike text, it is not necessary to hyperlink the image for the behavior to function.

A drawback of displaying information in the status bar is that the area is relatively inconspicuous, and some users may overlook it. In some browsers, users can hide the status bar.

CREATE A STATUS BAR MESSAGE

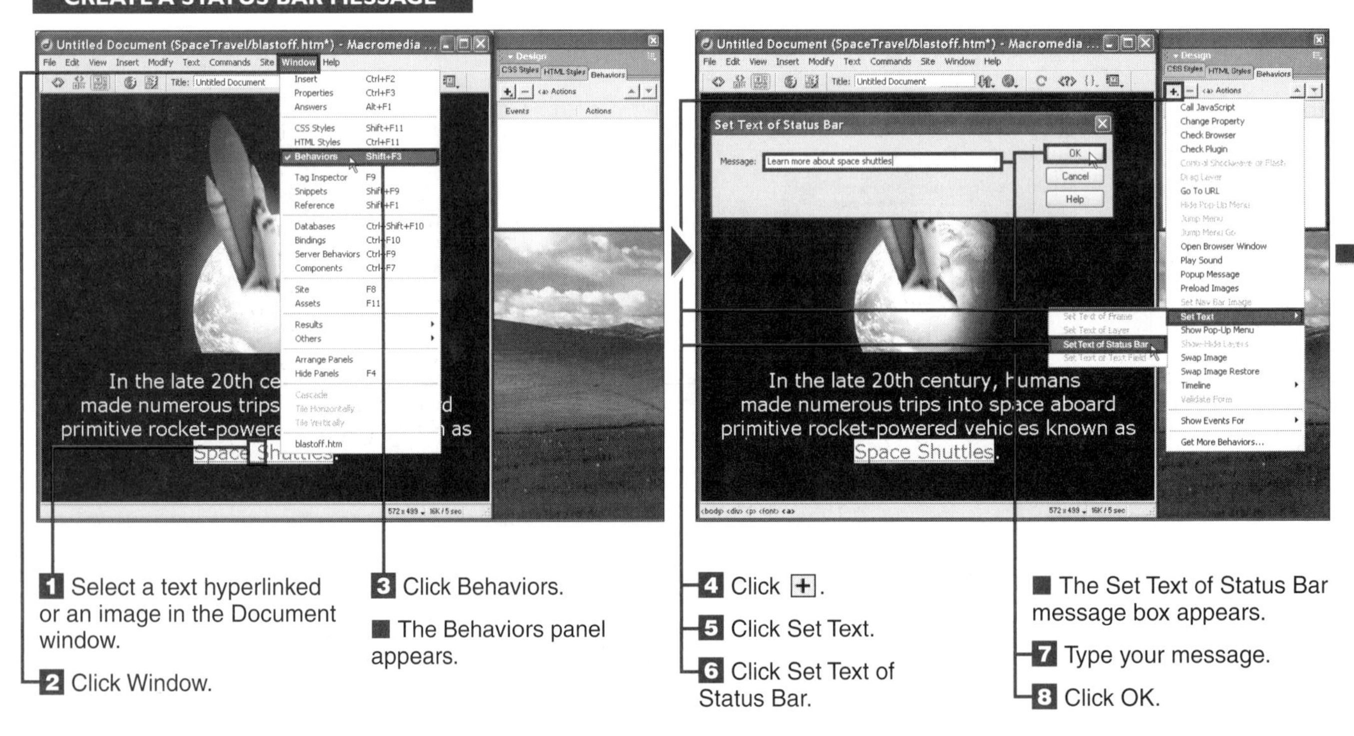

1 Select a text hyperlinked or an image in the Document window.

2 Click Window.

3 Click Behaviors.

■ The Behaviors panel appears.

4 Click [+].

5 Click Set Text.

6 Click Set Text of Status Bar.

■ The Set Text of Status Bar message box appears.

7 Type your message.

8 Click OK.

Can I make special information appear in my status bar message?

✔ You can add special JavaScript code enclosed in braces to make certain information appear. For example, `{window.location}` causes the current page's URL to appear. `{new Date()}` displays the date.

What happens if my message is too long to fit in the browser's status bar?

✔ The message still appears. But in most browsers it is cut off on the right.

How do I cause the status bar message to disappear when I roll the cursor off my object?

✔ You need to define a complementary `onMouseOut` action for your object. Repeat the steps in this task, but specify a blank message and use the `onMouseOut` event. Doing this causes the message to disappear when you roll off the object.

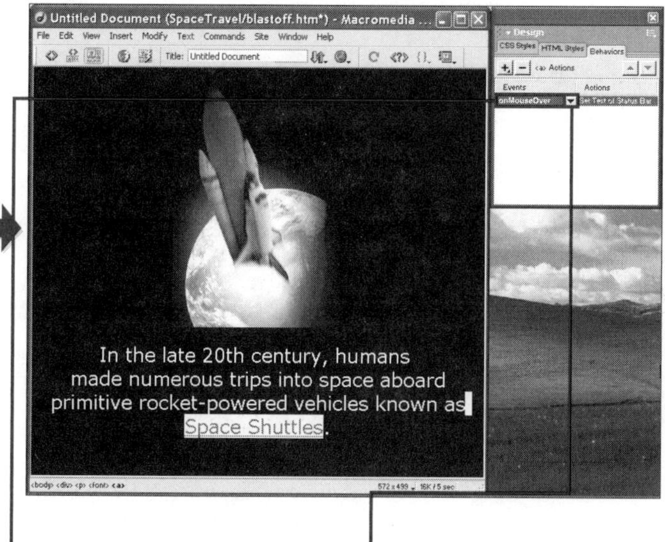

■ The default event is `onMouseOver`. This means passing the cursor over the selected object triggers the message.

■ You can click ▼ to select a different trigger event.

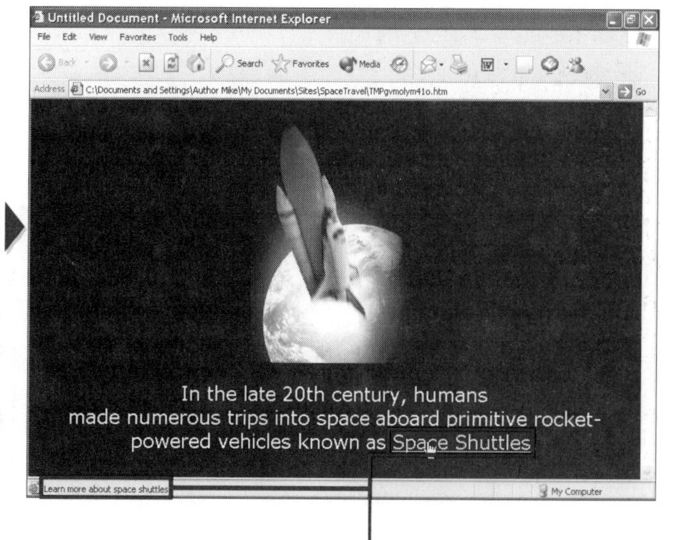

9 Preview the page in a Web browser.

Note: To preview a page in a Web browser, see page 58.

■ When you pass the cursor over the page element, the message appears.

VALIDATE A FORM

Dreamweaver helps you follow good form-building practices by validating the information the user submits before a form handler processes it. This validation can include checking that postal codes have the correct number of numeric characters and that e-mail addresses are in the correct format.

You can use a Dreamweaver behavior to check data submitted by a form and generate an alert if the data is not valid. The user can then re-enter the data and submit the form again. Validation helps keep potentially corrupt data out of your database.

This kind of form validation is known as *client-side validation*, because the check is done by the browser or client. An alternative is to validate the form data at the form handler, also called *server-side validation*. This is slower, because the form data must be sent to the Web server for processing, and more difficult to implement, because form handlers can be a challenge to write and debug. On the other hand, browsers that do not have JavaScript capability cannot have their form information validated by the Dreamweaver behavior.

VALIDATE A FORM

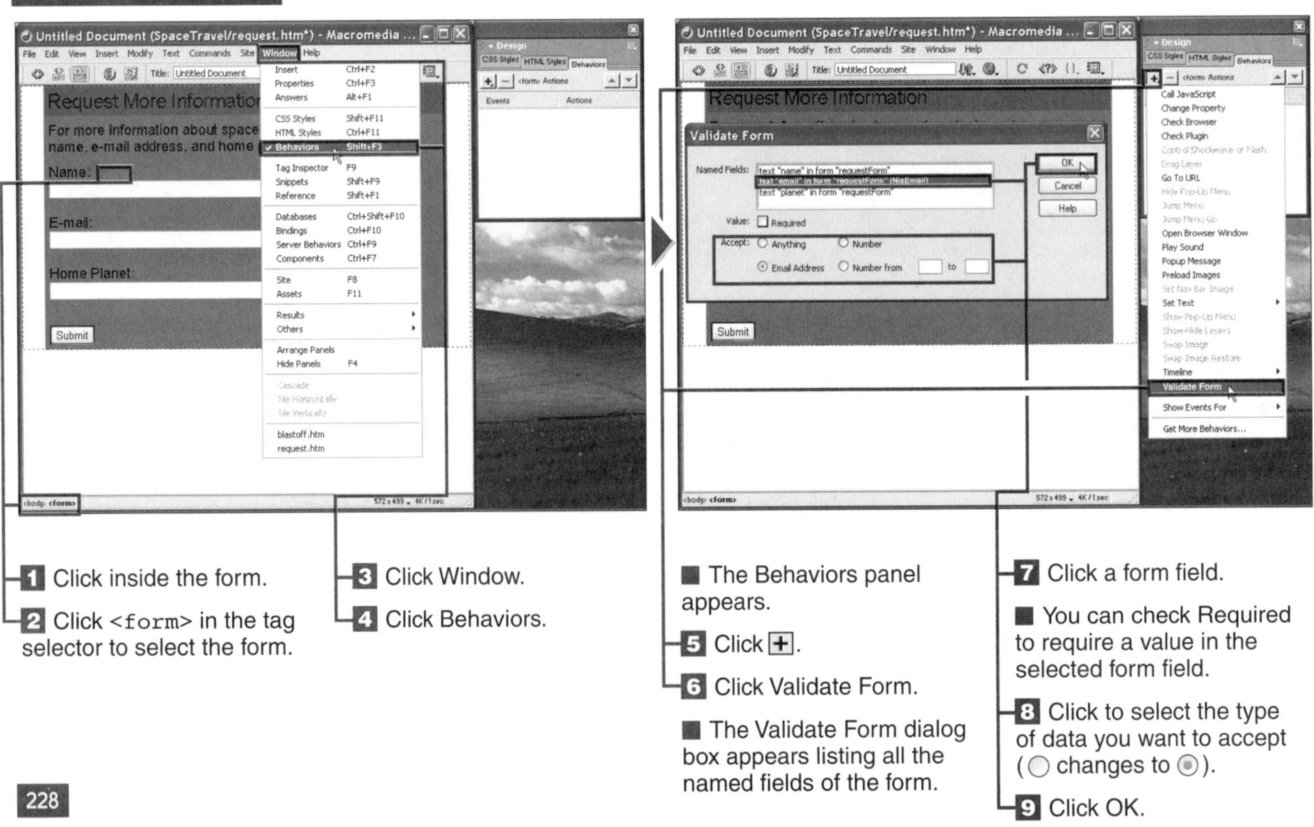

1 Click inside the form.

2 Click <form> in the tag selector to select the form.

3 Click Window.

4 Click Behaviors.

■ The Behaviors panel appears.

5 Click [+].

6 Click Validate Form.

■ The Validate Form dialog box appears listing all the named fields of the form.

7 Click a form field.

■ You can check Required to require a value in the selected form field.

8 Click to select the type of data you want to accept (○ changes to ◉).

9 Click OK.

What browser events should I use to trigger validation?

✔ If you need to validate a single field in a form, you can use the `onBlur` event to trigger validation. In this case, the validation occurs when the user clicks away from the field. If you need to validate multiple fields, you need to use `onSubmit` for the trigger. In this case, the validation occurs after the Submit button is clicked. Dreamweaver automatically applies `onBlur` if you select a single field and attach the validation behavior. It applies `onSubmit` if you select the entire form and apply the validation behavior.

Why is the Anything option made available in the Validate Form dialog box?

✔ If you select Anything and check Required, Dreamweaver checks to make sure *something* is entered in the field — and alerts the user if that field is empty. Without Required selected, the Anything selection is meaningless.

How does Dreamweaver determine if a field contains a number or an e-mail address?

✔ Dreamweaver's criteria for determining this are rudimentary. If Number is selected, Dreamweaver checks for nonnumeric characters — anything other than numbers and a single decimal point. E-mail addresses are validated with a simple check for an @ sign.

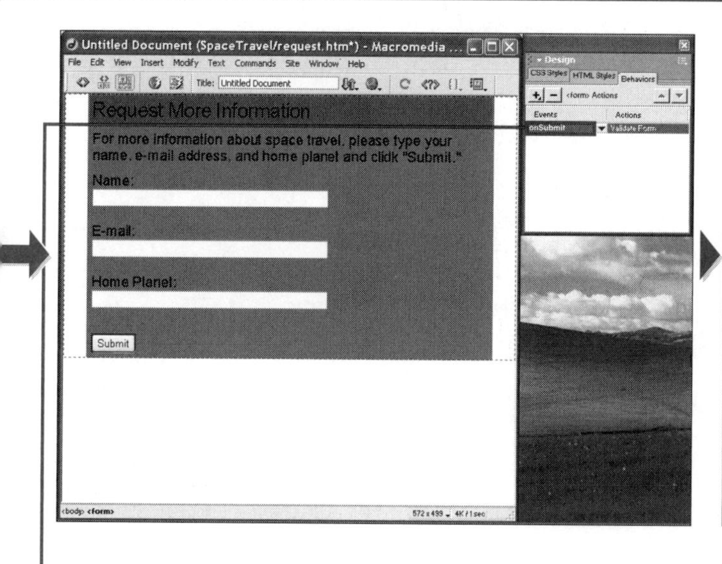

■ The default event when you apply validation to an entire form is `onSubmit`. When the user clicks the Submit button, the form is validated.

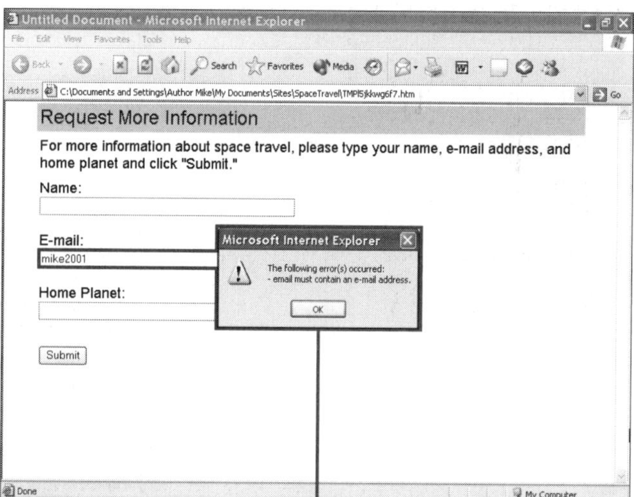

10 Preview the Web page in a browser.

Note: To preview a page in a Web browser, see page 58.

■ If you submit the form with invalid content in a field, the browser generates a pop-up alert.

■ In this example, an alert appears because an invalid e-mail address was entered.

OPEN A CUSTOMIZED BROWSER WINDOW

You can cause a hyperlink to open a new, customized browser window using a Dreamweaver behavior. You can tailor the window for viewing specialized content on your Web site. You can set various properties of the new window, including its dimensions, whether it has a menu bar or scroll bars, its name, and other attributes. By not including the typical attributes that appear in new browser windows, you can maximize the amount of content that can appear in the window.

One useful way to use customized windows is to size them to the dimensions of the image, movie, or other content that appears in the window. This way, the window can open over the existing page and act as a miniature console for viewing the content. Users can click the Close button on the window when they want to return to the original page.

The Open Browser Window behavior is similar to the one described on page 114. That feature uses the target hyperlink attribute rather than JavaScript to cause a hyperlink to open a new window.

OPEN A CUSTOMIZED BROWSER WINDOW

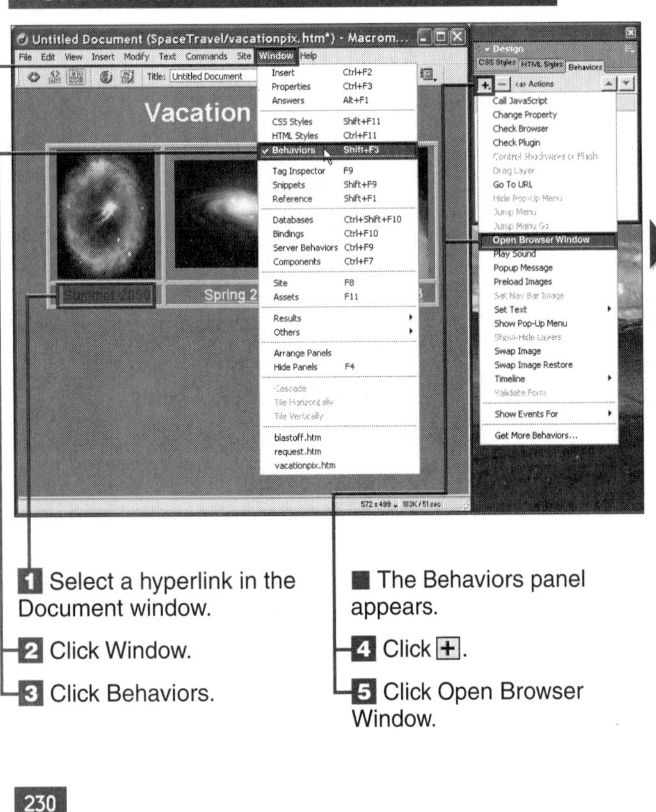

1 Select a hyperlink in the Document window.

2 Click Window.

3 Click Behaviors.

■ The Behaviors panel appears.

4 Click [+].

5 Click Open Browser Window.

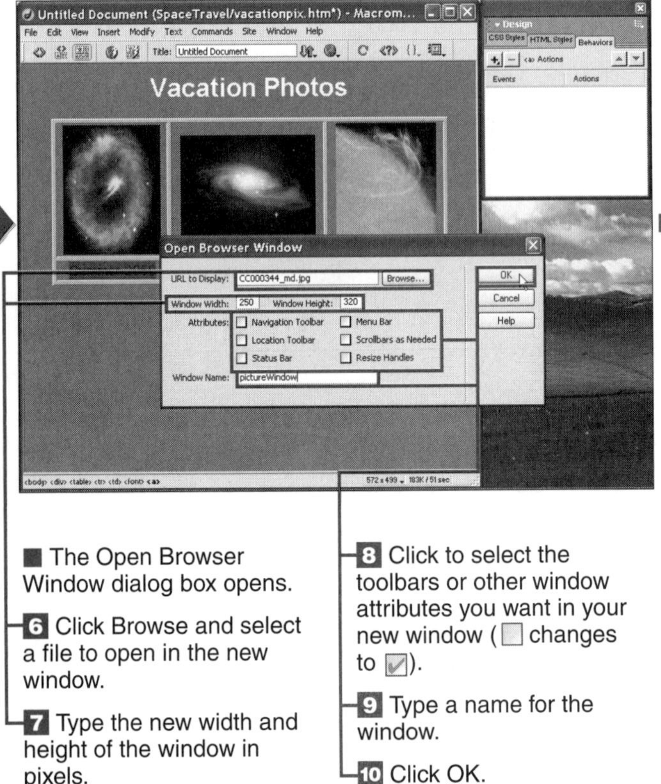

■ The Open Browser Window dialog box opens.

6 Click Browse and select a file to open in the new window.

7 Type the new width and height of the window in pixels.

8 Click to select the toolbars or other window attributes you want in your new window (☐ changes to ☑).

9 Type a name for the window.

10 Click OK.

What happens if I do not specify any attributes of the window?

✔ If you do not specify *any* attributes, the new window opens at the size and with the attributes of the window that spawned it — the current window. If you specify *some* attributes, such as just the window dimensions, all the other attributes that are not explicitly turned on are disabled.

What happens if I leave resize handles off of my new window?

✔ The user cannot resize the new window by clicking and dragging the bottom-right corner or by clicking the maximize button on the title bar.

Why is naming the window useful?

✔ Naming the window enables you to target the window with other hyperlinks in your site. Similar to having a set of hyperlinks in one frame open all their destination content in another frame, you can have a set of links in one window open all their content in another window.

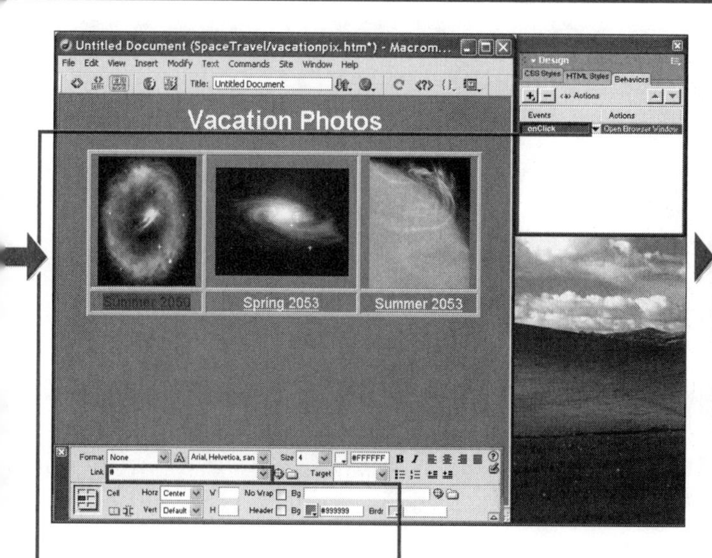

■ Check to make sure onClick is the trigger event. You may have to click ▼, click Show Events For, and then click 4.0 and Later Browsers to make it available.

11 Replace any existing hyperlink destination with a pound sign (#) to prevent files from opening in the old window.

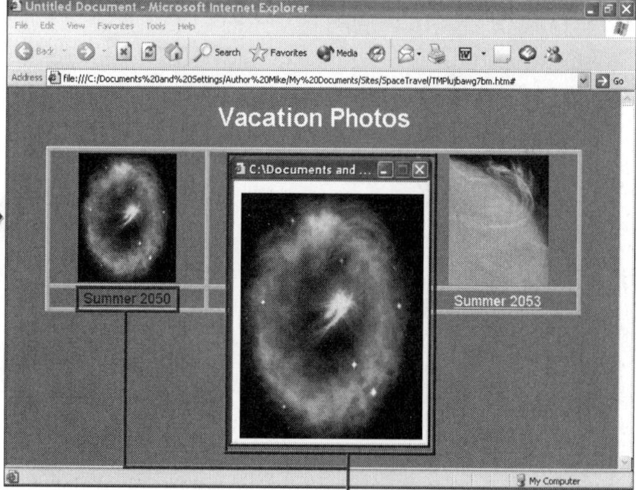

12 Preview the Web page in a browser.

Note: To preview a page in a Web browser, see page 58.

■ When you click the hyperlink, the new browser window appears with the specified file inside it.

CHECK THE BROWSER OF A USER

Designing a page that works equally well in all browsers is difficult, especially if you use advanced features, such as style sheets and layers. To get around this, you can use a behavior to check the brand and version of the browser, and then forward a user to a page built specifically for that browser.

For example, you want to feature layers-based content on your home page. But you also want to accommodate version 3 browsers, which cannot display layers. A possible solution is to create your home page without layers and place the layers version on a secondary page. Then you can have a behavior check the browser on the home page and forward users with version 4 or better to the secondary page while keeping users with other browsers where they are.

You can also use the check-browser feature to forward users of Netscape Navigator and Microsoft Internet Explorer to different pages. This option can be useful if you want to integrate design features that are specific to one or the other browser.

CHECK THE BROWSER OF A USER

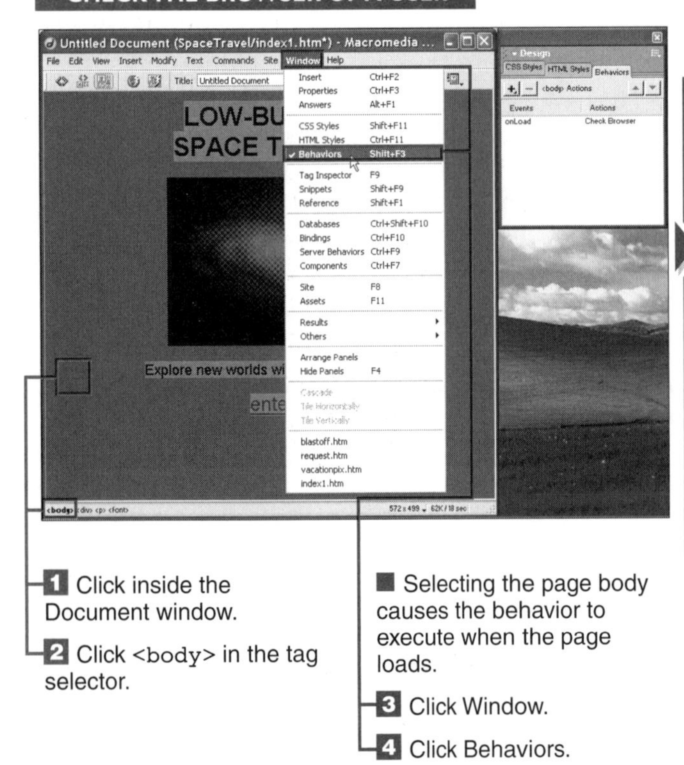

1 Click inside the Document window.

2 Click <body> in the tag selector.

■ Selecting the page body causes the behavior to execute when the page loads.

3 Click Window.

4 Click Behaviors.

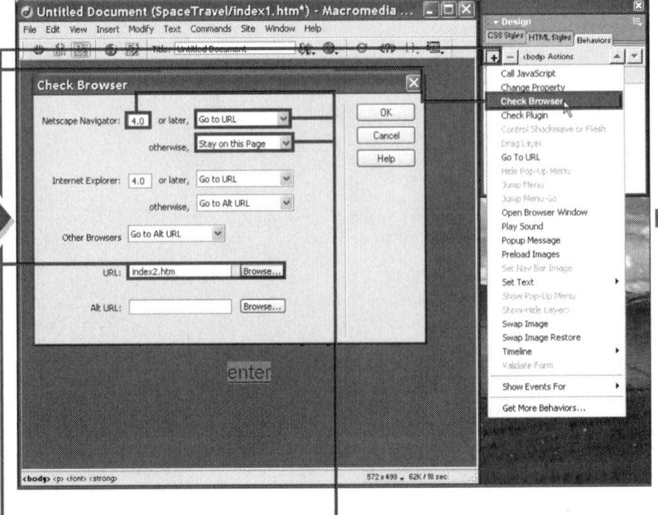

■ The Behaviors panel appears.

5 Click [+].

6 Click Check Browser.

7 Click Browse to select a destination page on your site.

■ If you want to send some users to a second page, click Browse to select the page. You can also type an external URL.

8 Type a Netscape Navigator version to test for.

9 Click [v] to select destinations for the test.

What other browsers are there besides Microsoft Internet Explorer and Netscape Navigator?

✔ Although the vast majority of Web users have one of the "big two" browsers, some may use America Online's browser, which is based on Internet Explorer; Opera, available for all platforms; Lynx, which is text-based, for Windows, UNIX, and DOS; iCab, for Macintosh; WebTV; and others.

Can I use a behavior to check a browser for plugins?

✔ Yes. Similar to the Check Browser behavior, you can use a behavior to check for multimedia plug-ins installed in a browser. The predefined tests for the behavior let you check for Flash, Shockwave, LiveAudio, Windows Media Player, and QuickTime in Netscape Navigator. In Internet Explorer (Windows), only the Flash and Shockwave tests work. In Internet Explorer (Mac), you cannot check for any plug-ins.

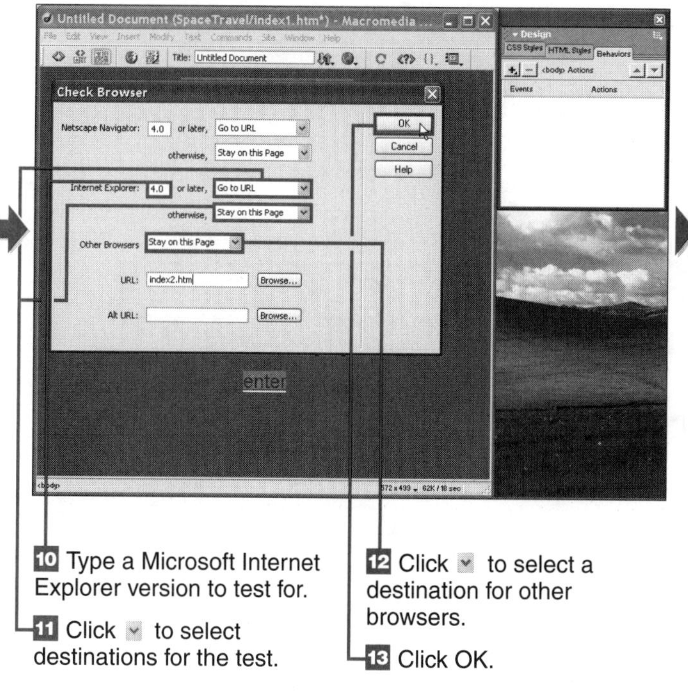

10 Type a Microsoft Internet Explorer version to test for.

11 Click ▾ to select destinations for the test.

12 Click ▾ to select a destination for other browsers.

13 Click OK.

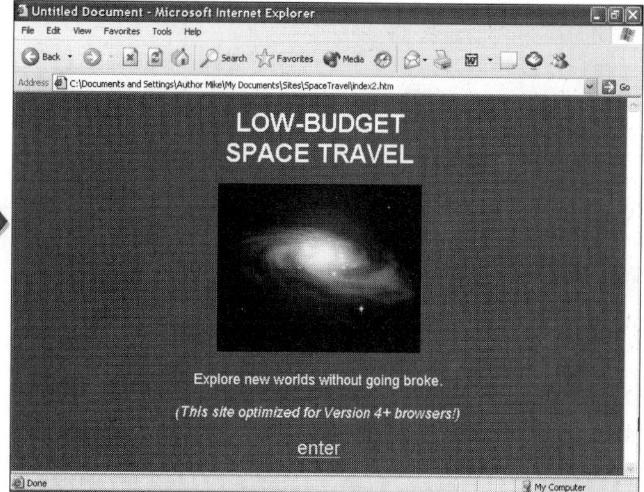

14 Preview the page in a Web browser.

Note: To preview a page in a Web browser, see page 58.

■ When the Web page opens in a Web browser, the browser loads the original page, checks the browser's brand and version, and forwards the user to a new page if required.

■ In this example, the Web page is opened in Microsoft Internet Explorer 6. The browser is forwarded to a custom page.

DEBUG JAVASCRIPT

Debugging your *JavaScript* enables you to catch errors in your programming and save users from experiencing broken features on your site. JavaScript is a programming language that you can use to add interactivity to your Web page. Unlike HTML, which is a *markup language* used for formatting Web pages, JavaScript is a full-fledged programming language that can be challenging to write and difficult to get working perfectly.

Dreamweaver provides a JavaScript debugger that helps you pinpoint any errors in your JavaScript code. The debugger can also help you fix your JavaScript by letting you step through code line by line and examine the program's variables as it executes.

The debugger needs a browser running to operate. It can work with Netscape Navigator and Microsoft Internet Explorer on Windows, and Netscape Navigator on Macintosh. To debug your page, you view the page in a browser and the JavaScript code in a special Dreamweaver window.

Dreamweaver writes JavaScript code when you add behaviors to your page. You can use the debugger to analyze this code. You can also use the debugger to check any custom JavaScript that you have added to your page yourself.

DEBUG JAVASCRIPT

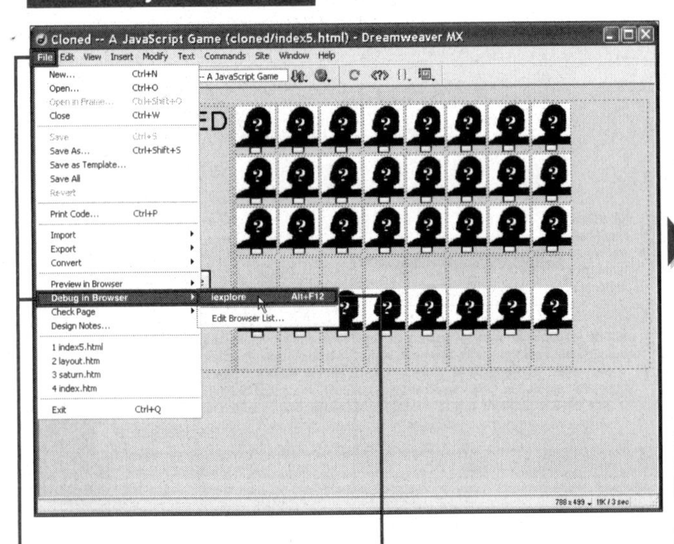

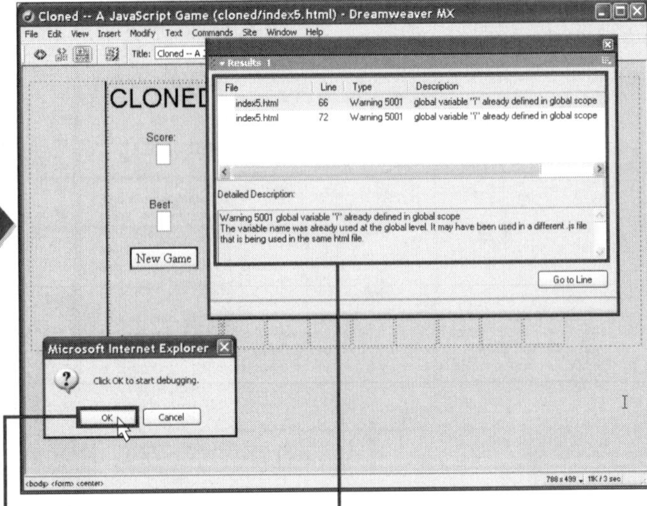

1 Open a file that contains JavaScript.

2 Click File.

3 Click Debug in Browser.

4 Click a browser.

Note: You may initially see dialog boxes asking if you want to grant Dreamweaver access to your browser. Click the buttons to give it access.

■ An alert box appears.

5 Click OK to start the debugger.

6 Click OK if Dreamweaver displays a dialog box asking you to set a breakpoint.

■ Dreamweaver checks the syntax of your JavaScript. It displays any errors that it finds in a separate window.

What are breakpoints?

✔ *Breakpoints* are triggers that you can set at specific lines of your JavaScript code. When the JavaScript debugger encounters a breakpoint, it pauses. Breakpoints let you examine variables at a point in time during the execution of your JavaScript.

How do I stop code execution in progress?

✔ You can click ▮ to stop your JavaScript from executing.

How do I step through my code one statement at a time?

✔ You can use the button to step through your code one statement at a time. When you hit a function call, you can click to step into (execute) the function and monitor how it runs. You can click to step out of (exit) a function.

How do I remove the breakpoints that I have defined in the debugger?

✔ You can click to delete all your breakpoints.

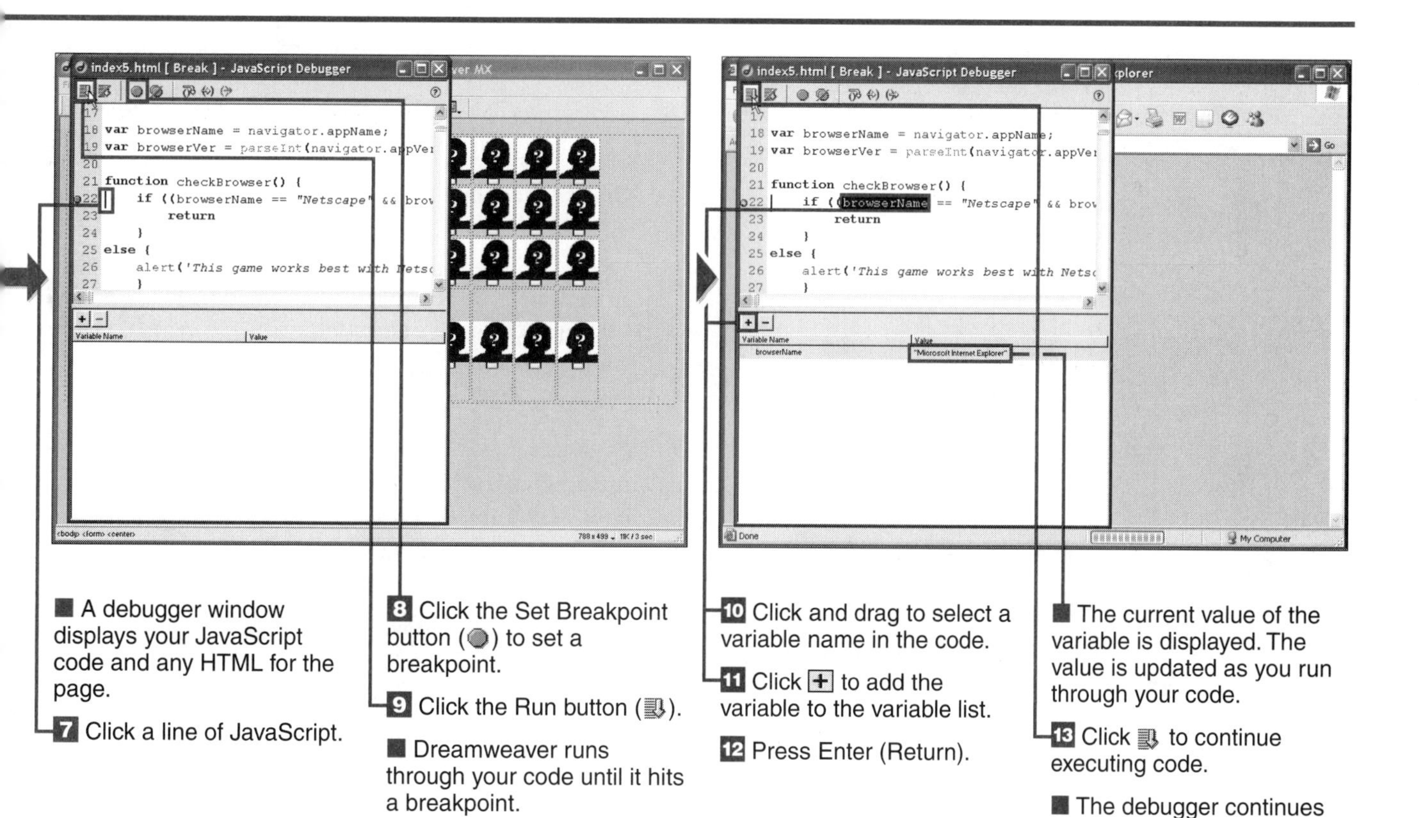

■ A debugger window displays your JavaScript code and any HTML for the page.

7 Click a line of JavaScript.

8 Click the Set Breakpoint button (●) to set a breakpoint.

9 Click the Run button ().

■ Dreamweaver runs through your code until it hits a breakpoint.

10 Click and drag to select a variable name in the code.

11 Click + to add the variable to the variable list.

12 Press Enter (Return).

■ The current value of the variable is displayed. The value is updated as you run through your code.

13 Click to continue executing code.

■ The debugger continues to the next breakpoint.

INTRODUCTION TO TIMELINES

Timelines are an easy way to introduce movement to an otherwise static Web page. They allow you to move text and images on your page in straight or curved paths by changing the properties of Web page layers. Dreamweaver lets you create these effects quickly with a full-featured Timelines inspector.

Animate Your Pages

Timelines enable you to manipulate the position, visibility, and other attributes of a Web page's layers over time. For an introduction to layers, see Chapter 12. You can use timelines to make images float across a page, cause overlapping layers of text to shuffle positions, or create tables that appear and disappear. Because timelines rely on layers, timeline animation works only in Version 4.0 or later browsers.

Combine HTML and JavaScript

You create timeline animations with JavaScript, which can change the HTML and style-sheet properties of a page over time. This combining of JavaScript, style sheets, and HTML is also known as Dynamic HTML. You define the characteristics of a timeline using the Timelines inspector; Dreamweaver then writes the JavaScript code behind the scenes to create the animation.

Create Timeline Frames

You define the action that occurs in a timeline animation as a sequence of frames. Typically, you have 10 to 15 frames for every second of animation. Each frame contains information about the layer being animated at a moment in time. Usually, you define just a few of the frames — the so-called *keyframes* — in a timeline yourself. Dreamweaver fills in the rest, basing the other frames off the keyframe information you provide.

USING THE TIMELINES INSPECTOR

The Timelines inspector lets you create animations by specifying the position and other characteristics of layers on your page at different times. You can click Window, Others, and then Timelines to open the inspector.

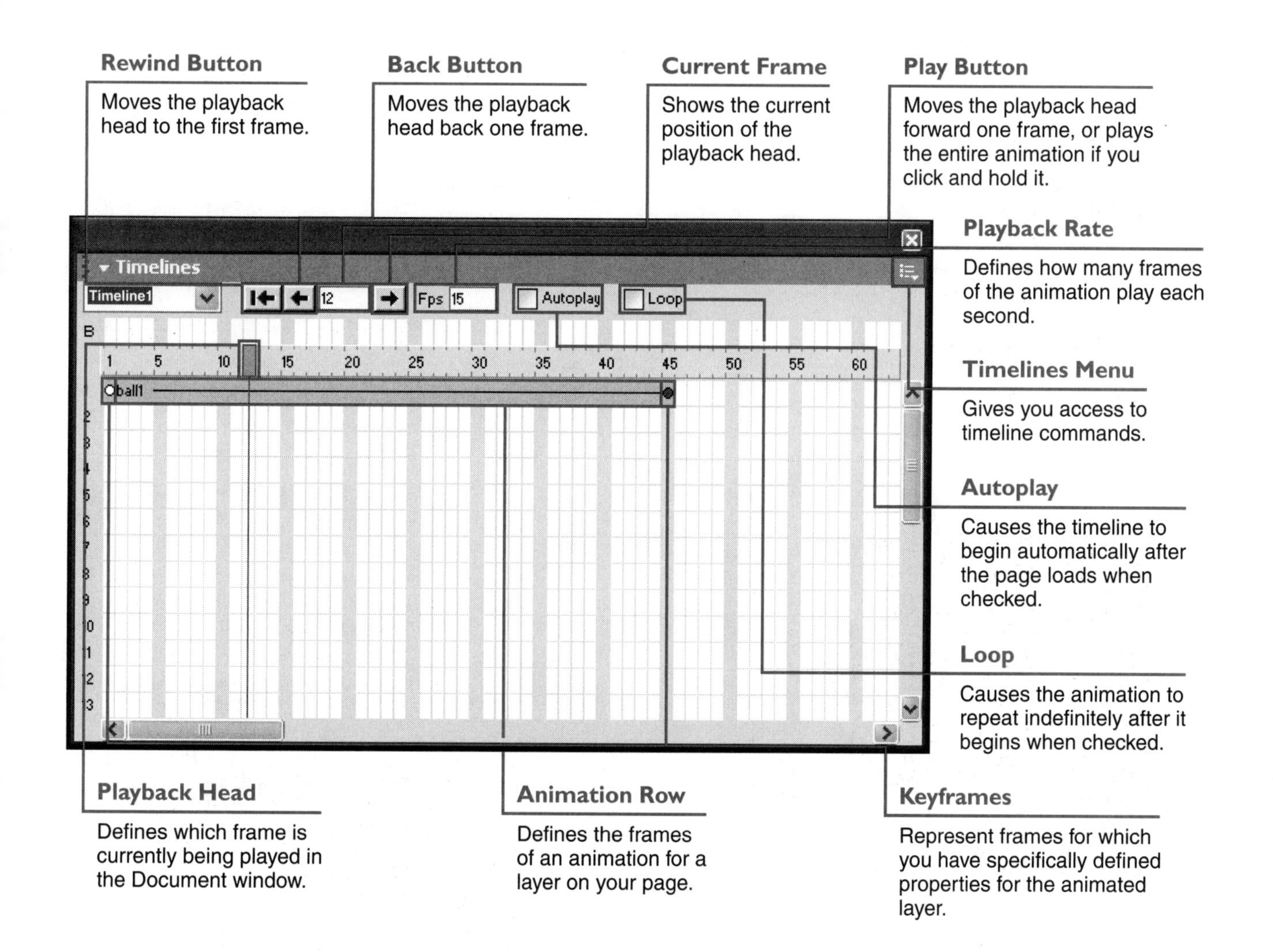
Rewind Button
Moves the playback head to the first frame.
Back Button
Moves the playback head back one frame.
Current Frame
Shows the current position of the playback head.
Play Button
Moves the playback head forward one frame, or plays the entire animation if you click and hold it.
Playback Rate
Defines how many frames of the animation play each second.
Timelines Menu
Gives you access to timeline commands.
Autoplay
Causes the timeline to begin automatically after the page loads when checked.
Loop
Causes the animation to repeat indefinitely after it begins when checked.
Playback Head
Defines which frame is currently being played in the Document window.
Animation Row
Defines the frames of an animation for a layer on your page.
Keyframes
Represent frames for which you have specifically defined properties for the animated layer.
Timelines
Timeline1
12
Fps 15
Autoplay
Loop
B
1 5 10 15 20 25 30 35 40 45 50 55 60
ball1

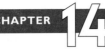

CREATE A STRAIGHT-LINE ANIMATION

You can create a timeline animation that moves a layer in a straight line on your page. A *straight-line animation* is a quick and easy way to enliven a page that otherwise consists of static text and images.

Creating a straight-line animation involves defining two keyframes: one at the beginning of the timeline's animation bar, and one at the end. The beginning keyframe specifies the position of your layer at the start of the animation. The end keyframe specifies the position of the layer at the end of the animation. Dreamweaver fills in position information for the frames in between.

You can change the speed of the animation by adjusting the length of the animation bar or the timeline's frame rate. See page 244 for more information.

Because you can fill a layer with any type of page element — including text, images, tables, and multimedia — you can turn practically anything you can put on a Web page into an animation. To learn more about adding layers to your page and filling them with content, see Chapter 12.

CREATE A STRAIGHT-LINE ANIMATION

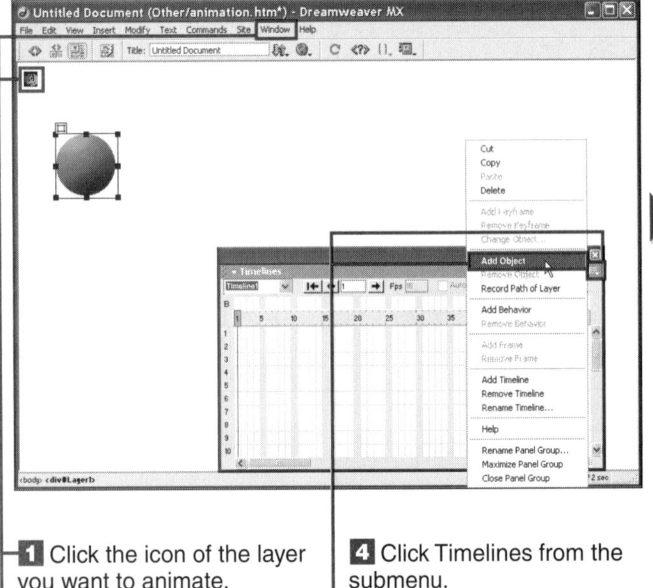

1 Click the icon of the layer you want to animate.

Note: To add a layer to your page, see page 216.

2 Click Window.

3 Click Others from the drop-down menu.

4 Click Timelines from the submenu.

■ The Timelines inspector opens.

5 Click to open the Timelines menu.

6 Click Add Object.

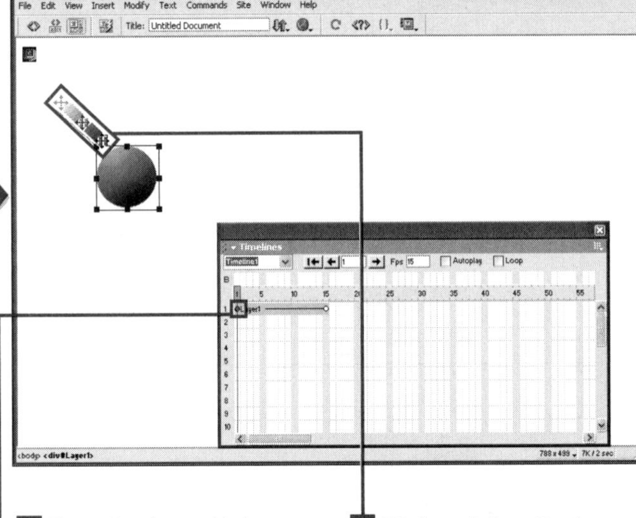

7 If an alert box with layer attribute information appears, click OK.

8 Click the keyframe at the beginning of the animation bar.

9 Click and drag the layer to its initial position.

Does the position of the animation on the page change with the size of the browser window?

✔ You define timeline animations using absolute coordinates, which means that their positions do not change with changes in the size of the browser window. This means that if you place animations on the far right of your page, they could potentially not be visible to users viewing your site on smaller monitors.

Can I create several straight-line animations on a single Web page?

✔ Yes. Put each piece of content that you want to animate in its own layer and then define an animation bar in the Timelines inspector for each layer. To add each additional animation bar to the Timelines inspector, click a layer and use the Add Object command in the Timelines menu. You can place animation bars on different rows in the inspector, which allows the animations to play simultaneously on the page. You can also place the bars one after the other on the same row, which causes the animations to play sequentially. You can click and drag the animation bars in the inspector to change their positions.

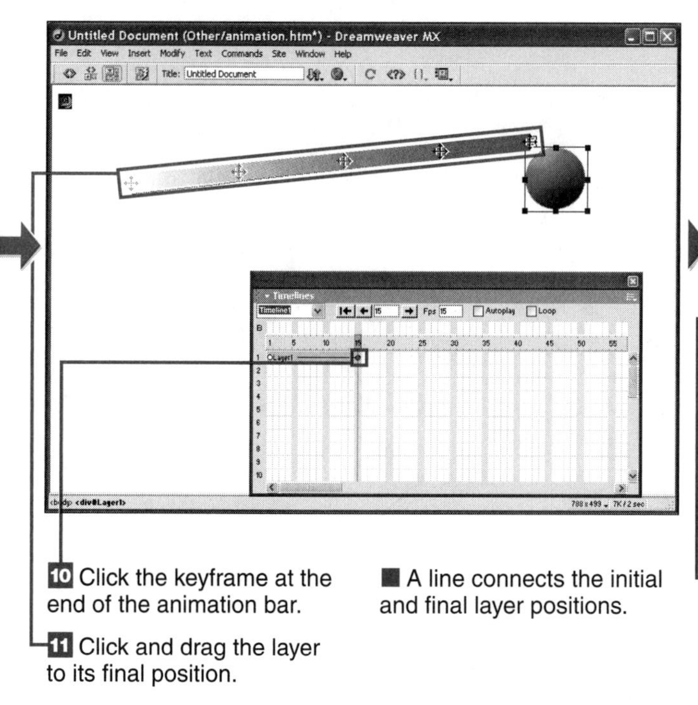

10 Click the keyframe at the end of the animation bar.

11 Click and drag the layer to its final position.

■ A line connects the initial and final layer positions.

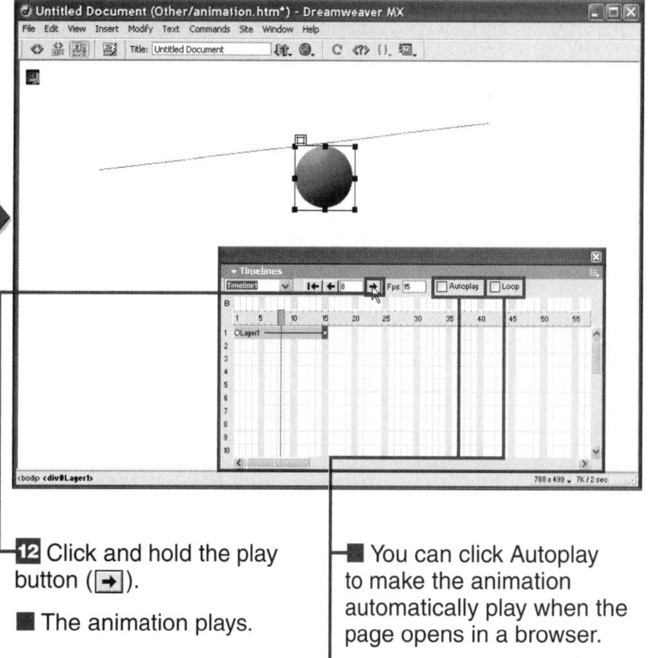

12 Click and hold the play button (➔).

■ The animation plays.

■ You can click Autoplay to make the animation automatically play when the page opens in a browser.

■ You can click Loop to make the animation repeat indefinitely after it starts.

CREATE AN ANIMATION BY DRAGGING A PATH

While some of the animations you may want to create involve movement in straight lines, others may involve more complex paths that include loops and curves. To create these animations, you can drag a layer along the intended path and have Dreamweaver record the path as you go.

Dreamweaver creates the animation bar for you in the inspector, inserting the appropriate keyframes where the path changes direction. After you record your path, you can edit it by moving the playback head to a keyframe, and then repositioning the layer in the Document window.

Recording a path can be a great timesaver, because describing an animation that includes loops or curves can require you to insert many keyframes and carefully position your layer for each one.

Creating an acceptable recording can also be a challenge, however, because Dreamweaver records not only the position of the layer as you drag but also the speed at which you move it. If you speed up and slow down as you move your layer, you can end up with a jerky animation that looks unnatural.

CREATE AN ANIMATION BY DRAGGING A PATH

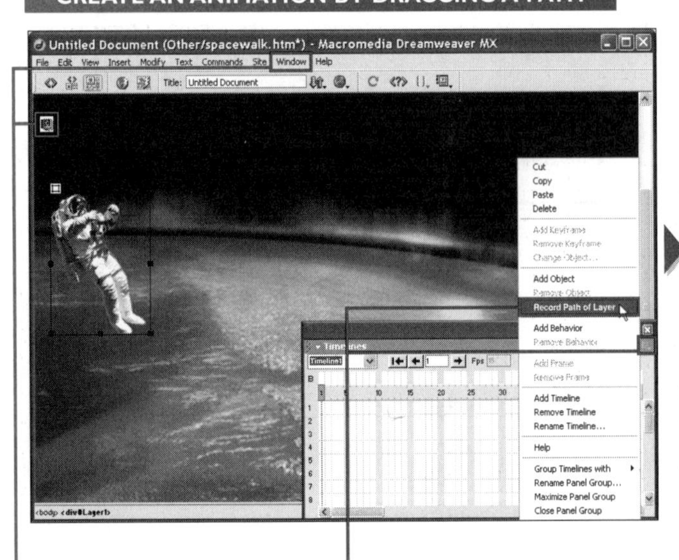

1 Click the icon of the layer you want to animate.

Note: To add a layer to your page, see page 216.

2 Click Window.

3 Click Others from the drop-down menu.

4 Click Timelines from the submenu.

■ The Timelines inspector opens.

5 Click ▤ to open the Timelines menu.

6 Click Record Path of Layer.

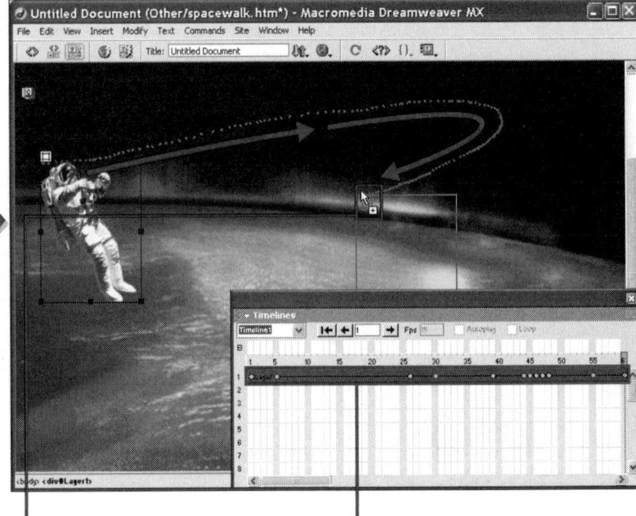

7 Click and drag the layer along the intended animation path.

8 If, after dragging, an alert box with layer attribute information appears, click OK.

■ Dreamweaver creates an animation bar that describes the path that was recorded.

Can I cause a layer to rotate using timelines?

✔ While the path of a timeline animation can contain curves and loops, you cannot use timelines to actually rotate the content that is inside a layer. The content in the layer that is being animated must stay perpendicular to the browser window as it moves. One way to put rotating content on your page is to create it as an animated GIF file. You can create animated GIFs in Macromedia Fireworks.

How can I change the speed of a recorded animation?

✔ If you want to slow down an animation, increase the length of the animation bar by clicking the last keyframe on the bar and dragging right. If you want to speed it up, decrease the length of the animation bar by clicking the last keyframe on the bar and dragging left. For more information, see page 244.

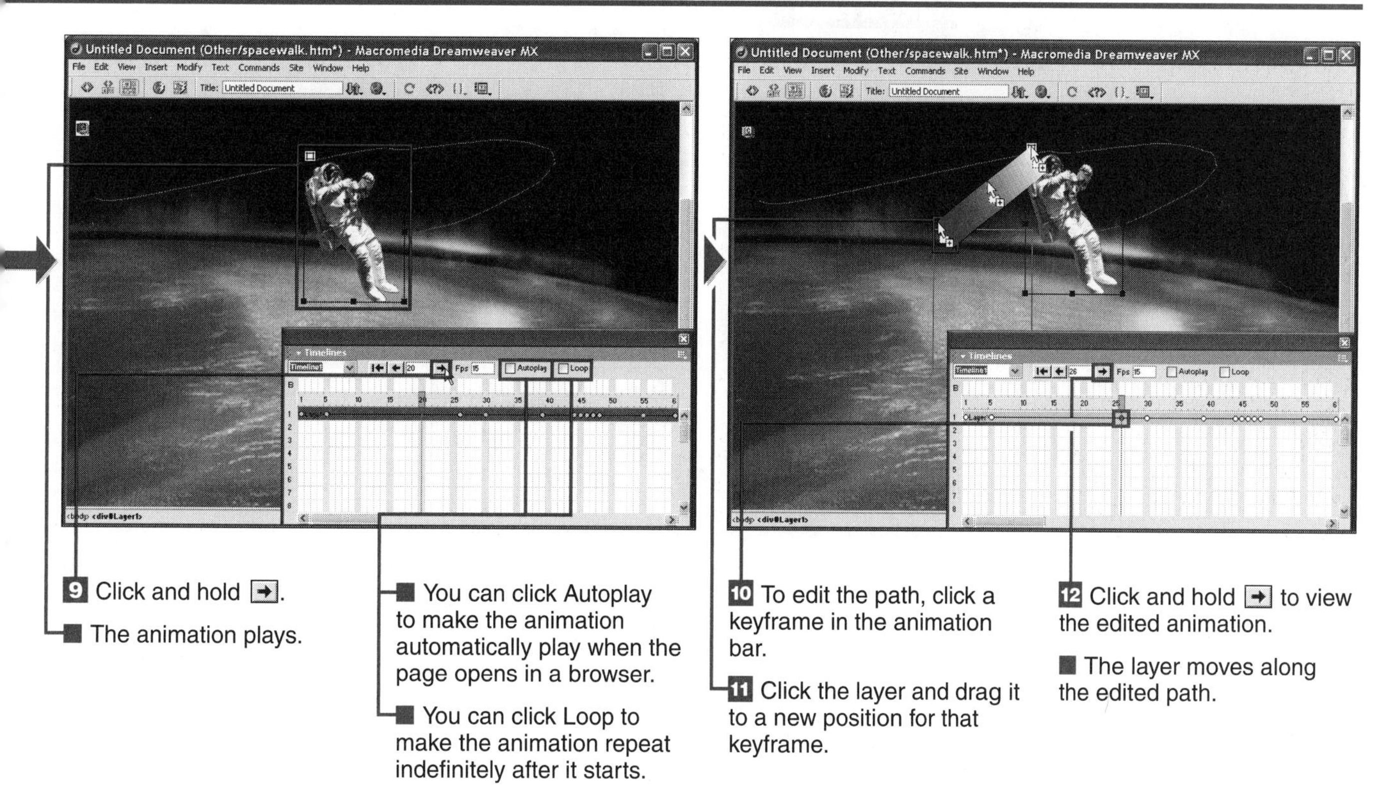

9 Click and hold ➔.

■ The animation plays.

■ You can click Autoplay to make the animation automatically play when the page opens in a browser.

■ You can click Loop to make the animation repeat indefinitely after it starts.

10 To edit the path, click a keyframe in the animation bar.

11 Click the layer and drag it to a new position for that keyframe.

12 Click and hold ➔ to view the edited animation.

■ The layer moves along the edited path.

CHANGE LAYER PROPERTIES IN TIMELINES

You can change the visibility, dimensions, and Z-index of a layer over time to achieve interesting animated effects on your Web page. You can do this by making adjustments in the Properties inspector at different keyframes in your timeline.

Changing visibility enables you to make elements in your page appear or disappear at different times, or flash on and off repeatedly. You can combine changes of visibility with changes in position to create layered content that flashes as it moves across the page.

Changing dimensions of a layer in a timeline can make the layer gradually expand or shrink in size. If the Overflow value of a layer is set to hidden, shrinking a layer over time can cause content to gradually disappear as the layer closes around it. You can set a layer's Overflow value in the Property inspector.

The *Z-index* refers to the relative position a layer assumes when it is stacked with other layers. The greater the Z-index, the higher the layer is in the stack. You can change the Z-index in a timeline to shuffle stacked layers on your page.

CHANGE LAYER PROPERTIES IN TIMELINES

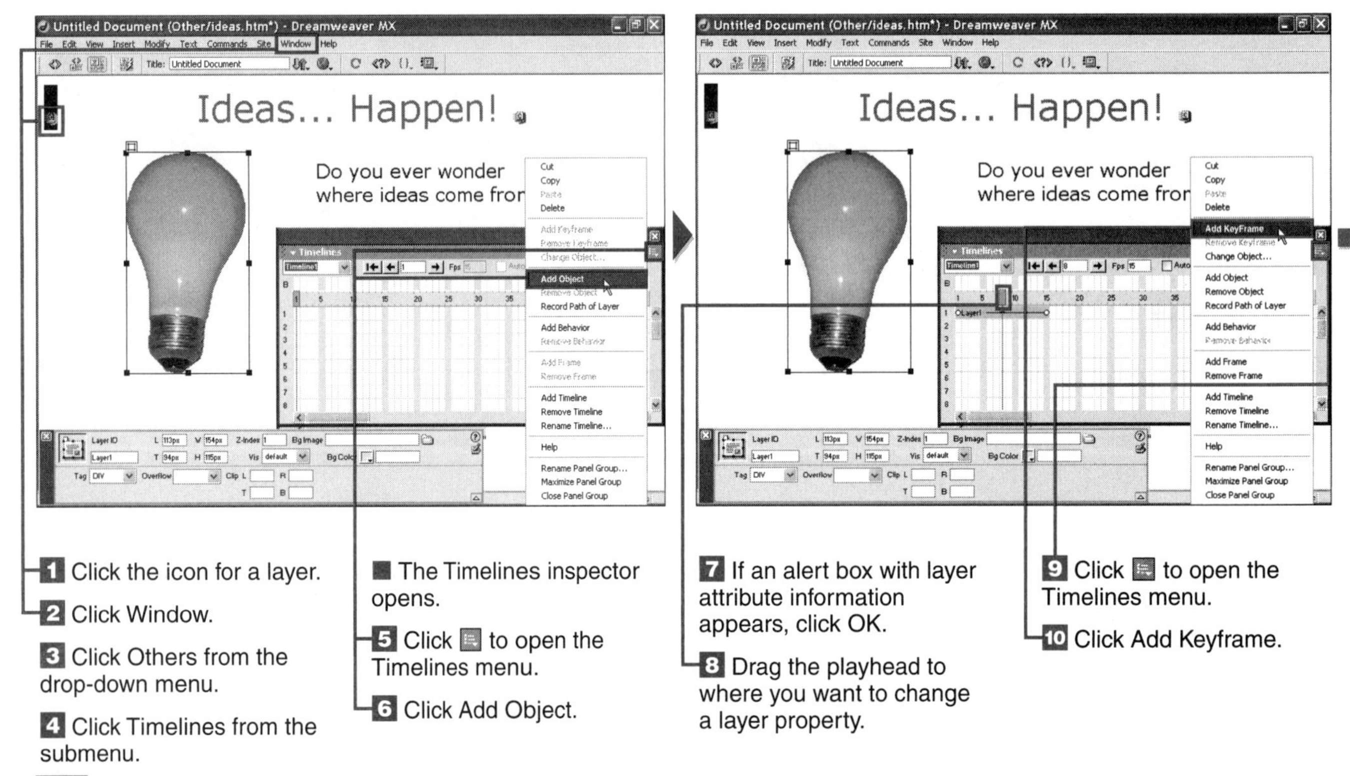

1 Click the icon for a layer.

2 Click Window.

3 Click Others from the drop-down menu.

4 Click Timelines from the submenu.

■ The Timelines inspector opens.

5 Click ▤ to open the Timelines menu.

6 Click Add Object.

7 If an alert box with layer attribute information appears, click OK.

8 Drag the playhead to where you want to change a layer property.

9 Click ▤ to open the Timelines menu.

10 Click Add Keyframe.

How can I create labels that pop up when the user rolls the cursor over images on my page?

✔ You can create a pop-up label for an image by using a hidden layer, a timeline, and a behavior. First, create the label using a layer. For example, place text into a layer that has a background color and set the visibility of the layer to hidden. Then create a timeline that makes the hidden layer visible. Finally, define a behavior that triggers the timeline when the cursor rolls over the image. For information about triggering timelines, see page 246.

What Z-index values should I give my layers?

✔ Z-indexes come into play only when layers overlap. When they do overlap, what matters is not the exact Z-index value, but what the value is relative to the Z-indexes of other layers. For example, if you want to use a timeline to move a layer whose Z-index is 1 beneath a layer whose Z-index is 5, you need to switch the Z-index of the first layer to something greater than 5. Z-indexes of 6 and 60 have the same effect.

11 With the new keyframe selected, make changes to the layer in the Property inspector.

■ In this example, the layer's visibility is turned off in the middle of the animation.

■ You can select Autoplay to start the animation when the page opens.

■ You can select Loop to make the animation repeat indefinitely.

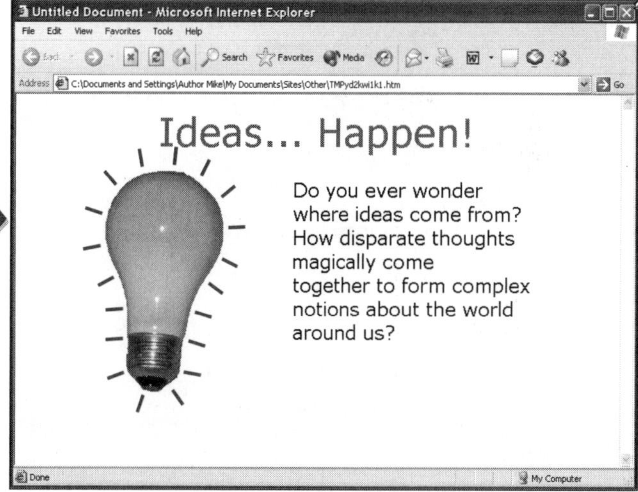

12 Preview the Web page in a browser.

Note: To preview a page in a Web browser, see page 58.

■ In this example, the object flashes on and off indefinitely.

CHANGE ANIMATION SPEED

You can speed up or slow down a timeline animation by changing the frame rate for the animation or by adjusting the number of frames that make up the animation. This allows you to fine tune how your animations play out when you test them in browsers.

You can change the rate at which the frames are displayed in the Timelines inspector. If the frame rate is increased and the number of frames of the animation stays the same, the animation runs faster. Conversely, if you decrease the frame rate, the animation slows down. The default animation speed in the Timelines inspector is 15 frames per second (fps).

You can also change the number of frames in an animation by increasing or decreasing the length of its animation bar. Increasing the animation bar's size means the browser has to play more frames to display the same animation. If the frame rate stays the same, the animation runs slower. Decreasing the size of the animation bar has the opposite effect: Fewer frames are played and the animation speeds up.

CHANGE ANIMATION SPEED

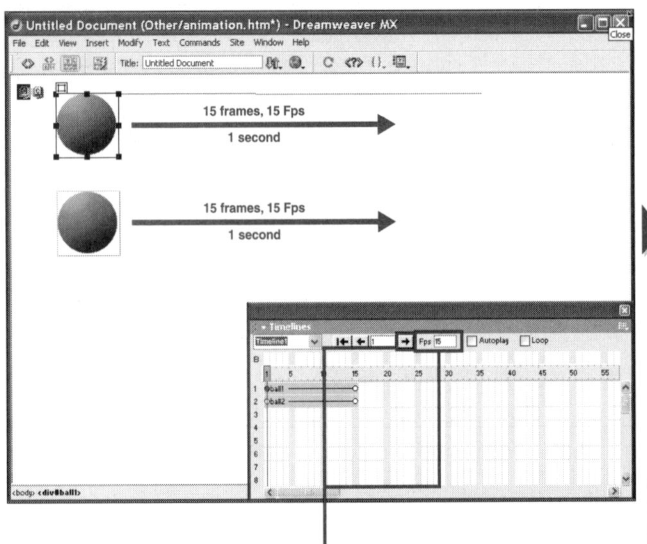

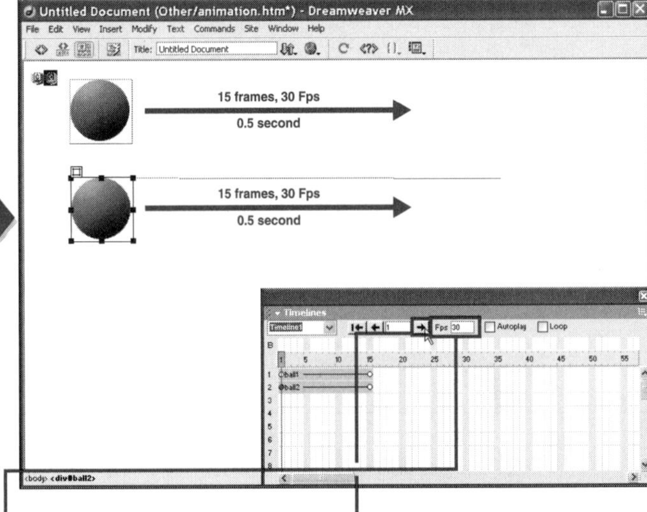

CHANGE THE FRAME RATE

1 Create two timeline animations on a page.

Note: To create a timeline animation, see pages 238 to 241.

■ In this example, two layers have parallel paths and animation bars of equal lengths. Both animations move at 15 frames per second.

2 To preview the timeline animations, click and hold ➔.

3 Type a new Fps value for the animations.

■ A higher value increases their speed. A lower value decreases their speed.

■ The change in the Fps rate affects all the animations in the timeline equally.

4 To preview the modified animations, click and hold ➔.

How high should I set my frame rate for animations?

✔ Most browsers running on average computer systems cannot display animations at rates faster than 15 frames per second. Most likely, you may want to use this rate as your ceiling. If you are running many animations on a page and want to make sure all users can play them without having performance issues, you may want to decrease the frame rate to less than 15 fps. As a comparison, 30 fps is the standard frame rate for video, and 24 fps is standard for film.

What happens when a browser cannot display an animation at the specified frame rate?

✔ The browser still plays all the frames in the animation, but it just plays them at a slower speed. It does not skip frames to make up for lost time.

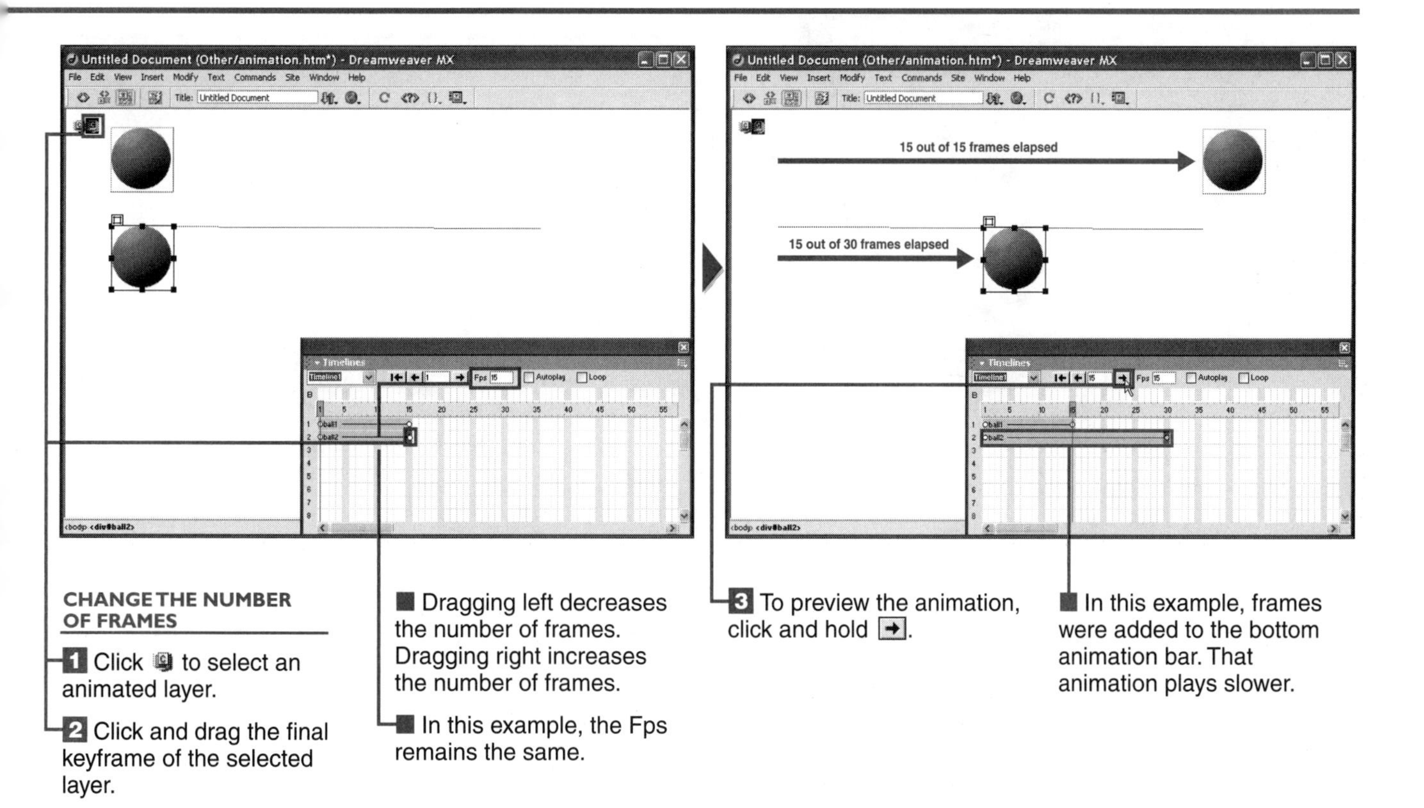

CHANGE THE NUMBER OF FRAMES

1 Click to select an animated layer.

2 Click and drag the final keyframe of the selected layer.

■ Dragging left decreases the number of frames. Dragging right increases the number of frames.

■ In this example, the Fps remains the same.

3 To preview the animation, click and hold ➔.

■ In this example, frames were added to the bottom animation bar. That animation plays slower.

TRIGGER AN ANIMATION WITH A BEHAVIOR

You can combine Dreamweaver behaviors and timelines so that clicking on an image or a hyperlink in your page starts an animation. This is an alternative to selecting Autoplay in the Timelines inspector, which causes an animation to start automatically when a page loads. By mixing behaviors and timelines, you can enable images on your pages to interact with one another in interesting ways.

To create a behavior-triggered animation, you first create your timeline. See page 238 or 240 for more information. Then you add an image or text hyperlink to your page that serves as the trigger when clicked, and you assign the Start Timeline behavior for it. If you use an image, it is usually a good idea to make it look like a clickable button, or to label it so that the user knows what to do.

A similar Stop Timeline behavior stops a timeline animation in progress. This enables you to create a simple VCR-like interface for an animation on your page. Just associate the Start Timeline behavior with a Start hyperlink or image, and the Stop Timeline behavior with a Stop hyperlink or image.

TRIGGER AN ANIMATION WITH A BEHAVIOR

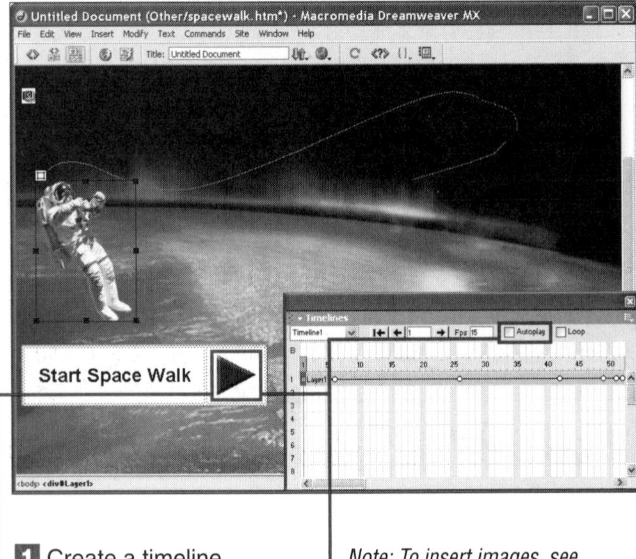

1 Create a timeline animation.

Note: To create a timeline animation, see pages 238 to 241.

2 Insert an image to serve as a clickable trigger for the animation.

Note: To insert images, see page 86.

3 Uncheck Autoplay (☑ changes to ☐).

4 Click the image.

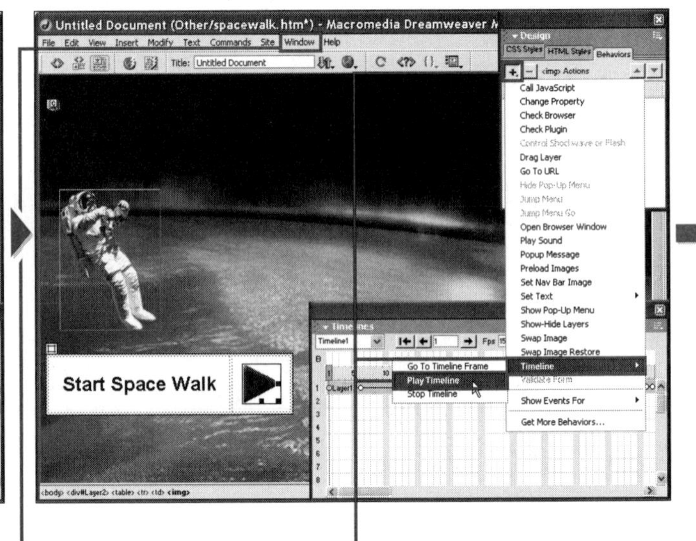

5 Click Window.

6 Click Others from the drop-down menu.

7 Click Behaviors from the submenu.

■ The Behaviors panel appears.

8 Click [+].

9 Click Timeline.

10 Click Play Timeline.

Can I make other events start my animation?

✔ After you have defined the behavior that starts the animation, you can select from a variety of trigger events in the Behaviors inspector. Just click the behavior, and then click ▾ to select an event. For example, `onDblClick` makes double-clicking the object start the animation. `onMouseOver` starts the animation when the cursor rolls over the object.

How do I remove a trigger that has been applied to an animation?

✔ You can remove the trigger by selecting the object in the Document window that does the triggering, clicking the behavior in the Behaviors panel, and pressing Delete. You can then assign the triggering behavior to another object on the page or make the animation autoplay by clicking the animation bar and selecting the Autoplay in the Timelines inspector.

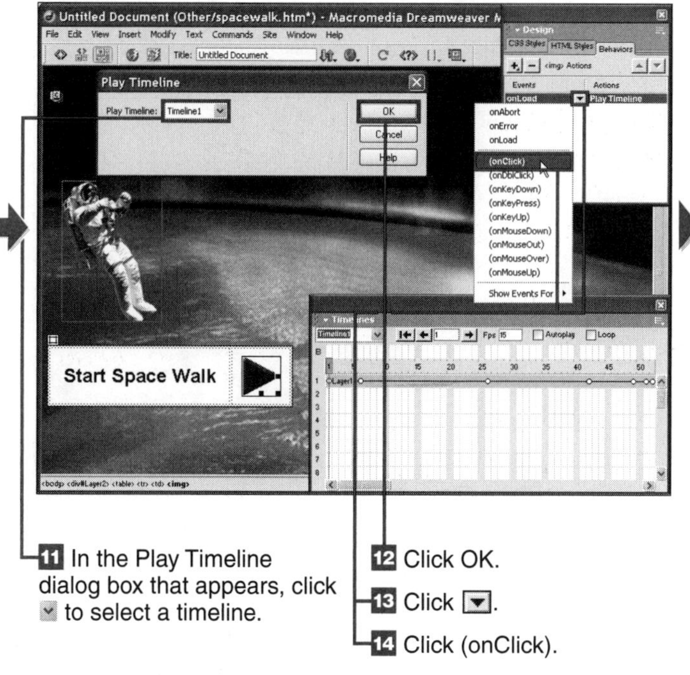

11 In the Play Timeline dialog box that appears, click ▾ to select a timeline.

12 Click OK.

13 Click ▾.

14 Click (onClick).

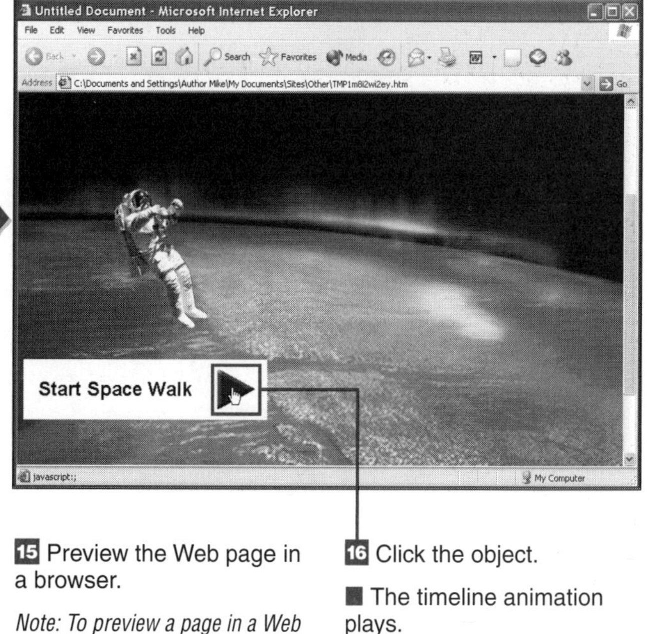

15 Preview the Web page in a browser.

Note: To preview a page in a Web browser, see page 58.

16 Click the object.

■ The timeline animation plays.

SECTION IV

15) PUBLISHING A WEB SITE

16) MAINTAINING YOUR SITE

MANAGING YOUR FINISHED SITE

PUBLISH YOUR WEB SITE

To make the pages that you have built in Dreamweaver accessible to other people on the Web, you must transfer them to a *Web server.* A Web server is an Internet-connected computer running special software that enables it to distribute, or serve, files to Web browsers. Most people publish their Web pages on servers maintained by their Internet service provider (ISP) or company.

Dreamweaver includes tools that enable you to connect to a Web server and transfer your Web documents to it.

Steps for Publishing Your Web Site

Publishing your site content using Dreamweaver involves the following steps:

1 Specify where on your computer the site files are kept. You do this by defining a local folder, which is covered in Chapter 4.

2 Specify the Web server to which you want to publish your files. You do this by defining a remote site. See page 254.

3 Connect to the Web server and transfer the files. The Dreamweaver Site window gives you a user-friendly interface for organizing your files and transferring them to the remote site.

After uploading your site, you can update it by editing the copies of the site files, which are on your computer in your local folder, and then transferring those updated copies to the Web server, which is the same as the remote site.

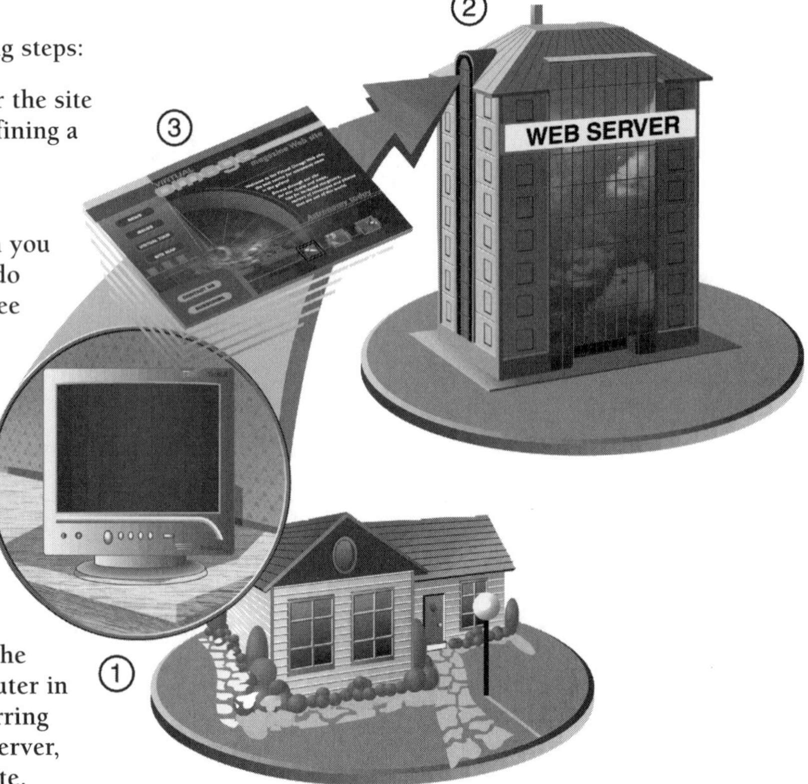

USING THE SITE WINDOW

The Site window lets you view the organization of all of the files in your site. It is also where you upload local files to the remote site and download remote files to the local site. To open the Site window, click Site and then Site Files.

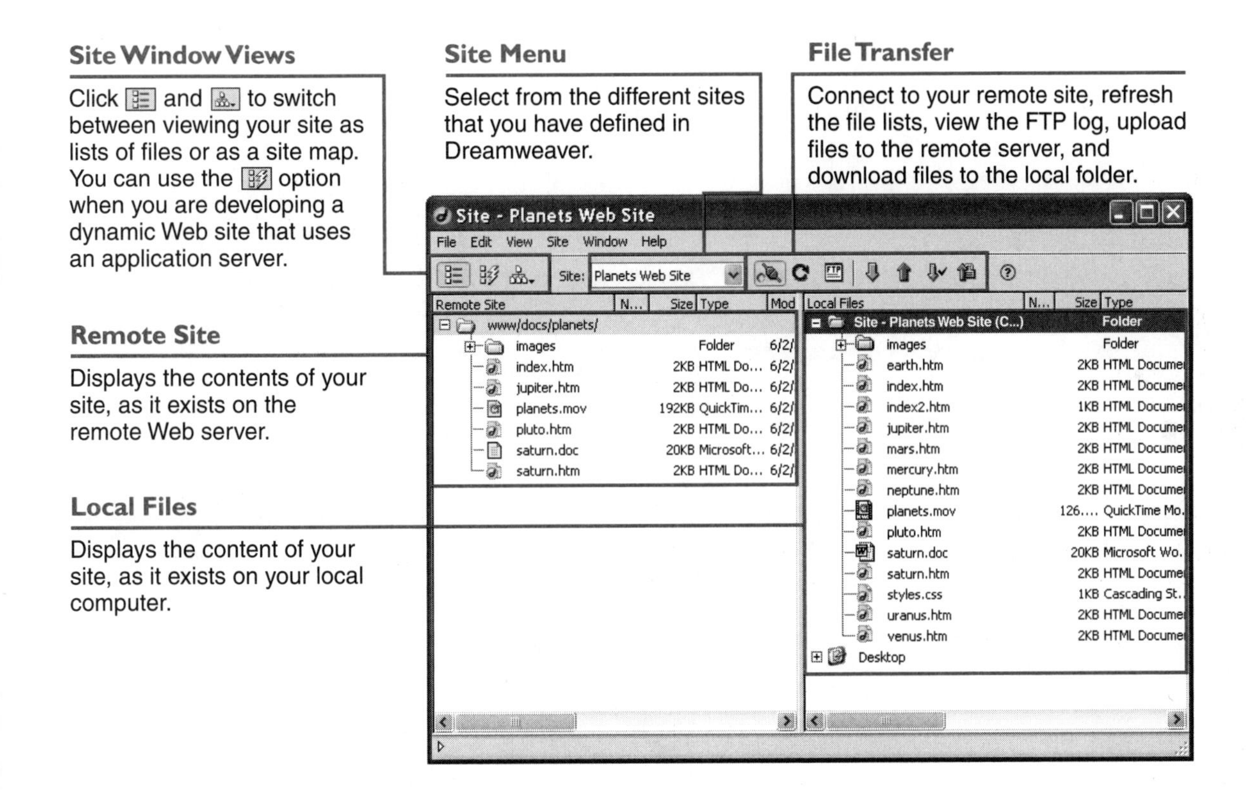

Site Window Views
Click and to switch between viewing your site as lists of files or as a site map. You can use the option when you are developing a dynamic Web site that uses an application server.
Site Menu
Select from the different sites that you have defined in Dreamweaver.
File Transfer
Connect to your remote site, refresh the file lists, view the FTP log, upload files to the remote server, and download files to the local folder.
Remote Site
Displays the contents of your site, as it exists on the remote Web server.
Local Files
Displays the content of your site, as it exists on your local computer.
Site - Planets Web Site
File Edit View Site Window Help
Site: Planets Web Site
Remote Site
Local Files
www/docs/planets/
Site - Planets Web Site (C...)
images
index.htm
jupiter.htm
planets.mov
pluto.htm
saturn.doc
saturn.htm
earth.htm
index2.htm
mars.htm
mercury.htm
neptune.htm
styles.css
uranus.htm
venus.htm
Desktop

ORGANIZE FILES AND FOLDERS

You can use the Site window to organize the elements that make up your local and remote sites. The window lets you create and delete files and folders, as well as move files between folders. It also updates page links in your HTML when you move a file.

Creating subfolders to organize files of a similar type can be useful if you have a large Web site. Most developers at a minimum create an images subfolder in which to store JPEG, GIF, and PNG image files. Dreamweaver automatically creates subfolders such as Templates and Library to store special files associated with a site.

When you move files into and out of folders, you will need to update the hyperlinks and image references on those pages because document-relative references will no longer be valid. Dreamweaver keeps track of any affected code when you rearrange files, and updates it for you after you move a file. This file tracking is a key advantage to moving your files in the Site window rather than through your computer's file-management system.

ORGANIZE FILES AND FOLDERS

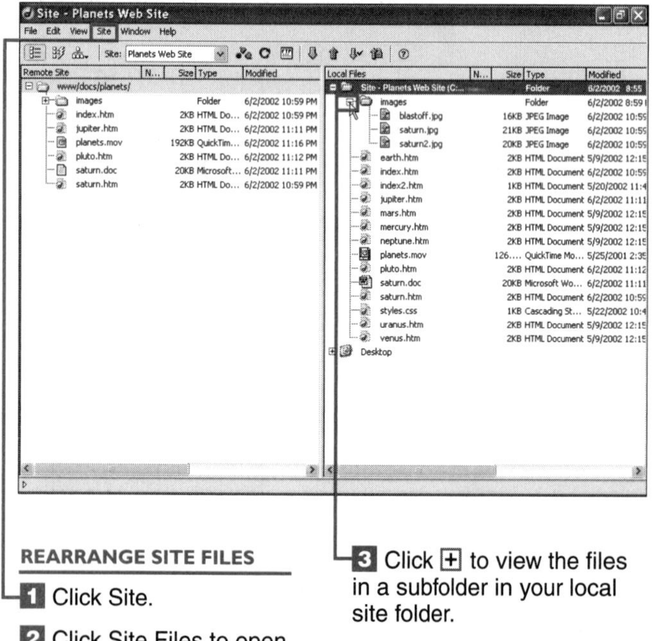

REARRANGE SITE FILES

1 Click Site.

2 Click Site Files to open the Site window.

3 Click ⊞ to view the files in a subfolder in your local site folder.

■ The ⊞ turns to ⊟ and the folder contents display. You can click ⊟ to close the subfolder.

4 Click and drag a file from the local site folder into a subfolder.

■ Dreamweaver reorganizes the files in your local site folder.

■ If any links in your pages need updates, Dreamweaver asks if it should update them. Click Update to update your pages.

Note: Dreamweaver cannot automatically update your links if you move pages on your remote site.

How do I create a new file in the Site window?

✔ Click inside the local or remote file list. Click File and then New File. Dreamweaver creates a new HTML file that has an empty body. You can also right-click a list and select New File from the contextual menu that appears.

How do I delete a file in the Site window?

✔ Click a file in either the local or remote file list. Click File, and then click Delete. An alert box asks you to confirm the deletion. You can also right-click a list and select Delete from the contextual menu that appears.

How do I open a file from the Site window?

✔ Double-click the file in the local or remote file lists. If you open a remote file and edit it, you can only save the modified file to the local site. You cannot save directly to the remote site in Dreamweaver.

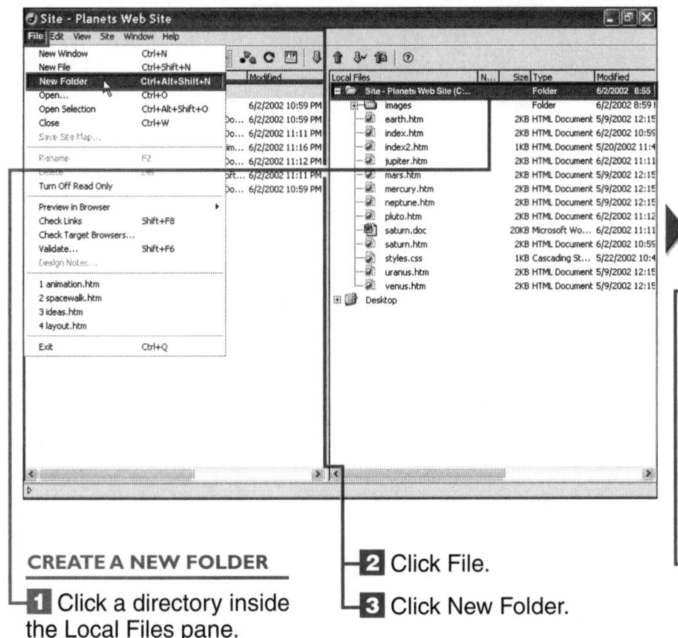

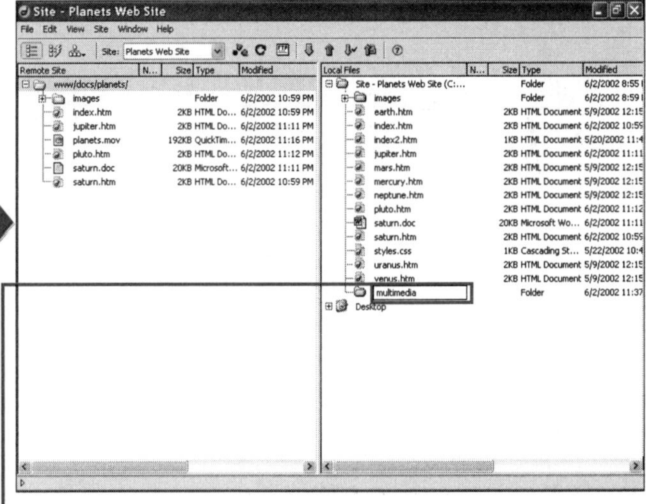

CREATE A NEW FOLDER

1 Click a directory inside the Local Files pane.

2 Click File.

3 Click New Folder.

4 Type a name for the new folder.

5 Press Enter (Return).

■ Dreamweaver creates a new folder.

■ To create a new folder on the remote site, click a directory inside the remote site and perform steps 2 to 5.

SET UP A REMOTE SITE

The *remote site* is the place where your site's files are made available to the rest of the world. You set up a remote site by specifying a directory on a Web server where your site will be hosted. Most remote sites are located on a Web server maintained by your Internet service provider or company.

Dreamweaver can connect to your remote site, transfer files there, and manage the files when you have to update them. To do these things, Dreamweaver needs certain technical information, including the name of the Web server, the login and password for the Web server account, and the directory on the server where you want to store the files. You enter this information in the Site Definition dialog box. After you enter the remote site information, see page 256 to access your Web server using Dreamweaver.

You can still build your local Web site without having set up a remote site. And while Dreamweaver's file-transfer capabilities are convenient, your can still upload Dreamweaver-built files to your server with a separate FTP program.

SET UP A REMOTE SITE

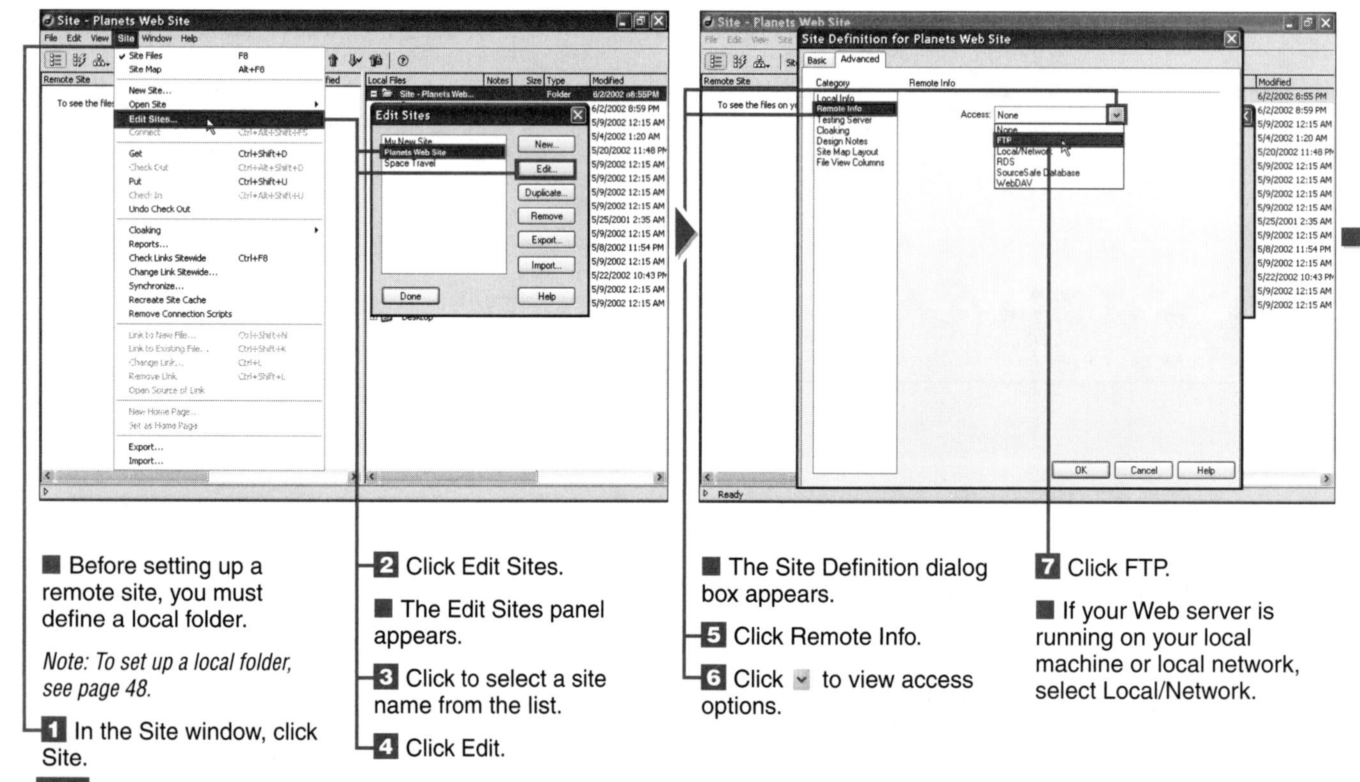

■ Before setting up a remote site, you must define a local folder.

Note: To set up a local folder, see page 48.

1 In the Site window, click Site.

2 Click Edit Sites.

■ The Edit Sites panel appears.

3 Click to select a site name from the list.

4 Click Edit.

■ The Site Definition dialog box appears.

5 Click Remote Info.

6 Click ▾ to view access options.

7 Click FTP.

■ If your Web server is running on your local machine or local network, select Local/Network.

What should I do if the computer I build my site on is also my Web server?

✔ You should select Local/Network from the Access menu in the Site Definition dialog box. You can then specify the local folder where the live site files are stored. In such a case, both your local and remote sites are on your local computer.

What are WebDAV and SourceSafe?

✔ WebDAV is an extension of the HTTP protocol that enables users to collaboratively edit files on remote Web servers. SourceSafe is a database application that offers similar capabilities. If you build sites using a WebDAV-enabled system or SourceSafe, you can have Dreamweaver connect to it when it needs to upload and download site files.

What is a firewall and how can it affect Dreamweaver?

✔ A *firewall* is a networking security system attached to a local-area network that controls information flowing in and out of the network. Sometimes a firewall can prevent Dreamweaver from connecting or transferring files to an external Web server. The Use Firewall and Passive FTP options in the Site Definition dialog box may remedy this. You can also click the Firewall Settings button to specify firewall-specific information in Preferences.

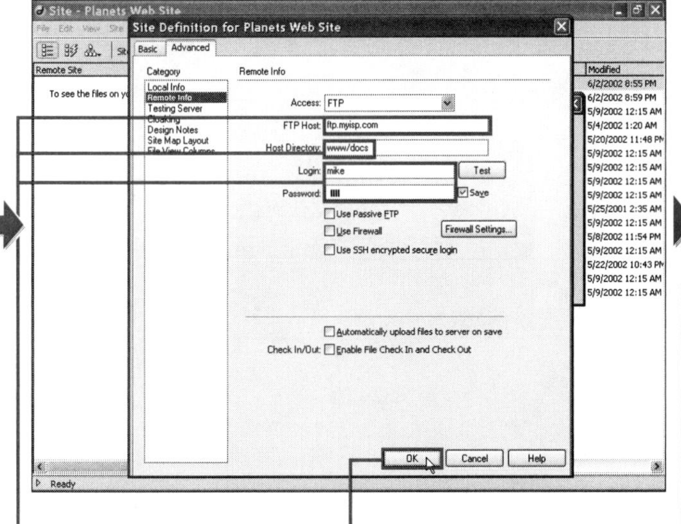

8 Type the name of the FTP host (Web server).

9 Type your site's directory path on the Web server.

10 Type your login and password.

■ Check Save to have Dreamweaver save your password.

■ You can click Test to verify your host directory, login, and password on the remote site.

11 Click OK.

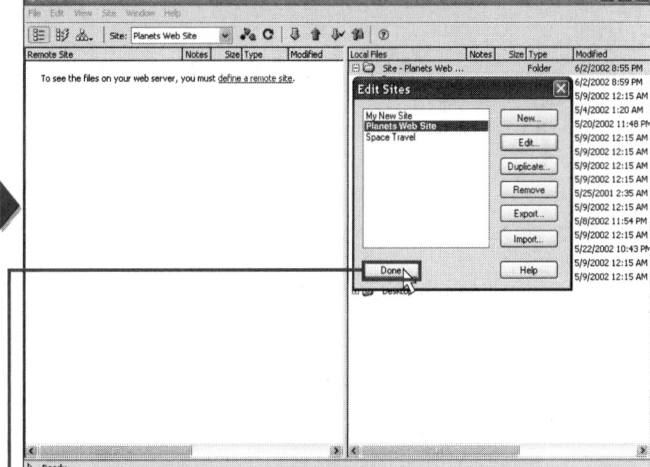

12 Click Done to close the Edit Sites dialog box.

Note: To access your remote site, see page 256.

CONNECT TO A REMOTE SITE

To transfer and manage files between your local folder and remote site, Dreamweaver must connect to a Web server. This requires several things to happen: Dreamweaver must make contact with the server, log in using your login and password, and then access the host directory.

If any of these steps fail — Dreamweaver cannot access the server, cannot log in, or cannot find the specified directory — Dreamweaver displays a warning informing you of its failure to connect. Failure can be the fault of either parties. The remote Web server might be down or information that you typed for your remote site might be invalid. If you continue to have trouble connecting, you should contact your Internet service provider to double check your site login information and verify that the server is online.

Dreamweaver connects to the remote Web server using *File Transfer Protocol* (FTP), which is the common standard for moving files between Internet-connected computers. Some of the Site window commands, such as Put, for upload, and Get, for download, correspond to actual FTP commands. *HyperText Transfer Protocol*, or HTTP, which transmits information between Web browsers and servers, is a related standard.

CONNECT TO A REMOTE SITE

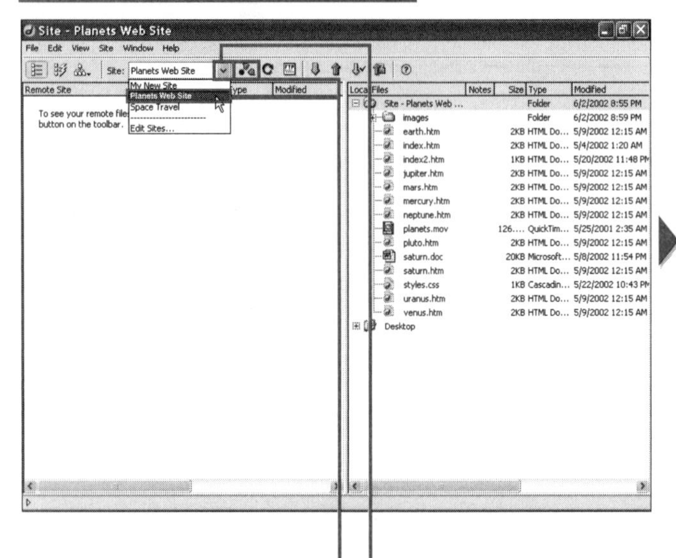

■ Before connecting, you must set up a local folder and a remote site.

Note: To set up a local folder, see page 48. To set up a remote site, see page 254.

1 In the Site window, click the Site ⌄.

2 Click a Web site.

3 Click the connect button.

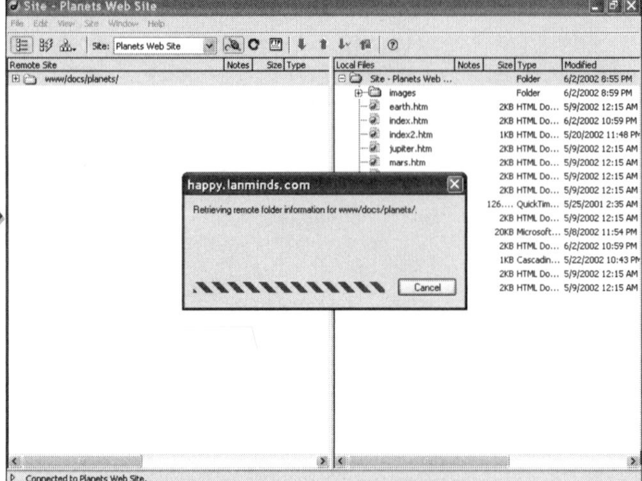

■ Dreamweaver attempts to connect to the remote site.

■ If it cannot connect to the site, Dreamweaver alerts you with a dialog box. If you have trouble connecting, double-check the host information you entered for the remote site.

How do I keep Dreamweaver from disconnecting from the Web server prematurely?

✔ You can access Preferences under the Edit menu and select the Site category. There, you can adjust the time that Dreamweaver lets pass between commands before it logs you off of the server — the default is 30 minutes. Web servers also have a similar setting on their end, so the server, not Dreamweaver, may log you off.

Can I use a separate FTP program to transfer pages that I create in Dreamweaver to my Web site?

✔ Yes. But using a separate tool means you will not get the benefit of some of the site management tools that Dreamweaver offers, such as the ability to collaboratively check files in and out. See Chapter 16 for more about these tools.

What if I do not know the host directory for my site?

✔ You can leave that field blank in the Site Definition dialog box when you set up your remote site. Dreamweaver will open the default folder on the server when it connects, which may or may not be the correct place to store your files. Most servers require you to store your files inside a folder named public_html or www.

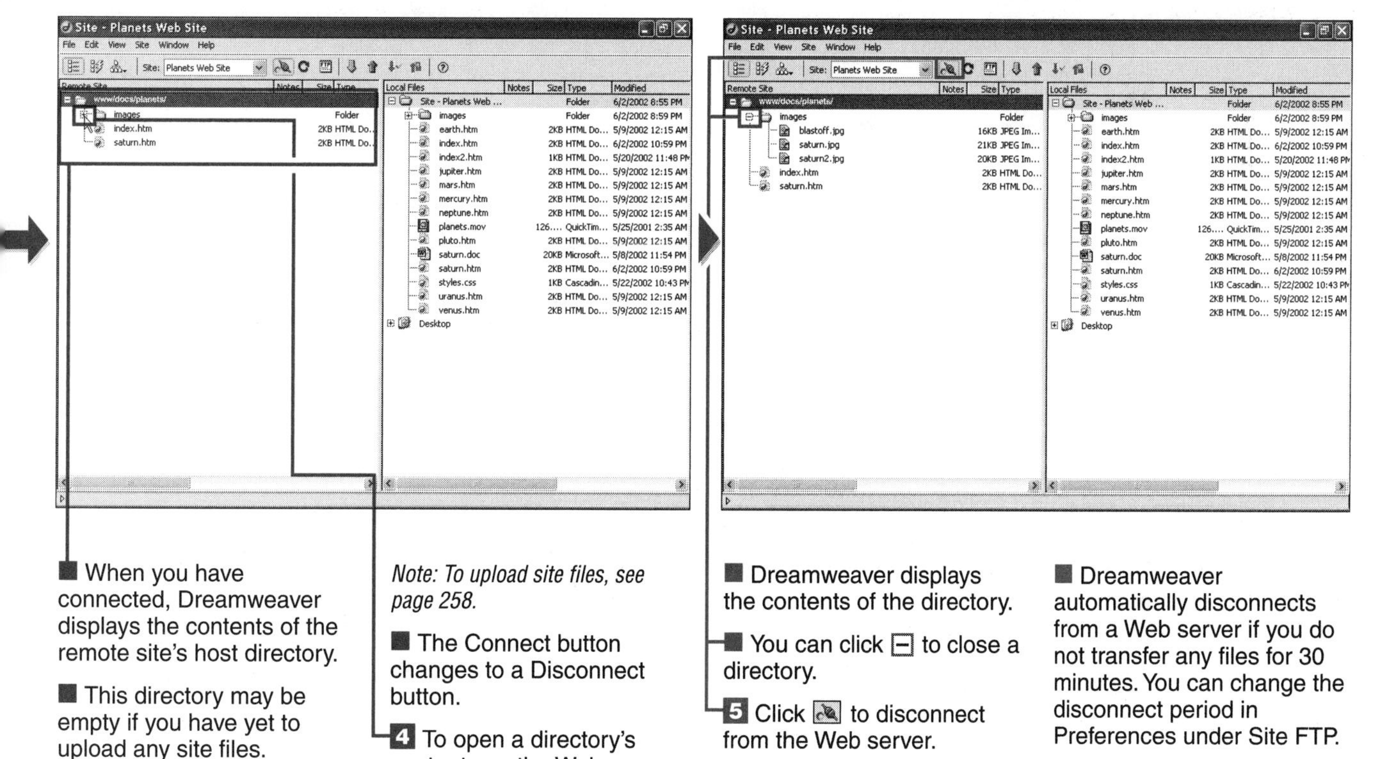

■ When you have connected, Dreamweaver displays the contents of the remote site's host directory.

■ This directory may be empty if you have yet to upload any site files.

Note: To upload site files, see page 258.

■ The Connect button changes to a Disconnect button.

4 To open a directory's contents on the Web server, click ⊞.

■ Dreamweaver displays the contents of the directory.

■ You can click ⊟ to close a directory.

5 Click the Disconnect button to disconnect from the Web server.

■ Dreamweaver automatically disconnects from a Web server if you do not transfer any files for 30 minutes. You can change the disconnect period in Preferences under Site FTP.

UPLOAD AND DOWNLOAD FILES

The Dreamweaver Site window makes transferring files between your local and remote sites easy. Clicking local files or folders in the right pane and then clicking uploads files to the remote Web server. Clicking remote files or folders in the left pane and then clicking downloads files to your local computer. You can even click the local root folder and transfer your entire site to your remote site all at once.

If you try to upload a file that has unsaved changes, Dreamweaver displays an alert and enables you to save those changes first. Dreamweaver also offers to transfer dependent files when you upload a Web page. Dependent files can be images and framed pages that are referenced by the page's HTML. When you upload a page for the first time, you usually want to also upload dependent files.

Dreamweaver includes a Check In/Check Out feature that flags site files when they have been downloaded from the remote site for editing. This feature is convenient when many people are collaborating to build a site. See Chapter 16 for details about site management.

UPLOAD AND DOWNLOAD FILES

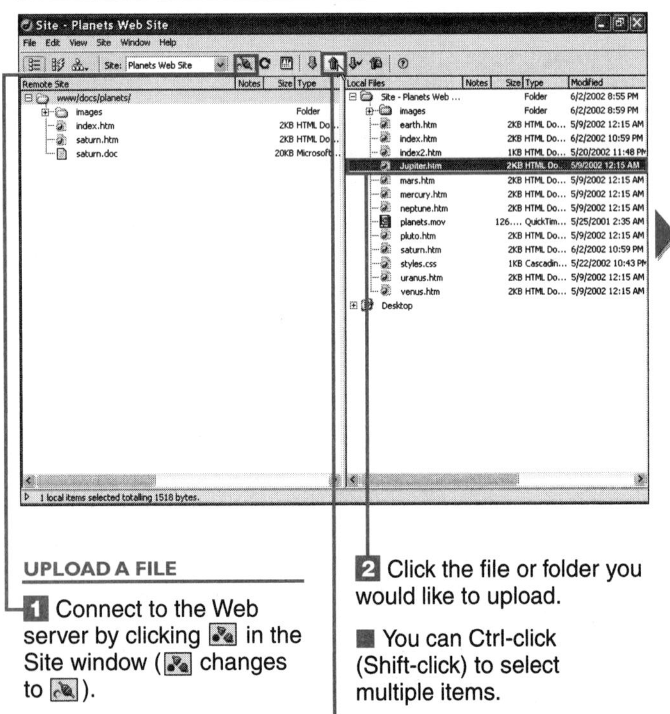

UPLOAD A FILE

1 Connect to the Web server by clicking in the Site window (changes to).

Note: For more on connecting to a remote site, see page 256.

2 Click the file or folder you would like to upload.

■ You can Ctrl-click (Shift-click) to select multiple items.

3 Click the Put button ( ).

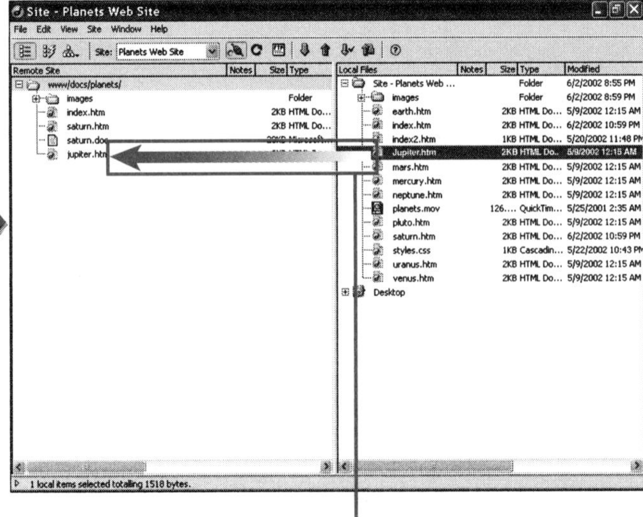

■ An alert may appear asking if you want to include *dependent files*. Dependent files are images and other files referenced in the page's HTML code. Click Yes if you would like to upload the dependent files.

■ Dreamweaver transfers the file or folder from your local site on the Web server to the remote site.

How do I stop a file transfer in progress?

✔ You can click the Cancel button in the dialog box that appears while a transfer is in progress. You can also press Esc (⌘+.).

How do I exclude certain site files from site-wide operations such as batch transfers?

✔ You can exclude files by placing them in a separate directory and then *cloaking* that directory. Right-click the directory in the Site window, click Cloaking, and then click Cloak. Cloaked files will not be transferred when performing a batch upload of the entire local folder.

Where does Dreamweaver log errors that occur during transfer?

✔ Dreamweaver logs all transfer activity, including errors, in an FTP log. You can view it by clicking the View Site FTP Log button ( ).

What happens if I change my Internet service provider and need to move my site to a different server?

✔ You will need to change your remote site settings to enable Dreamweaver to connect to the new service provider's server. Your local site settings can stay the same.

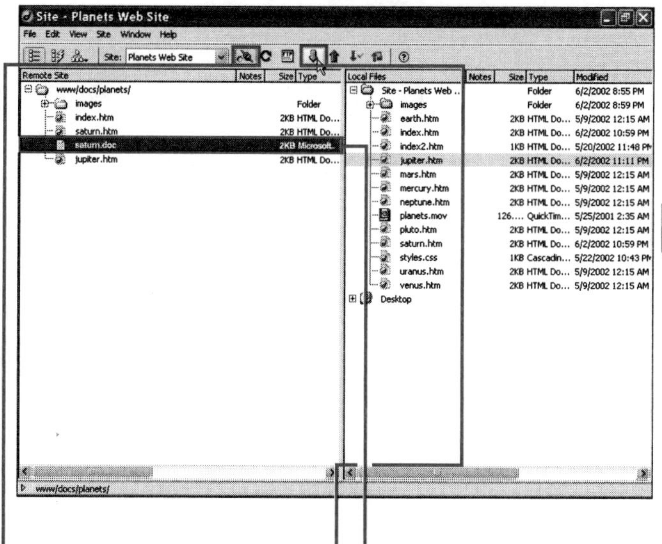

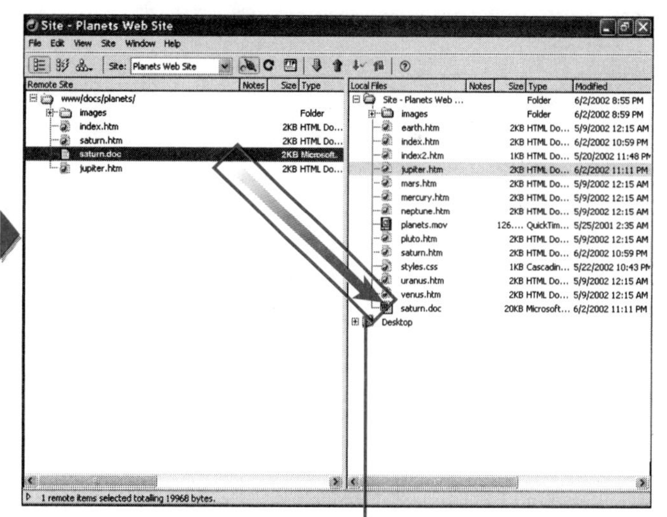

DOWNLOAD A FILE

1 Connect to the Web server by clicking in the Site window (changes to).

Note: For more on connecting to a remote site, see page 256.

2 Click the file or folder you would like to download.

■ You can Ctrl-click (Shift-click) to select multiple items.

3 Click the Get button ( ).

■ Dreamweaver asks if you want to include *dependent files*. Dependent files are images and other files that are referenced in the page's HTML. Click Yes if you would like to download the dependent files.

■ Dreamweaver transfers the file or folder from the remote site on the Web server to the local site.

USING THE SITE MAP

Users can get a visual representation of the structure of a site with a Site Map. A Site Map view lays out the different pages of a site in flowchart form, with arrows between them representing links. It also highlights pages that have broken internal links.

Initially, the Site Map displays your site two levels deep, starting with the page you define as the home page. You can modify the view by opening sublevels below individual pages, or by resetting the home page.

Dreamweaver gives you an option of saving the Site Map as a BMP file, which can be useful if you need to give a slide-show presentation about the site or document the site on paper.

Besides serving as a visual tool, you can also perform management duties via the Site Map view. Many of the tasks you can perform in the Site window, such as updating links, can also be done when the Site Map is displayed. See page 272.

You can also create links with the Site Map open. Just click and drag the point-to-file icon (⊕) from a file in the Site Map to a file in the local site list.

USING THE SITE MAP

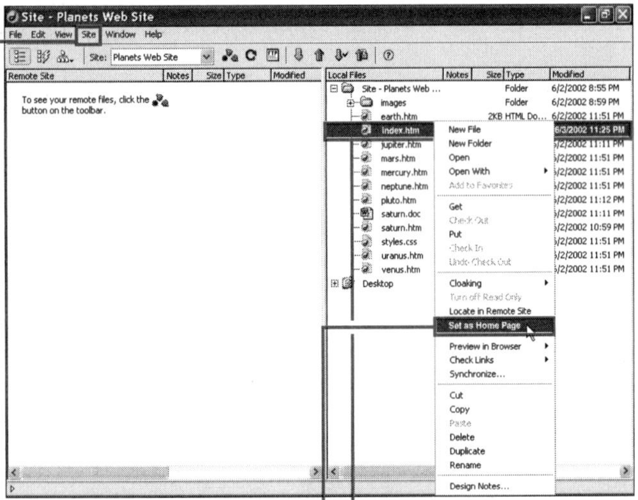

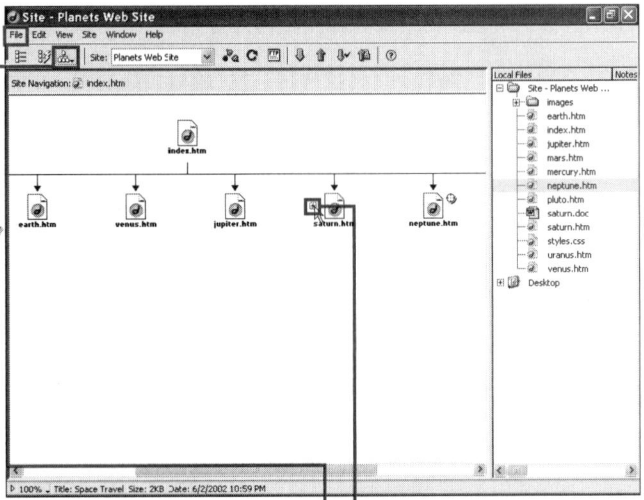

1 Click Site.

2 Click Site Files.

■ To create a site map in Dreamweaver, you must first define your site's home page. It serves as the root file of your Site Map.

3 In the Local Files pane, right-click (Control-click) the file you want to have serve as your home page.

4 Click Set As Home Page in the pop-up menu.

5 Click the Site Map button (🖧).

■ Dreamweaver displays a Site Map in the left pane. By default, the Site Map displays the site structure two levels deep beginning from the home page.

6 To view files below the second level, click ⊞.

■ To save the Site Map as a BMP image, click File and then Save Site Map.

How can I view a subset of the Site Map, starting from a particular page?

✔ Click the page that you want to serve as the map root. Click View, and then View as Root. Or click Site, SiteMap View, and then View as Root (Macintosh). The Site Map redraws with the selected file at the top of the map.

How do I temporarily hide a part of my Site Map?

✔ You can hide files in your Site Map by clicking the files, and then clicking View, and then Show/Hide Link (Windows). Or click Site, Site Map View, and then Show/Hide Link (Macintosh).

How do I unhide files in my Site Map?

✔ First click View and then Show Files Marked as Hidden (Windows). Or click Site, Site Map View, and then Show Files Marked as Hidden (Macintosh). You can then select the hidden files, which appear with their filenames italicized, and use the Show/Hide Link command.

How do I change the labels in the Site Map?

✔ Click View and then Show Page Titles to switch between file name and page title labels underneath the site pages.

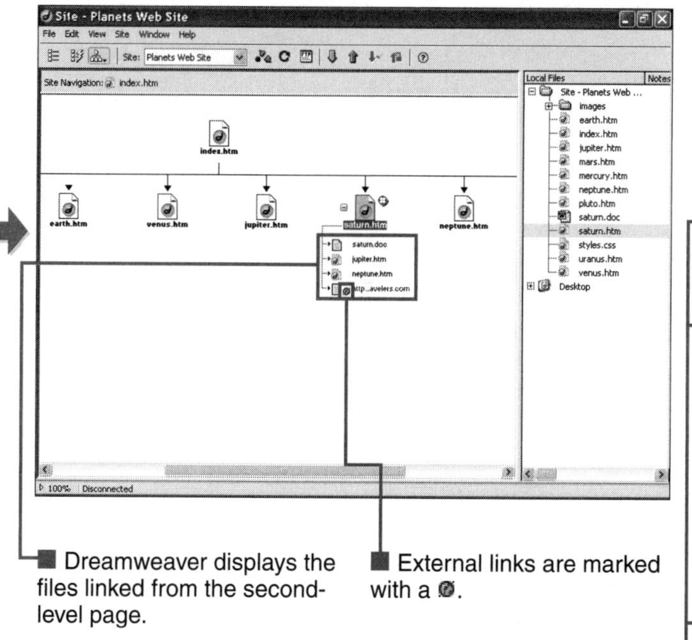

■ Dreamweaver displays the files linked from the second-level page.

■ External links are marked with a ⊘.

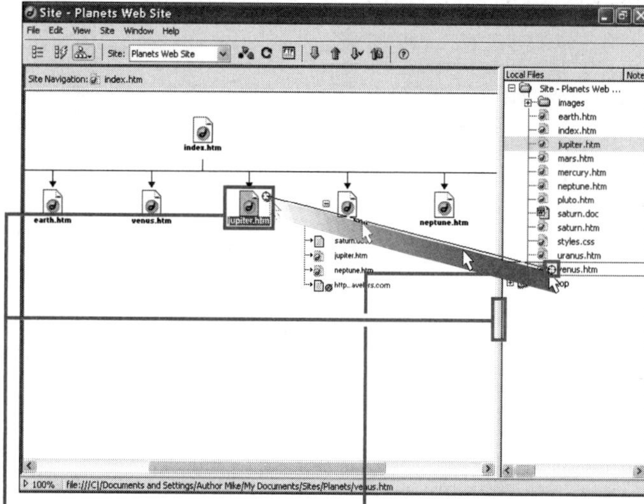

CREATE A LINK USING THE SITE MAP

1 Click and drag the Site window border to display both the Site Map and the Local Files.

2 Click a file in the Site Map. This page will contain the link.

3 Click and drag ⊕ to the destination file in the local site.

■ A new link is added to the bottom of the page selected in the Site Map. You can double-click the page to open it.

MANAGE SITE ASSETS

A large Web site can include hundreds of images, external links, multimedia files, and other features spread across hundreds of Web pages. The Assets panel provides a central place where you can view and manage these important elements that appear in your site. Dreamweaver compiles the images, colors, and other elements into categorized lists that you can view in one place, even though in reality the elements may be spread over many different directories and pages.

Items in the Assets panel are organized into various categories. GIF, JPG, and PNG images are stored in an *Images* category. The *Colors* category includes text, background, and link colors, as well as style-sheet colors. The *URLs* category is where external Web addresses that are linked to your site are kept. JavaScript features are stored in the *Scripts* category. There are also categories for Flash movies, Shockwave movies, and other movie files.

Dreamweaver stores templates and library items in the Assets panel as well. These features help you manage repeated layouts and content in your site. For more information about templates and library items, see Chapter 11.

Dreamweaver populates the Assets panel by searching through the files of a site for recognized file types and HTML code. It adds references to recognized items to the panel. Files are not duplicated when they are added to the Assets panel.

MANAGE SITE ASSETS

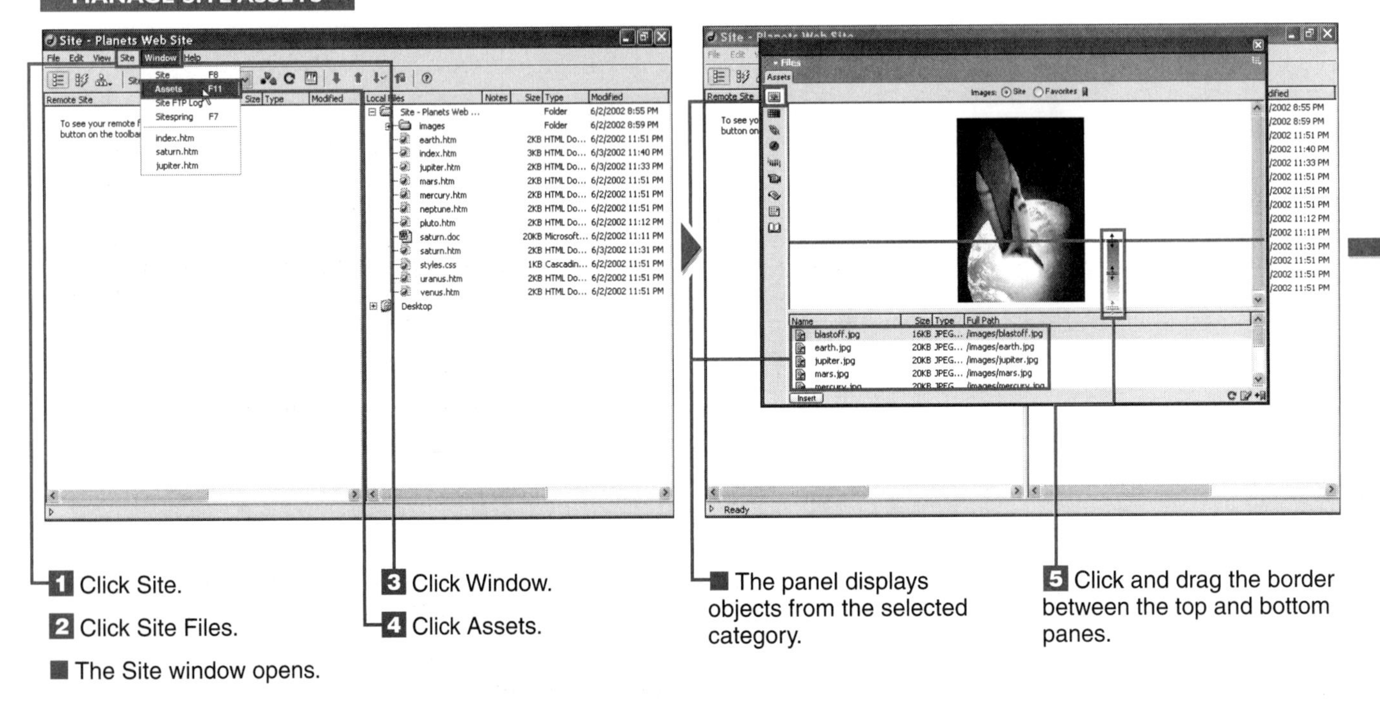

1 Click Site.

2 Click Site Files.

■ The Site window opens.

3 Click Window.

4 Click Assets.

■ The panel displays objects from the selected category.

5 Click and drag the border between the top and bottom panes.

How can I find out where an asset is in the site file structure?

✔ You can select the item in the Assets panel and select Locate in Site from the Assets panel menu. The Site window opens with the item highlighted.

Can I preview multimedia in the Assets panel?

✔ You can preview QuickTime movies. Click [icon], select a QuickTime file, and click [icon].

How do I refresh the Assets panel lists?

✔ You can click the Refresh button ([C]) in the bottom right of the panel. This updates the panel and adds or removes assets that you have recently added or removed from your site. If items still do not display properly, you can Ctrl-click (Alt-click) the [C] button and Dreamweaver rebuilds its site cache from scratch and refreshes the Assets panel.

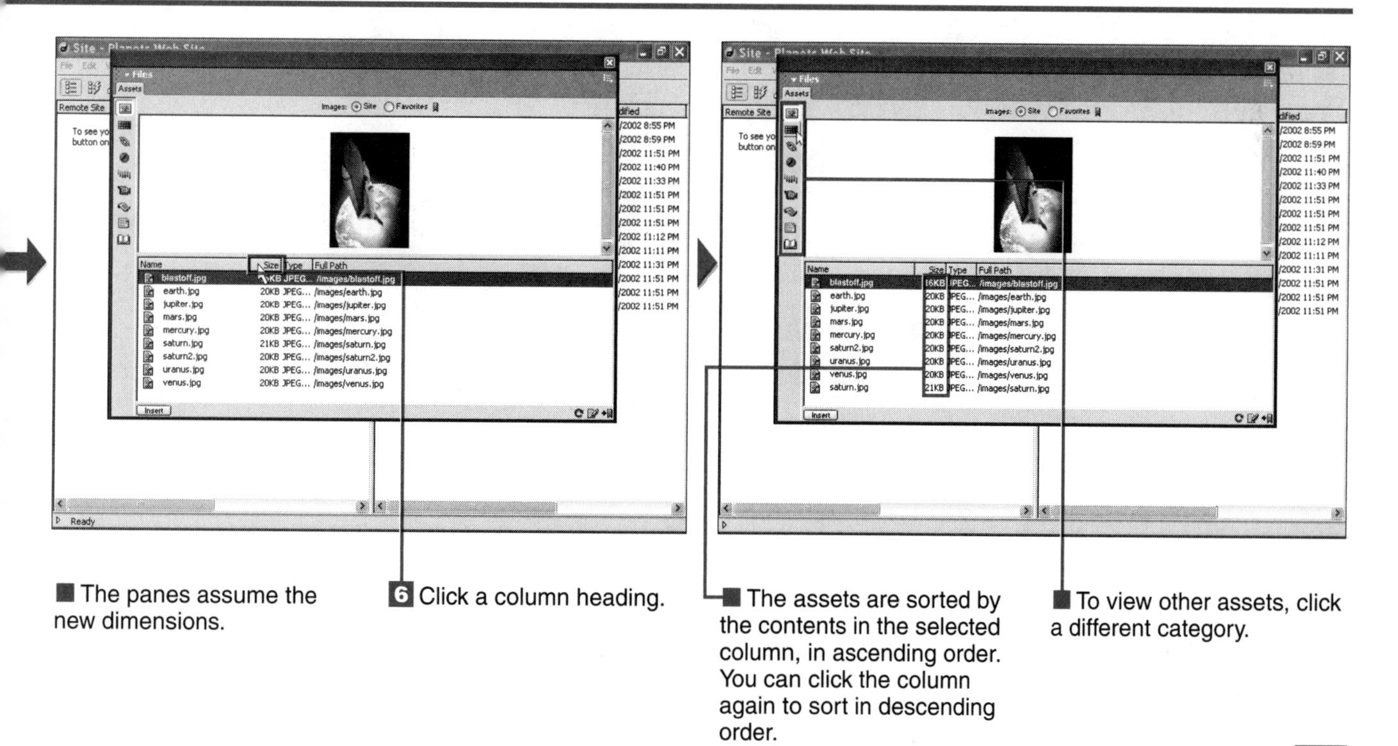

■ The panes assume the new dimensions.

6 Click a column heading.

■ The assets are sorted by the contents in the selected column, in ascending order. You can click the column again to sort in descending order.

■ To view other assets, click a different category.

ADD CONTENT USING THE ASSETS PANEL

The Assets panel offers a faster, more convenient way of adding objects such as images and multimedia files to your site pages. Normally you add these objects by selecting a command or clicking a button in the Objects panel and then searching through the file structure of your site. With the Assets panel, you can drag and drop the file from the panel, or select it in the list and click the Insert button.

The Assets panel features also let you apply colors to your page and create external links. You can select text in the Document window and drag and drop a color asset onto the text to change its color. If you add a color asset to your page to an insertion point rather than to a selected object, any text that you subsequently type at that insertion point will appear in that color. Similarly, you can drag a URL from the Assets panel to a selected piece of text or image to create a new external hyperlink.

ADD CONTENT USING THE ASSETS PANEL

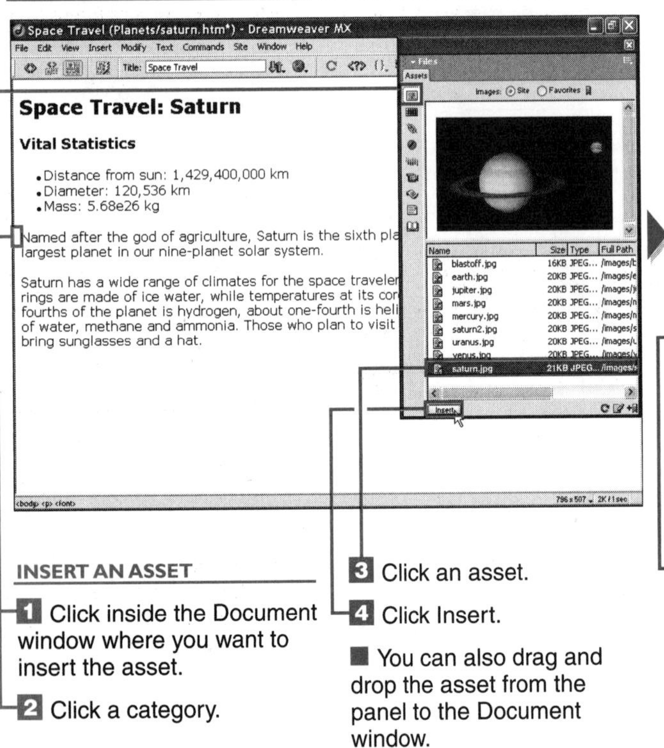

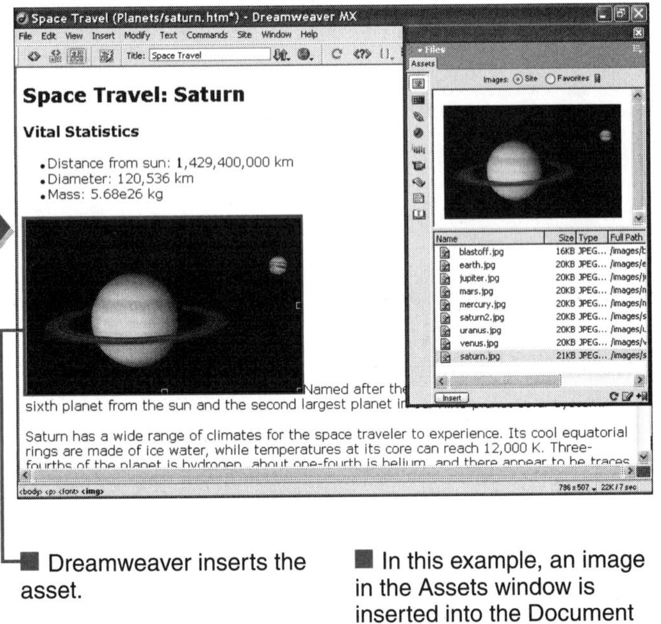

INSERT AN ASSET

1 Click inside the Document window where you want to insert the asset.

2 Click a category.

3 Click an asset.

4 Click Insert.

■ You can also drag and drop the asset from the panel to the Document window.

■ Dreamweaver inserts the asset.

■ In this example, an image in the Assets window is inserted into the Document window.

How do I copy assets from one site to another?

✔ Select one or more items in the Assets panel, click Copy to Site in the Assets panel drop-down menu, and click a site to copy to. The assets appear in the Favorites list under the same category in the other site.

Is there an easy way to tell if the colors I am using on a Web site are all Web safe?

✔ The Assets panel specifies which colors are safe and which are not safe under the Colors category.

How can I edit an asset?

✔ You can double-click most assets in the Assets panel to edit them. For templates and library items, Dreamweaver opens a new Document window for editing the item. For items such as images and multimedia, Dreamweaver launches an external editing application, if one is available for the file type. For example, double-clicking a GIF image opens the image in Macromedia Fireworks if you have the application installed.

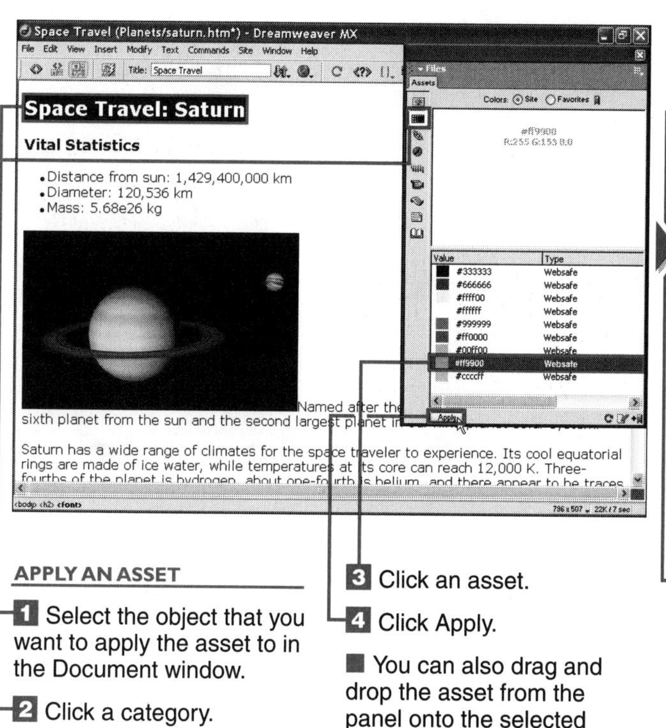

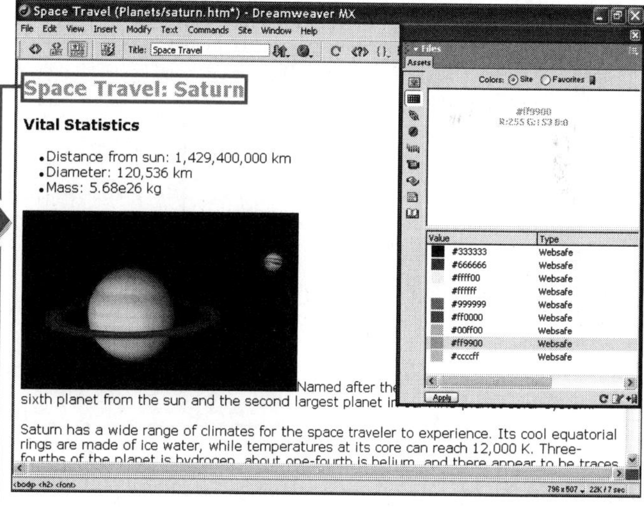

APPLY AN ASSET

1 Select the object that you want to apply the asset to in the Document window.

2 Click a category.

3 Click an asset.

4 Click Apply.

■ You can also drag and drop the asset from the panel onto the selected object in the Document window.

■ Dreamweaver applies the asset.

■ In this example, a color in the Assets panel was applied to text in the Document window.

SPECIFY FAVORITE ASSETS

For a large site that has lots of content and complicated page designs, the number of items that appear in the Assets panel can become cumbersome. To make the assets lists more manageable, you can segregate assets that you use often into a Favorites list inside their category. Then you have the option of viewing all the items in a category, or just a subset — your favorites. You choose between the two views by clicking the Site and Favorites radio buttons at the top of the Assets panel. Assets that are defined as favorites show up in both views — Site and Favorites.

You can also give the assets in your Favorites folder nicknames by right-clicking (Control-clicking) the name and selecting Edit Nickname. Nicknames can be useful for assets that normally have names that are not descriptive, such as colors defined using a hexadecimal code.

You can further group assets that are in a Favorites list by moving them into folders. To create a folder inside Favorites, open a Favorites list and then click . You can add Favorites items to the folder by dragging and dropping them onto the folder.

SPECIFY FAVORITE ASSETS

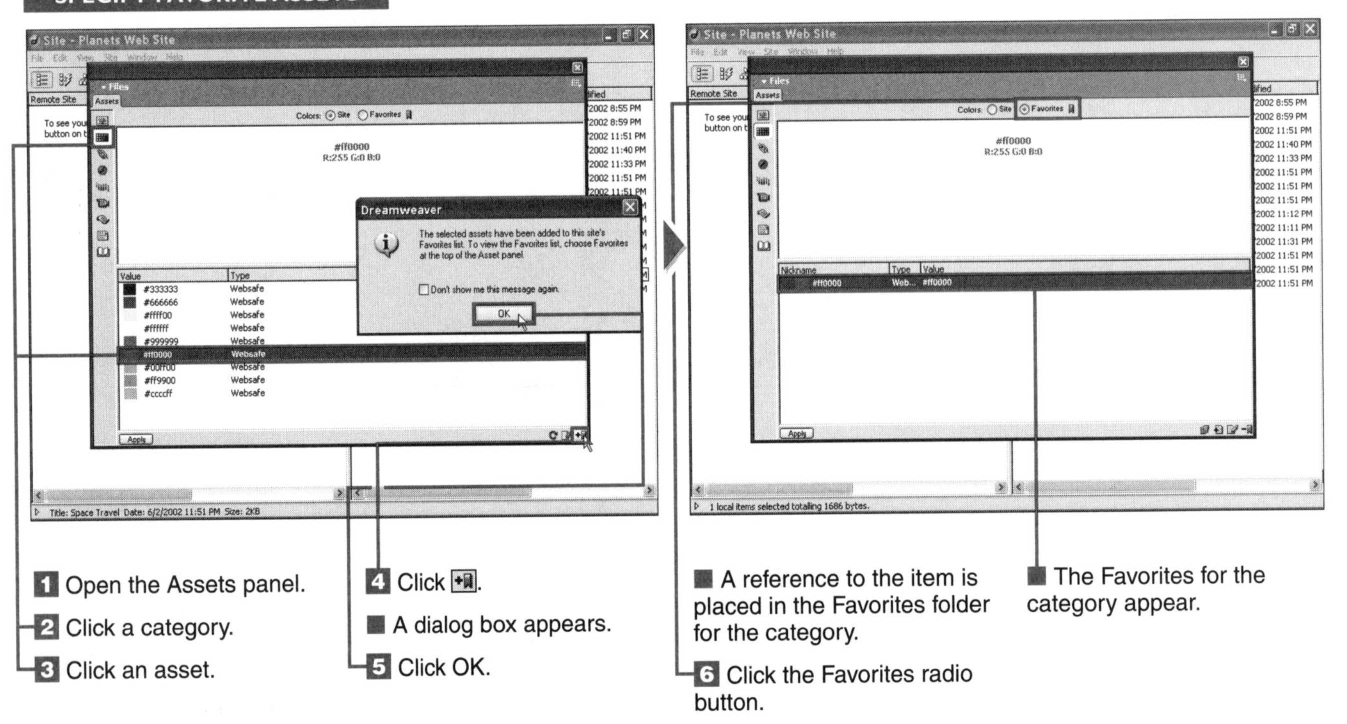

1 Open the Assets panel.

2 Click a category.

3 Click an asset.

4 Click .

■ A dialog box appears.

5 Click OK.

■ A reference to the item is placed in the Favorites folder for the category.

6 Click the Favorites radio button.

■ The Favorites for the category appear.

How do I remove an item from the Assets panel entirely?

✔ You cannot remove an asset while in the Assets panel itself. You need to open the Site window and delete the file from there. When you return to the Assets panel and click [C], the asset is gone.

Can I specify favorites for all of my assets?

✔ The Templates and Library categories cannot have Favorites. All the other categories of assets can.

Can I add an element to a Favorites list more than once?

✔ Yes. You may want to do this if you would like to refer to it by more than one nickname.

How do I remove an asset from my Favorites?

✔ View your Favorites, select the asset, and click [-] in the lower right of the panel.

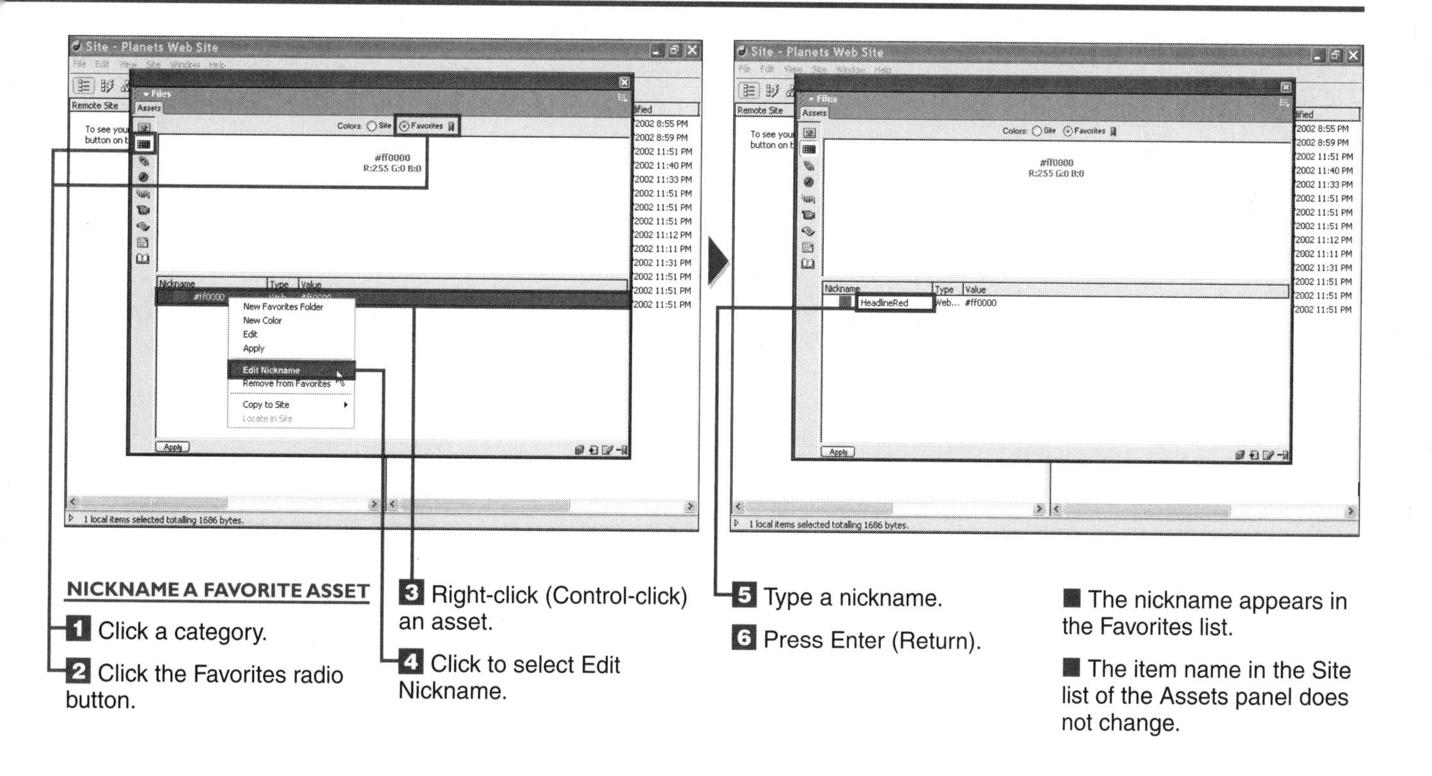

NICKNAME A FAVORITE ASSET

1 Click a category.

2 Click the Favorites radio button.

3 Right-click (Control-click) an asset.

4 Click to select Edit Nickname.

5 Type a nickname.

6 Press Enter (Return).

■ The nickname appears in the Favorites list.

■ The item name in the Site list of the Assets panel does not change.

CHECK A PAGE IN OR OUT

The Check In/Check Out system in Dreamweaver enables more than one developer to work collaboratively on a Web site. With the system turned on, Dreamweaver keeps track of which files in the site are being worked on and by whom. It also controls which files in your local site can be changed, depending on whether you have the file checked out.

In the Site window, a checked out file has a check next to it. The check is green if you checked out the file. It is red if someone else checked it out. To edit a file, you need to check it out from the Site window. Otherwise, the file is read-only in your local site, meaning you cannot change it.

You click a special button (⇩✓) in the Site window to check out a file.

You can also specify in the remote site settings that files are automatically checked out when they are double-clicked in the Site window. This can help keep two people from unintentionally making edits to a file at the same time.

CHECK A PAGE IN OR OUT

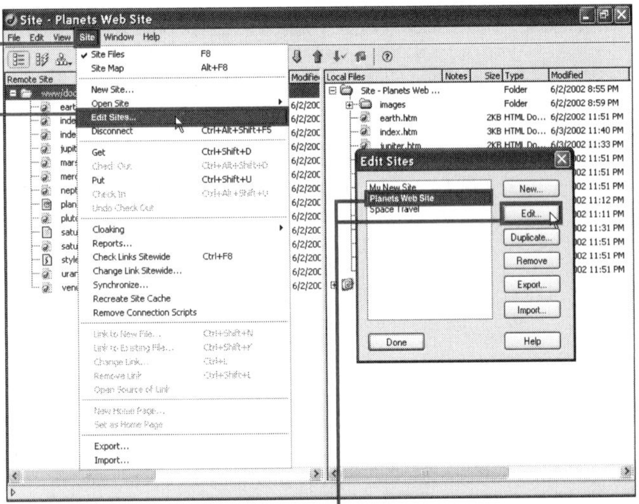

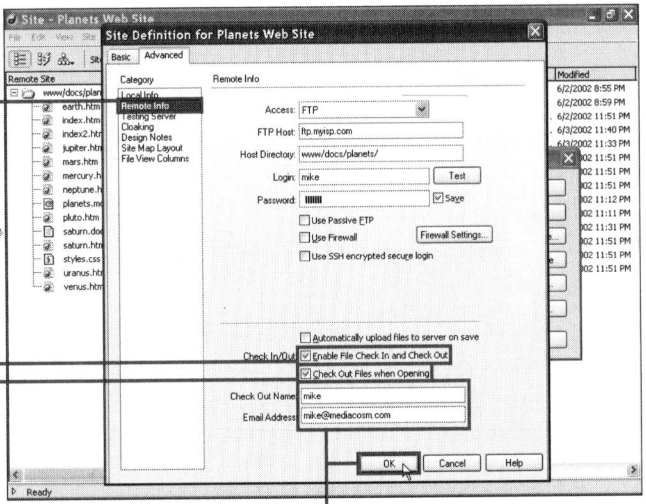

ENABLE CHECK IN/CHECK OUT

1 Click Site.

2 Click Edit Sites.

3 Click a site.

4 Click Edit.

5 Click Remote Info.

6 Click Enable File Check In and Check Out.

7 Click to select Check Out Files when Opening (☐ changes to ☑).

8 Type your name and e-mail address.

9 Click OK.

10 Click Done in the Define Sites dialog box.

How does Dreamweaver lock a file on the remote server?

✔ When you check out a file, Dreamweaver creates a temporary .LCK file that is stored in the remote folder while the page is checked out. The file contains information about who has checked the file out. Dreamweaver does not display the .LCK files in the Site window, but you can see them if you access your remote site with an FTP client program.

How do I contact the person who has checked out a file from a site?

✔ Each person working on a site can enter their name and e-mail address in the remote site information for that site. When a file is checked out, this information is displayed as a link next to the file in the Site window under the Checked Out By heading. Clicking the link opens an e-mail composition window with the name of the person who checked out the file in the To field.

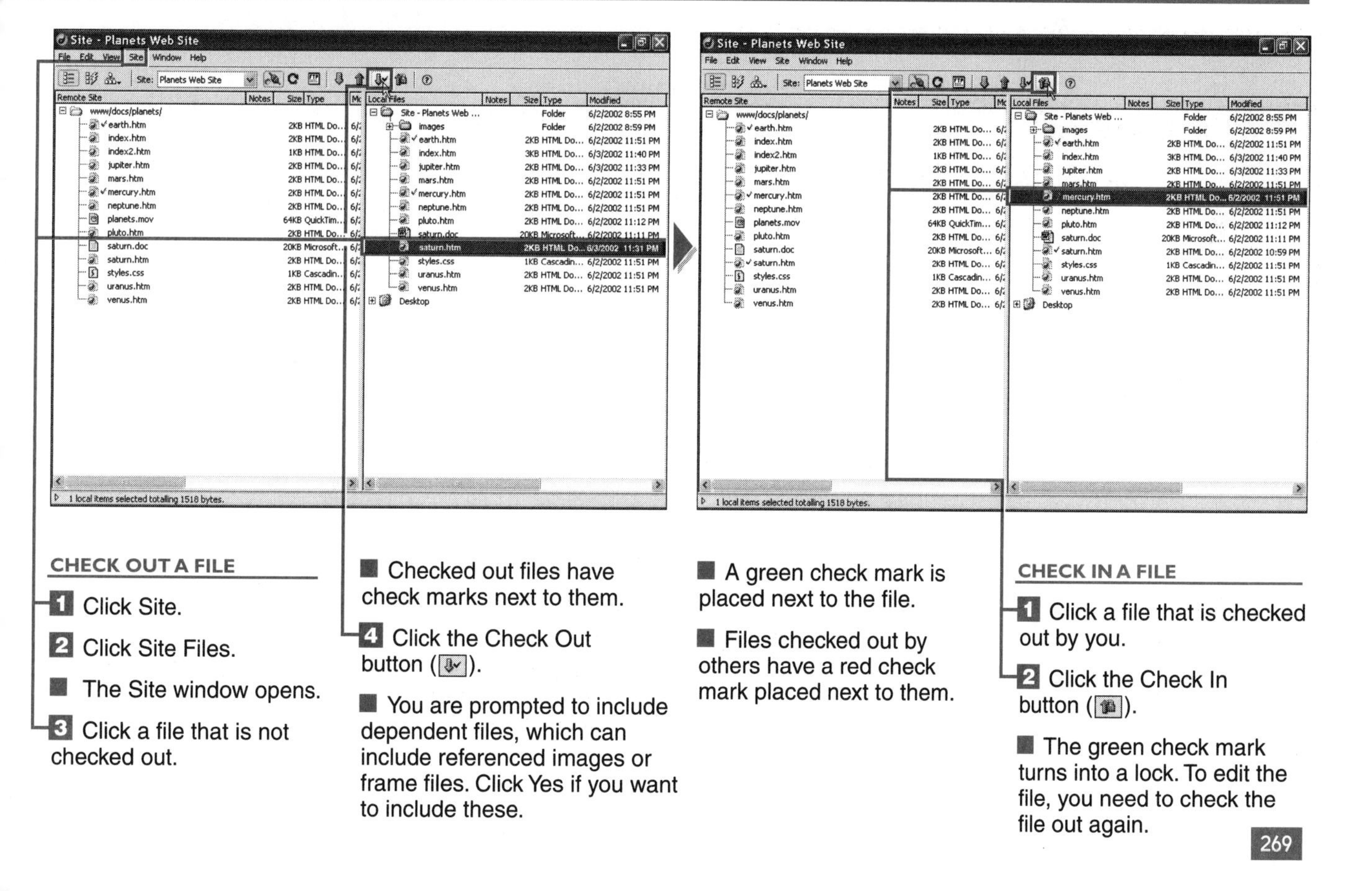

CHECK OUT A FILE

1 Click Site.

2 Click Site Files.

■ The Site window opens.

3 Click a file that is not checked out.

■ Checked out files have check marks next to them.

4 Click the Check Out button (⇩✓).

■ You are prompted to include dependent files, which can include referenced images or frame files. Click Yes if you want to include these.

■ A green check mark is placed next to the file.

■ Files checked out by others have a red check mark placed next to them.

CHECK IN A FILE

1 Click a file that is checked out by you.

2 Click the Check In button (🔒).

■ The green check mark turns into a lock. To edit the file, you need to check the file out again.

MAKE DESIGN NOTES

You can attach accessory information — such as editing history and an author name — to your Web pages with Design Notes in Dreamweaver. Such notes are especially useful if you are working on a site collaboratively, letting you update the development status of a page every time you edit it. Other users can view the Design Notes of a page by double-clicking an icon next to the page in the Site window.

Design Notes are also useful if you are working alone to develop your site. For example, you can use them to specify where the original design specs for each page are stored on your hard drive.

Design Notes offer a more secure alternative to adding extra information to your Web page files than HTML comments. Although they do not show up in the browser window when a page is opened, HTML comments can still be viewed if the page's source code is examined. Design Notes are stored separately from the HTML files themselves.

Macromedia Fireworks also makes use of Design Notes. When you import a graphic from Fireworks into Dreamweaver, Dreamweaver will import any Design Notes that are attached.

MAKE DESIGN NOTES

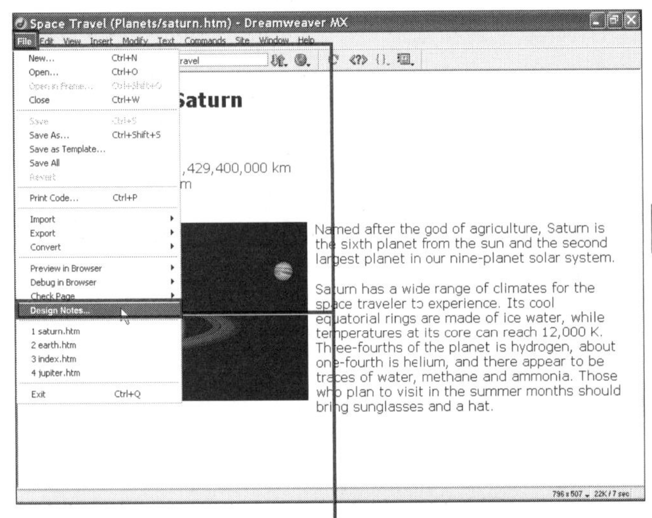

■ Design Notes are turned on by default when you create a site. You can turn them off in your site definition settings.

1 Open the page to which you want to attach Design Notes.

2 Click File.

3 Click Design Notes.

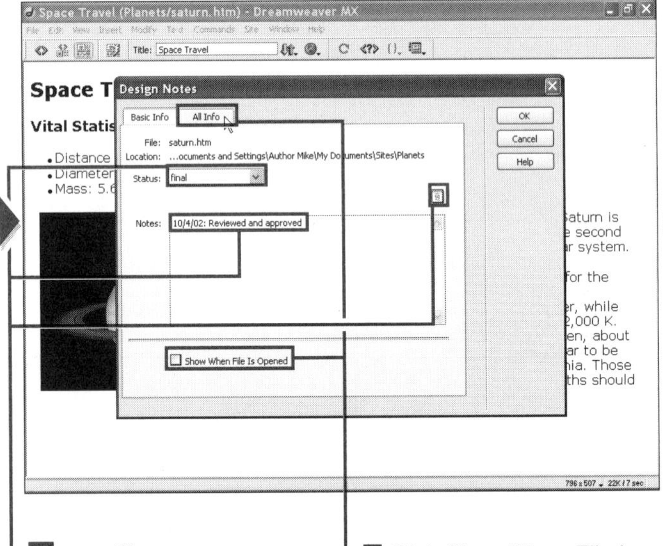

4 Click ▾ to select a status for the page.

5 Type any notes that are relevant to the page's development.

■ Click the Date button (▦) to enter the current date in the Notes field.

■ Click Show When File is Opened to automatically show any Design Notes when a file is opened.

6 Click the All Info tab.

How do I add Design Notes to an object on my page?

✔ Right-click (Control-click) the object in the Document window. In the contextual menu that appears, click Design Notes. You can then add notes to the object, just as you can to a page.

How are Design Notes stored in my site?

✔ Dreamweaver saves the information for Design Notes as XML files and stores them in a folder called _notes in your local site folder. The folder does not appear in the Site window.

Can I specify that Design Notes not be uploaded to the remote site?

✔ If you want your Design Notes kept private and accessible only to you, you can keep them from being uploaded to the remote site. Open the Site Definition dialog box for your site by clicking Site and then Edit Sites. Select your site and click Edit. Click the Design Notes category, and then unclick Upload Design Notes for Sharing.

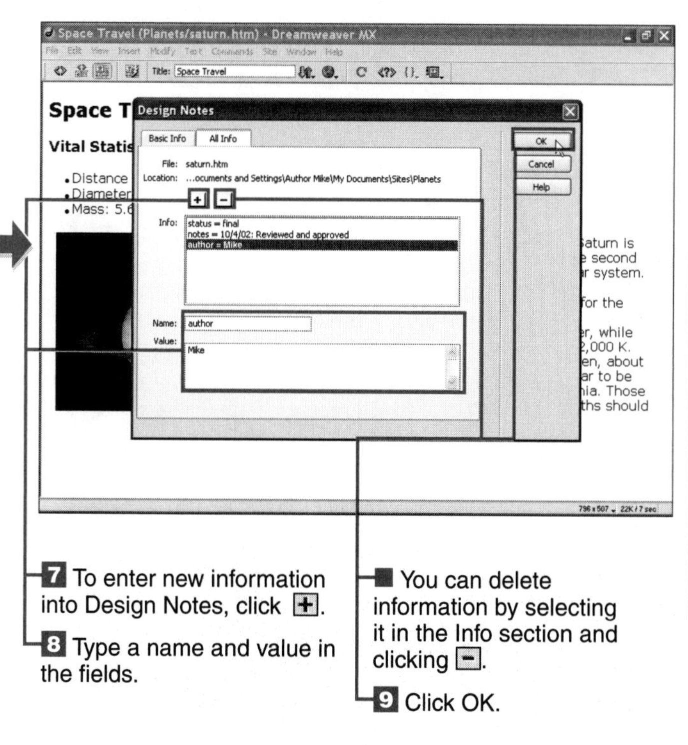

7 To enter new information into Design Notes, click [+].

8 Type a name and value in the fields.

■ You can delete information by selecting it in the Info section and clicking [−].

9 Click OK.

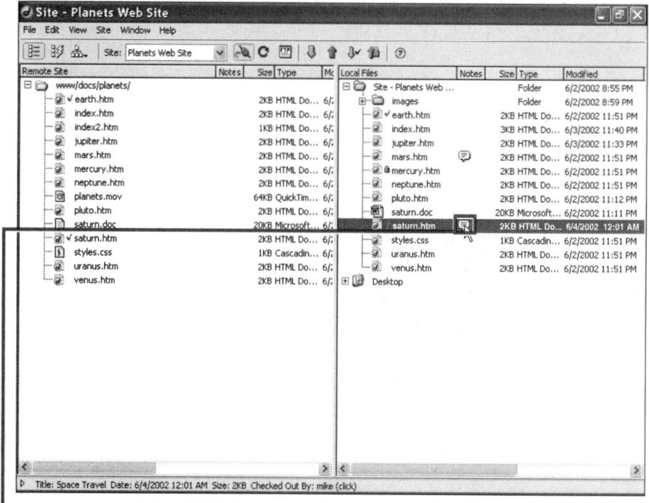

VIEW DESIGN NOTES

1 From the Site window, double-click [Design Notes icon] next to a file.

■ The Design Notes for that file open.

■ You can also click File and then Design Notes when a page is open in the Document window.

RUN A SITE REPORT

To make a quick assessment of your Dreamweaver work, you can generate reports on a page, several pages, or an entire site. The reports can tell you if there are HTML errors that need correcting and if there is descriptive information such as image alt text and page titles that are empty. The reports can also include checkout and Design Notes information for files.

After a report has been run, you can save the results as an XML file, which can be imported into a database or spreadsheet for further analysis.

After running a site report, you can use the Clean Up HTML command to fix the code errors that were found. You can also open files to add titles and alt text where these are missing. Adding descriptive titles and alt text to all your pages can potentially increase their visibility on search engines.

Some items in the report results are linked to information in the Reference panel, which gives you more information about how to fix problems in your site.

RUN A SITE REPORT

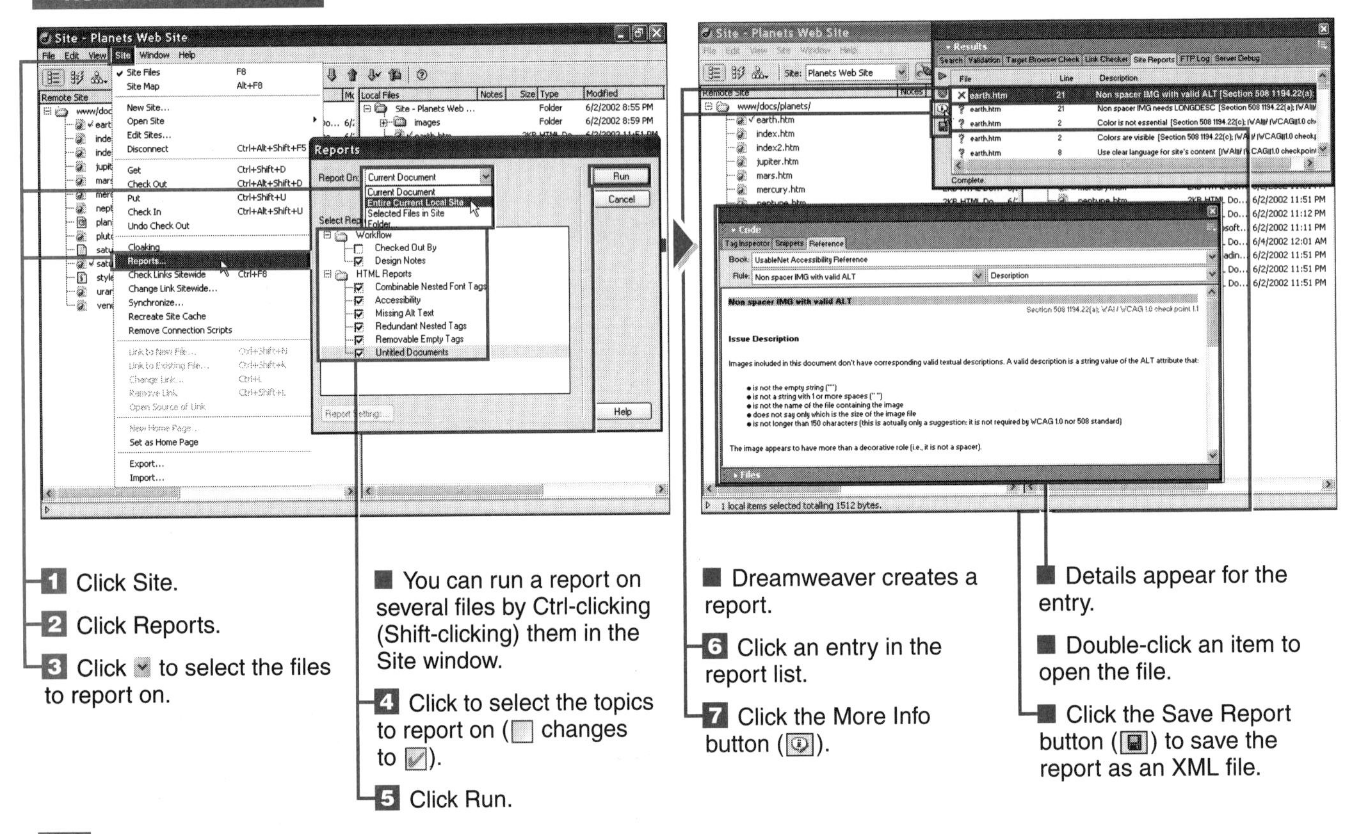

1 Click Site.

2 Click Reports.

3 Click ▾ to select the files to report on.

■ You can run a report on several files by Ctrl-clicking (Shift-clicking) them in the Site window.

4 Click to select the topics to report on (☐ changes to ☑).

5 Click Run.

■ Dreamweaver creates a report.

6 Click an entry in the report list.

7 Click the More Info button (ⓘ).

■ Details appear for the entry.

■ Double-click an item to open the file.

■ Click the Save Report button (💾) to save the report as an XML file.

CHANGE A LINK SITEWIDE

You can keep all the hyperlinks in your site up to date quickly and easily using the Change Link Sitewide command. It lets you search for and replace hyperlink references when those references require fixing or updating. Hyperlinks can break when you delete or rename files on your site, or when pages that you link to externally get deleted or renamed.

The Change Link Sitewide command is useful if you have content on your page that changes on a regular basis, such as a page that displays a monthly schedule. The Change Link Sitewide command can let you easily update links to a new schedule file each month.

This command is also useful if you point to an external Web page in several places on your site, and the address of that page changes. You can update the links to that page by entering full URLs into the Change Link Sitewide dialog box.

You can also use the command to change e-mail (mailto:) links, which can come in handy if a contact e-mail address for a site changes.

CHANGE A LINK SITEWIDE

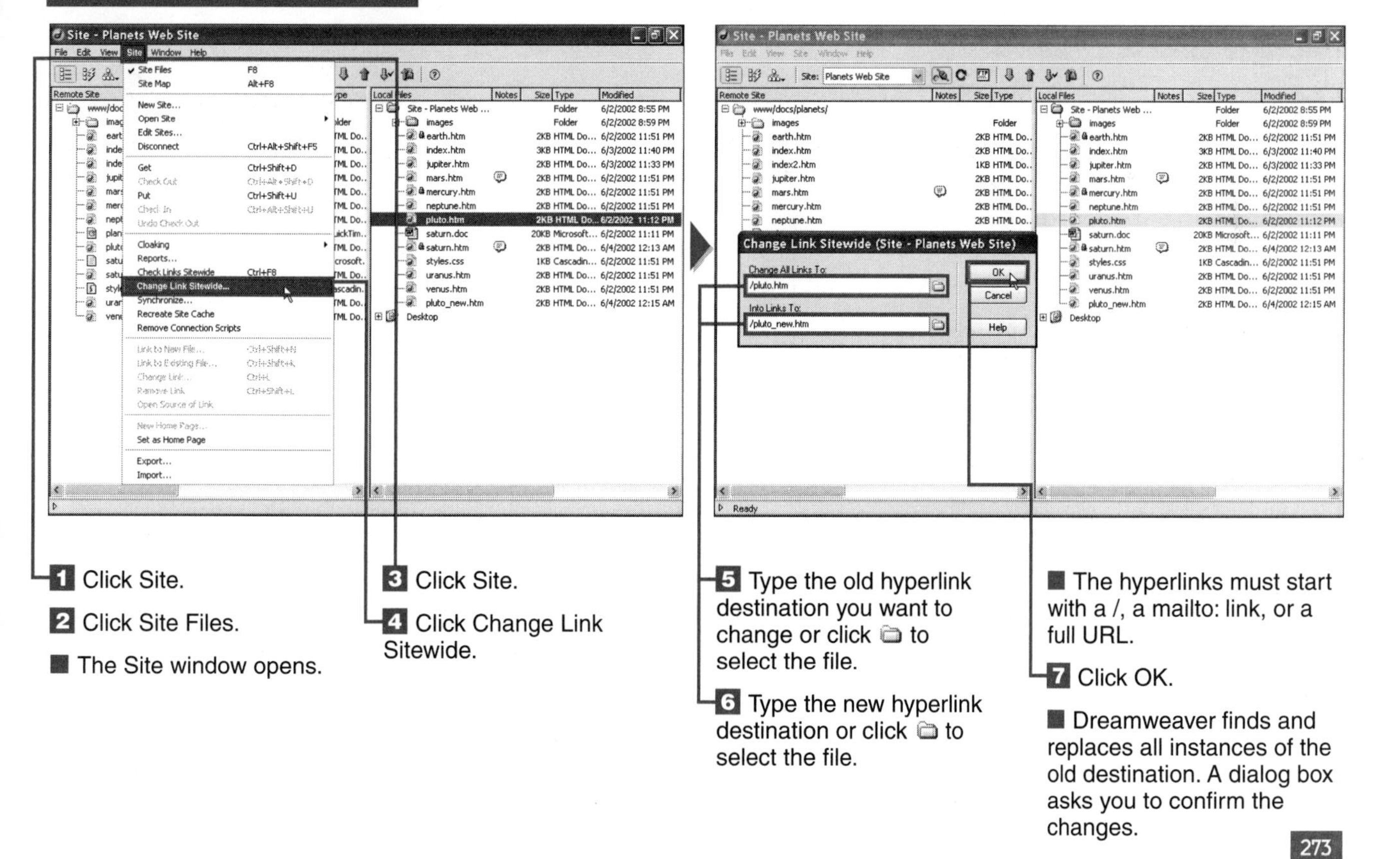

1 Click Site.

2 Click Site Files.

■ The Site window opens.

3 Click Site.

4 Click Change Link Sitewide.

5 Type the old hyperlink destination you want to change or click 🗀 to select the file.

6 Type the new hyperlink destination or click 🗀 to select the file.

■ The hyperlinks must start with a /, a mailto: link, or a full URL.

7 Click OK.

■ Dreamweaver finds and replaces all instances of the old destination. A dialog box asks you to confirm the changes.

FIND AND REPLACE TEXT

With the Find and Replace feature in Dreamweaver, you can search for text on your Web page, text in your source code, or specific HTML tags in your pages. You can also perform searches across the current document, a set of selected documents, a folder, or the entire site. After searching, you can replace some or all of the instances where your search query was found.

The Find and Replace feature is a powerful tool for making changes to text elements that repeat across many pages. A search query might be something as small as a copyright date in a page footer or something as complex as a nested HTML table.

The HTML tag search allows you to specifically remove, replace, or edit the tags or attributes of tags in your pages. There is also an advanced text search that lets you find text only if it appears inside a specific HTML tag.

You can add even more power to your Find and Replace queries with Regular Expressions, which allow you to add wild card characters to your search queries. See page 276 for more information.

FIND AND REPLACE TEXT

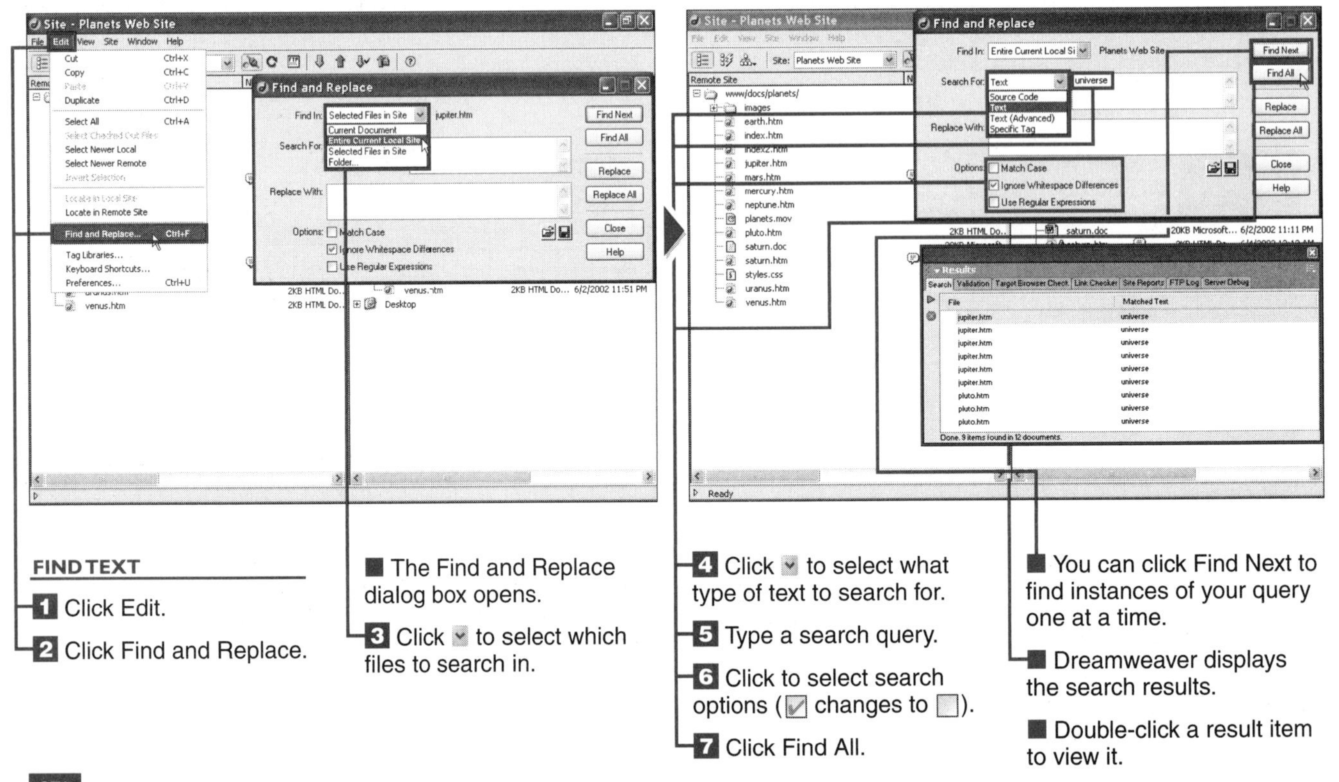

FIND TEXT

1 Click Edit.

2 Click Find and Replace.

■ The Find and Replace dialog box opens.

3 Click ▾ to select which files to search in.

4 Click ▾ to select what type of text to search for.

5 Type a search query.

6 Click to select search options (☑ changes to ☐).

7 Click Find All.

■ You can click Find Next to find instances of your query one at a time.

■ Dreamweaver displays the search results.

■ Double-click a result item to view it.

How do I search through a select group of files in my site?

✔ Ctrl-click (Shift-click) the files in the Site window before performing the Find and Replace. Be sure to choose Selected Files in Site in the Find In menu. Clicking Find All searches for text in only the files you selected.

Do searches of the source code find JavaScript and style-sheet code?

✔ Yes. They find any text that is in a page's source code, which can include JavaScript and style-sheet code.

Why might I want to find and replace an HTML attribute?

✔ You can replace attributes to achieve many things. You can change the alignment of the contents of a table, changing `align="center"` to `align="right"` in `<td>` tags. You can change the color of specific text in your page, changing `color="red"` to `color="green"` in `<font>` tags. Or you can change the page background color across your site, changing `bgcolor="black"` to `bgcolor="white"` in `<body>` tags).

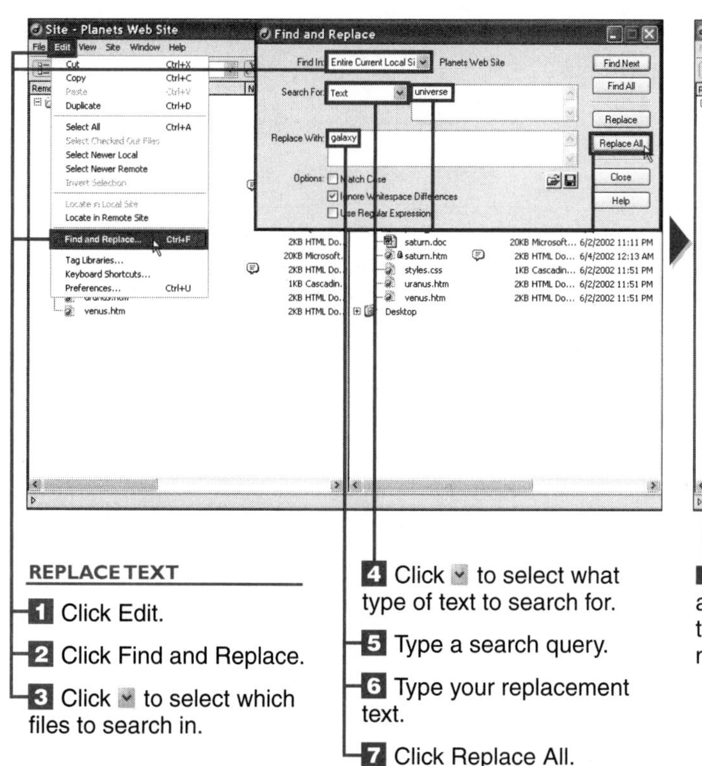

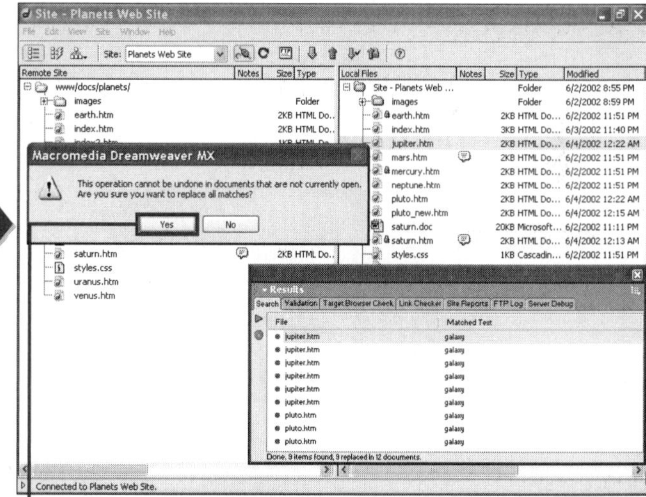

REPLACE TEXT

1 Click Edit.

2 Click Find and Replace.

3 Click ▾ to select which files to search in.

4 Click ▾ to select what type of text to search for.

5 Type a search query.

6 Type your replacement text.

7 Click Replace All.

■ An alert box may appear asking if you want to replace text in documents that are not open. Click Yes.

■ A Results panel appears displaying the results of the replace.

SEARCH FOR PATTERNS OF TEXT

There may be times when you want to search for a *pattern* of text in your pages rather than a specific string of letters. You can perform these more complicated kinds of searches in Dreamweaver by using regular expressions, which allow you to substitute special wild-card characters in your search queries.

Some common regular-expression symbols include `*`, which matches the character it follows 0 or more times; `+`, which matches the character it follows 1 or more times; and `?`, which matches the character it follows 0 or 1 time.

With regular expressions turned on, the query `eb*` matches `eb` in `web`, `ebb` in `webby`, and `e` in `went`. The query `eb+` matches `eb` in `web` and `ebb` in `webby`, but nothing in `went` because for `eb+`, patterns must contain at least one `b`.

Other special symbols include `.`, which matches any single character, `\w`, which matches any alphanumeric character, and, which matches the beginning of a line. With regular expressions turned on, the query `^M.*` matches all the lines in a document that begin with `M`.

Optionally, you can use parentheses in your search query to specify patterns that you can then reference in your replacement text. You reference the patterns using `$1` for the first set of parentheses, `$2` for the second, and so on.

SEARCH FOR PATTERNS OF TEXT

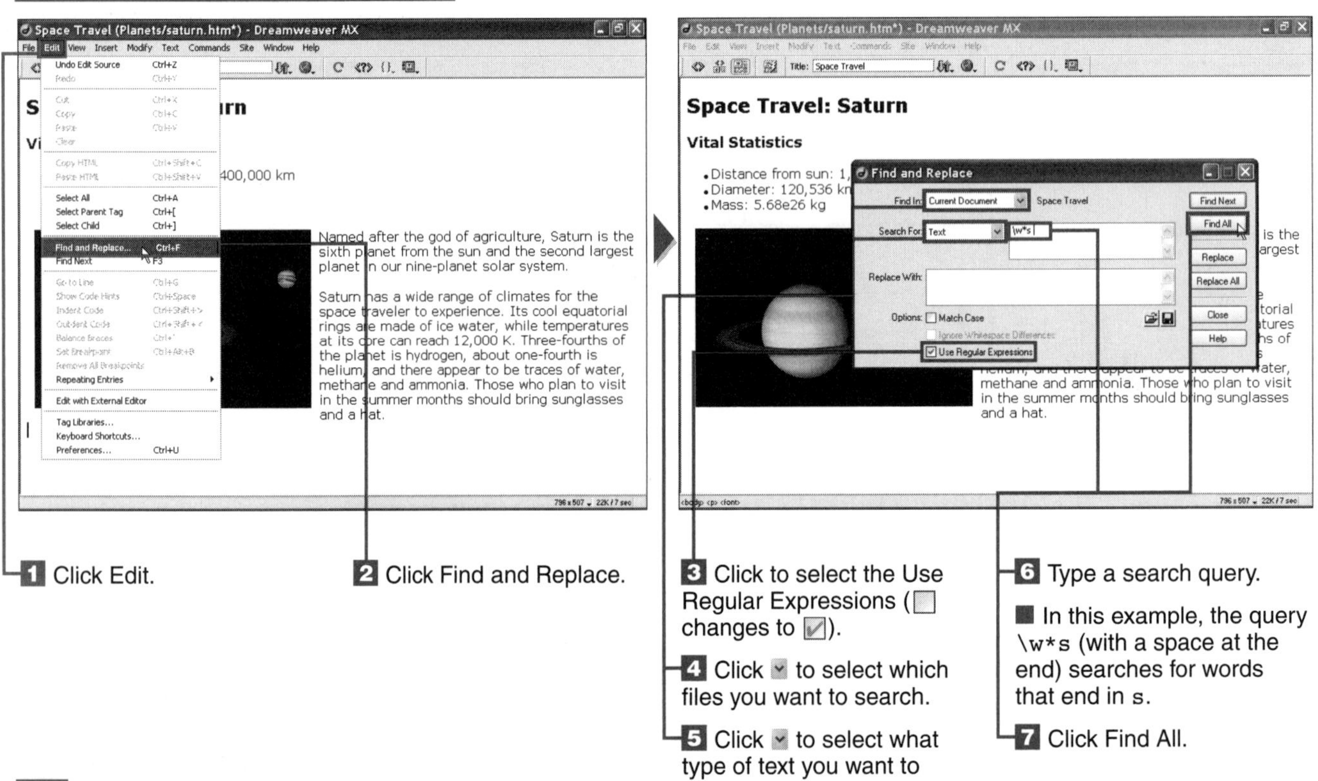

1 Click Edit.

2 Click Find and Replace.

3 Click to select the Use Regular Expressions (☐ changes to ☑).

4 Click ▾ to select which files you want to search.

5 Click ▾ to select what type of text you want to search.

6 Type a search query.

■ In this example, the query `\w*s` (with a space at the end) searches for words that end in `s`.

7 Click Find All.

With regular expressions turned on, how do I search for characters in my code that have a special meaning, such as * or ? ?

✔ You must escape these characters with a preceding \ (for example, * or \?). A preceding backslash tells Dreamweaver to treat characters such as * and ? as regular characters in a query.

How can I save my search patterns?

✔ You can save a search pattern by clicking [save icon] in the Find and Replace dialog box. This can be handy if you have a complicated regular-expression search that you might want to use again. Clicking [open icon] lets you access search patterns that you have saved.

How do I specify white space in a regular expression?

✔ There are various special characters that match different types of white space:

\r matches a carriage return
\t matches a tab
\s matches any single white-space character (space, carriage return, tab, and so on)

These special characters can be mixed with others. For example, \s+ matches one or more white-space characters.

Can I match the beginning or end of a line in my search patterns?

✔ Yes. ^ matches the beginning of a line while $ matches the end of a line.

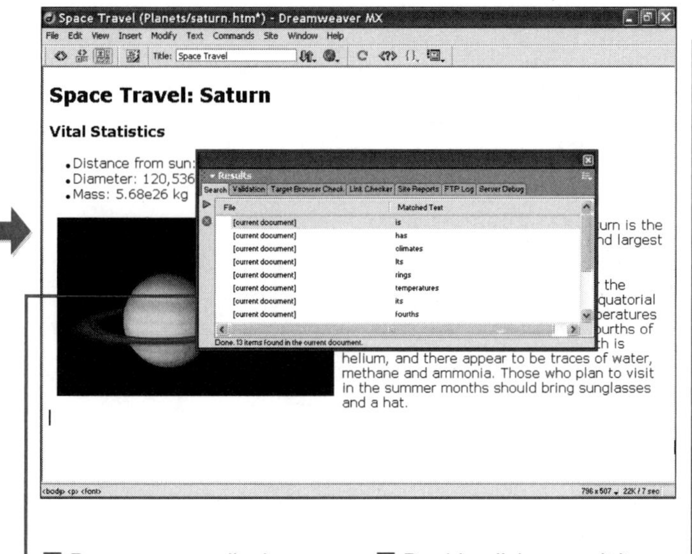

■ Dreamweaver displays a Results panel listing any successful searches.

■ Double-click a result item to view it.

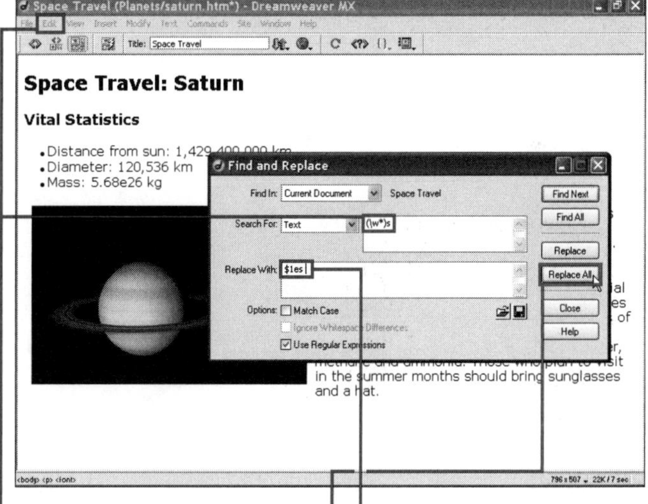

REPLACE A PATTERN

1 Click Edit.

2 Click Find and Replace.

3 Type a search query.

■ Parentheses mark a pattern to be referenced in the replacement text.

4 Type your replacement text. In this example, $1 will substitute the pattern in the first set of parentheses.

5 Click Replace All.

■ Dreamweaver performs the Find and Replace.

SECTION V

17) SETTING UP A DYNAMIC SITE

18) DISPLAYING DYNAMIC DATA

19) ADVANCED DYNAMIC TOPICS

CREATING A DYNAMIC SITE

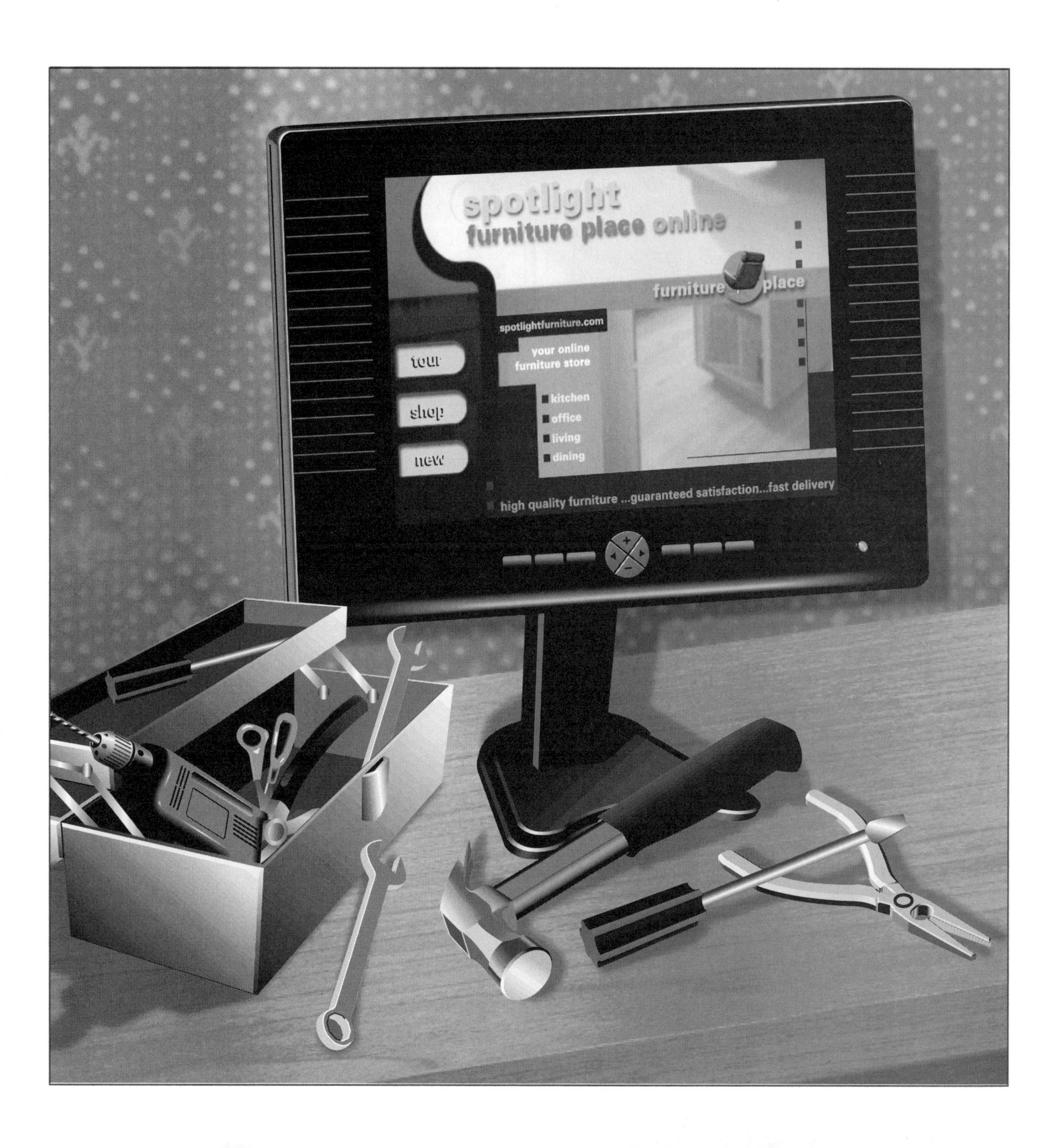

INTRODUCTION TO DYNAMIC SITES

Dynamic Web pages enable you to create richer, more flexible, and more responsive sites by restyling and adding content to pages at the time a user requests them. Dynamic sites are more complicated to build than static sites, because their pages are more challenging to code and serving them requires additional software. However, they have numerous advantages, including a better experience for site visitors as well as easier maintenance for the developer.

Dreamweaver lets you create dynamic sites that work with a variety of dynamic technologies. This chapter covers how to create dynamic sites in general, with examples created for Macromedia's ColdFusion MX dynamic platform.

Static Sites

A dynamic site is different from a static site, whose pages contain content completely determined by its HTML and other static code. With a *static site*, the code that resides on the Web server is the same code that the browser receives — the pages do not undergo special processing like dynamic pages do, and no new content is added at the time of a page request. The first sixteen chapters in this book focus on building static pages, which include HTML and additional code such as JavaScript and style sheets.

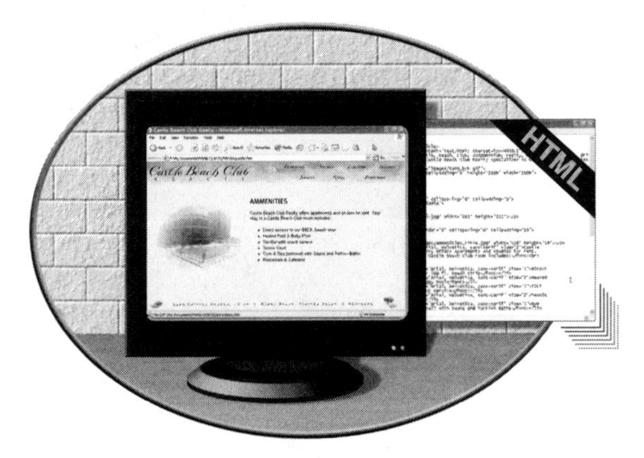

Going Dynamic

Static pages are usually sufficient for sites featuring limited amounts of information that rarely changes. Examples include a personal site with journal entries and vacation images, or a small business site that features product descriptions and information about how to contact the company. However, when you are publishing large amounts of information that changes often, like many newspaper sites do, or an e-commerce site that sells many products online, it is usually necessary to introduce dynamic features into your pages.

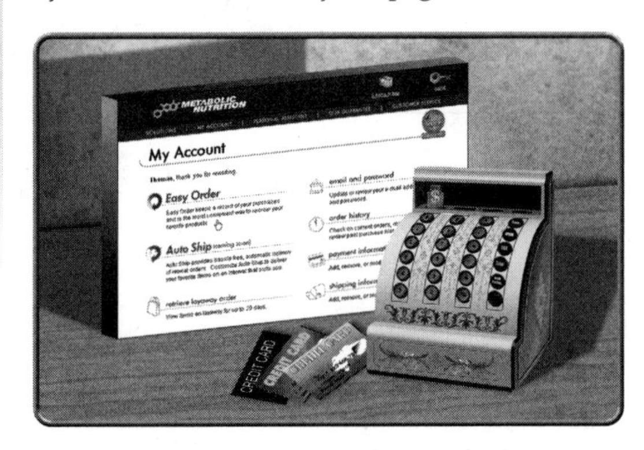

Dynamic Parts

Dynamic sites involve several additional elements compared to static sites. First, their pages include dynamic code that specifies what parts of a page need to be built dynamically by the server. Whereas the main job of HTML code is to determine how content is organized and formatted on your pages, dynamic code determines what content is displayed and from where it is retrieved. Dynamic sites also require an application server to process the dynamic code and insert the dynamic content. Finally, dynamic sites need to connect to a database where they can retrieve the content for their pages. Typically it is the application server that connects the site with the database.

Easier Maintenance

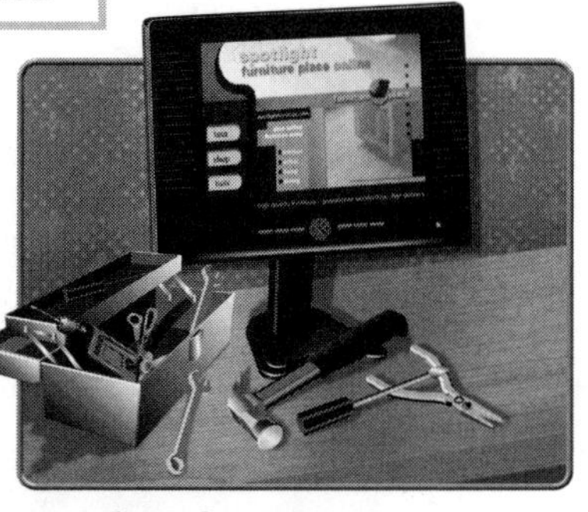

Dynamic Web sites can be challenging to create initially, because they involve coding in more complex languages than HTML, deploying special application software, and setting up and maintaining a database. But after you have created a dynamic Web site, it can be easier to maintain because you can make updates by editing the content in your database instead of having to rewrite the HTML in your Web pages. Dynamic sites can also be set to change their content automatically without the developer being involved. A dynamic site can run itself.

Better User Experience

One advantage to running a dynamic Web site is it can be easier for users to find what they are looking for. For example, dynamic sites can take search queries from users, use those queries to search massive databases of information, and then build custom pages for the user that contain relevant results. This is essentially how search engines work, as do large e-commerce companies that sell many, many products, such as Amazon.com. These sites could never offer such rich information with static pages.

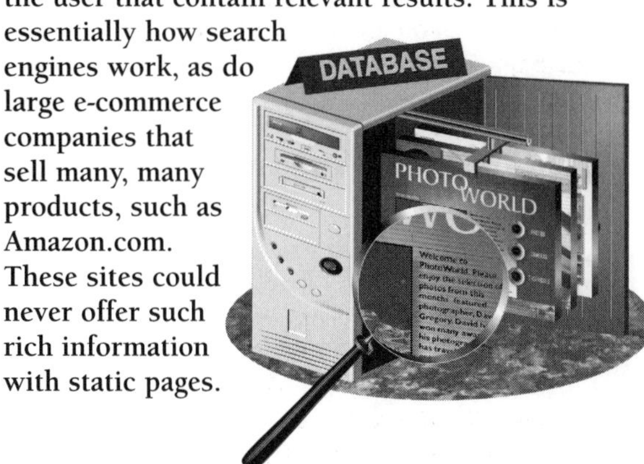

Dynamic Sites and Dreamweaver

Dreamweaver MX has a host of features that help you develop dynamic Web pages quickly and easily. It allows you to insert dynamic code into your pages, often without having to write any of the code by hand. You specify the functionality of the dynamic code using dialog boxes, and then Dreamweaver inserts the code for you behind the scenes. Additionally, Dreamweaver includes tools that allow you to seamlessly connect with application servers and databases to view stores of dynamic content for your pages. Dreamweaver supports many popular Web application platforms, which means you can create sites using tools that have been proven on thousand of sites already on the Web.

INTRODUCTION TO APPLICATION SERVERS

The real brains behind a dynamic Web site is the *application server*, which is the software that handles the processing of dynamic code on a Web page and interacts with databases to retrieve and insert dynamic content. To develop dynamic sites in Dreamweaver, you must first install an application server. Without an application server, Dreamweaver has no way to access dynamic data or test dynamic pages. Dreamweaver supports a variety of popular server technologies, including ColdFusion, ASP, ASP.NET, JSP, and PHP.

Serving Dynamic Pages

Serving a static Web page is a simple process: A Web server receives a page request from a browser, the Web server locates the file in its file system, and the Web server sends the browser the page. When a Web server receives a request for a dynamic page, the process is more complicated. By definition, a raw dynamic page includes undetermined information that can vary depending on the user requesting the page, the referring page, what information is currently in the database, and other factors.

Before a dynamic page can be sent to the browser, an application server must process it. The application server reads the dynamic code on the page, connects to the database to retrieve any required dynamic content, and then inserts that content into the page. The result is a page with dynamic content added that the Web server can send to the browser.

Types of Application Servers

Application servers vary in how they operate with Web servers. Often the application server software is separate from the Web server. That is the case with servers such as ColdFusion and Macromedia Jrun. While they usually run on the same computer as the Web server software, they are separate and distinct programs.

Other application servers are simply extensions of Web servers. These high-performance Web servers can process dynamic code themselves, without having to pass the files to a different program. Microsoft Internet Information Server is an example of such a server. It can process ASP and ASP.NET dynamic code.

Choose a Platform

The application server platform you choose depends on a variety of factors, including how you develop your site, what kind of Web server you use, and your budget. Dreamweaver supports various Web application platforms, but is most integrated with ColdFusion. The dynamic examples in this book use the ColdFusion MX platform. If you are serving your sites on a Microsoft Web server, you may want to use the ASP platform, because it is built into the Web server. PHP can be an attractive option for developers on a budget because it is an open-source technology, and many PHP tools can be downloaded free of charge.

How Everything Fits Together

1. A browser requests a page from a Web site.
2. If the page is static, the Web server sends the processed page to the browser. If the page is dynamic, the Web server passes the page to the application server for processing.
3. The application server processes the page, retrieving and inserting into the page any required database information.
4. The application server passes the processed page back to the Web server.
5. The Web server sends the processed page to the browser.

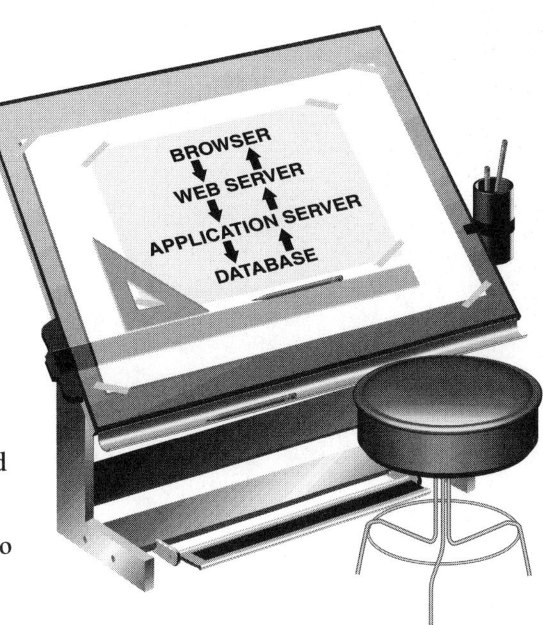

Dynamic Code

Dreamweaver has tools that let you create dynamic Web pages on a variety of platforms, including ColdFusion, ASP, ASP.NET, PHP, and JSP. Each platform has a dynamic coding language. For example, if you are coding a dynamic site that uses the ColdFusion platform, you insert ColdFusion Markup Language, or CFML, into your pages to create dynamic features. Similarly, if you are coding on the ASP platform, you insert ASP code.

You can create dynamic pages by writing the dynamic code by hand in Code View, just like you can create HTML code by hand. You can also create dynamic pages using many Dreamweaver commands, panels, and dialog boxes. This allows you to create dynamic elements visually in Design View and have Dreamweaver automatically insert the relevant dynamic code for you.

INTRODUCTION TO DATABASES

Simply defined, a *database* is a set of files that can store organized information. For the purposes of creating dynamic sites, databases store ASCII text that can be retrieved and inserted into dynamic Web pages. There are a variety of databases that you can use to power a dynamic site, from relatively simple file-based systems such as Microsoft Access to high-powered server-based systems such as Oracle.

In a dynamic Web site, it is the application server that connects to the database, retrieves relevant information, and inserts that information into your dynamic pages. Dreamweaver can access database information, but it does this by connecting to the application server. You view available databases in Dreamweaver in the Databases panel.

Tables

Information inside a database is stored in one or more *tables*, which are grid-like structures comprising columns and rows, similar to spreadsheets. Each table in a database stores a distinct type of information. In a company database, for example, one table might store employee information while another might store product inventory information. You can view the names of the tables that make up a database by opening the Databases panel and then opening one of the databases listed.

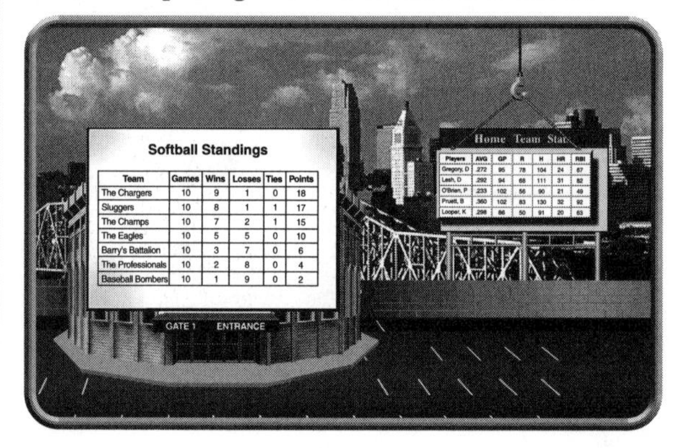

Database Columns

Every database table is made up of one or more *columns*. When you set up a table, you define the type of data that will be displayed in each column. For example, in an employee information table, one column might be defined as containing text for a last name, while another might be defined as containing an integer for an employee ID. How you define the datatypes of the columns limits the type of information you can retrieve and insert into your pages. You can view the columns in a table by opening the table in the Databases window. Individual elements of a column are sometimes referred to as *fields*.

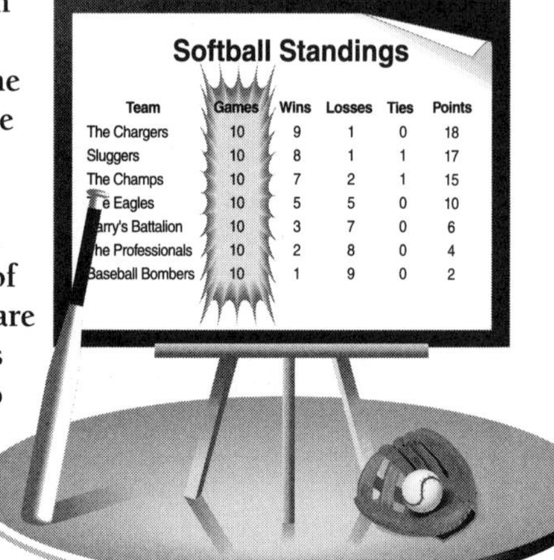

Database Rows

The data you store in a database table is organized as a series of *rows*. The size of a row depends on the number of columns in your table. In an employee table, for example, each row might include four columns of information: the employee's last name, first name, employee ID, and phone number. When displaying database information on your Web site, you can retrieve many rows of data or just a single row. You can also retrieve particular columns in a row. Individual rows are often referred to as *records*.

Softball Standings

Team	Games	Wins	Losses	Ties	Points
The Chargers	10	9	1	0	18
Sluggers	10	8	1	1	17
The Champs	10	7	2	1	15
The Eagles	10	5	5	0	10
Barry's Battalion	10	3	7	0	6
The Professionals	10	2	8	0	4
Baseball Bombers	10	1	9	0	2

Recordsets

To get data out of a database and display it in a Web page, you need to first define a *recordset*. A recordset specifies the database, table, and column information for the data that you want to insert into your page. When you create a recordset, Dreamweaver builds the appropriate SQL statement and inserts the statement into your Web page code. After you create a recordset for a page, you can insert data from the recordset. Dreamweaver's tools make it easy to create recordsets that insert an entire database table as an HTML table on your page, or just insert individual fields of data. To create a recordset, see Chapter 18.

SQL

When you need to interact with a database — whether it involves retrieving information, inserting information, or deleting information — you will probably interact with it using Structured Query Language, or *SQL*. SQL is a non-proprietary language for manipulating databases, and every major database platform supports it.

One advantage of SQL is that its statements are made up of descriptive English words:

```
SELECT first_name FROM Employees
WHERE id = 101
```

The above statement retrieves data from the first_name field of the Employees database wherever the value of the id field in that row equals 101.

When you build dynamic pages in Dreamweaver, you add SQL code to your pages. If you are using Dreamweaver's user-friendly commands, menus, and panels to interact with your database, you may never actually write the SQL code by hand; Dreamweaver writes it behind the scenes. To view SQL statements in your Web page code, switch to Code View.

INSTALL AND LOG INTO COLDFUSION

Installing and running ColdFusion on your computer enables you to create Web pages that can dynamically interact with databases and thereby tailor their content to different users. Sites powered by ColdFusion are known as *dynamic sites* because ColdFusion processes their pages before the Web server serves them, adding custom content that can vary depending on who is viewing them, the referring Web page, and other factors. Dreamweaver offers a variety of tools to quickly and easily create and test ColdFusion-enabled sites.

To install ColdFusion, you run the ColdFusion installer program, which is included on the CD-ROM that comes with this book. This setup program installs a fully functional developer version of ColdFusion MX for Windows. You can also download ColdFusion MX from the Macromedia Web site at www.macromedia.com. There is currently no version of ColdFusion MX available for the Macintosh.

In addition to installing the main ColdFusion application server, setting up ColdFusion installs a standalone Web server on your computer you can use to test your dynamic Web pages. The setup program also creates a special Web files folder where you store the ColdFusion-enabled Web pages to be served by the standalone server. The default location for the Web files folder is C:\CfusionMX\wwwroot\.

INSTALL AND LOG INTO COLDFUSION

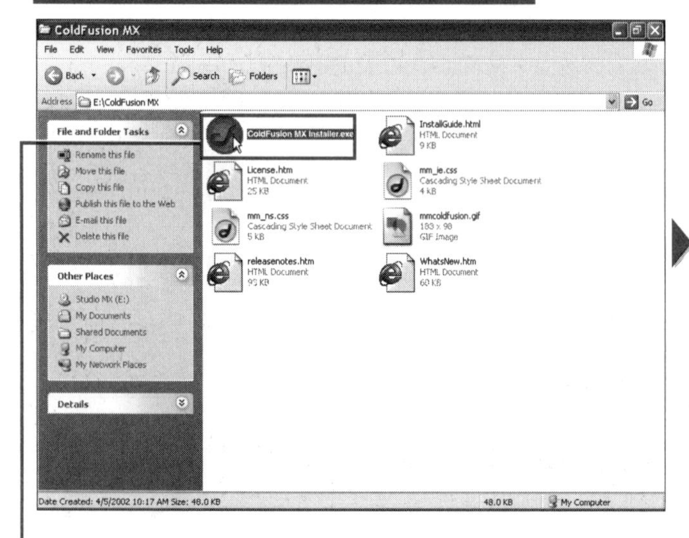

1 Double-click the ColdFusion application installer file.

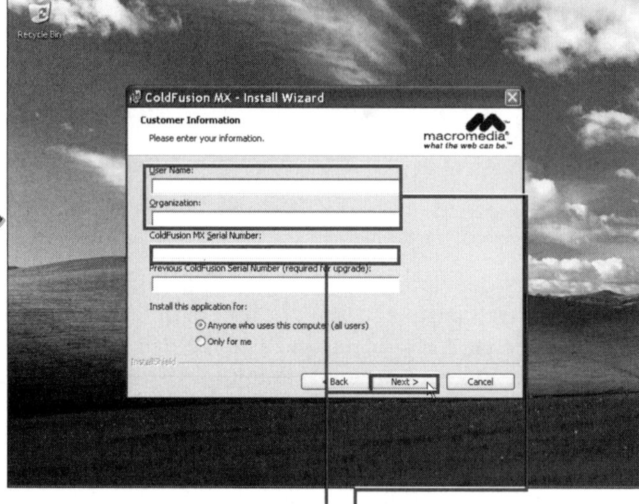

■ The ColdFusion Install Wizard opens.

2 Complete the initial screens, accepting the registration agreement.

3 Type your personal information.

4 Type your ColdFusion MX serial number.

5 Click Next.

How is the developer version of ColdFusion MX different from other versions?

✔ The developer version of ColdFusion MX, which is included on the book CD-ROM, expires after 30 days and thereafter only supports a single IP address. This makes the developer version fine for building and testing simple dynamic sites locally, but insufficient for deploying a live Web site. The professional and enterprise versions of ColdFusion MX allow you to serve a dynamic Web site to the rest of the world.

What port does the ColdFusion standalone Web server run on?

✔ The standalone Web server runs on port 8500. This means you need to append :8500 to the host name or IP address of URLs when you use the standalone Web server. For example:

http://localhost:8500/index.cfm

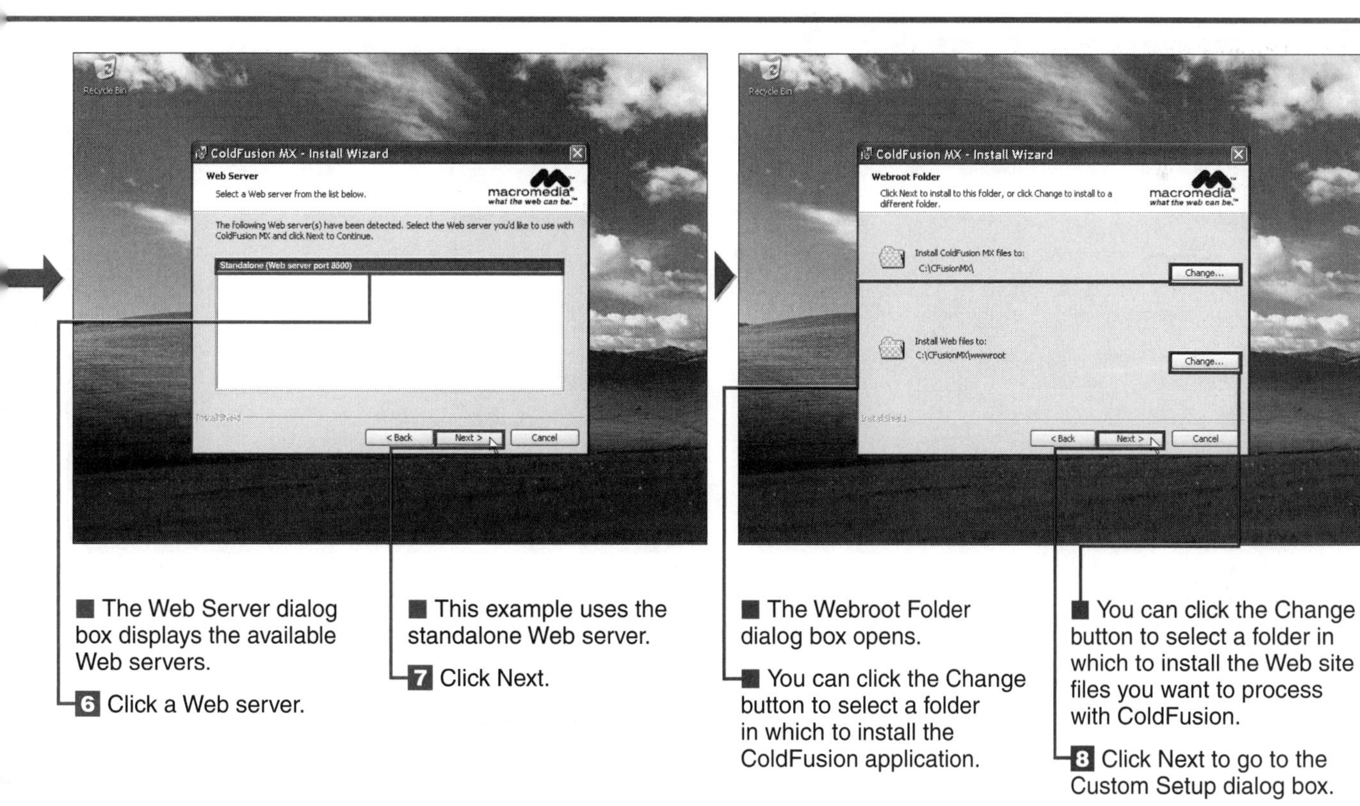

■ The Web Server dialog box displays the available Web servers.

6 Click a Web server.

■ This example uses the standalone Web server.

7 Click Next.

■ The Webroot Folder dialog box opens.

■ You can click the Change button to select a folder in which to install the ColdFusion application.

■ You can click the Change button to select a folder in which to install the Web site files you want to process with ColdFusion.

8 Click Next to go to the Custom Setup dialog box.

CONTINUED

INSTALL AND LOG INTO COLDFUSION (CONTINUED)

After it is installed, the ColdFusion program acts as an intermediary between the dynamic Web pages that you create in Dreamweaver and the databases that hold the dynamic content for your site. The job of ColdFusion is to process special code in your dynamic pages that determines what database content to retrieve, and then insert the content into the appropriates places in your pages. After ColdFusion processes the pages, a Web server can serve the pages to the end user.

Part of the ColdFusion setup includes defining passwords for administering ColdFusion and for Remote Data Source (RDS) access by programs such as Dreamweaver. You need to log in as an administrator to connect ColdFusion to the databases that contain your page content. The ColdFusion administrator runs in a Web browser. RDS access enables Dreamweaver to connect to ColdFusion and access information about the connected databases, so it can write the code to generate dynamic features on your pages.

After installation, you can change your administrator and RDS passwords by logging into ColdFusion and clicking links under the Security section of the navigation menu. ColdFusion also allows you to disable both passwords, if you prefer it not require them for access.

INSTALL AND LOG INTO COLDFUSION (CONTINUED)

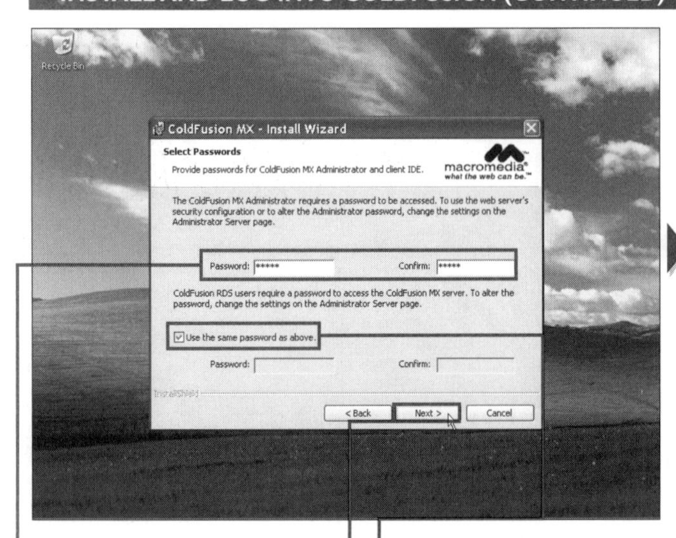

9 Click Next.

■ The Select Passwords dialog box appears.

10 Type an administrator password for managing ColdFusion.

11 Click Use the same password as above to specify the same password for RDS (☐ changes to ☑).

■ Dreamweaver uses the RDS password to connect to ColdFusion and access databases.

12 Click Next.

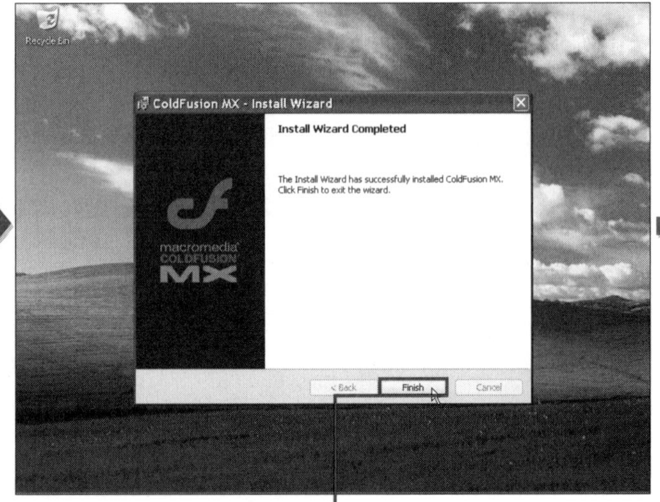

■ The Ready to Install Program dialog box appears.

13 Click Install.

■ The Install Wizard Completed dialog box appears.

14 Click Finish.

What Web servers does ColdFusion MX support?

✔ ColdFusion MX supports Microsoft Internet Information Services 4.0 and 5.x (Windows only), Apache 1.3.2x and later as well as 2.x, Netscape 3.6x, iPlanet 4.x and 6.x, Zeus 4.1 (Linux SuSE only), and the ColdFusion MX standalone Web server.

How do I get more information about how to use ColdFusion MX?

✔ This book covers only the basics of setting up ColdFusion MX with Dreamweaver and building a few simple dynamic pages. For more information about ColdFusion, click Help and then Using ColdFusion in Dreamweaver, or view the ColdFusion documentation.

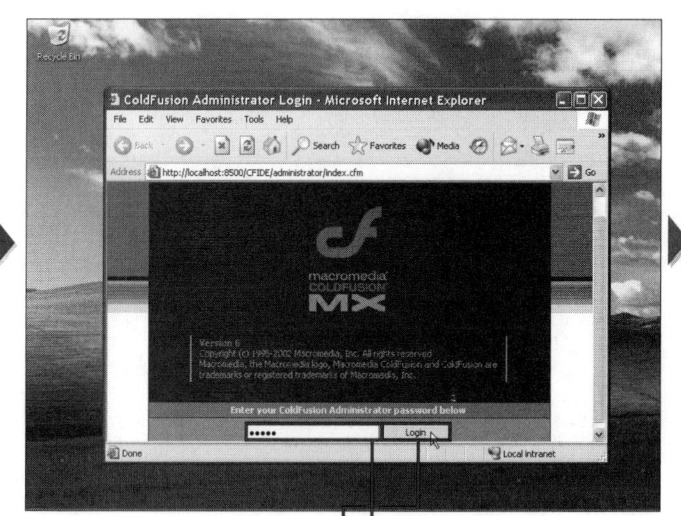

■ The ColdFusion login screen appears in a browser after installation is complete.

15 Type the ColdFusion administrator password.

16 Click Login to administer ColdFusion.

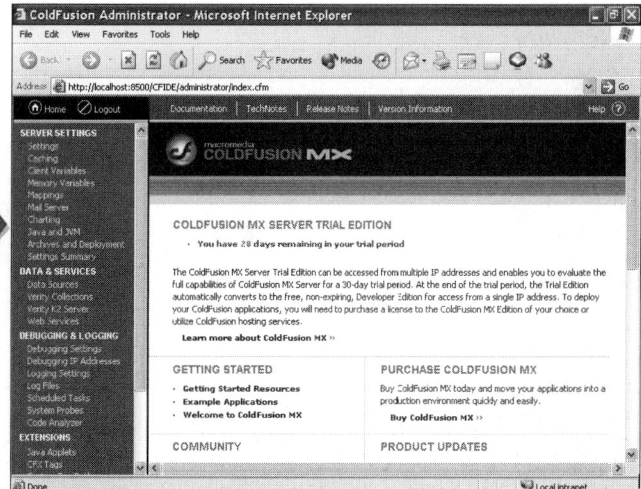

■ The ColdFusion administrator appears in a browser window.

■ You can click links to view and specify ColdFusion settings.

CONNECT COLDFUSION TO A DATABASE

You can connect your ColdFusion application server to a database to give your dynamic Web pages access to database information such as customer records, product descriptions, or news articles. After you establish this connection, your site can take advantage of much of the power that comes with running a dynamic site.

Connecting a ColdFusion application server to a database requires defining a *data source.* Defining a data source tells ColdFusion what type of database you are dealing with, for example, Microsoft Access or Oracle, and where it is stored on your local computer or network. After defining a data source, ColdFusion is able to access the database and all its contents, including data tables, stored procedures, and other elements.

Because Dreamweaver can communicate with ColdFusion, creating data sources also gives you access to databases as you build your dynamic pages in Dreamweaver. The data sources defined on your application server appear in the Databases panel in Dreamweaver. To connect Dreamweaver to the data sources of an application server, see page 298.

CONNECT COLDFUSION TO A DATABASE

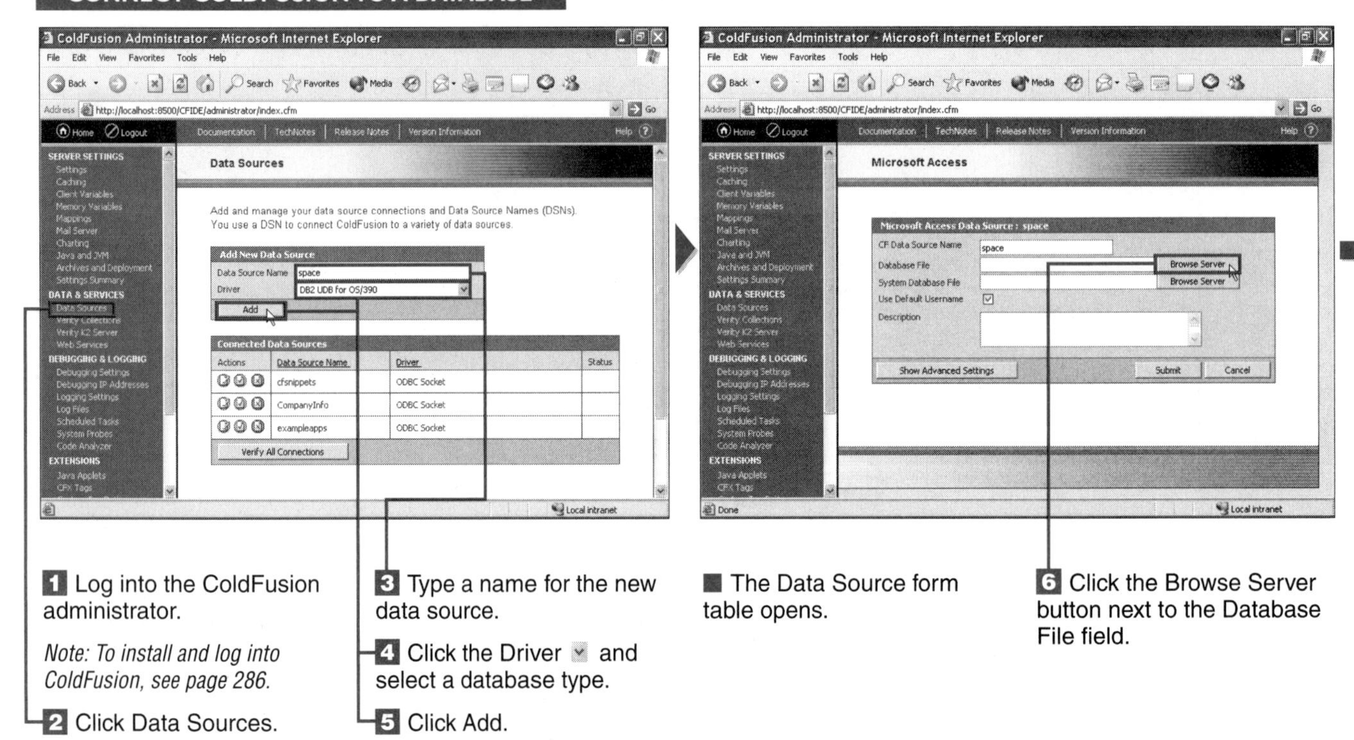

1 Log into the ColdFusion administrator.

Note: To install and log into ColdFusion, see page 286.

2 Click Data Sources.

3 Type a name for the new data source.

4 Click the Driver ▾ and select a database type.

5 Click Add.

■ The Data Source form table opens.

6 Click the Browse Server button next to the Database File field.

Can I access more than one database from a dynamic Web site?

✔ Yes. For each database, you need to create a separate data source in your application server.

What happens if I rename a data source?

✔ Pages that reference the old name will no longer work and will generate errors when accessed. It is a good idea not to change data source names if you are already using them for dynamic Web sites.

What if I move the database file that I have set up as a data source?

✔ The ColdFusion administrator displays an error when it tries to verify its connection to the data source. You also encounter errors if you try to access Web pages that retrieve information from the data source.

To fix this problem, click the name of the data source in the Data Sources section of the ColdFusion administrator. Click the Browse Server button to redefine where the data source is stored.

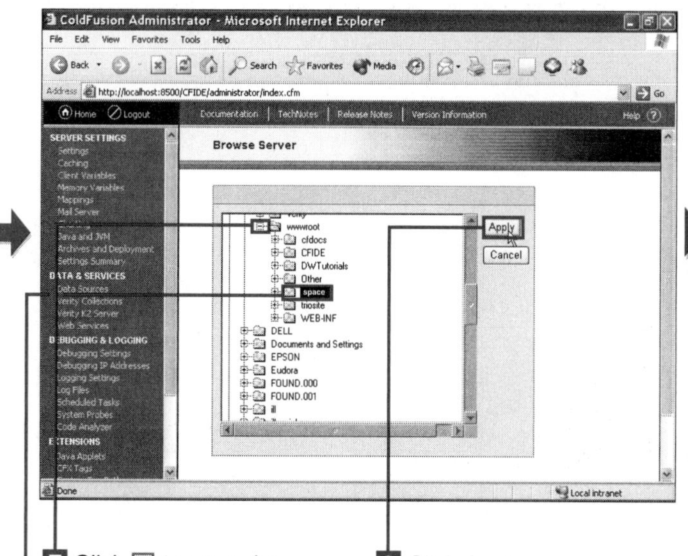

7 Click ⊞ to open the folders that contain your database file (⊞ changes to ⊟).

8 Click the database file.

9 Click Apply.

■ The Browse Server dialog box closes and returns you back to the Data Source form table.

10 Click Submit in the Data Source form table.

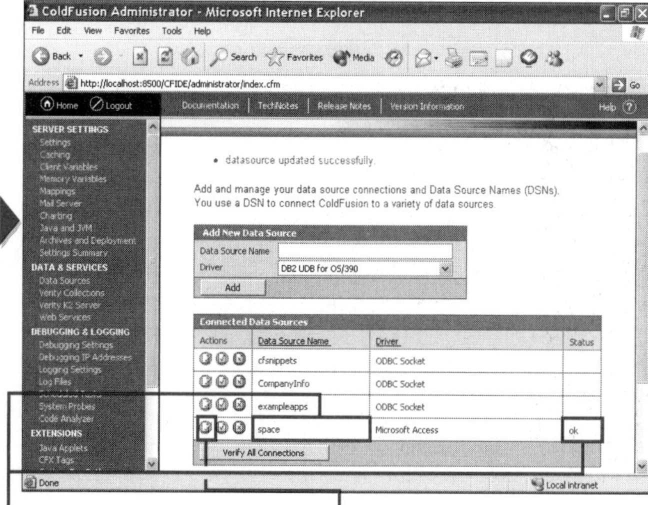

■ ColdFusion adds the database file to the Connected Data Sources list.

■ If ColdFusion connects to the file successfully, the Status registers OK.

■ If the Status is not OK, see your ColdFusion or database management documentation.

■ You can click ⓔ to edit the Data Source information.

SET UP A DYNAMIC SITE

To begin building and testing dynamic Web pages, you need to set up a dynamic Dreamweaver site. Setting up a dynamic site allows you to view and manage your site files in the Site window, just like you can for non-dynamic sites. Dynamic sites also require that you specify the location of a testing server, which allows you to preview your dynamic pages with any dynamic content inserted. The testing server can be your local computer, a development server on your network, or a production server where your site will go live.

Setting up a local folder for a dynamic site is similar to setting one up for a non-dynamic site. This is the folder where you store and manage your pages that are under development. You can create new files and subfolders in your local folder as your site grows. For more details about setting up a local folder, see Chapter 15.

Setting up a testing server requires that you have already installed an application server, such as ColdFusion, that can process your dynamic site files. In order to preview your dynamic site files in a browser, Dreamweaver needs to pass the files to the application server so it can insert the necessary database information into your Web page.

SET UP A DYNAMIC SITE

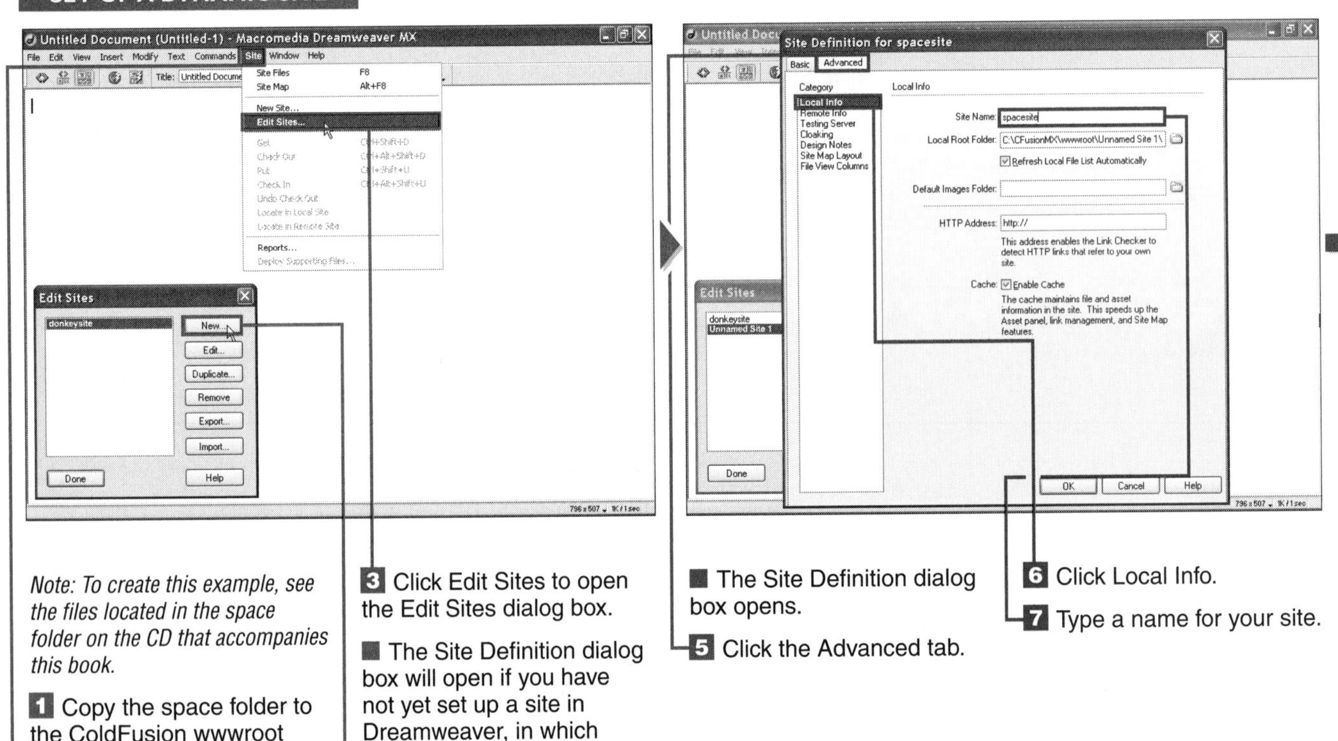

Note: To create this example, see the files located in the space folder on the CD that accompanies this book.

1 Copy the space folder to the ColdFusion wwwroot Web files folder.

2 Click Site.

3 Click Edit Sites to open the Edit Sites dialog box.

■ The Site Definition dialog box will open if you have not yet set up a site in Dreamweaver, in which case, skip to step 5.

4 Click New.

■ The Site Definition dialog box opens.

5 Click the Advanced tab.

6 Click Local Info.

7 Type a name for your site.

Can my remote server be my testing server?

✔ Yes. This is often the case, because both servers need to be running application server software to process your dynamic files. Having them be one and the same saves you the trouble of setting up and maintaining two application servers.

Can the testing server folder and local folder be the same location?

✔ Yes. You want to do this if you have an application server running on your local machine. In the example below, the two folders are the same location.

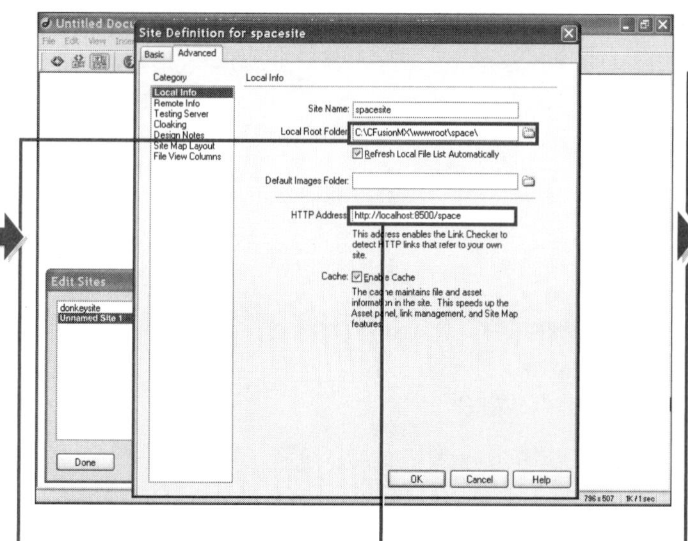

8 Click 🗀 to select a Local Root Folder.

■ For this example, specify the space folder as your Local Root Folder.

9 Type the Web server address followed by the site folder name.

■ This example has the address http://localhost:8500/space.

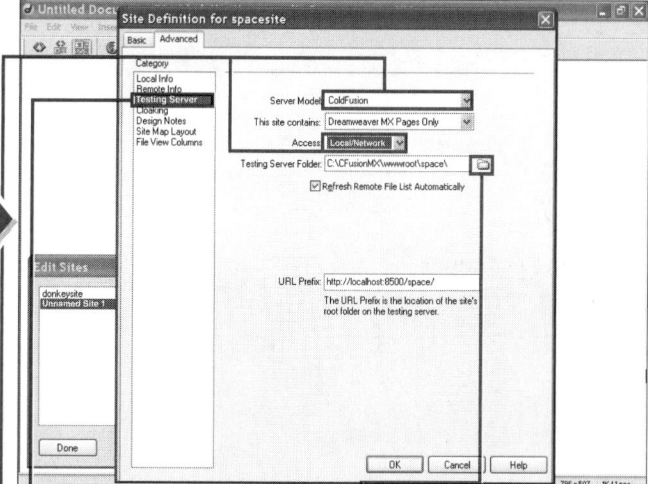

10 Click Testing Server.

11 Click ▾ to select an application server model.

■ For this example, select ColdFusion.

12 Click ▾ to select Local/Network access.

13 Click 🗀 to select where you want to store your Web files on the application server.

■ For this example, select C:\CfusionMX\wwwroot\space\.

CONTINUED

SET UP A DYNAMIC SITE (CONTINUED)

Setting up a testing server for your dynamic site allows you to see your dynamic pages as your end users will eventually see them — with the dynamic information from a database or other content source inserted in your pages. Without the processing, you would end up viewing dynamic code on your previewed pages rather than real information.

For the processing to happen correctly, Dreamweaver needs to know where to copy your dynamic files so that the testing server can read them. This is done by defining the Testing Server Folder, which specifies a directory relative to a drive on your local computer or on the network.

Dreamweaver also needs to know how a Web browser can access the testing server to preview the processed files, because all previewing in Dreamweaver is performed via a browser. This is done by defining URL Prefix information, which defines the testing server directory as a Web address beginning with http://. Both the Testing Server Folder and the URL Prefix should refer to the same folder on the testing server; otherwise dynamic pages will not be processed and previewed correctly.

SET UP A DYNAMIC SITE (CONTINUED)

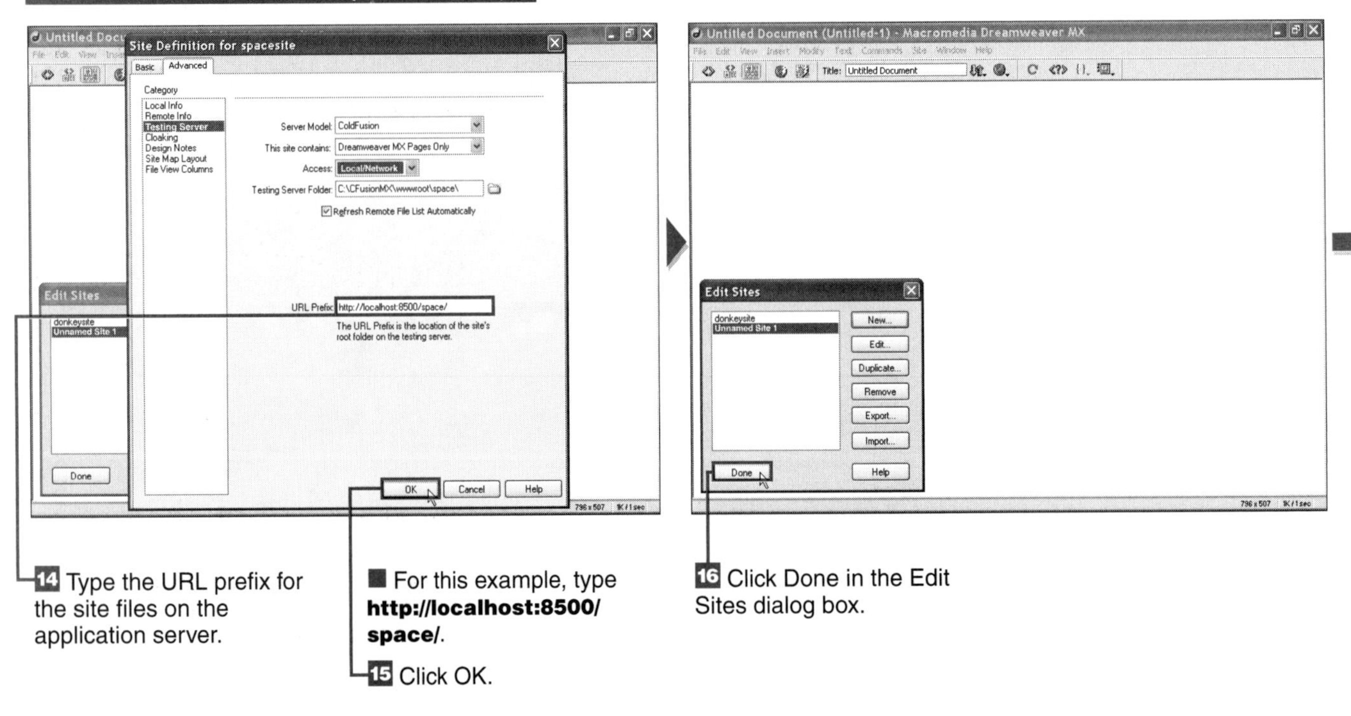

14 Type the URL prefix for the site files on the application server.

■ For this example, type **http://localhost:8500/space/**.

15 Click OK.

16 Click Done in the Edit Sites dialog box.

What if I am using the ColdFusion standalone server as my testing server?

✔ If you use the standalone server to test your files, be sure to specify the ColdFusion wwwroot folder as your Testing Server Folder. Also, make sure you specify the port 8500 on your URL Prefix. For example:

http://localhost:8500/mysite/

What is a localhost?

✔ *Localhost* is the URL server name you must specify when your browser or Dreamweaver is accessing a Web server running on your local computer. Accessing the localhost means you are viewing Web files served from your own computer, instead of a remote computer somewhere on the network.

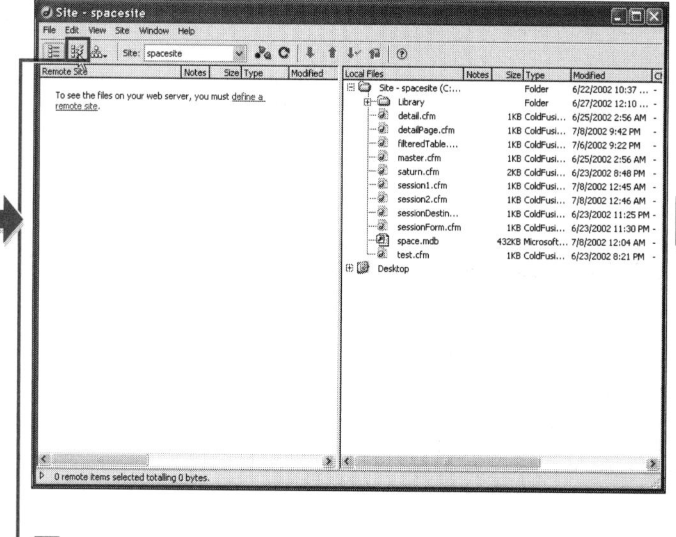

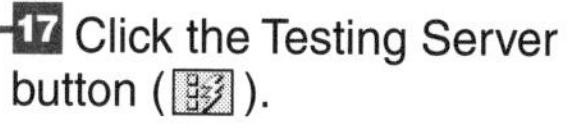

17 Click the Testing Server button ( ).

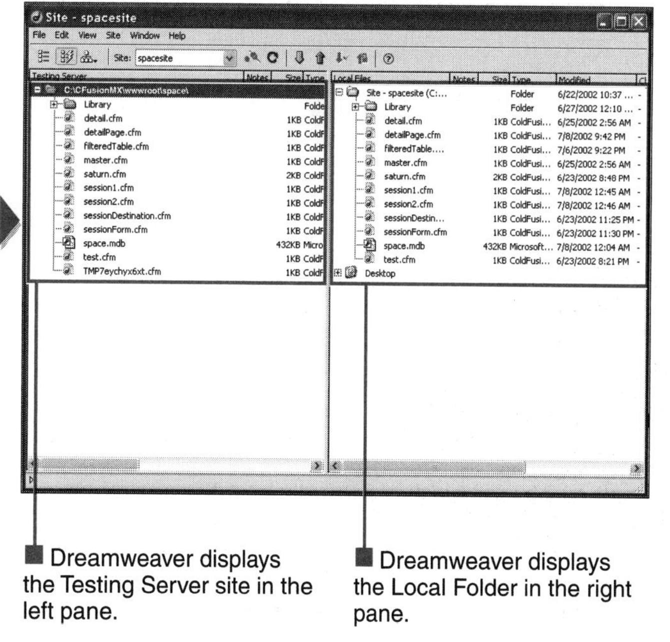

■ Dreamweaver displays the Testing Server site in the left pane.

■ Dreamweaver displays the Local Folder in the right pane.

CREATE A NEW DYNAMIC PAGE

You can create a blank page in a new Document window to use as a starting point for your dynamic Web pages. Dreamweaver lets you create starter pages for all the server types that it supports, including ColdFusion, Active Server Pages (ASP), ASP.NET, Java Server Pages (JSP), and PHP. When you create a new dynamic page, Dreamweaver suggests a file type and file extension that match your dynamic Dreamweaver site.

ColdFusion is Macromedia's Web application platform for their MX series of products. The dynamic Web-page examples in this book work with ColdFusion dynamic pages and a ColdFusion application server. ColdFusion pages include ColdFusion Markup Language (CFML), which tells the ColdFusion application server what database information to include in site pages. After you create a new dynamic ColdFusion page, you can use visual commands in Dreamweaver to specify dynamic features. Dreamweaver writes the CFML code behind the scenes.

ASP and ASP.NET pages are based on Microsoft technology, and work with Microsoft Web servers such as Internet Information Services (IIS) and Personal Web Server (PWS). JSP pages are Java-based, and work with the Macromedia JRun application server and other JSP-enabled servers. PHP pages are based on an open-source technology, and work with PHP application servers.

CREATE A NEW DYNAMIC PAGE

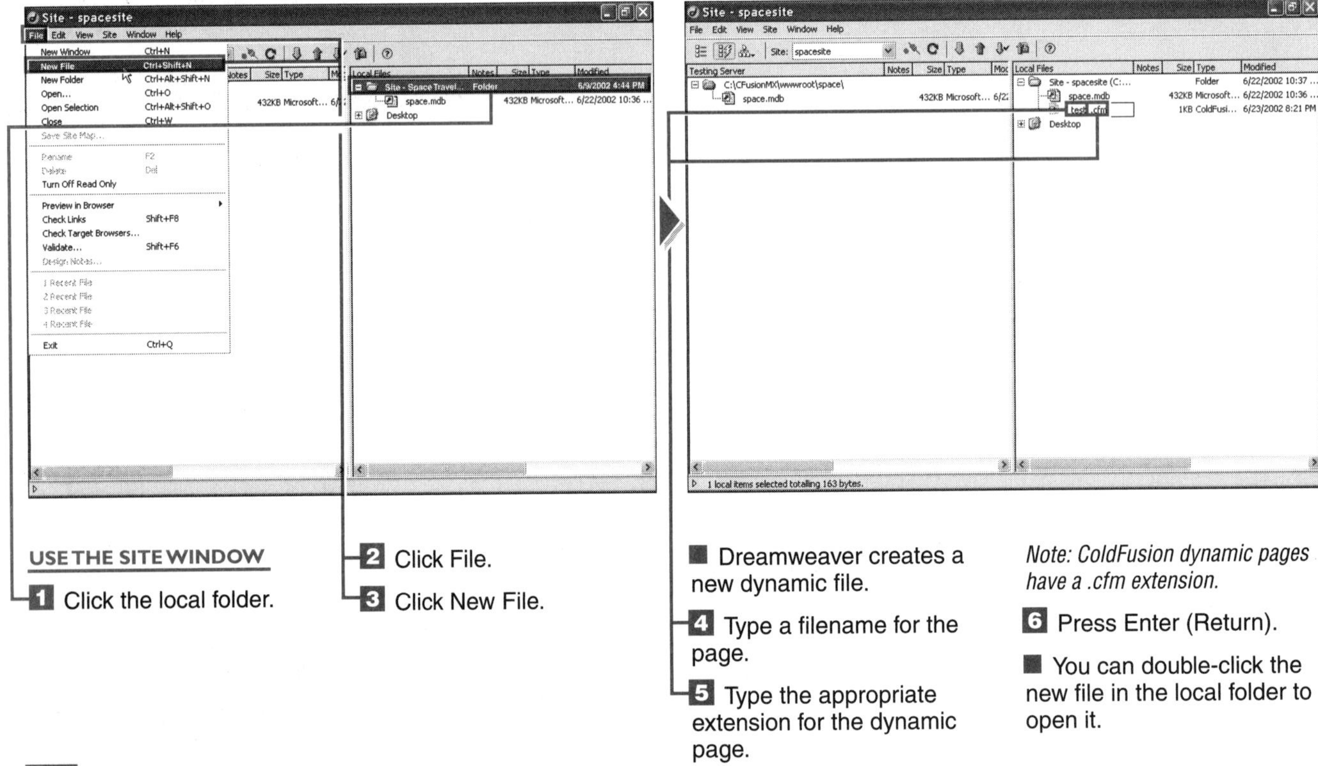

USE THE SITE WINDOW

1. Click the local folder.
2. Click File.
3. Click New File.

■ Dreamweaver creates a new dynamic file.

4. Type a filename for the page.
5. Type the appropriate extension for the dynamic page.

Note: ColdFusion dynamic pages have a .cfm extension.

6. Press Enter (Return).

■ You can double-click the new file in the local folder to open it.

How do new dynamic pages differ from normal pages?

✔ Most dynamic pages created in the New Document dialog box include special code at the top of the page that designates the page type. Web servers and application servers can read the code and then process the page appropriately. For example, ASP JavaScript pages include the following first line of code:

```
<%@LANGUAGE="JAVASCRIPT"
CODEPAGE="1252"%>
```

How can I create other advanced page types in Dreamweaver?

✔ In the New Document dialog box, there is an Other category that allows you to create a variety of other page types such as ActionScript, Java, WML, and others.

How do I create a new Dreamweaver template page that supports dynamic code?

✔ You can create a template for a dynamic page by clicking File, then New, and then clicking the Template Page category. You can create a template for all the types of dynamic pages that Dreamweaver supports, such as ColdFusion, ASP, and so on. Dreamweaver templates are special starter pages that include editable and non-editable areas. For more information about templates, see Chapter 11.

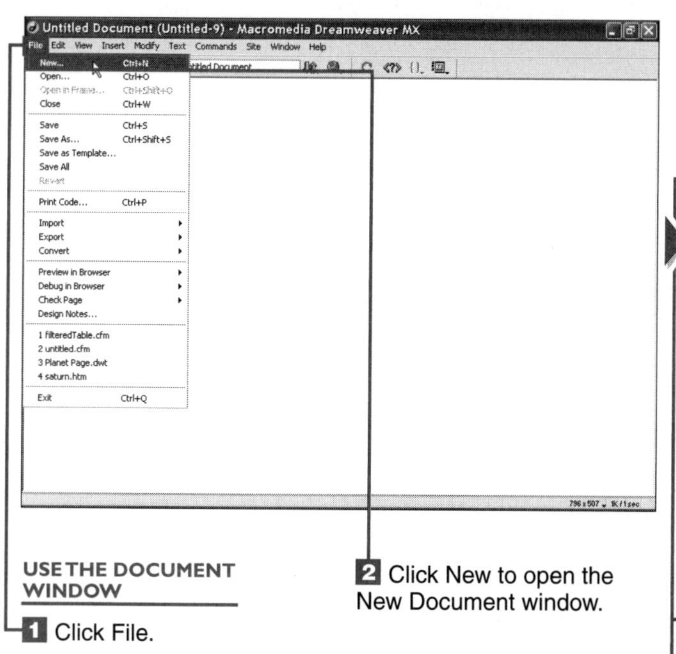

USE THE DOCUMENT WINDOW

1 Click File.

2 Click New to open the New Document window.

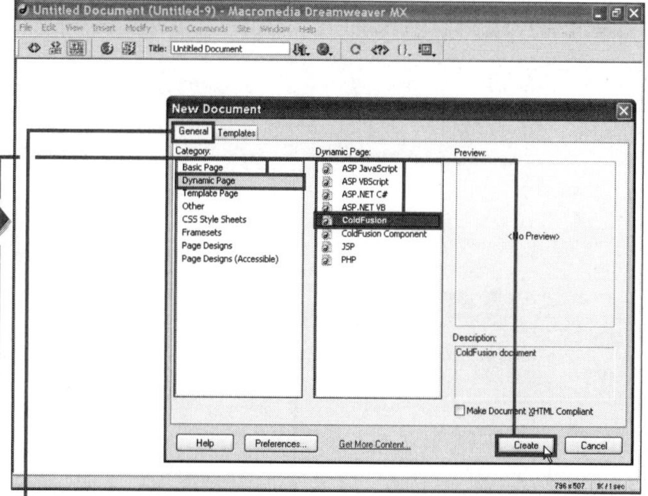

3 Click the General tab.

4 Click Dynamic Page.

5 Click a dynamic page type.

6 Click Create.

■ Dreamweaver opens the new dynamic page.

■ Save your dynamic page with the appropriate extension.

Note: ColdFusion dynamic pages have a .cfm extension.

CONNECT A SITE TO A DATABASE

You can connect your site to a database in Dreamweaver to access stored data and insert it into your Web pages. Connecting to a database is the key initial step in setting up a dynamic site after setting up your application server and defining your testing server.

To connect to a database in a ColdFusion environment, the database needs to have been defined as a ColdFusion data source. Defining a data source connects the ColdFusion application server to the database, which makes it possible to connect Dreamweaver to the same database.

Dreamweaver must communicate with ColdFusion to access its data sources, and to do this it needs to log in to ColdFusion using Remote Data Source, or RDS, login information. You specify the RDS login information when you install ColdFusion. After logging in, Dreamweaver displays the accessible data sources in the Database panel. Databases are specific to a Dreamweaver site, so after you connect to a database, you can access that database from all the pages in a site.

CONNECT A SITE TO A DATABASE

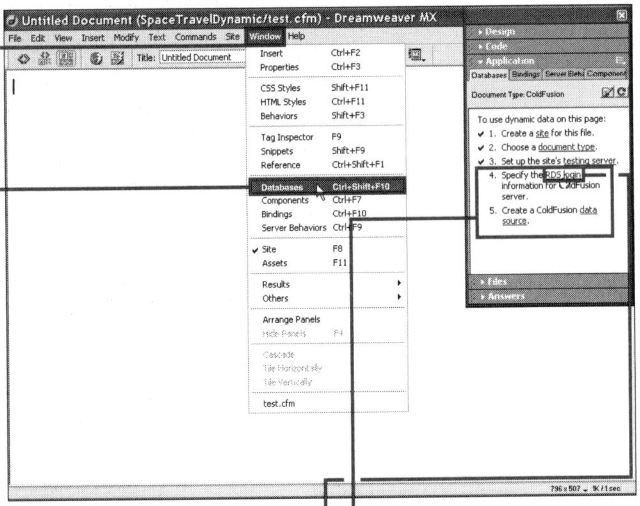

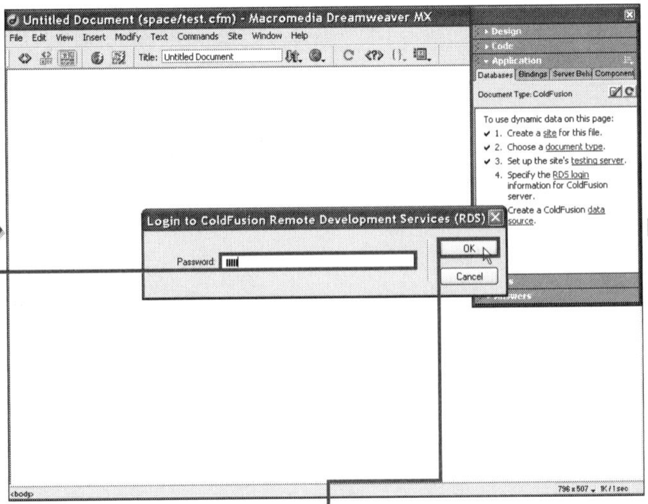

1 Open a page in your dynamic site.

2 Click Window.

3 Click Databases.

■ The Databases panel appears.

■ If you have connected ColdFusion to the appropriate database and set up your dynamic Dreamweaver site, only steps 4 to 5 in the Databases window should be unchecked.

4 Click RDS Login.

■ A Login dialog box appears.

5 Type your ColdFusion RDS login.

Note: To set your RDS login (password), see page 288.

6 Click OK.

What are some common database column types?

✔ If you open a table in the Databases panel, you will see datatypes listed next to the column names. The following are some common datatypes.

CHAR, VARCHAR: for text information

INTEGER: for positive or negative integers numbers such as 1 and -3

FLOAT: for positive or negative numbers with a decimal such as 1.1 and –3.14

DATE: for date information such as '2002-12-25'

TIME: for time information such as 10:30:45

What information about connected databases can I view in the Databases panel?

✔ You can open the databases in the Databases panel to view their associated tables and stored procedures. Tables are the structures that contain the data in a database; you can view column names and datatypes for a table inside the Database panel. Stored procedures are pieces of SQL code that you can store along with your database. Some application servers can run them to perform more complicated operations on a database.

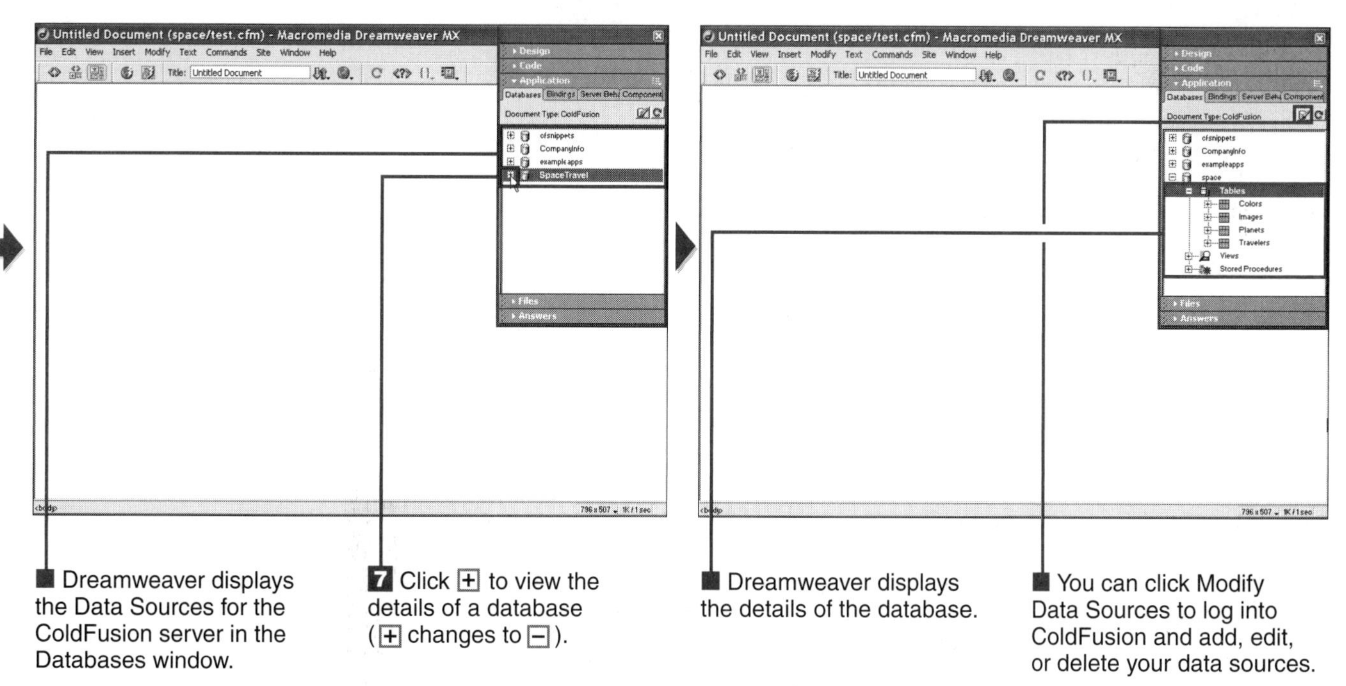

■ Dreamweaver displays the Data Sources for the ColdFusion server in the Databases window.

Note: To set up a data source, see page 290.

7 Click ⊞ to view the details of a database (⊞ changes to ⊟).

■ Dreamweaver displays the details of the database.

■ You can click Modify Data Sources to log into ColdFusion and add, edit, or delete your data sources.

DEFINE A RECORDSET

Before you can insert dynamic content into a Dreamweaver page, you must define a *recordset* for that page. A recordset specifies the database, table, and column information for the data that you want to insert into your dynamic site.

Dreamweaver gives you an easy-to-use interface for creating a recordset. Using text fields and drop-down menus, you define the name of a database, what table in the database to access, and what records to retrieve. After you define the recordset and associate it with a Web page, you can insert content from the recordset in the page. See pages 304 to 307 for more information. Recordsets you define for a Web page show up in the Bindings panel.

You can define multiple recordsets for a Web page. You need to do this if you want to insert different types of dynamic content on a single page. Recordsets are page specific, which means you cannot use a recordset that you define for one page for the other pages in your site unless you copy the recordset between pages.

DEFINE A RECORDSET

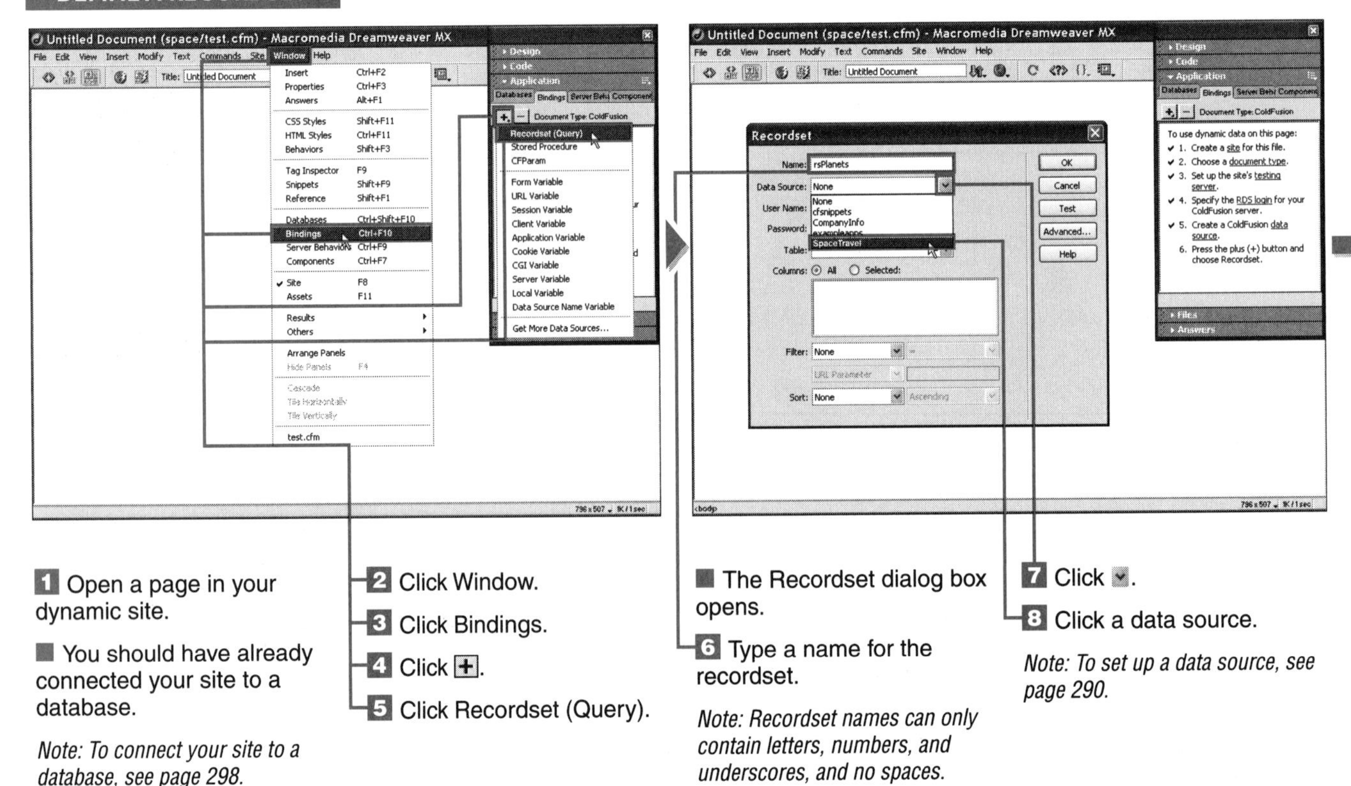

1 Open a page in your dynamic site.

■ You should have already connected your site to a database.

Note: To connect your site to a database, see page 298.

2 Click Window.

3 Click Bindings.

4 Click [+].

5 Click Recordset (Query).

■ The Recordset dialog box opens.

6 Type a name for the recordset.

Note: Recordset names can only contain letters, numbers, and underscores, and no spaces.

7 Click [▾].

8 Click a data source.

Note: To set up a data source, see page 290.

How do I copy a recordset from one page to another?

✔ Right-click the recordset in the Bindings panel. Click Copy from the menu that appears. Then open the page you want to copy the recordset to, right-click (Control-click) the Bindings panel, and click Paste from the menu that appears.

How do I edit or delete a recordset?

✔ You can double-click a recordset in the Bindings panel to edit it. The Recordset dialog box opens, enabling you to change the settings. To delete a recordset, click it in the Bindings panel and click ⊟.

How does Dreamweaver code a recordset in a Web page?

✔ When you define a recordset for a page, Dreamweaver inserts the definition for the recordset at the top of the page's HTML code. If you are building ColdFusion pages, the code includes a `cfquery` tag and an SQL query that specifies what in the database to retrieve. For more about viewing Web page code, see Chapter 3.

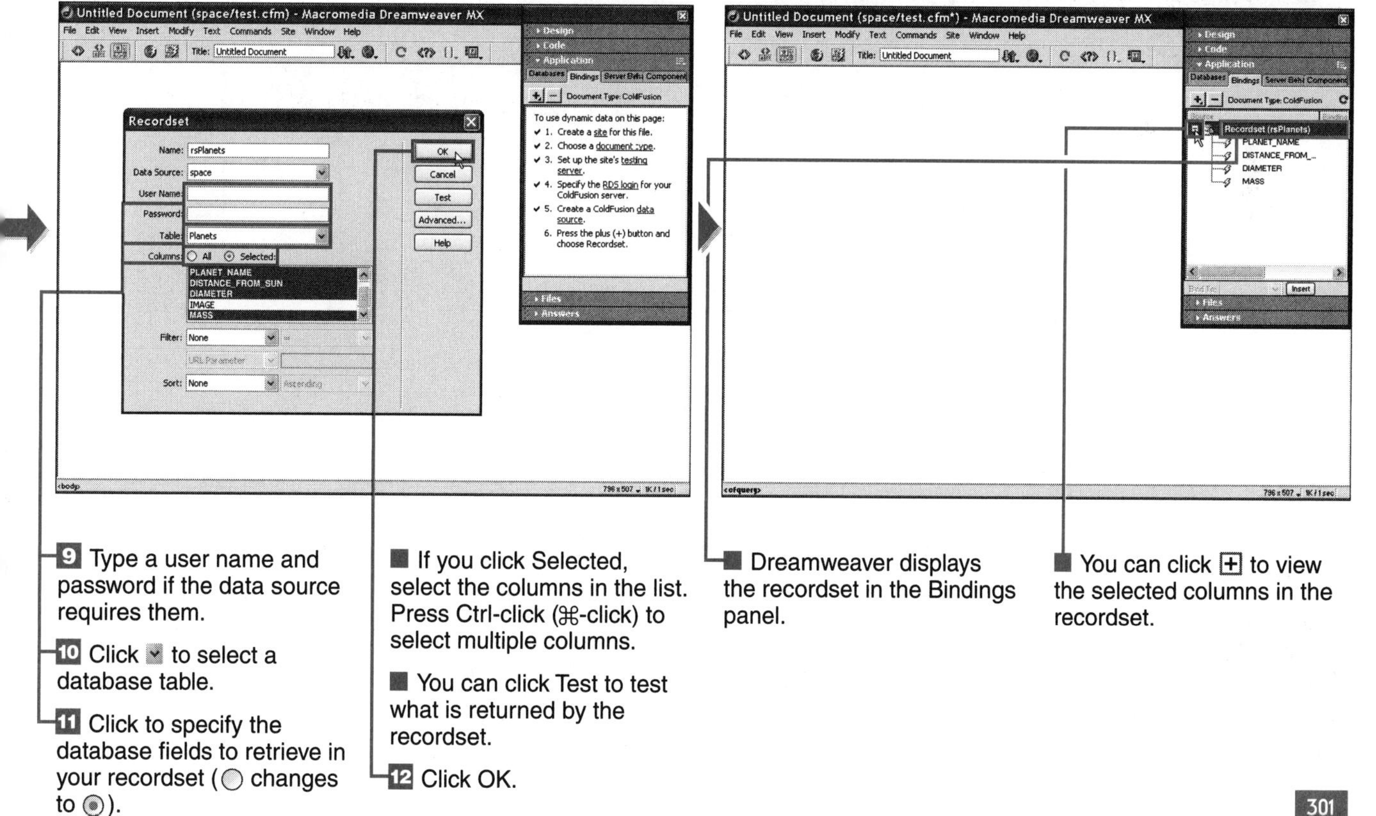

9 Type a user name and password if the data source requires them.

10 Click ▾ to select a database table.

11 Click to specify the database fields to retrieve in your recordset (○ changes to ◉).

■ If you click Selected, select the columns in the list. Press Ctrl-click (⌘-click) to select multiple columns.

■ You can click Test to test what is returned by the recordset.

12 Click OK.

■ Dreamweaver displays the recordset in the Bindings panel.

■ You can click ⊞ to view the selected columns in the recordset.

USING A FILTER IN A RECORDSET

Sometimes you want to retrieve very specific data from a database and insert it into your page. Using filters in your recordset definitions allows you to do this. For example, filters enable you to retrieve just the record in a database that includes a specific piece of text, or only records that include numbers within a particular range.

To create a filter, you set up a test case for data within a particular database column. There are many different kinds of tests you can set up, which makes filters very powerful tools.

For example, suppose you are interested in accessing records from an employee database that contain a particular last name. Different types of filters enable you to display this information. You can create a filter that explicitly tests for a specific last name, for example, last name equals Smith. You can create a filter that tests for a last name submitted in an HTML form, for example, last name equals the value of the LastName form field. You can also create a filter that tests for a last name passed on a referring page's link URL, for example, last name equals the value of the LastName URL variable.

USING A FILTER IN A RECORDSET

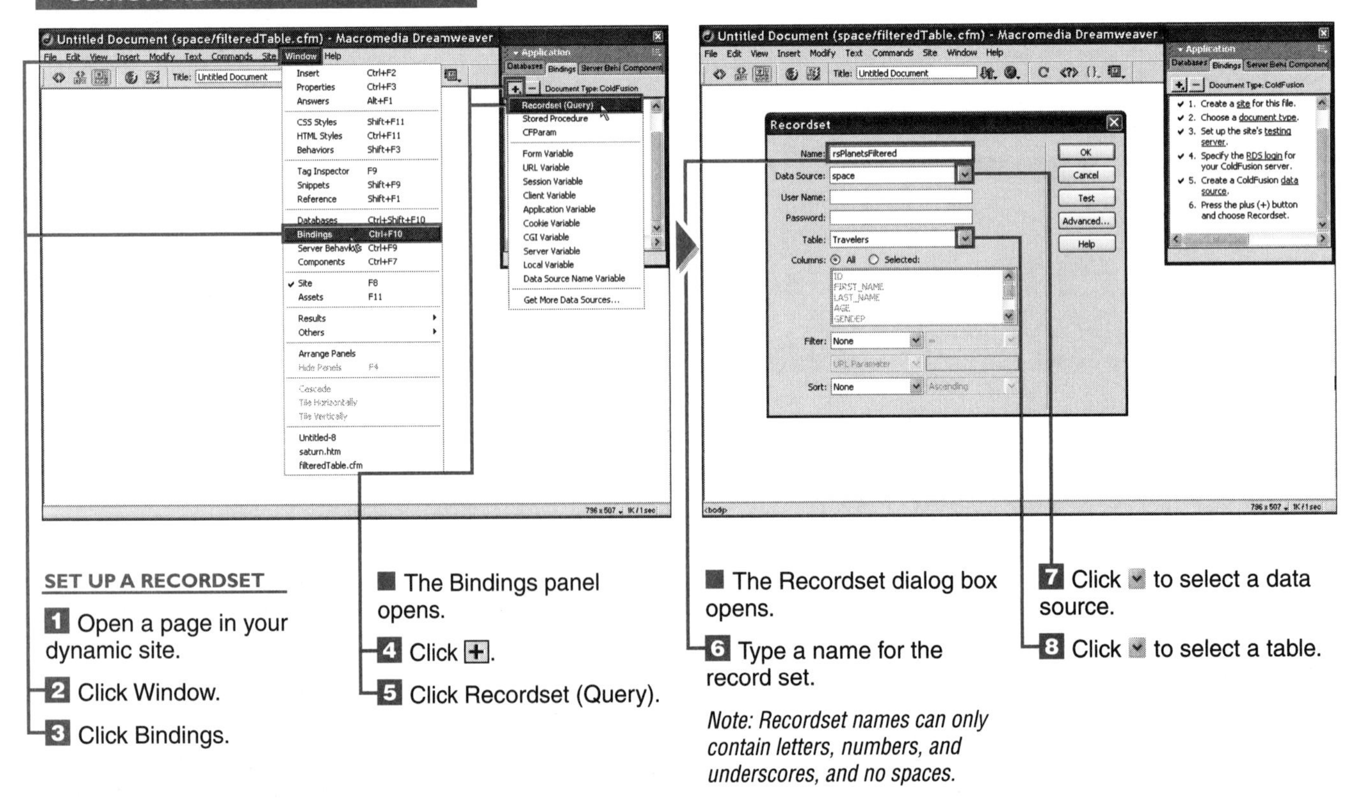

SET UP A RECORDSET

1 Open a page in your dynamic site.

2 Click Window.

3 Click Bindings.

■ The Bindings panel opens.

4 Click [+].

5 Click Recordset (Query).

■ The Recordset dialog box opens.

6 Type a name for the record set.

Note: Recordset names can only contain letters, numbers, and underscores, and no spaces.

7 Click [▼] to select a data source.

8 Click [▼] to select a table.

How can variables on URLs help me create dynamically generated product pages?

✔ Passing variables on a URL is a common strategy used on e-commerce sites. You can include a product ID as a variable on a link's URL. Then you can create a recordset that retrieves product database information based on that ID.

This lets you create a single dynamic product page capable of displaying information about many different products. The links

`http://www.wiley.com./product.cfm? ID=101`

and

`http://www.wiley.com./product.cfm? ID=102`

can generate different product pages.

How are variables passed to a Web page on a link URL?

✔ Variable information can be passed to a Web page on a link URL by adding a ? after the URL filename and then adding one or more variable/value pairs. For example, the URL

`http://www.wiley.com/index.cfm? Author=Mike`

includes the variable `Author` whose value is `Mike`. Application servers such as ColdFusion can access these variables and use them to determine the type of dynamic content retrieved from a database. You can pass multiple variable/value pairs by separating the pairs with & symbols.

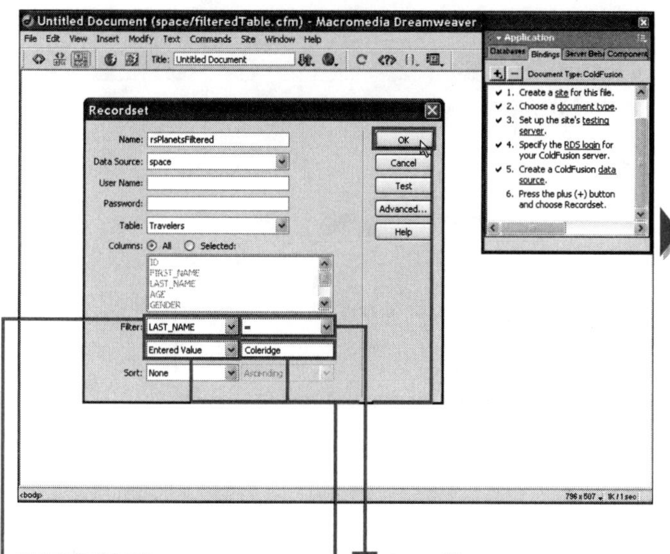

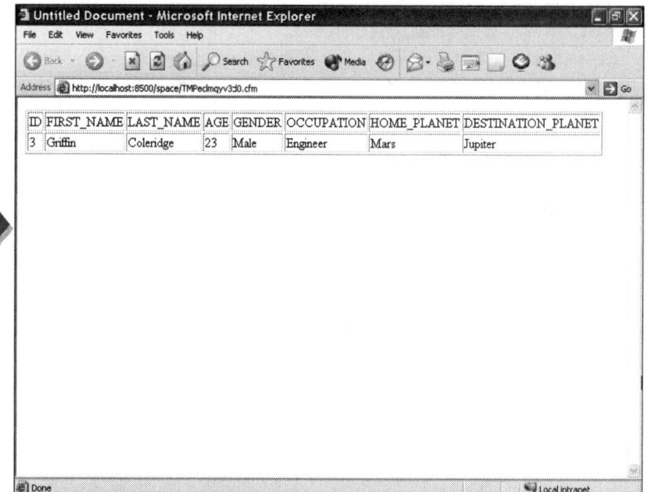

FILTER BY AN ENTERED VALUE

9 Click ▾ to select a database column to test.

■ You may select any column from the selected table.

10 Click ▾ to select an operator.

11 Click ▾ to select Entered Value.

12 Type a test value.

13 Click OK.

14 Display the filtered recordset as a dynamic table.

Note: To display a dynamic table, see page 306.

■ This example returns records where the LAST_NAME field is equal to Coleridge.

■ You may repeat steps 9 to 13 to filter against another value, such as a URL Parameter or a Form Variable.

■ When testing against a URL Parameter or Form Variable, you enter the name of the parameter or variable in step 12.

DISPLAY A DYNAMIC TABLE

You can insert multiple rows and columns of database information into your Web page by creating a dynamic table. Dreamweaver displays this information as an HTML table. Dynamic tables allow you to display large amounts of information such as customer lists and product inventory.

You can insert a dynamic table only after you define a recordset, which specifies the group of records that the application server should retrieve from a database. See page 300.

Dreamweaver allows you to customize a dynamic table by limiting the number of records displayed at a given time on a page. Dreamweaver can automatically build navigation that lets a user page forward and backward through the rest of the information in the recordset. For details, see page 308.

You can edit the look and feel of the HTML table that contains your dynamic information just as you would a regular HTML table. You can change background colors, cell padding and spacing, border visibility, and other attributes. For more information about formatting HTML tables, see Chapter 8.

DISPLAY A DYNAMIC TABLE

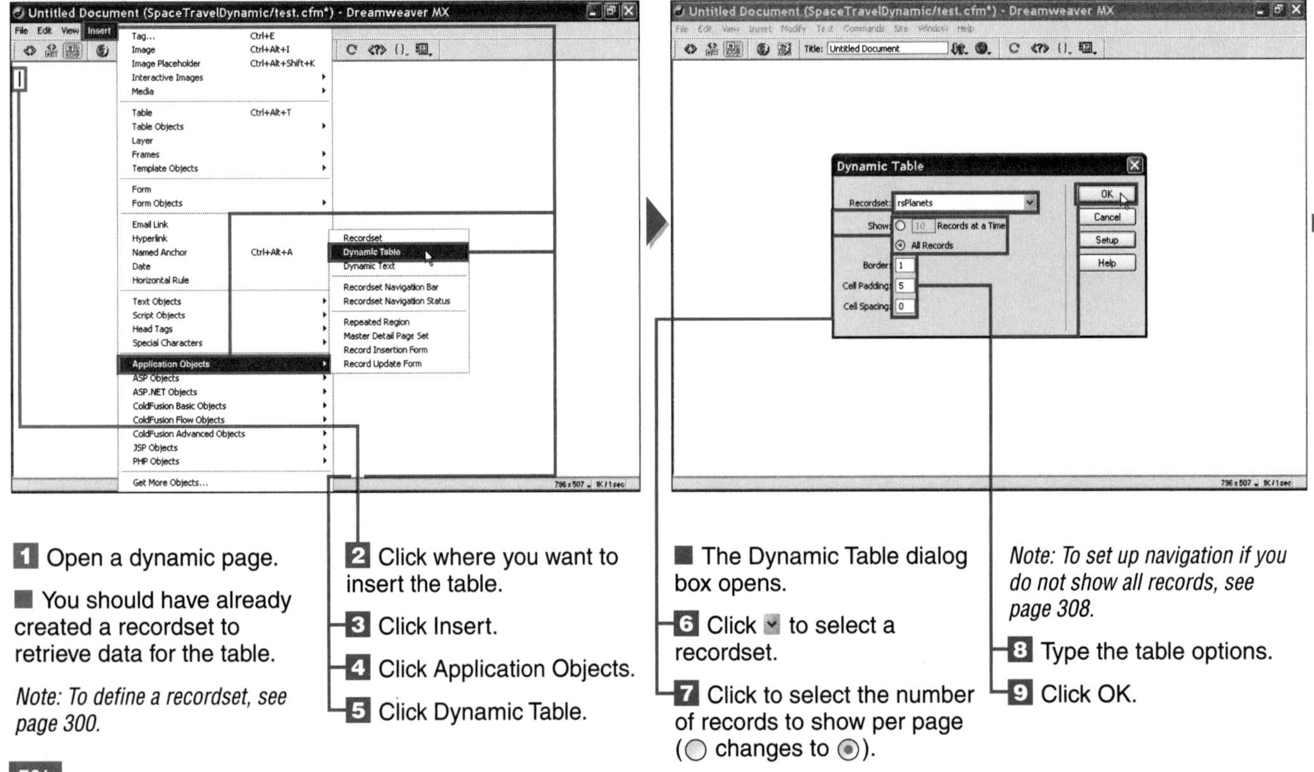

1 Open a dynamic page.

■ You should have already created a recordset to retrieve data for the table.

Note: To define a recordset, see page 300.

2 Click where you want to insert the table.

3 Click Insert.

4 Click Application Objects.

5 Click Dynamic Table.

■ The Dynamic Table dialog box opens.

6 Click ▾ to select a recordset.

7 Click to select the number of records to show per page (○ changes to ◉).

Note: To set up navigation if you do not show all records, see page 308.

8 Type the table options.

9 Click OK.

How do I sort information that is displayed in a dynamic table?

✔ You can specify a sorting scheme for dynamic table data when you create the recordset for the table. The Recordset dialog box allows you to sort by a particular column in ascending or descending order. Sorting works for both text and numeric data.

How do I create a recordset by writing my own SQL code?

✔ Every recordset you define includes SQL code for communicating with the database. You can click the Advanced button in the Recordset dialog box to write or edit the SQL code for a recordset. If you define a recordset and then switch to the advanced interface, Dreamweaver displays the current SQL code for your recordset.

How can I display all the data from a database table in my Web page?

✔ Create a recordset that retrieves all the table information by selecting all the columns when you define the recordset and do not include filtering. Then insert a dynamic table that displays all the records from that recordset. All the columns and rows from the table display as an HTML table. To display more than one table from a database on a page, you can define multiple recordsets and insert more than one dynamic table.

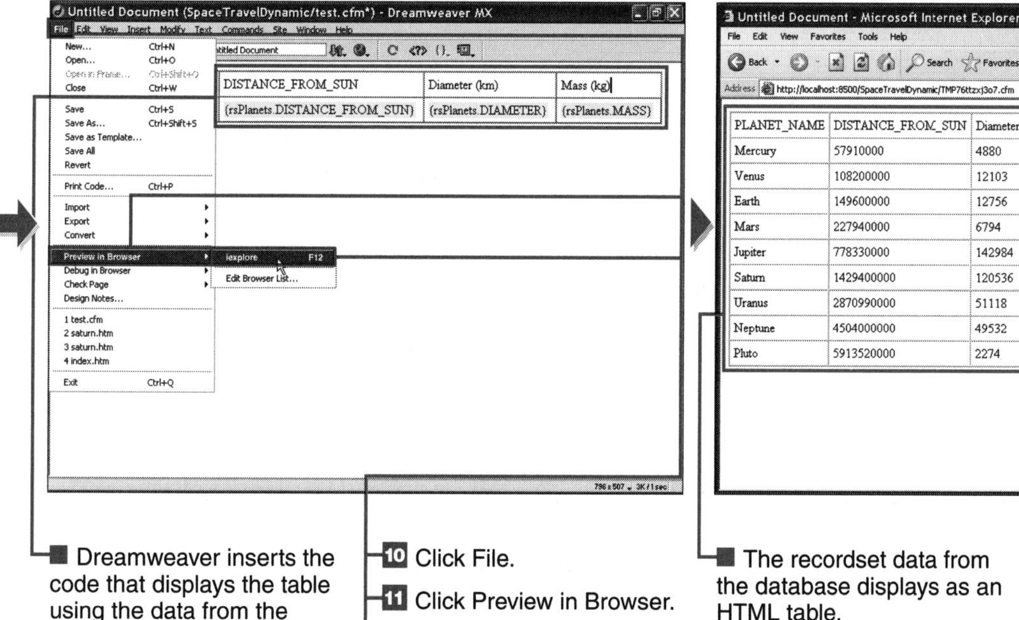

■ Dreamweaver inserts the code that displays the table using the data from the recordset.

■ You can edit the table headings, which by default are the table column names.

10 Click File.

11 Click Preview in Browser.

12 Click a browser.

■ The recordset data from the database displays as an HTML table.

DISPLAY DYNAMIC TEXT

You can insert a single piece of dynamic text into your page from a recordset listed in the Bindings panel. This enables you to insert user names, prices, contact information, and even blocks of HTML code. Anything you can save as ASCII text and store in a database you can insert as dynamic text.

Displaying pieces of dynamic text is an alternative to displaying multiple rows and columns from a database. See page 306 for more information.

Inserting small pieces of dynamic text is a way to easily convert a static site into a simple dynamic site. You can select static elements in your existing pages, such as headlines, navigation elements, or footers, and replace them with dynamic references to text from a database.

Note that if you use the same recordset for inserting dynamic text as you do for a dynamic table, you may end up with unpredictable results. For example, if you insert a last name column from an employee recordset, and that column contains multiple employee records, the application server will insert only one of those last names when you insert it as dynamic text. You can limit the number of records that a recordset retrieves by adding a filter. To add a filter, see page 302.

DISPLAY DYNAMIC TEXT

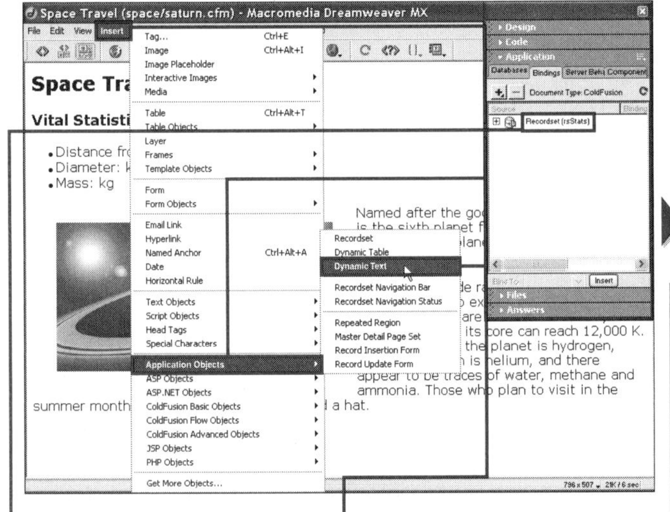

1 Open a dynamic page.

■ You should have already created a recordset to retrieve data for the dynamic text.

Note: To define a recordset, see page 300.

2 Click where to insert the text or select the text you want to replace.

3 Click Insert.

4 Click Application Objects.

5 Click Dynamic Text.

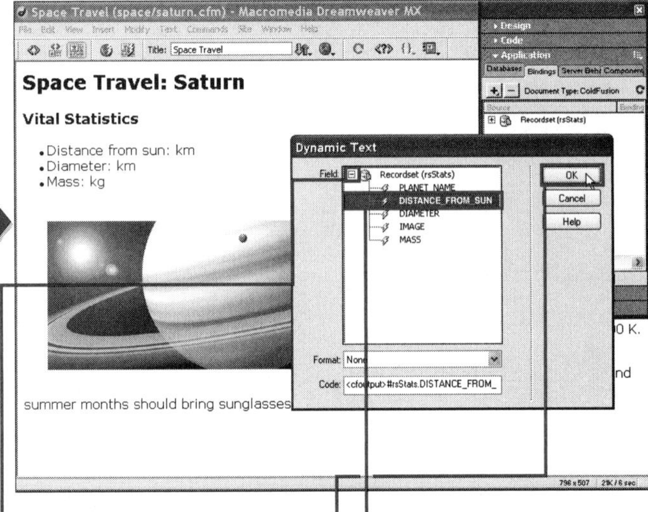

■ The Dynamic Text dialog box displays the data available.

■ You can click ⊞ to open a recordset or other database structure (⊞ changes to ⊟).

6 Click a dynamic text field from the list.

Note: For more about formatting, see page 310.

7 Click OK.

What are other ways to insert dynamic data from the Binding panel?

✔ You can select data in the Bindings panel and click the Insert button at the bottom of the panel. You can also click and drag data from the Binding panel to the Document window.

Is there an alternative to previewing dynamic Web pages in a browser?

✔ Dreamweaver's Live Data View is an alternative to previewing dynamic Web pages in a browser. Click the Live Data View button (▣) in the toolbar. Dreamweaver replaces the dynamic references in the page with dynamic data retrieved from the testing server.

How can I change the dynamic code that appears in Design View?

✔ When Dreamweaver adds dynamic content to a page, it adds special dynamic code that the application server processes. This information can take up a lot of space in your page and distort the layout in Design View. You can specify that Dreamweaver insert a shorter placeholder, {}, by clicking Edit and then Preferences to open the Preferences dialog box. Click the Invisible Elements category and then select {} from the Show Dynamic Text As menu.

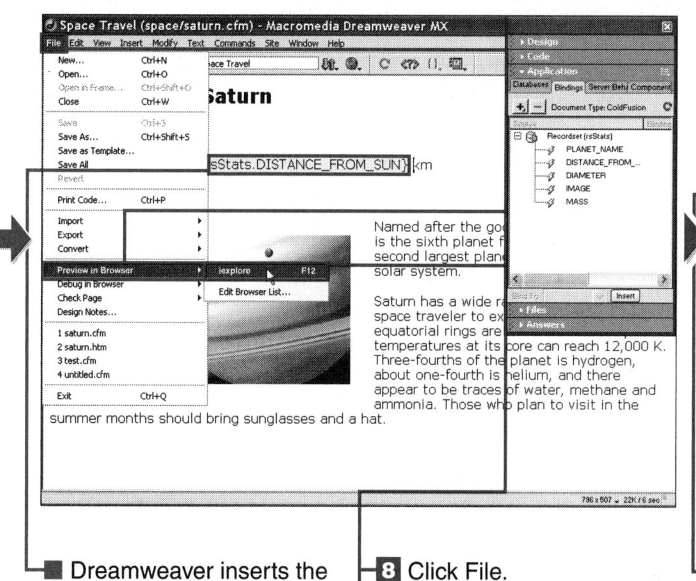

■ Dreamweaver inserts the code that displays the dynamic text.

8 Click File.

9 Click Preview in Browser.

10 Click a browser.

■ The dynamic text from the database displays.

■ If you insert text from a recordset column that has multiple rows, only one field displays.

Note: You can limit your column information to a single piece of data using filters. To use filters, see page 302.

ADD NAVIGATION TO A DYNAMIC TABLE

You can enable your site visitors to navigate through records from a database by adding navigational links above or below a dynamic table. With navigation inserted, users can click a forward link to view more records, click a backward link to view previous records, or click links to view records at the start or end of the recordset.

Dreamweaver's navigation bar feature saves you from having to create navigation images, add and link those images on your Web page, and write the dynamic code that tells the application server what records to display in the dynamic table. A navigation bar is especially useful for viewing recordsets that contain a large number of records.

You can display the navigation bar as predefined images or text. After you insert a navigation bar, you can customize it by replacing images or stylizing the text links.

You want to use a navigation bar only for dynamic tables that display fewer than the total number of records in a recordset. You specify the number of records that a dynamic table displays when you insert the table. See page 306 for details.

ADD NAVIGATION TO A DYNAMIC TABLE

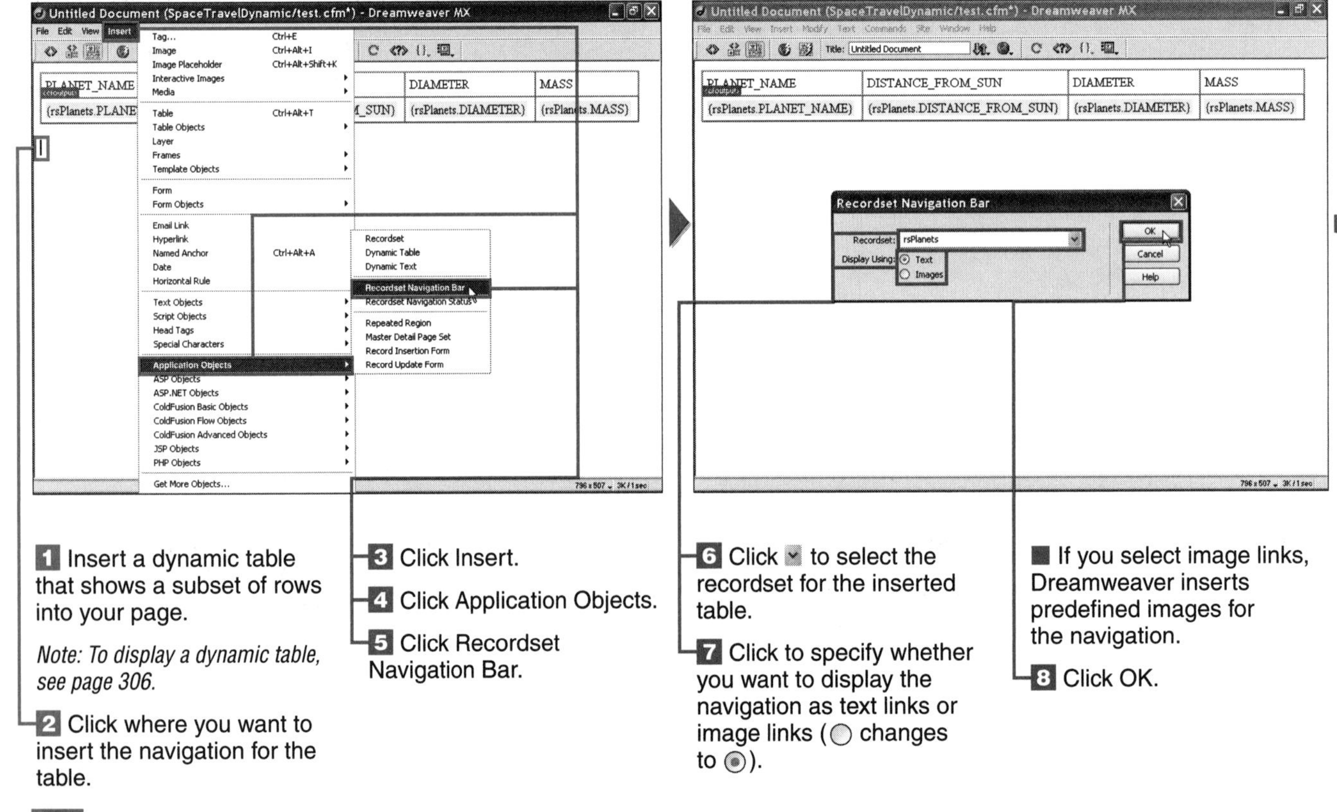

1 Insert a dynamic table that shows a subset of rows into your page.

Note: To display a dynamic table, see page 306.

2 Click where you want to insert the navigation for the table.

3 Click Insert.

4 Click Application Objects.

5 Click Recordset Navigation Bar.

6 Click ▾ to select the recordset for the inserted table.

7 Click to specify whether you want to display the navigation as text links or image links (○ changes to ◉).

■ If you select image links, Dreamweaver inserts predefined images for the navigation.

8 Click OK.

How do I change the images in the navigation bar?

✔ You can change the images just as you do other images on a Web page. In Design View, click an image, click the button next to the Src text field in the Properties inspector, and then select a replacement image in the dialog box that appears. When editing the navigation, be sure not to change any of the dynamic code that surrounds the images. This code keeps track of the records currently on display and determines what records to display in the next dynamic table.

How do I add page counter information to my navigation bar?

✔ You can add counter information by clicking Insert, Application Objects, and then Recordset Navigation Status. This inserts a number corresponding to the current page in the recordset and the total number of pages in the set. Such information offers the user context as they navigate through records in a dynamic table. The counter works only when you have a navigation bar on the page.

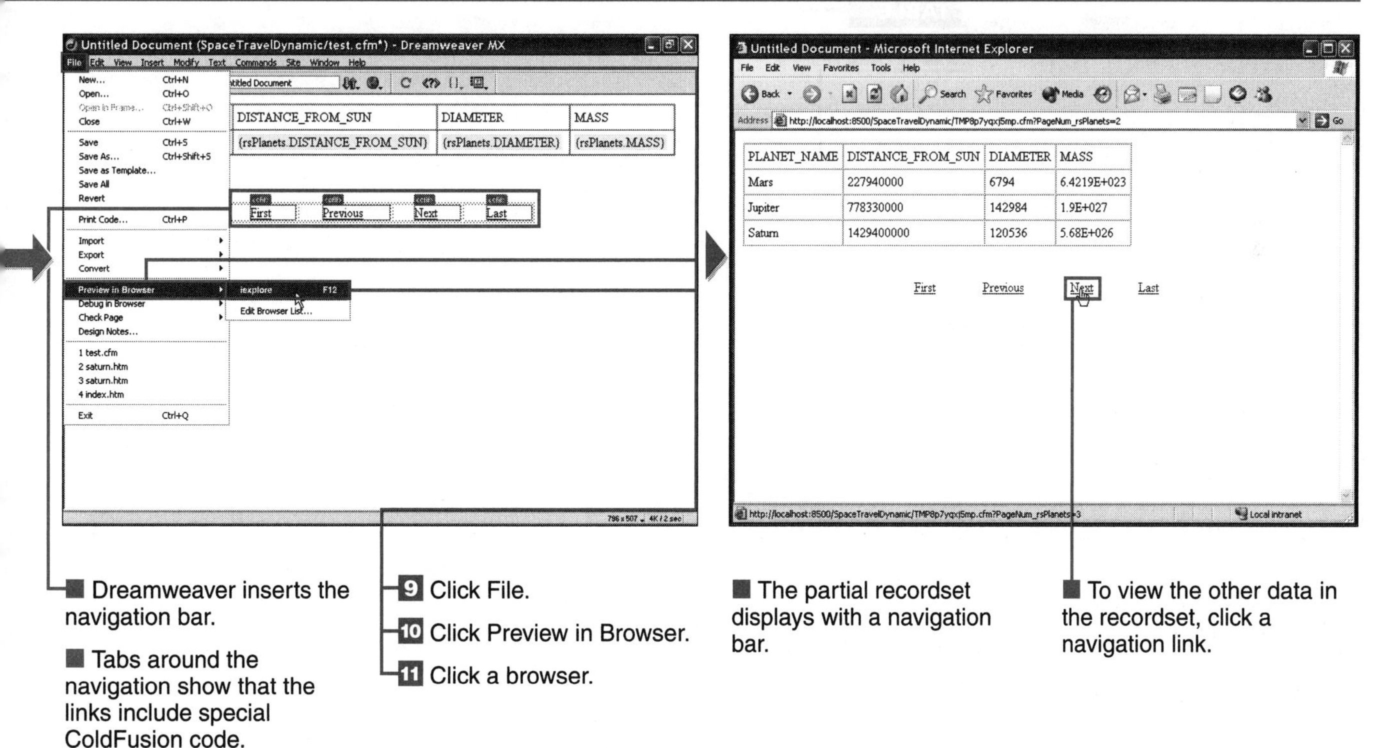

■ Dreamweaver inserts the navigation bar.

■ Tabs around the navigation show that the links include special ColdFusion code.

9 Click File.

10 Click Preview in Browser.

11 Click a browser.

■ The partial recordset displays with a navigation bar.

■ To view the other data in the recordset, click a navigation link.

FORMAT DYNAMIC TABLE DATA

When you insert dynamic information from a database into a Web page, Dreamweaver displays the data just as it was saved in the database. To change the way this data displays, you can apply one of you application server's predefined data formats. They enable you to effectively display time, currency, complex numbers, percentages, and other specially formatted data. You can choose a format that makes the most sense given your audience and your page's design.

To apply a format to dynamic data, select the data in the Document window and open the Bindings panel. You can select from various formatting options in the Format drop-down menu. The application server applies the formatting after it retrieves the data from the database, but before it inserts the data into the Web page.

Make sure the formats you apply to your data are appropriate for the datatype. For example, certain time formatting makes sense for number data but not for text data. You can check your formatted data by testing the page in a browser. See page 58 for details.

FORMAT DYNAMIC TABLE DATA

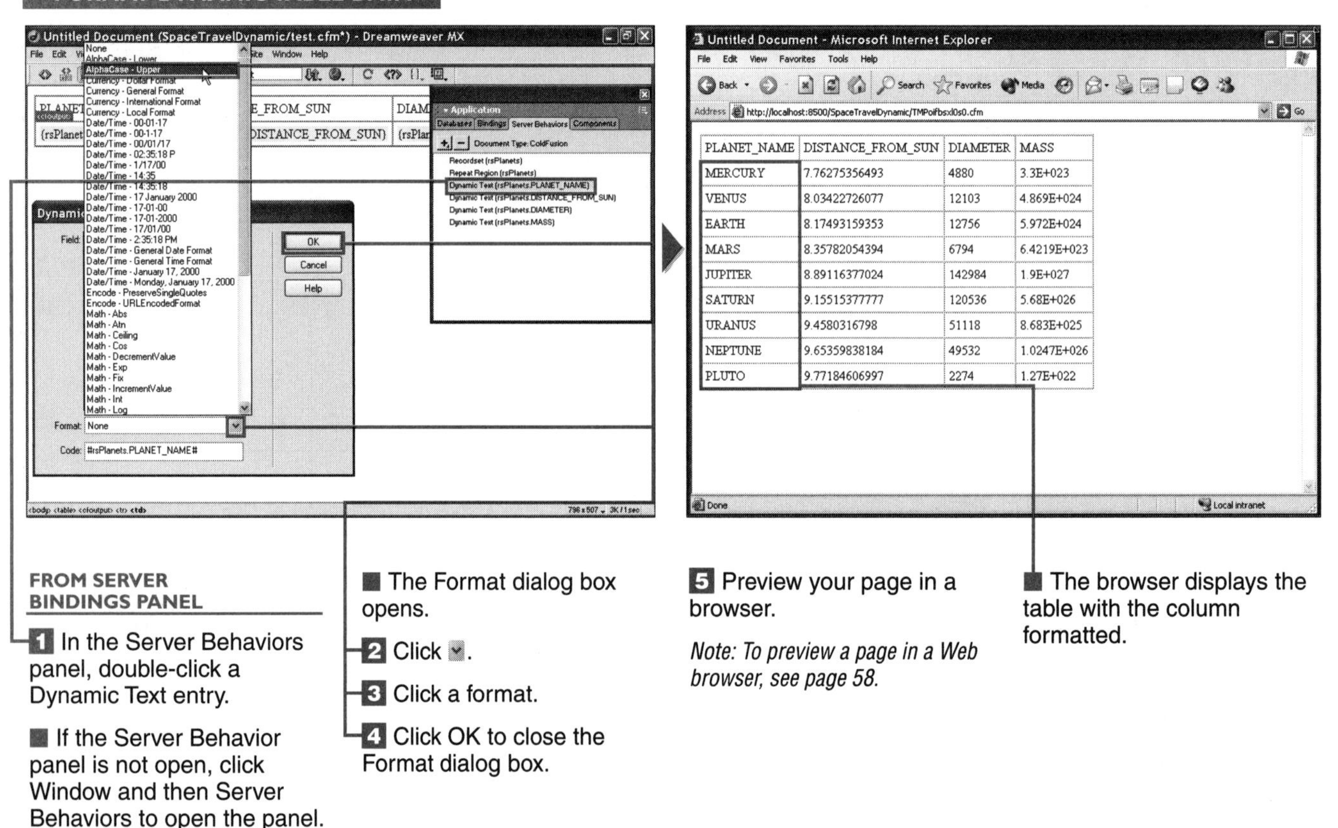

FROM SERVER BINDINGS PANEL

1 In the Server Behaviors panel, double-click a Dynamic Text entry.

■ If the Server Behavior panel is not open, click Window and then Server Behaviors to open the panel.

■ The Format dialog box opens.

2 Click ▾.

3 Click a format.

4 Click OK to close the Format dialog box.

5 Preview your page in a browser.

Note: To preview a page in a Web browser, see page 58.

■ The browser displays the table with the column formatted.

How do I trim extra whitespace from my data?

✔ In ColdFusion, you can format the data with one of several Trim formats. They get rid of whitespace on the left, on the right, or on both sides. There is also a Trim format that removes carriage return characters.

How do I restrict the decimal places in numeric dynamic data?

✔ For ColdFusion documents, there is a predefined format for two decimal places. There is also a currency format that converts a number to two decimal places.

How do I format for a 24-hour time?

✔ ColdFusion includes 24-hour time formats with and without minutes.

How are formats applied in the code?

✔ Here is an example of formatted ColdFusion data:

```
#UCase(rsPlanets.PLANET_
NAME)#
```

The format is applied as a ColdFusion function, with the dynamic data as its argument.

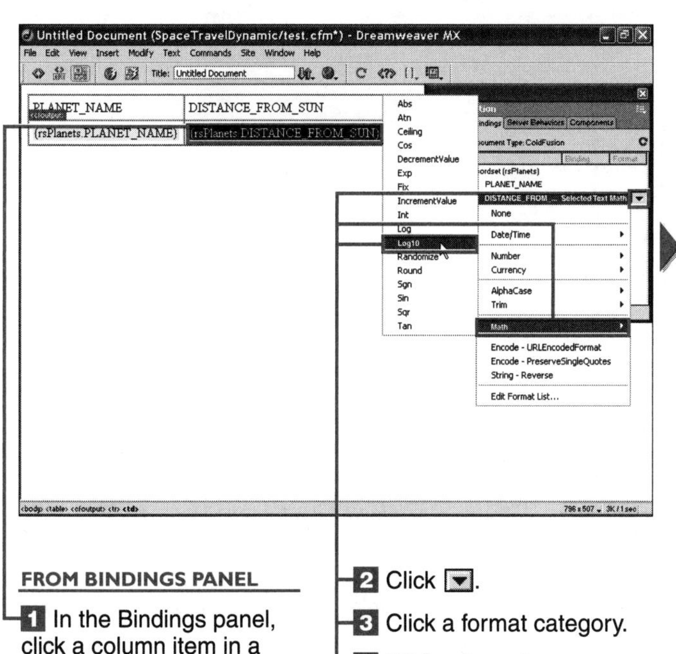

Untitled Document - Microsoft Internet Explorer

PLANET_NAME	DISTANCE_FROM_SUN	DIAMETER	MASS
MERCURY	7.76275356493	4880	3.3E+023
VENUS	8.03422726077	12103	4.869E+024
EARTH	8.17493159353	12756	5.972E+024
MARS	8.35782054394	6794	6.4219E+023
JUPITER	8.89116377024	142984	1.9E+027
SATURN	9.15515377777	120536	5.68E+026
URANUS	9.4580316798	51118	8.683E+025
NEPTUNE	9.65359838184	49532	1.0247E+026
PLUTO	9.77184606997	2274	1.27E+022

FROM BINDINGS PANEL

1 In the Bindings panel, click a column item in a table.

■ If the Bindings panel is not open, click Window and then Bindings to open the panel.

2 Click ▼.

3 Click a format category.

4 Click a format.

5 Preview your page in a browser.

Note: To preview a page in a Web browser, see page 58.

■ The browser displays the table with the column formatted.

CREATE A SEARCH/RESULTS PAGE SET

You can create an HTML form using form objects found in the Insert panel to allow users to submit information about what data they want to view from your database. You can also build a results page that processes the form information and displays only data that matches the search query. Building the results page requires defining a filtered recordset, then displaying the recordset as a dynamic table. Creating such a search/results page set is useful when you have a large database of information, such as a customer list or product catalog, and want to enable users to view specific records from it.

Creating a search page puts to work many of the features introduced in Chapter 9. A standard search form includes a text field that allows a user to type in the information they are interested in viewing. Alternatively, the input element could be a menu, list, or set of radio buttons or check boxes that allows a user to pick from several predefined inputs. The form also includes a Submit button that sends the information to the results page.

You can stylize the search form by placing the form elements in an HTML table that has colored backgrounds, borders, and other features. To learn about validating search submissions and to ensure users submit the correct type of information, see Chapter 13.

CREATE A SEARCH/RESULTS PAGE SET

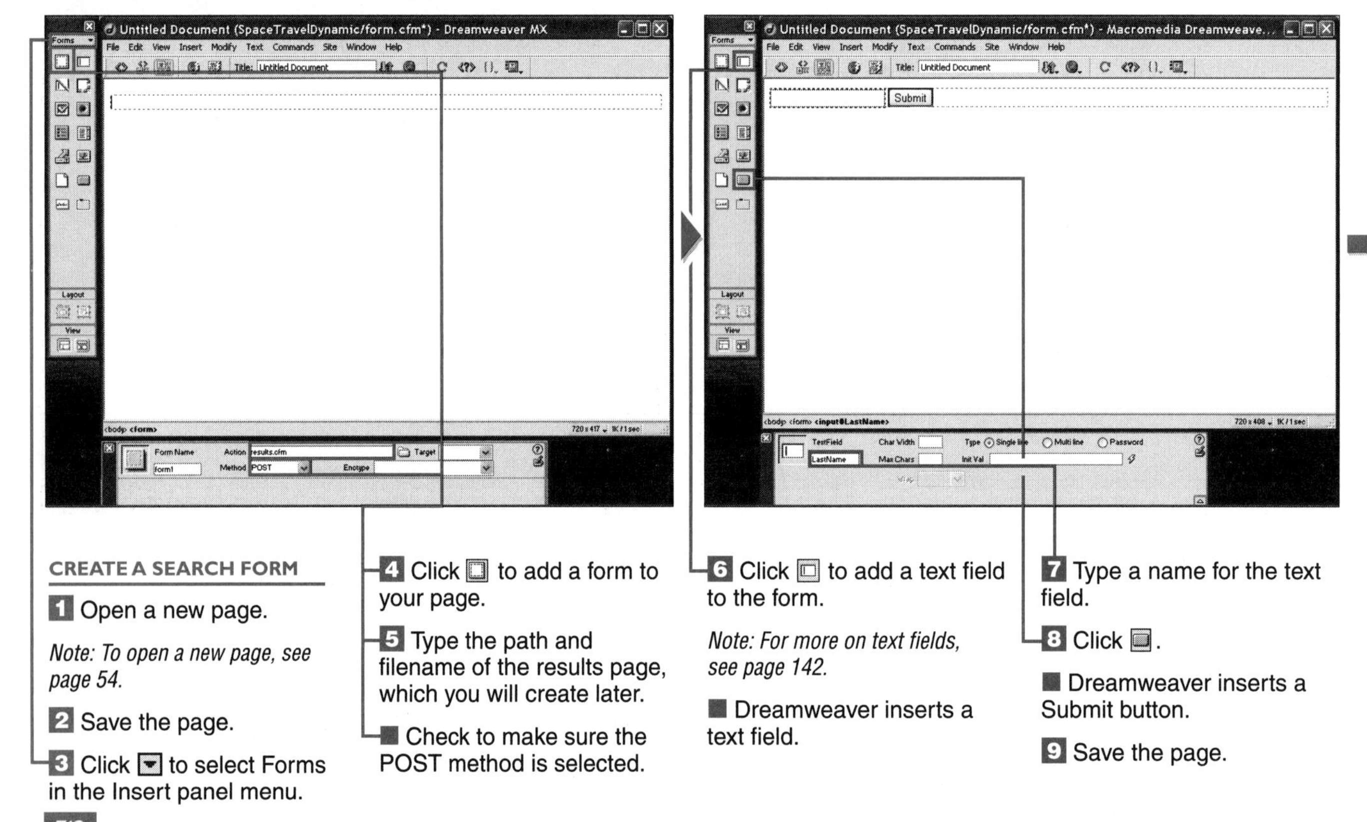

CREATE A SEARCH FORM

1 Open a new page.

Note: To open a new page, see page 54.

2 Save the page.

3 Click ▾ to select Forms in the Insert panel menu.

4 Click to add a form to your page.

5 Type the path and filename of the results page, which you will create later.

■ Check to make sure the POST method is selected.

6 Click to add a text field to the form.

Note: For more on text fields, see page 142.

■ Dreamweaver inserts a text field.

7 Type a name for the text field.

8 Click .

■ Dreamweaver inserts a Submit button.

9 Save the page.

Can I make the search page open the results page in a new window?

✔ Yes. Click inside your form and then click the <form> tag in the tag selector in the lower left corner of the Document window. Then select _blank in the Target drop-down menu in the Properties inspector. This causes the results page to open inside a new browser window.

What if a search query returns no results from the database?

✔ The dynamic table on the results page displays as empty. Only the table headings display. If you are ambitious, you can write custom dynamic code to display a No results found message. See your application server documentation for details.

Can I restrict the text that users can enter in the search box?

✔ You can use form validation to restrict the information that users can enter into the search box. Dreamweaver's behaviors offer limited features that check form fields for numbers, e-mail addresses, and whether the field is empty. See Chapter 13 for more information. Most application servers offer built-in form validation features as well. See your application server documentation for details.

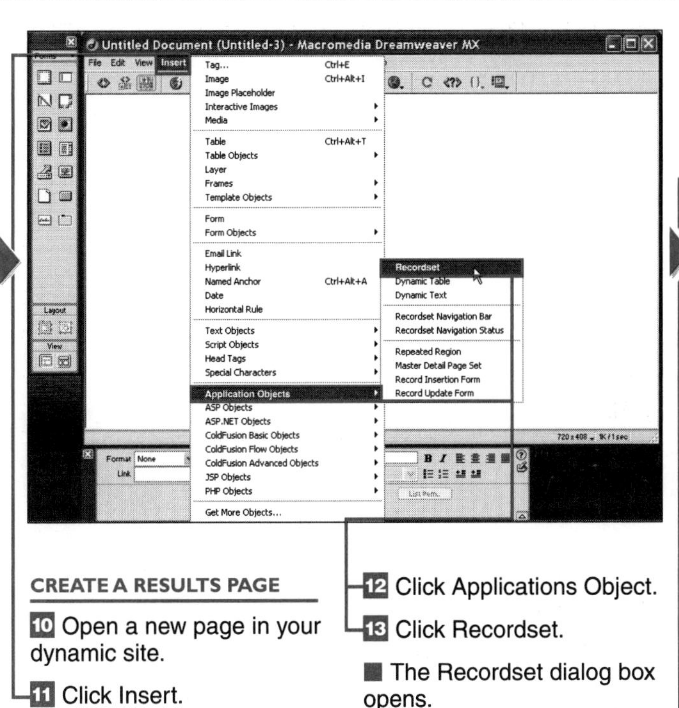

CREATE A RESULTS PAGE

10 Open a new page in your dynamic site.

11 Click Insert.

12 Click Applications Object.

13 Click Recordset.

■ The Recordset dialog box opens.

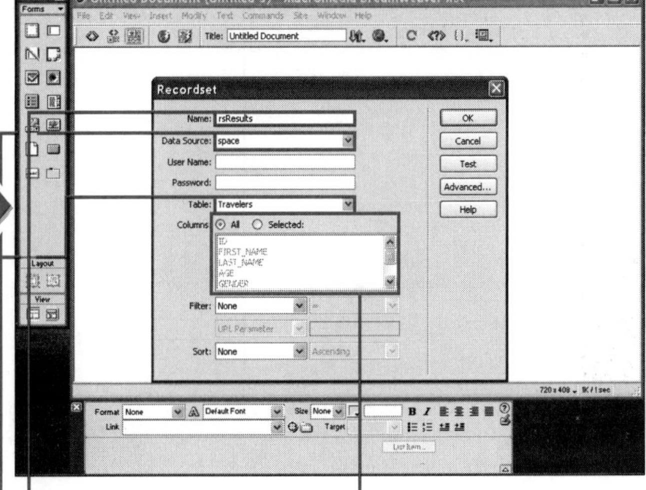

14 Type a name for the recordset.

15 Click ▾ to select a data source.

16 Click ▾ to select a table.

17 Click to select the columns to display (○ changes to ◉).

■ If you choose the Selected Columns radio button, you must highlight the columns in the field below.

CONTINUED

CREATE A SEARCH/RESULTS PAGE SET (CONTINUED)

In a search/results page set, the results page displays a dynamic table listing only the database information that matches the search query submitted by an HTML form. A dynamic table enables you to display the data similar to how the data is organized in the database — as a table of rows and columns.

To create the dynamic results table, the application server first retrieves the data to be searched as a recordset. Then it filters the recordset by comparing data from one of the recordset columns to the search query. For more information about recordsets and recordset filters, see Chapter 18.

The search example below is simple — it includes only one search parameter, which the user enters in the text field of the HTML form, and it compares this parameter with only one column in a database table. You can build more complicated search systems that accept more than one input from the user, and search more than one of the database columns. To create this in Dreamweaver, you have to create a more advanced type of recordset that includes custom SQL code. To learn more about these types of recordsets and SQL, see Dreamweaver's documentation.

CREATE A SEARCH/RESULTS PAGE SET (CONTINUED)

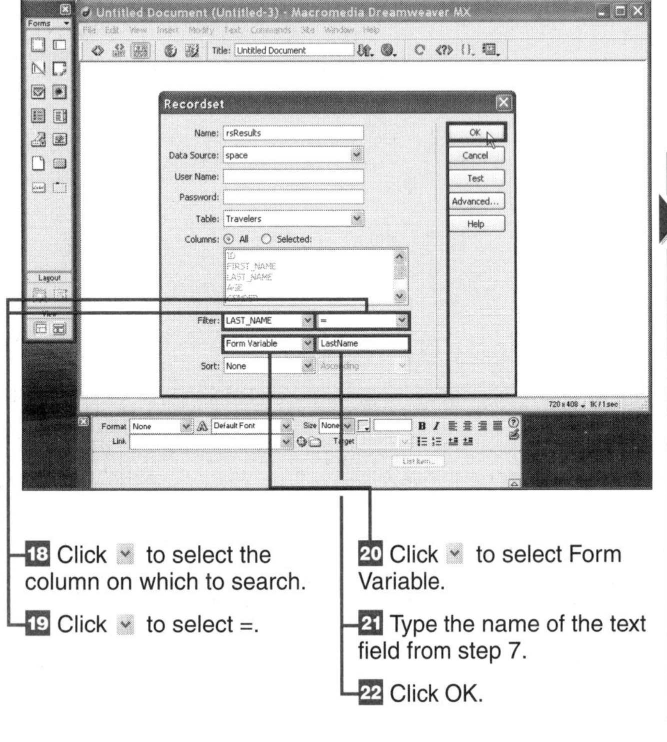

18 Click ▾ to select the column on which to search.

19 Click ▾ to select =.

20 Click ▾ to select Form Variable.

21 Type the name of the text field from step 7.

22 Click OK.

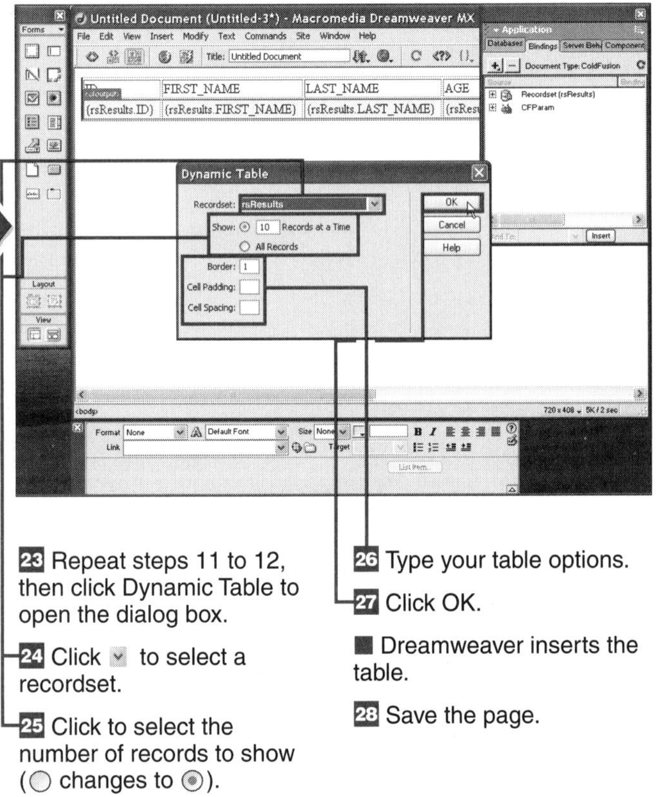

23 Repeat steps 11 to 12, then click Dynamic Table to open the dialog box.

24 Click ▾ to select a recordset.

25 Click to select the number of records to show (◯ changes to ◉).

26 Type your table options.

27 Click OK.

■ Dreamweaver inserts the table.

28 Save the page.

What does the SQL code that produces a search result look like?

✔ To retrieve a list of results for a database search, Dreamweaver writes a SQL statement that accesses specific columns in a database table and then filters the database records using the search text. The SQL statement below selects the columns for the first name, last name, occupation, and home planet from a Travelers database table. Then it filters the records using text from the form field named LastName:

```
SELECT FIRST_NAME,
LAST_NAME, OCCUPATION,
HOME_PLANET FROM Travelers
WHERE LAST_NAME =
'#FORM.LastName#'
```

What can I add to my search form to make it user friendly?

✔ Our example below creates the bare minimum required for a search/results page set to work. To make your search form user friendly, you can add a label to the text entry field so that users know what to type, and text above the form explaining any restrictions there are, if any, on such things as case and number of characters allowed in the text field.

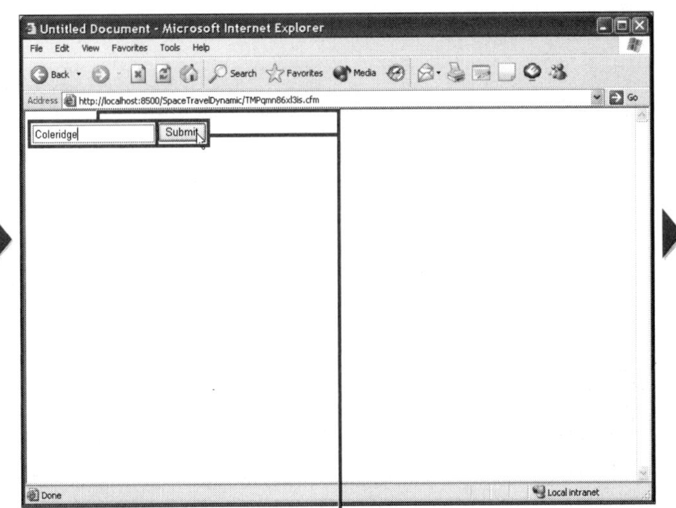

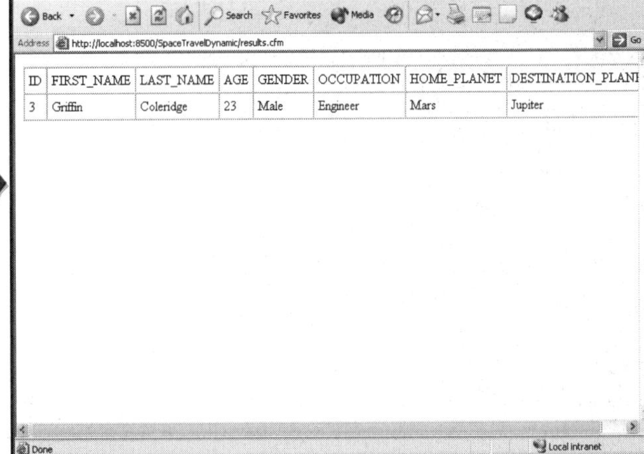

TEST THE SEARCH FORM

29 Switch back to the search form page.

30 Preview the page in a browser.

Note: To preview a page in a Web browser, see page 58.

■ The search form displays.

31 Type a search term in the text field.

32 Click Submit.

■ If the search term is found in the column specified in step 18, the results page displays the searched record.

■ If the search produced no results, a heading row displays with no records below it.

ADD DATA TO A DATABASE

You can create an HTML form that inserts a new record into a database. Creating such a Web-based interface for inserting records can help you maintain a large store of data without having to access a complicated database management system. It also offers a way to add interactive features that store and display information from site visitors to your Web pages. A site guestbook is one such feature.

The Record Insertion Form command lets you specify which table in your available databases you want to add to and which fields in the table you want to update. You can create a form that inserts data into all the fields in a record, or just a subset of the fields. You also specify what kind of input elements should be used for the form, such as text fields, menus, lists, and other elements. See Chapter 9 for more about creating HTML forms.

After clicking the OK button, Dreamweaver adds the form to your page with accompanying dynamic code that inserts the information into the database after the user clicks the Submit button.

ADD DATA TO A DATABASE

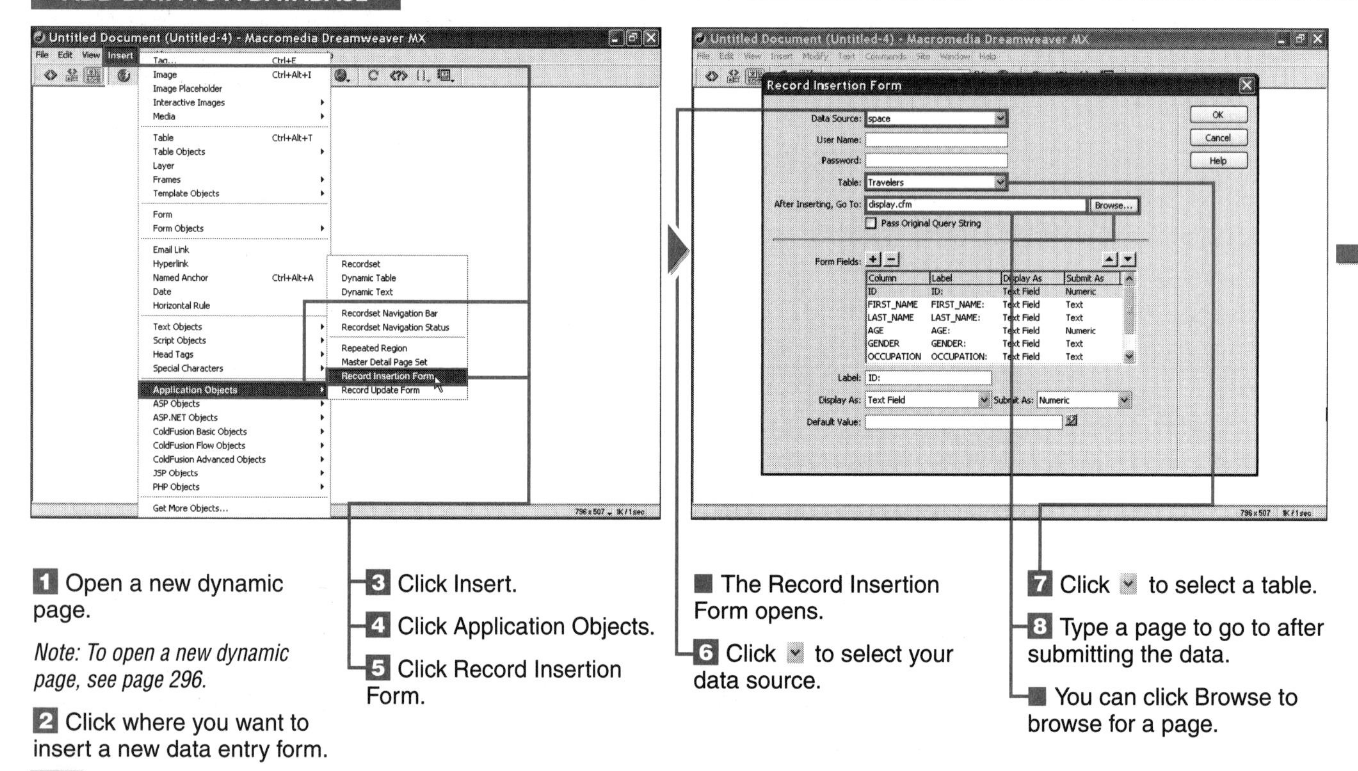

1 Open a new dynamic page.

Note: To open a new dynamic page, see page 296.

2 Click where you want to insert a new data entry form.

3 Click Insert.

4 Click Application Objects.

5 Click Record Insertion Form.

■ The Record Insertion Form opens.

6 Click ▾ to select your data source.

7 Click ▾ to select a table.

8 Type a page to go to after submitting the data.

■ You can click Browse to browse for a page.

When building a form that adds to a database, what fields do I want to remove from a form?

✔ Your database may include ID columns that are automatically created by the database when a new record is inserted. You want to remove those from the HTML form that the user submits. Check your database management documentation for details.

How do I specify a default value in the record insertion form that cannot be changed by the user?

✔ You can create a hidden form field, which allows you to specify a fixed value that Dreamweaver submits to the form handler for a given field. Dreamweaver hides the hidden field code from the user in the source HTML. Hidden fields are added at the end of the record insertion form.

How important is form validation when adding to a database?

✔ It is a good idea to add at least some basic validation. If the type of data that a user submits conflicts with the type of data the database field is designed to hold, the application server adds nothing to the database and displays an ugly error message on the results page. You can add validation to a form using a Dreamweaver behavior. See Chapter 13 for details. Some application servers also offer form validation features as well.

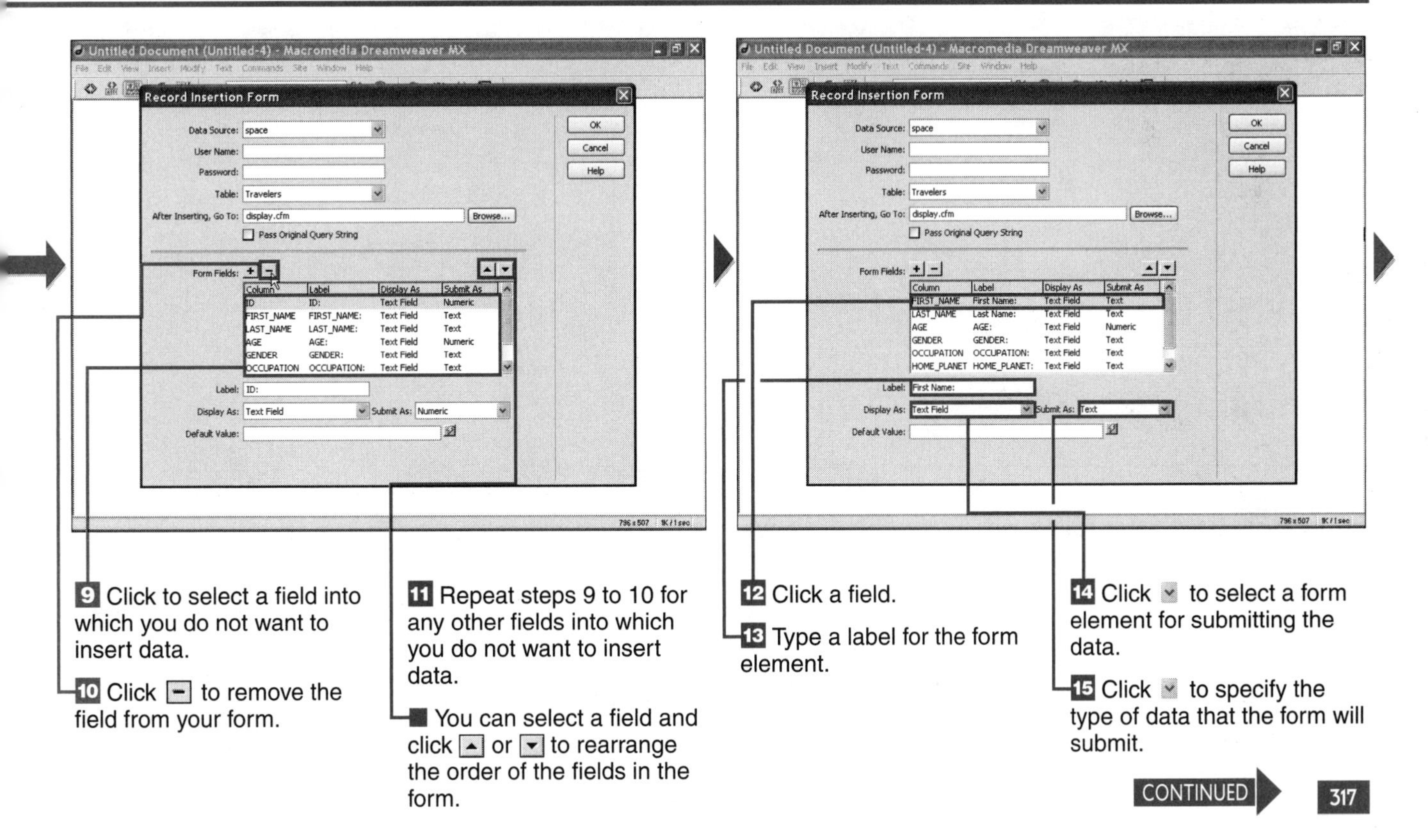

9 Click to select a field into which you do not want to insert data.

10 Click ⊟ to remove the field from your form.

11 Repeat steps 9 to 10 for any other fields into which you do not want to insert data.

■ You can select a field and click ▲ or ▼ to rearrange the order of the fields in the form.

12 Click a field.

13 Type a label for the form element.

14 Click ▾ to select a form element for submitting the data.

15 Click ▾ to specify the type of data that the form will submit.

CONTINUED

ADD DATA TO A DATABASE (CONTINUED)

Creating a Web page that adds information to a database reverses the flow of dynamic information in your Web site. By allowing an HTML form to insert information into a database, you can collect important information from your site visitors and have it immediately available to other pages in your site. Other pages can access the new information and display it dynamically in table or text form.

When creating the record insertion form that adds to a database, you specify what page the user is forwarded to after submitting the form. This page can serve as a confirmation page that announces that the form has been submitted successfully. Alternatively, the page can display the updated database table to show the new data in place.

To create a page that displays the updated information, you first must create a recordset that retrieves the newly updated table. Then you display the recordset as a dynamic table in your page. To define a recordset, see page 300. To display a dynamic table, see page 306.

ADD DATA TO A DATABASE (CONTINUED)

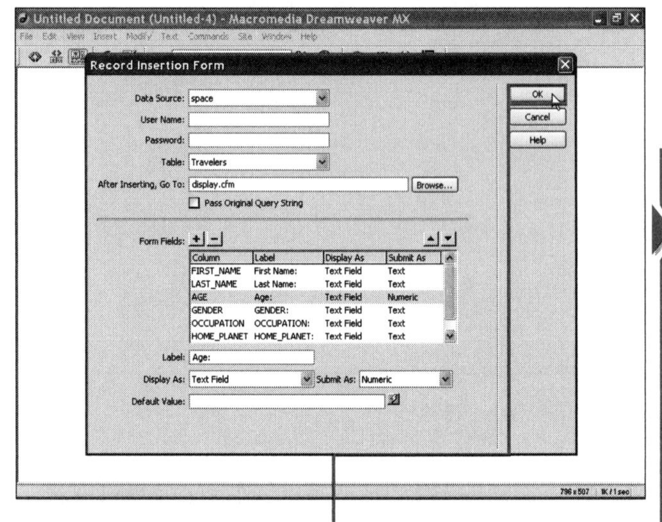

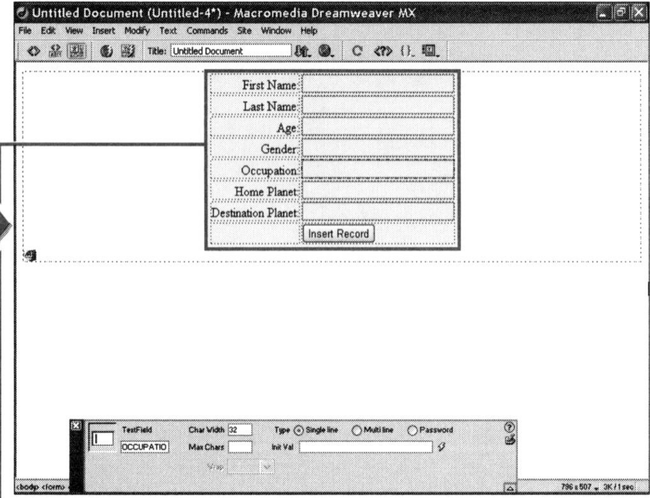

16 Repeat steps 12 to 15 for all the fields in your form.

■ There may be additional options to configure for some form elements such as menus and radio buttons.

17 Click OK.

■ Dreamweaver inserts the form into the page.

■ You can click a form input element to view its properties in the Properties inspector.

Note: Click Window and then Properties to open the Properties inspector.

How can I enable a user to easily enter multiple entries into a database?

✔ You can make the submission form also the confirmation page, which results in the HTML form submitting to itself. After users submit a new record, they see a new blank form where they can add another record. This saves them from having to click the Back button to return to the input page.

How do I edit a record insertion form after I create it and add it to a page?

✔ Click Window and then Server Behaviors to open the Server Behaviors panel. Double-click the Insert Record entry. An Insert Record dialog box appears allowing you to change settings such as what data type each field is submitted as and what page is displayed after submission. You can even change the database table into which the form inserts.

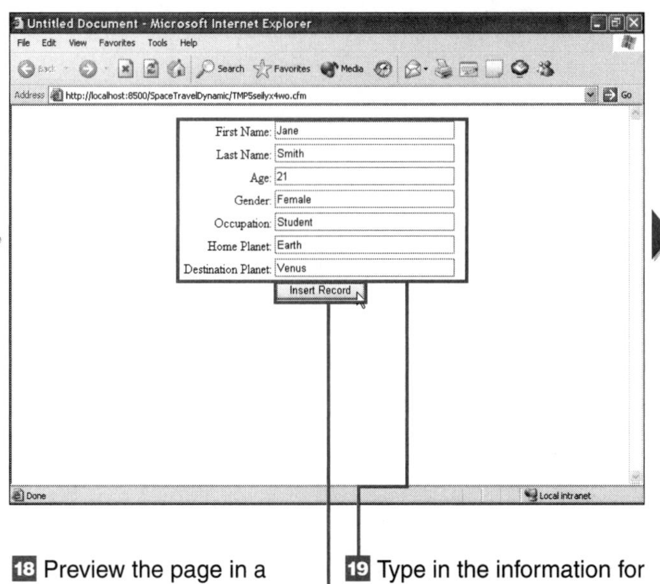

Untitled Document - Microsoft Internet Explorer

http://localhost:8500/SpaceTravelDynamic/display.cfm

FIRST_NAME	LAST_NAME	AGE	GENDER	OCCUPATION	HOME_PLANET	DESTINATION_PLANET
Mike	Wooldridge	34	Male	Astronaut	Earth	Saturn
Linda	Corazon	42	Female	Veterinarian	Earth	Venus
Griffin	Coleridge	23	Male	Engineer	Mars	Jupiter
Lucy	Springhaven	13	Female	Student	Venus	Neptune
Belle	Waggsworth	21	Female	Paralegal	Earth	Pluto
Jane	Smith	21	Female	Student	Earth	Venus

18 Preview the page in a browser.

Note: To preview the page in a Web browser, see page 58.

19 Type in the information for the new database record.

20 Click Insert Record.

■ The page you specified in step 8 appears.

■ In this example, the page displays records from the updated table, including the newly inserted record.

Note: To display a dynamic table, see page 306.

CREATE A MASTER DETAIL PAGE SET

With a master/detail page set, you can present dynamic information to site visitors at two different levels of detail. The master page lists a summary of all the records in a database table as an HTML table. Each record in the master list is associated with a detail page, which displays the complete information about a record. The detail pages are linked from the master page by hyperlinks in one of the HTML table columns.

Master/detail pages are useful for displaying product information on e-commerce sites. The master page displays a list of the product names, while the detail pages list complete information about each product such as descriptions and prices. Master/detail pages are also useful for organizing employee or address book information, with the master page listing first and last names, and the detail pages listing addresses, phone numbers, and other personal information.

You can use a master/detail page set as the basis of a Frequently Asked Questions (FAQ) system for your site. The master page can display a table of question hyperlinks, while each detail page displays a question and an answer.

CREATE A MASTER DETAIL PAGE SET

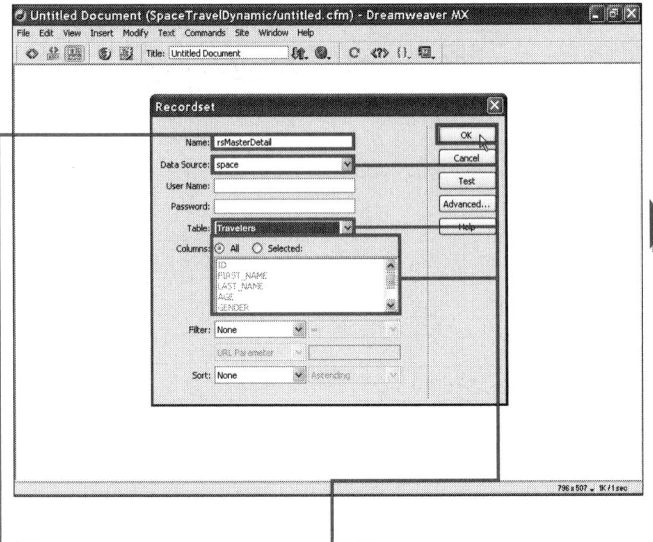

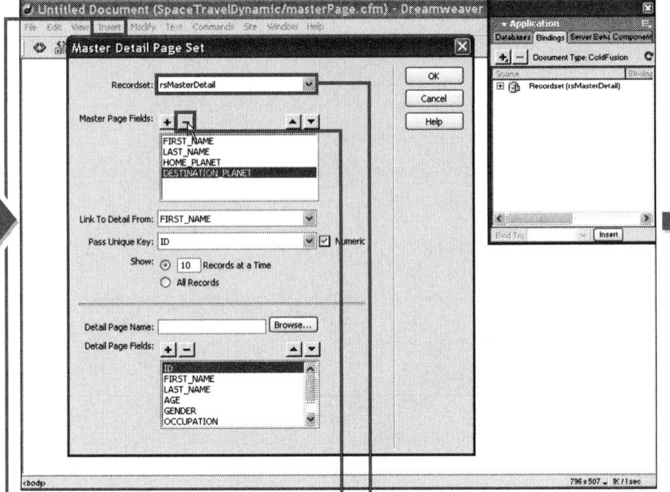

1 Open a new dynamic page as your master page.

Note: To open a new dynamic page, see page 296.

2 Open the Recordset dialog box.

3 Name the recordset.

4 Click ▾ to select a data source.

5 Click ▾ to select a table.

6 Click to select any columns you want to display on the master *or* detail pages.

7 Click OK.

8 Save the master page.

9 Click Insert.

10 Click Applications Object.

11 Click Master Detail Page Set.

12 Click ▾ to select the recordset that you just created.

13 Click a field you do not want to display on the master page.

14 Click ⊟ to delete the field.

Why would I want to use an ID field as the key for a master/detail page set?

✔ Because an ID field in a database table usually contains a value that is unique for a given record. Using an ID field as the key in your master/detail pages helps ensure that there is only one database record for each link on the master page. If you specify a field that is not unique, a detail page could display details for more than one record.

How can I allow users to add to the information in my master/detail page set?

✔ You can add a form to your dynamic site that inserts records into your database table. For each record inserted, an additional item appears on the master page. See pages 316 to 319 for information on how to create such a form.

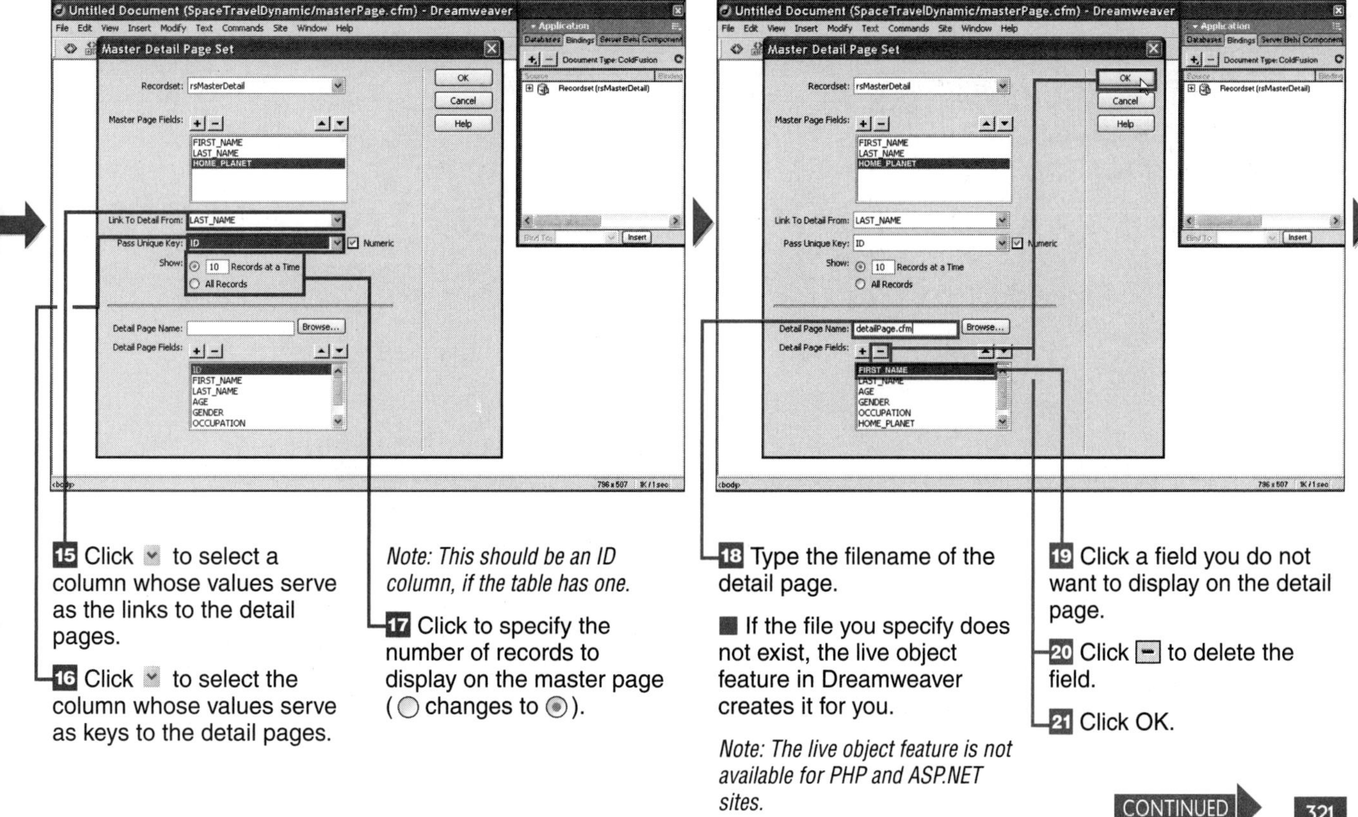

15 Click ▾ to select a column whose values serve as the links to the detail pages.

16 Click ▾ to select the column whose values serve as keys to the detail pages.

Note: This should be an ID column, if the table has one.

17 Click to specify the number of records to display on the master page (◯ changes to ◉).

18 Type the filename of the detail page.

■ If the file you specify does not exist, the live object feature in Dreamweaver creates it for you.

Note: The live object feature is not available for PHP and ASP.NET sites.

19 Click a field you do not want to display on the detail page.

20 Click ▭ to delete the field.

21 Click OK.

CREATE A MASTER DETAIL PAGE SET (CONTINUED)

Both the master and detail pages include dynamic tables, with the master table displaying some information from *all* the records in the table, and the detail page displaying all the fields from a *single record*. Generating these two dynamic tables makes use of the recordset you define at the beginning of this task. Dreamweaver applies different filters to the recordset to display different tables.

If the database table involved contains a large amount of records, you can limit the number of records displayed on the master page, and then add navigation to allow the user to page through the list. To add navigation to a dynamic table, see page 308.

The key to linking the master page to the detail pages is to pass a variable/value pair on each master page hyperlink URL. The variable information enables the detail page to filter the information in the recordset and retrieve only the record for the clicked product. For more information about how information is passed on a URL, see page 302.

CREATE A MASTER DETAIL PAGE SET (CONTINUED)

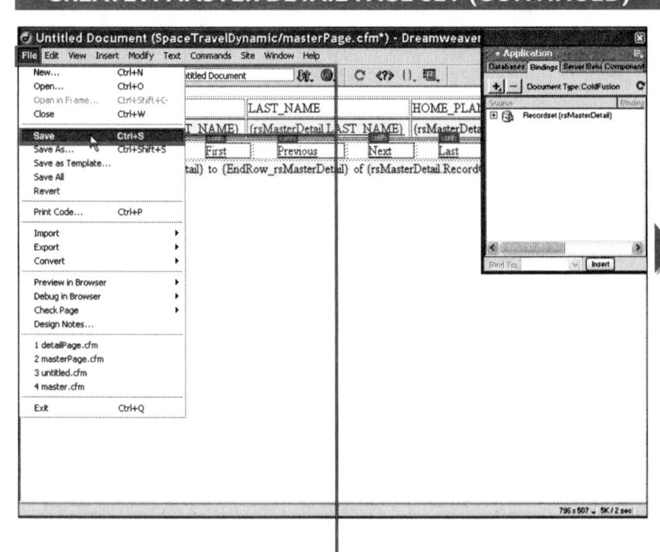

■ Dreamweaver inserts the dynamic code into the master page.

■ Dreamweaver also creates a detail page, if needed, and inserts the dynamic code into it.

22 Click File.

23 Click Save.

■ Dreamweaver saves the master page.

24 Click Window.

25 Click the name of the detail page to view it.

■ If the file is not open, you can open it using the File menu or Site window.

26 Save the detail page.

■ Dreamweaver saves the detail page.

How do I create a link back to the master page from the detail page?

✔ Most of the time, users will want the option to view multiple detail pages from the master page. A link from the results page to the master page gives users an alternative to clicking the browser back button. To create a link, type the link text on the detail page and select it. Click the Src button in the Properties inspector, and then select the master page from the dialog box that appears.

How do I make the detail pages open in new windows?

✔ On the master page, select the dynamic code in the column that has the hyperlink. In the Properties inspector, select _blank in the Target drop-down menu. This opens each detail page that a user clicks in a new window. See Chapter 6 for more details.

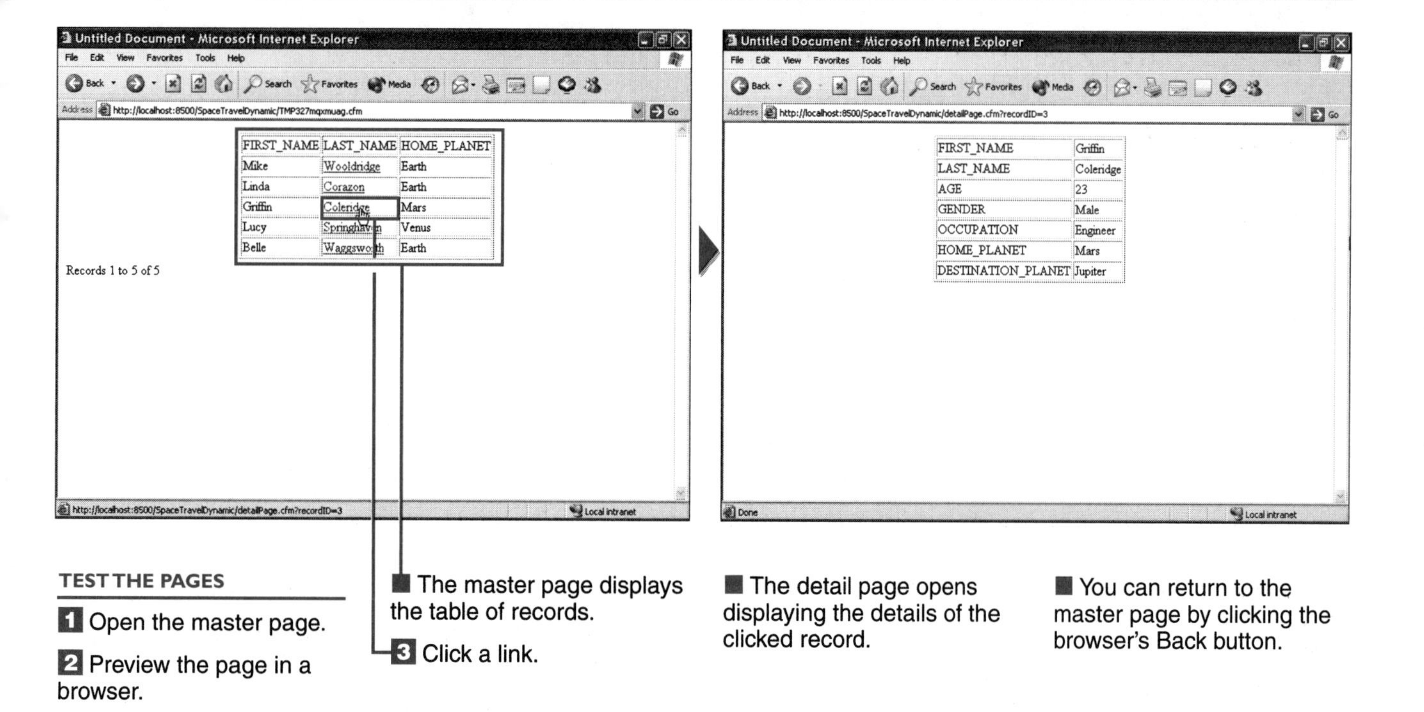

TEST THE PAGES

1 Open the master page.

2 Preview the page in a browser.

Note: To preview a page in a Web browser, see page 58.

■ The master page displays the table of records.

3 Click a link.

■ The detail page opens displaying the details of the clicked record.

■ You can return to the master page by clicking the browser's Back button.

STORE SESSION INFORMATION

You can temporarily save data about users as they view different pages on your Web site as session information. You can then use this information to customize your dynamic pages as the user clicks from page to page.

Dreamweaver makes it easy to store such session variables and then access them to make decisions about what dynamic data is displayed on a Web site. Storing session information helps you tailor a site to a visitor's preferences, and can save visitors from having to enter certain information repeatedly while they view different pages on a site.

Session information can come from different places. As in the example below, you can create a form on your page that gathers data from the user and then posts the data to a destination page. The destination page can store the data as a session variable. You can also store data gathered from link URLs and HTTP environment variables as session variables. After the application stores a session variable, all the pages in the site can access the information throughout the duration of the user visit.

STORE SESSION INFORMATION

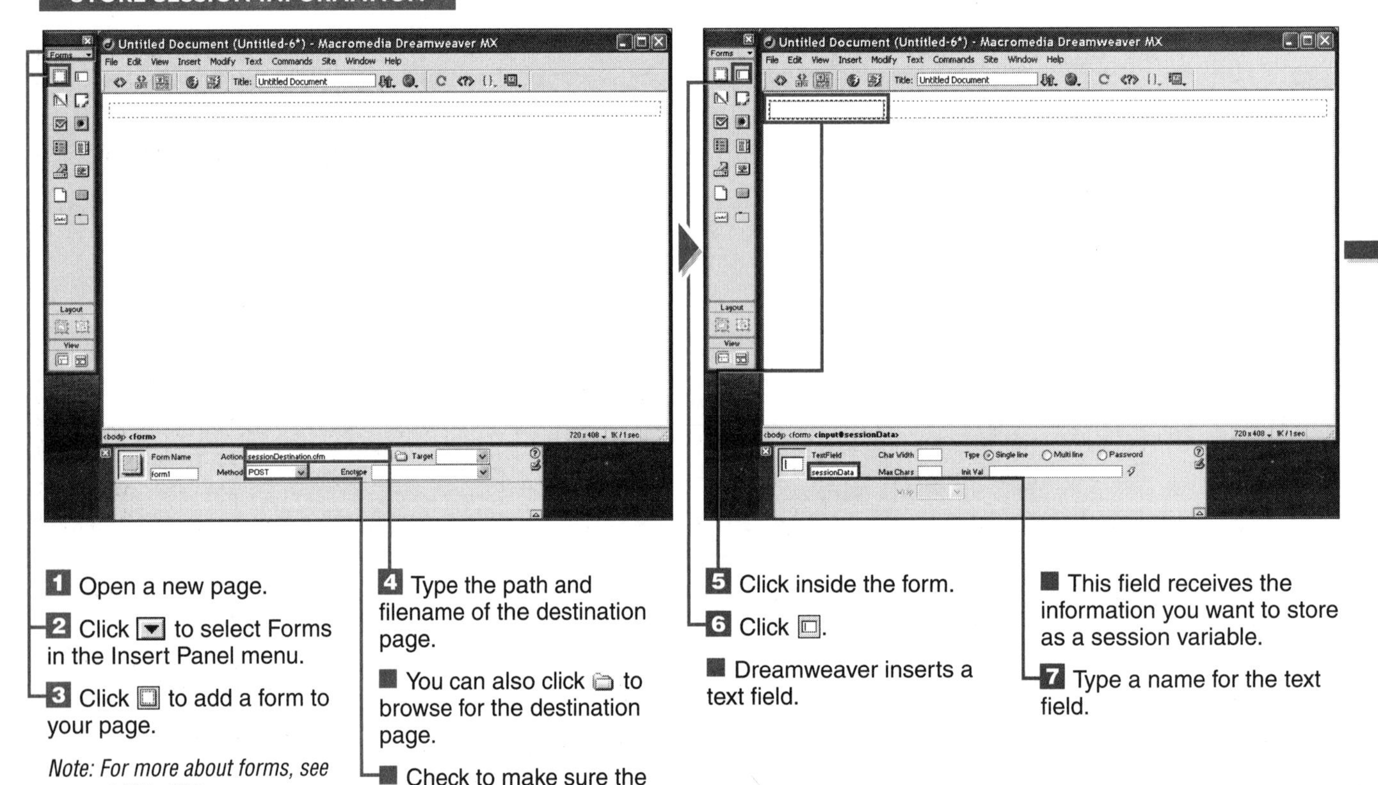

1 Open a new page.

2 Click ▾ to select Forms in the Insert Panel menu.

3 Click ▢ to add a form to your page.

Note: For more about forms, see pages 140 to 159.

4 Type the path and filename of the destination page.

■ You can also click ▢ to browse for the destination page.

■ Check to make sure the POST method is selected.

5 Click inside the form.

6 Click ▢.

■ Dreamweaver inserts a text field.

■ This field receives the information you want to store as a session variable.

7 Type a name for the text field.

How do I specify how much inactivity should be interpreted as an end of a session?

✔ This varies depending on the application used to serve the dynamic site. For ColdFusion MX, you can set this value by logging into the administrator area and clicking Memory Variables. The default length of time for a session timing out in ColdFusion MX is 20 minutes.

Can I filter a recordset based on the value of a session variable?

✔ Yes. In the Filter area of the Recordset dialog box, you can specify that the application server filter the recordset using a session variable.

How does an application server define a session?

✔ A session begins when a user accesses the first Web page in a site. This can be any page in the site, not just the home page. A session ends after a certain length of inactivity by the user, which usually means that the user has left the site. A session can also end after a user explicitly terminates a session by clicking a Log off link.

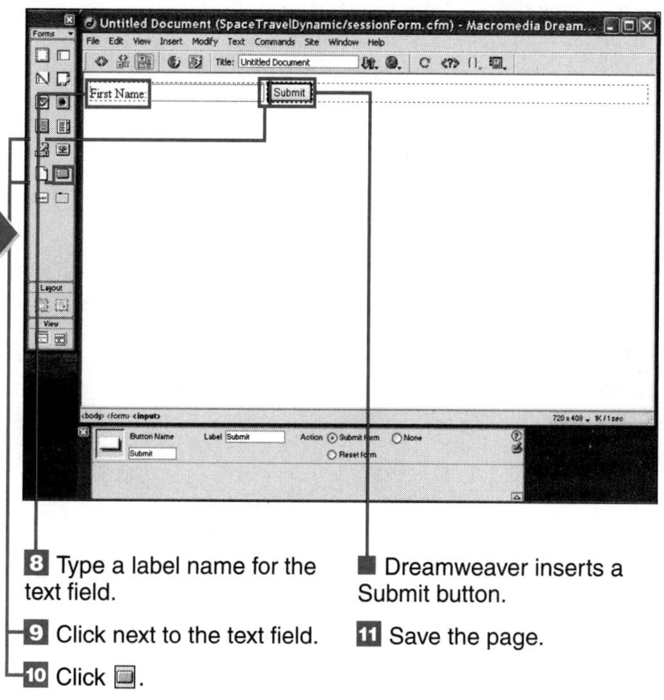

8 Type a label name for the text field.

9 Click next to the text field.

10 Click .

■ Dreamweaver inserts a Submit button.

11 Save the page.

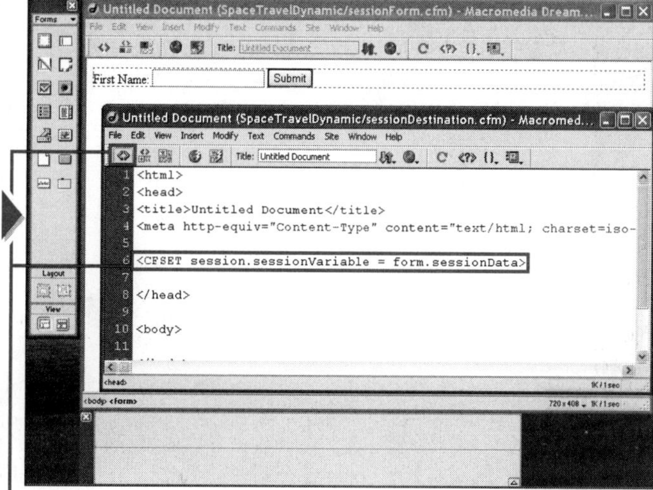

12 Open a new page.

13 Save the page as the filename from step 4.

14 Click .

15 Between the <HEAD> and </HEAD> tags, type **<CFSET session.Variable1 = form.Variable2>**.

■ *Variable1* is the stored session variable.

■ *Variable2* is the text field name defined in step 7.

16 Save the page.

RETRIEVE SESSION INFORMATION

You can retrieve stored session information for a user and use the information to customize the look and feel of your dynamic site or determine what kind of content a user can view. You can add session variables that you have stored in a page to the Bindings panel, which allows you to easily insert the variables into your site pages without having to write dynamic code by hand.

Typically, session information is stored after a user submits the information via a form or when a user clicks a link that includes session information on the URL. In the example below, a page stores the first name information from a form as a session variable. The page then immediately retrieves the stored session information and displays it on the page.

Working with session information is similar to what happens in the section "Add Data to a Database," where the application server retrieves information from an HTML form and stores it in a database table. Except with session information, instead of storing it permanently in a database file, the application server saves the information temporarily as session variables in memory. The information stays saved only for the duration of the user's visit to the site.

RETRIEVE A SESSION VARIABLE

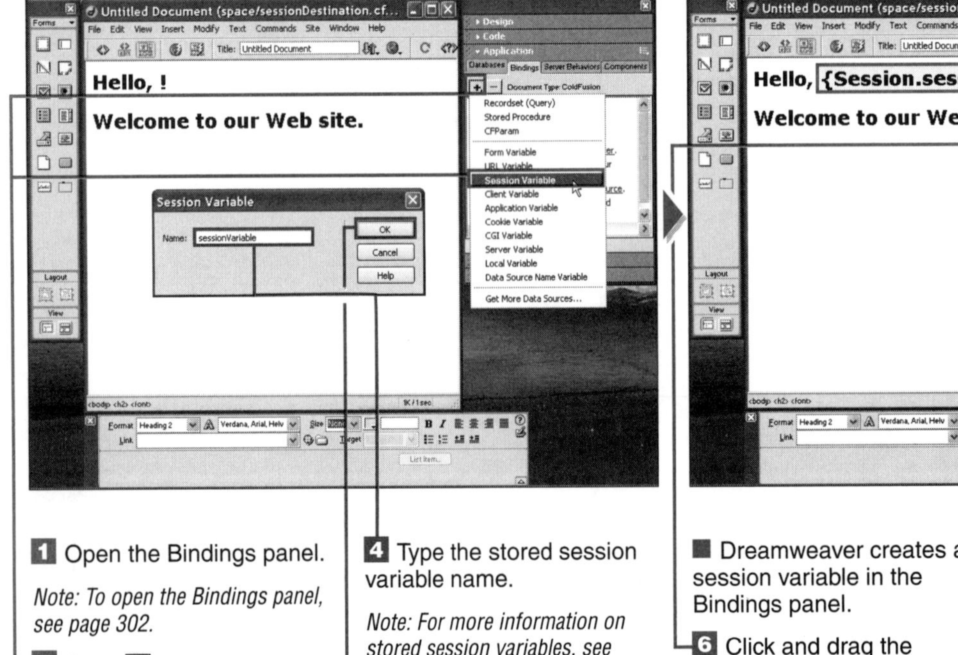

1 Open the Bindings panel.

Note: To open the Bindings panel, see page 302.

2 Click ⊞.

3 Click Session Variable.

■ The Session Variable dialog box opens.

4 Type the stored session variable name.

Note: For more information on stored session variables, see page 324.

5 Click OK.

■ Dreamweaver creates a session variable in the Bindings panel.

6 Click and drag the session variable to where you want its value to appear in the Document window.

■ Dreamweaver adds the dynamic code to display the session variable value.

Can every user have session variables assigned to them?

✔ Part of tracking a user session involves setting a unique cookie value in a user's browser that distinguishes them from other site users. You cannot store session information about users that have browsers that do not support cookies, or that have cookies turned off.

How can I save information about a user across separate site visits?

✔ You can save such information as *client information* on your application server. Client information is associated with a particular user and browser, and is not erased after the user leaves the site. For more information, see the documentation for your application server.

How can I use a URL to store session information?

✔ Create a link whose URL contains a ? followed by a variable/value pair that you want to store. For example, the following link passes a variable named ID that has a value of 101:

http://www.wiley.com/index.cfm?ID=12

In ColdFusion, you store this information as an ID session variable by typing the following between the <HEAD> and </HEAD> tags on the destination page:

```
<CFSET session.ID=url.ID>
```

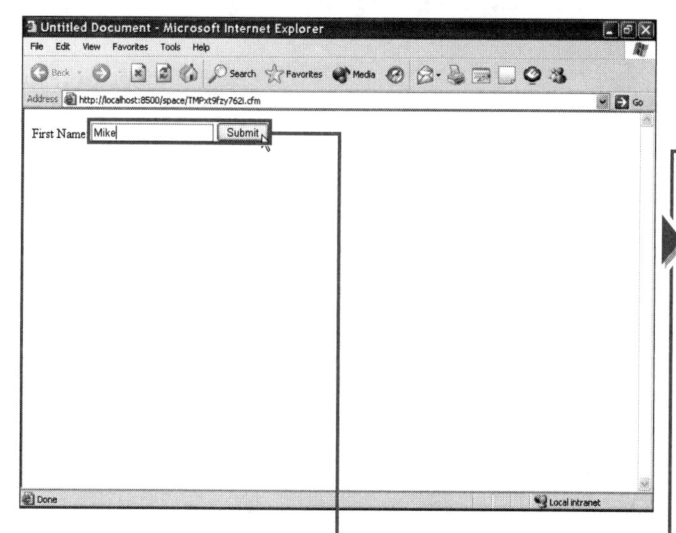

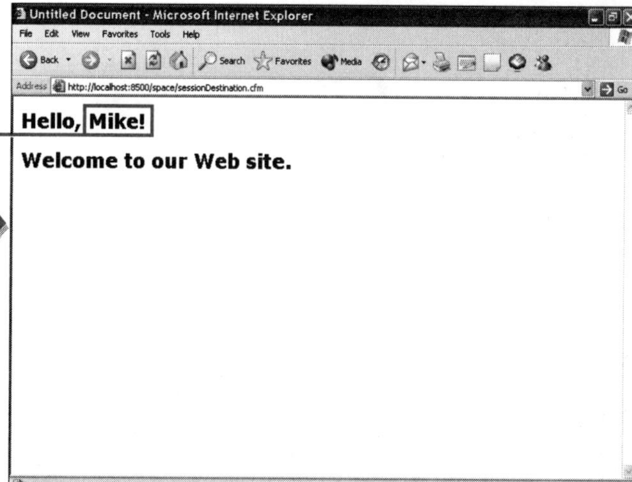

TEST THE PAGE

1 Open the page that accepts the session information from the user.

Note: To set up this page, see page 324.

2 Preview the page in a browser.

Note: To preview a page in a Web browser, see page 58.

■ The page displays in a browser.

3 Submit the session information.

■ In this example, the destination page accepts the session information and stores it.

■ The page also displays the session information.

■ After the session information is stored, any page that the user visits during a session can access the session information.

SECTION VI

20) GETTING STARTED WITH FLASH MX

21) CREATING SHAPES AND OBJECTS

MASTERING FLASH MX BASICS

22) ENHANCING AND EDITING OBJECTS

23) WORKING WITH IMPORTED GRAPHICS AND VIDEO

24) WORKING WITH TEXT

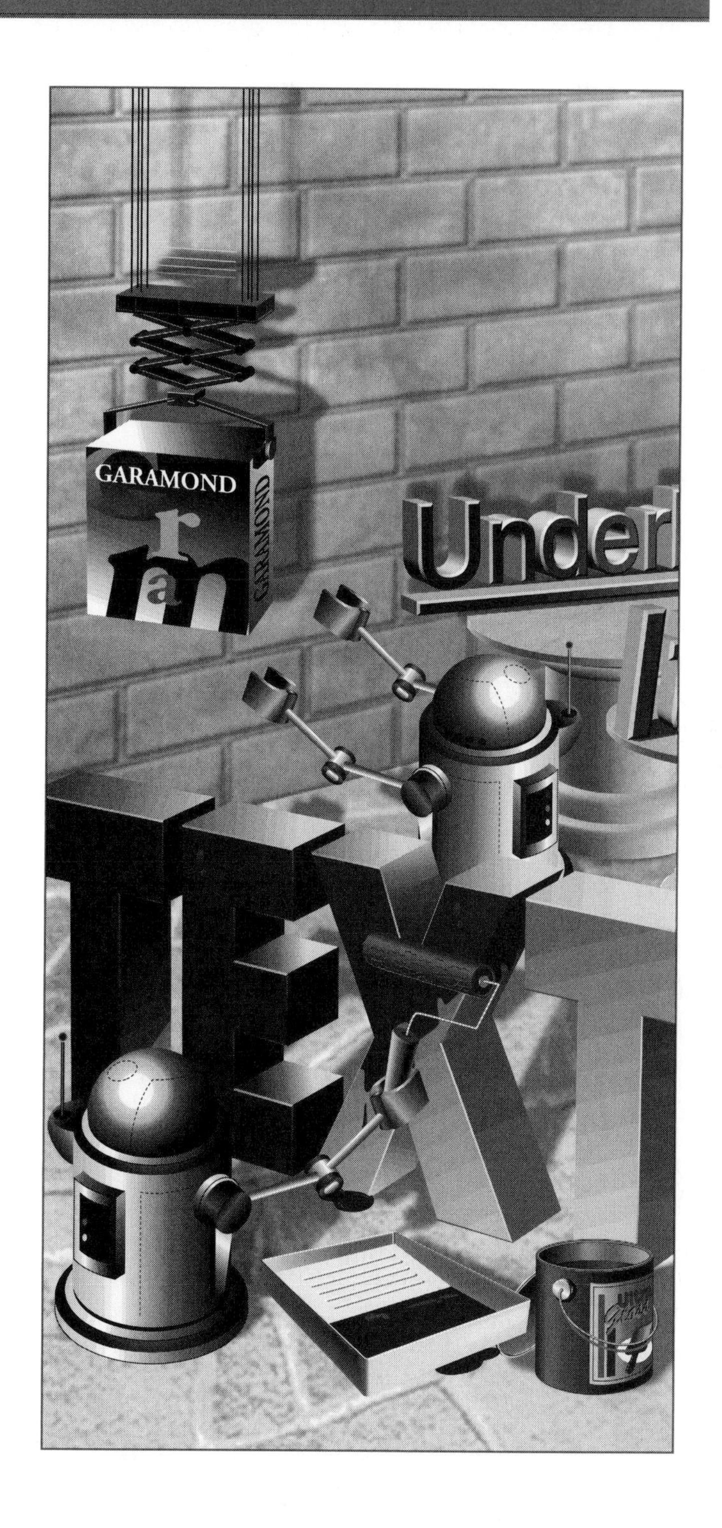

INTRODUCTION TO FLASH MX

Macromedia Flash has quickly become the standard for creating lively vector art and animation on the Web, and the latest version — Flash MX — offers more versatility and workflow enhancements than ever before.

Flash MX is the perfect tool for both new and experienced Web page designers who want to create expressive, dynamic Web page elements. With the program's many tools, you can add interactivity to page elements such as banner ads and navigation buttons, and you can animate graphic objects, create cartoons and movies, and coordinate accompanying sounds.

Flash humbly started out as another program. Originally called *Future Splash Animator,* the program was designed to help make and animate vector art. Macromedia purchased the program in 1997, changed its name to *Flash,* and marketed it for the Web. It has experienced phenomenal growth ever since and is now the number one delivery system for rich media on the Web.

Features of Flash MX

Flash MX is a versatile multimedia authoring program, featuring a collection of tools you can use to create Web pages and applications as well as dynamic animations and vector-based graphics. Previous versions of Flash are known for giving users the ability to create compact, vector-based graphics and animations for quick delivery over the Web.

The latest version of the program — Flash MX — offers greater support of other file types, including the addition of video support. With the help of the Sorenson Spark codec, a compression/decompression process for compressing video, Flash MX can stream and play source video clips as well as allow you to edit video just as you edit other objects in Flash.

Using Vector-Based Graphics

Most graphics you encounter on the Web are *raster graphics*, such as JPEGs and GIFs. Raster graphics use a series of horizontal lines that vary in intensity and color to display an image. Raster graphics, due to their size, take longer to display on a Web page. Every Web surfer has experienced the frustration of waiting for raster graphics to display.

Vector-based graphics, such as those you can create in Flash, are much smaller in file size. Vector-based graphics use mathematical coordinates to define an image. As such, the image is much easier to scale and is incredibly compact in size. Vector graphics display much faster on a downloading Web page and are a much more efficient method of delivering images over the Internet.

Animate with Flash

Flash frames enable you to animate graphics that you create with Flash or any other graphic-editing program. You can easily animate graphic objects, buttons, and even text. You can create mini-movies that play on Web pages or as self-extracting files.

The animation techniques used in Flash are based on animation techniques employed by early cartoonists. Animators of yesteryear painstakingly drew graphic objects onto transparent cells and stacked the cells to create a single image for a single movie frame. They reused images that stayed the same throughout the animation, such as backgrounds, and added new images whenever there was a key change in the animation sequence. Flash works in a similar fashion, allowing you to layer objects to create backgrounds and reuse objects throughout a movie.

Add Sound

Flash has controls for adding and manipulating sound files. You can include sound effects or music files with an animation for added pizzazz and interest. For example, you can add a background sound to play along with your movie, or a narration that corresponds with several movie frames. You can also add sound effect clips to various parts of your animations or buttons, such as a clicking noise the user hears when he clicks a button in your movie.

Add Interactivity

You can also create interactive Web page features using Flash. For example, you can create a button that performs an action as soon as the user moves the mouse pointer over it, or a menu that, when activated, animates several menu choices. You can use Flash to create interactive elements, such as forms or search engines, or complex interactive elements such as games. With a little imagination and skill using Flash MX, you can create all kinds of interactive elements.

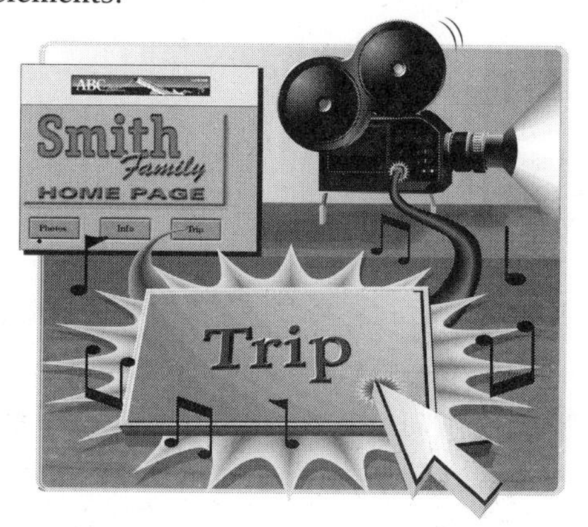

NAVIGATE THE FLASH MX WINDOW

The Flash MX program window has several components for working with graphics and movies. Take time to familiarize yourself with the on-screen elements. The Flash MX program window varies slightly in appearance between the Windows version and the Mac version, but the features and tools all work the same.

FLASH MX IN THE WINDOWS ENVIRONMENT

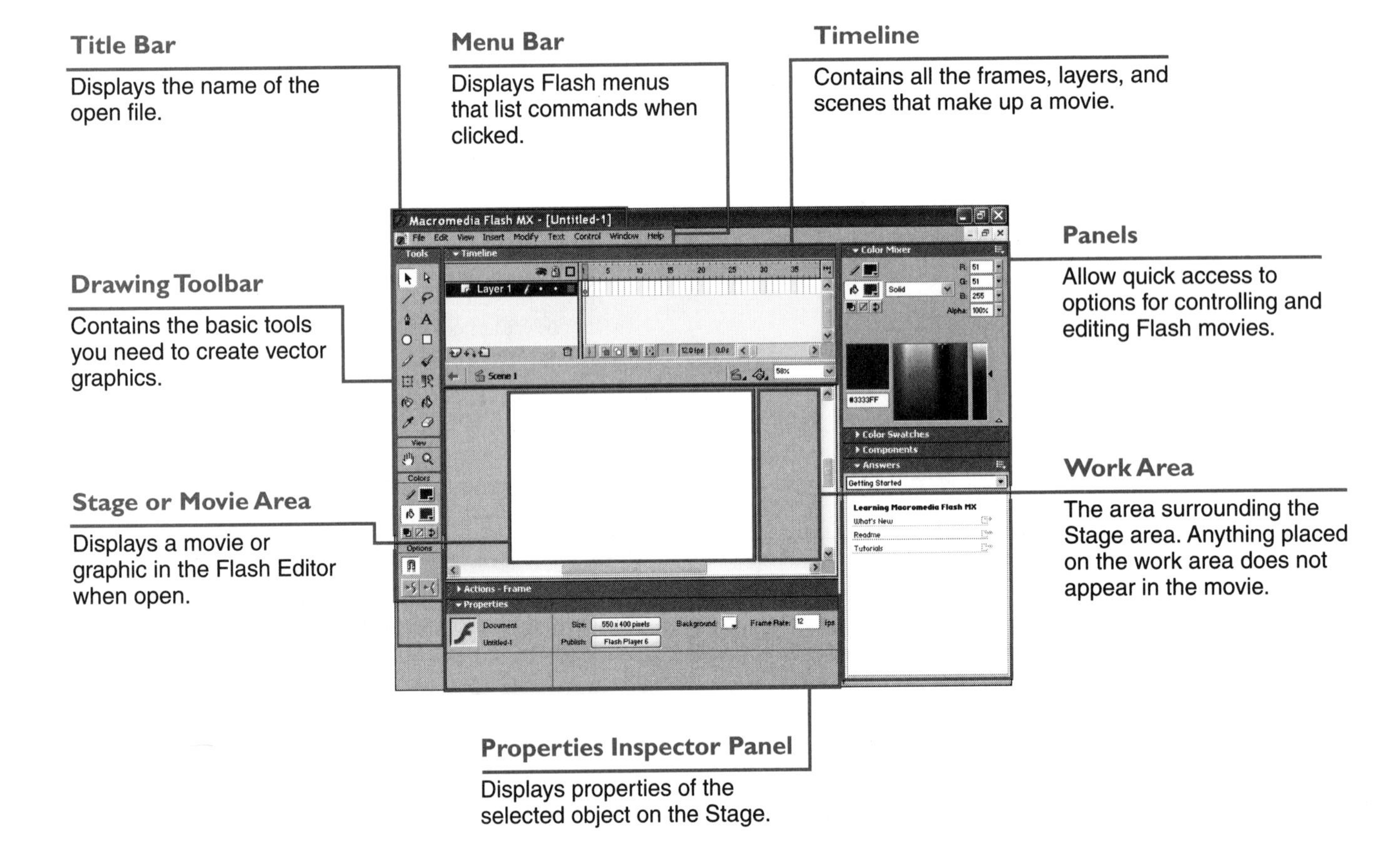
Title Bar
Displays the name of the open file.
Menu Bar
Displays Flash menus that list commands when clicked.
Timeline
Contains all the frames, layers, and scenes that make up a movie.
Panels
Allow quick access to options for controlling and editing Flash movies.
Drawing Toolbar
Contains the basic tools you need to create vector graphics.
Work Area
The area surrounding the Stage area. Anything placed on the work area does not appear in the movie.
Stage or Movie Area
Displays a movie or graphic in the Flash Editor when open.
Properties Inspector Panel
Displays properties of the selected object on the Stage.
Macromedia Flash MX - [Untitled-1]
File Edit View Insert Modify Text Control Window Help
Timeline
Layer 1
Scene 1
Color Mixer
Color Swatches
Components
Answers
Getting Started
Learning Macromedia Flash MX
What's New
Readme
Tutorials
Actions - Frame
Properties

FLASH MX IN THE MACINTOSH ENVIRONMENT

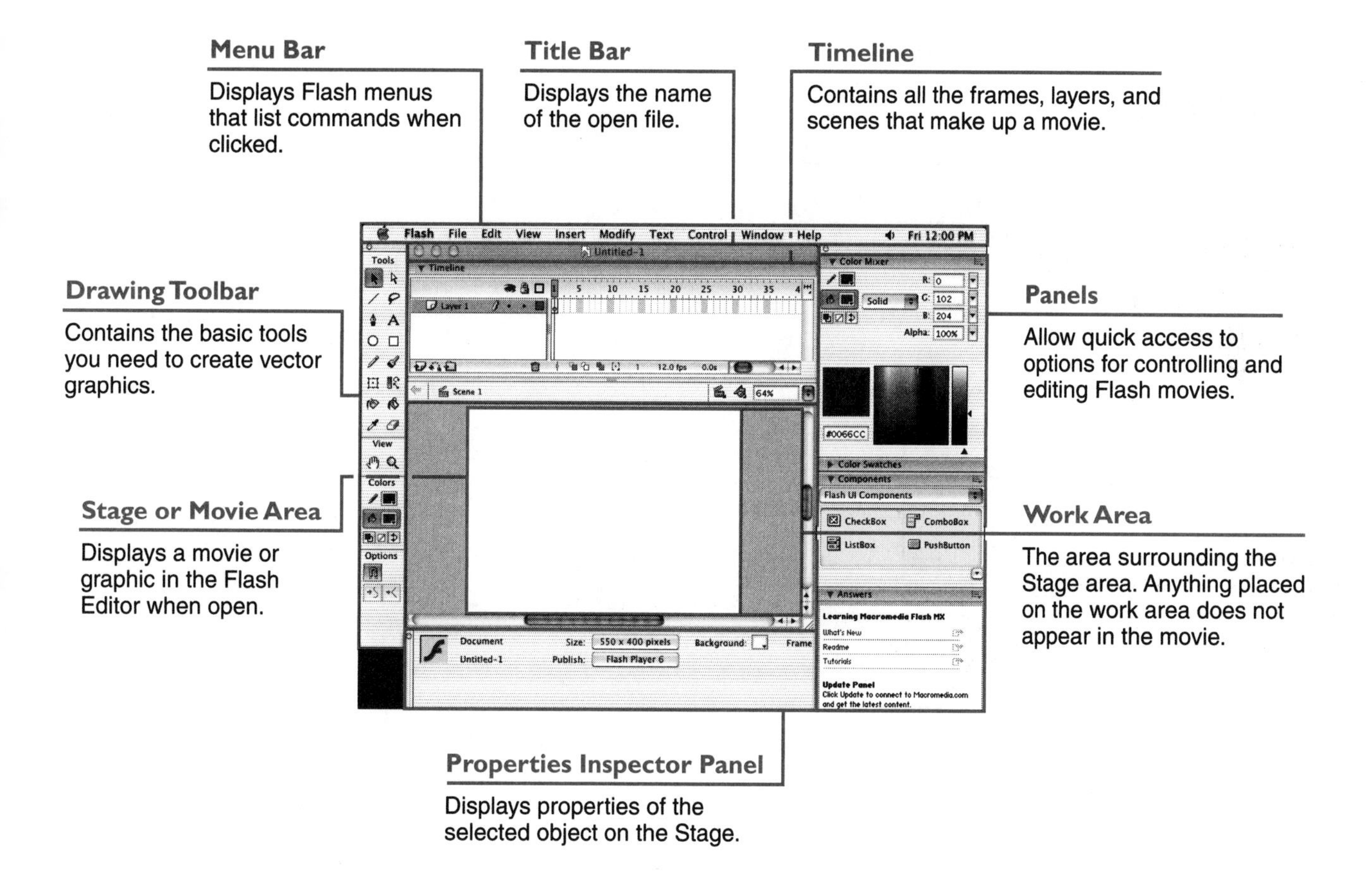
Menu Bar
Displays Flash menus that list commands when clicked.
Title Bar
Displays the name of the open file.
Timeline
Contains all the frames, layers, and scenes that make up a movie.
Drawing Toolbar
Contains the basic tools you need to create vector graphics.
Panels
Allow quick access to options for controlling and editing Flash movies.
Stage or Movie Area
Displays a movie or graphic in the Flash Editor when open.
Work Area
The area surrounding the Stage area. Anything placed on the work area does not appear in the movie.
Properties Inspector Panel
Displays properties of the selected object on the Stage.

OPEN A FLASH FILE

Flash files are called *documents* or *movies*. When you save a file, you can open it and work on it again. Flash files can be as simple as a drawing you have created using the Flash drawing tools, or as complex as an animation sequence consisting of scenes and interactive elements.

There are several ways to access Flash files you have previously saved. Flash keeps track of the last four files you have worked with and lists them at the bottom of the File menu. You can display the menu and select the file you want to open.

To open other Flash files, use the Open dialog box. The Open dialog box in Flash works similarly to the Open dialog box found in other programs. You can open Flash files of all types, including files created using older versions of Flash.

You can also start a new file whenever you want. Every new file you start in Flash MX uses a default Stage size. To learn more about setting the Stage dimensions, see page 344 later in this chapter.

OPEN A FLASH FILE

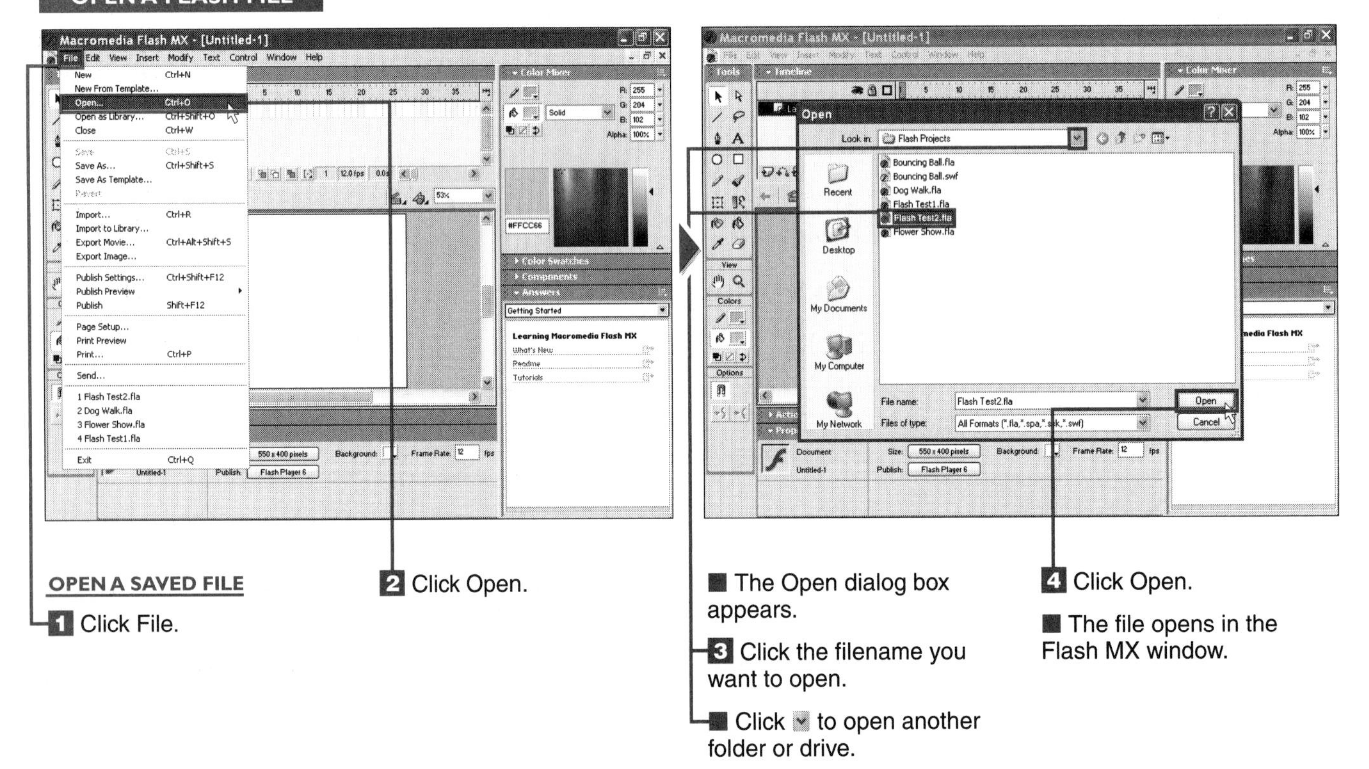

OPEN A SAVED FILE

1 Click File.

2 Click Open.

■ The Open dialog box appears.

3 Click the filename you want to open.

■ Click ▾ to open another folder or drive.

4 Click Open.

■ The file opens in the Flash MX window.

Why does Flash MX not show a Main toolbar?

✔ By default, Flash MX does not show the Main toolbar. To display the Main toolbar, click Window, Toolbar, and then Main. You can display the Main toolbar to quickly access common commands, such as Open and Save.

Is there a limit to how many Flash files I can have open?

✔ No. However, the more files you open, the slower your computer becomes. Graphics files, such as those you author in Flash MX, can take up more processing power than other programs. Unless you are sharing data between the files, close Flash files you are no longer using.

Can I open other file types besides Flash files?

✔ To open other file formats, such as QuickTime movies, use the Import command. Click File and then Import. This opens the Import dialog box, which looks just like the Open dialog box. From there, you can locate the file type and import it into Flash MX.

If I have two Flash files open, can I borrow items from one to use in the other?

✔ You can borrow items from another file using the Open as Library command; however, you cannot borrow items if the file you are borrowing from is open. You must first close the file before applying the Open as Library command. See Chapter 26 to learn more about the Library feature.

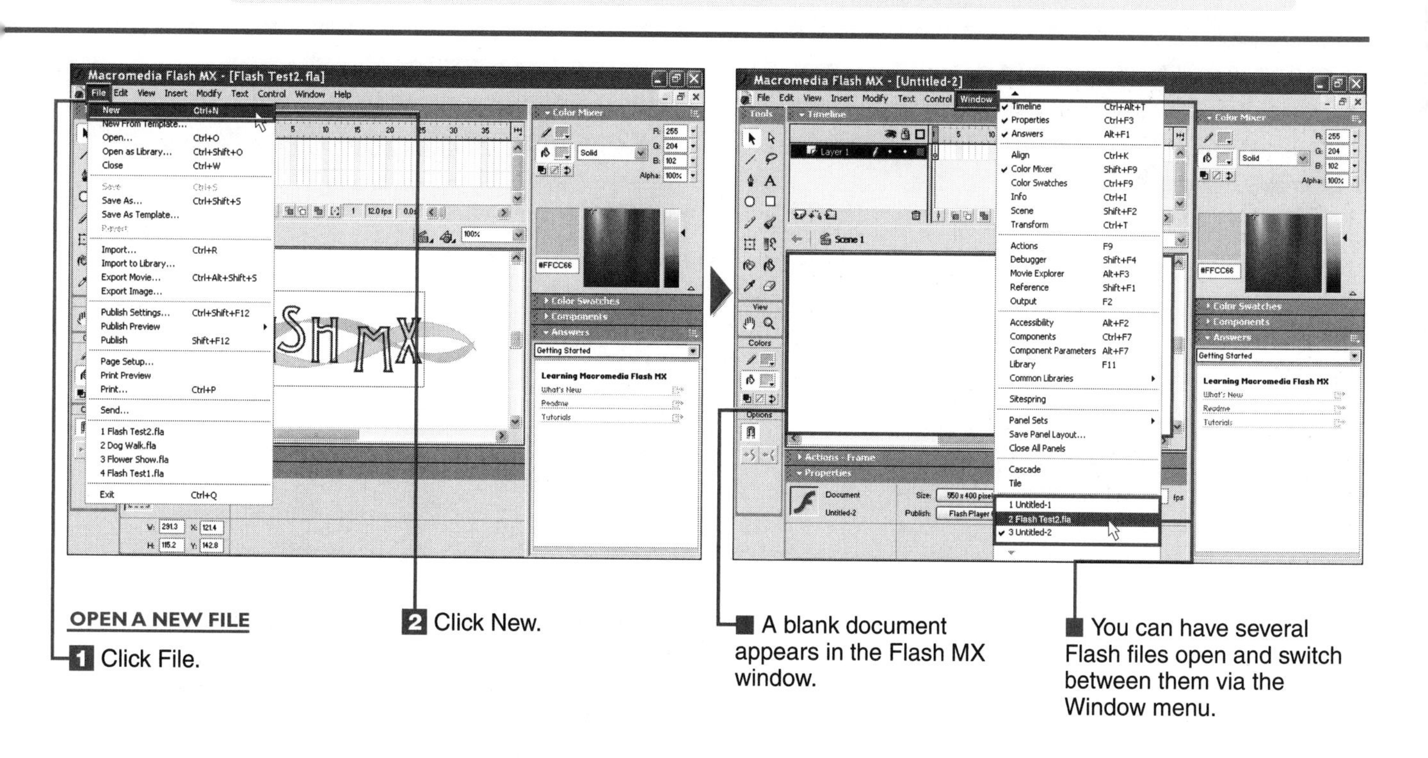

OPEN A NEW FILE

1 Click File.

2 Click New.

■ A blank document appears in the Flash MX window.

■ You can have several Flash files open and switch between them via the Window menu.

SAVE AND CLOSE A FLASH FILE

As you create movies in Flash MX, you need to save the files before closing in order to work on them again. By default, all Flash files are saved in the FLA format. After you have completed a Flash movie, you can publish it to a Web page or to a self-extracting file, both of which use another file format. To learn more about the Flash MX publishing options, see Chapter 34.

To perform a simple save and name your file, use the Save As dialog box. From there, you can enter the name that you want to use for the file and save the file to a specific folder or drive.

You can close Flash files that you are no longer using to free up memory on your computer. When closing files, you can close just the file or both the file and the Flash MX program. If you have not saved your changes yet, you will be prompted to do so.

It is a good practice to save your work often. Flash MX does not offer an automatic save feature, so it is up to you as the Flash author to save your work frequently in case of power surges or outages.

SAVE A FILE

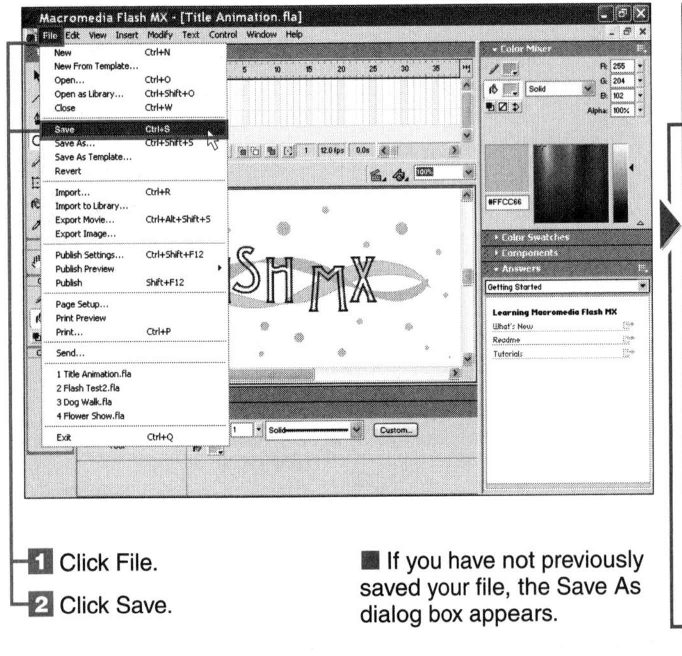

1 Click File.

2 Click Save.

■ If you have not previously saved your file, the Save As dialog box appears.

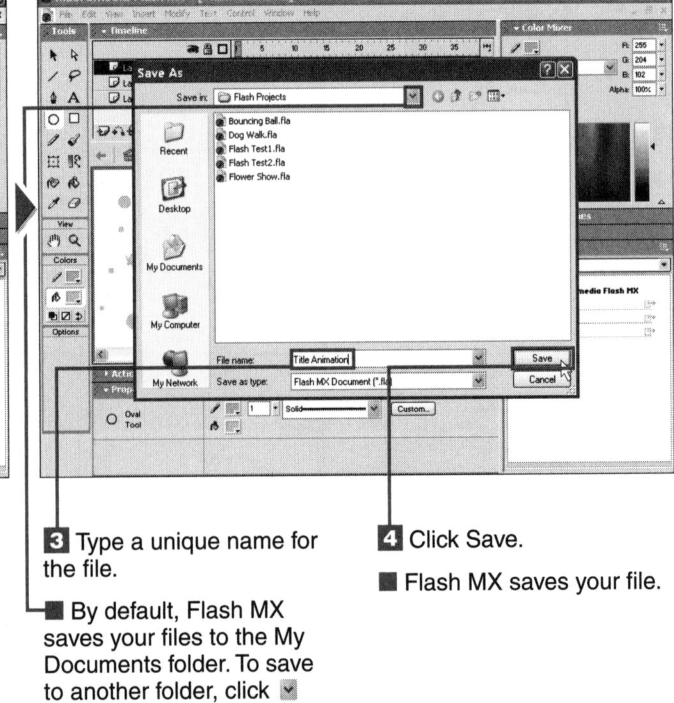

3 Type a unique name for the file.

■ By default, Flash MX saves your files to the My Documents folder. To save to another folder, click ▾ and select another location.

4 Click Save.

■ Flash MX saves your file.

How do I save a previously saved file under a new name?

✔ You can copy a previously saved file and save it under a new filename. You can then make changes to the copied file without worrying about changing the original file. To do so, click File and then Save As. This opens the Save As dialog box. Enter a new name for the file and click Save.

What is the keyboard shortcut for saving a file?

✔ You can press Ctrl + S (⌘ + S) to quickly save a file.

Can I save a Flash file in another file format?

✔ Yes; however, you cannot use the Save command unless you want to save as a Flash 5 file. Instead, you must use the Export Movie command. For example, if you prefer to save a file as a QuickTime movie or a Windows AVI file, click File and then Export Movie to open the Export dialog box. Click the Save as Type ▾ and select another file type from the list. Give the file a unique filename and click Save.

CLOSE A FILE

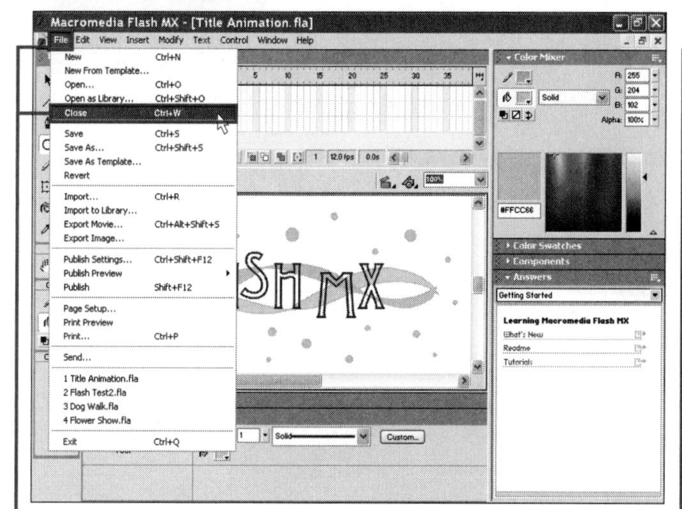

1 Save your file.

2 Click File.

3 Click Close.

Note: If you have not saved your changes, Flash prompts you to do so with a dialog box. Click Yes.

■ Flash closes the file you were working on, but the program window remains open.

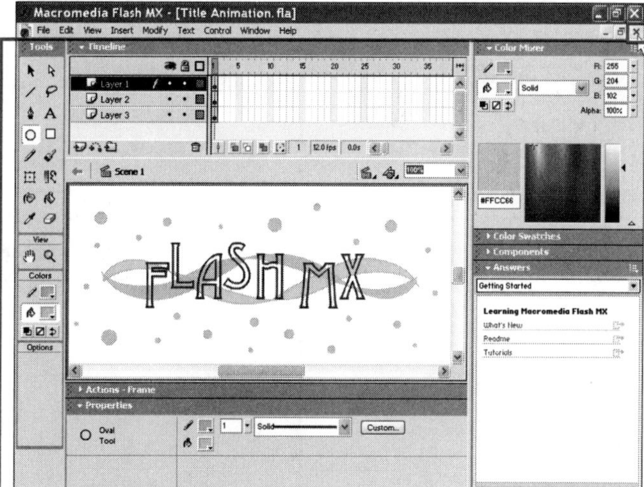

USING THE CLOSE BUTTON

1 Save your file.

Note: To save a file, see page 336.

2 Click ×.

Note: If you have not saved your changes, Flash prompts you to do so with a dialog box. Click Yes.

■ Flash closes the file.

Note: Clicking the program window's ☒ button instead of the file's × button closes the Flash MX application entirely.

USING A FLASH TEMPLATE

You can use a template to speed up document creation in Flash MX. Design templates can help you build specialized content for your projects. New to Flash MX, you can create your own templates or utilize built-in templates.

Flash MX installs with a library of sample templates in seven different categories: Ads, Broadcast, Menus, Mobile Devices, Photo Slideshow, Presentation, and Quiz. Each category includes a variety of elements, such as banner ads, drop-down menus, presentation styles, and more. You can pick and choose which template elements you want to use.

For example, you can use the 468 x 60 banner under the Ads category to help you create a Web page banner measuring 468 x 60 pixels. This particular banner size follows the Interactive Advertising Bureau (IAB) guidelines for creating effective advertising on the Web. In other words, you can rest assured that your banner size meets the IAB standards, which is a commonly accepted format found throughout the Web.

After applying a template, you can add your elements and formatting and then save your work. You can also use a blank template or modify an existing template and save the file as a unique template to use again and again.

USING A FLASH TEMPLATE

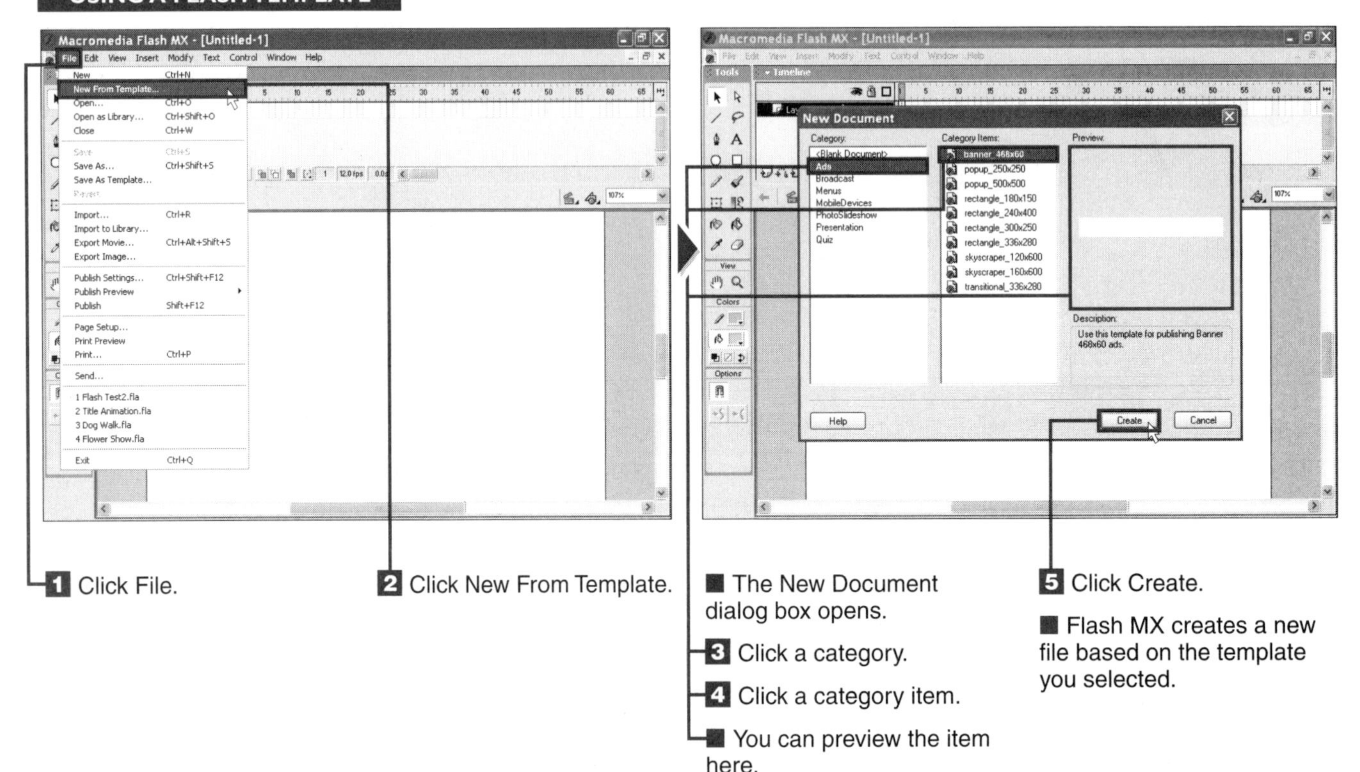

1 Click File.

2 Click New From Template.

■ The New Document dialog box opens.

3 Click a category.

4 Click a category item.

■ You can preview the item here.

5 Click Create.

■ Flash MX creates a new file based on the template you selected.

What should I do with the template instructions?

✔ When you assign a new template, an instructional guide layer appears on the Stage and in the Timeline detailing how to use the template. The instructions are merely an interactive tutorial to help you learn more about the template. You can click the Continue arrow to view more details. After you read about the template, you can delete or hide the guide layer.

Do I have to type a description for the new template?

✔ No, but doing so may help you remember what is on the template. The description appears in the New Document dialog box when you click the template.

How do I hide the template's guide layer?

✔ Although the guide layer does not appear in your final project, you can hide the layer so you can more easily see and work on the template. Click the guide layer's Show/Hide column in the Timeline (⊡ changes to ☒). To work on another layer in the template, click the layer name. See Chapter 25 to learn more about working with layers in the Timeline.

Can I delete the instructional guide layer instead of hiding it?

✔ Yes. Click the guide layer name in the Timeline and then click Delete (🗑). The guide layer is removed from your project.

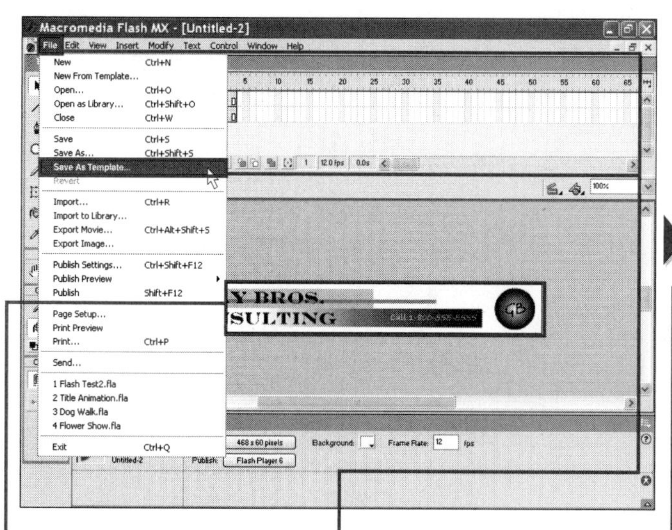

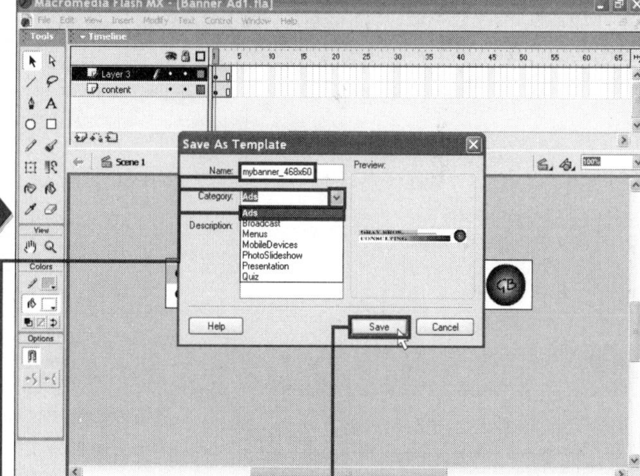

SAVE YOUR OWN TEMPLATE

1 Create a document or modify a template, including all the elements and formatting you want to save.

2 Click File.

3 Click Save As Template.

■ The Save As Template dialog box opens.

4 Type a unique name for the template.

5 Click the Category ▾.

6 Click a category.

■ You can also type in a description for the new template.

7 Click Save.

■ Flash saves the template.

UNDERSTANDING THE FLASH TIMELINE

The Flash Timeline contains the frames, layers, and scenes that make up a movie. You can use the Timeline to organize and control your movies.

By default, the Timeline appears docked near the top of the program window. If you are new to Flash, take a moment and familiarize yourself with the Timeline elements.

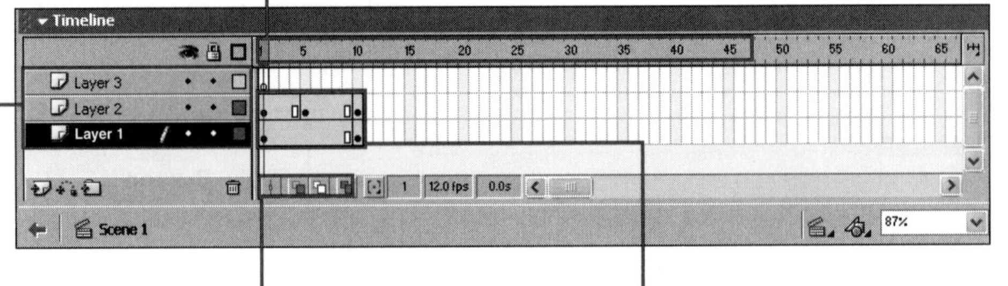

Frame Numbers

Frames appear in chronological order in the Timeline, and each frame has a number.

Layers

Use *layers* to organize artwork, animation, sound, and interactive elements. Layers enable you to keep pieces of artwork separate. Flash MX combines them to form a cohesive image. For example, a company logo might include a layer of text and another layer with a graphic shape.

Timeline Buttons

Scattered around the Timeline are buttons for controlling frames, layers, and movies.

Frames

Flash divides lengths of time in a movie into *frames*. Frames enable you to control what appears in animation sequences and which sounds play.

Playhead and Frame Display

The *Playhead*, also called the Current Frame Indicator, marks the current frame displayed on the Stage.

Click a frame to display its contents on the Stage and move the Playhead. You can also drag the Playhead across the frames to simulate the animation on the Stage.

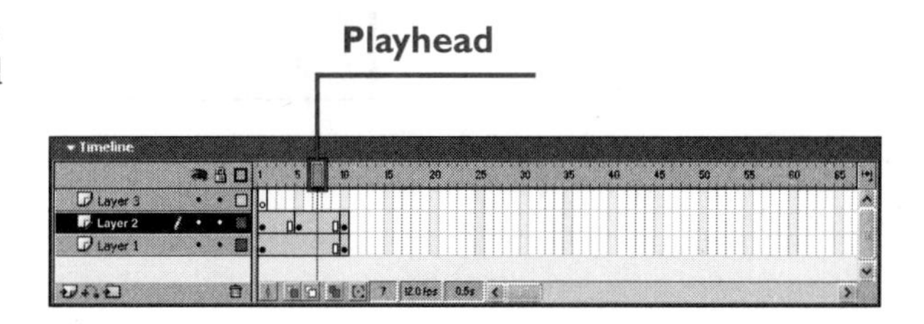

Layers and Layer Buttons

You can have numerous layers in a single frame. Newer layers are listed at the top of the layer stack. Layers help you to organize graphics as well as create backgrounds and masking effects.

Directly above the layer names are icons that represent the status of the layer, such as whether a layer is hidden, locked, or outlined on the Flash Stage. Below the layers are buttons for adding and deleting layers. For more information on working with the Timeline layers, see Chapter 25.

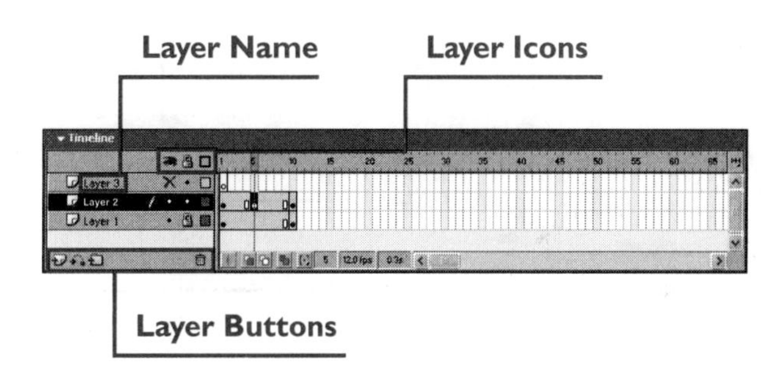

Timeline Controls

Click the Timeline button (![]) to display a drop-down menu of customizing options that control how Flash MX displays the frames. For example, you can enlarge or shrink the frame size. This is particularly helpful if you are having trouble seeing the individual frames on the Timeline.

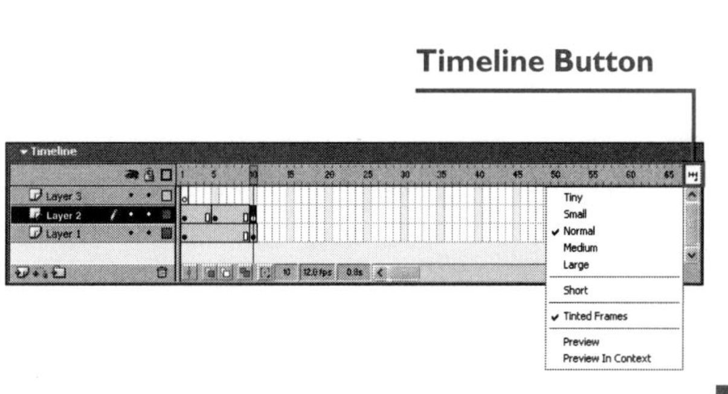

MOVE AND DOCK THE TIMELINE

You can use the Timeline to view frames and content in your Flash movies. The Flash MX Timeline is an essential tool for animating graphics. By default, the Timeline appears at the top of the work area; however, you can move the Timeline around the program window or dock it to any side of the window.

You may prefer to move the Timeline out of the way when you are drawing on the Stage, thus giving you more room to draw. In this case, you can hide the Timeline and redisplay it when you need it. Flash Timelines and panels are collapsible, which means you can reduce the Timeline or panel window to a title bar and quickly expand its full contents again by clicking the title bar.

Or you may prefer the Timeline docked in another position. For example, a vertical docking enables you to see all the layers in the Timeline but decreases the number of frames visible.

When the Timeline is not docked, it appears to float as its own window. You can drag the Timeline's drag area to move the Timeline window around on-screen. You can click the window's Close button (☒) to close the floating Timeline entirely.

MOVE THE TIMELINE

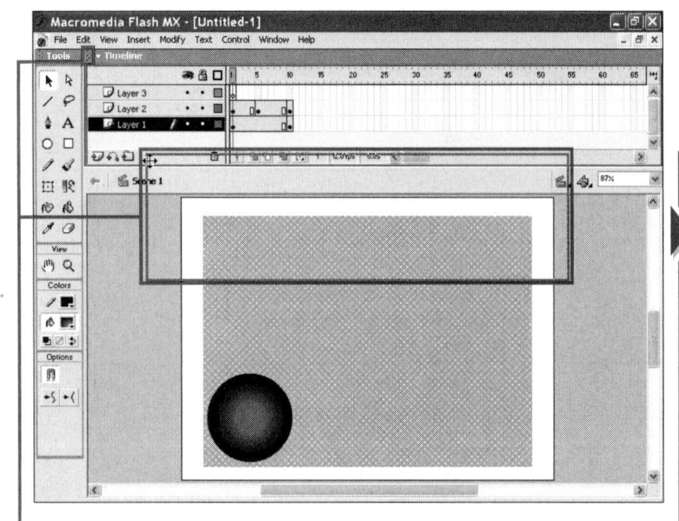

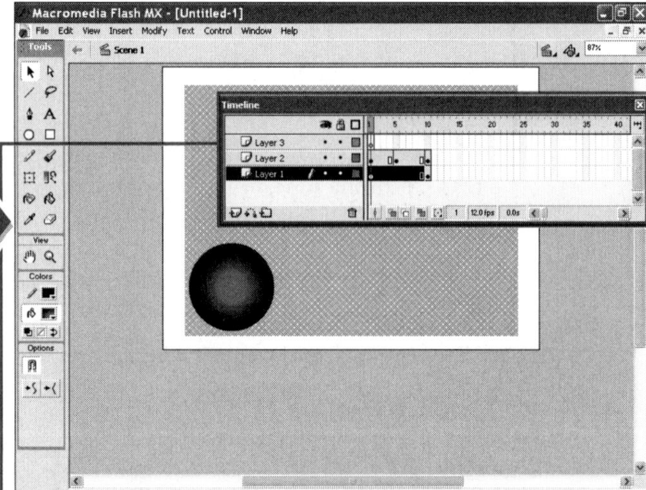

1 Click and drag the Timeline's drag area (↖ changes to ✥).

■ As you drag, an outline of the Timeline moves away from its docked position.

Note: You can use this same technique to undock and move panels, too.

2 When you have positioned the Timeline where you want it on-screen, release the mouse button.

■ The Timeline is repositioned.

Can I collapse the Timeline?

✔ Yes, you can collapse program elements, such as the Timeline and panels, in Flash MX. You can collapse the Timeline by clicking the Timeline's title bar to increase your drawing room. To expand the Timeline, click the title bar again.

How can I hide the Timeline entirely?

✔ You can completely remove the Timeline from the screen by hiding the Timeline. Click View and then Timeline. This turns off the Timeline display on-screen. You can also use the keyboard shortcuts Ctrl + Alt + T (Option + ⌘ + T) to toggle the Timeline on or off.

Can I customize my Timeline?

✔ Flash MX offers you several customization settings you can use to control the Timeline's appearance. For example, you can enlarge the size of the frames or shorten the layer/frame height. To do so, click ⊞ to reveal a drop-down menu of Timeline controls and select the customizing feature you want to apply.

Hoc can I resize the Timeline?

✔ You can drag the bottom border edge to resize the Timeline.

DOCK THE TIMELINE

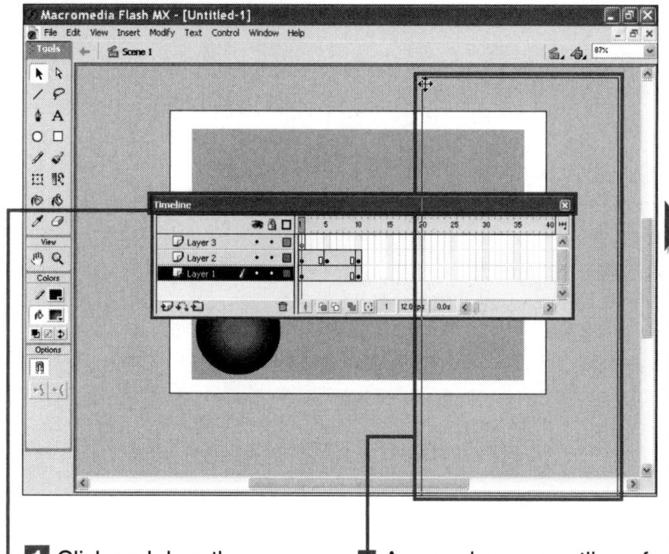

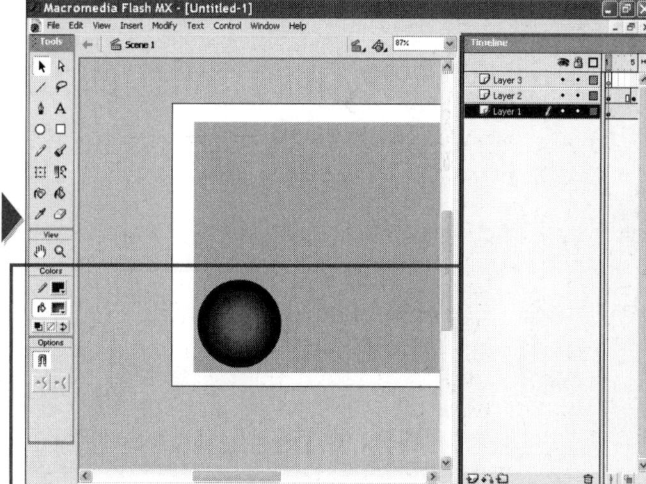

1 Click and drag the Timeline's title bar area to the window edge where you want to dock it.

■ As you drag, an outline of the Timeline moves with the mouse pointer.

2 Release the mouse button.

■ The Timeline docks and resizes to fit the horizontal or vertical space in the program window.

Note: This example shows the Timeline docked on the right side of the screen. Notice this arrangement does not leave much room to view Timeline frames.

CHANGE THE STAGE SIZE

The *Stage* is the on-screen area where you can view the contents of a frame and draw graphic objects. You can control the size and appearance of the Stage.

The size of the Stage determines the size of your Flash movie screen. You can specify exactly how big you want the movie screen to be by designating the screen's width and height in the Document Properties dialog box. By default, Flash sets the Stage size at 550 x 400 pixels for every movie file you create. If you do not want to use the default size, you must set your own dimensions. The very minimum size you can set is 1 x 1 pixels, and the maximum is 2,880 x 2,880 pixels.

It is a good idea to set your movie Stage size before adding content to your frames. If you set a size after creating your movie, you may end up needing to reposition objects in your movie to fit the Stage size.

The Document Properties dialog box offers two Match options you can use to help you determine Stage size if you do not want to enter a specific measurement: Match Printer or Match Contents. Use the Printer button to change the dimension settings to the maximum print area allowed on your printer. Use the Contents button to set the Stage dimensions to fit all the content with an equal amount of space all around.

CHANGE THE STAGE SIZE

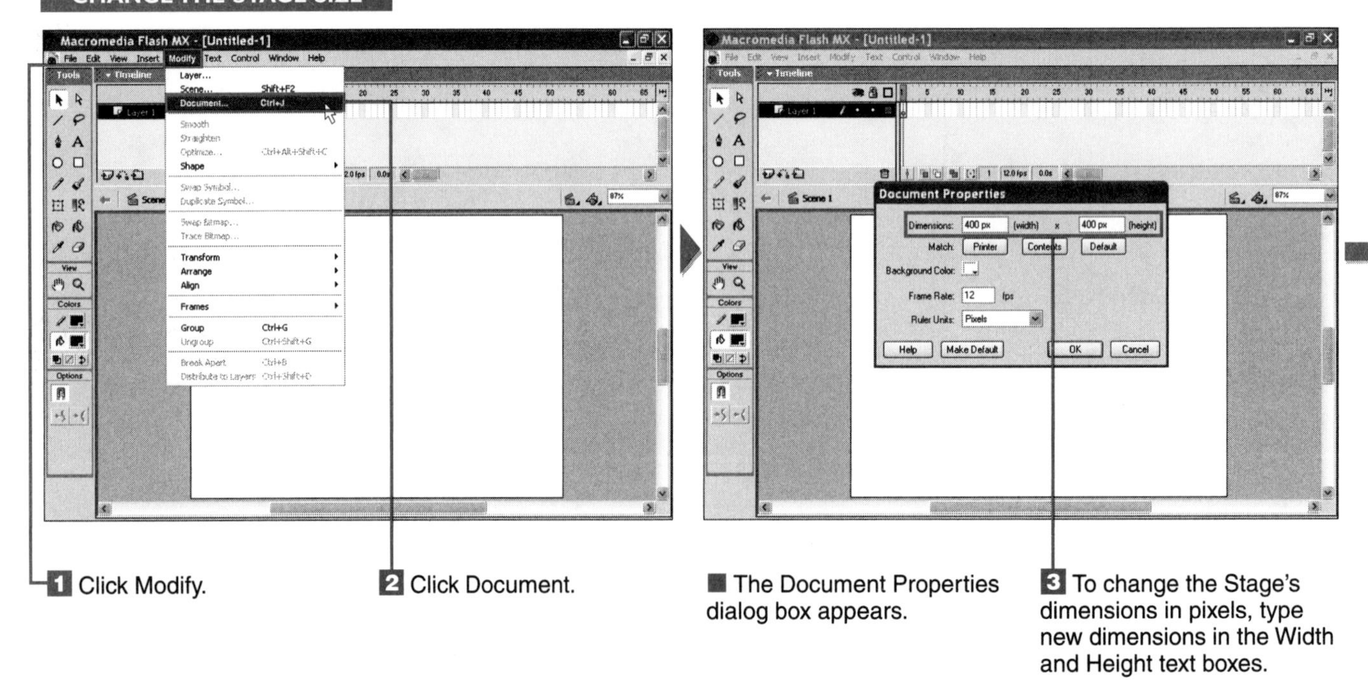

1 Click Modify.

2 Click Document.

■ The Document Properties dialog box appears.

3 To change the Stage's dimensions in pixels, type new dimensions in the Width and Height text boxes.

How do I specify different units of measurement for the Stage?

✔ From the Document Properties dialog box, click the Ruler Units ▾ and then click on the unit of measurement you want to apply. The unit of measurement immediately changes in the Width and Height text boxes, and you can now set the appropriate measurements.

How can I save the Stage settings for future movies?

✔ Use the Make Default button in the Document Properties dialog box to save your settings as the default Stage measurements for all Flash movies. Any new Flash project files you create will use the new measurements.

How do I set a new background color?

✔ By default, the Stage background color is set to white. To set another color as a background, click the Background Color button (□) in the Document Properties dialog box. A pop-up palette of color choices appears. Click the color you want to apply. The color you choose is used throughout your movie as the Stage background color.

Can I use the Property inspector to set the Stage size?

✔ Yes. In the Property inspector, click the Size button to quickly open the Document Properties dialog box and set a new size for the Stage.

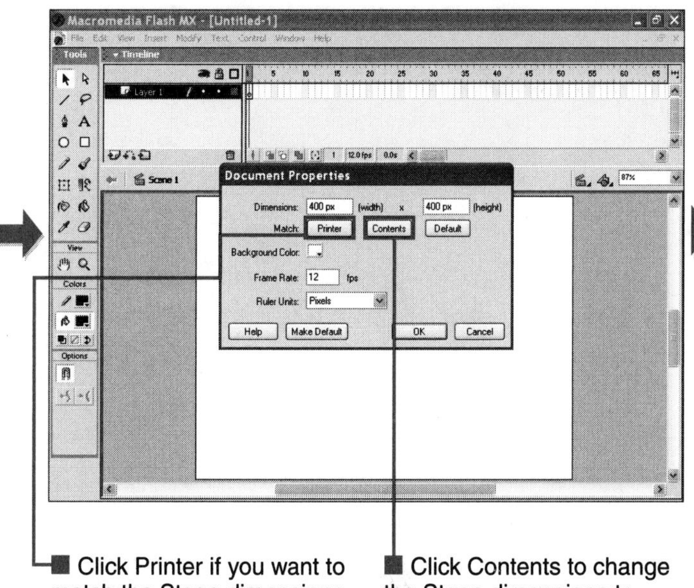

■ Click Printer if you want to match the Stage dimensions to the maximum available print area size used for your printer.

■ Click Contents to change the Stage dimensions to match the contents of your movie with equal spacing all around.

Note: Click Default to return the Stage size to the default size.

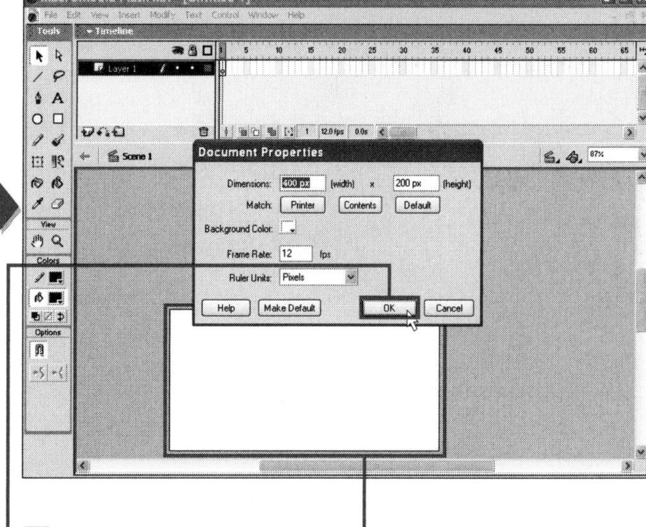

4 Click OK.

■ Flash MX resizes the Stage area according to your new settings.

USING THE PROPERTY INSPECTOR PANEL

You can use the Property Inspector panel to see the properties of the object you are currently working with on the Stage and make changes to those properties when applicable. The Property inspector is new to Flash MX and offers you quick and easy access to property controls.

The Property inspector acts as a panel, which can be collapsed, hidden from view, or moved. By default, the Property inspector is docked at the bottom of the Flash MX program window.

Depending on what object you select on the Stage, the Property inspector changes to reflect the properties associated with the object. For example, if you click on text, the Property inspector displays text properties, such as font and size. If you click on a graphic object, such as shape, the Property inspector displays properties related to the shape, such as stroke and fill colors.

If an object includes numerous properties, the Property inspector grows in size. You can choose to collapse the properties and view only the most important properties, thus freeing up some more viewable area of the Stage.

USING THE PROPERTY INSPECTOR PANEL

COLLAPSE AND EXPAND THE PROPERTY INSPECTOR

1 Click the Collapse button (▼ changes to ▶).

Note: It is a good idea to collapse the Property inspector when not in use to free up workspace.

Note: This example shows the text properties listed in the Property inspector.

■ The Property inspector collapses.

2 To expand the panel again, click the Expand button (▶ changes to ▼).

Can I close the Property inspector entirely?

✔ Yes. To close any panel, click the panel's Options Menu control (☰) to display a pop-up menu, then click Close Panel. The Property inspector closes completely. You can also right-click the panel's title bar and click Close Panel. To reopen the panel again, click the Window menu and click Properties.

Is there a quicker way to expand or collapse the Property inspector?

✔ Yes. You can press Ctrl + F3 (⌘ + F3) to toggle the Property inspector open or closed. You can also click on the panel's title bar to toggle the panel open or closed.

Can I move the Property inspector?

✔ Yes. Like all panels in Flash MX, you can move the Property inspector to create a floating panel or you can dock the panel on another side of the screen. To move the panel, click and drag the drag area, the upper left corner of the panel. To collapse a floating panel, click the panel's title bar. To expand it again, click the bar again.

How can I change the Stage background color using the Property inspector?

✔ Click the Background button (■) and click another color from the pop-up palette that appears.

SHOW AND HIDE PROPERTIES

1 Click the Expand/Collapse button (▲). (▲ changes to ▼.)

■ A portion of the Property inspector collapses.

2 To view all properties again, click ▼ again (▼ changes to ▲).

WORK WITH PANELS

You can use the Flash MX panels to access additional controls. Flash MX offers over a dozen different panels, each displaying options related to a specific task. For example, the Color Mixer panel enables you to change the stroke or fill color of a selected object on the Stage. Panels can appear docked on the far right side of the program window or they can appear as floating panels.

When you open Flash MX for the first time, the Default Layout panel set appears. This panel set includes the Color Mixer, Color Swatches, Components, and Answers panels docked on the right side of the screen. You can replace the Default Layout panel set with another panel set. Flash MX installs with three Designer panel sets and three Developer panel sets.

Each panel set includes a different combination of useful panels you might want to have open on-screen. All panel sets include the Property inspector and Actions panel. You can also rearrange panels and create your own panel set to use over and over again.

You can move and dock panels as you like in Flash MX. You can also close panels to free up on-screen workspace.

WORK WITH PANELS

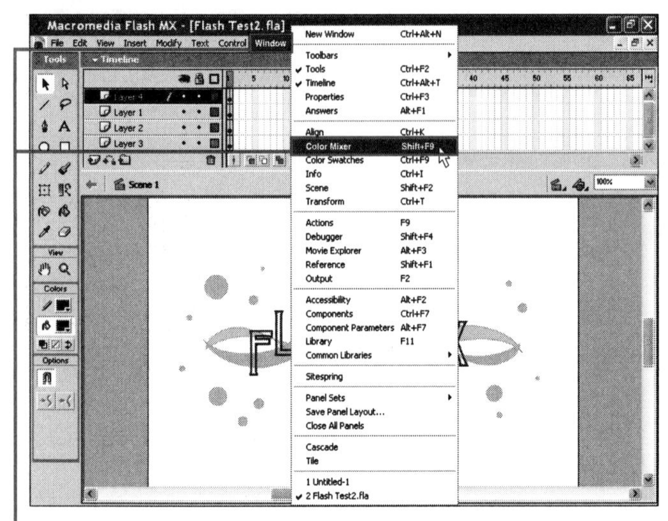

OPEN PANELS

1 Click Window.

2 Click the panel you want to open.

Note: A check mark next to the panel name indicates the panel is open; no check mark means the panel is closed.

■ The panel appears on-screen.

CLOSE PANELS

1 Click Window.

2 Click the panel you want to close.

■ The panel closes.

■ To collapse a panel instead of close it, click the Collapse button (▼ changes to ▶).

Note: Closing panels frees up on-screen workspace.

Can I completely remove a panel from the program window?

✔ Yes. Click the panel's Options Menu control ( ) to display a pop-up menu, and then click Close Panel. You can also right-click on the panel's title bar and click Close Panel. The panel closes completely. To reopen it again, click the Window menu and click the panel you want to open.

Can I undock a panel?

✔ Yes. Click and drag the panel's drag area, the upper left corner of the panel. To collapse a floating panel, simply click the panel's title bar. To expand it again, click the bar again.

Can I resize a panel?

✔ Yes. Move the mouse pointer over the edge of the panel (changes to ⟷), and then drag the panel border to a new size.

How do I make my own panel set?

✔ Display the panels you want to save as a set. Click Window, and then click Save Panel Layout. This opens the Save Panel Layout dialog box. Type a name for the panel set and click OK. The panel set is now available in the list of panels to apply when needed.

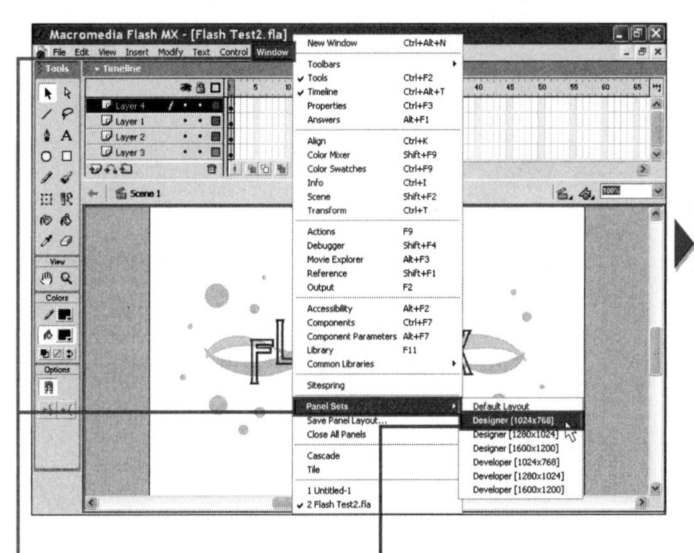

OPEN A PANEL SET

1 Click Window.

2 Click Panel Sets.

3 Click the panel set you want to apply.

■ The panel set appears on-screen.

FIND HELP WITH FLASH

When you run across a program feature or technique that you do not understand, consult the Flash Help system. The Flash MX help files offer a wide variety of topics ranging from basic Flash features, such as how to use on-screen buttons and drawing tools, to advanced features, such as how to write scripts using ActionScript. The Flash help files include a full reference dictionary of ActionScript commands, as well as tutorials that step you through common Flash tasks.

To fully utilize the Help features, you must have an Internet connection and access to a Web browser. For example, when you access the offline Help HTML page, your default browser window automatically opens, and you can peruse a variety of Flash MX topics. Other features, such as the Flash Support Center, require an Internet connection in order to log on to the Macromedia Web site.

When you install Flash MX, a number of lessons and sample Flash files are loaded onto your computer. You can use these features to help you learn the program.

FIND HELP WITH FLASH

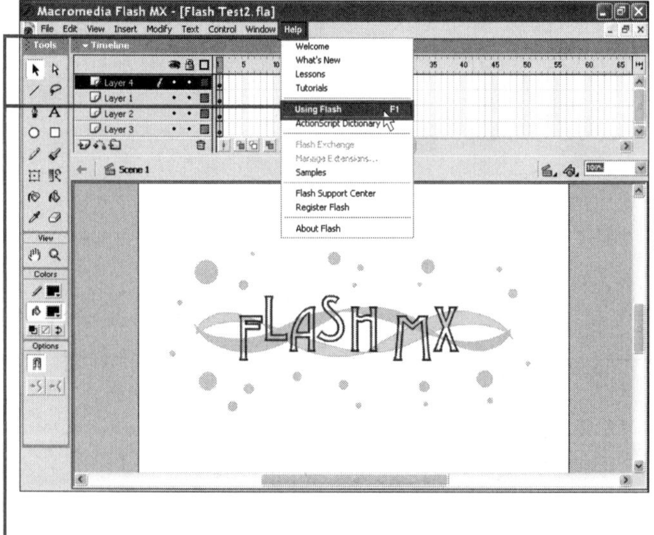

1 Click Help.

2 Click Using Flash.

■ To access the sample movies or lessons, you can click Samples or Lessons in the Help menu.

■ Your Web browser launches immediately and displays an offline Web page.

3 Click the Using Flash link to reveal Flash topic headings.

4 Click a topic heading to reveal topics.

■ Scroll through the topics and follow links to the information you want.

5 Click a topic to display the information.

6 To search for a specific Flash topic, click Search.

How does the Answers panel work?

✔ You can use the Answers panel to access Flash MX tutorials and learn about new features. Simply click a link to open an offline Web page.

How would I use the sample files?

✔ Flash ships with a large number of sample movie files that you can study to help you learn how the program works as well as a variety of things you can do with it. When you click Samples from the Help menu, a Web page opens displaying links to various sample files. You can click a link to view the sample.

What is the difference between lessons and tutorials?

✔ The Help menu has commands for both Lessons and Tutorials. Lessons are a set of interactive mini-windows you can view from the Flash MX program window. The lessons cover a variety of topics, including drawing, layers, and animation. You can progress through each lesson, step by step. Tutorials start out like lessons, but when you click a specific tutorial, your Web browser opens and displays the information from the Flash help files.

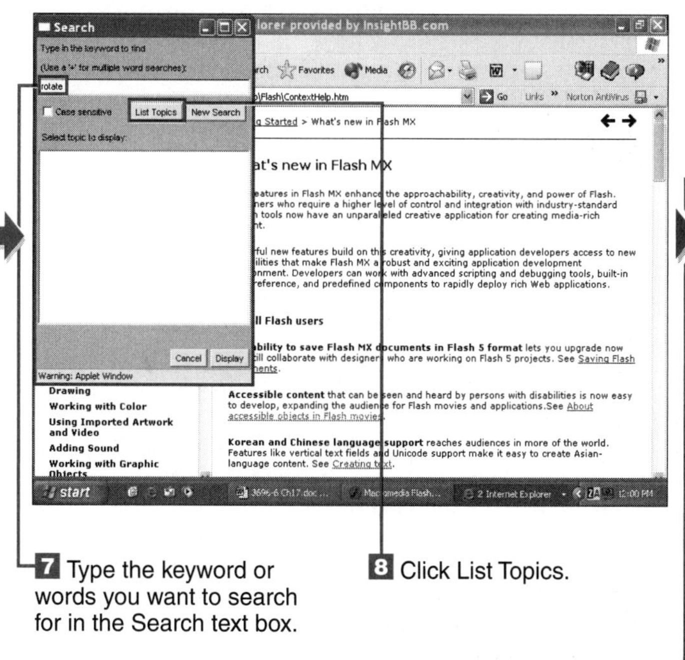

7 Type the keyword or words you want to search for in the Search text box.

8 Click List Topics.

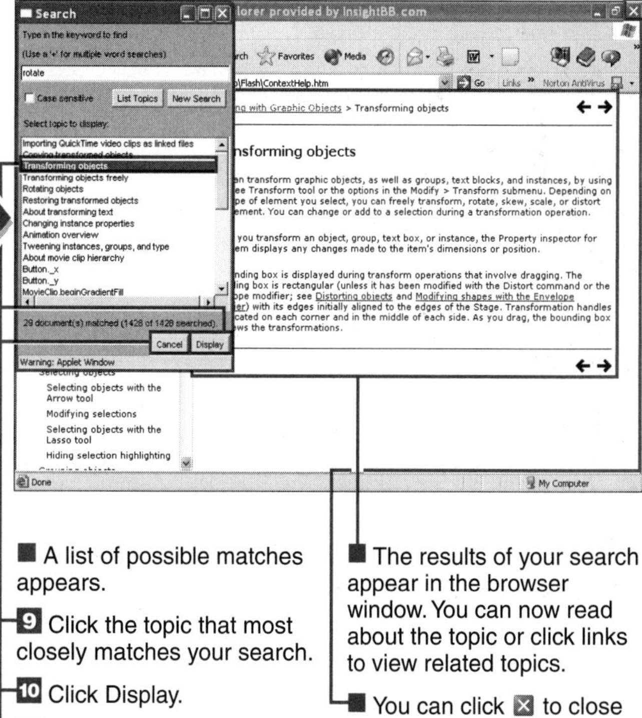

■ A list of possible matches appears.

9 Click the topic that most closely matches your search.

10 Click Display.

11 Click Cancel to close the Search window.

■ The results of your search appear in the browser window. You can now read about the topic or click links to view related topics.

■ You can click ☒ to close the Browser window and return to Flash MX.

INTRODUCTION TO FLASH OBJECTS

You can create all kinds of drawings in Flash MX. The program includes a variety of tools for creating simple shapes or complex images to use in your Flash movies.

Drawings you create in Flash MX are composed of lines, called *strokes*, and solid colors that fill the interior of connected lines. An item you draw, such as a single square or a collection of images, is called an *object*. With the tools found on the Drawing toolbar, you can create simple objects, such as shapes, or complex objects that involve layers, grouped elements, and more.

If you have worked with other drawing programs, such as Macromedia FreeHand, you will find the drawing features in Flash MX familiar. For example, you can use the Pencil tool to draw freeform lines or the Line tool to draw straight lines. You can combine simple objects to create complex drawings or remove parts of shapes and lines to create new shapes. You can change the color, scale, and positioning of an object.

Whether you are an experienced graphic designer or are just learning to create graphics with a computer, Flash drawing tools are ample for making detailed drawings or simple objects.

Shape Recognition

It is not always easy to draw with a mouse, but Flash makes it simpler with shape recognition. Draw a rough idea of a shape, and Flash automatically cleans it up for you. For example, if you draw a round shape and connect the line to the start of the shape, Flash assumes you are drawing an oval and automatically adjusts the drawing to conform to a circular shape. Shape recognition is turned on by default, but you can turn the feature off if you do not want Flash to guess at what you are trying to draw on-screen.

Segments

When you draw overlapping lines or shapes, the areas that overlap divide the image into segments. For example, if you draw a straight line through the middle of an oval shape, the line is divided into three sections: the section that falls outside the left side of the oval, the section that goes through the middle of the oval, and the section that falls outside the right side of the oval. You can use the Arrow tool to manipulate any of the three line segments separately, if needed. If the oval shape includes a fill color in the middle, the fill is also divided into two segments by the line. You can edit each fill segment as well.

Import Graphics

You do not have to rely on your drawing skills to create objects for your movies. You can also import graphics from other programs and manipulate them with the Flash drawing tools. You can find out about importing graphic objects in Chapter 23.

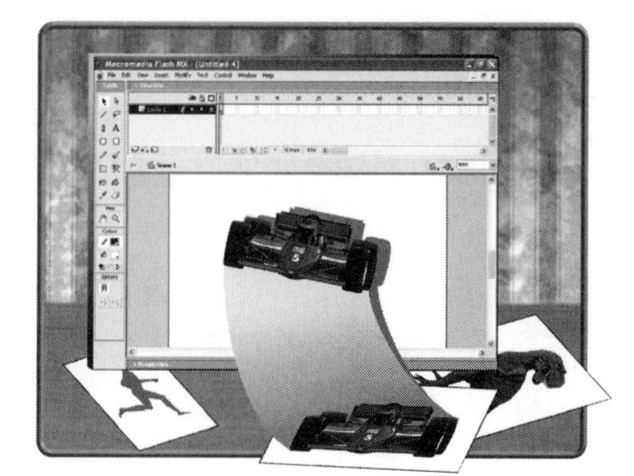

Drawing Levels

When working with objects on the Flash Stage, there are two levels: the *stage* level and the *overlay* level. The stage level is the bottom level on the Stage, and any objects you place there can interact. For example, a line and a shape can connect. Stage-level objects include anything you draw with the drawing tools.

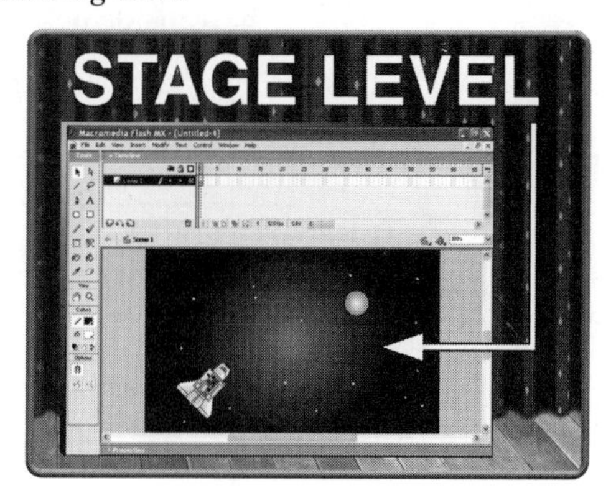

The overlay level is like a transparent sheet of paper on top of the stage level. Any object you place on the overlay level floats on top and does not interact with stage-level objects. Overlay-level objects include items you group together to act as a single unit, symbols you create for reuse throughout your movie, text blocks, and imported graphics.

As you work with objects in Flash MX, it is important to distinguish between the two levels. You may find yourself trying to make two objects interact that are actually located on two different levels.

You can make objects from different levels interact by using the Break Apart command. This command makes it easy to break apart overlay-level objects and turn them into stage-level objects that you can manipulate and edit. For example, you can turn text into graphic shapes that you can resize and rotate.

Drawing levels should not be confused with Flash layers, which allow you to place objects, animations, and actions on different layers to organize your movie.

ACQUAINT YOURSELF WITH THE DRAWING TOOLBAR

You can use the tools on the Drawing toolbar to create and work with text and graphic objects. By default, the Drawing toolbar is docked vertically on the far left side of the Flash MX program window, allowing you handy access to the many tools you need for creating objects on the Stage.

Before you start using the tools, take a moment to acquaint yourself with each tool and its function.

To hide the Drawing toolbar at any time, click Window and then Tools.

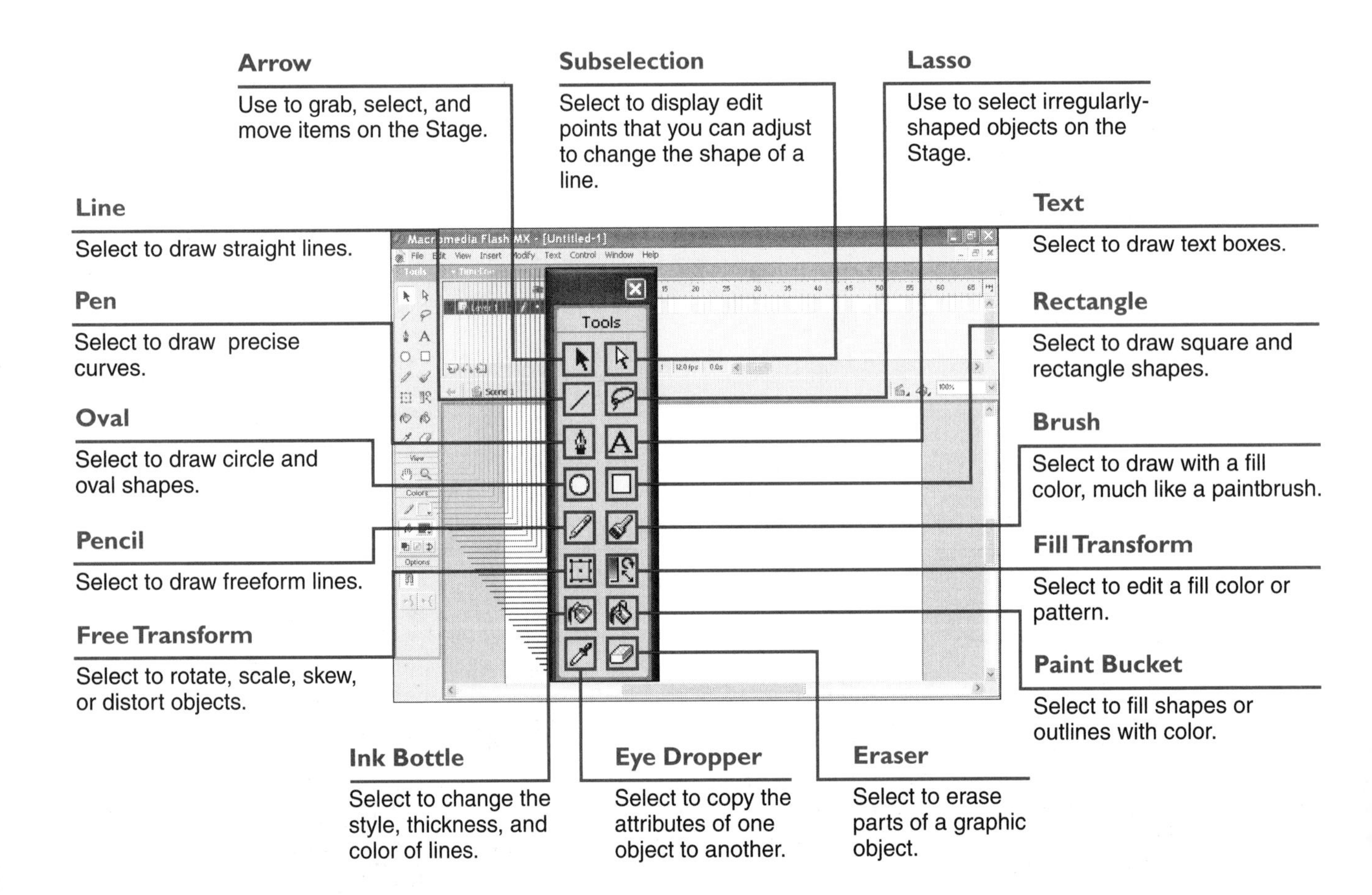
Arrow
Use to grab, select, and move items on the Stage.
Subselection
Select to display edit points that you can adjust to change the shape of a line.
Lasso
Use to select irregularly-shaped objects on the Stage.
Line
Select to draw straight lines.
Text
Select to draw text boxes.
Pen
Select to draw precise curves.
Rectangle
Select to draw square and rectangle shapes.
Oval
Select to draw circle and oval shapes.
Brush
Select to draw with a fill color, much like a paintbrush.
Pencil
Select to draw freeform lines.
Fill Transform
Select to edit a fill color or pattern.
Free Transform
Select to rotate, scale, skew, or distort objects.
Paint Bucket
Select to fill shapes or outlines with color.
Ink Bottle
Select to change the style, thickness, and color of lines.
Eye Dropper
Select to copy the attributes of one object to another.
Eraser
Select to erase parts of a graphic object.
Macromedia Flash MX - [Untitled-1]
Tools

Using the View Tools

You can use the View tools on the Drawing toolbar to change your view of the Stage area. The View tools include the Hand tool and the Zoom tool.

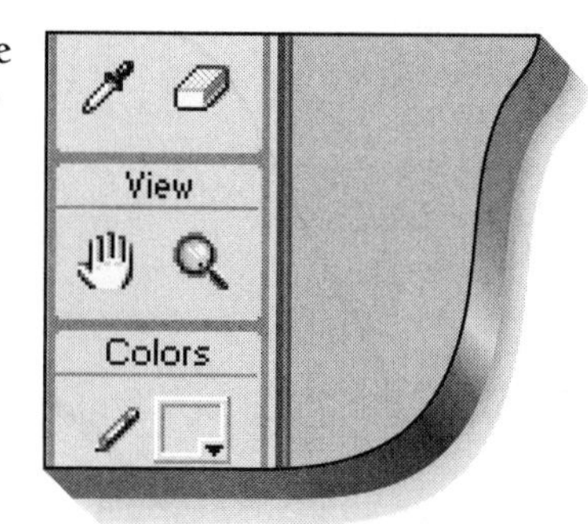

You can use the Hand tool (✋) to move your view of the objects on the Stage or in the work area by dragging the Hand tool on the Stage.

You can use the Zoom tool to magnify your view of an object on the Stage or zoom out for a view from afar. Simply click the Zoom Tool button (🔍), click a view option from the Options tray (Enlarge or Reduce), and then click over the Stage. The more you click, the greater (or lesser) your magnification.

To zoom in or out by a magnification percentage, use the Zoom box at the top of the Stage area. Click ▾ and then click a zoom percentage. You can also type an exact zoom percentage directly in the Zoom box.

You can also find additional zoom tools in the View menu. Click View and then click Zoom In or Zoom Out. Or click View, Magnification, and then select from the list of magnification levels.

Using the Color Tools

You can use the Color tools to define line and fill colors for objects you draw on the Stage. You can click the Stroke Color button (✏■) to display a palette of colors for lines. To select a color, drag the mouse pointer over your color choice and click to select the color.

To choose a fill color, click the Fill Color button (■), drag the mouse pointer over your color choice, and click to select the color.

Use the buttons directly below the Stroke and Fill Color tools to quickly modify an object's color. Click the Black and White button (■) to change the line color to black and the fill color to white. Click the No Color button (☒) to draw shapes without outlines or borders. Or click the Swap Colors button (⇅) to switch the line color to the fill color and vice versa.

Using the Option Tools

Some of the drawing tools you select may offer modifiers that enable you to set additional controls for the tool. Any modifiers associated with a tool appear in the Options tray at the bottom of the toolbar. If you click the Brush tool (🖌), additional option buttons appear for selecting brush size, shape, and paint mode. If you click the Eraser tool (⌫), additional options appear for controlling the eraser shape.

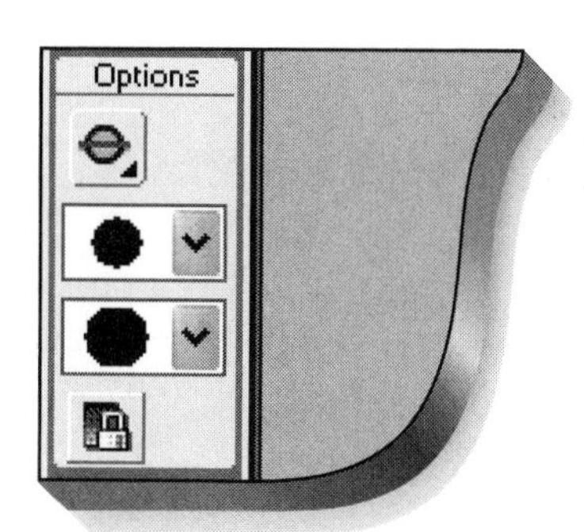

DRAW LINE SEGMENTS

You can draw all sorts of objects to use in your Flash movies and animations with lines. Lines, called *strokes* in Flash MX, can connect with other lines and shapes to create an image or shape.

The easiest way to draw straight lines in Flash is to use the Line tool. The Line tool draws perfectly straight lines. You control where the line starts and where the line stops.

To draw a freeform line, use the Pencil tool. The Pencil tool has three pencil modes that control how a line is drawn: Straighten, Smooth, or Ink.

By selecting the Straighten mode, any line you draw on the Stage straightens itself after you release the mouse button. By selecting the Smooth mode, your curved lines appear smooth. By selecting the Ink mode, the line you draw stays as is; no straightening or smoothing occurs.

The tool you choose to draw a line segment depends on the outcome you expect to create. You can use the Line tool for drawing objects or shapes with edges. You can use the Pencil tool to create curves.

DRAW LINE SEGMENTS

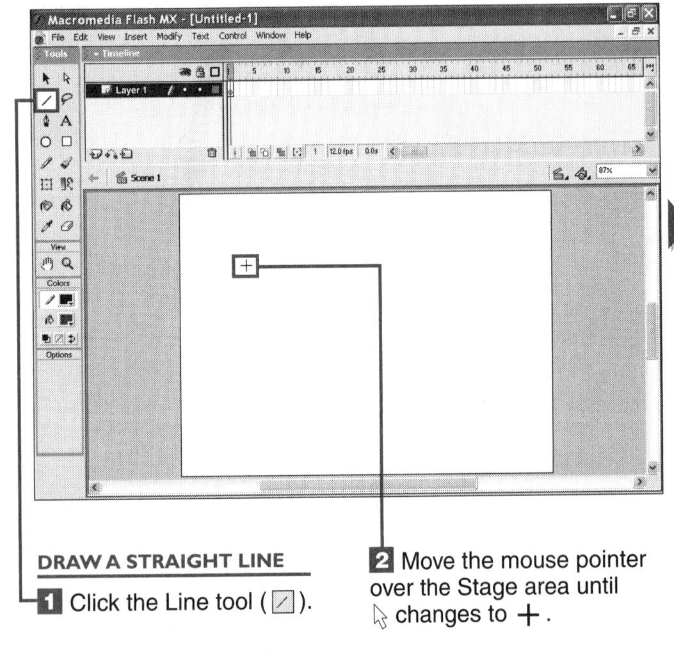

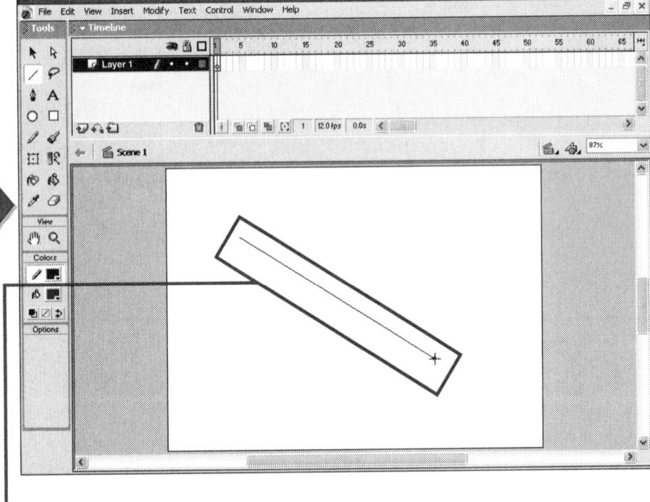

DRAW A STRAIGHT LINE

1 Click the Line tool (⁄).

2 Move the mouse pointer over the Stage area until ↖ changes to +.

3 Click and drag to draw a line of the desired length.

4 Release the mouse button.

■ The line is complete.

How do I control the line thickness?

✔ You can set a line thickness before you start drawing the actual line segment. Open the Property inspector, if it is not already open. See Chapter 20 to learn more about this panel. The Property inspector displays options for controlling line thickness, style, and color. To change the thickness, drag the thickness slider up or down. You can apply a new line thickness to an existing line by first selecting the line and then dragging the slider.

How do I keep a straight line vertical or horizontal?

✔ Using the Line tool, hold down shift and draw a line that is pretty much vertical or horizontal. Flash MX makes the line perfectly vertical or horizontal. The shift trick also works when drawing a 45-degree line.

When I draw with the Line tool, why does Flash try to connect the lines for me?

✔ Shape recognition is automatic. To disable the feature, click Edit, Preferences, and then click the Editing tab. Next, click the Recognize Shapes ▾ and click Off. Finally, click OK to close the Preferences dialog box.

Can I use a ruler to help draw my lines?

✔ Flash MX has two features to help you with objects you draw on the Stage: rulers and gridlines. To turn the rulers on, click View and then Rulers. Horizontal and vertical rulers appear around the work area. To turn on gridlines, click View, Grid, and then Show Grid.

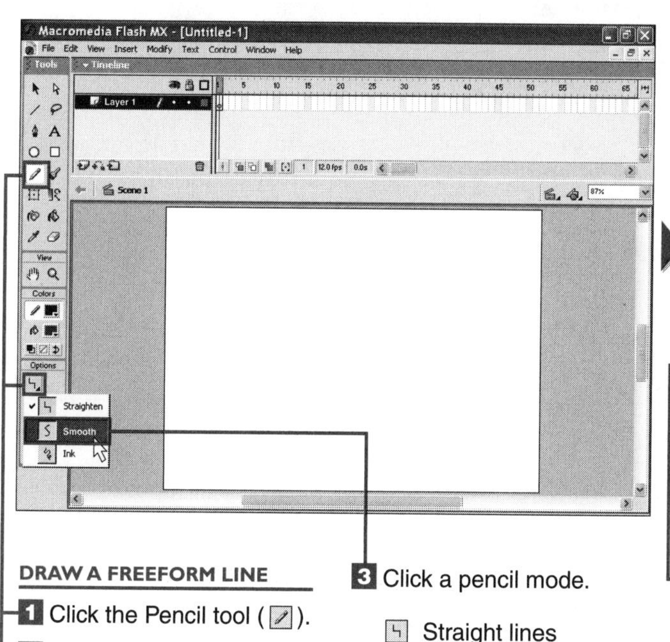

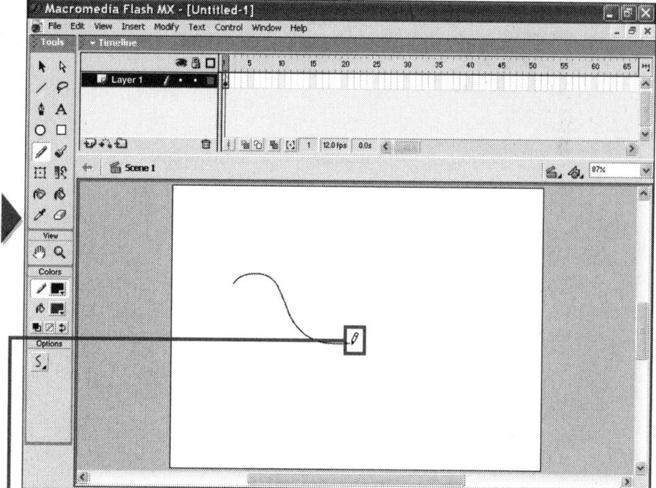

DRAW A FREEFORM LINE

1 Click the Pencil tool ( ).

2 Click the Pencil Mode button ( ).

3 Click a pencil mode.

- Straight lines
- Curvy lines
- Freeform lines

4 Click and drag the cursor on the Stage to draw the line (changes to).

5 Release the mouse button.

■ The line is complete. If you use the Straighten or Smooth mode, the line becomes straight or smooth, respectively.

FORMAT LINE SEGMENTS

You can quickly format or change the attributes of line segments you draw in Flash MX. By default, lines you draw on the Stage are solid black and 1-point thick. You can control the thickness, style, and color of a line by using the formatting controls found in the Property inspector.

You can set the formatting options before you draw a line, or you can assign formatting to an existing line. For example, you might want to change the formatting for a particular line segment in a drawing, or you might want to draw a new line that is precisely 5 points thick and dashed. Use the Property inspector options to set the exact formatting you want.

You can use the options in the Property inspector to set the formatting of lines drawn with the Line, Pen, or Pencil tool and any outlines drawn with the shape tools. Depending on the tool you select, the options that appear in the Property inspector vary.

See page 356 to find out more about drawing lines on the Stage. See page 366 to find out more about the shape tools.

FORMAT LINE SEGMENTS

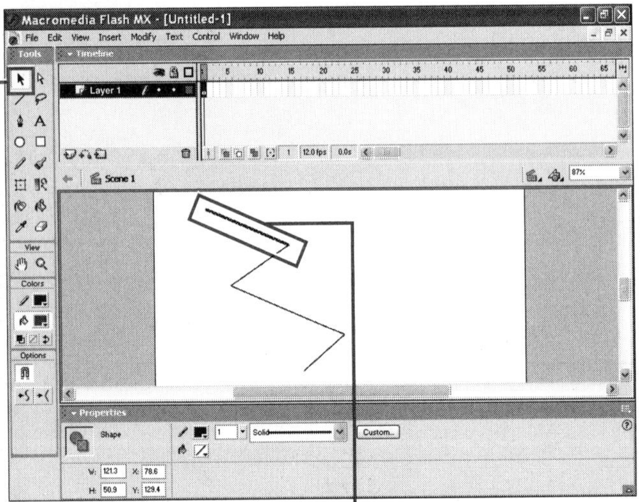

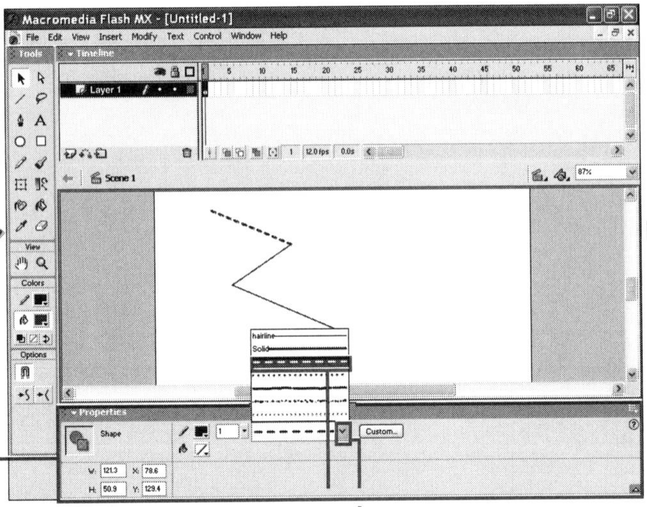

1 Click .

2 Click the line segment you want to format.

Note: To learn more about selecting objects on the Stage, see page 372.

3 If the Property inspector is not visible, display it.

Note: To display and hide the Property inspector, see page 346.

4 Click the Stroke Style .

5 Click a stroke style.

■ The line changes to your specifications.

Can I set the formatting options before actually drawing a line segment?

✔ You can change the formatting options in the Property inspector before you start drawing the line segment. If you know you want to draw a 10-point thick green line, you can set the formatting before you draw. The Property inspector settings stay in effect until you decide to change them.

How do I select all the line segments at once to change formatting?

✔ Right-click (Control-click) over a line segment, and then click Select All from the pop-up menu. Flash selects all the line segments you have drawn and any changes you make to the formatting affect all the lines.

How do I straighten a curved line?

✔ First, select the line segment you want to edit and then click Modify and Straighten. You may have to select this command several times to get the effect you want. You can also click ( ) in the Options tray at the bottom of the Drawing toolbar. See page 364 for more information.

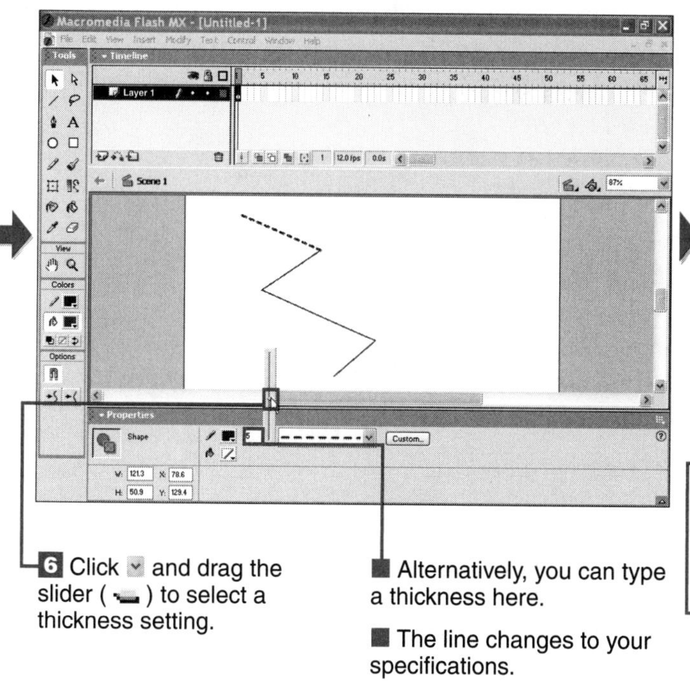

6 Click ( ) and drag the slider ( ) to select a thickness setting.

■ Alternatively, you can type a thickness here.

■ The line changes to your specifications.

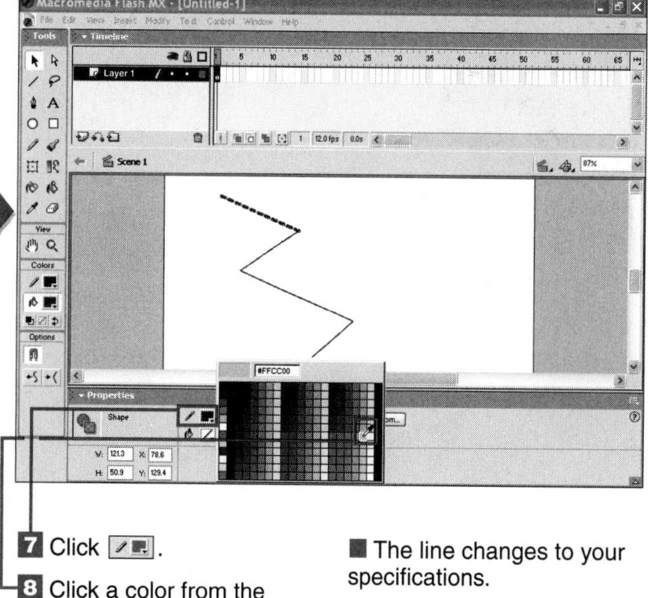

7 Click ( ).

8 Click a color from the palette.

■ The line changes to your specifications.

DRAW A CUSTOM LINE

You can select a line style and customize its appearance by using the options in the Stroke Style dialog box. This dialog box offers a variety of line styles ranging from dots to dashes to waves, thus allowing you to create unique or specialized line styles. With the options in the Stroke Style dialog box, you can specify how closely or loosely the dots or dashes appear, creating a multitude of line styles for your line segments.

Depending on the style you select, such as Dotted or Ragged, additional customizing options appear in the Stroke Style dialog box. For example, if you choose a Ragged line style, you can additionally set the wave pattern, height, length, and thickness.

The preview area of the Stroke Style dialog box enables you to see an example of what the selected options will look like when applied to a line. Experiment with the various dialog box settings to create just the right line style for your Flash drawing.

DRAW A CUSTOM LINE

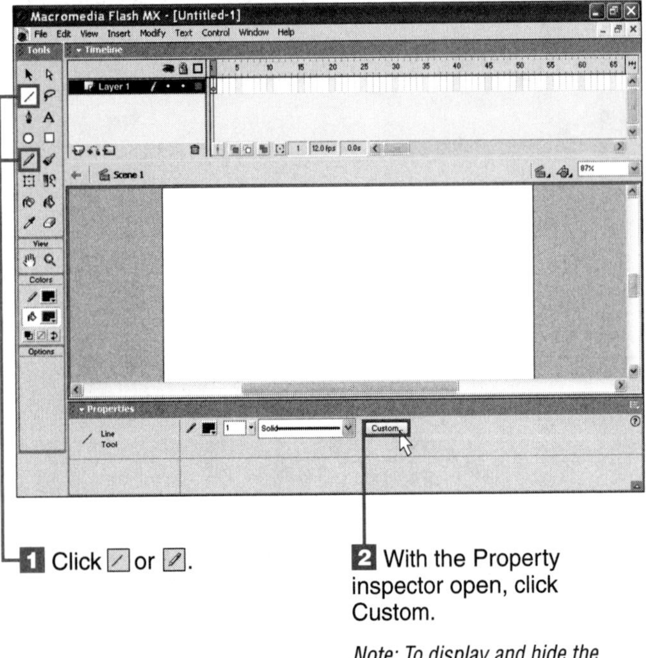

1 Click or .

2 With the Property inspector open, click Custom.

Note: To display and hide the Property inspector, see page 346.

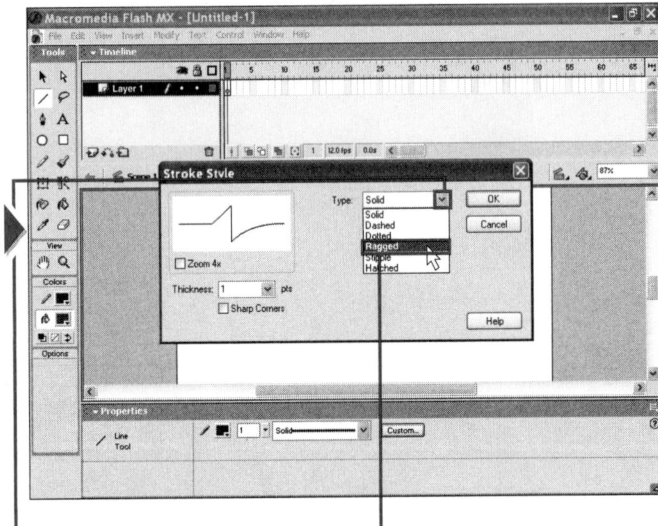

■ The Stroke Style dialog box opens.

3 Click the Type .

4 Click a line style.

■ Depending on the style you select, additional customizing options appear.

How do I fix a mistake?

✔ To undo your last action, such as drawing a line segment, just click the Edit menu and click undo. If you change your mind and want the action back, click the Edit menu and click Redo.

How do I smooth my line style?

✔ You can further customize your line segment by using the Arrow tool's Smooth feature in the Options tray on the Drawing toolbar. See page 364 for more information.

Can I turn off the shape recognition feature?

✔ Yes. By default, Flash's shape recognition feature tries to determine what sort of object you are drawing and completes the shape for you. If you draw an open-ended triangle using the Pencil tool, for example, Flash assumes that you want to draw a triangle and completes the shape. To keep the program from doing so, click Edit and then Preferences. This opens the Preferences dialog box. Click the Editing tab, click the Recognize Shapes ▾, and select Off. Click OK to exit the dialog box.

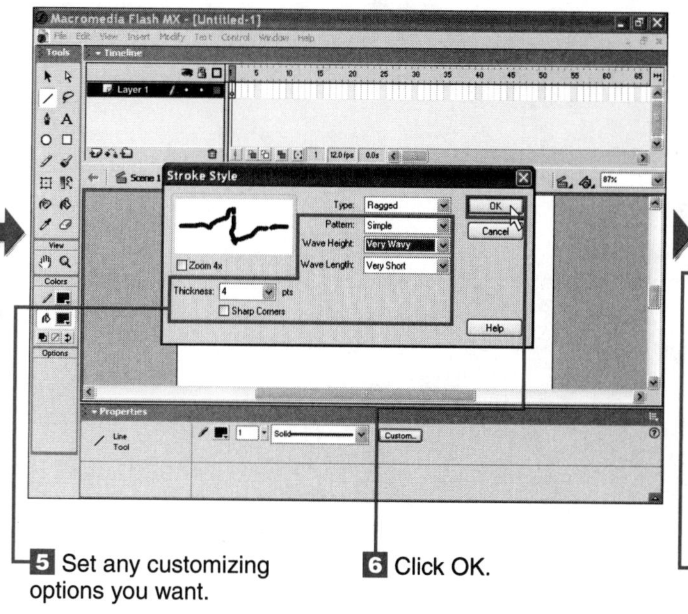

5 Set any customizing options you want.

6 Click OK.

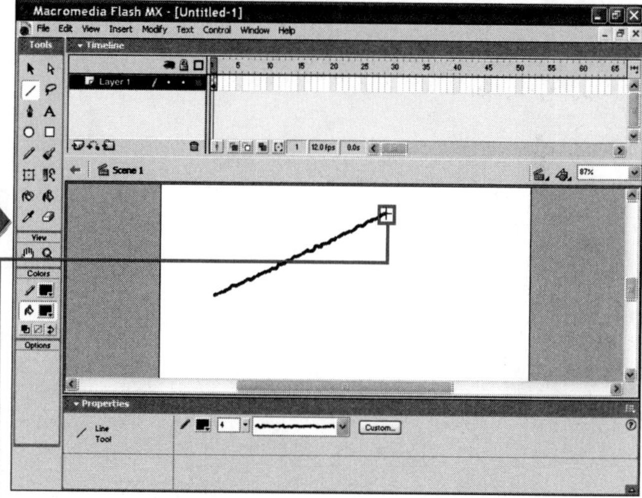

7 Click and drag to draw your custom line on the Stage.

■ The line appears with your specifications.

DRAW CURVES WITH THE PEN TOOL

You can draw precise lines and curves using the Pen tool. Using this tool takes some getting used to, but with a little practice, you can draw curves like a pro.

You can use a couple of techniques to draw lines with the Pen tool. The quickest way to draw curved lines is to drag the Pen tool along with its curve bar on the Flash Stage. The *curve bar* is a straight line with two solid points at either end. You can rotate the curve bar to create different degrees of curvature for the line. The key to creating just the right curve is learning to drag the curve bar in the correct direction. This technique takes a bit of practice, so be sure to experiment in a new file to get the hang of it.

Lines created with the Pen tool are composed of points. The points appear as dots on the line segment and represent segments or changes in the line's curvature. To keep adding to the line, keep clicking away from the end of the line segment to add length to the line itself. If you create a loop in the line, Flash MX immediately fills the closed loop with a fill color. If you do not want a fill color in a loop, be sure to set the Fill Color to No Color before drawing with the Pen tool.

DRAW CURVES WITH THE PEN TOOL

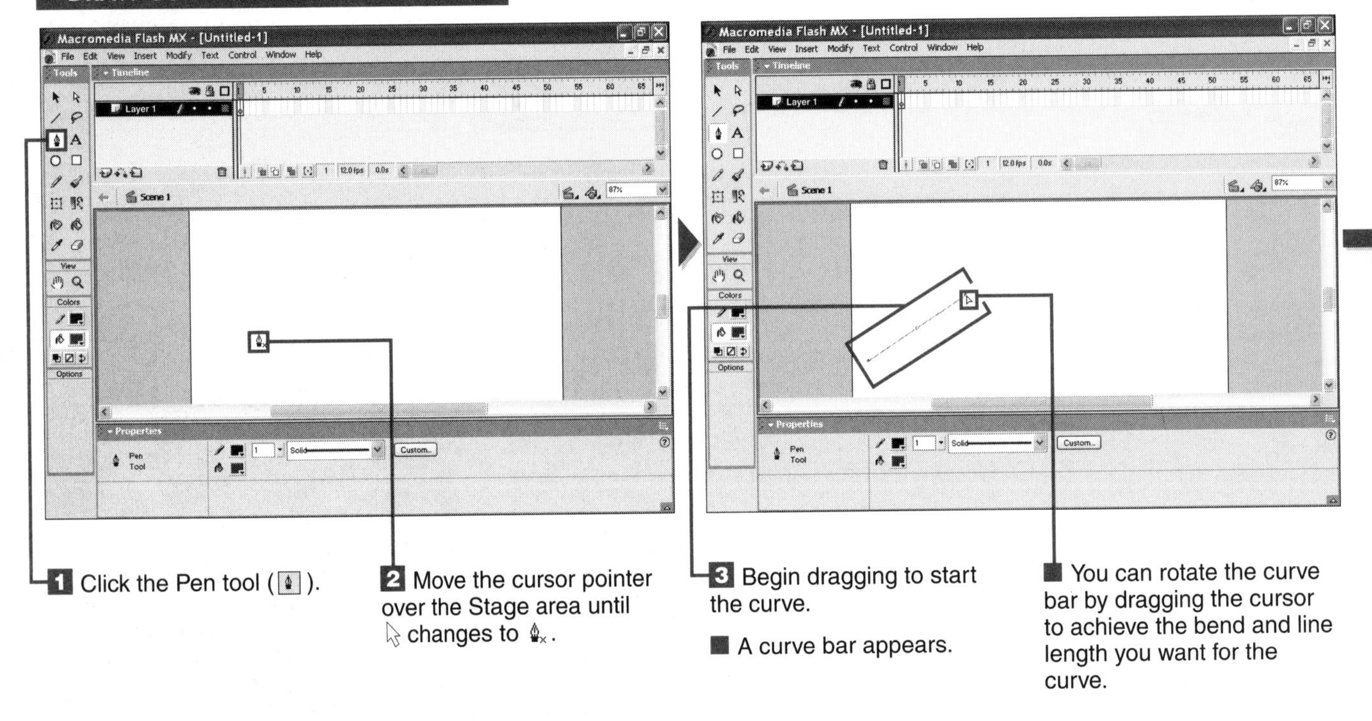

1 Click the Pen tool ( ).

2 Move the cursor pointer over the Stage area until ↖ changes to ✒ₓ.

3 Begin dragging to start the curve.

■ A curve bar appears.

■ You can rotate the curve bar by dragging the cursor to achieve the bend and line length you want for the curve.

How can I edit points on a curved line?

✔ Use the Subselection tool to make changes to a curved line you have created using the Pen tool. Click [Subselection tool] and move the cursor over an edit point on the line or at the end of the line. Drag to reposition and reshape the line or curve.

Is there a way to constrain the degree of curvature?

✔ Yes. You can press and hold down Shift while dragging the Pen tool to keep the curves at 45-degree angles.

Can I customize the Pen tool?

✔ Yes, you can control how the tool's pointer appears on-screen, how you want the lines displayed, and more. Click Edit and then Preferences (Flash, then Preferences). Click the Editing tab. Click Show Pen Preview (☑ changes to ☐) if you want to see the resulting line segment as you draw. Click Show Solid Points (☑ changes to ☐) if you prefer to see line points as solid dots. Click Show Precise Cursors (☑ changes to ☐) to change the tool's pointer icon to a crosshair. Click OK to exit.

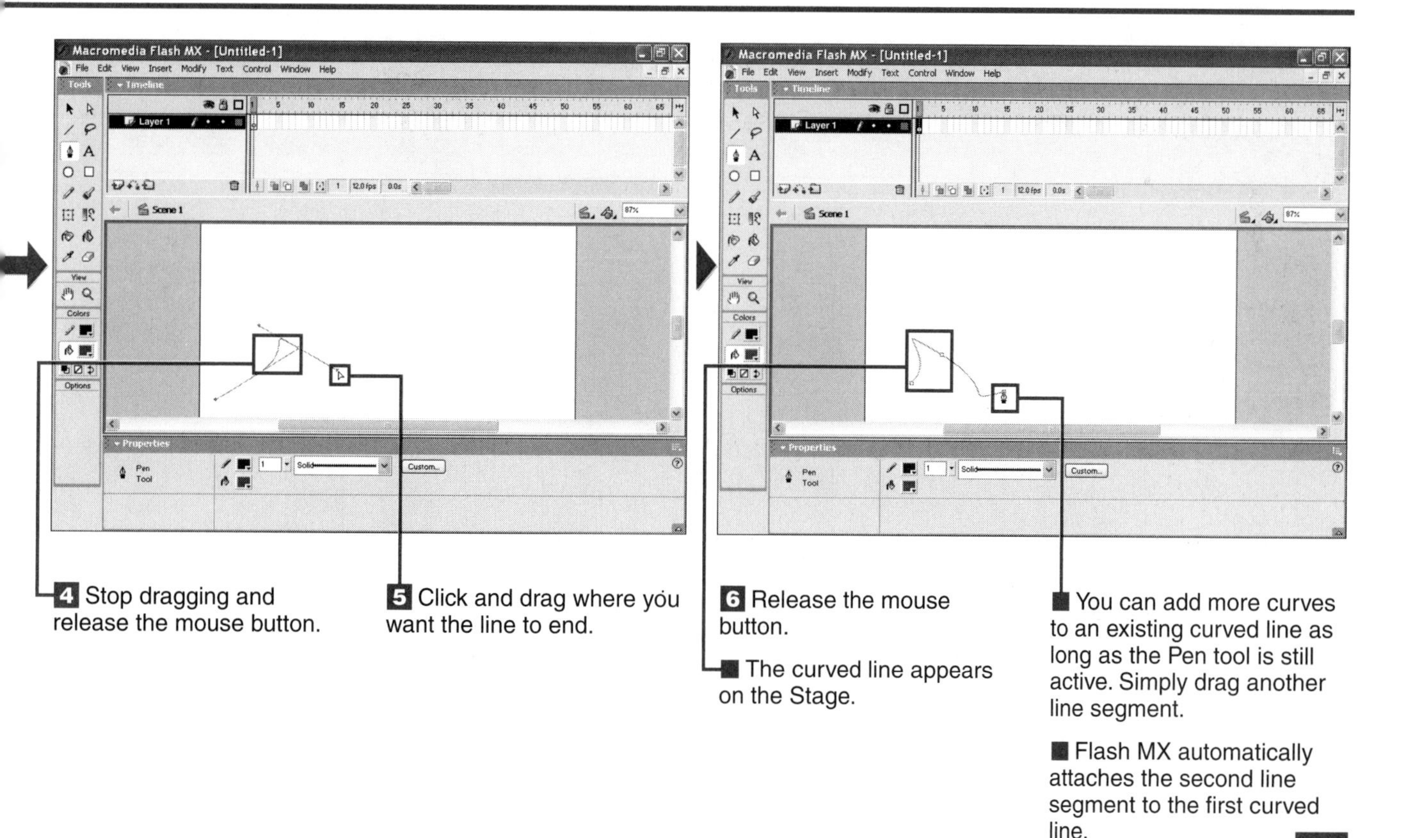

4 Stop dragging and release the mouse button.

5 Click and drag where you want the line to end.

6 Release the mouse button.

■ The curved line appears on the Stage.

■ You can add more curves to an existing curved line as long as the Pen tool is still active. Simply drag another line segment.

■ Flash MX automatically attaches the second line segment to the first curved line.

SMOOTH OR STRAIGHTEN LINE SEGMENTS

You can create subtle or dramatic changes in your drawing by smoothing or straightening the line segments you draw. For example, perhaps you have painstakingly drawn a tree with several curving branches. You now decide a few of your branches need some modifications. You can use the Arrow tool's Smooth or Straighten option buttons on the Drawing toolbar to adjust your lines.

The Smooth feature can take a curved line and smoothen it as much or little as you need. Use the Smooth feature to smooth out rough corners or edges on a line or curve. You can apply the option repeatedly until you get just the right look for a line segment.

The Straighten feature turns a curvy line into a straight one. Like the Smooth feature, you can apply the Straighten feature as much as you need to get the desired effect. Keep in mind that you can straighten only rough and curved lines — straightening an already straight line has no effect.

In addition to the Smooth and Straighten tools on the Drawing toolbar, you can also find the commands on the Modify menu.

SMOOTH OR STRAIGHTEN LINE SEGMENTS

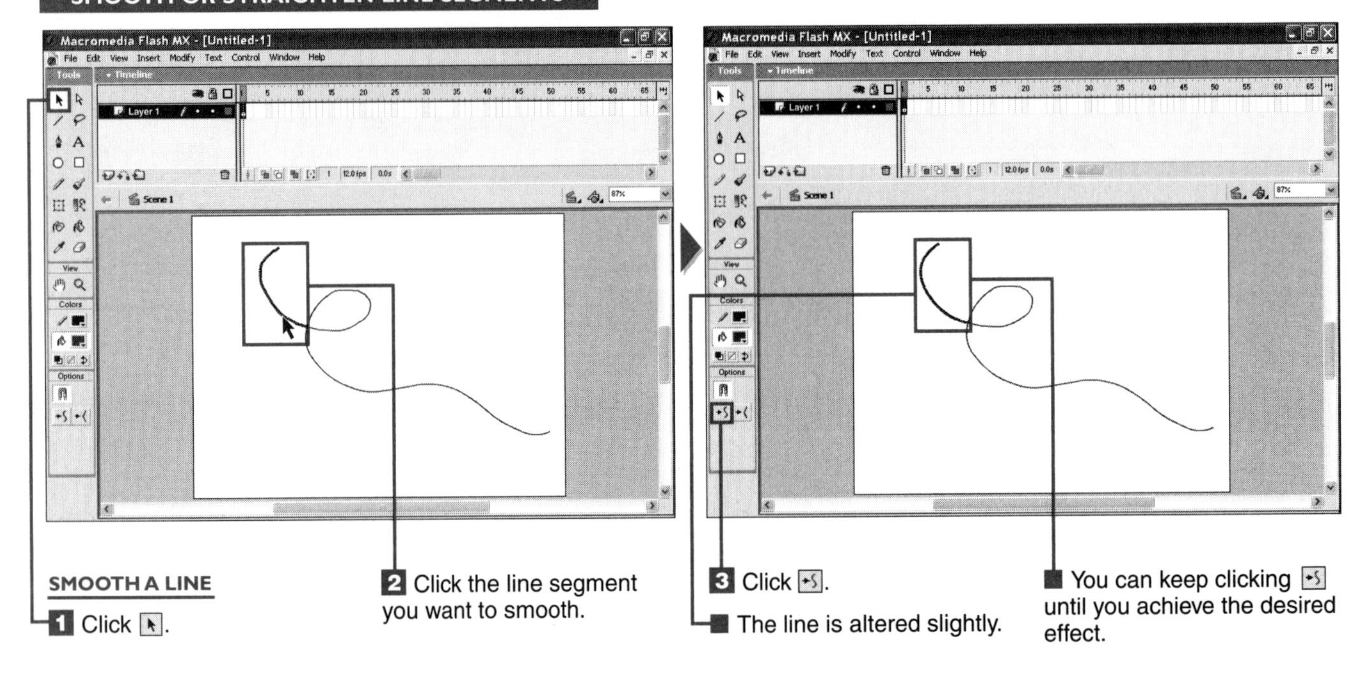

SMOOTH A LINE

1 Click .

2 Click the line segment you want to smooth.

3 Click .

■ The line is altered slightly.

■ You can keep clicking until you achieve the desired effect.

Can I draw in Smooth or Straighten mode?

✔ Yes. When you draw lines with the Pencil tool, you can preselect the Smooth or Straighten mode. See page 356 for more information.

Should I use the set of Smooth buttons on the Drawing toolbar or the set on the Main toolbar?

✔ You can use either set. One set is located at the bottom of the Drawing toolbar in the Options tray. This set displays only when you select the Arrow tool. The other set is located in the Main toolbar at the top of the program window. However, the Main toolbar does not display by default. To display it, click Window, Toolbars, and then Main.

Why do my curved lines appear so rough?

✔ A previous user may have made some adjustments to the program's preferences. You can adjust settings for drawing lines and shapes through the Preferences dialog box. Click Edit and then Preferences. This opens the Preferences dialog box. Click the Editing tab, click the Smooth Curves ▾, and then select Normal. Click OK to exit the dialog box and apply the new setting.

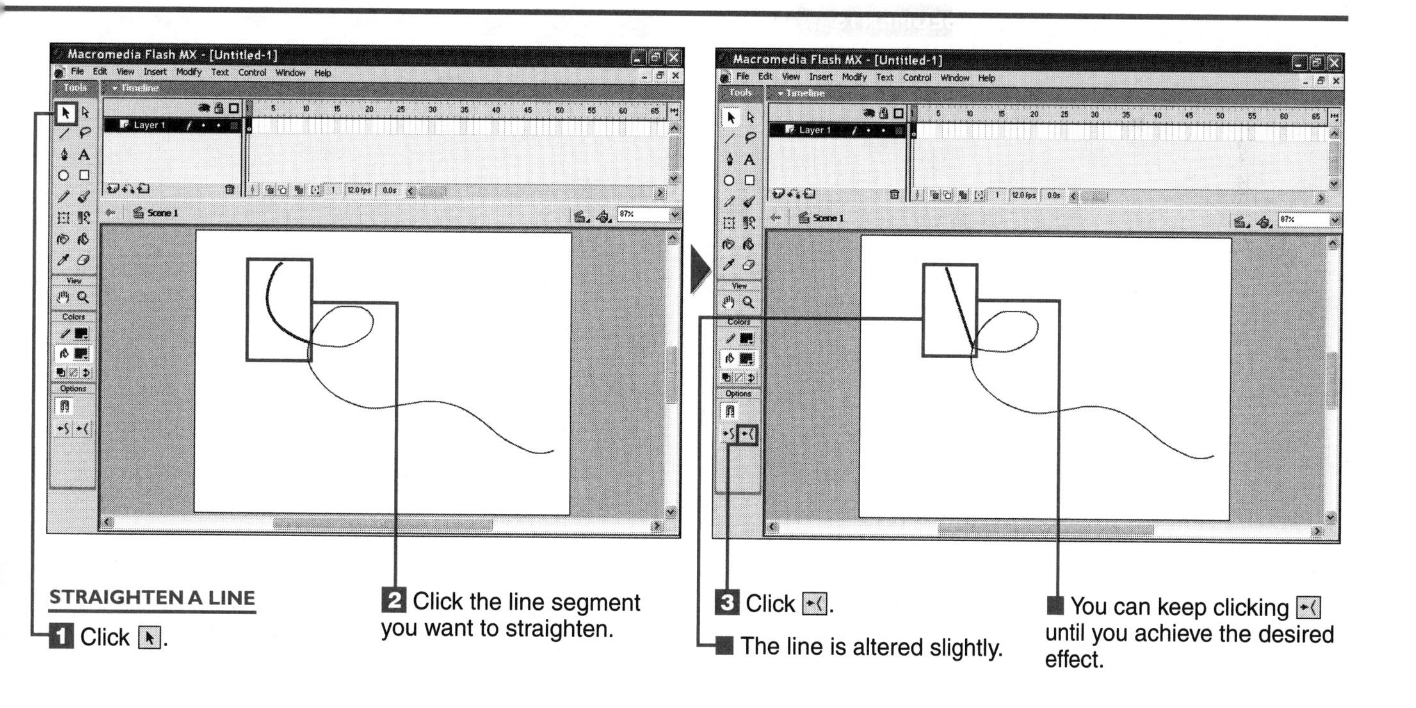

STRAIGHTEN A LINE

1 Click ↖.

2 Click the line segment you want to straighten.

3 Click ⁺‹.

■ The line is altered slightly.

■ You can keep clicking ⁺‹ until you achieve the desired effect.

DRAW OVAL AND RECTANGLE SHAPES

You can use shapes to create drawings, buttons, and other graphic objects in Flash MX. After you draw a shape, you can fill it with a color or pattern. You can create shapes using many of the tools found on the Drawing toolbar, such as the Pencil or Line tool, just by connecting or closing the lines. For more uniform shapes, such as circles, ovals, squares, and rectangles, you can use the Oval or Rectangle tools.

The Oval tool can create all kinds of oval or circular shapes. You can overlap the shapes to create more shapes. The Rectangle tool is used to create all kinds of rectangular or square shapes. These, too, can be overlapped to make more shapes.

You can choose to draw an oval or rectangle shape with or without a fill. A *fill* is the color or pattern that fills up the inside of your shape. By default, a fill color is selected. You can turn the Fill off or choose another color from the Fill Color palette. You can also change the fill later. See the section "Fill Objects with the Paint Bucket Tool" in this chapter.

DRAW OVAL AND RECTANGLE SHAPES

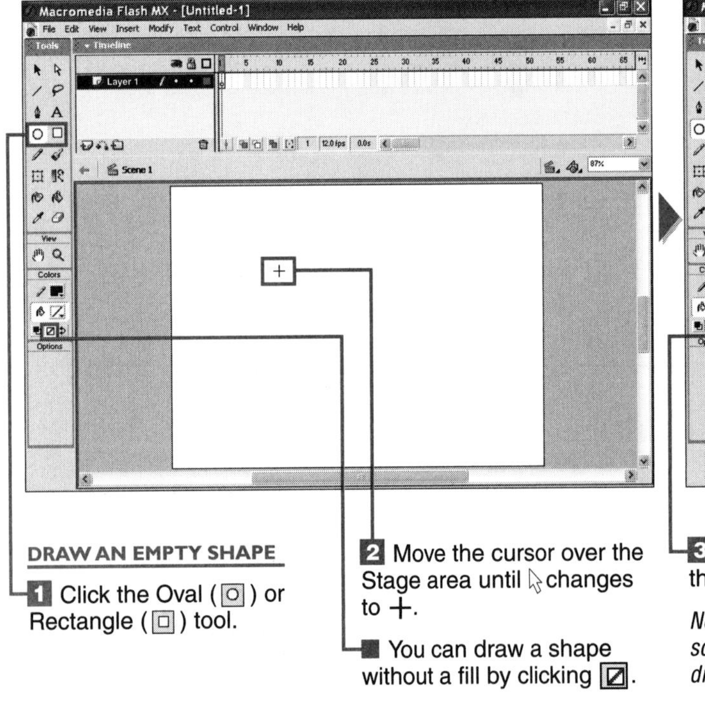

DRAW AN EMPTY SHAPE

1 Click the Oval (◯) or Rectangle (□) tool.

2 Move the cursor over the Stage area until ↖ changes to +.

■ You can draw a shape without a fill by clicking ☒.

3 Click and drag to draw the shape you want.

Note: To draw a perfect circle or square, hold down Shift as you draw the shape.

4 Release the mouse button.

■ The shape is complete.

Can I open a Fill Color dialog box?

✔ Yes, you can open the Fill Color dialog box if you want to spend time choosing colors or create a custom color. Click the Fill Color button on the Drawing toolbar, and then click the Color button in the upper right corner of the Color palette to open the Color dialog box. You can then click a color to use as a fill and click OK.

Is there another way to assign a fill color?

✔ Yes. You can use the Color Mixer panel to display the Color palette and use the panel's Fill Color button to change fill colors. You can then leave the panel open and use it when you need it. See page 348 to learn how to open and close Flash MX panels.

How do I draw a rectangle with rounded corners?

✔ By default, all rectangular shapes you draw with the Rectangle tool have sharp corners. You can create rounded corners by using the Rectangle options. Click ▢ on the Drawing toolbar and then click ◰ in the Options area. The Rectangle Settings dialog box appears. Type a corner radius setting, such as 10 points, and click OK. Draw your rectangle shape with rounded corners. To draw regular corners again, enter 0 as the radius setting.

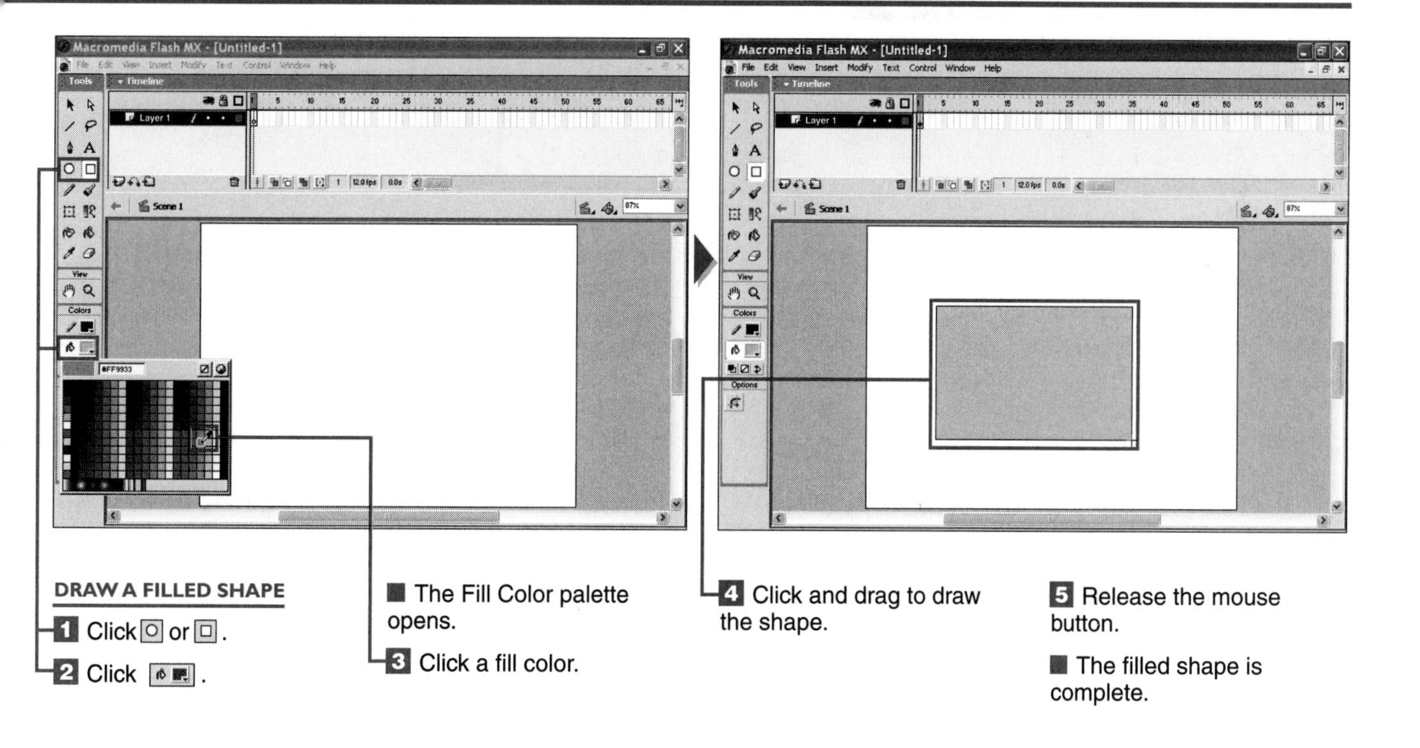

DRAW A FILLED SHAPE

1 Click ○ or ▢.

2 Click ◈■.

■ The Fill Color palette opens.

3 Click a fill color.

4 Click and drag to draw the shape.

5 Release the mouse button.

■ The filled shape is complete.

DRAW OBJECTS WITH THE BRUSH TOOL

You can use the Brush tool to draw with brush strokes, much like a paintbrush. You can use brushstrokes to create a variety of shapes and images on the Flash Stage. You can also control the size and shape of the brush as well as how the brush strokes appear on the Stage.

The Brush tool is handy when you want to draw varying sizes of freeform strokes on the Stage. You can choose a specific color to use with the Brush tool by first selecting a color from the Fill Color palette. See page 366 to learn about using the Fill Color palette.

After you select the Brush tool, several Brush modifiers appear in the Options tray at the bottom of the Drawing toolbar. You can use the modifiers to change the brush shape and size, as well as how the brush strokes interact with objects on the Stage. For example, some of the brush sizes enable you to create calligraphy effects, while the shapes allow you to create large brushstrokes or small brushstrokes in a drawing. With a modifier, you can choose to paint behind or in front of an existing shape on the Stage. Be sure to test all the Brush tool modifiers to see what kind of interesting effects you can create.

DRAW OBJECTS WITH THE BRUSH TOOL

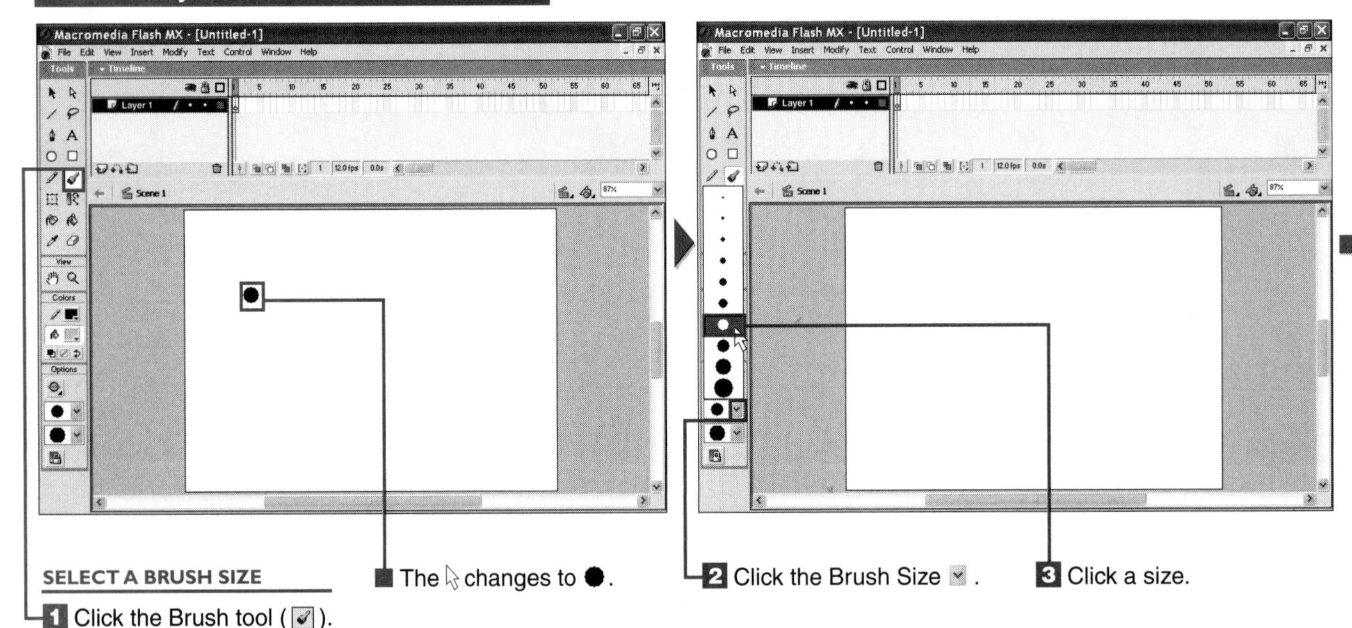

SELECT A BRUSH SIZE

1 Click the Brush tool (✓).

■ The ↖ changes to ●.

2 Click the Brush Size ▾.

3 Click a size.

How do I brush in just one direction?

✔ If you press and hold Shift while dragging the Brush tool on the Stage, the tool allows you to draw only in a horizontal or vertical direction.

How do I use the Brush tool with a pressure-sensitive tablet?

✔ If you use a pressure-sensitive tablet to draw, you will see an extra modifier for the Brush tool at the bottom of the Drawing toolbar. Use the Pressure modifier to activate a finer degree of sensitivity in the Brush tool when drawing. This feature toggles on or off.

What do the brush modes do?

✔ You find the five brush modes by clicking the Brush Mode button ( ) at the bottom of the Drawing toolbar. Paint Normal lets you paint over anything on the Stage. Paint Fills paints inside fills but not on lines. Paint Behind paints beneath any existing objects on the Stage. Paint Selection paints only inside the selected area. Paint Inside begins a brush stroke inside a fill area without affecting any lines.

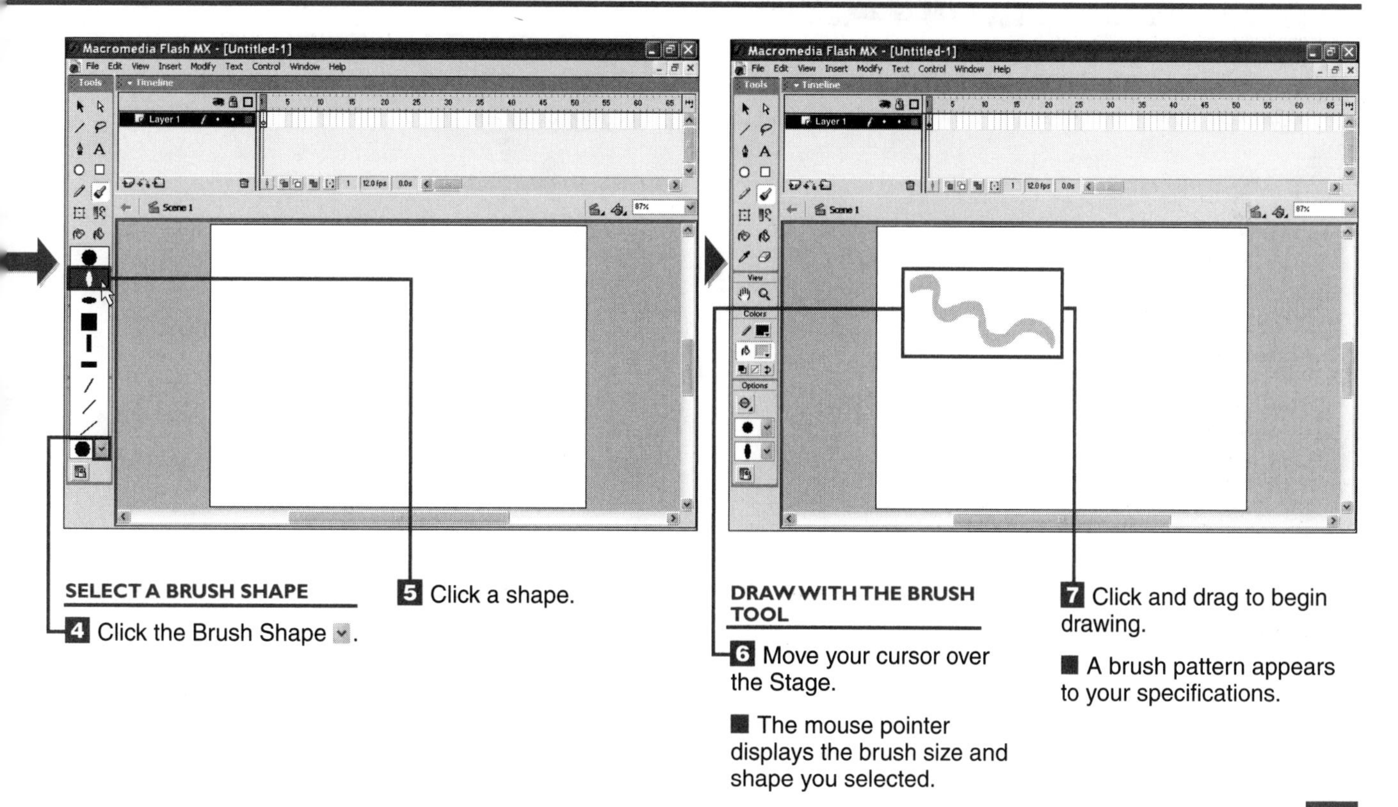

SELECT A BRUSH SHAPE

4 Click the Brush Shape .

5 Click a shape.

DRAW WITH THE BRUSH TOOL

6 Move your cursor over the Stage.

■ The mouse pointer displays the brush size and shape you selected.

7 Click and drag to begin drawing.

■ A brush pattern appears to your specifications.

FILL OBJECTS WITH THE PAINT BUCKET TOOL

You can use the Paint Bucket tool to quickly fill in objects, such as shapes and outlines. You can fill objects with a color, a gradient effect, or even a bitmap picture. The Flash Color palette comes with numerous colors and shades, as well as several built-in gradient effects to choose from.

The Paint Bucket tool uses the same Fill Color palette as the other drawing tools. The palette shows all the available colors plus some gradient effects. The Fill Color palette is a common feature among most drawing programs, so if you have used a color palette with other programs, you will find that the Flash Color palette works the same way.

When you select a color from the palette, you can then fill the inside of any closed shape with the selected color. If you try to fill a shape that is not closed, or has gaps in the line segments that comprise the shape, the fill color cannot fill the shape. Likewise, you cannot use the Paint Bucket to add color to the document background. You must set a background color using the Document Properties dialog box instead.

FILL OBJECTS WITH THE PAINT BUCKET TOOL

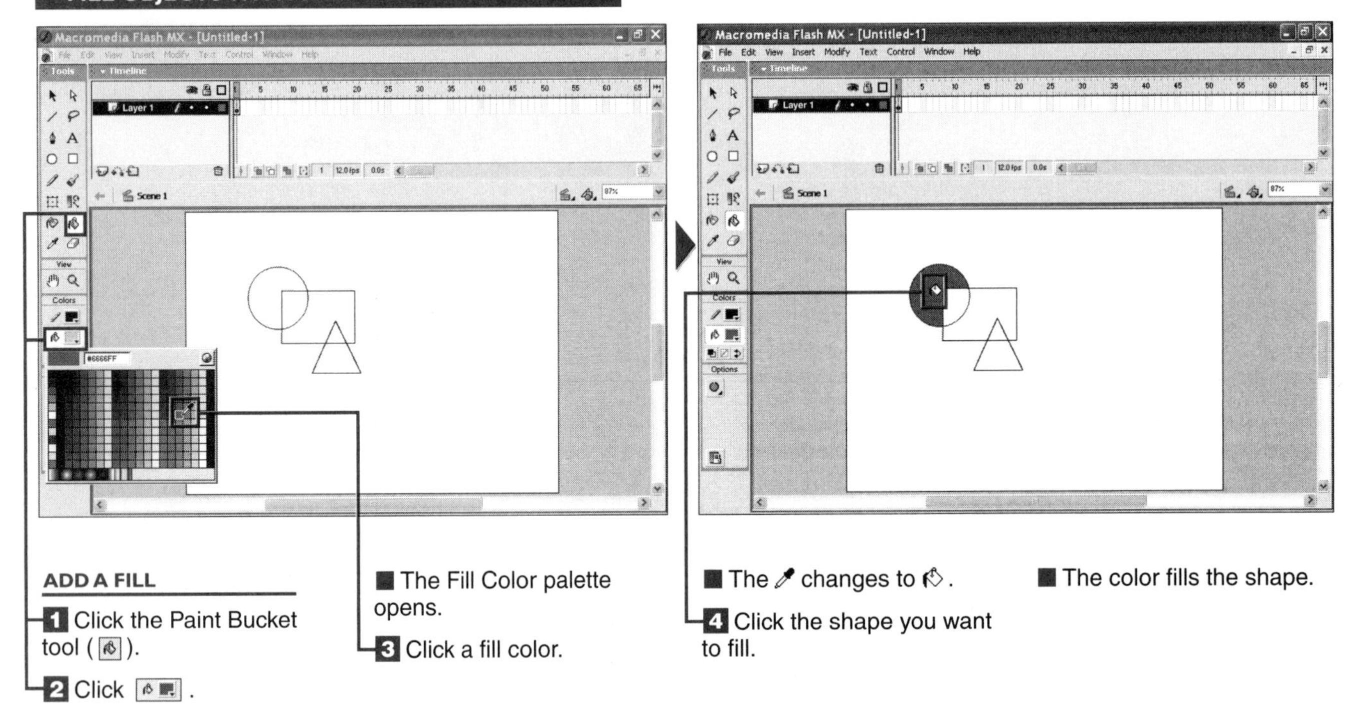

ADD A FILL

1 Click the Paint Bucket tool ([icon]).

2 Click [icon].

■ The Fill Color palette opens.

3 Click a fill color.

■ The [icon] changes to [icon].

4 Click the shape you want to fill.

■ The color fills the shape.

What is a gradient effect?

✔ A *gradient effect* is a color effect that shows one or several colors of different intensities, often creating a three-dimensional effect. With Flash, you can create a *linear* gradient effect that intensifies color shading from left to right or top to bottom. You can also create a *radial* gradient effect that intensifies color shading from the middle to the outer edges or vice versa. To find out more about creating new gradient effects, see page 390.

What does the Gap Size modifier do?

✔ When you select the Paint Bucket tool, the Gap Size modifier ( ) appears in the Options tray at the bottom of the Drawing toolbar. Click to display a menu list of four settings. These settings determine how the Paint Bucket tool treats any gaps that appear in the shape you are trying to fill. However, for very large gaps, you may need to close them yourself before applying the fill color.

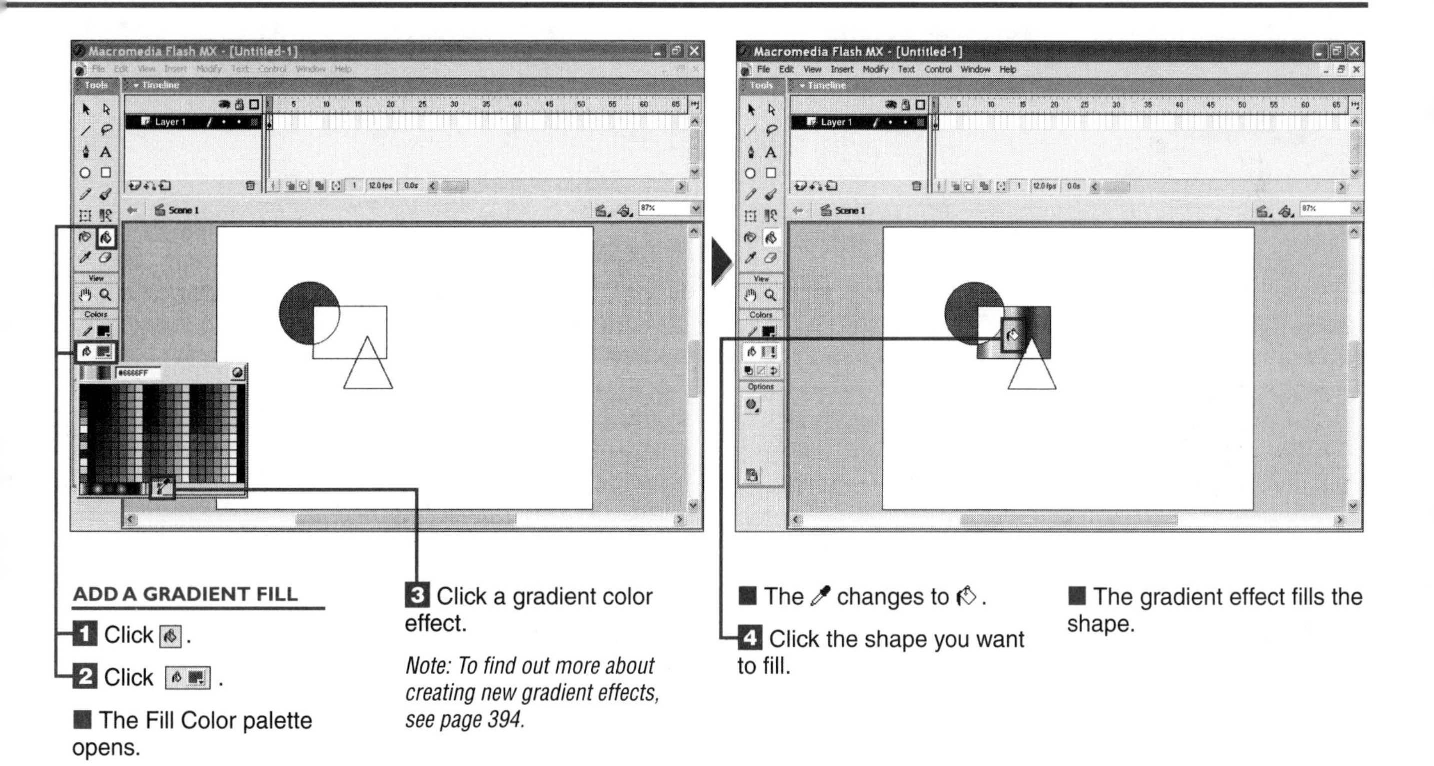

ADD A GRADIENT FILL

1 Click .

2 Click .

■ The Fill Color palette opens.

3 Click a gradient color effect.

Note: To find out more about creating new gradient effects, see page 394.

■ The changes to .

4 Click the shape you want to fill.

■ The gradient effect fills the shape.

SELECT OBJECTS

To work with objects you draw or place on the Flash Stage, you must first select them. For example, you might want to change the color of a line outlining a shape or modify the curve of a particular line segment. Or, you may want to group several lines and shapes into a single object to save as a symbol in your movie. In order to do so, you must first select the line segment you want to edit. The more lines and shapes you place on the Stage, the trickier it is to select only the ones you want.

There are several techniques you can employ to select objects on-screen. You can use the Arrow tool to quickly select any single object, such as a line segment or fill. To select several objects, such as a couple of shapes or an entire drawing, you can drag a frame, also called a *marquee*, around the items. Flash MX selects anything inside the selection frame. Any edits you make affect all the items within the selection frame.

When editing fill shapes, you can select both the fill and the border. If you click just the border, you cannot make changes to the fill.

SELECT OBJECTS

CLICK TO SELECT OBJECTS

1 Click [Arrow tool].

2 Move the [pointer] over the object you want to select, and then click.

■ You can select a fill and its surrounding line border by double-clicking the fill.

Note: When working with multiple layers, click the layer containing the object you want to select, and then click the object. To learn more about layers, see page 436.

■ Selected objects appear highlighted with a pattern.

■ You can now edit the object.

How do I select multiple objects?

✔ Hold down the Shift while clicking objects when you want to select more than one at a time. For example, if a line is comprised of several segments, you can select all of them for editing. Click [selection arrow], then hold the Shift, and click each line segment you want to select.

How do I unselect a selected object?

✔ Just click anywhere outside the selected object. You can also press Esc on the keyboard.

Is there a fast way to select everything on the Stage?

✔ Yes. Click the Edit menu and click Select All. You can also press Ctrl + A (⌘ + A) on the keyboard.

How do I select just a fill and not its border?

✔ Simply click the fill to select it. To select both the fill and the fill's border, double-click the fill.

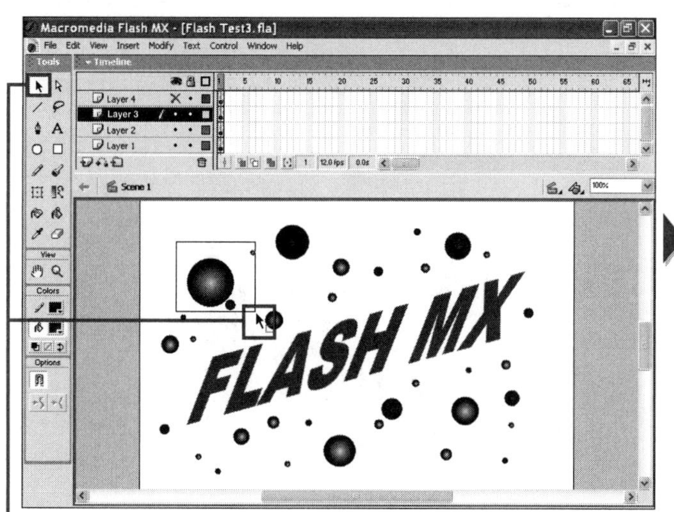

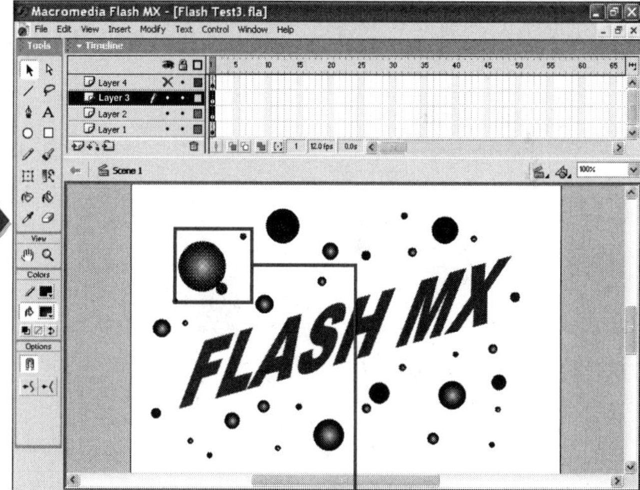

SELECT BY DRAGGING

1 Click [selection arrow].

2 Click and drag a square selection box around the object you want to select.

Note: When working with multiple layers, click the layer containing the object you want to select, and then click the object. To learn more about layers, see page 436.

3 Release the mouse button.

■ Flash selects everything inside the selection box.

CONTINUED

SELECT OBJECTS (CONTINUED)

If you are working with several irregularly-shaped objects, it is not always easy to select a specific item or line. For example, you may have several circle shapes that overlap and need to select only one section; or perhaps you have several objects drawn closely together, but want to select only one object. You can use the Lasso tool to help you select irregular objects.

The Lasso tool draws a freehand rope around the item you want to select. This allows you to select an oddly-shaped object or just a small portion of an object. You must drag the Lasso tool completely around the item you want to select. You drag the loop closed to complete the rope, so be sure to end the dragging procedure in the same place you started from. Flash MX selects anything inside the roped area. Using the Lasso tool takes a steady hand and a bit of practice. If you make a mistake and lasso a part of the drawing you do not want to select, you can click on-screen and start the lassoing process again.

If you choose not to work with any object you select on the Flash Stage, you can click outside the selected object to deselect the items.

SELECT OBJECTS (CONTINUED)

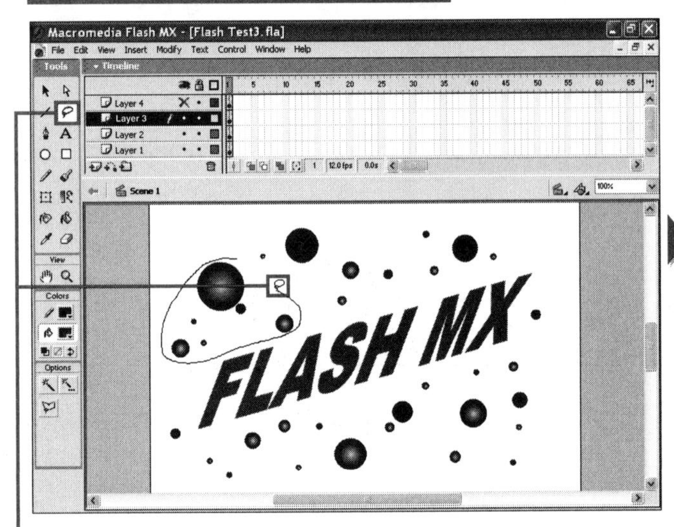

LASSO AN OBJECT

1 To select an irregularly-shaped object, click [lasso icon].

■ When you move the [pointer icon] over the Stage area, it changes to a [lasso icon].

2 Click and drag the lasso completely around the object until you reach the point where you started.

Note: When working with multiple layers, click the layer containing the object you want to select, and then click the object. To learn more about layers, see page 436.

3 Release the mouse button.

■ Flash highlights anything inside the lasso shape.

How can I select complex shapes?

✔ You may find drawing around irregular items with the lasso difficult. Use the Lasso tool's Polygon Mode modifier to help. Click [lasso icon], and then click [polygon icon] in the Options tray. Now click your way around the object you want to select. Every click creates a connected line to the last click. To turn off the Polygon Mode, double-click.

What does the Magic Wand modifier do?

✔ The Magic Wand modifier ([magic wand icon]) appears in the Options tray when you select [lasso icon]. You use it with broken apart bitmap images to help you select areas within the image for modifications. See Chapter 23 to learn more about bitmap images in Flash MX.

Can I customize the Magic Wand settings?

✔ You can customize two Magic Wand modifier settings, the Threshold setting and the Smoothing setting, by clicking [magic wand properties icon]. Alter the Threshold setting to define color values of adjacent colors to be included in the Lasso selection, and adjust the Smoothing setting to specify the degree of smoothing (similar to antialiasing) of the edges of the selected area.

Can I select objects on multiple layers in my movie?

✔ Yes. It does not matter which layer contains the objects you select on the Stage. You can press and hold the Shift key while clicking items on different layers.

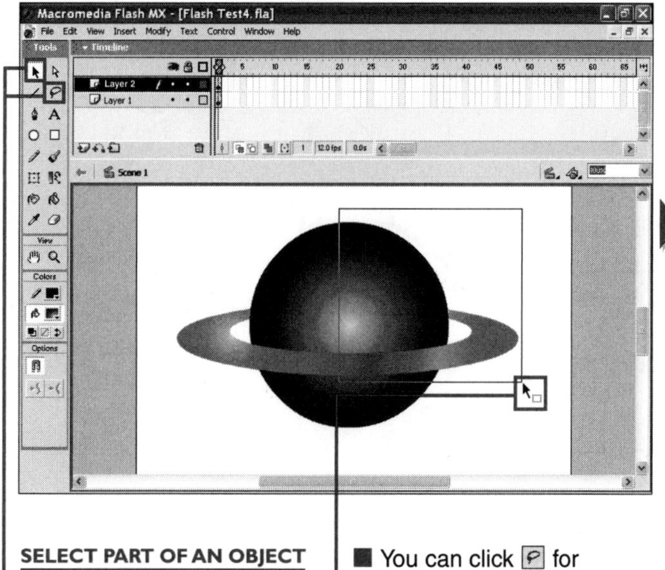

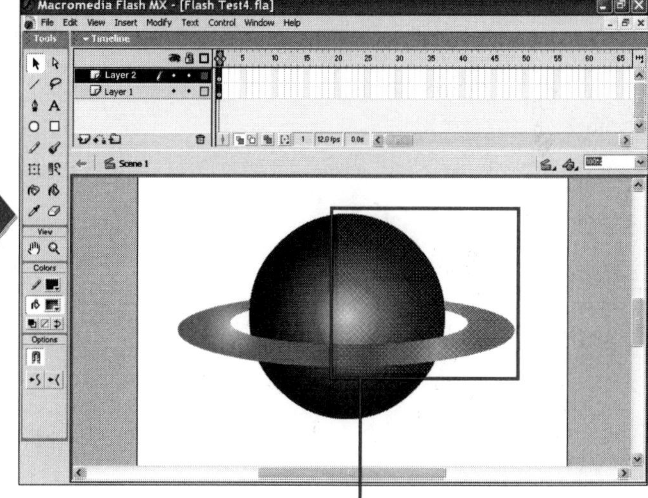

SELECT PART OF AN OBJECT

1 Click [arrow icon] or [lasso icon].

■ You can click [arrow icon] for simple shapes or lines.

■ You can click [lasso icon] for irregularly-shaped objects.

2 Drag the pointer to surround the object part you want to select.

3 Release the mouse button.

■ Flash MX selects everything inside the area.

MOVE AND COPY OBJECTS

You can easily reposition objects on the Flash Stage to change your drawing. Flash lets you quickly move an object from one area to another. You can also make copies of the original object. For example, you may need to move a shape to the left side of the Stage or copy the shape to create a new shape.

Moving and copying in Flash MX works the same way as moving and copying items in other programs, using the Cut, Copy, and Paste commands. In Flash, the Cut, Copy, and Paste commands are available as toolbar buttons on the Main toolbar or as menu commands on the Edit menu.

You can move an object by dragging it around the Stage using the mouse, or you can activate the standard Cut and Paste commands. Dragging an object is the quickest way to place it where you want it to go. To work with any object, you must first select it on the Stage. This tells Flash exactly which object you want to edit.

Copying an object places a duplicate of the selected object on the Stage. You can then move the duplicate to the desired location.

MOVE AN OBJECT

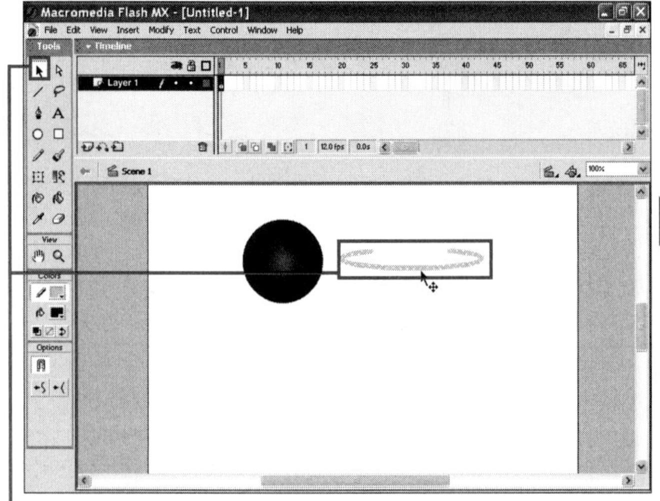

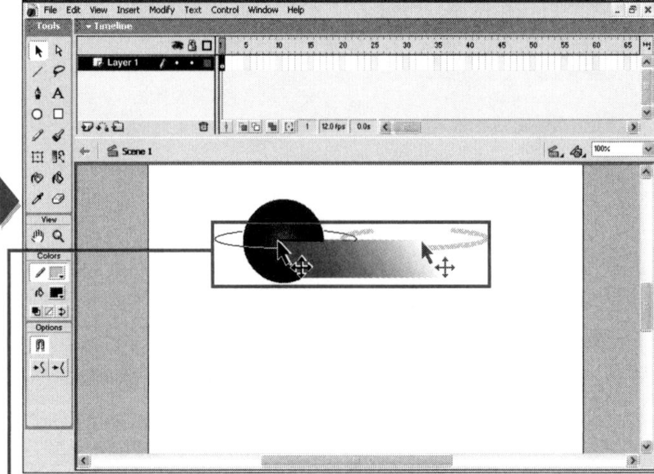

1 Click (arrow tool).

2 Click the object you want to move.

■ A ✥ appears next to the (arrow pointer).

Note: When working with multiple layers, click the layer containing the object you want to select, and then click the object. To learn more about layers, see page 436.

3 Click and drag the object to a new position.

4 Release the mouse button.

■ Your object moves to the location you selected.

Are the Cut, Copy, and Paste keyboard shortcuts the same in Flash MX?

✔ Yes. Whether you are using Mac or Windows, the keyboard shortcuts work the same way in Flash MX as they do in most other programs.

Press Ctrl + X (⌘ + X) to cut an object and place it on the Clipboard.

Press Ctrl + V (⌘ + V) to paste an object.

Press Ctrl + C (⌘ + C) to place a duplicate of a selected object onto the Clipboard.

Can I precisely control where I position an object?

✔ For more precise positioning controls, open the Align panel. Click Window, then Align to open the Align panel where you can find a variety of controls for positioning an object precisely on the Stage. To learn more about using the alignment controls, see page 404. You can also set *x* and *y* positioning values for a selected object in the Property Inspector. See page 346 to learn more about the Property Inspector.

COPY AN OBJECT

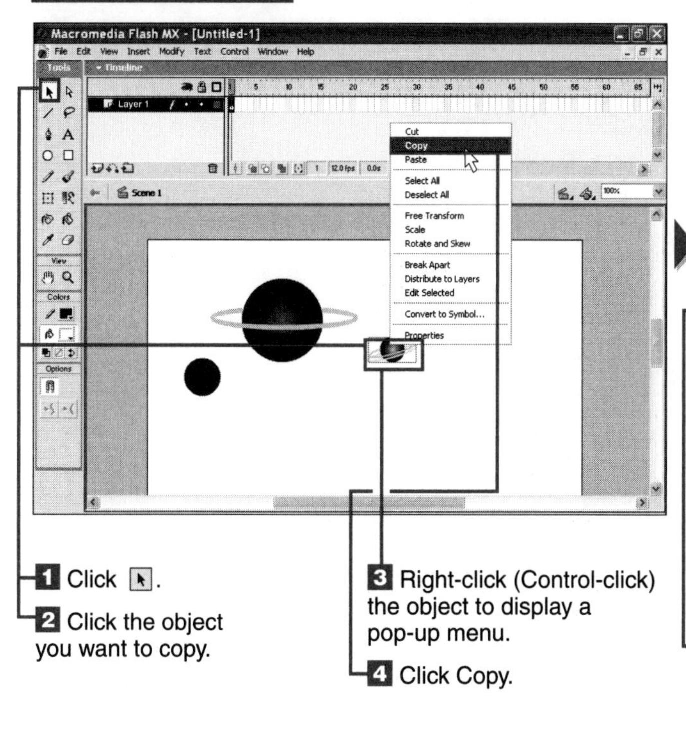

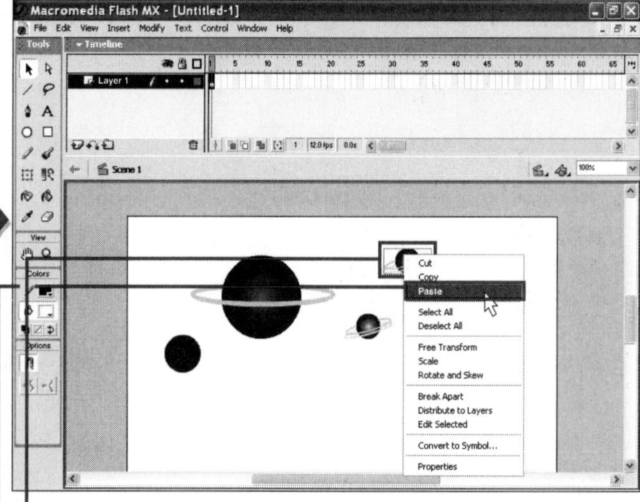

1 Click ⬉.

2 Click the object you want to copy.

3 Right-click (Control-click) the object to display a pop-up menu.

4 Click Copy.

5 Right-click (Control-click) a blank area on the Stage.

6 Click Paste.

Note: If you want to place the copy exactly where the original appears, click the Paste in Place command.

■ A copy of the object appears.

■ You may need to move the copy to the exact place you want it on the Stage.

EDIT LINE SEGMENTS

You can edit or modify a line segment by adjusting its length or reshaping its curve. Editing line segments enables you to change the appearance of your drawing. For example, you might want to change the angle of a line, extend a curved line to make it appear longer, or just simply make the curve more curvy.

You can edit any line segment by altering its end points. Dragging an end point shortens or lengthens the line. Unlike other editing techniques, you do not need to first select the line in order to modify its end points.

You can edit a line's shape by dragging the area between the line's end points. Depending on the direction you drag, the line seemingly bends along with the pointer as you drag. When you release the mouse button, the line immediately takes on the new curvature. For example, if you click and drag the middle of a line in an upwards direction on the Stage, Flash curves the middle section of the line upwards, thus creating a bulge or hill in the middle of the line. If you drag the middle of the line in a downwards direction, Flash curves the line downwards, thus creating a valley or dip in the middle of the line.

EDIT LINE SEGMENTS

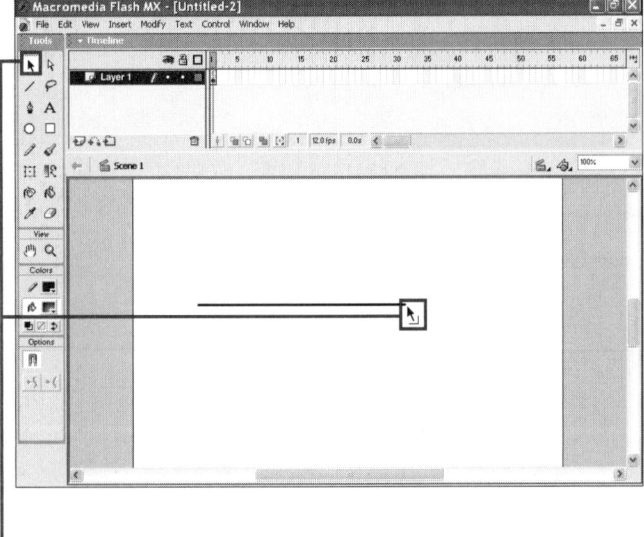

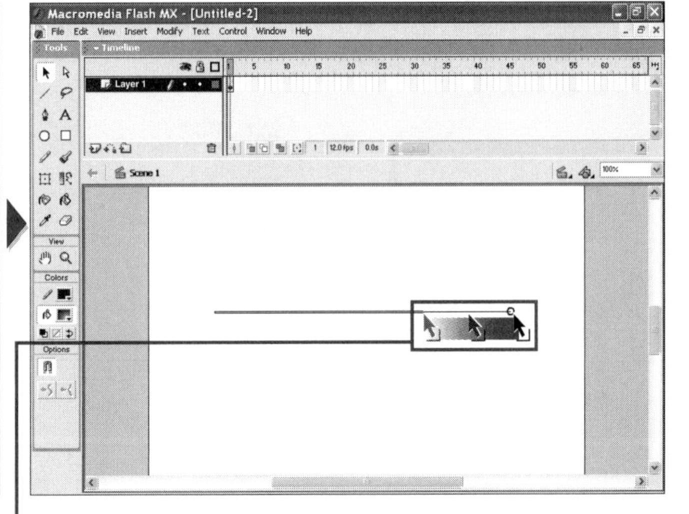

RESIZE A LINE SEGMENT

1 Click ⬚.

2 Position the ↖ over the end of the line.

Note: Do not click the line to select it.

■ A ⌟ appears next to the ↖.

3 Drag the end of the line to shorten or lengthen the segment.

■ As you drag the ⌟ in any direction, you can change the angle of the line.

4 Release the mouse button.

■ Flash MX resizes the line.

How do I draw perfect vertical and horizontal lines?

✔ It is not always easy to hold a steady hand while you draw a line on the Stage. You can draw perfectly straight horizontal and vertical lines if you hold the Shift down while dragging the Line tool across the Stage.

Can I see precise edit points on a line?

✔ Yes. Click [arrow icon] and then click the line. Edit points appear at either end of the line, and if the line consists of more than one segment, edit points also appear at each change of segment. You can drag any edit point to reshape the line.

How do I edit a line's color or thickness?

✔ You can find settings for changing line color, thickness, and style in the Property inspector. See Chapter 21 to learn more about assigning line-formatting attributes. See Chapter 20 to learn more about using the Property inspector.

How can I best measure line segments?

✔ You can turn on the ruler feature to help you gauge the length of line segments you draw on the Stage. Click Rulers from the View menu to turn on the rulers. Follow the same steps to turn the rulers off again.

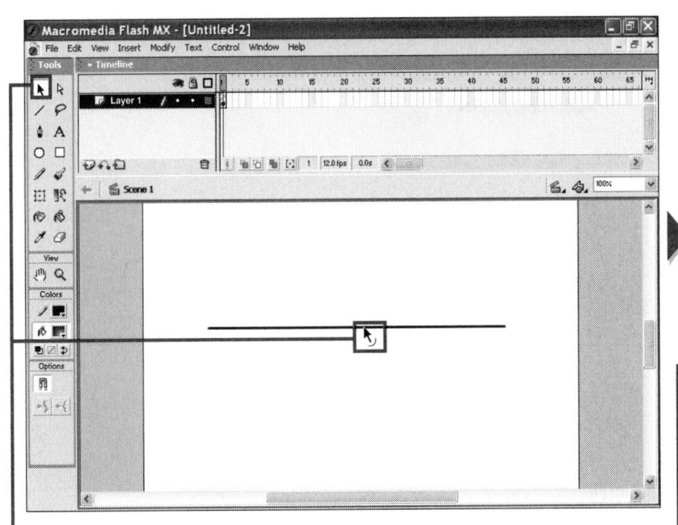

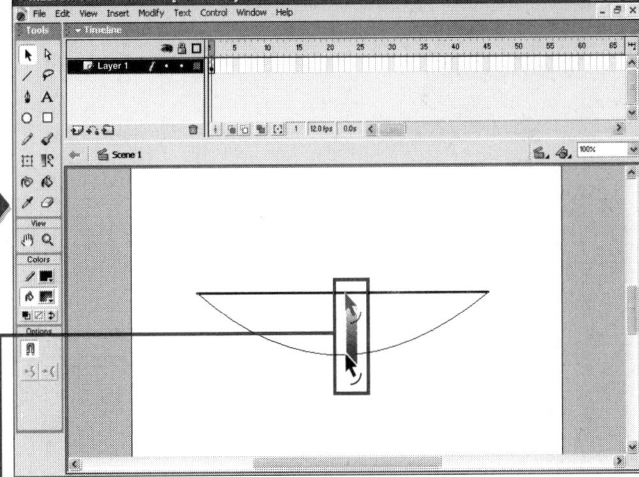

RESHAPE A LINE SEGMENT

1 Click [arrow icon].

2 Position the [pointer] over the area of the line that you want to curve.

Note: Do not click the line to select it.

■ A [curve icon] appears next to the [pointer].

3 Drag the line to add or reshape the curve.

4 Release the mouse button.

■ Flash MX reshapes the line.

EDIT FILLS

With Flash MX, you can change a fill shape by adjusting the sides of the fill. A *fill* is a color or pattern that fills a closed outline or shape. Changing the fill color can change the appearance of a shape or object on the Stage. You can also change the fill color at any time to create additional changes to the shape or object.

You can easily adjust the edges of a fill to create new and unusual shapes. The fastest way to change a shape's edge is to drag it. Depending on the direction you drag, the shape's edge may curve or straighten. If the fill shape includes an outline border, the border is modified as well. You do not have to select the entire fill in order to adjust the fill edges.

In addition to changing the fill's edges, you can also change the fill color. Using the Fill Color palette, you can assign a new color or gradient effect. You must, however, select the fill first in order to apply a new color. As long as the fill is highlighted on the Stage, you can continue trying different colors from the Fill Color palette. Flash MX applies each color you select immediately to the fill.

EDIT FILLS

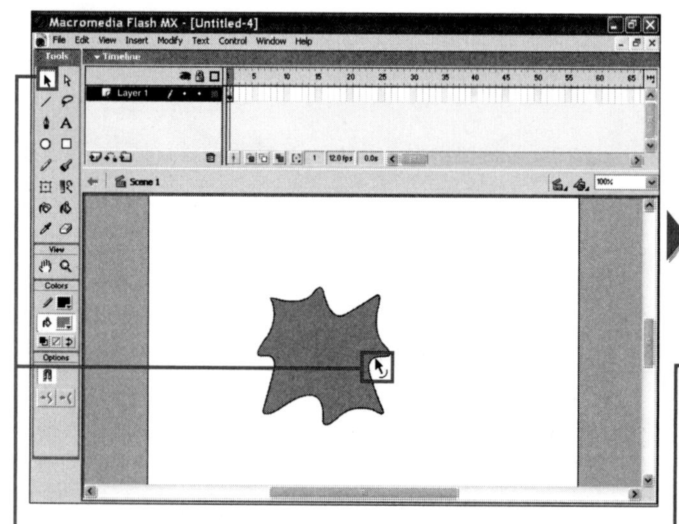

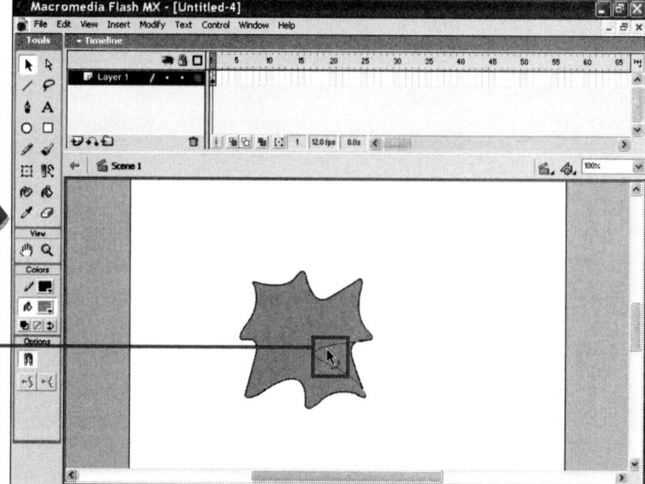

RESHAPE A FILL

1 Click [arrow tool].

2 Move the [pointer] over the edge of the fill.

Note: Do not select the fill.

■ A ◡ appears next to the [pointer].

3 Drag the fill's edge in or out to reshape the fill.

Can I adjust edit points on a fill outline?

✔ Yes. Click [icon], and then click on the fill shape's outline. This displays edit points on the outline that surrounds the fill. You can then drag an edit point to change the shape of both the fill outline as well as the fill itself.

My fill object does not include strokes. Can I add an outline around the fill?

✔ Yes. Click the [icon] tool, and then click the edge of the object. To set stroke properties, such as line thickness, before applying the outline, open the Property inspector and set stroke properties first.

Are there other ways to edit fill shapes?

✔ You can find additional Shape commands on the Modify menu that can help you edit fills. For example, to soften a fill's edges, select the fill, and then click Modify, Shape, and then Soften Fill Edges. From the Soften Fill Edges dialog box, adjust the settings and click OK. Experiment with the settings to see what sort of effects you can create. See Chapter 21 to learn more about drawing simple shapes in Flash MX.

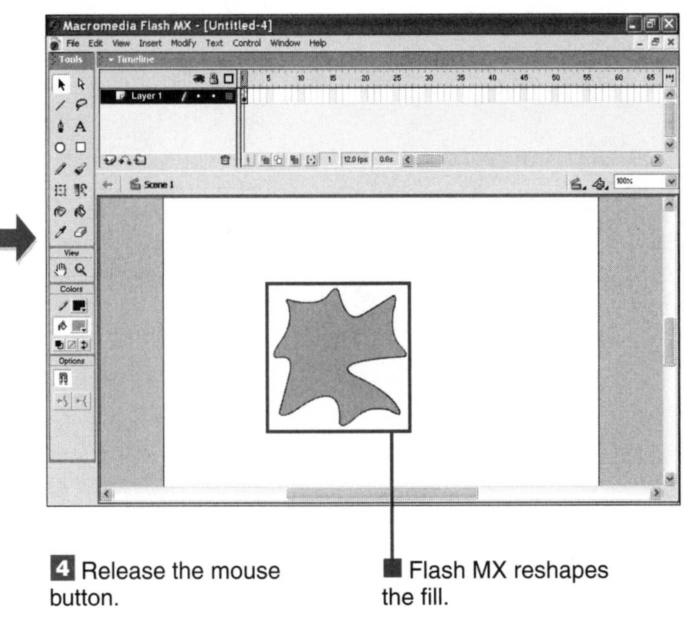

4 Release the mouse button.

■ Flash MX reshapes the fill.

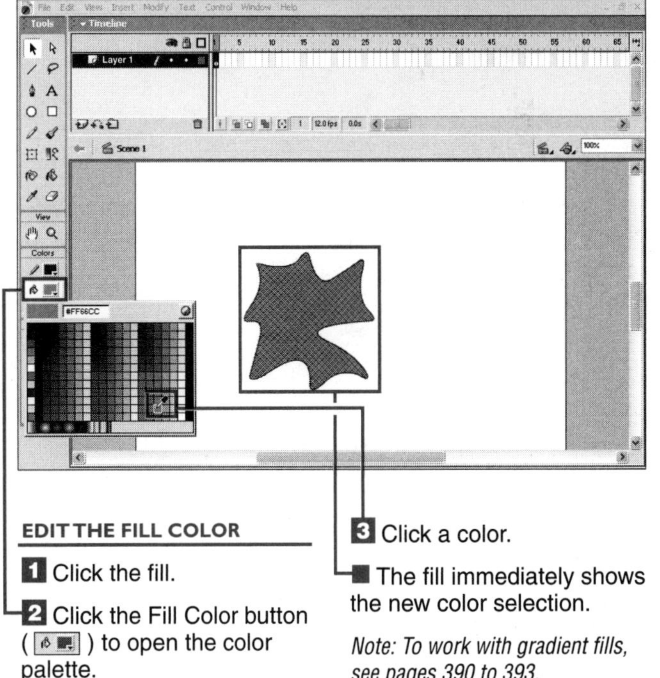

EDIT THE FILL COLOR

1 Click the fill.

2 Click the Fill Color button ([icon]) to open the color palette.

3 Click a color.

■ The fill immediately shows the new color selection.

Note: To work with gradient fills, see pages 390 to 393.

EDIT OBJECTS WITH THE FREE TRANSFORM TOOL

You can use the new Free Transform tool to alter existing shapes on the Stage and create new shapes to use in your animations and Flash movies. The Free Transform tool, located on the Drawing toolbar, includes four modifier tools: Rotate and Skew, Scale, Distort, and Envelope.

You can apply the Rotate and Skew and the Scale modifiers to objects you create or import. You can use the Rotate and Skew modifier to rotate an object or skew the appearance of an object. For example, you might rotate a photograph you import into Flash.

You can use the Scale modifier to resize objects using *edit points*, also called *handles*. The direction you drag an edit point determines whether the object grows or shrinks in size, or whether the object's overall shape distorts. For example, if you drag any corner edit point, Flash scales the object in proportion to its original size. If you drag a center edit point on any side of the selected object, the object appears to stretch or condense, depending on which way you drag the mouse.

You can apply the Distort and Envelope modifiers to objects you draw in Flash. You can use the Distort modifier to alter various points along the object's edges to distort the object's appearance.

EDIT OBJECTS WITH THE FREE TRANSFORM TOOL

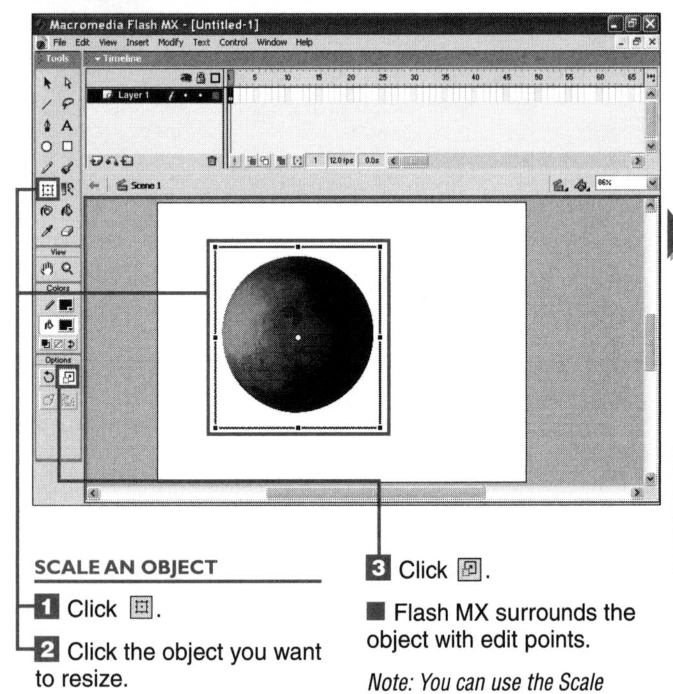

SCALE AN OBJECT

1 Click .

2 Click the object you want to resize.

3 Click .

■ Flash MX surrounds the object with edit points.

Note: You can use the Scale modifier to resize objects you draw and objects you import.

4 Drag an edit point to scale the object.

■ Drag corner edit points to resize the object but keep its proportions.

■ Drag middle edit points to stretch or compress an object, distorting its shape.

5 Release the mouse button.

■ The object resizes.

What happens if I resize an item beyond the Stage?

✔ In some cases, the object you resize may reach beyond the Stage area. Not to worry, the object is still there. You may need to zoom out to see the object. You can move the item back onto the Stage or resize the Stage to fit the larger object. Any part of the object that hangs off the Stage is still considered in the work area; however, the part may not be visible when you play your Flash movie. To resize the Stage area, see page 344.

How do I set a precise size?

✔ If you need to size an object to a precise measurement, use the Info panel. Open the Info panel by clicking Window, Info. Here you can set a precise size for the object using the width (W) and height (H) text boxes. Simply type the measurements you want, and then click outside the panel to see the changes take effect.

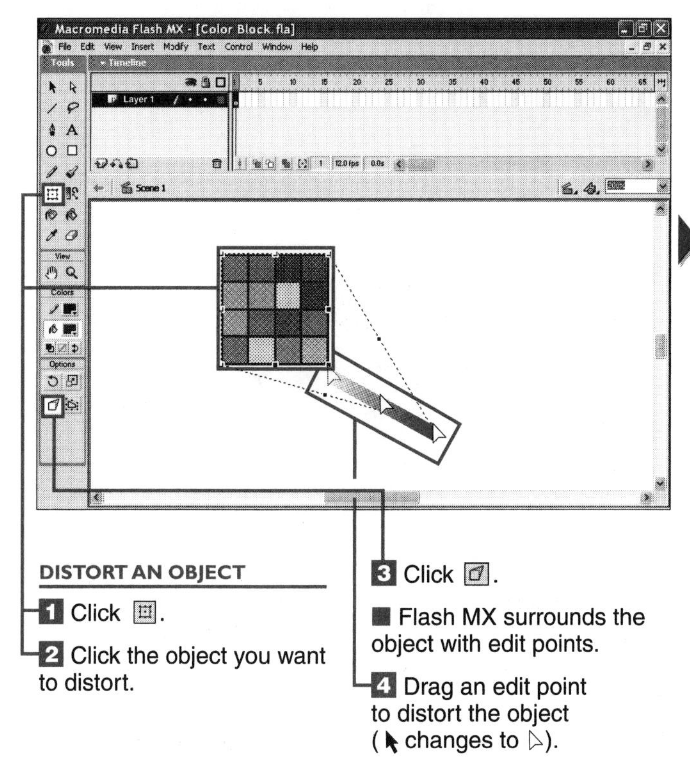

DISTORT AN OBJECT

1 Click ⊞.

2 Click the object you want to distort.

3 Click ◿.

■ Flash MX surrounds the object with edit points.

4 Drag an edit point to distort the object (↖ changes to ▷).

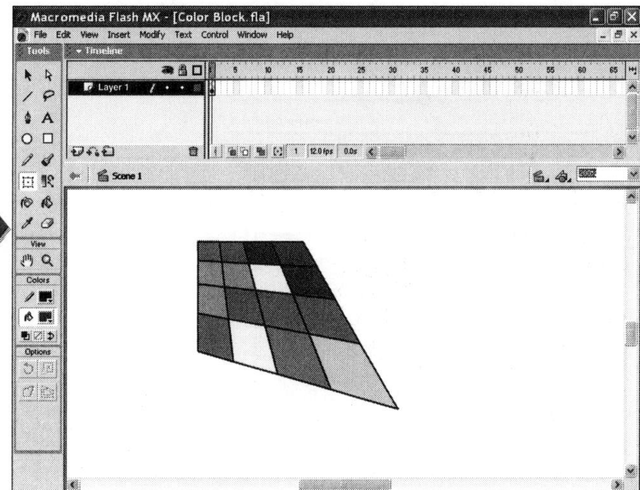

5 Release the mouse button.

■ The object redraws.

CONTINUED

EDIT OBJECTS WITH THE FREE TRANSFORM TOOL (CONTINUED)

You can use the Free Transform tool's skew and envelope features to warp and distort an object or shape, which is useful for creating morphed elements for animations. The skew feature is part of the Rotate and Skew modifier. You can learn how to use the rotate portion of the feature in the next section. The skew feature allows you to distort an object or shape by slanting it on one or both axes.

The Envelope modifier allows you to enclose the shape with an envelope of edit points and then use the points to control the shape effect. The Envelope modifier uses two types of edit points: regular edit points and tangent handles. Regular edit points are square and when manipulated, can change the corners and sides of an object. Tangent handles are circles that adjust additional points along the edges of a selected object.

You can use the Envelope modifier only to change shapes you create in Flash MX. You cannot use the feature to alter symbols, bitmaps, text boxes, or video objects.

EDIT OBJECTS WITH THE FREE TRANSFORM TOOL (CONTINUED)

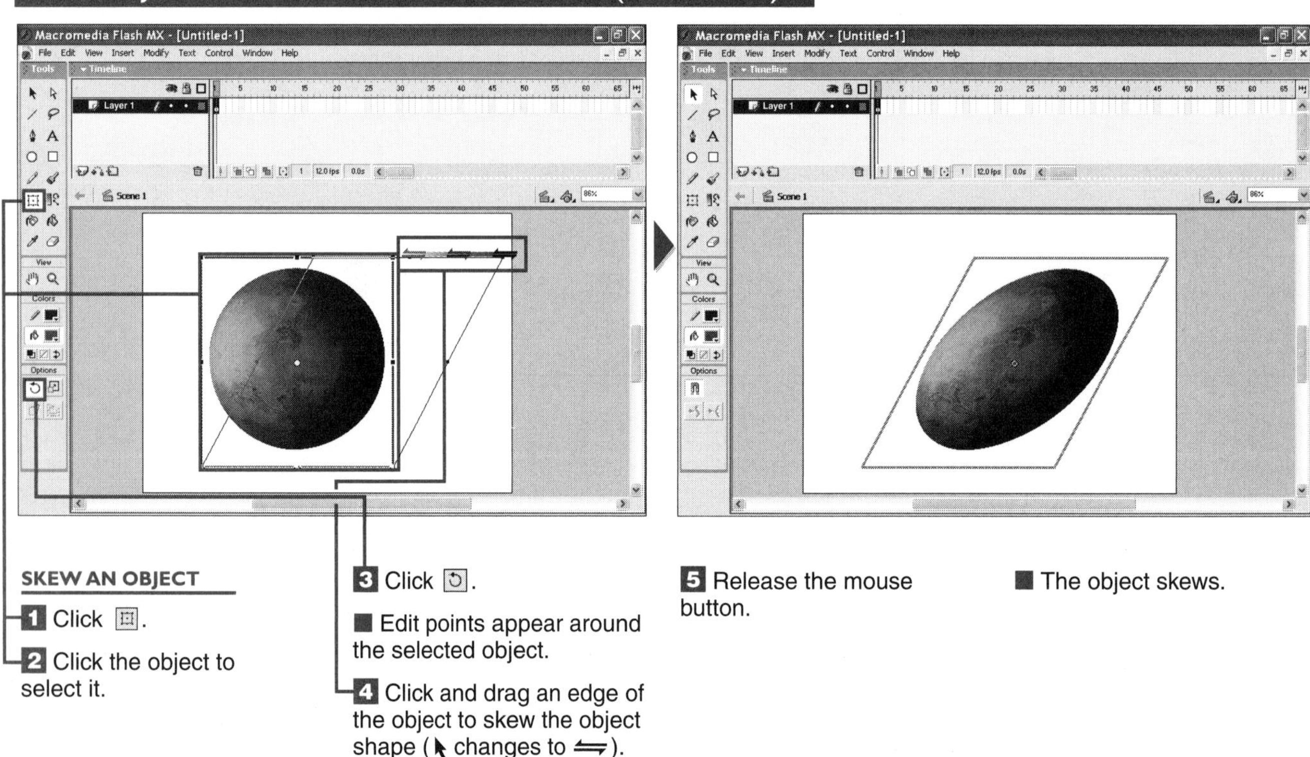

SKEW AN OBJECT

1 Click ⬚.

2 Click the object to select it.

3 Click ↻.

■ Edit points appear around the selected object.

4 Click and drag an edge of the object to skew the object shape (↖ changes to ⇋).

5 Release the mouse button.

■ The object skews.

How do I distort text in Flash MX?

✔ Using the Break Apart command, you can break apart the strokes and fills that make up the letters in a word or words, and then use the Envelope modifier to distort the shape of the text. To do so, click the text box, and then click Modify, Break Apart. Repeat this step two more times, and then you can apply the Envelope modifier. See Chapter 24 to learn more about working with the Text tool.

How do I turn on the Flash MX grid?

✔ Click the View menu, and then click Grid, Show Grid. The grid can help you align objects you draw or add to the Flash Stage. To hide the grid again, repeat this step.

I am having trouble seeing the edit points with the Envelope modifier. How can I make the edit points easier to see?

✔ Change the Stage background color by clicking Modify and then Document to open the Document Properties dialog box. Click Background Color and click a darker color from the Color palette. Click OK to apply it to the Stage. When you finish using the Envelope modifier, you can revisit these steps to return to the original document color again. You can also use the Background Color button in the Property inspector.

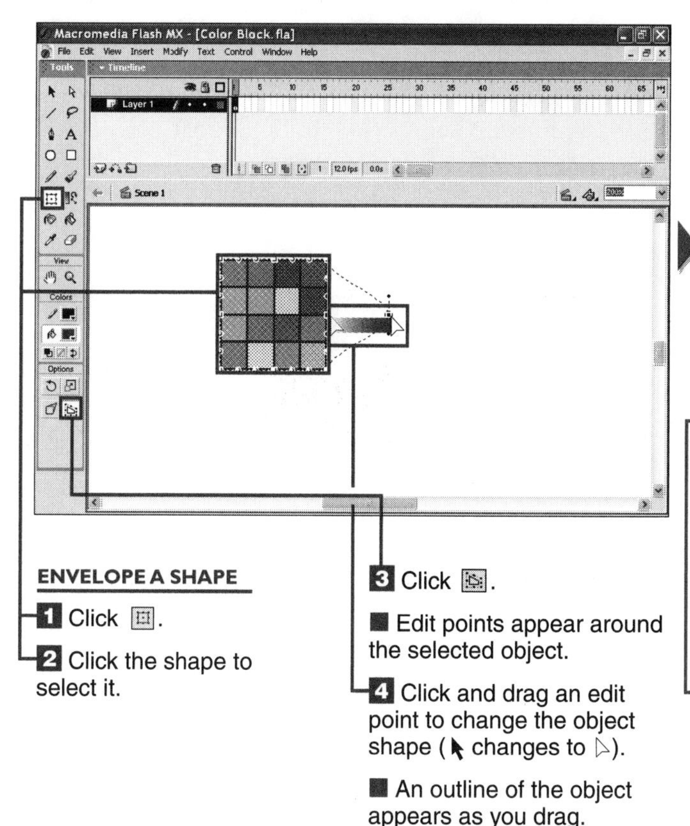

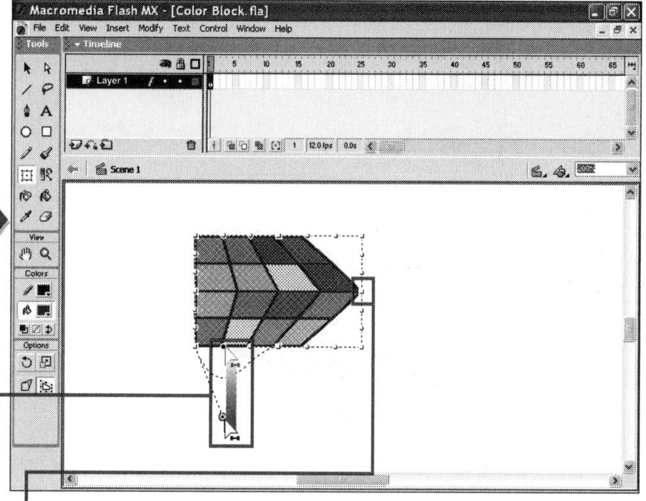

ENVELOPE A SHAPE

1 Click ⌗.

2 Click the shape to select it.

3 Click ⌗.

■ Edit points appear around the selected object.

4 Click and drag an edit point to change the object shape (↖ changes to ▷).

■ An outline of the object appears as you drag.

5 Release the mouse button.

■ The object reshapes.

6 Click and drag a tangent point to change the object shape (↖ changes to ▷).

■ An outline of the object appears as you drag.

7 Release the mouse button.

■ The object reshapes.

ROTATE AND FLIP OBJECTS

Not every shape or line you draw has to remain the same on the Stage. You can reorient objects to create different looks. You can spin an object based on its center point, or you can flip an object vertically or horizontally. Both actions enable you to quickly change an object's position in a drawing.

When you rotate an object on the Stage, you use the edit points, also called rotation handles, to reorient the object. You can achieve different degrees of rotation depending on the direction in which you drag an edit point on-screen. The Rotate modifier is part of the new Free Transform tool on the Drawing toolbar. You can rotate objects you draw as well as objects you import into Flash.

When you flip an object, there are no edit points. Flash MX automatically reorients the object in the position you indicate. You can flip an object horizontally or vertically. The Flip command flips an object 180 degrees. You might use the flip command to switch the direction of a photograph or shape on the Stage. This example shows how to rotate and flip a selected object on the Stage.

ROTATE AN OBJECT

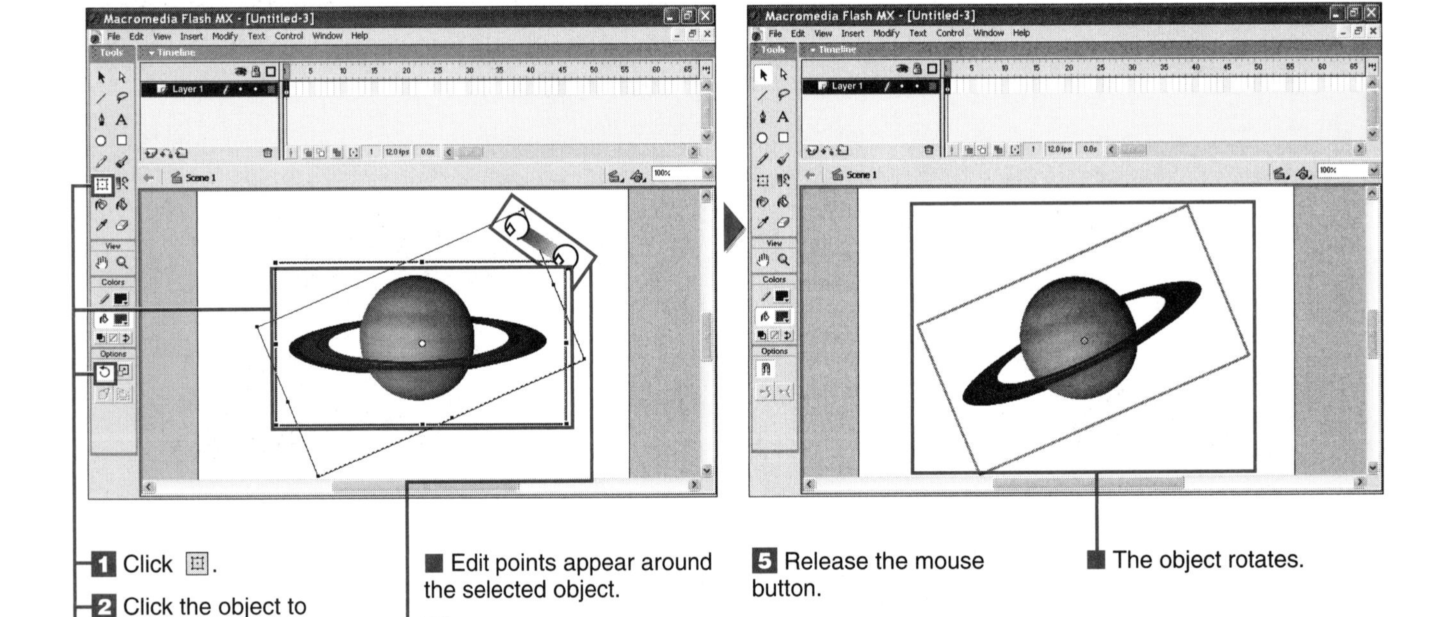

1 Click ⬚.

2 Click the object to select it.

3 Click ↻.

■ Edit points appear around the selected object.

4 Click and drag an edit point to rotate the object (↖ changes to ↻).

■ An outline of the object appears as you rotate.

5 Release the mouse button.

■ The object rotates.

Can I change an object's center point?

✔ For most objects, the center point is truly the object's center. But there are times when you want the center point to reference another part of the object. To change an object's center point, select the object, and then click . The center point appears as a tiny circle icon in the middle of the selected object. Drag the center point icon to a new location. Note that this works only on overlay-level, not stage-level, objects. See Chapter 21 to learn more about drawing levels.

Can I enter a precise degree of rotation?

✔ Yes. You can use the Transform panel to specify an exact rotation. Click Window, and then click Transform to open the panel. Click the Rotate option and type a degree of rotation in the text box. Flash MX immediately rotates the object on the Stage.

FLIP AN OBJECT

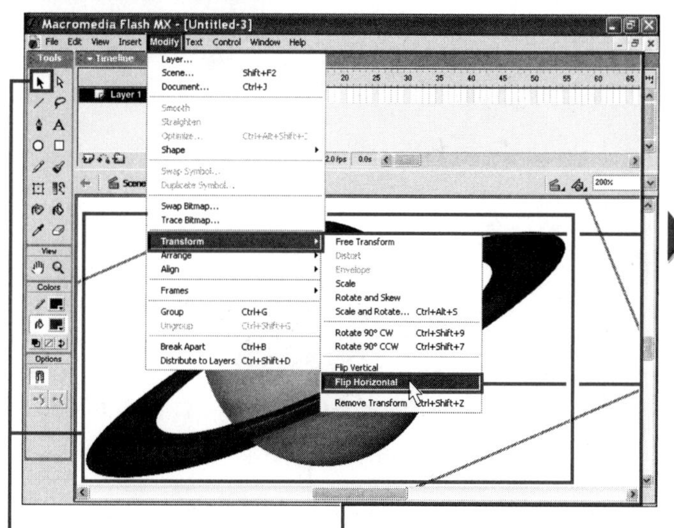

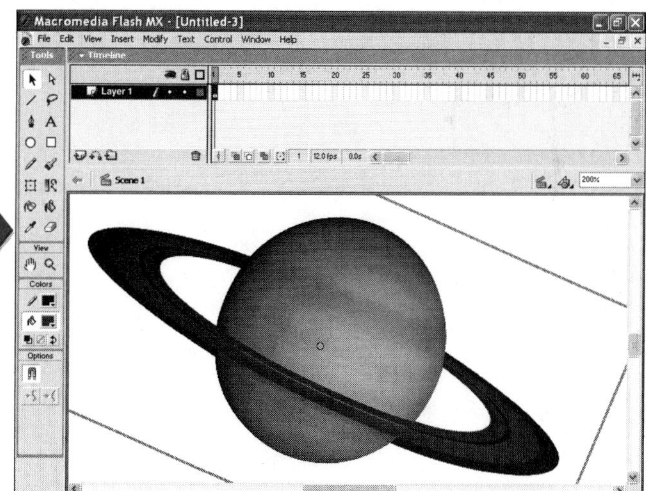

1 Click .

2 Click the object to select it.

Note: To select objects, see page 372.

3 Click Modify.

4 Click Transform.

5 Click Flip Vertical or Flip Horizontal.

■ The object flips on the Stage.

USING THE ERASER TOOL

You can use the Eraser tool to erase stray parts of a drawing or object, or you can use it to create new shapes within an object. The Eraser tool has several modifiers you can use to control how the tool works.

The Eraser tool does not really draw or paint, but rather it eliminates drawings or parts of drawings from the Stage. You can specify a shape for the Eraser as it moves around on the Stage. For example, perhaps you need to erase only a small piece of a line at the edge of a drawing. Such a task requires a small Eraser shape. A larger Eraser shape may end up erasing parts of your drawing that you do not want to erase.

Use the Eraser tool to erase strokes and fills on the stage level. You cannot erase grouped objects, symbols, or text blocks unless you apply the Break Apart command and make the items part of the stage level rather than the overlay level. See Chapter 21 to learn more about drawing levels in Flash.

If you accidentally erase part of the drawing, you can apply the Undo command to quickly reverse the effect.

USING THE ERASER TOOL

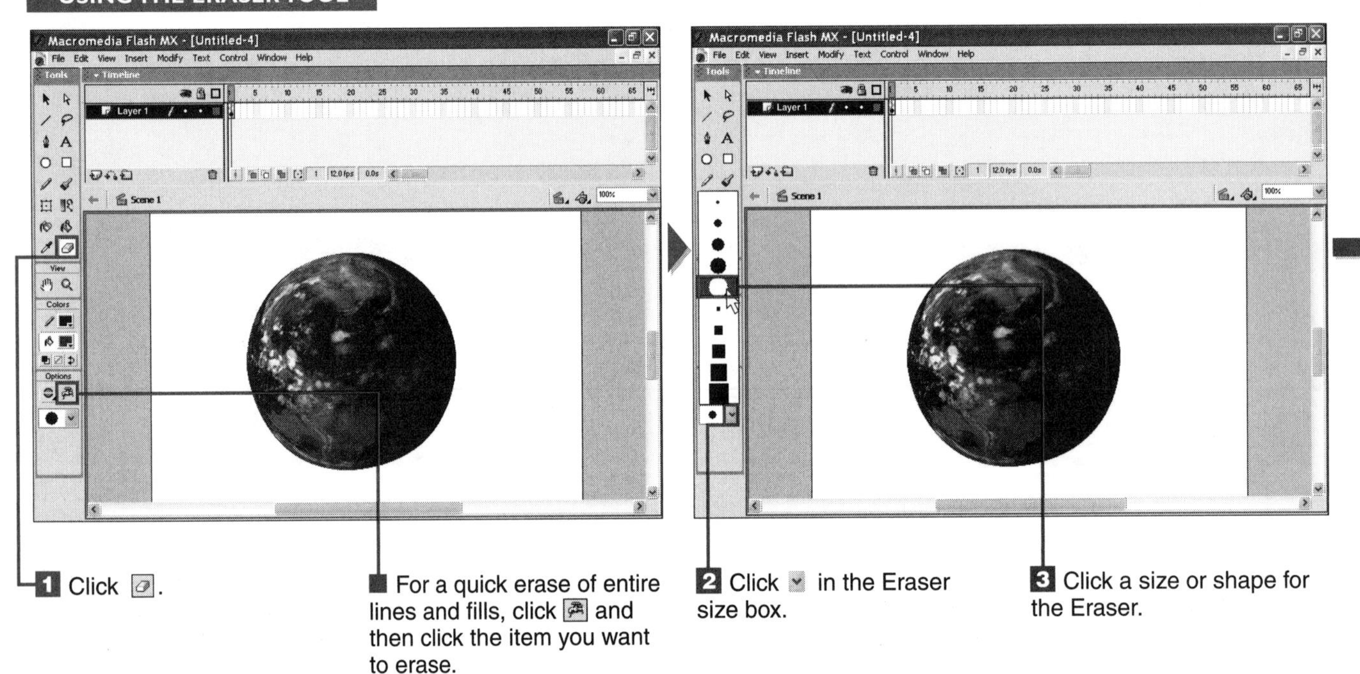

1 Click [Eraser tool icon].

■ For a quick erase of entire lines and fills, click [Faucet icon] and then click the item you want to erase.

2 Click [drop-down arrow] in the Eraser size box.

3 Click a size or shape for the Eraser.

How does the Eraser differ from a white fill?

✔ When you use the Eraser tool, you are literally erasing strokes and fills on the Stage. When you paint with the Brush tool using the white fill color, you are not erasing, but rather adding a shape to the Stage. Even though you cannot see the shape, because it is painted white and blends with the Stage background color, the shape is still there, and you can select and manipulate it. When you erase something on the Stage, it is permanently gone.

What do the Eraser modifiers do?

✔ You can use one of five modifiers with the Eraser tool. Click the button in the Options tray at the bottom of the Drawing toolbar to view the five modifiers. Erase Normal lets you erase over anything on the Stage. Erase Fills erases inside fill areas but not lines. Erase Lines erases only lines. Erase Selected Fills does just that — erases only the selected fill. Erase Inside erases only inside the selected area.

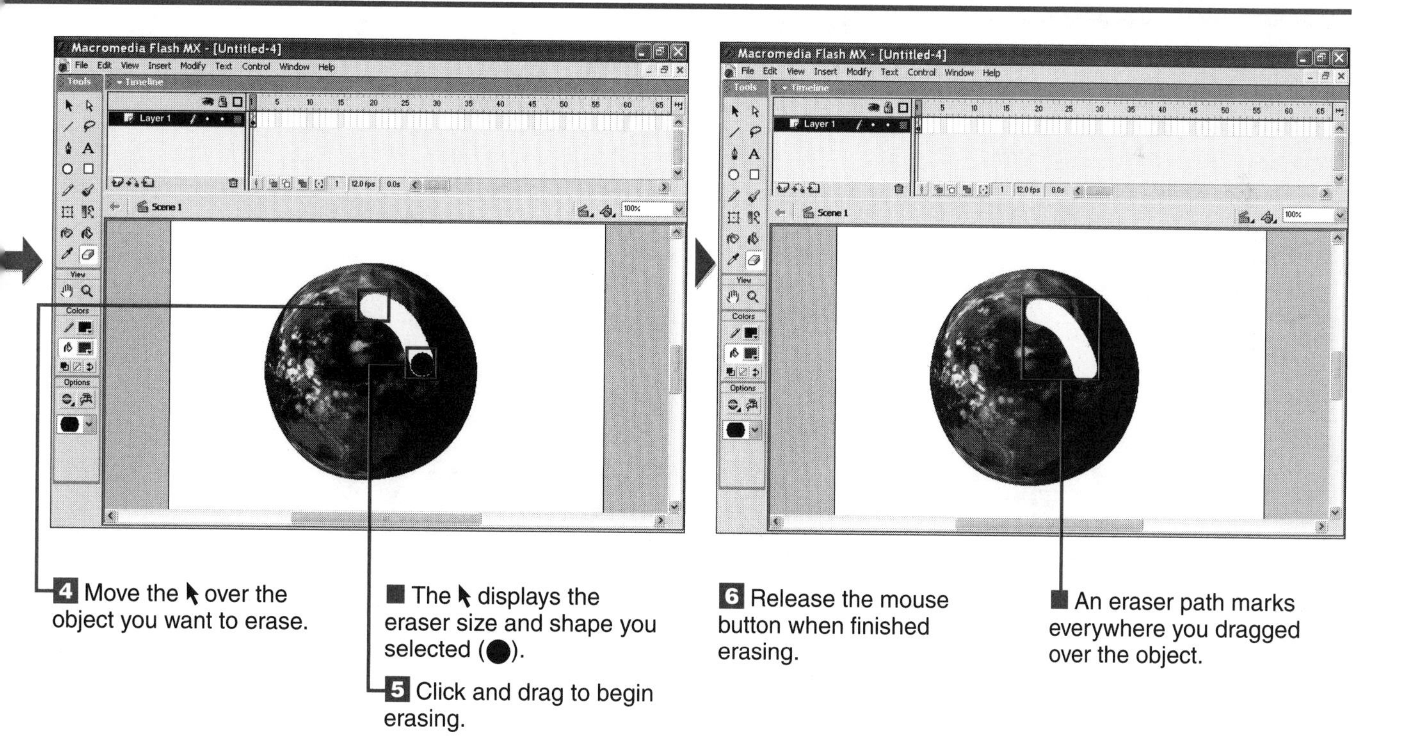

4 Move the over the object you want to erase.

■ The displays the eraser size and shape you selected (●).

5 Click and drag to begin erasing.

6 Release the mouse button when finished erasing.

■ An eraser path marks everywhere you dragged over the object.

WORK WITH GRADIENT EFFECTS

You can use gradient effects to add depth and dimension to your Flash drawings. A *gradient* effect is a band of blended color or shading. In Flash MX, you can apply a gradient effect as a fill to any shape.

By default, the Fill Color palette offers several gradient effects you can use. There are three vertical color bar effects, called *linear gradients*, and four circle gradient effects, called *radial gradients* you can choose from the color palette. If you do not like the default choices, you can create your own linear or radial gradient effect.

You can save time if you plan out which colors you want to use in a gradient and decide which type of gradient you want to apply. For example, if you want to create an illusion of depth and apply it to an interactive button you have created, experiment with a radial gradient.

This example shows you how to assign a default gradient effect from the Fill Color palette as well as customize a new gradient. You can use the steps in the example to apply any gradient effect.

WORK WITH GRADIENT EFFECTS

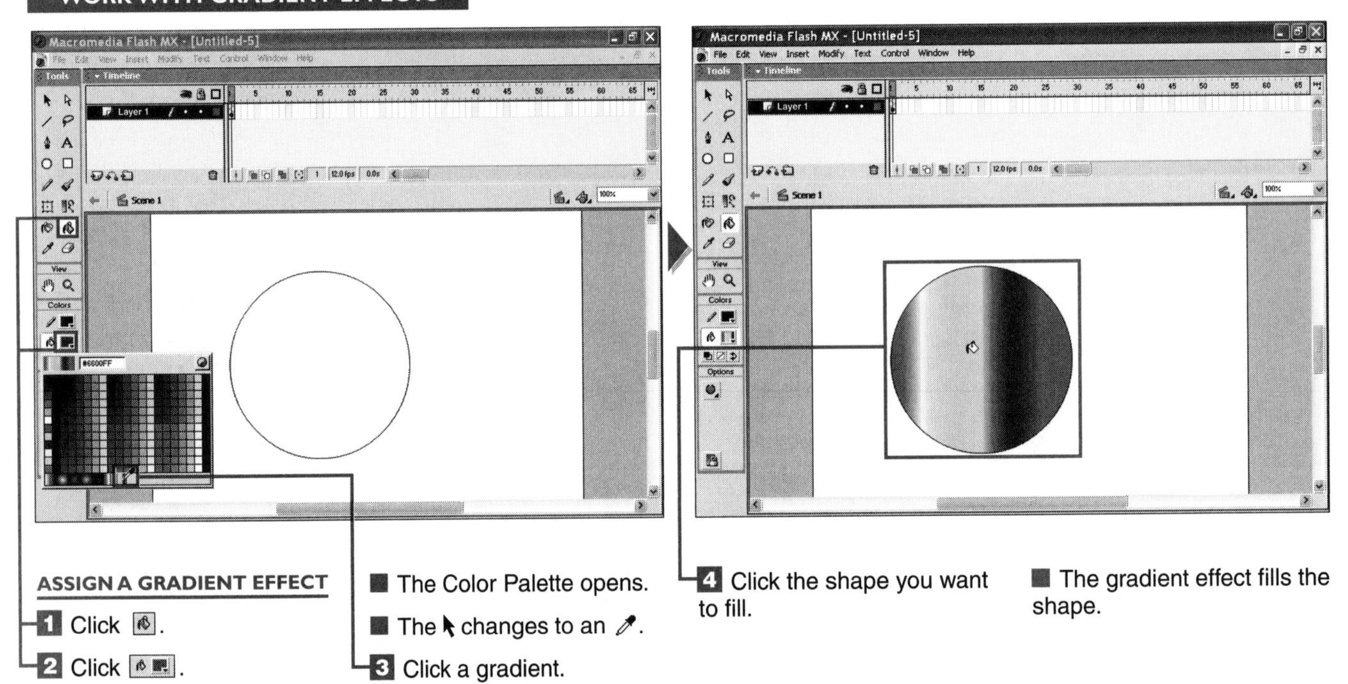

ASSIGN A GRADIENT EFFECT

1 Click .

2 Click .

■ The Color Palette opens.

■ The changes to an .

3 Click a gradient.

4 Click the shape you want to fill.

■ The gradient effect fills the shape.

What makes a gradient effect?

✔ The term *gradient* refers to an effect in which two or more colors graduate in color intensity from one color to another. For example, a two-color gradient effect might show the color red blending into yellow from the left to the right. The middle area of the effect shows the subtle blending of the two colors. You can create gradient effects in Flash that blend colors from left to right. Gradient effects can also create a three-dimensional appearance. You can create a radial effect that intensifies color from the middle to the outer edges, or from the outer edges to the middle.

Can I use a gradient as a Brush color?

✔ Yes. You can assign a gradient as the color you use with the Brush tool. You can specify a gradient effect from the Fill Color palette before you begin using the Brush tool, or you can use the Paint Bucket to fill the painted shape after you have drawn it on the Stage.

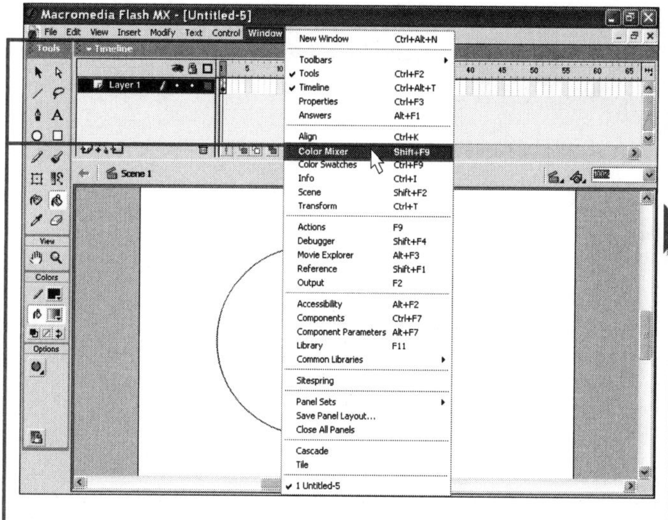

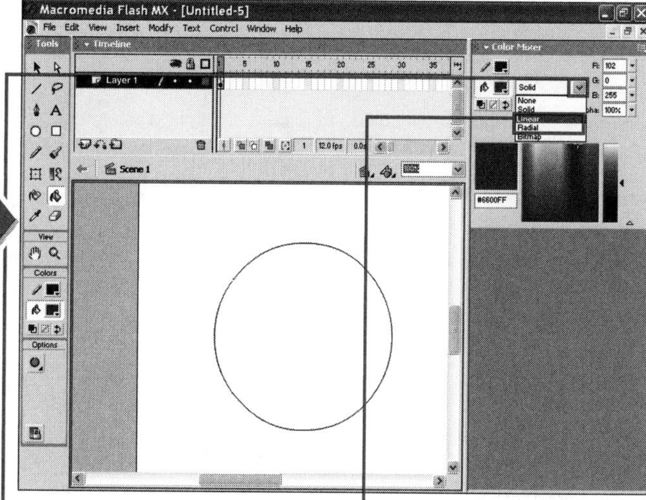

CREATE A NEW GRADIENT

1 Click Window.

2 Click Color Mixer.

■ The Color Mixer panel opens.

Note: To work with Flash MX panels, see page 348.

3 Click the Fill Style .

4 Select Radial Gradient or Linear Gradient.

CONTINUED

WORK WITH GRADIENT EFFECTS (CONTINUED)

Using the tools associated with the Color Mixer panel, you can customize your own unique gradient effect. You might prefer a certain color combination and arrangement in a gradient or need to match the colors of existing HTML elements on a Web page. After you create the customized gradient effect, you can save it and access it again throughout your project.

You can change the properties of the gradient you create by adjusting different colors and color markers creating color intensity bandwidths. Color markers are the tiny icons beneath the gradient bar in the Color Mixer panel. By dragging a marker on the gradient bar, you can create different areas of intensity in the gradient effect.

To get a feel for how the customizing effect works, start with one color and adjust the marker left and right across the color bar in the Color Mixer panel. Flash MX does not limit you to the number of colors you use in the gradient, and after you create the gradient just the way you want it, you can save it as a swatch in the color palette to reuse again. You can add and subtract additional color markers as needed to create just the right effect.

WORK WITH GRADIENT EFFECTS (CONTINUED)

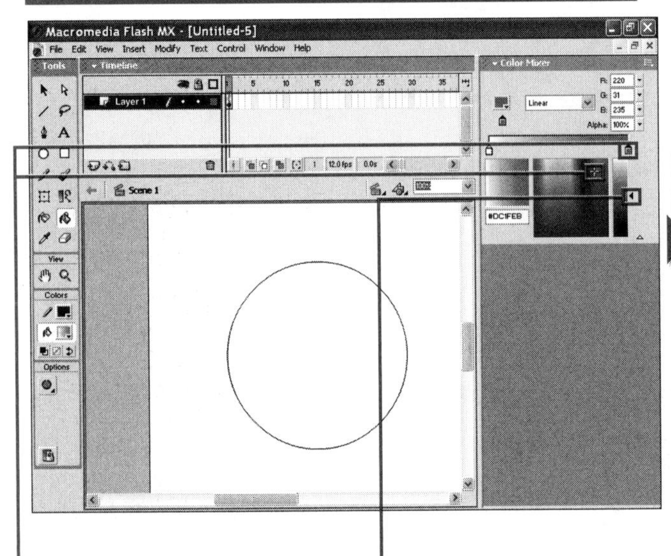

CHANGE GRADIENT COLOR

5 Click the color marker (⌂) you want to change.

6 Click a color.

7 Click a color shade.

■ The gradient bar changes color.

ADJUST COLOR INTENSITY

8 Drag the ⌂ left or right to adjust the color intensity bandwidth on the gradient.

■ To add another ⌂ to the effect, click below the gradient bar.

■ To remove a ⌂, drag it off the panel.

■ You can continue creating the gradient effect by adding color markers, assigning colors, and dragging the markers to change the intensity.

How do I control the highlighting of a radial gradient?

✔ Radial gradient fills, when used with the Paint Bucket tool, are controlled by where you click on the shape. Click left of center to make the fill highlighted on the left, or click center to highlight the center of the fill.

Can I make changes to an existing gradient in the palette?

✔ Yes. You can select an existing gradient effect and make modifications. From the Color Mixer panel, click the gradient swatch you want to edit. You can now make changes to the color markers or intensities and save the edits as a new gradient color swatch.

Can I delete a customized gradient effect I no longer need?

✔ Yes. Click Window, and then Color Swatches to display the Color Swatches panel. Click on the gradient effect swatch you want to delete. Click at the top of the panel and click Delete Swatch. Flash MX permanently deletes the gradient effect from all color palettes.

How do I close the Color Mixer panel?

✔ You can click the panel's Options Menu button ( ) and then click Close Panel.

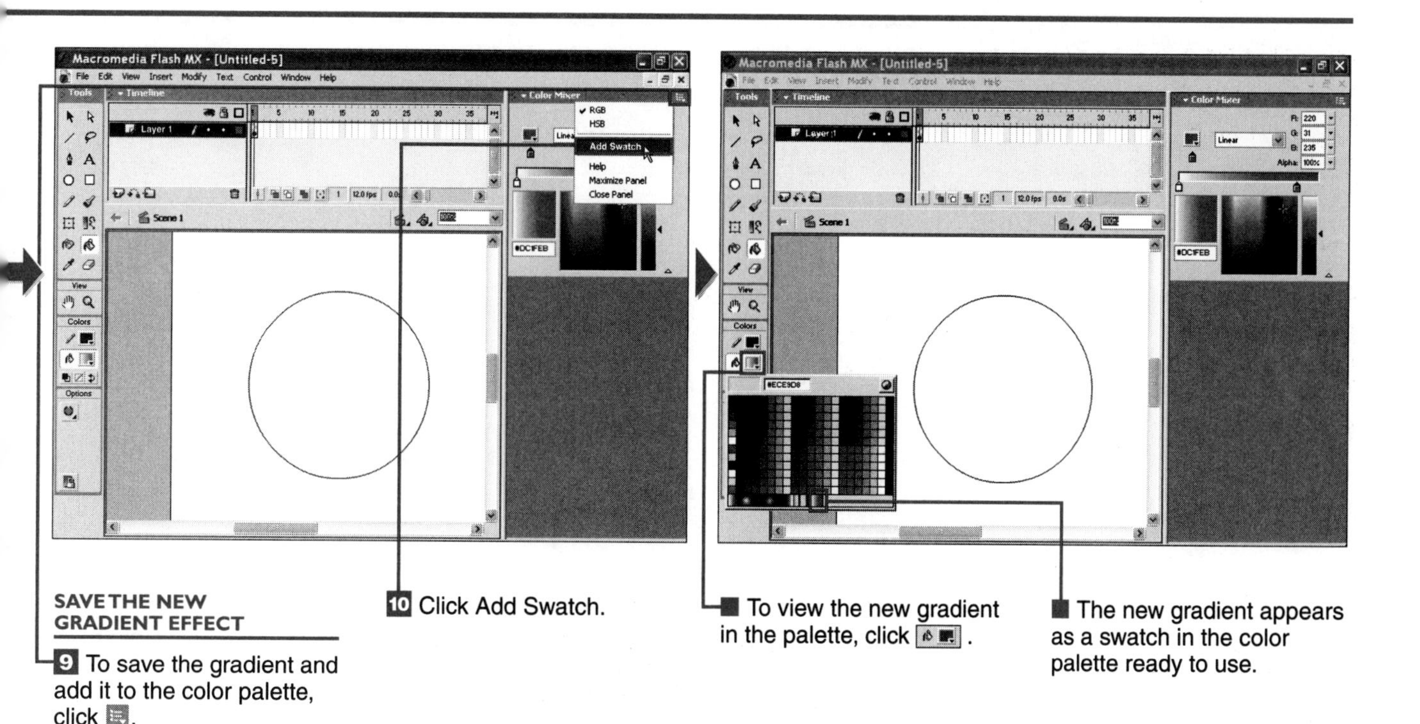

SAVE THE NEW GRADIENT EFFECT

9 To save the gradient and add it to the color palette, click .

10 Click Add Swatch.

■ To view the new gradient in the palette, click .

■ The new gradient appears as a swatch in the color palette ready to use.

TRANSFORM A GRADIENT FILL

You can use the new Fill Transform tool on the Drawing toolbar to transform gradient fills and bitmap fills. Gradient fills blend two or more colors to create a dimensional effect, while bitmap fills utilize an image or pattern as the fill instead of a color. The Fill Transform tool is new to Flash MX and allows you to change the appearance of fills, most noticeably, gradient fills.

For example, by default, a radiant fill radiates the fill color from the middle of the fill. With one gradient color appearing lighter than the other, the radiant fill makes the object appear to be highlighted by an off-stage light source. With the Fill Transform tool, you can change the position of the radiant, called the *center point*, thus changing where the highlight appears on the object.

You can also change the angle of the gradient, thus changing the angle of the imaginary light source shining upon the object. You can also change the position of the fill as it appears around the center point.

You can also fill an image or pattern into a closed shape or outline and use the Fill Transform to modify the appearance of the bitmap fill. To create a bitmap fill, see page 412.

TRANSFORM A GRADIENT FILL

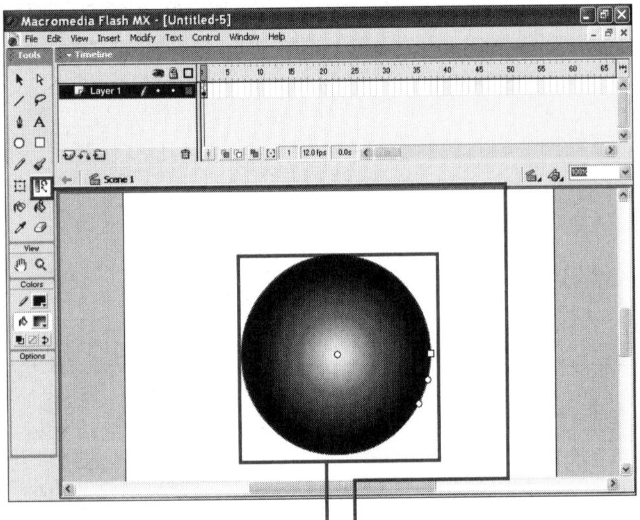

1 Assign a gradient fill to an object or shape.

Note: To assign a gradient effect, see page 390.

2 Click [Fill Transform tool icon].

3 Click the fill.

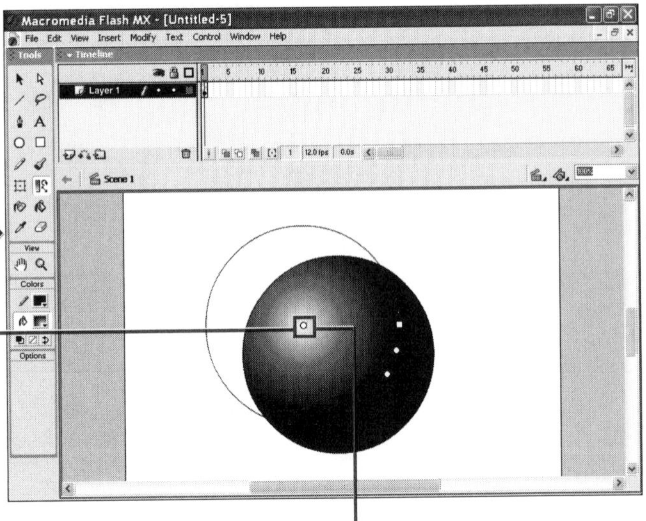

■ Four edit point controls appear on the fill.

4 Drag an edit point to transform the fill.

■ Use the center point to change the position of the highlight.

■ In this example, the center point moves up and left.

How do I get rid of the transformation?

✔ Click the Edit menu and click Undo. The Undo command immediately reverses the last edit you made. You may need to repeat Undo several times to return the fill to the status you started with. A faster way of undoing edits is to press Ctrl + Z (⌘ + Z) on the keyboard.

My fill shape takes up the entire Stage, and I cannot see the fill's edit points. How do I view the edit points to transform the fill?

✔ Click the View menu, and then click Work Area. You can also click the View menu, click Magnification, and click a zoom level to zoom out and see more of the work area.

What does the Lock Fill option do?

✔ You can use the Lock Fill modifier to lock a gradient or bitmap fill and make it seem to extend beyond the Stage. For example, if you have several shapes across the Stage, you can lock the fill and make the gradient fill each shape with a different portion of the gradient effect, much like a mask effect. To use the modifier, simply click a gradient and click the Lock Fill modifier ( ).

Can I replace a transformed gradient fill with another gradient?

✔ Yes. Any edits to the fill are applied to the new fill you add.

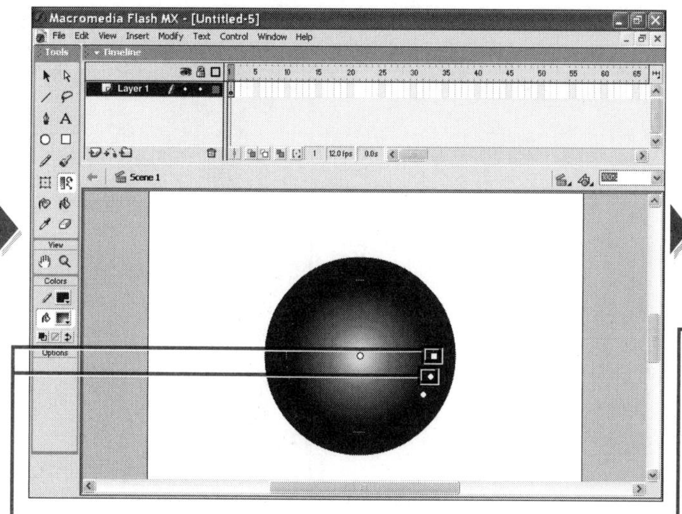

■ Use the width point to change the shape of the gradient effect.

■ Use the scale point to change the size or radius of the gradient effect.

■ In this example, the scale point is moved inward in the radial gradient.

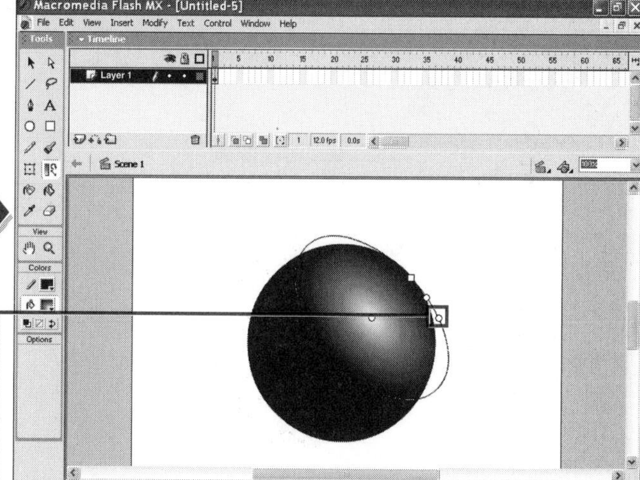

■ Use the rotation point to change the angle of the gradient.

■ In this example, both the center point and width are adjusted, and the rotation point is moved to change the angle of light.

EDIT A COLOR SET

You can customize the colors you use in Flash MX and create a unique color set to suit the projects you build. Flash comes with a default color set, but you can make new color sets based on the default set by removing colors you do not need for a particular project. You can then save the edited color set as a new color set for use in other Flash projects. You save color sets with the .clr file extension.

For example, if you are designing Flash elements for a Web page, you may need to match the color scheme of an existing site. By setting up a customized color set, you can be sure to use only the colors that match the existing color scheme.

You can mix colors and edit color sets using the Color Swatches panel. When working with colors, keep in mind that Flash MX handles colors differently across platforms (Windows and Mac). Computer systems and monitors also display colors differently, and older equipment is often incapable of displaying full color. Ultimately, this means that browsers may not always have the same colors available for Web page display as the colors you painstakingly choose for your Flash creations.

EDIT A COLOR SET

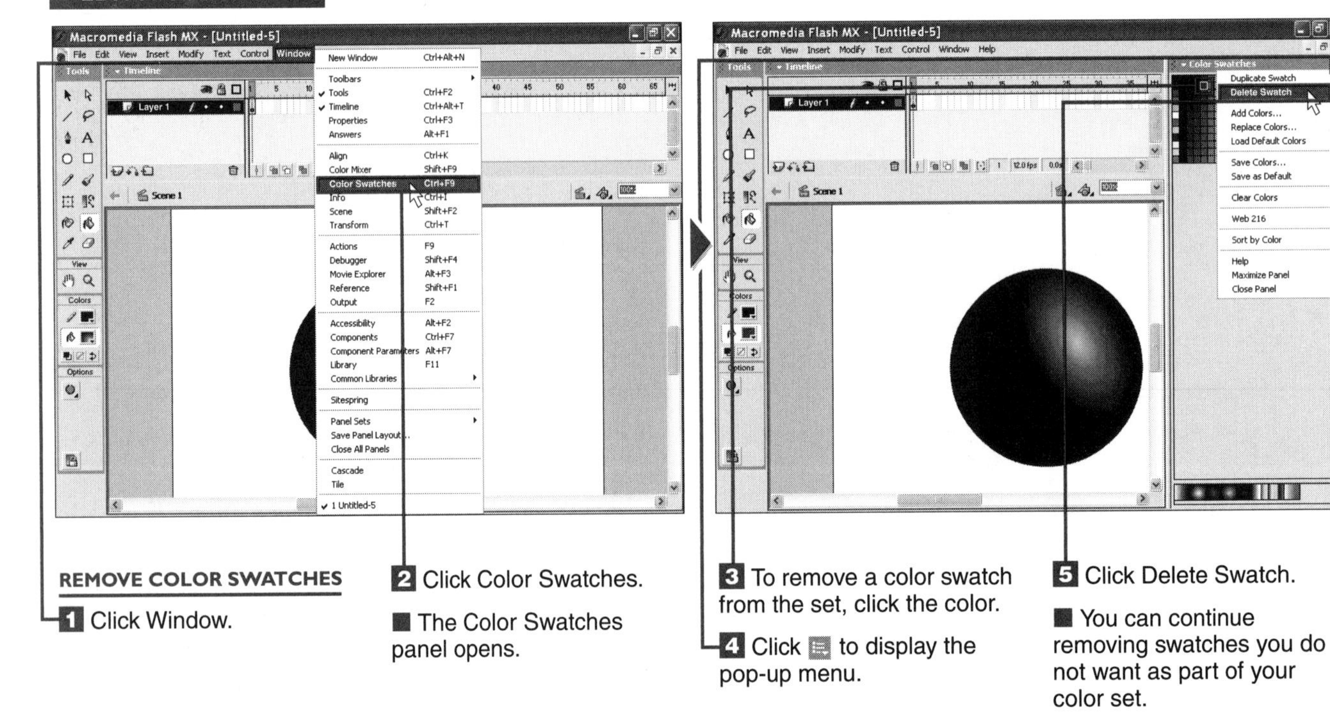

REMOVE COLOR SWATCHES

1 Click Window.

2 Click Color Swatches.

■ The Color Swatches panel opens.

3 To remove a color swatch from the set, click the color.

4 Click ☰ to display the pop-up menu.

5 Click Delete Swatch.

■ You can continue removing swatches you do not want as part of your color set.

Which colors should I use for Web page designs?

✔ Because different computers handle color differently, designers have come up with a Web Safe color palette. The Web Safe palette consists of 216 colors that Web designers find are consistent in both Windows and Mac platforms for all the major Web browser programs. To use the Web Safe palette in Flash, open the Swatches panel, click in the upper-right corner of the palette, and then click Web 216. Using the Web 216 color palette assures that your color selections are suitable for all browsers.

How do I load a color set?

✔ After you create a color set, you can reuse it in any Flash file. Open the Color Swatches panel, click the button in the upper-right corner of the panel, and click Replace Colors from the pop-up menu. This opens the Import Color Swatch dialog box. Locate the color set file you want to use, select it, and click Open.

SAVE THE EDITED COLOR SET

6 Click the to display the pop-up menu.

7 Click Save Colors.

■ The Export Color Swatch dialog box opens.

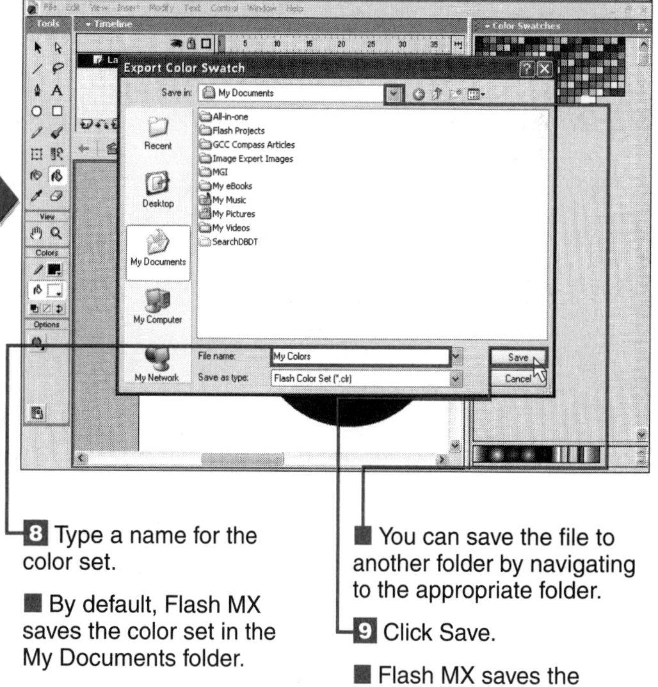

8 Type a name for the color set.

■ By default, Flash MX saves the color set in the My Documents folder.

■ You can save the file to another folder by navigating to the appropriate folder.

9 Click Save.

■ Flash MX saves the edited color set.

COPY ATTRIBUTES

You can use the Eyedropper tool to quickly copy attributes from one object to another. Copying attributes, rather than reassigning them one at a time, can save you time and effort. The Eyedropper tool copies fill and line attributes and enables you to copy the same formatting to other fills and lines.

The Eyedropper tool works a bit differently in Flash MX as compared to similar tools in other applications. Much like a real life eyedropper, the Eyedropper tool absorbs the formatting you apply to a particular line or shape. When it is not over a line or fill, the Eyedropper icon looks the same as the icon Flash uses to select a fill color. Move the Eyedropper over a line and a tiny pencil appears next to the dropper icon. The pencil icon lets you know you are hovering the Eyedropper over a stroke. When you click the Eyedropper, it absorbs the formatting applied to the stroke.

After picking up the attributes you want to copy, the Eyedropper becomes an ink bottle icon. You can then move the Eyedropper over the Stage and drop the same formatting onto another line.

COPY ATTRIBUTES

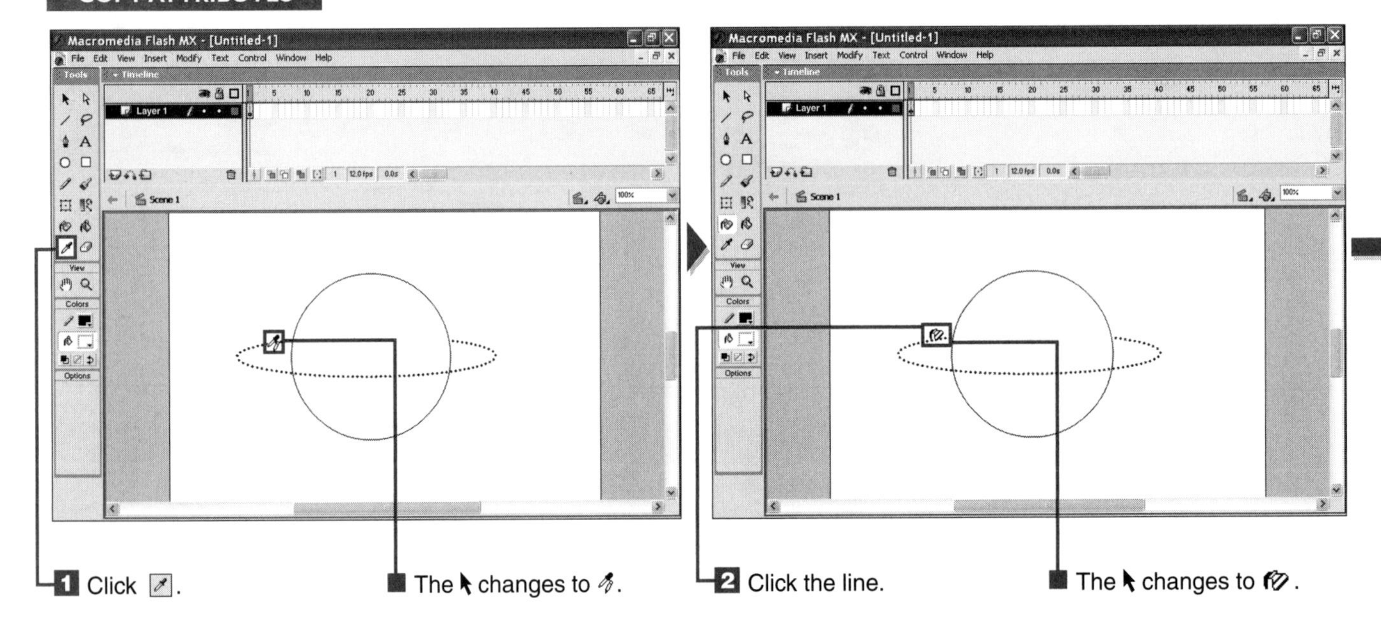

1 Click [Eyedropper].

■ The [arrow] changes to [eyedropper with pencil].

2 Click the line.

■ The [arrow] changes to [ink bottle].

Can I copy fill attributes, too?

✔ You can copy fill attributes just like you copy line attributes. When you move the eyedropper over a fill, a tiny brush appears next to it to show that you are over a fill. Click the eyedropper to absorb the fill formatting. Move the eyedropper over the fill you want to reformat and click again. Flash immediately changes the second fill to match the first.

My Eyedropper tool does not work. Why not?

✔ When copying line attributes, you cannot use the Ink Bottle on grouped lines. Be sure to ungroup the lines first and then try copying the line attributes to each line. To group and ungroup objects, see page 400.

Can I copy attributes before I draw another line or fill on the Stage?

✔ You can use the Eyedropper to copy the attributes of an existing line or fill, and the Line Color and Fill Color buttons change to reflect the formatting you assign to the object. You can then select a tool and draw on the Stage. The new object you draw has the same attributes as the original object.

Can I copy a bitmap fill without the Eyedropper tool?

✔ Yes. Make sure you break apart the bitmap before applying the Eyedropper.

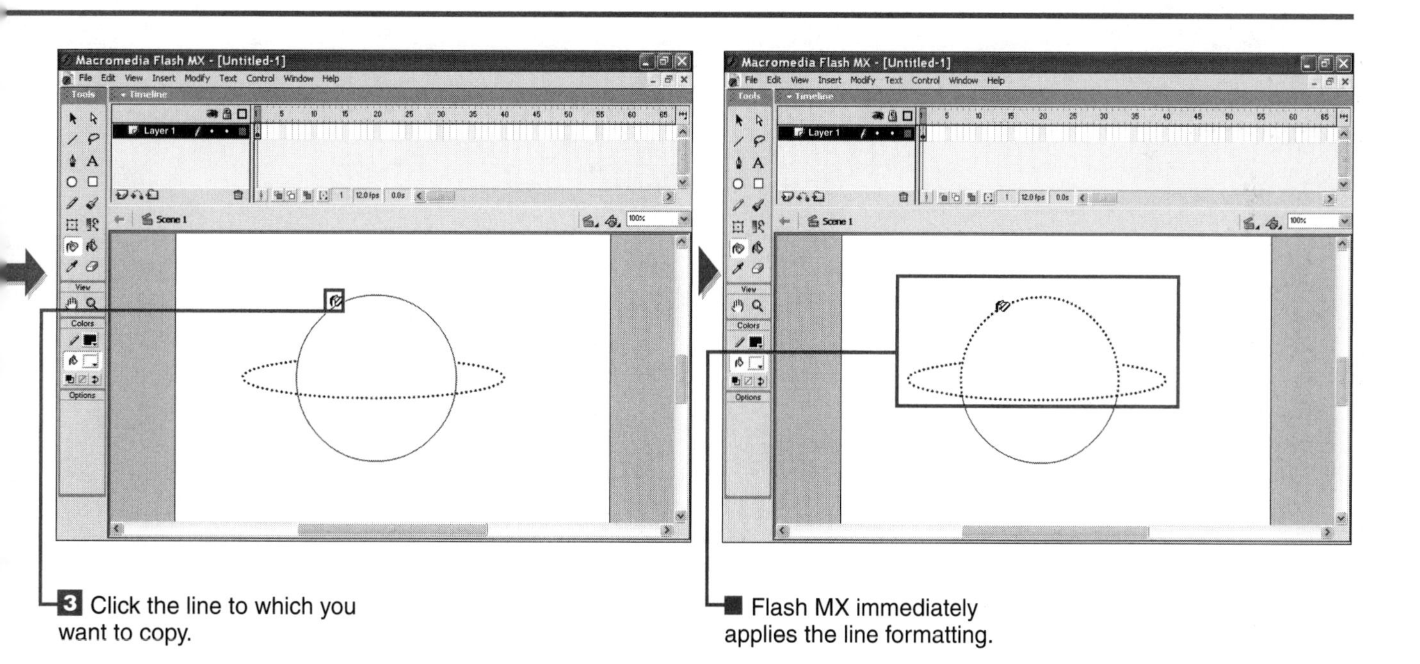

3 Click the line to which you want to copy.

■ Flash MX immediately applies the line formatting.

GROUP OBJECTS

You can work on multiple items at the same time by placing the objects in a group. A group enables you to treat the items as a single unit. Any edits you make affect all items in the group.

You place grouped objects on the overlay drawing level in Flash MX. Grouped objects do not interact with objects on the stage level. See Chapter 21 to learn more about drawing levels.

One of the prime benefits of grouping several objects is that you can move them all at once on the Stage instead of moving one object at a time. Grouping is also helpful when you want to keep related objects together, such as the elements that create a logo. For example, your logo might include a background box, a text box, and several freeform lines. After you design or create the logo on the Flash Stage and layer the objects just the way you want them, turn the objects into a group. You can ungroup the objects again to edit them individually. See page 402 to learn about stacking layers.

GROUP OBJECTS

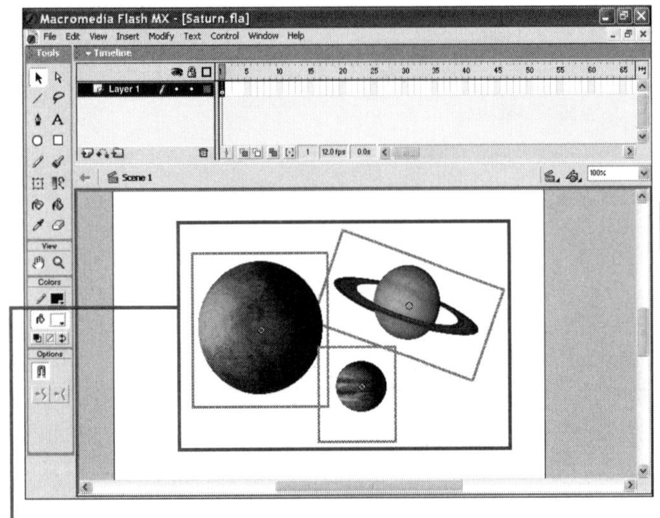

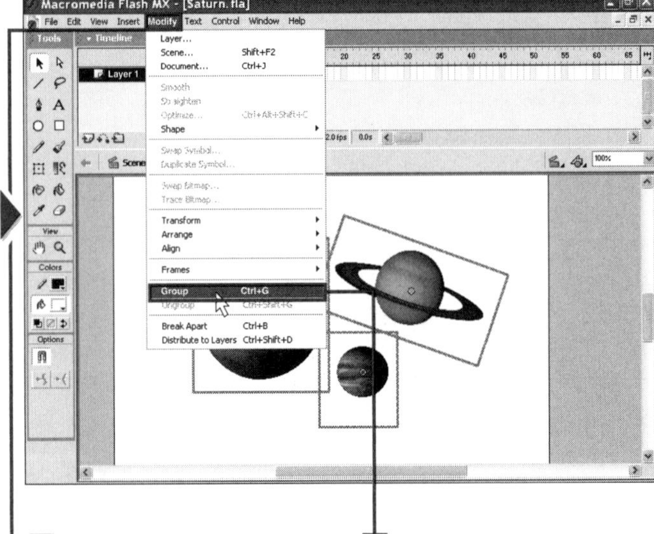

CREATE A GROUP

1 Select all the objects you want to include in a group.

Note: To select objects, see page 372.

■ You can select multiple items by pressing and holding Shift while clicking each item.

2 Click Modify.

3 Click Group.

How can I avoid accidentally changing a group?

✔ If you worry about accidentally moving or changing a group, you can lock it. Click Modify, Arrange, and then Lock. To unlock the group again, click Modify, Arrange, and then Unlock.

How is grouping different from stacking?

✔ Grouping sticks objects together so that they act as one object. Stacking allows you to move different grouped objects to the background or foreground, or somewhere in between.

Can I have a group of one?

✔ Yes. You can turn one object into a group to move it to the overlay level and keep it from interacting with other objects on the stage level.

How do I edit a group?

✔ Click [selection tool], and then double-click on the group you want to edit. Everything else on the Stage dims except for the items in the selected group. After editing the group, double-click anywhere outside the group.

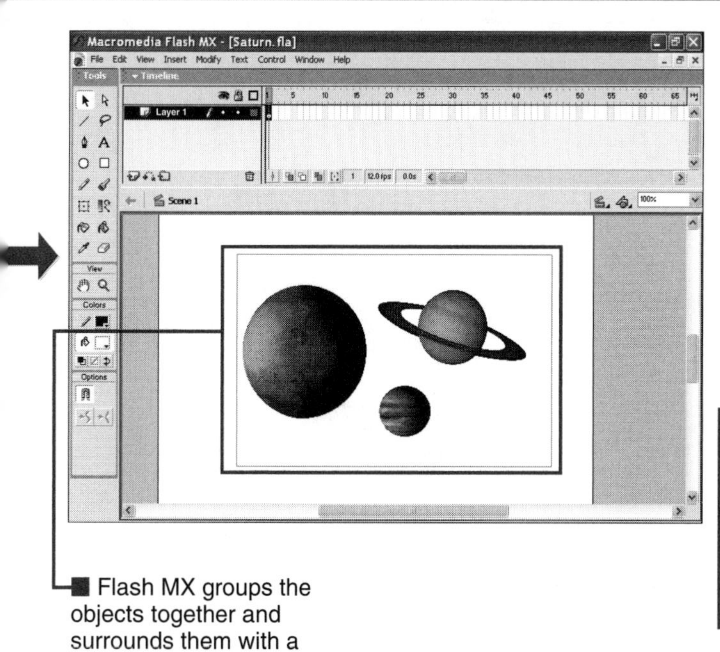

■ Flash MX groups the objects together and surrounds them with a blue box.

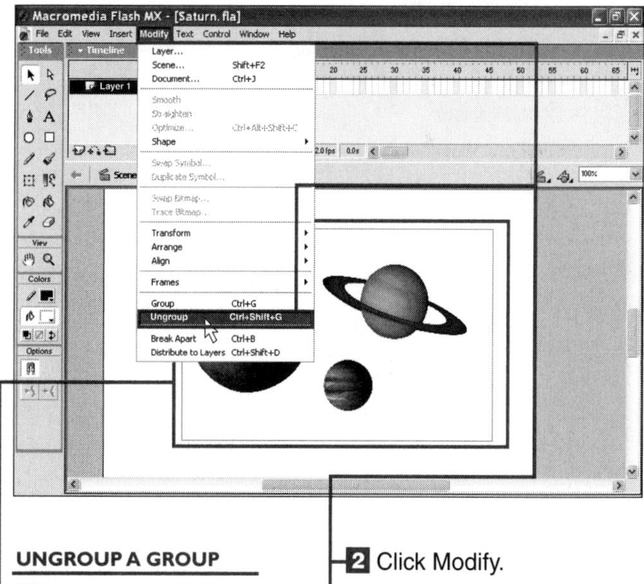

UNGROUP A GROUP

1 Select the group you want to ungroup.

Note: To select objects, see page 372.

2 Click Modify.

3 Click Ungroup.

■ Flash MX ungroups the objects.

STACK OBJECTS

You can stack objects you add to the Flash Stage to change the appearance of drawings. You may need to stack a circle shape on top of a horizontal line to create a logo or you may stack several objects over one another to create the illusion of depth in drawing.

When placing objects over other objects, you can control exactly where an object appears in the stack. You can place an object at the very back of a stack, at the very front, or somewhere in-between.

Stacking works only with grouped objects. Flash MX places grouped objects — whether the group consists of several objects or just one — on the overlay level, which means that they always appear stacked on top of objects that are located on the stage level.

When stacking grouped objects, you can move them to several different layers. These layers are invisible on the Flash Stage, but quickly become apparent when you move one group over another and reorder their placement in the stack. Stacking placement involves moving elements from the front of the stack to the very back, with several levels in between.

STACK OBJECTS

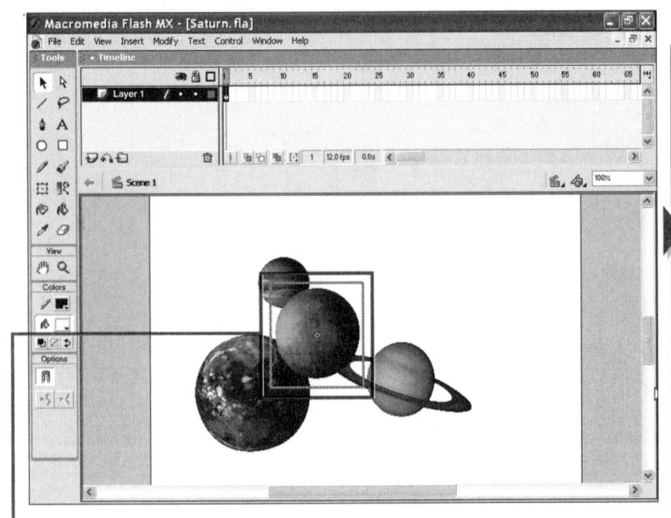

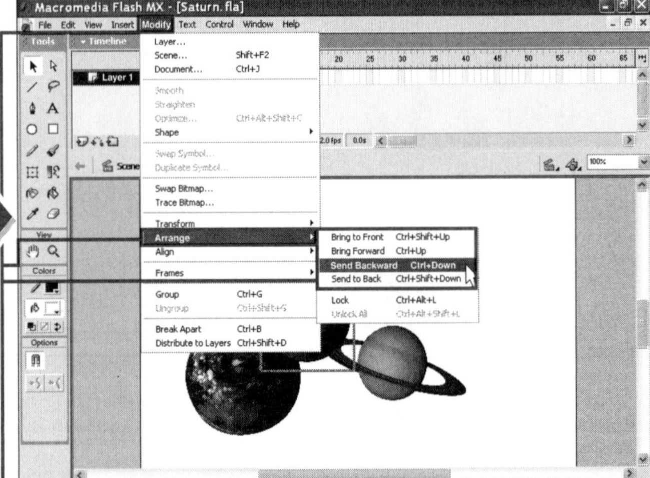

1 Select the symbol or group you want to reorder.

Note: To select objects, see page 372.

2 Click Modify.

3 Click Arrange.

4 Select whether you want to send the object to the front or back of the stack.

■ To send an object to the very back of the stack, click Send to Back.

■ To bring an object to the very front of the stack, click Bring to Front.

Is there a shortcut to moving an object up or back a layer in a stack?

✔ Yes. You can use keyboard shortcuts to quickly reposition an object in a stack.

Press Ctrl + ▲ (⌘ + ▲) to move an object up one layer.

Press Ctrl + Shift + ▲ (⌘ + Shift + ▲) to move an object directly to the top of the stack.

Press Ctrl + ▼ (⌘ + ▼) to move an object back a layer.

Press Ctrl + Shift + ▼ (⌘ + Shift + ▼) to move an object directly to the back of the stack.

Can I stack objects located on the stage level?

✔ No. You cannot apply the stacking commands to objects on the stage level; if you try, they do not work. Objects you place on the stage level interact, which means if you move a shape over a line, the line is covered. If you move the shape again, the line is no longer there; it has become a part of the shape. Stacking works only on objects you place on the overlay level.

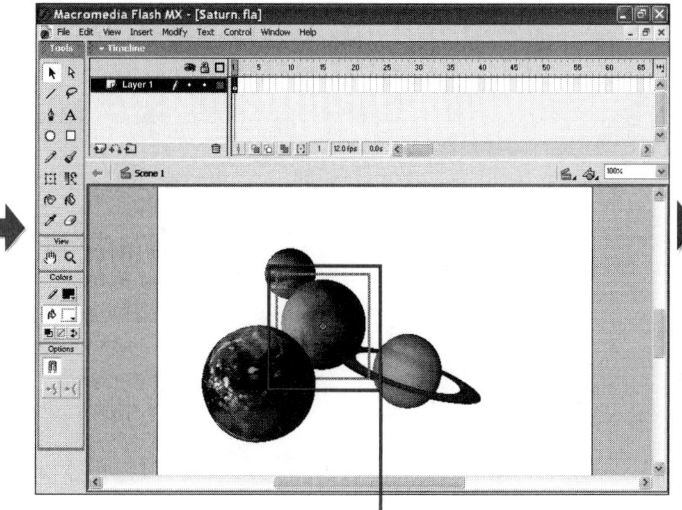

■ The object now relocates in the stacking order.

■ In this example, the selected planet moves back in the stack.

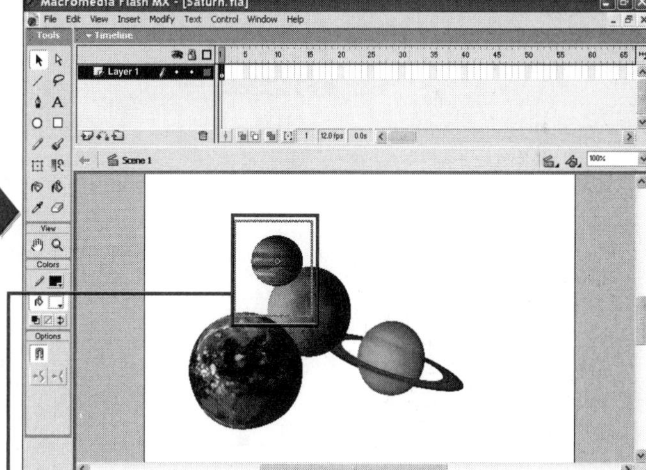

■ In this example, the selected planet moves forward in the stack.

ALIGN OBJECTS

You can control the alignment of objects you add to the Stage, whether they are shapes you draw or graphics you import. Changing object alignment can change the appearance of your drawing.

You can control precisely where an object sits on the Stage with the Align panel tools. You can align objects vertically and horizontally by their edges or centers. You can align objects to objects with the edges of the Stage, or even control the amount of space between the objects.

The alignment commands come in handy when you are trying to position several objects on the Stage and dragging them around manually does not seem to create the results you want. Although the Flash rulers and grid can help you line things up on the Stage, applying alignment options are much faster and easier.

You can find a variety of options just a quick click away in the Align panel. For example, the Align panel has a set of buttons for controlling horizontal alignment on the Stage and another set of buttons for controlling vertical alignment. You can open and display the Align panel for as long as you need it on the Stage. Like the other panels available in Flash MX, you can move, resize, and collapse the panel as needed to free up workspace onscreen.

ALIGN OBJECTS

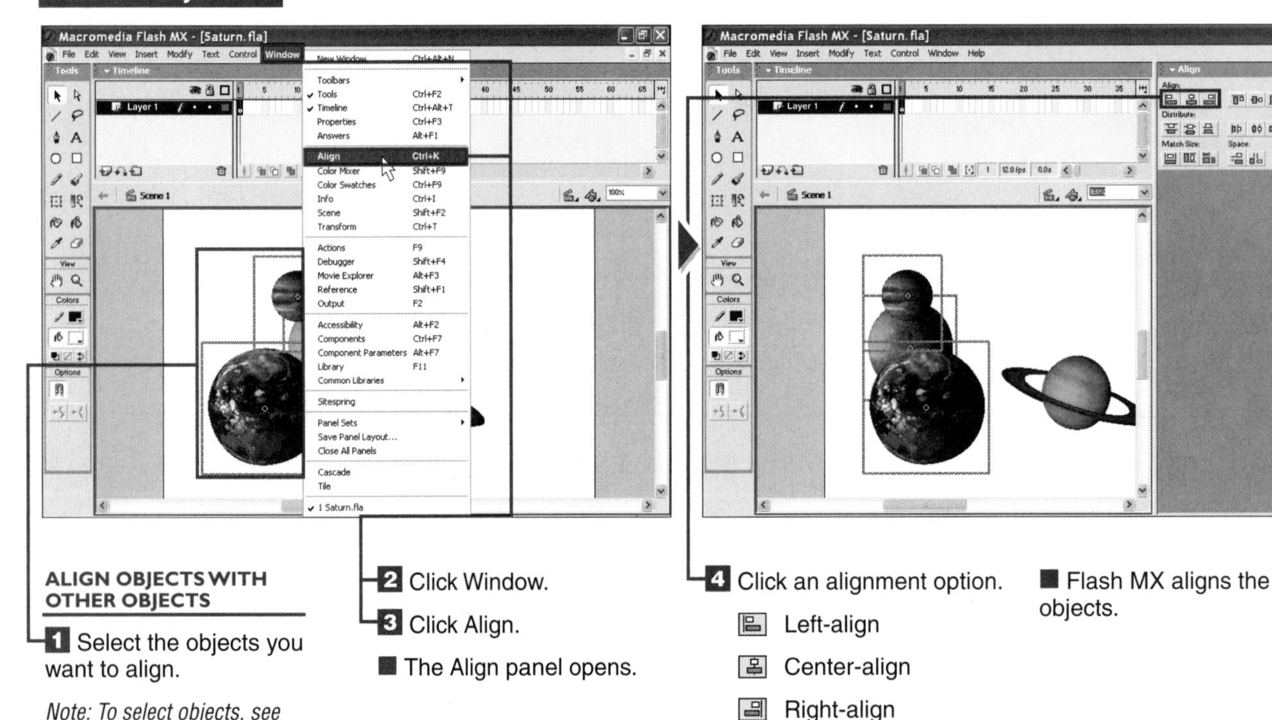

ALIGN OBJECTS WITH OTHER OBJECTS

1 Select the objects you want to align.

Note: To select objects, see page 372.

2 Click Window.

3 Click Align.

■ The Align panel opens.

4 Click an alignment option.

- Left-align
- Center-align
- Right-align

■ Flash MX aligns the objects.

How can I use the Match Size buttons?

✔ You can use the Match Size buttons in the Align panel to make two or more objects the same size on the Stage. For example, if you have two circles of differing sizes, you can select them both and click the sizing option you want to apply.

- Click to make the two objects equal in width.
- Click to make the two objects the same height.
- Click to make the objects match in dimensions.

How can I use the Space buttons?

✔ You can use the Space buttons in the Align panel to space two or more objects evenly on the Stage.

- Click to space the objects evenly, vertically on the Stage.
- Click to space the objects evenly, horizontally on the Stage.

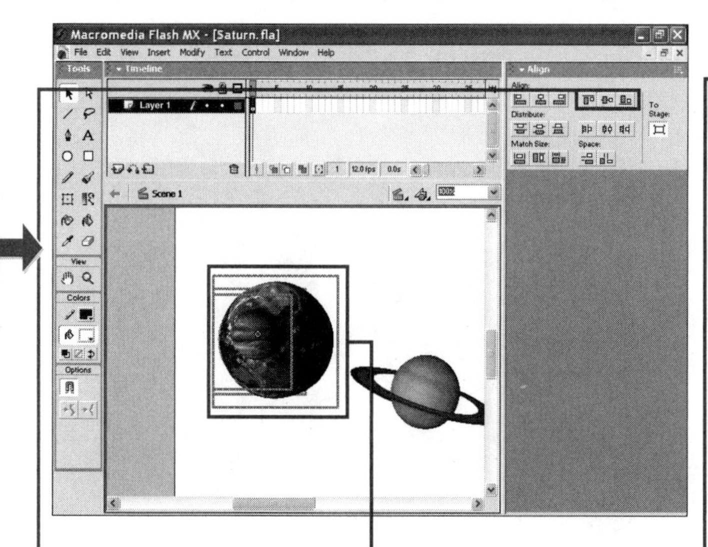

■ To align the objects vertically, click a vertical alignment.

- Top-align
- Center vertically
- Bottom-align

■ Flash MX aligns the objects to the Stage.

■ In this example, the selected objects align vertically centered.

ALIGN OBJECTS WITH THE STAGE

1 Select the objects you want to align.

2 Repeat steps 2 to 3 on the previous page to open the Align panel.

3 Click .

4 Click an alignment option.

■ Flash MX aligns the objects to the Stage.

■ In this example, the selected objects line up on the far left edge of the Stage.

INTRODUCTION TO VECTOR AND BITMAP IMAGES

You can create your own vector graphics in Flash MX or import graphics from other sources for use in your movies. Vector graphics are the native file types of Flash, so anything you draw by using the Flash drawing tools is a vector graphic. You can also import vector graphics from other vector graphics programs, such as Macromedia FreeHand, Adobe Illustrator, or vector graphics from earlier versions of Flash.

Vector graphics created in Flash MX produce the highest graphic quality in the Flash movies you export. Other graphics file types that you import into Flash are known as *bitmap* images. It is important to understand the basic differences between vector and bitmap file formats before you begin importing graphics from other programs.

Bitmap Graphics

Until recently, bitmap graphics, also called *raster* graphics, were the traditional way to illustrate Web pages. While bitmap images offer a great deal of detail, their file sizes are often large, requiring a lot of bandwidth when transferred across a network or the Internet.

Bitmap graphics are made of square dots called *pixels*. The dots are arranged in a grid pattern, and each dot includes information about its color and position. Most bitmap images use thousands of pixels. A single bitmap file must contain information that maps out the placement and color of each pixel to redisplay the image. The resulting file size is extremely large.

To illustrate this concept, try drawing a simple yellow smiley face in a bitmap drawing program and save the file in the bitmap file format. The resulting file size is likely to consume well over 100,000 bytes or 100 kilobytes. If you draw the same smiley face in Flash MX and save it as a Flash movie, the file consumes about 11 kilobytes.

Vector Graphics

Vector graphics use mathematical equations, or *vectors*, to define an image's shape, color, position, and size. Vector instructions tell how to display an image based on lines and curves (or arcs). The use of equations instead of pixels makes the image file size the same, regardless of whether the image is large or small. The vector file need only contain the mathematical data that describes the line and curve properties. This data tells the computer how to display the lines and curves that make up an image, including colors and size.

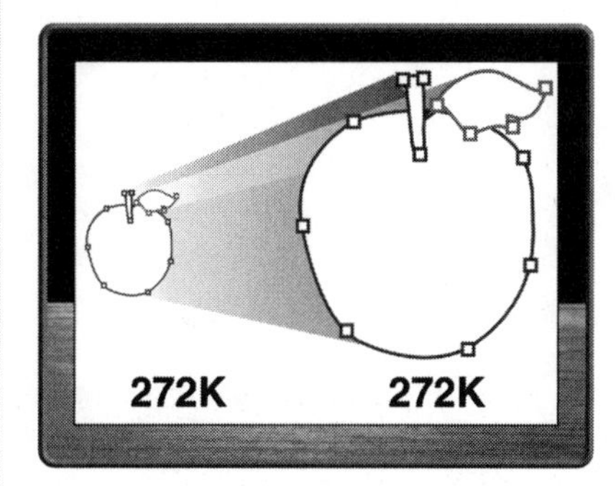

Technically, bitmap images use mathematical data, too, but the data includes instructions for each dot in the image, resulting in a much larger file size. The data that describes a vector graphic merely instructs how to display lines and arcs based on mathematical formulas along with coordinates for where the lines and arcs are placed. The result is a graphic file that is much more versatile.

You can easily scale vector graphics, unlike bitmap graphics. Because of their smaller file size, vector graphics download much more quickly onto Web pages. This is a big plus for Web page designers.

Import Graphics

Flash MX supports a variety of graphic-file formats, both bitmap and vector. Flash supports the following bitmap file types: Graphic Interchange Format (GIF), animated GIF, Joint Photographic Experts Group (JPEG/JPG), Portable Network Graphic (PNG), and Windows Bitmap (BMP, DIB). Flash supports the following vector file types: Adobe Illustrator AI or EPS, Windows Metafile (WMF) and Enhanced Metafile (EMF), PICT, PCT, and Flash Player files SWF and SPL. Flash also supports multimedia and a few AutoCAD file formats, such as QuickTime Movie (MOV) and AutoCAD DXF (DXF).

If QuickTime 4 or later is installed on your computer, Flash MX can support additional vector and bitmap file types, such as MacPaint (PNTG), Photoshop (PSD), Pict (PCT, PIC), QuickTime (QTIF), Silicon Graphics Image (SGI), and Tiff (TIF).

Although you can certainly use bitmap graphics in your Flash projects, just remember that they are not as scalable, and they increase file size. To avoid these issues, you can convert an imported bitmap graphic into a vector graphic or use other Flash tools to optimize the graphic's file size.

There are several ways to import a graphic, whether it is a bitmap or vector image. If you are using Windows, you can copy and paste images using the Windows Clipboard. Another way to import graphics is to use the Import command.

IMPORT GRAPHICS

You can import graphics, including vector or bitmap graphics, from other sources to use in Flash MX. You can use imported graphics to add to an existing drawing you create in Flash, or in animations you build for export to the Web or other sources. For example, you may have a product logo created in Macromedia's FreeHand program that you want to place in a Flash movie, or you might want to use a clipart image from the Web in a Flash drawing. You can manipulate imported images with Flash MX commands.

When you import a graphic, Flash immediately places it on the Stage in the current frame. Flash also automatically adds the graphic to the movie's Library. Flash treats imported graphics as a group. For example, if you import a detailed graphic, you can initially move and resize it as a single piece, not as separate elements.

In addition to importing graphics, you can also use the Paste command to paste graphics you cut or copy from other programs. The Cut, Copy, and Paste commands work the same way in Flash MX that they do in other programs.

IMPORT GRAPHICS

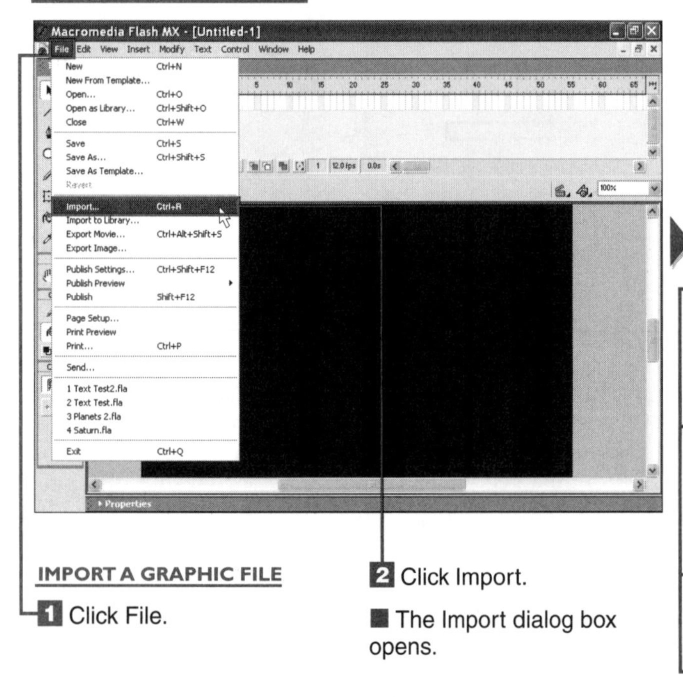

IMPORT A GRAPHIC FILE

1 Click File.

2 Click Import.

■ The Import dialog box opens.

3 Navigate to the file you want to import and click the filename.

■ You can click ▾ and select a file type, if you cannot locate the file you want.

4 Click Open.

■ Flash MX places the graphic on the Stage as a grouped object.

Note: To learn more about working with grouped objects, see page 400.

How do I remove an imported file I no longer want to include in my movie?

✔ To remove an imported file, open the Library window and delete the file. Click the Window menu, and then click Library. Click the imported file in the list and click 🗑. Flash MX removes the file. To learn more about the Flash MX Library feature, see pages 446 to 459.

Can I import a series of images?

✔ Yes. If you want to include a series of images in sequential keyframes, such as animation sequence in PICT format, you can easily import all the files at once. Flash MX recognizes sequentially numbered files in the Import dialog box and offers to import the entire sequence. Click Yes to do so or click No to import only the selected file.

Can I reuse the same bitmap graphic without importing each time?

✔ Yes. You do not have to repeat the import procedure to reuse the same image. Any time you import a graphic, Flash MX immediately adds it to its library for use in other frames in your movie. To view the Library, click Window, and then click Library. To learn more about using Library images, see pages 446 to 459.

How can I use imported graphics found in other Flash files?

✔ You can access another Flash file's library to share graphics by clicking the File menu and clicking Open as Library. Then double-click the file to open the library.

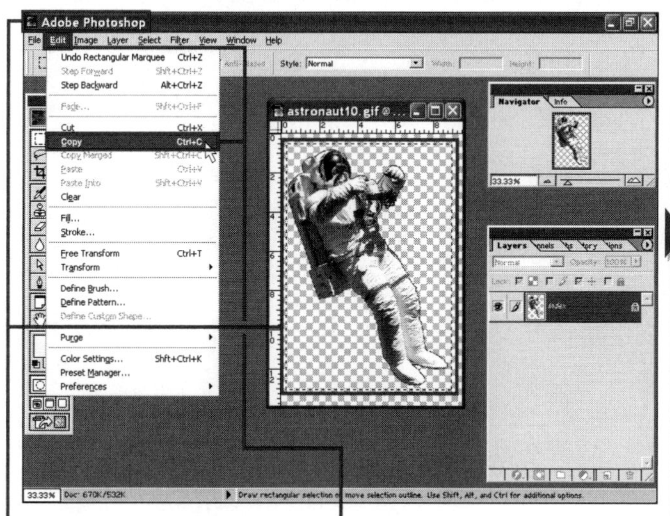

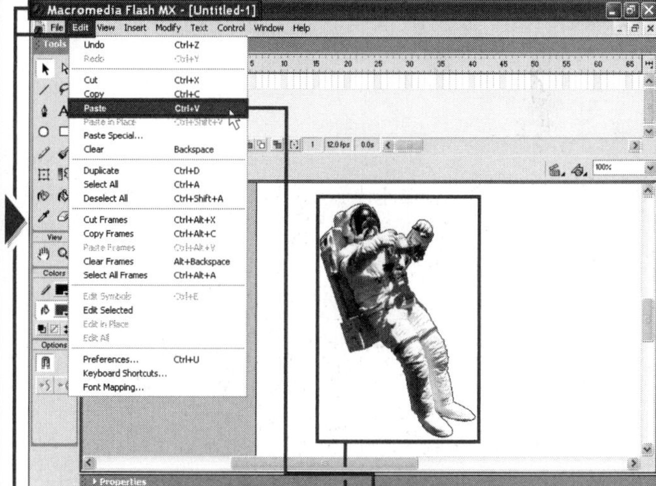

COPY AND PASTE A GRAPHIC

1 Open the graphic you want to copy.

2 Click the graphic.

■ In most programs, selection handles surround the selected object.

3 Click Edit.

4 Click Copy.

5 Switch back to Flash MX.

6 Click Edit.

7 Click Paste.

■ Flash MX pastes the graphic onto the Stage area.

CONVERT BITMAPS INTO VECTOR GRAPHICS

You can use the Trace Bitmap command to convert a bitmap graphic into a Flash MX vector graphic object. Turning a bitmap graphic into a vector graphic can minimize the file size and enable you to use the Flash MX tools to manipulate the graphic. Keep in mind, however, that changing the file format may lose some of the detail or photo-realism exhibited by the original bitmap image.

When you apply the Trace Bitmap command, you have an opportunity to adjust several parameters that define the rendering of the image, including how Flash MX handles the color variances, pixel size translation, and the smoothness of curves or sharpness of corners. These parameters can help you manage how closely the bitmap image matches the vector graphic image.

During conversion, Flash MX examines how the pixels in the bitmap relate to one another. You can specify a color threshold setting that instructs Flash how to treat bordering pixels of the same or similar colors. A higher color threshold setting groups subtle color changes into a single vector object, thus decreasing the number of overall colors in the image. A lower setting results in more vector objects, yet more colors display in the image.

For most images, the default settings work fine. You can experiment with the settings to create different looks.

CONVERT BITMAPS INTO VECTOR GRAPHICS

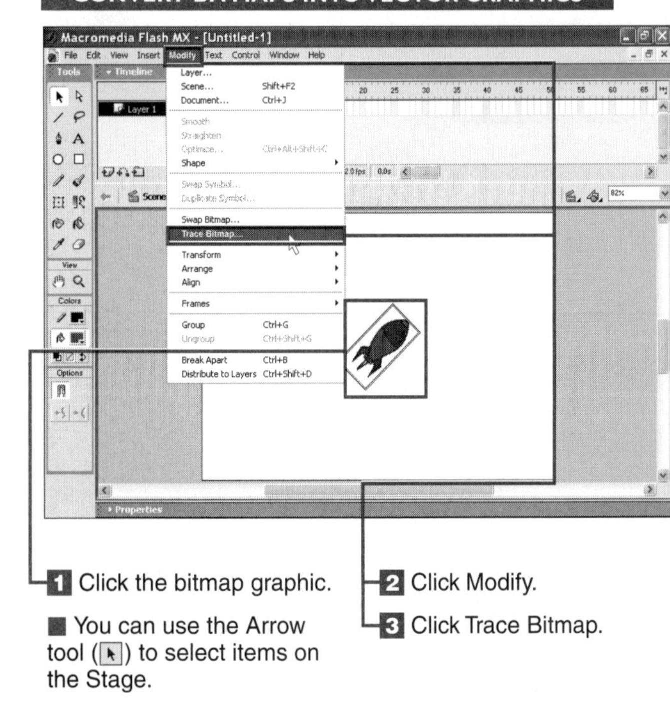

1 Click the bitmap graphic.

■ You can use the Arrow tool (↖) to select items on the Stage.

2 Click Modify.

3 Click Trace Bitmap.

■ The Trace Bitmap dialog box opens.

4 Type a value that determines the amount of color variance between neighboring pixels.

■ A smaller value results in many vector shapes; a larger value results in fewer vectors.

5 Type a minimum pixel radius.

What if my graphic does not look quite like the original?

✔ When applying the Trace Bitmap controls, you might need to experiment with the settings in the Trace Bitmap dialog box to get the results you want. Start with the default settings. If those do not work, click the Edit menu, click Undo, and try again. Make a few adjustments, such as changing color variance or pixel radius values.

Does converting a bitmap reduce its file size?

✔ Yes, if you do not set the Trace Bitmap threshold settings too low. If the bitmap is a complex drawing with lots of colors and shapes, low threshold settings may result in a larger vector file size. Try to find a balance when adjusting the threshold settings.

How does the Color Threshold setting work?

✔ It determines the number of colors converted into vectors. For example, perhaps your image is of a boat on water, and the water is made up of three shades of blue. A high color threshold setting may result in a single vector object for the water, or one shade of blue. If you set the color threshold too low, the color of the water ends up as dozens of vector objects, one for each shade change in the image.

Why specify a pixel radius?

✔ The minimum pixel radius you define in the Minimum Area field of the Trace Bitmap dialog box tells Flash the number of nearby pixels it should consider when assigning a color to a pixel during the conversion process.

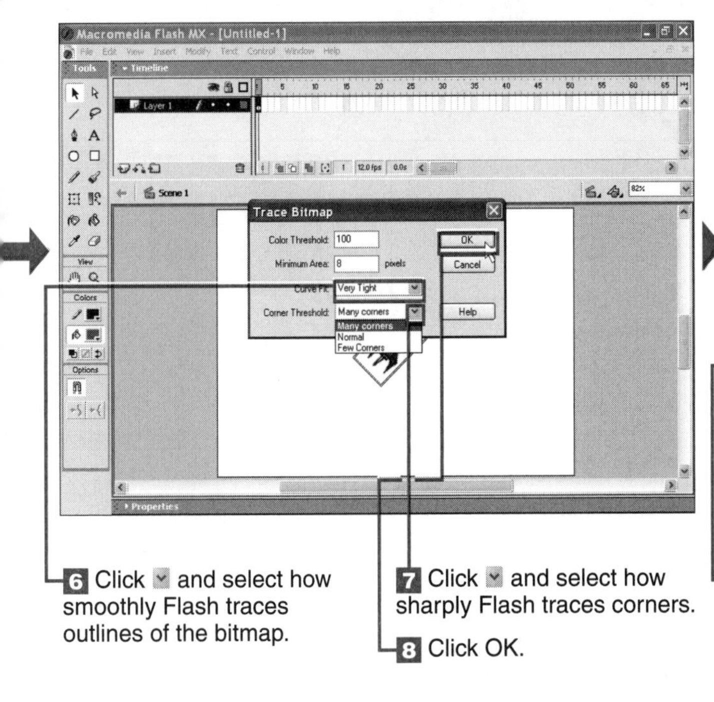

6 Click and select how smoothly Flash traces outlines of the bitmap.

7 Click and select how sharply Flash traces corners.

8 Click OK.

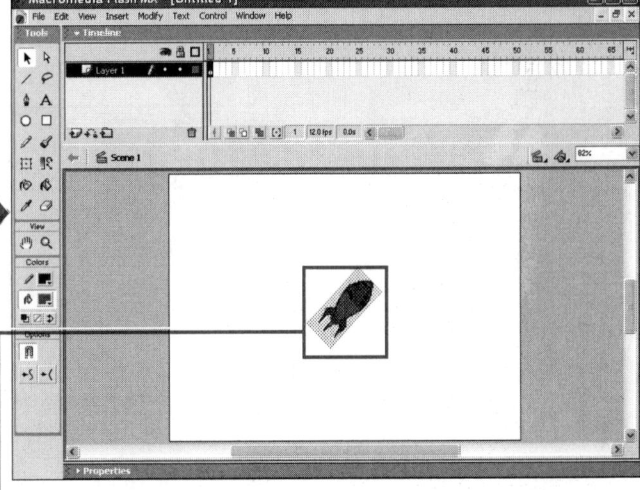

■ Flash MX traces the graphic. When finished, Flash MX replaces the bitmap with vector shapes. By default, Flash MX selects all the vector shapes.

■ You can now edit the various vector shapes that comprise the graphic to make changes to the graphic's appearance.

TURN BITMAPS INTO FILLS

You can turn a bitmap image into a fill for use with Flash drawing tools that use fills, such as the Oval, Rectangle, or Brush. *Fills* are solid colors or patterns that fill a shape. Conventional fills include colors and gradient effects. You can also use a bitmap image, such as a photo, as a fill. Depending on the size of the shape, Flash repeats the image within the shape, called *tiling*.

Bitmap photos make good fills. For example, you might have a photo of a face that you fill into an oval shape or a photo that makes a good repeat background pattern. You can use a variety of bitmap fills to create texture and depth in your Flash MX drawings.

To prepare a bitmap image as a fill, you must use the Break Apart command. This command converts the image into separate pieces.

After you separate the image, you can use the Eyedropper tool to duplicate the image as a fill. Using layers in your Flash Timeline helps you organize different elements in your movie, such as bitmaps you turn into fills.

TURN BITMAPS INTO FILLS

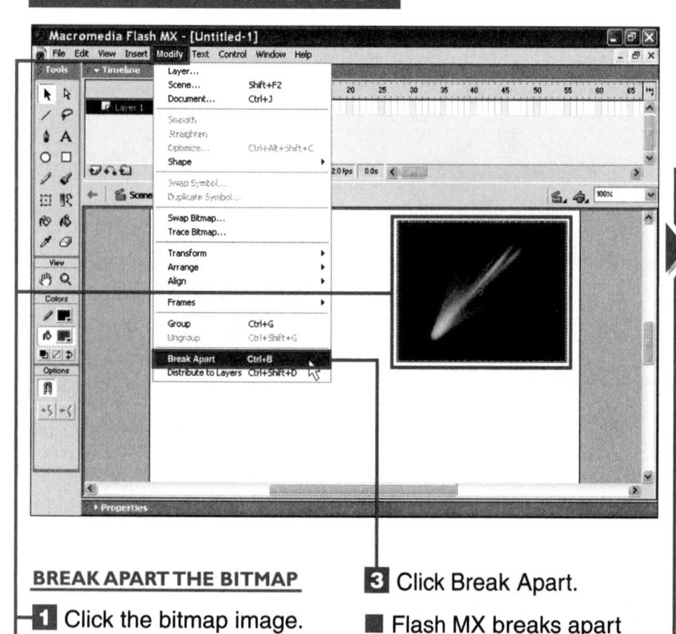

BREAK APART THE BITMAP

1 Click the bitmap image.

2 Click Modify.

3 Click Break Apart.

■ Flash MX breaks apart the image into the individual elements that comprise the image.

TURN THE BITMAP INTO A FILL

4 Select the drawing tool of your choice to create a shape you want to fill.

5 Draw a shape on the Stage to contain the bitmap fill.

■ You can place the new shape on another layer to help you keep objects organized.

Note: To learn more about working with layers in Flash MX, *see page 436.*

What types of edits can I perform on the bitmap fill?

✔ You can edit a bitmap fill just as you can any other fill, including rotating the image and scaling it to another size. See page 380 to learn more about editing Flash fills.

How do I use a bitmap fill with the Brush tool?

✔ Turn the bitmap into a fill following the steps in this section. Click the Brush tool (), select a brush size or shape, and then draw brush strokes on the Stage. Everywhere you draw, Flash uses the bitmap image as your paint color. To learn more about the Brush tool and its options, see page 368.

How do I use a bitmap image as a tiled pattern?

✔ Click the Window menu and click Color Mixer to open the Color Mixer panel. Click the Fill Style and select Bitmap. Click the image you want to use, and then click the Paint Bucket tool (). You can now fill any shape with a tiled pattern of the bitmap image.

How do I edit the position of a bitmap fill?

✔ Use the Fill Transform tool () to make changes to the way in which the fill is positioned within a shape.

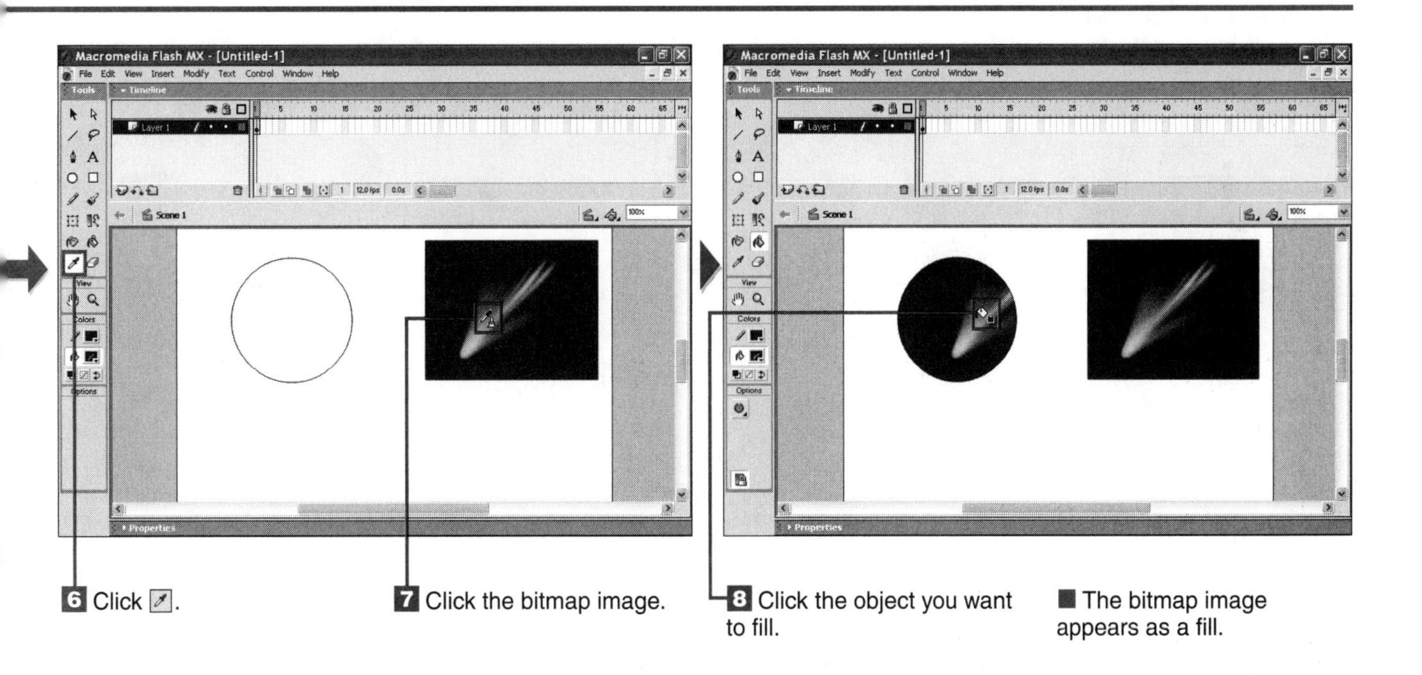

6 Click .

7 Click the bitmap image.

8 Click the object you want to fill.

■ The bitmap image appears as a fill.

IMPORT VIDEO CLIPS

You can import video clips from other sources into your Flash projects. For example, you can embed a video clip into a Flash movie, making the clip a part of the movie much like an imported graphic. As soon as you import a video clip, Flash adds it to the Stage and to the Library. You can use multiple instances of the video clip throughout your project.

Flash MX uses the Sorenson Spark *codec* — short for compression/decompression — a video encoder/decoder that compresses video to play at lower bandwidth without losing video quality. With the Sorenson Spark codec, video compression is determined by video content, which means a motionless scene in a video clip takes up less bandwidth than one involving a lot of action, such as a sporting event.

Video objects require the same number of frames equal to their length when you add the video clip to a Flash frame. For example, if a clip is 500 frames in length, it will require 500 timeline frames in Flash.

Flash MX supports Windows Media (ASF or WMV), Digital Video (DVI or DV), MPEG (MPG), Video for Windows (AVI), and QuickTime (MOV) video file formats.

IMPORT VIDEO CLIPS

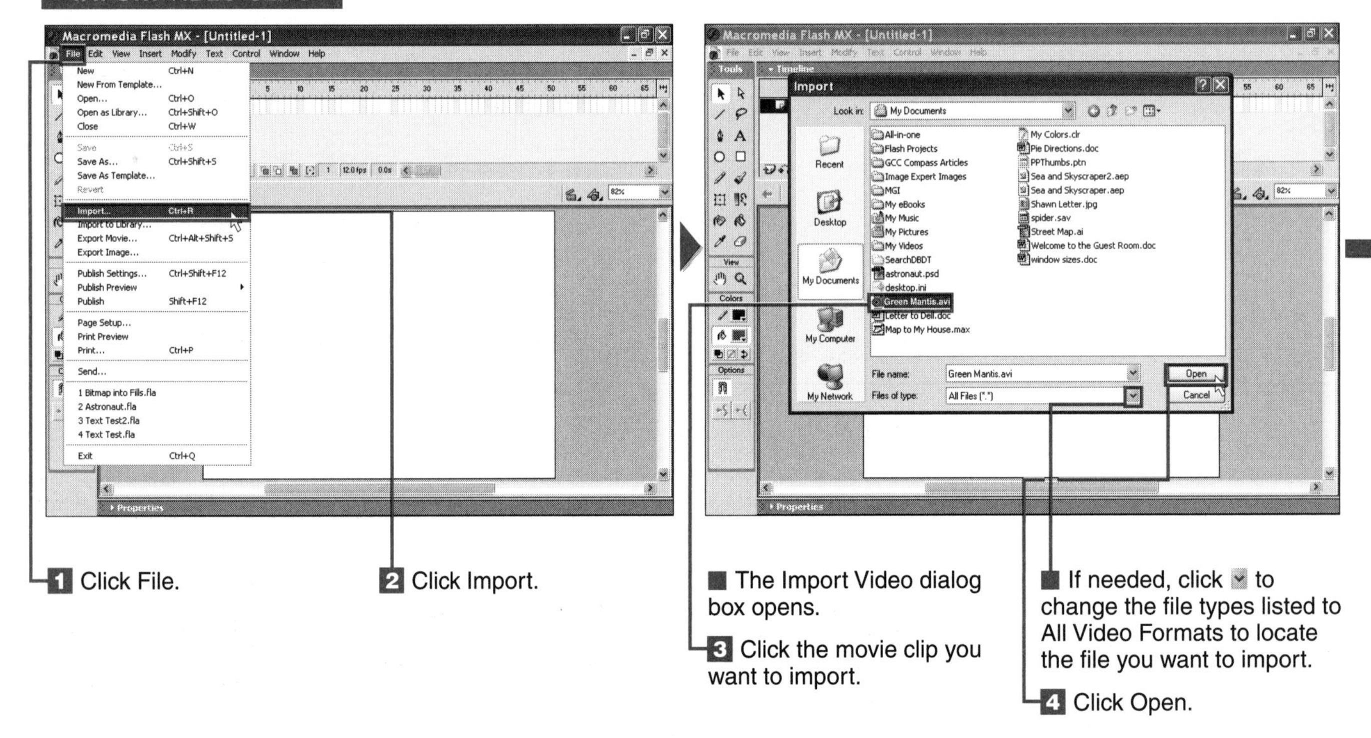
Macromedia Flash MX - [Untitled-1]
Import
Green Mantis.avi
Open
Cancel
1 Click File.
2 Click Import.
■ The Import Video dialog box opens.
3 Click the movie clip you want to import.
■ If needed, click ▾ to change the file types listed to All Video Formats to locate the file you want to import.
4 Click Open.

What frame ratio should I use?

✔ By default, a frame ratio of 1:2 gives you one video frame per two Flash frames. This ratio halves the size of the clip. A ratio of 1:1 gives you one video frame per one Flash frame, but the resulting timeline is larger.

Can I choose not to import or synchronize audio?

✔ Yes. To forego any associated audio entirely, deselect the Import Audio check box (☐ changes to ☑). If the clip has no audio, the option is not available.

How does the Keyframe Interval setting work?

✔ With video compression, the first video frame in the clip is treated as a keyframe, and the keyframe interval setting controls the frequency of subsequent keyframes. An interval of 30 stores a complete frame every 30 frames in the clip. An interval of 1 stores a complete frame for every frame in the clip, allowing no inter-frame compression but compressing each frame individually. If your video clip is very small in size, an interval setting of 1 is fine.

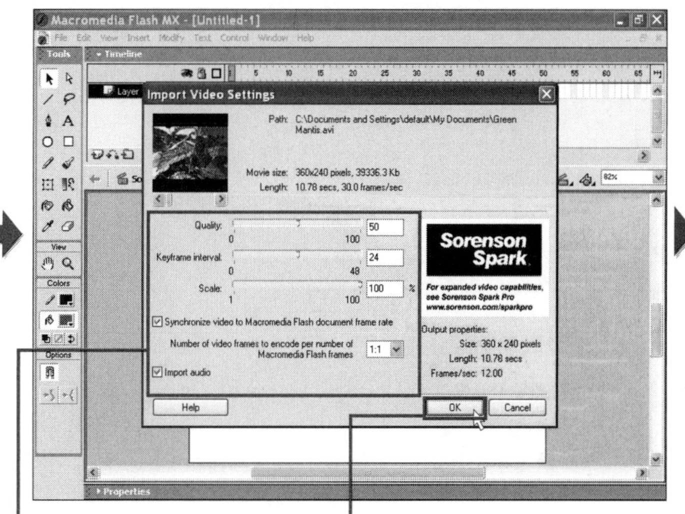

■ The Import Video Settings dialog box opens.

5 Change any settings, as needed.

■ Drag the Quality slider to control the level of compression.

■ Drag the Keyframe Interval slider to control the frequency of video clip keyframes.

■ Drag the Scale slider to reduce the dimensions of the video.

6 Click OK.

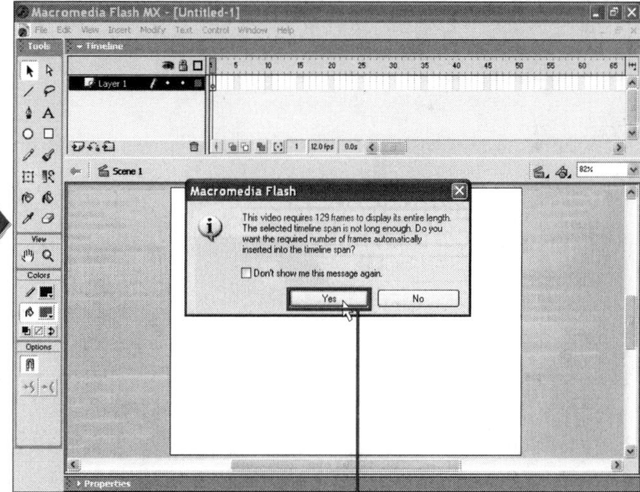

■ A prompt box appears if the imported clip contains more frames than you are currently using in the Flash Timeline.

7 Click Yes.

■ Flash MX adds the clip to the Stage and adds it as an embedded video in the Flash Library.

ADD TEXT WITH THE TEXT TOOL

You can use the Text tool on the Drawing toolbar to add text to a Flash movie. Like graphic objects you add to the Stage, you can animate text objects as well.

You can use three types of text elements in Flash: *static*, *dynamic*, or *input* text. Static text, the default text property, is text that does not change — you edit the text the way you want it, and it appears the same way in your Flash movie. Dynamic text is used for text fields you insert into your project that change in value or update, such as stock quotes or weather temperature. Input text is text entered into a field by the user, such as an interactive form. Dynamic and input text are often used with Flash ActionScripts.

You add text to the Stage in text boxes, which you can reposition or resize as needed. You can use two methods to create a text box. One method is to click the Stage where you want the box to appear and start typing. This creates what Flash calls an extending text block. Another method is to define the text box size first by dragging its dimensions on the Stage. This is called a fixed text block. When you create a text box on the Stage, Flash MX applies the text attributes or formatting you assigned to previously added text boxes.

ADD TEXT WITH THE TEXT TOOL

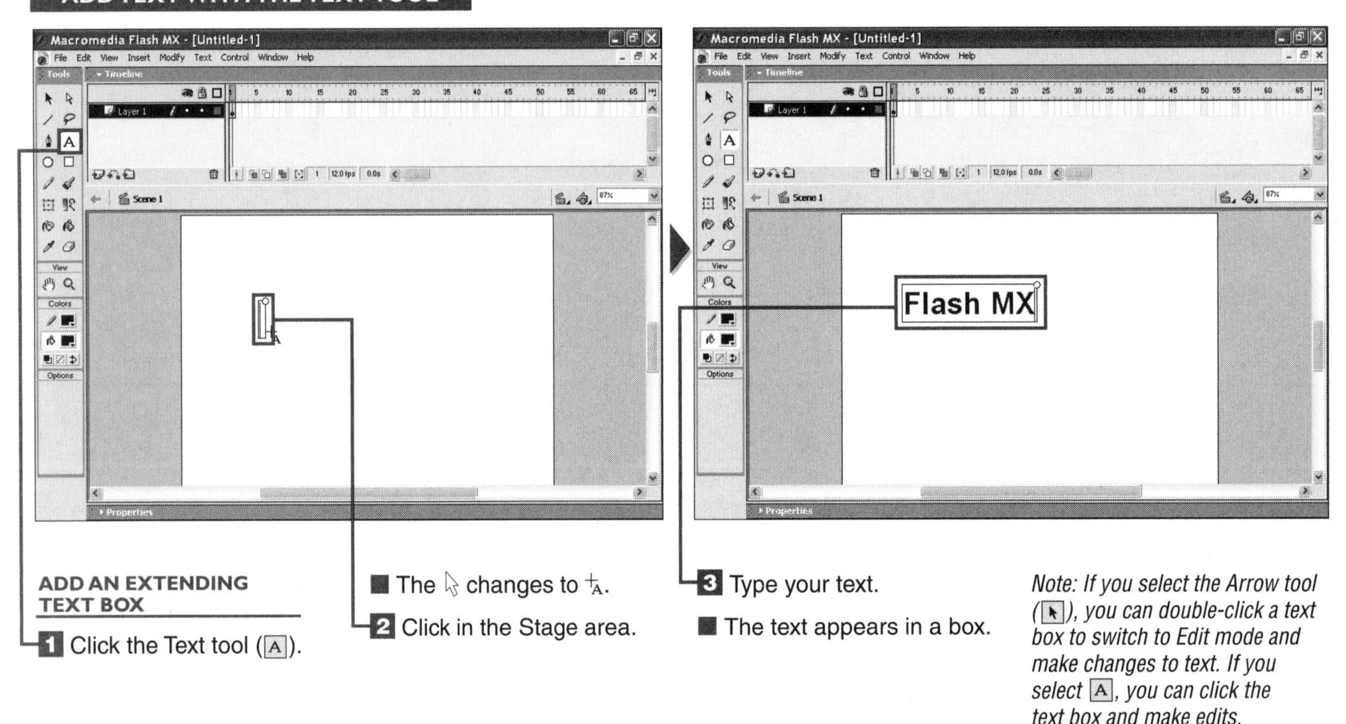

ADD AN EXTENDING TEXT BOX

1. Click the Text tool (A).

■ The arrow pointer changes to the text cursor.

2. Click in the Stage area.

3. Type your text.

■ The text appears in a box.

Note: If you select the Arrow tool (arrow), you can double-click a text box to switch to Edit mode and make changes to text. If you select A, you can click the text box and make edits.

What is the difference between an extending text box and a fixed text box?

✔ When you type text into an extending text box, text does not wrap. The width of the text box keeps expanding as you type characters. With a fixed text box, you specify a width, and when the text you are typing reaches the end of the block, it wraps to start a new line, increasing the depth of the text box. To visually discern between which method you used to create the text box, look at the icon in the upper-right corner of the text box. Extending text boxes display a tiny circle icon (○), and fixed block text boxes have a tiny square icon (□).

How do I turn an extending text box into a fixed text box?

✔ Double-click the text box and move the mouse pointer over ○ in the upper-right corner of the text box. Drag ↔ to the right and release the mouse button. The extending text box is now a fixed text box. Note that you cannot turn fixed text boxes into extending text boxes.

How do I change the text type to dynamic or input?

✔ Select the text box, then open the Property inspector, click the Text Type ▾, and click a text type. To display and hide the Property inspector, see page 346.

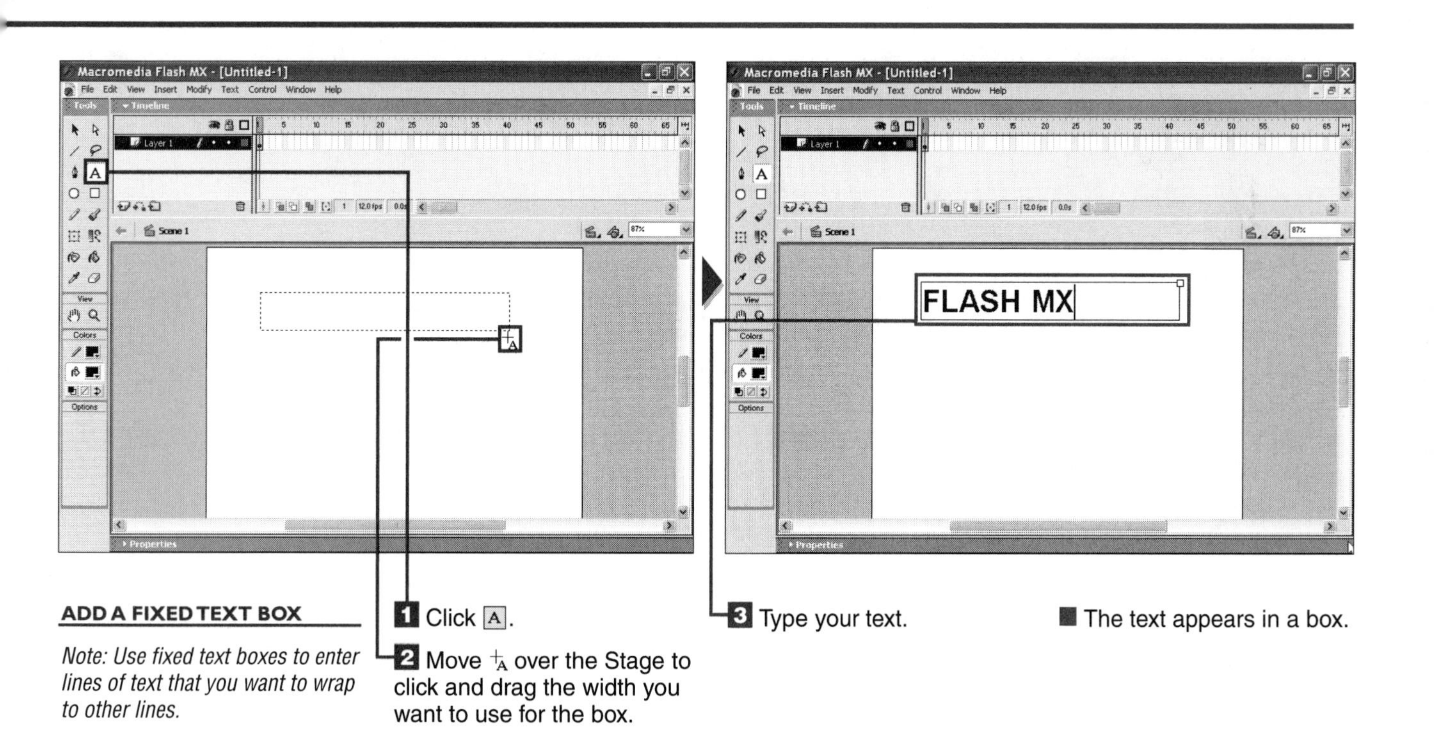

ADD A FIXED TEXT BOX

Note: Use fixed text boxes to enter lines of text that you want to wrap to other lines.

1 Click A.

2 Move ⁺A over the Stage to click and drag the width you want to use for the box.

3 Type your text.

■ The text appears in a box.

FORMAT TEXT

You can format text in your Flash movie to change the impact or appearance of words and characters. You can easily format text by using the Property inspector. It has all the controls for changing text attributes located in one convenient panel. You can quickly change the font, font size, font color, and spacing.

You can choose text attributes before you start typing in text or apply formatting to existing text. Leave the Property inspector open on-screen to keep the formatting controls handy as you work with text on the Stage.

The Property inspector offers many of the same formatting controls you find in word processing programs. For example, you can click the Bold button to make your text boldface. When you click the Font drop-down list, you will see the names and samples of available fonts you can use before applying it to your text. See page 346 to learn more about using the Property inspector.

Regardless of which attributes you assign to your text, it is important that the text is legible. While animation effects can add pizzazz to any message, the effects should never take precedence over the readability of your text.

FORMAT TEXT

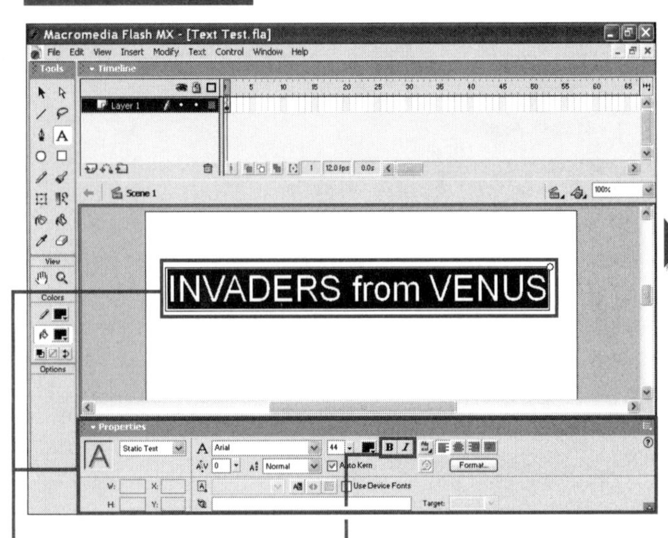

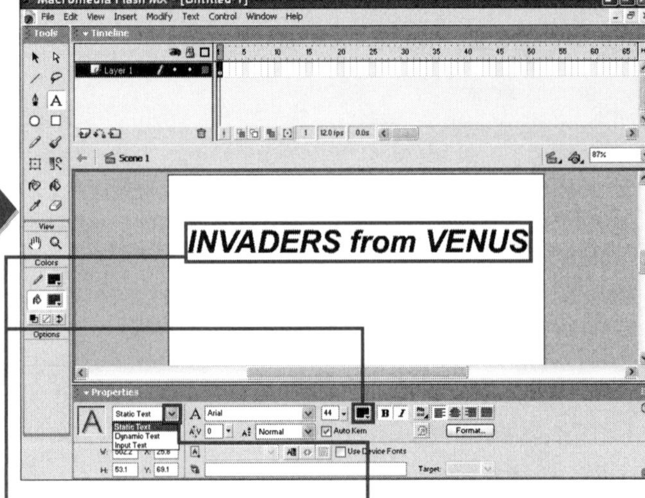

CREATE BOLD AND ITALICS

1 Open the Property inspector.

Note: To display and hide the Property inspector, see page 346.

2 Highlight the text you want to format.

Note: If you select A, you can click the text box and make edits. If you select ↖, you can double-click a text box and make edits.

3 Click B to apply bold or click I to apply italic.

■ The text changes appearance.

■ You can click the Text Fill Color button (■) to open the Color palette and choose another color for the selected text.

■ To change the text type from static to dynamic or input, click the Text Type ▾ and click another text type.

Do I have to use the Property inspector to format text?

✔ You can also find text formatting controls in the Text menu. For example, to change the font, click Text, Font, and then click a font from the menu list that appears.

When would I use dynamic or input text?

✔ You can use dynamic and input text boxes to display dynamically updating text in your Flash project, such as user input boxes, text retrieved from a database, or a variable value obtained from a function within your movie or an external script. Dynamic and input text is commonly used with Flash Actions. See Chapters 31 and 32 to learn more about Actions and ActionScript.

What types of fonts does Flash MX support?

✔ Flash MX supports TrueType and bitmap fonts and Type 1 PostScript fonts. Flash also includes device fonts (sans serif, serif, and typewriter) that, when exported, instruct the Flash Player to use equivalent fonts found on the target computer. Device fonts take up less movie size than other fonts because Flash does not have to embed information about each font when exporting.

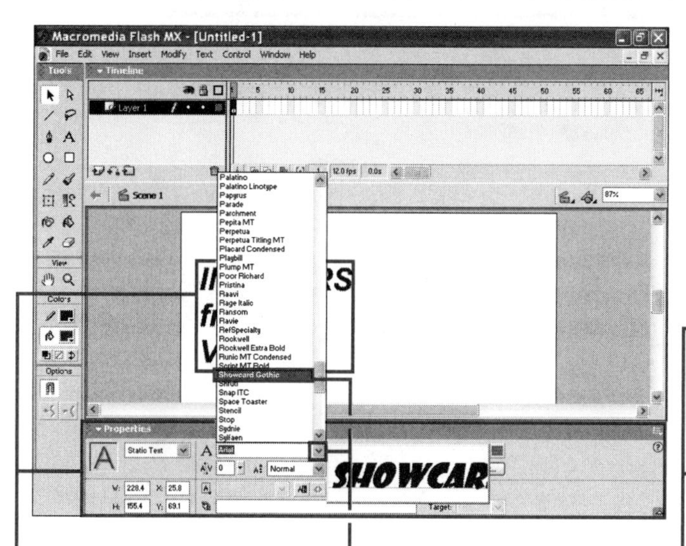

CHANGE THE TEXT FONT

1 Open the Property inspector.

Note: To display and hide the Property inspector, see page 346.

2 Select the text you want to format.

3 Click the Font ▾.

■ A list of available fonts appears, along with a sample box.

4 Click a font name.

■ The text changes font type.

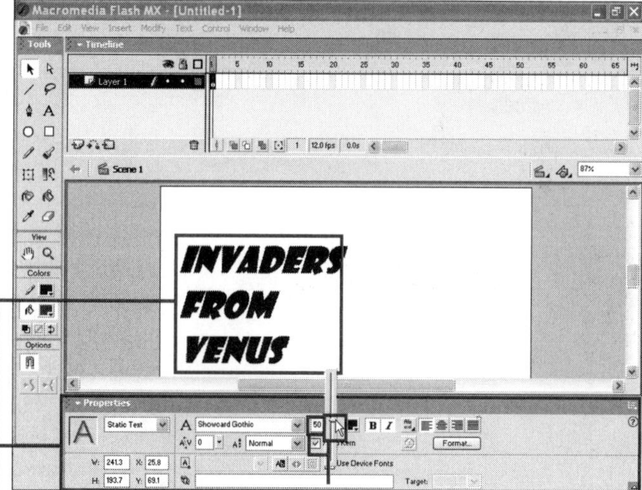

CHANGE THE FONT SIZE

1 Open the Property inspector.

Note: To display and hide the Property inspector, see page 346.

2 Select the text you want to format.

3 Click the Size ▾.

4 Select a new size by dragging the slider.

■ You can also type the exact size in the Size box.

■ The text changes size.

ALIGN AND KERN TEXT

You can control the position of text within a text box using the alignment options found in the Property inspector or on the Text menu. Alignment options include setting horizontal controls for the positioning of text, such as left, center, right, or fully justified.

Left alignment moves the text to the far-left side of the text box. Right alignment moves the text to the right side. Center alignment centers the text between the left and right edges of the text box. Fully justified text spaces out the text evenly between the left and right edges so that both margins are flush with the edges of the text box. To set margins for text boxes, see page 422.

Another way to control the positioning of text is with kerning, called tracking in Flash MX. *Kerning* refers to the spacing of characters. By changing the kerning setting, you can create text effects such as word characters condensed together or pulled apart. You can find kerning controls in the Property inspector.

To apply alignment or kerning options to a text box, you must first select the text. Any previous alignment or kerning settings are applied automatically to new text boxes you add.

ALIGN TEXT

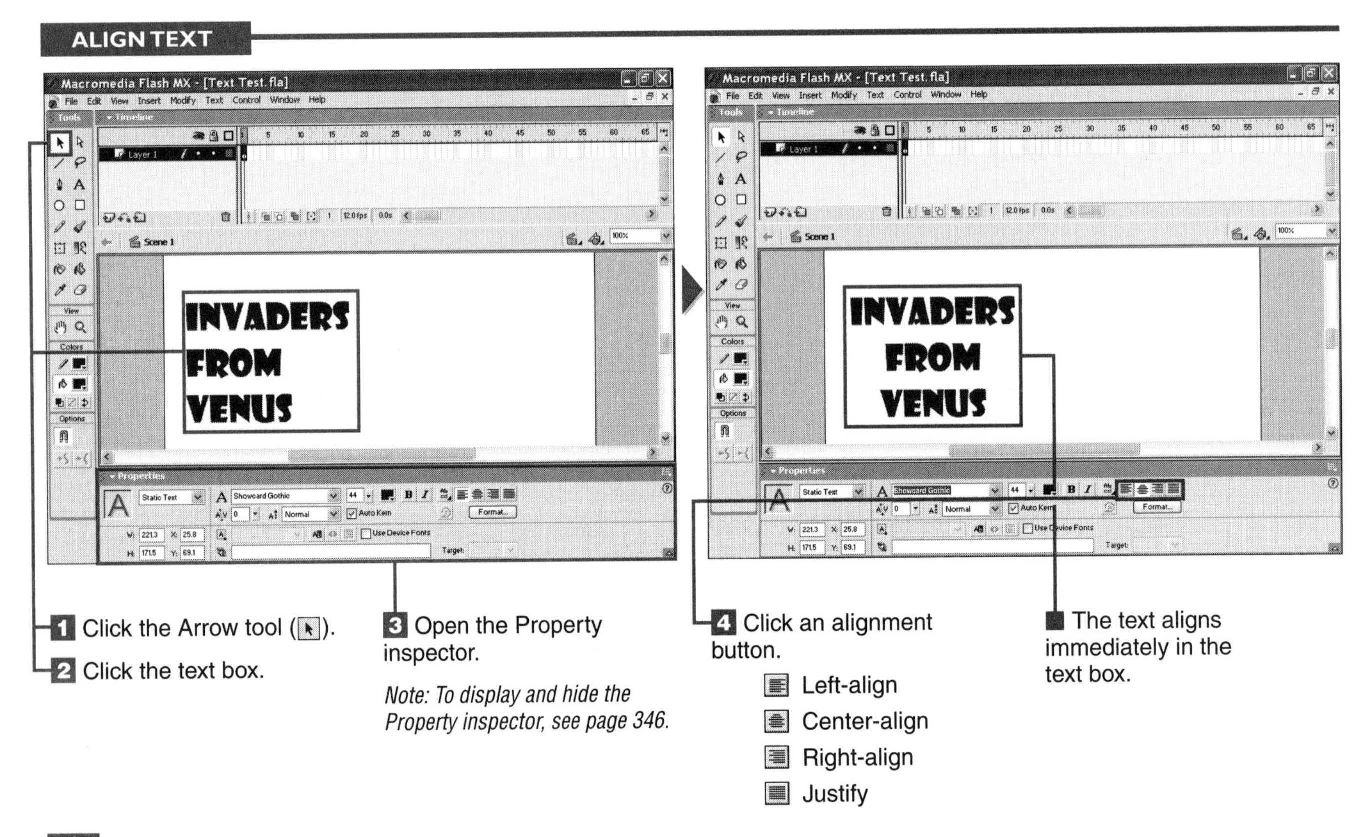

1 Click the Arrow tool (↖).

2 Click the text box.

3 Open the Property inspector.

Note: To display and hide the Property inspector, see page 346.

4 Click an alignment button.

- Left-align
- Center-align
- Right-align
- Justify

■ The text aligns immediately in the text box.

Does the Property inspector save my current formatting settings?

✔ The Property inspector retains your last formatting settings as long as you have Flash MX open. If you add another text box to the Stage, the text appears using the current attributes you previously assigned. The next time you open Flash MX and the Property inspector again, the default settings are in effect until you change them.

How do I fix a formatting mistake?

✔ Click the Edit menu and click Undo to quickly undo the last formatting command you applied.

How do I copy attributes from one text box to another?

✔ Click [arrow icon] and then the text box containing the text to which you want to copy attributes. Click the Eyedropper tool ([eyedropper icon]) on the Drawing toolbar and then click the text box containing the attributes you want to copy. The attributes are immediately copied.

Do I have to use the Property inspector to align text?

✔ No, you can use the Text menu to align text. Click the Text menu, click Align, and then click the alignment you want to apply.

KERN TEXT

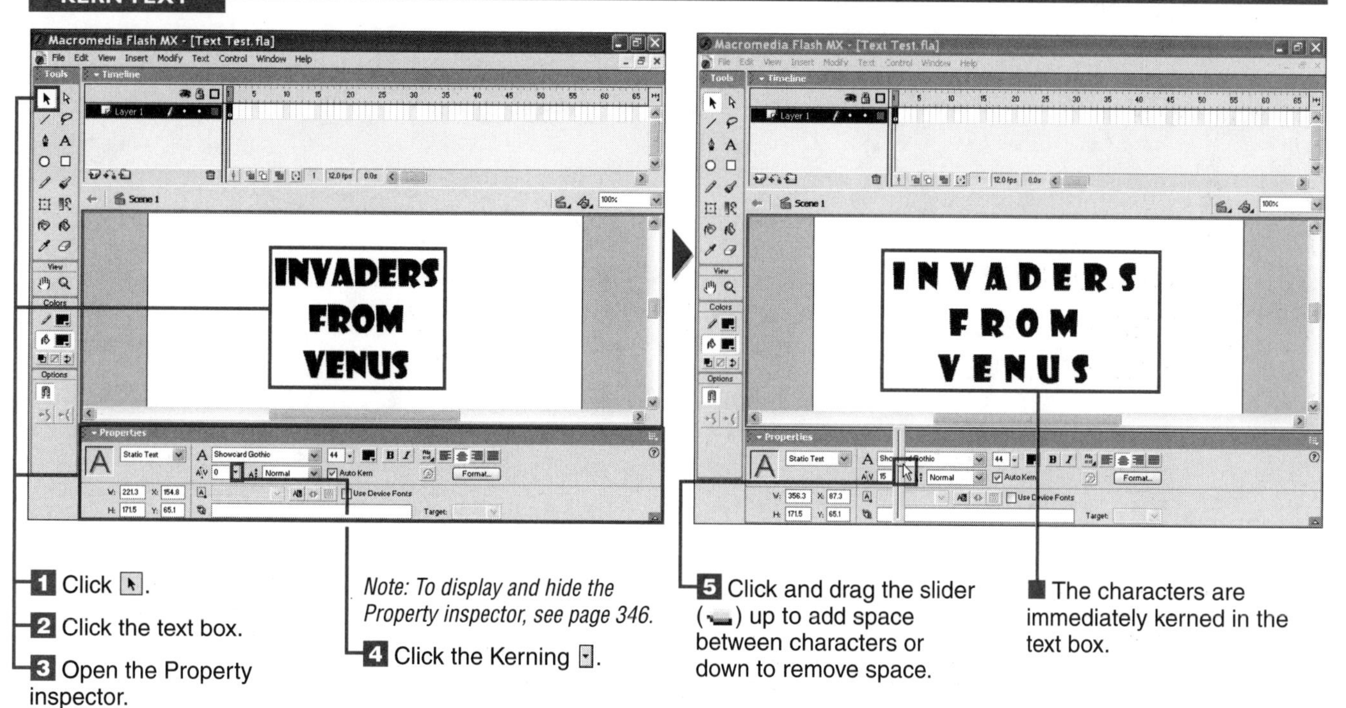

1 Click [arrow icon].

2 Click the text box.

3 Open the Property inspector.

Note: To display and hide the Property inspector, see page 346.

4 Click the Kerning [dropdown icon].

5 Click and drag the slider ([slider icon]) up to add space between characters or down to remove space.

■ The characters are immediately kerned in the text box.

SET TEXT BOX MARGINS AND INDENTS

Set margins and indents within text boxes for greater control of text positioning in your Flash movies. You can find margin and indent commands in the Format Options dialog box. This dialog box is accessible through the Property inspector.

Margins define the distance between the edge of the text box and the text inside. For example, if a text box appears next to another graphic object on the Stage, you may want to specify a margin within the text box to make sure the text does not appear too close to the bordering graphic. You can define left and right margins in Flash, as well as top and bottom margins.

Indents are used to control where a line of text sits within the margins. For example, you might choose to indent the first line in a paragraph by several pixels or points.

In addition to margin and indent controls, the Property inspector also has controls for line spacing. Line spacing is the distance between lines of text. Increase the line spacing to add space between lines or decrease the spacing to bring the lines closer together.

SET THE MARGINS

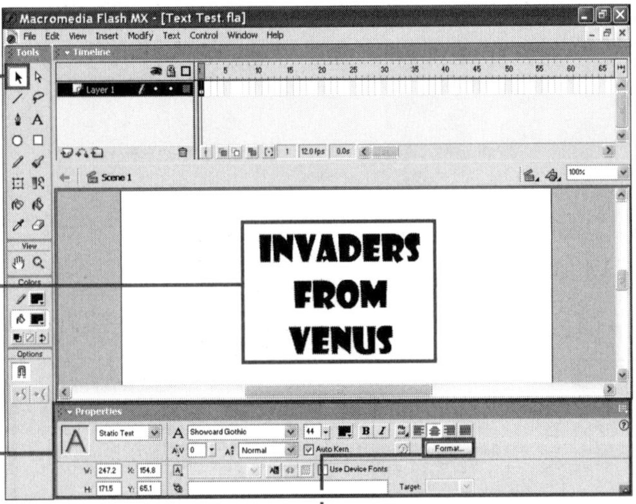

1 Click the Arrow tool.

2 Click the text box.

3 Open the Property inspector.

Note: To display and hide the Property inspector, see page 346.

4 Click Format.

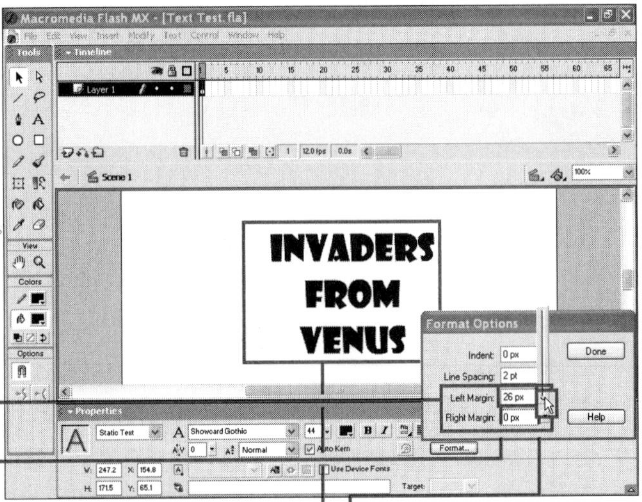

■ The Format Options dialog box opens.

5 Set the left or right margin.

■ You can type a value in the margin text box.

■ You can also click the arrow and drag the slider to the desired position.

■ The margin immediately changes in the text box.

How do I change the margin's unit of measurement?

✔ By default, Flash assumes you want to work with pixels as your unit of measurement, but you can change it to the unit of your choice, such as points or inches. Click Modify and then Document. This opens the Document Properties dialog box. You can also press Ctrl + M (⌘ + J) to open the dialog box. Click ▾ of the Ruler Units box and select the appropriate units. Click OK to close the dialog box. When you open the Property inspector, the margin values reflect the unit of measurement you defined.

Would I use the Line Spacing slider to set superscript or subscript characters in Flash MX?

✔ No, the Line Spacing slider cannot be used on individual characters — only entire lines. Instead, to set superscript or subscript characters, first select the text. Next, display the Property inspector. Click the Character Position ▾. A list of choices appears. Click Superscript or Subscript, and the attribute is immediately applied.

SET AN INDENT

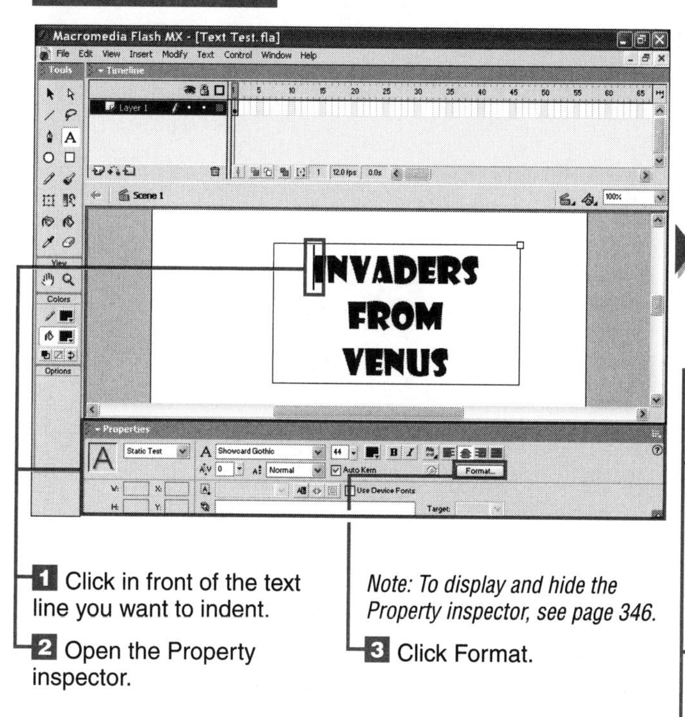

1 Click in front of the text line you want to indent.

2 Open the Property inspector.

Note: To display and hide the Property inspector, see page 346.

3 Click Format.

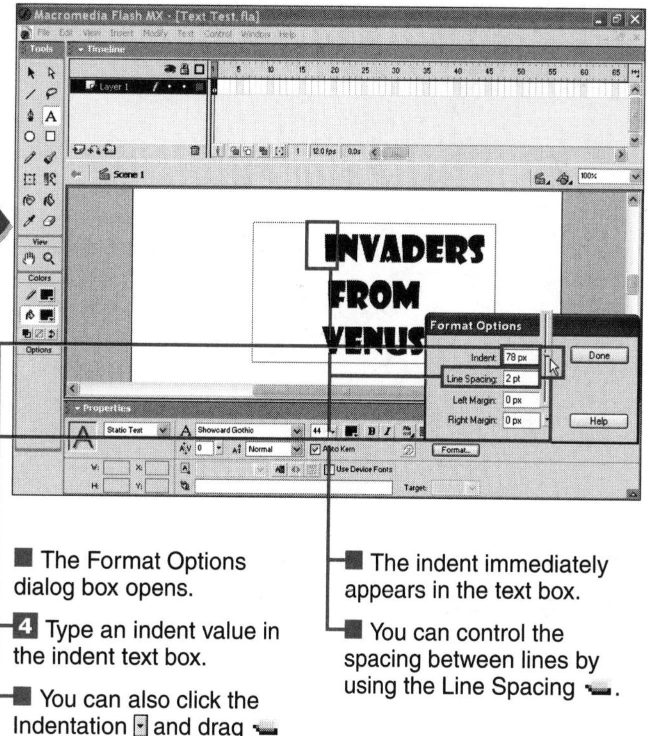

■ The Format Options dialog box opens.

4 Type an indent value in the indent text box.

■ You can also click the Indentation ▾ and drag ▬ to change the number.

■ The indent immediately appears in the text box.

■ You can control the spacing between lines by using the Line Spacing ▬.

MOVE AND RESIZE TEXT BOXES

You can move text boxes around on the Flash Stage or resize them as needed. Text boxes are as mobile and scalable as other objects you add to the Stage.

You can position a text box anywhere on the Stage. Or you can move a text box off the Stage onto the work area, the gray area that surrounds the Stage. Nothing you place in the work area appears in your Flash movie. However, you can move items to the work area and move them back onto the Stage when you need them, such as when you want to place an item into a particular Flash frame. See Chapter 29 to learn more about working with frames.

When you resize a text box, the existing text inside is resized depending on the direction you choose to scale the box. When you select a text box, a small handle appears in the upper right corner of the box. You can use this handle to drag the text box to a new size. Any font sizes you have previously set for the text are overridden. If you want the text set at a certain size, you must manually change the font size again after you scale the text box.

MOVE A TEXT BOX

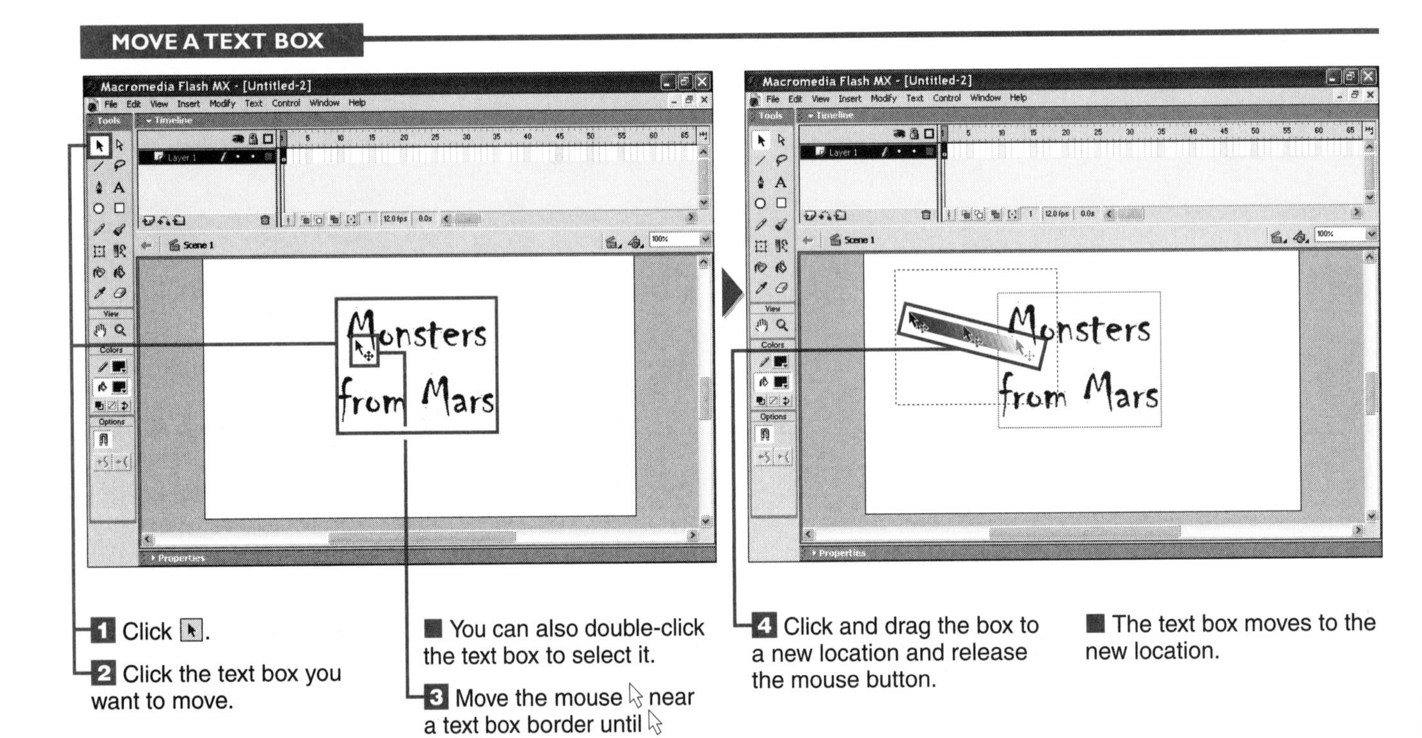

1 Click .

2 Click the text box you want to move.

■ You can also double-click the text box to select it.

3 Move the mouse near a text box border until changes to .

4 Click and drag the box to a new location and release the mouse button.

■ The text box moves to the new location.

Can I rotate or resize a text box?

✔ Yes. First select the text box and then click [icon], and then click [icon] or [icon] on the Drawing toolbar. Click and drag an edit point to rotate or resize the text box. You can find out more about rotating or resizing objects on page 382.

Can I move a text box off the Stage?

✔ Yes, you can move a text box to the work area surrounding the Stage and move it back when you want it to appear in the movie.

Can I change the text direction?

✔ Yes, if the text is static text, you can make the text read vertically or even backwards. With the text box selected, click the Change Direction of Text button ([icon]) in the Property inspector to reveal a pop-up menu of text directions. Click the one you want, and the new setting is immediately applied.

RESIZE A TEXT BOX

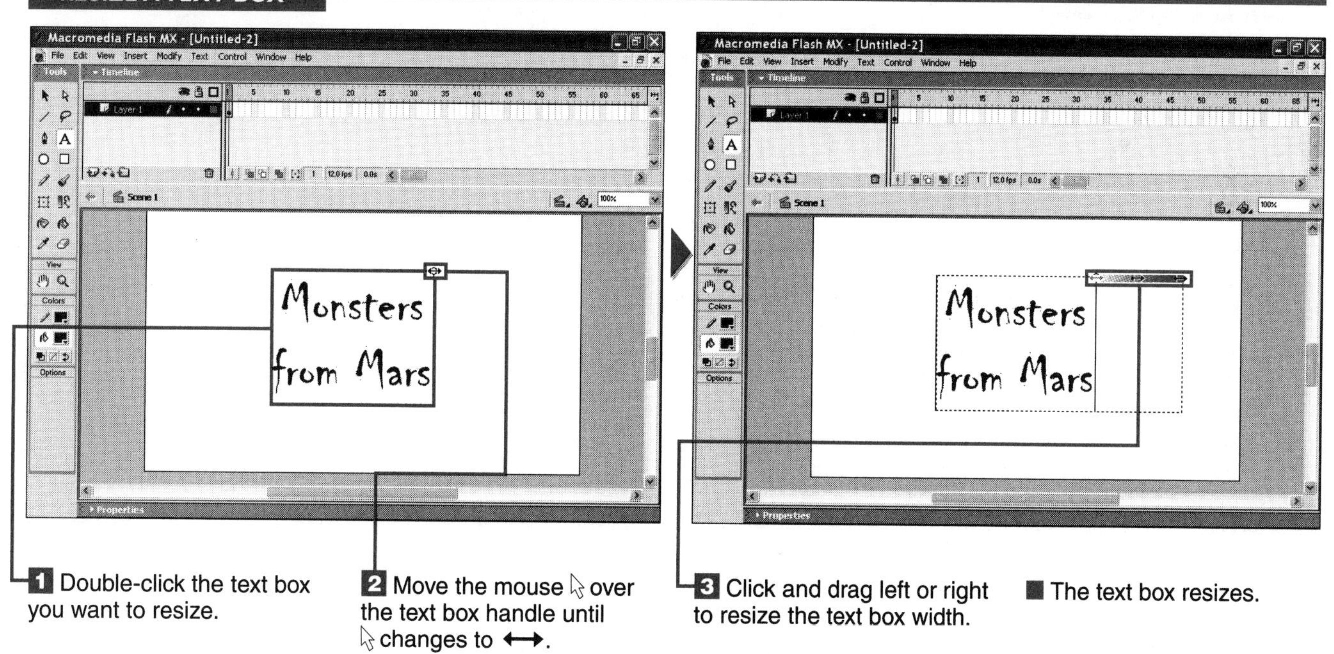

1 Double-click the text box you want to resize.

2 Move the mouse [pointer] over the text box handle until [pointer] changes to ⟷.

3 Click and drag left or right to resize the text box width.

■ The text box resizes.

BREAK APART TEXT

You can use the Break Apart command to turn text into graphics and then manipulate the text with the various Flash drawing and editing tools. For example, you can break apart text into separate blocks and distribute them to different layers in your animation, or you can break text apart to make modifications on each character in a word.

When you apply the Break Apart command to a text block, Flash MX treats the text as mini-text blocks or graphic shapes. Apply the command once to turn text into individual text blocks, one for each character in the text. Apply the command a second time to convert the text into shapes. You can then modify the text shapes as you do other shapes you draw in Flash MX. See Chapters 21 and 22 to learn more about the Flash drawing tools.

After you apply the Break Apart command to a text block, you can no longer edit the text, such as change the font or font size. For that reason, be sure you apply all the text formatting you want to use before applying the Break Apart command.

BREAK APART TEXT

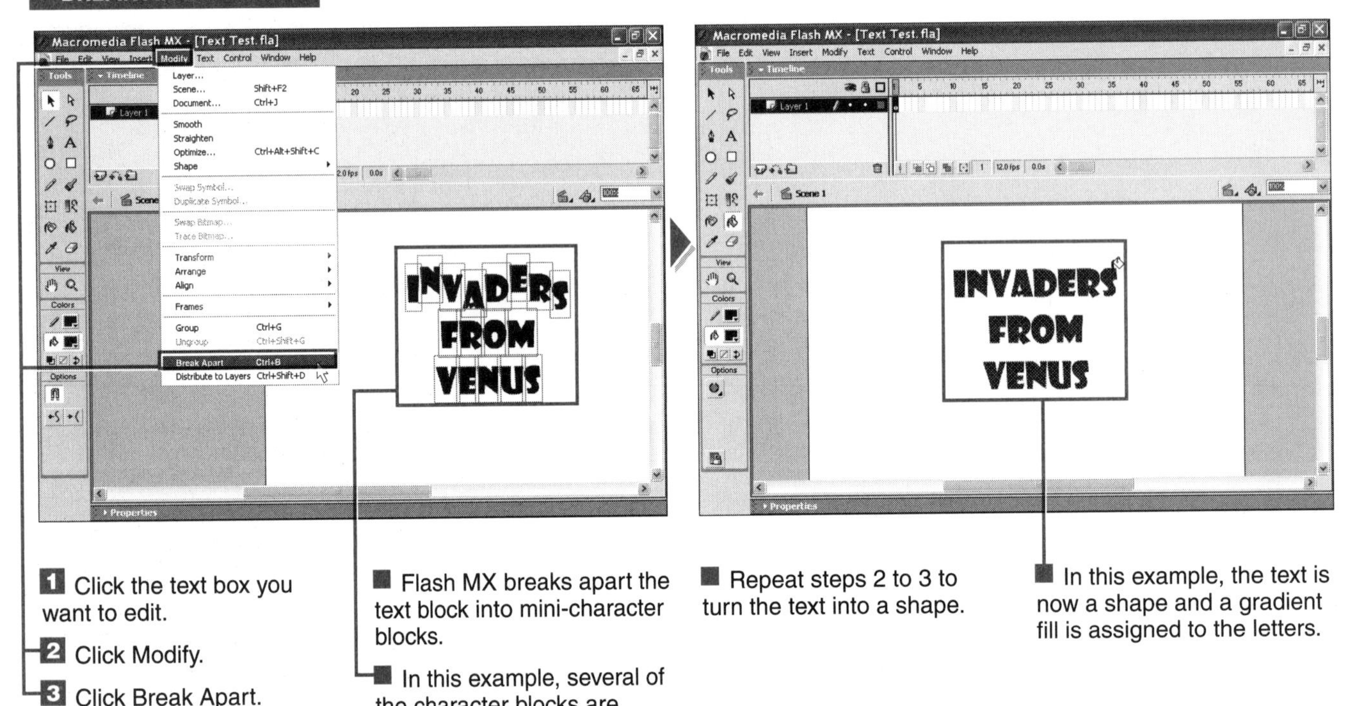

1 Click the text box you want to edit.

2 Click Modify.

3 Click Break Apart.

■ Flash MX breaks apart the text block into mini-character blocks.

■ In this example, several of the character blocks are repositioned.

■ Repeat steps 2 to 3 to turn the text into a shape.

■ In this example, the text is now a shape and a gradient fill is assigned to the letters.

DISTORT TEXT

You can use the Free Transform tool's Envelope modifier to distort the appearance of text in a Flash project. For example, you can make the text appear as a wave or exaggerate the size of some letters while keeping the other letters the same, or you can make the text seem to follow a path.

In order to use the Envelope modifier, you must apply the Break Apart command to your text box. After you apply this command to a text block, you cannot edit the text formatting again.

The Envelope modifier, new to Flash MX, allows you to enclose the text shape with an envelope of edit points and then use the points to control the shape effect. The Envelope modifier uses two types of edit points: regular edit points and tangent handles. Regular edit points are square and, when manipulated, can change the corners and sides of an object. Tangent handles are circles that adjust additional points along the edges of a selected object. Experiment with dragging both types of edit points to create different distortions with your text.

DISTORT TEXT

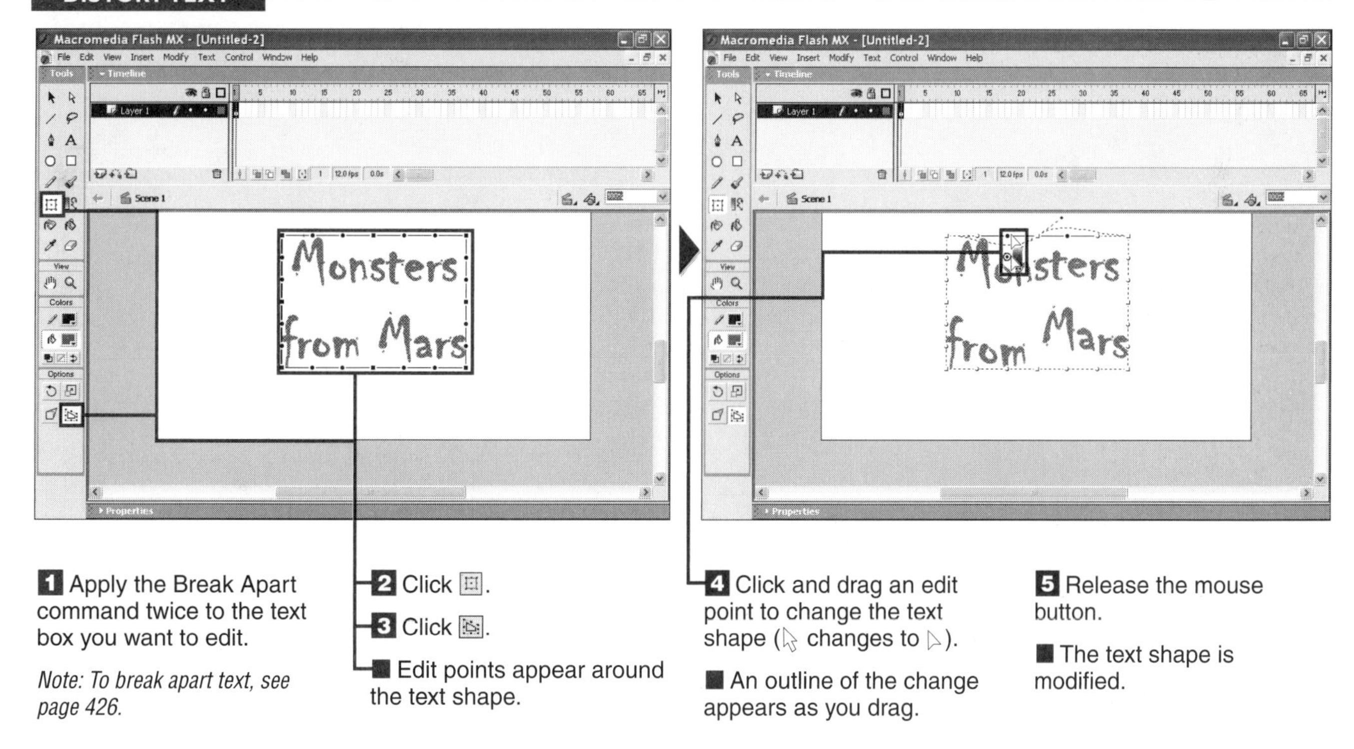

1 Apply the Break Apart command twice to the text box you want to edit.

Note: To break apart text, see page 426.

2 Click ⬚.

3 Click ⬚.

■ Edit points appear around the text shape.

4 Click and drag an edit point to change the text shape (↖ changes to ▷).

■ An outline of the change appears as you drag.

5 Release the mouse button.

■ The text shape is modified.

SECTION VII

25) WORKING WITH LAYERS

26) WORKING WITH FLASH SYMBOLS AND INSTANCES

27) CREATING INTERACTIVE BUTTONS

28) ADDING SOUND

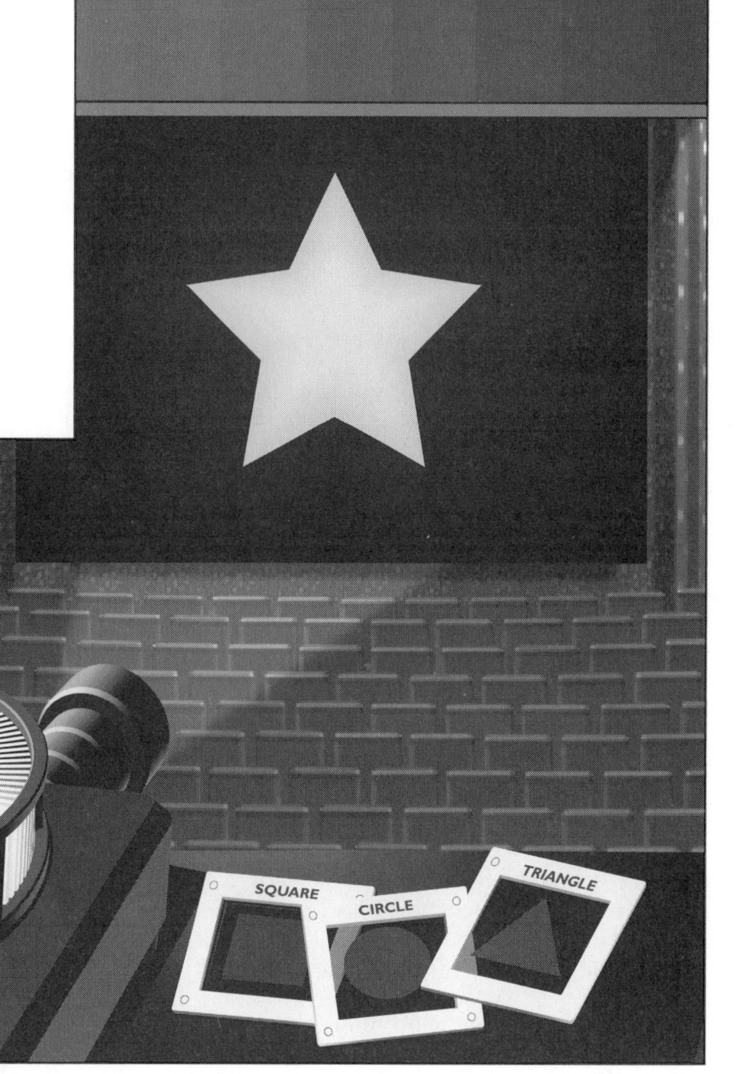

INTRODUCTION TO LAYERS

The key to working with graphic objects and animation in Flash MX is *layers*. A layer is a like a transparent sheet or overlay in your movie. Layers can help you organize elements and add depth to your Flash projects. By default, every time you create a new Flash MX file, the Timeline starts out with one layer. The layer name appears on the left side of the Flash Timeline.

You can add new layers as needed and change their order around in the Timeline. Each layer has its own Timeline containing frames.

To learn more about the Flash Timeline, see page 340.

You can have as many layers as you need in Flash, but you can work on only one layer at a time. You can use layers to accomplish several different tasks.

Organize Layers

You can use layers to help you organize elements in your project. The bigger your project, the more elements it is likely to contain. Rather than placing all of these elements in a single layer, which makes them more difficult to locate and edit, you can insert the elements into separate layers and name each layer with a descriptive name that tells what is in the layer. You can now organize layers into folders with Flash MX. For example, you might have a very complex movie that uses sound, animation, buttons, and actions. To help keep your movie organized, place the sound clip in a layer named Sound. Create your animation effect in a layer named MyMovie or Animation. When you add a button to the movie, place it in a new layer named Button. Any actions you assign to the button should be kept in another layer named Actions.

Layers can also help you keep track of the various pieces, such as related elements of an animation sequence. You can place related objects in a single layer to keep them together, making it easier to find them later.

For example, if your Flash movie uses a company logo, you might place all the elements related to the logo in a single layer and name the layer Logo.

You can edit objects in one layer without affecting objects in another layer. For example, if you place all the logo elements in a single layer, any edits you make to the logo elements do not affect objects in other layers. This keeps you from accidentally changing items you do not want to change. You can also lock a layer to make sure no edits occur to its contents.

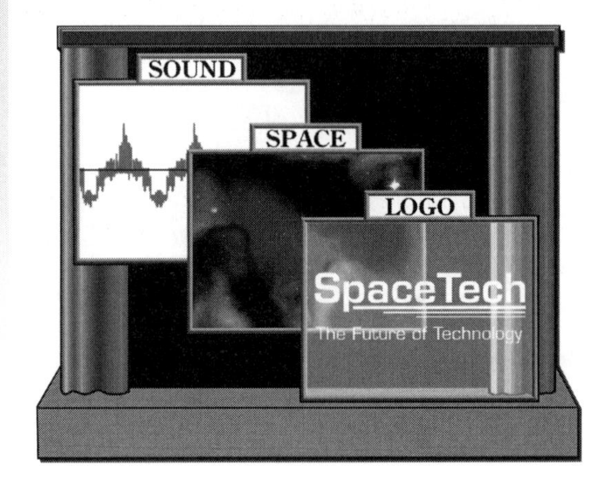

Add Depth with Layers

Layers act similarly to transparent sheets of paper or plastic when you stack one on top of another. Flash stacks layers from top to bottom. Each layer lets you see through to the layer below. As you add more layers to the Timeline, existing layers move down in the stack to appear behind new layers. Items you place in the top layer appear in front of items placed in a bottom layer. You might place a background in the bottom layer and add other objects to subsequent layers to create a feeling of depth.

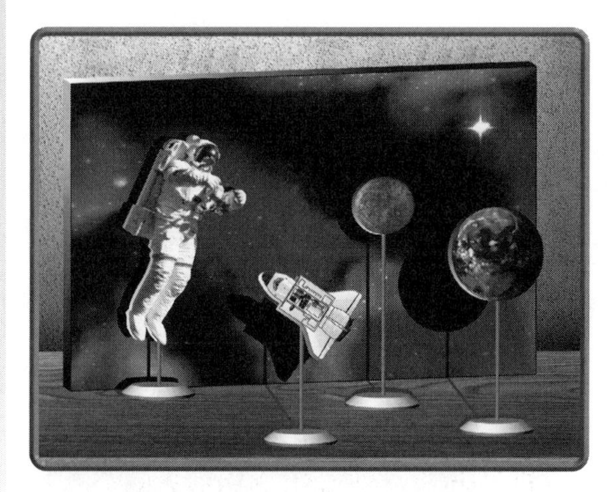

Flash makes it easy to rearrange layers in the Timeline. You can move a layer by dragging it to a new location in the Timeline and dropping it in place. For example, you might move a back layer to the top of the stack by dragging it from the bottom of the layer list to the top. Moving layers around does not affect the layer's contents, only the stacking order of the contents on the Stage.

Types of Layers

There are several different kinds of layers in Flash. A *plain layer* holds various elements such as graphics, sounds, and movie clips. Flash classifies plain layers as *normal* layer types, which are the most commonly used layers.

A *guide layers* is another type of layer. Guides can help you with the layout and positioning of objects in other layers. You most often use guides with *motion tween animations*, animation effects that follow a specified path in your Flash movie. See Chapter 30 to learn more about creating motion tween animations.

The third type of layer is a *mask layer*. Mask layers enable you to hide elements in underlying layers from view. You create a hole, as it were, in the mask layer that lets you view layers below. You might make the hole in the shape of a circle, square, or other type of outline. Any objects in the layers beneath the mask that fall into the shape of the hole appear. Flash masks anything lying outside the hole from view.

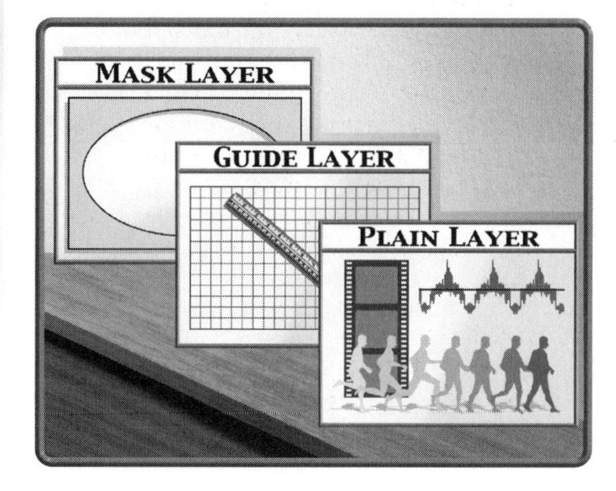

ADD AND DELETE LAYERS

When you create a new movie or scene, Flash MX starts with a single layer in the Timeline. You can add layers to the Timeline or delete layers you no longer need. Additional layers do not affect the file size, so you can add and delete as many layers as your project requires.

Use layers to organize objects in your Flash project. For example, you might devote a layer to the background image that you require for your Flash movie. You might add another layer on top of the background layer that plays an animation sequence. You may then include another layer that holds all the sound clips related to your movie. You can add as many layers as your project requires.

Layers can help you keep track of related items in your movie. For example, you might want to place all the objects you use for a logo in a single layer, and all the objects for a product illustration in another layer.

You can also use layers to add depth to your drawings. Layers are stacked from top to bottom in the Timeline. The layer at the bottom of the Timeline listing appears at the bottom of the layer stack. You can add and delete layers in the stack to change the stacking order.

ADD A LAYER

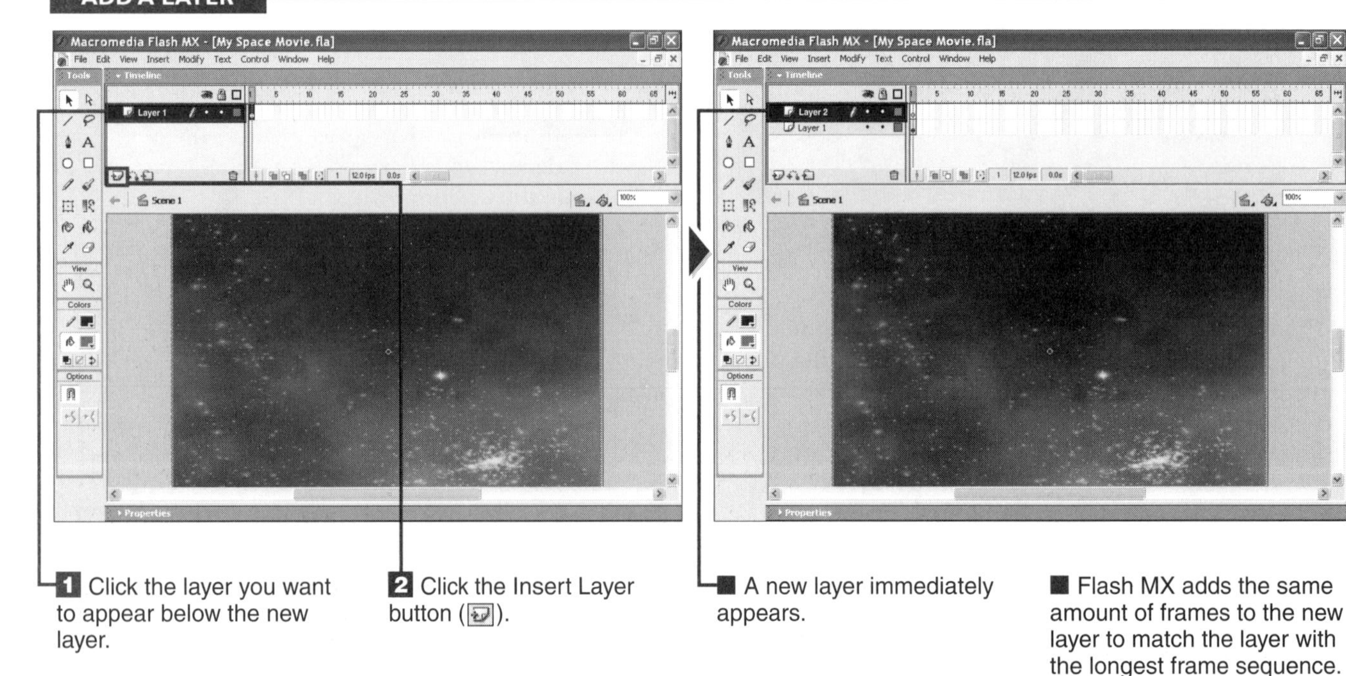

1 Click the layer you want to appear below the new layer.

2 Click the Insert Layer button (🗋).

■ A new layer immediately appears.

■ Flash MX adds the same amount of frames to the new layer to match the layer with the longest frame sequence.

Are there other ways to add layers?

✔ Yes. You can click the Insert menu and click Layer, or you can right-click a layer name and click Insert Layer from the pop-up menu. Remember, Flash MX adds a new layer directly above the active layer.

Can I drag a layer to the Trash icon (🗑) to delete it?

✔ Yes. You can quickly drag any selected layer over the 🗑 icon on the Timeline and drop it to delete it. This method saves you a step because you do not have to first select the layer, and then click 🗑.

How do I hide a layer in Flash MX?

✔ You can hide a layer to move it out of view. Simply click on the tiny bullet (•) under the eye icon (👁) for the layer you want to hide. The bullet changes to a red ☒, and Flash hides the layer from view on the Stage. Click ☒ to show the layer again.

How can I retrieve a layer that was accidentally deleted?

✔ Click the Edit menu and click Undo. Follow this step immediately after deleting the layer. If you use the Undo command after performing several other tasks, you must activate the command several times to retrieve the deleted layer.

DELETE A LAYER

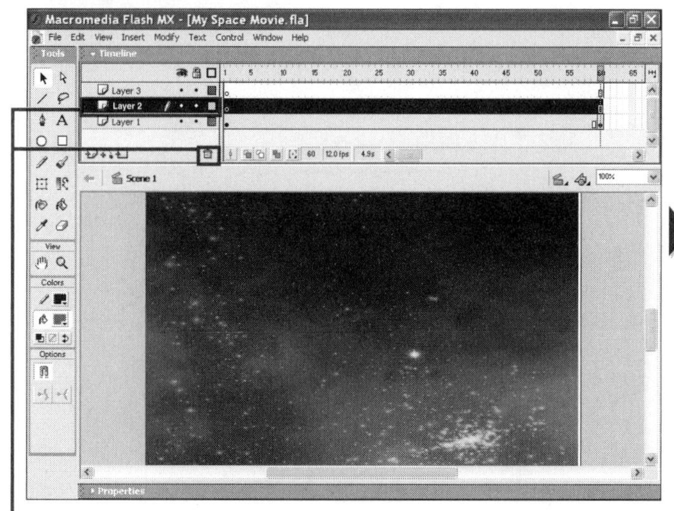

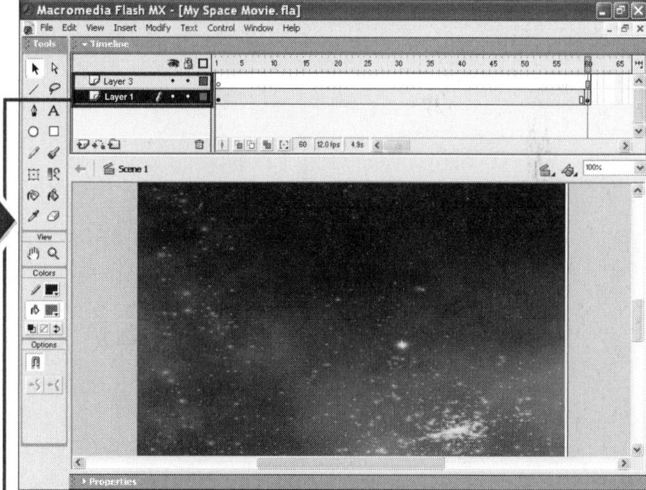

1 Click the layer you want to delete.

2 Click the Delete Layer button (🗑).

■ You can delete more than one layer by clicking the first layer you want to remove, pressing Ctrl (⌘) while clicking other layers, and then clicking 🗑.

■ The layer disappears from the Timeline.

Note: If you accidentally delete the wrong layer, you can click the Edit menu and click Undo.

SET LAYER PROPERTIES

You can define the aspects of any given layer through the Layer Properties dialog box, a one-stop shop for controlling a layer's name, function, and appearance. The more you work with layers in Flash MX, the more necessary it is to change layer properties.

You assign layer properties to the currently selected layer in the Flash Timeline. An important option you can apply to a layer is to change its name. By naming different layers in your Timeline, you can more easily keep track of their contents and position. By default, Flash MX names layers with numbers, such as Layer 1, Layer 2, and so on. Layer names can use upper- and lowercase letters.

You also have the option of hiding the layer to get its contents out of the way. To keep the layer's contents safe from editing, you can lock the layer.

The Layer Properties dialog box also has options for changing the layer type, such as turning a normal layer into a guide layer. It also has options for changing how you view layers. You can view a layer's contents as colored outlines on the Stage, or change the height of the layer as it appears in the Timeline.

SET LAYER PROPERTIES

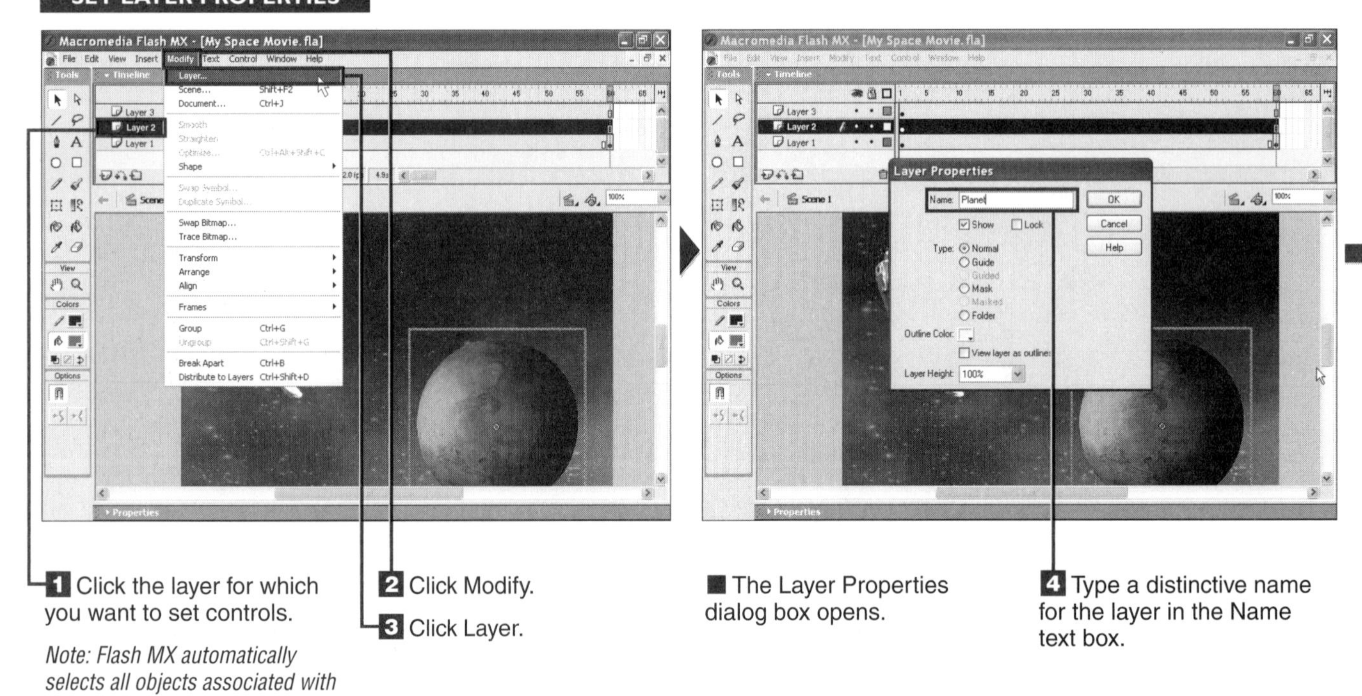

1 Click the layer for which you want to set controls.

Note: Flash MX automatically selects all objects associated with the selected layer.

2 Click Modify.

3 Click Layer.

■ The Layer Properties dialog box opens.

4 Type a distinctive name for the layer in the Name text box.

Is there a shortcut to the Layer Properties dialog box?

✔ Yes. Right-click (Control-click) the layer name and click Properties from the pop-up menu.

What happens when I choose an outline color?

✔ The outlining feature helps you to assess exactly which objects on the Stage are in the current layer by assigning colors. From the Layer Properties dialog box, click the Outline Color button (▭) to display a palette of available colors. Click the color you want to use. Flash MX outlines all objects associated with the layer in that color.

What are layer types?

✔ By default, all layers you add to the Timeline are *normal*, which means all the objects in the layer appear in the movie. Objects in guide layers do not appear in the movie. You can use a regular *guide* layer for reference points and alignment. A *guided layer* is a layer you link to a regular guide layer. A *mask* layer hides any layers you link to it. A *masked layer* links to the mask layer. To change the layer type, click a type in the Layer Properties dialog box. To learn more about layer folders see page 440.

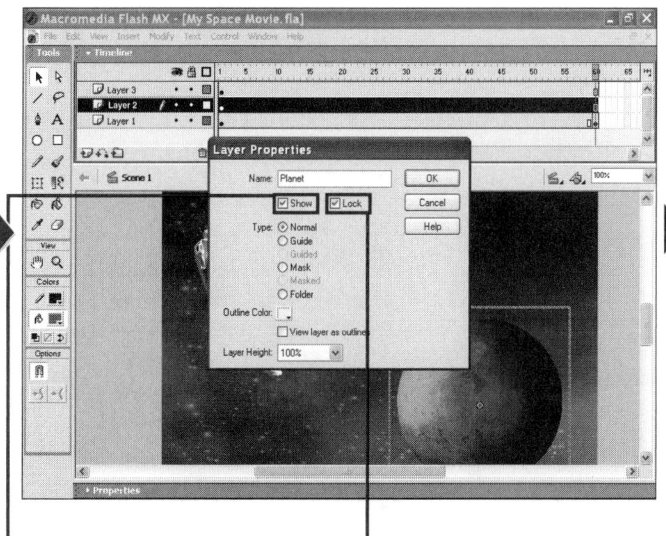

5 Change the desired layer property.

■ To make the layer visible in the Timeline, you can leave the Show check box checked (☐ changes to ☑).

■ To lock the layer to prevent changes, you can click the Lock check box (☐ changes to ☑).

■ You can select a layer type (○ changes to ◉).

■ To enlarge the layer height, you can click ▾ and select a percentage.

■ An enlarged height is useful for viewing sound waveforms in the layer.

6 Click OK.

■ The layer properties change to your specifications.

WORK WITH LAYERS IN THE TIMELINE

Flash MX makes it easy to control layers in the Timeline. You can quickly rename a layer, hide a layer, or lock a layer to prevent unnecessary changes without having to open a separate dialog box. The Timeline has buttons and toggles that you can use to control a layer with a quick click.

For example, you may want to hide a layer to remove the layer objects from view on the Stage and focus on other objects you want to edit. If you leave the layer in view and click an object on the layer by mistake, you may end up editing something you did not mean to change.

The bar above the layer names list has three icons that help you discern the status of each layer. Each icon indicates a specific status setting for the column below it. For example, the eye icon column indicates whether the layer is visible. The lock icon tells you whether the layer is locked. The outline icon enables you to view a layer's contents as outlines on the Flash Stage. All three of the icon categories for each layer can be toggled on or off.

In addition to controlling layer status, you can also quickly name layers in the Timeline by entering new labels directly on the layer name list.

WORK WITH LAYERS IN THE TIMELINE

RENAME A LAYER

1 Double-click the layer name.

2 Type a new name.

3 Press Enter (Return).

■ The layer's name changes.

HIDE A LAYER

1 Click ⊡ beneath the eye icon column.

Can I lock multiple layers?

✔ Yes. Right-click (Control-click) the layer you want to remain unlocked. Click Lock Others from the pop-up menu.

Can I enlarge the size of a layer?

✔ All layers you add to the Timeline use a default size; however, you can enlarge a layer to better view its contents. This is useful when a frame contains a sound clip. To enlarge the layer height, right-click (Control-click) the layer name and click Properties to open the Layer Properties dialog box. Click the Layer Height ▾ and choose a percentage. Click OK to apply the new size.

How can I tell which objects are in which layer?

✔ You can choose to view layer contents as outlines, making it easy to distinguish the objects from other layers. Click ☐ under the square icon column (☐ changes to ☐). Flash MX outlines all objects in the layer in the same color as the square you clicked.

How do I view a long list of layers?

✔ Use the scroll bar on the far right side of the Timeline to scroll through a long list of layer names and view their frames.

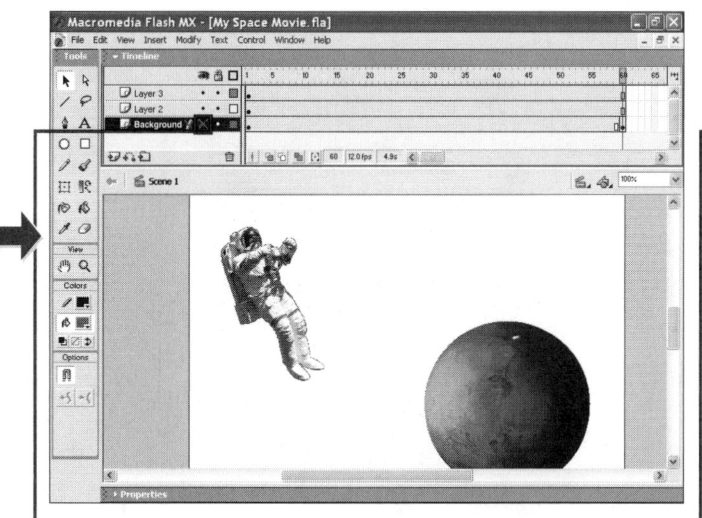

■ All the objects in the layer become invisible (• changes to ☒).

■ To make the layer objects visible again, you can click ☒ under the eye icon column (☒ changes to •).

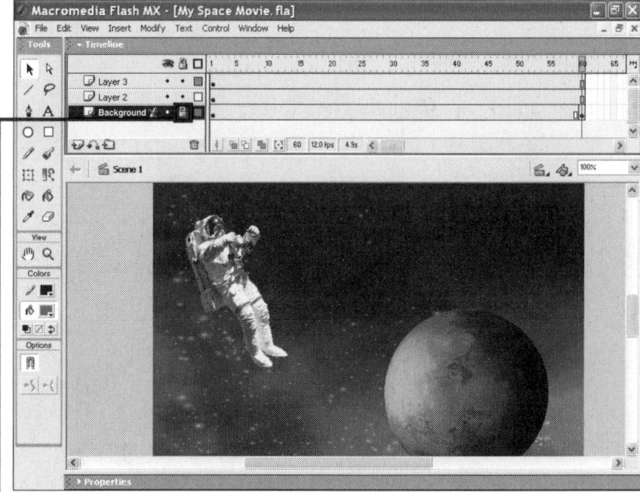

LOCK A LAYER

1 Under the padlock icon column, click the layer's bullet (• changes to 🔒).

■ Flash MX locks the layer and you cannot edit the contents.

■ To unlock a layer, click the layer's padlock icon (🔒 changes to •).

STACK LAYERS

To rearrange how objects appear in your Flash project, you can stack Flash layers in a manner similar to the way you stack objects in a drawing. Flash layers act like sheets of transparent plastic or film. Depending on the placement of the layers, objects can appear in front of or behind objects in other layers.

For example, if you have a layer containing background elements, you can move it to the back of the layer stack. Any object you insert onto layers stacked on top of the background layer appears on top of the background itself. Stacking layers in this manner creates the illusion of depth in your movie.

You can change the order of a layer by moving it up or down in placement in the layer list on the Flash Timeline. The layer at the top of the list appears at the top of the stack, while the layer at the bottom of the list appears at the bottom of the stack. When changing stacking order, you can move a single layer or you can move multiple layers up or down in the layer list. You cannot move a locked layer. You can, however, move hidden layers.

STACK LAYERS

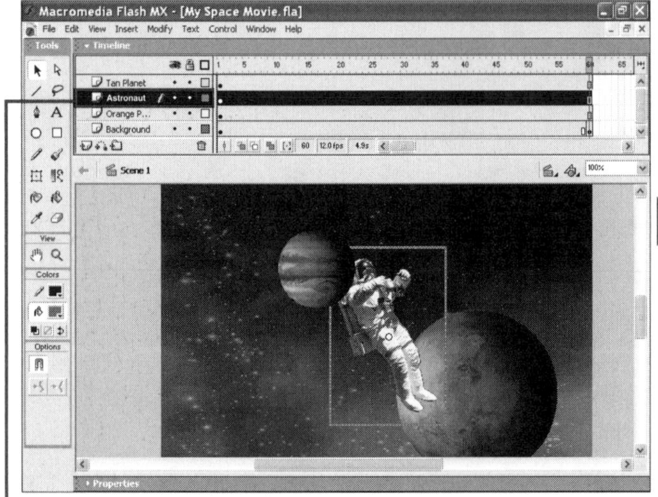

1 Click the layer you want to move.

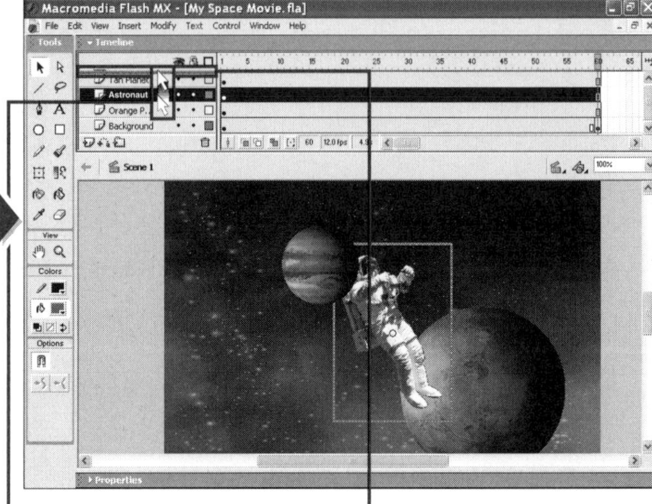

2 Drag the layer up or down to its new location in the stack.

■ An insertion point appears, showing where the dragged layer will rest.

Why can I not see all my layers?

✔ The more layers you add to the Timeline, the longer the list of layer names become. Not all the layers stay in view. Use the scroll bar at the far right end of the Timeline to scroll up and down the layer list to view other layers. You can also use the new Flash MX layer folders to organize layers in the Timeline. To organize your layers for viewing, see page 440.

Can I copy a layer?

✔ Yes. Click the layer you want to copy. Click the Edit menu and click Copy. Click the new layer, click the Edit menu, and then click Paste. Flash MX copies the contents of the first layer and places them in the second layer, slightly offset.

How can I see more layers at a time in my Timeline?

✔ You can resize the Timeline to see more of your layers. Move the ↖ over the bottom border of the Timeline until the ↖ changes to ÷. Click and drag the border down to increase the size of the Timeline. This enables you to see more of the layers in the Timeline. You can also undock and resize the Timeline. To learn more about working with the Timeline, see page 340.

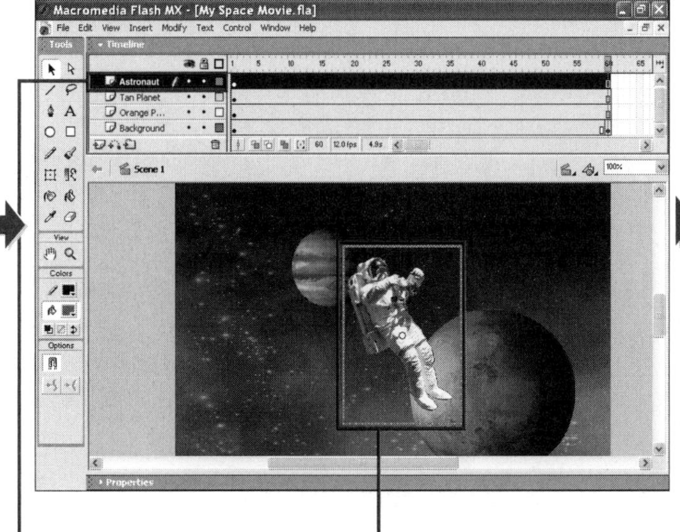

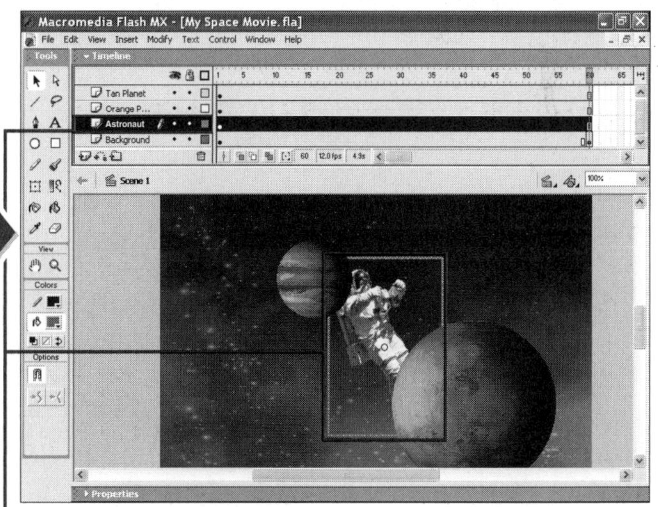

3 Release the mouse button.

■ The layer assumes its new position.

■ In this example, the layer moves up in the stacking order. Any objects in the layer now appear on top of all the other layer objects.

■ In this example, the layer moves down in the stacking order. Any objects in the layer now appear below other top layer objects.

ORGANIZE LAYERS INTO FOLDERS

You can use layer folders to organize the numerous layers you use in a Flash project. Layer folders are new to Flash MX, but a greatly needed addition to help bring order to the multitude of layers typically found in Flash animations.

Layer folders act just like the folders found on the hard drive of your computer. For example, if you have several layers pertaining to a particular animation sequence, you can place all the related layers into one layer folder on the Flash Timeline. This makes it much easier to find a layer for editing later. Layer folders are identified in the Timeline by tiny folder icons next to the folder names.

Layer folders can expand and collapse to allow you to view or hide the layer folder content. Collapsing layers you are not currently using can tidy up the Timeline. You can also nest layer folders in other layer folders.

When you add a new layer folder to the Timeline, Flash MX assigns a default name. You can rename folders to describe their contents. To keep your movies organized and prevent confusion later in a project, it is a good practice to name all layers and their folders within the Timeline.

ORGANIZE LAYERS INTO FOLDERS

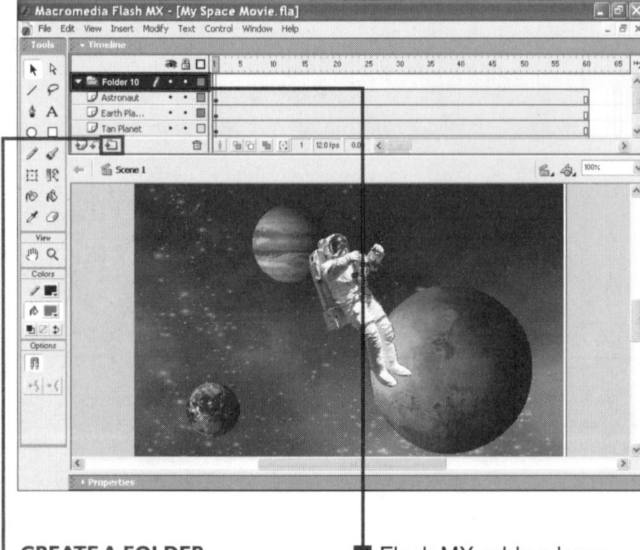

CREATE A FOLDER

1 Click the Insert Layer Folder button ( ).

■ Flash MX adds a layer folder to the Timeline.

■ You can also click the Insert menu and click Layer Folder.

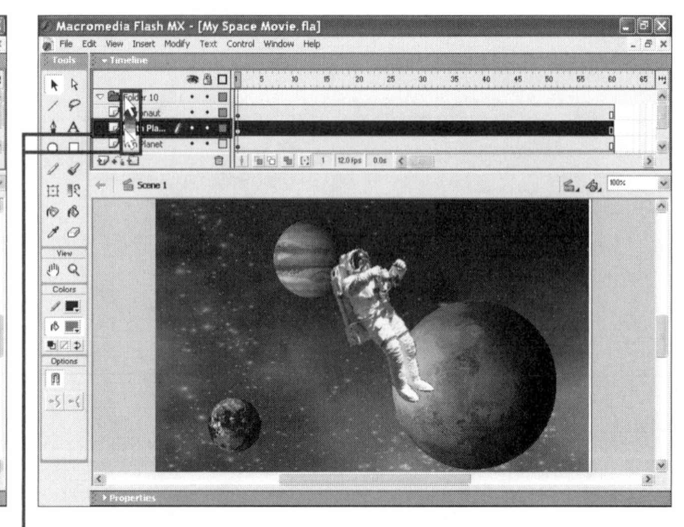

ADD A LAYER TO A FOLDER

1 Click the layer you want to move into a folder.

2 Drag the layer over the folder.

3 Release the mouse button.

■ The layer moves to the layer folder.

Can I move a folder in the stacking order?

✔ Yes. You can move layer folders just as you move layers. Drag the folder name up or down in the Timeline to change the stacking order of the folder. See page 436 to learn more.

How do I remove a layer from a folder?

✔ Display the content of the folder layer, drag the layer you want to remove from the folder, and then drop it where you want it to appear in the layer stacking order. To remove the layer completely from the Timeline, click the layer name and click 🗑.

Can I lock a layer folder?

✔ Yes. You can lock and hide layer folders just as you can lock and hide layers. Locking a folder locks all the layers included within the folder. Click the folder layer's bullet (• changes to 🔒). Flash MX locks the folder and any layers associated with the folder.

How do I delete a layer folder I no longer need?

✔ You can click the layer folder, then click the 🗑 icon. However, any layers included in the folder are also deleted.

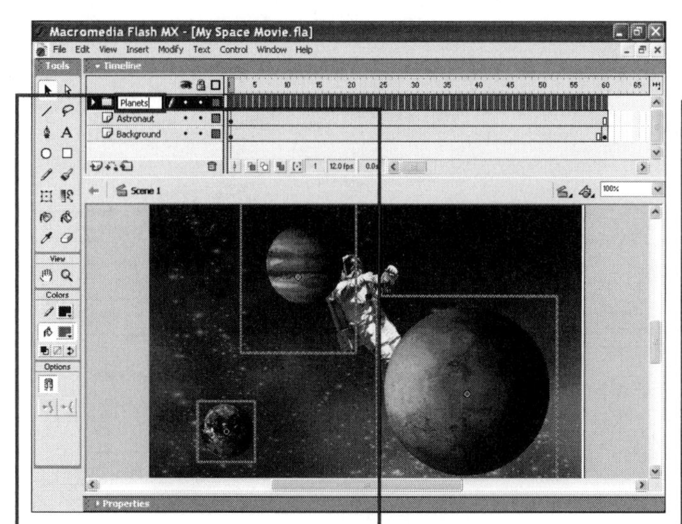

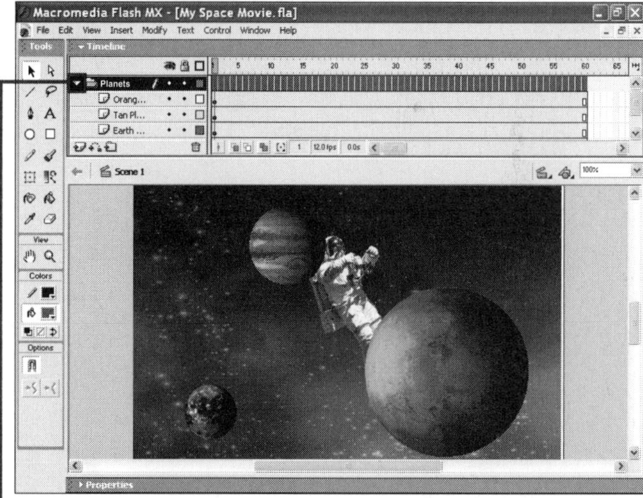

RENAME A FOLDER

1 Double-click the layer folder name you want to rename.

2 Type a new name.

3 Press Enter (Return).

■ The layer folder renames.

EXPAND A FOLDER

1 Click the layer folder's Expand icon (▶). (▶ changes to ▼).

■ Layers associated with the folder are now hidden.

■ Click the layer folder's Collapse icon (▼) to view the folder's contents again (▼ changes to ▶).

ADD GUIDE LAYERS

Guide layers help you position objects. There are two types of guide layers in Flash: *plain* and *motion*. A plain guide layer can help you position objects on the Stage, but it does not appear in your final movie. A plain guide layer can enable you to keep your layout consistent, trace objects that you draw, or generally assist you in lining things up.

You use a motion guide layer to animate an object to a path on the Flash Stage. For example, you can create a motion guide layer that specifies a path of flight for a bee in another layer. A motion guide layer contains the animation path that links to an object in another layer. Flash MX exports motion guide layers with the movie, but the guide layers are not visible in the movie. See Chapter 30 to learn more about creating a motion tween animation.

Flash MX notes all guide layers in the Timeline with a unique icon. Plain guide layers are noted with a T-square icon, while motion guide layers are noted with a dotted arch icon. You can move guide and motion guide layers around in the Timeline just like regular layers. However, when you move a motion guide layer, the associated layer moves as well. Because plain guide layers are not associated with a specific layer, you can move them freely within the Timeline layer stacking order.

ADD GUIDE LAYERS

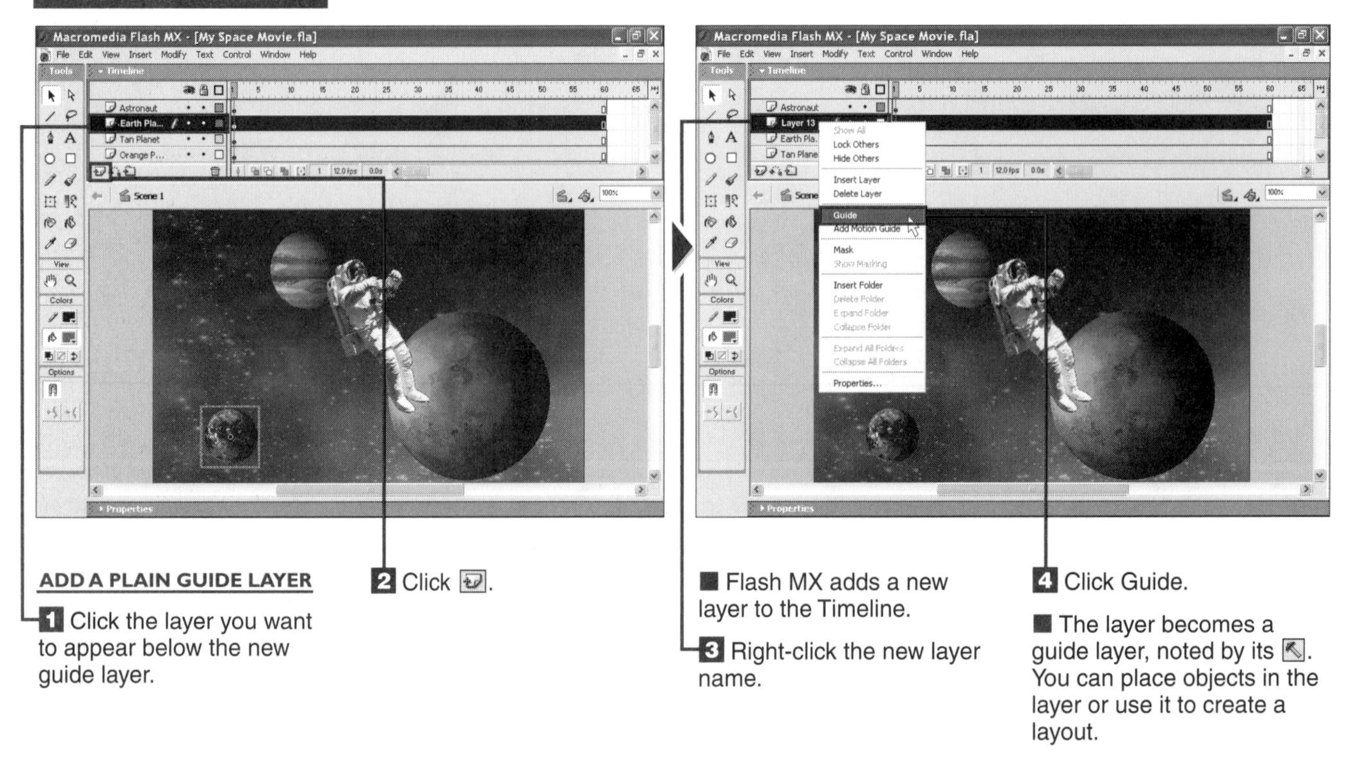

ADD A PLAIN GUIDE LAYER

1 Click the layer you want to appear below the new guide layer.

2 Click .

■ Flash MX adds a new layer to the Timeline.

3 Right-click the new layer name.

4 Click Guide.

■ The layer becomes a guide layer, noted by its . You can place objects in the layer or use it to create a layout.

Why is it Flash will not let me add a motion guide layer?

✔ Flash MX will not allow you to add a motion guide layer to an existing guide layer. Make sure you click the regular layer to which you want to assign a motion guide and then add the motion guide layer.

Can I lock my guide layer in place?

✔ Yes. In fact, it is a good idea to always lock and motion guide layers in place so you do not accidentally move anything in them. To lock a layer, click [•] on the Timeline. To unlock the layer again, click [🔒] again.

How exactly does a motion guide layer work?

✔ Flash MX links motion guide layers to layers containing objects you want to animate along a given path. The motion guide layer contains the path, and you can link it to one or more layers. The motion guide layer always appears directly above the layer (or layers) to which it links. To learn more about animating in Flash MX, see Chapter 29.

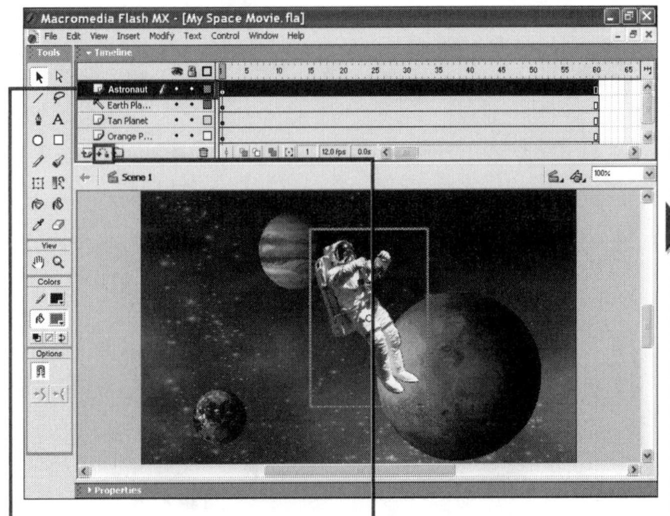

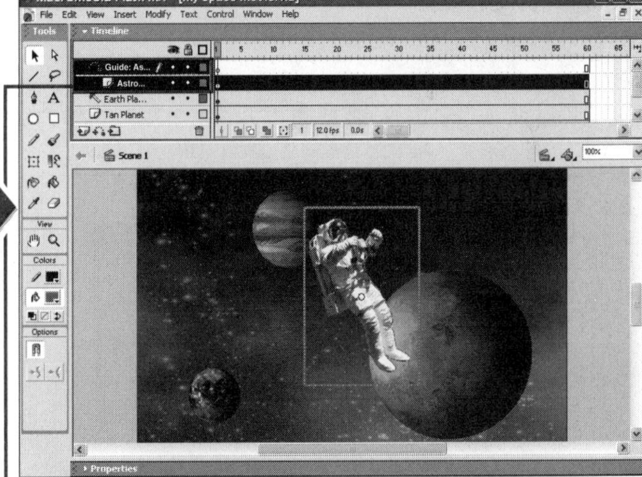

ADD A MOTION GUIDE LAYER

1 Click the layer you want to link to a motion guide layer.

2 Click the Add Motion Guide button ( ).

■ Flash MX adds the motion guide layer to the Timeline and links it to the layer you selected.

■ You can distinguish a guide layer by its unique icon ( ).

ADD AND CREATE A MASK LAYER

You can use mask layers to hide various elements in underlying layers. A mask is much like a stencil you tape to a wall. Only certain portions of the underlying layer appear through the mask design, while other parts of the layer are hidden, or *masked*. Flash MX links masked layers to layers and exports them in the final movie file.

You might create a mask layer that has a filled square shape in the middle that acts like a window to the layer below. The hole or square shape lets you see anything directly beneath, but the remainder of the mask layer hides anything that lies out of view of the hole.

Mask layers appear with a unique icon on the Timeline. You can link a mask layer only to the layer directly below it. Mask layers can contain only one fill shape, symbol, or object to use as a window.

By default, any layer you turn into a mask layer is automatically locked. To work with the layer to create a mask, you must first unlock the mask layer. Once you complete the mask, you can lock the layer again to prevent any accidental changes to the layer content.

ADD AND CREATE A MASK LAYER

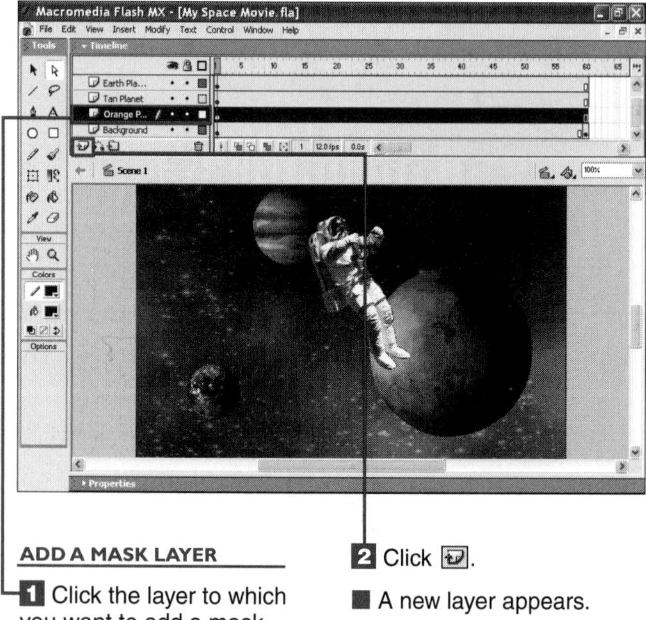

ADD A MASK LAYER

1 Click the layer to which you want to add a mask.

2 Click .

■ A new layer appears.

3 Right-click (Control-click) the new layer's name.

4 Click Mask.

■ Flash MX marks the layer as a mask layer, locks it against any changes, and links it to the layer below.

Why can I not see the mask effect?

✔ Probably because you unlocked the layer. You must first lock the mask layer in order to see the mask effect. You can also see the effect if you run the movie in test mode — click the Control menu and click Test Movie. The Flash Player window opens and runs the movie. Click the window's ☒ to return to the Flash MX program window.

Can I convert a mask layer into a regular layer?

✔ You can convert a mask layer back into a normal layer by opening the Layer Properties dialog box. Right-click (Control-click) the mask layer and click Properties. This opens the Layer Properties dialog box. Click Normal, then click OK. Flash resets the layer to normal status.

What sort of fill should I draw for my mask shape?

✔ You can use any kind of fill color or pattern to create the mask shape. Regardless of what makes up your fill, Flash MX treats the shape as a window to the linked layer below. For that reason, you might consider using a transparent fill rather than a solid so you can see through the fill to the layer below and position it correctly on the Stage. If you choose a gradient effect for a fill, the mask will still appear completely transparent.

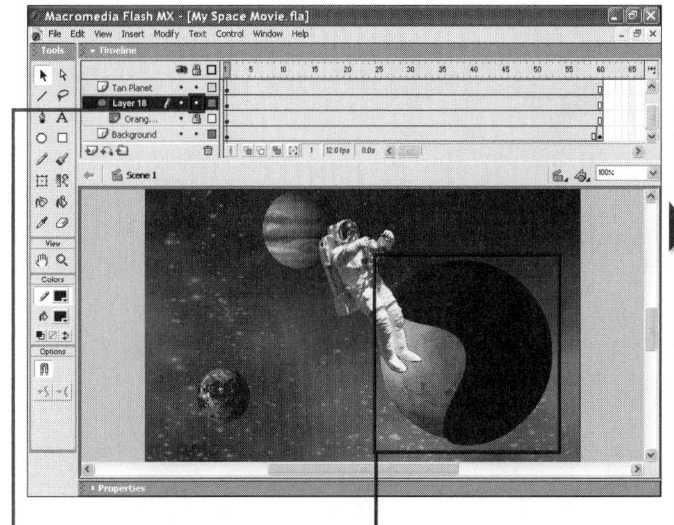

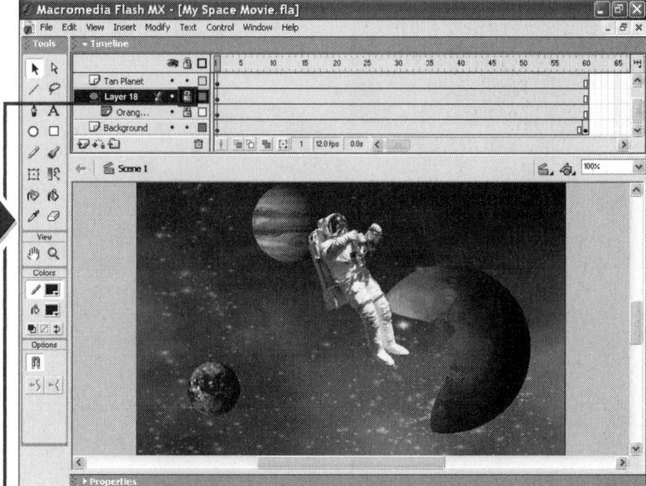

CREATE A MASK

1 Click 🔒 to unlock the mask layer (🔒 changes to •).

2 Draw a fill shape on the Stage over the area you want to view in the layer below.

■ In this example, an oval fill shape is modified slightly to create another shape.

3 Lock the mask layer.

Note: To lock a layer, see page 437.

■ You can now see the masking effect.

Note: Anything appearing outside the fill shape is masked out.

UNDERSTANDING SYMBOLS AND INSTANCES

In Flash MX, a *symbol* is a reusable element you can store in the Flash Library. You can repeatedly use a symbol throughout your movie by inserting an *instance* of the symbol in the frame in which you want it to appear. An instance is a copy of the original symbol.

Storing Movie Elements

Every file you create in Flash MX has a Library that stores elements you want to reuse in your project. You can manage these elements from the Library window by organizing them into related folders, much like organizing files on the hard drive of your computer.

The Library window is a separate window or panel you can open inside the Flash MX program window. You can open and close the Library as you work with various symbols. The Library window lists the symbols stored with your file alphabetically. You can drag symbols from the Library and drop them onto the Stage to use in a movie. You can also add and delete symbols as needed. See the section "Using the Flash Library" to learn more about using this feature.

Flash Symbols

A *symbol* is any graphical element you store in the Flash Library. A symbol can be a drawing you create with the Flash drawing tools, a graphic you create in another program, or a rollover button. Symbols are also sound clips or movie or video clips. You can even treat text as symbols in your project.

When you import a graphic, Flash MX automatically classifies a symbol and adds it to the file's Library. With other graphics you create from scratch, you must first define them as symbols in order to place them in the file's Library. You can convert existing graphical elements into symbols using the Convert to Symbol command, or you can use the Symbol editor to create new symbols.

You can edit symbols in Symbol-Edit mode. Flash MX reflects any changes you make to a symbol in Symbol-Edit mode in the symbol that appears in the Library window. Flash also updates any instances of the symbol in the Flash Timeline.

Instances

Anytime you insert a copy of the symbol into your project, you are inserting an *instance*. The instance references the original so you do not greatly affect the file size each time you reuse a symbol. The original symbol stays in the Library, unaffected by how you use or edit the instance. Any edits you make to an instance are good only for that one occurrence of the instance in your movie.

You can use as many instances of a symbol in your project as you like. You can also use symbols from other Flash files.

TYPES OF SYMBOLS

You can reuse symbols to create animation in your Flash movies. Every time you reuse a symbol, you must specify how you want the symbol to behave. Flash classifies symbols, or *behaviors*, into three types: graphics, movie clips, or buttons.

Graphic Symbols

You can create *graphic* symbols or import graphics from other programs to use in Flash. You can make graphic symbols as simple as a shape or as complex as a highly detailed drawing. You can also turn text into graphic symbols that you can manipulate and animate in your movies. To learn more about drawing graphic objects in Flash, see Chapter 21. To learn how to create text in Flash, see Chapter 24.

Button Symbols

You can save interactive buttons, also called *rollover buttons*, as symbols, and reuse them by associating different actions to the same button. You can use graphics or movie clips as buttons. You can make a button a simple shape or a complex graphic. You can also create hidden buttons, which look like the rest of the movie, but which the user must find and click to start another action. You can use just about anything as a button in Flash MX.

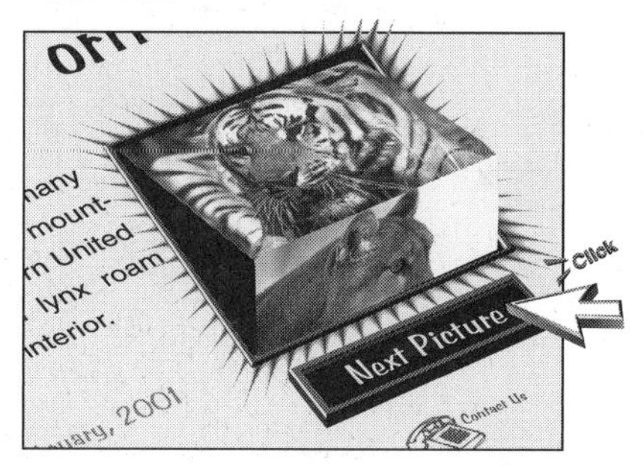

Button symbols react to mouse cursor movements in your Flash movies. Mouse cursor movements include rolling over the button, pressing the button, and releasing the button. By altering the button's state, you can clue users in to the button's presence. To learn more creating buttons in Flash, see Chapter 27.

Movie Clip Symbols

Independent of the main movie's timeline, *movie clip* symbols are mini-movies that reside inside the main Flash movie file and utilize timelines of their own. For example, instead of building a sequence into your main movie timeline, you can create a short animation, make a movie clip symbol of it, and reuse it in your movie. When you define a short animation sequence as a movie clip symbol, you can easily keep track of it, edit it separately from your main movie, and drop it into place whenever you want it to play. To learn more about creating animations in Flash, see Chapters 29 and 30.

USING THE FLASH LIBRARY

A Flash project can contain hundreds of graphics, sounds, interactive buttons, and video and movie clips. The Flash Library can help you organize these elements. For example, you can store related symbols in the same folder, create new folders, or delete folders and symbols you no longer need. You can organize symbols in the Library much like you organize files on your computer.

Every time you import a graphic image into a Flash file, convert a graphic element into a symbol, or add a new sound to a frame, Flash MX adds it to the file's Library. In effect, the Library is a compendium of your movie's contents.

When you open the Library, it appears as a panel or window within the Flash MX program window. You can move the Library around on-screen, or hide it when you no longer need to use it. You can enlarge the Library window to view more details about its contents and use the scroll bars to view different symbols in the list. You can also preview what a symbol looks like before adding it to the Stage.

You can also click the title bar of the Library window to expand and collapse the window. This enables you to view or hide content as necessary.

USING THE FLASH LIBRARY

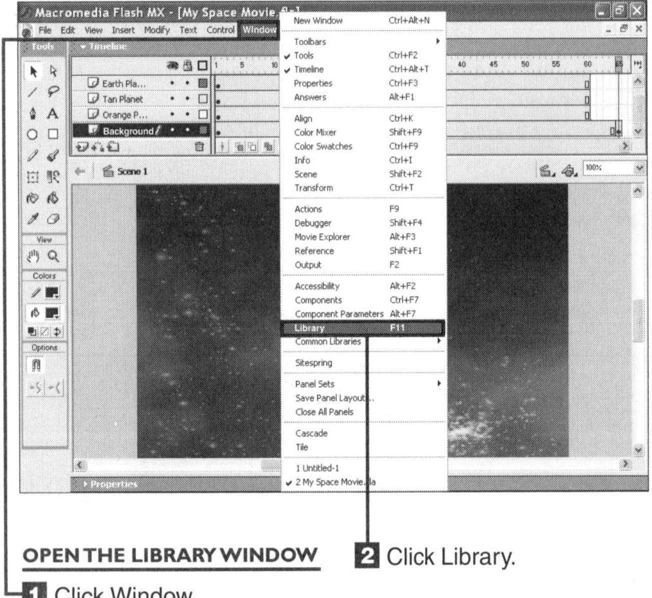

OPEN THE LIBRARY WINDOW

1 Click Window.

2 Click Library.

■ The Library window appears.

■ You can click the Wide Library View button (□) to display the full Library window.

■ You can return the window to Narrow state by clicking Narrow Library View button (▯).

Can I use symbols from another movie's Library?

✔ You can easily insert symbols into your current project from another file's library. Click the File menu and click Open as Library. The Open as Library dialog box appears. Click the filename, and then click Open. The Library window opens listing the other file's symbols. Drag the symbol you want to use onto the Stage.

Does Flash offer a faster way to open the Library window?

✔ Yes. You can press F11 on the keyboard to quickly summon the Library at any time.

How do I place a symbol from the Library onto the Stage?

✔ From the Library window, locate the symbol you want to use, and then drag it from the Library and drop it onto the Stage.

How do I close the Library window?

✔ You can leave the Library window open as long as you need it, or you can hide it again by clicking the window's Close button (☒).

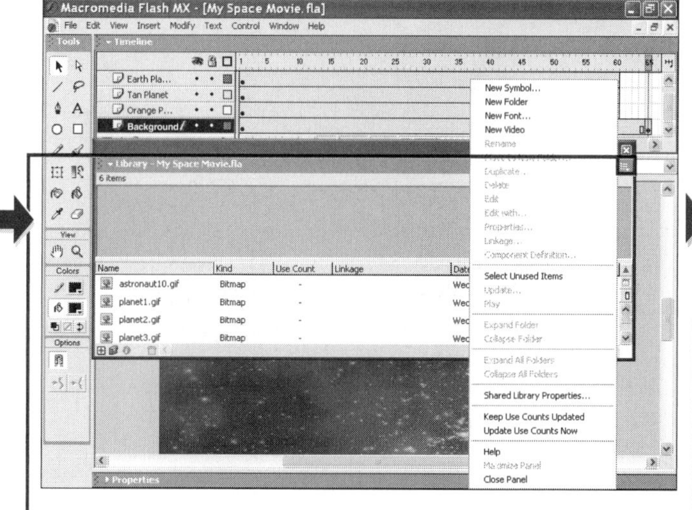

■ You can click ▤ next to the Options box to display a pop-up menu of commands related to Library tasks and items.

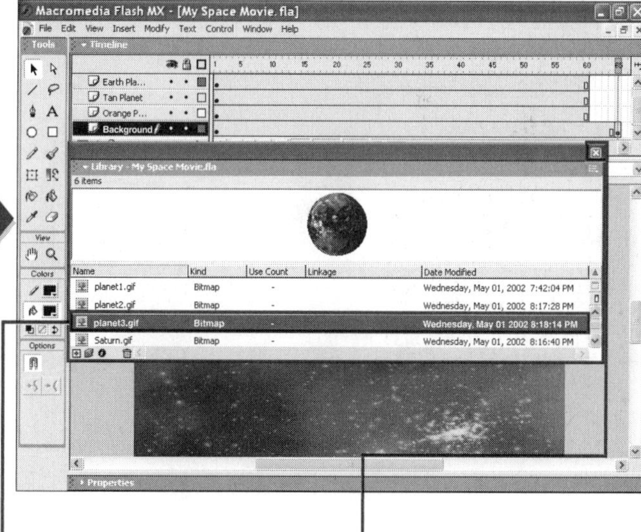

■ You can preview an item in the Library by clicking the item.

3 Click ☒.

■ Flash MX closes the Library window.

CONTINUED

USING THE FLASH LIBRARY (CONTINUED)

To organize all of your symbols, you can store them in folders. You might have a folder containing symbols you use in a company logo, and another folder containing symbols you use in an animation sequence. You can name and rename folders any way you like. You can add and delete folders and move symbols from one folder to another. You can also delete symbols from the Library that you no longer need.

The Library folders display like any other folder on your computer. Open the folder to view its contents or hide the contents and view only the folder name. When you open a folder, you can see every symbol it contains. The icon next to the symbol name in the Library window indicates the symbol type. For example, a speaker icon indicates the symbol is a sound clip symbol, while an icon with three tiny shapes indicates a graphic symbol.

Folders and symbols are listed alphabetically in the Library window. When you move items around from one folder to another, the items are also listed alphabetically within the folder.

USING THE FLASH LIBRARY (CONTINUED)

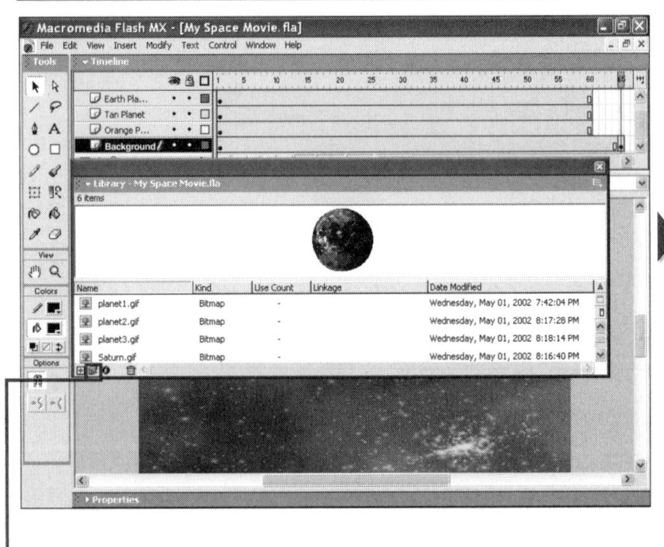

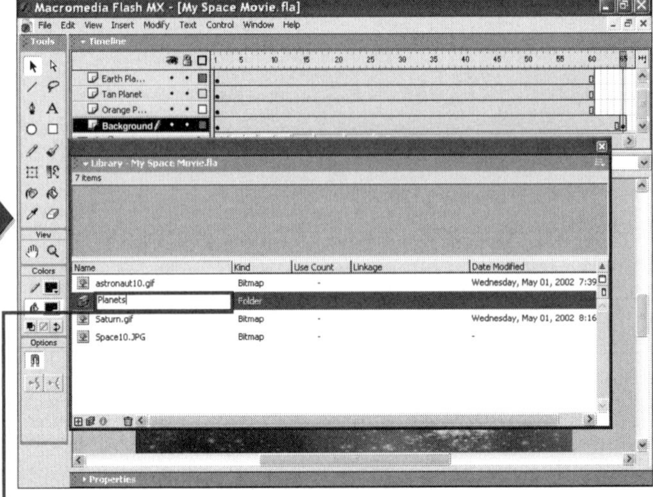

CREATE A NEW FOLDER

1 In the Library window, click the New Folder button ( ).

■ Flash MX adds a new folder to the list.

2 Type a name for the folder.

3 Press Enter (Return).

■ Flash MX creates a new folder.

How do I rename a folder?

✔ Double-click the folder name in the Library window to highlight the folder name. Type a new name, press Enter, and Flash MX applies the new name. You can use this technique to rename symbols in the Library window.

Do I have to widen the Library window?

✔ No. You widen it only if you want to see more content details. You may find it easier to leave the window narrow to easily see the Flash Stage contents and to drag symbols from the window onto the Stage.

Can I delete a folder I no longer need?

✔ Yes, but make sure it does not contain any symbols you want to keep or are currently using in the Flash file. After you delete a folder, Flash MX deletes its contents, along with any instances you use in your Flash animation. To delete a folder, click it, and then click the Delete icon (🗑) at the bottom of the Library window. Flash MX warns you that you are about to permanently delete the folder and its contents. Click Delete, and Flash MX removes the folder from the Library list.

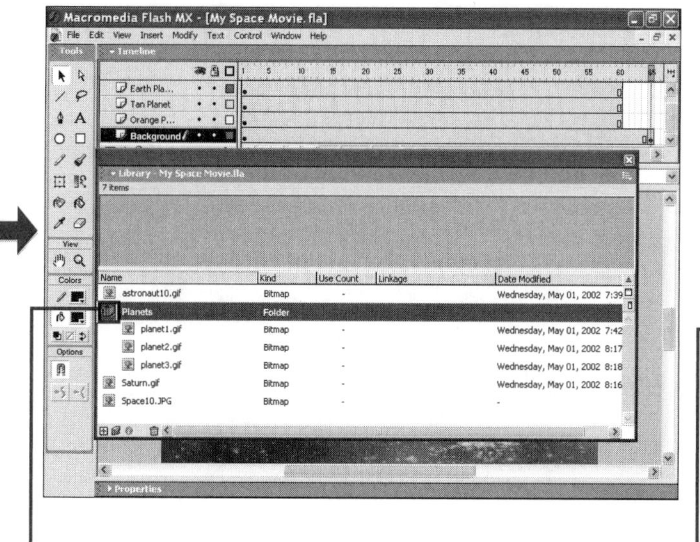

■ To view a the contents of a folder, you can double-click the Folder icon (📁).

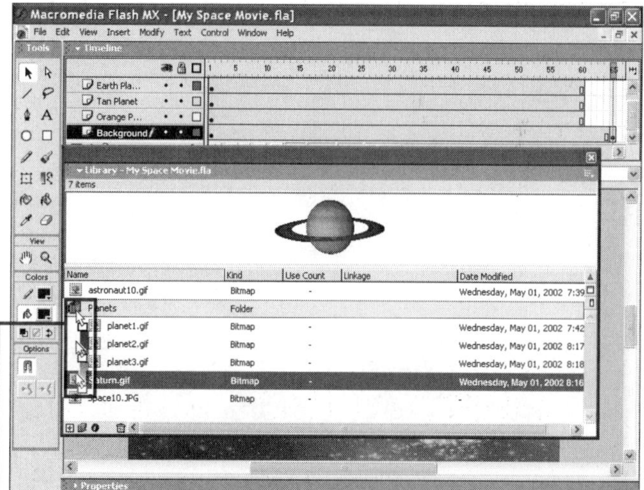

MOVE A SYMBOL

1 Drag the symbol over the 📁.

2 Release the mouse button.

■ The symbol moves into the folder.

CREATE A SYMBOL

You can easily turn any object you draw on the Flash Stage into a symbol you can reuse throughout your project. You can also convert any existing drawing or graphical element into a symbol. When you save an item as a symbol, Flash MX stores it in the file's Library. When you reuse the symbol, you are using an *instance* or copy of the original symbol.

There are three types of behaviors you can assign to a symbol: graphic, movie clip, or button. The behavior you assign depends on what you want to do with the symbol.

By turning graphical elements into symbols, you can considerably reduce the file's size. Converting an element into a symbol places it in the file's Library. Any time you want to use the symbol elsewhere in your Flash project, you can place an instance of the symbol onto the Stage. The instance contains information that references the original symbol. The referencing data takes up much less file size than a complete set of instructions for drawing the symbol each time you want it to appear in your project.

CREATE A SYMBOL

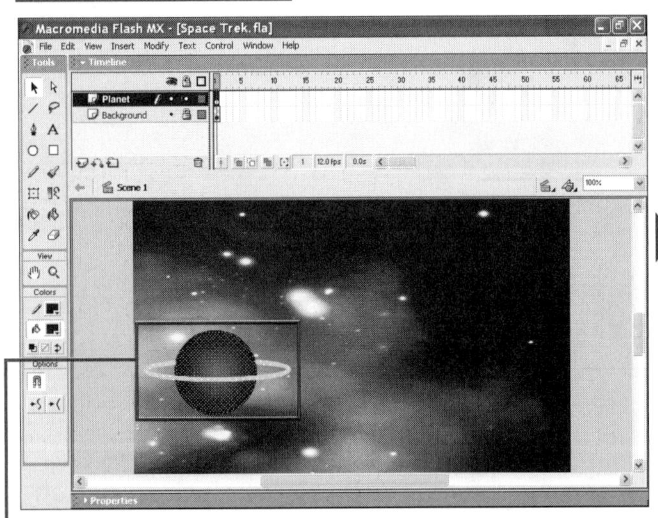

CONVERT AN OBJECT TO A SYMBOL

1 Select the objects on the Stage you want to convert into a symbol.

Note: To select objects, see page 372.

■ To select multiple objects, you can hold down Shift while clicking each object.

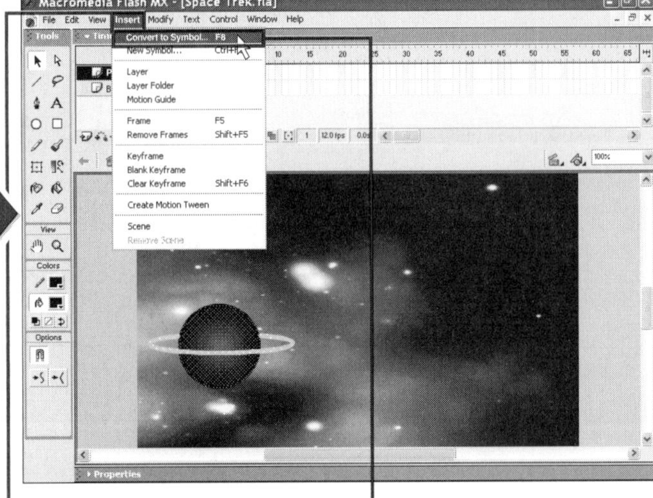

2 Click Insert.

3 Click Convert to Symbol.

How do I create a symbol from scratch?

✔ Rather than converting an object into a symbol, you can switch to Symbol-Edit mode and create a new symbol. Click the Insert menu, and click New Symbol. Type a name for the symbol and assign a behavior, such as Graphic, and then click OK. Flash MX immediately switches you to Symbol-Edit mode, and you can use the drawing tools to create a new symbol. The symbol's name appears above the Stage area. To save the symbol and exit Symbol-Edit mode, click the Scene Name link to the left of the symbol name.

Can I create a duplicate symbol?

✔ Yes. For example, you might want to copy a symbol and change it ever so slightly in one frame of your Flash movie. From the Library window, right-click the symbol you want to duplicate. Click Duplicate. Type a new name and assign a behavior and click OK. Now you can edit the copy of the symbol without affecting the original.

Is there a shortcut for converting objects into symbols?

✔ Yes, you can press F8 on the keyboard to open the Convert to Symbol dialog box and convert objects into symbols.

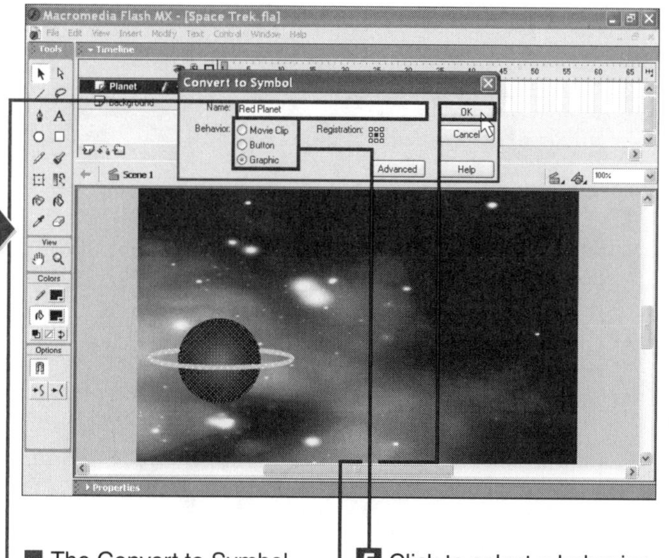

■ The Convert to Symbol dialog box opens.

4 Type a name for the symbol.

5 Click to select a behavior to assign to the symbol (○ changes to ◉).

6 Click OK.

■ Flash MX adds the symbol to the Library for the file.

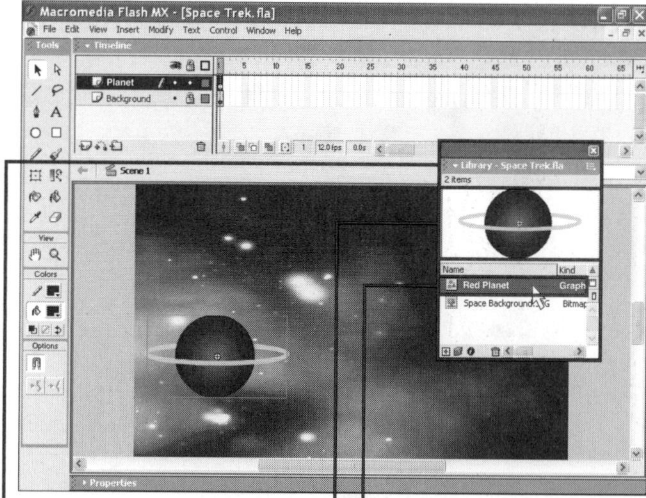

PREVIEW THE SYMBOL

1 Open the Library window.

Note: To open and close the Library window, see page 448.

2 Click the symbol name.

■ The symbol appears in the top section of the Library window.

INSERT AN INSTANCE

To reuse a symbol in your Flash project, you can place an instance of it on the Stage. An *instance* is a copy of the original symbol. The copy references the original instead of redrawing the object completely. This method of referencing a vector object for reuse is much more efficient than copying an object over and over again in a file. To learn how to create an original symbol, see page 452.

When copying an object, you are copying the entire set of instructions that tells the computer how to draw the object. With the Flash MX method, the symbol instance merely points to the original symbol without needing a complete set of instructions for re-creating the object. This greatly decreases the movie's file size.

You can place as many instances as you like throughout your Flash movie or just in a single frame. You can also make edits to an instance without affecting the original symbol. For example, you might want to change the appearance or shape of the object.

You can insert instances of graphics, movie clips, and buttons onto the Stage. When you add an instance, a circled crosshair icon appears in the middle of the instance. This icon represents the instance on the Stage. Some instances may not be entirely visible on the Stage, but you still see the circled crosshair icon representing the instance. For example, some movie clips do not start out with full graphics, but a fade in effect. Sound instances do not employ the crosshair icon when added to the Stage.

INSERT AN INSTANCE

1 Click the frame and layer where you want to insert the instance.

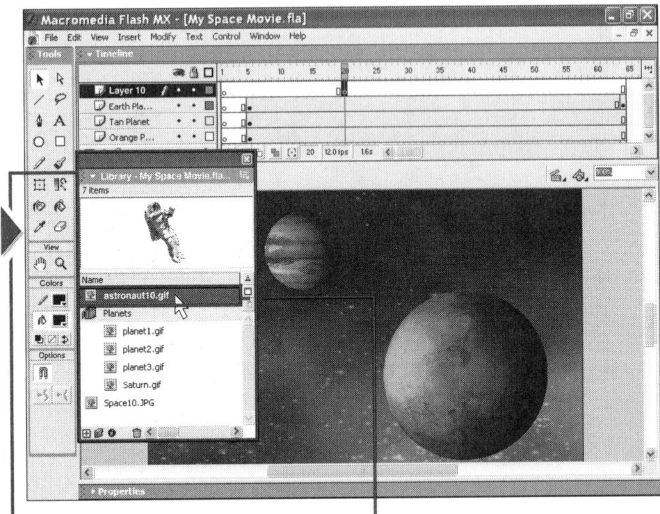

2 Open the Library window.

Note: To open the Library window, see page 448.

3 Click the name of the symbol.

Can I replace one instance with another?

✔ Yes. First click the symbol you want to replace, and then open the Property inspector. Click Swap Symbol. Click the replacement symbol from the Swap Symbol dialog box and click OK. See page 346 to learn more about viewing the Property inspector.

Flash MX does not let me place an instance in a regular frame. Why not?

✔ You can place an instance only in a keyframe in the Flash Timeline. You are not allowed to place instances in regular frames. To learn more about how frames work in the Timeline, see Chapter 29.

I made a mistake. How do I remove an instance?

✔ If you change your mind about placing an instance on the Stage, you can undo your action with the Undo command. Click the Edit menu and click Undo to immediately reverse your last action in Flash MX. To redo the action again, click the Edit menu and click Redo. You can also press Ctrl + Z (⌘ + Z) and Ctrl + Y (⌘ + Y) to activate the Undo and Redo commands.

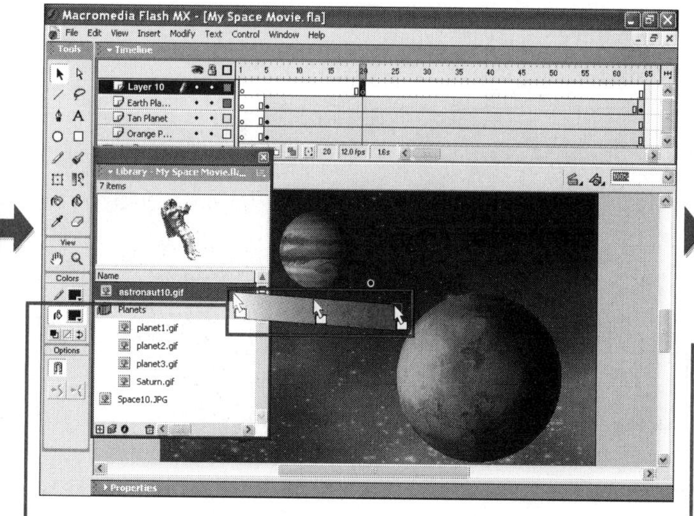

4 Drag the symbol from the Library window.

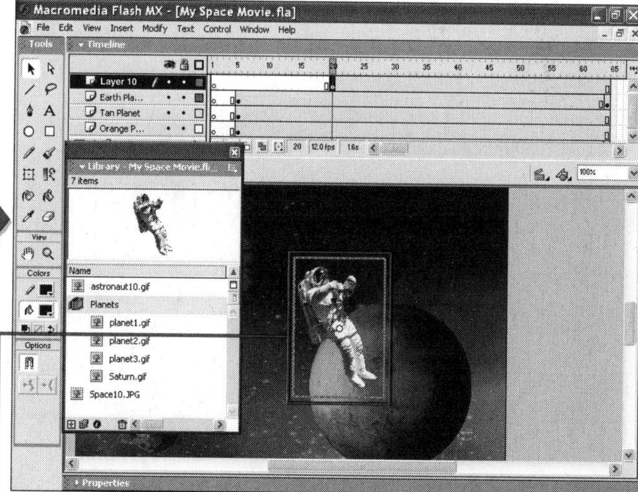

5 Drop the instance on the Stage.

■ An instance of the symbol now appears on the Stage.

MODIFY AN INSTANCE

After you place a symbol instance on the Stage, you can change the way it appears without changing the original symbol. For example, you can change its color or make it appear transparent.

When you make changes to an instance in the Property inspector, you use several tools to modify its properties. For example, you can change the object's behavior by turning a graphic symbol into a movie clip or a button. You can also experiment by fine-tuning an instance's brightness, tint, or transparency, all of which are color effects.

The Brightness option enables you to adjust the brightness level of the instance, ranging from 100% dark (black) to 100% light (white).

You use the Tint option to change the hue of the instance. You can choose from a palette of colors or specify exact RGB values for red, green, and blue.

The Alpha option allows you to change the transparency of the instance to make it appear faded or transparent.

Use the Advanced option to modify both color and transparency settings in value.

If you want to modify every instance of the symbol in your movie, you must make changes to the original symbol.

MODIFY AN INSTANCE

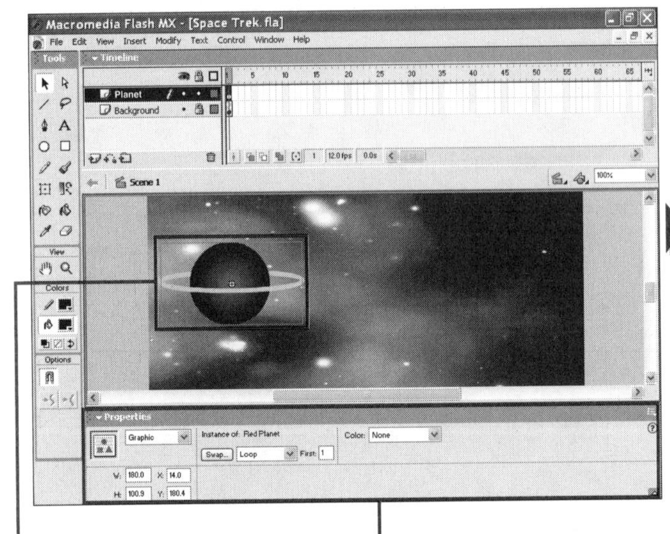

1 Click the instance you want to modify.

2 Open the Property inspector.

Note: To display and hide the Property inspector, see page 346.

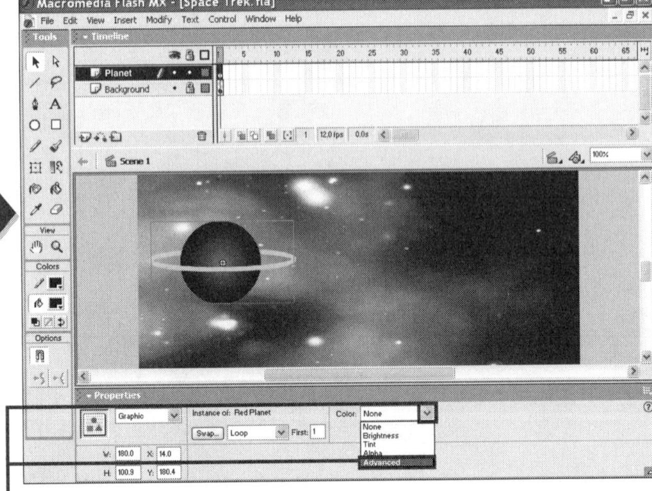

3 Click the Color ▾.

4 Click Advanced.

■ The Settings button appears in the Property inspector when you select the Advanced option.

How do I make the instance transparent?

✔ To make an instance appear transparent, change its Alpha setting. Click the Color ▾ in the Property inspector and click Alpha. Flash MX displays a slider for adjusting the Alpha setting. You can also follow steps 1 to 3 below and open the Advanced Effect dialog box to drag the Alpha slider to the transparency level you want to apply. Click OK to apply the effect.

Can I test how my edits affect the movie?

✔ Yes. As you edit an instance, you might want to see the results of your edits before exiting Symbol-Edit mode. Click Control, Test Movie to run the movie and check the appearance of the instance.

Can I edit the symbol instead of just the instance?

✔ Yes. When you edit a symbol rather than an instance, Flash MX updates every appearance of the symbol throughout the entire movie. To learn more about editing symbols, see page 458.

Can I name an instance?

✔ You can name a movie clip instance and use the name in your action variables. Click inside the Name text box in the Property inspector and type a name. This works only for movie clip instances. See Chapter 31 to learn more about Flash actions.

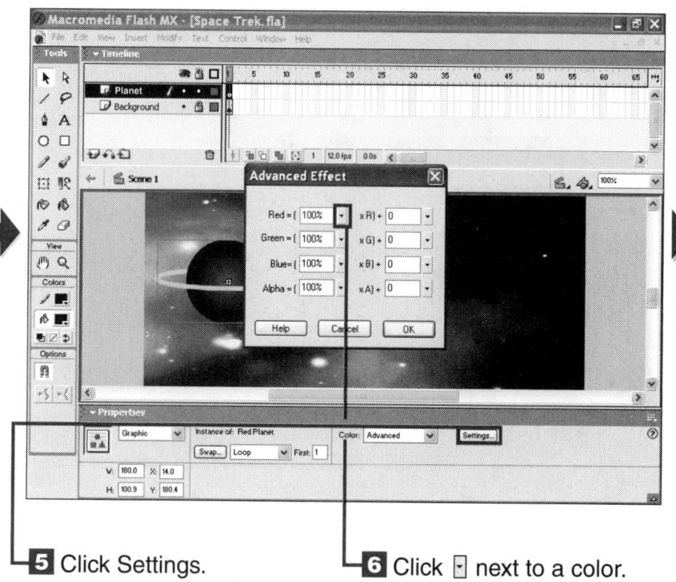

5 Click Settings.

■ The Advanced Effect dialog box opens.

6 Click ▾ next to a color.

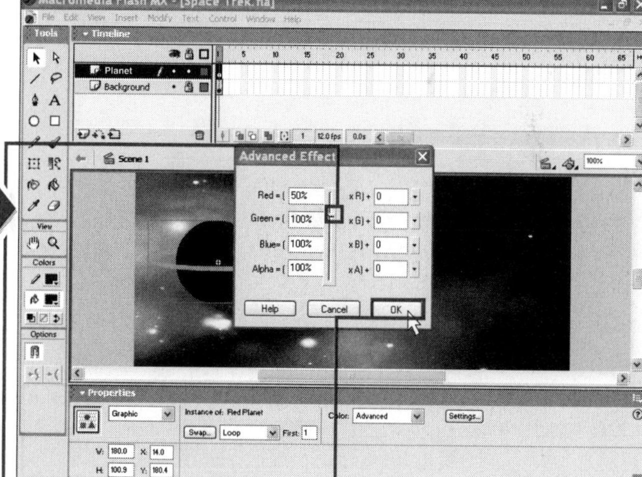

■ A slider bar (▬) appears.

7 Drag ▬ to a new color setting.

■ The selected object changes color as you drag ▬ .

■ You can experiment with the various color settings to achieve the color effect you want.

8 Click OK.

■ Flash MX applies the new settings.

EDIT SYMBOLS

You can edit symbols stored in the Library for your Flash file. Editing symbols may include changing a symbol appearance slightly, such as adjusting a line or shape, or perhaps assigning another color. You can make changes to the original symbol, and Flash MX automatically updates all instances of it in your movie. This can save you considerable time and effort.

You can edit symbols in Symbol-Edit mode or in a new window. You can edit graphic, movie clip, and button symbols in Symbol-Edit mode. When in Symbol-Edit mode, Flash MX locks the other objects on the Stage to prevent accidental changes. This means you cannot edit other symbols or objects on the Stage area, only the selected symbol.

Flash MX lets you easily switch back and forth between timelines and edit modes. You can click the Scene name or use the Edit Symbols and Edit Scene buttons.

It is not always easy to discern whether you are in Symbol-Edit mode. The easiest way to tell is to look for the symbol name at the top of the Stage, to the right of the scene name. When you edit in a new window, only the symbol you want to edit appears.

You can return to Symbol-Edit mode at any time to adjust a symbol globally throughout your movie.

EDIT SYMBOLS

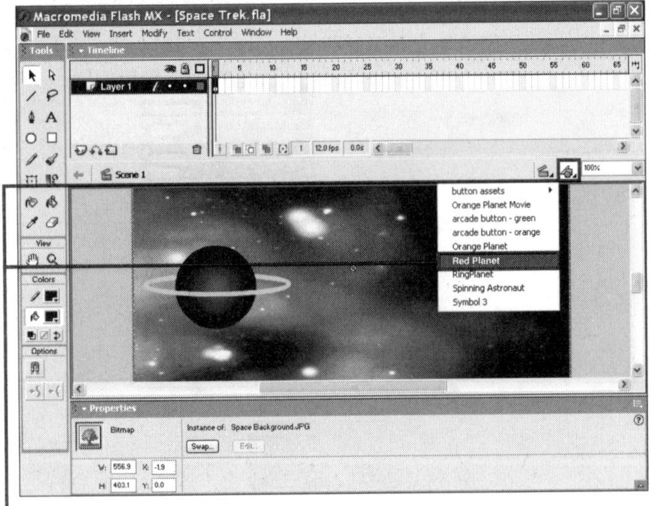

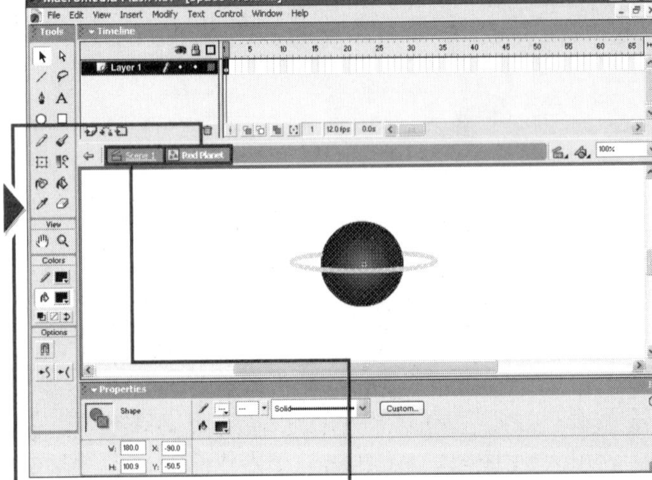

SYMBOL-EDIT MODE

1 Click the Edit Symbols button ( ).

2 Click the name of the symbol you want to edit.

■ You can also double-click the symbol to switch to Symbol-Edit mode.

■ Flash MX switches to Symbol-Edit mode.

■ If the symbol name appears at the top of the Stage, you are in Symbol-Edit mode.

3 Edit the symbol as needed.

■ You can use the Flash drawing tools to make changes to the object, such as changing the fill color or adjusting a line segment.

Note: To learn more about editing objects, see Chapter 22.

4 Click the scene name to return to Movie-Edit mode.

How do I remove a symbol I no longer want?

✔ First make sure you do not use the symbol anywhere in your Flash movie. When you delete a symbol, Flash MX removes any instances of the symbol. Open the Library window and then select the symbol you want to remove. Click 🗑. A warning prompt box appears asking you to confirm the deletion. Note, after you delete a symbol, you cannot undo the action. To continue, click Delete and Flash MX permanently removes the symbol from the file's Library.

Flash MX does not let me edit my symbol. Why not?

✔ Depending on the complexity of the symbol, you may need to first apply the Break Apart or Ungroup command. The Break Apart command breaks the symbol down into its most basic construction — lines and fills. You can then edit a single line or fill. The Ungroup command ungroups a grouped object. You can find the Break Apart and Ungroup commands on the Modify menu. See Chapter 24 to learn more about using these commands.

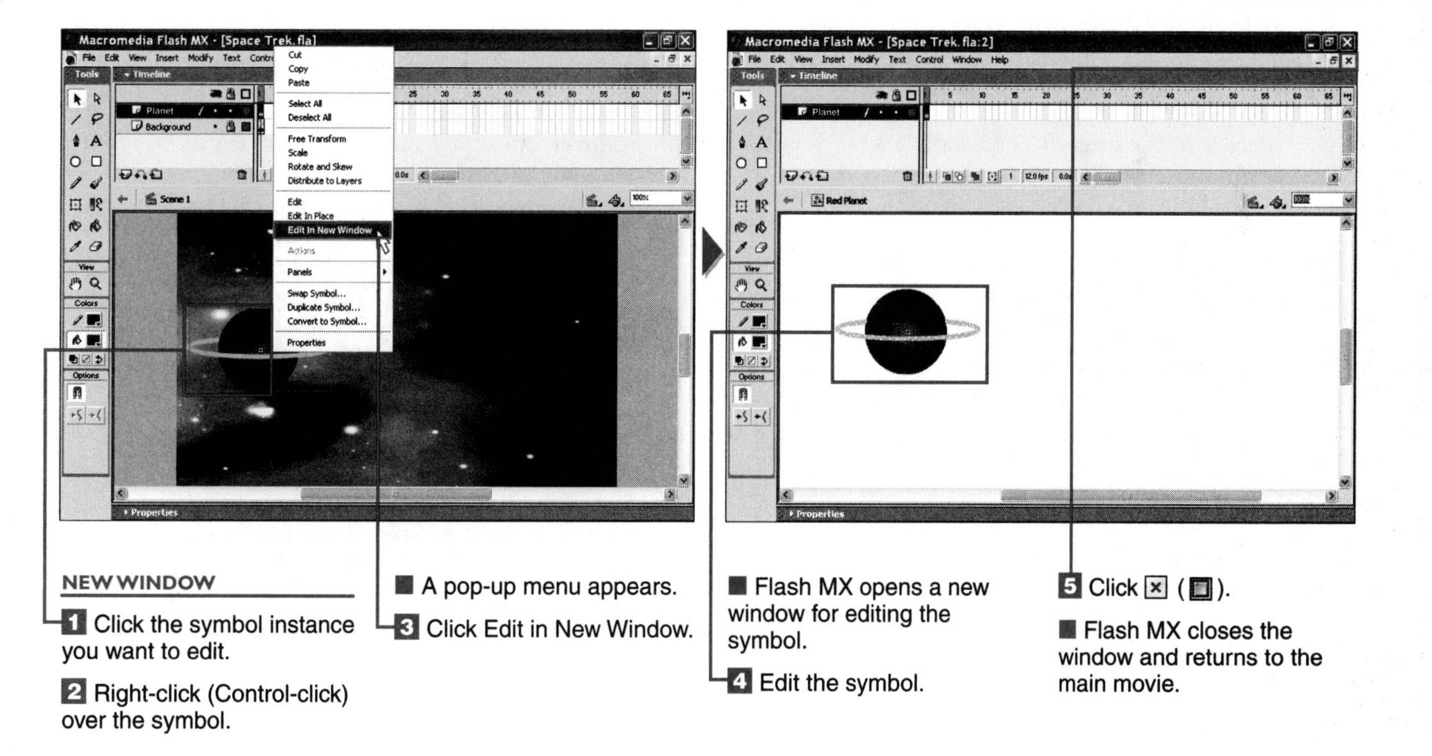

NEW WINDOW

1 Click the symbol instance you want to edit.

2 Right-click (Control-click) over the symbol.

■ A pop-up menu appears.

3 Click Edit in New Window.

■ Flash MX opens a new window for editing the symbol.

4 Edit the symbol.

5 Click ☒ (▣).

■ Flash MX closes the window and returns to the main movie.

INTRODUCTION TO FLASH BUTTONS

You can use rollover buttons to enable users to interact with your Flash movies. A rollover button is a simple button that changes in appearance when the user rolls the mouse pointer over it, and changes appearance again when the user clicks it.

You can create buttons in Flash that are static or animated.

Buttons are a distinct symbol type in Flash MX. Buttons use four specific frame states or stages that control the various points of interaction with the mouse. You can assign actions to your buttons that instruct Flash on how to react when activated by the user.

Buttons are a popular way to add interactivity to Web pages and forms. For example, you can include movie control buttons that allow users to stop the movie or start playing it again.

Buttons As Symbols

Buttons are a type of symbol to which Flash MX assigns *behaviors*. The behaviors are based on what happens when the mouse pointer interacts with the button. You can assign Flash actions to a button that trigger an action, such as stopping the movie.

You can turn any symbol you create in Flash into a button symbol, or you can create a new button from scratch. You might custom-make a button shape that includes text specific to the interactive task the user performs. Flash MX even comes with pre-drawn buttons you can use, found in the Buttons Library. You can also use different symbols for different stages of the button. For example, the button labeled Click Here may appear as a gray box when inactive but may become a cartoon character when the user moves the mouse over the button.

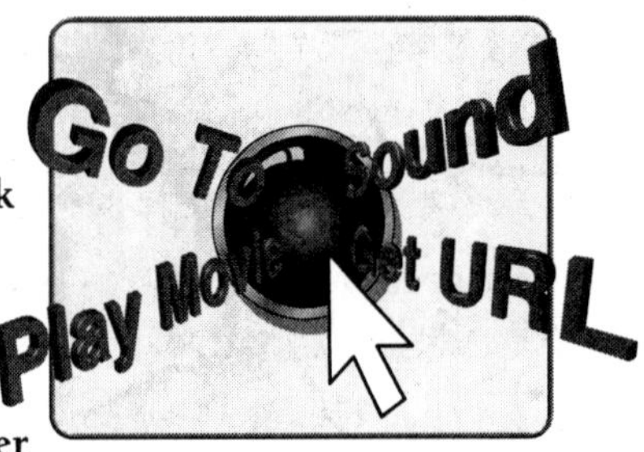

When you create a button, you need to think about how you want the button to behave when the user interacts with it. Do you want it static or animated? Do you want it to make a sound? What do you want to happen when the user rolls over the button, clicks the button, and releases the button? You can make buttons as complex or simple as you want. You must also determine the purpose of the button. When you activate the button, what happens? Does it play a movie, stop a movie, or open a form?

Button Stages

There are four stages to a button: inactive, rollover, click, and release. Each stage is uniquely identified in the button Timeline as the Up, Over, Down, and Hit frames. The four frames make up a mini-movie clip of the behavior of the button. A timeline of a button does not actually play like other Flash Timelines, but rather jumps to the appropriate frame directed by the user's mouse action.

The inactive stage, called the Up frame, is what the button looks like when not in use. For example, it may be an oval shape with the text Submit or Stop. The rollover stage, called the Over frame, is what the button looks like when the user rolls over it with the mouse. The click stage, called the Down frame, is what the button looks like when the user clicks it. The release stage, or Hit frame, is what the button looks like after the user has performed a click action. You can choose to make the button look the same for all four stages, or you can use different symbols for some or all of the stages.

You decide what symbol to use in each frame of a timeline of a button. If you use different symbols in each frame, with the exception of the Hit frame, the button appears animated.

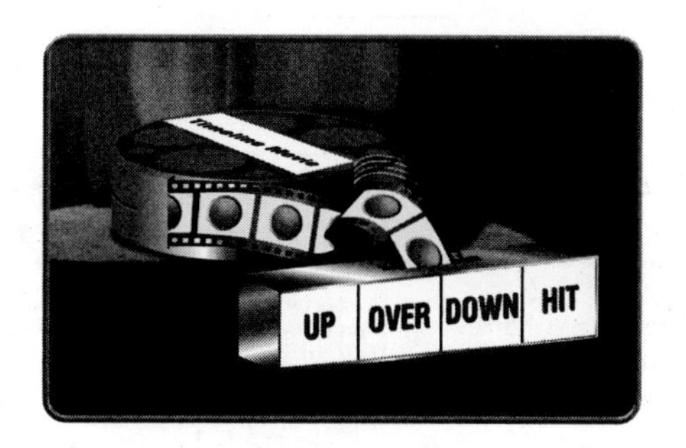

Up Frame

You use the Up frame to display the inactive button. This is the frame the user sees when the mouse pointer is not hovering over the button. By default, the Up frame already has a keyframe added in the timeline of the button.

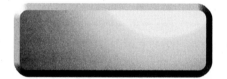

Over Frame

The Over frame displays what the button looks like when the mouse pointer moves, or rolls over the button. For example, you might make the button turn bright red or emit a sound when the user places the mouse pointer over it to indicate that the button is active.

Down Frame

The Down frame displays what the button looks like when a user clicks it. You can add a sound to the Down frame to indicate the button has been activated.

Hit Frame

The Hit frame defines the clickable button area or boundary as a whole. This frame is often the same size and shape as the image in the Over and Down frames. The Hit frame differs from the other button frames in that the user does not actually see it.

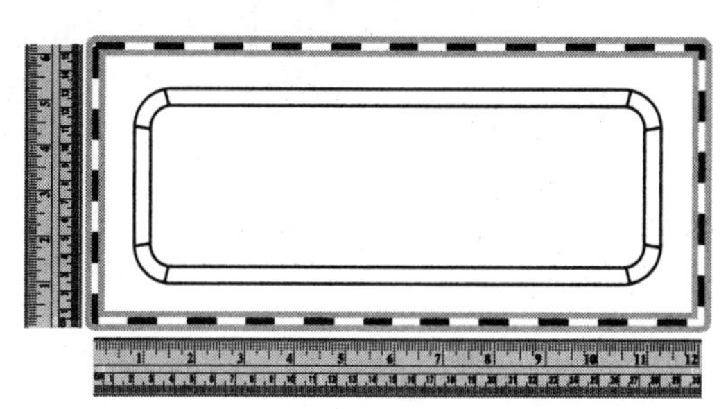

CREATE A BUTTON SYMBOL

You can create button symbols to add interactivity to your Flash movies. Buttons allow users to interact with movies by clicking to start or stop an action. You can create new buttons or turn any symbol into a button symbol in Flash MX. By assigning a button behavior to a symbol, you are turning it into an interactive element. You can then use the button in a movie frame, a Web page, or any other area where you want users to interact with your project. See page 460 to learn more about button basics.

When you create a button, it includes a timeline with four frames: Up, Over, Down, and Hit. You can assign an image or action to each of the four button states. You can make the image the same in each frame, or you can vary it to create the illusion of movement. You can make any object or drawing, such as a simple geometric shape, into a button that the user can easily identify and click. You may want to include a text block on the button shape that identifies the button or its purpose.

CREATE A BUTTON SYMBOL

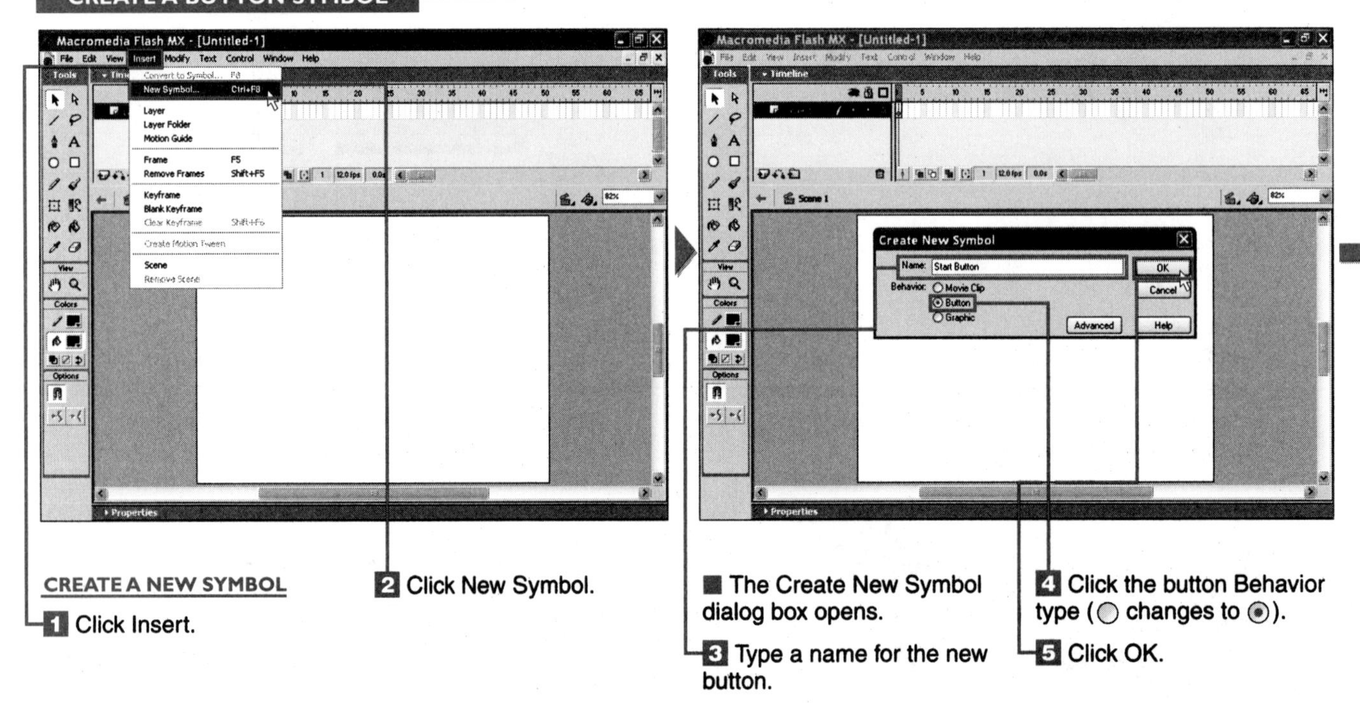

CREATE A NEW SYMBOL

1 Click Insert.

2 Click New Symbol.

■ The Create New Symbol dialog box opens.

3 Type a name for the new button.

4 Click the button Behavior type (◯ changes to ◉).

5 Click OK.

Does Flash MX have premade buttons I can use?

✔ Yes. Flash MX has several common libraries, including sounds and buttons. To display the Buttons Library, click Windows, Common Libraries, Buttons. The Buttons Library window appears. The Buttons Library works like the regular Library window. See page 448 to learn more about using the Library. Double-click a folder name to see a list of button types. You can preview a button by clicking its name. You can use a button from the Library simply by dragging it off the Library window onto the Stage.

Can I use a button from another Flash file?

✔ Yes. If you have stored a button symbol in another Flash project, you can open the other file's Library window and place an instance of the symbol on the Stage. Click the File menu and click Open As Shared Library. This displays the Open As Library dialog box. Double-click the Flash file you want to utilize. The associated Library window opens on-screen. You can now use any button symbol you have stored in the Library.

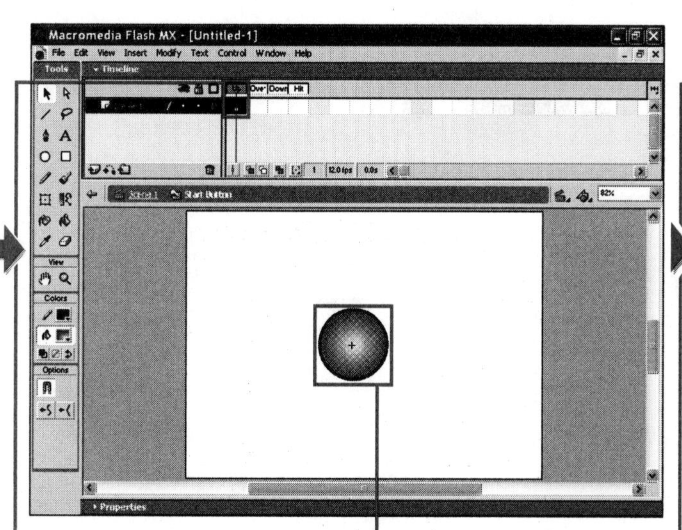

CREATE THE UP STATE

■ The timeline of the button opens in Symbol-Edit mode with four frames. You can now create a button state for each frame.

■ By default, Flash MX selects the Up frame and inserts a keyframe.

6 Create or place the object to use as a button on the Stage.

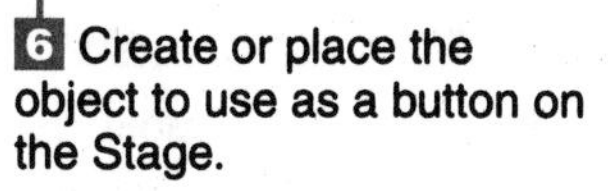

Note: To draw shapes, see Chapter 21. To import graphics, see page 408.

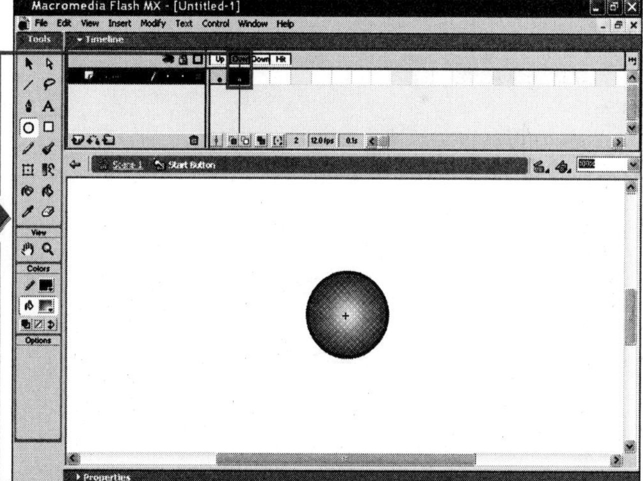

CREATE THE OVER STATE

7 Click the Over frame.

8 Insert a keyframe into the frame.

Note: To insert a keyframe, see page 510.

■ You can press F6 to insert a keyframe into the frame.

CONTINUED

CREATE A BUTTON SYMBOL (CONTINUED)

When deciding what you want your button to look like, consider your audience. Are they technologically perceptive enough to recognize the image you use as a button on-screen, or do you need to keep the button simple and easy to understand? Although it is sometimes tempting to use detailed drawings as buttons, simple geometric shapes are always reliable for a general audience. You can draw a new object to use as a button using any of the Flash drawing tools, or you can use an imported graphic as a button.

You can make even the simplest of buttons more exciting with a few variations. For example, if you duplicate the same object in each button frame, you can make minor changes so that the button appears different in each state. For example, you can change the color, scale, or shape for each keyframe.

Keep in mind that users do not see the Hit frame for a button. The Hit frame merely defines the button area. For that reason, it is not necessary to add or change the graphic for the Hit frame; however, it is important to make sure the Hit frame defines the size and boundary of the button itself.

CREATE A BUTTON SYMBOL (CONTINUED)

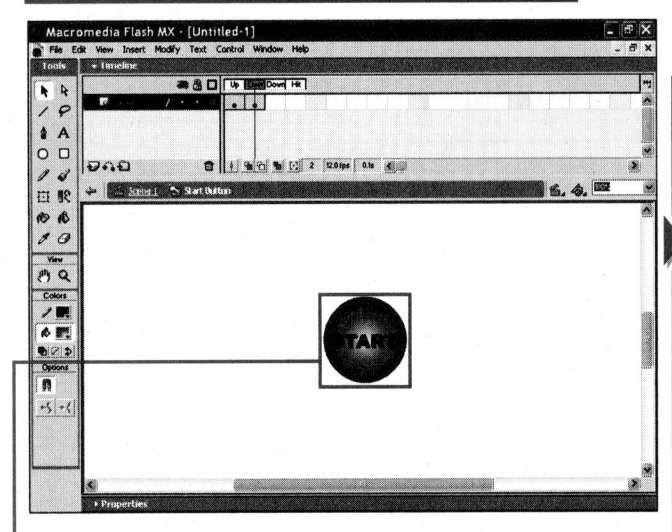

■ Flash MX duplicates the object from the Up keyframe.

■ You can make changes to the object.

■ In this example, a text box is added to describe the button.

Note: To add a text box, see page 416.

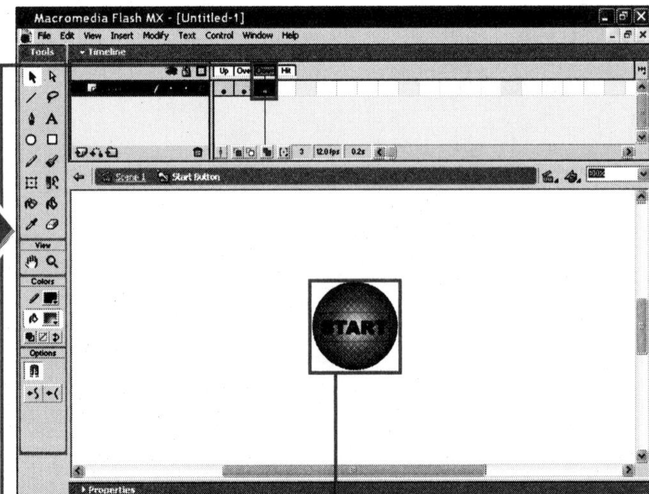

CREATE THE DOWN STATE

9 Click the Down frame.

10 Insert a keyframe into the frame.

Note: To insert a keyframe, see page 510.

■ You can press F6 to insert a keyframe into the frame.

■ Flash MX duplicates the object from the Over keyframe.

■ You can edit the object by adding a sound to the frame, or short animation.

How can I tell in which edit mode am I?

✔ There are two edit modes in Flash MX: Movie-Edit mode and Symbol-Edit mode. Flash switches you to Symbol-Edit mode when you create a button. You are in Symbol-Edit mode if you see the name of the symbol to the right of the Scene name at the top of the Stage. To exit Symbol-Edit mode at any time, just click the Scene name link. You can also exit Symbol-Edit mode by pressing Ctrl + E (⌘ + E).

How do I close the Library window?

✔ Click the window's Close button (☒).

How do I preview a button?

✔ In Symbol-Edit mode, click the button's Up frame, and then press Enter (Return). Watch the Stage as Flash plays through the four button frames. Any changes made to frames appear during playback.

You can preview the button in Movie-Edit mode by pressing Ctrl + Alt + B (⌘ + Option + B) to activate the button on the Stage and moving the mouse pointer over the button and clicking it to see the rollover capabilities.

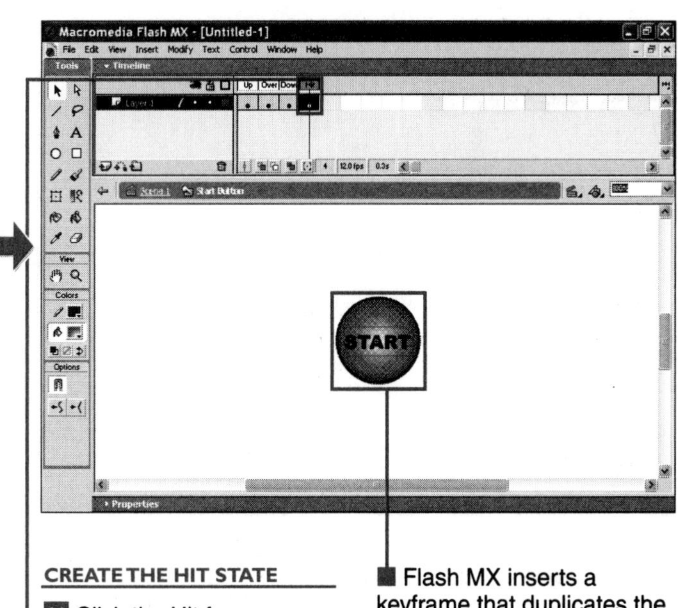

CREATE THE HIT STATE

11 Click the Hit frame.

12 Insert a keyframe into the frame.

Note: Press F6 to quickly insert a keyframe.

■ Flash MX inserts a keyframe that duplicates the Down frame object.

■ Users cannot see the object contained in the Hit frame.

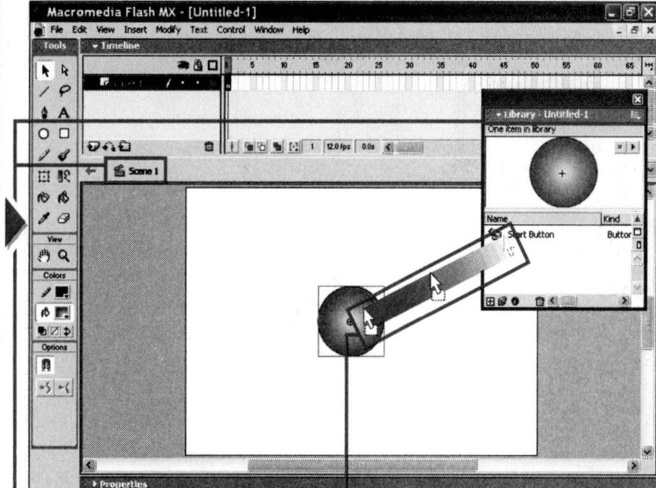

PLACE THE BUTTON ON THE STAGE

13 Click the Scene name to return to Movie-Edit mode.

14 Open the Library.

Note: To open the Library window, see page 448.

15 Click and drag the button from the Library to the Stage.

■ The newly created button appears on the Stage.

CREATE SHAPE-CHANGING BUTTONS

You can create shape-changing buttons in your Flash movies for added graphical impact. Buttons are a great way to add interactivity to your Flash movies, and shape-changing buttons can make an ordinary button much more dynamic.

Although a simple geometric shape makes a good button, you can jazz up a button to create the illusion of movement or animation. To do this, you can change the object you use for each button state. For example, an ordinary circle shape button might become a flower when the user rolls over it with the mouse. It might change into an entire bouquet when the user clicks on it with the mouse.

Creating a shape-changing button requires four different shapes. The Up, Over, and Down frames can each have a different shape, but the Hit frame needs a shape that encompasses all three of the other shapes. Although a user does not view the Hit frame, it defines the size of the button. See page 462 to learn more about creating buttons.

To create a shape for each different button state, you must add keyframes to signify a change in the button state. A regular keyframe merely repeats the content of the previous keyframe, while a blank keyframe allows you to create brand new content. You can learn more about keyframes in Chapter 29.

CREATE SHAPE-CHANGING BUTTONS

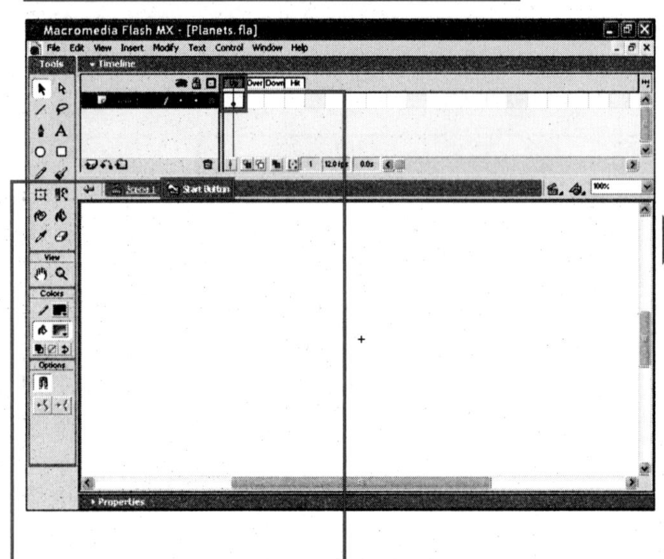

CREATE A NEW BUTTON

1 Create a new button symbol.

Note: To create a new symbol, see pages 462 to 465.

■ Flash MX switches to Symbol-Edit mode, and the button's name appears at the top of the Stage.

■ Flash MX selects the Up frame by default when you switch to Symbol-Edit mode.

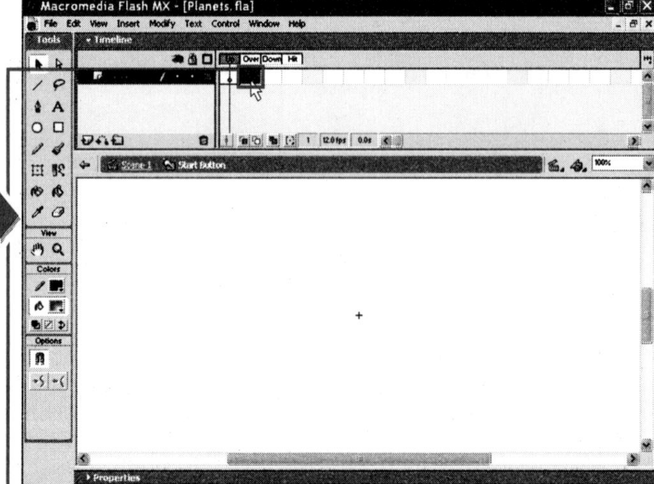

2 Click the Over frame.

How do I view a newly created button in Movie-Edit mode?

✔ You create buttons in Symbol-Edit mode. When you finish and return to Movie-Edit mode, you do not see the button symbol unless you place an instance of the button symbol onto the Flash Stage. Open the Library window and drag the button onto the Stage.

How do I toggle between Symbol-Edit and Movie-Edit mode?

✔ You can quickly toggle back and forth between editing modes using a keyboard shortcut. Press Ctrl + E (⌘ + E).

Can I use layers in my button?

✔ Yes. The button's timeline works just like the main timeline in Movie-Edit mode. You can add different layers to your button to organize various objects. For example, if your button includes a text block, you may want to place the text on another layer. Or if your button uses a sound, you can place the sound clip on a separate layer from the graphic. You can add, delete, and rename layers in Symbol-Edit mode just as you do in Movie-Edit mode. See Chapter 25 to learn more about using layers in Flash MX.

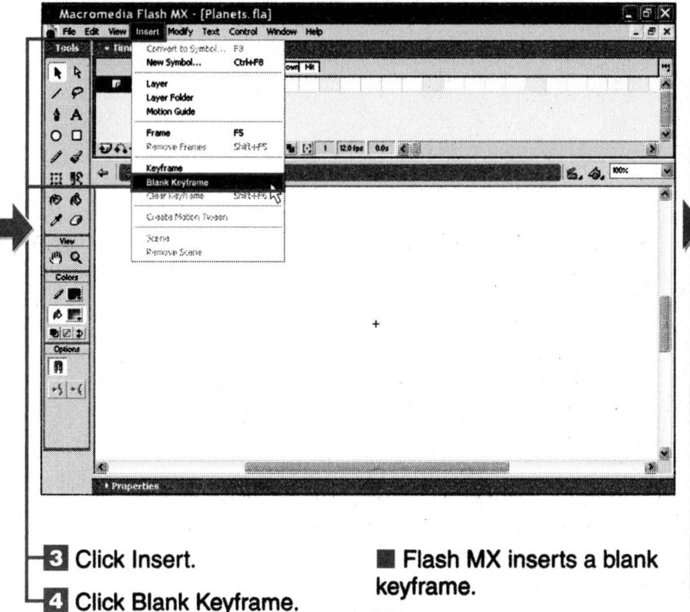

3 Click Insert.

4 Click Blank Keyframe.

■ Flash MX inserts a blank keyframe.

5 Repeat steps 3 to 4 to add blank keyframes to the Down and Hit frames.

CREATE THE UP STATE

6 Click the Up frame to select it.

7 Create a new object or place an existing object on the Stage.

CONTINUED

CREATE SHAPE-CHANGING BUTTONS (CONTINUED)

If the image of a button stays the same for all four frames in the timeline, the button looks the same regardless of how the user interacts with the button. In other words, users cannot distinguish between its active and inactive states. Changing the image for each button state gives users some idea of the status of the button object. Users can see a difference when the mouse pointer hovers over a live button or when the button is clicked.

Shape-changing buttons can add pizzazz to Web pages. For example, you might create a button that blends in with the page, only to come alive with a different shape as soon as the user rolls over it with the mouse. This type of button becomes a *hot spot* — an area for which the user must hunt in order to activate the control.

Common switches also make good shape-changing buttons. For example, in its inactive state, a button might look like a common light switch resembling the Off setting, but when the user clicks the button, it changes to resemble the On setting of the toggle. You can come up with all sorts of interesting shapes to use as buttons in Flash MX.

CREATE SHAPE-CHANGING BUTTONS (CONTINUED)

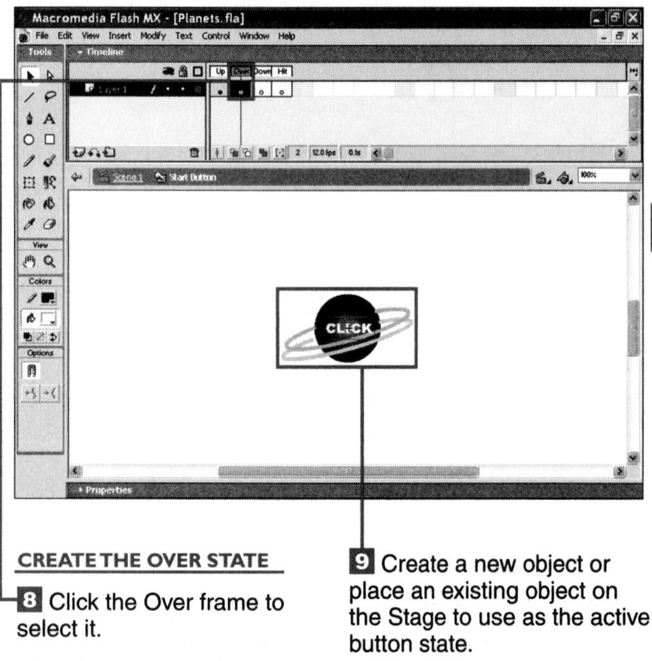

CREATE THE OVER STATE

8 Click the Over frame to select it.

9 Create a new object or place an existing object on the Stage to use as the active button state.

■ The object must differ from the object placed in the Up frame.

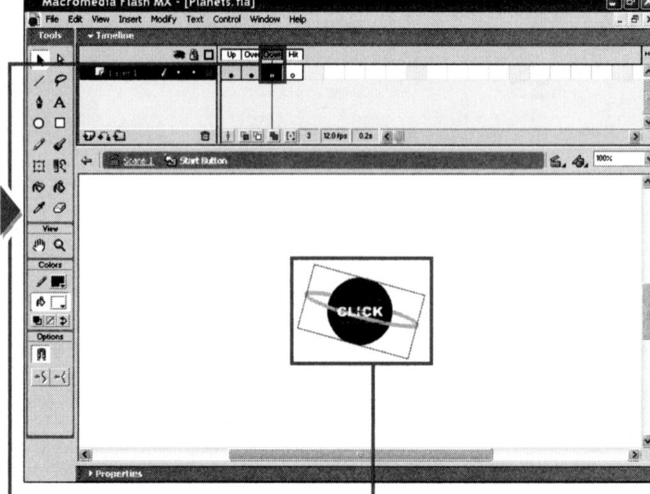

CREATE THE DOWN STATE

10 Click the Down frame to select it.

11 Create another new object or place an existing object on the Stage.

■ Make this object differ from the other two objects used in the previous frames.

Why do I need to draw a shape in the Hit frame?

✔ Although the Hit frame is invisible to the user, it defines the active area of the button, making it essential to the button's operation. You must make the object you draw big enough to encompass the largest object in the other button frames. If you do not, a user may click an area of the button that does not activate. If you have trouble guessing how large of an area to define, click [icon] to see outlines of the shapes on all the other frames. Click [icon] again to turn the feature off.

How do I make changes to a button?

✔ Double-click the button symbol to return to Symbol-Edit mode and make changes to the objects in each button timeline frame. For example, you may decide to use a different shape in your shape-changing button. After modifying your button, remember to check the Hit frame to make sure the defining shape size encompasses any new shapes in the other frames.

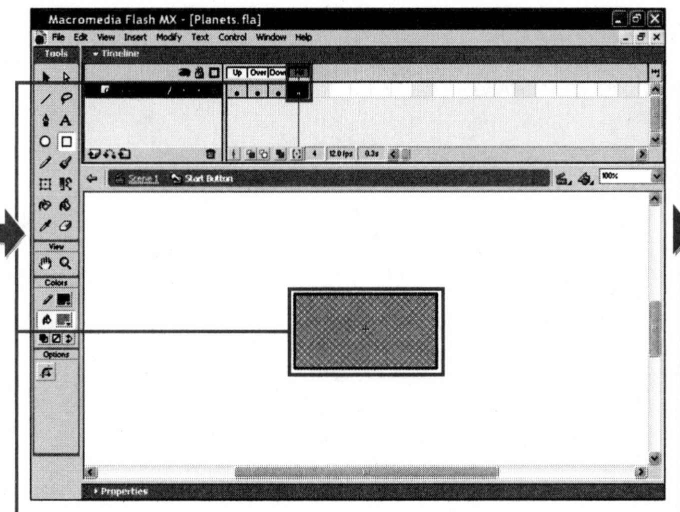

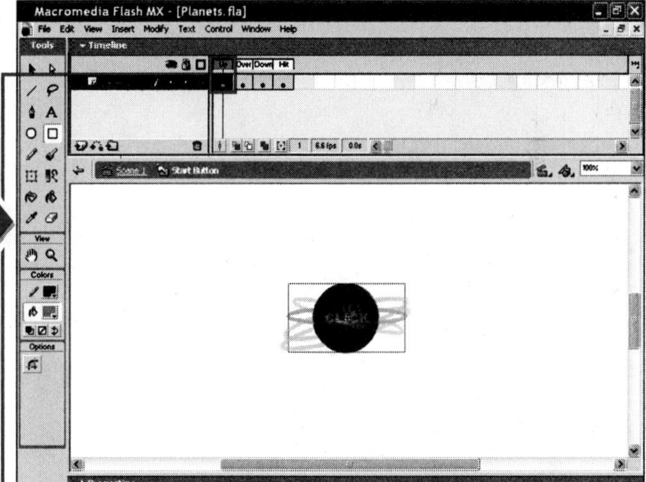

CREATE THE HIT STATE

12 Click the Hit frame.

13 Draw a geometric shape large enough to encompass the largest object size used in your button frames.

Note: If you do not define the Hit frame area properly, the user cannot interact with the button. Users cannot see the Hit frame's contents, but they are essential to the button's operation.

PREVIEW THE BUTTON

14 Click the Up frame to select it.

15 Press Enter (Return).

■ On the Stage, Flash MX plays through the four button frames, and you can see the changing button states.

ADD ANIMATION TO A BUTTON

You can create impressive animation effects for buttons to make your buttons seem to spring to life with user interaction. Animation effects create the illusion of motion or movement. For example, you can make a button glow when the mouse pointer hovers over it, or animate the button with a cartoon that includes sound, such as a character dancing around and singing. Spinning buttons, jumping buttons, and flashing buttons are all good examples of animation effects you can apply to help draw the user's attention to interactive buttons.

You can save animations you create in Flash as movie clips, one of the three symbol behavior types used in Flash MX. Short movie clips work best for button animations. You can learn more about creating animations and saving them as movie clips in Chapter 29.

Flash MX makes it easy to place movie clips into your button frames. Movie clips add far more animation to a button than shape-changing buttons does. You must first create a movie clip or import one and then assign it to a button state. Movie clips use their own timelines, which means that they play at their own pace. The button remains animated as long as the clip plays.

ADD ANIMATION TO A BUTTON

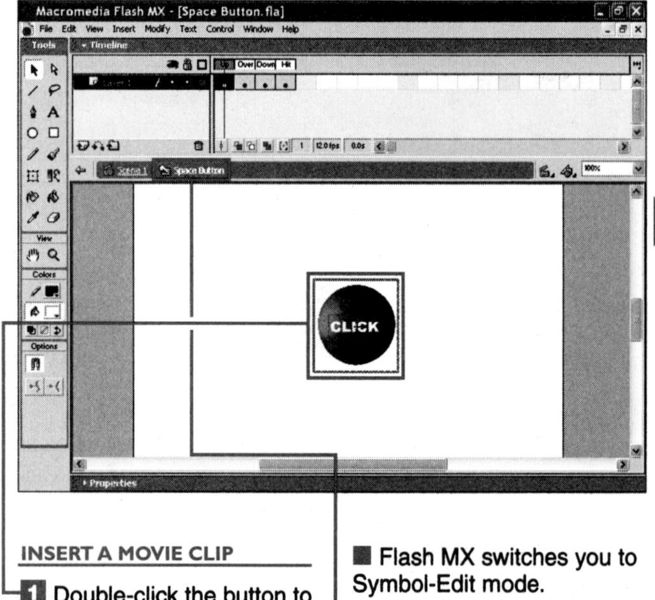

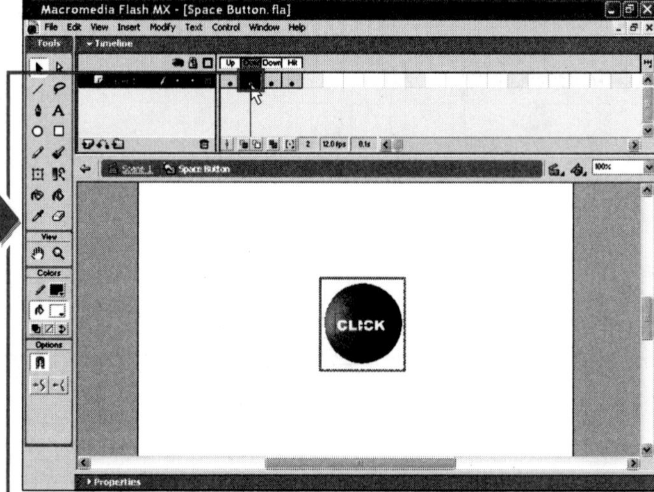

INSERT A MOVIE CLIP

1. Double-click the button to which you want to add an animation.

■ Flash MX switches you to Symbol-Edit mode.

■ The name of the button appears above the Stage.

2. Click the frame to which you want to add an animation, such as the Up, Over, or Down frame.

Note: The Hit frame is not seen by the user, so it is not useful to animate this frame.

Should I add my movie clip to another layer in my button timeline?

✔ You can utilize as many layers and layer folders as you need with a button to keep the various elements organized, including movie clips you add to the button. To learn more about Timeline layers, see Chapter 25.

Is there a limit to the length of a button animation?

✔ No. However, remember that the purpose of your button is for user interaction. When you add a long animation sequence to a button state, you keep the user waiting to complete the action. It is a good idea to keep animation sequences short when applying them to buttons.

Can I use an animation clip from another Flash file?

✔ Yes. Click the File menu and click Open as Library. Locate the Flash file containing the clip you want to use, and then double-click the filename. This opens the other file's Library on-screen, and you can drag the clip you want to use onto the Stage.

Can I minimize the Library window to move it out of the way?

✔ You can click the Library window title bar to minimize the window, or you can press F11 to quickly toggle the Library window open and closed.

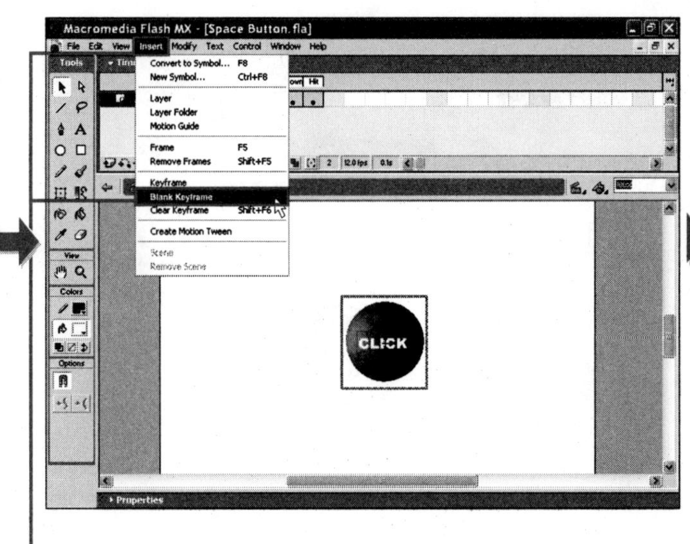

3 Click Insert.

4 Click Blank Keyframe.

■ Flash MX inserts a blank keyframe.

Note: If the frame already has an object, press Shift + F6 to clear the existing keyframe and object.

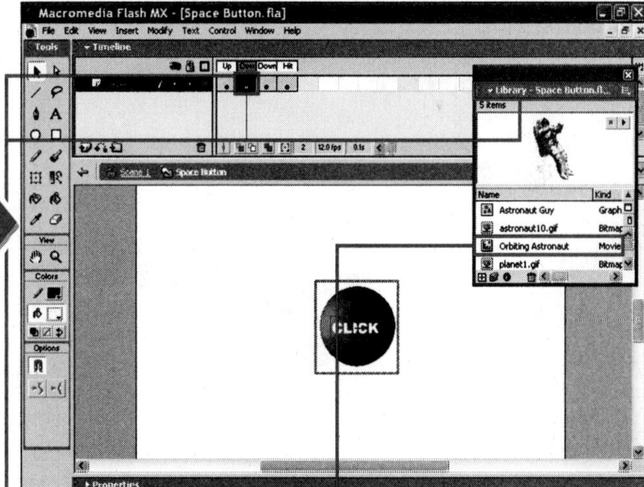

5 Click again the frame to which you want to add the animation.

6 Open the Library window.

Note: To open the Library window, see page 448.

7 Click the movie clip that you want to insert to select the clip.

CONTINUED

ADD ANIMATION TO A BUTTON (CONTINUED)

You can add a movie clip to the Up, Over, or Down button states. For example, you might want the user to see a spinning leaf when the button is inactive — the Up state. Or you might want the leaf object to spin only when the user rolls over the button with the mouse, thus adding animation to the Over state. You might play the animation when the user actually clicks the mouse button — the Down state. The only frame you do not want to animate is the Hit frame because its contents are not visible to the user.

It is more common to see movie clips added to the Over and Down states than the Up state. Users are more likely to expect animations when actually interacting with the button.

You can use animation sequences you create in Flash MX or animations authored in other programs. Be sure to test your movie clips to make sure they work the way you want before importing them into a Flash button frame. Testing beforehand may save you some time and effort later.

Avoid using animations that play too long. The user may not be patient enough to wait through a long animation sequence, especially upon repeat use of a button.

ADD ANIMATION TO A BUTTON (CONTINUED)

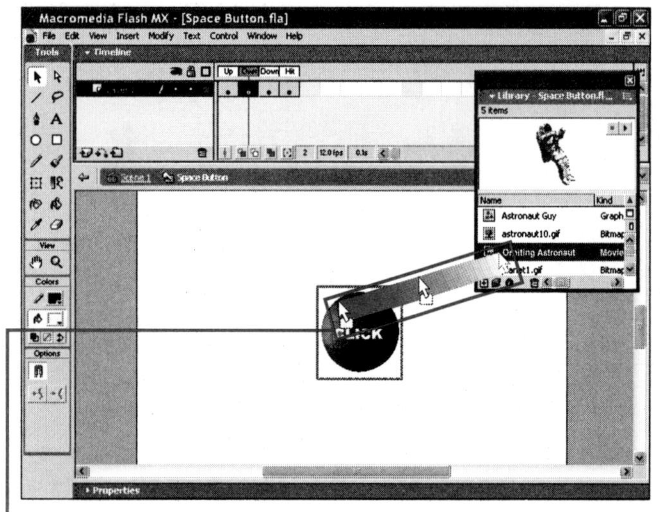

8 Click and drag the movie clip from the Library window and place it on the Stage where the button appears.

■ Flash MX places an instance of the clip on the Stage.

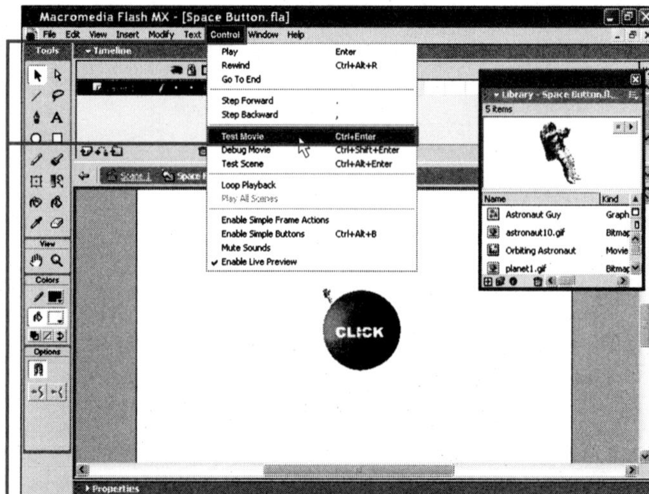

TEST THE MOVIE CLIP

1 Click Control.

2 Click Test Movie.

Note: To test the button states within the button timeline, press Enter (Return).

Can I add sounds to button frames?

✔ Yes. You can add sound clips to button frames the same way you add movie clips. Try adding a sound from Flash's Sound Library. Start by clicking on a frame. Next, click the Window menu, click Common Libraries, and then Sounds. The Sounds Library opens. In the Sounds Library window, click the sound clip and drag it to the button area on the Stage. A sound wave appears in the frame. You can press Enter to test the button sequence. See page 484 to learn more about adding sounds to frames.

How do I preview the animated button in Movie-Edit mode?

✔ When you press Ctrl + Alt + B (⌘ + option + B) to preview a button's rollover capabilities in Movie-Edit mode, any movie clips you added to button frames do not run. Instead, you see the first frame of the movie clip. To see the fully animated button, click Control and then click Test Movie. This opens up the Flash Player window inside the Flash program window and plays the animation. Click the Player window's ☒ to exit and return to the Flash Stage.

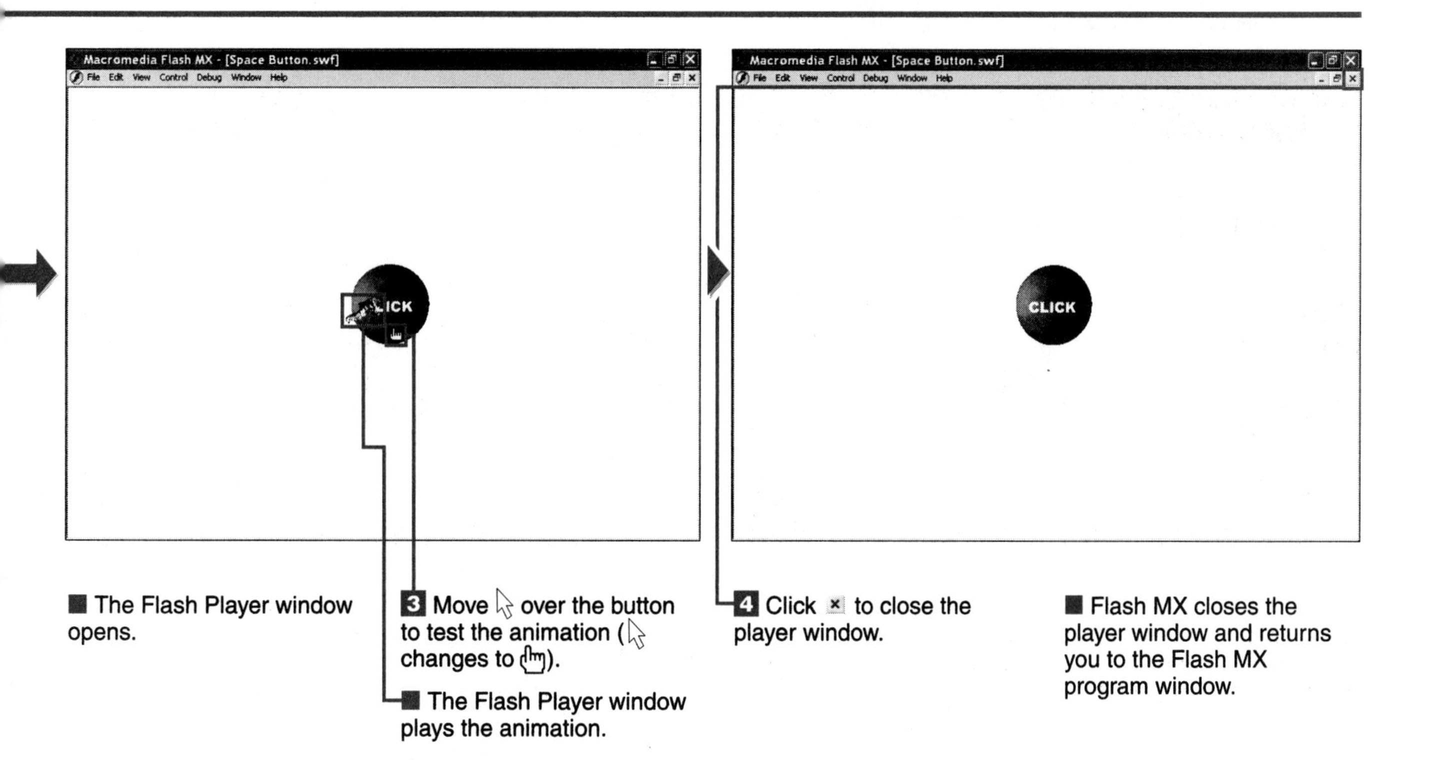

■ The Flash Player window opens.

3 Move the pointer over the button to test the animation (the pointer changes to a hand).

■ The Flash Player window plays the animation.

4 Click ☒ to close the player window.

■ Flash MX closes the player window and returns you to the Flash MX program window.

ASSIGN BUTTON ACTIONS

You can add more interactivity to your buttons using Flash actions. Actions are simply sets of instructions that tell Flash to carry out a task. Actions can be as simple as stopping the movie from playing. You can assign all kinds of actions to buttons you create in Flash MX.

Buttons already use built-in actions, such as moving immediately to the Down frame when a user clicks the button. You can add other Flash actions to your buttons. For example, you can add a Play action to a button so that a movie clip starts playing when the user clicks the button, or a Stop action that enables the user to stop a movie that is in progress. You can also assign actions that tell Flash to jump to a specific Web page when the user clicks a button.

You assign actions, also called *frame actions*, to individual frames in your movie's timeline. An action is a behavior, such as stopping a movie, and is triggered by an *event*, such as a mouse click. See Chapter 31 to learn more about assigning actions. In the case of buttons, you can assign frame actions that determine how the user interacts with the button. You add frame actions in Movie-Edit mode, not Symbol-Edit mode, and you add them to the frame containing the button. Always test any actions you assign to make sure they work as expected.

ASSIGN BUTTON ACTIONS

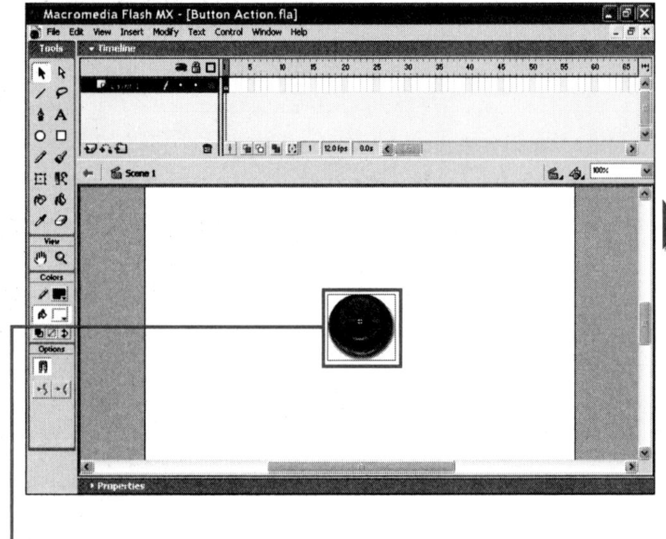

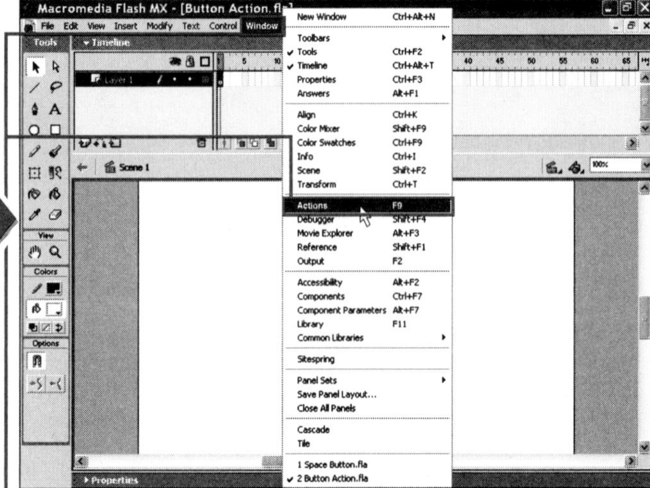

ADD AN ACTION TO A BUTTON

1 Click the button symbol to which you want to add an action.

2 Click Window.

3 Click Actions.

■ The Actions-Button panel opens.

What types of actions are good for buttons?

✔ The `goto` action jumps the user to a particular frame or scene in your movie. The `getURL` action jumps the user to a Web page. The `play` action starts playing a specified movie clip. The `stop` action stops a movie in progress. You can use this action in a presentation to allow users to stop and read the screen or ask questions.

I cannot select my button on the Flash Stage. Why?

✔ If Flash displays the button animation sequence when you move your ↖ over the button, you have the Enable Simple Buttons feature active. Press Ctrl + Alt + B (⌘ + option + B) to disable the feature and then click the button to select it.

What is an event handler?

✔ An *event handler*, such as the On Mouse Event, manages the action. You can recognize On Mouse Events in the Actions panel by the word *on*, such as *on release* preceding the action name. The words following the word *on* set the parameters for the event. Click the appropriate check boxes in the Actions panel to specify which event you want.

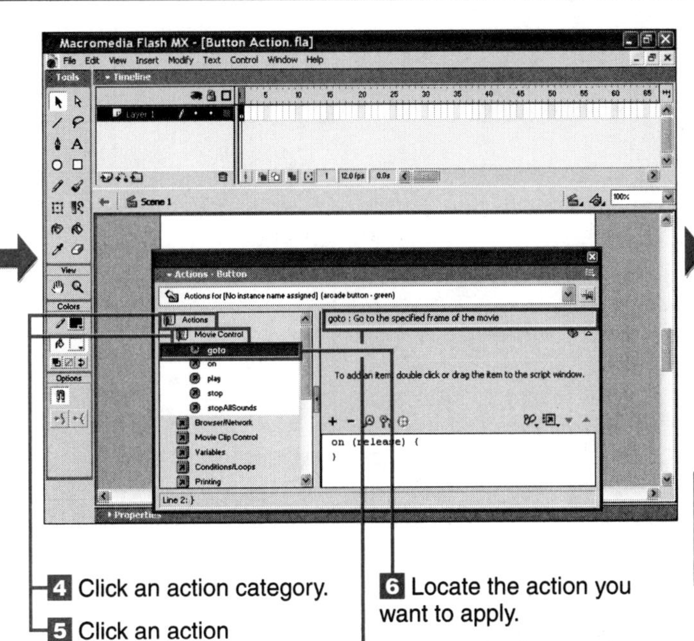

4 Click an action category.

5 Click an action subcategory.

6 Locate the action you want to apply.

■ Flash MX displays the action description here.

Note: To learn more about Flash actions, see Chapter 31.

7 Click and drag the action from the list and drop it in the Actions list box.

■ You can also double-click the action name to immediately place it in the Actions list box.

CONTINUED

ASSIGN BUTTON ACTIONS (CONTINUED)

Flash actions are simplified programming scripts that instruct Flash MX how to perform a certain task, such as activating a Web page link or stopping a sound clip. Actions are based on ActionScript, a programming language unique to Flash MX. Using this basic programming language, actions include command strings to spell out exactly what action Flash MX must perform. Most button actions require input from the user, such as moving the mouse over the button or clicking the button. You do not have to know programming in order to use Flash actions. To learn more about adding actions to your movies, see Chapter 31.

You do not need to know how to write programming scripts in order to assign actions to buttons. Flash MX includes numerous actions you can assign and define parameters for without having to type scripts or codes.

In addition to the action you assign, Flash MX also automatically assigns a special event handler, called the On Mouse Event action, to the button. The On Mouse Event action acts as a manager to make sure whatever action you assign works properly with the button actions that are already built-in to the symbol type.

ASSIGN BUTTON ACTIONS (CONTINUED)

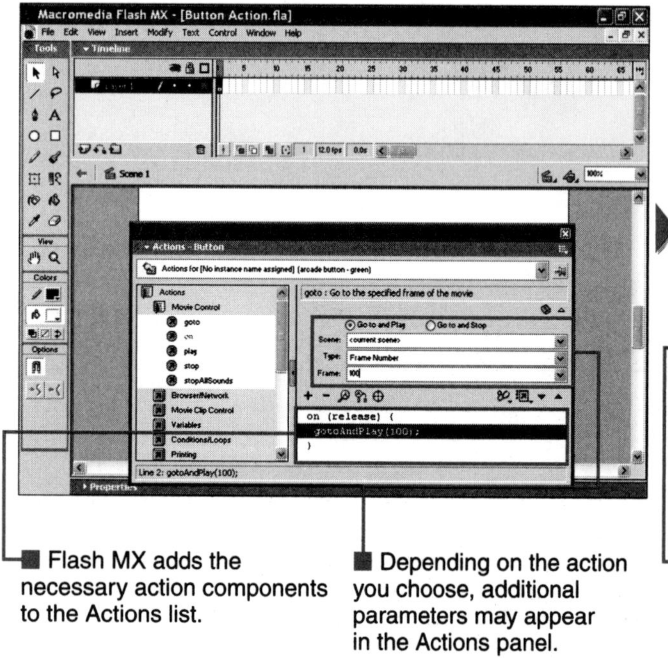

■ Flash MX adds the necessary action components to the Actions list.

■ Depending on the action you choose, additional parameters may appear in the Actions panel.

■ You can change any parameter settings, as necessary.

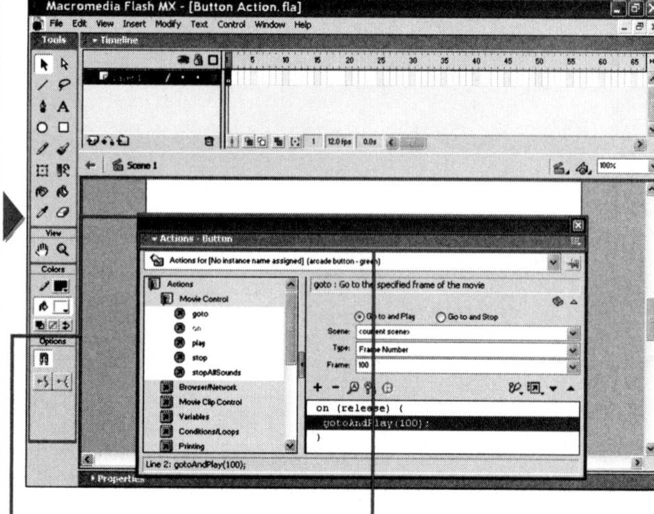

8 Click ☒ to close the Actions panel.

■ You can also click the panel's title bar to minimize the panel.

How do I edit an action assigned to a button?

✔ You can perform edits to your button actions in the Actions-Button panel. Click the line you want to edit in the Actions list. Depending on the action, a variety of parameters appear at the bottom of the box. You can make changes to those parameters, if necessary. To remove an action component from the Actions list, click the line you want to delete and then click ⊟. To add an action, click ⊞ and then click another action.

Can I add multiple actions to a button?

✔ Yes. You can use the Actions-Button panel to add more actions to a button, either before or after an existing action. For example, you can add multiple actions to occur within one set of On/End actions, and Flash triggers all of the actions by a single mouse event.

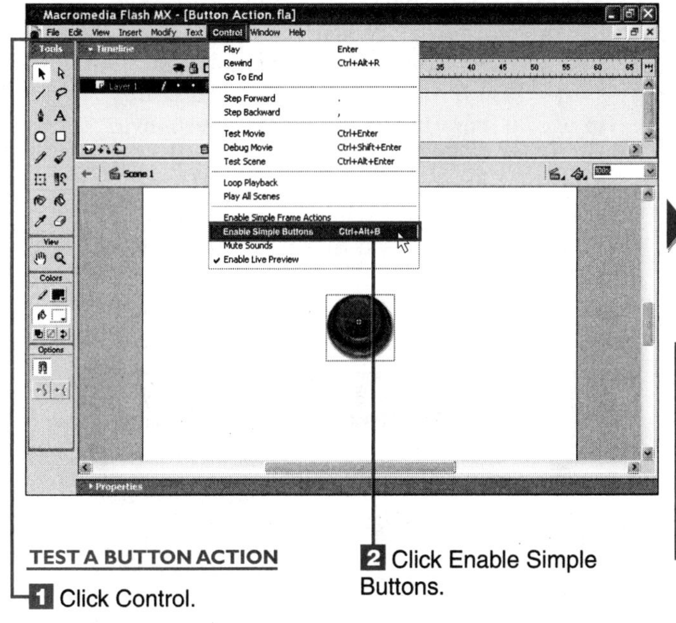

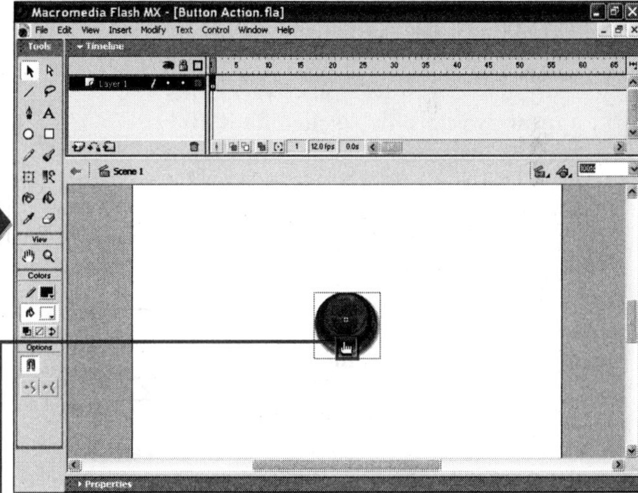

TEST A BUTTON ACTION

1 Click Control.

2 Click Enable Simple Buttons.

■ You can now move ⇖ over the button (⇖ changes to ☝) and click to see the associated action.

INTRODUCTION TO FLASH MX SOUNDS

Adding sound to your Flash MX projects is like adding icing to a cake. With sounds, you can help convey your message and give your movies a polished edge. You can make your sounds as simple as short sound-effect clips, or as complex as coordinating background music. Sounds can include voice narrations, musical scores, and sound effects, such as a doorbell ringing or a thunderclap.

You can assign a sound that continues to play throughout your Flash movie, or synchronize a sound to play with specific frames. You can assign sound clips to buttons to make them more interactive. You can apply sounds to enhance your Flash presentations, movies, cartoons, and other projects in a variety of useful ways.

Digital Sounds

Although invisible, sounds are made of waves that vary in frequency and amplitude. Digital sounds are visually represented as *waveforms*. Waveforms appear as vertically stacked lines of varying heights resembling the output from a seismic chart of an earthquake. The more intense the sound, the taller and denser the waveform line measurement.

For computer usage, sounds are transformed into mathematical equations called *digital sampling*. Digital quality is measured by how many samples exist in a single second of the sound. This is called the *sampling rate*. Sampling rates are expressed in *kilohertz* (kHz). Higher sampling rates result in larger files and clearer sound. Typically, sampling size is measured in 8, 16, or 24 bits. When planning sounds for your Flash movie, remember that larger sound clips take longer to download.

Sounds Are Symbols

You can import sound clips into Flash MX to use in your movies. When you import sounds Flash treats them as symbols and stores them in the Library. When you want to use an imported sound clip in your movie, you place an instance of the sound in the Timeline where you want it to go. Like graphics and button symbols, you can use sound clip instances throughout your movie as many times as necessary. Because an instance references the original symbol, the overall file does not increase greatly in size.

Add Sounds to Layers

You can add sounds to your Flash MX movie frames in the same way that you add other frame content, such as graphics and buttons. Although you can add only one sound per frame in Flash, you can use multiple layers for different sounds. For example, to play multiple sounds at the same time, you can add new sounds to the same movie frame, but assign them to different layers.

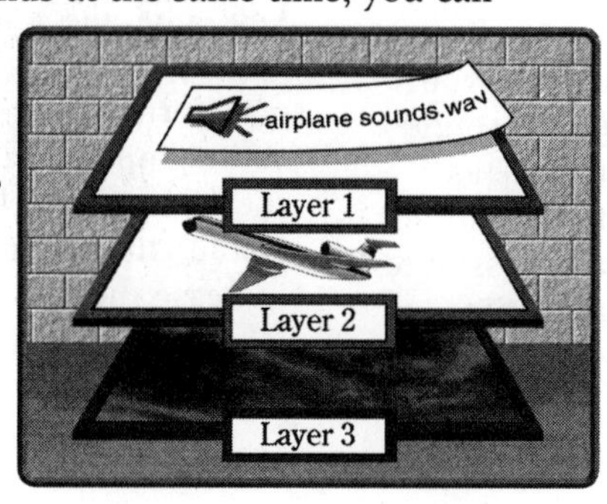

Types of Sounds

All sounds you add in Flash MX, whether music, narration, or sound effects, fall into two categories: *event driven* and *streamed.* An action in your movie triggers event-driven sounds, and they must be downloaded completely before playing. You assign an event sound to start playing on a specific keyframe, and it continues to play independently of the Timeline for your movie. If the event sound is longer than your movie, it continues to play even when your movie stops. You can use event sounds when you do not want to synchronize a sound clip with frames in your movie.

Streamed sounds download as they are needed, and start playing even if the entire clip has not yet finished downloading. Flash MX synchronizes streamed sounds with the frames of your movie and, in fact, attempts to keep any created animation in sync with the streamed sound. Streaming sound works best for sounds you intend to play over the Internet.

When assigning event or streamed sounds, you can use the options in the Properties inspector to specify the sound type. Flash MX offers four sync options — event, stream, start, and stop — based on what you want the sound to do.

Sound File Formats

Flash recognizes a large variety of sound file formats. You can import WAV, AIFF, MP3, and QuickTime file formats into your movies. If you have QuickTime 4 or later, you can also import a few additional sound file formats, including Sun AU and Sound Designer II. When importing sound effects, Flash MX works best with 16-bit sounds.

You can export the audio you use in your Flash movies as MP3 format, or you can compress it as ADPCM, MP3, or RAW. You can find compression options for sounds available in the Publish Settings dialog box.

You can check the file format for any sound clip using the Sound Properties dialog box. The dialog box offers detailed information about the sound clip, including file size and compression assigned to the clip.

IMPORT A SOUND FILE

Although you cannot record sounds in Flash MX, you can import sounds from other sources for use with your movies. For example, you can download an MP3 file from the Internet and add it to a movie, or import a saved recording to play with a Flash button. Flash MX supports popular sound file formats, such as WAV and AIFF. Sound files are called sound *clips* in Flash MX.

When assigning sounds in Flash, you add them to keyframes the same way you add graphics and buttons. Before you can add a sound to a frame, you must first import it into the Library of your movie. When you import a sound file, Flash MX treats the file as a symbol and stores it in the Library. You can use copies, called *instances*, of the sound clip as many times as you want throughout your movie.

You can also use sound clips saved in other Flash files.

When you add a sound to a keyframe, the sound does not appear on the Stage. Rather, a waveform representation of the sound appears in the Timeline for the layer in which you add the sound clip. You may need to increase the size of your Timeline layers to better see the waveform.

IMPORT A SOUND FILE

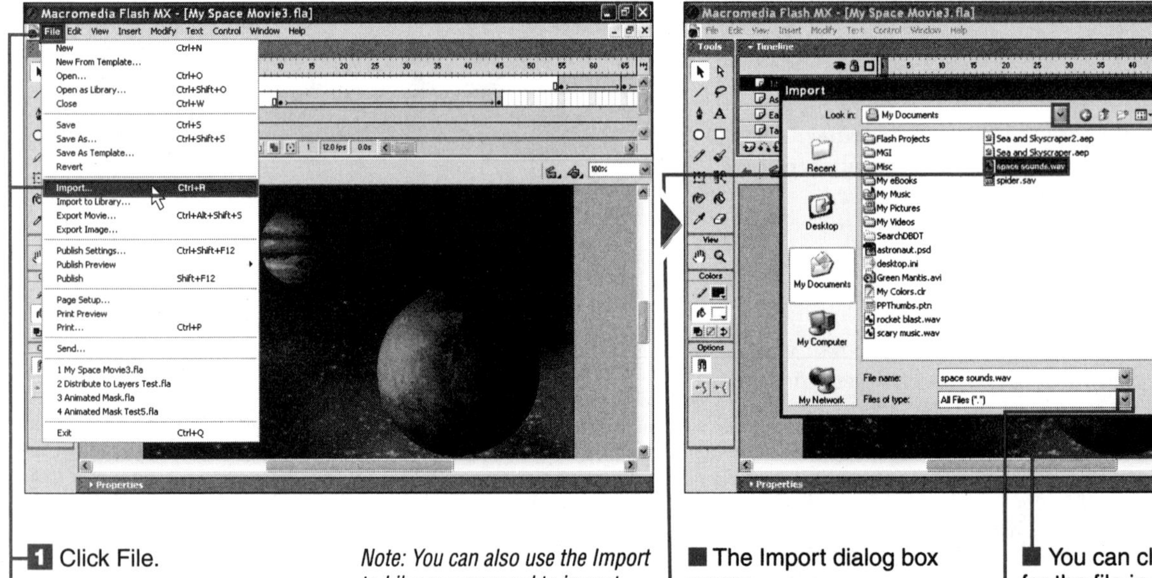

1 Click File.

2 Click Import.

Note: You can also use the Import to Library command to import sound files.

■ The Import dialog box opens.

3 Click the sound file you want to import.

■ You can click ▾ to look for the file in another folder or drive.

■ You can click ▾ to look for a particular type of sound file.

Do I need to worry about the size of my sound file?

✔ When you use large sound files, such as background music for your movie, these sound files take longer to download when users are accessing Flash files from your Web site. It is a good idea to make sure that your sound files are as short as you can possibly make them. Trim off excess parts of the file or plan to use an audio clip that loops in your movie.

Can I rename a sound I import?

✔ Yes. Open the Library window and double-click the sound clip you want to rename. Type a new name and press Enter. Flash MX assigns the new name to the sound clip.

Does Flash MX have any sounds I can use?

✔ Yes, Flash MX has several common libraries from which you can borrow items, including one for sounds. To display the Sounds Library, select the Window menu, click Common Libraries, and then click Sounds. You can preview a sound by clicking the name of the sound and then clicking the Play button (▶). To use a sound, you can drag it from the Library window onto the Stage.

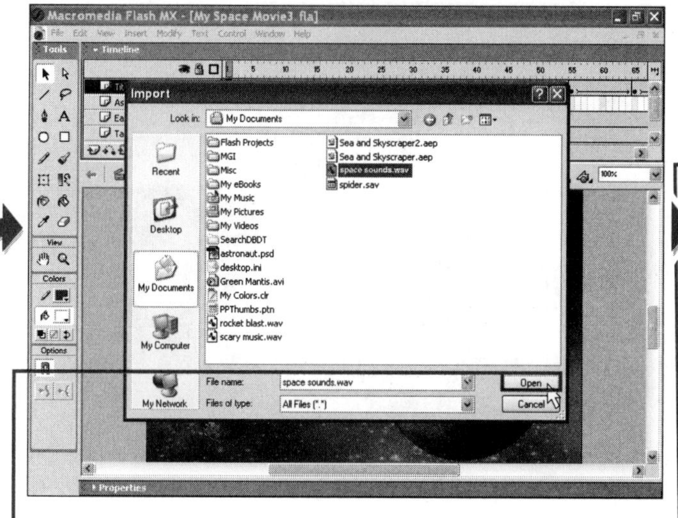

4 Click Open.

■ Flash MX imports the sound file and places it in the Library.

Note: The sound clip is added to the movie after you place an instance of the sound in a frame. To assign a sound to a frame, see page 484.

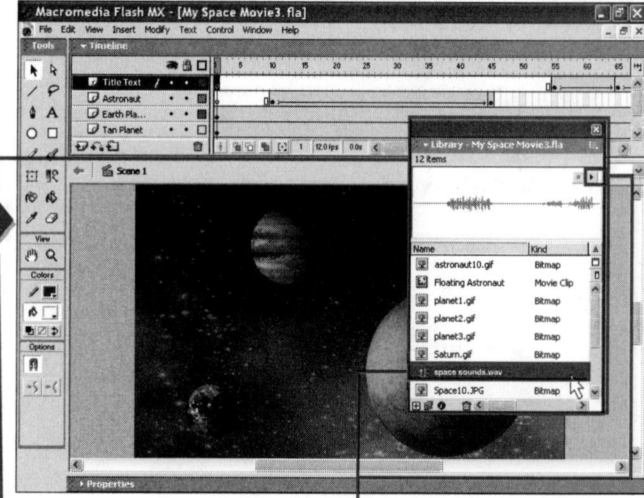

5 Open the Library window to view the imported sound clip.

Note: To open and close the Library window, see page 448.

■ You can preview the sound clip in the Library window by clicking the sound and clicking the Play button (▶).

ADD A SOUND LAYER

You can use Flash layers to organize sounds and separate them from other elements in your movie. Layers appear in the Flash Timeline. You can use layers to hold sounds, graphics, and animations. Like graphics, you assign sounds to frames in the Timeline.

By keeping your sound clips on a separate layer, you can more easily locate the sounds in your Flash movie and see how they relate to items in other layers. Placing sounds in separate layers also lets you more easily edit them later. When you place sounds on separate layers, you can treat these layers as audio channels in your Flash movie. You can also give a sound layer a distinct name so that you immediately recognize its contents. It is good practice to name all the layers you add to the Timeline to better describe the layer content.

Flash MX allows for multiple sound layers in your movie. For example, you can use one layer for special effects sounds, like a doorbell ringing, and another layer for background music. When you run a Flash movie, any overlapping sound layers play together.

ADD A SOUND LAYER

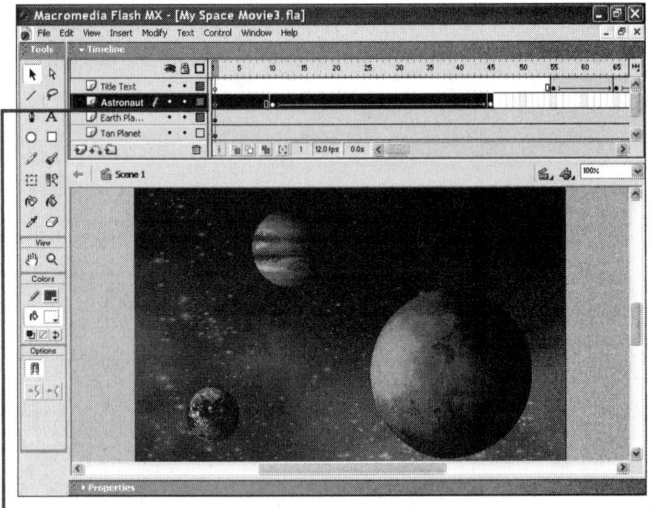

1 Click the layer below where you want to insert a new layer.

■ Flash MX always adds a new layer to the Timeline directly above the active layer.

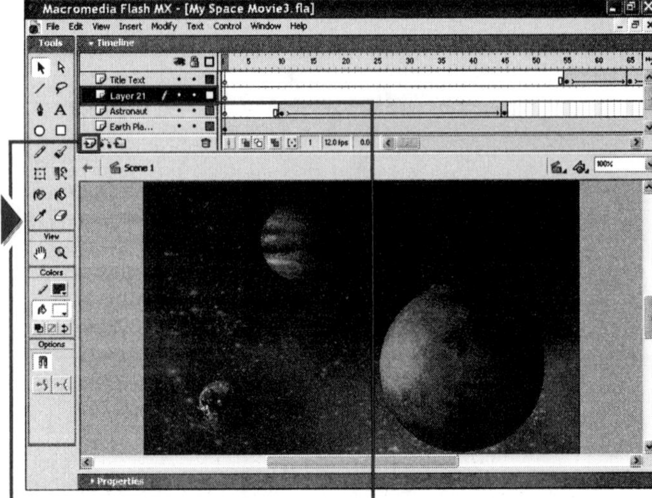

2 Click the Insert Layer button (📄).

■ A new layer appears on top of the active layer.

Can I make a soundtrack layer?

✔ Although Flash MX uses no official soundtrack layer, you can organize multiple sound layers and place them in a layer folder labeled Soundtrack. By placing all of your sound layers in a layer folder, you can quickly see the organization of sound files in your Flash movie.

How can I tell which object is on which layer?

✔ You can view your layer contents as outlines on the Stage. Click the Colored Square (□) under the square icon column in the Timeline (□ changes to □). Flash MX outlines all objects on the layer in the same color as the square you clicked.

Can I enlarge the size of my sound layer?

✔ Yes. Enlarging a layer that contains a sound clip enables you to easily view the waveform image of the sound in the Timeline. To enlarge the layer height, right-click the layer name and click Properties. This opens the Layer Properties dialog box. Click the Layer Height drop-down arrow and choose a percentage. Click OK to close the dialog box and apply the new size.

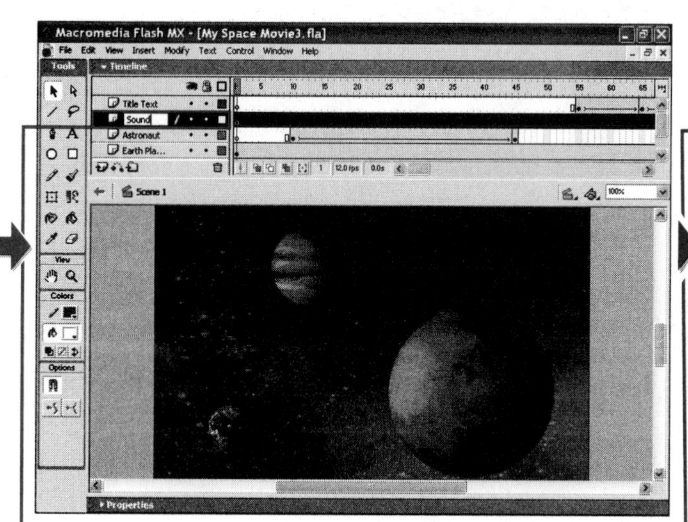

3 To give the layer a distinct name, double-click the default layer name.

4 Type a name that identifies this layer as a sound layer.

5 Press Enter (Return).

■ Flash MX saves the new layer name.

■ To make the sound layer easier to find, drag the layer to the top or bottom of the Timeline layer stack.

Note: To learn more about working with layers in the Timeline, see page 436.

ASSIGN A SOUND TO A FRAME

You can enliven any animation sequence by adding a single sound effect or an entire soundtrack. You save sound files as instances that you can insert into frames on the Timeline and use throughout your movie. Flash MX represents sounds as waveforms in Flash frames.

Sound files appear as symbols when you import them to the Flash Library. You can drag a sound clip from the Library out onto the Stage to assign it to any keyframe in your movie. After it is on the Stage, Flash MX gives no visual representation of the sound. Instead, a *waveform*, an image of vertical lines representing the digital sampling of the sound, appears in the Timeline frame. Unlike a graphic or button symbol, sound clips do not appear on the Stage. Depending on the length of the sound file, the sound may play through several frames of your movie.

You can use two methods to assign a sound to a frame. You can place an instance of the sound clip on the Stage for a selected frame using the Library window, or you can use the Sound drop-down list in the Property inspector. The method you choose may depend on which feature is displayed in the Flash MX program window.

ASSIGN A SOUND TO A FRAME

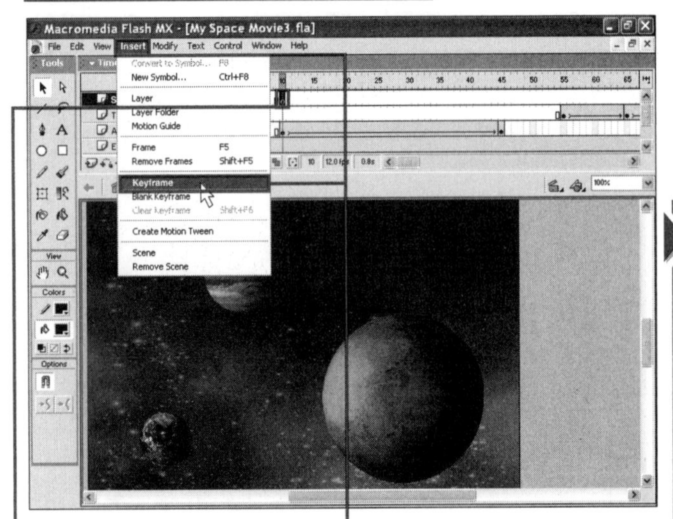

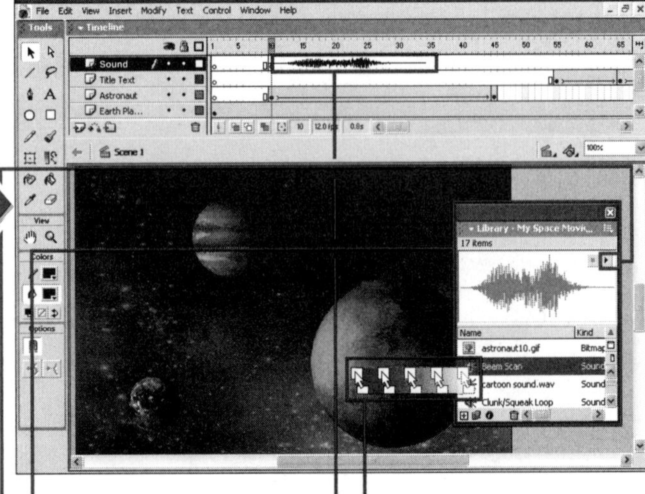

ADD A SOUND USING THE LIBRARY WINDOW

1 Click the frame to which you want to add a sound.

Note: To organize your sounds, you can add them to a layer that you create specifically for sound clips.

2 Click Insert.

3 Click Keyframe.

■ Flash MX inserts a keyframe icon in the frame.

Note: To learn more about working with keyframes in the Timeline, see Chapter 29.

4 Open the Library window.

Note: To open and close the Library window, see page 448.

5 Click to select the sound clip you want to use.

■ You can click the Play button (▶) to preview the sound in the Library window.

6 Click and drag the sound clip from the Library and drop it onto the Stage (changes to).

■ Flash MX adds the sound to the frame and the waveform for the sound appears in the frame.

How do I know which sound is which?

✔ Because sounds appear as waveforms in the Timeline, it is not easy to determine exactly which sound is which. One way you can quickly tell is to hover your mouse pointer directly over the waveform. A tooltip appears with the name of the sound.

Can I use sound clips from the Library of another movie?

✔ Yes. Click the File menu and click Open as Library. The Open as Library dialog box appears. Click the filename and then click Open. The Library window opens, listing the symbols in the other file. Drag the sound clip you want to use from the Library window onto the Stage.

Why does the waveform of my sound appear compressed into one frame?

✔ If you assign a sound file to a keyframe that appears at the end of your movie, or if you have yet to add additional frames or keyframes to your movie, the waveform of the sound appears only in the frame in which you assigned it. This makes the waveform appear compressed in the frame.

I tried to borrow a sound from another file's Library, but it did not work. Why not?

✔ You must close the file containing the sound clip that you want to use before sharing it with a new file.

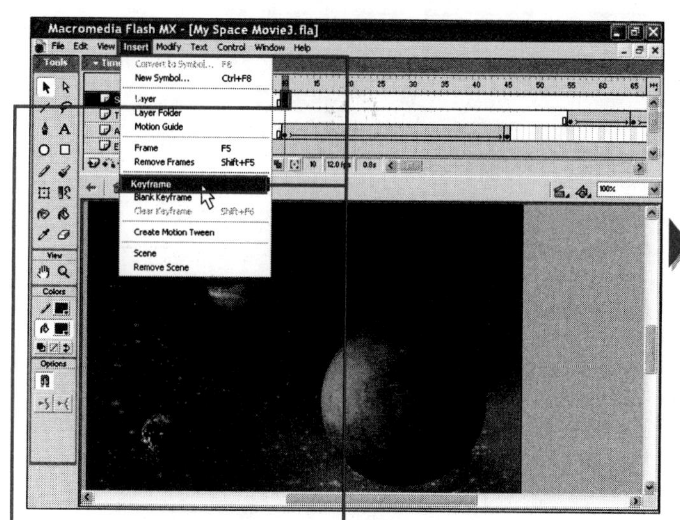

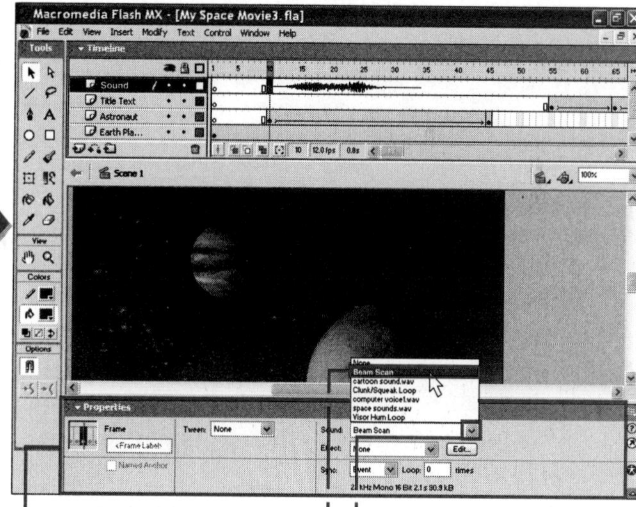

ADD A SOUND USING THE PROPERTY INSPECTOR

1 Click the frame to which you want to add a sound.

Note: To organize your sounds, you can add them to a layer that you create specifically for sound clips.

2 Click Insert.

3 Click Keyframe

■ Flash MX inserts a keyframe icon in the frame.

Note: To learn more about working with keyframes in the Timeline, see Chapter 29.

4 Open the Property inspector.

Note: To open and close the Property inspector, see page 346.

5 Click the Sound ▾.

6 Click to select the sound you want to assign.

ASSIGN A SOUND TO A BUTTON

You can use sound to call attention to the buttons in your movie or on your Web page. When you add sounds to buttons, you make the buttons more interactive and your Web page or movie livelier.

For example, you can add a clicking sound that the user hears after clicking a button. If your buttons are part of a graphic or page background, adding a sound to the rollover state of a button helps users find the button on the page.

When you add multiple sounds to your buttons, you make them even more interactive and exciting. You can add a different sound to each button state, such as a chime effect that plays when the user rolls over the button with the mouse, and a click effect when the user actually clicks on the button. It is not necessary to add a sound to the Hit state because the user never sees or interacts with this button state.

When assigning a sound to a button, you should create a separate layer for the sound. You can add layers to the button timeline just as you add layers to the main Timeline.

ASSIGN A SOUND TO A BUTTON

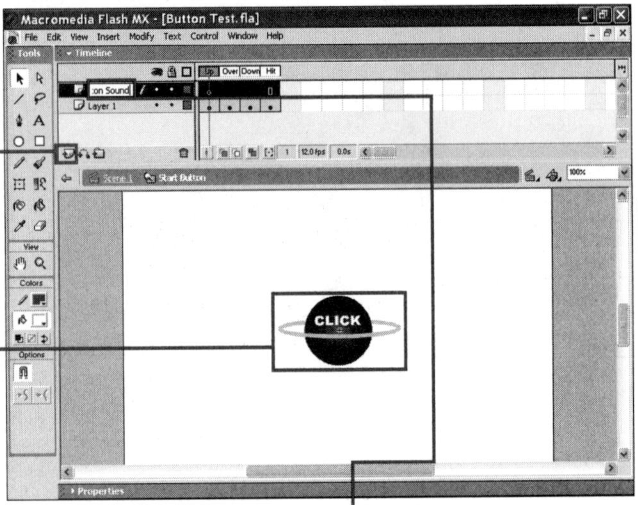

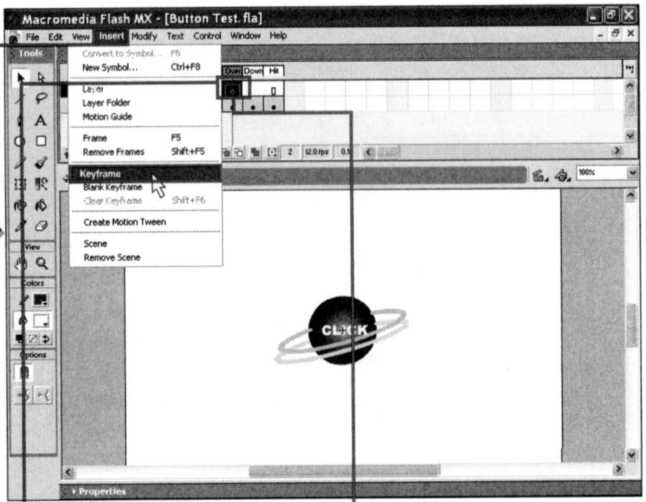

SET A BUTTON SOUND

1 Double-click the button to which you want to add a sound in symbol-edit mode.

2 Click [icon] to add a new layer to the button timeline.

3 Type a name for the layer.

Note: To learn more about working with layers in Flash MX, see Chapter 25.

4 Click the frame to which you want to add a sound.

5 Click Insert.

6 Click Keyframe.

■ Flash MX inserts a keyframe icon in the frame.

Note: To learn more about working with keyframes in the Timeline, see Chapter 29.

Flash does not let me add a sound to a frame. Why not?

✔ You can add sounds to only keyframes, not to regular frames in the Timeline. Be sure you insert a keyframe first before attempting to add the sound.

To which button should I assign a sound?

✔ The most practical frames to use when assigning sounds are the Over and Down frames. For example, you might want the button to beep when the user rolls over the button with the mouse pointer. To do this, assign a sound to the Over frame. You might also want the button to make another type of sound when the user actually clicks it. To do this, assign a sound to the Down frame.

I want to share my imported sounds with other Flash files. Is there an easy way to do this?

✔ Yes. You can create a sample library of your own files to share clips and graphics with other Flash projects you create. Create a Flash file that contains all the shared elements in the Library window. When you save the file, save it to the Libraries folder located in First Run folder among the Flash program files and folders. When you restart Flash MX, the new sample file is added to the list of common libraries under the Window menu. See Chapter 26 to learn more about working with the Library window, symbols, and instances.

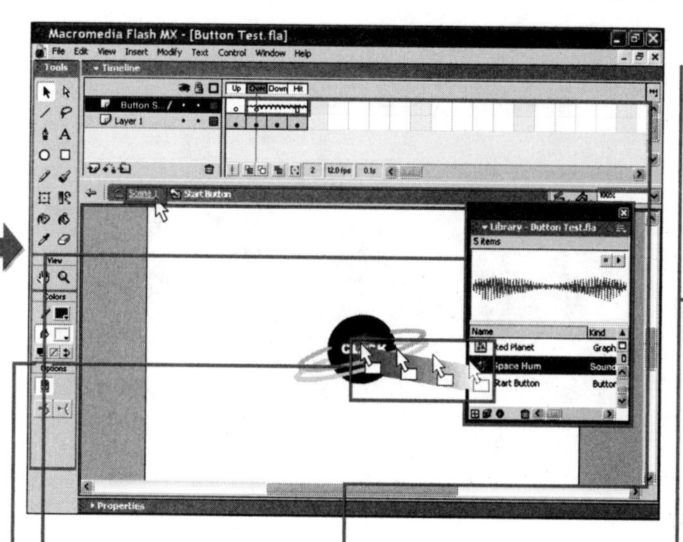

7 Open the Library window.

Note: To open and close the Library window, see page 448.

8 Click to select the sound clip you want to use.

9 Click and drag the sound clip from the Library and drop it onto the Stage.

Note: To use the Property inspector to assign a sound, see page 485.

■ Flash MX adds the waveform to the frame.

10 Click the scene name to return to movie-edit mode.

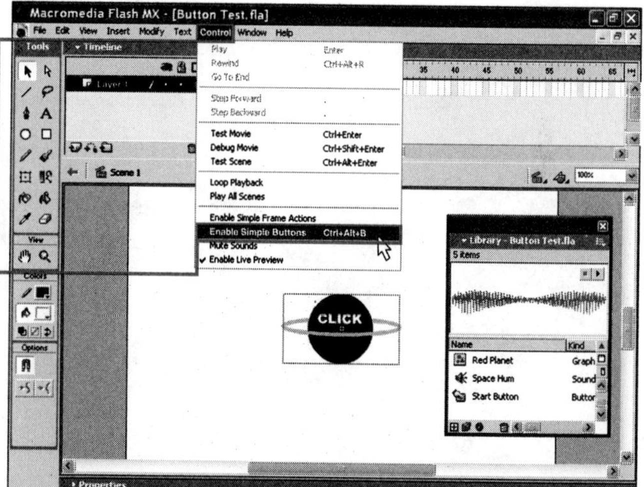

TEST THE BUTTON SOUND

1 Click Control.

2 Click Enable Simple Buttons.

■ You can move over the button or click the button to hear the assigned sound.

CREATE EVENT SOUNDS

You can assign an event-driven sound in your Flash MX project that is triggered by an action. Event sounds can be triggered when the playhead reaches the frame containing the event sound or by Flash actions you assign to your movies, such as a `play` action assigned to a button. Actions are sets of instructions that tell Flash what to do.

Event sounds play in their entirety and in their own Timeline. The user must completely download the sound before playing it. By default, Flash MX treats all sounds that you add as event sounds unless you specify another type.

You can use event sounds to include background music in your movie. Keep in mind, however, that if the sound file is longer than your movie, the sound keeps playing until it ends or encounters a stop command. If your movie happens to loop and the event sound does not stop by the time the movie reaches its starting point again, Flash plays two instances of the sound at the same time. This overlapping of sounds does not create a very harmonious effect in the movie, so be sure to time the length of your event sound before setting your movie to loop status.

CREATE EVENT SOUNDS

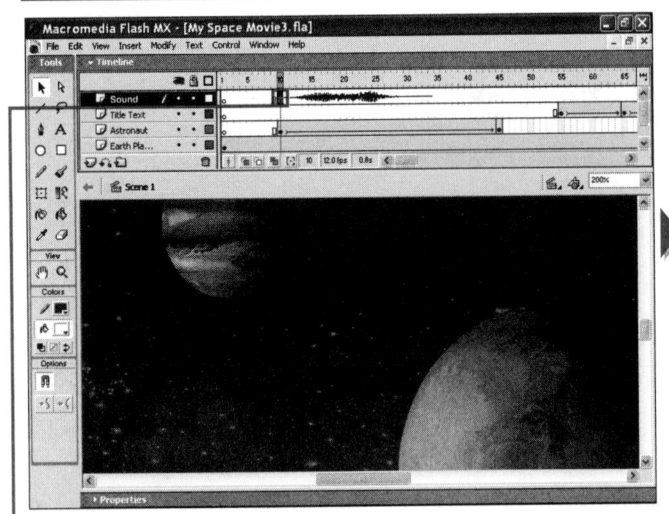

TURN A SOUND INTO AN EVENT SOUND

1 Click the frame containing the sound you want to change.

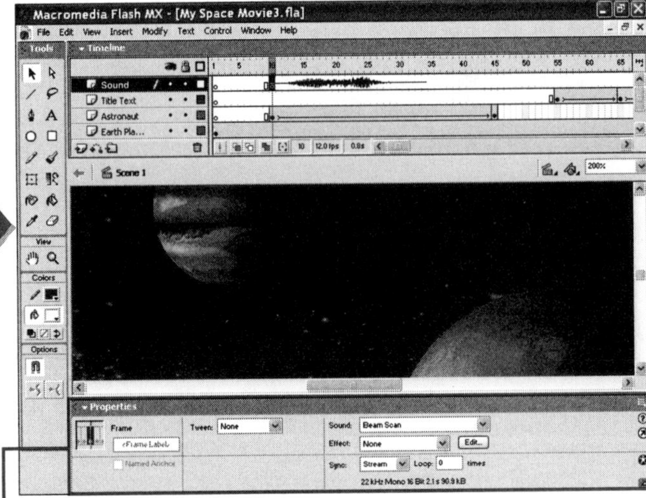

2 Open the Property inspector.

Note: To open and close the Property inspector, see page 346.

What types of sounds work best as event sounds?

✔ For best results in Flash MX, assign event sounds to short sound clips. Sound effects, like a handclap or a bell ringing, work well as event sounds. Long clips, such as an entire song, work best as streamed sounds.

How do I unassign an event sound?

✔ To remove a sound you no longer want, you can use the Properties inspector. With the Properties inspector open, click the Sound ▾, and click None. Flash MX removes the sound from the frame.

Can I overlap event sounds, or start two sounds simultaneously?

✔ Yes. Although you can only insert one sound per frame, you can use multiple layers to play sounds at the same time or to overlap them. For example, you might place one event sound in a sound layer labeled Sound 1 and assign the sound to frame 1. You can create a second layer and name it Sound 2, and place another sound in frame 5 of this new layer. The sounds overlap even if one starts slightly later than the other.

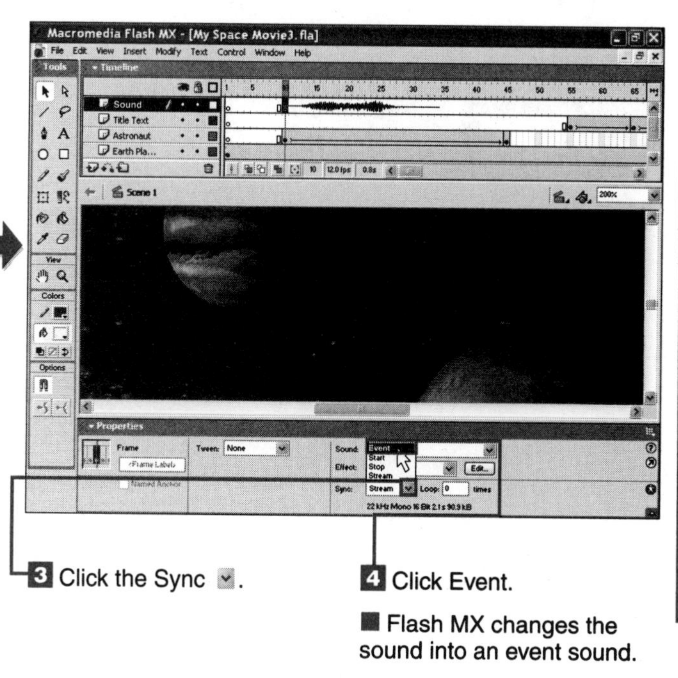

3 Click the Sync ▾.

4 Click Event.

■ Flash MX changes the sound into an event sound.

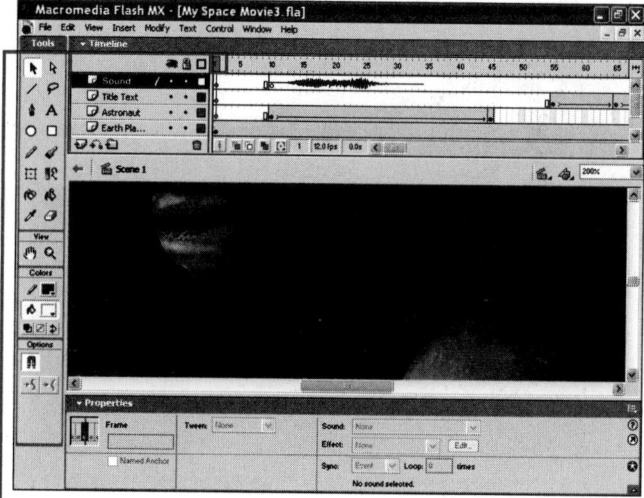

TEST THE SOUND

1 Click the first frame in your movie.

2 Press Enter (Return).

■ The movie plays. When the movie reaches the selected frame, the sound plays.

Note: To test movies in the Flash Player window, see page 630.

ASSIGN START SOUNDS

You can use the Flash start sound control to start a new instance of a sound in your movie. This is helpful when you want to synchronize a sound with your animation.

Start sounds act just like event sounds with one important difference: if an instance of the sound happens to be playing already, which can happen if your movie loops, the start sound does not restart itself. In the case of event sounds, however, a second instance of the sound starts playing regardless of whether a current instance plays. This means that you can have two or more instances of the same sound playing at different stages. Needless to say, this does not always sound harmonious. When you assign the start sound, you avoid this problem; you hear only one instance of the sound, not a doubling of the same sound.

You can use the Property inspector to turn an event sound into a start sound. Remember, all sound clips you add to movie frames are classified as event sounds by default. In addition to options for changing the sound status, the Property inspector also offers options for looping and editing the sound.

ASSIGN START SOUNDS

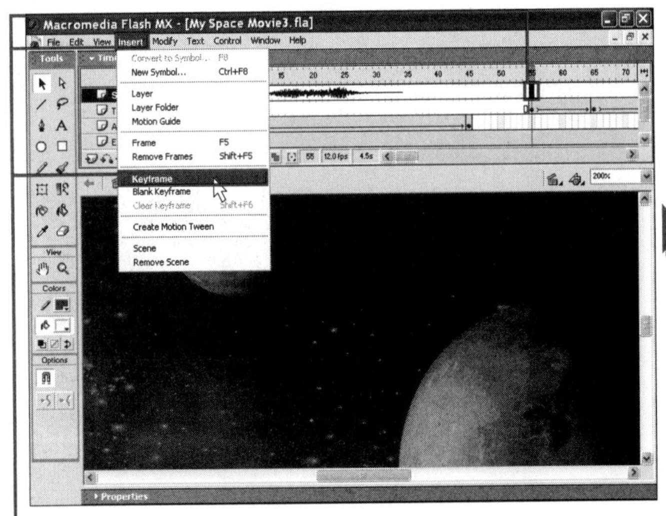

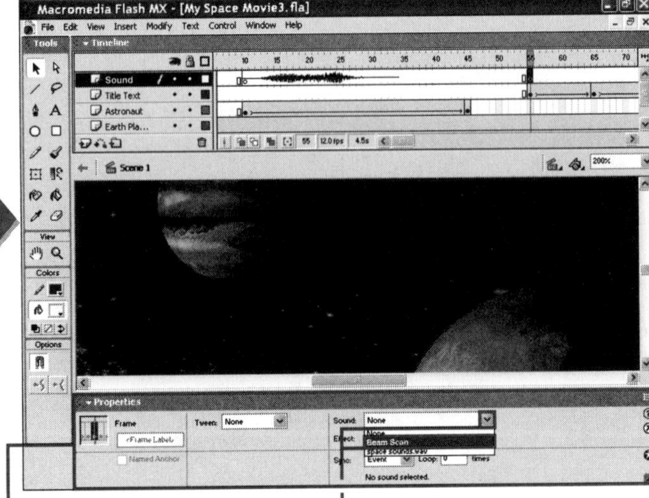

SET A START SOUND

1. Click the frame where you want the sound to start.
2. Click Insert.
3. Click Keyframe.

■ Flash MX inserts a keyframe icon in the frame.

Note: To learn more about working with keyframes in the Timeline, see Chapter 29.

4. Open the Property inspector.

Note: To open and close the Property inspector, see page 346.

5. Click the Sound ▾.
6. Click to select the sound you want to start.

How can I control the volume of a sound?

✔ You can find volume effects controls in the Property inspector. Click the Effect ▾ to view the available settings. For example, to make the sound fade in, click the Fade In setting. You can learn more about editing sounds on page 498.

Can I reassign the sync type of a sound?

✔ Yes. You can easily redesignate a sync type for any sound in your movie. Simply open the Property inspector, click the Sync ▾ and apply another sync type to the selected frame containing the sound you want to change.

What does the Loop option do?

✔ The Loop option loops the sound. You can set your sound clip to loop by typing the number of times you want the loop to occur in the Loop text box located in the Property inspector. For example, if you want the clip to keep playing indefinitely, input a large number, such as 50 or 75.

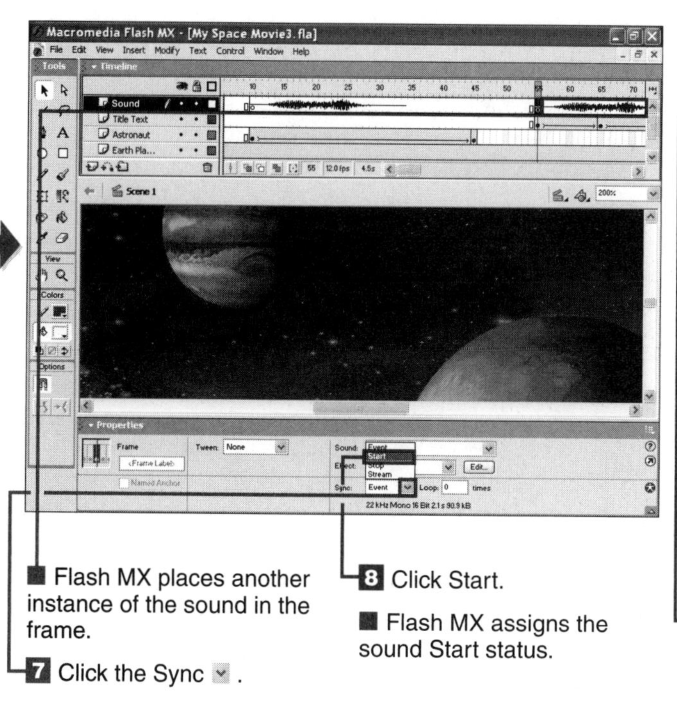

■ Flash MX places another instance of the sound in the frame.

7 Click the Sync ▾ .

8 Click Start.

■ Flash MX assigns the sound Start status.

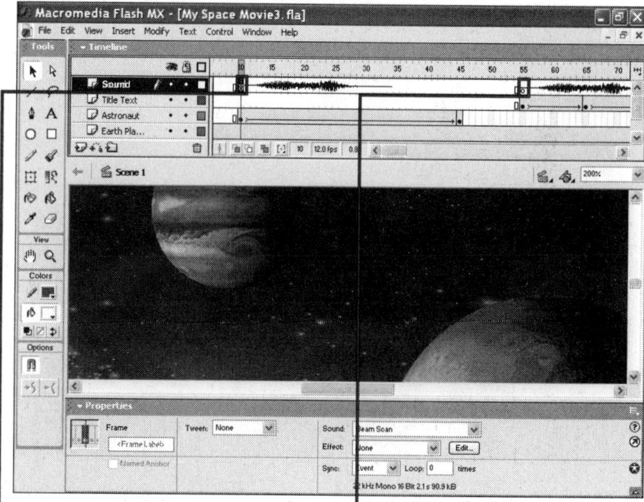

TEST THE START SOUND

1 Click a frame at the beginning of the movie or before the start sound keyframe.

2 Press Enter (Return).

■ The movie plays. When it reaches the frame with the start sound, the sound plays again.

Note: To test movies in the Flash Player window, see page 630.

ASSIGN STOP SOUNDS

You can stop a sound before it reaches the end by inserting a stop sound. A stop sound is simply an instruction that tells Flash MX to quit playing a specific event sound. For example, if your animation ends on a particular frame, but your sound clip goes on much longer, you can place a stop sound in the frame to end the sound.

You use stop sounds in conjunction with event sounds. If you have a long sound clip playing as a background in your movie, you can stop it at a certain point in your movie by placing a stop sound in the frame where you want the sound to end. For example, you might stop a background sound in order to hear a narration clip or a sound effect.

You can use the Property inspector to assign a stop status to a sound. The Sync drop-down list includes the four synchronization types you can assign to sounds in your movies, including the Stop status.

You can also use the Stop All Sounds action to stop sounds in your movie. You can use actions when you want to create more complex instructions for how Flash MX handles movie clips. See Chapter 31 to learn how to add actions in Flash.

ASSIGN STOP SOUNDS

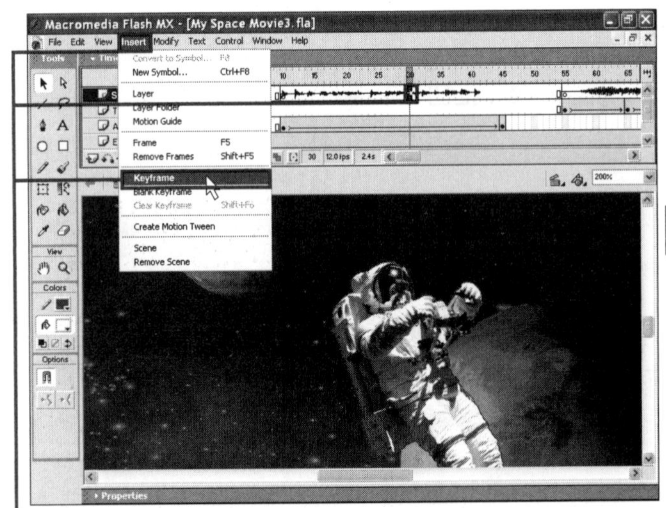

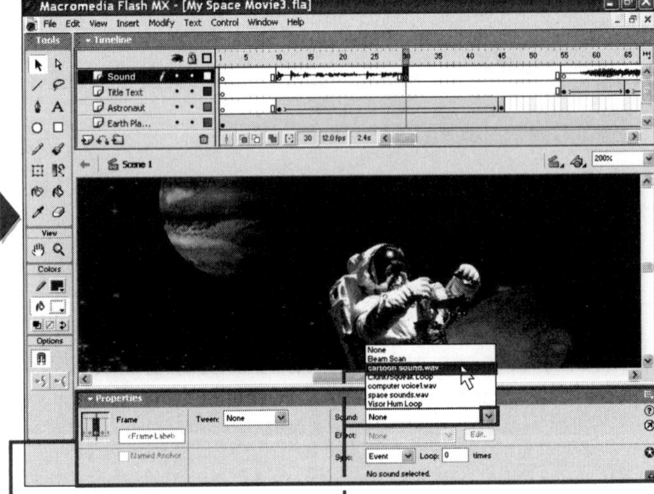

SET A STOP SOUND

1 Click the frame where you want the sound to stop.

2 Click Insert.

3 Click Keyframe.

■ Flash MX inserts a keyframe icon in the frame.

Note: To learn more about working with keyframes in the Timeline, see Chapter 29.

4 Open the Property inspector.

Note: To open and close the Property inspector, see page 346.

5 Click the Sound ▾.

6 Click to select the sound you want to stop.

Do I have to assign the stop sound in the same layer as the sound I am stopping?

✔ You do not have to assign a stop command to the same layer containing the sound you want to stop. The command immediately stops any playback of the sound regardless of where you assign the sound.

How do I stop a streaming sound?

✔ Insert a blank keyframe in the sound layer at the point in your movie where you want the sound to end. You can press F7 to insert a blank keyframe, or you can click the Insert menu and click Blank keyframe. See Chapter 29 to learn more about working with frame types in Flash MX.

Can I stop all the sounds playing in my movie?

✔ Yes. First select the keyframe in which you want to add the action. Select Window, and then click Actions. When the Actions panel appears, select Actions, Movie Control and click stopAllSounds. Flash MX adds the command to the actions list box. When you test your movie, all sounds stop when Flash MX reaches the frame containing the action. See Chapter 31 to learn more about using the Actions panel.

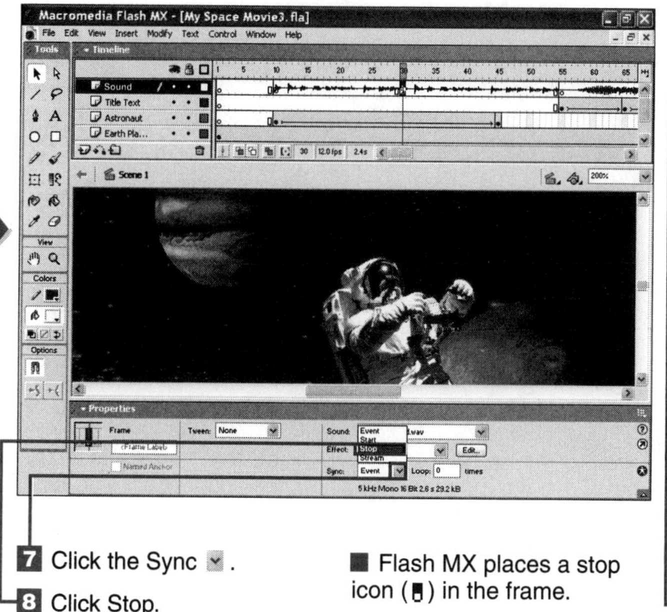

7 Click the Sync ▾.

8 Click Stop.

■ Flash MX places a stop icon (▮) in the frame.

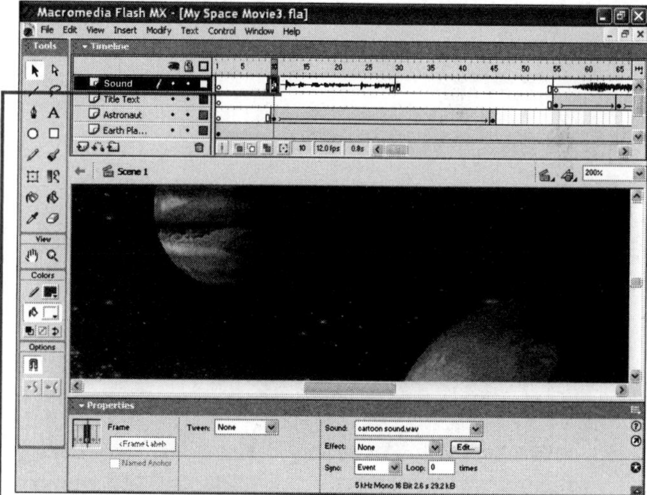

TEST THE STOP SOUND

1 Click a frame at the beginning of the movie or before the stop sound keyframe.

2 Press Enter (Return).

■ The movie plays. When it reaches the frame with the stop sound, the sound stops playing.

Note: To test movies in the Flash Player window, see page 630.

ASSIGN STREAMING SOUNDS

You can use *streaming* sounds for Flash MX movies you place on Web pages to synchronize the sounds with animation. This enables users to hear the sound as soon as the streaming or downloading starts, as Flash breaks the sound into smaller units for easier downloading. Streaming sounds are good for long sound files, such as musical soundtracks. The sound starts streaming as the page downloads, so the user does not have to wait for the entire file to finish downloading.

With streaming sound, Flash MX synchronizes the frames in your movie with the sound clip. If your sound is a bit slow in downloading, the frames slow down as well. The synchronization forces Flash to keep your animation at the same pace as your sound. Occasionally, the sound may play much faster than Flash can display the individual frames, resulting in skipped frames. When your movie ends, the streaming sound also stops.

You can use the Property inspector to turn a sound into a streaming sound. The Sync drop-down list includes the four synchronization types you can assign to sounds in your movies, including the Streaming sound status.

ASSIGN STREAMING SOUNDS

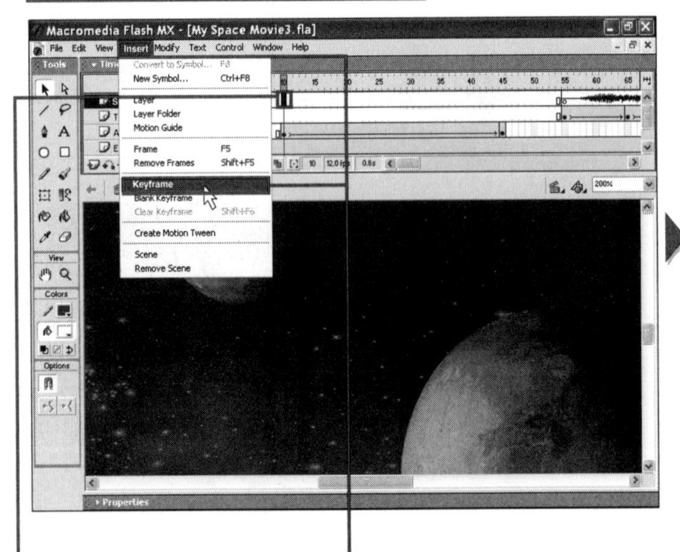

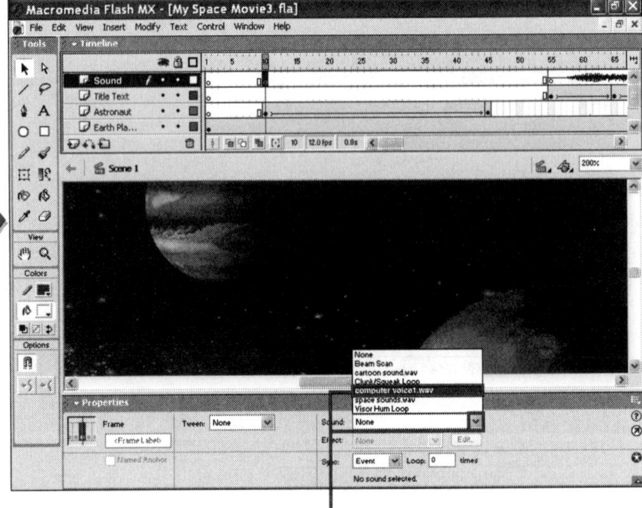

SET A STREAMING SOUND

1 Click the frame where you want to start the streaming sound.

2 Click Insert.

3 Click Keyframe.

■ Flash MX inserts a keyframe icon in the frame.

Note: To learn more about working with keyframes in the Timeline, see Chapter 29.

4 Open the Property inspector.

Note: To open and close the Property inspector, see page 346.

5 Click the Sound ▾.

6 Click to select the sound you want to make into a streaming sound.

What do I do if my streaming sound gets cut off too soon?

✔ You can try switching the units from seconds to frames. To do so, click Edit in the Properties inspector. The Edit Envelope dialog box opens to reveal the sound file. Click ▦ to set the unit scale to Frames and click ☒ to close the dialog box. Play the movie again to test it.

Where can I find detailed information about a sound clip?

✔ You can view details about a sound clip in the Property inspector. From the Sound drop-down list, click to select the sound. The Property inspector lists the kilohertz, channels, bits, duration, and file size for the sound.

Does the frame rate of my movie affect my sounds?

✔ Yes, particularly for longer-playing sounds. For example, if your movie uses the default frame rate of 12 frames per second (fps), a 30-second sound consumes 360 frames in your movie. If you change the frame rate to 18 fps, the sound uses 540 frames. The frame rate and the length of your sound factor into how your movie plays. To change the frame rate of your movie, click the Modify menu and then click Document. This opens the Document Properties dialog box where you can change the frame rate for your movie.

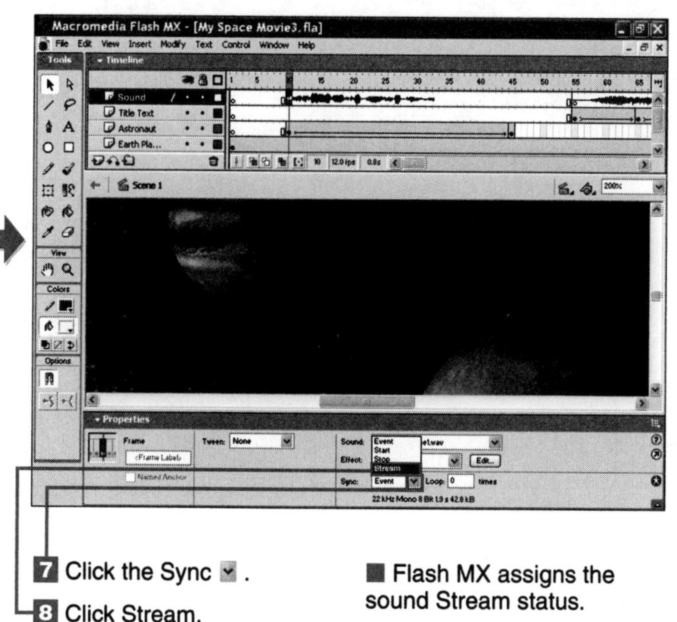

7 Click the Sync ▾.

8 Click Stream.

■ Flash MX assigns the sound Stream status.

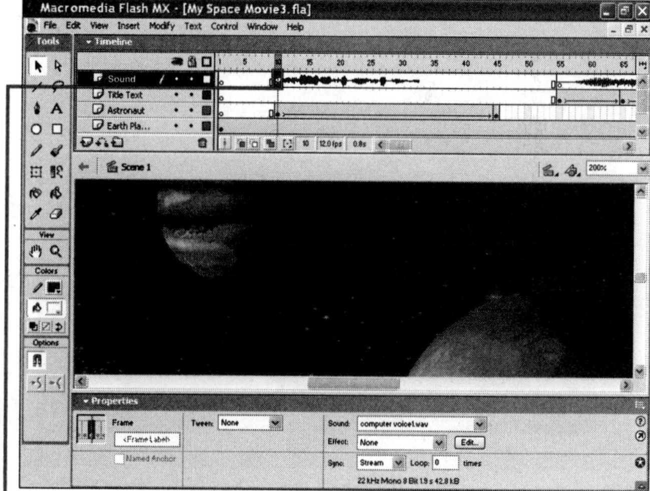

TEST THE STREAMING SOUND

1 Click a frame at the beginning of the movie or the keyframe at the start of the streaming sound.

2 Press Enter (Return).

■ The movie plays. When it reaches the frame with the streaming sound, the sound starts playing.

Note: To test movies in the Flash Player window, see page 630.

LOOP SOUNDS

You can make a sound play over and over again in your movie with the Loop command. Looping means to play the sound repeatedly, as many times as you like. You can choose to loop event and streaming sounds in your Flash MX movies.

When you loop a sound, you are only using one instance of the sound throughout your movie. To set the number of times you want a sound to repeat, use the Loop field in the Property inspector. The number you type dictates how many times the sound repeats. If the Loop field is set to 0, the sound plays through one time. If you type a setting of 5, Flash loops the sound five times from start to finish. If you specify a loop setting that exceeds the length of your movie and the sound is an event sound, the sound continues to play even after your movie stops. For that reason, it is important to test any loop setting you input to make sure that it is compatible with the running time of your movie.

Use caution when looping streaming sounds. When you loop streaming sounds, Flash adds frames to a movie, thus creating a larger file size.

LOOP SOUNDS

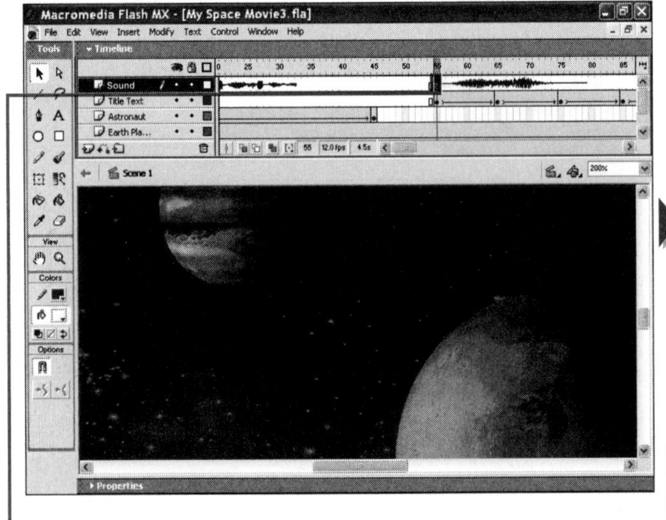

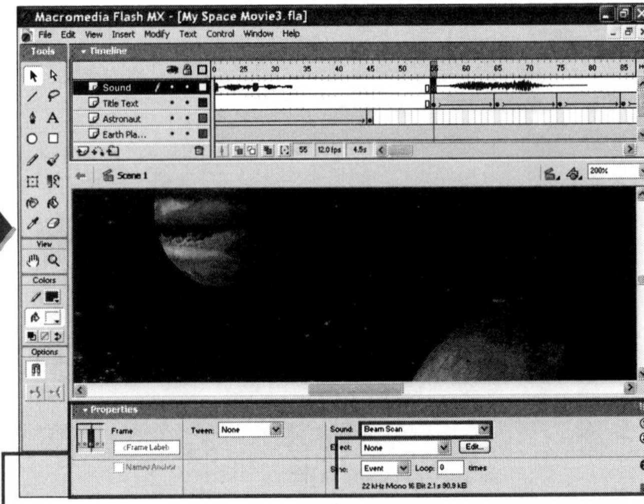

SET A LOOP SOUND

1 Click the frame containing the sound to which you want to set a loop option.

2 Open the Property inspector.

Note: To open and close the Property inspector, see page 346.

3 Click the Sound .

4 Click to select the sound you want to loop.

What if I want the sound to loop to the end of the movie?

✔ If you have set a streaming sound, you can set the loop to a high number, like 30 or 40. Flash MX does not loop the sound that many times, but the sound keeps looping until the end of the movie.

How do I change the properties of a sound?

✔ You can change any properties of a sound through the Library window. Display the Library window and click the sound you want to change. Click (i) to open the Sound Properties dialog box. Here you can view information about the sound file and set export compression for the sound.

How do I update a sound I use throughout my movie?

✔ While testing your movie, you may want to edit a sound you use frequently throughout the movie. From the Library window, select the sound you want to edit, and then click the Options menu. Choose Edit With or Edit With QuickTime Player. You can then edit the sound with the sound-editing program you choose. When you save the sound file, Flash MX updates every instance of it throughout your movie.

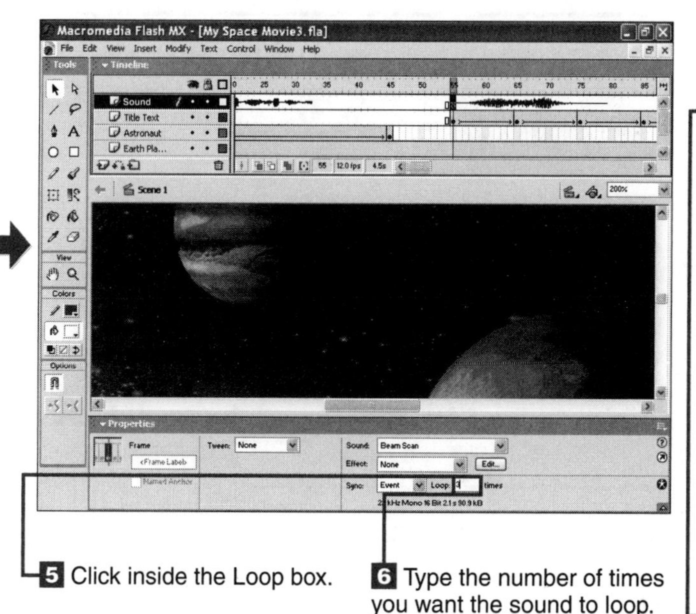

5 Click inside the Loop box.

6 Type the number of times you want the sound to loop.

TEST THE LOOP EFFECT

1 Click a frame at the beginning of the movie or the keyframe at the start of the looping sound.

2 Press Enter (Return).

■ The movie plays. When it reaches the frame with the looping sound, Flash loops the sound as many times as you specified.

Note: To test movies in the Flash Player window, see page 630.

EDIT SOUNDS

You can use volume controls in Flash MX to improve the way sound is integrated into your movie. Sound-editing controls enable you to fade sounds in or out, or make sounds move from one speaker to another in a stereo setup, to define start and end points for sounds, or to adjust the volume at different points in the sound. These controls can help you make your sound files smaller in size by defining the exact point at which a sound starts to play, or defining the point where the sound ends. For applying simple sound effects such as volume and stereo control, you can use the Effect drop-down list in the Property inspector. For additional editing controls, open the Edit Envelope dialog box.

When you import a sound into Flash MX, the file includes information about the length, volume, and stereo settings of the sound. You can fine-tune these settings using the Edit Envelope dialog box.

The Edit Envelope dialog box displays your sound as a waveform with both left and right audio channels. You can click the waveform in either channel and drag edit points, called envelope handles, to adjust the volume and length of the sound.

EDIT SOUNDS

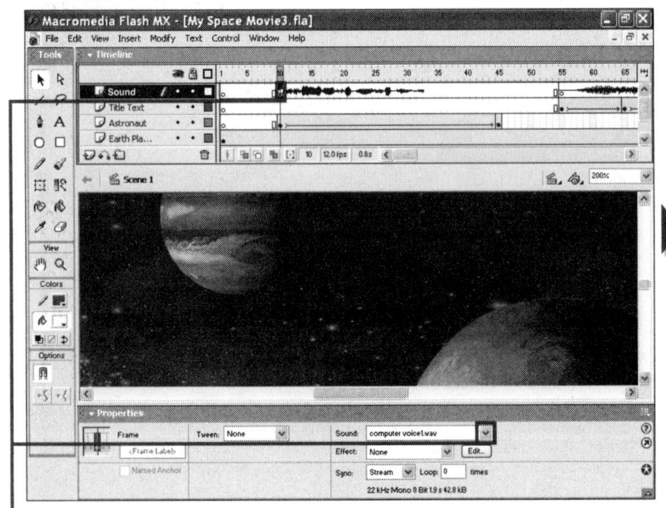

1 Click the frame containing the sound to which you want to apply a sound effect.

2 In the Property inspector, click the Sound ▾.

3 Click to select the sound to which you want to apply sound effects.

Note: To open and close the Property inspector, see page 346.

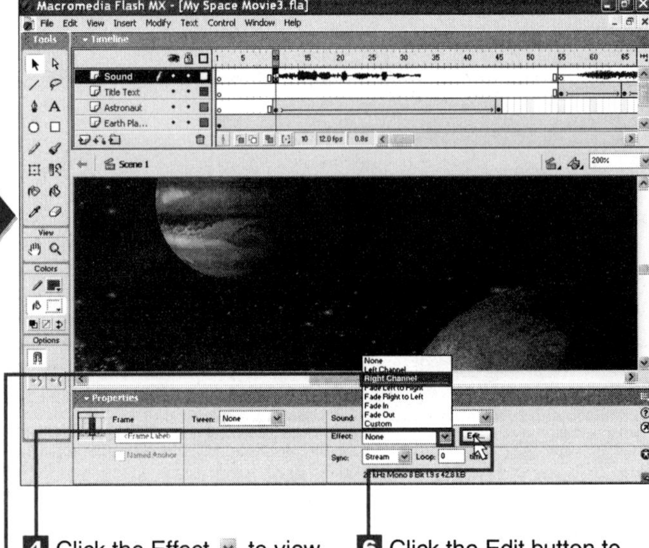

4 Click the Effect ▾ to view effects.

5 Click the Effect you want to apply.

■ Flash MX applies the effect to the sound.

6 Click the Edit button to edit the volume.

■ The Edit Envelope dialog box opens.

How do I create start and end points for my sound?

✔ To create a new start point for your sound, drag the Time In control marker, located at the far left side of the Sound Timeline bar separating the two channels in the Edit Envelope dialog box. To create a new end point, drag the Time Out control marker, located at the far right side of the Sound Timeline bar separating the two channels.

How many envelope handles can I use on a channel?

✔ You can add up to eight envelope handles to either channel and drag them up or down to adjust the sound volume.

What are audio channels?

✔ Flash MX audio channels simulate stereo audio channels that make sounds move from one speaker to the other. The top waveform box in the Edit Envelope dialog box represents the Right channel, the bottom box represents the Left channel.

Can I change the panning for a sound channel?

✔ Yes. Panning refers to the stereo effects of a sound. To create panning effects for your movie, you can adjust the volume by dragging envelope handles in either audio channel in the Edit Envelope dialog box.

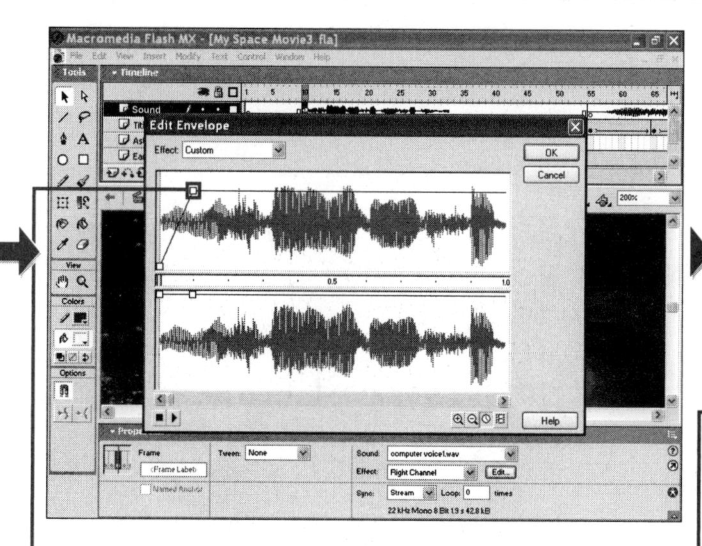

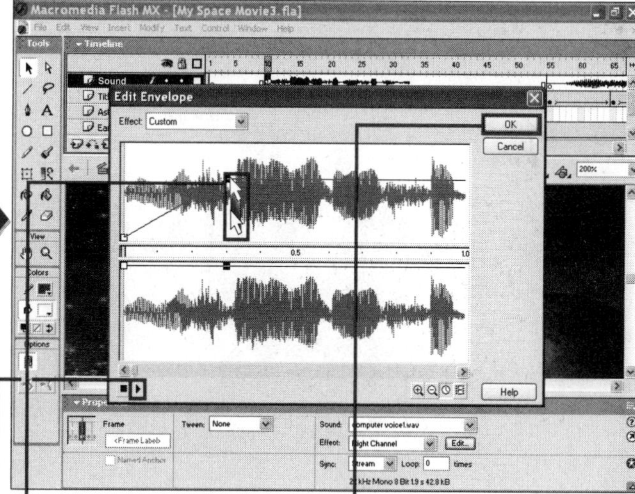

7 Click the waveform channel you want to edit.

■ Flash MX places an envelope handle (□) on the waveform.

Note: You can add up to eight handles to either channel for editing.

8 Click and drag the handle up or down to adjust the volume of the sound.

9 Click the Play button (▶) to hear the edit play.

■ You can continue adjusting the handles to edit the sound as needed.

10 When finished editing the sound, click OK.

Note: For greater sound-editing controls, you might need a full-featured sound-editing program.

■ Flash applies the edits to the selected sound.

SET AUDIO OUTPUT FOR EXPORT

You can control how you export sounds in your Flash MX files. Flash MX provides you with options for optimizing your sound files for export in the Publish Settings dialog box. Options include settings for compressing your sounds in ADPCM, MP3, or RAW format.

By default, Flash exports sounds in MP3 format using a bit rate of 16 Kbps. MP3 is the emerging standard for distributing audio on the Internet and has been available since Flash 4. MP3 efficiently compresses audio files, resulting in high bit rates and small file sizes.

The ADPCM compression format enables you to convert stereo to mono, which cuts down on the movie file size. The RAW format enables you to export your movie sounds without using any sound compression, which is fine if you export your movie to a floppy disk or CD-ROM.

The Publish Settings dialog box has options for controlling both event and streaming sounds. You can specify exactly how you want to compress the sounds in your movie for export. You can also change the settings for bit rate and quality. If you do not reset any sound options in the Publish Settings dialog box, Flash exports the file using the default settings.

SET AUDIO OUTPUT FOR EXPORT

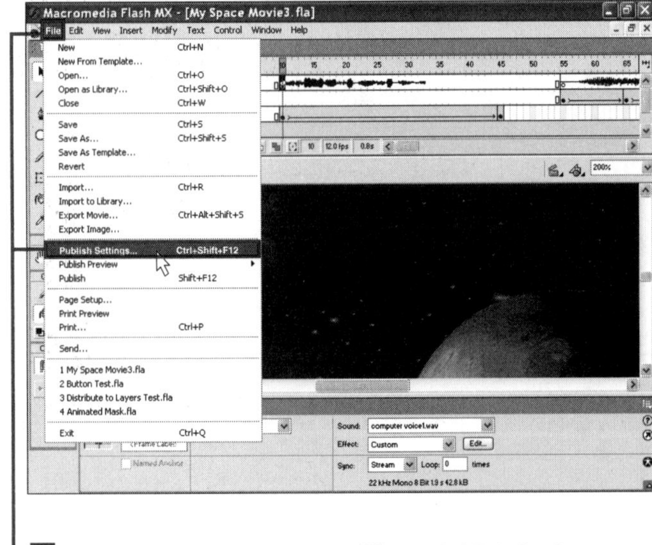

1 Click File.

2 Click Publish Settings.

■ The Publish Settings dialog box opens.

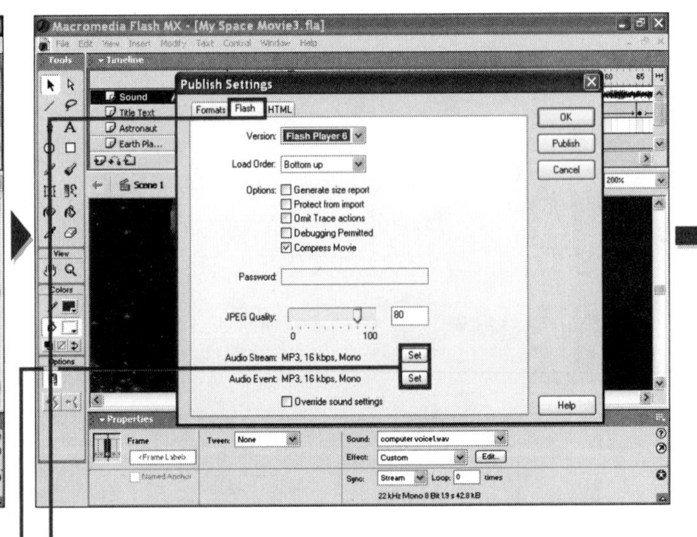

3 Click the Flash tab.

4 Click the Set button corresponding to the audio type you want to control.

Note: You can control the export quality of both streaming and event sounds.

Note: Clicking either Set button opens the Sound Settings dialog box.

What can I do to minimize the file size of my movie?

✔ You can do several things, particularly with the sound portions of your file. If you loop event sounds, use short sound clips. Avoid making streaming sounds loop. You can also get more out of the same sounds in a movie if you apply some editing techniques, such as fading sound in or out at different keyframes.

What is a good bit rate for MP3?

✔ For large music files, use a setting of 64 Kbps. For speech or voice files, use 24 or 32 Kbps. To set near-CD quality, use a setting of 112 or 128 Kbps. Use 16 Kbps settings for simple button sounds, or larger audio sounds where quality is not crucial.

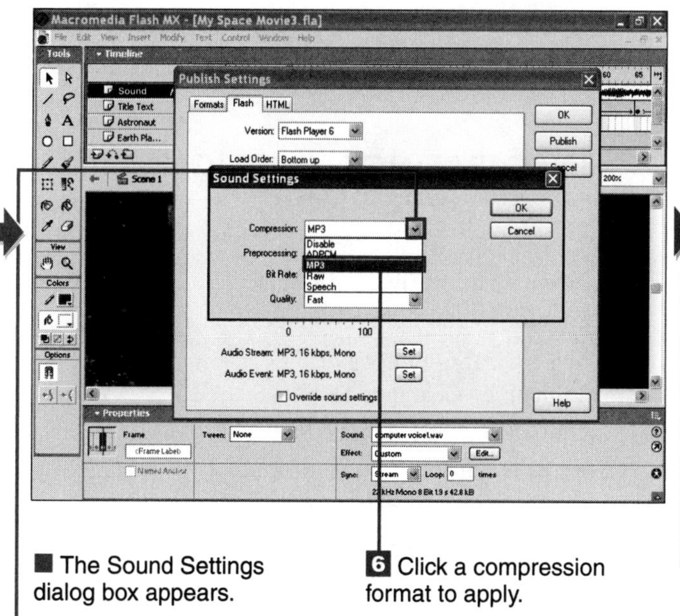

■ The Sound Settings dialog box appears.

5 Click ▾ to view available compression formats.

6 Click a compression format to apply.

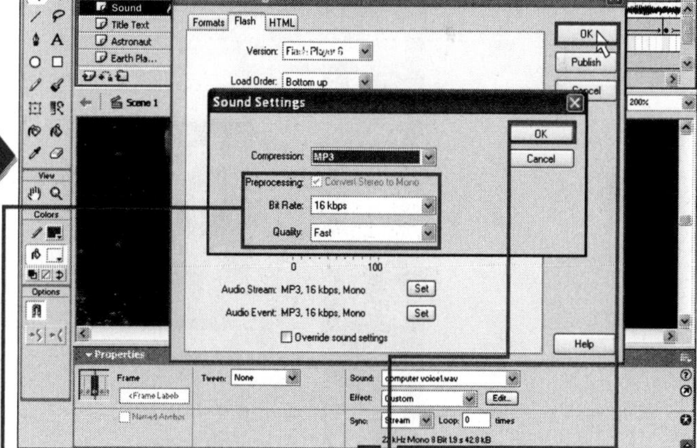

■ Depending on the format you select, the remaining options in the Sound Settings dialog box reflect settings associated with your selection.

Note: You can make changes to the remaining settings.

7 Click OK to close the Sound Settings dialog box.

8 Click OK.

■ The Publish Settings dialog box closes and Flash MX saves your settings.

SECTION VIII

29) CREATING ANIMATION IN FLASH

30) CREATING ANIMATION BY TWEENING

ANIMATING IN FLASH

INTRODUCTION TO ANIMATION

Animation features are one of the most exciting aspects of Flash MX. You can animate objects, synchronize the animation with sounds, add backgrounds, animate buttons, and much more. After you complete a Flash animation, you can place it on a Web page or distribute it for others to view.

Using Animations

You can use Flash animations to present a lively message or to simply entertain. Animations you create in Flash MX can make a Web site come to life. For example, you can create a cartoon to play in the banner for your site, or animate buttons for the user to click. You can make your company logo grow in size, or make your company tagline glow. You can create interactive presentations with instructions on how to complete workplace tasks, or make an online tutorial for clients that explains your latest product developments and applications.

You can create animation effects for all kinds of elements associated with Web pages, such as an animated preloader timer that displays how long it takes to complete a download or an animated cursor that users can click to view different parts of your site. The various ways you can use animations are limitless, and with the powerful Flash animation tools, you can create a site equal to your vision.

Work with Animations

Animation is simply a change that occurs between two or more frames in a movie. Animation effects use frames to hold illustrated scenes or objects. The scene or object changes slightly from frame to frame to create the illusion of movement.

The change can be the slight movement of an object from one area on the screen to another, or it can be in the color, intensity, size or shape of the object. Any change you make to an object makes it appear to be animated during playback of your movie. For example, you might have an animation of a ball bouncing. Each frame displays a "snapshot" of the ball in various bouncing positions. When you play the animation back, each frame appears for less than a moment before the next frame replaces it. The effect is a ball that seems to bounce.

Back in the early days of animating, cartoonists and other animators painted objects and scenery on transparent cels. The cels were stacked to create an image. A movie camera then took a snapshot of that image to create a single frame. The animators reused some of the cels for the next frame, such as backgrounds, and changed other cels to create the movement of an object across the foreground. The end result was a strip of film that, when played back through a projector, created the illusion of movement.

Flash MX uses similar principles today to create animations. Instead of transparent cels, you add content to frames and layers in a digital Timeline, and then stack the layers to create depth. Anytime you want the content to change, you can add keyframes to the Timeline and vary the position or appearance of the content. When the animation, or movie, is played back, the content appears to move.

Instead of using a film projector for playback, Flash movies use a Flash Player application. The Flash Player is a special program designed to view Flash content.

Using frames and layers, you can create simple or sophisticated animation effects for your Web site or Flash files to distribute to others. To learn more about distributing movies using the Flash Player, see Chapter 34.

Types of Animation

You can apply animation in one of two ways in Flash MX: you can create animation manually frame-by-frame, or you can let Flash help you create the illusion of motion through a process called tweened animation.

Frame-by-frame animation, as its name implies, involves creating the illusion of movement by subtly changing the appearance of the content of your movie from frame to frame. This method of animation gives you a great deal of control over how the content changes across the Flash Timeline. You determine how much of a change appears from one frame to the next, whether it is very slight or very pronounced. Keep in mind when creating frame-by-frame animations that this type of animation increases the file size of the movie.

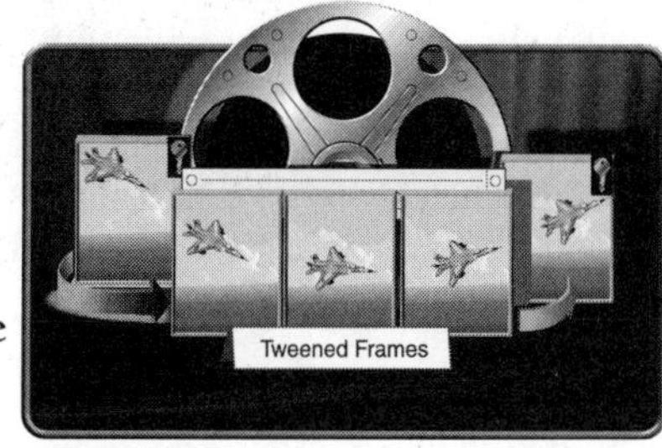

Tweened animation is the second method of animation in Flash MX. With tweened animation, you tell Flash to calculate the in-between frame content from one keyframe to the next keyframe. Flash then draws the in-between frame changes to get from the first keyframe to the next. The term tweened comes from this process of in-between framing.

Tweened animation is faster, easier to edit, and consumes less file size. This is because Flash MX does all the hard work for you by describing the subtle changes between frames mathematically.

INTRODUCTION TO FRAMES

Frames are the backbone of your animation effects. When you start a new Flash file, it opens with a single layer and hundreds of frames, called placeholder frames, in the Timeline. Before you start animating objects, you need to understand how frames work.

Frame Rates

The number of frames you use in your Flash movie combined with the speed at which they play determines the length of your movie. By default, new Flash MX files you create use a frame rate of 12 frames per second, or 12 fps. You can set a frame rate higher or lower than the default if needed.

The default frame rate is well suited for playing movies on the Web. Compared to television frame rates of 30 frames per second, and movie frame rates of 24 frames per second, a Flash animation frame rate of 12 frames per second may seem a bit slow. However, assigning a faster frame rate may result in smoother play, but it requires a computer that can keep up with the speed and it requires more frames in the animation, thus increasing the size of your movie. Anything slower than 12 fps will cause the movie to appear jumpy when played.

Because there are so many different types of computer processors used today, many of which cannot process higher frame rates, using a common frame rate is the best way to reach the widest audience for your movies. When you set a frame rate in Flash MX, you are setting the maximum rate at which the movie can play. There is no minimum rate, which means slower computers may play the movie slower than the frame rate you assign.

Types of Frames

Frames appear as tiny boxes in the Flash MX Timeline. You can work with several different types of frames in the Timeline: placeholder frames, keyframes, static or regular frames, and tweened frames. A placeholder frame is merely an empty frame that has no content. When your movie reaches an empty frame, it stops playing. With the exception of the first frame in a new layer, frames are all placeholders until you assign them to another frame type.

Keyframes

A *keyframe* defines a change in animation, such as an object moving or taking on a new appearance. Because keyframes are the only frames that define key changes in a movie, they are crucial in creating your animation effects. By default, Flash MX inserts a blank keyframe for you in the first frame of every new layer you add to the Timeline. You can add and delete keyframes as needed. Keyframes are identified with black bullets in the Timeline.

When you add a keyframe, Flash duplicates the content from the previous keyframe and inserts it in the new keyframe. This technique makes it easy to tweak the contents slightly to create the illusion of movement between frames. If the content of the previous keyframe is blank, for example, the new keyframe shows nothing, but if the previous keyframe held an object, the new keyframe holds the same object. To create animation, you can move the second object slightly.

Tweened Frames

You can use tweened frames to create tweened animation effects in Flash MX. With tweening, Flash calculates the number of frames between two keyframes to create movement.

Tweened frames have an arrow extending between the start and end keyframes in the tween effect. In addition, all of the frames associated with a tween effect, including keyframes, are shaded in another tint. Learn more about creating tweened frames in Chapter 30.

Regular Frames

Another type of frame you use in Flash is the *static frame*. Static frames (or *regular frames*) display the same content as the previous frame in the Timeline. Static frames must be preceded by a keyframe. Static frames are used to hold content that you want to remain visible until you add another keyframe in the layer.

For example, if your movie has five static frames between two keyframes, all five frames between the two keyframes will show the same content as the first keyframe. If you make a change to the content in the first keyframe, all the static frames that appear after it will reflect the change as well.

Placing static frames between keyframes slows down the speed at which the animation plays in your movie. For example, if five static frames between two keyframes seems too fast during playback, you can add more static frames to the sequence to slow down the animation effect.

SET MOVIE DIMENSIONS AND SPEED

You can specify the size and speed of a movie before you begin building the animation you want the movie to contain. You can use the Document Properties dialog box to set movie size and speed. Taking time to set the movie dimensions and speed now will save you time and prevent headaches later. If you resize the movie after you have created it, you may find yourself having to reposition elements on numerous layers to make things fit.

The vertical and horizontal dimensions of the stage determine the size of your movie, which in turn specifies the size of the screen used to play the movie. You can make your movie any size, but most users prefer to keep the size relative to the largest objects in the movie.

The play speed of a movie is measured by the number of frames per second, or *fps*. By default, Flash MX assigns a frame rate of 12 fps, a good setting for animation delivered over the Web. You can set a higher rate as needed, but setting the rate too high will cause the images to blur. Set the rate too low and the animation may appear choppy.

SET MOVIE DIMENSIONS AND SPEED

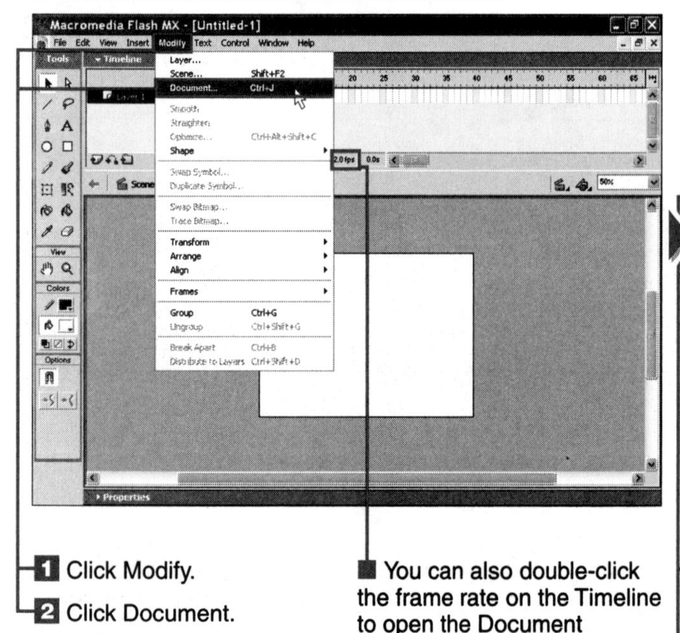

1 Click Modify.

2 Click Document.

■ You can also double-click the frame rate on the Timeline to open the Document Properties dialog box.

■ The Document Properties dialog box opens.

3 Type the number of frames per second you want the movie to play in the Frame Rate text box.

Note: If you use a higher fps setting, slower computers might not be able to play back your movie properly.

What is the maximum frame rate I can use?

✔ The maximum rate you should set is 24 fps, unless you are exporting your movie as a QuickTime or Windows AVI video file, which can handle higher rates without consuming computer processor power. If you set a higher frame rate, slower computers struggle to play at such speeds.

Can I vary the frame rate throughout my movie?

✔ No. After you set a frame rate, that rate is in effect for the entire movie file. You can, however, vary the speed of animation sequences by adding or removing frames.

Can I tell which frame rate is in effect without opening the Document Properties dialog box?

✔ Yes. Look at the status bar at the bottom of the Timeline. The status bar displays the current frame number, frame rate, and elapsed time for the movie. You can quickly open the document box by double-clicking the frame rate number in the status bar of the Timeline.

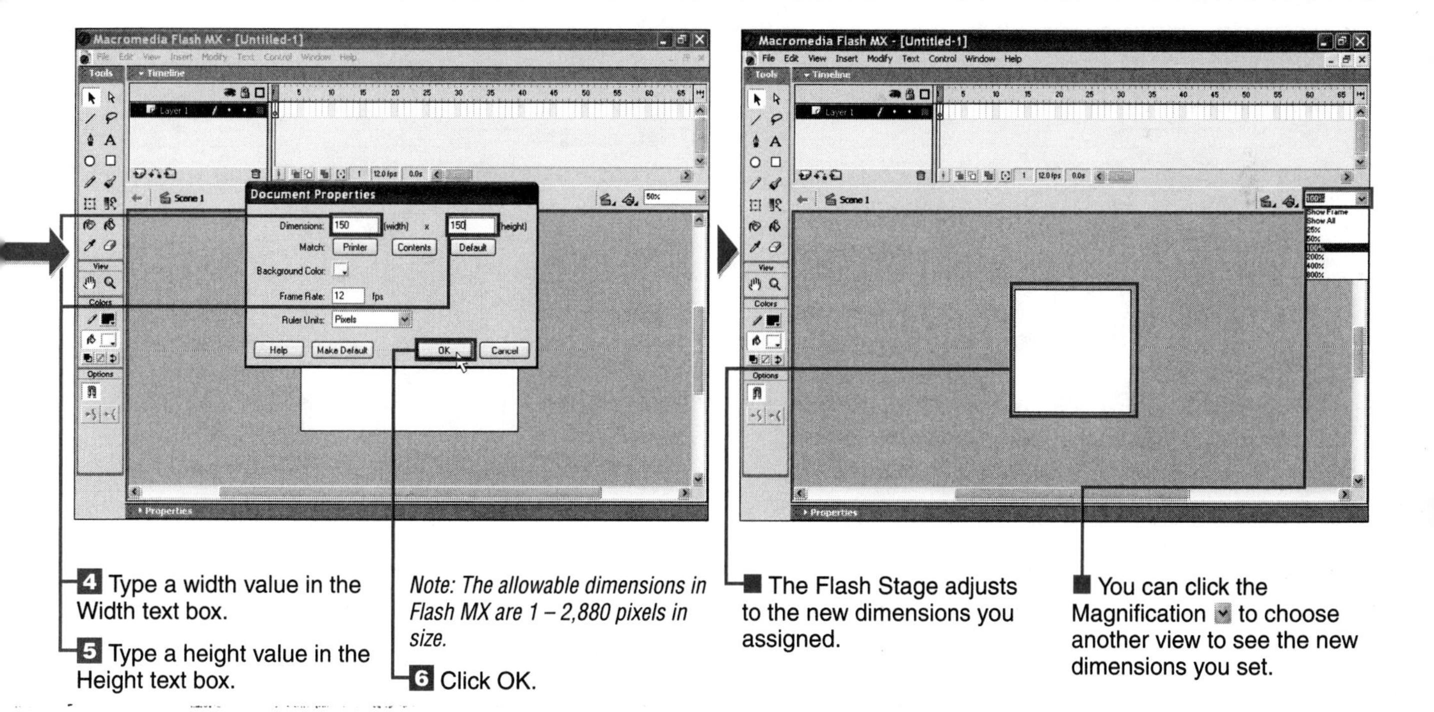

4 Type a width value in the Width text box.

5 Type a height value in the Height text box.

Note: The allowable dimensions in Flash MX are 1 – 2,880 pixels in size.

6 Click OK.

■ The Flash Stage adjusts to the new dimensions you assigned.

■ You can click the Magnification ▾ to choose another view to see the new dimensions you set.

ADD FRAMES

You can add frames to add content and length to your Flash movies. When you add a new layer or start a new file, Flash MX starts with one keyframe in the Timeline and many placeholder frames.

Adding frames is as easy as adding pages to a document. Flash lets you specify exactly which kind of frame to add and allows you to add as many frames as you need. You can add keyframes, regular frames, and blank keyframes, and you can add more than one at a time.

You add keyframes to define changes in the appearance of your animation, such as changing the placement or color of an object. When you add a keyframe, Flash copies the contents of the previous keyframe, which you can then edit to create a change in the animation sequence.

You can also add regular frames, to repeat the content of the keyframe preceding them. Regular frames help extend the animation effect between keyframes. You can also add regular frames to slow down the change that occurs between two keyframes. For example, in an animation sequence of a bouncing ball, you can add regular frames to a bounce sequence to make the effect seem to slow down.

ADD FRAMES

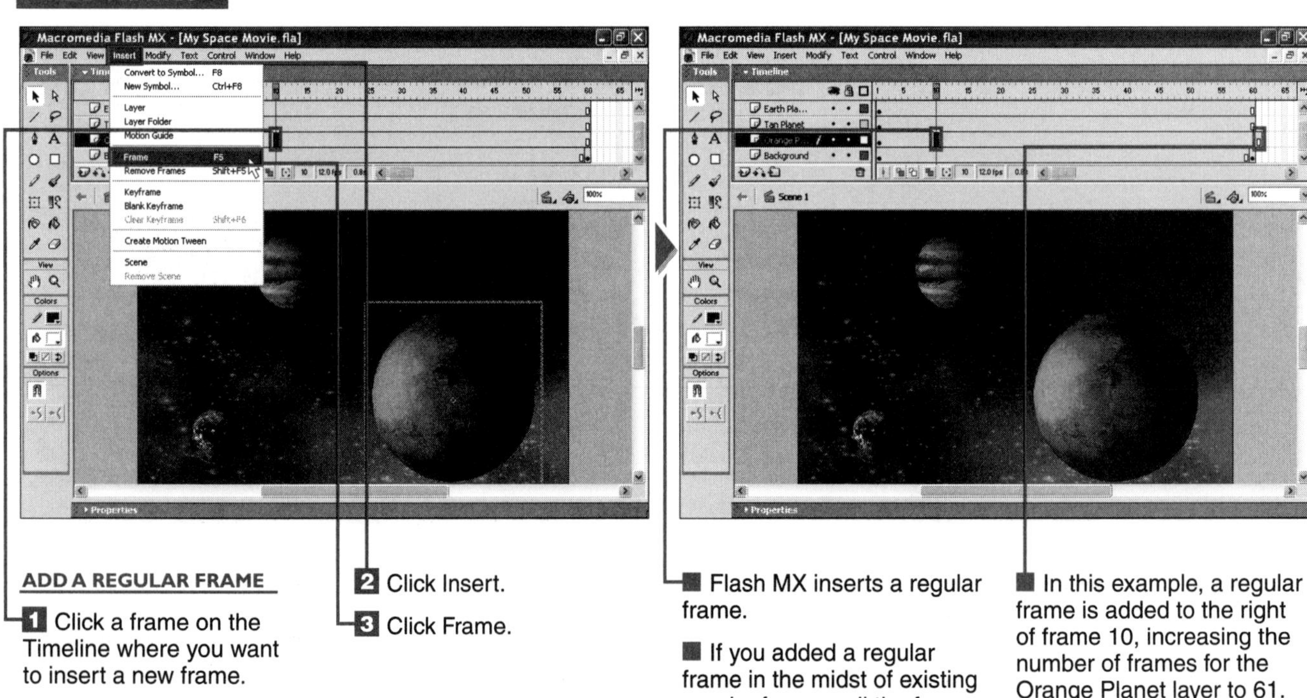

ADD A REGULAR FRAME

1 Click a frame on the Timeline where you want to insert a new frame.

2 Click Insert.

3 Click Frame.

■ Flash MX inserts a regular frame.

■ If you added a regular frame in the midst of existing regular frames, all the frames to the right of the insertion move over to make room for the new frame.

■ In this example, a regular frame is added to the right of frame 10, increasing the number of frames for the Orange Planet layer to 61.

How can I tell which frames are which in the Timeline?

✔ You can identify Flash frames by the following characteristics:

- Keyframes with content appear with a solid bullet in the Timeline.
- Blank keyframes, which have no content added yet, appear as a hollow box in the preceding frame.
- In-between frames that contain content appear tinted or grayed on the Timeline.
- In-between frames without content appear as a block of white.
- Empty frames appear white.

Can I undo a frame I just added?

✔ Yes. You can click the Edit menu and click Undo to remove a newly added frame, however, you must activate the Undo command twice to completely remove the added frame.

Can I add frames to a motion tween?

✔ Yes. Tweened animation frames work the same way as frame-by-frame animation frames. You can add keyframes and regular frames as needed. See Chapter 30 for more about creating tweened animations.

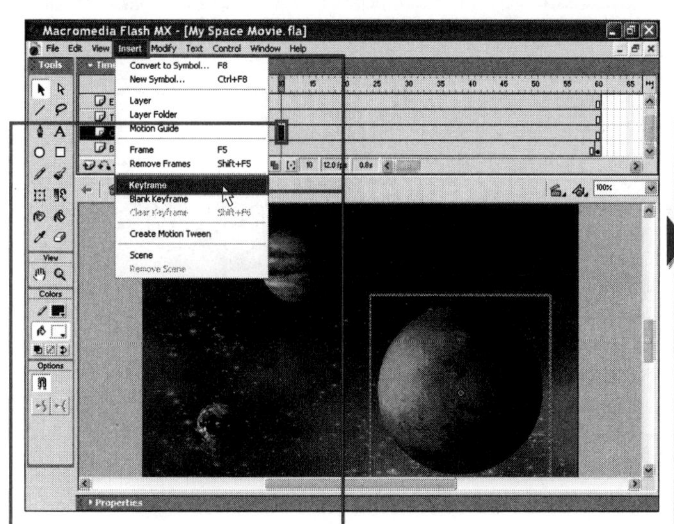

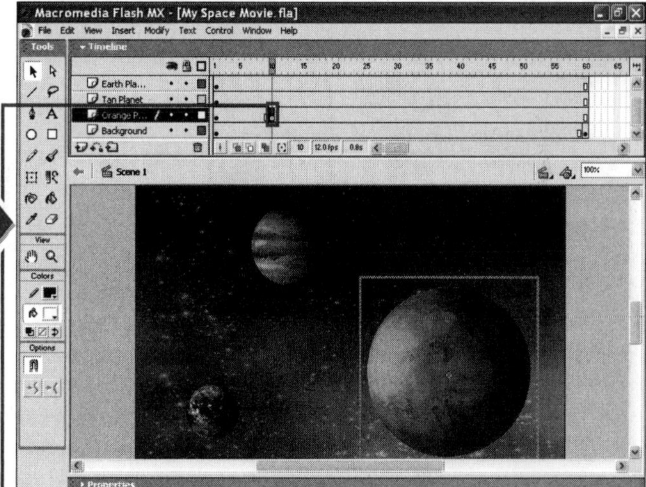

ADD A KEYFRAME

1 Click the frame on the Timeline which you want to turn into a keyframe.

Note: To select a single frame within a group of frames, press Ctrl (⌘) while clicking the frame.

2 Click Insert.

3 Click Keyframe.

■ Flash MX inserts a keyframe, marked by a solid bullet in the Timeline.

■ If the frame you selected in step 1 was a regular frame, Flash MX converts it to a keyframe.

■ If the frame was an empty frame, Flash MX inserts regular frames in between the last regular frame or keyframe up to the frame you clicked in step 1.

CONTINUED

ADD FRAMES (CONTINUED)

You can add different types of frames to each layer in the Timeline of your movie. You can add a blank keyframe when you want to introduce new content in your movie. Unlike a default keyframe, which copies the content from the previous keyframe in the sequence, a blank keyframe is completely empty of content. You often insert a blank keyframe when you want to start a new animation segment in your movie.

You can also add multiple frames at a time in Flash MX. This technique is useful when you are creating an animation sequence that needs to be extended in the Timeline in order to play more slowly in playback. Rather than insert one regular frame at a time, you can insert multiple frames, such as five frames at once.

You can also delete frames you no longer need or change the status of a frame from a keyframe to a regular frame. To delete or change the status of a frame, see page 516.

ADD FRAMES (CONTINUED)

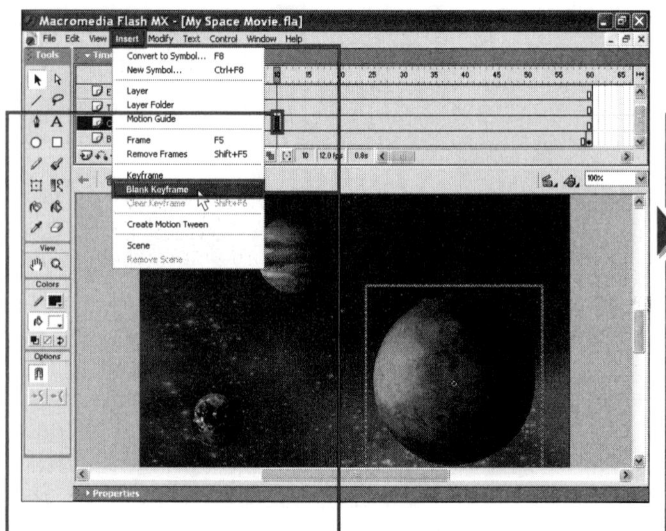

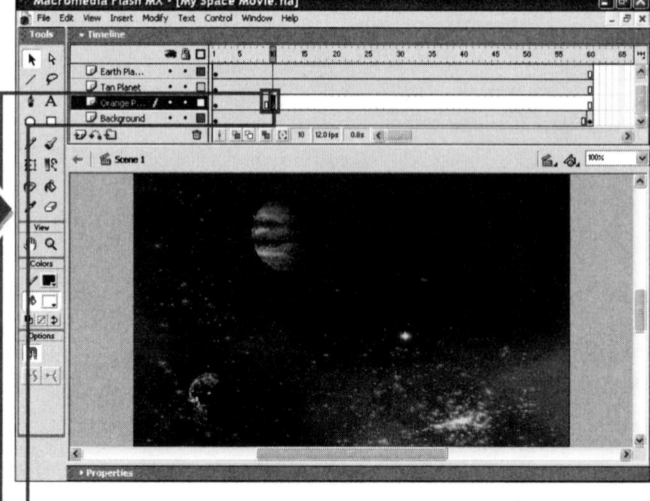

ADD A BLANK KEYFRAME

1 Click a frame on the Timeline where you want to insert a blank keyframe.

Note: To select a single frame within a group of frames, press Ctrl (⌘) while clicking the frame.

2 Click Insert.

3 Click Blank Keyframe.

■ Flash MX inserts a blank keyframe.

■ A hollow box precedes the blank keyframe.

Note: In this example, a blank keyframe is inserted in the midst of existing frames, thus creating blank frames after the blank keyframe.

Can I change the size of the Timeline frames?

✔ You can change the size of the frames in the Timeline using the Timeline Options menu. By default, the frames appear in Normal size. To change the size of the frames, click the Timeline Options Menu button ( ). Click the frame size you want to apply. You can change the size to Tiny or Small to fit more frames in the Timeline view, or select Medium or Large to make the frames easier to see. The Preview options let you see thumbnails of frame content in the Timeline.

Is there another shortcut for adding frames?

✔ Yes. You can right-click a frame to view a pop-up list of commands related to frames, including the commands for inserting different types of frames. Simply make your selection from the shortcut menu and the frame is added.

Can I resize the Timeline to view more layers?

✔ Yes. You can drag the bottom border of the Timeline to increase its size.

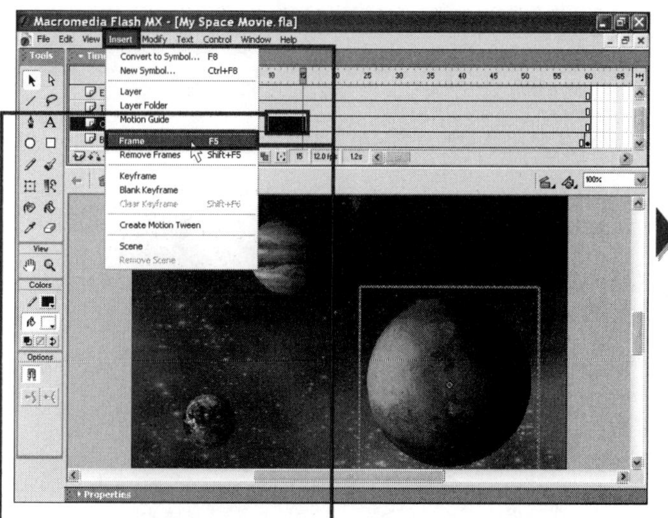

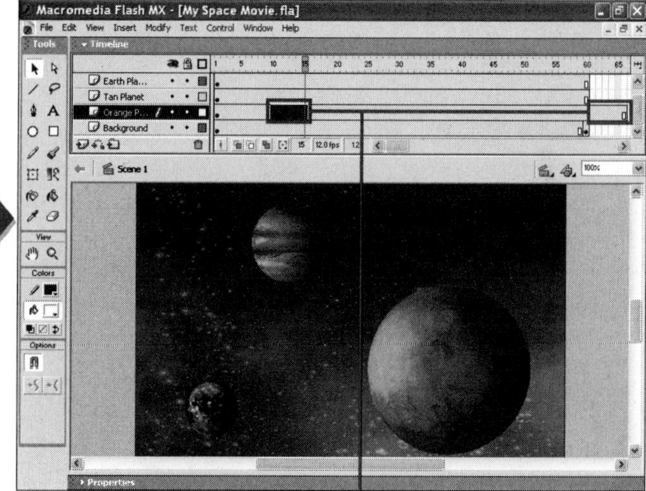

ADD MULTIPLE FRAMES

1 Click to select two or more frames.

■ To select multiple frames, click the first frame in the range, press and hold down Shift, and click the last frame in the range.

Note: To select frames, see page 514.

2 Click Insert.

3 Click Frame to insert regular frames.

■ You can click Keyframe or Blank Keyframe to make the new frames all keyframes.

■ Flash MX inserts the same number of new frames and lengthens the movie by the same number of frames.

SELECT FRAMES

You can select frames in the Flash Timeline in order to add content or to edit the frames. You must also select frames in order to remove them from the Timeline. You can use a couple of selection techniques when working with frames.

When you select a single frame, it appears highlighted in the Timeline and the frame number appears in the status bar at the bottom of the Timeline. The playhead also appears directly above the selected frame. When you select multiple frames, the number of the last frame in the group appears on the Timeline status bar.

Selecting keyframes and placeholder frames that have no content is easy, but selecting in-between frames is a bit more difficult. Individual frames that are part of an animation sequence, such as a tweened animation, are not selected with a simple click. In fact, when you click an in-between frame, the surrounding range of frames are also selected. You can use keyboard shortcuts to select a single frame from within a range of frames, as shown in the steps below.

To deselect a selected frame or range of frames, simply click anywhere outside the selected frames. Flash MX immediately deselects the frames.

SELECT FRAMES

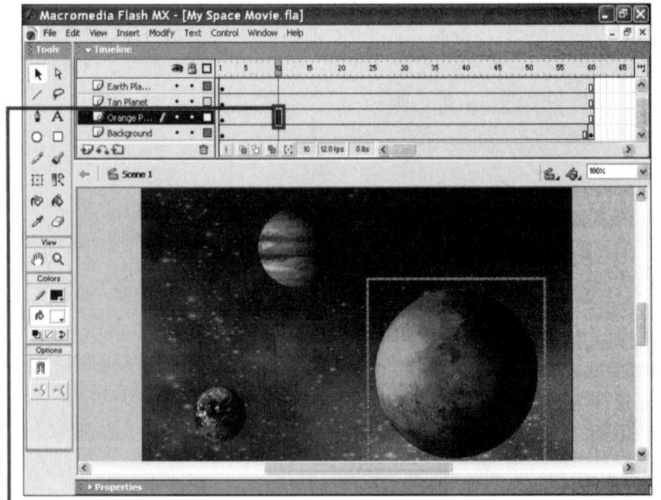

SELECT A SINGLE FRAME

1 Click the frame to select it.

■ Flash MX highlights the frame in the Timeline.

Note: If you have difficulty selecting a regular frame between two keyframes, press and hold Ctrl (⌘), and then click the frame you want to select.

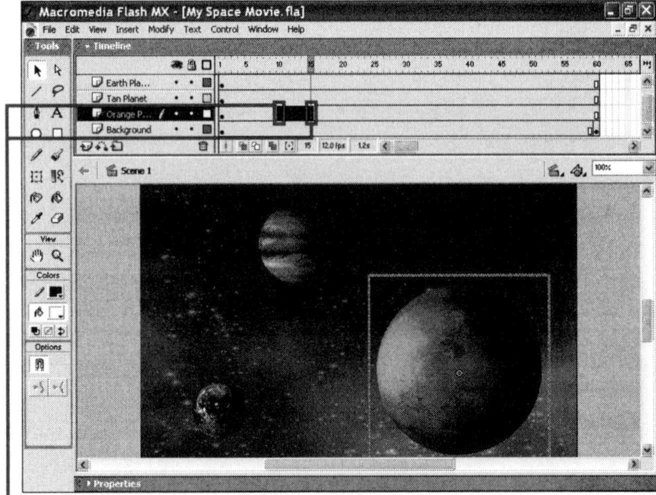

SELECT MULTIPLE FRAMES

1 Click the first frame in the range of frames you want to select.

2 Press and hold down Shift and click the last frame in the range.

■ Flash MX selects all the frames in-between.

■ To select multiple frames between two keyframes, click anywhere between the two keyframes.

MODIFY FRAME PROPERTIES

You can use the Property inspector to define properties for frames, such as labels and tweening status. Each frame type you add in Flash includes default properties.

By default, you identify a frame by the frame number. However, the longer and more complex your movie, the more you may need to identify frames by descriptive labels. A label can help you immediately recognize the contents of a frame.

You can use frame labels to organize frames with actions, frames with animation effects, and so on. Frame labels appear on the Timeline with tiny red flag icons. Depending on the length of the label, some labels appear cut off. You can view the full frame label by moving the mouse pointer over the label to display a tooltip box.

In addition to labels, you can also change the animation status of a frame. By default, frames are static unless you add animation and assign tweening status. Tweening status is a special frame status for creating motion in an animation sequence. When you select a tweening status, additional options appear in the Property inspector, such as controls for tween speed or ease, rotation, path orientation, and more.

MODIFY FRAME PROPERTIES

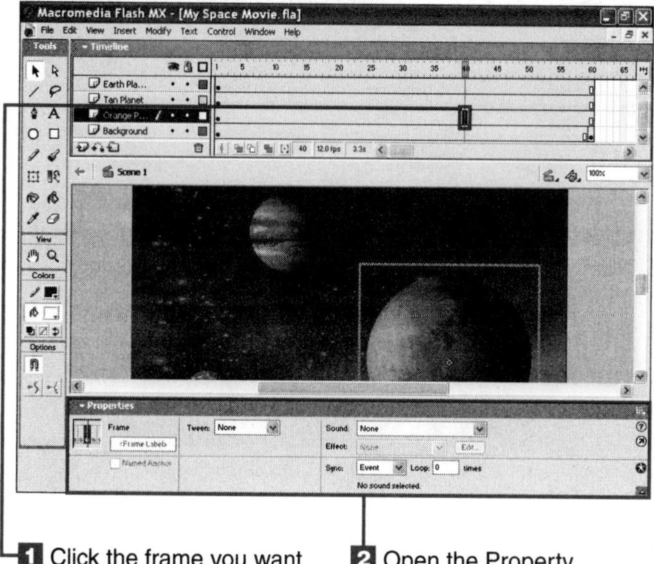

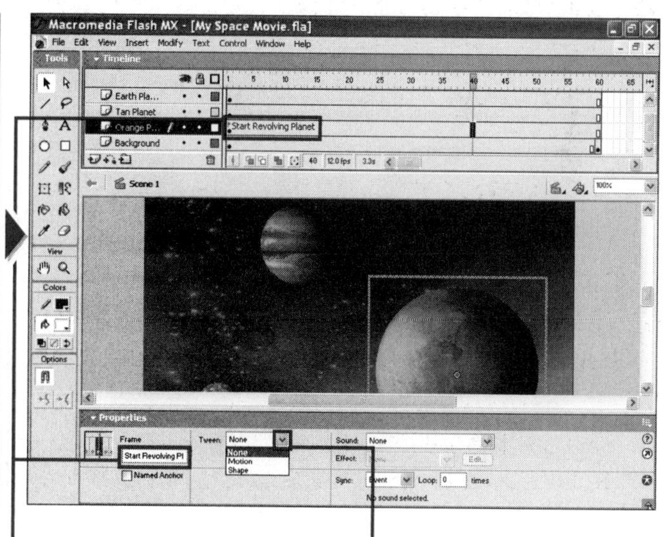

1 Click the frame you want to modify.

2 Open the Property inspector panel.

Note: To open and close the Property inspector, see page 346.

3 Type a label for the frame.

■ The label appears in the Timeline.

4 Click ▾ to change the frame tween.

■ The new frame type is assigned.

Note: To learn more about tweening, see Chapter 30.

DELETE FRAMES OR CHANGE KEYFRAME STATUS

You can remove frames you no longer need or change them to a type of frame that you can use. For example, you may decide a particular animation sequence between two keyframes runs too slowly during playback. You can remove several regular frames to speed up the sequence. Or you might make a drastic change in your animation and decide you no longer need a particular keyframe in the sequence.

You can use the Remove Frames command to remove a single frame or several frames completely from the Timeline. To remove a keyframe from the Timeline, you must select both the keyframe and all the in-between frames associated with it; otherwise, the Remove Frames command does not successfully remove the keyframe.

Instead of removing a keyframe completely, however, you can change the status of the keyframe by using the Clear Keyframe command. This command removes the keyframe status of the frame and demotes it to a regular frame. When you change the status of a keyframe, all in-between frames are altered as well.

DELETE FRAMES

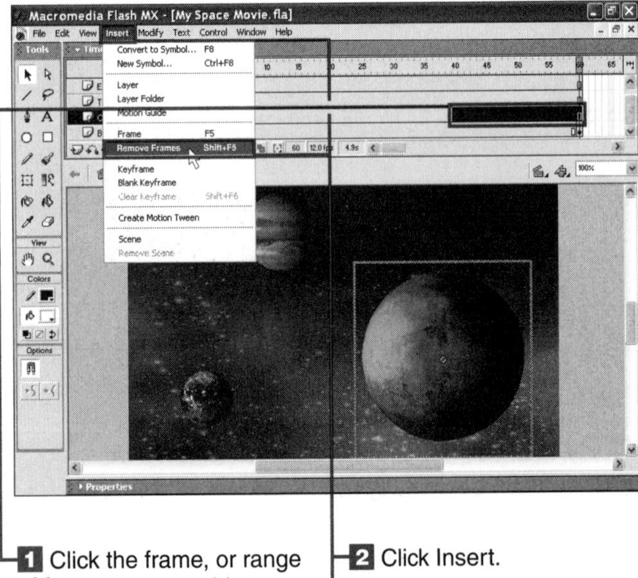

1 Click the frame, or range of frames, you want to delete.

2 Click Insert.

3 Click Remove Frames.

Note: To select a single frame within a group of frames, press Ctrl (⌘) while clicking the frame.

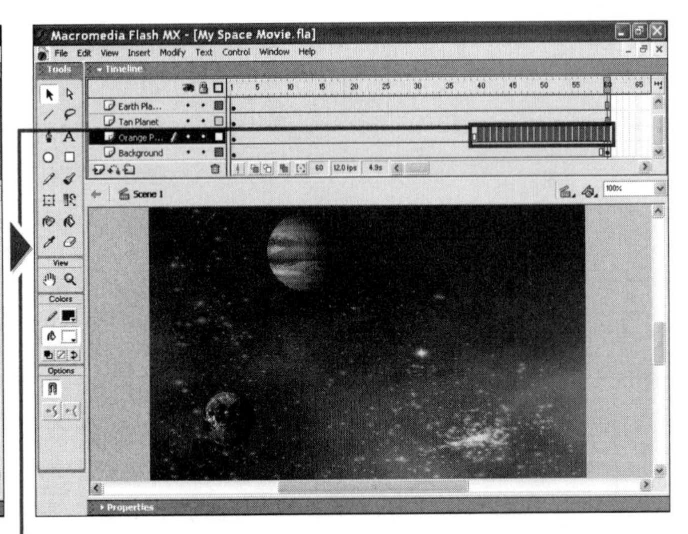

■ Flash MX removes the frame and any existing frames to the right move over to fill the void.

Note: To select multiple frames within a group of frames, press Ctrl (⌘) while clicking the frames.

Can I remove a range of frames?

✔ Yes. First select the range of frames you want to delete by clicking the first frame in the group, and then dragging to highlight the remaining frames. After all the frames in the range are selected, you can apply the Remove Frames command.

If I delete a frame, is the frame label removed as well?

✔ Yes. Any time you remove a frame from the Timeline, any associated frame labels are removed as well.

Can I undo a frame deletion?

✔ Yes. If you click the Edit menu and click Undo immediately after removing a frame, Flash MX undoes the action.

Why does Flash MX prevent me from clicking a frame?

✔ If you are trying to remove a regular frame between two keyframes, you may have difficulty selecting a single frame. Press and hold down Ctrl (⌘) and click the frame you want to remove.

CHANGE KEYFRAME STATUS

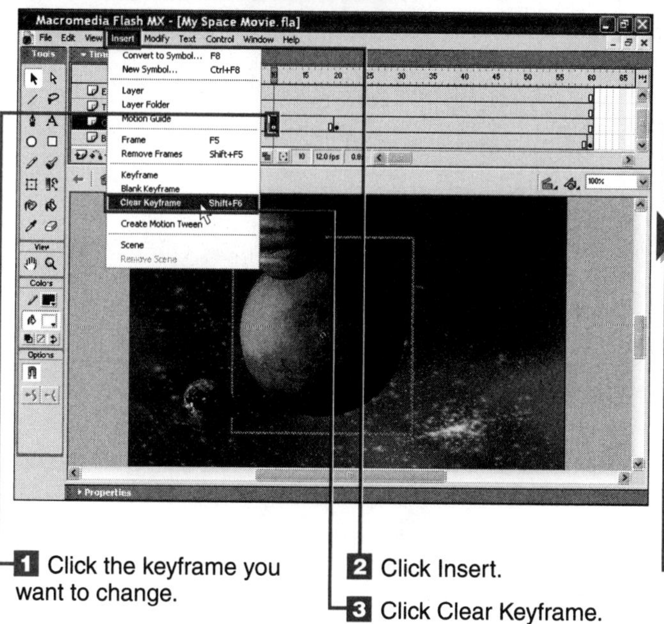

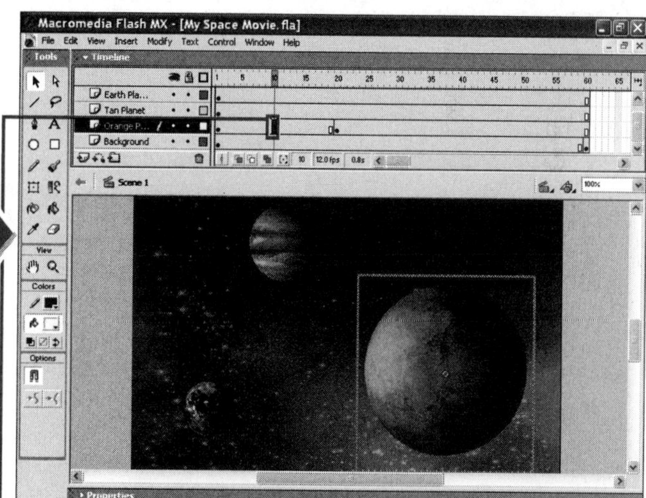

1 Click the keyframe you want to change.

2 Click Insert.

3 Click Clear Keyframe.

■ Flash MX converts the frame to a regular frame, and changes the frame to match the contents of the previous keyframe.

Note: You cannot change the status of the first keyframe in a layer.

CREATE FRAME-BY-FRAME ANIMATION

You can create the illusion of movement in a Flash movie by changing the placement or appearance of the Stage content from keyframe to keyframe in the Flash Timeline. This type of animation is called, appropriately, frame-by-frame animation. With frame-by-frame animation, you control exactly how your content changes from one keyframe to the next. It is important that the object, or objects, in the frames experience some sort of change, whether that change involves a different color, size, or placement on the Stage. Without any changes, your animation sequence will not appear animated.

You can add an animation sequence to any layer in your movie, and you can use one sequence right after another. For example, you might start your movie with a fade-in animation of your company logo, then jump to a completely different animation detailing a new product or service.

You can animate an object using as many keyframes as you need. The placement of those keyframes in the Timeline is entirely up to you. You can place one keyframe right after another, or you can space them out with regular frames in between. The more regular frames that appear between two keyframes, the slower the animation effect. Less regular frames between keyframes speeds up the effect. The example below shows you how to use six keyframes to build a frame-by-frame animation.

CREATE FRAME-BY-FRAME ANIMATION

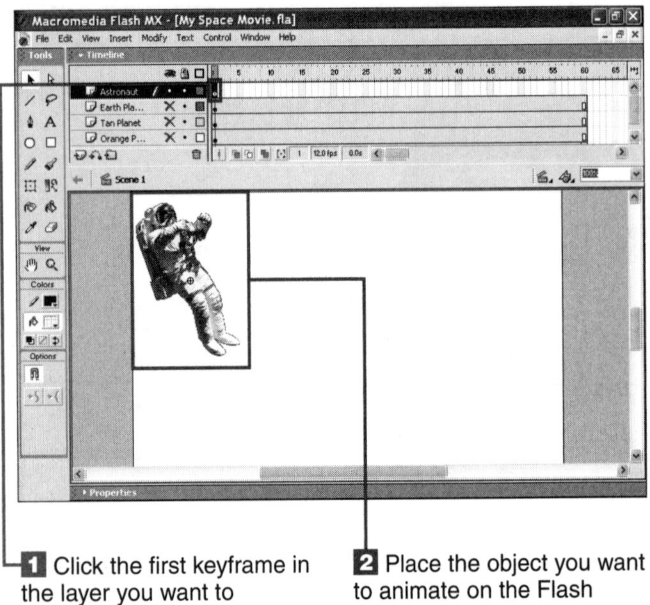

1 Click the first keyframe in the layer you want to animate.

2 Place the object you want to animate on the Flash Stage.

■ You can add an instance of a symbol from the Library to animate, or you can use the drawing tools to create an object.

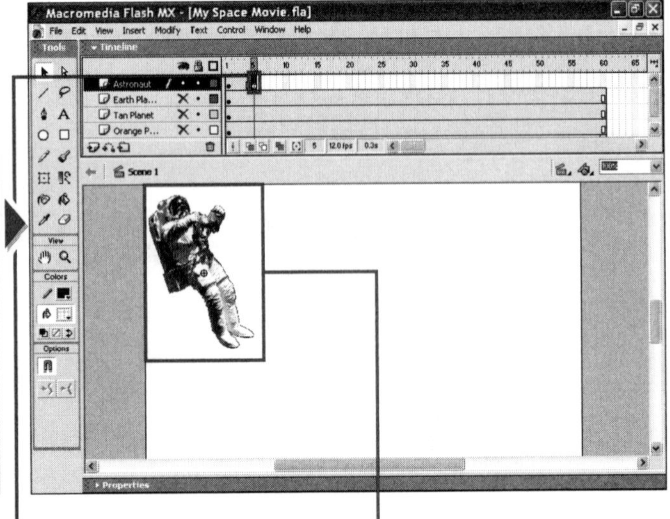

3 Click the next frame in the Timeline where you want to continue the animation.

Note: You can continue the animation in the very next frame, or space the animation out with a few regular frames in between.

■ Flash MX inserts a keyframe that duplicates the previous keyframe's contents.

Can I add in-between frames to the animation?

✔ Yes. To slow down the animation sequence, especially if the changes between keyframes are happening too fast to see very well, just add regular frames between keyframes in your frame-by-frame animation. To add in-between frames, first click a keyframe, then click the Insert menu, and click Frame or press F5 on the keyboard. Flash MX adds a regular frame after the keyframe. You can keep adding more regular frames to achieve the effect you want. When you play back the movie, the animation appears to slow down.

How do I edit a symbol as I create the animation?

✔ To make changes to a symbol you use in your movie, first select the keyframe where you want to introduce a change. To open the symbol in symbol-edit mode, double-click the symbol. After editing, click the Scene name to return to movie-edit mode. You can switch back and forth between edit modes as needed when creating your animation sequence. Editing a symbol changes every use of the symbol in the animation. Editing an instance of the symbol affects only that instance.

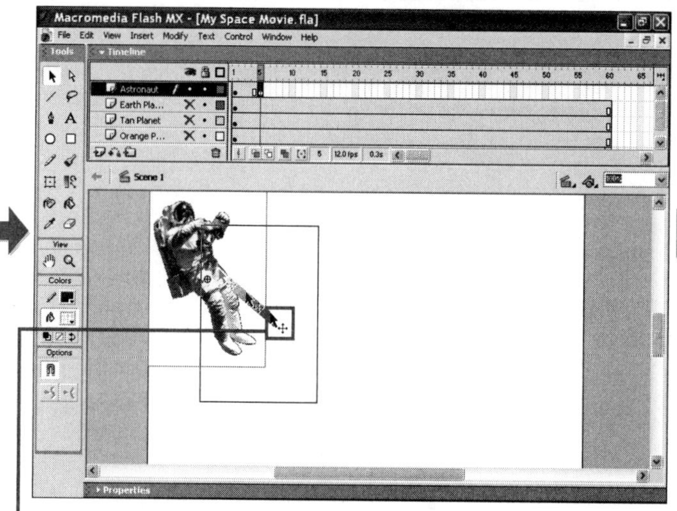

4 Change the object slightly to animate.

■ You can move the object slightly on the Stage, or change the appearance of an object, such as color or size.

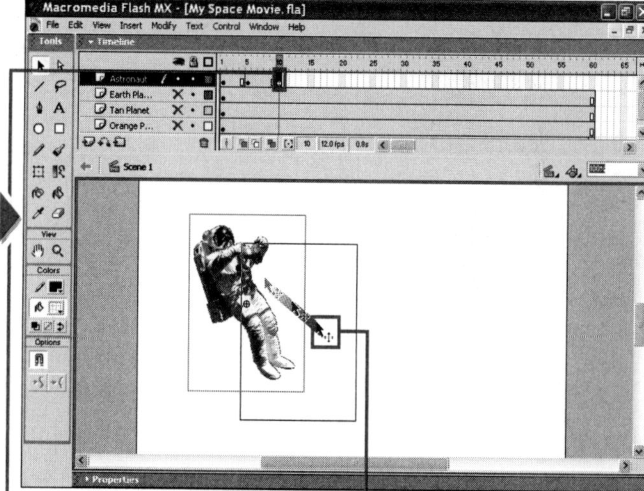

5 Click the next frame in the layer and add a keyframe.

■ Flash MX inserts a keyframe that duplicates the contents of the second keyframe.

6 Change the object appearance or position slightly to differ from the previous keyframe contents.

CONTINUED

CREATE FRAME-BY-FRAME ANIMATION (CONTINUED)

You can create all kinds of animation effects using frame-by-frame animation techniques. For example, a simple circle can become a bouncing ball if moved strategically around the Stage in each frame of the movie. A text box can appear to glow if you change the text color and boldness from one keyframe to the next.

If you are new to Flash MX, you can quickly learn the principles of frame-by-frame animation by creating a simple animation sequence, such as making an object move across the Flash Stage. The example in this section shows how to create the illusion of an astronaut moving through space by moving the astronaut slightly down the Stage in each keyframe. By the last keyframe, the astronaut reaches the bottom. When the animation is played back, the astronaut appears to drop from the top-left corner to the bottom-right corner.

You can animate an object on or off the Stage. By starting the animation sequence in the work area surrounding the Stage and moving the object onto the Stage, you create the illusion of the object entering into the frame. Objects placed in the work area do not appear in the published or exported movie.

CREATE FRAME-BY-FRAME ANIMATION (CONTINUED)

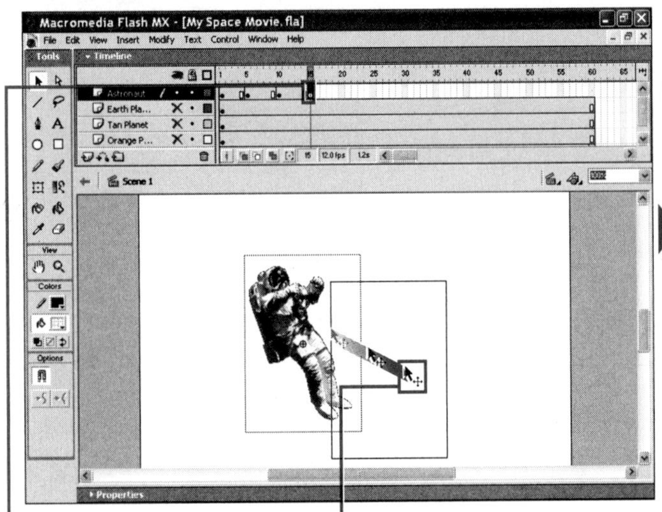

7 Click the next frame in the layer to which you want to change the animation and add a keyframe.

■ Flash MX inserts a keyframe that duplicates the contents of the previous keyframe.

8 Change the object again so it varies from the previous keyframe.

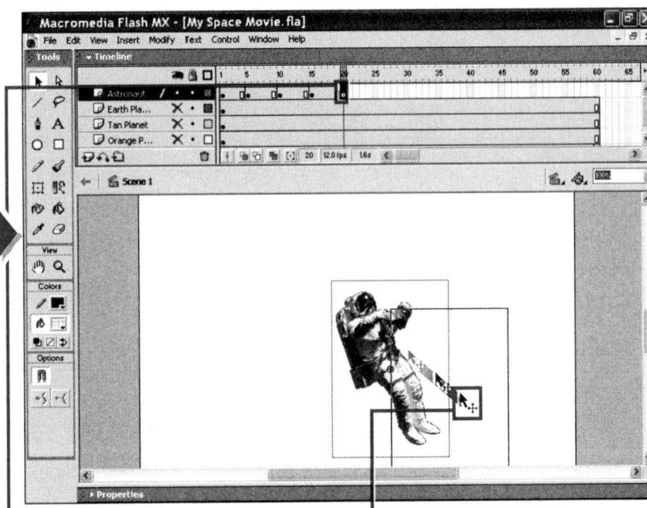

9 Click the next frame in the layer and add a keyframe.

■ Flash MX inserts a keyframe that duplicates the contents of the fourth keyframe.

10 Change the object again.

How do I know where to reposition an object on the Stage?

✔ You can use gridlines to help you control how an object moves around the Stage. To turn on the Flash gridlines, click the View menu, click Grid, and then click Show Grid. Flash MX turns on the gridlines on the Stage area. With gridlines visible, you can clearly see the placement of objects on the Stage. To hide the gridlines, click View, then click Grid, and click Show Grid.

What does the Snap To Objects feature do?

✔ When the Snap to Objects button (🧲) is clicked, Flash MX automatically aligns objects to each other on the Stage. This feature is activated by default; however, you can turn it off or on as needed as you move items around on the Stage area. When the feature is activated and you also turn on gridlines, you can quickly align objects on the Stage to the nearest gridline as you move them.

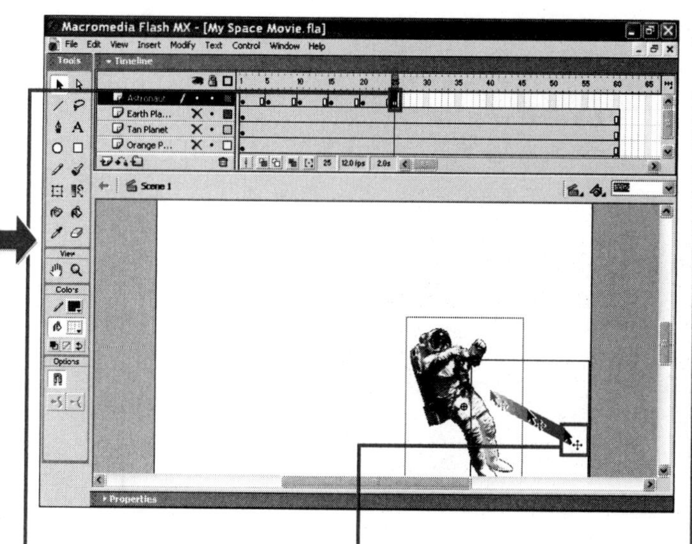

11 Click the next frame in the layer and add a final keyframe.

■ Flash MX inserts a keyframe that duplicates the contents of the fifth keyframe.

12 Change the object again to complete the final stage of the animation sequence.

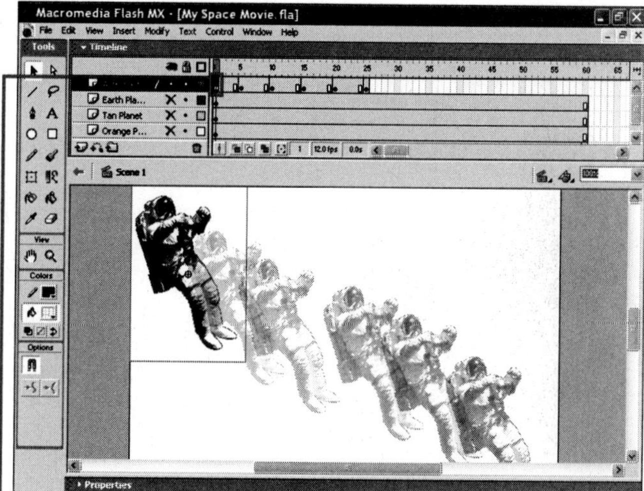

PLAY BACK THE MOVIE

1 Click the first keyframe in the layer containing the animation sequence.

Note: You can also drag the playhead to the first frame of any layer to play the movie.

2 Press Enter (Return).

■ Flash MX plays the entire animation sequence.

ONION-SKINNING AN ANIMATION

You can use the onion-skinning feature of Flash MX to quickly assess the positioning of objects in surrounding frames in your movie. By viewing the placement of objects in other frames, you can more clearly determine how you want to position the object in the frame in which you are working. This is particularly useful when creating an animation sequence in which object placement is crucial to the appearance of the animation.

The name *onion-skinning* refers to the effect of seeing the contents of other frames as shaded layers — like the translucent layers of an onion — in context to the current frame.

Onion-skinning offers two modes of display: dimmed content or outlined content. The objects in the frames surrounding the current frame are displayed as dimmed — the default option — or outlined objects, but regardless of the choice, the contents of the current frame are fully displayed. This allows you to see multiple frames and how their movements relate to the current frame.

You may need to change the magnification of your view in order to see the onion-skinned objects on the Stage. You can use the Zoom drop-down list in the top right corner of the Stage to change your view magnification level at any time during the animation process.

ONION-SKINNING AN ANIMATION

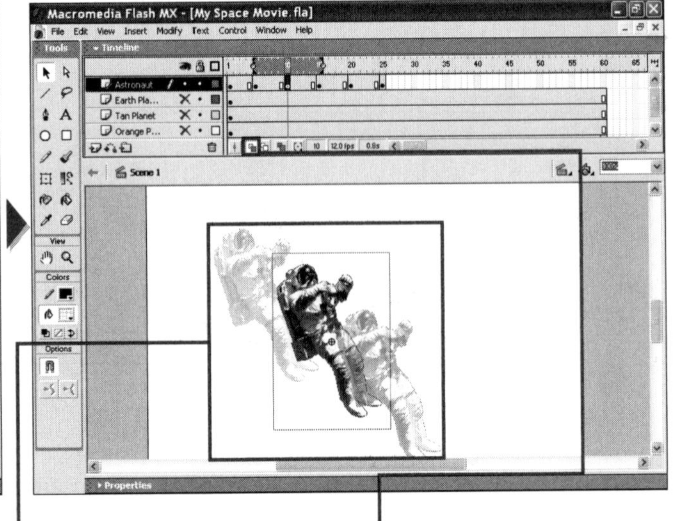

TURN ON ONION-SKINNING

1 Click a frame in your animation sequence.

2 Click the Onion Skin button (▣) at the bottom of the Flash Timeline.

Note: If the Timeline is closed, you can click the View menu and click Timeline to open it again.

■ Flash MX displays dimmed images from the surrounding frames and places onion-skin markers at the top of the Timeline.

■ To turn off onion-skinning, you can click ▣ again.

Can I edit the onion-skin frames?

✔ No. You cannot edit the onion-skin frames unless you click [icon]. When you make the other frames editable, you can select and move the onion-skin objects to fine-tune the animation sequence.

In what kinds of situations does onion-skinning work best?

✔ When you need to track the positioning of an object as it moves across the Stage, onion-skinning will definitely assist you in showing the placement of the object in each frame of the sequence. However, if, for example, an object stays in one spot but changes in color, the onion-skinning feature will not be of great benefit.

Can I play back my movie with the onion-skin feature turned on?

✔ Yes. However, the onion-skinning will turn off while the movie plays. Click in the first frame of your movie and then press Enter. Flash MX plays the movie on the Stage. When it reaches the last frame, the onion-skin feature becomes active again.

Why can I not see onion-skins for objects on a locked layer?

✔ Flash MX does not allow onion-skinning for locked or hidden layers. You must unlock or view hidden layers to onion-skin their contents.

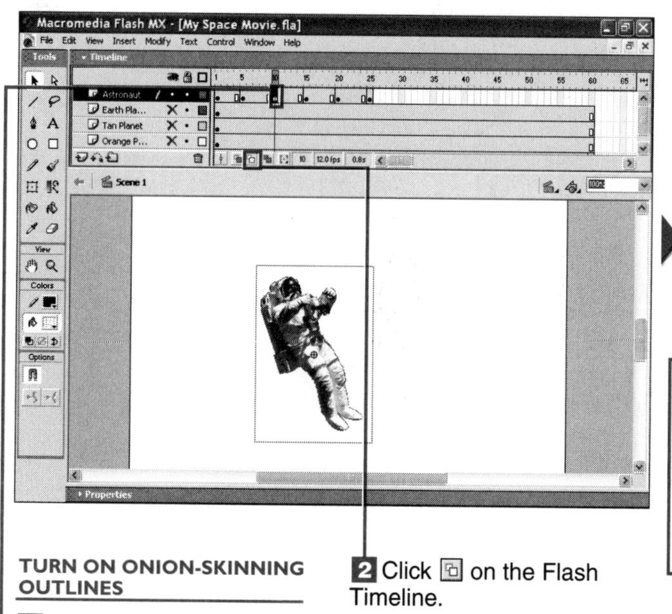

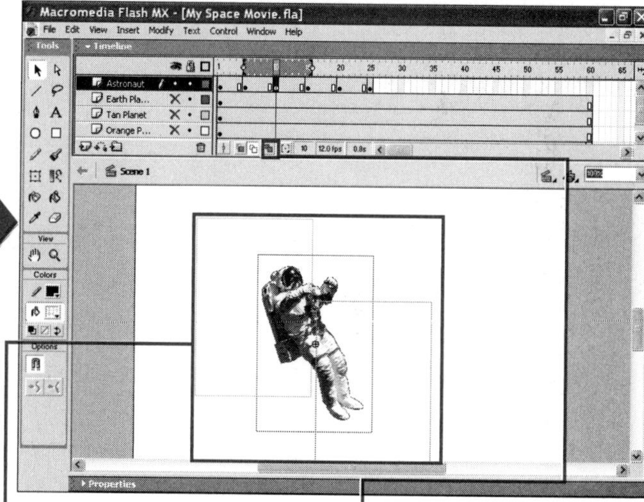

TURN ON ONION-SKINNING OUTLINES

1 Click a frame in your animation sequence.

2 Click [icon] on the Flash Timeline.

■ Flash MX displays outlines of the images from the surrounding frames and places onion-skin markers at the top of the Timeline.

■ To make the content of the onion-skin frames editable, click [icon].

CONTINUED

ONION-SKINNING AN ANIMATION (CONTINUED)

The onion-skinning features makes it easier for you to gauge the changes needed to create your animations. You can control which frames appear in onion-skin mode using the onion-skin markers that appear on the Timeline. You can manually adjust the markers as needed. You can also control the markers using the Modify Onion Markers pop-up menu.

The Modify Onion Markers pop-up menu displays several choices for controlling markers on the Timeline: Always Show Markers, Anchor Onion, Onion 2, Onion 5, and Onion All. The Always Show Markers option leaves the onion-skinning markers on, even when onion-skinning is turned off. The Anchor Onion option enables you to lock the markers in place, even as you view frames at the other end of the Timeline.

Both the Onion 2 and Onion 5 options display the corresponding number of frames before or after the current frame. For example, if you choose Onion 5, Flash sets the markers to show 5 frames on either side of the current frame. To onion-skin all the frames in the movie, use the Onion All option.

ONION-SKINNING AN ANIMATION (CONTINUED)

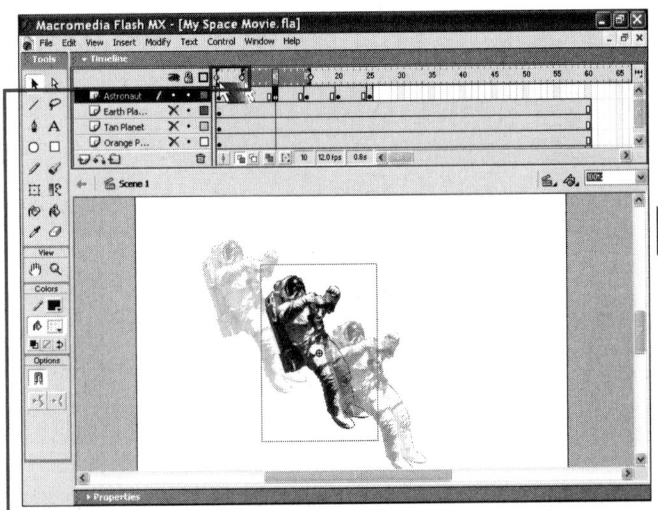

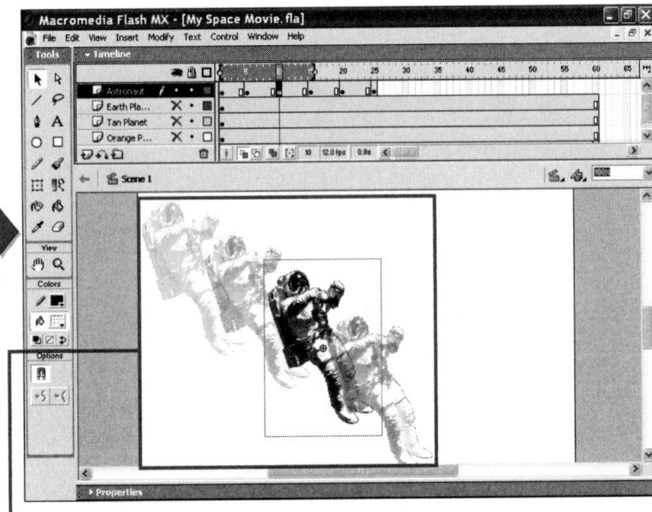

MOVE THE ONION-SKIN MARKERS

1 To view more or less frames with onion-skinning, you can click and drag an onion-skin marker left or right.

■ Flash MX adds or subtracts the additional frames from the view.

What should I keep in mind when adjusting the onion-skin markers?

✔ Remember that the greater the range of frames you onion-skin, the more difficult it might be to discern the image and which frame is associated with which onion-skin outline. This is particularly true of animation effects that do not involve a great deal of movement.

Can I apply onion-skinning to all the frames and layers in my movie?

✔ Yes. Click [icon] to display a pop-up menu of marker options. Click Onion All. This causes Flash MX to onion-skin all the frames in all the layers in your movie.

How do I make the onion-skin markers stay in place?

✔ If you click in another frame, the onion-skin markers move in position relative to the frame you are in. To keep them anchored in their original locations, click [icon], and then click Anchor Onion. This command keeps the markers from adjusting when you click in different frames.

Can I apply onion-skinning to an off-stage symbol?

✔ Yes. You can view onion-skinning for objects that animate into the work area.

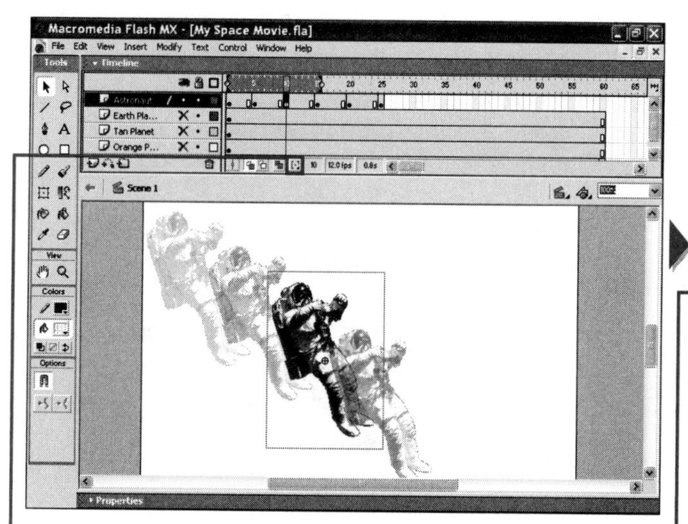

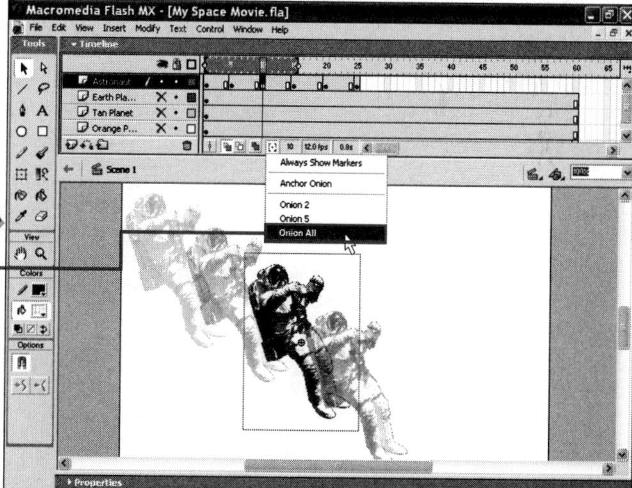

CHANGE THE MARKER DISPLAY

1 To change how the onion-skin markers appear on the Timeline, click [icon].

■ The Modify menu appears with options for changing the marker display.

2 Click the marker setting you want to apply.

PREVIEW A FLASH ANIMATION

You can preview the animations you create in Flash to see how the various effects are working. You can click an animation sequence one frame at a time to see the contents of each frame, but a faster way to check the sequence is to play the movie. A quick way to test the movie is to move the playhead to the first frame and press Enter (Return). Flash MX plays your movie on the Stage.

Alternatively, you may wish to see the movie as your audience will see it. To do this, you can use the Test Movie mode to open the built-in Flash Player within the Flash MX program window. This option allows you to see the movie without the surrounding Timeline, layers, and drawing tools. Using this feature, you can preview animation in the Flash Player window as many times as you like, and then exit the player and return to the Flash MX program window.

When using the built-in player, the regular Flash MX menu controls are not available. Instead, you see the Flash Player controls for testing and playing the movie.

PREVIEW A FLASH ANIMATION

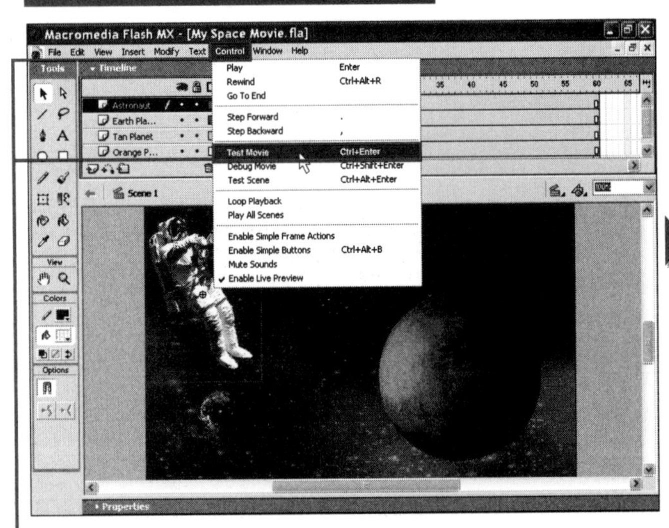

1 Click Control.

2 Click Test Movie.

■ Flash MX exports your movie to the Flash Player and plays the animation.

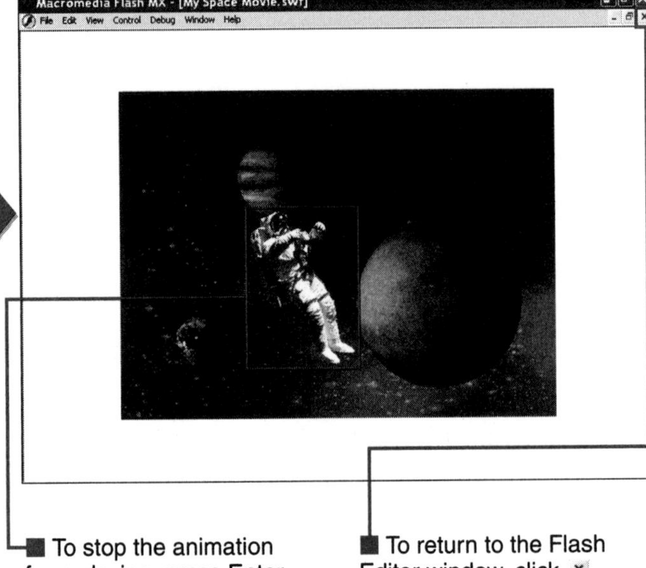

■ To stop the animation from playing, press Enter (Return).

■ To return to the Flash Editor window, click ×.

ADJUST THE ANIMATION SPEED

You can use regular frames in your movie to adjust the speed of an animation sequence. Although the frame rate is constant throughout a Flash movie, you can make the animation appear to slow or speed up by adding or subtracting frames in the layer containing the animation. Adding regular frames to an animation sequence extends the length of time over which the sequence plays back.

For example, if a particular section of your animation seems to run too quickly during playback, you can slow it down by inserting regular frames between two keyframes. In the example of the floating astronaut animation sequence, a regular frame is added immediately after a keyframe. By adding in-between frames rather than keyframes, you do not increase the file size of the movie.

You may need to add several regular frames before a change in animation speed becomes noticeable. Adding one or two regular frames may not be enough. Adding five or more may create the effect you want. It does not really matter where you add the regular frames, just as long as you add them somewhere between two keyframes.

ADJUST THE ANIMATION SPEED

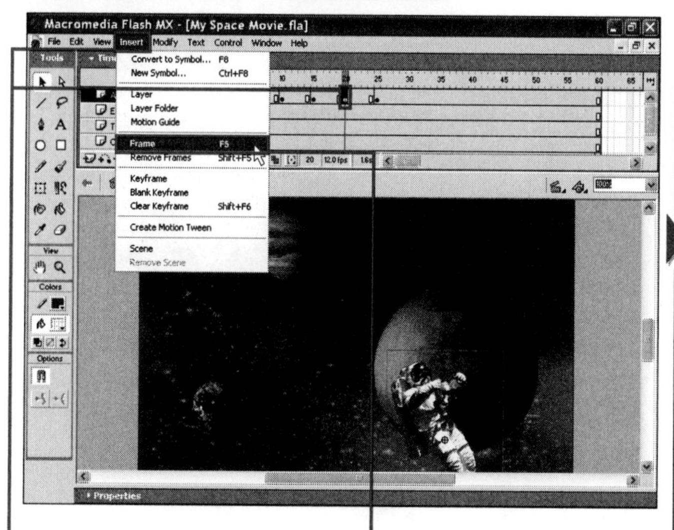

1 Click the keyframe you want to add frames to.

2 Click Insert.

3 Click Frame.

■ You can also press F5 to add a frame to the Timeline.

■ Flash MX adds a frame after the keyframe.

■ Because adding just one regular frame is not always enough, repeat steps 2 to 3 as needed to add more frames to the sequence.

■ To test the animation, click the first frame in the Timeline and press Enter (Return).

MOVE AND COPY FRAMES

You can move and copy frames in your animation sequence to change the way in which it plays. Moving and copying frames is just one way you can edit your Flash movie. For example, you may want to move a keyframe forward or backward in the Timeline, or to copy multiple regular frames and paste them between two keyframes.

You cannot copy frames in the same way you copy other objects in Flash MX; you must use the Copy Frames and Paste Frames commands found in the Edit menu. Using the standard Copy and Paste commands does not work.

If you are familiar with using the drag-and-drop feature in other programs, you will find that it works the same way in Flash MX. Using the drag-and-drop feature, you can drag frames around on the Timeline and drop them into new locations. You can also drag a frame to another layer. You can even select multiple frames and relocate them as a group by dragging them around the Timeline.

If you accidentally move or copy frames you did not mean to edit, you can always activate the Undo command to quickly reverse the move or copy. Found in the Edit menu, the Undo command always undoes your last action.

MOVE AND COPY FRAMES

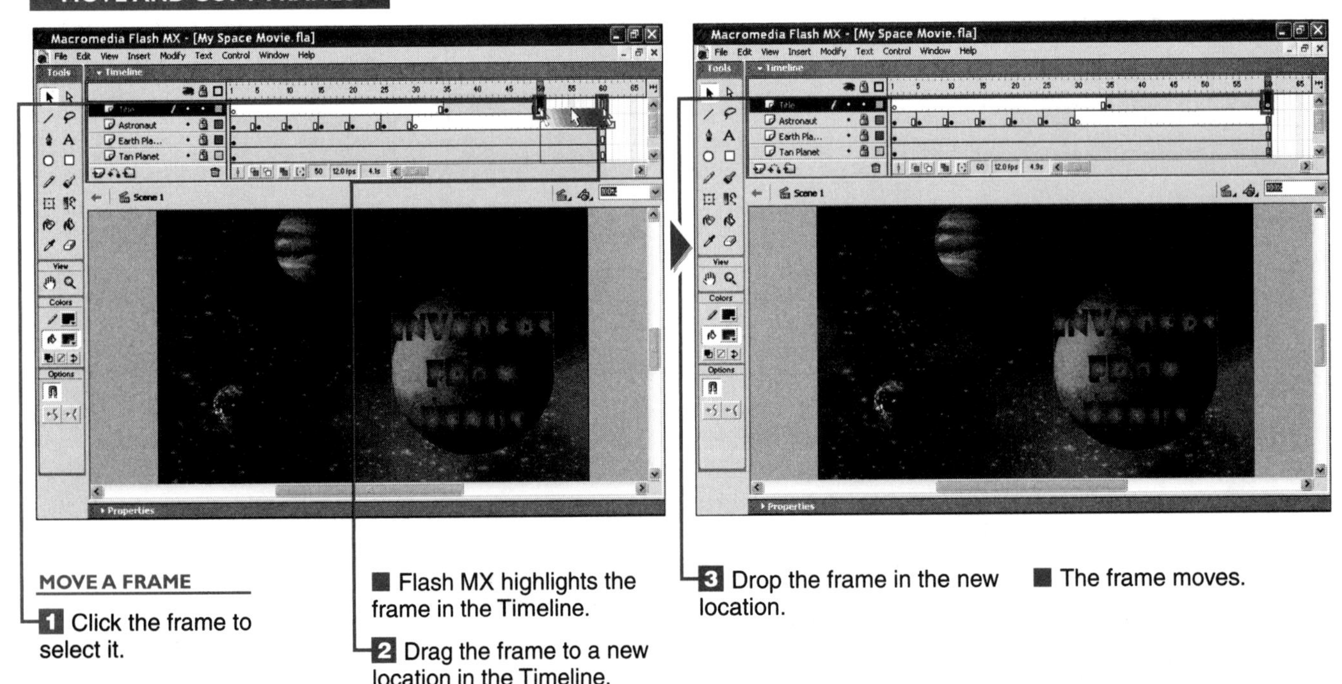

MOVE A FRAME

1 Click the frame to select it.

■ Flash MX highlights the frame in the Timeline.

2 Drag the frame to a new location in the Timeline.

3 Drop the frame in the new location.

■ The frame moves.

What do I do if I pasted a copy in the wrong place?

✔ Anytime you make a mistake in Flash MX, click the Edit menu and click Undo to undo your last action. This command only works if you click the button immediately after performing the action. If you perform another action before activating the Undo command, Flash MX undoes the most recent action, and the previous action is lost.

Can I use the drag-and-drop technique to copy frames?

✔ Yes. First select the frame or frames you want to copy. Press and hold Alt (Option) and then drag the frame or frames and drop them into the new location on the Timeline. Flash MX will duplicate the frames.

Can I drag an end keyframe to extend an animation?

✔ Yes. Dragging an end keyframe in your animation sequence can quickly lengthen or shorten an animation, depending on which direction you drag. For example, to extend your animation sequence, you can drag a keyframe to the right a couple of frames and Flash MX will automatically add in-between frames for you.

How do I delete frames entirely?

✔ Select the regular frame or frames you want to delete, click the Insert menu and click Remove Frames. You can also press Shift + F5 on the keyboard to remove regular frames.

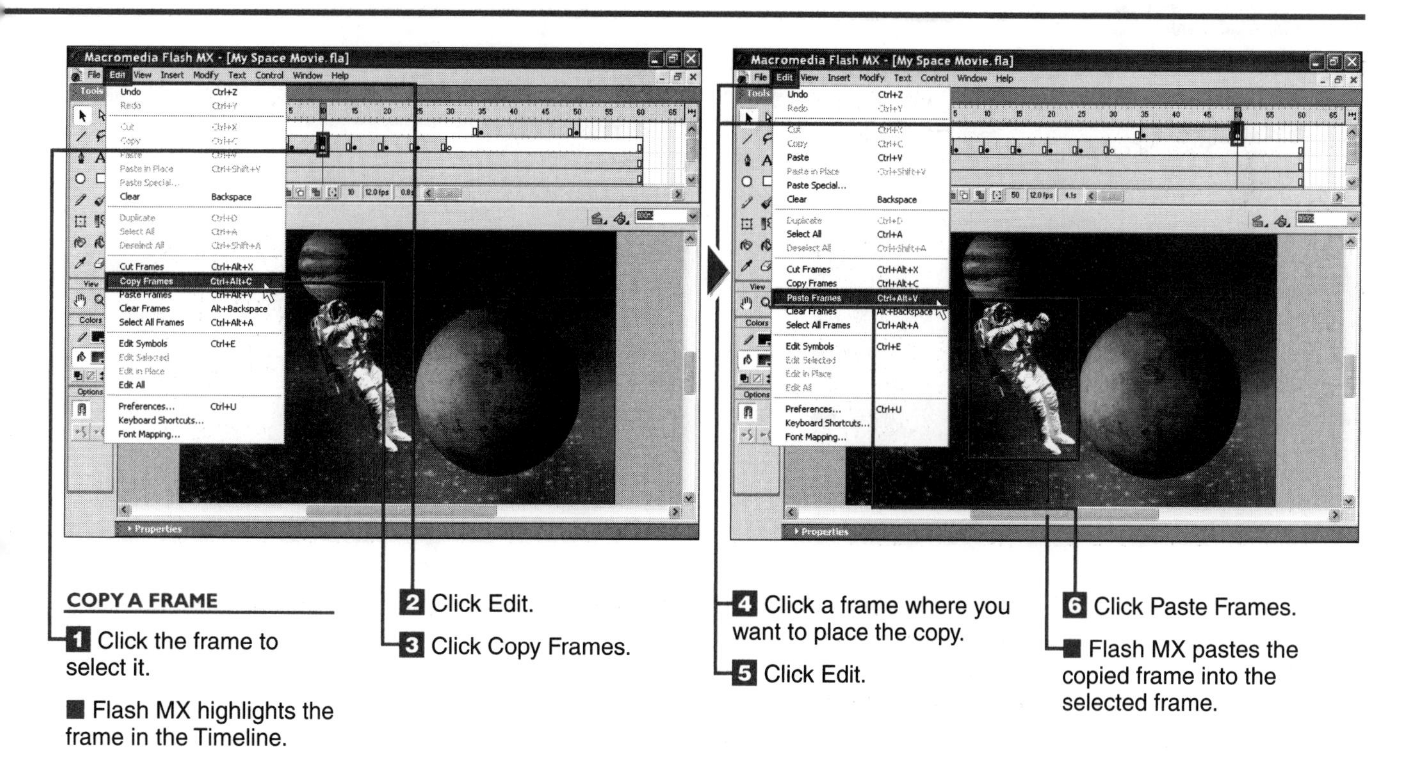

COPY A FRAME

1 Click the frame to select it.

■ Flash MX highlights the frame in the Timeline.

2 Click Edit.

3 Click Copy Frames.

4 Click a frame where you want to place the copy.

5 Click Edit.

6 Click Paste Frames.

■ Flash MX pastes the copied frame into the selected frame.

CREATE SCENES

You can create scenes in your movie to organize your animations. When you are working with a very long movie, you can break up the movie into smaller sections called *scenes*. Scenes are blocks of animation frames turned into their own independent Timelines. Rather than scrolling around long Timelines and trying to keep track of where you are in the movie, you can break your movie into smaller, manageable scenes that you can work with individually.

For example, one scene might include frames 1–50, and another scene might include frames 51–75. The scenes are still part of the overall movie, but are now readily organized into sections that you can label and rearrange as needed. You can even use Flash actions to jump to different scenes. When you start a new project, by default, Flash MX creates a new scene, labeled Scene 1. You can rename this scene and add others as you need them.

The current name of the scene appears at the top of the Timeline. During playback, the scenes are played in the order in which they are listed in the Scene panel. You can quickly access scenes for editing using the Edit Scene button at the top of the Stage area.

CREATE SCENES

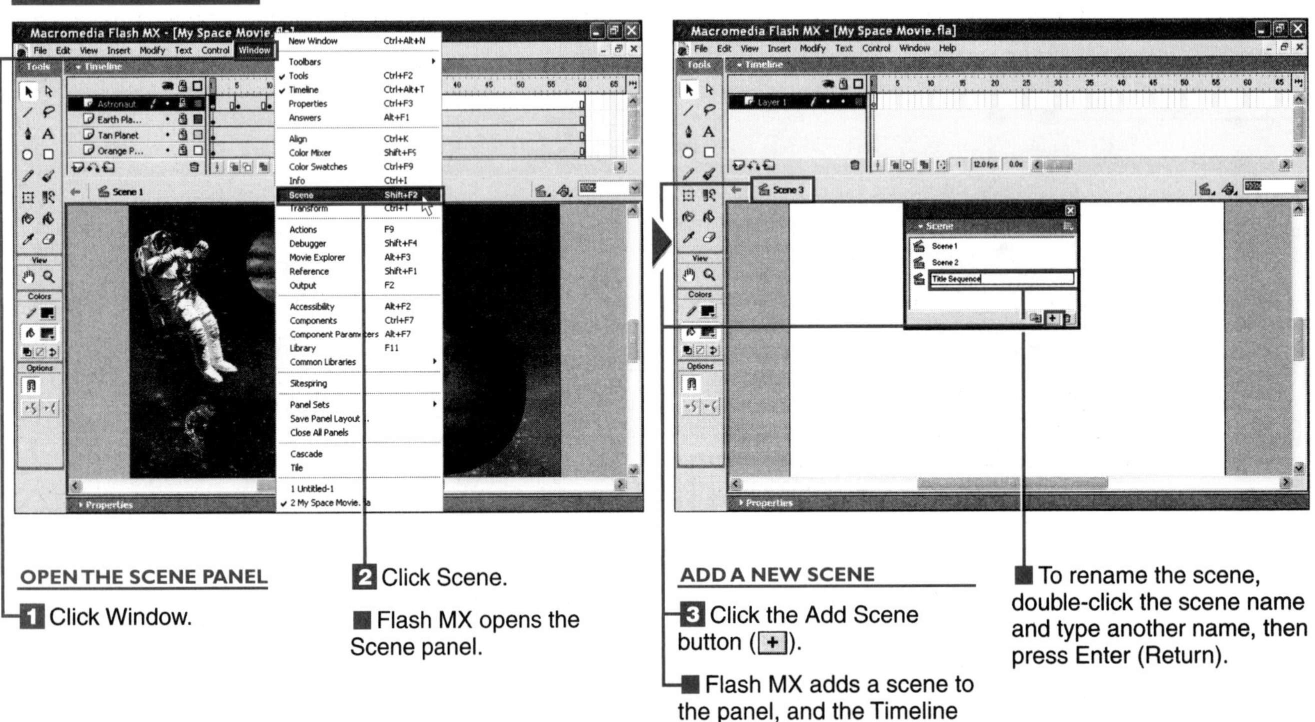

OPEN THE SCENE PANEL

1 Click Window.

2 Click Scene.

■ Flash MX opens the Scene panel.

ADD A NEW SCENE

3 Click the Add Scene button (+).

■ Flash MX adds a scene to the panel, and the Timeline switches to the new scene.

■ To rename the scene, double-click the scene name and type another name, then press Enter (Return).

How do I rearrange the scene order?

✔ You can move scenes around using the Scene panel. Open the Scene panel to display a list of all the available scenes by following steps 1 to 3 in this section. Click the scene you want to move. Click and drag the scene to a new location in the list. Release the mouse button and the scenes are reordered.

How do I delete a scene?

✔ You can delete scenes from the Scene panel. Select the scene you want to remove, then click the Delete button (🗑) at the bottom of the Scene panel. If the Scene panel is not open, you can delete the current scene showing in the Timeline by clicking the Insert menu and selecting Remove Scene.

Can I tell Flash MX to stop the movie after a particular scene?

✔ Yes. You can assign Flash actions to your scenes just like you assign actions to frames. For example, you can add a Stop action to the last frame in a scene to stop the movie, and any remaining scenes do not play. To learn more about actions, see Chapter 31.

Can I duplicate a scene?

✔ Yes. Click the scene you want to copy in the Scene panel, then click the Duplicate Scene button at the bottom of the panel. A copy of the scene is added to the panel. You can rename and edit the scene as needed.

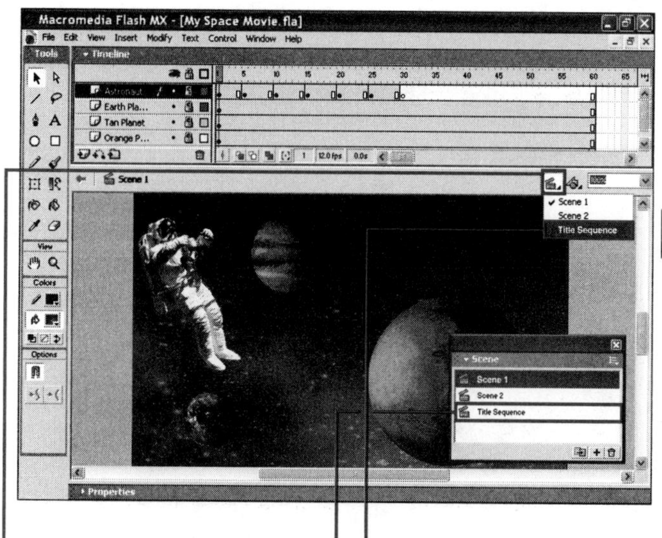

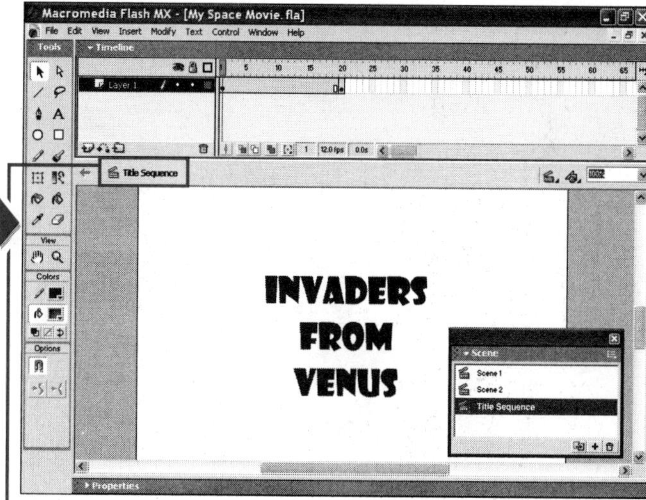

SWITCH BETWEEN SCENES

1 Click the Edit Scene button (🎬).

■ Flash MX displays a pop-up menu listing all the available scenes.

2 Click the scene you want to view.

■ If the Scene panel is open, you can also click on the scene name you want to view.

■ Flash MX switches to the scene you selected.

SAVE AN ANIMATION AS A MOVIE CLIP

You can save an animation sequence as a movie clip that you can use again elsewhere in your movie. When you save an animation sequence, Flash MX saves it as a movie clip symbol. Movie clip symbols are just one of the three symbol types you can create in Flash MX. Movie clips utilize their own timelines apart from the main movie Timeline.

As with graphic and button symbols, you can place a movie clip symbol on the Stage for any frame. When Flash MX reaches that frame during playback, it plays the movie clip animation. You can also reference movie clips in Flash actions you add to your movie.

You can assign a distinctive name to your movie clip so that you can easily find it and use it again. As a symbol, the movie clip is added to the Library of the file, a collection of all the symbols that are part of the project.

As a symbol, you can edit the movie clip and all uses of the clip in your movie are updated as well. Because the movie clip is treated as a symbol, multiple uses of the clip in your movie do not increase the file size of the movie.

SAVE AN ANIMATION AS A MOVIE CLIP

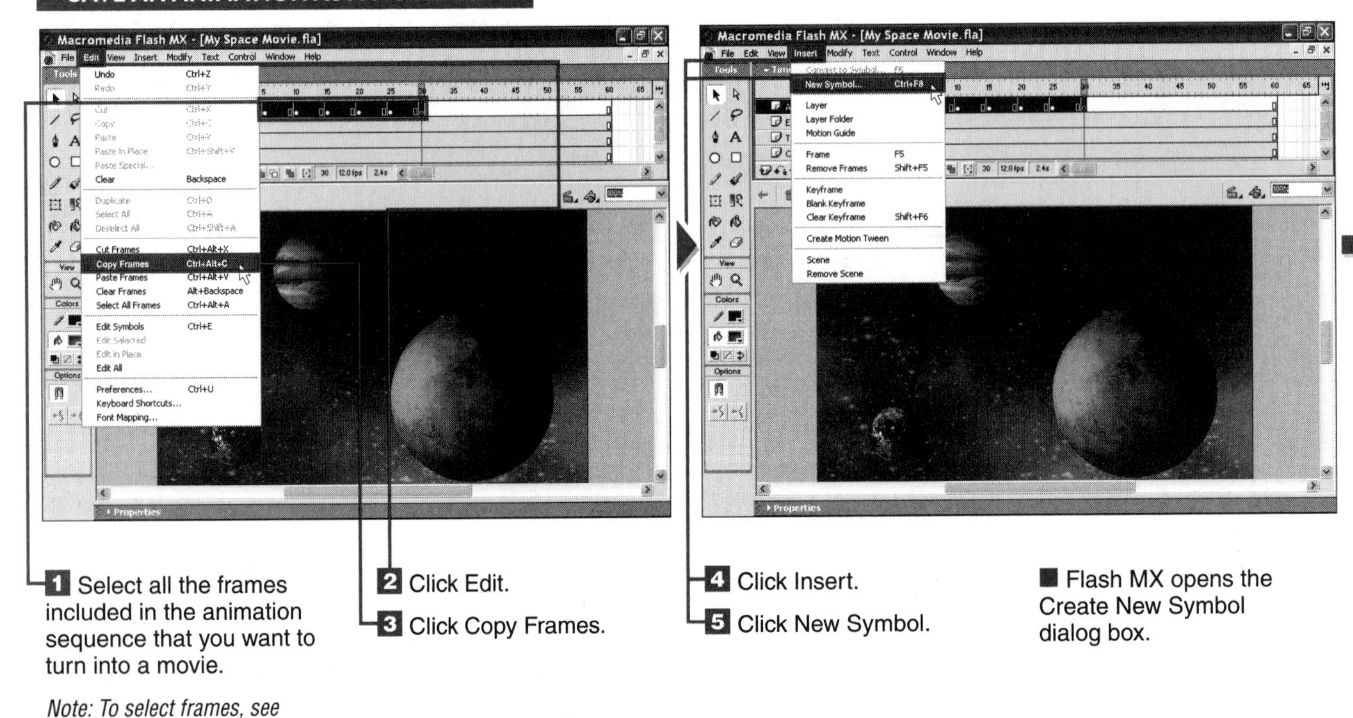

1 Select all the frames included in the animation sequence that you want to turn into a movie.

Note: To select frames, see page 514.

2 Click Edit.

3 Click Copy Frames.

4 Click Insert.

5 Click New Symbol.

■ Flash MX opens the Create New Symbol dialog box.

How do I place a movie clip in my movie?

✔ You can place movie clips into your movie just as you place any other item saved in the Flash Library: Click the frame where you want to insert the clip. Open the Library window and drag the movie clip from the Library window to the Stage. You can turn any animation effect, including frame-by-frame motion and shape tweens, into movie clips.

Does Flash MX have any premade clips I can study?

✔ Yes. Flash MX installs with a couple of movie clips you can use to help you learn how animation techniques work. To locate the clips, open the Help menu and click Samples.

How do I save an existing clip as a new clip?

✔ You can use the Convert to Symbol command to save an existing movie clip as a new movie clip symbol. One purpose for doing this is to alter the clip slightly and use it again elsewhere in your movie. On the Flash Stage, select the clip you want to save, and then click the Insert menu and select Convert to Symbol. Enter a new name for the clip and click OK. The clip is added to the Library of the movie. You can now edit it and use it in your movie.

Is there a shortcut to the Create New Symbol dialog box?

✔ Yes. You can press Ctrl + F8 (⌘ + F8) to summon the dialog box and create a new movie clip.

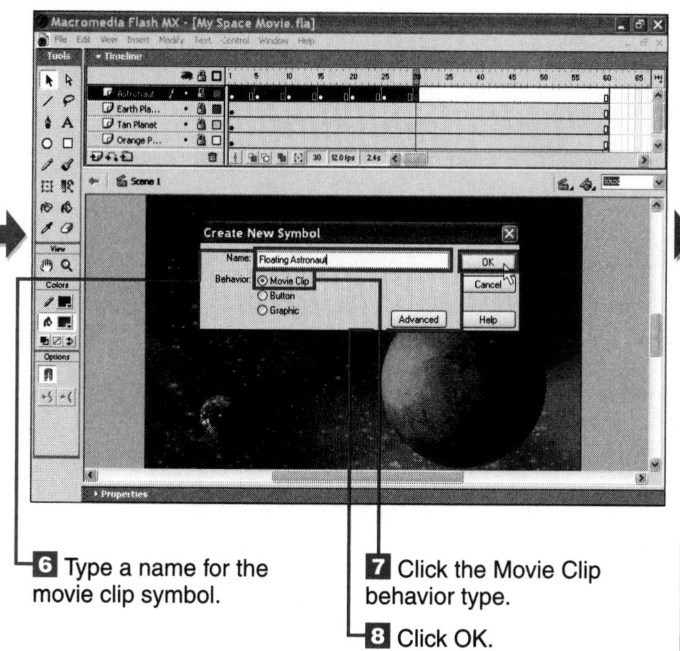

6 Type a name for the movie clip symbol.

7 Click the Movie Clip behavior type.

8 Click OK.

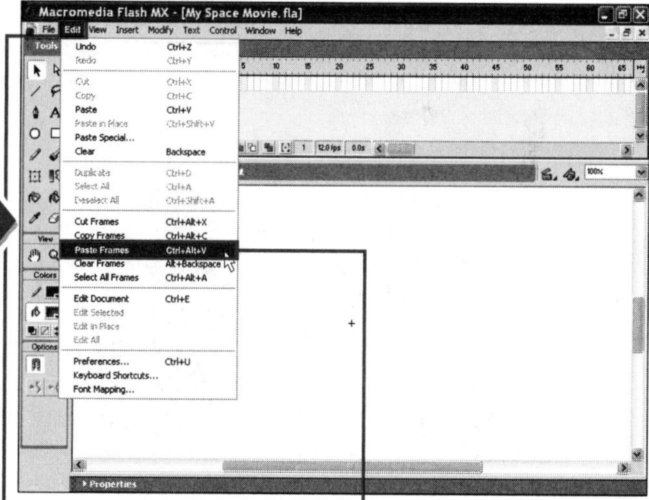

■ Flash MX switches you to symbol-edit mode.

9 Click frame 1 if it is not already selected.

10 Click Edit.

11 Click Paste Frames.

■ Flash MX copies the animation into the movie clip Timeline and saves the clip as a symbol in the Movie Library.

USING THE MOVIE EXPLORER

You can use the Movie Explorer feature to help you organize and view the contents of your movie. This feature, like many of the other panels in Flash MX, offers you easy access to the elements of your movie, such as symbols and clips. You can use the Movie Explorer panel to find out which actions are assigned or search for a specific item in your movie.

All the elements associated with your Flash file are listed in a hierarchical manner in the Movie Explorer panel, much like the files in your computer are listed in Windows Explorer or in the MacOS Finder. You can search for a specific item in your movie using the Find field at the top of the panel.

You can also choose exactly which movie elements to view in the list box of the panel using the Show buttons at the top of the panel.

The Movie Explorer feature can help you analyze the elements in movies created by other users. Because the Movie Explorer lists all the hidden clips and actions contained in a movie, you can examine the various elements that comprise the movie and find out how the author pieced together his or her creation.

USING THE MOVIE EXPLORER

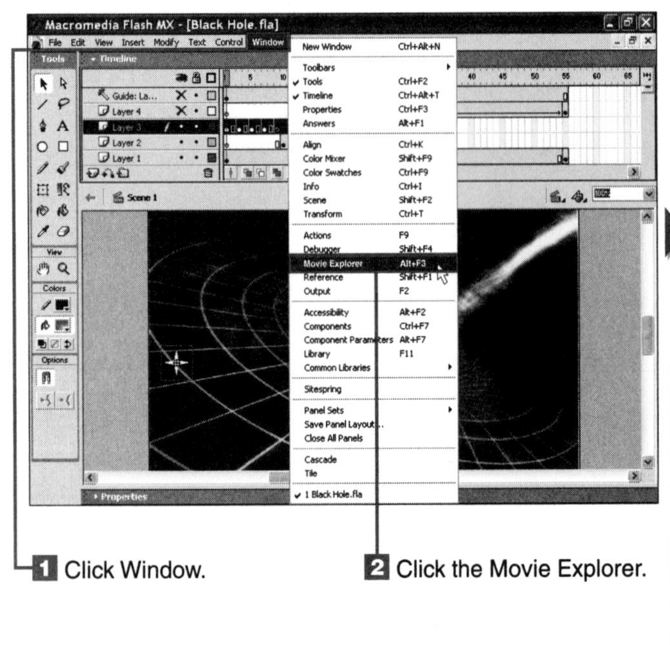

1 Click Window.

2 Click the Movie Explorer.

■ Flash MX opens the Movie Explorer panel.

■ Click ⊞ to expand a list element.

■ Click ⊟ to collapse a list element.

■ Select an item in the list to see the full path location of the item in your movie. Flash MX also scrolls to that location in the Timeline.

3 Click ☒ to hide the panel again.

Can I filter which items appear in the Movie Explorer list box?

✔ Yes. Click any of the Show filter buttons at the top of the panel to show text, symbols, actions, sound, video and bitmaps, frames and layers. For example, click the Show button ( ) to display symbols used in your movie, including buttons, movie clips, and graphic symbols. Flash MX will show those items in the list box. You can expand and collapse the hierarchy as needed to help you view more items in the panel list box.

Can I customize my list view?

✔ Yes. Click the Customize button ( ) to open the Movie Explorer Settings dialog box. From here you can select which types of movie elements you want to view in the list box of the Movie Explorer. Click OK to close the dialog box and apply the new settings.

Can I collapse the panel and leave it open?

✔ Yes. The Movie Explorer panel can be collapsed and expanded just like all the other panels in Flash MX. Click the title bar of the panel to collapse and expand the panel.

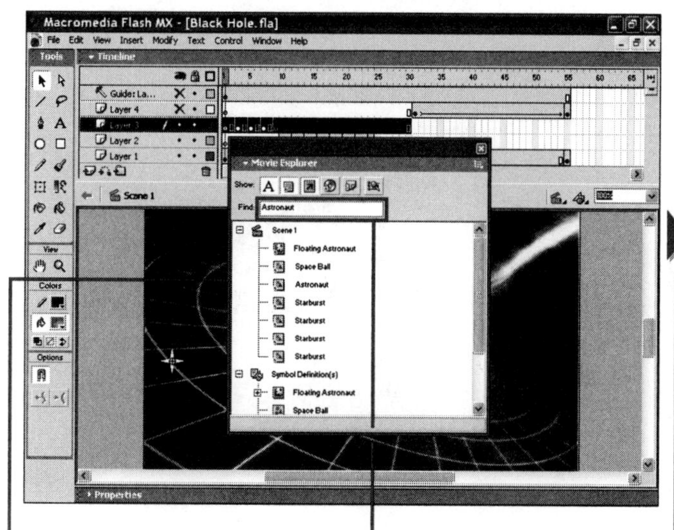

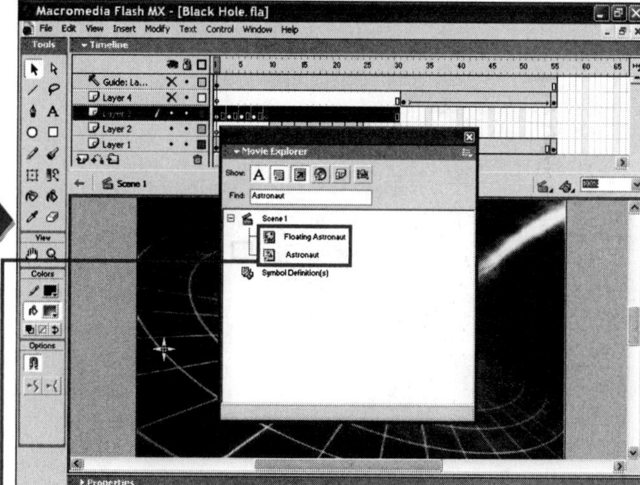

SEARCH FOR AN ITEM

1 Open the Movie Explorer panel.

Note: To open the Movie Explorer panel, perform steps 1 to 2 on the previous page.

2 Type the item name or description.

■ You can search for all kinds of elements in your movie, such as a frame number, an action or ActionScript string, or even a font.

■ Flash MX immediately performs a search for the item you entered and displays any matches in the list box.

CREATE A MOTION TWEEN

Flash MX can help you animate moving objects when you apply a motion tween. A *motion tween* is created when you define two points of movement in the Timeline with two keyframes, and then let Flash calculate all the in-between frames necessary to get from point A to point B. The term tween comes from the fact that Flash calculates the in-between frames.

Motion-tweened animations take up much less file space than frame-by-frame animations. Tweened animations are also much less labor-intensive than the frame-by-frame animation technique; you do not have to work so hard to make sure the object you are animating is placed just so for each frame in the animation sequence. Instead, tweened animation lets Flash MX do all the work regarding the placement of the animated object in each frame.

You can motion tween only symbols or grouped objects, and you can tween only one symbol per layer.

You cannot create a motion tween using an object or objects you have just drawn on the Stage. You must save the object or objects as a symbol, or group the items together first. If you try to assign tween status to an oval you draw on the Stage, the effect will not work properly.

Motion tween frames are marked by an arrow in the Timeline, making them easy to identify as they relate to other frames in a layer.

CREATE A MOTION TWEEN

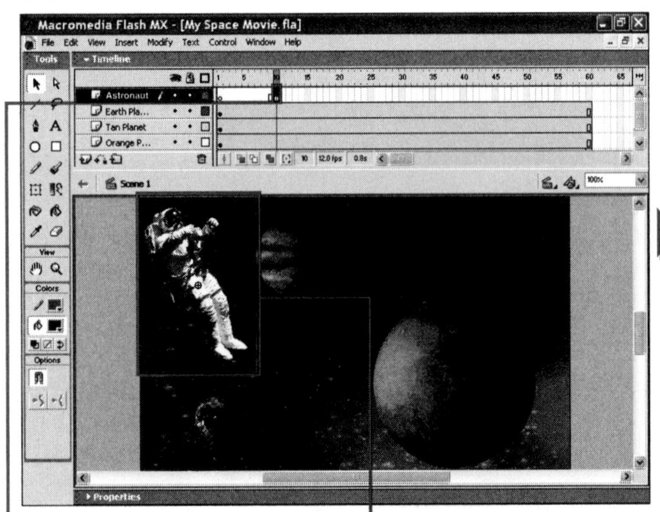

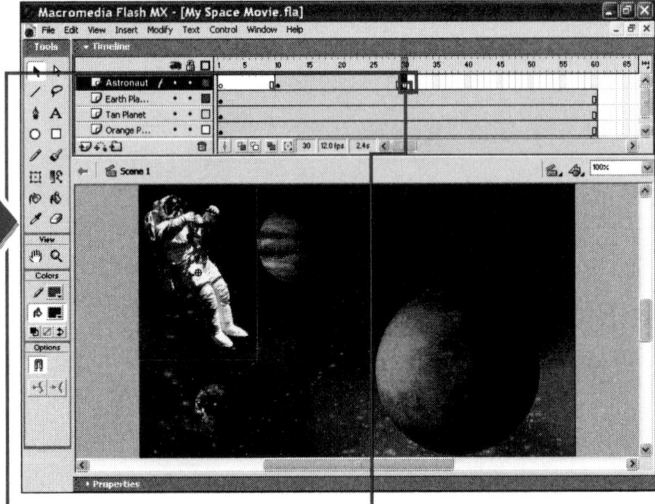

SELECT KEYFRAMES AND SYMBOL

1 Insert a keyframe where you want to start the motion tween.

Note: To add a frame, see page 510.

2 Place the symbol you want to animate on the Stage.

■ The position of the symbol is the starting point of the animation effect, such as a corner or side of the movie area.

3 Click the last frame you want to include in the motion tween.

4 Insert a keyframe.

■ You can press F6 to insert a keyframe.

When would I use a frame-by-frame animation as opposed to a motion tween animation?

✔ You can use a motion tween when you want Flash to calculate the changes between frames. You can use a frame-by-frame animation when you want complete control over the changes between keyframes. When you create a frame-by-frame animation, you manually input the changes made to each frame in the sequence. Manually creating an animation sequence results in a larger file size than the same sequence calculated with a motion tween.

What is the difference between a shape tween and a motion tween?

✔ With motion tweening, Flash calculates the changes for an object moving around the Stage. With shape tweening, Flash calculates the changes between an object that morphs into another object.

Can I add frames to a motion tween?

✔ Yes. The quickest way to add frames is to drag the end keyframe of the sequence right or left in the Timeline to lengthen or shorten the effect.

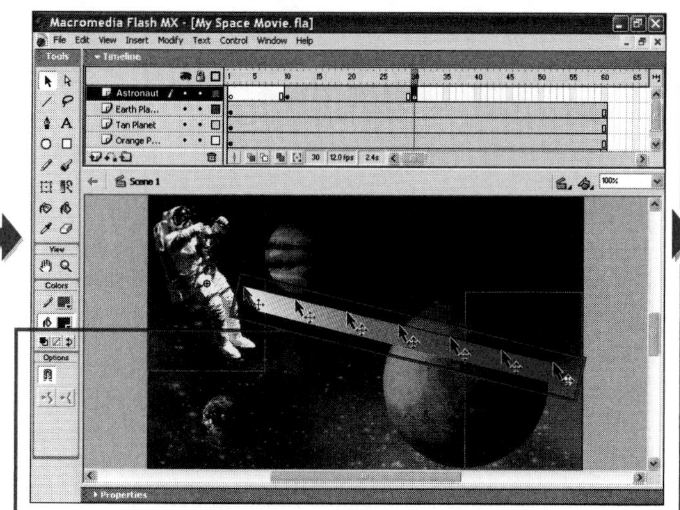

5 Move the symbol to the position on which you want the motion tween to end (for example, the other side of the Stage).

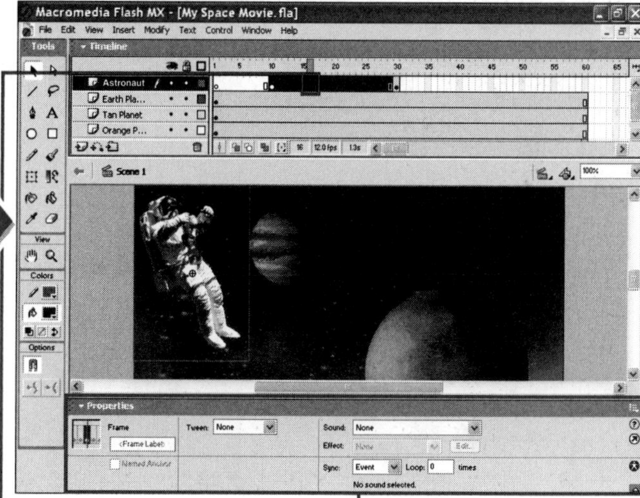

6 Click a frame between the two keyframes that make up your motion tween to select the frames.

Note: To select frames, see page 514.

7 Open the Property inspector.

Note: To open and close the Property inspector, see page 346.

CONTINUED

CREATE A MOTION TWEEN (CONTINUED)

You can assign as many motion tween segments as you like throughout your movie, or you can make your animation one long motion tween. Motion tweening works best for objects you want to move around the Flash Stage. For example, you can make a company logo seem to move across the top of the movie, or a cartoon character seem to walk around. In the movie demonstrated in the steps in this section, the animation focuses on an astronaut floating through space. You can apply the same principles to a logo or product picture. You determine where the logo starts and where it finishes, and then Flash MX supplies the necessary frames containing incremental changes to make the object appear to move from one spot to another.

The number of in-between frames is determined by your placement of the second keyframe in the sequence. If you insert the second keyframe only a couple of frames away from the first keyframe, you do not see a very smooth motion tween. You should allow five or more frames between your reference keyframes to create a smooth motion tween effect.

CREATE A MOTION TWEEN (CONTINUED)

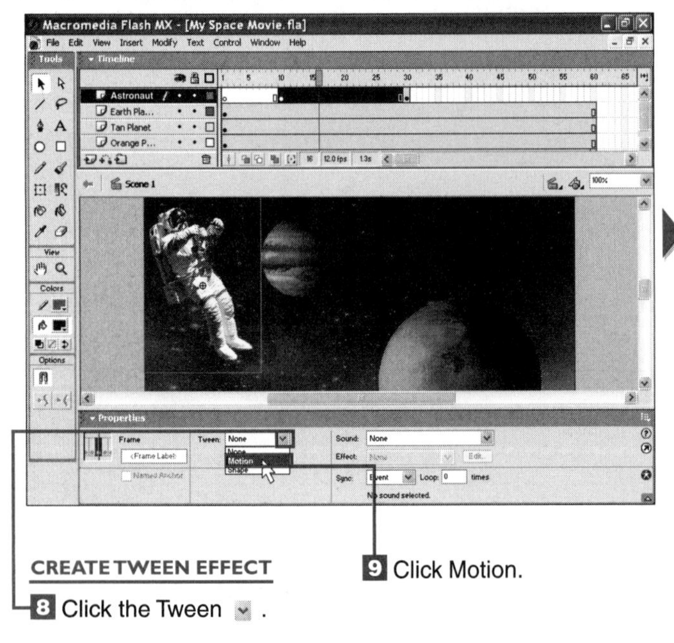

CREATE TWEEN EFFECT

8 Click the Tween ▾.

9 Click Motion.

■ Flash MX calculates the in-between changes the symbol must undergo to move from the first keyframe to the next keyframe.

■ Flash MX adds a motion tween arrow (↣) from the first keyframe in the tween effect to the last keyframe in the tween effect.

Can I see the incremental changes on the in-between frames?

✔ Yes. If you turn on the onion skin feature, you can see the incremental changes in the frames surrounding the current frame. Click at the bottom of the Timeline to activate the feature.

Can I add keyframes to a motion tween?

✔ Yes. You can add keyframes to make important changes in the motion tween, such as changing the direction of the motion. Flash MX reconfigures the in-between frames to reflect changes in the new keyframes you add.

Can I create a motion tween as I go?

✔ You can start a motion tween without defining the end keyframe in the sequence. Click Insert, and then click Create Motion Tween. A dotted line appears in the frames, indicating a motion tween in progress, but not yet complete. In the final frame of the sequence, move the symbol on the Stage to where you want the animation to end. Flash MX automatically assigns keyframe status to the frame and marks the in-between frames with an arrow to show the motion tween is complete.

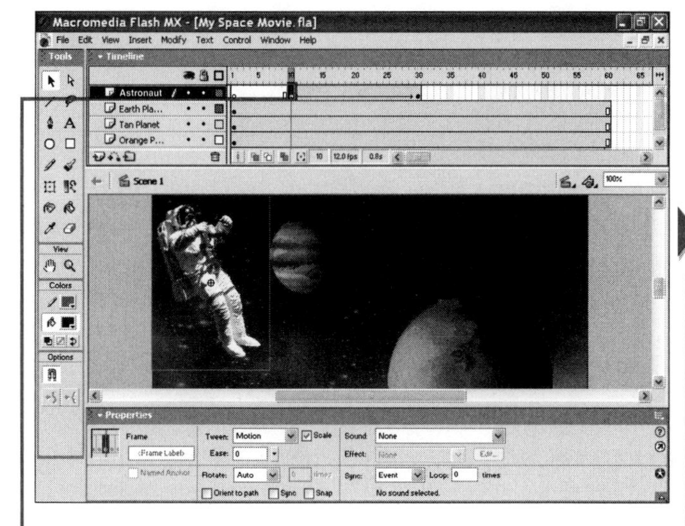

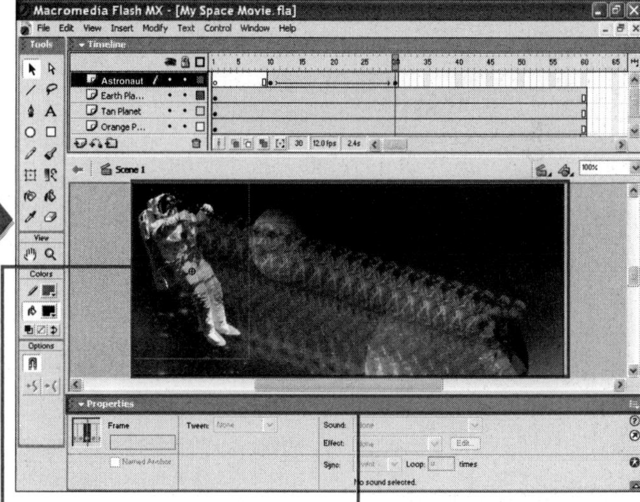

TEST THE TWEEN EFFECT

1 To view a motion tween in action, click in the first frame of the motion tween.

2 Press Enter (Return).

■ Flash MX plays the animation sequence.

■ Click the title bar of the panel to hide the Property inspector.

ANIMATE BY ROTATING A SYMBOL

You can rotate symbols to create quick and easy animations in your movie. Rotating animations move an object clockwise or counterclockwise on the Stage. Creating a rotating animation requires a series of keyframes in which you control how much rotation occurs in each keyframe. By assigning the animation sequence motion tween status, Flash MX calculates the in-between frames to create the rotation effect. The result is an animation in which the object appears to move in a clockwise or counterclockwise direction.

In Flash MX, you can create many types of objects that make good rotating animation effects. Shapes, lines, and text boxes all make good candidates for rotating. For example, you can make your corporate logo rotate at the top of your movie screen, or you can make a text box seem to rotate upside down and back. The steps in this section show how to rotate a text box, but you can apply the same steps to rotate any symbol on the Stage.

You can create your own rotation effects by animating the process frame-by-frame. However, assigning tween status to the sequence allows Flash to perform all the calculations for rotating the symbol for you, thus creating a smaller movie file size.

ANIMATE BY ROTATING A SYMBOL

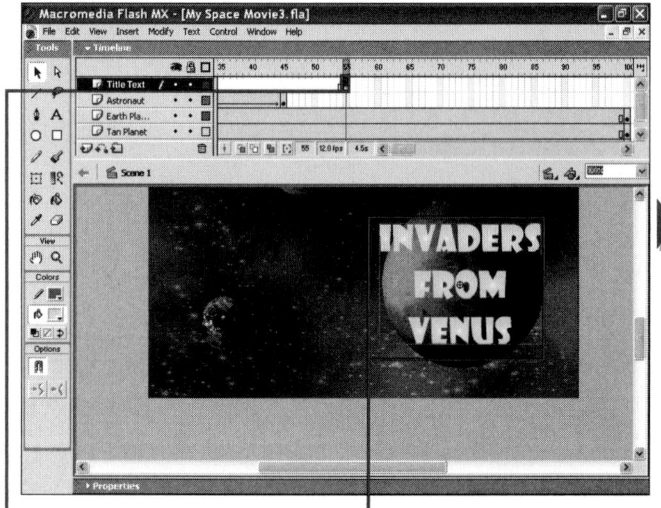

1 Insert a keyframe where you want to start the motion tween.

Note: To add a frame, see page 510.

2 Place the symbol you want to animate on the Stage.

Note: It is a good idea to place animations on a separate layer from the background of your movie.

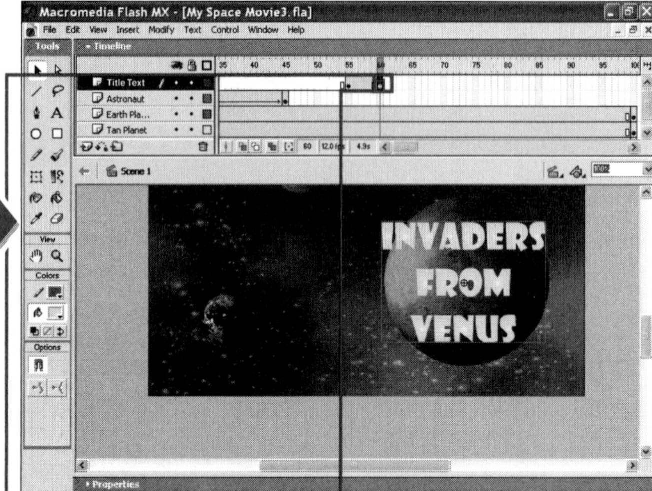

3 Click the next frame you want to include in the motion tween.

■ For example, you can start the rotation five frames later.

4 Insert a keyframe.

■ You can press F6 to insert a keyframe

Does it matter which direction I rotate the object?

✔ No. You can drag a rotation handle in any direction to start rotating the object. The direction you drag determines the direction of the rotation. For example, you may want your object to rotate counterclockwise. To do this, drag a rotation handle to the left. To rotate clockwise, drag the handle to the right. The rotation feature works best if you drag a corner handle versus a handle from the middle of the selected object.

Can I use the motion tween effect to rotate an object I draw on the Flash Stage?

✔ The Flash motion tween effect does not work with items you draw on the Stage. It does work with objects that you turn into symbols or that you group together. You can also motion tween text blocks. To turn objects you draw into symbols you can use with tweening, see page 452.

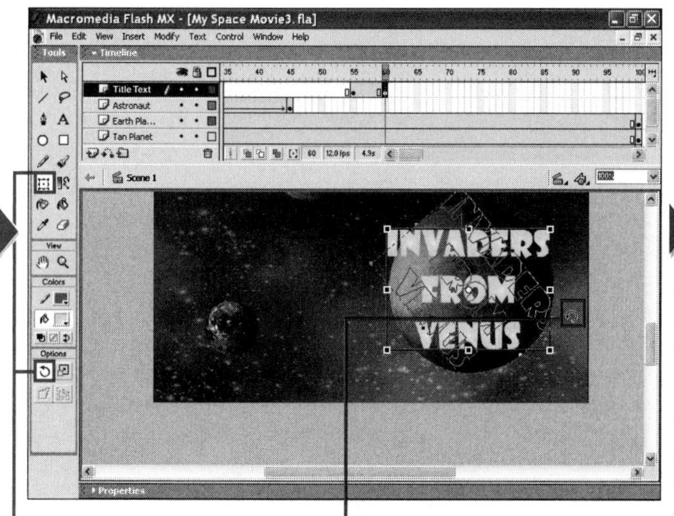

5 Click ⊡.

6 Click ⟳.

■ You can also click the Modify menu and click Transform, Rotate and Skew.

■ Flash MX surrounds the selected symbol with rotation handles, also called *edit points*.

7 Click and drag a rotation handle and rotate the symbol in the direction you want it to go.

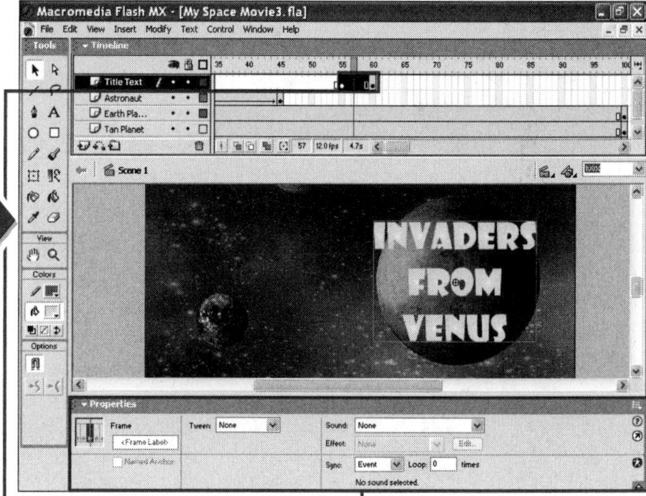

8 Click a frame between the two keyframes that make up your motion tween to select the frames.

Note: To select frames, see page 514.

9 Open the Property inspector.

Note: To open and close the Property inspector, see page 346.

CONTINUED

ANIMATE BY ROTATING A SYMBOL (CONTINUED)

When creating a rotating tween effect, you decide where to add keyframes at key points of the rotation. Flash MX cannot calculate the between frames without key spots that change the direction of the object in the rotation.

For example, if you rotate the symbol a full 360 degrees, you can change the rotation's progress by stretching it out over four keyframes, rotating the symbol 90 degrees each time. You can then add regular frames between the keyframes to lengthen the animation time. The end result is a symbol that rotates completely and smoothly from beginning to end.

You can use the Free Transform and the Rotate and Skew tools on the Drawing toolbar to change the degree of rotation in the motion tween. By clicking and dragging a rotation handle, or edit point, you can control whether the symbol rotates clockwise or counterclockwise.

When deciding a rotation direction, you may need to consider the type of symbol and animation you want to create. For example, if you are animating a turning wheel on a car, the wheel looks the most natural when rotating counterclockwise. If you animate the wheels in a clockwise position, the car appears to be going backwards.

ANIMATE BY ROTATING A SYMBOL (CONTINUED)

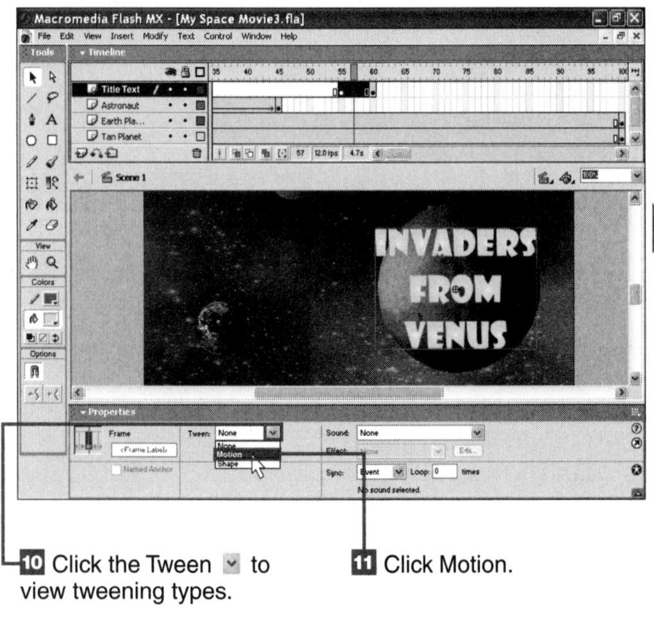

10 Click the Tween ▾ to view tweening types.

11 Click Motion.

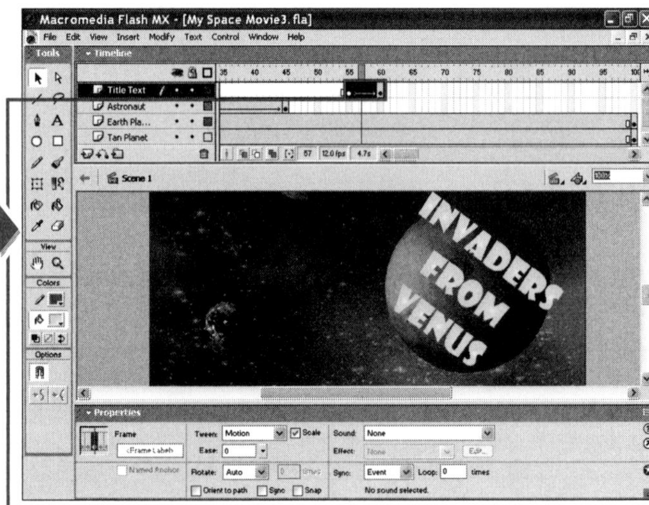

■ Flash MX calculates the in-between changes the symbol must undergo between keyframes. Flash also adds a motion tween arrow (⤚⟶) to the frames.

Can I tell Flash MX to rotate the symbol for me?

✔ Yes. Flash can help you with the rotation process if you prefer not to do it manually. From the Properties inspector, click the Rotate ▾, and then select a rotation direction. You can select CW for clockwise or CCW for counterclockwise. Next to the Rotate option, type the number of rotations you want to occur. Start with 1 to see whether you like the effect. When the movie plays, Flash MX rotates the symbol in the direction you specified.

How do I make the object seem to keep rotating?

✔ You can repeat the animation sequence of your movie by copying the rotation sequence and adding it to the end of the movie as many times as needed. You can also set the sequence to loop with the Go To and Play actions. See Chapter 31 to learn more about Flash actions.

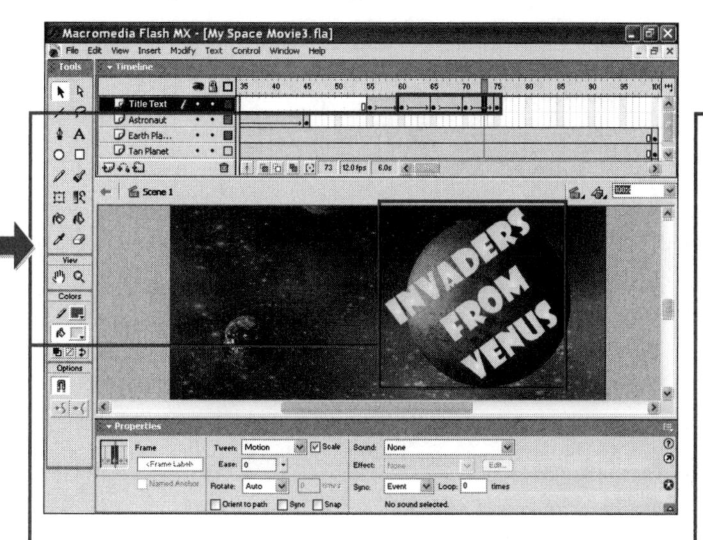

12 Repeat steps 3 to 11 to continue rotating the symbol.

■ You can make the symbol complete a full rotation.

Note: To ensure the motion tween stays in effect with additional keyframes you add, be sure to select both the start and end keyframes in the tween before applying Motion tween status.

TEST THE ROTATION EFFECT

1 To view the rotating effect, click in the first frame of the motion tween.

2 Press Enter.

■ Flash MX plays the animation sequence.

ANIMATE BY SPINNING A SYMBOL

You can create an animation effect that makes a symbol appear to spin in your Flash movie. Spinning effects are a quick way to animate an object in your movie. A spinning symbol rotates clockwise or counterclockwise a full 360 degrees. Unlike a rotating symbol in which you must define key points of change in the rotation, you can tell Flash MX to spin the symbol and calculate the necessary in-between frames to create the spin.

With a spin effect, you only need two keyframes to create the motion tween. The rotated object starts and ends up at the same spot, so the two keyframes that begin and end the effect remain the same. You just tell Flash MX which direction to spin the object. Flash MX then calculates all the incremental changes that must occur in the in-between frames to create the illusion of spinning.

You can apply the spinning symbol effect to a variety of objects. For example, if your movie features an airplane, you might animate the propeller with the spinning effect. If you are illustrating the passage of time in a scene, you might create a clock with spinning hands.

ANIMATE BY SPINNING A SYMBOL

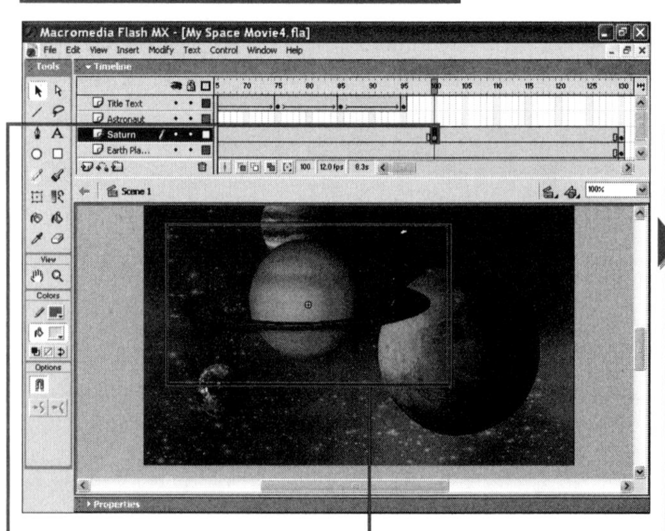

CREATE THE TWEEN EFFECT

1 Insert a keyframe where you want to start the spin motion tween in your movie Timeline.

Note: To add a frame, see page 510.

2 Place the symbol you want to animate on the Stage.

3 Click the end frame in which you want to conclude the motion tween.

4 Insert a keyframe.

■ You can press F6 to insert a keyframe.

Does it matter in which direction the symbol spins?

✔ No. If you let Flash pick a direction, it chooses the rotation that involves the least amount of change from frame to frame. This method creates a smoother animation sequence. To instruct Flash MX to handle the rotation, leave the Auto option selected.

My spinning effect happens too fast during playback. What can I do?

✔ You can add more regular frames between keyframes to slow down the animation effect. Try adding five or more frames and play back the movie again.

How do I make the motion tween continue past the end keyframe?

✔ If you plan to continue the motion tween, make sure you select the end and start keyframes, and in-between frames in the sequence. Click the end keyframe in the range. Next, press and hold down the Shift key while clicking to the left of the end keyframe. This should select all the frames in the motion tween. To stop a motion tween sequence, click the last keyframe in the sequence, and then assign None using the Tween setting in the Property inspector.

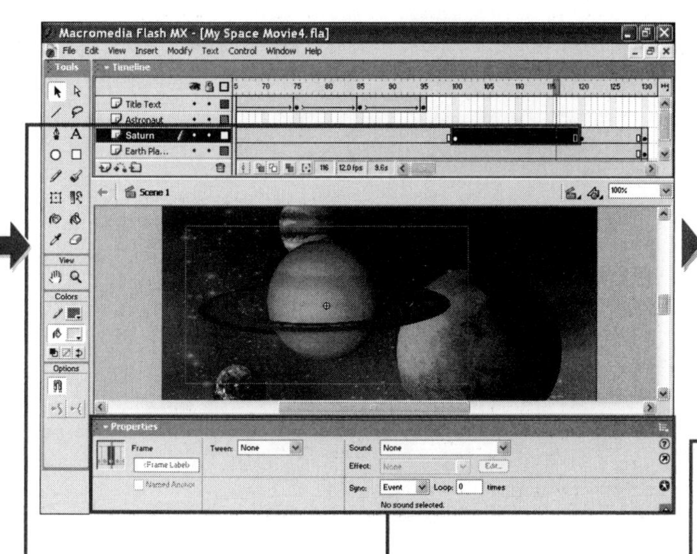

5 Double-click a frame between the two keyframes that make up your motion tween to select the frames.

6 Open the Property inspector.

Note: To open and close the Property inspector, see page 346.

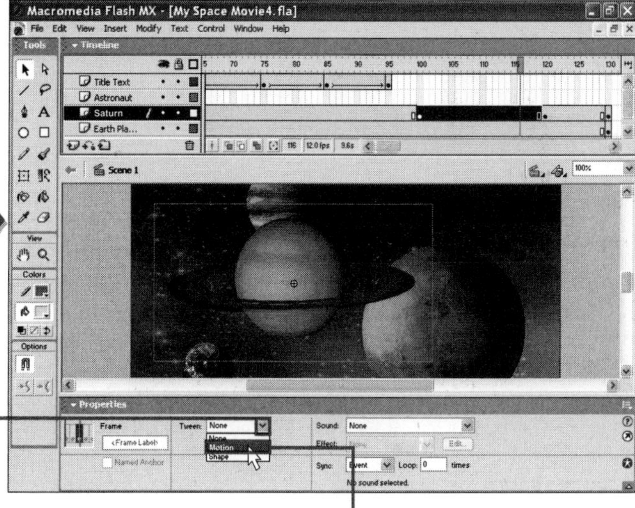

7 Click the Tween ⌄ to view tweening types.

8 Click Motion.

■ Flash MX adds a motion tween arrow (⟼) to the selected frames.

CONTINUED

ANIMATE BY SPINNING A SYMBOL (CONTINUED)

You can use the Rotation controls to spin items such as corporate logos or text blocks. By assigning a motion tween effect, Flash MX takes care of the hard work of incrementing the content of each frame in the sequence for you. You can specify how many times the symbol rotates between the two keyframes, and exactly which direction it goes.

The steps below use an example of a ringed planet as a spinning object. You can apply the same principles to other objects you create or add to the Flash Stage, such as a wheel, a button, or a star shape. You can also import artwork from another program and make it spin in your Flash movie.

As with rotating a symbol manually, the direction of a spinning object may be a factor you must consider when determining which way to spin the effect. You may need to consider the type of symbol and animation you want to create. If you are animating a turning wheel on a car, the wheel looks the most natural when spinning counterclockwise. If you spin the wheels in a clockwise position, the car appears to be going backwards.

ANIMATE BY SPINNING A SYMBOL (CONTINUED)

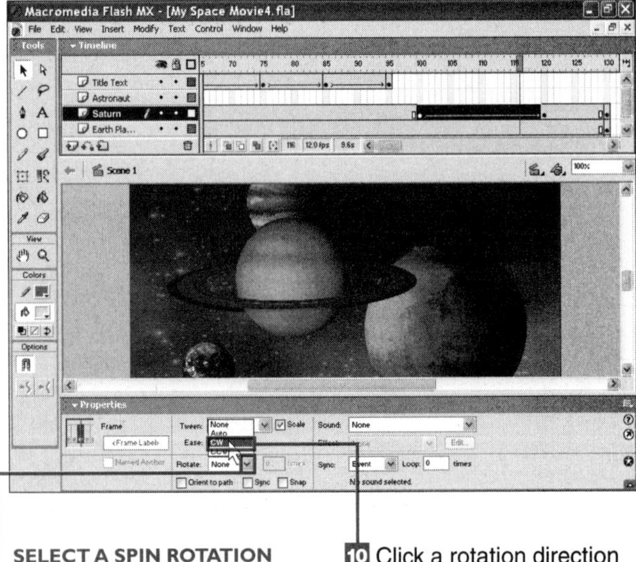

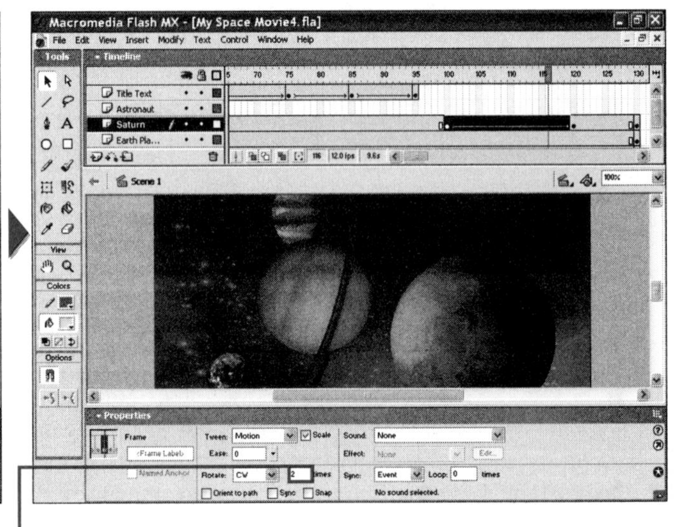

SELECT A SPIN ROTATION

9 Click the Rotate ▾ to view rotation types.

10 Click a rotation direction for the spin.

■ You can choose CW to spin the symbol clockwise.

■ You can choose CCW to spin the symbol counterclockwise.

11 Type the number of times you want the rotation to occur.

■ Flash MX calculates the in-between changes the symbol must undergo to move from the first keyframe to the next keyframe.

How can I see the spin effect play more than once?

✔ You can use the Test Movie feature to see your spin effect play more than once. Click the Control menu and click Test Movie. By default, the Flash Player is set to loop a movie within the Flash program window. To stop the animation at any time, press Enter.

What does the Auto rotate setting do?

✔ The Auto option setting rotates the selected object in the direction using the least amount of motion. You can choose Auto from the Rotate menu in the Property inspector to have Flash MX determine the rotation for you.

Can I control how quickly the object starts spinning?

✔ Yes. Use the Ease setting in the Property inspector to adjust the speed of the start of the spinning effect of your motion tween. You can drag the Ease slider up to accelerate the spin or down to slow it down.

How do I return the sequence to a static state?

✔ To reset the motion tween, click the Rotate ▾ in the Property inspector, and then click None. This resets the tween to a non-rotating, or static state.

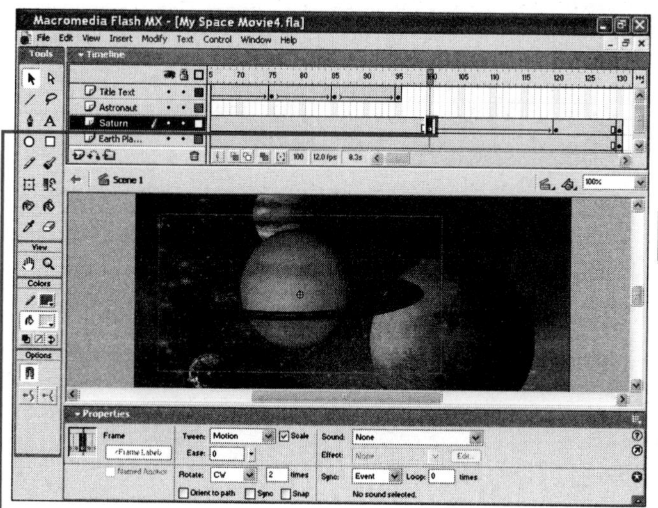

VIEW THE SPIN

1 To view a motion tween in action, click in the first frame of the motion tween.

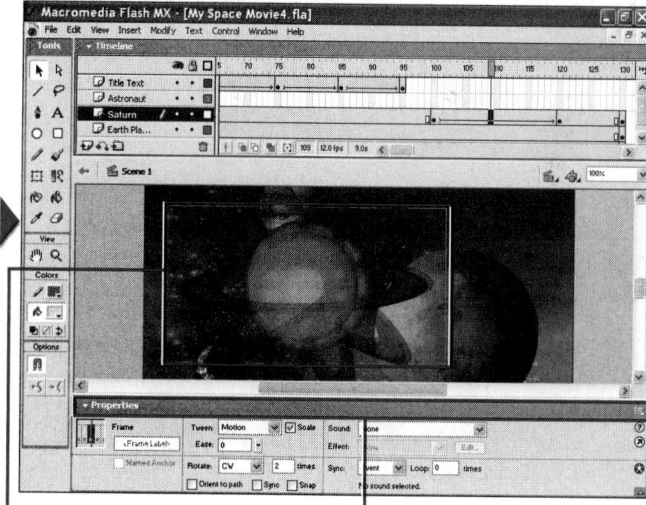

2 Press Enter (Return).

■ Flash MX plays the animation sequence.

■ You can click the panel's title bar to hide the Property inspector.

ANIMATE BY CHANGING SYMBOL SIZE

You can use the motion tween technique to create an animation effect that makes a symbol appear to grow or shrink in size. You define two keyframes, one of which includes the symbol scaled to a new size. With the motion tween effect applied, Flash MX fills in all the in-between frames with the incremental changes needed to create the illusion of growth or shrinkage.

You can animate size changes to create depth in an animation. For example, to create distance in a drawing, you might make a symbol seem very small in the background. As the symbol moves into the foreground, it grows in size, making it look closer.

You can use the same scaling tools from the Flash drawing tools to resize symbols for animation effects. The Scale command can be found as a button on the Main toolbar as well as a button at the bottom of the Drawing toolbar when the Free Transform tool is selected.

To help keep your animations organized, consider placing them on a separate layer from the movie background layer in the Flash Timeline. By placing an animation sequence on a different layer, you can easily locate the animation sequence and make edits to it without accidentally changing other elements, such as background elements, in the movie. To add layers to the timeline, see page 432.

ANIMATE BY CHANGING SYMBOL SIZE

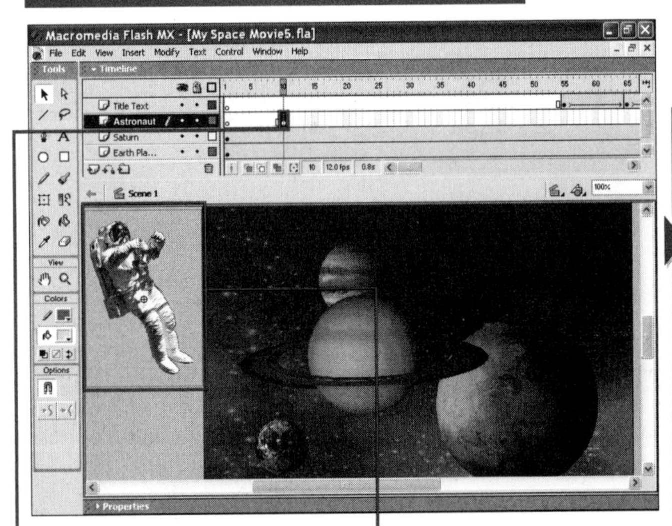

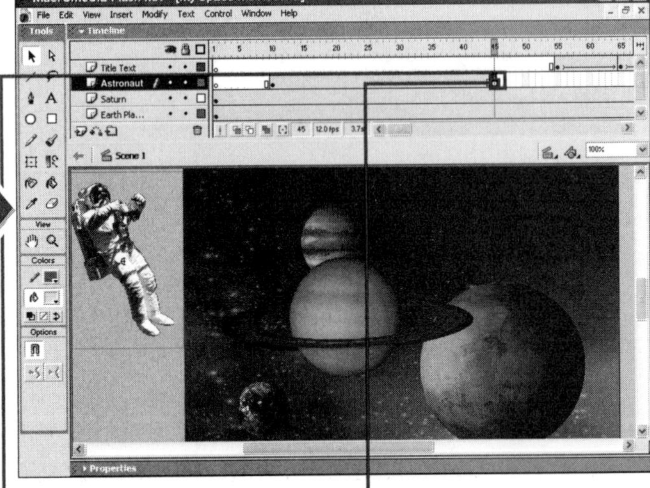

CREATE THE TWEEN EFFECT

1 Insert a keyframe where you want to start the motion tween.

Note: To add a frame, see page 510.

2 Place the symbol you want to animate on the Stage.

■ In this example, the animation starts off-screen in the work area before appearing on the Stage.

3 Click the end frame in which you want to conclude the motion tween.

■ In this example, the astronaut appears to shrink in the course of 35 frames.

4 Insert a keyframe.

■ You can press F6 to quickly insert a keyframe.

How can I tell what size changes Flash MX makes in my motion tween?

✔ You can use the Onion Skin tool to see the changes in the frames that surround the current frame. To turn on the feature, click at the bottom of the Timeline. After you activate the onion skin feature, you can drag the onion skin markers left or right to include other frames in the view.

Which Scale edit point should I drag?

✔ For best results, drag a corner edit point. Dragging the corner edit point away from the object makes the object larger, while dragging the corner edit point toward the object makes the object smaller.

How does Flash MX break down my motion tween to get from one keyframe to the next?

✔ By default, Flash MX makes equal incremental changes to tween the object from the first keyframe in the sequence to the last keyframe. If few regular frames separate the two keyframes, the change in size is minimal and appears quickly during playback. Adding a few regular frames to extend the animation effect slows it down during playback.

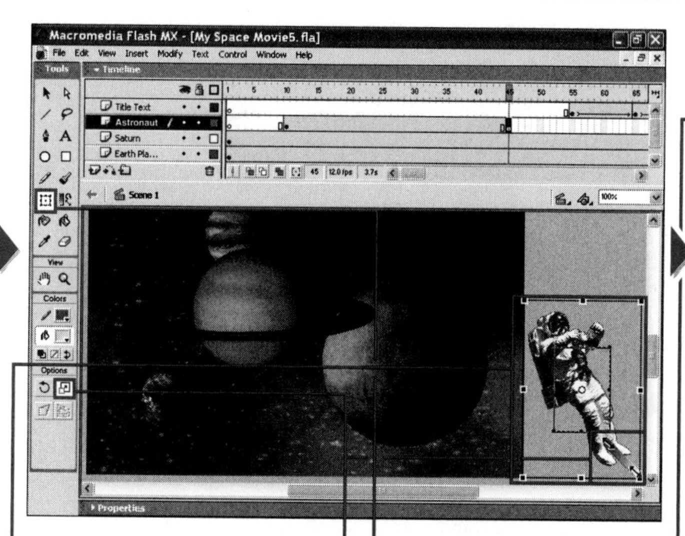

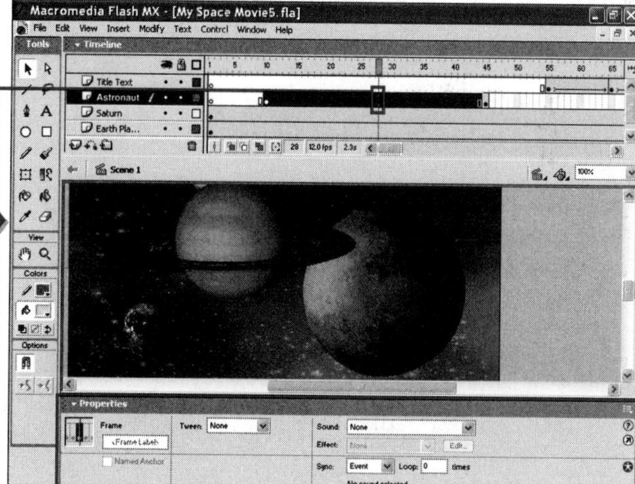

RESIZE THE SYMBOL

5 Select the symbol and place it where you want it to appear.

■ In this example, the animation ends off-screen in the work area after appearing on the Stage.

6 Click .

7 Click .

■ Flash MX surrounds the object with edit points, also called *handles*.

8 Click and drag a handle to resize the symbol.

9 Double-click a frame between the two keyframes that make up your motion tween.

10 Open the Property inspector.

Note: To open and close the Property inspector, see page 346.

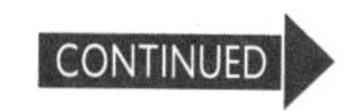

ANIMATE BY CHANGING SYMBOL SIZE (CONTINUED)

In addition to using the Scale tool to resize a symbol for your animation effect, you must also tell Flash MX the type of effect you want to create. You can do this by assigning the Scale option setting to your motion tween.

You can use the Scale option in the Property inspector to make symbols grow or shrink. The speed at which this occurs depends on how many frames you insert between the two defining keyframes. You can experiment with the number of regular frames to create just the right animation speed. For example, if your motion tween uses five in-between frames, adding five more slows down the tween effect. This means that the object seems to grow or shrink at a slower pace.

You can combine the symbol sizing effect with other animation techniques in Flash MX to create all sorts of interesting visuals. For example, you can make a symbol seem to change size and move across the screen at the same time, or spin around the Stage. Or you can make the symbol change size over the course of a path. Do not hesitate to combine techniques to create just the right animation effects for your movies.

ANIMATE BY CHANGING SYMBOL SIZE (CONTINUED)

11 Click the Tween ▾ to view tweening types.

12 Click Motion.

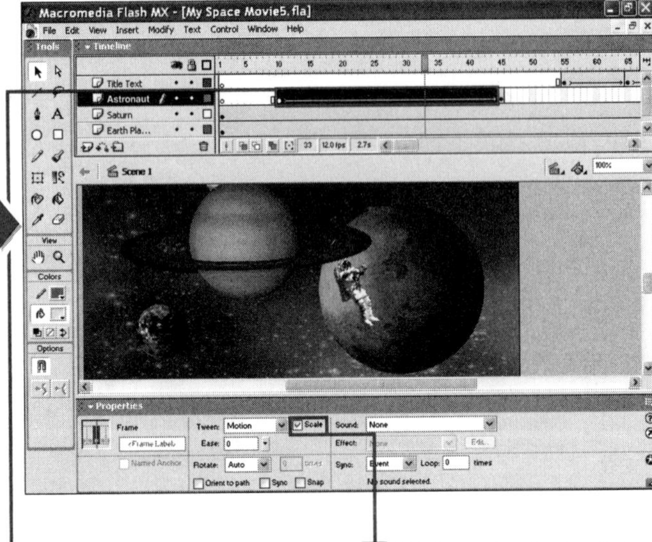

■ Flash MX adds a motion tween arrow (→) from the first keyframe in the tween effect to the last keyframe in the tween effect.

13 Click the Scale check box (☐ changes to ☑).

Can I both rotate and scale an object in a motion tween?

✔ Yes. To apply both rotation and scaling at the same time, click the Modify menu and click Transform, then click Scale and Rotate. This opens the Scale and Rotate dialog box. Enter values for both the percentage of scaling and the degree of rotation. Click OK and Flash applies both types of changes at once to the selected object.

Can I resize a movie clip symbol to create a similar animated scaling effect?

✔ No. When you add a movie clip symbol to the Stage and attempt to change the object size, the original clip changes as well.

My symbol does not grow or shrink very much. Why not?

✔ For a maximum tween effect, you need to make the final symbol in the tween sequence much smaller or larger than the symbol shown in the first keyframe. You should also allow plenty of regular keyframes in between the two anchor keyframes.

How do I make my object shrink back again to its original size?

✔ You can copy the entire sequence and apply the Reverse Frames command to make the object seem to shrink again after growing.

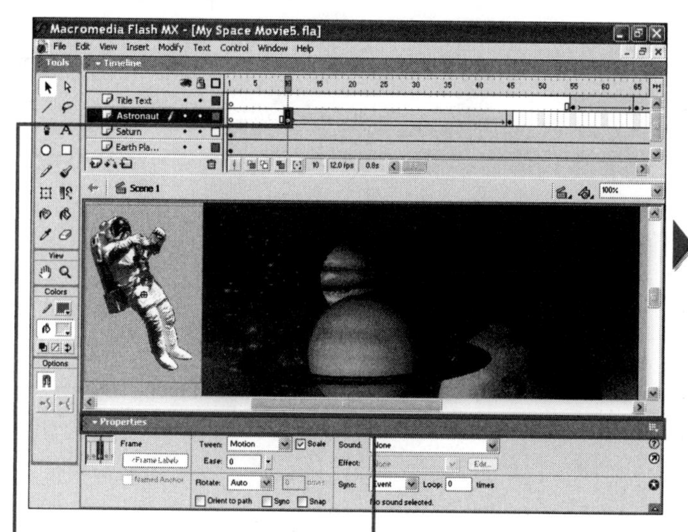

VIEW THE ANIMATION

1 To view a motion tween in action, click the first frame of the motion tween.

■ You can click the panel's title bar to hide the Property inspector.

2 Press Enter (Return).

■ Flash MX plays the animation sequence.

ANIMATE SYMBOLS ALONG A PATH

You can make a symbol follow a path you create in your Flash movie. A path is simply a line of direction you want the symbol to follow to create an animated sequence. You can animate symbols along a path to move objects around the Stage. For example, you might make a company logo follow a path to various text blocks you want the reader to see, or you might make a cartoon character seem to move along a path in a background image.

You create an animated path on a special layer called *motion guide layer*. Then, using the Flash motion tween technique and the motion layer guide, you define the start and end points in the sequence, draw a line that tells Flash exactly where you want the symbol to move, and then Flash calculates all the in-between frames for you. The motion guide layer is not visible when you export the movie.

Using the drawing tools, such as the Pencil tool or the Brush tool, you draw on the Stage exactly where you want the symbol to go. The symbol follows the path you specify. In the example shown below, the motion guide layer is used to define a flight path for a symbol of an astronaut in space.

ANIMATE SYMBOLS ALONG A PATH

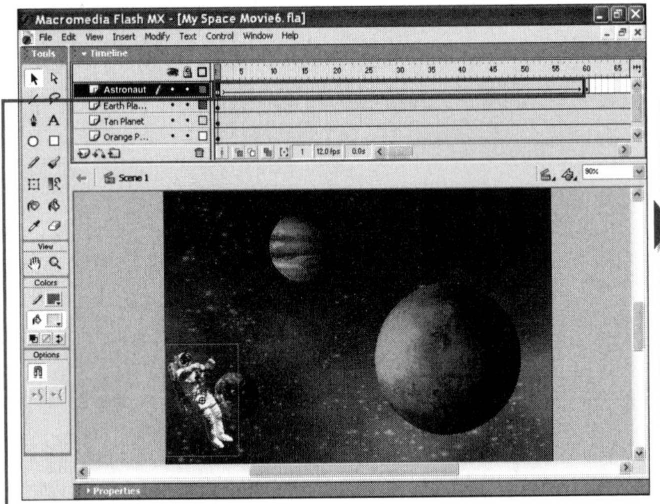

CREATE AND SELECT A TWEEN LAYER

1 Create a motion tween animation.

Note: To create a motion tween animation sequence, see page 536.

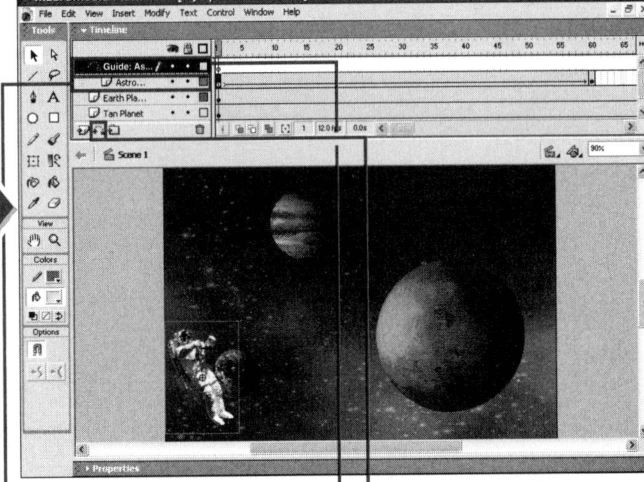

2 Click the layer containing the motion tween.

3 Click [icon].

■ Flash MX adds a motion guide layer directly above the layer containing the motion tween.

What Drawing tools can I use to define a path?

✔ You can use any of the following Drawing tools to add a path to the motion guide layer: Pencil, Brush, Line, Oval or Rectangle. For example, to make a symbol follow a perfect loop around the Stage, use the Oval tool to draw the motion path.

Do I have to start over if I make a mistake with my path line?

✔ It depends on which tool you use to draw the path. If you are connecting line segments with the Line tool, you can click the Edit menu and click Undo to undo a segment. If you are using the other drawing tools, you can activate the Undo command and start the path over again.

Does it matter which line color or thickness I use to draw the motion path?

✔ No. You can use any line color or attributes you like for the motion path. To make the line easy to see, consider using a thicker line style in a bright color. Before you start drawing the motion path, be sure to set the line attributes that you want in the Property inspector. To learn more about formatting lines, see Chapter 21.

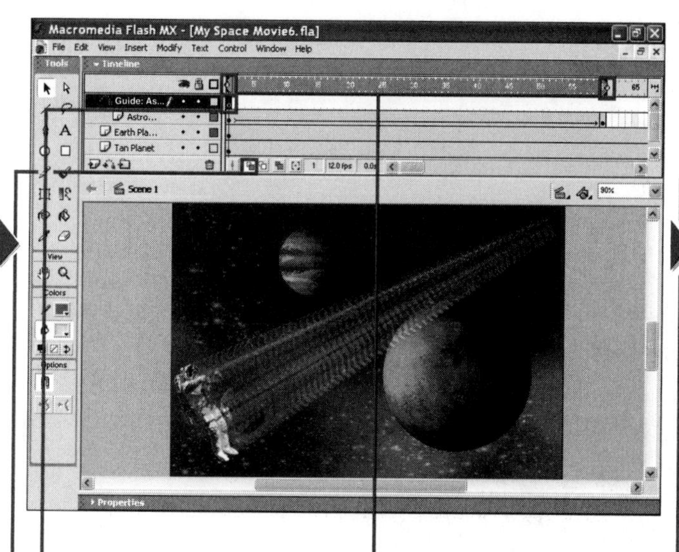

4 Click the motion guide layer's first frame.

5 Click the Onion Skin button ( ).

6 Click and drag the onion skin markers to include all the frames in the motion tween.

Note: For more information on the onion-skinning feature, see page 522.

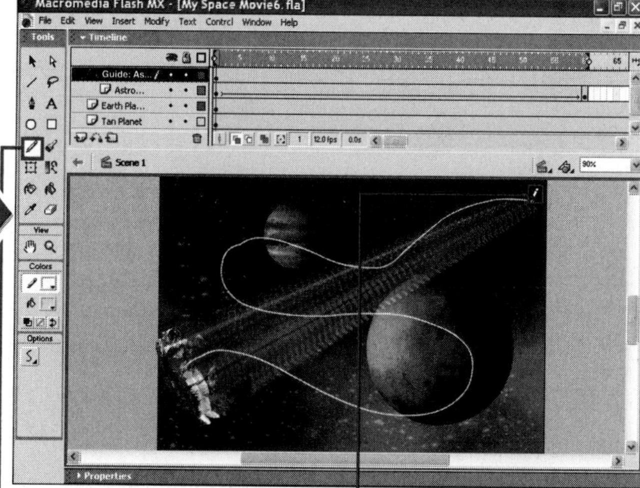

DRAW THE MOTION PATH

7 Click .

8 Draw a path from the center of the first motion tween symbol to the center of the last motion tween symbol.

Note: If you do not draw your path from center to center, the symbol cannot follow the motion path.

ANIMATE SYMBOLS ALONG A PATH (CONTINUED)

You can make your motion tween follow any type of path, whether it is extremely curvy, or it loops back on itself, or even if it falls out of the boundaries of the movie area. The motion guide path that you create does not appear in your final movie. Instead, the symbol appears to move along a path on its own accord.

When you draw your motion guide path, it is important that you not stop your path line when you reach the edge of the object you are animating, but continue it on to the middle of the object and then stop the path line. The path should be a continuous line in the movie.

In addition, you must also make sure that you select the Snap option in the Property inspector. This feature sticks the symbol to the path, much like a magnet. Without the Snap feature turned on, the symbol may not properly follow the path you have established. You can also control whether the symbol stays static when following the path, or orients itself to the path direction at all times.

ANIMATE SYMBOLS ALONG A PATH (CONTINUED)

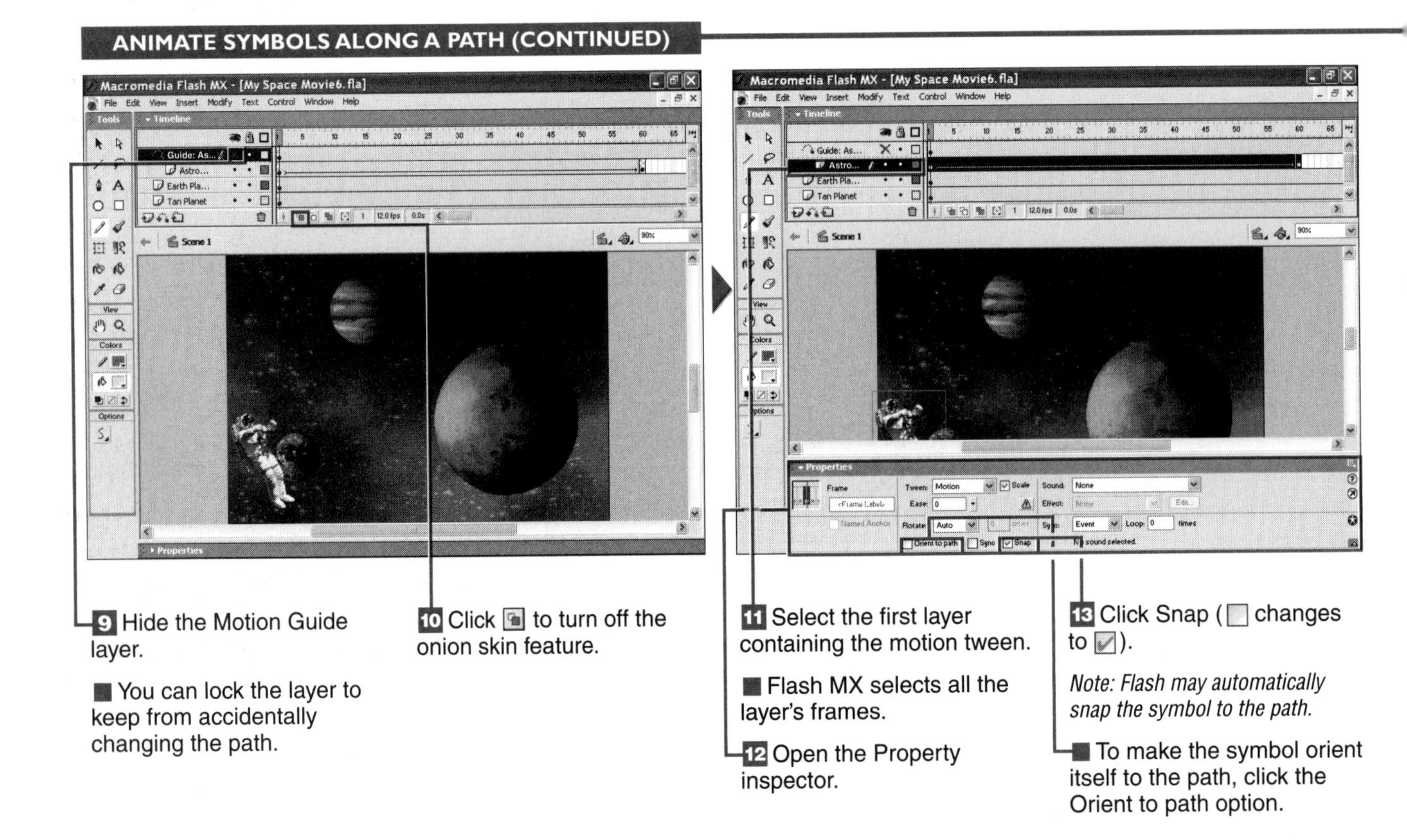

9 Hide the Motion Guide layer.

■ You can lock the layer to keep from accidentally changing the path.

10 Click ▣ to turn off the onion skin feature.

11 Select the first layer containing the motion tween.

■ Flash MX selects all the layer's frames.

12 Open the Property inspector.

13 Click Snap (☐ changes to ☑).

Note: Flash may automatically snap the symbol to the path.

■ To make the symbol orient itself to the path, click the Orient to path option.

Can I make my motion tween speed up?

✔ Yes. You can use the Ease setting in the Properties inspector to speed up the start of your motion tween as it follows the motion path. Drag the Ease slider up to start the object quickly along the motion path, or drag the slider down to slow the object down.

When I test my path, my symbol does not follow the path. Why not?

✔ Make sure you draw the path line so it starts and ends in the center of the object, and then click the Snap check box in the Property inspector. If you have trouble ending your path in the center of the object, use the onion skin feature to help you place the end of the path.

What does the Orient to path option do?

✔ The Orient to path option aligns the symbol to the path, regardless of which direction it goes. To make your symbol orient itself to the motion path you have drawn, click the Orient to path check box. Sometimes, the effect makes the movement of the symbol seem unnatural. To remedy the situation, you can insert extra keyframes in the animation sequence and rotate the symbol to where you want it on the path. Flash MX recalculates the in-between frames for you.

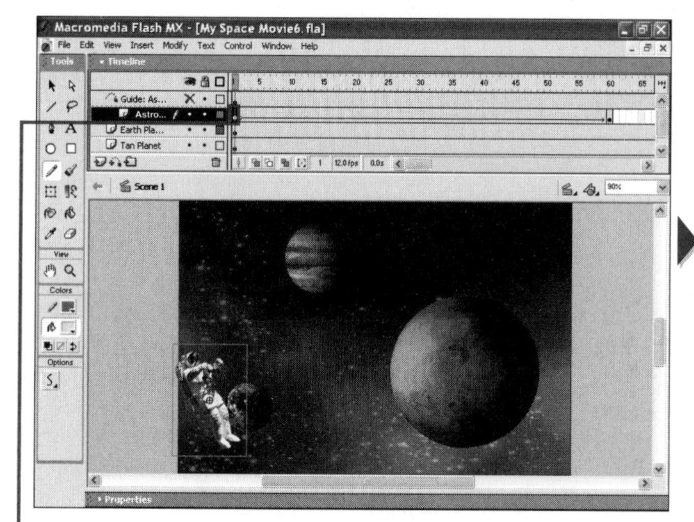

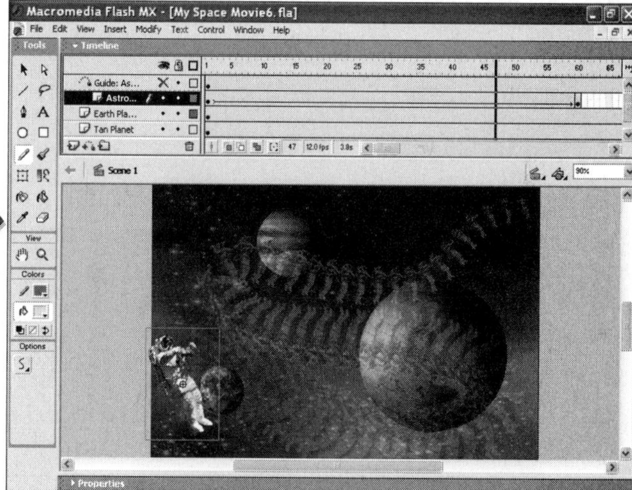

VIEW THE ANIMATION

1 Click in the first frame of the motion tween.

■ You can click the Property inspector title bar to hide the panel and view more of the Stage.

2 Press Enter (Return).

■ Flash MX plays the animation sequence along the motion path.

SET TWEEN SPEED

You can control the speed of a tweened animation by using the Flash MX Ease control. The Ease control eases the motion tween speed for the beginning or end of an animation sequence. The Ease control is found in the Property inspector.

One way you can slow down or speed up an animation sequence is by adding or subtracting frames. However, the addition or subtraction of regular frames between two keyframes does not affect tween speed. With a motion tween, Flash MX distributes the incremental changes between the two keyframes evenly over the regular frames, regardless of how many frames are in between. However, you can control the effects of a tween sequence using the Ease control.

The Ease control enables you to slow down or speed up the beginning or end of your tween effect. For example, perhaps you have a bumblebee symbol that lands on a flower symbol in your movie. You may prefer the bumblebee to fly quickly at the beginning of your motion tween, but slow down right before it lands on the flower symbol. You can change the Ease setting to adjust the motion tween speed.

SET TWEEN SPEED

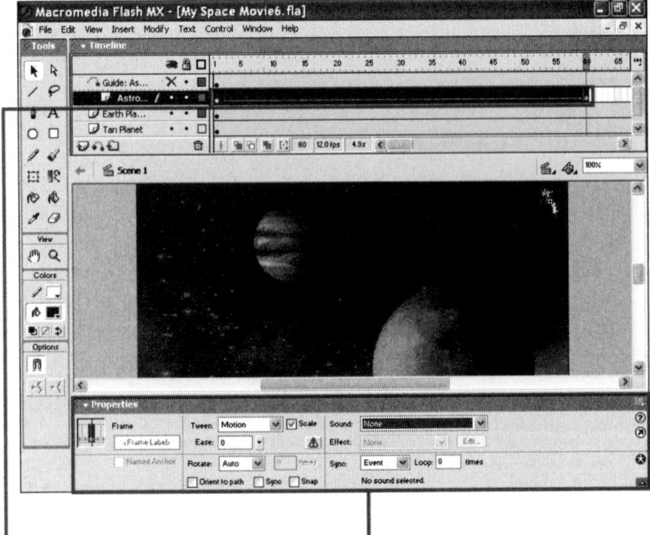

1 Select the frames containing the motion tween you want to adjust.

2 Open the Property inspector.

Note: To open and close the Property inspector, see page 346.

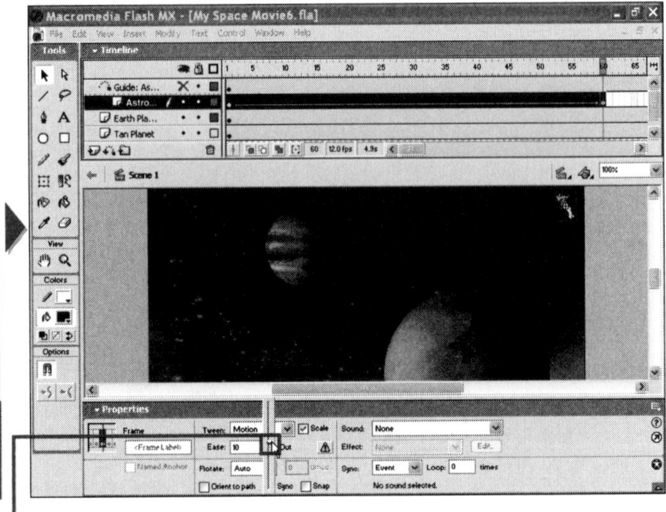

3 Click and drag the Ease slider to a new setting.

■ Drag the slider up to accelerate the tween speed.

■ Drag the slider down to decelerate the tween speed.

■ A zero value indicates a constant rate of speed.

Note: To test the new speed, click the first frame in the motion tween and press Enter (Return).

ADJUST SYMBOL OPACITY

You can control the opacity of an animated symbol instance by using the Alpha setting control. Opacity, also called the Alpha setting in Flash MX, is the level of transparency for a symbol in your movie. By default, all symbols are 100% opaque, which means they are completely solid in appearance. You can set another level of transparency using the Alpha control.

For example, you may want the symbol to appear to fade out at the end of a motion tween, or fade in at the beginning of the animation. Or you might want the symbol to remain somewhat opaque in order to see a background layer behind the symbol.

You can find the Alpha setting in the Property inspector. The Alpha setting allows you to change the opacity or alpha value of an instance in your Flash movie. Transparency in Flash MX is measured in a percentage range, with 100% being completely visible, or saturated, and 0% being completely transparent.

Can I change the brightness of a symbol in a motion tween?

✔ Yes. Click the symbol, and then click the Color ▾ in the Property inspector to find settings for controlling the Brightness of an instance or the color Tint of the object.

ADJUST SYMBOL OPACITY

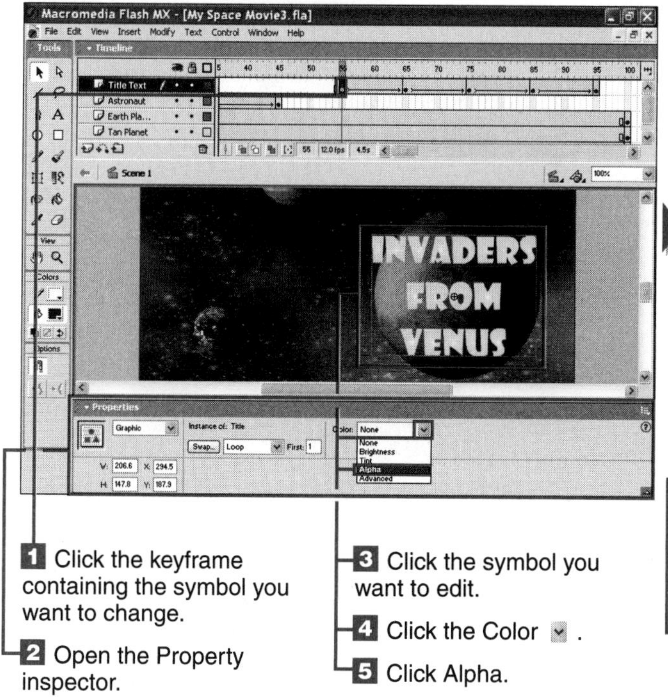

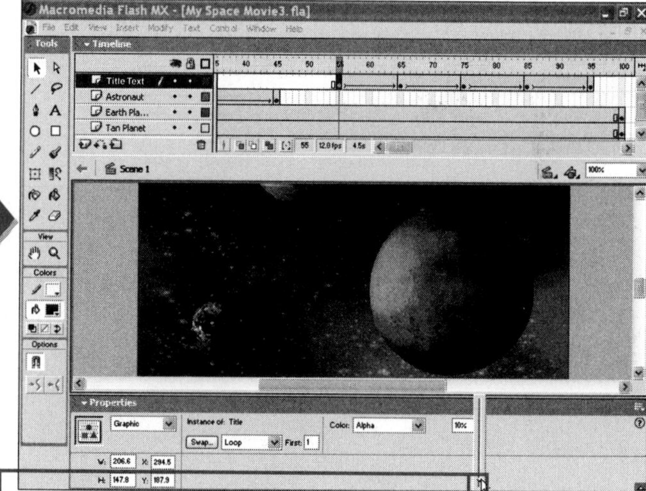

1 Click the keyframe containing the symbol you want to change.

2 Open the Property inspector.

Note: To open and close the Property inspector, see page 346.

3 Click the symbol you want to edit.

4 Click the Color ▾.

5 Click Alpha.

■ The Alpha setting option appears.

6 Drag the Alpha slider up or down to increase or decrease symbol opacity.

Note: To test the new speed, click the first frame in the motion tween and press Enter (Return).

CREATE A SHAPE TWEEN

You can create a shape tween to morph objects you draw on the Stage. Shape tweens enable you to create dynamic animations that change from one form to an entirely different form over the course of several frames. For example, you can morph a circle shape into a square or turn your company logo into a graphic depicting a product. Unlike other animations you create in Flash MX, shape tweening does not require the use of symbols or groups. You can animate any object you draw with the Drawing tools using the shape tween effect.

Like the motion tween effect, you define two keyframes when applying a shape tween. The first keyframe shows the beginning state of the object you want to morph. The last keyframe in the sequence shows the end state of the shape tween, the object in its morphed state. When the shape tween is applied, Flash MX calculates all the necessary frames in between to create the morphing effect. You cannot shape tween a symbol, text, or grouped object unless you apply the Break Apart command to break the objects into shapes. To apply the Break Apart command, see page 426.

CREATE A SHAPE TWEEN

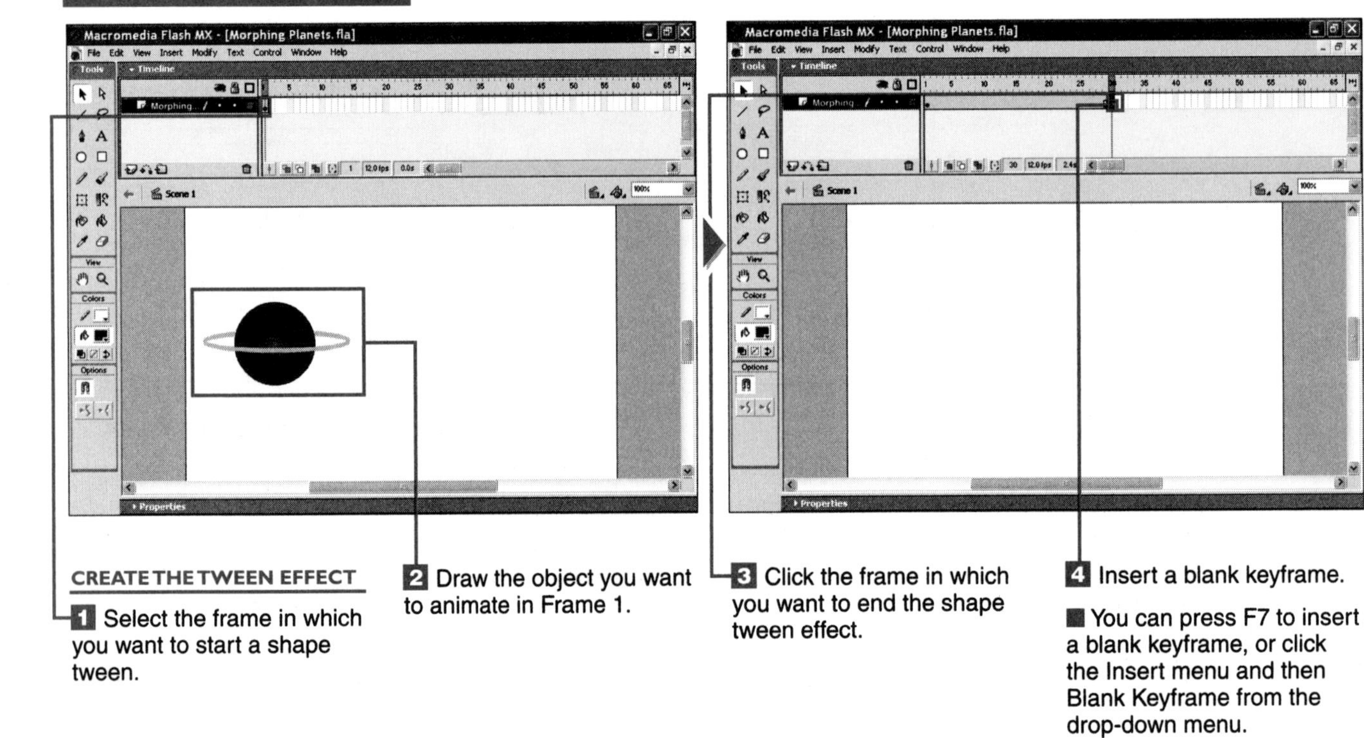

CREATE THE TWEEN EFFECT

1 Select the frame in which you want to start a shape tween.

2 Draw the object you want to animate in Frame 1.

3 Click the frame in which you want to end the shape tween effect.

4 Insert a blank keyframe.

■ You can press F7 to insert a blank keyframe, or click the Insert menu and then Blank Keyframe from the drop-down menu.

How is a shape tween different from a motion tween?

✔ With a motion tween, you can animate only symbols, grouped objects, or text blocks. With a shape tween, you can animate any object you draw on the Stage, and you do not have to save it as a symbol first or group it in order for Flash to create in-between frames. You cannot shape-tween a symbol or a group of objects. A motion tween is good for moving objects from one point to another, whereas you should use a shape tween when you want to morph the object into another object entirely.

Can I control the speed of the shape tween?

✔ Yes. By default, Flash MX spreads out the incremental changes in the shape tween effect evenly among the in-between frames. By applying the Ease control, however, you can speed up or slow down the beginning or end of the shape tween. The Ease control works the same way for shape tween animations as it does for motion tween animations. You can find the Ease control in the Property inspector. To learn more about using the Ease control, see page 556.

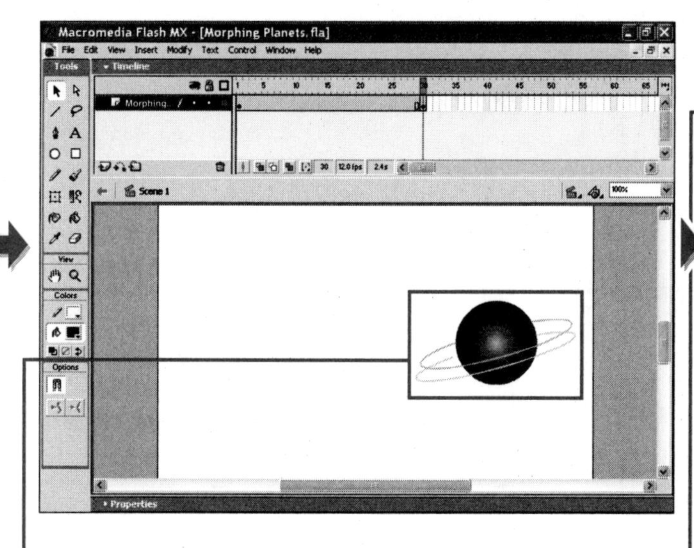

5 Draw the shape into which you want your image to morph, such as a variation of the first frame's shape, or an entirely different shape.

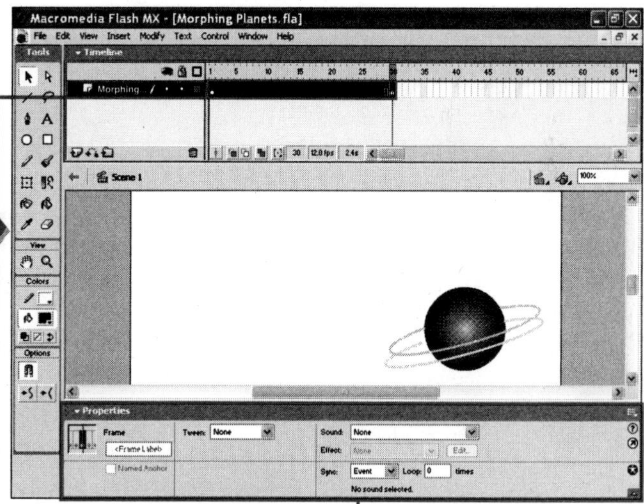

6 Click a frame in the tween sequence that contains the shape tween you want to create, or select the frames in the sequence.

Note: To select frames, see page 514.

7 Open the Property inspector.

Note: To open and close the Property inspector, see page 346.

CONTINUED

CREATE A SHAPE TWEEN (CONTINUED)

You can use shape tweens to morph between all kinds of objects you draw, including text that you turn into an object. *Morph* is a term derived from the word *metamorphose*, pertaining to a change from one state to another — like a cocoon to a butterfly. Morphing shapes is a common task for Web page animators. You can use as many shape tweens as you like in an animation, and you can start one right after the other in the Timeline.

For best results, tween one shape at a time in your Flash movie. Doing so gives you greater control over the object and the tween effect.

When defining a shape tween, the Properties inspector has a blending option to help you create just the right look for your effect. You can apply two types of blends to your shape: Distributive or Angular. If you apply a Distributive blend, Flash MX smoothes out the straight lines and sharp corners as your shape morphs. If you choose an Angular blend, Flash MX keeps all the sharp angles and lines intact during the tween.

Creating just the right effect may take a bit of practice. For best results, use objects you draw in Flash MX to change shapes.

CREATE A SHAPE TWEEN (CONTINUED)

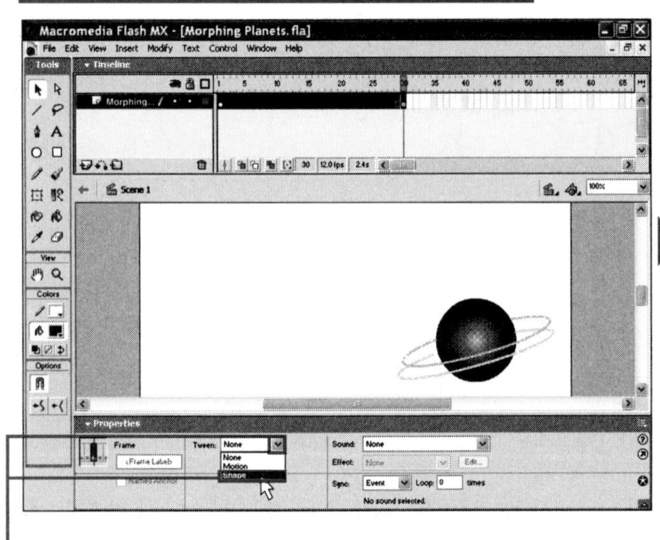

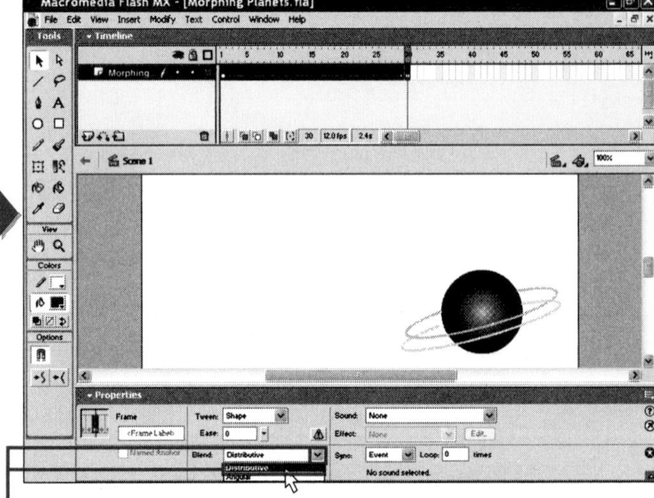

MORPH THE SHAPE

8 Click the Tween ▾ to view tweening types.

9 Click Shape.

■ Flash MX shades the selected frames green in the Timeline and adds a tween arrow from the first keyframe to the last.

10 Click ▾ to view blend types.

11 Click a blend type.

■ You can use the Distributive blend to smooth out lines in the in-between frames.

■ You can use the Angular blend to keep the sharp corners and straight lines that occur during the morph effect.

Can I use a symbol from the Library of my movie?

✔ Yes, but you must convert the symbol first. You cannot shape tween symbols, but you can take a symbol and break it apart into objects that the shape tween effect can morph. To turn a symbol into an object, do the following: place the symbol on the Stage, click Modify, and then click Break Apart.

Depending on how many groups of objects comprise the symbol, you may need to select the command several times to reach the last level of ungrouped objects.

Can I tween multiple shapes on the Stage?

✔ Yes. However, all the shapes must be on the same layer. Remember, Flash MX cannot tween symbols or grouped shapes. Flash also cannot shape tween raster or bitmap images.

Can I quickly lengthen my shape tween?

✔ Yes. Just drag the end keyframe to lengthen the tween effect. Flash MX automatically recalculates the new in-between frames for you.

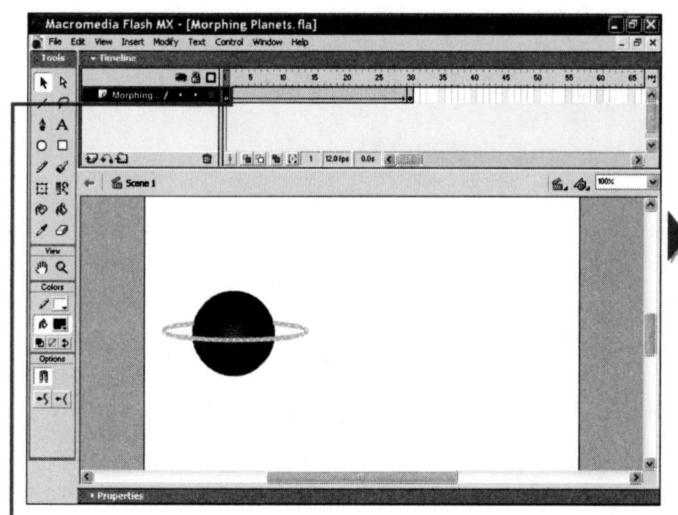

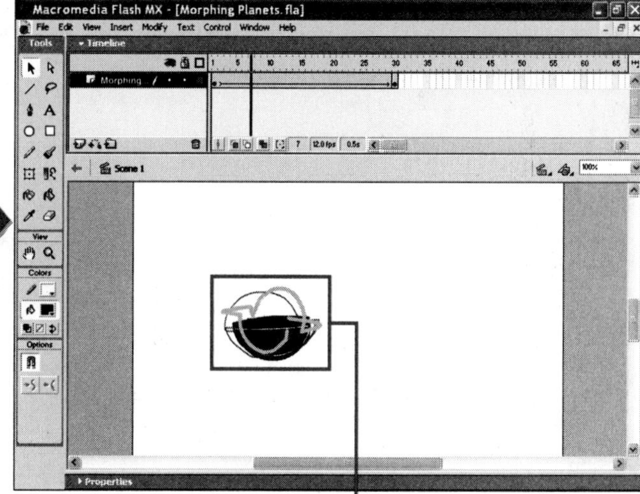

VIEW THE ANIMATION

1 To view a shape tween in action, click the first frame of the shape tween.

■ You can click the Property inspector title bar to hide the panel and view more of the Stage.

2 Press Enter (Return).

■ Flash MX plays the animation sequence.

ASSIGN SHAPE HINTS

You can have more control over the morphing process during a shape tween by using shape hints. Flash MX determines how to morph shapes during a shape tween by adding shape hints. A shape hint is a marker that identifies an area on the original shape that matches up with an area on the final shape and marks a crucial point of a change. Shape hints are labeled *a* through *z*, which means you can use up to 26 shape hints in a shape tween.

You can use shape hints to morph a particularly complex shape. For example, you can shape tween a company logo and turn it into a picture of your top-selling product, or you can shape tween a cartoon character into a completely different character for a Web page. When you assign shape hints to the object that you are morphing, Flash uses this information to determine the points of change.

Shape hints appear as tiny numbers in a circle icon, starting out yellow in the first keyframe of the sequence and turning green in the end keyframe. Shape hints are placed along the edges of the shape you are morphing, and must be placed in alphabetical order.

ASSIGN SHAPE HINTS

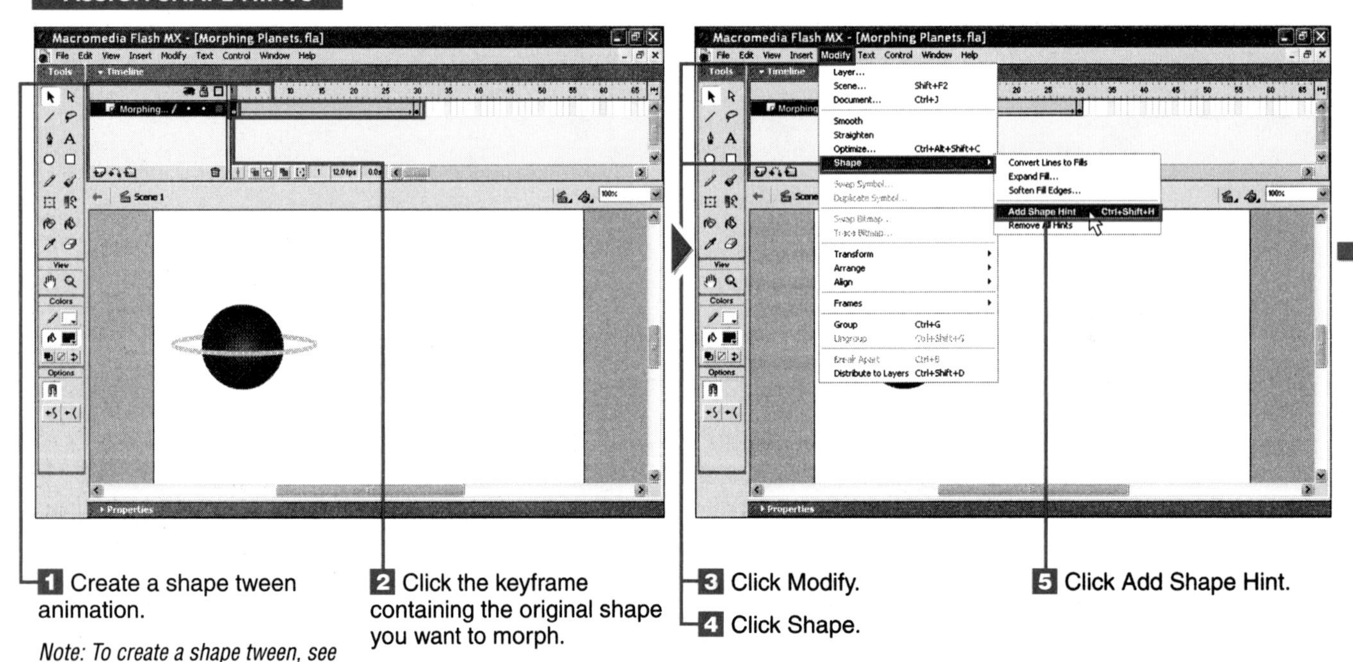

1 Create a shape tween animation.

Note: To create a shape tween, see page 558.

2 Click the keyframe containing the original shape you want to morph.

3 Click Modify.

4 Click Shape.

5 Click Add Shape Hint.

What can I do if my shape hints vary their positions between the first keyframe and the last?

✔ The onion skin feature enables you to see exactly where you place shape hints around an object between first and last keyframes. To use this feature, first make sure you have magnified your view so that you can easily see where you place the hints. Use the View drop-down list at the bottom of the Stage area to set a magnification. Next, turn on the onion skin feature and move the onion skin markers to show all the frames within the shape tween. Click to turn on the outlining feature.

What if shape hints still do not help create the morphing effect I am looking for?

✔ You can solve this problem by creating a few intermediate shapes that Flash MX can use to determine how to morph the shape. For example, if you are shape-tweening a complex shape that includes many details around the edges, you can add a few keyframes that contain key changes in the shape rather than relying on just a starting keyframe and an ending keyframe to complete the tween.

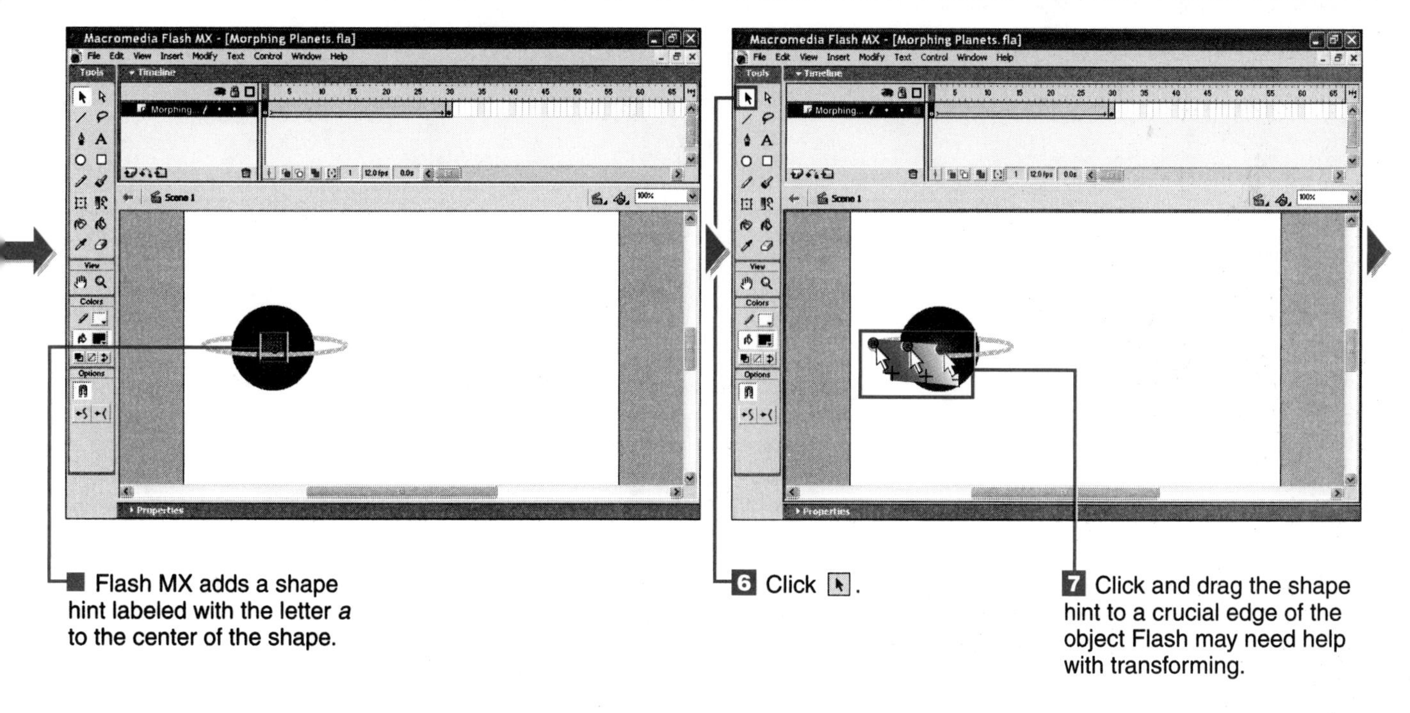

■ Flash MX adds a shape hint labeled with the letter *a* to the center of the shape.

6 Click .

7 Click and drag the shape hint to a crucial edge of the object Flash may need help with transforming.

CONTINUED

ASSIGN SHAPE HINTS (CONTINUED)

The more shape hints you add to the shape tween, the smoother the morphing transformation will be. You can use up to 26 hints on your shape. When determining where to place your shape hints, position them at key areas of change around the edges of the shape. For example, to morph a heart into a star shape, you can place shape hints at all the edges where the points of the star will appear as well as where points are recessed to create the star shape.

You must also make sure the shape hints you place around the object in the second keyframe correspond with the same order of shape hints on the object in the first keyframe. If you do not use the order that you used in the first keyframe, the effect does not work properly.

For best results, assign shape hints counterclockwise around the edges of the shape, starting with the top left corner of the shape. Use the onion skin feature to help you see how the shape changes across the animation sequence.

ASSIGN SHAPE HINTS (CONTINUED)

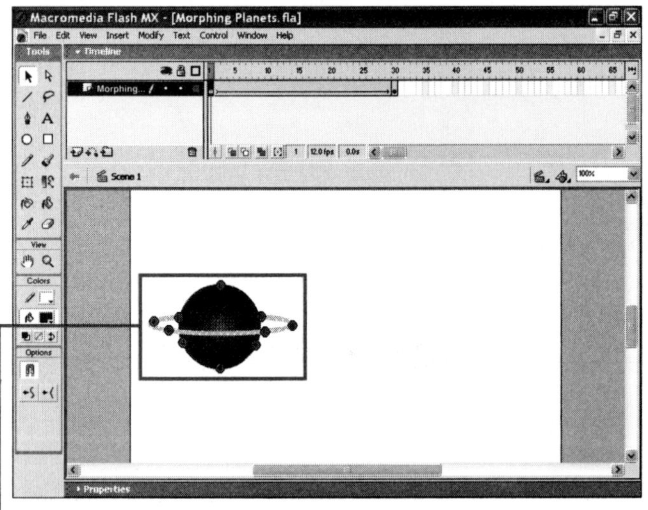

8 Repeat steps 3 to 7 to continue adding shape hints to other areas on the shape.

Note: For best results, arrange shape hints around the edge of the shape in alphabetical order going clockwise or counterclockwise.

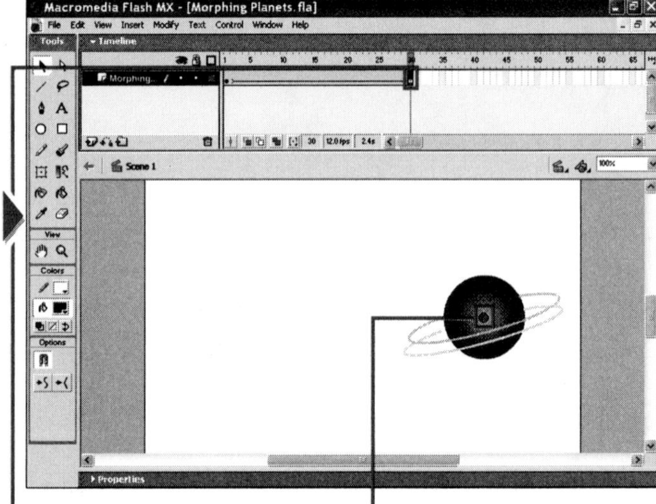

9 Click the last keyframe in the shape tween.

■ In this example, shape hints have been added to the final shape and stacked in the middle of the shape.

Can I see all the shape hints for my shape tween effect?

✔ Yes. Make sure that you are currently viewing the layer containing the tween effect. Click the View menu and click Show Shape Hints.

I am having trouble making sure I place the hints in the right place. What can I do?

✔ Although it is tedious, one way to keep your shape hints straight is to switch back and forth between the two keyframes as you add them. This way you can be sure you placed both hints in the same spot.

How do I remove a shape hint?

✔ To remove a shape hint, click and drag the shape hint completely off the Stage area. To rid the keyframe of all the shape hints, click the Modify menu and click Shape, then click Remove All Hints.

Can I check my shape tween progress in the Flash Player window?

✔ Yes. Click the Control menu and click Test Movie. Flash MX plays the animation in the Flash Player window. Click the Close button to return to the Flash MX program window.

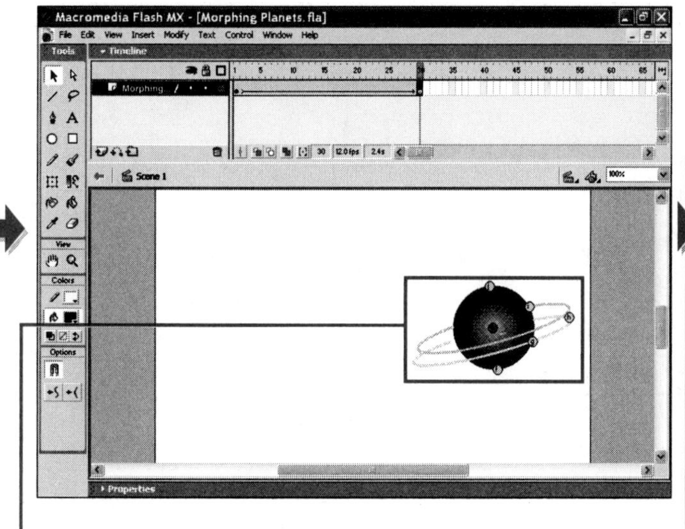

10 Click and drag each shape hint to the correct position around the final shape.

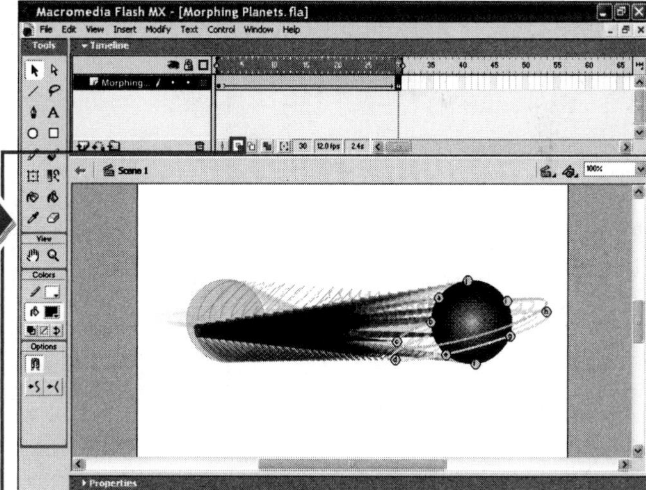

■ You can adjust the shape hints in the final frame as needed.

■ Clicking ▣ lets you see how the in-between frames morph the shape as directed by the shape hints.

■ To view the animation, click the first keyframe and press Enter (Return).

REVERSE FRAMES

You can reverse the order of your animation sequence with the Reverse Frames feature. This feature literally reverses the order of frames in your movie. With this feature, Flash MX enables you to copy a sequence of frames in a motion tween and paste them elsewhere in the Timeline, only in the reverse order. For example, if you create a motion tween that makes a symbol appear to grow in size, you can reverse the frame sequence to create the opposite effect. You can use the Reverse Frames feature when you need to repeat the animation sequence in the reverse without having to re-create the entire animation effect yourself.

The Reverse Frames feature allows you to save time creating an animation by reusing frames in your movie. For example, perhaps you have a flag logo that waves, or a candle symbol that has a flickering flame. You can copy the sequence and make it play in reverse. This saves you from having to create another animation sequence for the backwards effect. You can use the Reverse Frames feature to create a variety of animation effects in your movies.

REVERSE FRAMES

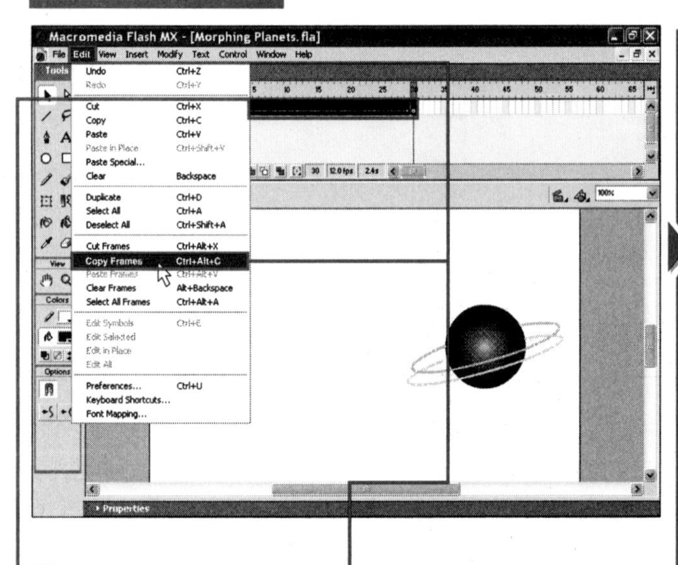

1 Select all the frames included in the animation sequence for which you want to create a reverse effect.

Note: Make sure you include the end keyframe in your selection.

■ If you have trouble selecting the sequence of frames, press and hold down Shift+Ctrl while clicking the frames.

2 Click Edit.

3 Click Copy Frames.

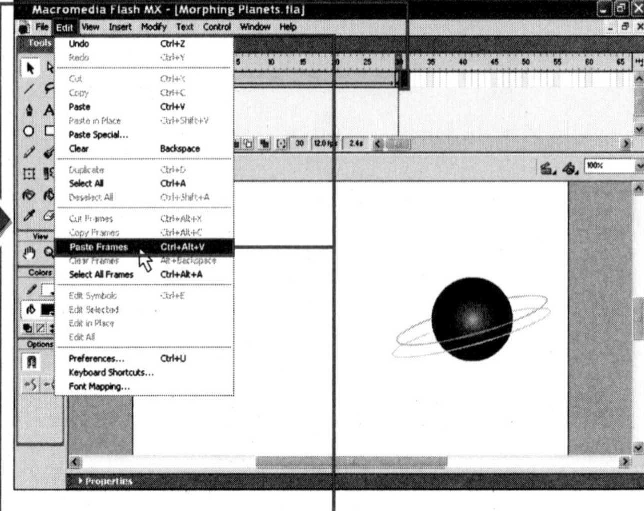

4 Click the frame where you want to insert the copied frames.

5 Click Edit.

6 Click Paste Frames.

How do I check to see whether the reverse frames work?

✔ You can check your movie by opening the Flash Player window. Click the Control menu and click Test Movie. The Flash Player window opens and plays the sequence. To stop the movie, press Enter. To close the Player window, click ✕.

How else can I activate the Reverse Frames command?

✔ Right-click the frame sequence and a pop-up menu appears with frame-related commands, including the Reverse Frames, Copy Frames, and Paste Frames commands.

How do I undo a reverse?

✔ You can immediately undo the Reverse Frames command if you click the Edit menu and click Undo. Make sure you do this immediately after you realize you are not happy with the animation results.

My shape is supposed to grow and shrink in size, but the reverse frames do not work. Why not?

✔ It is very important that you select the end keyframe in the tween sequence when you copy the frames. If you do not, the tween effect does not work properly.

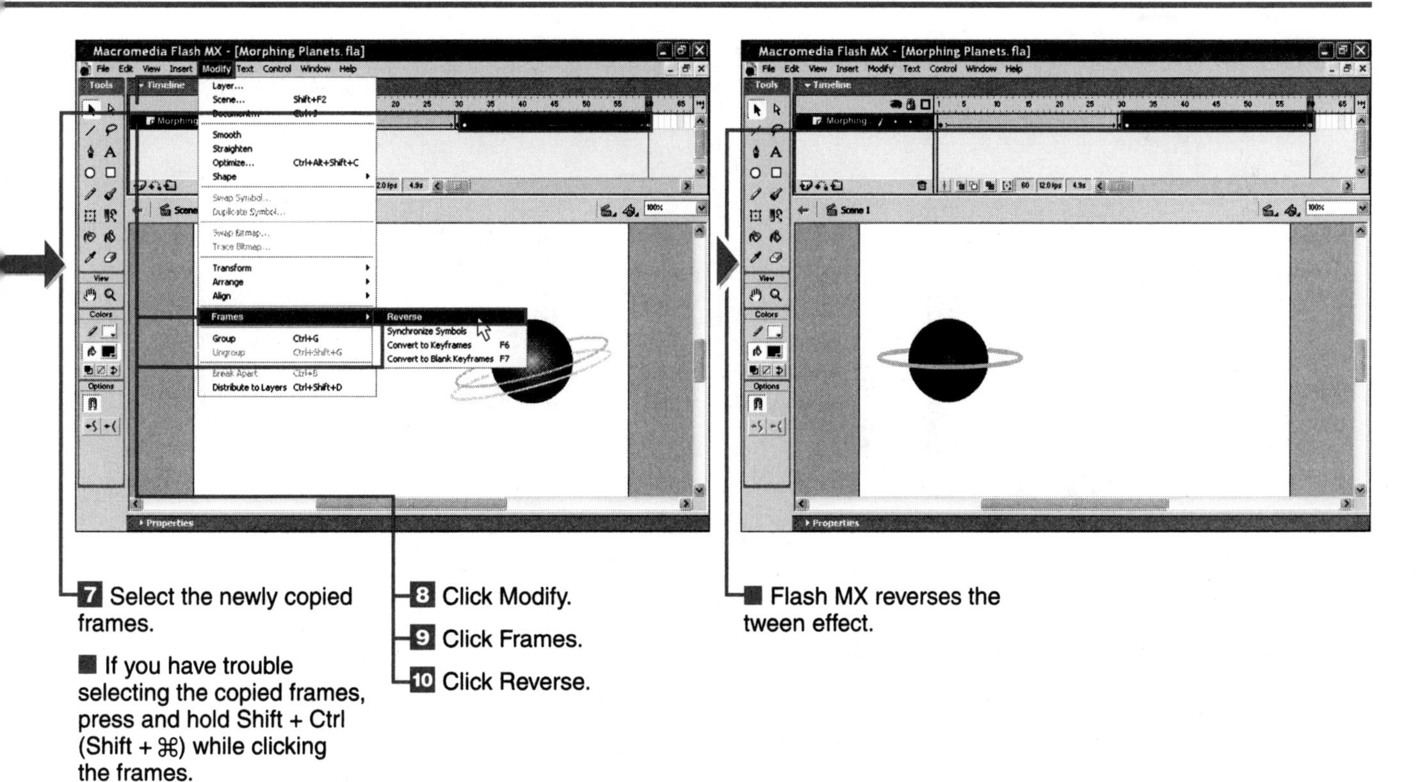

7 Select the newly copied frames.

■ If you have trouble selecting the copied frames, press and hold Shift + Ctrl (Shift + ⌘) while clicking the frames.

8 Click Modify.

9 Click Frames.

10 Click Reverse.

■ Flash MX reverses the tween effect.

ANIMATE A MASK

You can use mask layers to hide various elements on underlying layers in your Flash movies. In addition, you can animate a mask layer using any of the Flash animation techniques, such as a motion path or shape tween.

You can create an animated mask layer that acts as a moving window, exposing different parts of the underlying layer. This effect is similar to watching a landscape pass by through a car window. For example, you can draw an oval fill shape that acts as a window to the layer below the mask, and animate the window to move around the movie. The window lets you see anything directly beneath, but the remainder of the mask layer hides anything that lies out of view of the window.

You can assign a motion tween to a mask created from a symbol, an instance, or a grouped object. You can assign a shape tween to a mask you create with the Flash drawing tools. You cannot, however, animate a mask layer along a path.

You can use animated masks to create a spotlight effect on an underlying layer. You can even turn a movie clip into an animated mask.

ANIMATE A MASK

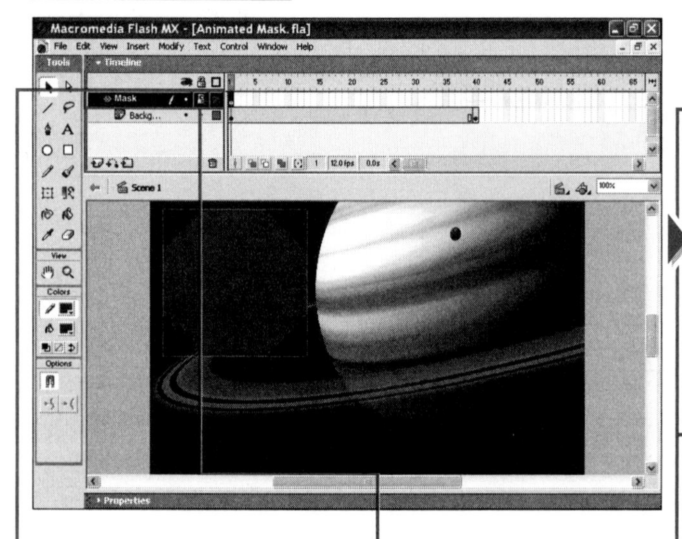

1 Click the mask layer you want to animate.

Note: To create a mask layer, see page 444.

2 Click the lock icon ( ) for the layer to unlock the mask layer.

3 Apply a motion or shape tween to the mask.

■ If the mask object is a graphic symbol, you can apply a motion tween.

■ If the mask object is a fill shape, you can apply a shape tween.

Note: To create a motion tween, see page 536. To create shape tween, see page 558.

Why can I not create a motion tween in my mask layer?

✔ You may be assigning the wrong tween type to your mask layer. Check and make sure you know what type of object you are using as a mask and then assign the appropriate motion tween type. You can only assign a motion tween to a mask that you create from a symbol, an instance, or an object group. You must assign a shape tween to a fill shape.

Can I use the mask to mask out more than one layer in my movie?

✔ Yes. Any layers placed directly between the original linked layer and the mask layer are also masked.

Why am I unable to play my animated mask?

✔ Flash MX will not play the animation if either the mask layer or the underlying layer is not locked. Click the lock icon (🔒) for both layers, and then play the animation.

Can I use two symbols in my animated mask layer?

✔ No. You cannot use more than one symbol as a mask. If your animation requires two mask symbols, try combining the two into one symbol.

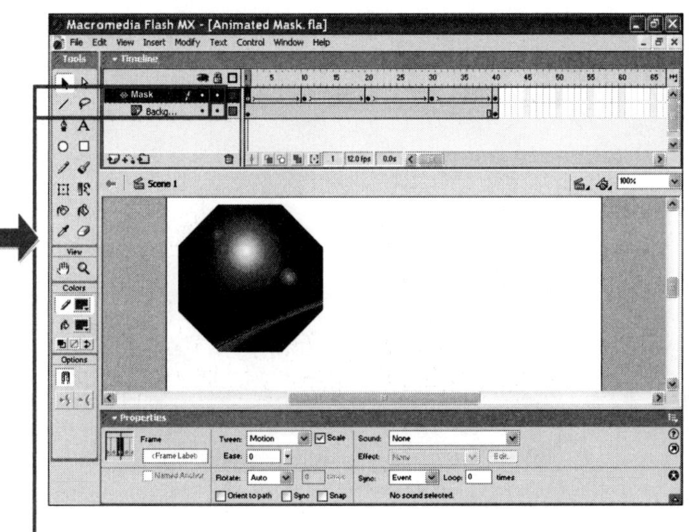

4 Click the unlock icon (▪) for the layer to lock the mask layer.

5 Click the unlock icon (▪) to lock the layer below the mask.

Note: See Chapter 25 to learn more about locking and hiding layers.

■ Flash MX masks the underlying layer.

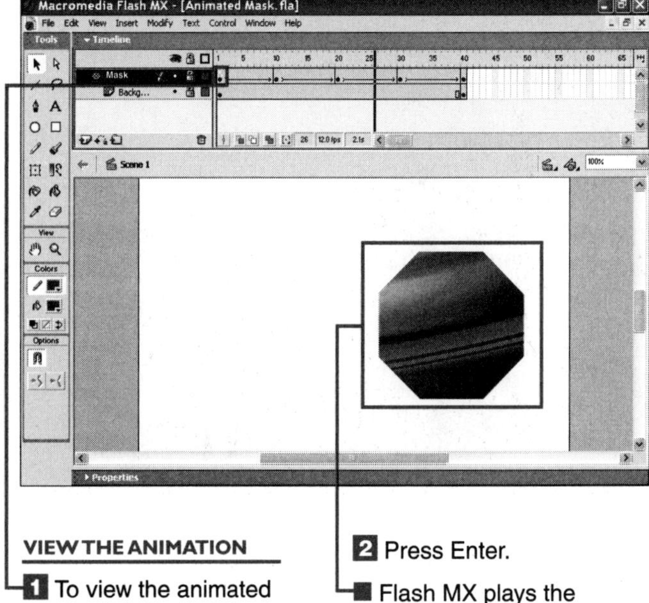

VIEW THE ANIMATION

1 To view the animated mask, click the first frame of the sequence.

2 Press Enter.

■ Flash MX plays the animation sequence.

DISTRIBUTE OBJECTS TO LAYERS

You can use the Distribute to Layers command to quickly distribute objects to different layers in your movie and then animate each object separately. For example, you can use this technique to animate individual letters in a company logo or animate a group of graphic objects with individual motion tweens.

New to Flash MX, the Distribute to Layers command can help you create a variety of layered animation effects. Used in conjunction with the Break Apart command, you can separate individual pieces from a whole and animate them separately; the Break Apart command literally breaks apart the selected object into editable pieces. If you apply the command to a text block, for example, you can break each character into a separate graphic object. To animate each character on its own, apply the Distribute to Layers command and each character is moved to a new layer separate from the remaining letters. From there, you can choose to assign motion or shape tweens to make the letters come alive.

You can apply the Break Apart command to a block of text. Other graphics and instances do not need to be broken apart first.

DISTRIBUTE OBJECTS TO LAYERS

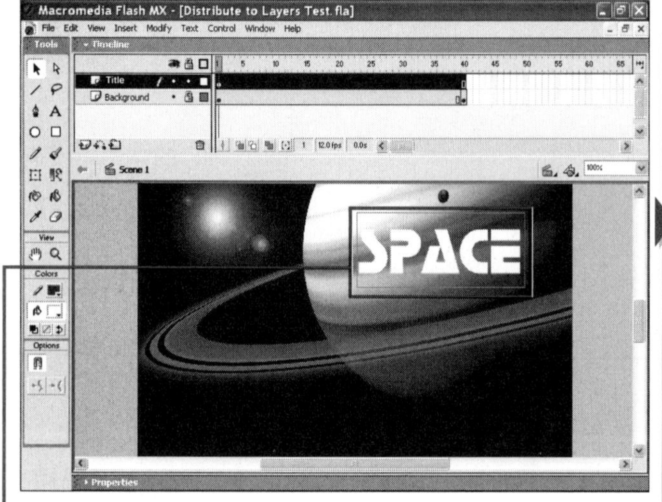

1 Click the object you want to break apart into separate layers.

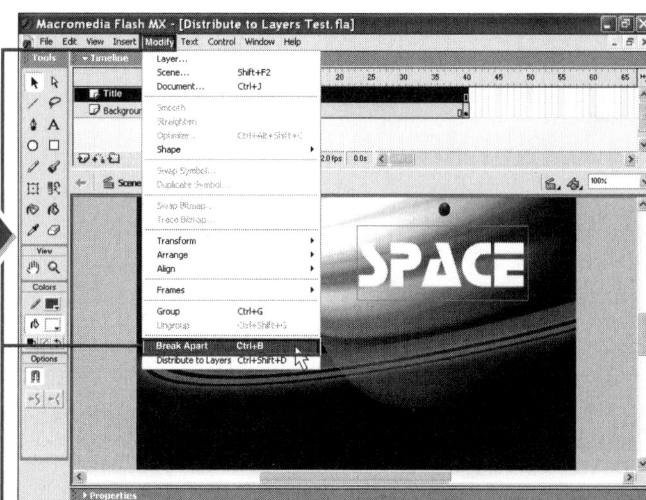

2 Click Modify.

3 Click Break Apart.

Note: Objects you create in Flash MX may not need the Break Apart command to distribute to layers.

■ Flash MX breaks apart the object.

How do I edit an object I distributed to layers?

✔ To edit a particular object on a layer, simply double-click the object to switch to symbol-edit mode and then make changes to the object. To return to movie-edit mode again, click the Scene name or the [←] located directly below the Timeline.

Is there a shortcut to the Distribute to Layers command?

✔ Yes. You can right-click (Control-click) the selected object and then click Distribute to Layers from the pop-up menu.

How do I tell which object is on which layer?

✔ Use the Show All Layers As Outlines column for each layer to help you color coordinate what object is on what layer. Click the layer you want to identify, and then click the [□] icon. Flash MX highlights the object in the designated color.

Can I regroup a word after applying the Distribute to Layers command?

✔ No. You cannot undo the command or group the letters again after distributing them to different layers.

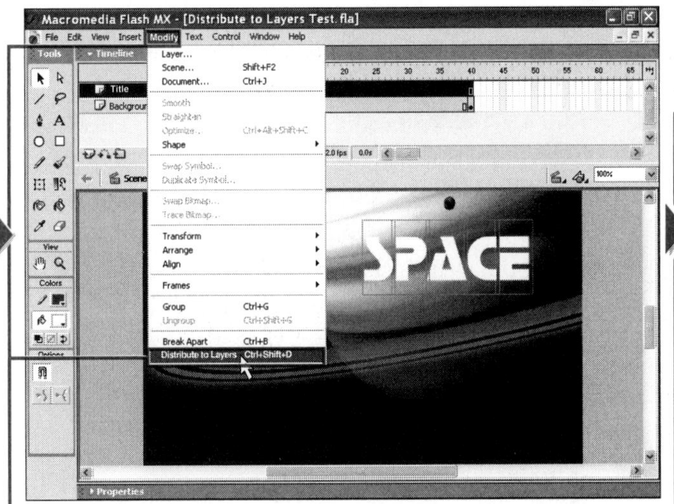

4 Click Modify.

5 Click Distribute to Layers.

Note: You must select all objects you want to distribute to layers before applying the command. If you clicked elsewhere on the Stage after using the Break Apart command, you must select all the objects again.

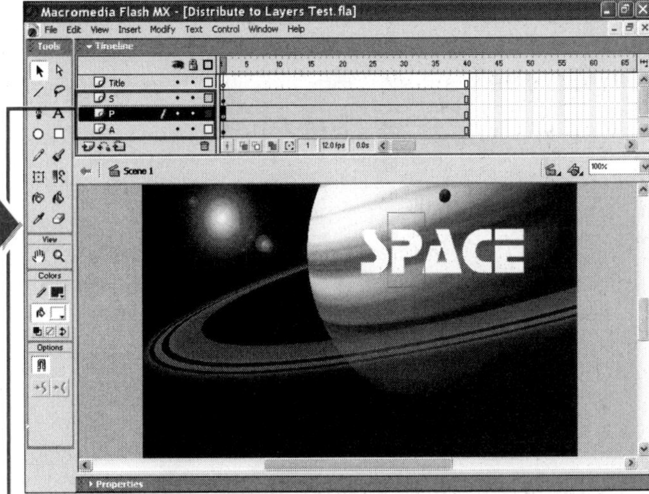

■ Flash MX distributes each object to a separate layer.

■ In this example, Flash placed each letter on a layer and named the layer accordingly.

■ You can now animate each object separately from the rest.

SECTION IX

31) ADDING FLASH ACTIONS

32) MAKING INTERACTIVE MOVIES

33) WORKING WITH FLASH MX COMPONENTS

BUILDING INTERACTIVE ELEMENTS

INTRODUCTION TO FLASH ACTIONS

You can add interactivity to your Flash movies by assigning an action, or behavior, to a frame, or to a button or movie clip instance. Actions are based on principles of cause and effect. For example, the action of clicking a button is a cause, while stopping a movie is the effect, or the behavior, of the action.

You can add actions to frames, buttons, and movie clips in Flash MX. You can also add Flash actions in different levels of complexity. You can add frame actions to give you greater control over how a movie or movie clip plays. You can add button actions that enable users to interact via a button. Or you can add complex actions that require parameters that enable users to interact with elements in your movie.

Although Flash MX offers hundreds of actions, this chapter focuses on the common navigational actions you can use in your own Flash movies.

Actions and ActionScript

Flash actions are built on a programming language called ActionScript. This scripting language allows you to write instructions that control a movie. If you know how to write scripts, you can write your own actions in Flash MX. However, you do not need to know a scripting language to create actions. Flash MX includes hundreds of prewritten scripts, or actions, you can assign.

ActionScript is comprised of statements, sentences composed of code based on the ActionScript language. When you assemble several statements, you create a script. You can also control parts of the script by specifying parameters. For example, you can use the Go To action to go to and play a particular frame in your movie. When assigning this action, you set the parameter for the action by designating a particular frame.

Using Actions in Flash MX

You use the Actions panel to add actions to frames, buttons, or movie clips — mini-movies within the main movie. When adding actions to movie clips, you add them to frames or buttons within the movie clip.

When you assign an action, Flash MX adds it to a list of actions for that particular frame or button. This list is called an action list or script. Flash MX then executes the actions in the list based on the order in which they appear.

The occurrence that triggers an action is called an event. An event might be a click of a button or reaching a certain frame in your movie. The result of the action is the target.

Events

Anything that causes an action is called an event. In Flash terminology, an event triggers an action in your movie. Flash MX recognizes several types of events: mouse events, or button actions, keyboard events, clip events, and frame events, also called frame actions. For example, a mouse event occurs when a user interacts with a button, such as moving the mouse pointer over the button or clicking the button, or when a user interacts with an instance in the movie. Keyboard events occur when a user presses a keyboard key; keyboard events are typically assigned to buttons. Clip events control movie clips. Frame events are placed in keyframes in your movie and trigger actions that occur at certain points in the Timeline of the movie.

Targets

A target is the object affected by the action. Targets are directed most often toward the current movie, called the *default target*. Other targets include movies, called the Tell Target, or a browser application, called an *external target*. For example, you might place a button in your movie that, when clicked, opens a Web page.

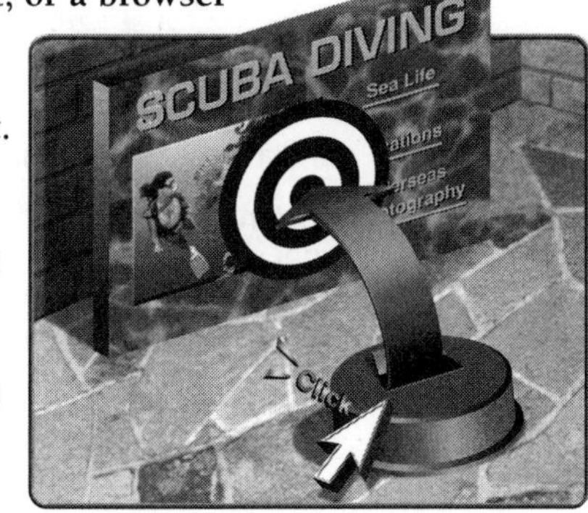

Event Handlers

Event handlers manage events. Event handlers tell Flash when to perform an action and make sure the action carries out the task as planned. When you assign an action, Flash MX automatically includes an event handler. If you assign a button action, the On Mouse Event handler is included, and if you assign a frame action, the On Clip Event handler is included. You can recognize an event handler in the actions list by the word *on* followed by the type of event.

Types of Actions

Flash groups actions into categories in the Actions panel. The most common actions include navigational actions, such as Go To and Play and Stop; browser actions such as Get URL and Load Movie; and movie clip control actions. For example, you might place a button in your movie that a user can click to stop the movie. By assigning a button with the Stop action in a movie frame containing a large amount of text, you enable users to stop the movie to read the text. You can assign a Play action to another button in the same frame so that users can click the Play button to continue with the movie.

You can use the Load Movie action to jump users to a Web page. For example, you can include a frame at the end of your movie that links to a particular page on your Web site, or you can assign the action to a button the user can click to view the page. In a similar fashion, you can use the Load Movie action to load another movie at the end of your main movie.

USING THE ACTIONS PANEL

You can use the Actions panel to add actions and write ActionScript for your Flash movies. Actions enable you to add interactivity to your movies.

The Actions panel is part of the default panel set, and appears docked at the bottom of the screen or as a floating panel.

The Actions panel uses two modes for entering actions: Normal editing mode and Expert editing mode. In Normal mode, Flash MX automatically corrects the syntax of your action script, but in Expert mode you are on your own. Any mistakes you make typing in scripts are not corrected automatically. Unless you are experienced at writing scripts, Normal mode works best for quickly entering and editing actions.

The left pane of the Actions panel lists all the categories and actions available. After you choose an action to add, it is listed in the right pane along with any parameters you specify to further define the action.

The categorization of actions in Flash MX differs slightly from previous versions of Flash. If you have trouble finding a specific action, you can now access a complete alphabetical listing of all available actions in the Index located in the Actions panel toolbox.

USING THE ACTIONS PANEL

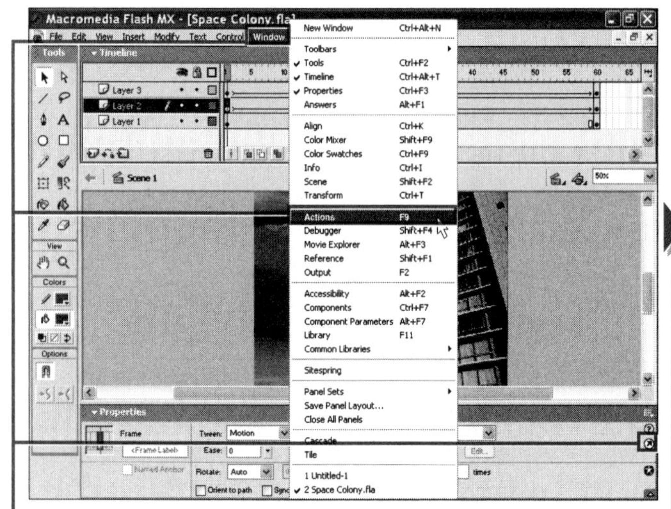

1. Click Window.
2. Click Actions.

■ If the Property inspector is open, you can also click the Edit Action Script button (⊡) to open the Actions panel.

Note: You can move and resize the Actions panel like other panels in Flash MX. For more information on panels, see page 348.

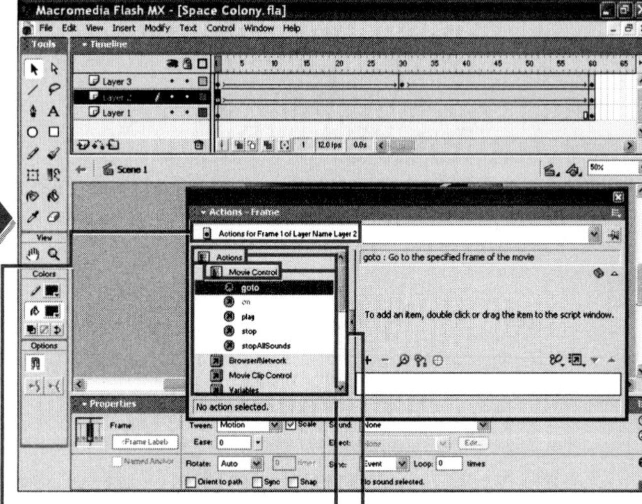

■ The Actions panel opens.

■ The Actions panel in this figure shows Normal editing mode.

■ The current frame or object is listed here.

■ The toolbox lists categories, subcategories, and actions.

■ Click a category to see associated subcategories or actions.

■ Click a subcategory to see a list of actions.

How do I know which action does what?

✔ In Normal mode, you can select an action from the toolbox pane and Flash gives a brief explanation about the action at the top of the right pane. For example, click the Actions category, click the Movie Control category, and then click goto. The following description appears: Go to the specified frame of the movie.

Where can I find additional commands for working with the Actions panel?

✔ You can click the Options menu button (▤), located in the upper right corner of the Actions panel, to reveal a list of related commands.

Can I move the Actions panel out of the way?

✔ Yes. You can move and resize the Actions panel just as you can any other panels available in Flash MX. You can also dock the panel. Click the title bar of the panel to quickly hide or display the panel contents.

Is there a faster way to open the Actions panel?

✔ Yes. You can press F9 on the keyboard to quickly summon the panel at any time.

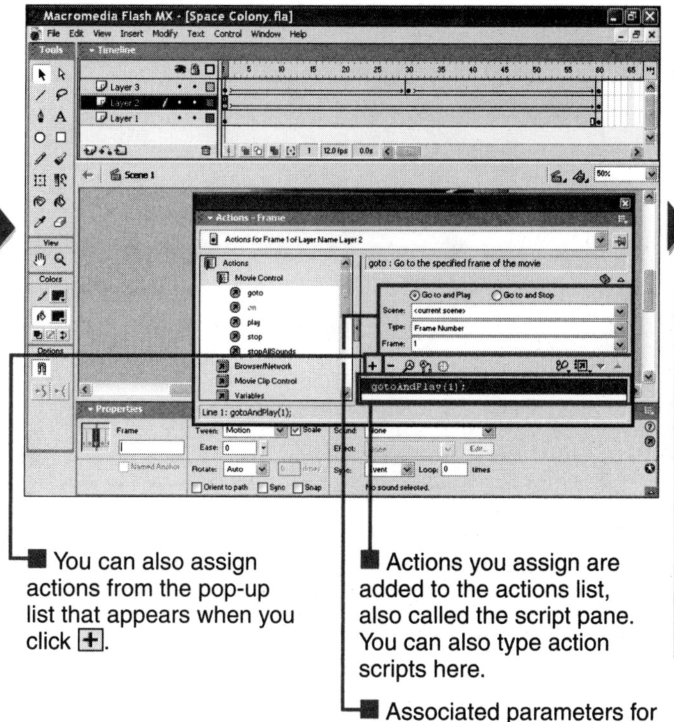

■ You can also assign actions from the pop-up list that appears when you click ⊞.

■ Actions you assign are added to the actions list, also called the script pane. You can also type action scripts here.

■ Associated parameters for the action you assign appear here.

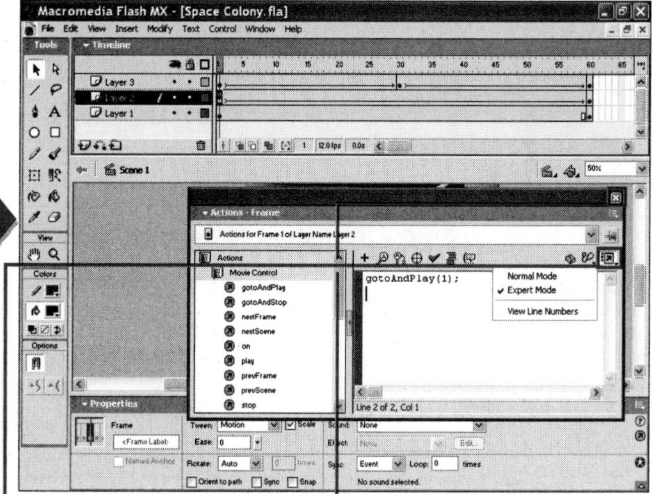

■ The Actions panel in this figure shows Expert editing mode.

■ You can use the View Options menu (▣) to switch back and forth between Normal and Expert mode.

Note: Flash does not automatically correct invalid action statements in Expert mode as it does in Normal mode. Normal mode works best for new Flash users.

■ To close the Actions panel, click ⊠.

ADD ACTIONS TO FRAMES

You can use the Actions panel to add actions to your movie. Frames can include multiple actions, but you can only assign an action one frame at a time. You add actions to the action script of a frame, a list of actions associated with the frame. Flash MX performs the actions in the order they appear in the list.

Flash MX groups the types of actions available into categories in the left pane, called the toolbox, of the Actions panel. Each category acts as a folder containing additional subcategories and lists of related actions. You can collapse and expand categories to see associated actions. You can also assign actions with the Plus Sign pop-up list, which also lists actions by categories and subcategories.

When you assign an action, it appears in the actions list on the right side of the Actions panel. As soon as you assign an action to a frame, the frame is marked with a tiny icon of the letter *a*, for action in the Timeline. After assigning an action to a frame, you can return to the Actions panel and make changes to the action as needed.

ADD ACTIONS TO FRAMES

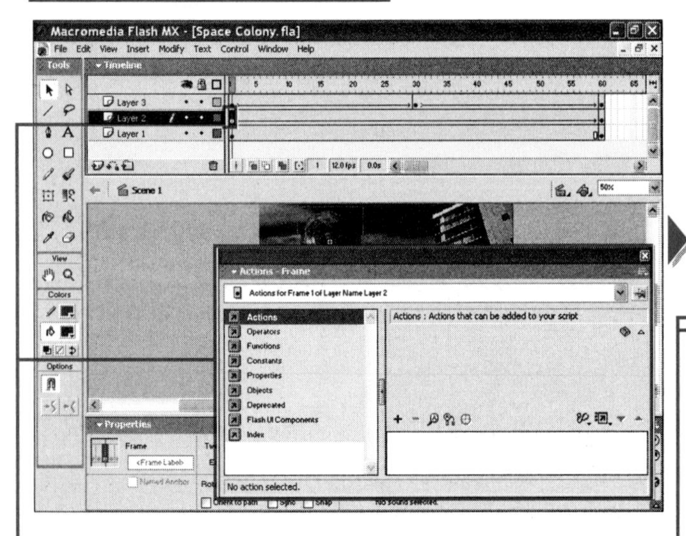

1 Select the frame to which you want to add an action.

2 Open the Actions panel.

Note: To open and close the Actions panel, see page 576.

3 Click an action category.

4 Click a subcategory.

■ Most categories include subcategories.

5 Double-click the action you want to add or drag it from the list and drop it in the actions list.

■ You can also click + to display a pop-up list of categories and actions to assign.

How do I organize actions in my movie?

✔ To help you clearly identify actions you assign to frames, consider creating a layer specifically for actions in your movie. This technique simplifies the process of finding the action you want to edit. To add a layer to the Timeline, click [icon]. A new layer appears above the current layer. You can rename the layer or move it to another position in the layer stack. See Chapter 25 to learn more about layers.

Where can I find a list of all the available actions in Flash MX?

✔ Click the Index category in the Actions panel to reveal an alphabetized list of actions.

How do I remove an action from my movie?

✔ Click the frame containing the action you want to delete and then open the Actions panel. From the actions list, select the action statement you want to remove. Click [icon]. The action is removed from the list.

Can I edit an action?

✔ Yes. To make changes to the parameters of an action, open the Actions panel and select the action statement for the action you want to modify. You can then make changes to the parameters as needed.

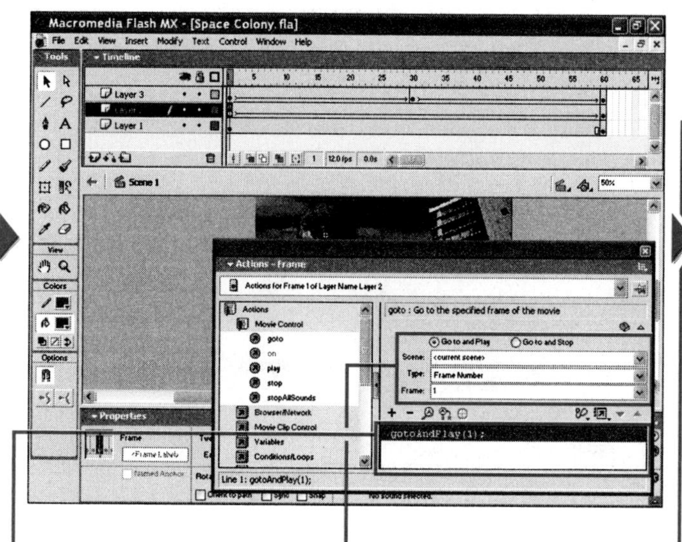

■ Flash MX adds the action to the actions list, also called the script pane.

■ Depending on the action you select, the Actions panel might reveal parameters you can set to further define the action.

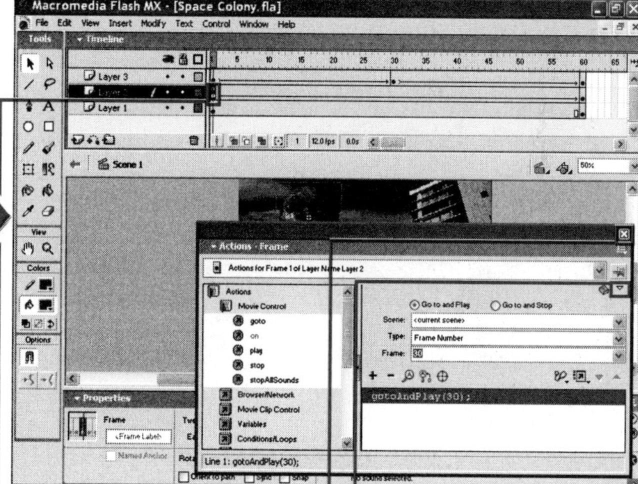

■ Flash MX also adds a tiny letter *a* to indicate that an action is assigned to the frame.

■ When you play the movie, Flash MX carries out the frame action you assigned.

■ Click [icon] to collapse the action description area. You can click [icon] again to expand the panel again.

6 When you are finished adding actions, click [icon] to close the Actions panel.

ADD ACTIONS TO MOVIE CLIPS

You can add actions to movie clip instances that appear in your main movie. Movie clips are mini-movies that use their own timelines, and act like any other symbol you place on the Stage, such as graphics or buttons.

Your main movie can be comprised of numerous mini-movies. For example, you may have an animation sequence of a moving car that includes movie clips for making each wheel rotate. To make the car seem to animate from parked status to moving, you can target the movie clips that comprise the wheels of the car and start the rotation of each wheel.

You can use the Actions panel to add actions to your movie clips. Any actions you attach to a movie clip instance apply only to that instance, not the original movie clip. Movie clip actions respond to the event `onClipEvent`, much like button actions respond to *on* events, such as `on release`.

When assigning actions to movie clip instances, it is important to name them. You can then target the clip you want by targeting the action to the instance name. You can assign instance names through the Property inspector.

ADD ACTIONS TO MOVIE CLIPS

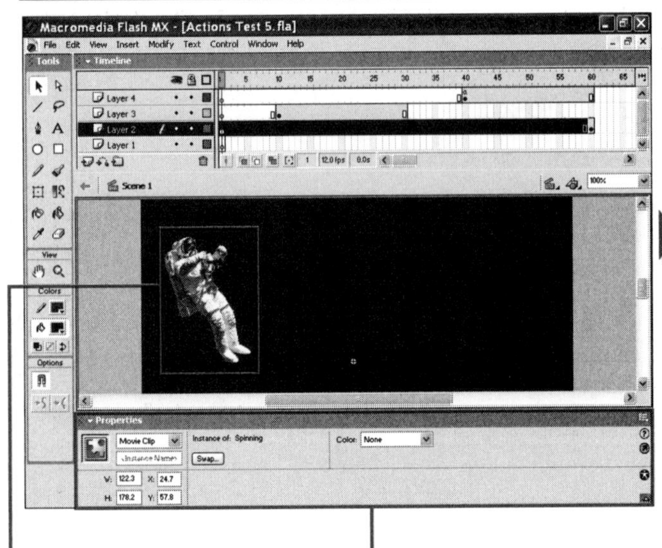

1 Click the movie clip instance to which you want to add an action

2 Open the Property inspector.

Note: To open and close the Property inspector, see page 346.

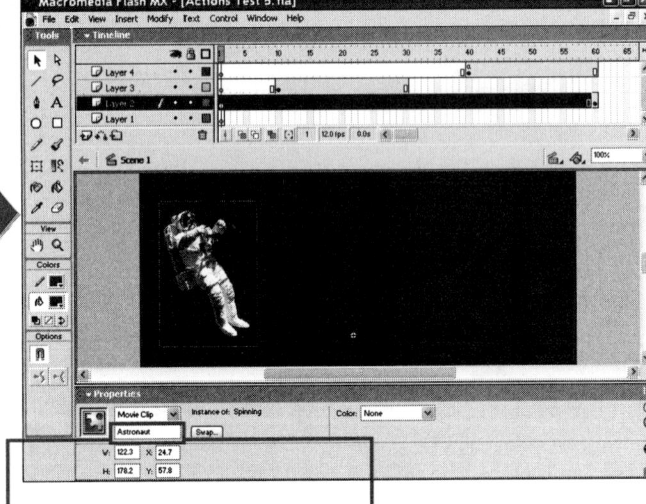

3 Click the instance name field.

4 Type a new name for the instance.

5 Press Enter (Return).

Which category in the Actions panel lists movie clip actions?

✔ Flash MX groups the majority of movie clip actions under the Movie Clip Control subcategory in the Actions panel, under the Actions category.

Can I assign multiple actions to a movie clip?

✔ Yes. You can use the `with` action, found under the Variables subcategory, to address a single movie clip and apply numerous actions to the clip. You define the target clip once and then assign the actions you want, essentially nesting them within the targeted clip for Flash to carry out.

How do movie clips differ from graphic or button instances?

✔ Movie clips are independent movies and, as such, they play all their frames when an instance of the clip is added to the Stage, whether it is 1 frame or 100. Movie clips also loop unless you add a Stop action to the last frame of the clip. Unlike graphic instances, movie clip instances do not play when you scrub, or drag, the playhead of the Timeline. To see clips play, you must open the Flash Player window; click the Control menu and click Test Movie to open the player.

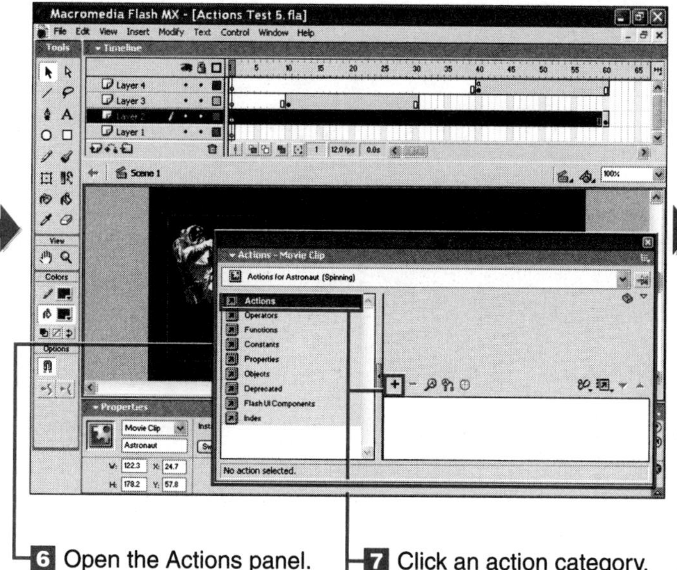

6 Open the Actions panel.

Note: To open and close the Actions panel, see page 576.

7 Click an action category.

■ You can also click ⊞ to open a pop-up list of actions.

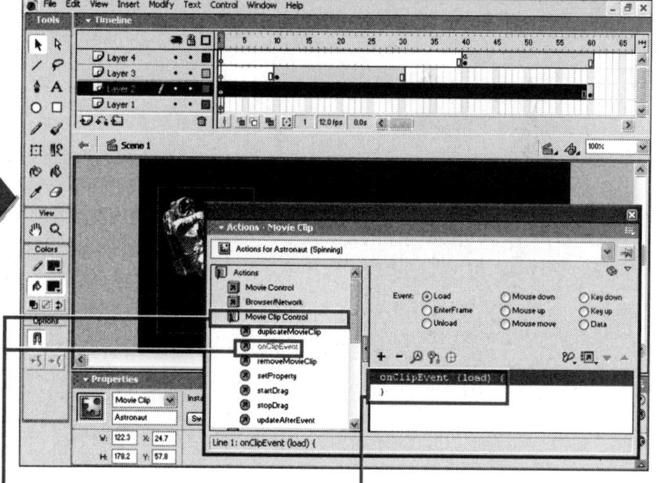

8 Click a subcategory.

■ Most categories include subcategories.

9 Double-click the action you want to add.

■ Flash MX assigns the action to the clip and you can set parameters as needed.

■ When finished adding actions, close or hide the Actions panel.

ASSIGN GO TO ACTIONS

You can assign a Go To action that tells Flash to start playing a particular frame in your movie. You can use the Go To action with frames, buttons, or movie clips. When Flash MX follows a Go To action, it jumps to, or goes to, a specified target frame.

The Go To action includes parameters you can define to play a specific frame. When you assign the Go To action using the Actions panel, you can enter either a frame number or a label as the target frame.

The Go To action has two variations: Go To and Play, or Go To and Stop. The Go To and Play parameter is used by default. With this parameter active, Flash goes to the frame you specify and immediately starts playing the movie from there. If you deselect the Go To and Play check box, the action statement reads Go To and Stop. This means Flash will stop playing the movie when it jumps to the designated frame.

The Go To and Play option is commonly used to loop a movie. For example, you can place the action on the last frame of the movie to tell Flash to start playing the movie again.

ASSIGN GO TO ACTIONS

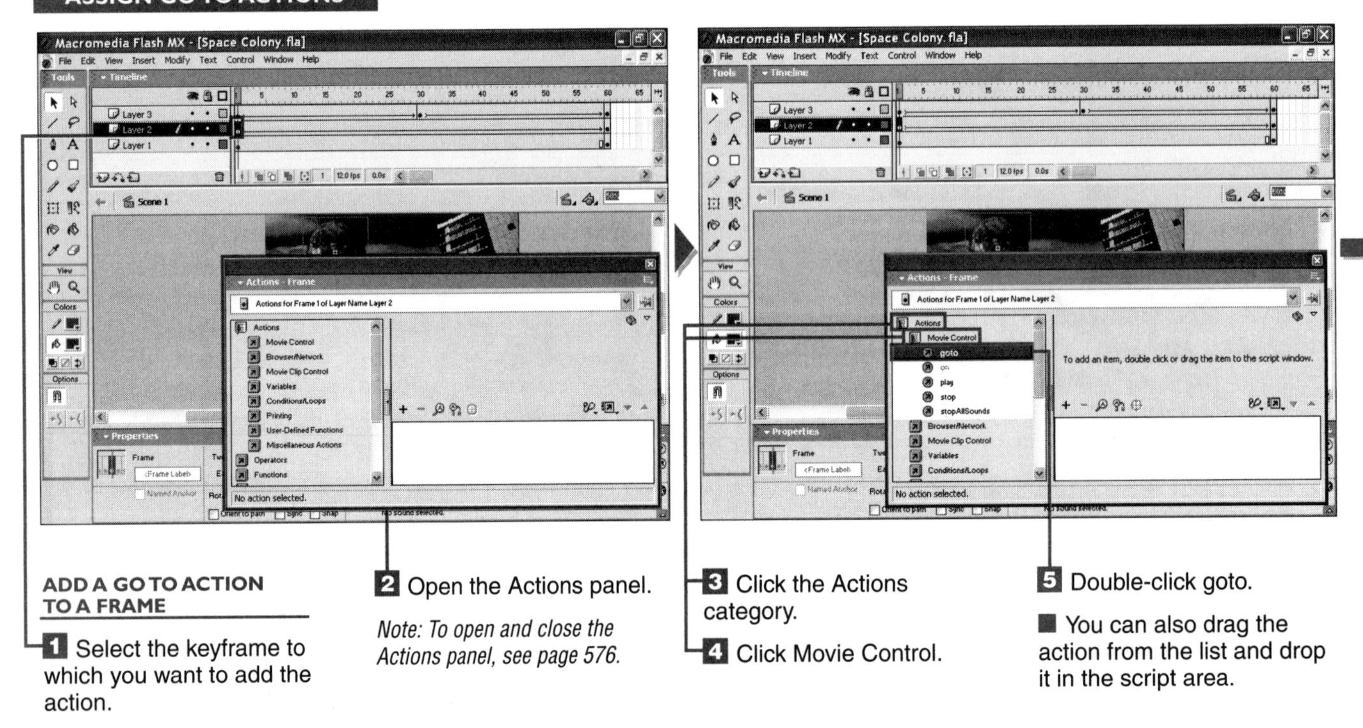

ADD A GO TO ACTION TO A FRAME

1 Select the keyframe to which you want to add the action.

2 Open the Actions panel.

Note: To open and close the Actions panel, see page 576.

3 Click the Actions category.

4 Click Movie Control.

5 Double-click goto.

■ You can also drag the action from the list and drop it in the script area.

My Go To action is not working. Why not?

✔ Click the frame to which you assigned the action and display the Actions panel. Check the parameters to make sure you referenced a valid frame in the movie, and make sure you did not select the Go To and Stop parameter by mistake.

How do I jump to the previous frame?

✔ Click the Type parameter and choose Previous Frame. This causes the movie Timeline to jump back to the frame preceding the frame in which you added this action.

Do I need to label my frames?

✔ Although you can refer to any frame by its number, it is a good idea to label frames with distinct titles that describe the content of the frame. Labeling frames is particularly helpful with longer Flash movies. You can use labels to tell you when a key change occurs in an animation, or to indicate a new element that appears in the movie. To learn more about assigning labels to frames, see Chapter 29.

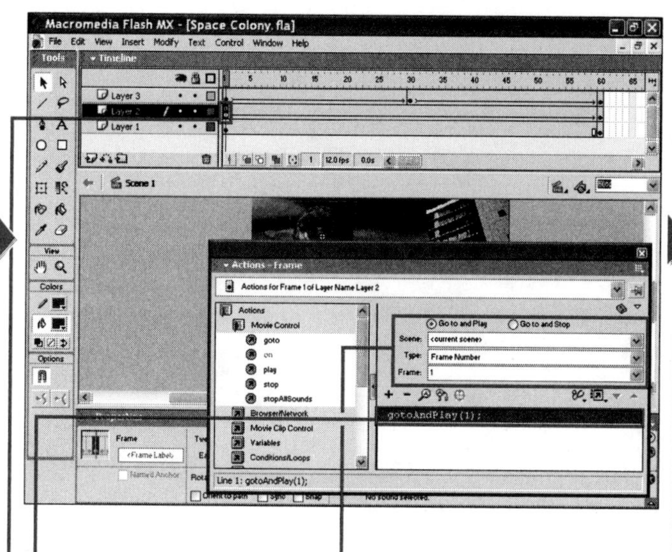

■ Flash MX adds the action to the actions list.

■ Flash MX also adds a tiny letter *a* to indicate that an action is assigned to the frame.

Note: If you assign an action to a button, Flash does not display the tiny letter a.

■ Parameters associated with the Go To action appear above the script area.

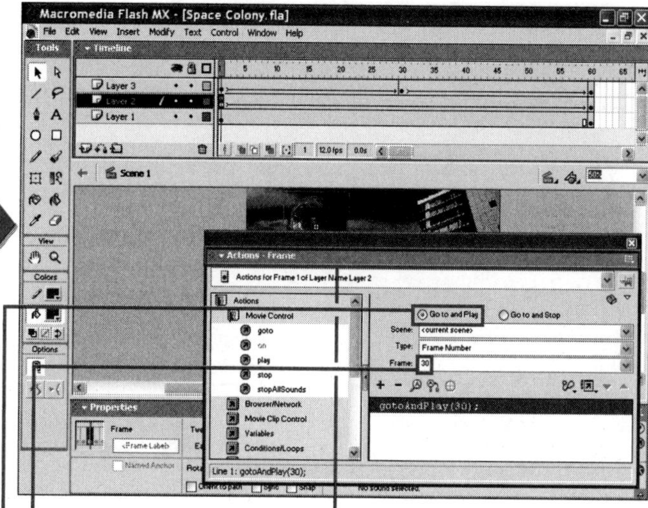

6 Type the number of the frame you want to go to in the Frame text box.

■ You can click the Go To and Play option to make the movie continue playing when it jumps to the designated frame.

■ You can click the Go To and Stop option to go to the designated frame and stop.

7 Click the Actions panel title bar to hide the panel.

■ When you play the movie, Flash MX follows the frame action you assigned.

ASSIGN GO TO ACTIONS (CONTINUED)

You can reference scenes in a Go To action. Scenes are simply organized sections of your Flash movie. You can specify a scene name in the Go To action parameters. When you assign a Go To action, Flash MX follows the instruction while playing the movie and jumps to the scene you referenced.

You can also define the Go To action to go to a specific expression you may have written in ActionScript. For example, you may write a script that calculates a frame number and then set a Go To action to jump to the destination frame.

If you edit your movie later, for example, add or delete frames or entire scenes, be sure to update any Go To actions to reference the correct frames or scenes. If you fail to update the Go To action, the action may not go to the correct frame.

Always test your movies after you add an action to any frame or button. Testing the action helps you determine if you have set the correct parameters. You can test the actions in the Flash Player window or play them on the Stage using the Enable Simple Frame Actions command located on the Control menu.

ASSIGN GO TO ACTIONS (CONTINUED)

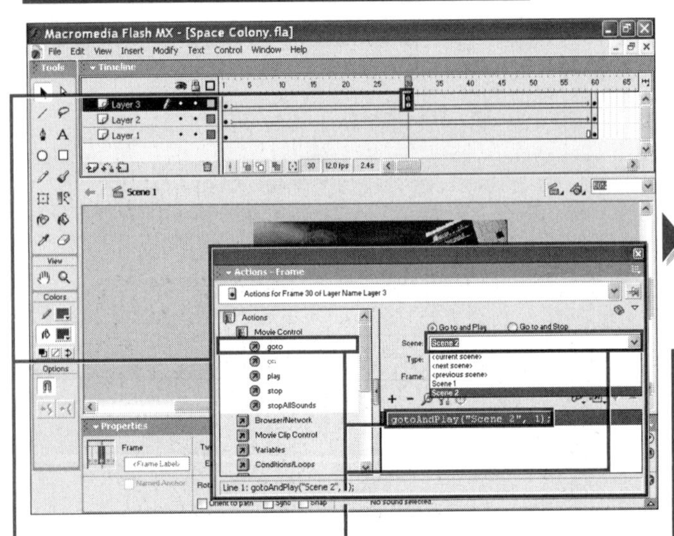

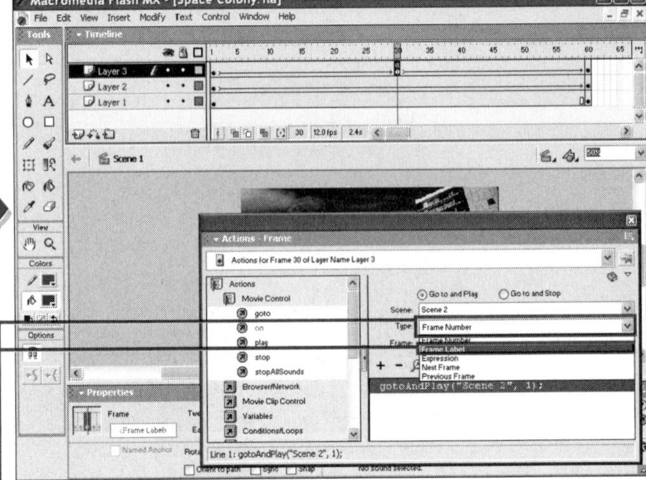

ADD A GO TO ACTION TO A SCENE

1 Select the keyframe to which you want to add the action.

2 Open the Actions panel.

Note: To open and close the Actions panel, see page 576.

3 Add a Go To action to the actions list.

4 Type the scene name or click the ▾ and click the scene name.

■ To go to a specific frame label instead of a frame number, click the Type ▾ and select Frame Label, then type the label into the Frame text box.

■ When you play the movie, Flash MX follows the frame action you assigned.

Can I reference a scene in the Go To parameters that I have not created yet?

✔ Yes. You can plan ahead and reference scenes you have not yet created in your movie. If the scene is still not available when you play the movie, Flash MX ignores the Go To command because it does not reference a legitimate frame in your movie.

Can I go to a specific frame in another scene?

✔ Yes. First enter the name of the scene in the Scene text box, then click the Type box and choose a Frame Number or Frame Label. If you choose a Frame Number type, you must then enter the frame number. If you choose a Frame Label type, you must enter the label.

Can I test my action out on the Stage?

✔ Yes, if you turn on the Enable Simple Frame Actions feature. Click the Control menu and then click Enable Simple Frame Actions. A check mark next to the command name means the feature is on; no check mark means the feature is off. It is a good idea to turn the feature off when not in use or Flash will engage the Go To command as you work with the frames in your Timeline.

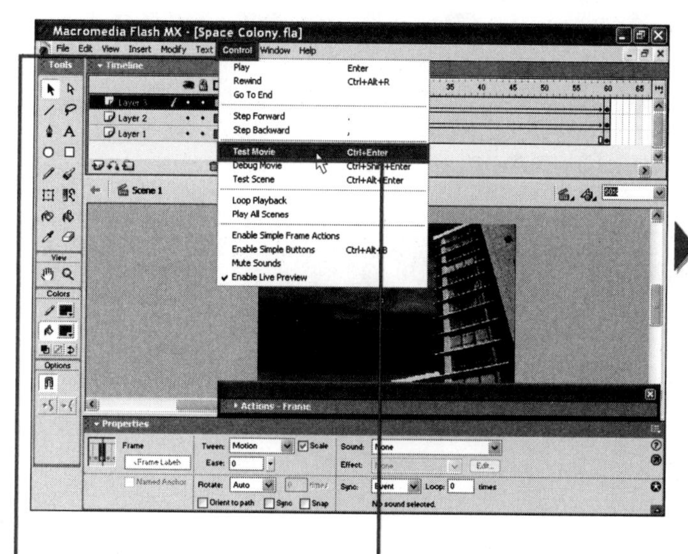

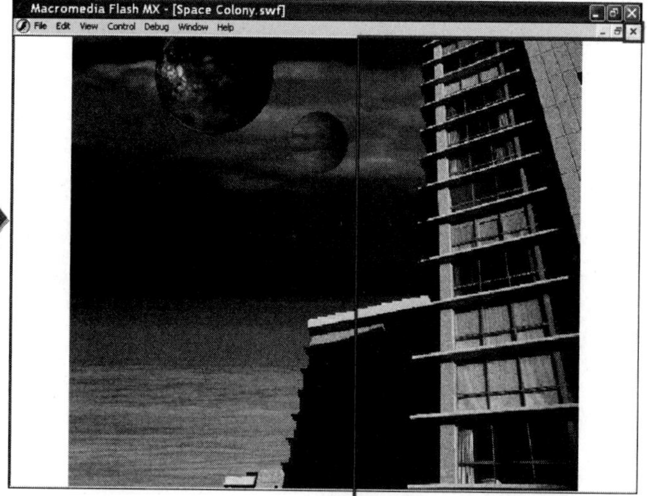

TEST THE GO TO ACTION

1 Click Control.

2 Click Test Movie.

■ Flash MX opens the Flash Player window and plays the movie.

3 Click ✕ to exit the Flash Player window.

ASSIGN STOP AND PLAY ACTIONS

You can assign a Stop action to stop a movie from playing, or you can assign a Play action to play it again. The Stop and Play actions do not offer any parameters you can set. Both actions do exactly as their name implies.

For example, perhaps one of the keyframes in your movie is text heavy and you want to enable the user to pause and read the text. You can create a button and assign a Stop action that enables the user to stop the movie, and assign a Play action to another button that lets the user play the movie again.

Stop and Play actions are two of the basic Flash navigation and interaction buttons. The Stop and Play actions are commonly used with buttons. If you add a Stop action to a frame, you must add a Play action to start the movie playing again. The steps below demonstrate how to add a Stop action and a Play action to two different buttons in a movie. You can add these same actions to other scenarios in your movie.

ASSIGN STOP AND PLAY ACTIONS

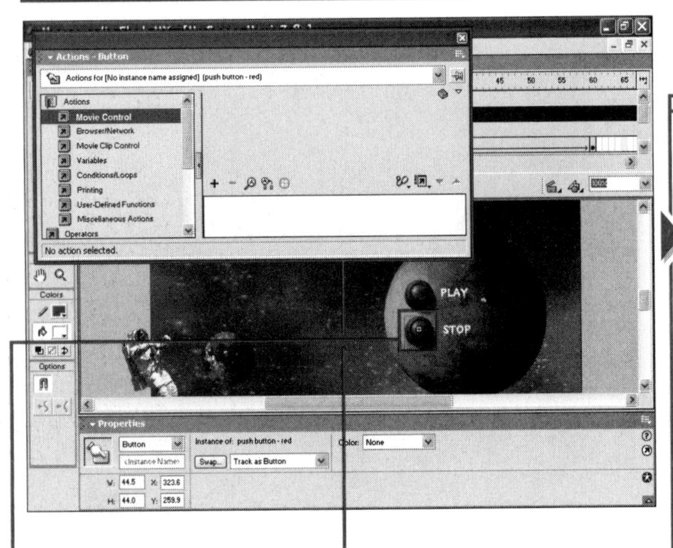

ADD A STOP ACTION TO A BUTTON

1 Click the button to which you want to add a Stop action.

Note: To create buttons, see Chapter 27.

2 Open the Actions panel.

Note: To open and close the Actions panel, see page 576.

3 Click the Actions category.

4 Click Movie Control.

5 Double-click stop.

■ You can also drag the action from the list and drop it in the script area.

How do I assign a Stop action to a frame?

✔ To assign a Stop action to a frame rather than a button, simply click the frame to which you want the action assigned and then add the action.

Does a Play action in a scene affect the rest of the Timeline of the movie?

✔ A scene has its own independent Timeline separate from the rest of the Timeline of the movie. If you add a Play action to a frame in that scene, it does not affect the Timeline of the main movie.

What is the difference between frame actions and button actions?

✔ Actions can be applied to frames or buttons. Frame actions are assigned to frames and control how a movie plays. Button actions are assigned to buttons and require input from the user. For example, a Stop action assigned to a button enables the user to stop a movie by clicking the button to which the action is assigned. You can assign Stop and Play actions to frames or buttons, although button actions require user input in order to carry out the action.

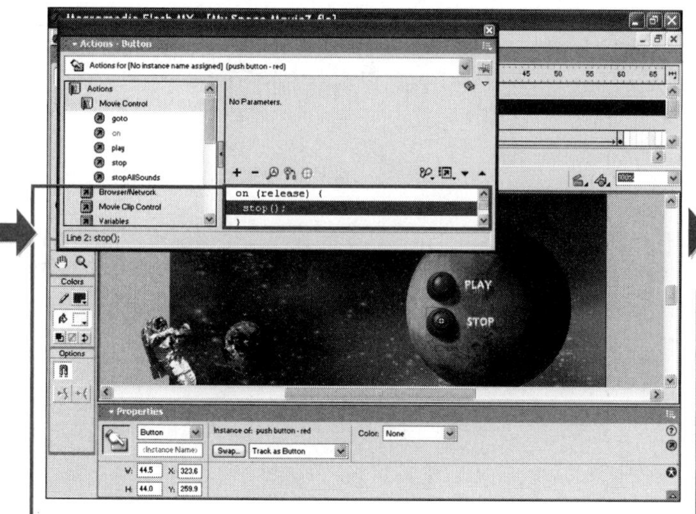

■ Flash MX adds the action to the actions list.

■ No parameters are available for the Stop action.

Note: If you assign an action to a button, Flash does not display the tiny letter a in the Timeline.

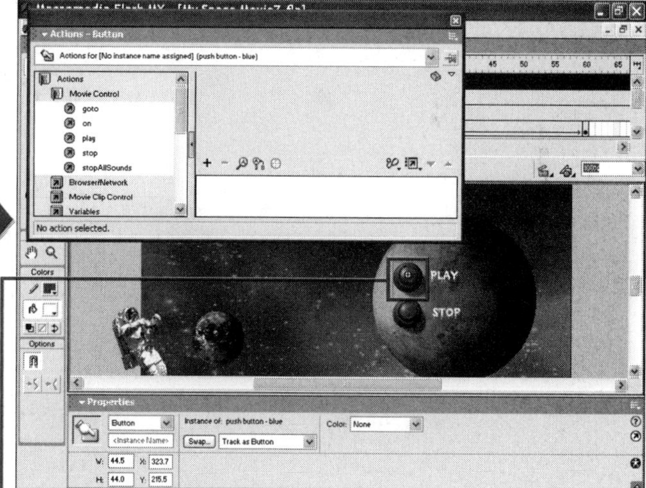

ADD A PLAY ACTION TO A BUTTON

6 Click the button to which you want to add a Play action.

ASSIGN STOP AND PLAY ACTIONS (CONTINUED)

You can assign the Stop and Play actions to give users control over the playback of your movie. Stop and Play actions act much like the controls found on a VCR or CD player. In many cases, you will want to use the two commands together because the Stop action ceases the movie from playing while the Play action starts a movie previously stopped with the Stop action. The Play action plays the movie based on the assigned frame rate, measured in frames per second.

You can assign the Stop and Play actions to any object you want to use as a button in your movie. However, keep your audience in mind when designing buttons, and make sure your buttons are clearly marked as to their purpose, either with a label or a symbol that identifies the action. Flash MX comes with a variety of premade buttons you can use in your movies, including navigation buttons for Stop and Play. The premade buttons include matching designs, and many of the buttons look like control buttons the user might find on a VCR or CD player.

ASSIGN STOP AND PLAY ACTIONS (CONTINUED)

7 With the Actions panel still open, double-click play.

■ You can also drag the action from the list and drop it in the script area.

■ Flash MX adds the action to the actions list.

■ No parameters are available for the Play action.

Note: If you assign an action to a button, Flash does not display the tiny letter a in the Timeline.

8 Hide or close the Actions panel.

■ You can click the title bar to collapse the panel or click ☒ to close the panel.

Can I resize the type in the actions list?

✔ If you have trouble reading the small type in the actions list, you can resize it. To do so, click ▤ to display a pop-up menu. Click Preferences to open the Preferences dialog box. Under the Actions Editor tab, you can change the font and size. Click OK when finished to return to the Actions panel; Flash MX updates the actions list text.

To which layer should I add an action?

✔ Although you can add actions to the current layer along with your animation, it is a good idea to employ a separate layer just for actions.

Does Flash MX support a Pause action?

✔ No. However, a Stop action acts like a pause action in that your movie stops playing and rests on the frame to which the Stop action is activated. You can place a Stop action at the start of a movie to keep the movie from playing automatically when opened as a self-playing projector file. See Chapter 34 to learn more about publishing Flash movies.

TEST THE ACTIONS

1 Click Control.

2 Click Test Movie.

■ Flash MX opens the Flash Player window and plays the movie.

3 Click the buttons to perform the Stop and Play actions.

4 Click ✕ to exit the Player window.

LOAD A NEW MOVIE

You can use the Load Movie action to start a movie file within your current movie. With the Load Movie action, you can create layered animation action, or replace the current movie with another movie.

For example, suppose that you create a movie of a wooded background. In the middle of the movie, you can load a movie of a man walking. By loading the walking man in the middle of the woods movie, you can combine the two movies to make it look as if the man is walking through the woods.

The Load Movie action makes it easier for users to download your movie. For example, you might have a long movie comprised of four sections. If a user wants to skip the first three sections and view only the fourth, the Load Movie action provides the user a way of directly accessing the fourth section to view.

When defining the parameters for the Load Movie action, you can specify a directory path using the URL parameter or you can specify a location level or target. You can also use the target parameter to replace a movie clip with another, or to create a stack of movies that play together.

LOAD A NEW MOVIE

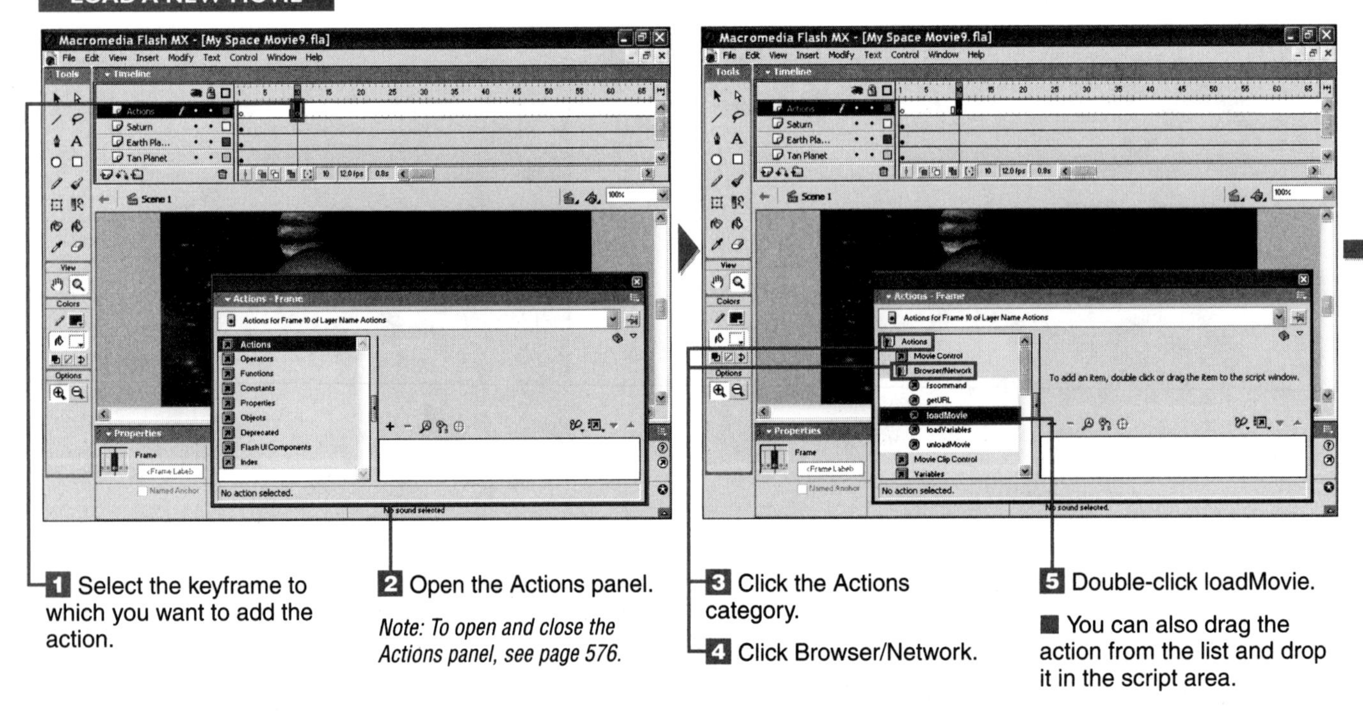

1 Select the keyframe to which you want to add the action.

2 Open the Actions panel.

Note: To open and close the Actions panel, see page 576.

3 Click the Actions category.

4 Click Browser/Network.

5 Double-click loadMovie.

■ You can also drag the action from the list and drop it in the script area.

What are movie levels?

✔ Flash MX plays multiple movies as levels. The current movie always plays at level 0. When you play a second movie with the Load Movie action, it plays at the level you designate, level 1 or higher. A movie set to play at level 2 appears on top of movies at levels 1 and 0. If you specify level 0 for the location level with the Load Movie action, the new movie replaces the existing movie. If you assign another level, the new movie plays on top of the existing movie.

Can I open the movie in a separate browser window?

✔ Yes. You can use the Get URL action to load a new movie file which plays in a separate browser window. Follow the steps below, but select the Get URL action instead of the Load Movie action. In the parameters, type the path to the movie file you want to load in the URL text box. In the Window text box, type **_blank**. Leave the Variables text box in the default state — Don't send.

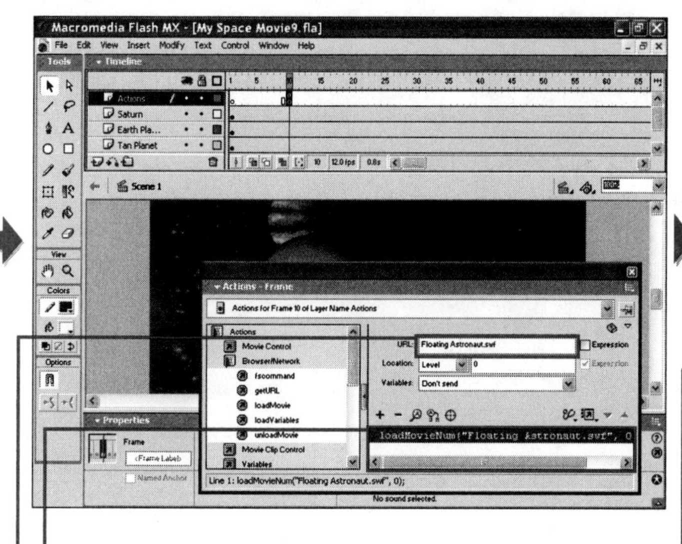

■ Flash MX adds the action to the actions list.

6 Click in the URL box.

7 Type the name of the movie file you want to load.

Note: You can type a relative path, which includes just the filename and extension, or you can enter an absolute path to the movie. An absolute path includes the drive and folder where the file is located.

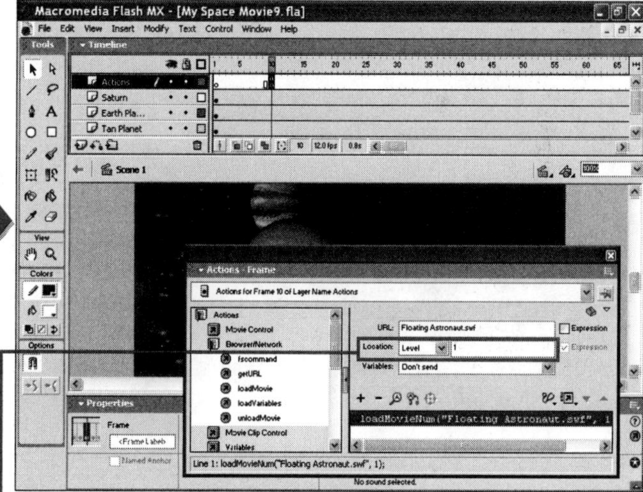

8 Select a location parameter for your movie.

■ Leave the Location level set to 0 if you want the new movie to replace the current movie.

■ To make the new movie play on top of the current movie, type **1** or higher in the Location level text box.

■ You can test the action by playing the movie in the Flash Player window.

ASSIGN A GET URL ACTION

You can use the Get URL action to take users to other files or Web pages. The action serves as an HTML hyperlink. You can also use this action to open a file or movie in a new browser window. For example, you can insert a Get URL action in a standalone Flash Player projector movie, which, when activated, opens a browser window and downloads the specified HTML page.

Another way to employ this action is to send variable data, such as data entered into your movie by a user, to a specified URL. For example, you can use the action to send data from a Flash form to a CGI script for processing.

There are four different targets you can specify in the parameters of the Get URL action: `_self` opens the designated HTML page in the current frame of the browser window; `_blank` opens the designated file in a completely new browser window; `_parent` opens the page in the parent of the current browser; and `_top` opens the page in the top-level frame of the current window.

In the steps demonstrated in this section, you learn how to assign a Get URL action to a button in your Flash movie that opens a file in a new browser window.

ASSIGN A GET URL ACTION

1 Click the button to which you want to add a Get URL action.

2 Open the Actions panel.

Note: To open and close the Actions panel, see page 576.

3 Click Actions.

4 Click Browser/Network.

5 Double-click getURL.

What do I need to know about using URLs with the Get URL action?

✔ URL stands for Uniform Resource Locator, the standard way of addressing files on the Internet. There are two types of URLs: absolute and relative. An absolute URL is a complete address, including the protocol needed to open the file, such as www.hungryminds.com. A relative URL is a shorthand version of the address, such as mymovieclip.swf. With a relative address, you are telling Flash MX to look for the file in a relative location, such as the current folder.

How does the syntax of a Get URL action statement work?

✔ Most scripting statements start with a keyword that identifies the action, such as `if` or `gotoAndPlay`. Data between curly brackets (`{}`) lists the action and parameters that need to be carried out. If you have more than one action, a semicolon separates each action in your actions list. Quotation marks appear around values in your action statement, while parentheses encompass any unusual aspects of the script.

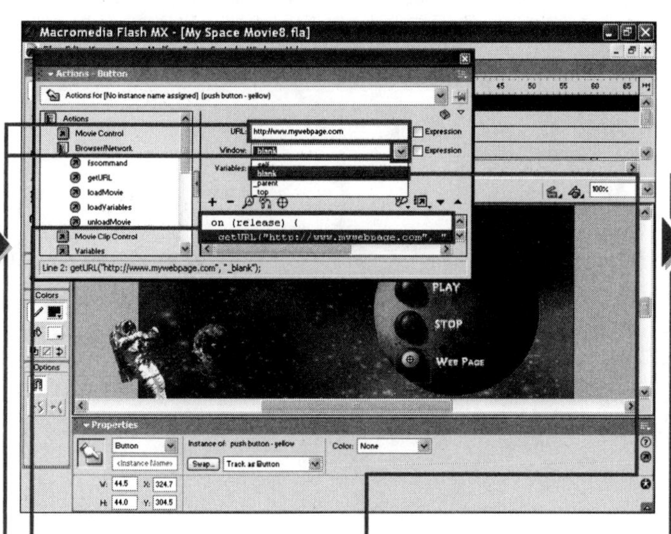

■ Flash MX adds the action to the actions list.

6 Click in the URL box and type the name or path of the file or Web page you want to open.

7 Click the Window ▾.

8 Click one of the four targets.

■ In this example, the `_blank` target is entered in the parameter to open the file in another browser window.

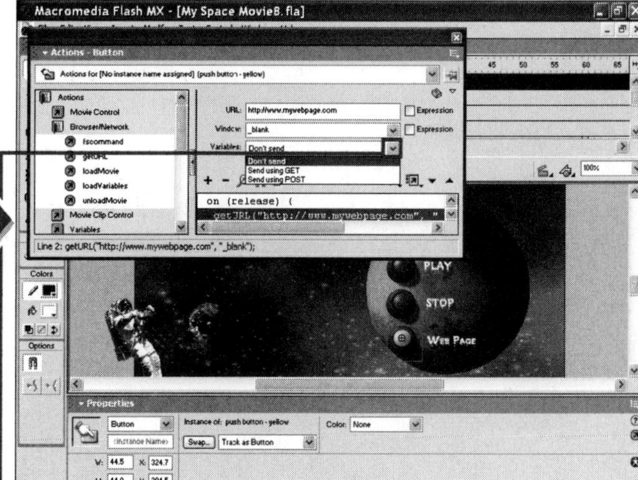

■ You can also click the Variable ▾ and specify where you want any associated variables sent.

■ Set to Don't send if you do not want to pass any variables to the target.

■ Set to Send using GET or Send using POST to send any variable data to a database or an e-mail message.

■ When you test the action, Flash loads the URL you specified when you click the button.

CONTROL THE FLASH PLAYER WITH THE FS COMMAND

You can use the FS Command to make your Flash movie communicate with a browser or with other programs that run Flash movies, including the standalone Flash Player or projector. The FS Command allows you to code your movie to interact with JavaScript used with HTML pages.

For example, you can add an FS Command that tells the Flash Player to make the movie fill the screen or hide the menu bar of the player. You can define two parameters when assigning the FS Command: command and arguments. Commands include FullScreen, AllowScale, ShowMenu, Exec, and Quit. Arguments include True/False conditions.

If you use the FullScreen command with your FS Command action, a `true` argument sets the player window to full-screen mode without a menu bar. If you assign this action to a button, your action statement may look like this:

```
on(release) {
fscommand ("fullscreen",
"true");
}
```

If a `false` argument is used, the player window shows the movie in the size specified in the Flash Movie Properties dialog box.

The steps below can be modified to apply to any FS Command.

CONTROL THE FLASH PLAYER WITH THE FS COMMAND

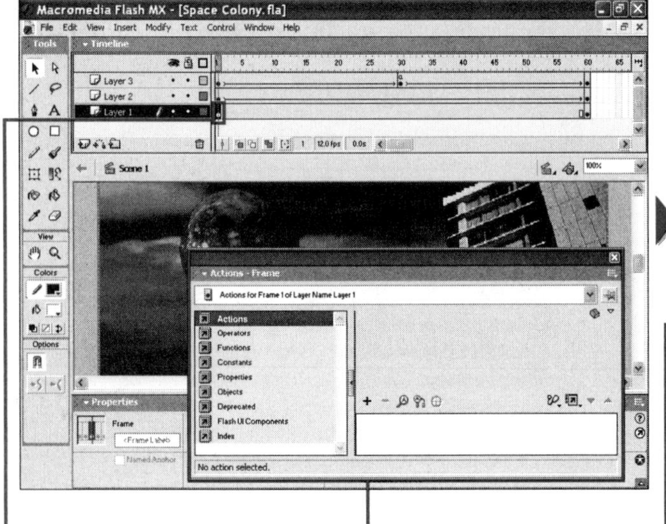

1 Select the first keyframe to which you want to assign the FS Command.

■ You can also assign the action to a button or movie clip instance.

2 Open the Actions panel.

Note: To open and close the Actions panel, see page 576.

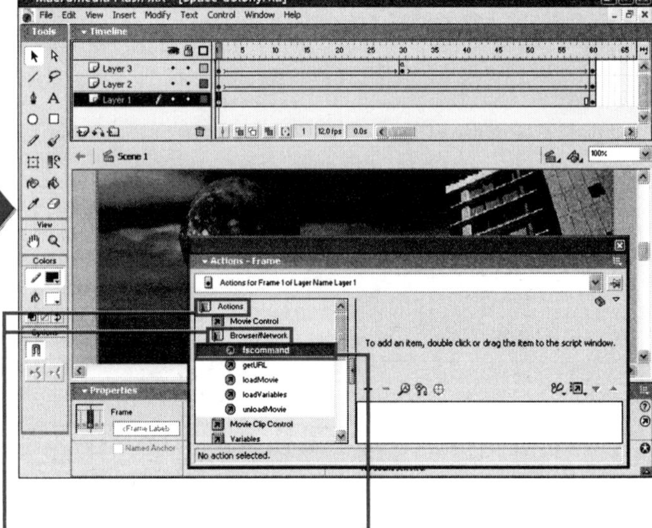

3 Click Actions.

4 Click Browser/Network.

5 Double-click fscommand.

Can I play my movies on alternative players besides the Flash Player?

✔ Your Flash movies play best with the Macromedia Flash Player, but you can also play them in other players. For example, you can use the Java edition of the Flash Player if you are using a Java-compatible browser. You can also play your Flash files as RealFlash — the makers of RealPlayer — presentations on the Web. QuickTime also supports Flash files.

What exactly is a Flash Projector?

✔ A projector is a standalone executable program for playing SWF files. Use a projector if the person you are sharing a Flash movie with does not have the Flash Player installed.

What do the other FS Commands do?

✔ The steps below show how to use the FullScreen FS Command. There are four other commands you can specify. You can use the AllowScale command to enable users to scale your Flash movie. A false value for this command constrains the movie to the sizes you set up in the Movie Properties dialog box. You can use the ShowMenu command to toggle the menu bar on or off in the player window. You can use the Exec command to open another executable file inside the player window. You can use the Quit command to close the player window.

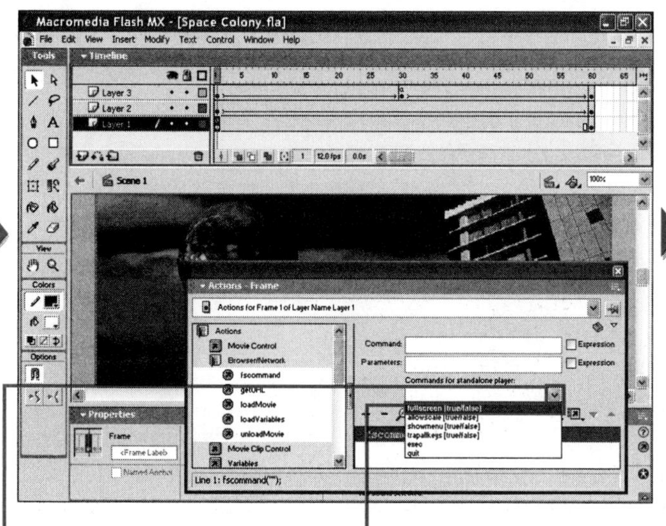

■ Flash MX adds the action to the actions list.

6 Click the Commands for Standalone Player ▾ to display a list of options.

7 Click an FS Command. In this example, fullscreen [true/false] is selected.

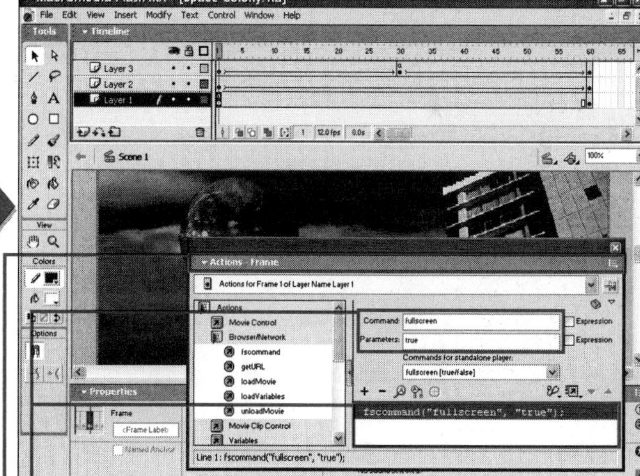

■ Flash MX adds the parameters to the actions list box.

8 Click the panel title bar to hide the Actions panel, or click ☒ to close the panel entirely.

■ You can now publish your movie as a standalone player projector and test the action.

Note: To learn more about publishing movies and using the projector, see page 630.

CHANGE ACTION ORDER

You can have more than one action assigned to a frame or button. All actions are listed in the actions list in the Actions panel. Although you can only add one action at a time, you can change the order of your actions list at any time.

When you add more than one action to a frame, Flash MX executes the actions in the order they appear in the actions list. You can reorder the actions as necessary. For example, if you want to move a Stop action before a Play action, you can use the arrow buttons in the panel to reorder the two actions.

The more actions you assign, the more important their order may be when Flash carries out the script instructions. If an action is out of order, the script will not play the way you expect it to. If a script does not perform correctly, you can revisit the Actions panel and check the order in which the actions appear in the list. You may need to move your statements around to follow a logical flow.

CHANGE ACTION ORDER

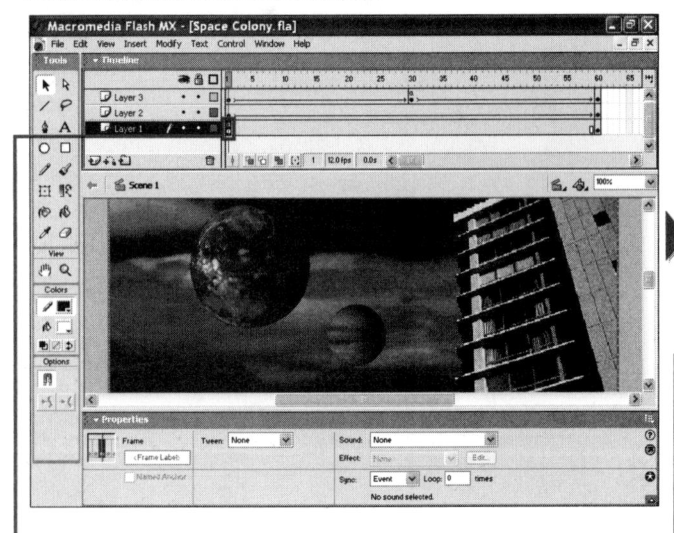

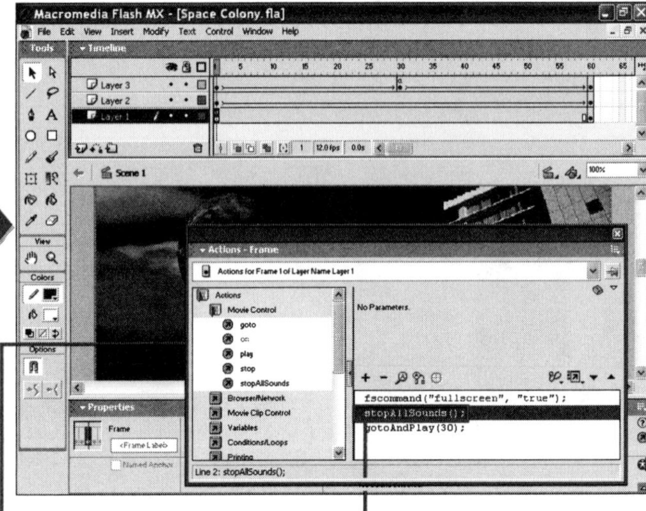

1 Select the frame containing the actions you want to reorder.

2 Open the Actions panel.

Note: To open and close the Actions panel, see page 576.

3 Click the action you want to move.

■ If your list is long, you can resize the panel to view more of the actions list.

Can I delete an action I no longer want?

✔ Yes. First, in the Actions panel, select the action statement in the actions list. Next, click the [−] button. Flash MX removes the action from the list, and the action is no longer a part of the frame or button.

Can I cut, copy, and paste actions in the Actions panel?

✔ Yes. Click an action statement to select it, then right-click (Control-click) to display a pop-up menu containing the cut, copy, and paste commands. You can use these commands to move statements around in the list.

Can I drag and drop action statements?

✔ Yes. Another way to edit the action order is to drag a selected action statement up or down in the actions list and drop the action statement when it reaches the desired location. You can also drag a new action onto the list, or remove actions you no longer want by dragging them off the list.

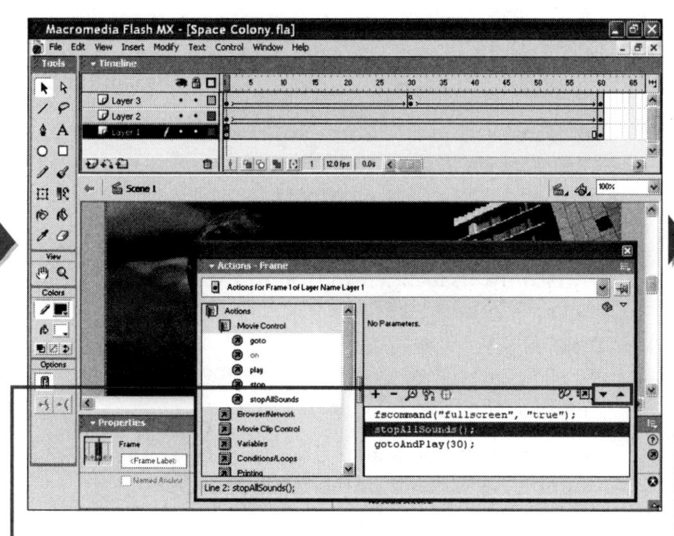

4 Click a reorder option.

■ Click [▼] to move the action down one line in the list.

■ Click [▲] to move the action up one line in the list.

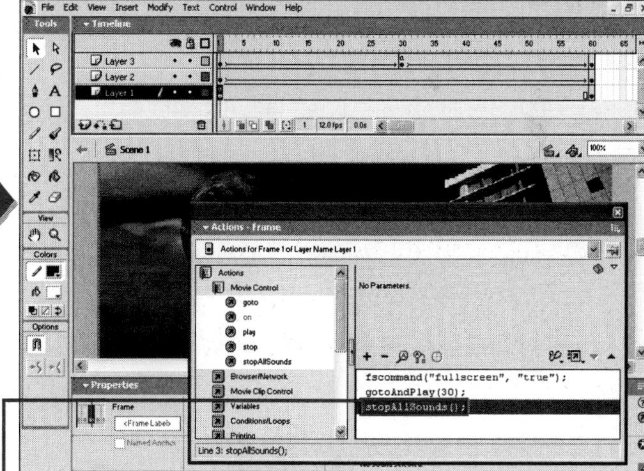

■ Flash MX moves the action up or down as directed.

■ You can click [▼] or [▲] as many times as needed to move the action line.

■ Close or hide the Actions panel when finished.

INTRODUCTION TO COMPLEX ACTIONS

You can add complex interactivity to your Flash MX movies to enable users to manipulate objects, input type, and access files that are not part of the original movie. Interactive movies utilize Flash actions — sets of instructions that tell the movie what to do if a certain event occurs. Depending on the complexity of the action, you can also define parameters that set up controls for the action. For example, you might have an interactive action that uses a dynamic text box in your Flash movie, enabling a user to enter their name, after which Flash generates a message using the name, such as Hello Dave, Welcome to my Web site!

You can break down actions into several levels of complexity in Flash MX. Frame actions give you greater control over how a movie plays. Button actions enable users to interact with your movie via a button. Complex actions use parameters that enable others to interact with elements in your movie.

Code Actions in ActionScript

Flash actions are written in ActionScript. This programming language, similar to JavaScript, uses object-oriented scripting. Though technically not a true programming language, ActionScript is an assortment of scripting commands which add interactivity to objects in your Flash movies. Simply put, you can use ActionScript programming language as a tool to define how your movie behaves and how other users interact with the movie.

You do not need to know ActionScript or any other programming language to create actions in Flash MX. If you are well versed in scripting languages, such as JavaScript, you can certainly employ your knowledge to write scripts in Flash. If you are new to writing scripts, you can still create scripts that add interactivity to your project based on action commands available in the Actions panel.

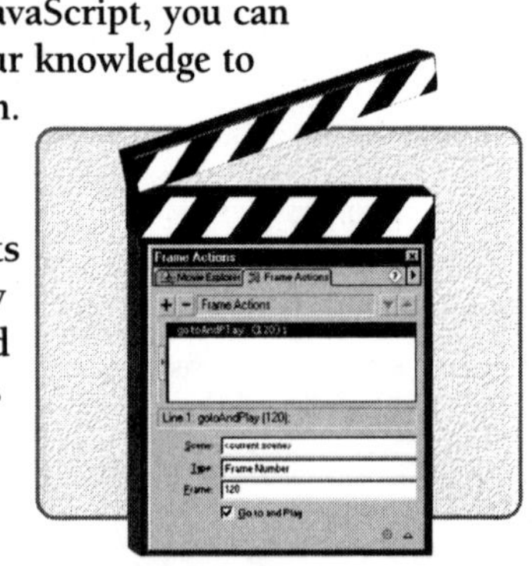

Enter Scripting Code

Scripting languages are based on codes that look similar to this:

```
on (release) { setProperty
("myMovieClip", _visible, 0);
```

This code changes the visibility of a movie clip, named myMovieClip, when the user presses the associated button in the Flash movie. The `setProperty` action has parameters for setting a level of visibility, in this case a setting of zero, which makes the clip invisible.

Script coding, such as the script used in the example, is written in the Actions panel in the actions list box, also called the script pane. You can write scripts in both Normal and Expert modes in the Actions panel. While Flash MX ensures scripts are written properly in Normal mode, in Expert mode, you are on your own. For that reason, you may want to confine your script building to Normal mode unless you are an experienced programmer and feel comfortable writing your own scripts.

Types of Flash Actions

The Actions panel categorizes Flash actions into eight main groups: Actions, Operators, Functions, Constants, Properties, Objects, Deprecated, and Flash UI Components. The panel also lists every available action in an Index. Each group category includes subcategories. For example, the Actions category lists subcategories for Movie Control, Browser/Network, and Movie Clip Control. You can find associated actions listed under each subcategory. All the basic actions, such as those you use for navigating in the movie, are found in the Actions category.

You can find all the necessary elements for building scripts in the remaining groups of actions in the Actions panel. For example, the Operators category lists operators for comparing and combining values, such as mathematical operators. The Functions category lists built-in functions such as `True`, `False`, and `Random`. The Constants category lists global constants you can use in expressions. The Properties category lists characteristics you can set for your movies, such as dimensions.

The Objects group offers several predefined objects for manipulating objects or working with information entered by the user. The Deprecated category includes actions you can utilize when creating movies for Flash Player 4 format. The Flash UI Components category includes prebuilt user interface components you can add to your movies.

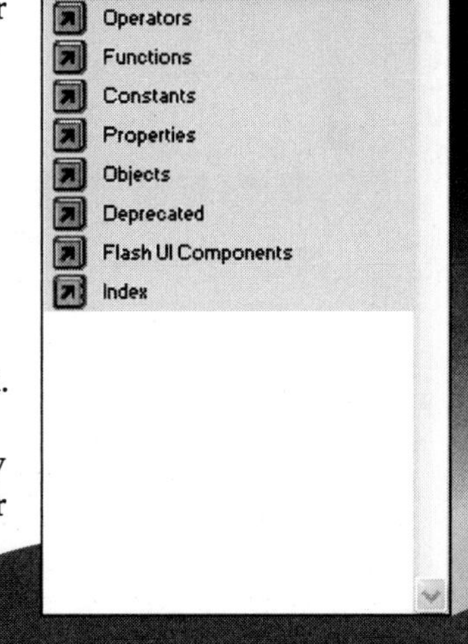

Using Expressions and Variables

When assigning actions in Flash MX, you can create formulas for manipulating data, called expressions, and holding places for changeable pieces of data, called variables. Expressions are any part of your Flash action that results in a value. An expression is a phrase that represents a result or evaluation. Variables are containers that hold values. Variable values can include numbers, test strings, and Boolean values.

Here is an example of an expression that evaluates which frame number to go to in a Flash movie:

```
on (release){
gotoAndPlay (5 + 10);
}
```

In this script expression, Flash evaluates 5 + 10 to arrive at frame number 15 and jumps to that particular frame in the movie.

When you plug in variables, the expression looks like this:

```
on (release){
luckyNumber = 5
secondLuckyNumber = 10
gotoAndPlay (luckyNumber +
secondLuckyNumber);
}
```

The variables in this script, luckyNumber and secondLuckyNumber, are used to accomplish the same thing as the first script example, jumping to a particular frame in the movie. Variable names always begin with a character and should describe the value you are collecting. The variables you define for an action determine the type of information a user inputs.

ADD A VARIABLE TEXT FIELD

You can use a variable text field to collect information from a user. Variable text is created from an editable text field, an interactive text box in your movie. Editable text fields appear in your Flash project and enable users to click inside and enter data. For example, you may use an input text box to enable users to type data in a form or survey. You can also use text fields to return ActionScript output, such as a message.

When you create an input text box for variable information, you assign a variable name to the box. This name describes the value that the user types into the box, such as name, favoriteColor or luckyNumber. You can then use the variable text field value in your Flash actions. For example, you can have a text field that collects the age of the user and name the variable age.

Variable names always begin with a character and are case-sensitive. To help you identify variable names in script coding, use a lowercase letter to start the name. You can assign variable names to text fields you create using the Text tool in Flash MX rather then assign a variable in the Actions panel.

ADD A VARIABLE TEXT FIELD

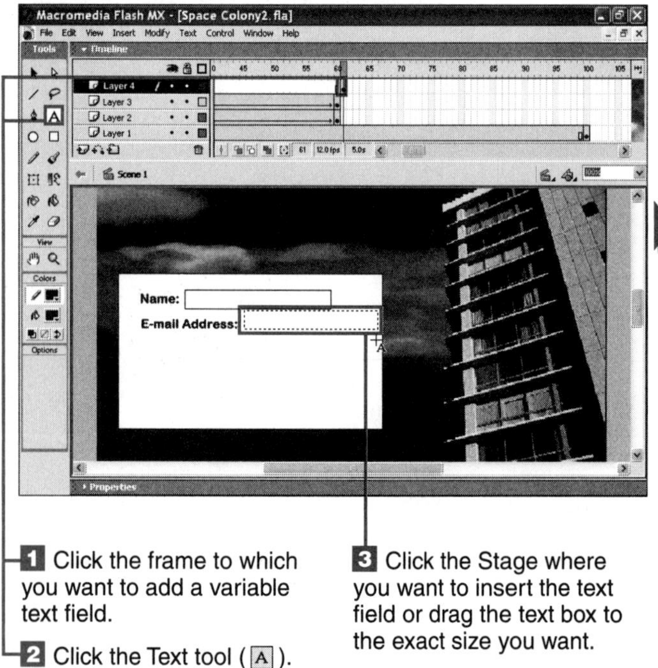

1 Click the frame to which you want to add a variable text field.

2 Click the Text tool (A).

3 Click the Stage where you want to insert the text field or drag the text box to the exact size you want.

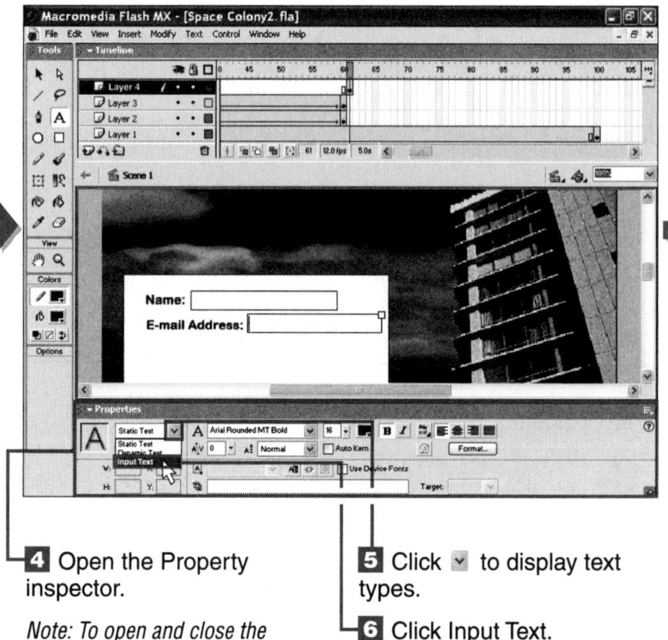

4 Open the Property inspector.

Note: To open and close the Property inspector, see page 346.

5 Click ▾ to display text types.

6 Click Input Text.

What types of text boxes can I use in Flash MX?

✔ Flash MX utilizes three types of text boxes: static, dynamic, and input. Use static text boxes to include text as part of your movie, such as a logo or product name. Use dynamic text boxes to display data that updates, such as stock quotes or basketball scores. Use input text boxes to collect interactive information from the user.

Can I format the text box for user input?

✔ Yes. Any formatting that you apply to the text box is what the user sees when they type data into the box. You can specify font, font size, font color, and more.

How do I specify a maximum character width?

✔ Enter a number in the Maximum Characters field in the Property inspector based on what you expect the user to type into the text field. For example, if the field is for an abbreviated state name, two characters are sufficient, but if the field is for the name of a person, twenty characters may be more appropriate.

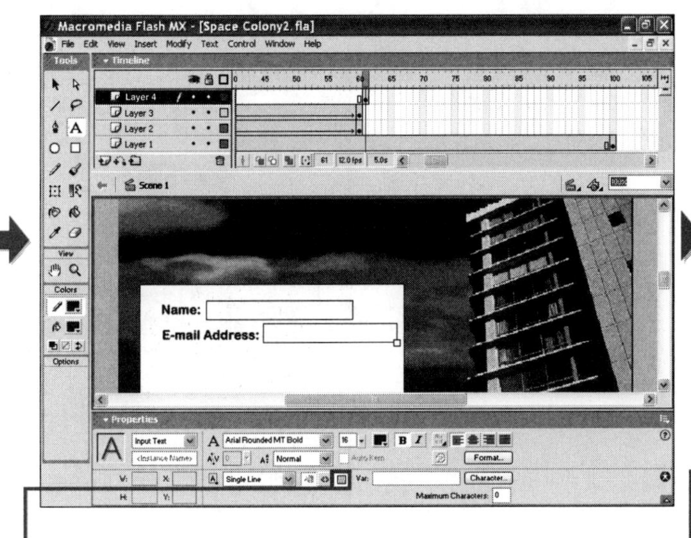

7 Click the Show Border Around Text button (▣).

■ Flash MX adds a border around the text field.

Note: When the text box is selected, a blue border surrounds the box. When you deselect the box, you can see the black border you assigned.

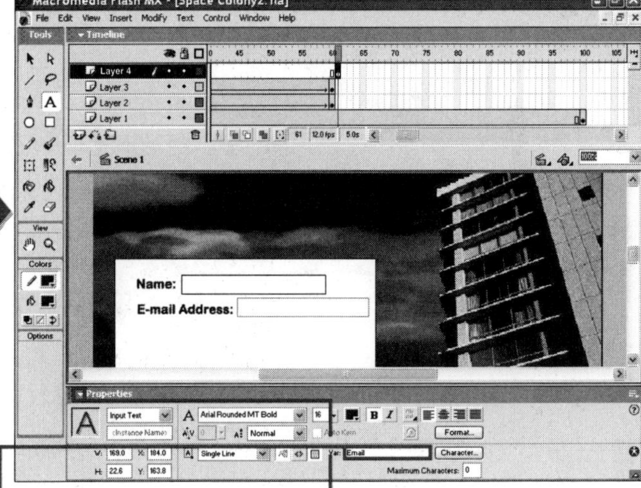

8 Click in the Variable box and type a name for the variable.

■ The variable text field is created.

■ You can hide the Property inspector by clicking ▾ (▾ changes to ▸).

ADD A VARIABLE TO GET A USER NAME

You can use variables in your action scripts as containers for values. Variables are a great way to create dynamic functionality in your movies. You can create a variable text field at the beginning of your movie that collects the name of the user. You can then add the variable to an expression that adds the name of the user to a greeting, such as Hi, Robin, welcome to my Web site. In this case, the variable is the user name, and the value is whatever text the person types into the field.

You can create a keyframe with a variable text field and a stop action that pauses the movie and allows the user time to type their name, then add a button the user can click to start the movie playing again. A few frames later, you can create a personalized greeting that takes the value entered into the variable and adds it to an expression you write that produces the personalized greeting.

Variables can store all kinds of values, such as numbers, text strings, and Boolean values — a type of value that analyzes conditions, such as true and false. You can assign variables to buttons, movie clip instances, or keyframes.

ADD A VARIABLE TO GET A USER NAME

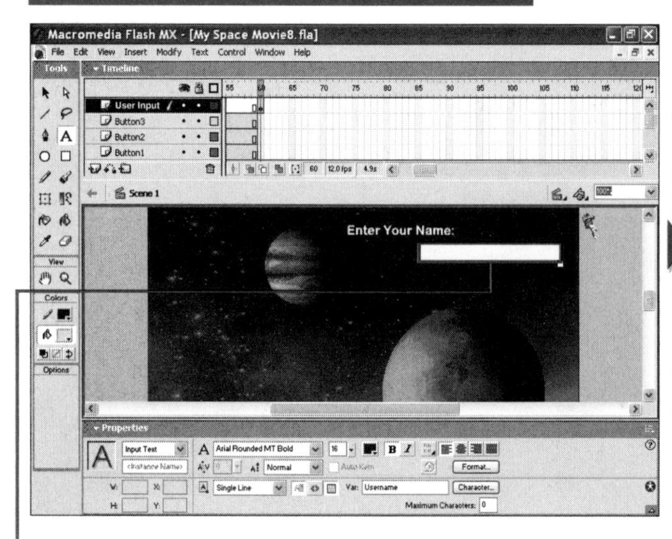

1 Create a variable text box.

Note: To add a variable text field, see page 600.

Note: Make sure you assign the box input status and a variable name.

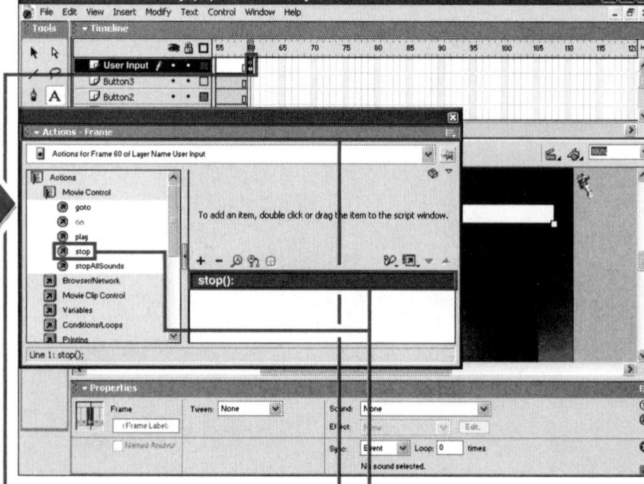

2 Click the frame.

3 Open the Actions panel.

■ You can click in the Property inspector to open the Actions panel, or press F9.

4 Add a Stop action to the frame.

Note: To add a Stop action, see page 586.

5 Click the title bar to hide the Actions panel.

When are keyboard events used?

✔ Many users automatically press Enter after typing text into a field rather than using the mouse to click another area onscreen. Consider this when creating variable text fields and buttons in your Flash movies. For example, if you create a Flash form, you can set the Tab key as the keypress variable so users can tab from field to field in the form. You can set a variety of event options to anticipate the various ways users interact with buttons.

Do I have to create a button from scratch?

✔ No. Flash MX comes with a library of premade buttons you can use in your movies. To add one to the library of your movie and place an instance on the Stage, click the Window menu, click Common Libraries, and then click Buttons. The Buttons Library window appears. Peruse the sample buttons and drag one out onto the Stage to add it to a frame and to the Library of your movie.

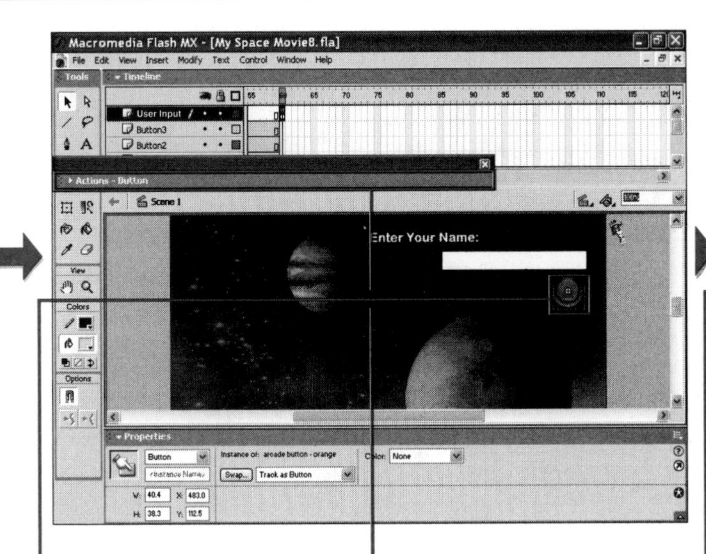

6 Add a button to the frame.

Note: To create a button, see page 462.

7 Click the title bar to display the Actions panel.

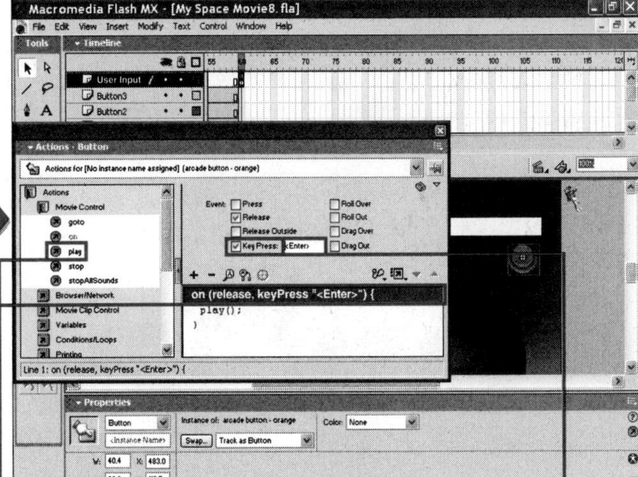

8 Assign a Play action to the selected button in the Actions panel.

Note: To add a Play action, see pages 586 to 589.

9 Click the first line of the Play action script.

10 Click the Key Press check box.

11 Click inside the Key Press field and press Enter (Return).

■ Flash MX automatically fills in the option.

CONTINUED

ADD A VARIABLE TO GET A USER NAME (CONTINUED)

After creating variables in your movie, you can use expressions to add values to variables and manipulate the values. In this example, you create an expression, or formula, that adds the name of the user to a general greeting. You can create any type of greeting you like for this task. The actual greeting text must appear in quotes in the Value text field.

When building expressions in the Actions panel, you create a formula with operators and text strings. An expression is simply a phrase that tells Flash what to do. Expressions can include numerous variables, operators, numbers, and text. Expressions can evaluate and carry out tasks, such as evaluating true/false conditions or adding numbers. To make any parameter in the Actions panel into an expression, you must click the Expression check box next to the appropriate field where applicable. This tells Flash to ignore the defaults and treat the entry as an expression.

When entering expressions, remember to place any information you want to appear in the actual movie within quote marks. Also be sure to include spaces and punctuation when needed.

ADD A VARIABLE TO GET A USER NAME (CONTINUED)

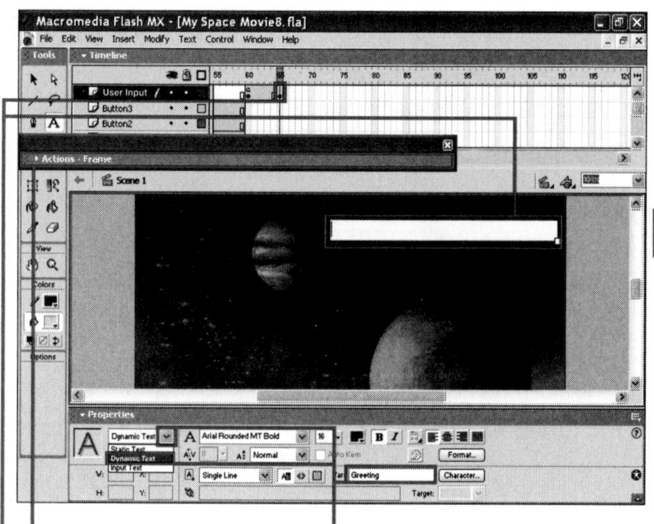

12 Click the title bar to hide the Actions panel.

13 Insert a blank keyframe where you want the personalized greeting to appear.

14 Add a text box to hold the personalized message.

15 Click the Text Type ▾.

16 Click Dynamic Text.

■ Flash MX assigns the box dynamic status, which means the user cannot edit it.

17 Type a variable name for the text box.

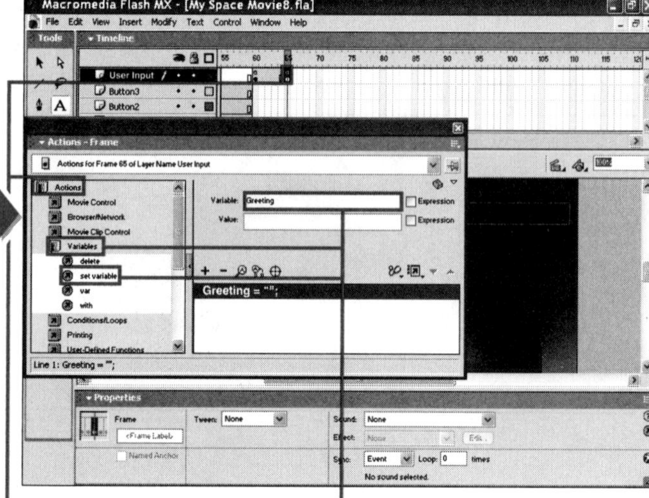

18 Click the keyframe.

19 Click the title bar to display the Actions panel.

20 Click Actions.

21 Click Variables.

22 Double-click set variable.

■ Flash MX adds the Set Variable to the actions list.

23 Type a name for the greeting variable.

Are there any rules to naming my variables?

✔ Yes. All variable names must begin with a character and cannot contain spaces or symbols, with the exception of the underscore symbol, or ActionScript keywords. Variable names are not case-sensitive, so it does not matter if you type lower or uppercase characters. Names such as myVariable or my_variable are good examples of valid variable names, while 1myVariable, or my#variable are invalid names. It is good practice to use descriptive names for your variables so you can easily identify them in your script code.

What can I do if I test my movie, but it does not work properly?

✔ First, make sure you followed the steps correctly. Open the Actions panel and check to make sure you used the correct variable names in the expression. Double check the spacing and punctuation of your expression. Text or numbers you want to appear in the movie must be enclosed in quotes. Also make sure you assigned Input status to the variable text field and Dynamic status to the message text field.

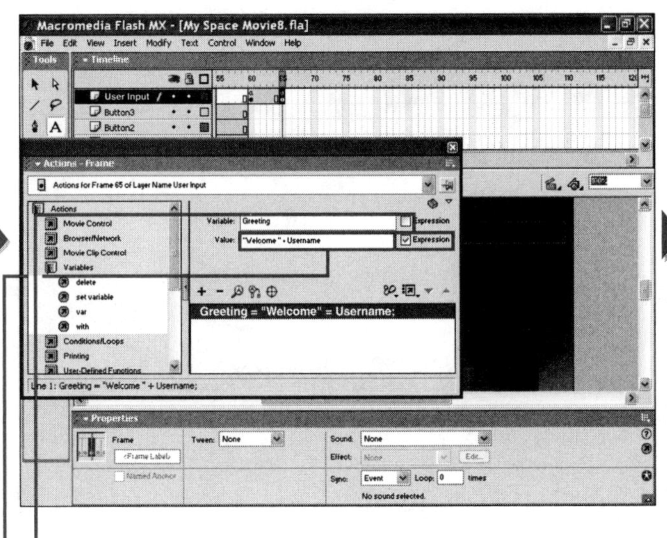

24 Click the Expression check box.

25 Type the greeting and expression in the Value field.

■ In this example, the expression reads "Welcome" + Username. Use the variable name you assigned in step 17 in place of "Username."

26 Add a Stop action to the frame.

Note: To add a Stop action, see page 586.

■ You can now test the movie to see if the variables work.

Note: To test movies in the Flash Player window, see page 630.

TARGET MOVIE CLIP TIMELINES

You can control and manipulate the individual Timelines of your movie clips by directing, or targeting, the specific movie clip instance for an action. In other words, you can control the Timelines of movies within your movie without having to assign the action to a specific Timeline. You just have to target the Timeline you want to control. The more complex your movies, the more likely they are to utilize separate interactive segments.

You can use the With action to both target a clip and tell Flash what to do with the clip. You can do this by specifying the instance name of the clip and then assigning the action you want Flash to perform on the clip. The With action is found in the Variables subcategory of the Actions category in the Actions panel.

When referencing targets, you use a directory structure. If a clip resides within another clip, you must indicate this in the target path, for example, `with ("Big Clip/MyClip1") {`. When you specify a target, you are identifying to Flash the object you are addressing. The With action must immediately follow the target path, within the ending curly bracket of the action statement.

TARGET MOVIE CLIP TIMELINES

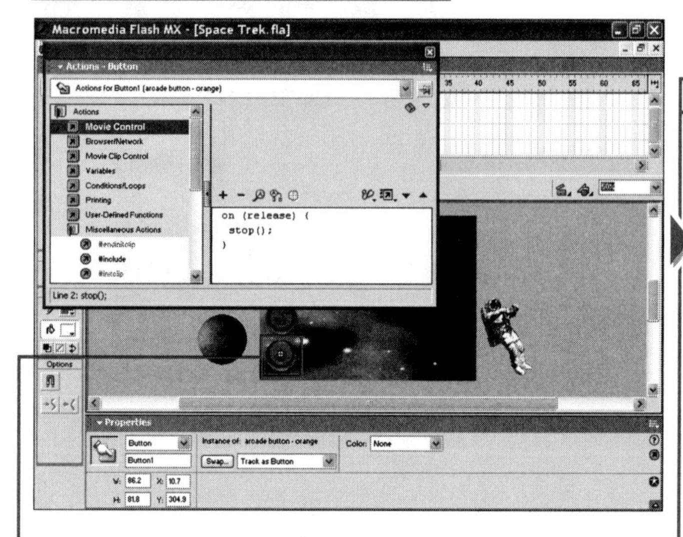

1 Click the instance to which you want to assign the action.

■ You can assign target actions to frames, buttons, or movie clips.

2 Open the Actions panel.

Note: To open and close the Actions panel, see page 576.

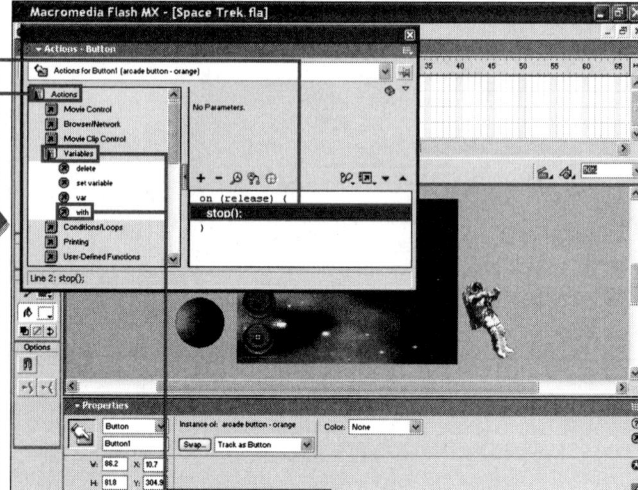

■ In this example, the button is assigned a stop action. To target a clip to stop, click the Stop action first.

3 Click Actions.

4 Click Variables.

5 Double-click with.

■ Flash MX adds the action to the actions list with the default `on release` statement.

Can I nest actions in Flash?

✔ Yes. Nesting actions within other actions is quite common for all programming languages. Nesting is when you place an action inside another action. Nested actions are indented in the actions list box in the Actions panel.

When I add the With and Stop actions to my button, the clip keeps playing when the button is clicked. Why?

✔ Make sure you first assign a Stop action to the button, then select the Stop action in the actions list and add the With action. Make sure you target the correct clip. Follow this with another Stop action that tells Flash what to do with the targeted clip. If the clip is nested, use the full path to the clip, such as BigClip.LittleClip. SmallestClip.

I want to target several different Timelines. Is there an easier way to do this in the Actions panel?

✔ Yes. You can use the Evaluate action to write an action statement that targets all the Timelines you want. Located under the Miscellaneous Actions subcategory, the Evaluate action allows you to type each target or instance name separated with a dot, such as `myClip1.myClip2.myClip3.stop ()`. You must enter the exact syntax, such as the Stop action in the example, plus the two parentheses. If you use the Target Path dialog box, Flash MX ensures the correct syntax is entered for you.

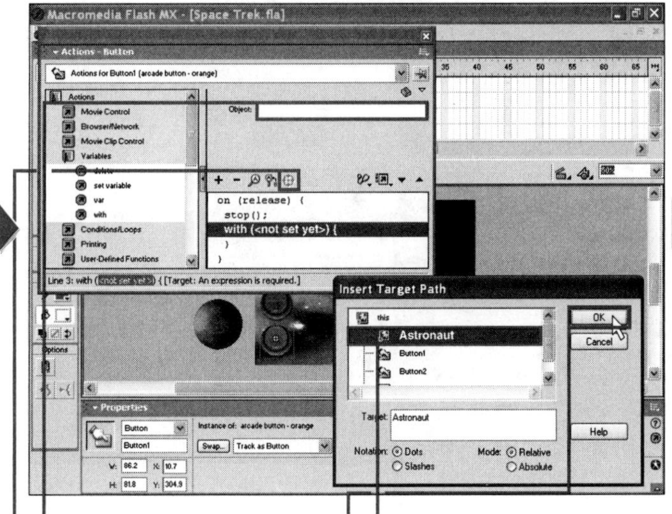

6 Click the Object text field.

7 Click the Insert Target Path button (⊕).

■ Flash MX opens the Insert Target Path dialog box, showing the hierarchy of your current movie.

8 Click a target movie clip in the directory tree for your file.

■ You can also type the target path in the Target text box.

9 Click OK.

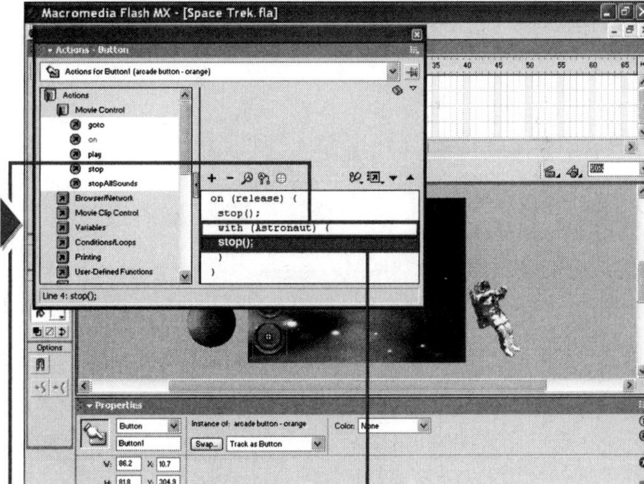

■ The target path is added to your actions list.

■ You can now add any additional actions to tell the movie clip what to do, such as Play or Stop.

■ In this example, a Stop action is added to the With action to stop the targeted movie clip's Timeline from playing.

Note: Movie clips loop continuously unless you include a Stop action.

CHANGE THE MOVIE CLIP PROPERTY

You can use actions to change movie clip properties. For example, you can rotate an instance of a movie clip in the middle of your main movie or change the opacity of the clip, also called the alpha value. You can also assign property changes to a button that the user clicks to see the changes occur in the movie.

All built-in properties, such as alpha or rotation, are preceded by an underscore in the ActionScript language, such as `_alpha`. Common built-in properties include positions, such as X position and Y position, height, width, and rotation. When you assign a value to a property, you type an equal sign followed by the value, for example,

```
myClip._alpha=50
```

This instruction tells Flash to make the `myClip` instance 50 percent transparent.

Flash MX lists properties under the Properties category in the Actions panel. You can add properties to the actions list and change their values as needed, targeting the clip instance you want to change.

Another way to change clip properties is with the Set Property action, a leftover action from previous versions of Flash. With the Set Property action, you can change properties using the action parameters.

CHANGE THE MOVIE CLIP PROPERTY

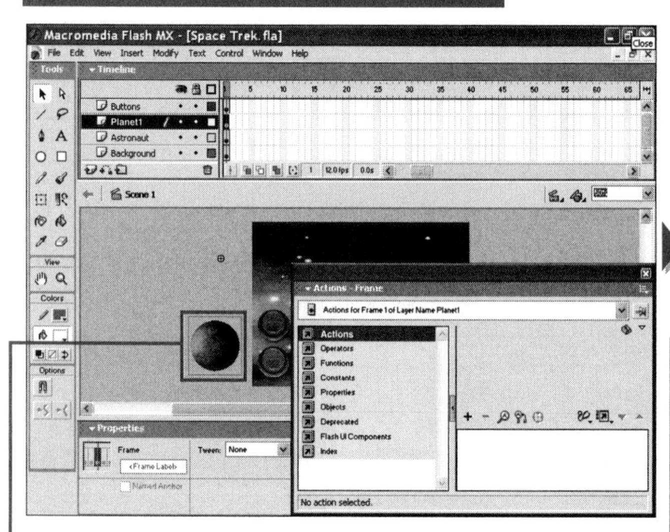

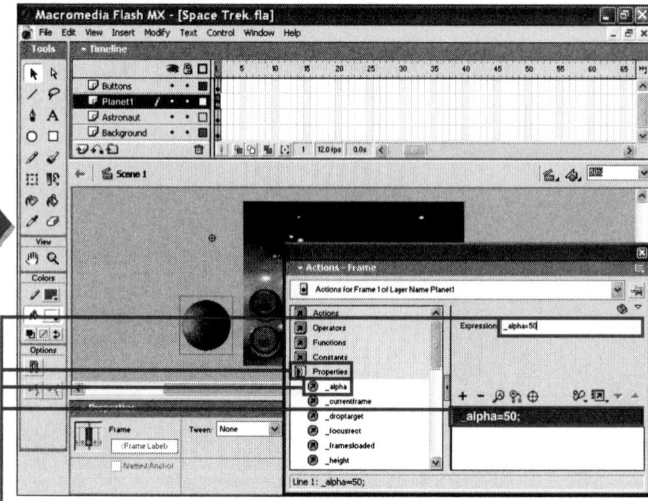

CHANGE A CLIP PROPERTY

1 Click the clip instance for which you want to change properties.

2 Open the Actions panel.

Note: To open and close the Actions panel, see page 576.

3 Click Properties.

4 Double-click the property you want to change.

■ Flash MX adds it to the actions list.

5 Edit the value or values as needed.

Note: You must type an equal sign before you enter a value in the Expression field.

■ You can now test the movie to see how the property change looks.

How do I assign a property change to a button that changes the movie clip when clicked?

✔ Start by placing instances of the button and the movie clip on the Stage. Then, assign the movie clip instance a name. Click the button instance and add an Evaluate action using the Actions panel, under Actions, Miscellaneous Actions. You can write an expression in the Expression text field that changes the clip property. The object property syntax is `object.property`. The first part of the syntax targets the instance name, followed by a dot, then the property, such as `myClip._alpha=50`. When you test the movie and click the button, the movie clip instance changes to 50 percent transparency.

What exactly is the alpha property?

✔ The alpha property controls the transparency of an instance or object in your movie. A value of 100 percent means the instance is completely visible, while a value of 0 percent means the instance is completely transparent. You can also set the alpha property for an object using the Property inspector.

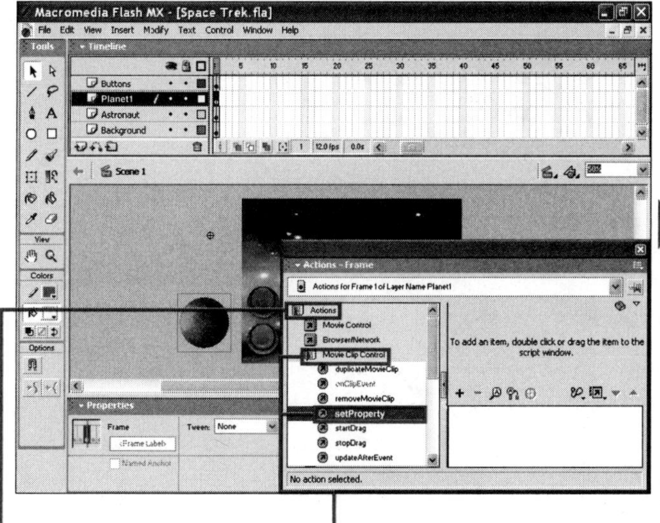

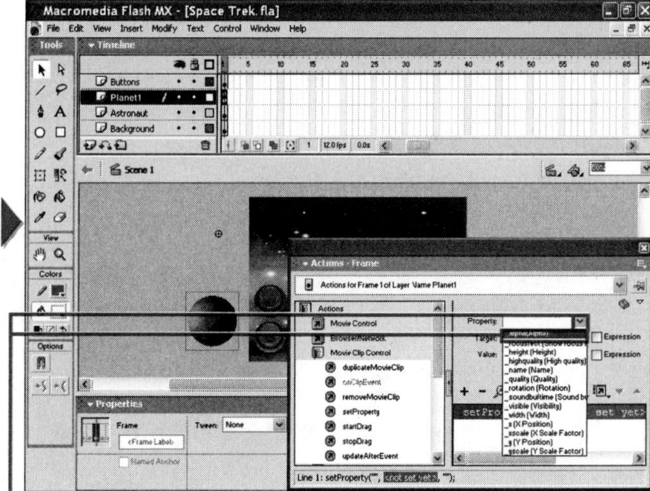

ASSIGN A SET PROPERTY ACTION

1 In the Actions panel, click Actions.

2 Click Movie Clip Control.

3 Double-click setProperty.

■ Flash MX adds the property to the actions list.

4 Click the Property ▾.

5 Click the property you want to modify, and make any necessary changes to the parameters.

■ Flash MX adds the property to the actions list.

6 Edit the value as needed.

CREATE A DRAGGABLE OBJECT

You can give users more interactivity with your movie by allowing them to drag objects around in the movie. The action of dragging and dropping onscreen objects is a staple of most computer games, and similar actions can make Web pages even more dynamic.

The easiest way to create draggable objects is to assign the Start Drag and Stop Drag actions to buttons. If you assign movie clips and text objects instance names, you can also add the Start Drag and Stop Drag actions to the instances, thus making them draggable objects as well.

When you assign an instance a unique name in Flash MX, you can then call upon that instance when targeting the instance for an action. You can assign a name to any instance you place on the Flash Stage using the Instance name field in the Property inspector.

For example, to turn a button into a draggable object, you can instruct Flash to make the button respond to both the pressing of the button, called the Press event, and the releasing of the button, called the Release event.

CREATE A DRAGGABLE OBJECT

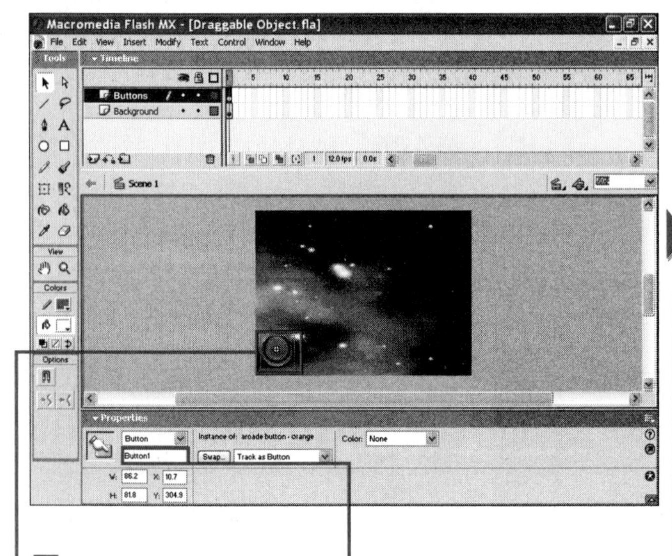

1 Click the button you want to turn into a draggable object.

2 Open the Property inspector.

Note: To open and close the Property inspector, see page 346.

3 Click inside the Instance Name field.

4 Type a name for the instance.

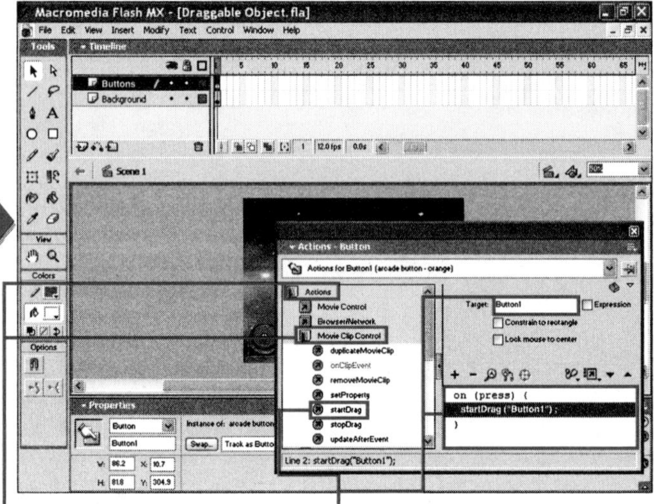

5 Open the Actions panel.

Note: To open and close the Actions panel, see page 576.

6 Click Actions.

7 Click Movie Clip Control.

8 Double-click startDrag.

■ Flash MX adds the Start Drag action to the actions list.

9 Type the instance name from step 4.

What if the user releases the mouse when it is not hovering over the dragging object?

✔ You can click the Release Outside parameter in the Stop Drag action to make the object stop dragging even if the user moves the mouse so quickly that it no longer hovers over the object.

Should I set any Start Drag parameters?

✔ When you click the Start Drag statement in the actions list, two parameters appear above. You can click the Lock Mouse to Center check box if you want the mouse to center on the object as it drags. Or you can click the Constrain to Rectangle check box to specify a draggable range area.

What happens if I do not give the button instance a name?

✔ Without an instance name, Flash MX treats the entire clip as a draggable object. However, if you place the Start Action on a button, you always need to specify an instance name.

Can I assign the Start Drag action to other objects in my movie?

✔ Yes, you can also assign the Start Drag action to other objects, such as movie clips and text objects.

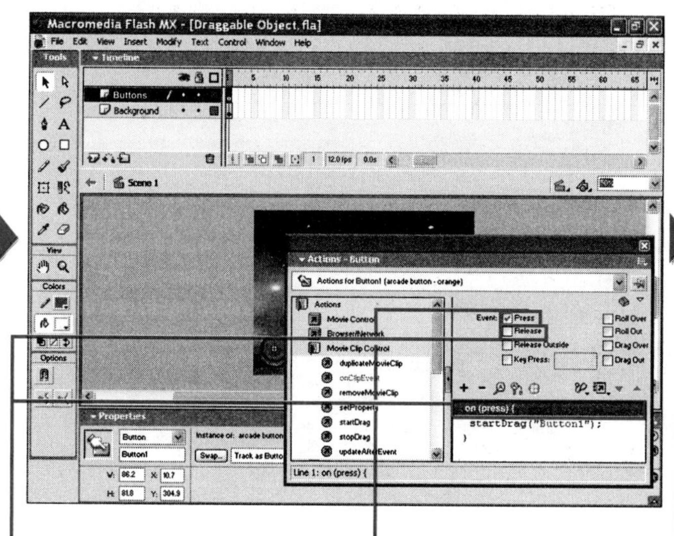

10 Click the first line of the startDrag code.

11 Click Release to deselect the parameter.

12 Click Press to select the parameter.

■ The button becomes draggable as soon as the user clicks it.

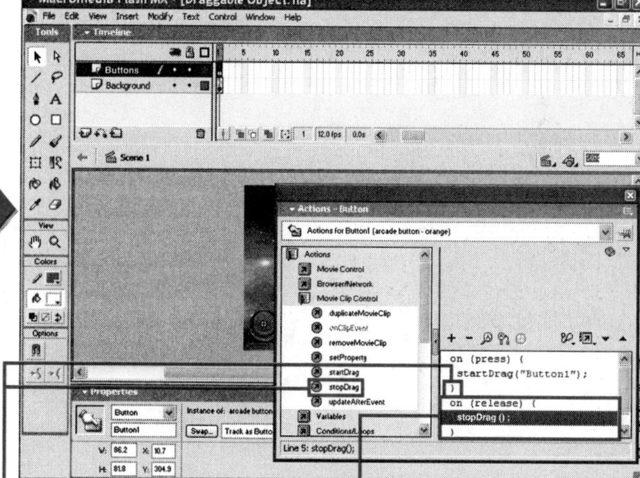

13 Click the last line of code in the actions list.

14 Double-click stopDrag.

■ Flash MX adds the Stop Drag action. This action makes the button undraggable when the user lets go of the mouse button.

■ You can now test the action in the Flash Player window.

USING THE DEBUGGER

Flash MX includes a Debugger tool you can use to help you test your movies, particularly all the actions and interactivity you add. Although you can fix problems in your action scripts by stepping through the script in the Actions panel one statement at a time, this can be a very tedious process if you have many actions listed. You can simultaneously check scripting problems and analyze your movie using the Debugger panel.

The Debugger does not fix bugs in your scripts; however, it does help you identify them. The Debugger only runs when you view a movie in the Flash Player window.

The Debugger lists all the objects in your movie along with a standard programming debugger pane. You can insert breakpoints to pause the Debugger at a particular line of code you want to test. When you play the movie, it pauses at the breakpoint and you can study the code or choose to step over the line of code and pause at the next line.

You can use the Properties, Variables, Locals, and Watch tabs to view various codes and parameters of the script. You can also make repairs to the code in the Debugger panel.

USING THE DEBUGGER

1 Click Control.

2 Click Debug Movie.

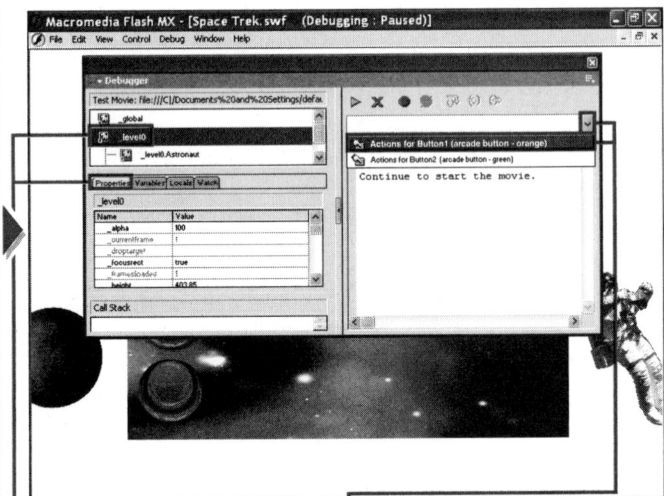

■ The Flash Player window opens along with the Debugger panel.

3 Click a movie clip.

4 Click the Properties tab to display the properties and variables of the movie clip.

■ You may need to resize the panes within the Debugger panel to view various items and resize the panel itself.

5 Click the Navigate ▾.

6 Click a script to check.

What does it mean when an Output window appears when I play my movie in the Flash Player window?

✔ The Output window appears automatically when Flash MX finds any errors in your script. You can also open the window by clicking Window, then Output. When you make note of the problem, you can revisit the Actions panel to make corrections. You can also click the Options Menu button to find options for copying the error message to a text file or print the message. You can click the Close button to close the Output window.

How do I know for sure if my script is being executed?

✔ You can run a Trace action to confirm that a script is working by outputting a custom message in the Output window when you test your movie in the Flash Player window. This message does not appear in your final movie, but merely helps you test script function. In the frame containing the action you want to trace, add a Trace action at the end of the script you want to test and define the parameters for the output message.

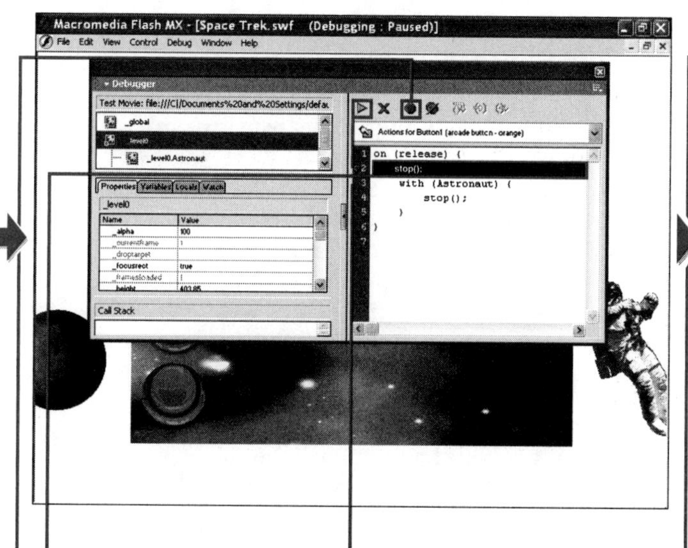

7 Click a line you want to check.

8 Click the Breakpoint button (●) to pause the movie at a particular line of code.

9 Click the Continue button (▷) to play and check the movie.

■ You can click the title bar to hide the Debugger panel and view the movie.

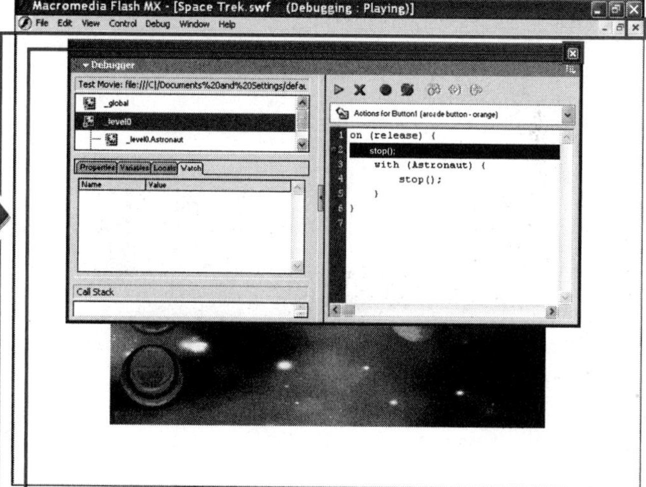

10 Click ☒ to close the Debugger panel.

11 Click ✕ to close the Flash Player window.

■ Flash returns you to the Flash MX program window.

INTRODUCTION TO COMPONENTS

You can use Flash MX components to add instant interactivity to your movie projects. Components are simply pre-built, complex movie clips for user interface elements such as radio buttons and list boxes.

User interface elements allow your viewers to interact with the movie in traditional ways, such as making selections from a combo box or check boxes, or clicking a submit button. You can use these elements to create forms, navigational buttons, and graphical user interfaces, or UIs, in Flash.

If you worked with previous versions of Flash, you may already be familiar with types of components, called Smart Clips. The new Flash MX components replace Smart Clips. Components offer built-in behaviors you can customize to create interesting user interface elements.

The beauty of components lies in the fact that you do not have to know programming code in order to create a user interface element for a movie. Even non-technical people can make components by building on the pre-existing scripts and parameters. Flash MX components are built on ActionScript code. To learn more about basic Flash actions and ActionScript, see Chapters 31 and 32.

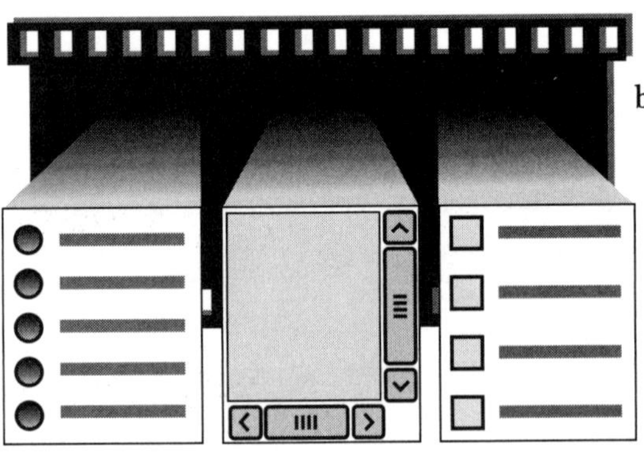

Types of Components

Flash MX components include the following common user interface elements: radio buttons, check boxes, push buttons, combo boxes, scroll panes, text scroll bars, and list boxes. Each of these elements are typically found in Web page forms and used for basic navigation.

You can add just one of these components to a movie, combine them, or use all of them to create a very simple user interface for a Web page form. For example, you might use the components on a survey form that gives you user feedback.

How Components Work

You can use the Components panel to add components to a Flash movie. Once you add a component to the Stage, you can customize the data contained within the component. For example, if you add a combo box that offers the user a drop-down list of menu choices, you can control exactly what menu choices appear in the list.

You use the Property Inspector to define the data that appears in components you add. When you select a component on the Stage and view the Property Inspector, two tabs appear for viewing the component's properties and for setting parameters for the component.

After adding components, you can assign actions and write scripts that tell Flash how to work with or process the user input. Writing functions for components takes practice. To learn more about ActionScript, see Chapter 32.

USING THE COMPONENTS PANEL

You can use the Components panel to add Flash MX components to your movies. Components are complex movie clips that include built-in actions for interacting with Flash movies.

You can quickly open the Components panel any time you need to add a component to the Stage. The Components panel is part of the default panel set that appears when you open Flash MX the very first time. You can also summon the panel separately to appear as a floating panel. To learn more about working with panels, see Chapter 20.

Once you add a component to your movie, you can populate it with your own content.

> **MASTER IT**
>
> **Can I move the panel out of the way?**
>
> ✔ Yes. You can move and resize the Components panel just as you can other panels available in Flash MX. Click the panel's title bar to quickly hide or display the panel contents. If the panel is docked, you can undock it and move it around the screen.

USING THE COMPONENTS PANEL

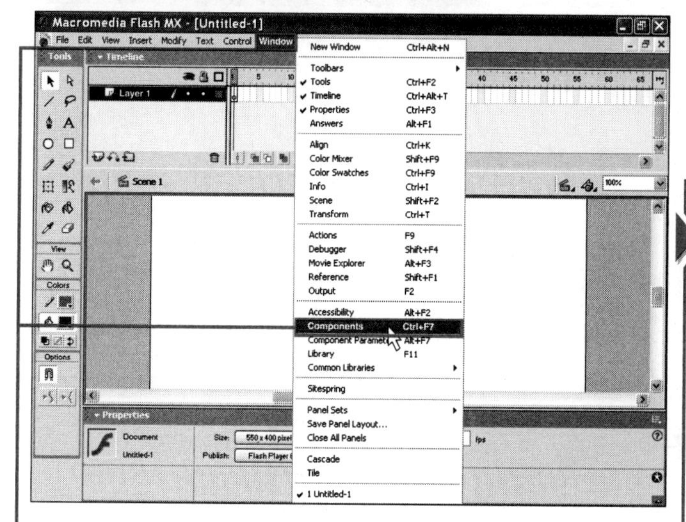

1 Click Window.

2 Click Components.

■ If your default panel set is open, you can access the docked Components panel on the right side of the program window.

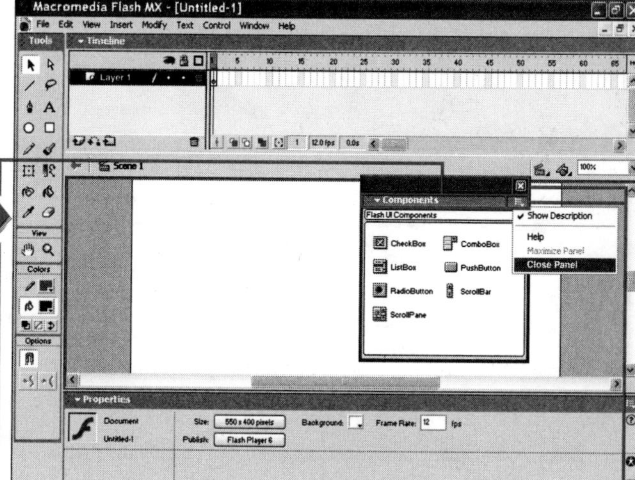

■ Flash MX opens the Components panel.

■ To hide the panel, click its title bar.

■ To close the panel, click the Options Menu button and click Close Panel.

■ You can also click the floating panel's Close button (☒) to close the panel.

ADD A COMBO BOX

You can include a combo box component in your movie to allow users to choose from a drop-down menu list of items. For example, you might include a combo box that allows users to choose a program version, state, or product. Combo boxes are commonly found on forms.

You determine what data to populate a combo box with, and the order in which the data appears. For example, a drop-down menu list of states might include abbreviations for each state listed alphabetically. A list of products might be random or alphabetized. You determine the order of list labels as well as their associated values.

Before adding a combo box, plan out the types of labels and values you want to include and how you want to use the values. Each selection in the drop-down list might link to a Web page or to a database on a Web server.

You can use the Components panel to add a combo box. See page 615 to display and close the panel when needed. After assigning a combo box, you can use the Property Inspector to add labels, values, and function to the component.

ADD A COMBO BOX

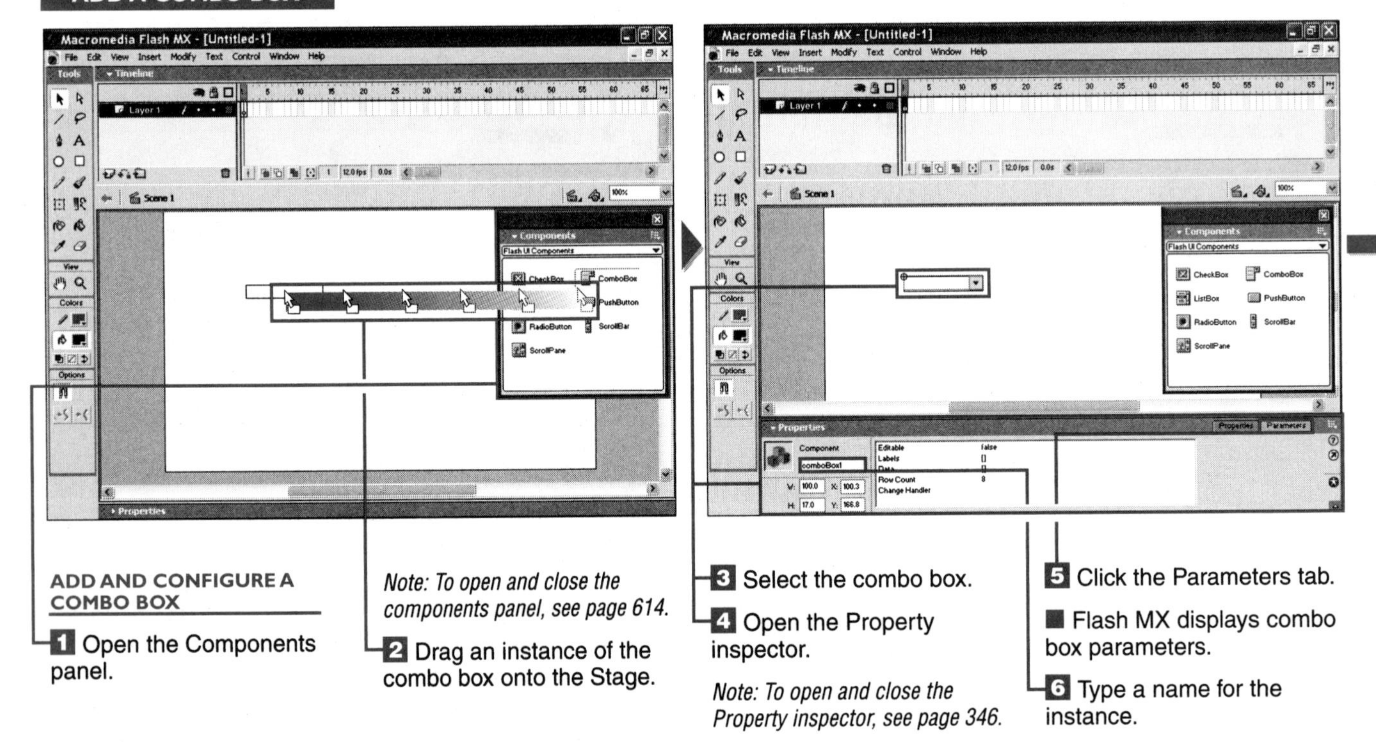

ADD AND CONFIGURE A COMBO BOX

1 Open the Components panel.

2 Drag an instance of the combo box onto the Stage.

Note: To open and close the components panel, see page 614.

3 Select the combo box.

4 Open the Property inspector.

Note: To open and close the Property inspector, see page 346.

5 Click the Parameters tab.

■ Flash MX displays combo box parameters.

6 Type a name for the instance.

Where can I find more Flash MX components?

✔ In addition to the seven components that come with Flash MX, you can also find components created by other users on the Macromedia Web site —www.macromedia.com/exchange/flash. Check back often to see what other types of components other Flash users create.

How do I widen my combo box menu list to fit my labels?

✔ To widen the length of your combo box, click the combo box on the Stage, open the Property Inspector, and click the Properties tab. Click in the Width text box, labeled with a W on the far left side of the panel, and type a new measurement or edit the default width. Press Enter and the box is resized.

Can I write my own components?

✔ Yes. If you know a bit about programming, you can write your own components using Flash ActionScript. Writing action scripts are beyond the scope of this book; however, you can learn more about ActionScript from the Flash MX help files. To learn the basics of actions and using the Actions panel, see Chapters 31 and 32.

What should the Editable parameter read?

✔ The default setting is False. This prevents anyone from typing in other text. It is a good idea to use the default setting as is unless you want users to enter additional text into the combo box.

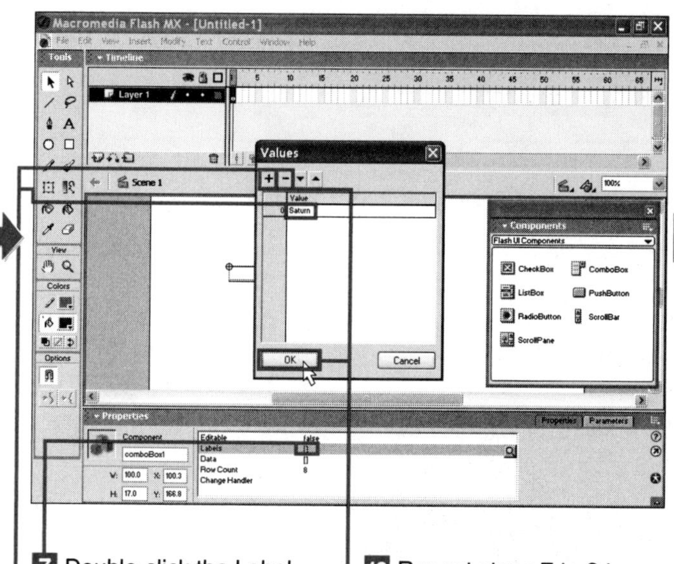

7 Double-click the Label field.

■ The Values dialog box opens.

8 Click the Plus button (+).

9 Type the first item label to appear in the list.

10 Repeat steps 7 to 8 to add more item labels.

■ You can click the Minus button (−) to remove an item.

■ You can click the Arrow buttons (▼ or ▲) to move an item.

11 Click OK.

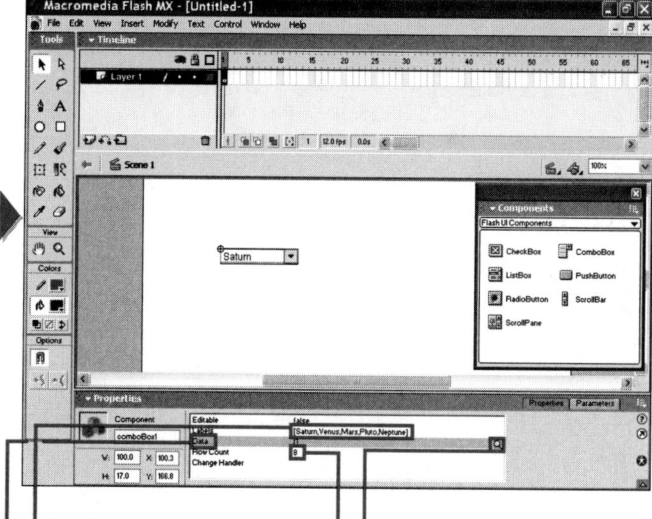

■ Flash MX adds the labels to the Labels field.

■ You can also enter values for each label by double-clicking the Data field and entering values in the Values dialog box.

■ You can also click the field you want to edit and click 🔍 to open the Values dialog box.

■ Unless your combo box requires more than eight lines, you can leave the default setting.

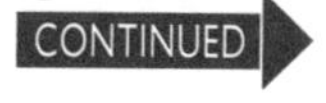
CONTINUED

ADD A COMBO BOX (CONTINUED)

After you add a combo box and define its parameters, you can assign a function called a Change Handler to a button that tells Flash how to process the choices the user makes. The Change Handler calls an ActionScript function. Unlike some of the other components, the combo box Change Handler only accepts a single value. When writing ActionScript to gather form data, use keyframes to contain your actions.

Writing functions for components is a bit tricky, however, the Actions panel can help. The Actions panel contains a category of actions dedicated to the Flash UI components.

The FcomboBox category lists methods associated with the combo box component. You can use the Get actions to create functions for the combo box. For example, you might write a statement that retrieves the label and data value of the item the user selects from the combo box instance named comboBox1 that looks like this:

```
trace
(comboBox1.getSelectedItem(
));
```

Or you might use the getValue method to find out the label of a selected item in the combo box, such as:

```
comboBox1.getValue()
```

Be sure to assign instance names to components so you can use them in functions.

ADD A COMBO BOX (CONTINUED)

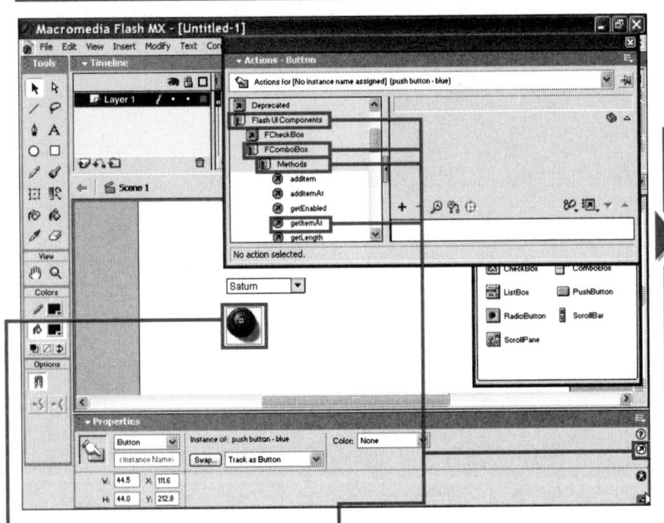

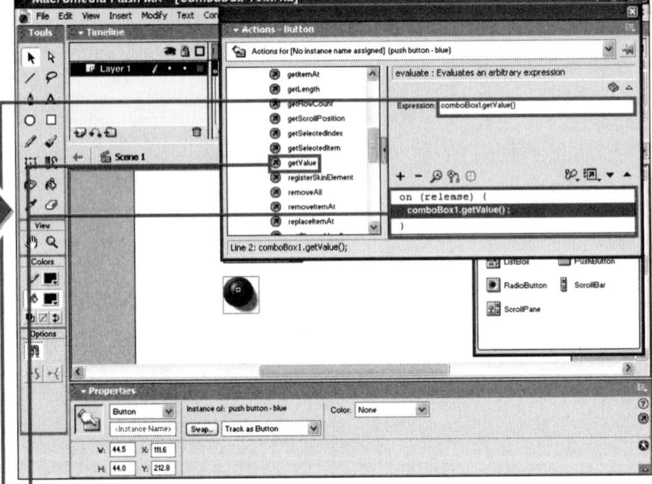

WRITE AN ACTION STATEMENT

1 Add a button to the Stage to process the combo box answer.

2 Select the button instance.

3 In the Property inspector, click [icon] to open the Actions panel.

4 Click Flash UI Components.

5 Click FComboBox.

6 Click Methods.

7 Double-click a method.

■ In this example, the `getValue` action returns the selected menu list item to appear as the selected choice in the combo box.

■ The instance name is typed before the method and a dot separates the two.

■ The `on Release` action is added by default when the `getValue` method is assigned.

How do I collect the results of my combo box?

✔ You can write a get results function to get the results of your combo box. For example, the following function gets the results of a combo box named food_box:

```
// get results from pg 2
function getResults() {
food_result =
food_box.getSelectedItem()
  .label;
selectedItem =
food_box.getSelectedIndex();
}
```

Writing script takes a lot of practice. Be sure to check out the components tutorials in the Flash Help files. Studying them can help you write functions for your own components.

Is there an action that tests my script?

✔ Yes. You can use the Trace action to check a script. For example, in Expert mode or in the expression field in Normal mode, you can type **trace (comboBox1.getSelectedItem());** and check the combo box from within the Flash Player window.

Is there a limit to how many combo boxes I can add to my movie?

✔ No. You can use as many as you like, but be sure to assign each one an instance name in order to tell Flash how to handle each one in scripts.

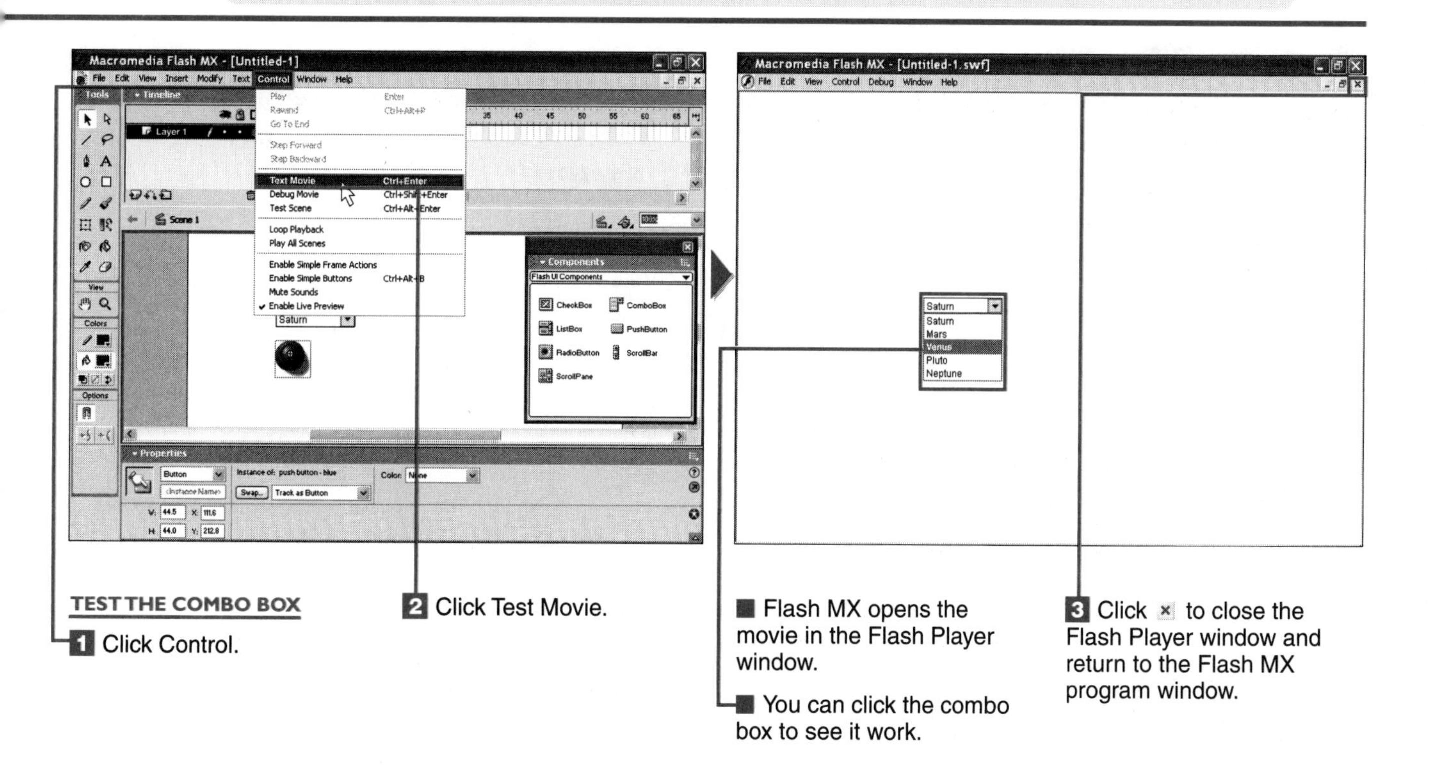

TEST THE COMBO BOX

1 Click Control.

2 Click Test Movie.

■ Flash MX opens the movie in the Flash Player window.

■ You can click the combo box to see it work.

3 Click ✕ to close the Flash Player window and return to the Flash MX program window.

ADD A RADIO BUTTON

You can add radio buttons to allow users to interact with your movie by clicking a choice. Like car radio buttons of old, the user can choose only one button at a time out of several. Use radio buttons to allow the user to make mutually exclusive choices, such as Yes or No, or Male or Female. Radio buttons are commonly found on forms.

Because radio buttons are typically used to offer two or more choices, you should plan on adding two or more buttons to the Stage. Plan out in advance how you want users to interact with the buttons and what choices you want them to make.

Radio buttons are just one of several user interface components that ship with Flash MX. You can combine radio buttons with other components to create interactive forms in your Flash movies. You can add radio buttons to the Stage using the Components panel. The panel works just like other panels in Flash MX and can be docked, moved around the program window, resized, hidden, and closed. After adding several radio buttons, you can link the components to an action that tells Flash how to carry out the user response.

ADD A RADIO BUTTON

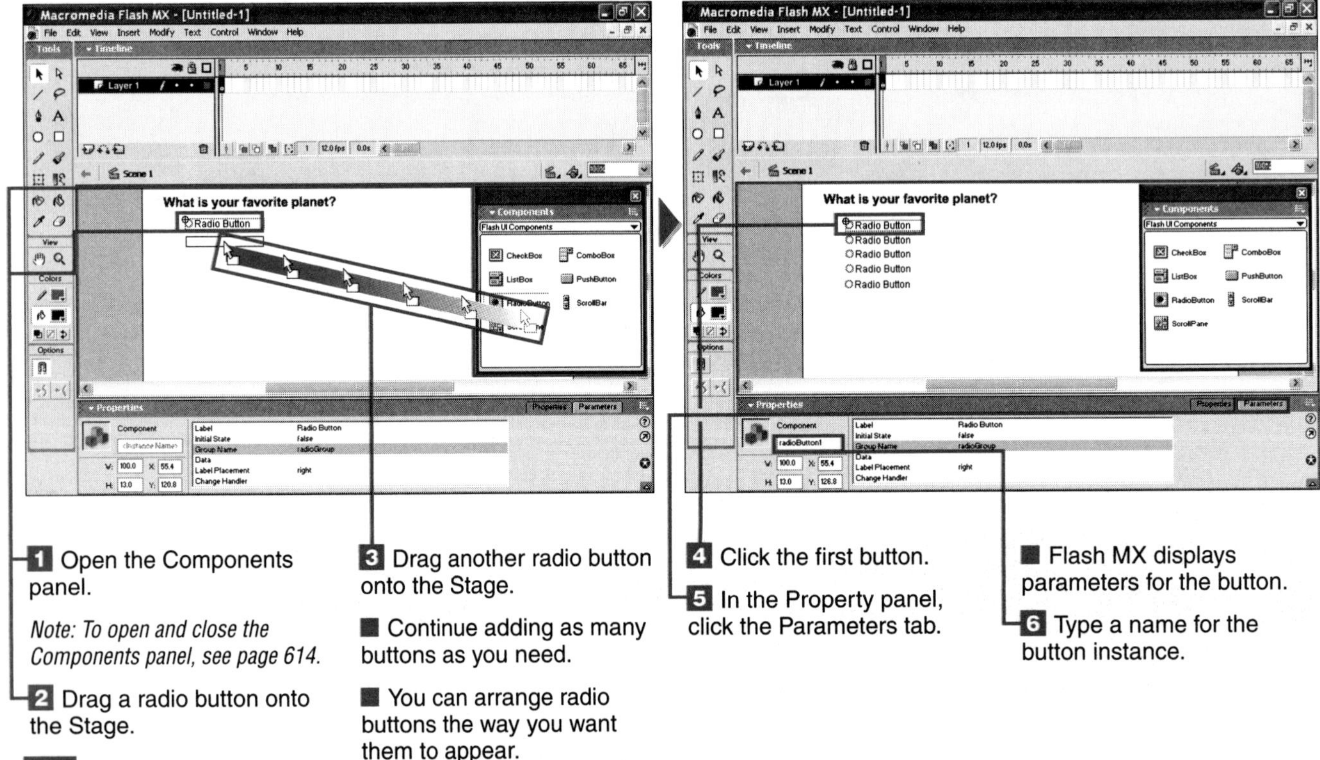

1 Open the Components panel.

Note: To open and close the Components panel, see page 614.

2 Drag a radio button onto the Stage.

3 Drag another radio button onto the Stage.

■ Continue adding as many buttons as you need.

■ You can arrange radio buttons the way you want them to appear.

4 Click the first button.

5 In the Property panel, click the Parameters tab.

■ Flash MX displays parameters for the button.

6 Type a name for the button instance.

How do I tell Flash MX to get a value from a selected radio button?

✔ You can use the `Get Value` action to determine which radio button the user clicks. To keep things simple, leave the group name of your radio buttons the same (radioGroup) or, if using more than one group in a movie, number them, such as radioGroup1, radioGroup2, and so on. For example, the following action finds out the label of a selected radio button:

```
radioGroup1.getValue().
```

Does it matter how I arrange my radio buttons?

✔ No. However, you should place them logically. For example, if you include a group of buttons on the Stage, locate them together rather than scattered randomly about the Stage. Both you and your intended audience will have an easier time viewing and using the buttons if they appear in a logical fashion on your form.

Can I preview the radio buttons on the Stage?

✔ Yes. Using the new Live Preview feature, you can see how your buttons will look in the published movie. Without the feature on, your components look like they did when you first added them to the Stage. Turn the feature on to see the actual labels you assigned. Click Control and then click Enable Live Preview. A check mark next to the command name means the command is active; no check mark means the feature is turned off.

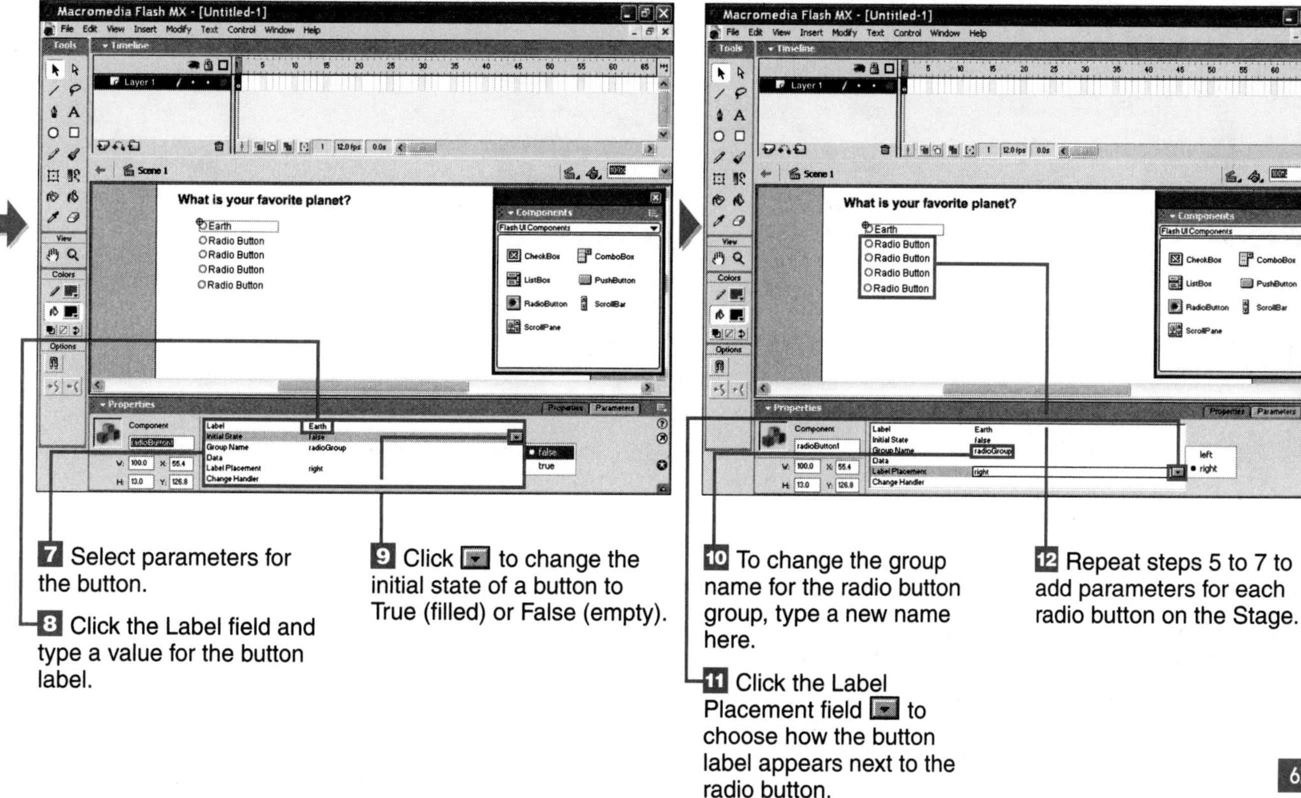

7 Select parameters for the button.

8 Click the Label field and type a value for the button label.

9 Click ▼ to change the initial state of a button to True (filled) or False (empty).

10 To change the group name for the radio button group, type a new name here.

11 Click the Label Placement field ▼ to choose how the button label appears next to the radio button.

12 Repeat steps 5 to 7 to add parameters for each radio button on the Stage.

ADD A CHECK BOX

You can add check boxes to allow users to interact with your movie by clicking a choice. For example, you might include a set of check boxes on a survey form that allow users to click which magazines they read or types of software they use.

Check boxes can be checked or unchecked by the user. If you add a group of check boxes, it allows users to make multiple choices. If you prefer your user makes only one choice out of many, use a radio button instead.

You can add check boxes to your movie using the Components panel. Once added to the Stage, you can use the Parameters tab in the Property Inspector to configure each check box, including assigning a label, initial value, and label placement.

After adding check boxes, you can use the ActionScript `Get Value` method to find out which check boxes the user enables. The value is either true, the check box is checked, or false, the check box is not checked.

ADD A CHECK BOX

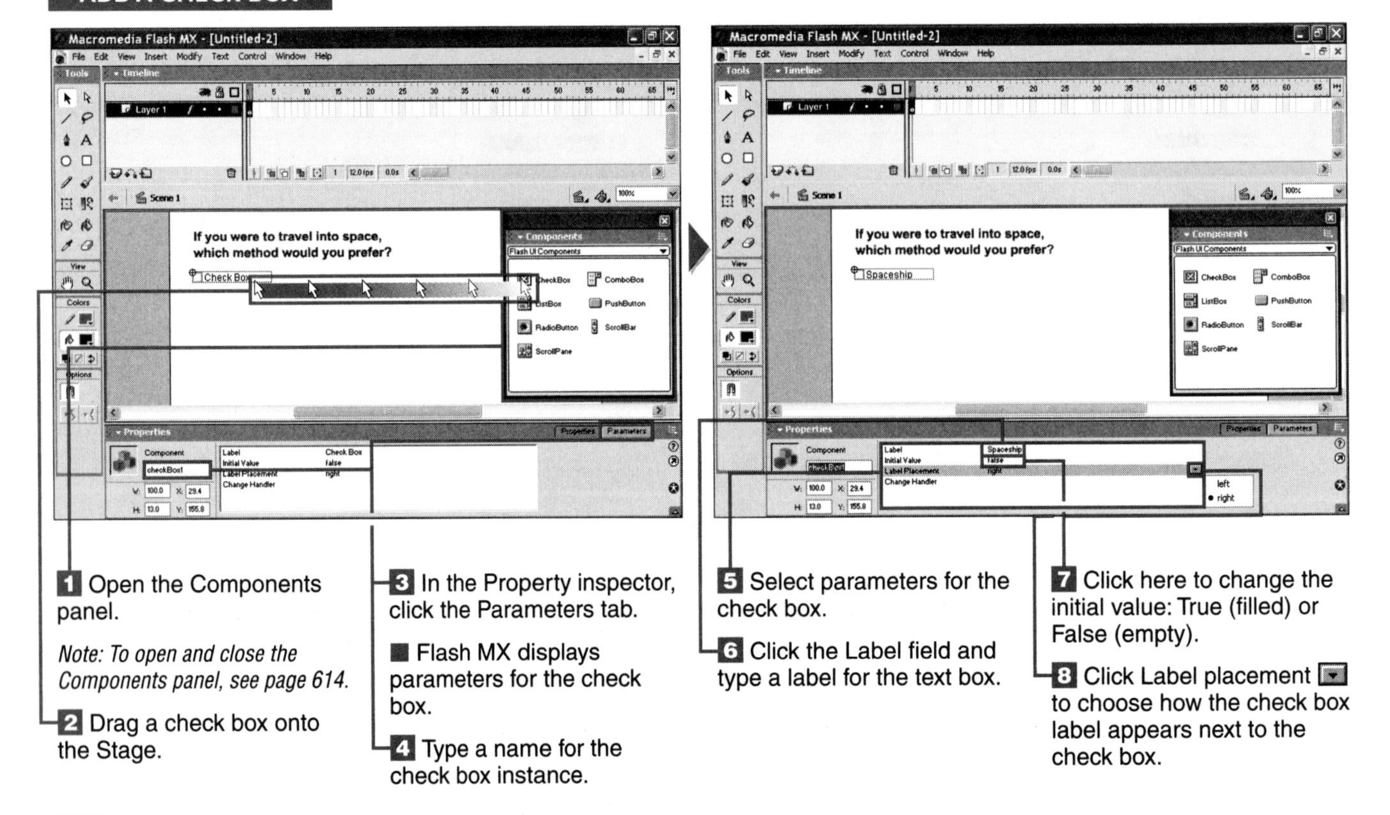

1 Open the Components panel.

Note: To open and close the Components panel, see page 614.

2 Drag a check box onto the Stage.

3 In the Property inspector, click the Parameters tab.

■ Flash MX displays parameters for the check box.

4 Type a name for the check box instance.

5 Select parameters for the check box.

6 Click the Label field and type a label for the text box.

7 Click here to change the initial value: True (filled) or False (empty).

8 Click Label placement ▼ to choose how the check box label appears next to the check box.

ADD A LIST BOX

You can add a list box to allow users to interact with your movie by scrolling through a list of choices and then clicking a choice. For example, you might include a list box when you want to include a long list of choices the user can make, such as a list of files or magazines. List boxes are commonly found on forms.

You can add list boxes to your movie using the Components panel.

Once added to the Stage, you can use the Parameters tab in the Property Inspector to configure the list box. Parameters include assigning labels for every item in the list and arranging labels in the list. The Select Multiple parameter allows for one choice or multiple choices by the user.

After adding a list box, you can use actions and write ActionScript functions that tell Flash how to handle the selections the user makes.

How do I make Flash list the user's selection at the top of the list box?

✔ Open the Actions panel and assign the getValue method. Do not forget to precede the method with the instance name. See page 616 to add component methods in the Actions panel. See page 576 to use the Actions panel in Flash MX.

ADD A LIST BOX

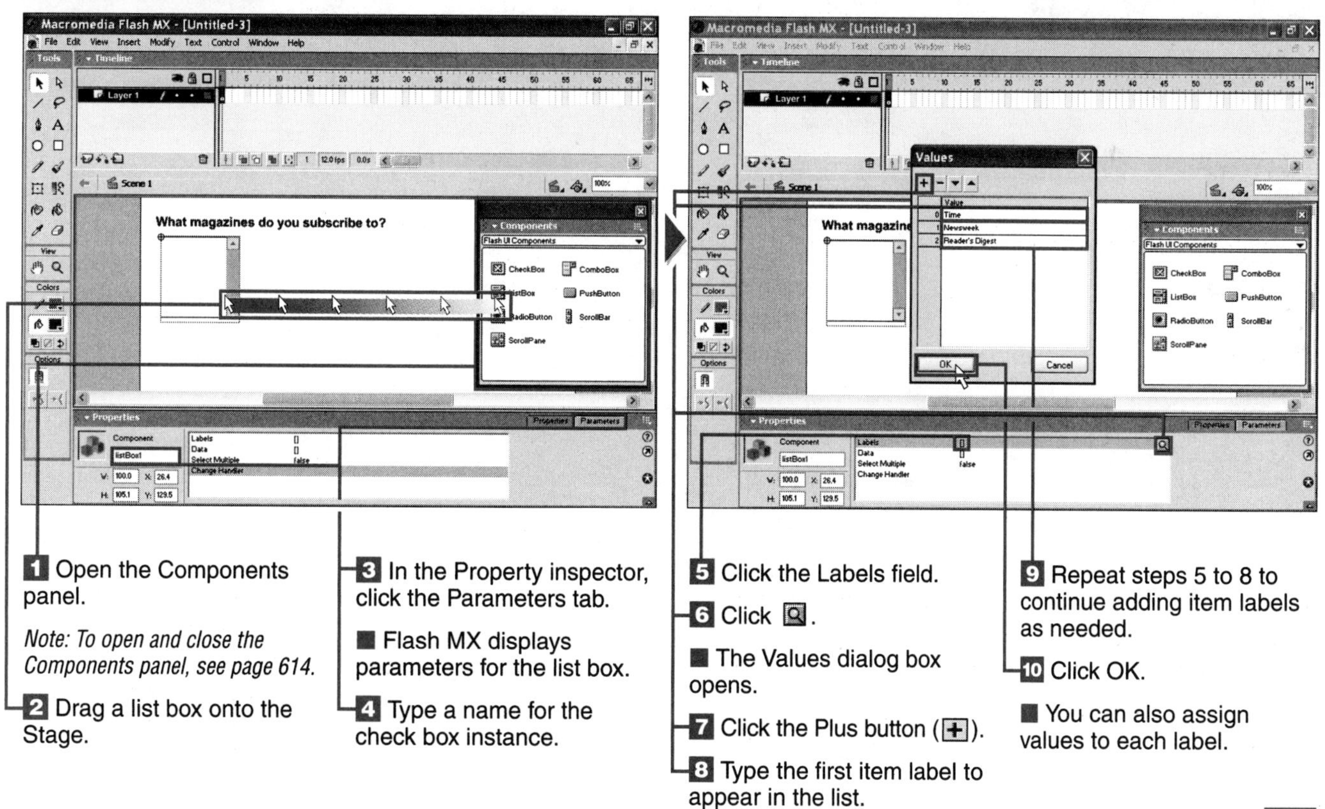

1 Open the Components panel.

Note: To open and close the Components panel, see page 614.

2 Drag a list box onto the Stage.

3 In the Property inspector, click the Parameters tab.

■ Flash MX displays parameters for the list box.

4 Type a name for the check box instance.

5 Click the Labels field.

6 Click 🔍.

■ The Values dialog box opens.

7 Click the Plus button (+).

8 Type the first item label to appear in the list.

9 Repeat steps 5 to 8 to continue adding item labels as needed.

10 Click OK.

■ You can also assign values to each label.

ADD A SCROLLING COMPONENT

Flash MX includes two types of scrollable components you can add to your movies. You can add a scroll pane that includes vertical and horizontal scroll bars to your movies that can hold other movie clips. You might use a scroll pane to display a large sized movie clip without taking up the same amount of space on your main movie's Stage. You can only display movie clips in a scroll pane.

You can add a scroll bar component to add vertical and horizontal scroll bars to input or dynamic text boxes. For example, if you add an input text box to a movie that needs to accept a lot of text entered by the user, you can use the scroll bar component to allow the user to scroll within the text box. The list box and combo box components already contain the scroll bar component.

MASTER IT

How do I display a JPG file in a scroll pane?

✔ Scroll panes can only be used to view movie clips. However, you can convert a JPG or other still image file into a movie clip using the Convert to Symbol command. Click the image on the Stage, then click Insert, Convert to Symbol. In the Convert to Symbol dialog box, assign the image movie clip status and a unique name. Click OK. You can now use the clip in a scroll pane.

ADD A SCROLLING COMPONENT

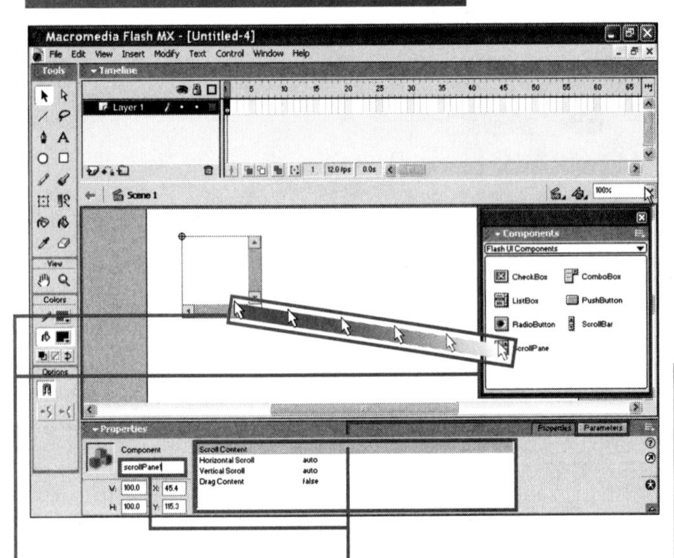

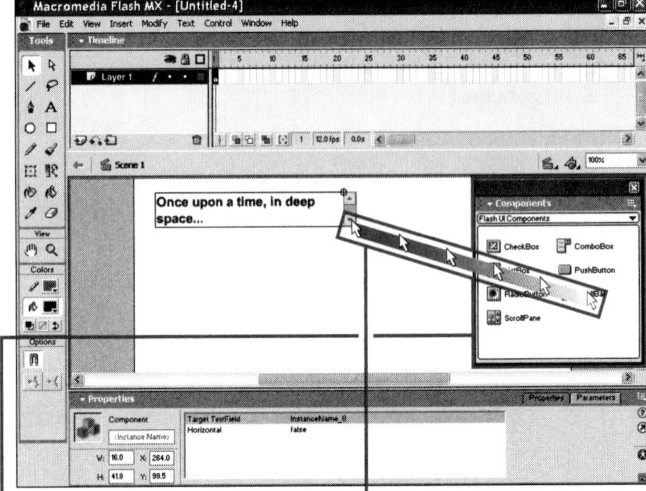

ADD A SCROLL PANE

1 Open the Components panel.

Note: To open and close the Components panel, see page 614.

2 Drag a scroll pane onto the Stage.

3 In the Property inspector, click the Parameters tab.

4 Type a name for the instance.

5 Set any parameters needed for the pane.

ADD A SCROLL BAR

1 Open the Components panel.

Note: To open and close the Components panel, see page 614.

2 Drag a scroll bar onto the Stage and drop it on the input or dynamic text box that needs a scroll bar.

■ Flash MX automatically docks the scroll bar to the text box.

3 Set any parameters needed for the scroll bar.

ADD A PUSH BUTTON

You can add a push button to your Flash form that accepts typical mouse clicks or keyboard presses. Once added to the Stage, you can specify a label that appears on the button, such as Click Here, Submit, or Continue.

Push buttons enable users to execute an action when the button is activated. For example, you might assign a callback function to a button that tells Flash what to do when the button is clicked, such as go to and stop on another frame.

You can add push buttons to your movie using the Components panel. Once added to the Stage, you can use the Parameters tab in the Property Inspector to configure each push button with a label.

You can also specify a parameter for a Click Handler — a scripted function that tells Flash exactly what to do once the button is pressed and released.

Which method should I use to tell Flash to what to do when the button is activated?

✔ You can use `FPushButton` methods to tell Flash how to handle push buttons. You can find the `FPushButton` methods under the Flash UI Components category in the Actions panel. The most common method is the `setClickHandler` method which specifies the function when the user releases the mouse button. See page 616 to use the Actions panel to add functions to components.

ADD A PUSH BUTTON

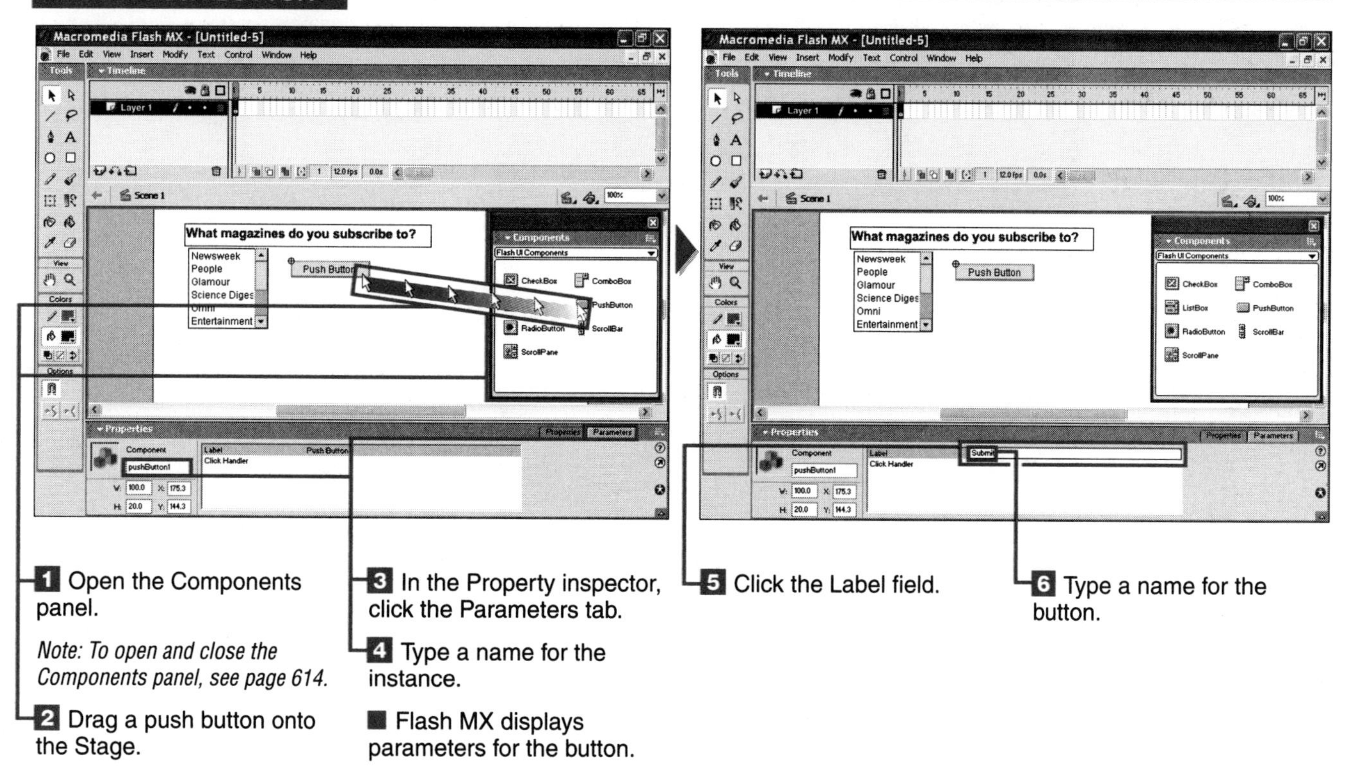

1 Open the Components panel.

Note: To open and close the Components panel, see page 614.

2 Drag a push button onto the Stage.

3 In the Property inspector, click the Parameters tab.

4 Type a name for the instance.

■ Flash MX displays parameters for the button.

5 Click the Label field.

6 Type a name for the button.

SECTION X

34) DISTRIBUTING FLASH MOVIES

FINALIZING YOUR PROJECT

INTRODUCTION TO DISTRIBUTION METHODS

You can distribute your Flash MX projects to an audience in several ways. You might publish a Flash movie to a Web page, save it as a QuickTime movie to send to another user via e-mail, or deliver the movie as a self-playing file. You can assign a distribution method using the Publish Settings dialog box, or you can export your movie as another file type using the Export Movie dialog box.

Start with an Authoring File

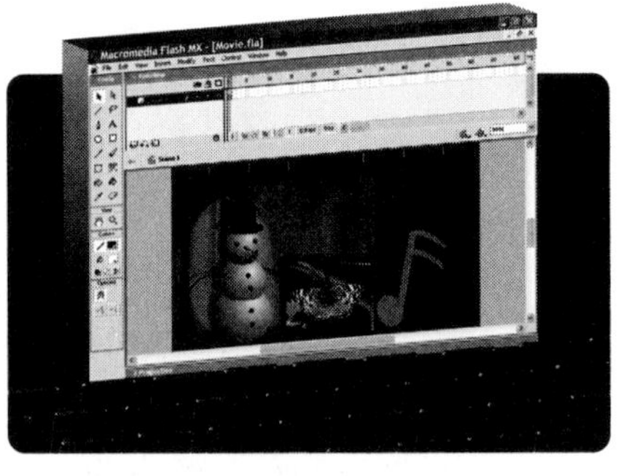

When you create content in Flash MX, you start by creating an *authoring file*. The authoring file is where you draw and animate your movie's content. This file contains all the elements that make up your movie, such as bitmap objects, sounds, symbols, buttons, text, and so on. The authoring file can be quite large in file size.

Any time you start a file in Flash MX, you are working with the authoring file for your movie. Authoring files use the .fla file extension.

Create an Export File

After you create the authoring file and get it working just the way you want, you can turn it into an *export file*. When you create an export file, you are creating a file that is separate from the authoring file. Flash MX offers two exporting features, Export Movie and Publish. The feature you select depends on what you want to do with your Flash content. When you export a movie using the Export Movie feature, you are exporting your file as a specific file type to be used in another program, such as QuickTime. When you publish a file, you are turning your content into a file type viewable from the Web. The process of publishing compresses the file contents, making it easier for others to view the file. The resulting file is uneditable, so you cannot change its contents. Published Flash movie files use the .swf file extension.

Export Formats

The Export feature enables you to save the file as another file format, such as a series of still images or an animated sequence. When exporting a Flash authoring file, keep in mind that you may lose all the vector-based information for the file, unless you choose to export to a vector-based format, such as Macromedia Freehand.

Flash MX Export File Formats

File Format	Extension
Adobe Illustrator	.ai
Animated GIF, GIF image	.gif
Bitmap	.bmp
DXF Sequence/AutoCad DXF Image	.dxf
Enhanced Metafile	.emf
EPS	.eps
FutureSplash Player	.spl
Generator Template	.swt
JPEG Sequence/JPEG image	.jpg
PICT Sequence	.pct
PNG Sequence/PNG Image	.png
QuickTime	.mov
WAV Audio	.wav
Windows AVI	.avi
Windows Metafile	.wmf

Publish in Flash Player Format

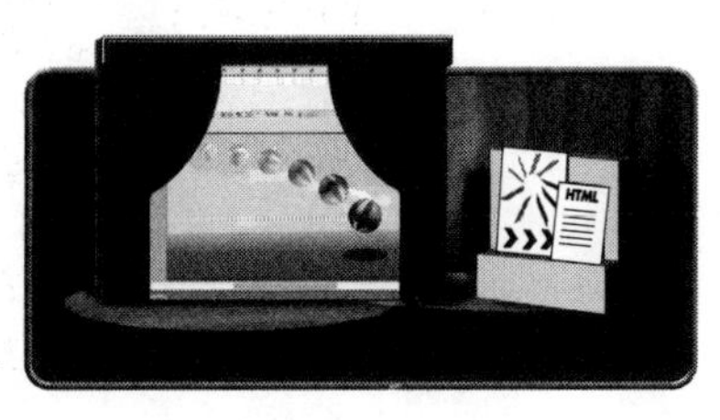

Your Flash MX creations really shine when you publish them in the original program format — Flash Player format. When you distribute a movie as a movie file, Flash saves it in the SWF file format, and the format requires the Flash Player application or plug-in for a user to view. The Flash Player is the most widely used player on the Web and comes preinstalled with most computers and most Web browsers today.

Use the Publish feature to quickly turn any Flash authoring file into SWF format. The Publish feature also generates the HTML code needed to make your movie or interactive creation ready for the Web.

Publish as a Projector

Another way to distribute your movie is to turn it into a *projector*. A projector is a standalone player that runs the movie without the need for another application. Use the Projector feature to distribute your Flash creations to users who do not have access to the Flash Player or plug-in.

Using the Bandwidth Profiler

When preparing a movie for publishing, Flash offers a handy tool to help you check for quality and optimal playback. The Bandwidth Profiler is a valuable tool that can help you fix problem areas that hold up your movie while downloading into the browser window. Use the Profiler to help you fix problems before you post the Flash file on a Web page.

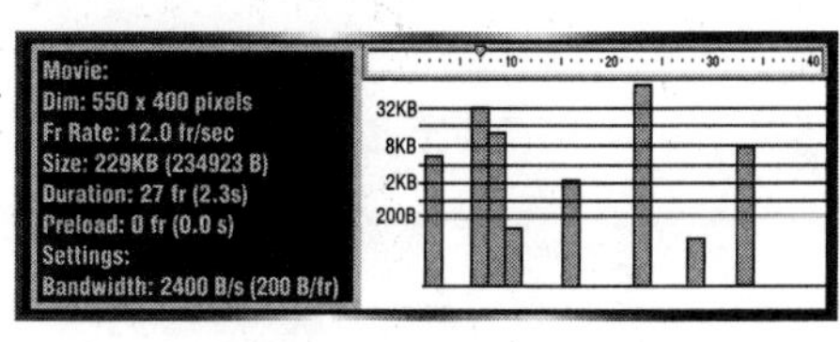

Printing Movie Content

You may find it useful to print out portions of your movie to distribute to members of a project team or to show to your boss. Flash comes with several options for preparing your movie frames for printing, all of which you will find located in the Page Setup dialog box (Windows) or the Print Margins dialog box (Mac).

PUBLISH A MOVIE

When you have completed a Flash movie, you can publish the movie to a Web page or file format you can share with others. You use two phases to publish your movie. First you prepare the files for publishing using the Publish Settings dialog box, then you publish the movie using the Flash Publish command.

By default, Flash MX is set up to publish your movie as an SWF file for the Web, but you can choose to publish in other formats. For example, you might publish your movie as a GIF, JPEG, or PNG image, or as a self-playing Windows or Mac file, or as a QuickTime movie.

In addition to choosing a format, the Publish Settings dialog box also offers you a chance to give the file a distinct name. The Publish Settings dialog box is set up to assign default names, but you can override the settings and enter your own unique filenames.

Depending on the format you select, you find additional publishing options among the other tabs in the Publish Settings dialog box. To learn more about setting additional publishing options, see page 640.

PUBLISH A MOVIE

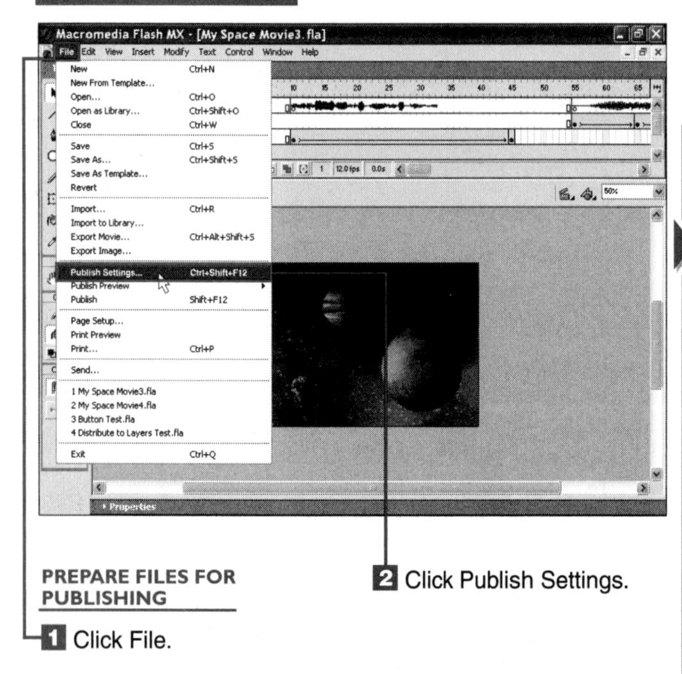

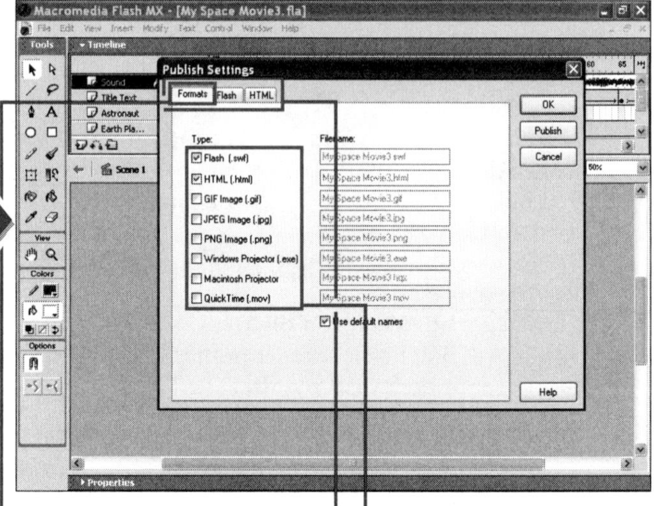

PREPARE FILES FOR PUBLISHING

1 Click File.

2 Click Publish Settings.

■ The Publish Settings dialog box appears.

Note: If you have already published your file, tabs from your last changes appear in the dialog box.

3 Click the Formats tab.

4 Click the Format option you want to use (☐ changes to ☑).

■ Depending on which format you select, additional tabs appear with options related to that format.

Can I publish a movie before I publish it?

✔ Yes. Testing your movie to check how it plays, especially in a browser, often is a good idea. Flash MX has a feature that lets you preview a movie in a browser window before you publish the movie. Click File. Click Publish Preview. Click Default. Flash MX opens the movie in your default Web browser.

How does the Publish feature differ from the Export Movie feature?

✔ You use the Publish feature specifically for publishing your work for use on the Web. The Export Movie feature enables you to save your Flash project as another file type, so you can use it in another program. To learn more about these features, see page 628.

Do I always have to publish a movie through the Publish Settings dialog box?

✔ No. If you want to publish the movie using the previous settings you set up in the Publish Settings dialog box, you can click the File menu and then click Publish. Flash MX does not give you a chance to name the file if you choose to publish directly and bypass the Publish Settings dialog box.

How do I specify another folder path in which to publish?

✔ If you use a Mac, you can type an absolute path, such as **HardDrive: Folder:file.swf**. If you use Windows, you must include slashes in the absolute path, such as **C:\Folder\file.swf**. For a relative path, use ..\ to target a folder.

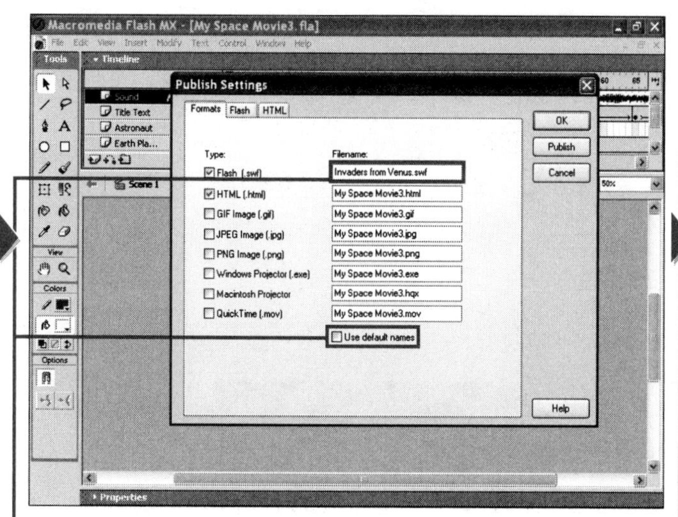

■ To assign a different filename other than the default supplied by Flash MX, you can click Use Default Names (☑ changes to ☐) and type a new filename in the format's text box.

■ Flash MX publishes your files to the My Documents folder unless you specify another folder and filename path in the Filename box.

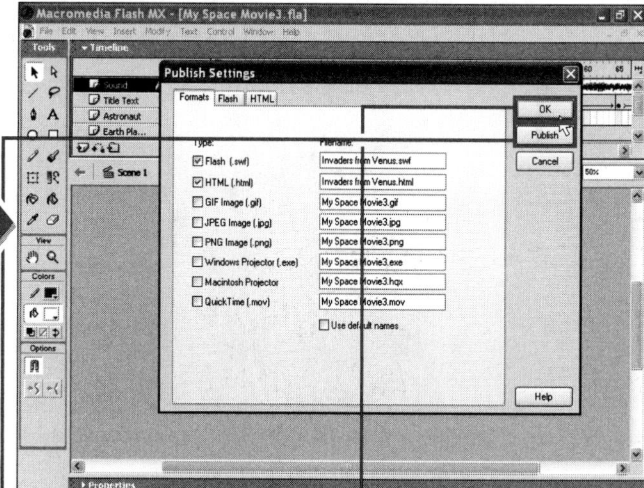

PUBLISH THE MOVIE

5 When you are ready to publish the movie using the settings you selected, click Publish.

■ Flash MX generates the necessary files for the movie.

6 Click OK to save the settings and close the Publish Settings dialog box.

PUBLISH A MOVIE IN HTML FORMAT

You can save a movie in HTML format, which is the most widely used format on the Web. In response, Flash MX creates an HTML page that displays your movie and a separate SWF movie file. In other words, the HTML document sets up browser settings and activates the movie.

When publishing to HTML format, Flash MX generates all the necessary HTML code for you, including the tags you need to view your page in both Microsoft Internet Explorer and Netscape Navigator. The HTML markup tags utilize the browser's built-in Flash Player. You can then upload the HTML document to your Web server.

Flash MX bases the HTML document you create on a template that contains basic HTML coding. By default, Flash MX assigns the Flash Only template, which is the simplest template to use to create an HTML document. You can choose from other templates, such as an image map, or if you know HTML code, you can customize the template. The steps in this section show you how to publish your movie to the default template.

Once you publish your movie, you can test the HTML page in your Web browser to see how your movie looks.

PUBLISH A MOVIE IN HTML FORMAT

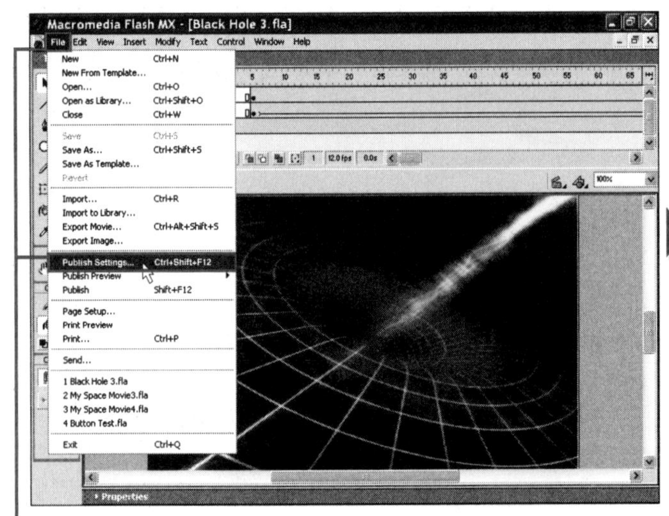

1 Click File.

2 Click Publish Settings.

■ The Publish Settings dialog box appears.

Note: If you have already published your file, tabs from your last changes appear in the dialog box.

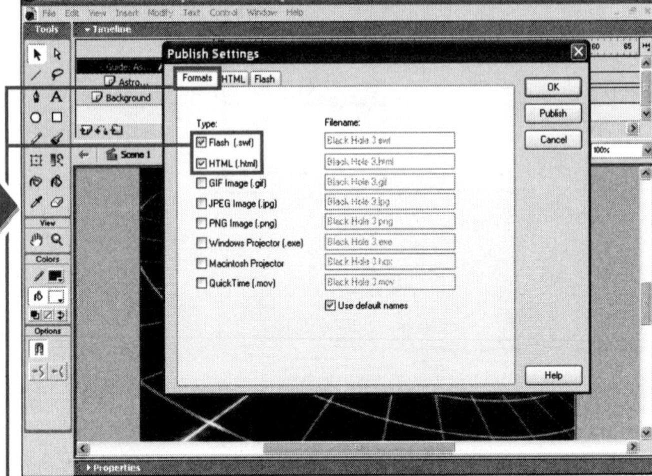

3 Click the Formats tab.

4 Click HTML format.

■ The Flash format (.swf) is selected by default.

Note: The Flash and HTML formats are selected by default the first time you use the Publish Settings dialog box.

Can I make my own HTML templates for Flash MX?

✔ Yes. You can set up your own HTML templates or customize existing templates. Be sure to save any HTML templates in the HTML subfolder within the Flash MX application folder on your computer system. Flash MX looks for all HTML templates in the HTML folder. The template must also include a title that starts with the recognized HTML title code `$TT`, such as `$TTMy` Template.

What HTML tags does Flash MX insert into the HTML document?

✔ The Publish feature inserts the tags necessary for playing a Flash movie file in the browser window, including the `OBJECT` tag for Microsoft's Internet Explorer browser and the `EMBED` tag for Netscape's Navigator browser. The `OBJECT`, `EMBED`, and `IMG` tags create the movie display window used to play the Flash movie.

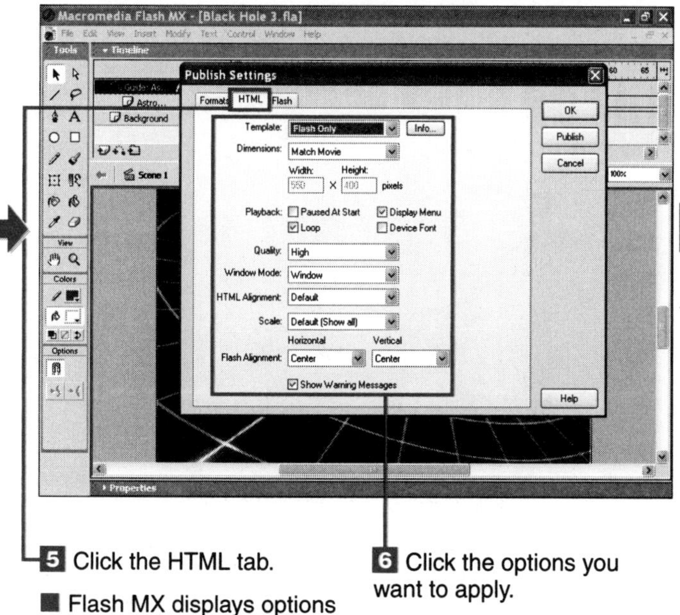

5 Click the HTML tab.

■ Flash MX displays options associated with generating a Web page, such as playback options and movie dimensions.

6 Click the options you want to apply.

■ The default Flash Only template allows other Flash users to view your movie. Users without the Flash plug-in cannot view the movie.

■ You can click the Template ▾ and select another template from the list.

PUBLISH A MOVIE IN HTML FORMAT (CONTINUED)

The HTML tab in the Publish Settings dialog box has a variety of options for controlling how your movie plays in the browser window. You can set alignment, dimensions, and even playback options. Any change you make to the settings overrides any previous settings for the file.

For example, you can specify an alignment placement for the movie on the Web page, such as Left, Center, or Right. You can also define the movie display window's dimensions. If you choose the Match Movie dimensions setting, Flash MX publishes the current movie size as the movie dimensions.

You can use the Playback options to control exactly how a movie starts, indicating whether the user starts the movie manually or if the movie loops continuously or not. The loop option is checked by default.

You can also specify new movie dimensions that differ from the movie's original screen size dimensions. If you do specify a size other than the default movie size, you must indicate how you want to scale the movie to fit in the dimensions you specify.

If you select the No Scale setting among the Scale options, you can prevent your movie from being scaled if the user resizes the Flash Player window.

PUBLISH A MOVIE IN HTML FORMAT (CONTINUED)

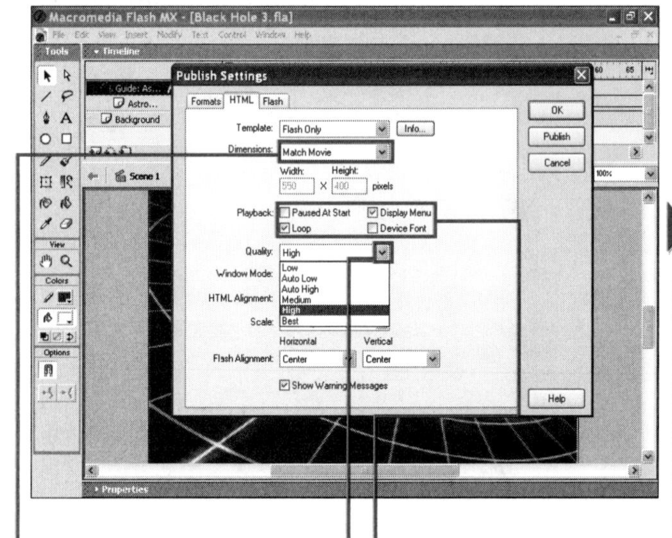

■ You can click the Dimensions ▾ to set width and height attribute values for the movie display window — the area where the Flash plug-in plays the movie.

■ You can click a Playback option to control how the movie plays on the Web page (☐ changes to ☑).

■ You can click the Quality ▾ and select options for controlling the image quality during playback.

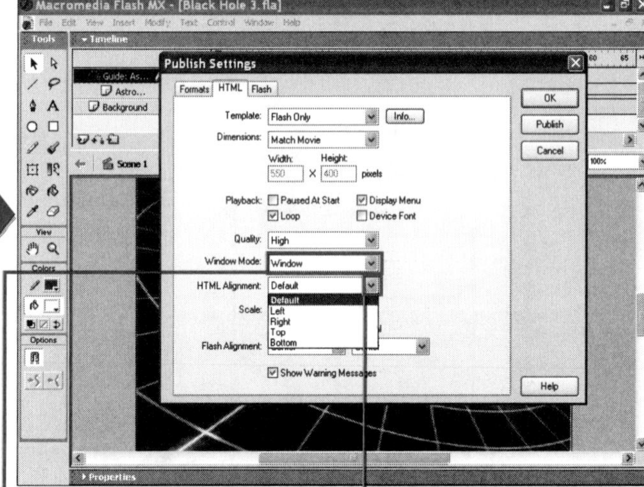

■ You can click the Window Mode ▾ and select options for playing your movie on a regular, opaque, or transparent background (Windows browsers only).

■ You can click the HTML Alignment ▾ and change the alignment of your movie as it relates to other Web page elements.

How do I make my movie full-size in the browser window?

✔ To make your Flash movie appear full-screen size in the browser window, click the in the Dimensions box. Select Percent. Type **100** as the percent values in the Width and Height text boxes.

How can I tell which HTML template does what?

✔ Select the template you want to know more about, then click the Info button in the Publish Settings dialog box to see a description of the selected template.

How do I view the source code for a Flash template?

✔ Open the template file, which Flash stores in the HTML subfolder within the Flash application folder, in SimpleText (Mac) or Notepad (Windows) to see the source code.

Can I see elements of my authoring file in the SWF file for my movie?

✔ No. When you publish your movie as a SWF file, you will not be able to see any of your authoring elements even if you open the SWF file in the Flash MX program window. You can only see your authoring elements in the FLA file.

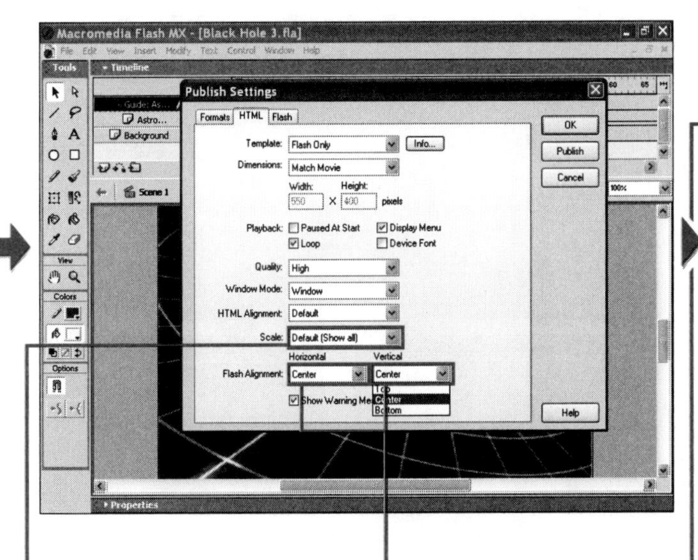

■ If you choose to set new dimensions for the movie, you can click the Scale to rescale movie elements to fit the new size.

■ You can click the Flash Alignment and designate how the movie aligns in the movie window area.

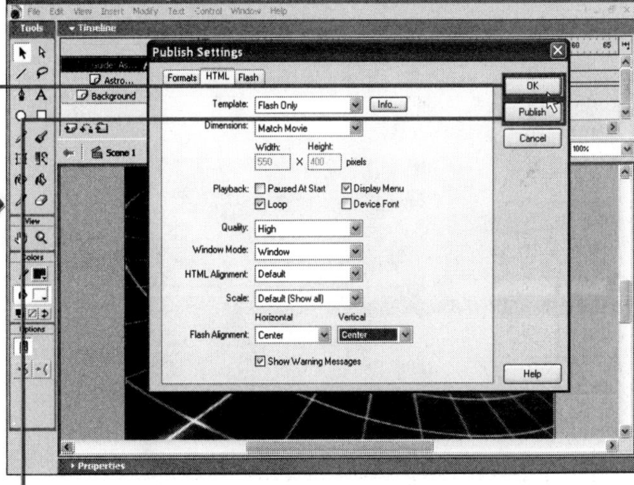

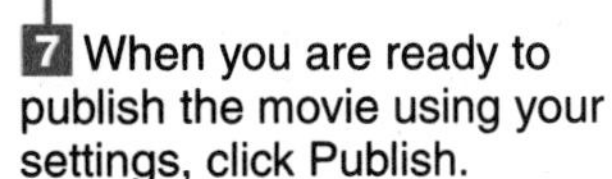

7 When you are ready to publish the movie using your settings, click Publish.

■ Flash MX generates the necessary files for the HTML document.

8 Click OK to save the settings.

Note: The files will, by default, be published to the same directory as the Flash authoring file (.fla).

CREATE A FLASH PROJECTOR

You can create a Flash movie that plays in its own Flash Player window without the benefit of another application, which means that anyone receiving the file does not need to install the Flash Player application. When you publish the movie as a Windows Projector or Macintosh Projector format, Flash MX publishes the movie as an executable file with an .exe extension.

Flash projectors are simply self-extracting, self-sufficient mini-applications designed to play movies in real time. Because the projector files are self-sufficient, you can easily place the files on disks to give directly to friends and colleagues, or send them as e-mail file attachments. The only catch is that you must publish the projector file to a format appropriate to the computer platform the end user needs. For example, if you want to send a Flash movie projector file to a friend who uses a Mac, make sure you publish the file to a Mac projector format (HQX) and not a Windows projector format (EXE).

Depending on the size of your movie, the Flash Projector file may be quite large, so you might need to compress the file using a program like WinZip before sending it as an e-mail attachment.

CREATE A FLASH PROJECTOR

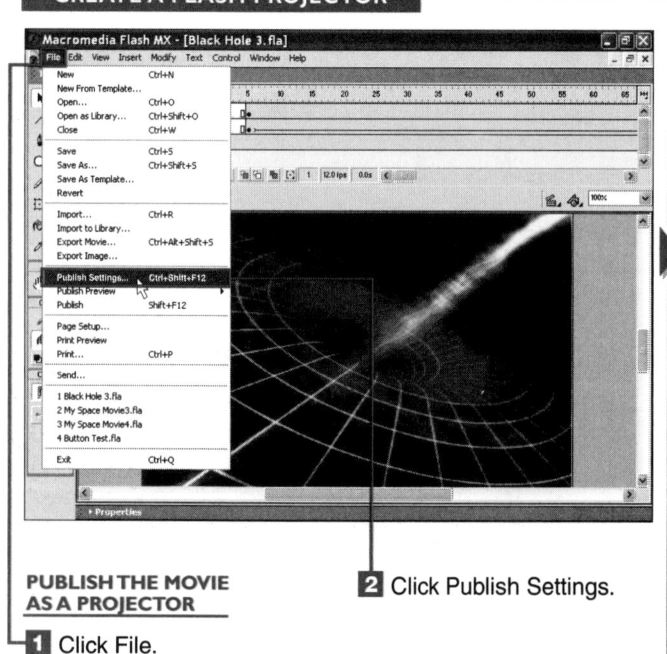

PUBLISH THE MOVIE AS A PROJECTOR

1 Click File.

2 Click Publish Settings.

■ Flash MX opens the Publish Settings dialog box.

Note: If you have already published your file, tabs from your last changes appear in the dialog box.

3 Click the Formats tab.

4 Click to select Windows Projector or Macintosh Projector as the format (☐ changes to ☑).

■ If you do not want to publish your movie for the Web, you can deselect the Flash and HTML format check boxes (☑ changes to ☐).

Can I rename the movie file?

✔ Yes. If you want a different name for the movie, deselect the Use Default Names check box (☑ changes to ☐) in the Publish Settings dialog box, and then type another name next to the movie format to which you are saving.

What is the difference between a standalone player and a projector?

✔ When you save a file as a Projector file, you are making an executable copy of your Flash movie. This file does not require a player or plug-in. It comes with everything necessary to run the movie. A regular SWF file packs only the movie data, not the player. Regular SWF files require the Flash Player in order to view the movie.

Do I need to worry about licensing my projector file?

✔ Macromedia allows free distribution of its Flash Player and Projector product. If you are distributing your movie for commercial purposes, however, you need to check the Macromedia Web site for information about crediting Macromedia. Visit www.macromedia.com/support/programs/mwm. You need to include the Made with Macromedia logo on your packaging and give proper credits on your credit screen.

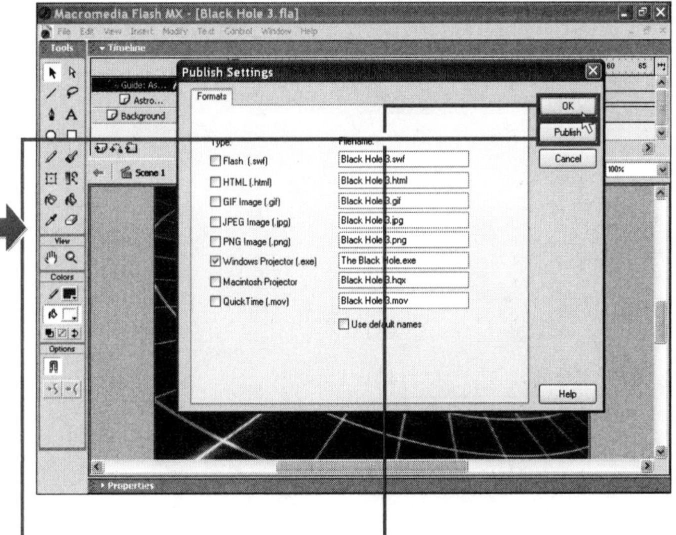

5 Click Publish.

■ Flash MX generates the necessary files for the movie with an .exe file extension.

6 Click OK.

■ The Publish Settings dialog box closes and Flash MX publishes the movie.

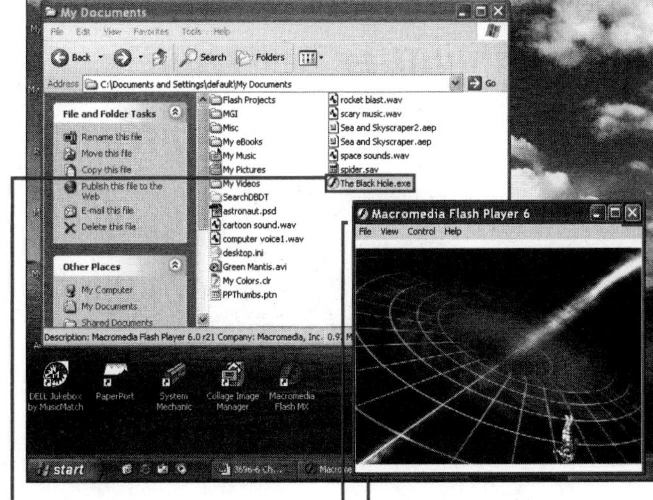

PLAY THE MOVIE

1 Test the movie by double-clicking its name.

■ The Flash Player window opens and plays the movie.

2 Click ☒ to close the window when the movie stops.

EXPORT TO ANOTHER FORMAT

You can easily export a Flash movie into another file format for use with other applications. For example, you might save your movie as a Windows AVI file or as a QuickTime file, or perhaps you want to save each frame as a bitmap sequence. Flash MX allows for over a dozen different file formats for export in both Windows and Mac platforms.

The Export feature of Flash MX differs from the Publish feature in that it creates editable Flash content. You use the Publish feature when you want to generate Web-based content. Unlike the Publish feature, Export savings are not saved with the movie file.

When exporting to other file formats, you can choose to export the entire Flash movie as an animated sequence or as still images. Depending on the file format, exporting may cause the loss of the Flash vector information, unless you export to a vector-based file format, such as Adobe Illustrator.

You can also use the Export Movie method to export SWF files rather than go through the Publish Movie settings to create a Flash Player file.

EXPORT TO ANOTHER FORMAT

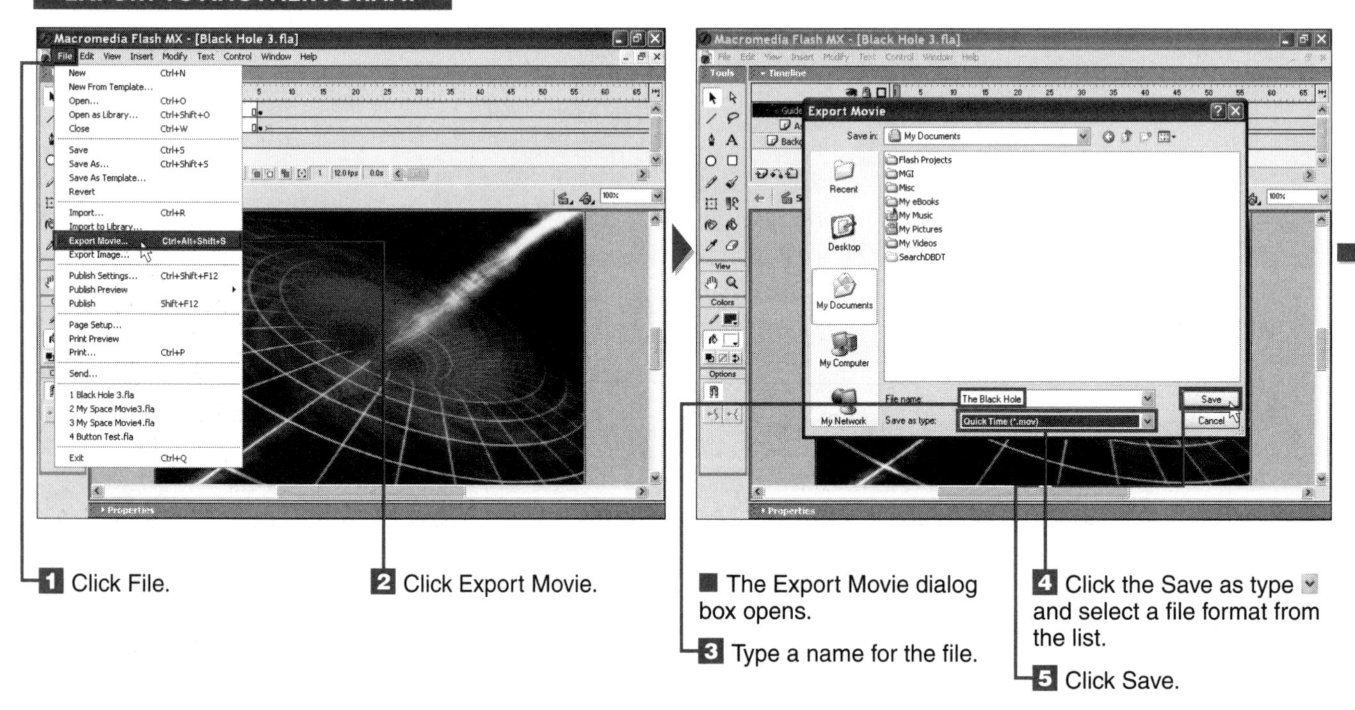

1 Click File.

2 Click Export Movie.

■ The Export Movie dialog box opens.

3 Type a name for the file.

4 Click the Save as type ▾ and select a file format from the list.

5 Click Save.

What is the difference between exporting a movie and publishing a movie?

✔ When you publish a movie, you can publish to Flash (SWF), Generator Template, HTML, GIF, JPEG, PNG, Windows Projector, Macintosh Projector, QuickTime, and RealPlayer formats. When you export a movie, you can save the file in over a dozen different file formats, such as Windows AVI or Animated GIF. The two features share some of the formats and options, but when you publish a movie as opposed to exporting it, Flash MX saves information about the movie's Publish settings along with the movie file. When you export a movie, you are saving it to a single format.

Can I export a single frame rather than an entire movie?

✔ Yes. First select the frame you want to save as an export file. Then click the File menu and click Export Image. This opens the Export Image dialog box. Give the file a distinct name and format type, then click Save. Depending on the format you select, additional parameters may appear for you to set.

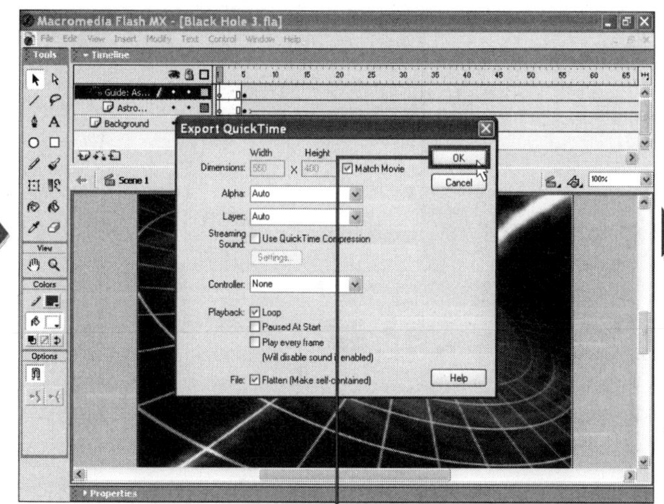

■ Depending on the file type you selected, an additional Export dialog box opens with options for size, sound, and video format. You can make any selections necessary.

6 Click OK.

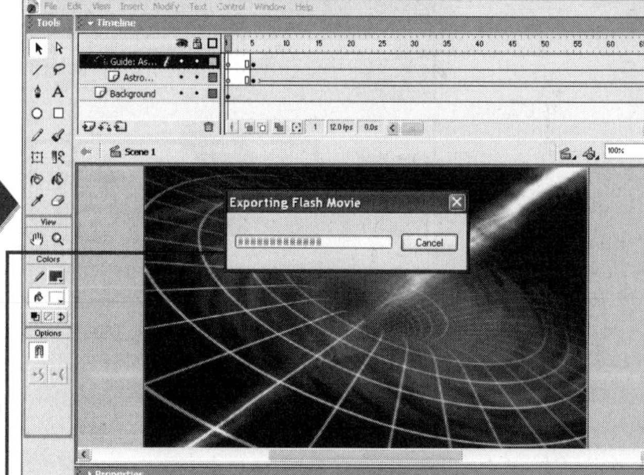

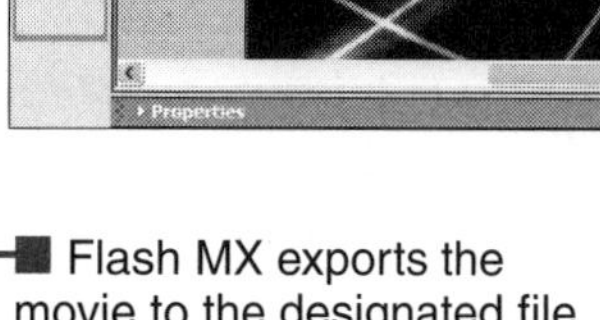

■ Flash MX exports the movie to the designated file type.

■ Depending on the file type you selected, another dialog box might open first. Make any selections necessary, and click OK to continue exporting.

Note: Interactive elements you include in your Flash movies might not export to other file formats properly.

PRINT MOVIE FRAMES

Some Flash projects may require you to print out a frame or series of frames. For example, you might print out frame content to show a storyboard of the movie. You can use the Page Setup dialog box (Windows) or Print Margins dialog box (Mac) to specify a layout for the storyboard, then use the Print dialog box to specify which pages to print.

You can specify a variety of printing options for frames. You can print a single frame and designate margins, alignment, page orientation, and paper size for the printout. You can print thumbnails — miniatures of your movie's frames — and print them as boxes or in a grid, or fit them all onto a single page of paper.

You can find frame and storyboarding options in the Page Setup dialog box (Windows) or Print Margins dialog box (Mac). The options in this dialog box can help you set up your frames for printing. To actually print the pages, you must activate the Print command by opening the Print dialog box and printing from there or clicking the Print button.

PRINT MOVIE FRAMES

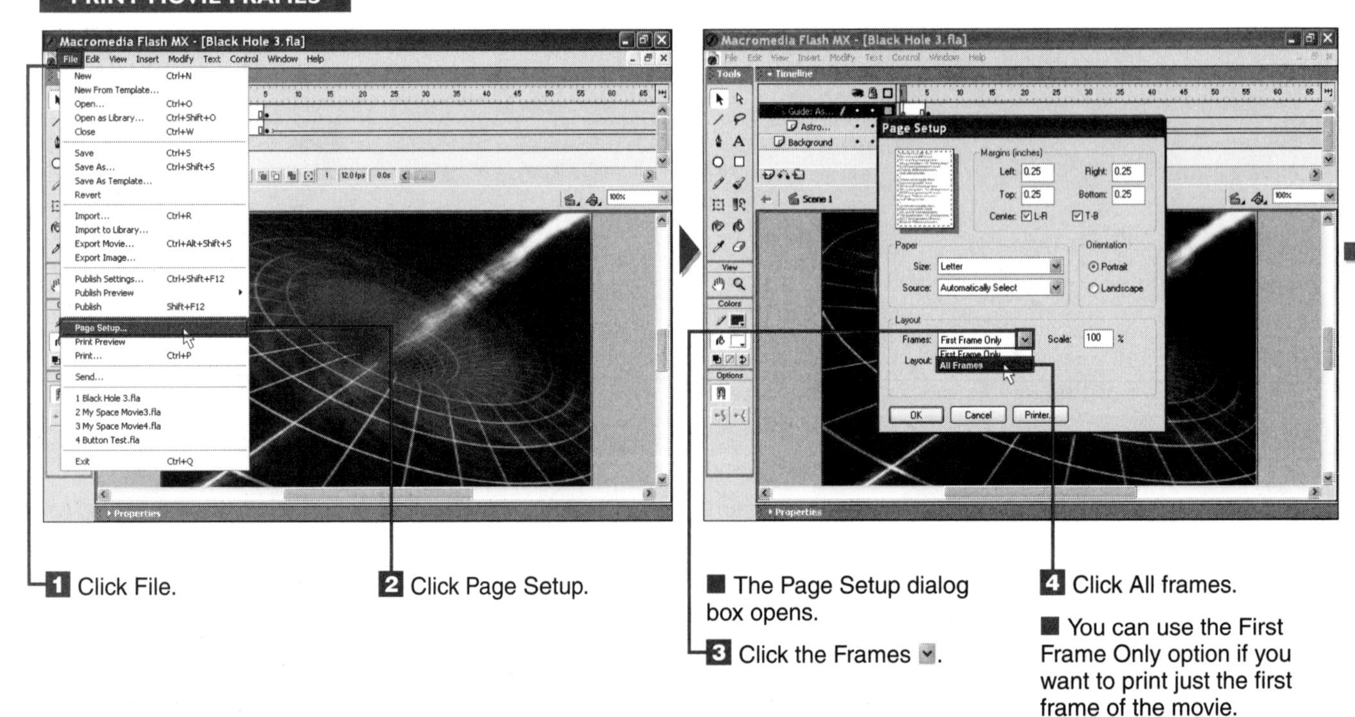

1 Click File.

2 Click Page Setup.

■ The Page Setup dialog box opens.

3 Click the Frames ▾.

4 Click All frames.

■ You can use the First Frame Only option if you want to print just the first frame of the movie.

Can I preview before I print?

✔ You can preview exactly how the frames and layout appear on the printed page using the Flash Print Preview feature. Click File, Print Preview to open the Print Preview window. Click the Print button to print the frames, or click the Close button to return to the Flash MX window.

Can I add labels to each printed frame?

✔ Yes. If you select one of the storyboard layout options in the Print dialog box, a Label frames check box appears. Click this check box (☐ changes to ☑) to print the scene and frame number for each frame you print out in the storyboard.

Will Flash MX print any symbols I have placed in the work area off of the Stage?

✔ No. Flash MX prints only the symbols and objects found on the Stage area of any given frame. If you move a symbol off the Stage to place in a later frame or insert later, the symbol does not display in your printout.

How can I avoid printing my main Timeline frames?

✔ You can add the label !#p to the first keyframe in the main Timeline. This dims the Print command when the movie is viewed in the Flash Player.

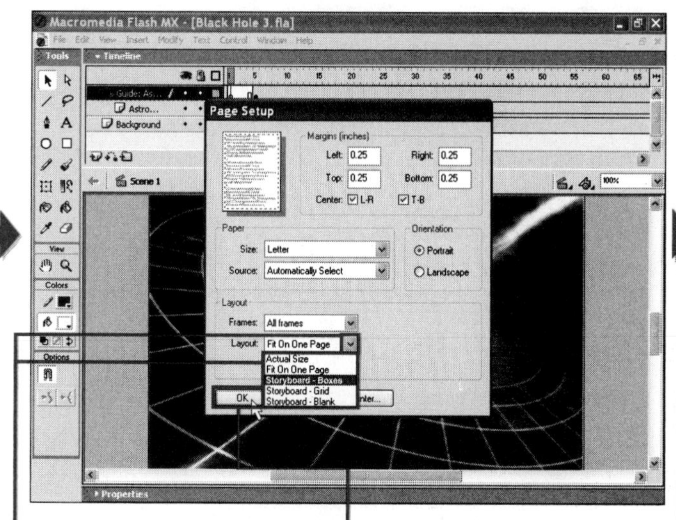

5 Click ▾ to view layout options.

6 Click an option.

■ You can select Storyboard-Boxes to print in storyboard boxes.

■ You can select Storyboard-Grid to print in a grid pattern.

■ You can select Storyboard-Blank to print only the graphic items of each frame.

7 Click OK.

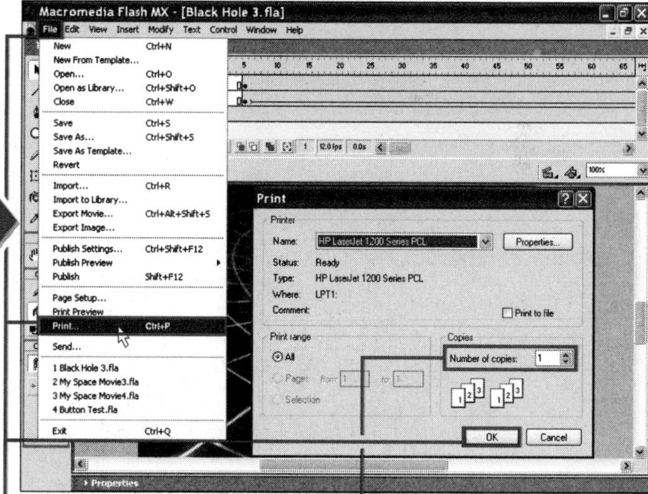

8 Click File.

9 Click Print.

■ The Print dialog box opens.

10 Click OK.

■ From within the Print dialog box, you can specify print options such as number of copies.

■ Flash MX prints the specified pages and layout.

PLAY A FLASH MOVIE IN FLASH

You can use the Flash Player to play your Flash movies. You can play movies from within Flash MX, or outside the confines of the Flash MX program window by using the Flash Player window. The Flash Player, version 6, is installed when you install Flash MX onto your computer.

Flash Players are also readily available with today's Web browsers, such as Microsoft Internet Explorer and Netscape Navigator. Computer manufacturers now ship many new machines with the latest version of the Flash Player preinstalled for your convenience. The Flash Player is an open standard widely used on the Internet today. It is also the most popular player technology, ranking above Java and Windows Media Player. Macromedia offers free Flash Player downloads available on their Web site.

The Flash Player is a separate application for viewing Flash multimedia files. As such, when you download a Flash file, it opens into its own window along with several menu commands for controlling how a movie plays. Depending on the movie settings, users may be able to resize the Flash Player window to enlarge their view of the movie. See page 638 to save your movies as Flash Player files (SWF).

PLAY A FLASH MOVIE IN FLASH

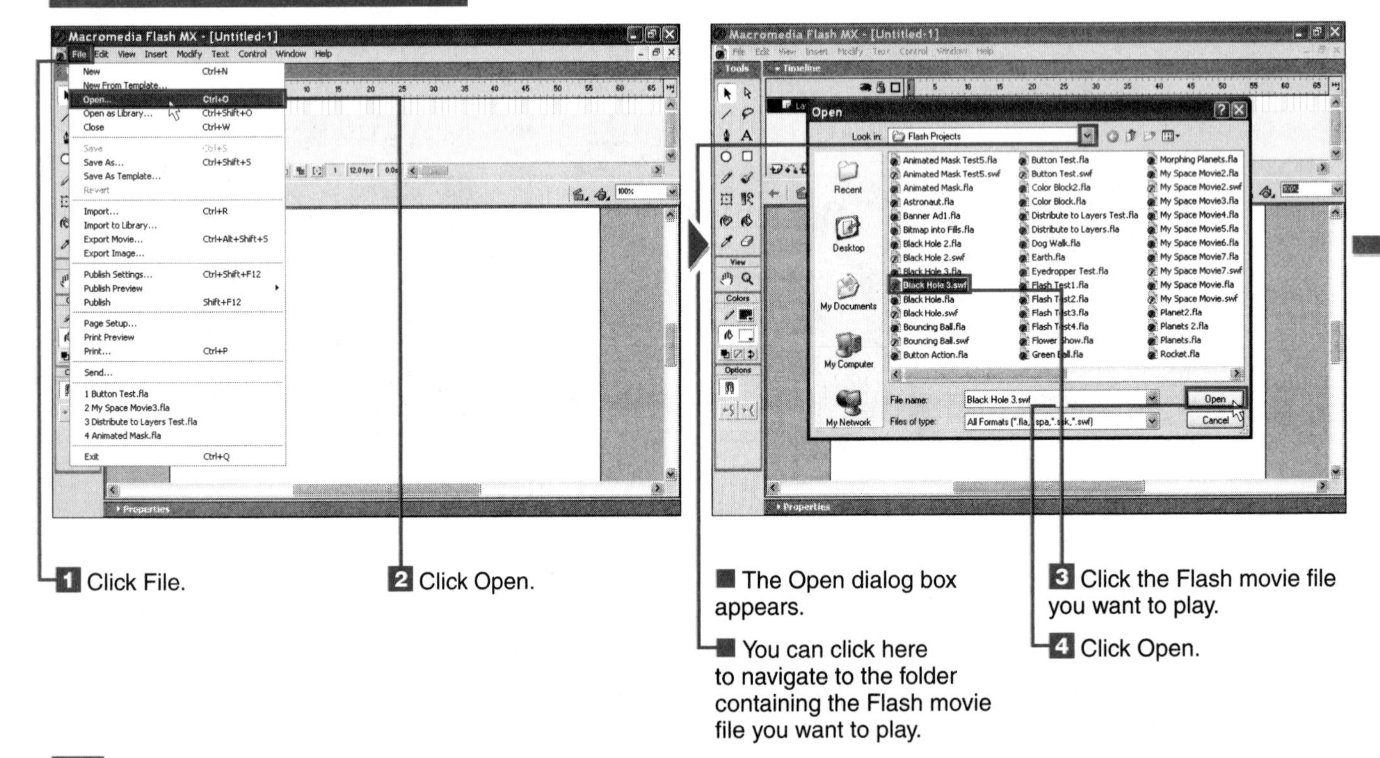

1 Click File.

2 Click Open.

■ The Open dialog box appears.

■ You can click here to navigate to the folder containing the Flash movie file you want to play.

3 Click the Flash movie file you want to play.

4 Click Open.

How do I stop the movie from looping?

✔ The Flash Player window has a few tools you can use to control how the movie plays. Click the Control menu to see the available commands. The Loop command is turned on by default. To deactivate the command, click Loop. To stop the movie from playing, click Stop or just press Enter.

How does the Player window differ from the test movie window?

✔ The Flash Player window and test movie window are one and the same. You can also open the Flash Player window by clicking the Control menu on the Flash menu bar and then selecting Test Movie. The Flash Player window opens and displays the current movie.

How do I open another movie to play in the Flash Player window?

✔ As long as you have the Flash Player window open, you can view other Flash movies as well. To view another movie, click the File menu, then click Open. Click the Browse button. Navigate to the next movie file you want to play. Double-click the movie filename. When you click OK, the movie starts playing.

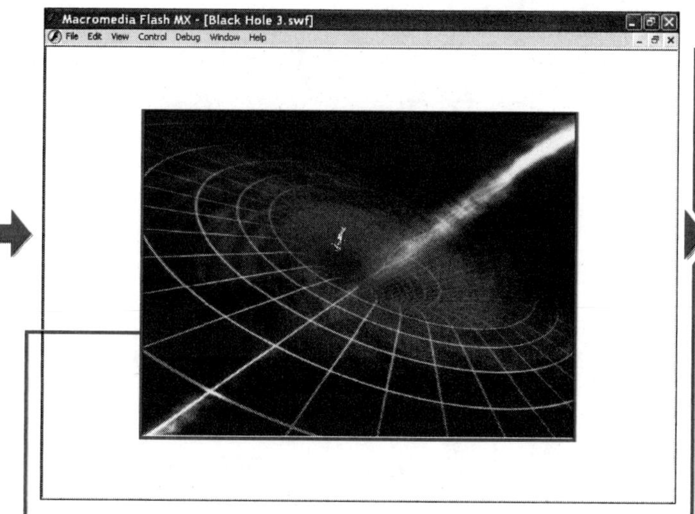

■ The Flash Player window opens and plays the movie.

Note: When opening the Flash Player from within the Flash MX program, the Player fits inside the Flash MX program window and has a separate set of window controls and menu commands.

■ To stop the movie, press Enter (Return).

■ To resume play, press Enter (Return) again.

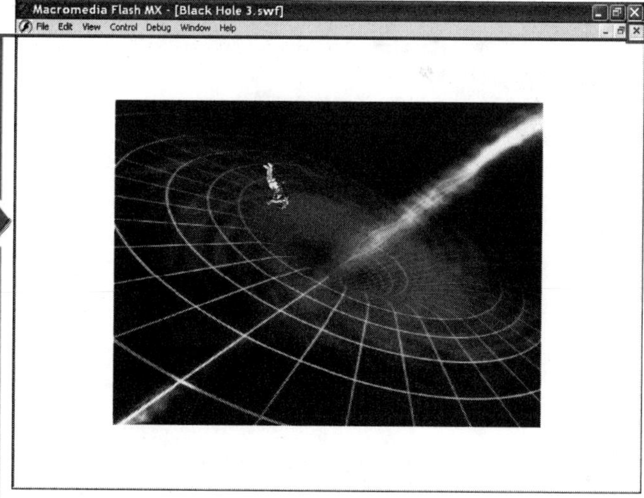

■ To close the movie, click ×.

■ The Flash Player application closes and you are returned to the Flash MX program window.

Note: To open a movie for editing, you must open the movie's FLA file.

PLAY A FLASH MOVIE IN A BROWSER

You can play a Flash MX movie using the browser's Flash plug-in. Playing a movie in a browser allows you to test your creation and make sure everything looks and acts according to your plans.

Flash Player 6 is the latest version of the plug-in currently available. Most browsers, such as Microsoft Internet Explorer and Netscape Navigator, include the Flash Player plug-in program for playing SWF files. Most Internet users can access Flash Web content without needing to download the Flash Player application separately, which makes the Flash Player the most widely used player on the Internet. Today's browsers and computer systems come with the Flash Player preinstalled.

If you place your Flash MX animations on a Web page, users are able to see them automatically, unless they are using a very old version of a browser. When you surf the Web, you encounter hundreds of Web pages that include Flash animations. Flash effects such as animated banners, interactive menus, and multimedia clips play automatically on the Web page. In this section, you learn how to play a Flash movie utilizing the built-in player in your browser.

PLAY A FLASH MOVIE IN A BROWSER

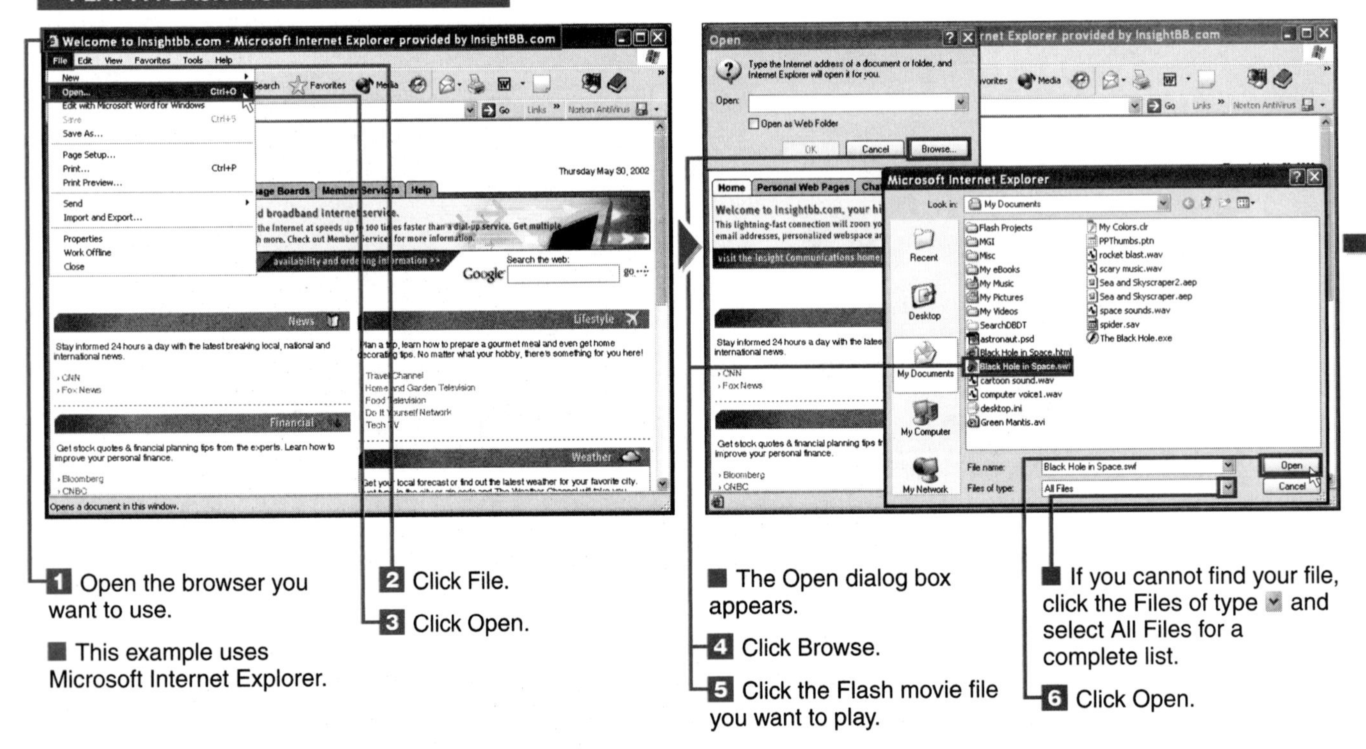

1 Open the browser you want to use.

■ This example uses Microsoft Internet Explorer.

2 Click File.

3 Click Open.

■ The Open dialog box appears.

4 Click Browse.

5 Click the Flash movie file you want to play.

■ If you cannot find your file, click the Files of type ▾ and select All Files for a complete list.

6 Click Open.

Can older browser versions view Flash movies?

✔ It depends on how old the version of the browser program is. The latest version of the Flash Player plug-in is version 6, which is supported in Netscape Navigator or Microsoft Internet Explorer. Earlier versions of these browsers do not include the Flash Player plug-in.

Do I have to view all Flash elements using the Flash Player window?

✔ No. Many of the interactive Web page elements created in Flash MX, such as animated banners, interactive menus, and buttons, are embedded in the Web page. These elements do not open a separate player window, but are a part of the Web page itself.

How do I control the screen size of a movie?

✔ The movie's screen size is set when you define the Stage area measurements. To learn how to set the Stage size, see page 344. You can also control the size of the movie display window that appears inside the browser window when a Flash movie plays. You can find movie-display controls in the Publish Settings dialog box. Learn more about these controls on page 640.

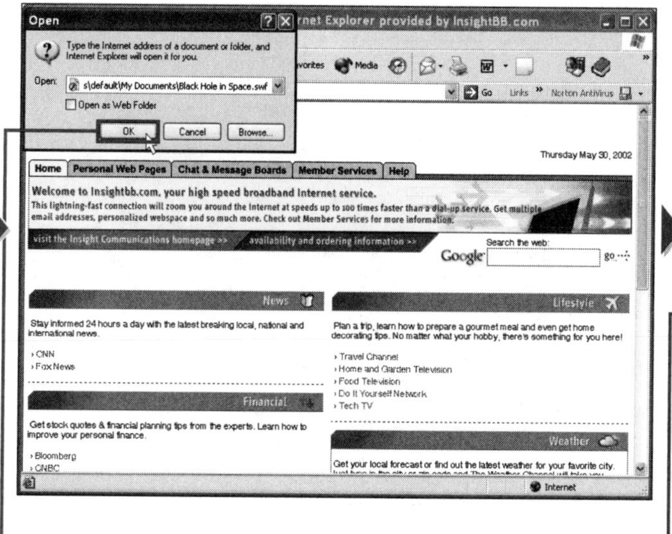

7 Click OK.

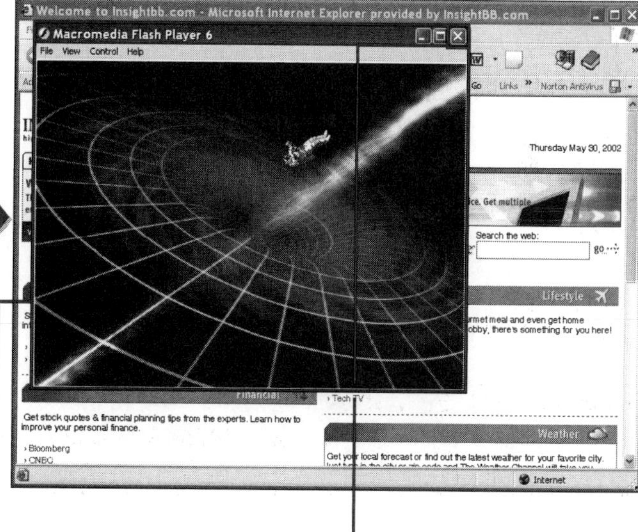

■ The Flash Player window opens and the movie plays.

■ To close the movie, click ☒.

TEST MOVIE BANDWIDTH

You can use the Flash Bandwidth Profiler to help you determine which movie frames might cause problems during playback on the Web. File size and the user's data-transfer rate affect how smoothly and quickly your movie downloads and plays. With the handy Bandwidth Profiler you can test your movies for maximum effect. The feature works in conjunction with the Flash Player window.

With the Bandwidth Profiler you can test six different modem speeds, and gauge which frames in your movie use the most bytes. This information helps you to see exactly where your movie might slow down during playback. For example, you can use the Bandwidth Profiler to simulate different modem speeds such as comparing how long a movie takes to download at 28.8 Kbps versus 36.6 Kbps.

When you activate the Bandwidth Profiler, it opens as a window at the top of the screen. The left section of the Profiler displays the different status areas you can check, such as the movie's dimensions and speed or the frame state. The right section displays a timeline and a graph detailing frame data.

TEST MOVIE BANDWIDTH

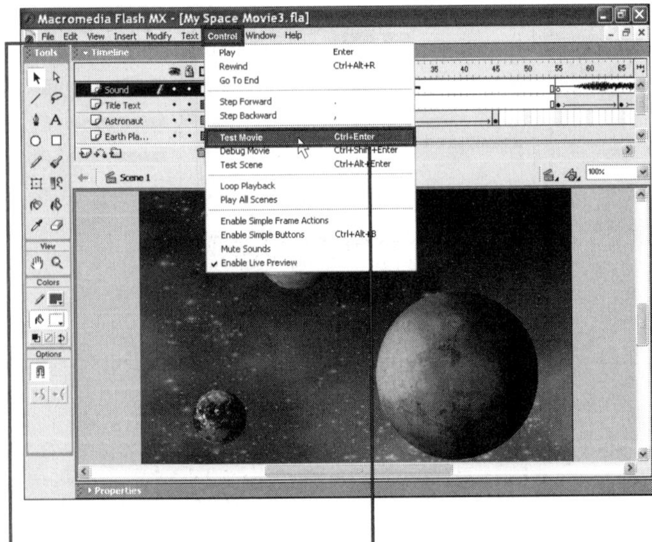

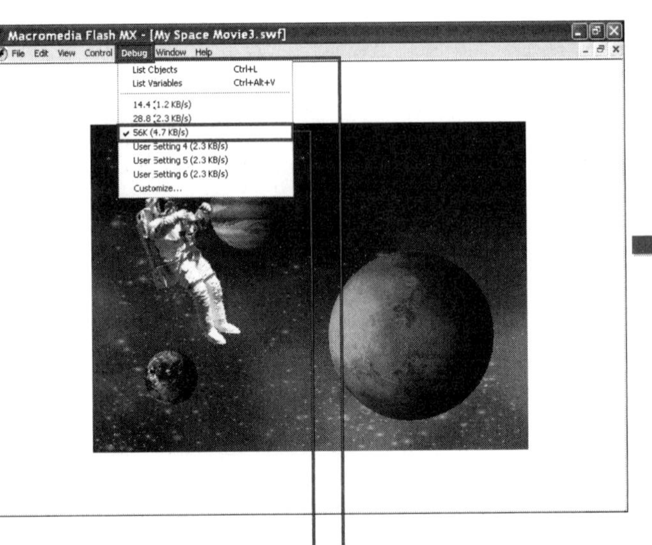

OPEN THE BANDWIDTH PROFILER

1 Click Control.

2 Click Test Movie.

■ Flash MX opens the Flash Player window and starts playing the movie.

3 Press Enter (Return) to stop the movie.

4 Click Debug.

5 Select a modem speed to test.

Can I customize the download speed I want to test?

✔ Yes. To customize the modem speed, click the Debug menu in the Flash Player window. Click Customize. Flash MX opens the Custom Modem Settings dialog box. Set a speed to simulate in the test. For example, you can change an existing speed setting's bit rate by typing in another bit rate. Or you can enter a custom speed in a User Setting box and a bit rate to test for that speed. Click OK to save your changes.

Can I save the test settings for use with another movie?

✔ Yes. Just leave the Bandwidth Profiler open in the Flash Player window. You can open another movie from the player window, or you can return to the player window at a later time and use the same Profiler settings. To open another movie without leaving the player window, click File, then click Open. Double-click the movie you want to view and it begins playing in the player window.

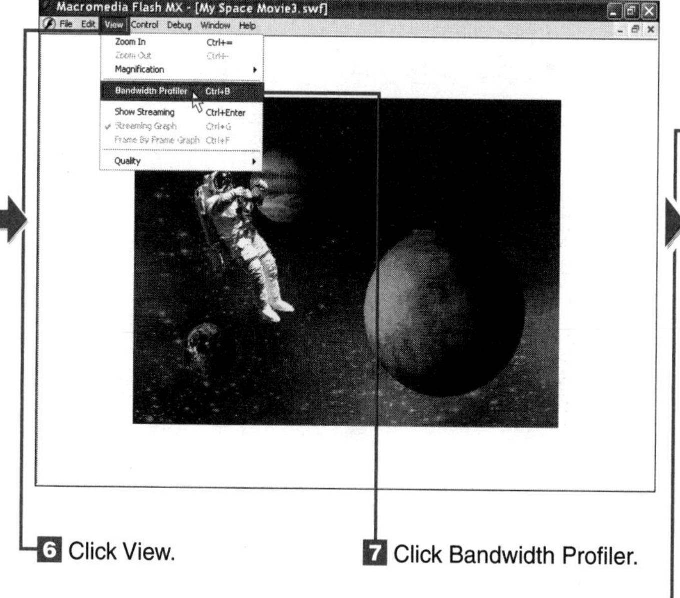

6 Click View.

7 Click Bandwidth Profiler.

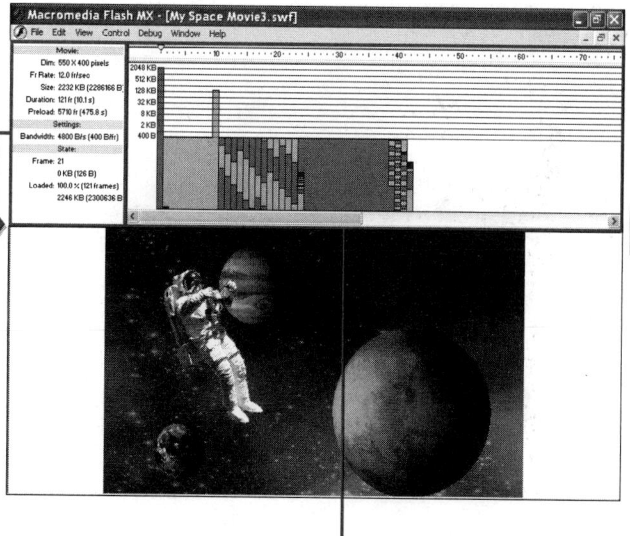

■ Flash MX displays the Bandwidth Profiler at the top of the window.

■ The left side of the Profiler shows information about the movie, such as file size and dimensions.

■ The bars on the right represent individual frames and the total size, in bytes, of data in the frame.

CONTINUED

TEST MOVIE BANDWIDTH (CONTINUED)

You can use two different views in the Flash Bandwidth Profiler to see how the frames play in your movie: Streaming Graph mode or Frame by Frame Graph mode. The default view is Streaming Graph mode. Depending on the view you select, the right section of the Profiler displays data differently.

A vertical bar on the graph represents a single frame in the movie. The bars correspond with the frame number shown in the timeline. In Streaming Graph mode, the alternating blocks of light and dark gray show relative byte size of each frame and the stack indicates how much data must download, or *stream*, into a browser window. Streaming Graph mode shows you the real-time performance of your Flash movie.

In Frame by Frame Graph mode, Flash profiles each frame side by side. If a frame's bar extends above the bottom red line of the graph, the Flash movie pauses to download the frame's data. Frame by Frame Graph mode shows you which frames are causing delays during movie downloads.

If you decide your movie needs to be optimized for greater speed, simplifying graphics by using symbols and grouped objects can help, as well as avoiding custom colors and too many gradient effects. Also limit the number of fonts you use with any text in your movies.

TEST MOVIE BANDWIDTH (CONTINUED)

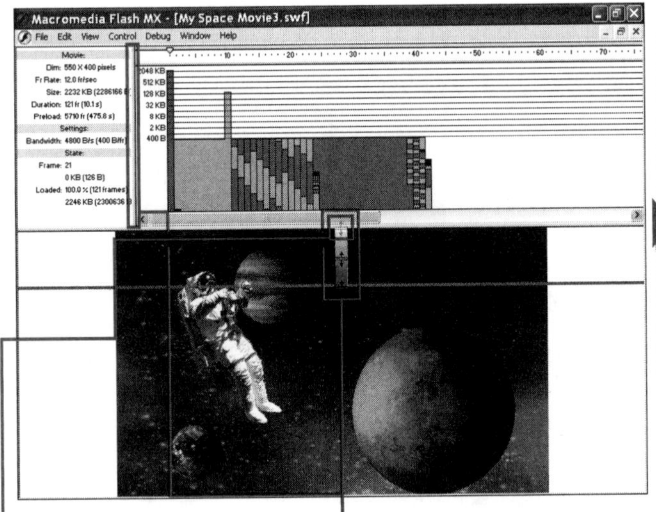

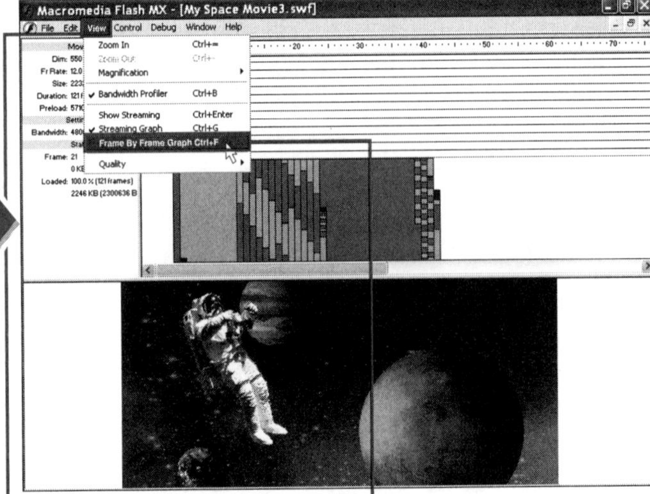

RESIZE THE GRAPH

■ To make sure you are viewing all the movie's information on the left side of the Profiler, resize the Profiler graph.

8 Move the pointer over the bottom border until the pointer turns into ÷.

9 Click and drag the border to resize the Profiler graph.

■ Flash MX resizes the Bandwidth Profiler.

■ You can also drag the border between the panels to resize panels.

CHANGE THE GRAPH VIEW

■ To check which frames might be causing a slow down, switch to Frame by Frame Graph mode.

10 Click View.

11 Click Frame by Frame Graph.

Does the Bandwidth Profiler test the exact modem speed?

✔ No. The Profiler estimates typical Internet connection speeds to estimate downloading time. Modem speeds are typically never full strength. For example, a 28.8 Kbps modem can download 3.5 kilobytes of data per second under perfect conditions, but in real life, there are no perfect conditions when connecting to the Internet. In real life conditions, a 28.8 Kbps modem is lucky to download 2.3 kilobytes of data per second. Flash gears each modem test speed setting in the Profiler towards real-life connection speeds.

How do I view a specific frame in the Profiler?

✔ Use the scroll bar arrows (◀ ▶) to move left or right in the Profiler Timeline at the top of the Profiler graph. To view a specific frame, drag the playhead to the frame, or click the playhead where you want it to go.

Is there a faster way to open the Profiler?

✔ Yes, press Ctrl + B (⌘ + B) in the Flash Player window.

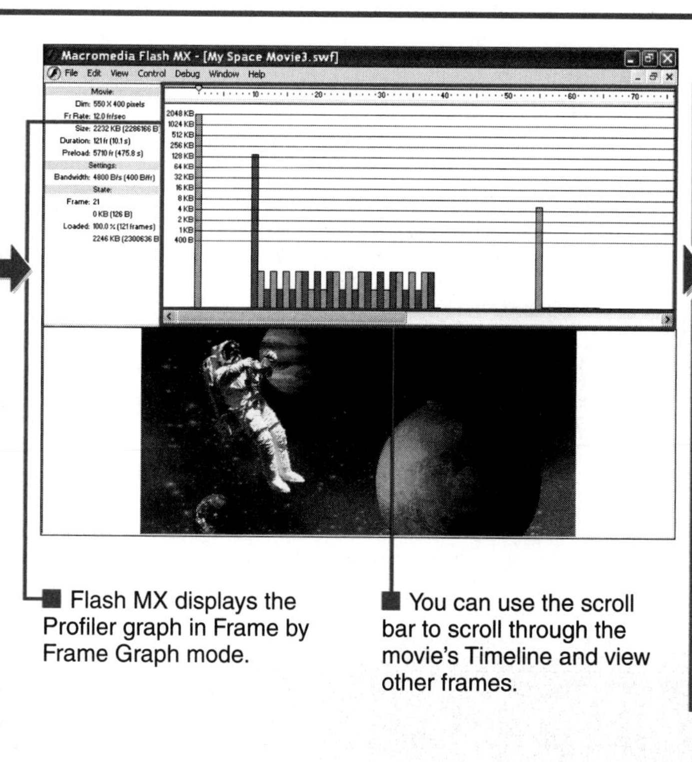

■ Flash MX displays the Profiler graph in Frame by Frame Graph mode.

■ You can use the scroll bar to scroll through the movie's Timeline and view other frames.

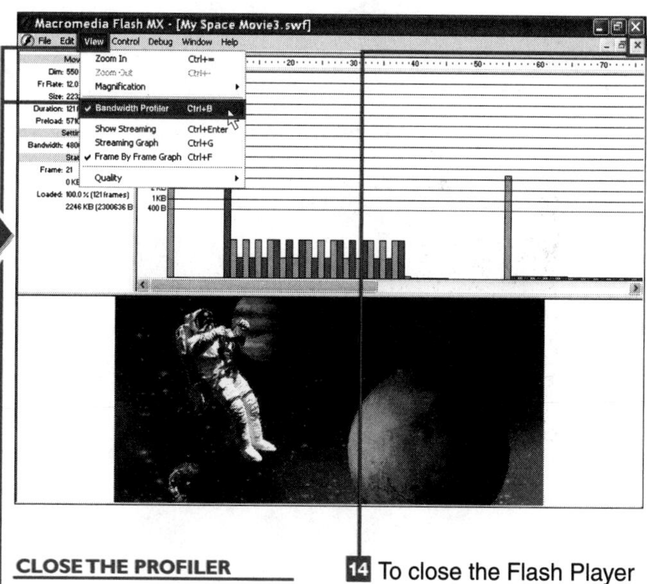

CLOSE THE PROFILER

12 To close the Bandwidth Profiler, click View.

13 Click Bandwidth Profiler.

14 To close the Flash Player window, click ×.

■ Flash MX closes the Bandwidth Profiler and the Player window.

SECTION XI

35) BUILDING INTERFACE CONTROLS

36) ENHANCING INTERACTIVITY WITH FLASH

37) CREATING SPECIAL EFFECTS IN FLASH

APPENDIX

ADVANCED FLASH

CREATE AN ANIMATED MENU

You can create an animated menu system that animates buttons or links in your Flash project. You can assign actions to the menu that animate the menu only when the user interacts with the menu object in the movie and closes when the user is not interacting directly. You can also set the menu up with a timer that tells the menu to close automatically if the user does not activate a menu item in the specified amount of time.

To create an animated menu, you must first build an animation of the menu sequence that shows the menu object opening and closing. You can use all kinds of shapes and objects as a menu. In the example shown below, three animated buttons comprise the menu, with each button containing a link to another Web page. The animation effect starts with a single button that animates into three separate buttons to create a menu of choices. Your own animated menu might include similar buttons that, when clicked, take the user to another area on a Web site or start another movie clip playing.

CREATE AN ANIMATED MENU

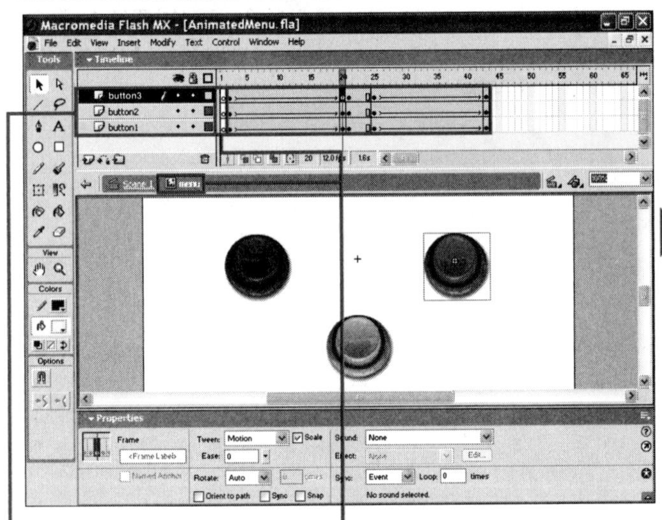

Note: To view a completed example, see the file AnimatedMenu.fla on the CD that accompanies this book.

1 Create an animation sequence to use as your animated menu.

■ Make sure the menu animates opening and closing.

2 Convert the animation into a movie clip symbol named **menu**.

■ You should leave the first frame of the movie clip reserved for the button or clip that triggers the menu.

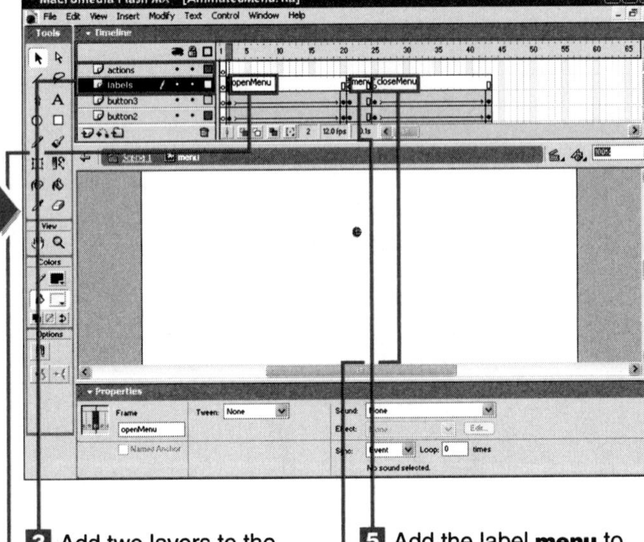

3 Add two layers to the movie clip symbol named **labels** and **actions**.

4 In the labels layer, add the label **openMenu** to the keyframe that starts the opening of the menu.

5 Add the label **menu** to the keyframe that shows the full menu displayed.

6 Add the label **closeMenu** to the keyframe that starts the menu closing.

When I try to type the second label in step 5, it replaces the first label I typed. What am I doing wrong?

✔ You forgot to add a keyframe first. You must add keyframes to the frame where you want a new label to appear. See Chapter 29 to learn more about adding keyframes to the Timeline.

Do I need to leave the first frame of the menu movie clip empty?

✔ Yes. If you want to allow the user to interact with a button or clip that starts the menu sequence, you must save a frame for the button or clip you intend to add later. If you forgot to leave the first frame empty, you can always return to the clip and insert a keyframe later.

Do I have to include labels for my animated menu?

✔ No. Adding labels is completely optional. However, labels can help you quickly see what is going on in the Timeline of your movie. In the example shown below, labels point out where each part of the animation sequence occurs so you know where to add actions later to control the sequence. To learn more about adding labels in Flash MX, see Chapter 29.

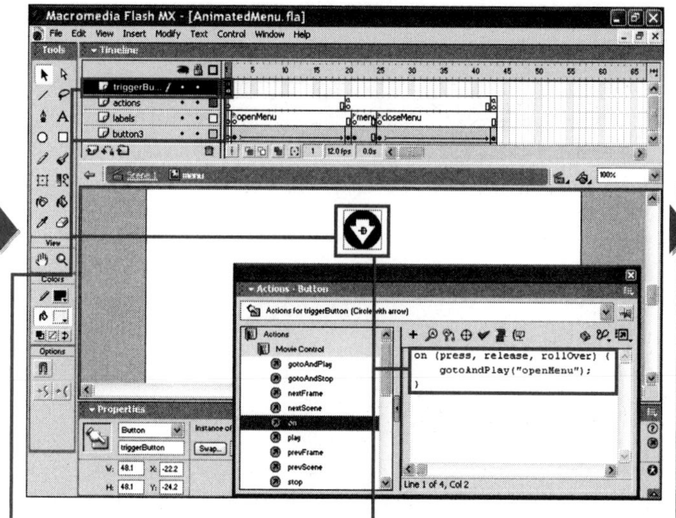

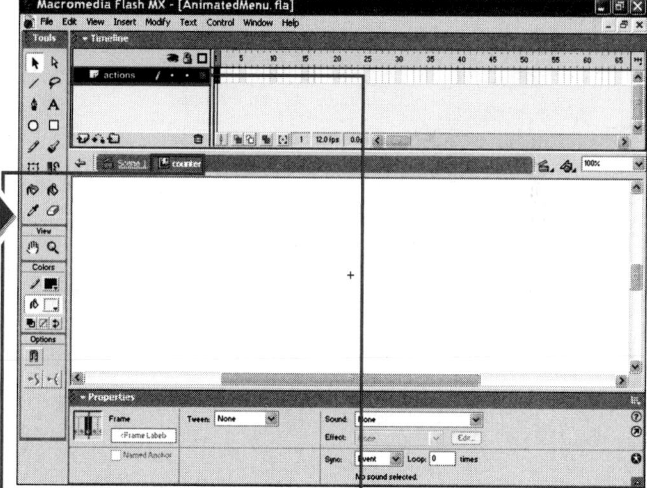

7 Add another layer named **triggerButton**.

8 Place a button in the first frame of the new layer that triggers the opening of the menu.

9 Click the frame and add a `stop` action.

10 Click the button and add an `on mouse` event action to the button that tells the movie to play when either pressed or rolled over, triggering the opening of the menu.

Note: To open and close the Actions panel, see page 576.

11 Create a new movie clip symbol within the menu movie clip and name it **counter**.

12 Add or rename a layer to the counter movie clip and name it **actions**.

CONTINUED

CREATE AN ANIMATED MENU (CONTINUED)

You can add the `var` and `if` actions to create a counter that tracks the number of seconds the user is not in contact with the animated menu. By including timeout functionality for a menu, you ensure that the user can concentrate on the clip or link activated by clicking a menu option rather than the animated menu itself.

You can create the counter effect by creating a separate movie clip that acts behind the scenes to count the number of seconds of user inaction. Because your frame rate is 12 frames per second by default, the counter movie clip needs to add 1 to the value of n, or once every second, after the variable checks the desired timeout limit. In the example shown below, the timeout limit is 5 seconds.

After creating the counter movie clip, you can add an instance of the clip to the spot in your menu movie where you want the activity of the user evaluated. Typically, you add the instance to the frame where the menu opening sequence is complete.

The complexity of this task requires typing script code using Expert mode. Be sure to type exactly what is shown in the figures below. If you mistype, the script will not run properly.

CREATE AN ANIMATED MENU (CONTINUED)

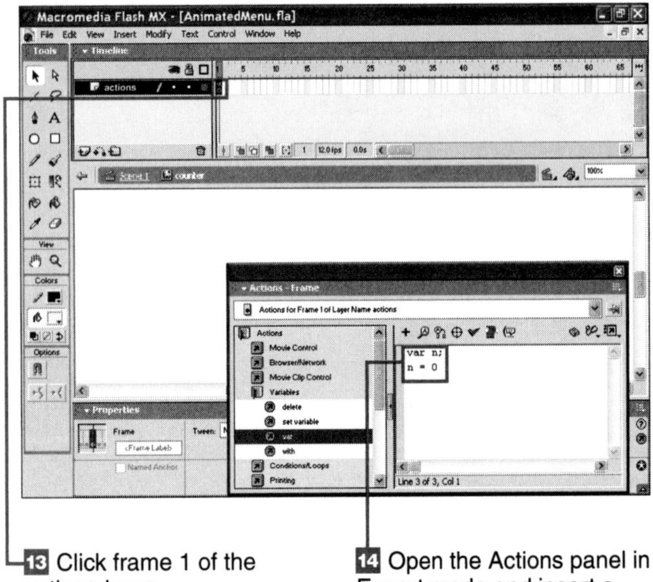

13 Click frame 1 of the actions layer.

14 Open the Actions panel in Expert mode and insert a `var` action setting a variable entitled `n` to an initial value of `0`.

Note: Do not forget to insert keyframes in order to assign an action to a frame.

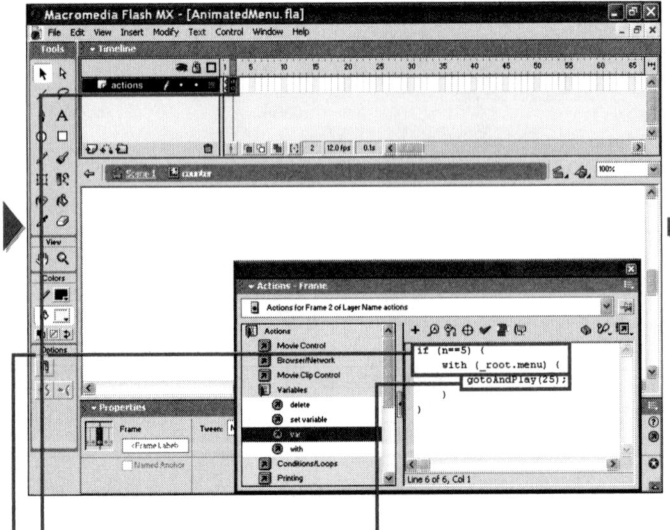

15 Click frame 2.

16 Add an `if` and `with` action using Expert mode to check if `n` is the number of seconds you want to leave the menu open if the user stops interacting with the menu.

17 If the time limit has been reached, instruct the menu to close by adding a `gotoAndPlay` action that sends the movie to the frame that starts the menu closing.

How do I switch Action panel modes?

✔ You can switch back and forth between Normal and Expert modes using the View Options button. Click ▣ and then click Expert mode or Normal mode in the panel.

Can I expand the actions list area to see more of the script I type?

✔ Yes. You can click the Expand button (▣) to expand the actions list and hide the action category pane. You can also resize the panel itself to view more of the script.

I do not want to use a button to open my animated menu. How can I trigger a menu to open from the first frame of my animation?

✔ You can use an invisible button in cases where you do not want to display a visible Menu Open button. For example, a developer might stop the playhead on the first frame of the animation that opens the menu system. An invisible button, which is simply a button containing only a Hit state, is placed over the top of the first frame. Then an action is added to the button that tells the menu to open when the user rolls over the desired area.

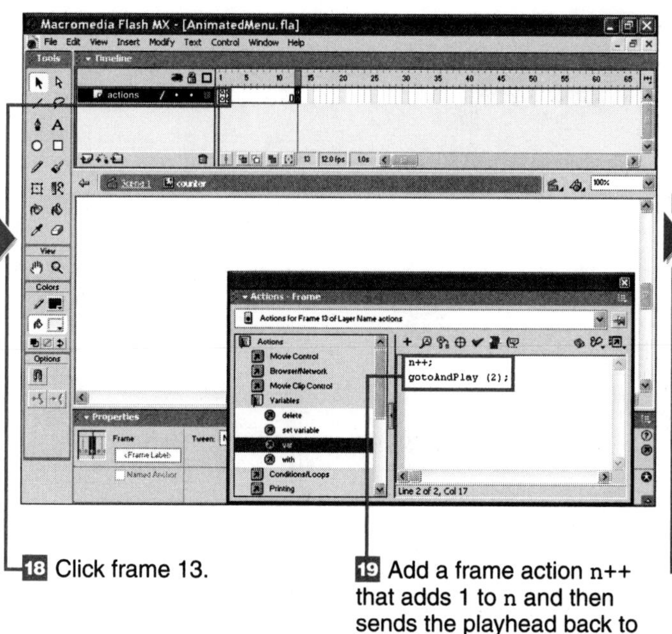

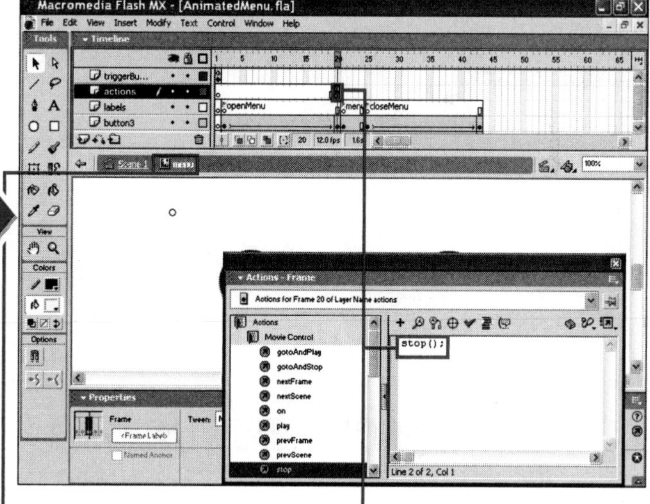

18 Click frame 13.

19 Add a frame action n++ that adds 1 to n and then sends the playhead back to frame 2 where the variable is checked for timeout again.

20 Return to the menu movie clip timeline.

21 In the actions layer, add a `stop` action to the frame where the menu completes the opening animation sequence.

CONTINUED

CREATE AN ANIMATED MENU (CONTINUED)

You can add actions to the buttons in your animated menu sequence that resets the value of n when the user is in contact with the buttons. This ensures that the menu does not close while the user is reading or using the menu system. In other words, when the user moves the mouse away from the menu buttons, the counter evaluates the amount of inactive time and activates the menu closing sequence.

The button actions include instructing Flash what to do when the user rolls over the button — called a *rollover*, as well as what to do when the user rolls off the button — called a *rollout*.

The `with` action specifies that you are performing actions using the counter movie clip instance. You must indicate the location of the clip you want to target with the `with` action. The location written in script includes the main movie timeline, `_root`, followed by the menu movie clip, `.menu`, followed by the counter movie clip, `.counter`.

To complete the functionality of the animated menu, you can add links or actions to the menu items later that, when clicked, take the user to a specified page or start a specified clip.

CREATE AN ANIMATED MENU (CONTINUED)

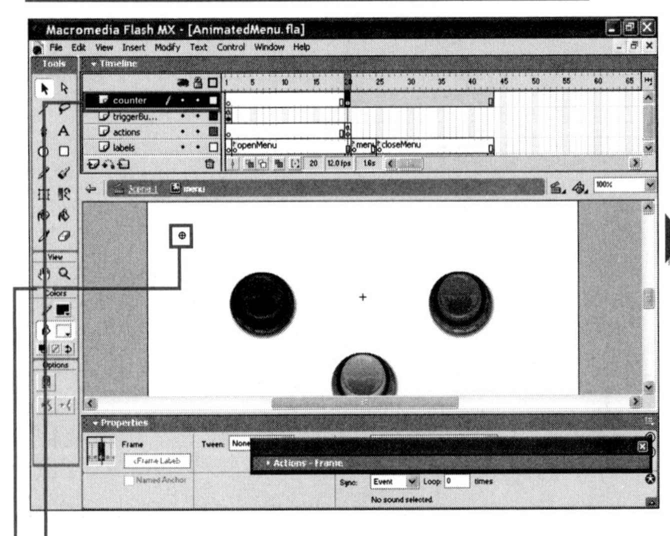

22 Add a new layer to the menu movie clip timeline named **counter**.

23 Insert an instance of the counter movie clip in the same frame as the `stop` action added in step 21.

■ Because the counter movie clip contains no graphics or shapes, the clip appears as a cross point icon on the Stage.

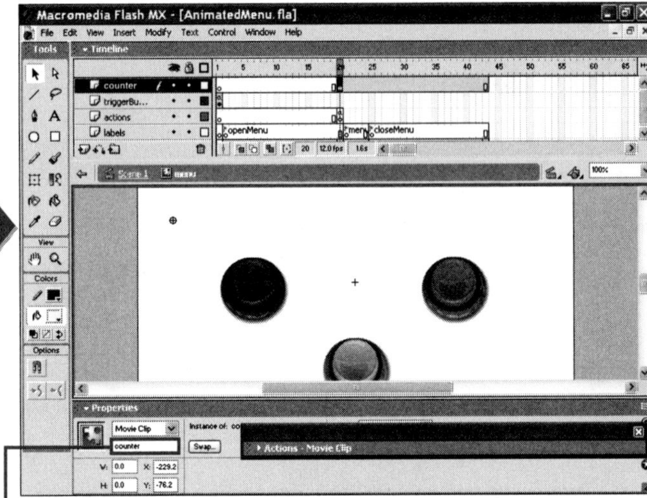

24 Name the instance **counter** in the Property inspector.

I want my menu buttons to link to Web pages. Where do I add the getURL action?

✔ You can add the `getURL` action at the end of the list of actions you typed in step 25. In the example shown, the button actions are added to the last frame of each animation sequence that shows the button open.

Flash MX does not let me add a button action. Why not?

✔ Make sure you click the button instance on the stage before trying to add an action to the button. If you click a frame instead, Flash MX thinks you are assigning frame actions.

In step 25, what does the `_root.menu.counter.n = 0` statement do?

✔ This statement sets the variable `n` of the counter movie clip instance. You assigned the instance a name in step 24 in order to reference the instance in the button action. Note the statement includes the full path of the instance, which includes the main movie timeline, the menu movie clip, and the counter movie clip instance name.

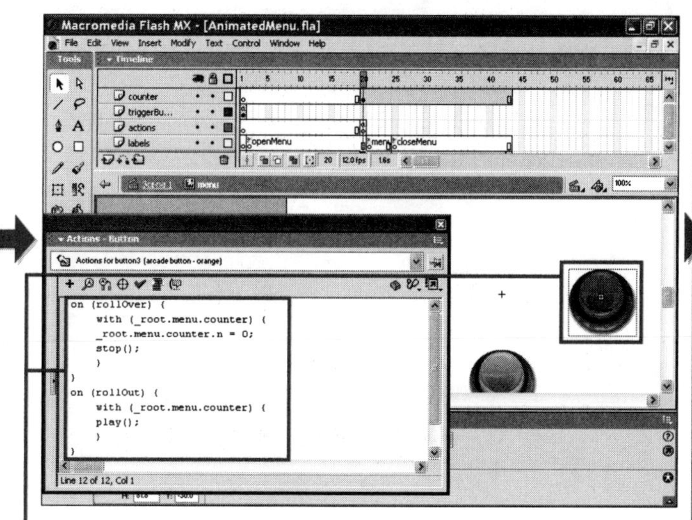

25 Add an object action to each button in your menu that resets the value of `n` when the user rolls over a button.

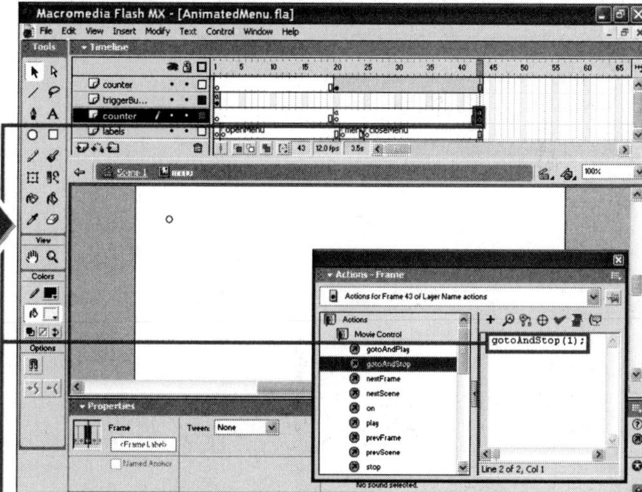

26 Add a `gotoAndStop` action to the last frame in the menu sequence that sends the playhead back to frame 1 in the menu movie clip.

■ You can test the animated menu in the Flash Player window.

Note: To test movies in the Flash Player window, see page 630.

CREATE A PRELOADER

You can add a preloader animation that plays while the user waits for a specific amount of data to load. Preloaders are commonly used on the Web today. A preloader mainly consists of a small animation and information concerning the state of the Web site.

Preloaders can be as simple as a text statement that tells users to wait while a movie downloads or as complex as an indicator bar that shows the user how much of the content has downloaded onto their computer.

Adding a preloader to a movie ensures that playback is not stopped due to bandwidth restrictions when your movie is played over the Web. Preloaders also give you a chance to communicate to the user in situations in which they might find themselves waiting for a Web site to download. A general statement declaring that the site is loading lets users know the site is not down, but just taking a moment to load.

When planning a preloader, keep in mind that the main purpose is to show or describe loading progress. Whether you choose to accurately represent the amount of data loaded is up to your discretion, but it is important that your preloader represent some sort of progress.

CREATE A PRELOADER

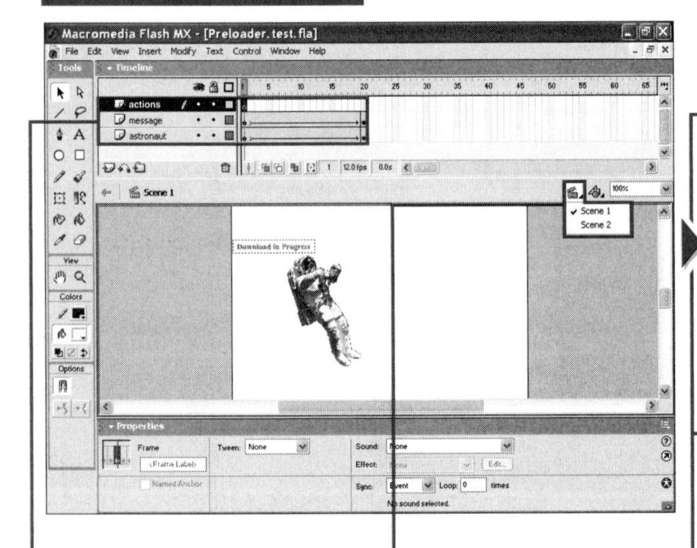

Note: To view a completed example, see the file Preloader.fla on the CD that accompanies this book.

1 Create two scenes in your movie, one for the preloader and the second for your main movie.

2 Create a preloader animation in Scene 1 that includes a layer named **actions**.

3 In the first frame of the action layer, add an `if` action.

■ You can find the `if` action under the Conditions/Loops subcategory in the Actions panel.

4 Add a `_framesloaded` action.

■ You can find the `_framesloaded` action under the Properties category in the Actions panel.

When I test the movie in the Flash Player window, I do not see the preloader animation. Why not?

✔ Your main movie may load too fast for the preloader effect to be seen. Try using the streaming option. From the Player window, click View, and then click Show Streaming. If you still do not see the preloader, try testing the Flash file on your Web site, or make sure the preloader animation is long enough to show the animation.

How do I test my preloader using a different bandwidth?

✔ From the Flash Player window, click the Debug menu and click a modem speed.

I want to use a progress bar in my preloader. What is the key to animating the bar to show progress?

✔ Make the bar into a motion tween animation anywhere from 15 to 20 frames in length that shows the bar growing from nothing to 100%. Then you can add a dynamic text box alongside or on top of the bar that displays the percentage of the download using a variable that takes the value of the current preloader scene, divides it by the total number of frames, multiplied by 100. Your statement might look like:

```
var percentage;
percentage=(_root.current
frame/20)*100
```

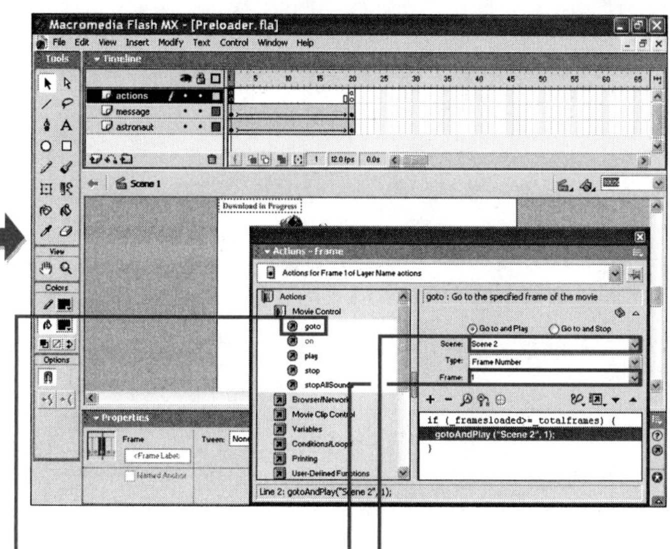

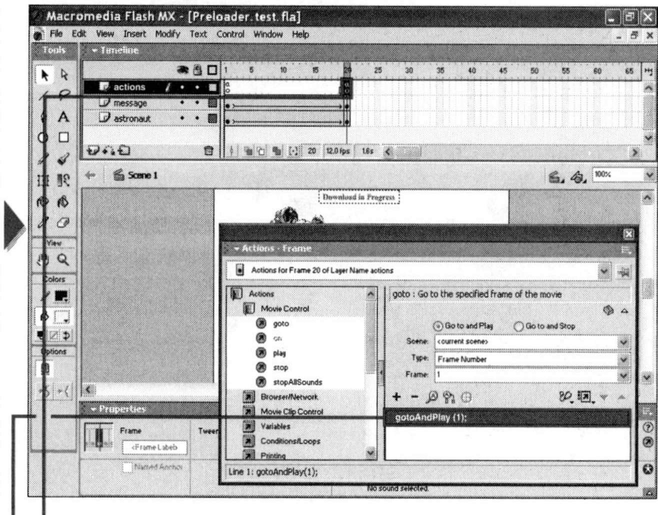

5 Add a goto action.

■ You can find the goto action under the Properties category in the Actions panel.

6 Click the Scene ▾ and select the main-movie scene.

7 Click the frame ▾ and select the frame parameter to the first frame in the main-movie scene.

8 Click the last frame in the preloader animation.

9 Add a goto action that loops the preloader animation back to frame 1 to play again if the main movie is still downloading.

■ Leave the Go to and Play option selected, as well as the default frame 1.

■ You can test the movie in the Flash Player window to see the preloader effect.

Note: To test movies in the Flash Player window, see page 630.

TURN A MOVIE CLIP INTO A CUSTOM CURSOR

You can create a customized cursor to use with your Flash movie or Flash-designed interface. You can use a movie clip to replace the standard cursor the user works with to point and click on items in a movie or in a user interface.

You can use an existing movie clip, or turn a graphic shape or object into a movie clip symbol to act as your custom cursor. If you are designing a Web page based on a theme, such as sports, you might turn a theme-related graphic into a cursor, such as a basketball or tennis racket.

To replace the standard cursor with a new one, you must utilize a mouse method in your ActionScript that hides the regular cursor. You can then summon the `startDrag` action to bring a new cursor object — a movie clip — to life.

When assigning the `startDrag` action, you can also define the parameters in which the custom cursor is visible. When you target the movie clip as an expression, you can enter values to determine the cursor range, including the left, top, right, and bottom border of the cursor area. If you do not define a range, the default range includes the entire screen.

TURN A MOVIE CLIP INTO A CUSTOM CURSOR

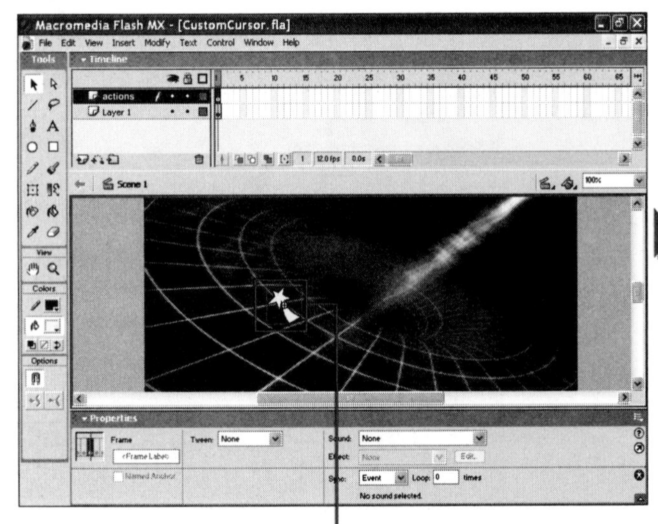

Note: To view a completed example, see the file CustomCursor.fla on the CD that accompanies this book.

1 Create a movie clip to use as a custom cursor in your main movie.

2 Add an instance of the cursor clip to the Stage.

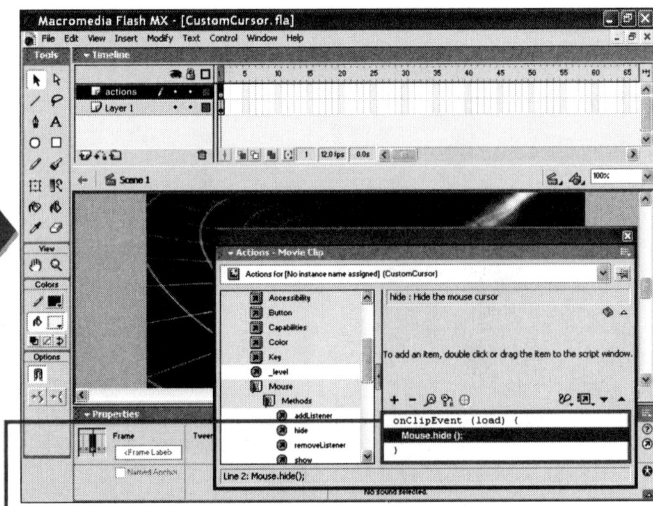

3 With the instance selected, add a `Mouse.hide` action.

■ You can find the `Mouse.hide` action under the Objects category, under the subcategory Movie, Mouse, Methods.

Can I track the position of the cursor within the movie?

✔ Yes. You can use a variable to track cursor position. For example, to track the x- and y-coordinates, add two dynamic text boxes and assign them variable names, such as xtextbox and ytextbox. Then add a set variable action that defines the variable for the x-coordinate and assigns the value _xmouse. Be sure to check the Expression check box for the value. Do the same for the y-coordinate, using the variable name and the value _ymouse. Your script might look like:

```
xtextbox = _xmouse;
ytextbox = _ymouse;
```

When I test the custom cursor effect in the Flash Player window, my cursor seems to move beneath existing buttons and objects on the movie. Why?

✔ You placed the custom cursor clip on a layer that appears beneath the layers containing the buttons or other objects in the movie. To ensure the custom cursor passes over the top of on-screen items, move the layer containing the custom cursor to the top of the layer stack in the Timeline. To reord layers in Flash MX, see page 440.

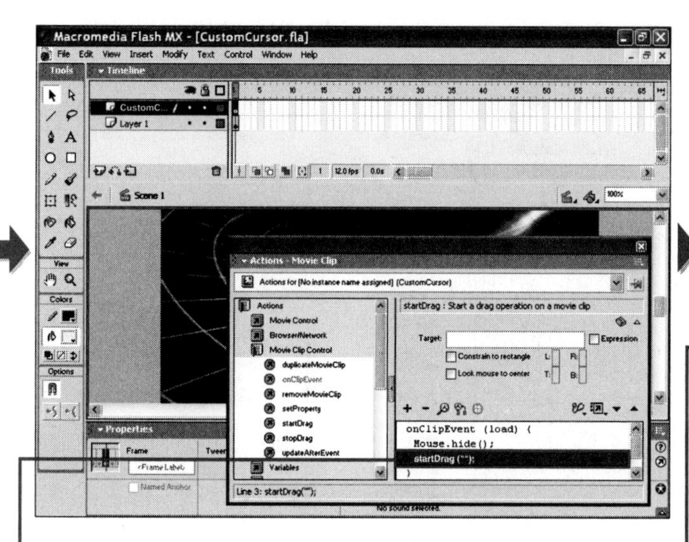

4 Add a `startDrag` action.

■ You can find the `startDrag` action under the Actions category, under the Movie Clip Control subcategory in the Actions panel.

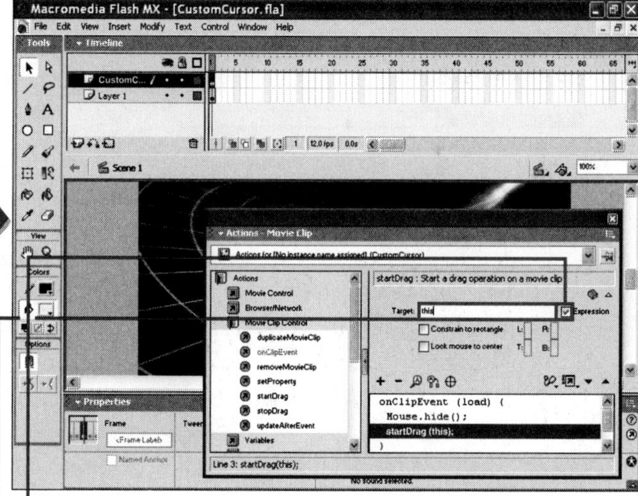

5 Click the Expression check box.

6 Type **this** in the Target field.

■ To limit cursor movement, type **true** in the Target field followed by four values to determine the area in which the cursor is active.

Note: Make sure you include commas after each value you enter in the target field, or the script will not work properly.

■ You can test the cursor in the Flash player window.

Note: To test movies in the Flash Player window, see page 630.

CREATE A WINDOW HIERARCHY

If you are creating a user interface in Flash MX, you can create a window hierarchy that allows windows to overlap in your movie. Window systems are commonly used for offering navigation, menus, and other controls to users.

In a window hierarchy, one window appears placed on top if two or more windows are open. Using a combination of two actions, `startDrag` and `swapDepths`, you can add functionality to a window that allows a user to drag the window around the screen as well as control the stacking order of the window as it relates to other objects in the movie.

You can use the `startDrag` action to make a draggable movie clip. The movie clip remains draggable until it encounters a `stopDrag` action or until it encounters another movie clip. You can only drag one clip at a time in Flash MX.

You can turn any graphic or shape into a draggable movie clip to use as a window in your movie. Most users associate windows as square shapes; however, you can use other shapes to mimic the design of your interface. In addition, you can add a Close or Minimize option to give your windows more functionality.

CREATE A WINDOW HIERARCHY

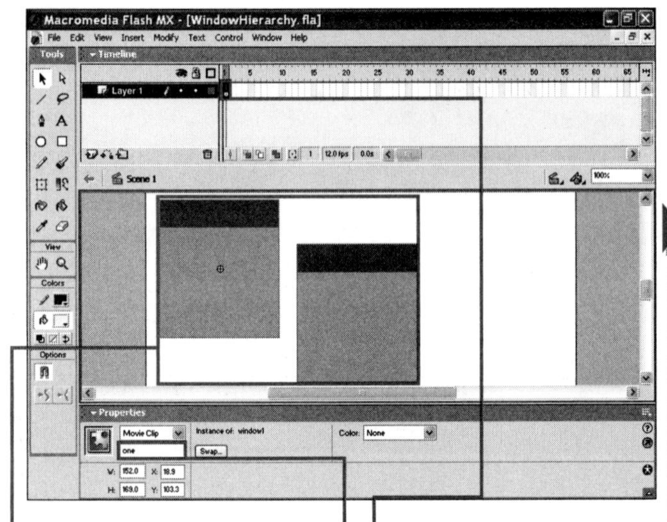

Note: To view a completed example, see the file WindowHierarchy.fla on the CD that accompanies this book.

1 Create two movie clip symbols named **window1** and **window2** to use as windows.

2 Place both window1 and window2 movie clips in frame 1 of the main Timeline.

3 Assign window1 the instance name of **one** and window2 an instance name of **two**.

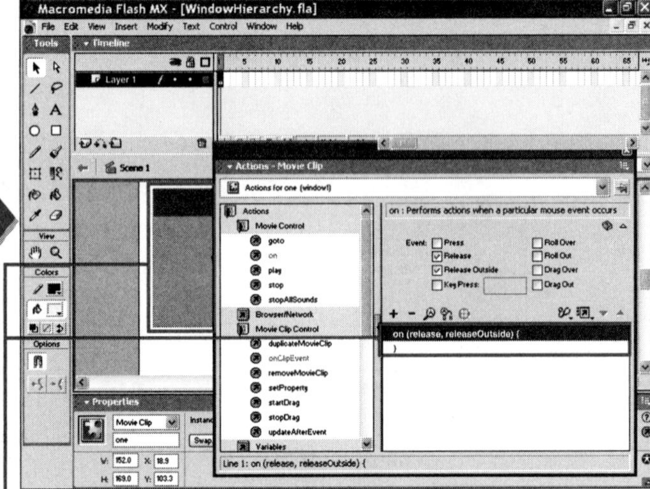

4 Add an on action to the window1 clip that drags the window when the user presses or releases the mouse button over the window or title bar.

■ You can find the on action under the Actions category, under the Movie Clip Control subcategory in the Actions panel.

Do I have to add the `startDrag` action to the title bar, or can I add it to the entire window?

✔ You do not have to target the title bar for the **`startDrag`** action; however, most users are familiar with how windows work in other interfaces and will instinctively try to drag your title bar to move it around in the movie.

Can I use a button as a title bar in my window movie clip symbols?

✔ Yes. By creating one button to use as a title bar in window1, you can copy the instance to create window2. Multiple uses of the same symbol do not increase file size. If you use a button as part of the window creation, you can target the button for dragging actions rather than the entire window.

How do I collapse a window?

✔ You can hide the contents of a window and display only the title bar by creating a frame in your movie that shows only the title bar. Use a Restore button or link to send the playhead to a frame where the window contents are displayed again.

How can I resize the Actions panel to view all the script code?

✔ You can click and drag the panel border to resize.

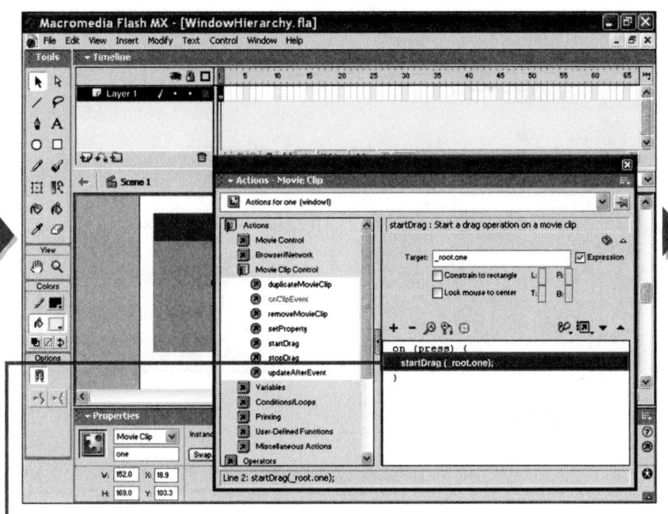

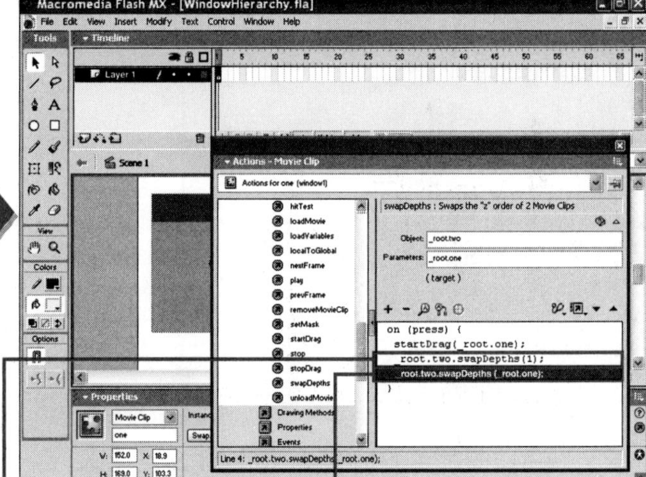

5 Add a `startDrag` action to the window1 clip that targets the instance name.

■ You can find the `startDrag` action under the Actions category, under the Movie Clip Control subcategory in the Actions panel.

6 Add a `swapDepths` action to the clip that swaps the depth value of window2 to 1.

■ To find the `swapDepths` action, click the Objects category, and then click Movie, Movie Clip, Methods.

Note: Do not forget to target the main movie, `_root`, in addition to the instance name.

7 Add another `swapDepths` action to swap the depth level of window2 with window1.

CONTINUED

CREATE A WINDOW HIERARCHY (CONTINUED)

You can use the `swapDepths` action to create a stacking order for the windows in your window hierarchy. The stacking order, also called the depth level, swaps one movie clip with another in Flash MX. Without the `swapDepths` action, the draggable window always remains at its current level, which means it might appear beneath other elements on the Stage even when you try to drag it on top of another window.

The key to using the `swapDepths` action is to target the full path to the window instance. The default `_root` name is used to tell Flash MX that the action affects the main movie, and then the targeted instance of the window movie clip. You assign two `swapDepth` actions to the instance, one to set the depth value to the first level, and the other to swap the depth level with the other window in the hierarchy.

To finish off the window hierarchy action, you must add an `on` action and a `stopDrag` action to the window that tells Flash to stop dragging the window when the user lets go of the mouse button. Remember, mouse actions are parameters for determining the stage at which you want the action to occur, such as press, release, and rollover.

CREATE A WINDOW HIERARCHY (CONTINUED)

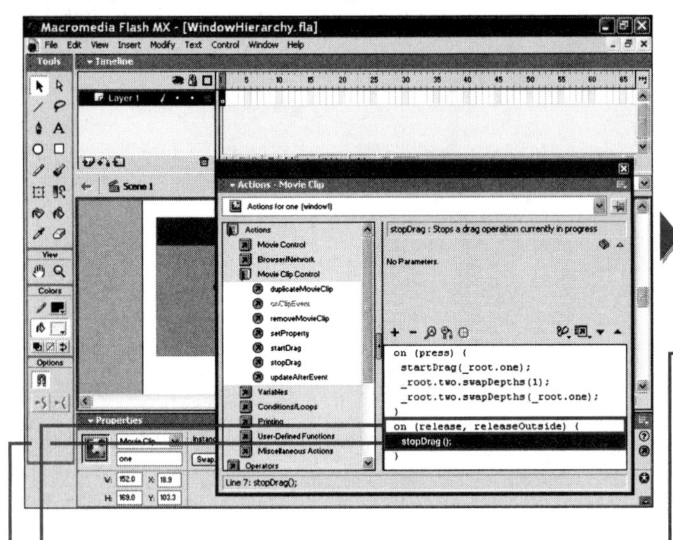

8 Add an `on` action to the window1 clip and set the parameter to `release` and `releaseOutside`.

9 Add a `stopDrag` action.

■ These two actions combine to tell Flash MX to stop the draggable window function when the user releases the mouse button.

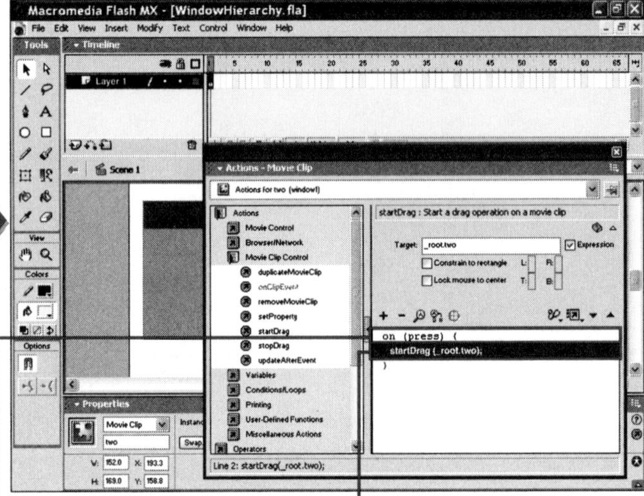

10 Add an `on` action to the window2 clip that drags the window when the user presses the mouse button over the window or title bar.

11 Add a `startDrag` action to the window2 clip that targets the instance name.

How do I close a window in the window hierarchy?

✔ So long as you have a means of opening the window after it is closed, you can use the instance `_visible` property to show and hide a movie clip. You can find the `_visible` property listed under the Properties category in the Actions panel.

When I test my window hierarchy, Flash does not let me stop dragging the window. Why?

✔ You forgot to add a `stopDrag` action and define the mouse action for when the action ceases. Be sure to add both an `on` action to define the mouse parameters and a `stopDrag` action to the end of your script.

How do I create a window hierarchy when using more than two windows?

✔ For instances when you have multiple windows, you need to have a method that tracks what depth level a given window is on. Remember, the `swapDepths` action only exchanges the current depth of the movie clip with a specified depth level. In order to have a complex hierarchy of multiple movie clips, set variable values that keep track of the depth levels and use the `swapDepths` action to exchange a clip's depth with the value of a given variable depth.

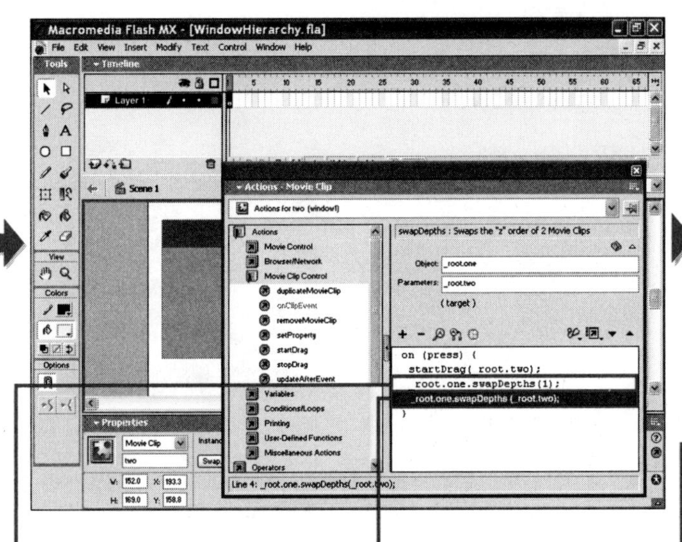

12 Add a `swapDepths` action to the window2 clip that swaps the depth value of window1 to 1.

Note: Do not forget to target the main movie, `_root`, in addition to the instance name.

13 Add another `swapDepths` action to swap the depth level of window1 with window2.

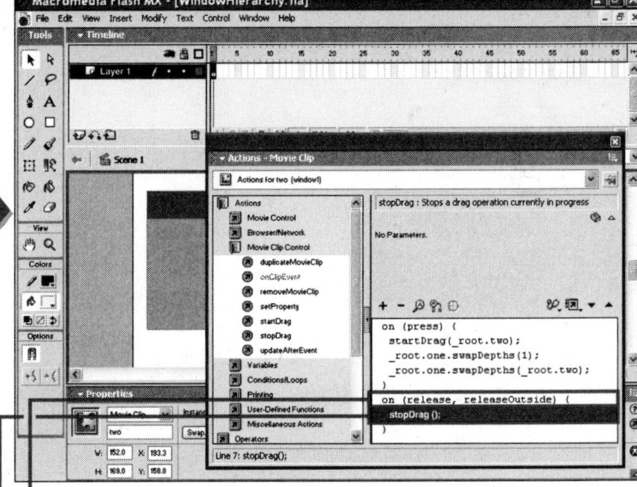

14 Add an `on` action to the window2 clip and set the parameter to `release` and `releaseOutside`.

15 Add a `stopDrag` action.

■ You can test the effect in the Flash Player window.

■ You can add other options to give the window more functionality.

Note: To test movies in the Flash Player window, see page 630.

ADD SOUND VOLUME CONTROLS

You can add controls to your Flash movie or interface that enable users to adjust the volume of a sound clip using the Sound object actions. The Sound object actions include built-in methods for controlling sounds.

When you import sounds into Flash MX, you can assign an identifier string to the sounds to use them later in Sound object actions. Whenever you want to add sounds and controls for the sounds in a movie, you can specify the sound identifier using the `attachSound` method for the particular sound you want to use.

You can find Sound object actions listed in the Actions panel under the Objects category, under the Movie subcategory and the Sound sub-subcategory.

In the example shown below, actions are added to buttons that start and stop a sound as well as to buttons that turn volume up or down. You can also add the same actions to sliders, also called slide bars, or other audio controls to allow users to adjust volume in a movie.

ADD SOUND VOLUME CONTROLS

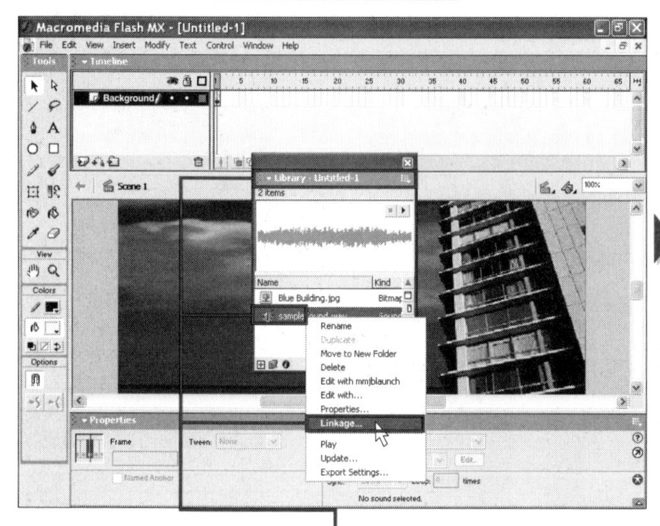

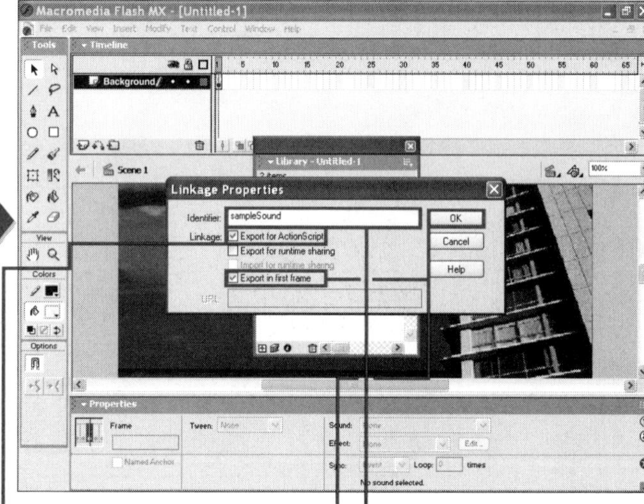

Note: To view a completed example, see the file SoundControls.fla on the CD that accompanies this book.

1 Import the sound clip you want to use into your movie.

Note: Choose a sound clip that plays longer than just a few frames in your movie.

2 Open the Library.

3 Right-click (Control-click) over the sound clip.

4 Click Linkage.

■ Flash MX opens the Linkage Properties dialog box.

5 Click Export for ActionScript.

6 Type an identifier name for the clip.

7 Click Export in first frame.

8 Click OK.

What sound formats can I import?

✔ You can import MP3, WAV, AIF, and AU sounds into Flash MX. You must have QuickTime 4 or 5 installed in order to import all of these formats.

My sound clip is rather large. Is there any way I can reduce the file size?

✔ One way to reduce file size is to trim any silence at the beginning or end of the audio clip. You can use the Edit Envelope dialog box in Flash MX to trim sounds. Learn more about this feature in Chapter 28.

How do I check the properties of my sound clip?

✔ You can check the properties of any sound file you have imported into Flash using the Sound Properties dialog box. From the Library window, right-click (Control-click) over the sound clip name and click Properties from the pop-up menu. This opens the Sound Properties dialog box, detailing information about the sound clip. To learn more about importing sound clips, see Chapter 28.

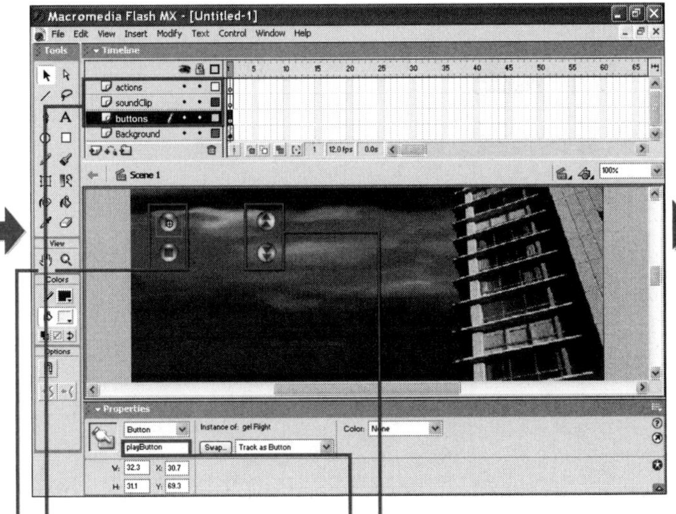

9 Add and label three layers in the Timeline: **buttons**, **soundClip**, and **actions**.

10 Create two buttons to use as controls to start and stop the sound and place instances of each on the Stage.

11 Create two more buttons to use as controls to adjust volume up or down.

12 Assign instance names to each button.

■ In this example, the names playButton, stopButton, upButton, and downButton are used.

13 Create a movie clip symbol named **soundClip**.

■ You may want to include a sound-related graphic or shape to give the clip a visual reference.

14 Add an instance of the soundClip to the Stage in the soundClip layer.

15 Name the movie clip instance **soundClip**.

ADD SOUND VOLUME CONTROLS (CONTINUED)

After assigning an identifier string to a sound clip, you can reference the identifier any time you want to add a control for the sound. You can do this by telling Flash MX to associate the sound with a variable using the `attachSound` action. Once attached, you can summon the sound for actions at any time by typing the variable name for the sound.

In addition to referencing a sound, you can use the `setVolume` action to change the volume level of the sound clip in your movie. Maximum volume level is 100, while a setting of 0 mutes the volume entirely. When assigning a volume to a button for controlling volume, first make sure the volume is set somewhere between the maximum and minimum levels. A middle setting allows the user to increase the volume as well as decrease the level using the volume control buttons.

You can use Normal mode in the Actions panel to enter Sound object actions, or you can type the scripts directly using Expert mode. The steps below show you how to enter script in Expert mode. When entering script code, be sure to follow ActionScript rules, being careful to include the proper syntax and punctuation.

ADD SOUND VOLUME CONTROLS (CONTINUED)

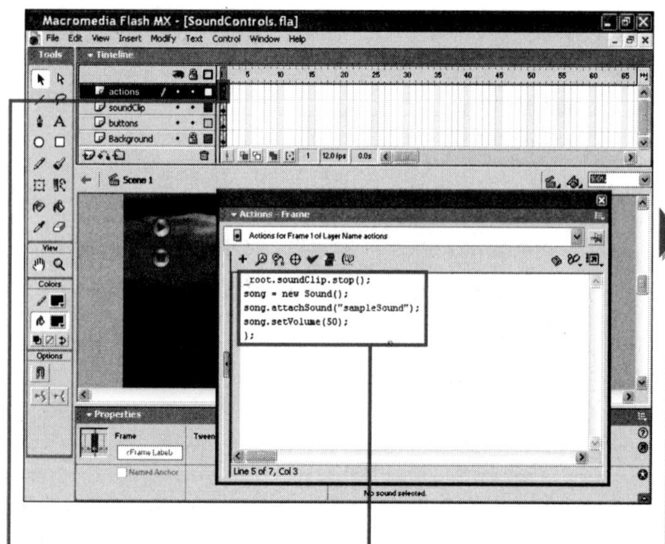

16 Click the first frame of the actions layer.

17 Open the Actions panel in Expert mode.

18 Type **_root.soundClip.stop(); song = newSound(); song.attachSound ("sampleSound"); song.setVolume(50);**.

■ The `setVolume` action sets the sound volume.

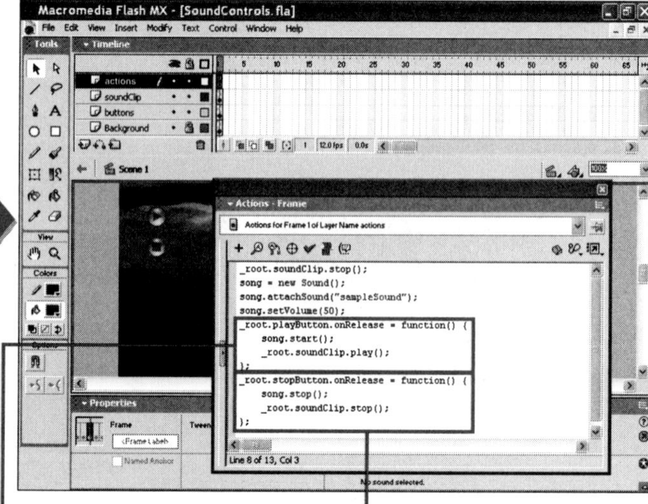

19 To assign the play action to the playButton in the movie, type **_root.playButton. onRelease = function () {song.start(); _root.soundClip.play();};**.

20 To assign the `stop` action to the stopButton in the movie, type **_root.stopButton. onRelease = function() {song.stop(); _root.soundClip.stop();};**.

Can I pan a sound clip?

✔ Yes. You can move the sound output from left to right speaker and vice versa using `getPan` and `setPan` actions. Advanced users can also manipulate both the balance and volume simultaneously using the `soundTransformObject` action.

Can I make a mono sound appear as a stereo sound?

✔ Yes. You can pan the left and right channels to create the illusion of a stereo sound. Mono sounds often sound cleaner in Flash MX than stereo sounds.

Which is the easiest method to add actions to my movies, the categories listed in the Actions panel or the Plus button?

✔ Either method does the same, so deciding on which one to use is simply a matter of preference. If you prefer to view more of the script area in the Actions panel, you might find it easier to hide the categories list and use the Plus button (+) to assign actions.

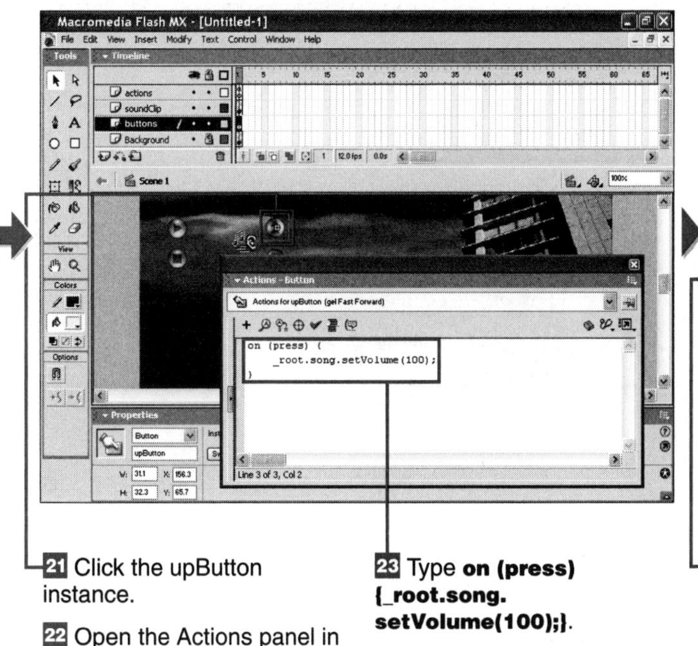

21 Click the upButton instance.

22 Open the Actions panel in Expert mode.

23 Type **on (press) {_root.song.setVolume(100);}**.

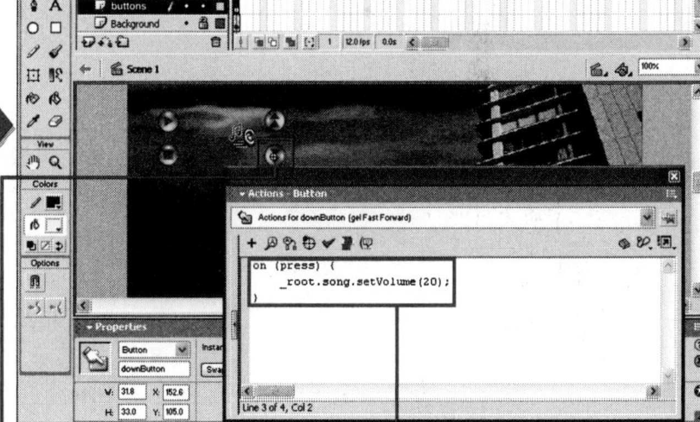

24 Click the downButton instance.

25 Open the Actions panel in Expert mode.

26 Type **on (press) {_root.song.setVolume(20);}**.

■ You can test the buttons and sound actions in the Flash Player window.

Note: To test movies in the Flash Player window, see page 630.

CREATE A PASSWORD IDENTIFICATION BOX

You can add a Password Identification box to your Flash movie that prompts users for a password to proceed. A Password Identification box uses a password text field and the `if` and `else` actions. When users encounter this box in a Flash file, they are prompted for a password. Depending on the string entered in the text field, the user is directed to various options you determine in advance.

When creating a Password Identification box, be sure to include some sort of text statement that tells the user whether the password is accepted. This lets users know what happened after they typed in the password. You should probably devote some time into thinking about what you want the users to know when they type in an incorrect password, whether it is as simple as *try again*, or *incorrect password* or information about how to get the correct password to use.

The steps in this section demonstrate how to add a Password Identification box using a variable text field, along with a button users can click to submit the password they type into the field. You can apply these same principles to add a Password Identification box to other types of projects you create in Flash MX.

CREATE A PASSWORD IDENTIFICATION BOX

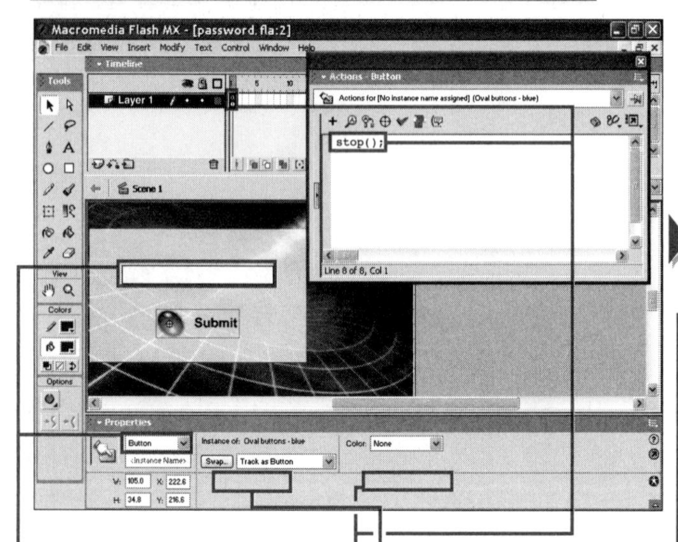

Note: To view a completed example, see the file password.fla on the CD that accompanies this book.

1 Add a text box to hold a password to frame 1.

2 In the Property inspector, click the Text Type and select Input.

3 Click the Line Type and select Password.

4 Assign the Variable name to **password** or another descriptive name.

5 In the Actions panel, add a `stop` action to frame 1.

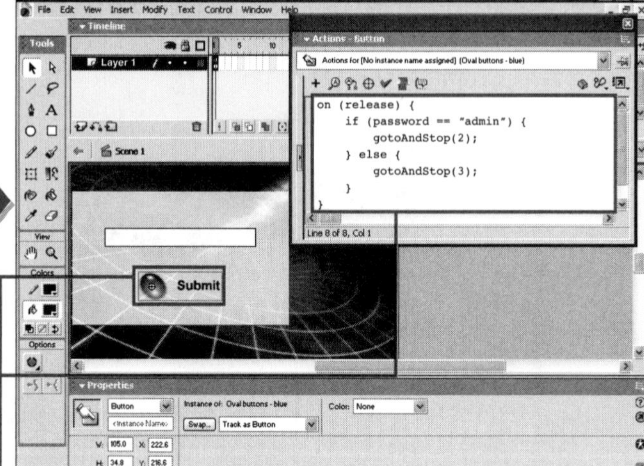

6 Create a submit button for the Password Identification feature.

7 Select the button.

8 Type the code that verifies the password.

■ This script uses an `if` action to define the string that the password must match.

■ In this example, the password admin is used.

Is the password protection 100 percent secure?

✔ No. A user can play through a Flash movie and disregard the `stop` actions. If you want to be completely secure, introduce a separate movie with the secret information and tell it to play during the `if` statement in the password movie. This way, if the user has disregarded the stop action, they still need the password to start the movie.

Can I create a Password Identification Box as a movie clip?

✔ Yes. Creating the Password Identification box as a movie clip symbol allows the designer greater flexibility. This method will allow you to utilize the same Password Identification feature at different points throughout your movie.

Does Flash MX have any premade buttons I can use?

✔ Yes. You do not have to create your own buttons to use in your Flash MX projects. You can use the buttons available in the Buttons Library. Click the Window menu and select Common Libraries, Buttons. This opens the Buttons Library and you can choose a button to assign.

Can I test my movie on the Stage without using the Flash Player window?

✔ You can test animations on the Stage, but it is best to test the movie in the Player Window to see what the user sees.

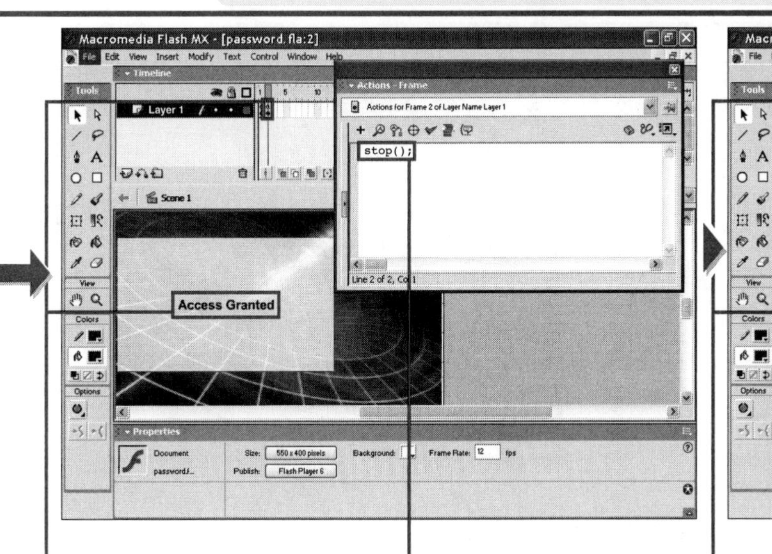

9 Add a keyframe to frame 2.

10 Add a static text box to the Stage that tells users that they have entered the correct password and now have access.

11 Type **stop ( ) ;** to assign a `stop` action to frame 2.

12 Add a keyframe to frame 3.

13 Add a static text box to the Stage that tells users that they have entered an incorrect password.

14 Assign a `stop` action to frame 3.

■ You can test your movie in the player window. Once you enter and submit a password, the movie will go to frame 2 if correct or frame 3 if incorrect.

COMBINE STRINGS GIVEN BY A USER

You can gather strings of data entered by the user and combine them to create a uniform statement. A string is a sequence of values, typically characters or numbers, that can be manipulated as a group in a programming script. You can join, or concatenate, strings to create an expression.

In the example in this section, you produce a variation of the family favorite *Mad Libs* and prompt the user for an adjective, a number, and a planet name and display a sentence using those words in it. This technique has an infinite amount of variations, including user identification and simplification of information.

The steps in this section involve the use of editable text fields, also called variable text fields, and the `Set variable` action. The `Set variable` action is assigned to a button to generate an expression using the values entered by the user. When you add a `Set variable` action, the `on (release)` event is added to the script automatically. You use static text boxes to give the user instructions on what to enter in the variable text fields.

You can format the variable text fields by using the text formatting options found in Flash MX. To learn more about formatting text, see Chapter 24.

COMBINE STRINGS GIVEN BY A USER

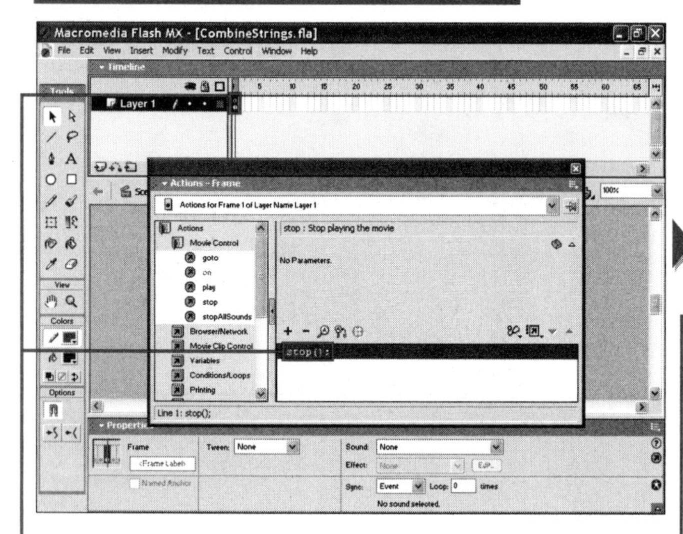

Note: To view a completed example, see the file CombineStrings.fla on the CD that accompanies this book.

1 In the Actions panel, add a `stop` action to frame 1 of the movie to which you want to add a combine strings technique.

■ You can close or minimize the Actions panel to better see the Stage for the next steps.

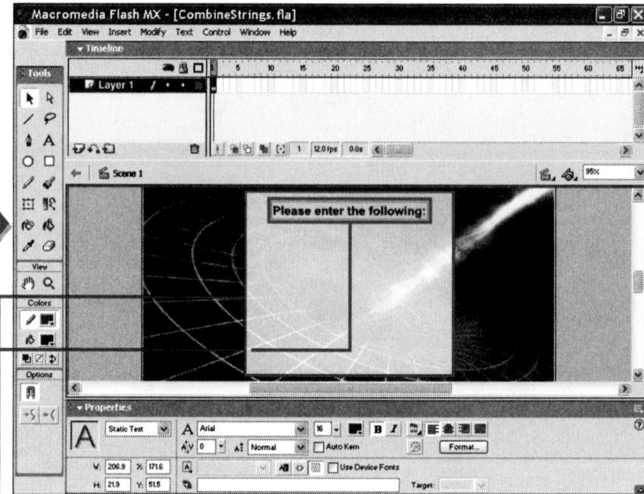

2 Create a box shape with a fill color.

Note: To draw and fill shapes, see Chapter 21.

3 Create a static text box at the top of the fill shape and type a set of instructions based on your movie.

■ In this example, the instructions read Please enter the following:.

Note: To add a text box, see page 416.

How long can the expression sentence be?

✔ There is no limit to the amount of text that goes into the expression, but you have to look out for two things: the punctuation as the expression gets longer is more difficult to troubleshoot, and the text field that holds the value has to correspond to the length of the expression or else text is cut off.

What can the user input into the text fields?

✔ They can basically put anything into the text fields. If you want to limit the possibilities that they can input, you must include an `if` action in the button statements telling them to insert a different value (for example, a number if they did not enter a number).

Why must I set text box types?

✔ Assign text types to your text boxes to tell Flash MX how to treat the boxes. You can choose from three different text types: static, dynamic, or input. Use static text for text that does not change in your movie. Use dynamic and input boxes for text boxes that reflect input or action statement results. You can change text box type using the drop-down list in the Property inspector. Be sure to select the text box first in order to view the properties for the text box listed in the Property inspector. To learn more about adding text boxes to your movies, see Chapter 24.

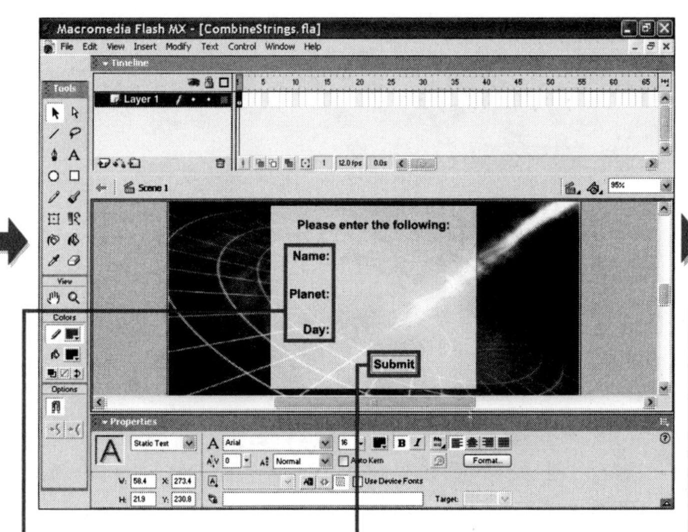

4 To the left side of the box, add three static text boxes, each containing a variable name.

■ In this example, the static text boxes contain Name, Planet, and Day as their variable names.

Note: Leave enough space for editable text fields to the right of the variable names.

5 At the bottom of the fill shape, add a static text box containing the word **Submit**.

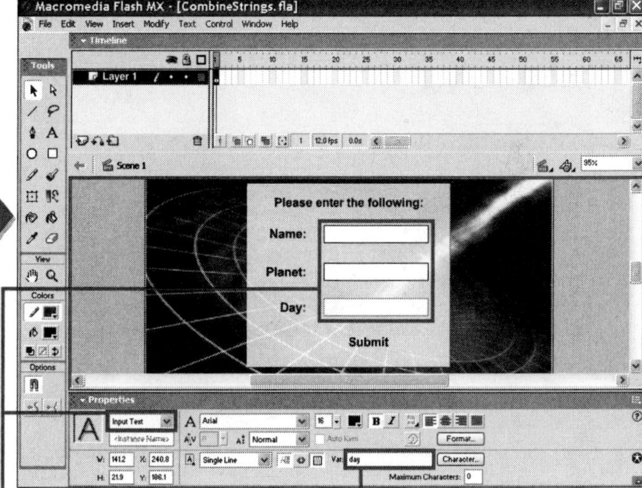

6 Add three input text boxes to the fill shape box, one beside each variable name.

7 In the Property inspector, click ▾ to assign each box Input Text type status.

8 Assign Variable names for each input text box, using the names you assigned in step 4.

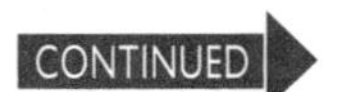

CONTINUED

COMBINE STRINGS GIVEN BY A USER (CONTINUED)

Text strings are a common type of variable value used in Flash MX actions. The term *string* is used in many programming languages, including Flash's ActionScript, to specify text values.

Text strings can use letters, spaces, punctuation, and numbers. For example, you may have a text string that asks the user something like *How are you today?* or *What is your favorite color?* You must enclose string values in quote marks, such as

```
lucky number = "7";
```

You can use the + operator to join strings. In the following statement, a personal greeting is generated.

```
greeting = "Hello," +
firstName;
```

Although lowercase and uppercase characters are not an issue in variable names, they are important in text strings. Text strings are literal, so if you type **HELLO**, the user sees all caps, but if you type **Hello**, the user sees an initial cap.

When using punctuation in a text string, be sure to include a space where necessary. In the greeting example, a comma follows the Hello string value, and a space appears before the end quote mark. Without the space, the word Hello would run into the user name:

```
Hello,Jane
```

instead of

```
Hello, Jane
```

COMBINE STRINGS GIVEN BY A USER (CONTINUED)

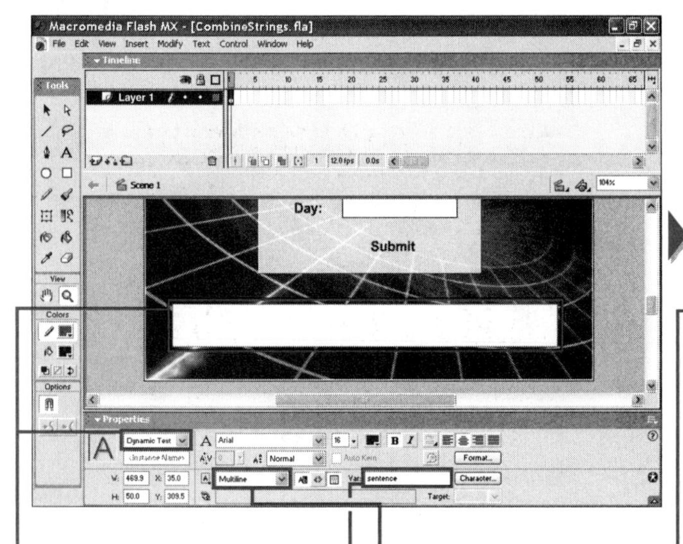

9 Add another text box field, outside of the filled shape, on the lower portion of the stage.

10 In the Property inspector, click ▾ to set the new text box's type to Dynamic Text.

11 Click ▾ to set the Line Type to Multiline.

12 Assign the Variable name **sentence**.

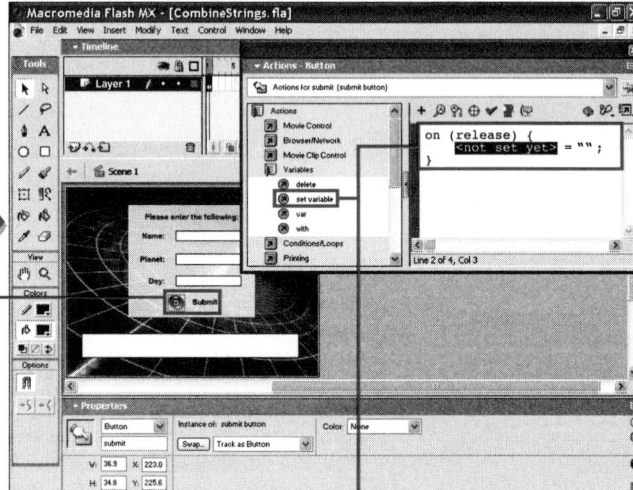

13 Create a new button or insert a button from the Buttons Library, placing it near the text box containing the word Submit.

Note: To create a button, see page 462.

14 In the Actions panel, add the `Set Variable` action to the button.

■ Flash MX automatically adds the `On (Release)` statement.

Can the user change the variables in the sentence after it is printed?

✔ After the Submit button has been pressed, the user can input different answers into the fields to change the sentence. Also, the designer can clear the text boxes after the Submit button has been pushed by adding another `Set variable` action for every variable you want cleared. Leave the value for these blank.

How do I include a quote mark in my text string if quote marks are essential to the expression?

✔ You can precede quotation marks with a backslash (\) character in the expression to include the special characters in your actual text string.

What if I include punctuation in my sentence that does not appear in the SWF file?

✔ This can happen if you have not embedded the needed font outlines in your Flash movie. To check which font outlines have been included, select the text box, and click the Character button in the Property inspector. This will open the Character Options dialog where you can select which font outlines you would like embedded in the movie.

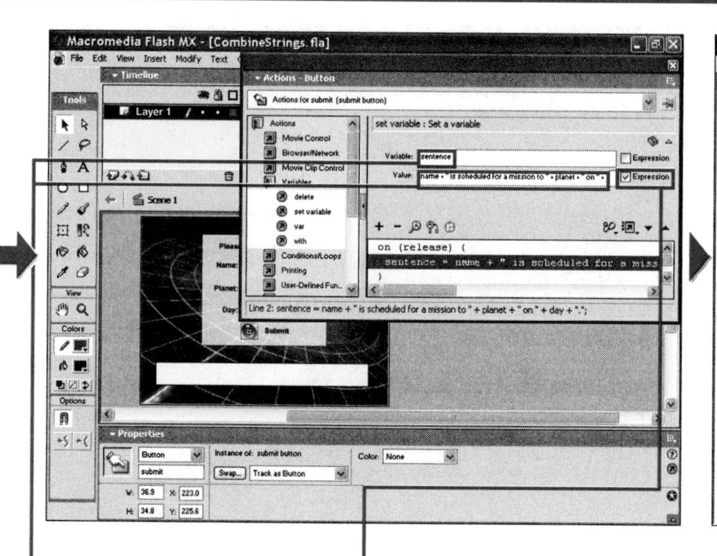

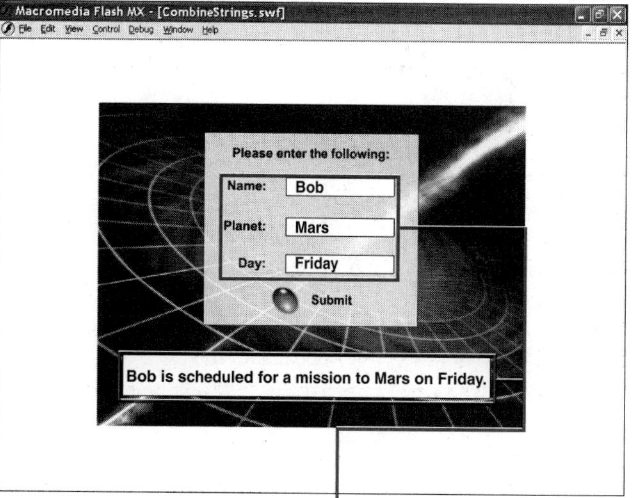

15 In the Variable field, type **sentence**.

16 In the Value field, type the expression **name + " is scheduled for a mission to " + planet + " on " + day + "."**

Note: Make sure that the punctuation is correct or else it may not read correctly.

■ Make sure the Expression check box is selected for the value.

■ You can now test your movie in the Flash Player window to see how the text string works.

Note: To test movies in the Flash Player window, see page 630.

■ When you type variable text into the text boxes and click the Submit button, the text string should result in a silly sentence.

REPLICATE A MOVIE RANDOMLY OR BY COMMAND

You can replicate a movie clip in a Flash MX movie to replay automatically in random areas on the Stage or by command. *Replicate* means to duplicate the movie clip either by a preprogrammed control or by a control activated by the user, such as a click of a button. One of the most common uses for this technique is in games you create in Flash MX. With a little imagination, you might come up with some other ways to employ this technique on a Web site or in a stand-alone Flash presentation.

A replicating movie plays in random positions on the Flash Stage. For example, when the user clicks the designated button, the clip duplicates itself and starts playing again in another area of the Stage while the first clip continues playing on its own.

When creating a movie clip to use as your replicating movie, try to create a clip that clearly shows some sort of animated action. The clip does not need to be very long in length.

The steps in this section involve using the `Duplicate Movie Clip` action as well as the `Set Variable` and `Properties` actions along with the `Random` expression to create a random replication effect.

REPLICATE A MOVIE RANDOMLY OR BY COMMAND

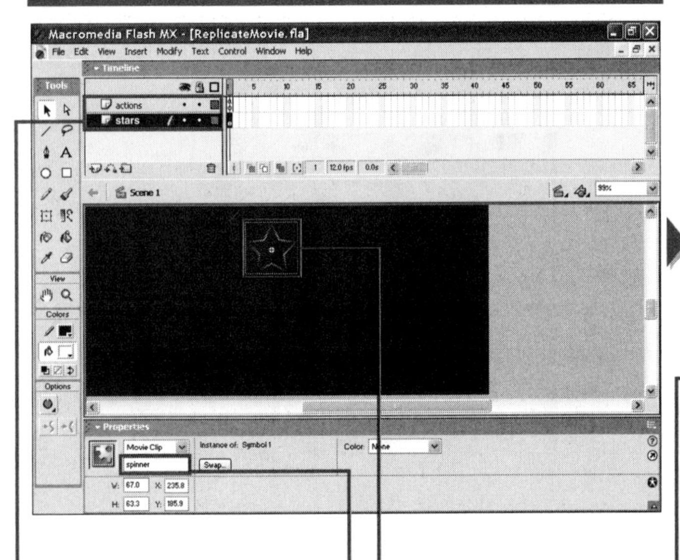

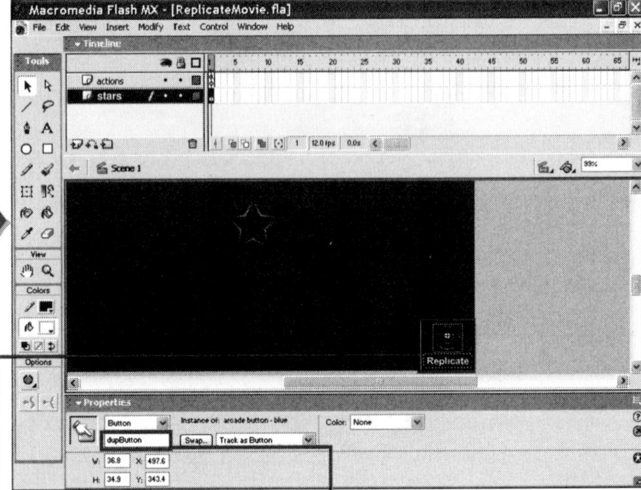

Note: To view a completed example, see the file ReplicateMovie.fla on the CD that accompanies this book.

1 In a new movie, create two layers named **action** and **stars**.

2 Place an instance of the movie clip you want to use as the replicating clip on the Stage.

3 In the Property inspector, assign an instance name to the movie clip.

4 Create a new button or use one from the Buttons Library and place it on the Stage.

Note: To create a button, see page 462.

Note: To use the Library, see page 448.

5 In the Property inspector, assign an instance name to the button.

Can I change other properties, too?

✔ Yes. You can change any of the properties (alpha, rotation, and so on) and randomize them as well, just by adding the `set property` value. To learn more about changing movie clip properties, see page 608.

Where can I learn more about writing ActionScript statements?

✔ Flash MX installs with help files dedicated to ActionScript. To access these files, click the Help menu and click ActionScript Dictionary. You can also use the Flash tutorials to help you learn more about ActionScript.

What do the numbers in the random statements mean?

✔ They are numbers that the random program can select between 0 and one less than the number you specify. 550 and 400 were selected because they were the dimensions of the default movie. You can make this number whatever you would like.

If you want to make a range not including 0, use this expression:

`Random(400)+75`

This creates a range between 75 and 475 to duplicate it in.

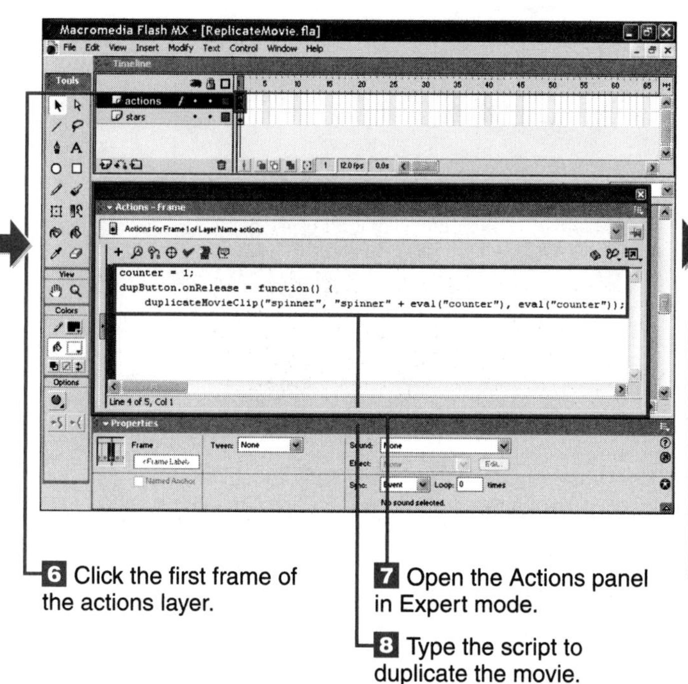

6 Click the first frame of the actions layer.

7 Open the Actions panel in Expert mode.

8 Type the script to duplicate the movie.

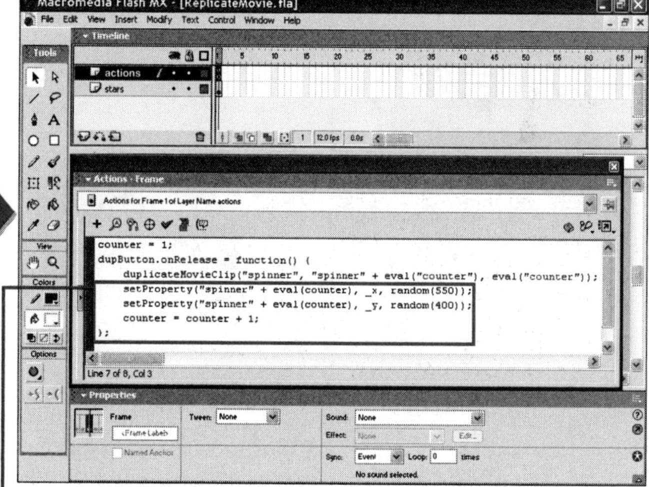

9 To set a random location for the duplicated movie clip, type the code to set new x and y coordinate values.

■ You can test the movie to see the effect.

Note: To test movies in the Flash Player window, see page 630.

MAKE A MOVIE CLIP ACT LIKE A BUTTON

You can make a movie clip act like a button that the user clicks to interact with the movie. You can use this technique in a number of ways, one of which is in a game scenario. For example, perhaps your Flash MX game uses a moving target that, when clicked, changes the action of the movie or adds to a list of hits. You could also make the clip act like a button for a stoppable movie embedded in another movie.

What makes this technique possible is that a movie clip can have a scripted response to many of the same events that a button uses to trigger an action. In the steps below, a `mouseDown` event is used to trigger an action. When the user clicks the movie clip, Flash MX is instructed to replace the clip with another clip. This action is assigned in order for a nested movie clip to change frames, or do whatever you, as the designer, want.

To make the switch occur, you must assign instance names to both the trigger clip and the replacement clip. Without instance names, Flash MX cannot tell on which clip to perform the action.

MAKE A MOVIE CLIP ACT LIKE A BUTTON

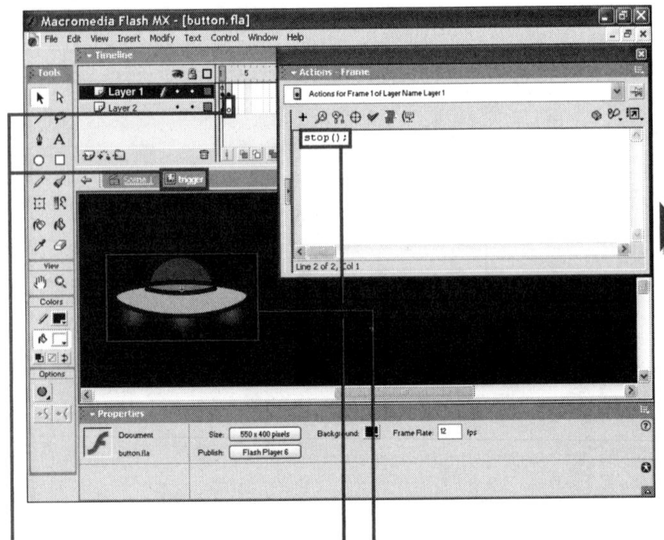

Note: To view a completed example, see the file button.fla on the CD that accompanies this book.

1 Create a movie clip symbol named **trigger**.

2 Insert a blank keyframe into frame 2.

3 In frame 1, create the object that you want to animate across the Stage and use to trigger the event.

4 Add a `stop` action to frame 1.

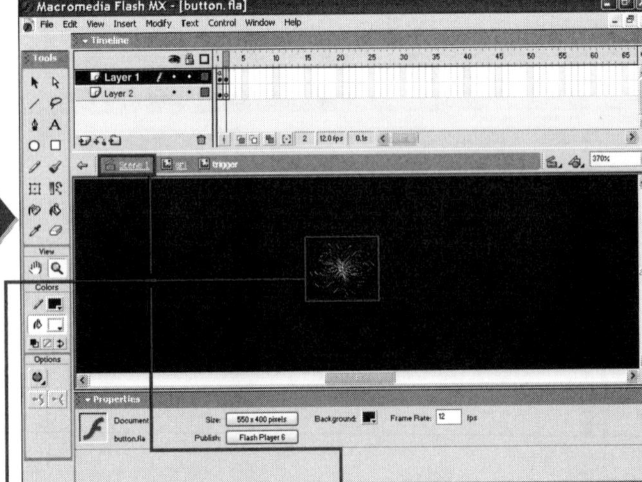

5 In frame 2, create the object, or insert the movie clip, that will appear after the user selects the object.

■ In this example, a click triggers an explosion graphic.

6 Click the scene name to return to the main movie.

Could I achieve a similar technique by using a button symbol?

✔ Yes. In this example, a button symbol could be used to trigger the event. In order for this technique to work, you need to nest the button within the movie clip. This will allow the button to follow the movie clip objects when animated.

Is there a faster way to switch between Normal and Expert modes in the Actions panel?

✔ Yes. You can press Ctrl+Shift+N (⌘+Shift+N) to quickly switch to Normal mode in the Actions panel. Press Ctrl+Shift+E (⌘+Shift+E) to switch to Expert mode.

Are there action events for movie clips that are not available for buttons?

✔ Yes. The movie clip symbol also uses the `Load`, `Enter Frame`, `Unload`, `Data` events. The `Load`, `Enter Frame`, and `Unload` events transpire automatically while the movie is playing, and they always occur in this order. The `Data` event occurs when a movie clip has received data from an external source.

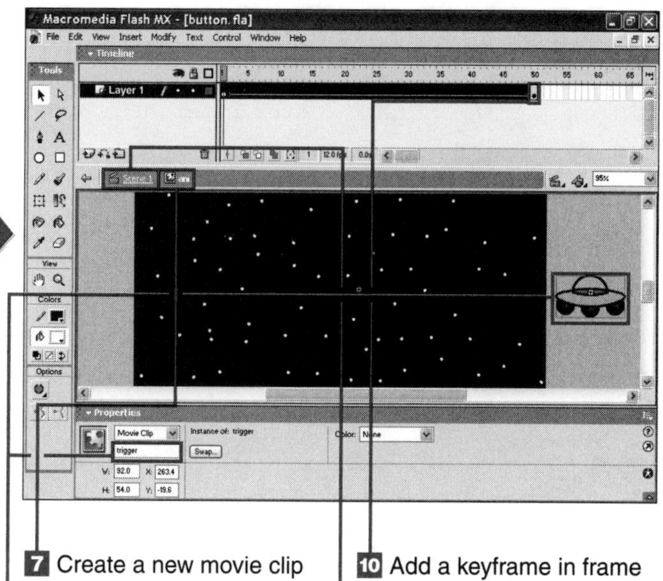

7 Create a new movie clip named **ani**.

8 Place an instance of the movie clip trigger on the right of the Stage.

9 In the Property inspector, assign the instance name as **trigger**.

10 Add a keyframe in frame 50, and move the instance to the left side of the stage.

11 Click the scene name to return to the main movie timeline.

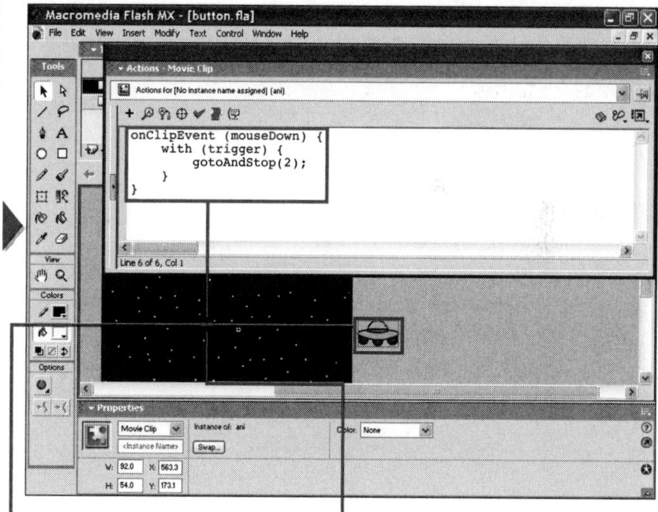

12 Place an instance of the movie clip ani on the Stage.

13 Select the ani instance.

14 Open the Actions panel in Expert mode.

15 Type the code that triggers Flash to replace the clip with another clip when clicked.

■ You can test the effect in the Flash Player window.

CREATE A GRAVITY EFFECT

You can create a gravity effect and attach it to an object or objects in your Flash MX movie. A gravity effect creates the illusion that a particular object on the Stage adheres to the laws of gravity. The user moves the object, and it immediately drops back to the bottom of the Stage with diminishing bounces as if controlled by gravity.

This is an interesting effect that you may wish to add to a game in which you want objects to appear to be affected by gravity. Not only can you use this technique in games, you can add this technique to objects in your Flash movie for the Web. For example, perhaps you are creating a Flash animation advertising an athletic store. You can attach the gravity effect to a basketball and have it bounce across the screen.

To build this effect following the steps in this section, you use a button to act as the object affected by gravity, then convert the button into a movie clip symbol. You can apply the same gravity effects to other objects you create in Flash MX, not just buttons.

CREATE A GRAVITY EFFECT

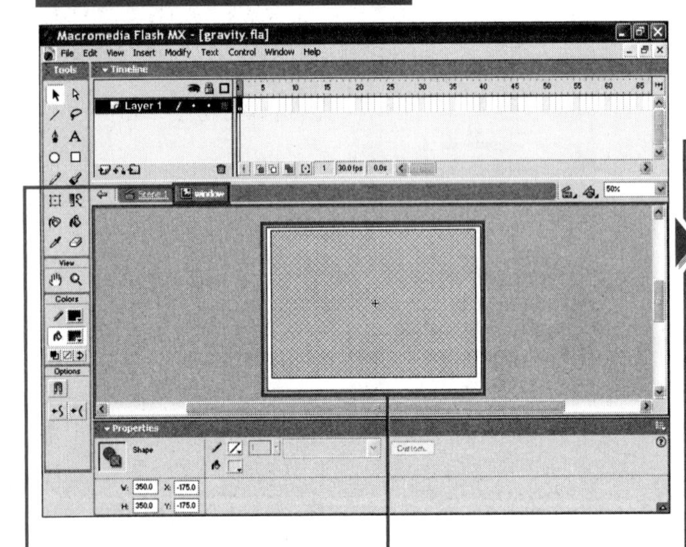

Note: To view a completed example, see the file gravity.fla on the CD that accompanies this book.

1 Create 3 layers and name as **ballplane**, **ball**, and **actions**.

2 Create a new movie clip and name as **window**.

3 In frame 1 of the movie clip, draw a rectangle 350 x 350 pixels.

■ You will use the rectangle size coordinates when setting x and y positions later in action statements.

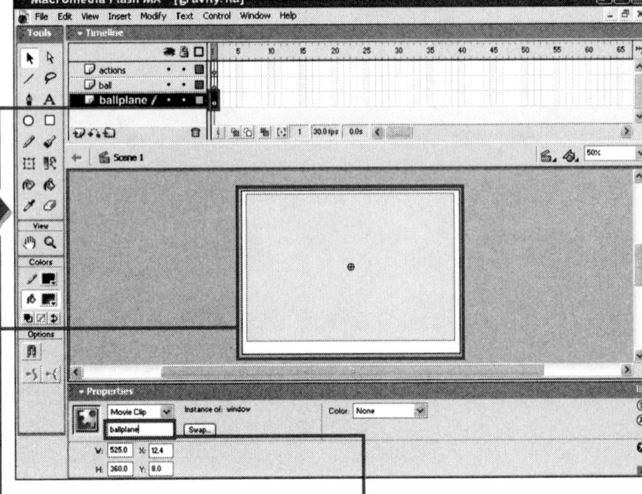

4 Return to the main movie and add the clip to the Stage in frame 1 of the ballplane layer.

Note: To add instances using the Library window, see page 454.

5 In the Property inspector, name the clip instance **ballplane**.

Can I change the way gravity affects the objects in my movie?

✔ Yes. By changing certain variable values you can change the way gravity affects your objects. You can change the gravity effect by increasing the gravity so the ball does not bounce nearly as much or not at all. You could also decrease the gravity effect so the ball is almost experiencing weightlessness. By making the gravity variable negative, you would make the ball bounce on the top part of the window rather than the bottom.

Where can I find the gravity constant?

✔ The gravity constant is found in frame 1 of the actions layer. By looking at the code used in this example, you discover that the gravity constant is 4. Another variable that affects the way the gravity works is the bounce variable. The closer the bounce variable gets to the value of 1, the more bounces you get before the ball stops. If the bounce variable is set to 1, the ball continuously bounces; if it is set to 0, the ball does not bounce at all.

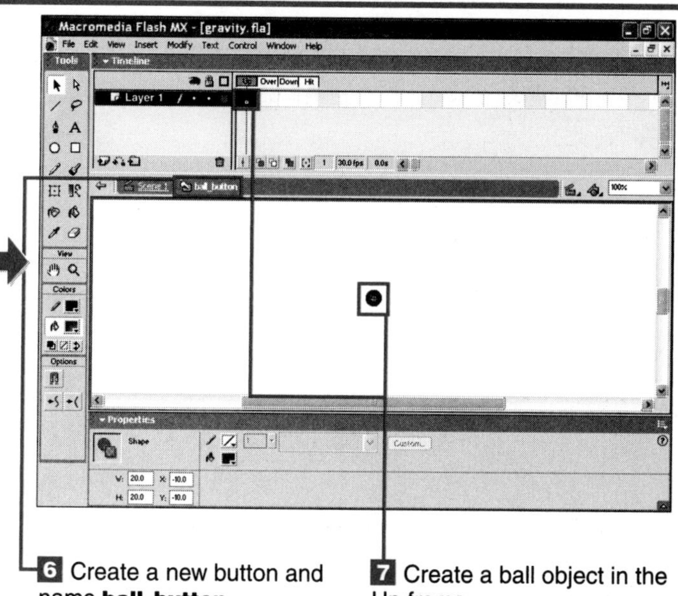

6 Create a new button and name **ball_button**.

Note: To create a button, see page 462.

7 Create a ball object in the Up frame.

■ This example shows a 20 x 20 pixel circle with a blue radial gradient fill.

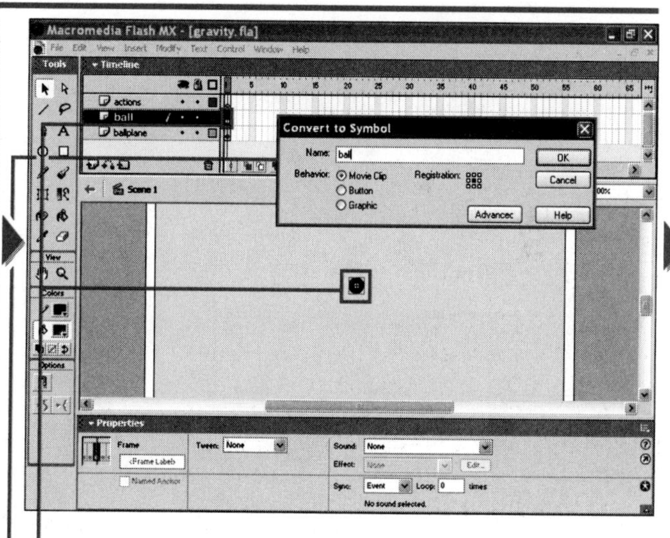

8 Return to the main movie and place an instance of the button into frame 1 of the ball layer.

9 Convert the ball button to a movie clip symbol and name it **ball**.

■ You can press F8 to quickly open the Convert to Symbol dialog box.

Note: To learn more about creating symbols in Flash MX, see Chapter 26.

CONTINUED

CREATE A GRAVITY EFFECT (CONTINUED)

You can write an ActionScript to develop a gravity effect for a selected object. Utilizing the `startDrag` action and setting position coordinates in the movie, you can build a script that controls the illusion of bounce for the object. In the example below, the script is attached to a raquetball-shaped object. When the racquetball is moved onto the window, the ball bounces up and down, eventually coming to a stop on the bottom.

When entering script code in the Actions panel, it is very important you type the code exactly as shown. Any mistakes you type will affect the outcome of the technique. Use Expert mode to type the statements in the Actions panel.

You can alter the ActionScript controlling the gravity effect to create your own custom gravity effect. Maybe you want your gravity to work by attracting things to the left of a screen, or maybe you want your gravity to effect things in a diagonal motion — the number of effects you can achieve is endless.

If you want to get really creative and advanced, you can take this movie and manipulate it into a miniature basketball or ball toss game. If you are into creating games, this is an important technique to learn because gravity affects everything.

CREATE A GRAVITY EFFECT (CONTINUED)

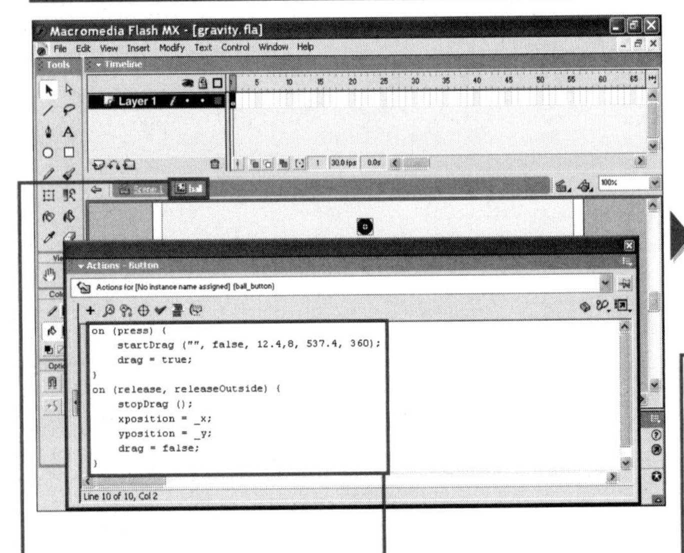

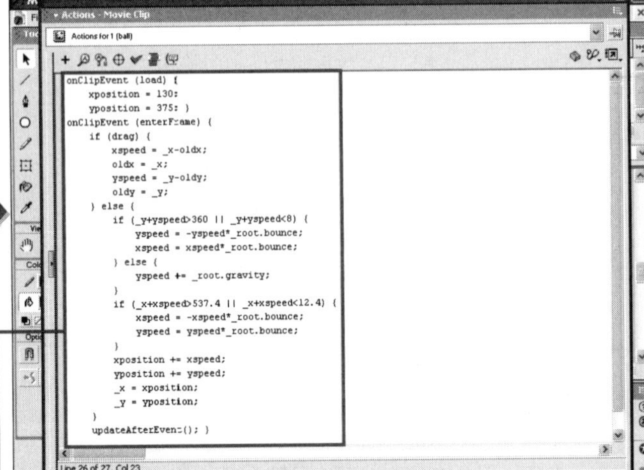

10 Open the ball movie clip in symbol-edit mode.

■ You can double-click the clip to quickly display the clip in symbol-edit mode.

11 Select frame 1.

12 Open the Actions panel in Expert mode and type the ActionScript shown in this figure.

■ You can press F9 to quickly open the Actions panel.

13 Return to the main movie and select the ball movie clip.

14 Open the Actions panel in Expert mode and type the ActionScript shown in this figure.

Note: You can resize the Actions panel to see more of the script pane. To learn more about the Actions panel, see page 576.

Note: To write ActionScripts, see Chapter 31.

How can I get the ball to bounce when I play my movie?

✔ If your movie does not work properly, there is probably an error in the code or a problem with one of the symbols. Because this technique contains many variables, the most likely place for errors to occur is in the code. You should check your code thoroughly for typos and other errors. You can use the Flash debugger to easily check your code. To use the debugger, see page 612. If, after you have reviewed your code and corrected any typos, your movie still fails to work, you should check the symbols. Verify that all symbols are correctly labeled and that each symbols is assigned the proper action.

Can I test ActionScripts on smaller test movies before adding them to my main movie?

✔ Yes. To save yourself a lot of frustration, you may want to develop a small movie to test little pieces of your ActionScript on while developing the main movie. Experiment with the ActionScript on the small movie until you are comfortable adding it to your main movie. Chances are that you will discover syntax errors as you test individual pieces of code on smaller movies before implementing them in your main movie.

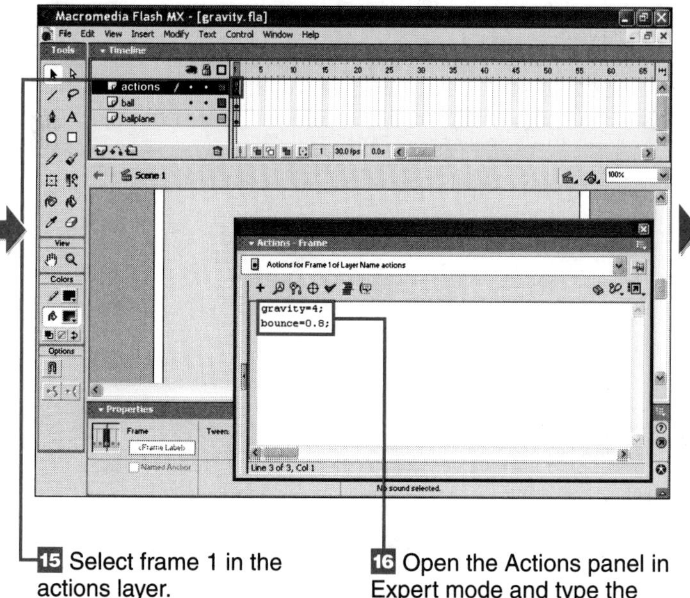

15 Select frame 1 in the actions layer.

16 Open the Actions panel in Expert mode and type the ActionScript shown in this figure.

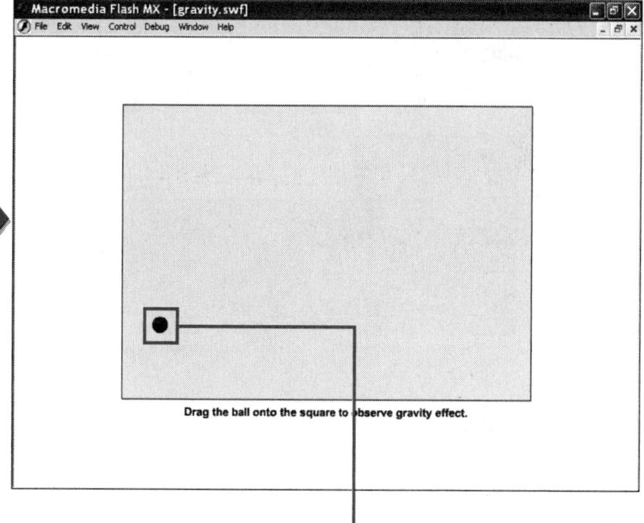

■ You can test the effect in the Flash Player window to see how the gravity effect works.

■ Drag the ball to the window area and drop it to see the gravity effect.

Note: To test movies in the Flash Player window, see page 630.

CREATE A MAGNIFYING GLASS EFFECT

You can create a magnifying glass effect that allows the user to magnify portions of your movie. Using the technique of masking layers, you can create the illusion of magnifying portions of an underlying image. The masking feature enables you to hide certain parts of your movie and make certain parts visible at a given time.

Basically, two layers are involved when masking: the content layer and the mask layer. You use the mask layer to hide the content layer. In order to see what is in the content layer, you need to create a window in your mask layer. Any shape, image, or content placed in the mask layer acts as a window to the content layer beneath it.

Mask layers appear with a unique icon on the movie Timeline and are always linked to the layer directly below the mask layer. To create a mask layer, see page 444.

In the steps below, the lens of a magnifying glass graphic acts as a mask in the movie. The lens shape is linked to the enlarged background image as a mask layer, enabling the lens to become a window to the enlarged background image.

CREATE A MAGNIFYING GLASS EFFECT

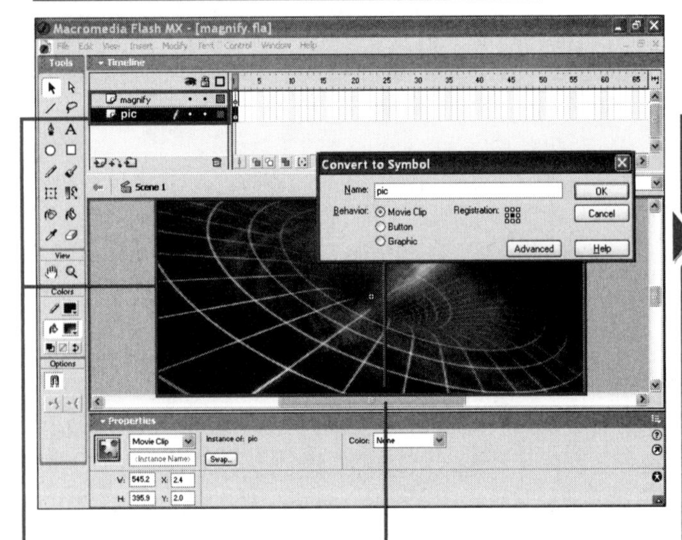

Note: To view a completed example, see the file magnify.fla on the CD that accompanies this book.

1 Create two layers and name as **magnify** and **pic**.

2 Add the image to be used as the magnified view to frame 1 of the pic layer.

3 Convert the image to a movie clip symbol and name as **pic**.

■ You can press F8 to open the Convert to Symbol dialog box.

Note: To learn more about creating symbols in Flash MX, see Chapter 26.

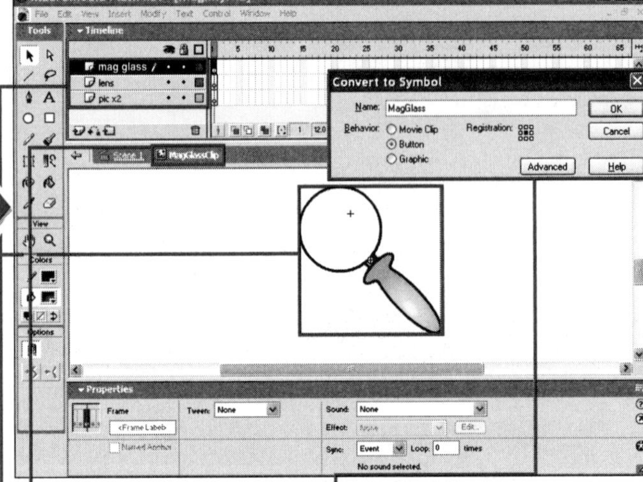

4 Create a new movie clip and name as **MagGlassClip**.

5 Add three layers and name as **mag glass**, **lens**, and **pic x2**.

6 Insert or create a magnifying glass graphic to use as a button into frame 1 of the mag glass layer.

■ The lens of the magnifying glass must not be filled.

7 Convert the magnifying glass to a button symbol and name as **MagGlass**.

■ You can press F8 to quickly open the Convert to Symbol dialog box.

How do I order my layers?

✔ Ordering your layers depends on what you are creating. Remember that any object you place in the top layer covers everything under it. There is no set of rules to how you order your layers, although the background layer should be on the bottom, and action layers are usually found on top because they do not contain any objects.

Should I lock my mask layer?

✔ You can lock the layer if you want to prevent accidental edits. It is good practice to lock your layers once you have created the layer items just the way you want them. You can click the Lock icon (🔒) for any layer to lock and unlock the layer. See Chapter 25 to learn more about layer features.

What is the importance of naming the layers?

✔ When working with small, simple Flash MX movies, you may not see the importance of labeling layers. When you start working with larger, more complex Flash movies, having layers labeled becomes very important. When editing symbols, figuring out what layer the symbol is in may be difficult without labeling. Labeling layers is more of an organizational tool for the creator. Labeling layers can also help others who may work on your Flash movies. To learn more about adding labels to layers, see Chapter 25.

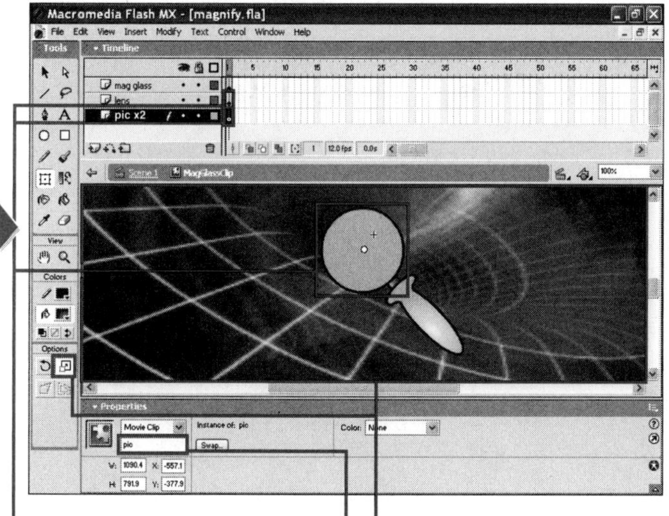

8 In frame 1 of the lens layer, create a filled circle shape the same size and position as the magnifying glass lens.

9 In frame 1 of the pic x2 layer, place an instance of the pic movie clip.

10 Scale the movie clip 200 percent.

■ This enlarges the image to create the magnified view.

11 In the Property inspector, name the instance **pic**.

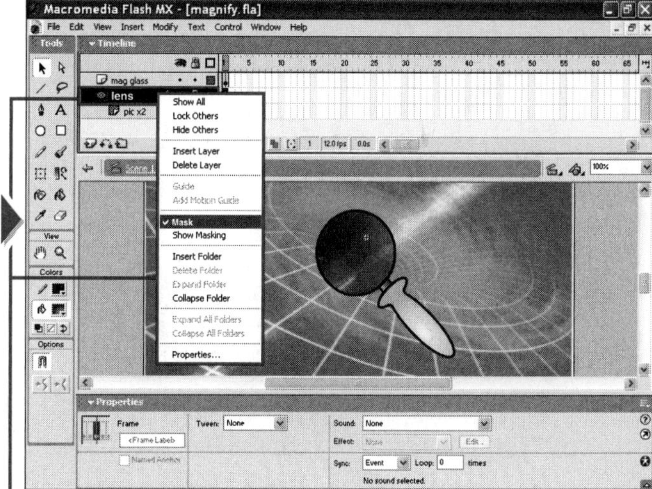

12 Convert the lens layer to a mask layer.

■ You can right-click over the layer and click Mask from the pop-up menu.

Note: To create a mask layer using the Layer Properties dialog box, see page 444.

■ The pic X2 layer will automatically be masked by the lens layer.

CREATE A MAGNIFYING GLASS EFFECT (CONTINUED)

You can turn the magnifying glass object into a draggable button in your movie. You can then use the `On Clip Event` action to define how the button behaves. Using variables for the magnification and coordinates for the clip position on the Stage, you can create a script that enables the user to drag the magnifying glass around the screen.

The key to creating this effect is to have the enlarged picture consistently show the portion of the image directly under the magnifying glass. This appearance is accomplished by dynamically moving the enlarged picture in the opposite direction as the magnifying glass.

The ActionScript contains five main variables — `lastX`, `lastY`, `picMoveX`, `picMoveY`, and `magnification` — that are used to calculate and control the position of both the magnifying glass and the enlarged picture. Variables `lastX` and `lastY` are used to contain the position of the magnifying glass, while the variables `picMoveX` and `picMoveY` contain the position of the enlarged picture. The `magnification` variable contains the factor by which we magnified the image. For example, if magnifier is set to 2, the picture is twice as large as the original. Because the image is twice as large, it must be moved twice as far.

CREATE A MAGNIFYING GLASS EFFECT (CONTINUED)

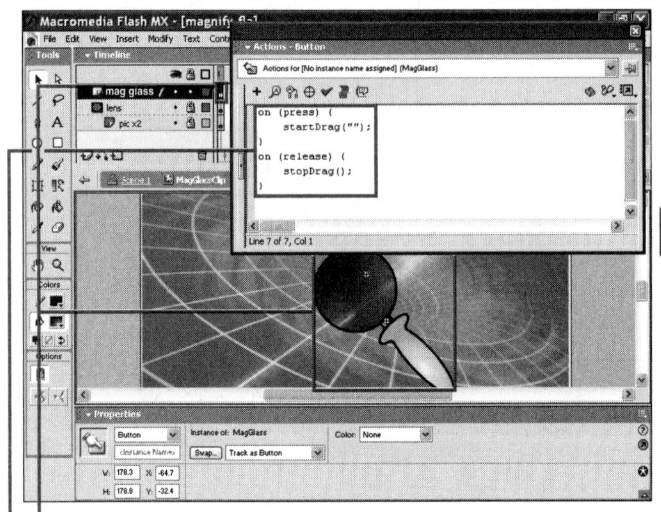

13 Select the magnifying glass button in frame 1 of the mag glass layer.

14 Open the Actions panel in Expert mode and type the ActionScript shown in the figure.

■ You can press F9 to quickly open the Actions panel.

■ This script adds a `startDrag` and `stopDrag` action to the button.

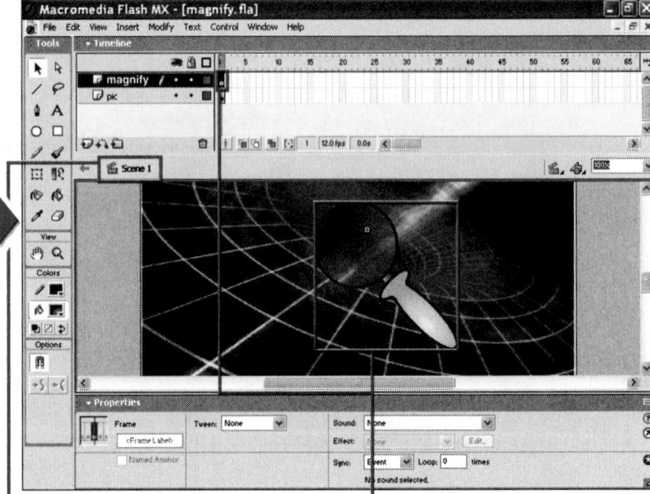

15 Return to the main movie.

■ You can click the Scene name to return to the main movie at any time.

16 Place an instance of the MagGlassClip into frame 1 of the magnify layer.

■ You will see the enlarged image through the lens of the magnifying glass.

What if I want to increase the magnification?

✔ In this example, the image is magnified by 200 percent; you may wish to increase the power of your magnifying glass. To increase the power of your magnifying glass, change the variable in step 10 from 200 percent to a higher number. Also be sure to change the magnification variable in the script used in step 16. For example, if you increase the magnification to 250 percent, change this variable to 2.5. Be aware that when you increase the size of an image, the viewer may not be able to recognize the object anymore. Instead of increasing the size of the image to be magnified, you may want to externally edit the image so that the image quality remains decent.

Do I have to use Expert mode to type in my scripts?

✔ No. You can add actions in Normal mode selecting from action categories and subcategories. If you know the exact script you want to use, you can speed up your script entry by typing it in using Expert mode.

Why have actions in a separate layer?

✔ Creating a layer specifically for assigning actions to frames can help to organize your work better. With all the motion tweens and other things going on in the timeline, a layer devoted just to actions makes finding and editing specific actions easier.

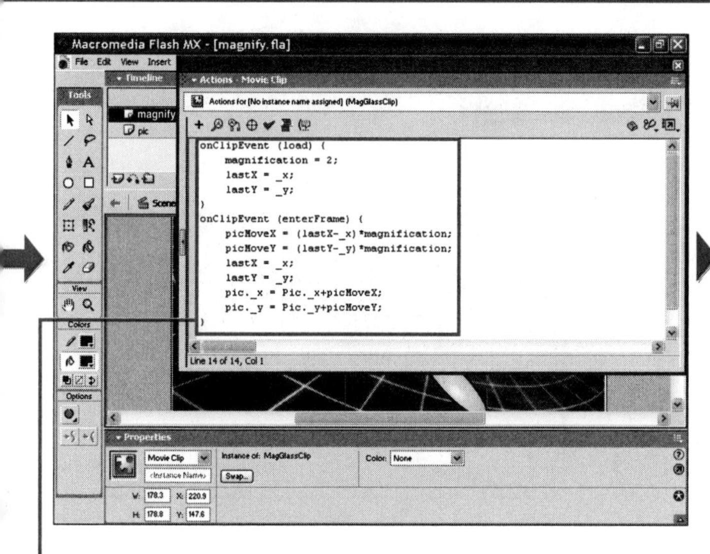

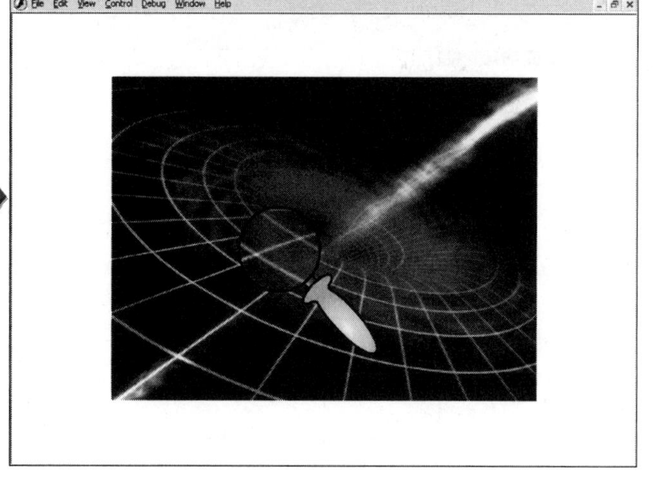

17 Select the MagGlassClip instance.

18 Open the Actions panel in Expert mode and type the ActionScript shown in the figure.

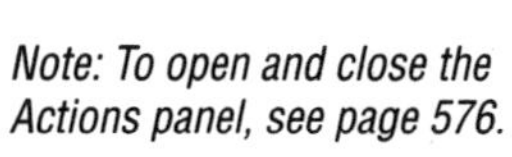
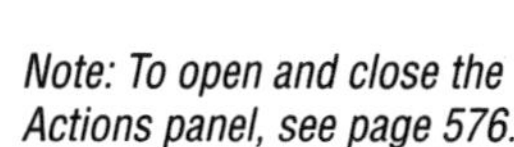

Note: To open and close the Actions panel, see page 576.

■ To see the effect, you can test your movie in the Flash Player window.

■ When you click and drag the magnifying glass, the image under the lens appears to magnify.

Note: To test movies in the Flash Player window, see page 630.

CREATE A FILMSTRIP EFFECT

You can use Flash MX to create a variety of navigational elements for Web pages. One such element is a scrolling bar of images that simulate an animated filmstrip. With a couple of quick ActionScript sequences, you can transform a static bar with images into a moving, eye-catching, effective method to get the attention of anyone visiting your Web site. With a couple of additional steps, the moving bar can become an interactive menu.

This effect works by showing an image and attaching a duplicate of the image to itself in a different level of the Flash MX movie. At any given time, you actually see the original picture and the duplicate of the picture. You cannot tell which image is the real image and which image is the duplicate. By duplicating itself and attaching itself to either end, a seamless, constant flow of images parade across the screen, creating the filmstrip effect.

You can use this technique to present different pages in your Web site, different products offered by your company, different departments in an organization, and so on. Before you begin, you must first decide how many images to use in the filmstrip effect. For best results, use enough images to space across the movie or page width horizontally.

CREATE A FILMSTRIP EFFECT

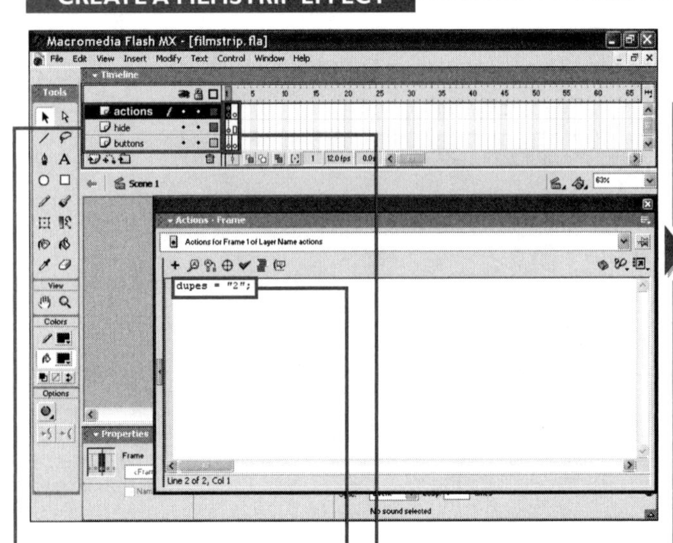

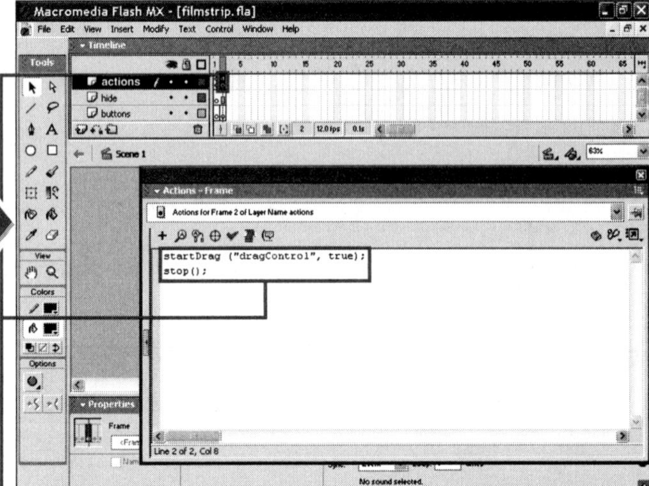

Note: To view a completed example, see the file filmstrip.fla on the CD that accompanies this book.

1. Create three layers and name as **buttons**, **hide**, and **actions**.

2. Add blank keyframes into frames 1 and 2 of each layer.

■ You can press F7 to add blank keyframes.

3. In frame 1 in the actions layer, open the Actions panel in Expert mode and type the script shown.

4. Click on frame 2 of the actions layer.

5. In the Actions panel, type the ActionScript shown in this figure.

Note: To learn more about writing ActionScripts, see Chapter 31.

Can I resize my images to create the filmstrip effect?

✔ Yes, however, use caution when manipulating graphics. Scaling a large image down 10 percent is going to affect the quality of the image when it is smaller. Using many images may drastically increase the loading time of your movie.

How do I collapse the categories pane of the Actions panel?

✔ You can click the narrow arrow button between the categories list and the script pane of the Actions panel to collapse (▼) or expand (▲) the categories list. You can collapse the list to see more of the script pane, or you can expand the list to view action categories and subcategories. The arrow button appears in both Normal and Expert modes.

What image sizes are good to use for the filmstrip effect?

✔ If your images are small, as in the example shown here, be sure to use many images. The effect does not work right with only two or three small images. If you do not have as many images as demonstrated in this example, you can expand the blocks on the side of the filmstrip to show less. Although this example does not work with two or three small pictures, it works with panoramic images.

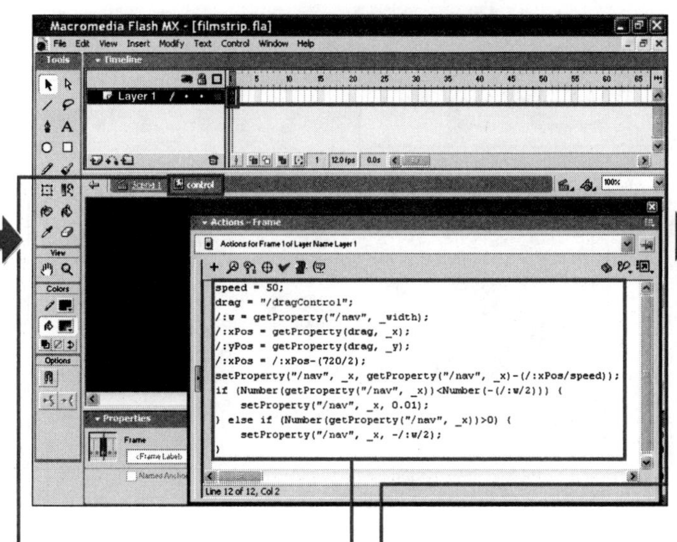

6 Create a new movie clip and name it **control**.

Note: To learn more about creating symbols in Flash MX, see Chapter 26.

7 Click on frame 1 in the control clip timeline.

8 Open the Actions panel in Expert mode and type the script shown in this figure.

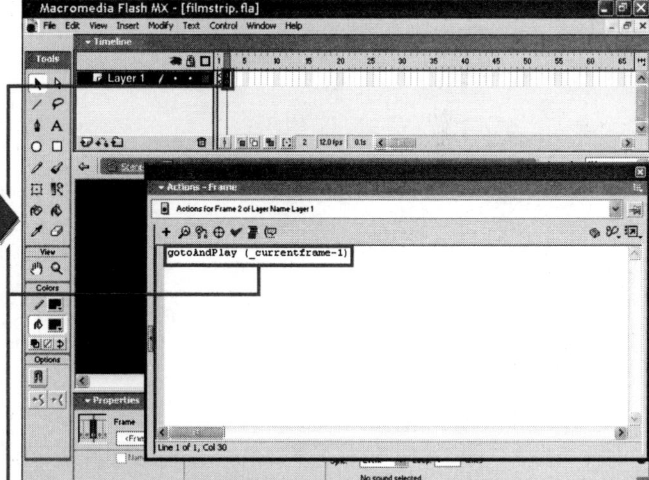

9 Insert a blank keyframe into frame 2.

■ You can press F7 to add a blank keyframe.

10 In the Actions panel, type the ActionScript shown in the figure.

■ You can close or minimize the Actions panel to better see the Stage for the next steps.

Note: To open and close the Actions panel, see page 576.

CONTINUED

CREATE A FILMSTRIP EFFECT (CONTINUED)

In the example shown in this section, the filmstrip effect can scroll horizontally to the left or to the right, depending on where the user moves the mouse pointer in the movie. If you want the filmstrip to move up and down instead of left and right, go into the ActionScript for the movie and change all the _x variables to _y and all of the _y to _x. After changing the code, you have to create a bar that consists of images stacked on top of each other instead of being side by side.

You can turn the filmstrip effect into an interactive menu. Instead of inserting static graphics into your bar, you can insert buttons the user can click to access other pages on your Web site or other actions that pertain to the movie.

In this example, each of the planet images are treated as button symbols. By assigning actions to the buttons, you can create a navigation menu with a filmstrip effect. For example, you may assign a `Get Url` action to each image that, when clicked, sends the user to another Web page.

CREATE A FILMSTRIP EFFECT (CONTINUED)

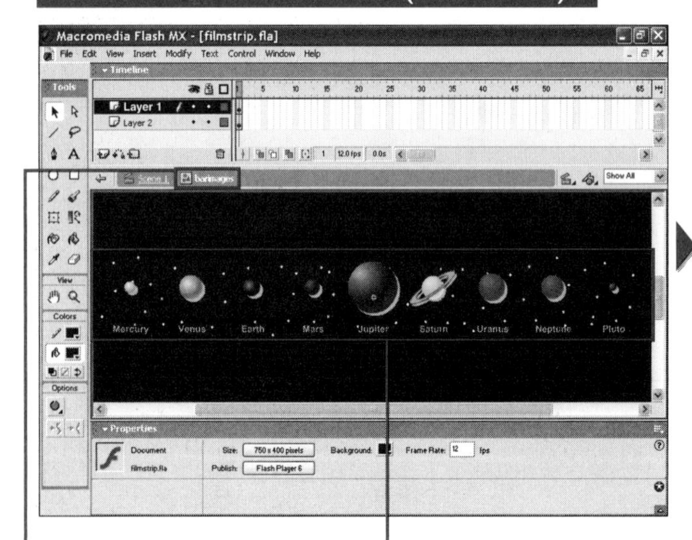

11 Return to the main movie and create a new graphic symbol and name as **bar images**.

■ This graphic is the image bar that scrolls across the screen.

12 Arrange the images as they will appear in the filmstrip.

■ The images will automatically repeat when they scroll.

Note: To learn more about creating symbols in Flash MX, see Chapter 26.

13 Return to the main movie and create a new movie clip symbol and name as **bar**.

14 Place an instance of bar images onto the Stage of the bar movie clip.

15 Return to the main movie and place an instance of the bar clip in frame 2 of the buttons layer.

16 Convert the bar clip to a movie clip and name as **slide bar**.

17 Select the slide bar clip and name the instance **nav**.

Why does the center of the movie clip that controls the direction of scroll seem off.

✔ There is a spot in the code where you need to enter the length, in pixels, of the bar you are scrolling. In frame 1 of the control movie clip there is a line that reads:

```
/:xPos = /:xPos-(720/2);
```

The number 720 is the width of the bar in pixels. You need to change this number to have the correct center point for scrolling.

How do I slow down the speed of this effect?

✔ You can change a variable that controls the speed of your scrolling filmstrip effect. The higher you make the speed variable, the slower your movie scrolls. The lower you make the variable, the faster your movie scrolls.

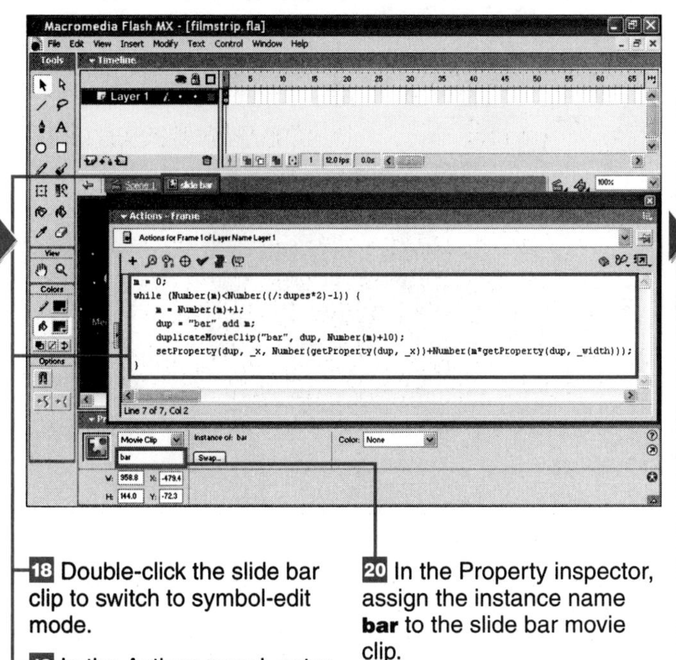

18 Double-click the slide bar clip to switch to symbol-edit mode.

19 In the Actions panel, enter the ActionScript for frame 1 of the slide bar movie clip shown in this figure.

20 In the Property inspector, assign the instance name **bar** to the slide bar movie clip.

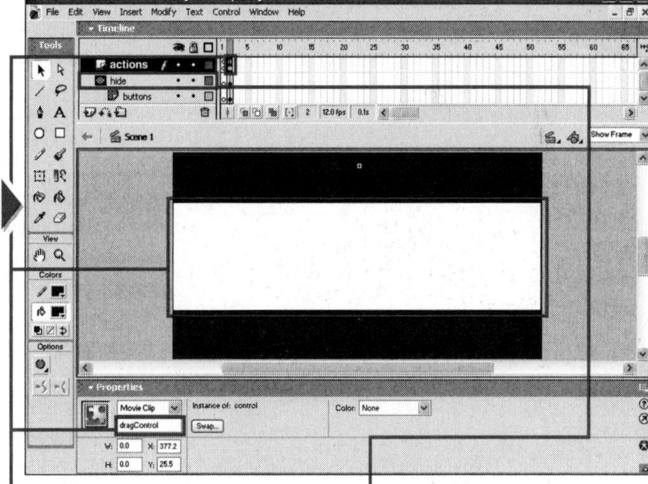

21 Return to the main movie and add the control movie clip to the Stage in frame 2 of the actions layer.

22 Type **dragControl** as the instance name.

23 In frame 2 of the hide layer, create a shape that covers the slide bar.

24 Convert the layer to a mask layer.

■ The hide layer automatically masks the buttons layer.

■ The effect is now ready to test in the Flash Player window.

CREATE A LASER-WRITING ANIMATION EFFECT

You can use Flash MX to create amazing special effects in your movies. In turn, you can place the movies on your Web page to wow your Web site visitors and increase traffic to your site. The laser-writing animation effect illustrated in this section simulates a laser writing text or drawing a simple graphic element. The effect is best used on a single character or illustration. Like text effects, it is important to remember that special effects such as these can increase file size and slow down playback if used in excess.

The following steps explain how to give the illusion that the animation sequence is laser-writing a single character. However, you are actually creating an animation sequence over the top of portions of the character that are revealed at the time the laser point passes over the given section. You can see another example of this special effect demonstrated on the sample Flash-based Web site included in this book. This effect can be seen at the end of the site introduction as the laser-writes the "V" part of the Visual logo. For simplicity's sake, the steps below use a circle instead of a V for the laser-writing effect.

CREATE A LASER-WRITING ANIMATION EFFECT

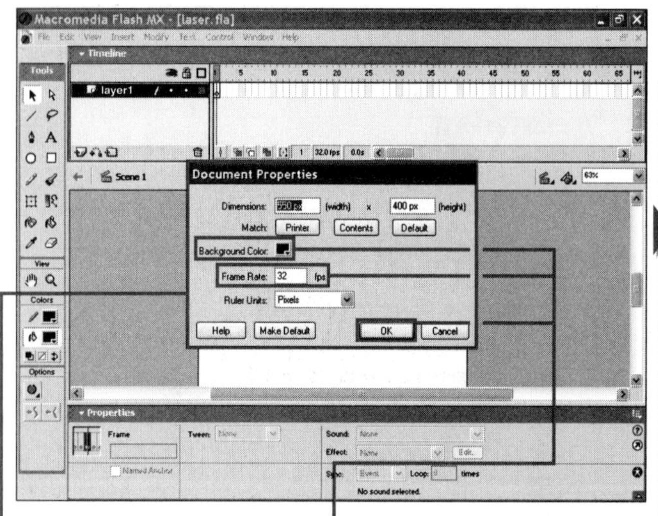

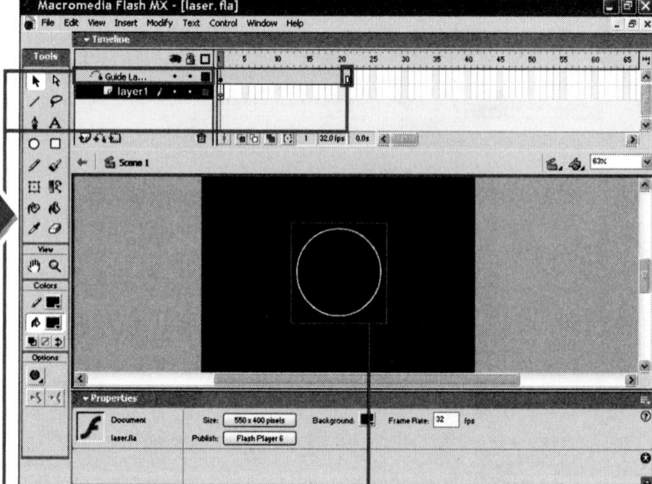

Note: To view a completed example, see the file laser.fla on the CD that accompanies this book.

1 Open the Document Properties dialog box.

■ You can press Ctrl+J (⌘+J) to quickly open the dialog box.

Note: To set movie properties, see page 346.

2 Change the Frame Rate to 32 fps.

3 Change the Background Color to black.

4 Click OK.

5 Add a guide layer to layer 1.

Note: To add a guide layer, see page 442.

6 Add a regular frame to frame 21 of the guide layer.

7 Using white as the outline color, draw a medium-sized circle on the Stage.

■ Do not include a fill with the circle.

■ When using text, choose a heavy, large font for the effect to be visible.

Can I make the laser light point appear to blink?

✔ Yes. You can adjust instance tint to make the effect appear to blink, resulting in a unique effect. To do this, you would convert your laser source to a symbol and modify each instance. For example, in frame 2 of your laser movie, you can insert a keyframe and change the tint of the light source instance to make it darker. Continue alternating tints, light and dark, for each instance of the light source. When you play back your movie, a blinking effect is created as your laser appears to write.

Should I lock my guide layer?

✔ Yes. Locking layers to prevent unnecessary changes — especially guide layers — is a good idea. To lock a layer, simply click the Lock icon bullet to the right of the layer name. A Lock icon appears over the bullet indicating the layer is now locked. You can not edit anything on the layer unless you unlock it again. See Chapter 25 to learn more about working with Flash layers.

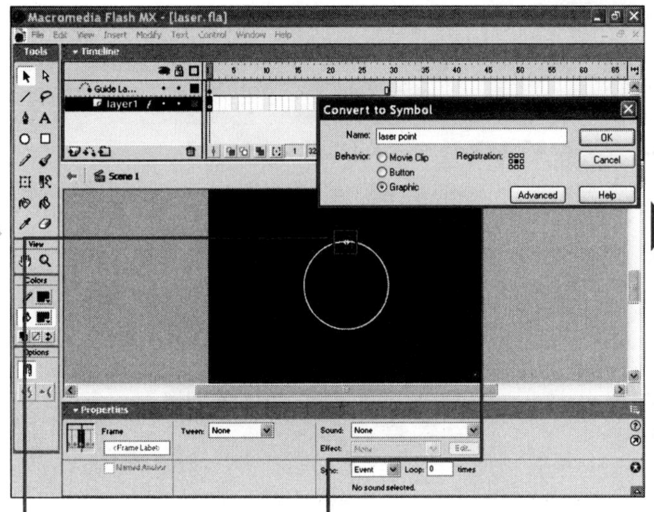

8 In layer 1, frame 1, create a circle shape to use as the laser light point.

■ In this example, the light point uses a gradient fill. The size of the point is about 10 x 10 pixels.

Note: To create a gradient fill, see page 370.

9 Select the laser light point, convert it into a graphic symbol, and name it **laser point**.

Note: To convert symbols, see page 458.

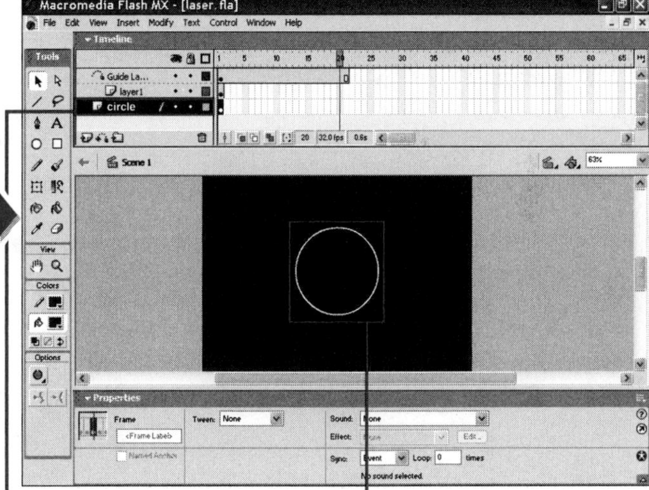

10 Add a new layer to the Timeline and name as **circle**.

Note: To add a layer, see page 432.

11 Copy and paste the circle from the guide layer and place it in the circle layer.

CREATE A LASER-WRITING ANIMATION EFFECT (CONTINUED)

You can use a guide layer for the light point animation which sets the stage for the effect. Guide layers help you position objects on the Stage.

To create the illusion of a point of light, you can animate a symbol in a revolution around the circle representing the character O while revealing three additional circles simultaneously. The actual illusion of a laser writing the O is created with four independently layered elements. The effect is accomplished by revealing portions of the image in each position the light point passes over. You can erase portions of the circle in correspondence with the position of the light point. Upon completion of a full revolution, the frame order of a given erased circle is reversed to represent the laser-writing. Keyframes are inserted in every frame of the circle layer in order that portions of the circle appear at the same rate as the animation of the light point located one layer up from the revealed circle. The sequence on the circle layer is then duplicated and displaced on the Timeline in two additional layers for use with different colored circles. The staggered animations of the three circles illustrate the burning effect of the laser.

CREATE A LASER-WRITING ANIMATION EFFECT (CONTINUED)

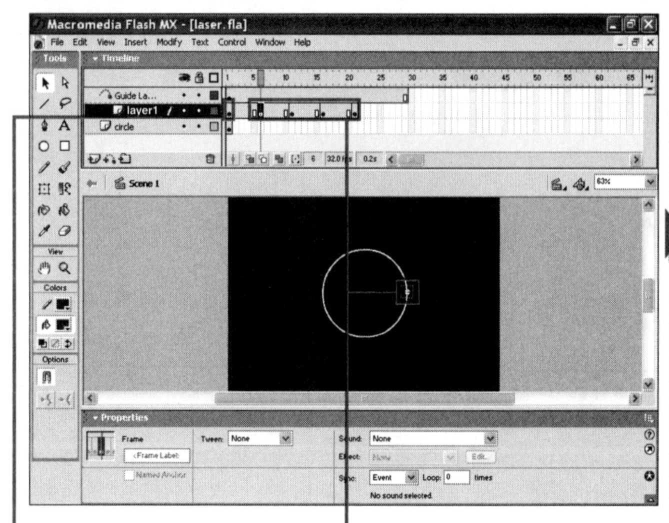

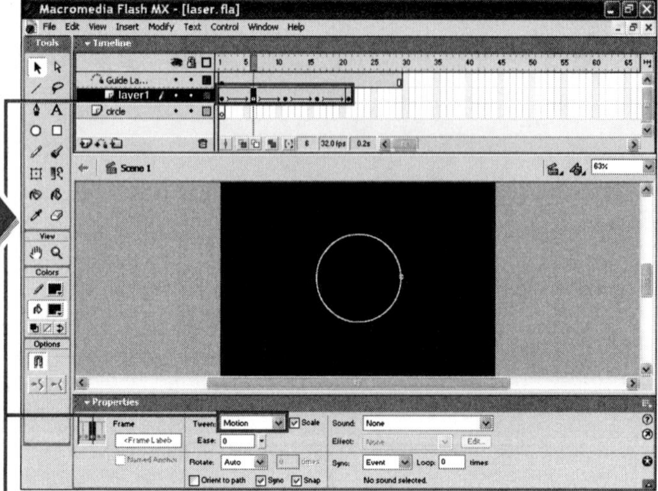

12 In layer 1, frame 1, place an instance of the laser point graphic on the top part of the circle.

Note: To insert an instance, see page 454.

13 Add keyframes to frames 6, 11,16, and 21, and move the laser light point in quarter increments around the circle in each keyframe.

■ For example, in frame 6, move the laser point a quarter around the circle, clockwise.

14 Create a motion tween between each keyframe, starting with frame 1 and ending on frame 21.

Note: To create a motion tween, see page 536.

■ This creates the effect of the laser point making one revolution around the circle.

How precise can I get with positioning content in Flash?

✔ The Info panel contains X and Y coordinate fields that allow you to enter exactly what coordinate you want to place your object on the Stage. Next to the X and Y fields in the panel is a diagram allowing you to pick whether the top, left corner of the object is placed at the coordinates specified or whether the center of the object is placed at the coordinates. If you have a hard time placing objects exactly where you want them using a mouse, this feature can be of great use to you. To open the Info panel, click Window, Info.

Does it matter which way I erase the circle parts?

✔ No. You can use any method you prefer to erase parts of the circle in step 16. You can use the Eraser tool (⌫) or any of its modifiers to erase the lines. To learn more about the available tools for erasing parts of your drawings, see Chapters 21 and 22.

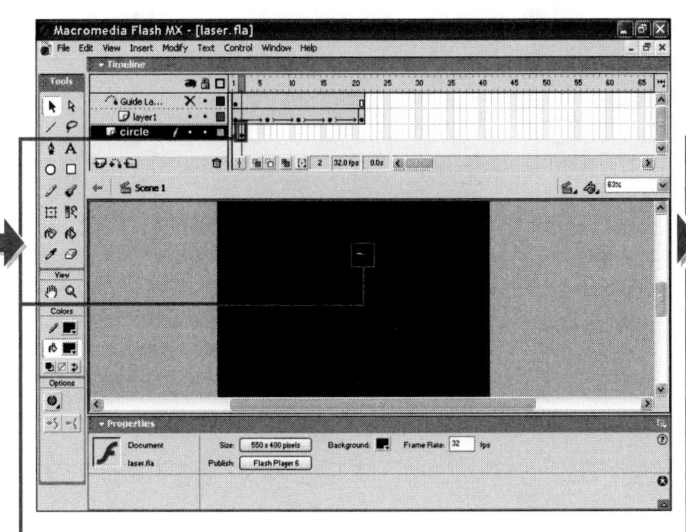

15 In the circle layer, add a new keyframe to frame 2.

16 Select and remove the portion of the circle that the laser has not moved over yet.

■ The easiest way to remove a portion of the circle outline is to use the Arrow tool to create a box around the part of the circle needing to be deleted, and delete it.

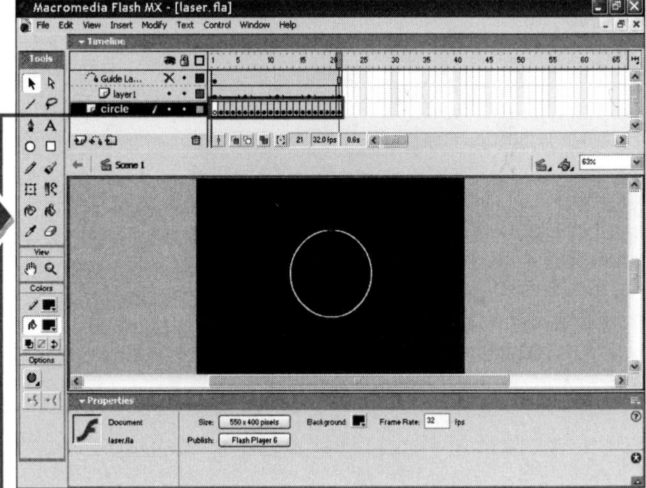

17 Repeat steps 15 to 16 to continue removing parts of the circle until you reach frame 21.

■ This creates the effect of the laser point drawing the circle.

CONTINUED

CREATE A LASER-WRITING ANIMATION EFFECT (CONTINUED)

The laser-writing technique can be used in other ways besides writing a text character. For example, you can use this method to laser-write any two-dimensional shape or illustration, such as a logo outline. After it is perfected, the laser-writing technique is a really eye-catching effect that is sure to impress anyone viewing your movie or Web page.

If you plan to apply this effect to multiple characters or words, however, be aware of what a time-consuming process this might be. You may want to think twice before using laser-writing on a wordy project. The same warning applies to complex shapes or objects. The simplest shapes and illustrations work best for this effect.

As you create the effect, be sure to test the movie as you go using the Flash Player window. You can also check your progress at any time by placing the playhead at the beginning of the movie and pressing Enter on the keyboard. Flash MX plays through the movie one time on the Stage. To learn more about previewing your work in Flash MX, see Chapter 34.

CREATE A LASER-WRITING ANIMATION EFFECT (CONTINUED)

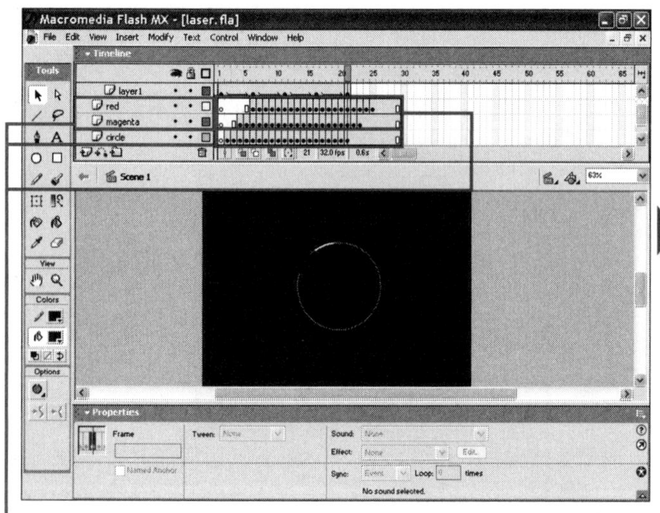

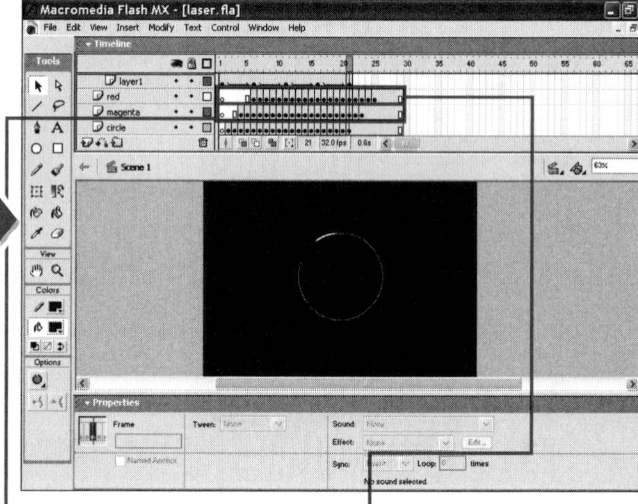

18 Add two new layers above the circle layer on the Timeline and name as **magenta** and **red**.

19 Select all frames in the circle layer and copy them.

20 Paste the frames into the red and magenta layers.

■ Stagger the pasted frames 2-3 frames down the Timeline. For example, in the magenta layer, paste the frames 2-3 frames down from where the content starts in the circle layer.

21 For each keyframe in the magenta layer, select the circle content and change its color from white to magenta.

22 Repeat step 21 for the red layer, changing the color from white to red.

■ This creates the effect of a laser writing a circle.

Note: To work with the color tools, see page 354.

Can I stagger the different colored layers more than two frames?

✔ Yes. You can stagger the colored layers of the laser effect to more or less than two frames. You may want to test out different amounts until you find the effect that you like the best. If you stagger them too much, the time between the burn and the glow stage is very long and it might lead away from the laser effect. You can experiment with the different settings to create just the right effect.

Can I use a different color besides red for my laser-writing effect?

✔ Yes. Although a red gradient fill color is used in this section, you can certainly assign another color for the effect. The general rule behind the colors is that the first layer stays white, the second layer should be white mixed with the color you want as a final result, and the last layer should be the color you want as your final result. By sticking to that general rule, you should be able to have your laser write in any color you choose.

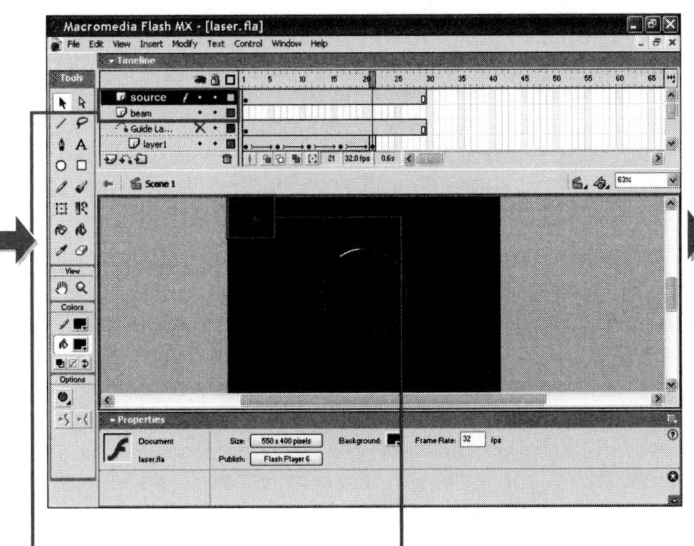

23 Add two more layers and name as **beam** and **source**.

■ Place the source layer at the top.

24 In the source layer, create a laser light source.

■ In this example, a large sphere was created with a red, radial gradient fill.

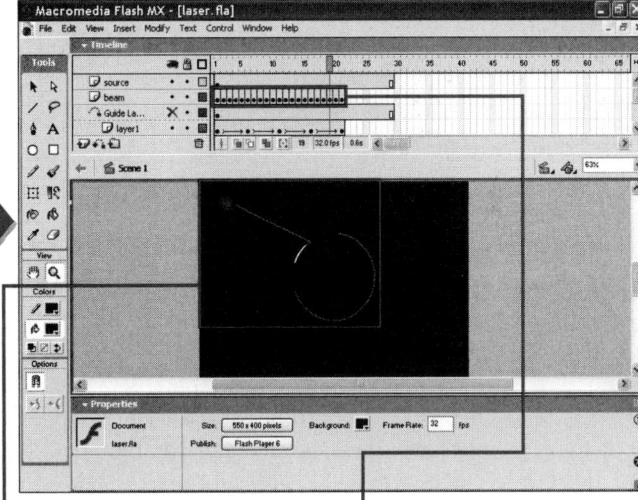

25 Use the Line tool (⁄) to connect the middle of the laser source to the laser point.

Note: To draw lines with ⁄, see page 356.

26 Continue adding blank keyframes to the beam layer that connect the source to the laser point until you have reached frame 21.

■ You can test the movie in the Flash Player to see the effect.

APPENDIX

WHAT'S ON THE CD-ROM

The CD-ROM disc included in this book contains many useful files and programs. Before installing any of the programs on the disc, make sure that a newer version of the program is not already installed on your computer. For information on installing different versions of the same program, contact the program's manufacturer.

SYSTEM REQUIREMENTS

To use the contents of the CD-ROM, your computer must be equipped with the following hardware and software:

- A PC with a Pentium or faster processor, or a Mac OS computer with a 68040 or faster processor.
- Microsoft Windows 98 or later, or Mac OS system software 7.6.6 or later.
- At least 128MB of total RAM installed on your computer (at least 64MB of free available system RAM on Windows 98 SE or higher PCs and Mac OS computers with PowerPC processors and 85MB of available disk space).
- A double-speed (2x) or faster CD-ROM drive.
- A sound card for PCs.
- A monitor capable of displaying at least 256 colors or grayscale.
- A modem with a speed of at least 14,400 bps.

AUTHORS' SAMPLE FILES

For Mac OS 9.1 and higher and Windows 98SE/NT/2000/ME/XP. These files contain all the sample code from the book in addition to a Flash-based interface. You can browse these files directly from the CD-ROM, or you can copy them to your hard drive and use them as the basis for your own projects. To find the files on the CD-ROM, open the D:\SAMPLE folder. To copy the files to your hard drive, just run the installation program D:\SAMPLES.EXE. The files will be placed on your hard drive at C:MasterVISUALLY.

WEB LINKS

http://www.macromedia.com

Additional information about Flash MX at the Macromedia Web site.

ACROBAT VERSION

This CD-ROM contains an e-version of this book that you can view and search using Adobe Acrobat Reader. You can also use the hyperlinks provided in the text to access all Web pages and Internet references in the book. You cannot print the pages or copy text from the Acrobat files. If you do not currently have Adobe Acrobat Reader 5 installed, the computer will prompt you to install the software. An evaluation version of Adobe Acrobat Reader is also included on the disc.

INSTALLING AND USING THE SOFTWARE

This CD-ROM disc contains several useful programs. Before installing a program from the CD, you should exit all other programs. In order to use most of the programs, you must accept the license agreement provided with the program. Make sure you read any ReadMe files provided with each program.

Program Versions

Shareware programs are fully functional, free trial versions of copyrighted programs. If you like a particular program, you can register with its author for a nominal fee and receive licenses, enhanced versions, and technical support.

Freeware programs are free, copyrighted games, applications, and utilities. You can copy them to as many computers as you like, but they have no technical support.

Trial, demo, or evaluation versions are usually limited either by time of functionality. For example, you may not be able to save projects using these versions.

For your convenience, the software titles on the CD are listed in alphabetic order.

Acrobat Reader

Freeware. For Windows. Acrobat Acrobat Reader lets you view the online version of this book. For more information on using Adobe Acrobat Reader, see page xxx. From Adobe Systems, Inc., www.adobe.com.

BBEdit Lite

For Macintosh. Freeware version.By Bare Bones Software. BBEdit is a popular text-based HTML editor. You can use BBEdit to edit the HTML documents that you create in Dreamweaver. This Lite version lacks some of the features available in the full version (BBEdit 6.1) but does not expire. For more information, visit www.bbedit.com.

BBEdit

For Macintosh. Demo version. By Bare Bones Software. BBEdit is a popular text-based HTML editor that you can use to edit the HTML documents that you create in Dreamweaver. This demo version is identical to the retail version but expires after 24 launches. For more information, visit www.bbedit.com.

Macromedia ColdFusion Server MX

For Win 95/98/NT/2000/Me. 30-day trial version. By Macromedia. ColdFusion Server MXis a full-featured Web application server that enables you to create dynamic Web sites that are database driven. This trial version expires after 30 days. For more information, visit www.macromedia.com/coldfusion.

Macromedia Dreamweaver MX

For Win 95/98/NT/2000/Me and Macintosh. 30-day trial version. By Macromedia. Dreamweaver MXis a full-featured application for designing, publishing, and maintaining Web pages. This trial version expires after 30 days. For more information, visit www.macromedia.com/dreamweaver.

Macromedia Fireworks MX

For Win 95/98/NT/2000/Me and Macintosh. 30-day trial version. By Macromedia. Fireworks MX lets you create, edit, and optimize images for use on your Web pages. You can create images in Fireworks and then add them to the pages that you build in Dreamweaver. This trial version expires after 30 days. For more information, visit www.macromedia.com/fireworks.

Macromedia Flash MX

For Win 98SE/NT/2000/Me/XP and Mac OS9.1 and higher. 30-day trial version. By Macromedia. Flash MX is the leading Web application development software. This trial version experies after 30 days. For more information, visit www.macromedia.com/flash.

Paint Shop Pro

For Win 95/98/NT/2000/Me. Evaluation version. By Jasc Software. Paint Shop Pro lets you create, edit, and optimize images for use on your Web pages. You can create images in Paint Shop Pro and then add them to the pages that you build in Dreamweaver. This evaluation version expires after 30 days. For more information, visit www.jasc.com.

TROUBLESHOOTING

We tried our best to compile programs that work on most computers with the minimum system requirements. Your computer, however, may differ and some programs may not work properly for some reason.

The two most likely problems are that you don't have enough memory (RAM) for the programs you want to use, or you have other programs running that are affecting installation or running of a program. If you get error messages like `Not-enough memory` or `Setup cannot continue`, try one or more of these methods and then try using the software again:

- Turn off any anti-virus software.
- Close all running programs.
- In Windows, close the CD-ROM interface and run demos or installations directly from Windows Explorer.
- Have your local computer store add more RAM to your computer.

If you still have trouble installing the items from the CD-ROM, please call the Wiley Customer Service phone number: 800-762-2974 (outside the U.S.: 317-572-3994) or email techsupdum@wiley.com.

USING THE E-VERSION OF THE BOOK

You can view *Master VISUALLY Dreamweaver MX and Flash MX* on your screen using the CD-ROM included at the back of this book. The CD-ROM allows you to search the contents of each chapter of the book for a specific word or phrase. The CD-ROM also provides a convenient way of keeping the book handy while traveling.

You must install Adobe Acrobat Reader on your computer before you can view the book on the CD-ROM. This program is provided on the disc. Acrobat Reader allows you to view Portable Document Format (PDF) files, which can display books and magazines on your screen exactly as they appear in printed form.

To view the contents of the book using Acrobat Reader, insert the CD-ROM into your drive. The autorun interface will appear. Navigate to the eBook, and open the book.pdf file. You may be required to install Acrobat Reader 5.0 on your computer, which you can do by following the simple intallation instructions. If you choose to disable the autorun interface, you can open the CD root menu and open the Resources folder, then open the eBook folder. In the window that appears, double-click the eBook.pdf icon.

USING THE E-VERSION OF THE BOOK

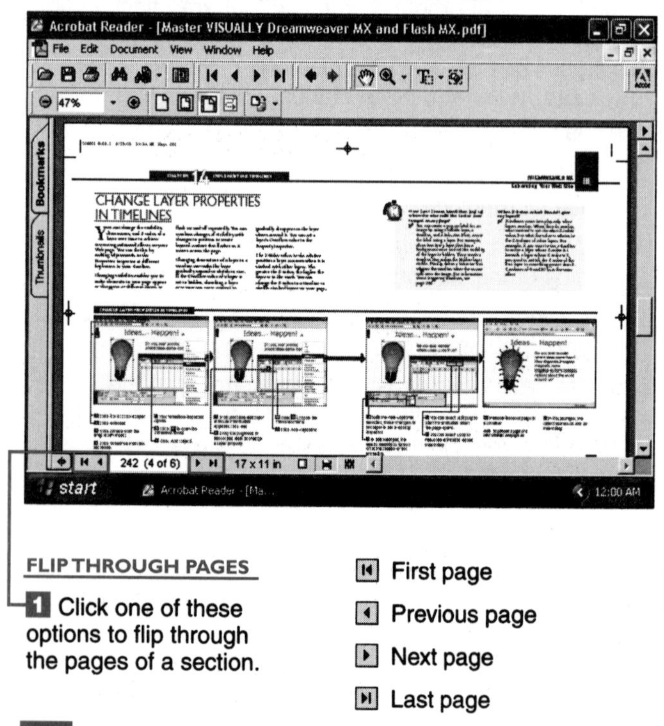

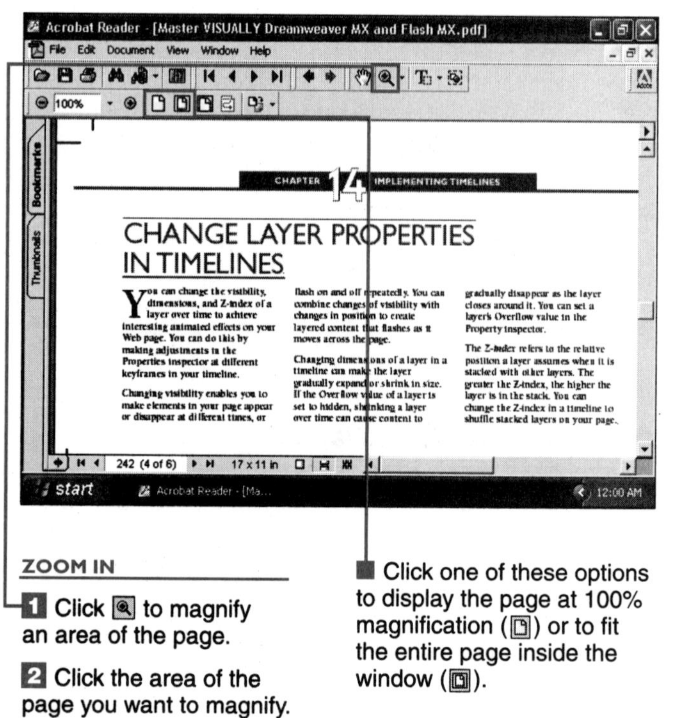

FLIP THROUGH PAGES

1 Click one of these options to flip through the pages of a section.

- First page
- Previous page
- Next page
- Last page

ZOOM IN

1 Click to magnify an area of the page.

2 Click the area of the page you want to magnify.

■ Click one of these options to display the page at 100% magnification or to fit the entire page inside the window.

How can I make searching the book more convenient?

✔ You can copy the .pdf files to your computer. Display the contents of the CD-ROM disc and then copy the PDFs folder from the CD to your hard drive. This allows you to easily access the contents of the book at any time.

When I search for text, the text Acrobat Reader highlights is difficult to read. How can I make highlighted text easier to read?

✔ You can turn off the font smoothing capabilities of Acrobat Reader to make highlighted text easier to read. In the Acrobat Reader window, display the Edit menu and choose Preferences. Click Display at the left side of the Preferences dialog box. In the Smoothing area, click Smooth Text (☑ changes to ☐) and then click OK.

How do I install Acrobat Reader?

✔ To install Acrobat Reader, insert the CD-ROM disc into your drive. In the screen that appears, click Software. Click Acrobat Reader and then click Install at the bottom of the screen. Then follow the instructions on your screen to install the program.

Can I use Acrobat Reader for anything else?

✔ Acrobat Reader is a popular and useful program. There are many files available on the Web that are designed to be viewed using Acrobat Reader. Look for files with the .pdf extension. For more information about Acrobat Reader, visit the Web site at www.adobe.com/ products/ acrobat/readermain.html.

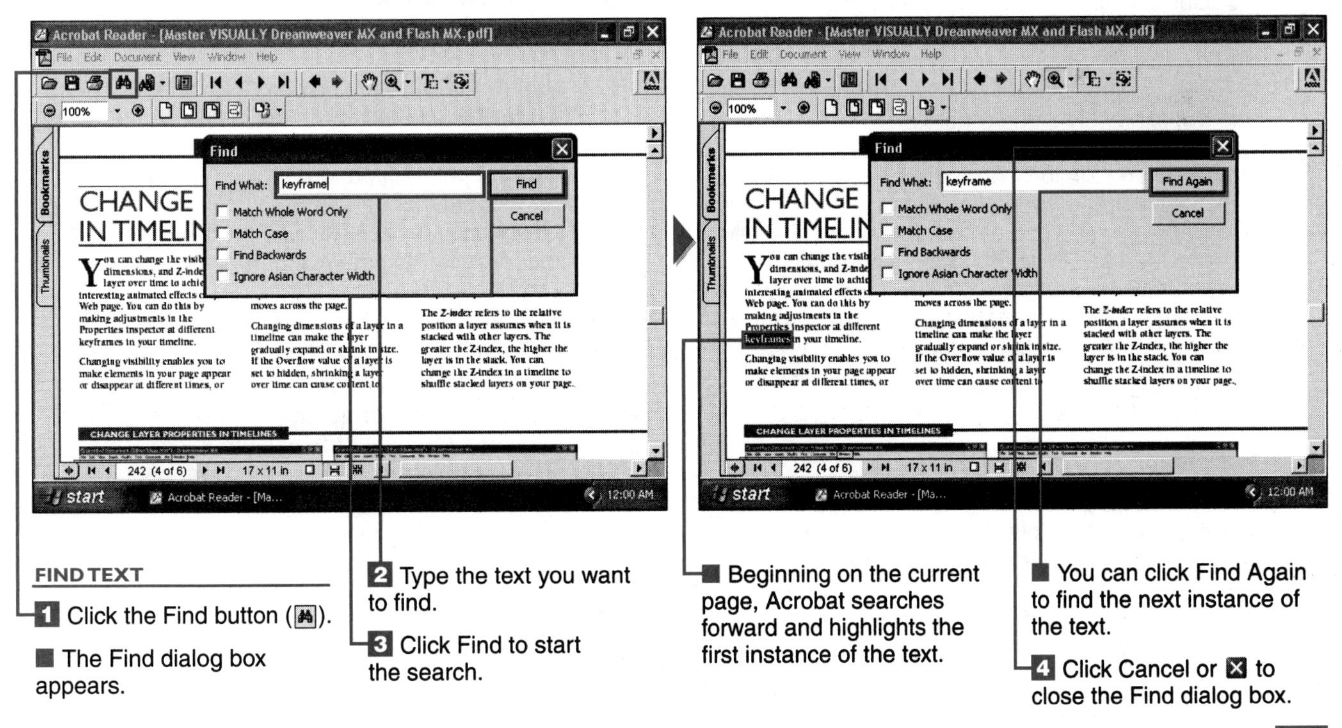

FIND TEXT

1 Click the Find button (🔍).

■ The Find dialog box appears.

2 Type the text you want to find.

3 Click Find to start the search.

■ Beginning on the current page, Acrobat searches forward and highlights the first instance of the text.

■ You can click Find Again to find the next instance of the text.

4 Click Cancel or ☒ to close the Find dialog box.

Wiley Publishing, Inc. End-User License Agreement

READ THIS. You should carefully read these terms and conditions before opening the software packet(s) included with this book "*Master VISUALLY Dreamweaver MX* and *Flash MX*". This is a license "Agreement" between you and Wiley Publishing, Inc. "WPI". By opening the accompanying software packet(s), you acknowledge that you have read and accept the following terms and conditions. If you do not agree and do not want to be bound by such terms and conditions, promptly return the Book and the unopened software packet(s) to the place you obtained them for a full refund.

1. **License Grant.** WPI grants to you (either an individual or entity) a nonexclusive license to use one copy of the enclosed software program(s) (collectively, the "Software" solely for your own personal or business purposes on a single computer (whether a standard computer or a workstation component of a multi-user network). The Software is in use on a computer when it is loaded into temporary memory (RAM) or installed into permanent memory (hard disk, CD-ROM, or other storage device). WPI reserves all rights not expressly granted herein.

2. **Ownership.** WPI is the owner of all right, title, and interest, including copyright, in and to the compilation of the Software recorded on the disk(s) or CD-ROM "Software Media". Copyright to the individual programs recorded on the Software Media is owned by the author or other authorized copyright owner of each program. Ownership of the Software and all proprietary rights relating thereto remain with WPI and its licensers.

3. **Restrictions On Use and Transfer.**

   (a) You may only (i) make one copy of the Software for backup or archival purposes, or (ii) transfer the Software to a single hard disk, provided that you keep the original for backup or archival purposes. You may not (i) rent or lease the Software, (ii) copy or reproduce the Software through a LAN or other network system or through any computer subscriber system or bulletin- board system, or (iii) modify, adapt, or create derivative works based on the Software.

   (b) You may not reverse engineer, decompile, or disassemble the Software. You may transfer the Software and user documentation on a permanent basis, provided that the transferee agrees to accept the terms and conditions of this Agreement and you retain no copies. If the Software is an update or has been updated, any transfer must include the most recent update and all prior versions.

4. **Restrictions on Use of Individual Programs.** You must follow the individual requirements and restrictions detailed for each individual program in the What's on the CD-ROM appendix of this Book. These limitations are also contained in the individual license agreements recorded on the Software Media. These limitations may include a requirement that after using the program for a specified period of time, the user must pay a registration fee or discontinue use. By opening the Software packet(s), you will be agreeing to abide by the licenses and restrictions for these individual programs that are detailed in the What's on the CD-ROM appendix and on the Software Media. None of the material on this Software Media or listed in this Book may ever be redistributed, in original or modified form, for commercial purposes.

5. **Limited Warranty.**

   (a) WPI warrants that the Software and Software Media are free from defects in materials and workmanship under normal use for a period of sixty (60) days from the date of purchase of this Book. If WPI receives notification within the warranty period of defects in materials or workmanship, WPI will replace the defective Software Media.

(b) WPI AND THE AUTHOR OF THE BOOK DISCLAIM ALL OTHER WARRANTIES, EXPRESS OR IMPLIED, INCLUDING WITHOUT LIMITATION IMPLIED WARRANTIES OF MERCHANTABILITY AND FITNESS FOR A PARTICULAR PURPOSE, WITH RESPECT TO THE SOFTWARE, THE PROGRAMS, THE SOURCE CODE CONTAINED THEREIN, AND/OR THE TECHNIQUES DESCRIBED IN THIS BOOK. WPI DOES NOT WARRANT THAT THE FUNCTIONS CONTAINED IN THE SOFTWARE WILL MEET YOUR REQUIREMENTS OR THAT THE OPERATION OF THE SOFTWARE WILL BE ERROR FREE.

(c) This limited warranty gives you specific legal rights, and you may have other rights that vary from jurisdiction to jurisdiction.

6. **Remedies.**

(a) WPI's entire liability and your exclusive remedy for defects in materials and workmanship shall be limited to replacement of the Software Media, which may be returned to WPI with a copy of your receipt at the following address: Software Media Fulfillment Department, Attn.: *Master VISUALLY Dreamweaver MX and Flash MX*, Wiley Publishing, Inc., 10475 Crosspoint Blvd., Indianapolis, IN 46256, or call 1-800-762-2974. Please allow four to six weeks for delivery. This Limited Warranty is void if failure of the Software Media has resulted from accident, abuse, or misapplication. Any replacement Software Media will be warranted for the remainder of the original warranty period or thirty (30) days, whichever is longer.

(b) In no event shall WPI or the author be liable for any damages whatsoever (including without limitation damages for loss of business profits, business interruption, loss of business information, or any other pecuniary loss) arising from the use of or inability to use the Book or the Software, even if WPI has been advised of the possibility of such damages.

(c) Because some jurisdictions do not allow the exclusion or limitation of liability for consequential or incidental damages, the above limitation or exclusion may not apply to you.

7. **U.S. Government Restricted Rights.** Use, duplication, or disclosure of the Software for or on behalf of the United States of America, its agencies and/or instrumentalities "U.S. Government" is subject to restrictions as stated in paragraph (c)(1)(ii) of the Rights in Technical Data and Computer Software clause of DFARS 252.227-7013, or subparagraphs (c) (1) and (2) of the Commercial Computer Software - Restricted Rights clause at FAR 52.227-19, and in similar clauses in the NASA FAR supplement, as applicable.

8. **General.** This Agreement constitutes the entire understanding of the parties and revokes and supersedes all prior agreements, oral or written, between them and may not be modified or amended except in a writing signed by both parties hereto that specifically refers to this Agreement. This Agreement shall take precedence over any other documents that may be in conflict herewith. If any one or more provisions contained in this Agreement are held by any court or tribunal to be invalid, illegal, or otherwise unenforceable, each and every other provision shall remain in full force and effect.

INDEX

Symbols

A

continued

B

continued

continued

E

G

H

J

M

N

O

continued

P

T

continued

U

V

continued

continued

X

Z

Disc Missing prior to 12.2.09 BKW (no disc listed in MARC record)